O'CONNOR'S TEXAS CIVIL FORMS

O'CONNOR'S
HOUSTON, TEXAS

O'CONNOR'S LITIGATION SERIES

Suggested cite form: *O'Connor's Texas Civil Forms* (2019)

42587034

O'CONNOR'S®

Print date: May 17, 2019
Printed in the United States of America

ISBN 978-1-53920-886-0

This book is intended to provide attorneys with current and accurate forms for Texas civil trials. The information in this book, however, may not be sufficient in dealing with a client's particular legal problem, and O'Connor's does not warrant or represent its suitability for this purpose. Attorneys using this book do so with the understanding that the information published in it should not be relied on as a substitute for independent research using original sources of authority.

Thank you for subscribing to this product. We welcome your feedback and suggestions at editors.us-legal@tr.com. Our reference attorneys are available to answer product questions and provide research assistance at 1-800-733-2889. To learn about related publications or to place an order, visit legalsolutions.thomsonreuters.com.

WHAT'S NEW IN THIS EDITION

This year's edition of ***O'Connor's Texas Civil Forms*** has been fully updated based on the most recent and pertinent decisions from the Texas Supreme Court and the courts of appeals. We also added and updated cross-references to ***O'Connor's Texas Rules * Civil Trials*** (2019), ***O'Connor's Texas Civil Appeals*** (2019), and ***Texas Rules of Evidence Handbook*** (2019) for procedural issues, to ***O'Connor's Texas Causes of Action*** (2019) for substantive issues, and to ***O'Connor's Texas Causes of Action Pleadings*** (2019) for additional forms on certain substantive topics.

RULE CHANGES

Since the 2018 edition was published, the Texas Supreme Court repealed Texas Rule of Civil Procedure 78a, which required a party to include a civil-case-information sheet with all petitions and applications filed in district and county-level courts. The Court also repealed Texas Rule of Civil Procedure 502.2(b), which required the civil-case-information sheet for all original petitions filed in justice court. Filing a case-information sheet is no longer necessary because the required information is recorded in the e-filing system; thus, these forms have been deleted from this edition. The orders for these repealed rules can be found on the Texas Supreme Court's website at www.txcourts.gov/supreme.

CONVENTIONS

The goal in writing this book was to provide trial attorneys with a comprehensive, well-organized set of forms. These forms follow the same organization as ***O'Connor's Texas Rules * Civil Trials*** (2019), and each form is numbered to correspond to the relevant chapter and section of that book. The forms are written in plain English. We have avoided legalese and removed the standard archaic conventions such as "To the Honorable Court" and "Wherefore, premises considered." We have shortened the forms by including the common elements (style of the case, certificate of service, etc.) in chapter 1, not as a part of each form. Each form refers you to other books in the O'Connor's series for issues of substantive and procedural law. In particular, we reference ***O'Connor's Texas Rules * Civil Trials*** (2019), ***O'Connor's Texas Causes of Action*** (2019), ***O'Connor's Texas Civil Appeals*** (2019), and ***O'Connor's Texas Causes of Action Pleadings*** (2019) with the shortened designations ***O'Connor's Texas Rules***, ***O'Connor's Texas COA***, ***O'Connor's Texas Appeals***, and ***O'Connor's Texas COA Pleadings***, respectively. Below each form we cite the relevant parts of these books so you can refer to them as authority in drafting your document.

If there is anything particularly important to think about before drafting or filing a pleading or motion, we include that information under the heading "NOTE" at the end of the form.

Because of the 2013 amendments to Texas Rule of Civil Procedure 190, there are now two sets of comments to the rule; thus, we have used "(1999)" or "(2013)" after each citation to a Rule 190 comment to specify which set we are referencing.

YOUR SUGGESTIONS

Thank you for subscribing to this product. We welcome your feedback and suggestions at editors.us-legal@tr.com.

CAVEAT

This book provides forms with citations to opinions that interpret the Texas Rules of Civil Procedure and Texas Rules of Evidence through the date of publication. Because there is no substitute for independent thinking, no form is a substitute for independent drafting. Although we have tried to indicate when additional argument and advocacy may be appropriate, only you can make that determination.

EDITORIAL & PRODUCTION STAFF

As always, the staff of O'Connor's worked hard to prepare this publication, both in its substance and in its layout. The people who worked on this edition of ***O'Connor's Texas Civil Forms*** are listed below.

EXECUTIVE EDITOR
Douglas Rosenzweig, J.D.

MANAGING LEGAL EDITOR
Kristen N. Ellis, J.D.

LEGAL EDITORS
Eun-Jeong Choi, J.D.
Victoria R. Guzman, J.D.
Kristen K. Sheils, J.D.

LEGAL EDITORIAL ASSISTANTS
Kalina Dalal, J.D.
Erin Gage, J.D.
Patrick M. Miller, J.D.

PRODUCTION MANAGER
Clare Jensen

PRODUCTION STAFF
Sara Rhodes Bean
Nicole E. Hammond
Marc A. Kashiwagi, J.D.
Rachel Kelly
Donna E. Vass

PROOFREADER
Sara Rhodes Bean

COPYEDITOR
David W. Schultz, J.D.

In the forms, italicized text in braces accompanied by a number—e.g., {❶ *name*}—indicates choices to make about the wording of a form. This worksheet is provided for writing in the information to be typed into the form. Other italicized items in braces, without numbers, are instructions and references that should be deleted in the final form.

To: ____________________ From: ____________________
Title of Form: ____________________ Number of Form: ____________________
Case Name: ____________________ Cause Number: ____________________
Party: ____________________ Adverse Party: ____________________

1 ____________________
2 ____________________
3 ____________________
4 ____________________
5 ____________________
6 ____________________
7 ____________________
8 ____________________
9 ____________________
10 ____________________
11 ____________________
12 ____________________
13 ____________________
14 ____________________
15 ____________________
16 ____________________
17 ____________________
18 ____________________
19 ____________________
20 ____________________
21 ____________________
22 ____________________

23 ______
24 ______
25 ______
26 ______
27 ______
28 ______
29 ______
30 ______
31 ______
32 ______
33 ______
34 ______
35 ______
36 ______
37 ______
38 ______
39 ______
40 ______
41 ______
42 ______
43 ______
44 ______
45 ______
46 ______
47 ______
48 ______
49 ______
50 ______

MASTER TABLE OF CONTENTS

TEXAS CIVIL FORMS

TABLE OF CONTENTS

CHAPTER 1. GENERAL TRIAL FORMS

TABLE OF CONTENTS

TABLE OF CONTENTS

TABLE OF CONTENTS

TABLE OF CONTENTS

CHAPTER 5. PRETRIAL MOTIONS

TABLE OF CONTENTS

CHAPTER 6. DISCOVERY

TABLE OF CONTENTS

TABLE OF CONTENTS

Table of Contents

TABLE OF CONTENTS

TABLE OF CONTENTS

TEXAS CIVIL FORMS

CHAPTER 1. GENERAL TRIAL FORMS

TABLE OF CONTENTS

TEXAS CIVIL FORMS

CHAPTER 1. GENERAL TRIAL FORMS

TABLE OF CONTENTS

{❶ *CAPTION*}

{❷ *State the nature of the motion, e.g., Defendant, Jane Smith, moves for sanctions against plaintiff, George Jones, for filing groundless pleadings in violation of Texas Civil Practice & Remedies Code section 9.011.*}

INTRODUCTION

1. {❸ *Identify the parties and state the basis of the suit and the relief sought.*}

BACKGROUND

2. {❹ *State facts relevant to the motion.*}

ARGUMENT & AUTHORITIES

3. {❺ *State the law that supports the request, applying it to the facts of the case.*}

CONCLUSION

4. {❻ *Summarize the motion.*}

PRAYER

5. {❼ *State the ruling the court should make.*}

SEE: Tex. R. Civ. P. 21
O'Connor's Texas Rules * Civil Trials (2019), "Motion," ch. 1-B, §2.2, p. 6; "Drafting motions," ch. 1-B, §4.1, p. 22

ADD: STYLE OF THE CASE – FORM 1B:2
SIGNATURE BLOCK – FORM 1B:3
VERIFICATION – FORM 1B:7, if necessary
CERTIFICATE OF CONFERENCE – FORM 1B:12, if necessary
CERTIFICATE OF SERVICE – FORM 1B:13

ATTACH: AFFIDAVIT – FORM 1B:8, if necessary
NOTICE OF HEARING OR SUBMISSION – FORM 1E:1
ORDER – FORM 1G:1
Exhibits, if necessary

NOTE: Each form in this book begins with a caption, which is the title of the form (e.g., Defendant's Motion for Summary Judgment). A motion should always have a caption that is useful to both the court and the clerk. See ***O'Connor's Texas Rules***, "Caption," ch. 1-B, §4.1.3, p. 23. If exhibits are attached or filed separately, the motion should incorporate them by reference.

A short motion (e.g., Request to Master for a Record) does not need to include a separate section for the conclusion, which merely summarizes the motion.

{*CHOOSE APPROPRIATE STYLE FOR COURT*}

{*District court*}

No. {❶ *cause number*}

{❷ *Name*}, Plaintiff,	§ § §	IN THE DISTRICT COURT
v.	§ §	OF {❸ ________} COUNTY, TEXAS
{❹ *Name*}, Defendant.	§ §	{❺ ___} JUDICIAL DISTRICT

{*County court*}

No. {❻ *cause number*}

{❼ *Name*}, Plaintiff,	§ § §	IN THE COUNTY COURT
v.	§ §	OF {❽ ________} COUNTY, TEXAS
{❾ *Name*}, Defendant.	§ §	COUNTY COURT NO. {❿ ___}

{*County court at law*}

No. {⓫ *cause number*}

{⓬ *Name*}, Plaintiff,	§ § §	IN THE COUNTY COURT AT LAW
v.	§ §	OF {⓭ ________} COUNTY, TEXAS
{⓮ *Name*}, Defendant.	§ § §	COUNTY COURT AT LAW NO. {⓯ ___}

{*Justice court*}

No. {16 *cause number*}

{17 *Name*}, Plaintiff,	§ § §	IN THE JUSTICE COURT
v.	§ §	OF {18 _______} COUNTY, TEXAS
{19 *Name*}, Defendant.	§ §	PRECINCT {20 ___}, PLACE {21 ____}

SEE: ***O'Connor's Texas Rules * Civil Trials*** (2019), "Style," ch. 1-B, §4.1.2, p. 22

NOTE: In the petition and the answer, all parties should be listed by their full names in the style of the case. In later documents, the list of parties may be shortened to the name of the first party followed by the inclusive term "et al." *See* ***Abramcik v. U.S. Home Corp.***, 792 S.W.2d 822, 824 (Tex.App.—Houston [14th Dist.] 1990, writ denied).

★

{*Signature block for sole practitioner*}

____
{❶ *Name of attorney for party*}
Texas Bar No. {❷ _____}
{❸ *Address 1*}
{❹ *Address 2*}
{❺ *City, state, zip code*}
Tel. {❻ ___________}
Fax {❼ ___________}
{❽ *E-mail address*}

ATTORNEY FOR {❾ *PARTY*},
{❿ *NAME OF PARTY*}

{*Signature block for law firm*}

{⓫ *Name of firm*}

By: ____________________________
{⓬ *Name of attorney for party*}
Texas Bar No. {⓭ _____}
{⓮ *Address 1*}
{⓯ *Address 2*}
{⓰ *City, state, zip code*}
Tel. {⓱ ___________}
Fax {⓲ ___________}
{⓳ *E-mail address*}

ATTORNEY FOR {⓴ *PARTY*}
{㉑ *NAME OF PARTY*}

{*Signature block for pro se litigant*}

Respectfully submitted,

____
{22 *Name of party*}

{23 *Address*}
{24 *City, state, zip code*}
Tel. {25 ____________}
Fax {26 ____________}
{27 *E-mail address*}

SEE: Tex. R. Civ. P. 7, 13, 45, 57
Tex. Civ. Prac. & Rem. Code §§9.011-9.014, 10.001 et seq.
O'Connor's Texas Rules * Civil Trials (2019), "Signature block," ch. 1-B, §3.2.12, p. 10

NOTE: Check the court's local rules, which may affect the form of the signature block.

When a party is filing a document, the document must be signed, and the signature block must include the e-mail address of the attorney or pro se litigant. Tex. R. Civ. P. 57. Pleadings that are e-filed must include an electronic signature. *See* Tex. R. Civ. P. 21(f)(7). See ***O'Connor's Texas Rules***, "Electronic signature," ch. 1-B, §3.2.12(2)(b), p. 11.

FORM 1B:4 SIGNATURE BLOCK – AGREED MOTIONS

{❶ *Name of firm if applicable*}

____

{❷ *Name of attorney for party*}
Texas Bar No. {❸ _____}
{❹ *Address 1*}
{❺ *Address 2*}
{❻ *City, state, zip code*}
Tel. {❼ ___________}
Fax {❽ ___________}
{❾ *E-mail address*}

ATTORNEY FOR {❿ *PARTY*},
{⓫ *NAME OF PARTY*}

{⓬ *Name of firm if applicable*}

____

{⓭ *Name of attorney for adverse party*}
Texas Bar No. {⓮ _____}
{⓯ *Address 1*}
{⓰ *Address 2*}
{⓱ *City, state, zip code*}
Tel. {⓲ ___________}
Fax {⓳ ___________}
{⓴ *E-mail address*}

ATTORNEY FOR {㉑ *ADVERSE PARTY*},
{㉒ *NAME OF ADVERSE PARTY*}

SEE: Tex. R. Civ. P. 7, 13, 45, 57
Tex. Civ. Prac. & Rem. Code §§9.011-9.014, 10.001 et seq.
O'Connor's Texas Rules * Civil Trials (2019), "Signature block," ch. 1-B, §3.2.12, p. 10

NOTE: This form can be modified if one of the parties is pro se. See FORM 1B:3.

____
PRESIDING JUDGE

APPROVED AS TO FORM ONLY:

{1 *Name of firm if applicable*}

____
{2 *Name of attorney for party*}
Texas Bar No. {3 _____}
{4 *Address 1*}
{5 *Address 2*}
{6 *City, state, zip code*}
Tel. {7 __________}
Fax {8 __________}
{9 *E-mail address*}

ATTORNEY FOR {10 *PARTY*},
{11 *NAME OF PARTY*}

{*ADD SIGNATURE LINES BELOW IF APPLICABLE*}

{12 *Name of firm if applicable*}

____
{13 *Name of attorney for adverse party*}
Texas Bar No. {14 _____}
{15 *Address 1*}
{16 *Address 2*}
{17 *City, state, zip code*}
Tel. {18 __________}
Fax {19 __________}
{20 *E-mail address*}

ATTORNEY FOR {21 *ADVERSE PARTY*},
{22 *NAME OF ADVERSE PARTY*}

SEE: Tex. R. Civ. P. 300-314
O'Connor's Texas Rules * Civil Trials (2019), "Signature line for attorneys," ch. 9-C, §4.13, p. 908

____
PRESIDING JUDGE

APPROVED AS TO FORM & SUBSTANCE:

{1 *Name of firm if applicable*}

____
{2 *Name of attorney for party*}
Texas Bar No. {3 _____}
{4 *Address 1*}
{5 *Address 2*}
{6 *City, state, zip code*}
Tel. {7 __________}
Fax {8 __________}
{9 *E-mail address*}

ATTORNEY FOR {10 *PARTY*},
{11 *NAME OF PARTY*}

{12 *Name of firm if applicable*}

____
{13 *Name of attorney for adverse party*}
Texas Bar No. {14 _____}
{15 *Address 1*}
{16 *Address 2*}
{17 *City, state, zip code*}
Tel. {18 __________}
Fax {19 __________}
{20 *E-mail address*}

ATTORNEY FOR {21 *ADVERSE PARTY*},
{22 *NAME OF ADVERSE PARTY*}

SEE: Tex. R. Civ. P. 300-314
O'Connor's Texas Rules * Civil Trials (2019), "Signature line for attorneys," ch. 9-C, §4.13, p. 908

VERIFICATION

STATE OF TEXAS §
{❶ _______} COUNTY §

Before me, the undersigned notary, on this day personally appeared {❷ *name of affiant*}, the affiant, whose identity is known to me. After I administered an oath, affiant testified as follows:

"My name is {❸ *name of affiant*}. I am capable of making this verification. I have read the {❹ *identify document by name; if verification is for only part of document, identify part, e.g., Defendant's Original Answer, paragraph 12*}. The facts stated in it are within my personal knowledge and are true and correct."

____
{❺ *Name of affiant*}

Sworn to and subscribed before me by {❻ *name of affiant*} on __________, 20___.

____
Notary Public in and for
the State of Texas

SEE: Tex. R. Civ. P. 14
Tex. R. Evid. 602
Tex. R. App. P. 10.2
Tex. Gov't Code §312.011(1)
O'Connor's Texas Rules * Civil Trials (2019), "Verification," ch. 1-B, §3.2.15, p. 12

NOTE: An e-filed document that must be sworn or notarized must include an electronic or scanned image of the necessary signatures. *See* Tex. R. Civ. P. 21(f)(7). For more information on e-filing requirements, see ***O'Connor's Texas Rules***, "E-filing," ch. 1-C, §4.1.1, p. 25.

In most instances, an unsworn declaration can be used instead of a verification. Tex. Civ. Prac. & Rem. Code §132.001(a). See FORM 1B:9.

AFFIDAVIT OF {❶ *NAME OF AFFIANT*}

STATE OF TEXAS §
{❷ ______} COUNTY §

Before me, the undersigned notary, on this day personally appeared {❸ *name of affiant*}, the affiant, whose identity is known to me. After I administered an oath, affiant testified as follows:

1. "My name is {❹ *name of affiant*}. I am over 18 years of age, of sound mind, and capable of making this affidavit. The facts stated in this affidavit are within my personal knowledge and are true and correct.

2. "{❺ *State facts to be sworn.*}"

____
{❻ *Name of affiant*}

Sworn to and subscribed before me by {❼ *name of affiant*} on __________, 20___.

____
Notary Public in and for
the State of Texas

SEE: Tex. R. Civ. P. 14
Tex. R. Evid. 601(a), 602
Tex. R. App. P. 10.2
Tex. Gov't Code §312.011(1)
O'Connor's Texas Rules * Civil Trials (2019), "Affidavits," ch. 1-B, §3.2.16, p. 12

ADD: STYLE OF THE CASE – FORM 1B:2

NOTE: An affidavit must show that it was made by a person who is competent to testify. *See* Tex. R. Evid. 601(a). See ***O'Connor's Texas Rules***, "Competency of witness," ch. 1-B, §3.2.16(2), p. 13.

In a summary-judgment proceeding, an affidavit must be made on personal knowledge, must set forth facts that would be admissible in evidence, and must show affirmatively that the affiant is competent to testify to the matters stated in the affidavit. Tex. R. Civ. P. 166a(f).

An e-filed document that must be sworn or notarized must include an electronic or scanned image of the necessary signatures. *See* Tex. R. Civ. P. 21(f)(7). For more information on e-filing requirements, see ***O'Connor's Texas Rules***, "E-filing," ch. 1-C, §4.1.1, p. 25.

In most instances, an unsworn declaration can be used instead of an affidavit. Tex. Civ. Prac. & Rem. Code §132.001(a). See FORM 1B:9.

Although Texas Government Code §312.011(1) requires that an affidavit be sworn, it does not specifically require a jurat. ***Mansions in the Forest, L.P. v. Montgomery Cty.***, 365 S.W.3d 314, 316 (Tex. 2012). Generally, an affiant includes a jurat to prove the written statement was made under oath before an authorized officer. *Id.* at 316-17. If there is no jurat, there must be other evidence present to show that the statement was sworn to before an authorized officer; otherwise, the statement is not an affidavit. *Id.* at 317.

UNSWORN DECLARATION OF {❶ *NAME OF DECLARANT*}

1. {❷ *Identify facts stated under penalty of perjury.*}

{*CHOOSE APPROPRIATE JURAT*}

{*Generally*}

"My name is {❸ *full name of declarant*}, my date of birth is {❹ *date of birth*}, and my address is {❺ *identify street, city, state, zip code, and country*}. I declare under penalty of perjury that the facts stated in this document are true and correct."

Executed in {❻ *name of county*} County, State of {❼ *name of state*}, on ________________, 20___.

____
{❽ *Name of declarant*}

{*Inmate*}

"My name is {❾ *full name of declarant*}, my date of birth is {❿ *date of birth*}, and {⓫ *my inmate identifying number is ______/I do not have an inmate identifying number*}. I am presently incarcerated in {⓬ *name of unit or county facility where incarcerated*} in {⓭ *identify facility's city, county, state, and zip code*}. I declare under penalty of perjury that the facts stated in this document are true and correct."

Executed on ________________, 20___.

____
{⓮ *Name of declarant*}

{*State employee*}

"My name is {⓯ *full name of declarant*}, and I am an employee of the following governmental agency: {⓰ *name of agency*}. I am executing this declaration as part of my assigned duties and responsibilities. I declare under penalty of perjury that the facts stated in this document are true and correct."

Executed in {⓱ *name of county*} County, State of {⓲ *name of state*}, on ________________, 20___.

____
{⓳ *Name of declarant*}

SEE: Tex. Civ. Prac. & Rem. Code §132.001
O'Connor's Texas Rules * Civil Trials (2019), "Unsworn declaration," ch. 1-B, §3.2.17, p. 14

ADD: STYLE OF THE CASE – FORM 1B:2

NOTE: Anyone—not just inmates—can use an unsworn declaration instead of a sworn declaration, verification, certification, oath, or affidavit required by statute or by rule, order, or requirement adopted as provided by law. Tex. Civ. Prac. & Rem. Code §132.001(a). For an instrument to qualify as an unsworn declaration, it must be in writing, be signed under penalty of perjury, and include a jurat in substantially the same form as above. *Id.* §132.001(c)-(f).

A person cannot make an unsworn declaration for (1) a lien filed with a county clerk, (2) an instrument concerning property filed with a county clerk, (3) an oath of office, (4) an oath taken before a specified official other than a notary public, or (5) a self-proved will executed on or after January 1, 2014. Tex. Civ. Prac. & Rem. Code §132.001(b) (#1-4); *see* Tex. Est. Code §21.005 (#5); Acts 2013, 83rd Leg., R.S., ch. 1136, §1, eff. Jan. 1, 2014 (same).

FORM 1B:10 JURAT – NOTARY

Sworn to and subscribed before me by {❶ *name of affiant*} on __________, 20___.

____
Notary Public in and for
the State of Texas

SEE: Tex. Gov't Code §§312.011(1), 406.013, 406.014
O'Connor's Texas Rules * Civil Trials (2019), "Jurat," ch. 1-B, §3.2.16(1)(e), p. 13

NOTE: A notary must authenticate all official acts with the seal of office. Tex. Gov't Code §406.013(a). Along with the words "Notary Public, State of Texas," the seal must include the notary's name, her identifying number, and the date her commission expires. *Id.*

A notary, other than a court clerk notarizing instruments for the court, must keep in a book or electronically a record of (1) the date of both the affidavit and the affidavit's notarization, (2) the affiant's name and mailing address, and (3) whether the affiant is personally known by the notary, was identified by a government-issued identification card or U.S. passport, or was introduced to the notary and, if so, the name and mailing address of the individual introducing the affiant. *See* Tex. Gov't Code §406.014(a)(1)-(a)(5), (e). For other information that must be kept by the notary, see Texas Government Code §406.014(a)(6)-(a)(9). Entries made by the notary are public information; any person can request a certified copy (for a fee) of any record of official acts in the notary's book of record. *Id.* §406.014(b), (c).

Online notarization is permissible, but a person who is appointed as an online notary public is subject to the same requirements as any other notary public. *See* Tex. Gov't Code §§406.105, 406.106.

Although Texas Government Code §312.011(1) requires that an affidavit be sworn, it does not specifically require a jurat. ***Mansions in the Forest, L.P. v. Montgomery Cty.***, 365 S.W.3d 314, 316 (Tex. 2012). Generally, an affiant includes a jurat to prove the written statement was made under oath before an authorized officer. *Id.* at 316-17. If there is no jurat, there must be other evidence present to show that the statement was sworn to before an authorized officer. *Id.* at 317.

FORM 1B:11 JURAT – UNSWORN DECLARATION

{*Generally*}

"My name is {❶ *full name of declarant*}, my date of birth is {❷ *date of birth*}, and my address is {❸ *address, including street, city, state, zip code, and country*}. I declare under penalty of perjury that the facts stated in this document are true and correct."

Executed in {❹ *name of county*} County, State of {❺ *name of state*}, on ______________, 20___.

____
{❻ *Name of declarant*}

{*Inmate*}

"My name is {❼ *full name of declarant*}, my date of birth is {❽ *date of birth*}, and {❾ *my inmate identifying number is ______/I do not have an inmate identifying number*}. I am presently incarcerated in {❿ *name of unit or county facility where incarcerated*} in {⓫ *identify facility's city, county, state, and zip code*}. I declare under penalty of perjury that the facts stated in this document are true and correct."

Executed on ________________, 20___.

____
{⓬ *Name of declarant*}

{*State employee*}

"My name is {⓭ *full name of declarant*}, and I am an employee of the following governmental agency: {⓮ *name of agency*}. I am executing this declaration as part of my assigned duties and responsibilities. I declare under penalty of perjury that the facts stated in this document are true and correct."

Executed in {⓯ *name of county*} County, State of {⓰ *name of state*}, on ______________, 20___.

____
{⓱ *Name of declarant*}

SEE: Tex. Civ. Prac. & Rem. Code §132.001
O'Connor's Texas Rules * Civil Trials **(2019), "Unsworn declaration," ch. 1-B, §3.2.17, p. 14**

NOTE: For an instrument to qualify as unsworn declaration, it must be in writing, signed under penalty of perjury, and include a jurat in substantially the same form as above. Tex. Civ. Prac. & Rem. Code §132.001(c), (d).

CERTIFICATE OF CONFERENCE

{*CERTIFICATE VERSION 1 – Tex. R. Civ. P. 191.2*}

I certify that a reasonable effort was made to resolve the dispute without the necessity of court intervention, and the effort failed. Tex. R. Civ. P. 191.2.

{*CERTIFICATE VERSION 2 – TARRANT COUNTY*}

I certify that

{*CHOOSE APPROPRIATE STATEMENT*}

Ⓐ I conferred with {❶ *name of opposing counsel*} on {❷ *date*}, and have made a reasonable effort to reach an agreement about {❸ *specify motion or other matter in dispute*} without the need for court intervention. We were unable to reach an agreement because {❹ *state reasons*}.

Ⓑ I did not confer with {❺ *name of opposing counsel*} on the merits of {❻ *specify motion or other matter in dispute*} because {❼ *state reasons for inability to confer*}.

Therefore, this matter is presented to the Court for determination.

{*CERTIFICATE VERSION 3 – DALLAS COUNTY*}

I certify that

{*CHOOSE APPROPRIATE STATEMENT*}

Ⓐ counsel for movant and counsel for respondent have personally conducted a conference at which there was a substantive discussion of every item presented to the Court in this motion and despite best efforts the counsel have not been able to resolve those matters presented.

Ⓑ counsel for movant has personally attempted to contact the counsel for respondent to resolve the matters presented as follows: {❽ *identify dates, times, methods of contact, and results*}. Counsel for the movant has caused to be delivered to counsel for respondent and counsel for respondent has received a copy of the proposed motion. At least one attempt to contact the counsel for respondent followed the receipt by counsel for respondent of the proposed motion. Counsel for respondent has failed to respond or attempt to resolve the matters presented.

C counsel for movant has personally attempted to contact counsel for respondent, as follows: {**9** *identify dates, times, methods of contact, and results*}. An emergency exists of such a nature that further delay would cause irreparable harm to the movant, as follows: {**10** *state details of emergency and harm*}.

D I, the undersigned attorney, hereby certify to the Court that I have conferred with opposing counsel in an effort to resolve the issues contained in this motion without the necessity of Court intervention, and opposing counsel has indicated that {**11** *he/she*} does not oppose this motion.

{*CHOOSE APPROPRIATE PARAGRAPH*}

{*For certificate version 1 & 2*}

Date: ______________, 20___

____
{**12** *Name of attorney*}

{*For certificate version 3*}

Certified to the Day of ______________, 20___, by

____
{**13** *Name of attorney*}

SEE: Tex. R. Civ. P. 3a, 191.2
Dallas Cty. Loc. R. 2.07
Tarrant Cty. Loc. R. 3.06(b)
O'Connor's Texas Rules * Civil Trials (2019), "Certificate of conference," ch. 6-A, §4.2, p. 517

NOTE: Version 1 of the certificate of conference must be included in all motions for discovery or requests for hearings relating to discovery. Tex. R. Civ. P. 191.2. Some local rules also require a certificate of conference on other motions. Version 2 substantially complies with Tarrant County Local Rule 3.06(b). Version 3 complies with Dallas County Local Rule 2.07, which requires the verbatim use of the language stated in the rule. The attorney should make sure the certificate complies with the local rules of the court where the suit is pending.

Nonparties who file motions objecting to discovery must also file a certificate. *See* ***United Servs. Auto. Ass'n v. Thomas***, 893 S.W.2d 628, 629-30 (Tex.App.—Corpus Christi 1994, writ denied).

CERTIFICATE OF SERVICE

{*CHOOSE APPROPRIATE INTRODUCTORY STATEMENT*}

{*For e-service*}

I certify that on {❶ *date*}, I served a copy of {❷ *name of document*} on the {❸ *party/parties*} listed below by electronic service and that the electronic transmission was reported as complete. My e-mail address is {❹ *e-mail address*}.

{*For other types of service*}

I certify that on {❺ *date*}, I served a copy of {❻ *name of document*} on the {❼ *party/parties*} listed below by {❽ *U.S. Mail/personal delivery by {me/my agent}/commercial delivery service by {identify type of delivery service, e.g., FedEx}/fax/e-mail/{identify other type of service}*}:

{❾ *Name of attorney or pro se party*}
{❿ *Address 1*}
{⓫ *Address 2*}
{⓬ *City, state, zip code*}
{⓭ *Add if appropriate: {Fax number}*}
{⓮ *Add if appropriate: {E-mail address}*}
Attorney for {⓯ *name of party*}, {⓰ *party*}

{*For multiple parties, repeat until all parties and methods of service are identified.*}

____
{⓱ *Name of attorney*}

SEE: Tex. R. Civ. P. 21(d), 21a(a)
O'Connor's Texas Rules * Civil Trials (2019), "Certificate of service," ch. 1-B, §3.2.13, p. 12; "Methods of service," ch. 1-D, §4.2, p. 41

NOTE: E-filing is mandatory for all nonjuvenile civil cases in most courts in all counties. *See* Tex. R. Civ. P. 21 cmt.; Tex.Sup.Ct. Order, Misc. Docket No. 13-9164 (Dec. 9, 2013). See ***O'Connor's Texas Rules***, "E-filing," ch. 1-C, §4.1.1, p. 25. If a document is e-filed, a party must serve it electronically through the electronic-filing manager (EFM), as long as the EFM has on file the e-mail address of the attorney or unrepresented party to be served. Tex. R. Civ. P. 21a(a)(1). If the e-mail address is not on file or if the document was not e-filed, a party may serve the document by (1) mail, (2) personal delivery, (3) commercial delivery, (4) fax, (5) e-mail, or (6) any other method as ordered by the court. Tex. R. Civ. P. 21a(a). See ***O'Connor's Texas Rules***, "Methods of service," ch. 1-D, §4.2, p. 41.

The certificate of service must be signed by the attorney or the party, not the attorney's secretary. *See* Tex. R. Civ. P. 21a(e). Pleadings that are e-filed or e-served must include an electronic signature. See ***O'Connor's Texas Rules***, "Electronic signature," ch. 1-B, §3.2.12(2)(b), p. 11.

Documents received by fax after 5:00 p.m. local time of the recipient are deemed served on the following day. Tex. R. Civ. P. 21a(b)(2). See ***O'Connor's Texas Rules***, "Fax," ch. 1-D, §6.4, p. 44.

Although the certificate of service does not need to specify the method of service used, this information should be included in case of a deadline dispute. *See* ***Approximately $14,980.00 v. State***, 261 S.W.3d 182, 187 (Tex.App.—Houston [14th Dist.] 2008, no pet.).

{❶ *PARTY*}'S NOTICE OF {❷ *CURRENT/CHANGE OF*} ADDRESS

{❸ *Party*}, {❹ *name*}, files this notice of {❺ *current/change of*} address with the court clerk as required by Texas Civil Practice & Remedies Code section 30.015.

{*CHOOSE APPROPRIATE STATEMENT*}

{❻ *Party*}'s current residence is {❼ *address*}.

{❽ *Party*}'s current business address is {❾ *address*}.

{❿ *Party*}'s {⓫ *residential/business*} address, {⓬ *identify former address*}, has changed. The new {⓭ *residential/business*} address is {⓮ *identify new address*}.

SEE: Tex. Civ. Prac. & Rem. Code §30.015
O'Connor's Texas Rules * Civil Trials (2019), "Notice of party's name & address," ch. 1-B, §3.2.18, p. 15

ADD: STYLE OF THE CASE – FORM 1B:2
SIGNATURE BLOCK – FORM 1B:3
CERTIFICATE OF SERVICE – FORM 1B:13

NOTE: Each party's name and address must be provided to the clerk in writing when the party files its initial pleading or within seven days after the clerk requests the information, and whenever the party changes its address. *See* Tex. Civ. Prac. & Rem. Code §30.015(a), (c), (d).

NOTICE OF CHANGE OF ATTORNEY'S ADDRESS

{❶ *Name of attorney*}, counsel for {❷ *name of party*}, notifies the Court and all counsel of record of {❸ *his/her*} change of address, effective {❹ *date*}. The new address is:

{❺ *Name of firm*}
{❻ *Address 1*}
{❼ *Address 2*}
{❽ *City, state, zip code*}
Tel. {❾ __________}
Fax {❿ __________}
{⓫ *E-mail address*}

SEE: ***O'Connor's Texas Rules * Civil Trials*** (2019), "Caution," ch. 1-H, §6.2, p. 64

ADD: STYLE OF THE CASE – FORM 1B:2
SIGNATURE BLOCK – FORM 1B:3
CERTIFICATE OF SERVICE – FORM 1B:13

DEFENDANT'S MOTION TO
DECLARE PLAINTIFF A VEXATIOUS LITIGANT

Defendant, {❶ *name*}, asks the Court to declare plaintiff a vexatious litigant, to stay the proceedings until the plaintiff provides security for defendant's reasonable expenses, and to prohibit the plaintiff from filing any new suit in Texas without first obtaining permission from a local administrative judge.

INTRODUCTION

1. Plaintiff, {❷ *name*}, sued defendant, {❸ *name*}, for {❹ *state basis of suit*}.

2. {❺ *State other relevant facts about the suit.*}

BACKGROUND

3. {❻ *State facts relevant to the motion.*}

ARGUMENT & AUTHORITIES

4. Under Texas Civil Practice & Remedies Code section 11.054, a plaintiff can be declared a vexatious litigant if the defendant shows there is no reasonable probability that the plaintiff will prevail in the current litigation and one of the following is true:

a. The plaintiff has commenced, prosecuted, or maintained at least five civil actions as a pro se party (excluding suits in small-claims court) in the seven years immediately before the date of this motion that were (1) finally determined against the plaintiff, (2) pending for at least two years without being brought to trial or hearing, or (3) determined by a court to be frivolous or groundless under state or federal law or rules of procedure. Tex. Civ. Prac. & Rem. Code §11.054(1).

b. Another civil action between the parties was finally determined against the plaintiff and the plaintiff, as a pro se party, has repeatedly relitigated or is attempting to relitigate against the same defendant the validity of either the final judgment or the same cause of action, claim, controversy, issues of fact, or issues of law. Tex. Civ. Prac. & Rem. Code §11.054(2).

c. The plaintiff has been declared a vexatious litigant by a state or federal court in an action based on the same or substantially similar facts, transactions, or occurrences. Tex. Civ. Prac. & Rem. Code §11.054(3).

5. If the Court finds that a plaintiff is a vexatious litigant under Texas Civil Practice & Remedies Code section 11.054, the Court (1) must order the plaintiff to post security to assure defendant that it will recover its reasonable expenses, including costs and attorney fees, should the case be dismissed on the merits, and (2) may sign an order prohibiting the plaintiff from filing any new civil action in Texas as a pro se party without first obtaining permission from a local administrative judge. *See* Tex. Civ. Prac. & Rem. Code §§11.055, 11.057, 11.101.

A. There is no reasonable probability that plaintiff will prevail.

6. There is no reasonable probability that plaintiff will prevail in this litigation against defendant. {❼ *Elaborate.*}

{*CHOOSE APPROPRIATE SECTIONS B-D*}

B. Five or more cases have been determined adversely against plaintiff since {❽ *date*}.

7. Since {❾ *date*}, plaintiff, as a pro se party, has commenced, prosecuted, and maintained {❿ *number*} civil actions that were determined adversely against {⓫ *him/her*}. {⓬ *Elaborate and identify civil actions commenced, prosecuted, or maintained by plaintiff.*}

C. Plaintiff is attempting to relitigate issues that were determined adversely against {⓭ *him/her*}.

8. Plaintiff, as a pro se party, is attempting to relitigate {⓮ *the validity of a final judgment/a cause of action/a claim/a controversy/an issue of fact/an issue of law*} that was determined adversely against {⓯ *him/her*} in an earlier action against defendant. {⓰ *Elaborate and identify earlier civil action involving plaintiff and defendant.*}

D. Plaintiff has been declared a vexatious litigant in an earlier action.

9. Plaintiff has been declared a vexatious litigant in an earlier action based on the same or substantially similar facts, transactions, or occurrences. {⓱ *Elaborate and identify earlier action in which plaintiff was declared a vexatious litigant.*}

RELIEF

10. To assure defendant that {⓲ *he/she/it*} will recover reasonable expenses (including costs and attorney fees) should plaintiff's case be dismissed on the merits, defendant asks the Court to order plaintiff to post security in the amount of ${⓳ *amount*} and to stay the proceedings until such payment is made.

Continued on next page

11. In addition to posting security, defendant also asks the Court to sign an order prohibiting plaintiff from filing any new litigation in Texas as a pro se party without first obtaining permission to sue from a local administrative judge.

CONCLUSION

12. {20 *Briefly summarize the motion.*}

PRAYER

13. For these reasons, defendant asks the Court to determine that plaintiff is a vexatious litigant, to stay the proceedings until plaintiff posts security in the amount of ${21 *amount*}, and to sign an order prohibiting plaintiff from filing any new litigation in Texas as a pro se party.

SEE: Tex. Civ. Prac. & Rem. Code §§11.051-11.057, 11.101-11.104
O'Connor's Texas Rules * Civil Trials (2019), "Vexatious litigant," ch. 1-B, §3.4, p. 16

ADD: STYLE OF THE CASE – FORM 1B:2
SIGNATURE BLOCK – FORM 1B:3
CERTIFICATE OF CONFERENCE – FORM 1B:12
CERTIFICATE OF SERVICE – FORM 1B:13

ATTACH: AFFIDAVIT – FORM 1B:8, if necessary
ORDER – FORM 1B:18
NOTICE OF HEARING OR SUBMISSION – FORM 1E:1

NOTE: A defendant must make this motion within 90 days after filing an original answer or a special appearance. Tex. Civ. Prac. & Rem. Code §11.051.

PLAINTIFF'S RESPONSE TO DEFENDANT'S
MOTION TO DECLARE PLAINTIFF A VEXATIOUS LITIGANT

Plaintiff, {❶ *name*}, asks the Court to deny defendant's motion to declare plaintiff a vexatious litigant.

INTRODUCTION

1. Plaintiff, {❷ *name*}, sued defendant, {❸ *name*}, for {❹ *state basis of suit*}.

2. {❺ *State other relevant facts about the suit.*}

BACKGROUND

3. {❻ *State facts relevant to the response.*}

ARGUMENT & AUTHORITIES

4. Under Texas Civil Practice & Remedies Code section 11.054, a plaintiff can be declared a vexatious litigant only if the defendant shows there is no reasonable probability that the plaintiff will prevail in the current litigation and one of the following is true:

a. The plaintiff has commenced, prosecuted, or maintained at least five civil actions as a pro se party (excluding suits in small-claims court) in the seven years immediately before the date of this motion that were (1) finally determined against the plaintiff, (2) pending for at least two years without being brought to trial or hearing, or (3) determined by a court to be frivolous or groundless under state or federal law or rules of procedure. Tex. Civ. Prac. & Rem. Code §11.054(1).

b. Another civil action between the parties was finally determined against the plaintiff and the plaintiff, as a pro se party, has repeatedly relitigated or is attempting to relitigate against the same defendant the validity of either the final judgment or the same cause of action, claim, controversy, issues of fact, or issues of law. Tex. Civ. Prac. & Rem. Code §11.054(2).

c. The plaintiff has been declared a vexatious litigant by a state or federal court in an action based on the same or substantially similar facts, transactions, or occurrences. Tex. Civ. Prac. & Rem. Code §11.054(3).

Continued on next page

{ADD PARAGRAPH 5 IF APPLICABLE}

5. A motion to declare a plaintiff a vexatious litigant under Texas Civil Practice & Remedies Code section 11.054 must be filed within 90 days after the defendant files its original answer or makes a special appearance. Tex. Civ. Prac. & Rem. Code §11.051.

{ADD SECTION A IF APPLICABLE}

A. Defendant's motion was untimely filed.

6. The Court should deny defendant's motion to declare plaintiff a vexatious litigant because the motion was untimely filed. On {❼ *date*}, defendant filed {❽ *an answer/a special appearance*}. On {❾ *date*}, defendant filed a motion to declare plaintiff a vexatious litigant, which is more than 90 days after the {❿ *an answer/a special appearance*} was filed.

B. Plaintiff has a reasonable probability of prevailing on the merits.

7. Contrary to defendant's motion, plaintiff has a reasonable probability of prevailing on the merits against defendant. {⓫ *Elaborate.*}

{CHOOSE APPROPRIATE SECTIONS C-E}

C. Five or more cases have not been determined adversely against plaintiff since {⓬ *date*}.

8. Contrary to defendant's motion, plaintiff has not commenced, prosecuted, or maintained at least five lawsuits as a pro se party over the past seven years that were determined adversely against {⓭ *him/her*}. {⓮ *Elaborate.*}

D. Plaintiff is not attempting to relitigate issues determined adversely against {⓯ *him/her*}.

9. Contrary to defendant's motion, plaintiff is not, as a pro se party, attempting to relitigate {⓰ *the validity of a final judgment/a cause of action/a claim/a controversy/an issue of fact/an issue of law*} that was determined adversely against plaintiff in an earlier action against defendant. {⓱ *Elaborate.*}

E. Plaintiff has not been declared a vexatious litigant in an earlier action.

10. Contrary to defendant's motion, plaintiff has not been declared a vexatious litigant by a state or federal court in an action based on the same or substantially similar facts, transactions, or occurrences. {⓲ *Elaborate.*}

CONCLUSION

11. {⓳ *Briefly summarize the response.*}

PRAYER

12. For these reasons, plaintiff asks the Court to deny defendant's motion to declare plaintiff a vexatious litigant.

SEE: Tex. Civ. Prac. & Rem. Code §§11.051-11.057, 11.101-11.104
O'Connor's Texas Rules * Civil Trials (2019), "Vexatious litigant," ch. 1-B, §3.4, p. 16

ADD: STYLE OF THE CASE – FORM 1B:2
SIGNATURE BLOCK – FORM 1B:3
CERTIFICATE OF SERVICE – FORM 1B:13

ATTACH: AFFIDAVIT – FORM 1B:8, if necessary
ORDER – FORM 1B:18

ORDER ON DEFENDANT'S MOTION TO DECLARE PLAINTIFF A VEXATIOUS LITIGANT

After considering defendant {❶ *name*}'s motion to declare plaintiff, {❷ *name*}, a vexatious litigant, plaintiff's response, the evidence presented at the hearing, and the arguments of counsel, the Court

{*CHOOSE APPROPRIATE ORDER*}

DENIES the motion.

GRANTS the motion, declares plaintiff a vexatious litigant, and orders as follows:

1. Plaintiff must furnish security for the benefit of defendant, {❸ *name*}, by {❹ *state how plaintiff is to provide security, e.g., posting a surety bond with the court clerk*} in the amount of ${❺ *amount*} by {❻ *date*}. The security is to assure payment to the defendant for reasonable expenses, including {❼ *his/her/its*} court costs and attorney fees, should the case be dismissed on the merits.

2. If plaintiff does not furnish security within the time limit set by this order, the Court will dismiss this suit with prejudice against plaintiff.

3. This suit will remain in abatement until plaintiff complies with this order or until it is dismissed by further order of this Court.

4. Plaintiff must not file as a pro se party any new litigation in a court in Texas against {❽ *state scope of prohibition, e.g., any party, the defendant and its agents, directors, officers, employees, heirs, assigns*} without first obtaining permission from the appropriate local administrative judge as required by Texas Civil Practice & Remedies Code section 11.102(a).

5. As required by Texas Civil Practice & Remedies Code section 11.104, the court clerk will provide a copy of this order to the Office of Court Administration of the Texas Judicial System.

SIGNED on _______________, 20___.

____
PRESIDING JUDGE

Form 1B:18 Vexatious Litigant – Order

SEE: Tex. Civ. Prac. & Rem. Code §§11.051-11.057, 11.101-11.104
O'Connor's Texas Rules * Civil Trials (2019), "Vexatious litigant," ch. 1-B, §3.4, p. 16

ADD: STYLE OF THE CASE – FORM 1B:2
CERTIFICATE OF SERVICE – FORM 1B:13, if proposed order served separately from motion or response

NOTE: If a district or statutory county court signs the order, the order applies to all Texas state courts; if a justice court or constitutional county court signs the order, the order applies only to the court that entered the order. *See* Tex. Civ. Prac. & Rem. Code §11.101(d), (e).

DEFENDANT'S NOTICE TO CLERK OF MISTAKEN FILING OF LITIGATION SUBJECT TO PREFILING ORDER

This notice is to inform the court clerk that on {❶ *date*}, the clerk mistakenly filed plaintiff {❷ *name*}'s suit against defendant, {❸ *name*}. Plaintiff, who is pro se, has previously been declared a vexatious litigant and is subject to a prefiling order, attached as Exhibit {❹ *letter*}, which prohibits {❺ *him/her*} from filing new litigation as a pro se party without first obtaining permission from the appropriate local administrative judge. Plaintiff has not obtained permission to file suit from the local administrative judge; thus, plaintiff's suit should not have been filed.

Defendant asks the clerk to notify the Court of the mistaken filing within one business day of receipt of this notice, as required by Texas Civil Practice & Remedies Code section 11.1035(b), so that the Court can immediately stay the litigation. Defendant further asks the Court to dismiss the suit if plaintiff does not obtain permission to file the suit from the appropriate local administrative judge within ten days after the filing of this notice.

SEE: Tex. Civ. Prac. & Rem. Code §§11.103, 11.1035
O'Connor's Texas Rules * Civil Trials (2019), "Vexatious litigant," ch. 1-B, §3.4, p. 16

ADD: STYLE OF THE CASE – FORM 1B:2
SIGNATURE BLOCK – FORM 1B:3
CERTIFICATE OF SERVICE – FORM 1B:13

ATTACH: Prefiling order

NOTE: If the court clerk mistakenly files pro se litigation subject to a prefiling order, any party can file with the clerk and serve on all parties to the litigation a notice showing that the plaintiff is a vexatious litigant required to obtain permission under Texas Civil Practice & Remedies Code §11.102. Tex. Civ. Prac. & Rem. Code §11.1035(a).

{[1] *PARTY*}'S MOTION TO EXTEND TIME

{[2] *Party*}, {[3] *name*}, asks the Court to extend the time to {[4] *describe required act*}, as allowed by Texas Rule of Civil Procedure 5.

INTRODUCTION

1. Plaintiff, {[5] *name*}, sued defendant, {[6] *name*}, for {[7] *state basis of suit*}.

2. {[8] *State other relevant facts about the suit.*}

BACKGROUND

3. {[9] *Describe the circumstances that triggered the act that party must perform.*}

4. {[10] *Party*} {[11] *must/was required to*} {[12] *describe required act*} by {[13] *date*}.

5. {[14] *State other facts relevant to the motion.*}

6. {[15] *Party*} asks the Court to extend the deadline until {[16] *date*}.

ARGUMENT & AUTHORITIES

{*CHOOSE APPROPRIATE PARAGRAPH 7*}

{*To request additional time before deadline*}

7. A court can grant a party an extension of time to perform an act "for cause shown" when the party seeks the extension before the deadline to act has expired. Tex. R. Civ. P. 5. {[17] *Party*} asks the Court to grant more time to {[18] *describe required act*} because {[19] *state facts that show cause, e.g., the area of law for the memorandum is complex and requires additional research that cannot be completed before the deadline*}.

{*To request additional time after deadline*}

7. A court can grant a party an extension of time to perform an act "for good cause" when the party seeks the extension after the deadline to act has expired. Tex. R. Civ. P. 5. {[20] *Party*} asks the Court to grant more time to {[21] *describe required act*} because {[22] *state facts that show good cause, e.g., the attorney was in a car accident and was unable to finish the response in time to file it by the deadline*}.

8. {[23] *Party*} requests an extension of time for the reasons stated in this motion, not to delay these proceedings.

Continued on next page

CONCLUSION

9. {㉔ *Briefly summarize the motion.*}

PRAYER

10. For these reasons, {㉕ *party*} asks the Court to set this motion for hearing and, after the hearing, grant {㉖ *his/her/its*} motion to extend the time to {㉗ *describe required act*} and extend the deadline until {㉘ *date*}.

SEE: Tex. R. Civ. P. 5
O'Connor's Texas Rules * Civil Trials (2019), "Motion to extend time," ch. 1-C, §9.1, p. 36

ADD: STYLE OF THE CASE – FORM 1B:2
SIGNATURE BLOCK – FORM 1B:3
CERTIFICATE OF CONFERENCE – FORM 1B:12, if necessary
CERTIFICATE OF SERVICE – FORM 1B:13

ATTACH: AFFIDAVIT – FORM 1B:8, if necessary
NOTICE OF HEARING OR SUBMISSION – FORM 1E:1
ORDER – FORM 1G:1

NOTE: If the motion states facts outside the record, it must be supported by an affidavit. For a motion to extend the time to respond to discovery, see FORM 6A:2. For a motion to delay a trial setting or hearing, see FORMS 5D:1 and 5D:2.

For good cause, a party can request to have the 45-day deadline for providing an English translation of foreign-language text shortened or extended. Tex. R. Evid. 1009(f).

{[1] *PARTY*}'S RESPONSE TO
{[2] *ADVERSE PARTY*}'S MOTION TO EXTEND TIME

{[3] *Party*}, {[4] *name*}, asks the Court to deny {[5] *adverse party*}'s motion to extend the time to {[6] *describe required act*}.

INTRODUCTION

1. Plaintiff, {[7] *name*}, sued defendant, {[8] *name*}, for {[9] *state basis of suit*}.

2. {[10] *State other relevant facts about the suit.*}

BACKGROUND

3. {[11] *Describe the circumstances that triggered the act that adverse party must perform.*}

4. {[12] *Adverse party*} {[13] *must/was required to*} {[14] *describe required act*} by {[15] *date*}. {[16] *Adverse party*} asked the Court to extend the deadline until {[17] *date*}.

5. {[18] *State other facts relevant to the response.*}

ARGUMENT & AUTHORITIES

{*CHOOSE APPROPRIATE PARAGRAPH 6*}

{*Request made before deadline*}

6. A court should not grant a party an extension of time to perform an act when the party seeks the extension before the deadline to act has expired unless the party shows cause for the extension. Tex. R. Civ. P. 5. The Court should deny {[19] *adverse party*}'s motion to extend time because the motion does not show cause for the extension. {[20] *Explain why adverse party's motion does not show any reason to extend time.*}

{*Request made after deadline*}

6. A court should not grant a party an extension of time to perform an act when the party seeks the extension after the deadline to act has expired unless the party shows good cause for the extension. Tex. R. Civ. P. 5. The Court should deny {[21] *adverse party*}'s motion to extend time because the motion does not show good cause for the extension. {[22] *Explain why adverse party's motion does not show good cause, e.g., the reasons amount to inexcusable neglect or intentional delay.*}

CONCLUSION

7. {[23] *Briefly summarize the response.*}

◄ *Continued on next page* ►

PRAYER

8. For these reasons, {㉔ *party*} asks the Court to deny {㉕ *adverse party*}'s motion to extend the time to {㉖ *describe required act*}.

SEE: Tex. R. Civ. P. 5
O'Connor's Texas Rules * Civil Trials (2019), "Motion to extend time," ch. 1-C, §9.1, p. 36

ADD: STYLE OF THE CASE – FORM 1B:2
SIGNATURE BLOCK – FORM 1B:3
CERTIFICATE OF CONFERENCE – FORM 1B:12, if necessary
CERTIFICATE OF SERVICE – FORM 1B:13

ATTACH: AFFIDAVIT – FORM 1B:8, if necessary
ORDER – FORM 1G:1

NOTE: If the response states facts outside the record, it must be supported by an affidavit.

NOTICE OF {❶ *HEARING ON/ SUBMISSION OF*} {❷ *PARTY*}'S {❸ *NAME OF MOTION*}

{*CHOOSE APPROPRIATE STATEMENT*}

{*For in-court hearing*}

The attached {❹ *name of motion*} has been filed and will be submitted to the Court for consideration at a hearing on {❺ *date*}, at {❻ *time*}.

{*For telephone hearing*}

The attached {❼ *name of motion*} has been filed and will be submitted to the Court for consideration at a telephone hearing on {❽ *date*}, at {❾ *time*}. Please contact the court clerk before this date to make arrangements for the hearing.

{*For submission without oral hearing*}

The attached {❿ *name of motion*} has been filed and will be submitted to the Court for consideration, without a hearing, on {⓫ *date*}. The Court will rule on the motion without a hearing unless you request one.

SEE: Tex. R. Jud. Admin. 7(a)(6)(b)
O'Connor's Texas Rules * Civil Trials (2019), "Notice of Hearing," ch. 1-E, §2, p. 47; "Hearing on Motion," ch. 1-E, §4, p. 48

ADD: STYLE OF THE CASE – FORM 1B:2
SIGNATURE BLOCK – FORM 1B:3
CERTIFICATE OF SERVICE – FORM 1B:13

NOTE: **The procedure for securing a hearing can differ from court to court, so check the court's local rules. For example, some courts require a party to request a hearing and submit an order setting a hearing date, while others require a party to set a motion for submission and then request a hearing.**

{❶ *PARTY*}'S REQUEST TO COURT REPORTER
TO MAKE A FULL RECORD & PRESERVE ALL NOTES

{❷ *Party*}, {❸ *name*}, asks the court reporter to make a full record of all hearings and to preserve the notes and recordings from all proceedings in this case.

INTRODUCTION

1. Plaintiff, {❹ *name*}, sued defendant, {❺ *name*}, for {❻ *state basis of suit*}.

2. {❼ *State other relevant facts about the suit.*}

3. A copy of this request has been served on the official court reporter, {❽ *name*}, and a copy has been filed with the records of this case.

MAKE A FULL RECORD

4. A court reporter is required to make a full record of the proceedings if requested to do so by a party. Tex. Gov't Code §52.046(a); *Nicholson v. Fifth Third Bank*, 226 S.W.3d 581, 583 (Tex. App.—Houston [1st Dist.] 2007, no pet.); *Nabelek v. Dist. Attorney of Harris Cty.*, 290 S.W.3d 222, 231 (Tex. App.—Houston [14th Dist.] 2005, pet. denied); *Langford v. State*, 129 S.W.3d 138, 139 (Tex. App.—Dallas 2003, no pet.).

5. {❾ *Party*} requests that the court reporter make a full record of all hearings in this case. This includes all pretrial hearings at which evidence is presented, the entire voir dire, all bench conferences, all evidence presented and objections made during hearings and trial, all orally recorded testimony played during trial, the charge conference, the jury argument, the hearing to receive the jury's verdict, and all post-trial hearings.

PRESERVE THE NOTES

6. On request, a court reporter is required to preserve the notes from a hearing or trial for three years from the date they were taken. Tex. Gov't Code §52.046(a)(4); *Piotrowski v. Minns*, 873 S.W.2d 368, 371 (Tex. 1993). When the proceedings are recorded, the court reporter has a duty to preserve the recordings and the reporter's logs for at least three years. *Walker v. Stefanic*, 898 S.W.2d 347, 349 (Tex. App.—San Antonio 1995, no writ).

7. {❿ *Party*} requests that the court reporter preserve the shorthand notes and any recordings of all hearings and the trial in this case for at least three years. Tex. Gov't Code §52.046(a)(4).

SEE: Tex. R. Civ. P. 263
Tex. R. App. P. 13.1(a)
Tex. Gov't Code §52.046(a)
Tex. Fam. Code §105.003(c)
O'Connor's Texas Rules * Civil Trials (2019), "Attend court & make record," ch. 1-E, §3.1, p. 47; "Preserve notes," ch. 1-E, §3.3, p. 48

ADD: STYLE OF THE CASE – FORM 1B:2
SIGNATURE BLOCK – FORM 1B:3
CERTIFICATE OF SERVICE – FORM 1B:13

NOTE: To avoid the loss or destruction of the reporter's record, request a transcript immediately after the hearing or other proceeding.

The appellate courts are split on whether a party or the court reporter bears the burden to ensure that trial proceedings are recorded. Some courts follow Texas Rule of Appellate Procedure 13.1(a), which requires the court reporter to make a record of the proceedings unless excused by an agreement of the parties. *E.g.*, ***Rittenhouse v. Sabine Valley Ctr. Found.***, 161 S.W.3d 157, 161-62 (Tex.App.—Texarkana 2005, no pet.). Other courts hold that Rule 13.1(a) is trumped by Texas Government Code §52.046(a), which requires the court reporter to make a record only if requested by a party. *E.g.*, ***Nicholson v. Fifth Third Bank***, 226 S.W.3d 581, 583 (Tex.App.—Houston [1st Dist.] 2007, no pet.). See ***O'Connor's Texas Rules***, "Attend court & make record," ch. 1-E, §3.1, p. 47.

{❶ *PARTY*}'S MOTION TO PRESERVE COURT REPORTER'S NOTES

{❷ *Party*}, {❸ *name*}, asks the Court for an order requiring the court reporter to preserve the notes and recordings from all proceedings in this case.

INTRODUCTION

1. Plaintiff, {❹ *name*}, sued defendant, {❺ *name*}, for {❻ *state basis of suit*}.

2. {❼ *State other relevant facts about the suit.*}

3. A copy of this motion has been served on the official court reporter, {❽ *name*}, and a copy has been filed in the records of this case.

BACKGROUND

4. {❾ *State facts relevant to the motion.*}

ARGUMENT & AUTHORITIES

5. After three years, a court reporter may dispose of notes or recordings if no party has taken steps to ensure that they are preserved, *See* Tex. Gov't Code §52.046(a)(4); *Piotrowski v. Minns*, 873 S.W.2d 368, 371 (Tex. 1993).

6. {❿ *Party*} served a request on the court reporter to preserve all notes and recordings for three years and filed it with the Court on {⓫ *date*}. The three-year period has almost expired, and this case has not been concluded. Thus, {⓬ *party*} asks the Court to sign an order requiring the court reporter to preserve the notes until this case is concluded.

PRAYER

7. For these reasons, {⓭ *party*} asks the Court to require the court reporter to preserve the notes and recordings from this case until the Court orders otherwise.

SEE: Tex. Gov't Code §52.046(a)(4)
Tex. Fam. Code §105.003(c)
O'Connor's Texas Rules * Civil Trials (2019), "Preserve notes," ch. 1-E, §3.3, p. 48

ADD: STYLE OF THE CASE – FORM 1B:2
SIGNATURE BLOCK – FORM 1B:3
CERTIFICATE OF SERVICE – FORM 1B:13

ATTACH: AFFIDAVIT – FORM 1B:8, if necessary
ORDER – FORM 1G:1

NOTE: To avoid the loss or destruction of the reporter's record, request a transcript immediately after the hearing or other proceeding.

ORDER ON {❶ *PARTY*}'S {❷ *NAME OF MOTION*}

After considering {❸ *party*} {❹ *name*}'s {❺ *name of motion*}

{*CHOOSE APPROPRIATE STATEMENT*}

Ⓐ and the response, the Court

Ⓑ , the response, and the evidence on file, the Court

Ⓒ , the response, the evidence on file, and arguments of counsel, the Court

Ⓓ , the response, and arguments of counsel, the Court

Ⓔ , the response, and arguments of counsel, and after receiving evidence in open court, the Court

{*CHOOSE APPROPRIATE ORDER*}

DENIES the motion.

GRANTS the motion and {❻ *identify the relief requested in the motion*}.

SIGNED on _______________, 20___.

____
PRESIDING JUDGE

SEE: ***O'Connor's Texas Rules * Civil Trials*** (2019), "Order," ch. 1-G, §4, p. 58

ADD: STYLE OF THE CASE – FORM 1B:2
CERTIFICATE OF SERVICE – FORM 1B:13, if proposed order served separately from motion or response

NOTE: Some rules require that findings be included in the order. *E.g.*, Tex. R. Civ. P. 13 (order must contain findings of good cause for sanctions). Other rules state that findings cannot be included in the order or judgment. *E.g.*, Tex. R. Civ. P. 299a (findings of fact cannot be included in judgment).

DESIGNATION OF {❶ *NAME*} AS ATTORNEY IN CHARGE

1. {❷ *Party*}, {❸ *name*}, designates {❹ *name of attorney*} as attorney in charge.

2. {❺ *Name of attorney*} will be responsible for this case and will be the attorney who receives all communications from the Court and other parties.

3. Notice of this designation has been provided to all other parties, as required by Texas Rule of Civil Procedure 21a.

SEE: Tex. R. Civ. P. 7, 8, 21a
O'Connor's Texas Rules * Civil Trials (2019), "Attorney in charge," ch. 1-H, §3.1, p. 62

ADD: STYLE OF THE CASE – FORM 1B:2
SIGNATURE BLOCK – FORM 1B:3
CERTIFICATE OF SERVICE – FORM 1B:13

NOTE: The attorney whose signature appears on the first pleading (and at the top of the signature block, if there is more than one attorney) is the "attorney in charge" for that party, unless another attorney is specifically designated. Tex. R. Civ. P. 8.

{❶ *NAME OF NONRESIDENT ATTORNEY*}'S MOTION PRO HAC VICE

I, {❷ *name of nonresident attorney*}, file this motion pro hac vice to appear before the Court, under the authority of the Rules Governing Admission to the Bar of Texas, Rule 19.

BACKGROUND

1. I am associated with {❸ *name of Texas attorney*}, who will personally participate in the hearings and trial of this case. {❹ *Name of Texas attorney*} is a practicing attorney and a member of the State Bar of Texas. {❺ *His/Her*} information is as follows:

Texas Bar No.: ____________________
Address: ____________________
Telephone: ____________________
Fax number: ____________________
E-mail: ____________________

{*CHOOSE APPROPRIATE PARAGRAPH 2*}

2. I am an active member in good standing with the State Bar of {❻ *name of state where licensed*} {❼ *add if appropriate: and the federal courts of {names of federal courts where licensed}*}.

2. I am not an active member but am in good standing with the State Bar of {❽ *name of state where licensed*} {❾ *add if appropriate: and the federal courts of {names of federal courts where licensed}*}.

{*CHOOSE APPROPRIATE PARAGRAPH 3*}

3. I have not been the subject of disciplinary action in the last five years by the bar or courts of any jurisdiction where I have been licensed.

3. The following are the disciplinary actions taken against me in the last five years: {❿ *identify and describe all disciplinary actions taken*}.

{*CHOOSE APPROPRIATE PARAGRAPH 4*}

4. I have not been denied admission to any state or federal court during the last five years.

4. I have been denied admission to the following courts during the last five years: {⓫ *identify and describe all denied admissions, including information for court to which admission was denied*}.

◄ *Continued on next page* ►

5. I am familiar with the State Bar Act, the State Bar Rules, and the Texas Disciplinary Rules of Professional Conduct governing the conduct of members of the State Bar of Texas. I will at all times abide by and comply with these rules as long as this case is pending and I have not withdrawn as counsel from the proceeding.

{*CHOOSE APPROPRIATE PARAGRAPH 6*}

6. I have not appeared or sought leave to appear in Texas courts in the last two years.

6. The cases in which I have appeared or sought leave to appear in Texas courts in the last two years are as follows:

Caption	Court	Cause No.

7. My office address, telephone number, fax number, and e-mail address are included below my signature.

PRAYER

8. For these reasons, I ask this Court to grant my motion pro hac vice and allow me to appear before this Court until the conclusion of this case.

____
{⓬ *Name of nonresident attorney*}
{⓭ *Name of state where licensed*}
Bar No. {⓮ *bar number*}
{⓯ *Address*}
{⓰ *City, state, zip code*}
Tel. {⓱ __________}
Fax {⓲ __________}
{⓳ *E-mail address*}

SEE: Tex. R. Civ. P. 7-14
Tex. Gov't Code §§81.102(b), 82.036
Rules Governing Admission to the Bar of Texas, Rule 19(a)
O'Connor's Texas Rules * Civil Trials (2019), "Nonresident attorneys," ch. 1-H, §2.2.1, p. 60

ADD: STYLE OF THE CASE – FORM 1B:2
VERIFICATION – FORM 1B:7
CERTIFICATE OF SERVICE – FORM 1B:13

ATTACH: NOTICE OF HEARING OR SUBMISSION – FORM 1E:1
MOTION IN SUPPORT – FORM 1H:3
ORDER – FORM 1H:4
Proof of fee payment

NOTE: A nonresident attorney requesting permission to appear in a Texas state court must pay a $250 fee for each case in which the attorney wants to participate. Tex. Gov't Code §82.0361(b). The nonresident attorney must pay the fee to the Board of Law Examiners before filing the motion pro hac vice. *Id.* Once payment is received, the Board of Law Examiners will send the attorney a nonresident acknowledgment letter, acknowledging that the fee has been paid. The letter will serve as proof of payment and should be attached to the motion. *See id.* §82.0361(f).

The Rules Governing Admission to the Bar of Texas, Rule 19, "Requirements for Participation in Texas Proceedings by a Non-Resident Attorney," can be found on the Texas Board of Law Examiners website at https://ble.texas.gov/rules.

{❶ *NAME OF TEXAS ATTORNEY*}'S MOTION IN SUPPORT OF
{❷ *NAME OF NONRESIDENT ATTORNEY*}'S MOTION PRO HAC VICE

I, {❸ *name of Texas attorney*}, file this motion in support of {❹ *name of nonresident attorney*}'s motion pro hac vice to appear before the Court.

BACKGROUND

1. I am associated with {❺ *name of nonresident attorney*} on this case. I am employed as an attorney on this case and will personally participate in the hearings and trial.

2. I am a practicing attorney and a member in good standing with the State Bar of Texas. My State Bar number, office address, telephone number, fax number, and e-mail address are included below my signature.

3. {❻ *Name of nonresident attorney*} is a reputable attorney in {❼ *his/her*} state, and I recommend that the Court permit {❽ *him/her*} to appear in this case.

PRAYER

4. For these reasons, I ask this Court to grant {❾ *name of nonresident attorney*}'s motion pro hac vice and allow {❿ *him/her*} to appear before this Court in this case.

SEE: Tex. R. Civ. P. 7-14
Tex. Gov't Code §§81.102(b), 82.036
Rules Governing Admission to the Bar of Texas, Rule 19(b)
O'Connor's Texas Rules * Civil Trials (2019), "Nonresident attorneys," ch. 1-H, §2.2.1, p. 60

ADD: STYLE OF THE CASE – FORM 1B:2
SIGNATURE BLOCK – FORM 1B:3
VERIFICATION – FORM 1B:7
CERTIFICATE OF SERVICE – FORM 1B:13

NOTE: The Rules Governing Admission to the Bar of Texas, Rule 19, "Requirements for Participation in Texas Proceedings by a Non-Resident Attorney," can be found on the Texas Board of Law Examiners website at https://ble.texas.gov/rules.

ORDER ON {❶ *NAME OF NONRESIDENT ATTORNEY*}'S MOTION PRO HAC VICE

After considering {❷ *name of nonresident attorney*}'s motion pro hac vice and {❸ *name of Texas attorney*}'s motion in support, the Court

{*CHOOSE APPROPRIATE ORDER*}

DENIES the motion.

GRANTS the motion and declares that {❹ *name of nonresident attorney*} is admitted to this Court pro hac vice with all the rights and privileges of an attorney in the State of Texas.

SIGNED on _______________, 20___.

____
PRESIDING JUDGE

SEE: Tex. R. Civ. P. 7-14
Tex. Gov't Code §§81.102(b), 82.036
Rules Governing Admission to the Bar of Texas, Rule 19(b)
O'Connor's Texas Rules * Civil Trials (2019), "Nonresident attorneys," ch. 1-H, §2.2.1, p. 60

ADD: STYLE OF THE CASE – FORM 1B:2
CERTIFICATE OF SERVICE – FORM 1B:13, if proposed order served separately from motion or response

{[1] *NAME OF SUPERVISING LAWYER*}'S MOTION
TO PERMIT THE APPEARANCE OF {[2] *NAME OF NONLAWYER*}

I, {[3] *name of supervising lawyer*}, file this motion to request that the Court permit {[4] *name of nonlawyer*} to appear before the Court on behalf of {[5] *party*}, {[6] *name*}.

QUALIFICATION OF {[7] *NAME OF NONLAWYER*}

{*CHOOSE APPLICABLE PARAGRAPH 1*}

1. {[8] *Name of nonlawyer*} is a qualified unlicensed law-school graduate.

1. {[9] *Name of nonlawyer*} is a qualified law student enrolled in a law school approved by the Texas Supreme Court.

WRITTEN CERTIFICATIONS

2. Attached as Exhibit {[10] *letter*} is the certification by Dean {[11] *name*} of {[12] *name of law school*}, an approved law school, which {[13] *name of nonlawyer*} {[14] *attends/attended*}, stating that the dean has no knowledge of any facts that prevent {[15] *name of nonlawyer*} from meeting the qualifications to take the State Bar examination.

{*CHOOSE APPROPRIATE PARAGRAPH 3*}

3. Dean {[16] *name*} also certified that {[17] *name of nonlawyer*} is a graduate of the law school. {[18] *He/She*} will {[19] *begin/continue*} supervised student practice during the interim between graduation and the first offering of the State Bar examination after {[20] *his/her*} graduation, and during the period after taking the State Bar examination for the first time but before receiving {[21] *his/her*} results.

3. Dean {[22] *name*} also certified that {[23] *name of nonlawyer*} has completed

{*CHOOSE APPROPRIATE STATEMENT*}

[A] two-thirds of the required curriculum for graduation as computed on an hourly basis and is not on scholastic probation.

[B] one-half of the required curriculum for graduation as computed on an hourly basis, is enrolled in a clinical legal-education course for which course credit is awarded, and is not on scholastic probation.

4. Attached as Exhibit {㉔ *letter*} is the certification by {㉕ *name of nonlawyer*} that {㉖ *he/she*} has read and is familiar with the Texas Code of Professional Responsibility, will abide by the Texas Code of Professional Responsibility in activities permitted by these rules, and subjects {㉗ *himself/herself*} to the grievance procedures of the State Bar of Texas.

CONDITIONS FOR APPROVAL

5. {㉘ *Party*}, {㉙ *name*}, has consented to the appearance of {㉚ *name of nonlawyer*} before the Court in this case.

6. A supervising attorney who is licensed to practice law in the State of Texas will accompany {㉛ *name of nonlawyer*} to all of the following: appearances for the purposes of trial, arguments on motions, depositions, and hearings or trials before any administrative tribunal or in any court.

7. The supervising attorney will sign all pleadings filed in this case.

RESPONSIBILITIES OF THE SUPERVISING ATTORNEY

8. As required by Texas Disciplinary Rules of Professional Conduct, Rule 5.03, Responsibilities Regarding Nonlawyer Assistants, and as the lawyer having direct supervisory authority over {㉜ *name of nonlawyer*}, I will make reasonable efforts to ensure that {㉝ *name of nonlawyer*}'s conduct is compatible with the professional obligations of a lawyer.

9. I recognize that I will be subject to discipline for any conduct of {㉞ *name of nonlawyer*} that would be a violation of the Texas Disciplinary Rules of Professional Conduct if I order, encourage, or permit the conduct or if I knowingly fail to take reasonable remedial action to avoid or mitigate the consequences of the nonlawyer's misconduct when I have knowledge of the misconduct.

10. I have been licensed as a lawyer by the Texas Supreme Court for more than three years.

11. I am registered with the General Counsel of the State Bar in compliance with the provisions of section VI of the Rules and Regulations Governing the Participation of Qualified Law Students and Qualified Unlicensed Law School Graduates in the Trial of Cases in Texas.

Continued on next page

12. I have demonstrated to the satisfaction of the General Counsel of the State Bar of Texas, by my personal affidavit and upon the certification of local bar officials, that I am skilled in the preparation and trial of cases; ethically, morally, professionally, and financially able to direct and supervise {35 *name of nonlawyer*}; and able to give {36 *him/her*} practical training in the trial of cases.

13. I will personally assume professional responsibility for the direct and immediate supervision of the professional work of {37 *name of nonlawyer*}.

14. I will not supervise at the same time more than four persons qualified as nonlawyers in compliance with the provisions of section V(A)(5) of the Rules and Regulations Governing the Participation of Qualified Law Students and Qualified Unlicensed Law School Graduates in the Trial of Cases in Texas.

{*CHOOSE APPROPRIATE PARAGRAPH 15*}

15. I will maintain professional malpractice and errors-and-omissions insurance covering {38 *name of nonlawyer*}.

15. I am a lawyer protected by governmental immunity in my employment as {39 *identify job, e.g., public prosecutor, assistant public prosecutor*}, so I do not need to maintain professional malpractice and errors-and-omissions insurance.

PRAYER

16. For these reasons, I ask this Court to permit {40 *name of nonlawyer*} to appear before this Court on behalf of {41 *party*}, {42 *name*}.

SEE: Tex. R. Civ. P. 7, 8
Tex. Gov't Code §81.102(b)
Tex. Disc. R. Prof. Conduct 5.02, 5.03
Rules & Regulations Governing the Participation of Qualified Law Students & Qualified Unlicensed Law School Graduates in the Trial of Cases in Texas
O'Connor's Texas Rules * Civil Trials (2019), "Law students & law-school graduates," ch. 1-H, §2.2.3, p. 61

ADD: STYLE OF THE CASE – FORM 1B:2
SIGNATURE BLOCK – FORM 1B:3
VERIFICATION – FORM 1B:7
CERTIFICATE OF SERVICE – FORM 1B:13

ATTACH: NOTICE OF HEARING OR SUBMISSION – FORM 1E:1
ORDER – FORM 1G:1
Certificate by dean of law school
Certificate by law student or law-school graduate

{❶ *NAME OF ATTORNEY*}'S MOTION TO WITHDRAW AS ATTORNEY IN CHARGE

{❷ *Name of withdrawing attorney*} asks this Court to allow {❸ *him/her*} to withdraw as attorney for {❹ *party*}, {❺ *name*}.

INTRODUCTION

1. Plaintiff, {❻ *name*}, sued defendant, {❼ *name*}, for {❽ *state basis of suit*}.

2. {❾ *State other relevant facts about the suit.*}

BACKGROUND

3. {❿ *State facts relevant to the motion.*}

ARGUMENT & AUTHORITIES

4. As required by Texas Rule of Civil Procedure 10, there is good cause for this Court to grant the motion to withdraw because {⓫ *specify reasons for withdrawal*}.

{*CHOOSE APPROPRIATE PARAGRAPHS 5-6*}

{*Withdrawal with substitution of attorney*}

5. {⓬ *Name of substitute attorney*} will be substituted as attorney for {⓭ *party*}. {⓮ *His/Her*} information is as follows:

Texas Bar No.: ____________
Address: ____________
Telephone: ____________
Fax number: ____________
E-mail: ____________

6. {⓯ *Party*} approves the withdrawal and substitution, which are not being done to delay this case.

{*Withdrawal without substitution of attorney*}

5. {⓰ *Name of withdrawing attorney*} has delivered a copy of this motion to {⓱ *party*} and has notified {⓲ *him/her/it*} in writing of {⓳ *his/her/its*} right to object to the motion.

6. {⓴ *Party*} {㉑ *consents/does not consent*} to this motion to withdraw.

◄ *Continued on next page* ►

{ADD PARAGRAPHS 7-8 IF NO SUBSTITUTION}

7. {[22] *Party*}'s last known address is {[23] *state last known address*}.

8. The following is a list of all pending settings and deadlines in this case: {[24] *identify all settings and deadlines*}.

CONCLUSION

9. {[25] *Briefly summarize the motion.*}

PRAYER

10. For these reasons, {[26] *name of withdrawing attorney*} asks this Court to grant {[27] *his/her*} motion to withdraw {[28] *add if appropriate: and substitute {name of substitute attorney} as attorney for {party}*}.

SEE: Tex. R. Civ. P. 10
O'Connor's Texas Rules * Civil Trials (2019), "Withdrawal by attorney," ch. 1-H, §7.2, p. 65

ADD: STYLE OF THE CASE – FORM 1B:2
SIGNATURE BLOCK – FORM 1B:3
VERIFICATION – FORM 1B:7
CERTIFICATE OF SERVICE – FORM 1B:13

ATTACH: NOTICE OF HEARING OR SUBMISSION – FORM 1E:1
ORDER – FORM 1H:7

NOTE: Texas Rule of Civil Procedure 10 does not define good cause, but courts generally view the Texas Disciplinary Rules of Professional Conduct as guidance for determining whether withdrawal is appropriate. *E.g.*, ***In re Marriage of Harrison***, 557 S.W.3d 99, 115-16 (Tex.App.—Houston [14th Dist.] 2018, pet. denied) (good cause for withdrawal based on Tex. Disciplinary R. of Prof'l Conduct 1.15 when attorney alleged that continued representation of client would cause her to violate disciplinary rules).

When the court grants a motion to withdraw and no attorney is substituted, the withdrawing attorney must immediately notify the party in writing of any additional settings or deadlines that the withdrawing attorney knows about at the time of withdrawal. Tex. R. Civ. P. 10.

If the attorney in charge withdraws and another attorney remains or is substituted, the new attorney must be designated as attorney in charge with notice to all other parties under Texas Rule of Civil Procedure 21a. Tex. R. Civ. P. 10. For designation of an attorney in charge, see FORM 1H:1.

ORDER ON {❶ *NAME OF ATTORNEY*}'S MOTION TO WITHDRAW

After considering {❷ *name of withdrawing attorney*}'s motion to withdraw as attorney in charge, the Court

GRANTS the motion and orders {❸ *name of withdrawing attorney*} withdrawn as attorney in charge for {❹ *party*}, {❺ *name*}.

{*INSERT IF APPROPRIATE*}

ORDERS that {❻ *name of substitute attorney*} be substituted as attorney in charge for {❼ *party*}.

SIGNED on _______________, 20___.

____
PRESIDING JUDGE

SEE: Tex. R. Civ. P. 10
O'Connor's Texas Rules * Civil Trials (2019), "Withdrawal by attorney," ch. 1-H, §7.2, p. 65

ADD: STYLE OF THE CASE – FORM 1B:2
CERTIFICATE OF SERVICE – FORM 1B:13, if proposed order served separately from motion

{[1] *PARTY*}'S MOTION REQUESTING
{[2] *NAME OF ATTORNEY*} TO SHOW AUTHORITY TO ACT

{[3] *Party*}, {[4] *name*}, files this verified motion requesting {[5] *name of attorney*} to show {[6] *his/her*} authority to {[7] *prosecute/defend*} this suit on behalf of {[8] *adverse party*}, {[9] *name*}, as allowed by Texas Rule of Civil Procedure 12.

INTRODUCTION

1. Plaintiff, {[10] *name*}, sued defendant, {[11] *name*}, for {[12] *state basis of suit*}.

2. {[13] *State other relevant facts about the suit.*}

BACKGROUND

3. {[14] *Party*} believes that {[15] *name of attorney*} is {[16] *prosecuting/defending*} this suit without the authority of {[17] *adverse party*}.

4. {[18] *State facts sufficient to support belief that the challenged attorney does not have the authority to represent the adverse party.*}

ARGUMENT & AUTHORITIES

5. When a party alleges that an attorney is prosecuting or defending a suit on behalf of another party without authority, the challenged attorney must appear before the court to show his or her authority to act. Tex. R. Civ. P. 12.

6. Under Rule 12, the Court should cite {[19] *name of attorney*} and require {[20] *him/her*} to appear for a hearing to show {[21] *his/her*} authority to {[22] *prosecute/defend*} on behalf of {[23] *adverse party*}.

CONCLUSION

7. {[24] *Briefly summarize the motion.*}

PRAYER

8. For these reasons, {[25] *party*} asks the Court to cite {[26] *name of attorney*} to appear before the Court and show {[27] *his/her*} authority to act on behalf of {[28] *adverse party*}.

SEE: Tex. R. Civ. P. 12
O'Connor's Texas Rules * Civil Trials (2019), "Attorney not authorized," ch. 1-H, §8.2.2(3), p. 72

ADD: STYLE OF THE CASE – FORM 1B:2
SIGNATURE BLOCK – FORM 1B:3
VERIFICATION – FORM 1B:7
CERTIFICATE OF SERVICE – FORM 1B:13

ATTACH: AFFIDAVIT – FORM 1B:8, if necessary
NOTICE OF HEARING OR SUBMISSION – FORM 1E:1
ORDER – FORM 1H:10

NOTE: This motion must be served on the challenged attorney at least ten days before the hearing. Tex. R. Civ. P. 12.

Generally, this motion should be filed before the parties announce ready for trial. Tex. R. Civ. P. 12. However, if a new attorney is substituted after the parties announce ready, the motion may be brought to challenge that attorney. *See **Air Park-Dallas Zoning Cmte. v. Crow-Billingsley Airpark, Ltd.***, 109 S.W.3d 900, 905-06 (Tex.App.—Dallas 2003, no pet.).

{[1] *NAME OF ATTORNEY*}'S RESPONSE TO
{[2] *ADVERSE PARTY*}'S MOTION TO SHOW AUTHORITY TO ACT

{[3] *Name of attorney*} files this response to {[4] *adverse party*} {[5] *name*}'s motion to show authority to act.

INTRODUCTION

1. Plaintiff, {[6] *name*}, sued defendant, {[7] *name*}, for {[8] *state basis of suit*}.

2. {[9] *State other relevant facts about the suit.*}

BACKGROUND

3. {[10] *State facts sufficient to show that the challenged attorney has authority to act on behalf of the party.*}

ARGUMENT & AUTHORITIES

4. When a party alleges that an attorney is prosecuting or defending a suit on behalf of another party without authority, the challenged attorney is required to appear before the court to show his or her authority to act. Tex. R. Civ. P. 12; *Boudreau v. Fed. Tr. Bank*, 115 S.W.3d 740, 741 (Tex. App.—Dallas 2003, pet. denied). Once the challenged attorney shows his or her authority, the court should allow the attorney to appear in the case. *See* Tex. R. Civ. P. 12; *Boudreau*, 115 S.W.3d at 741.

5. {[11] *Name of attorney*} has sufficient authority to {[12] *prosecute/defend*} this suit on behalf of {[13] *party*}. At a hearing, {[14] *name of attorney*} will provide the following evidence of {[15] *his/her*} authority to {[16] *prosecute/defend*} this suit on behalf of {[17] *party*}: {[18] *summarize evidence that will be presented at the hearing, e.g., a copy of the contract of employment and an affidavit from the client confirming that the attorney was retained*}.

CONCLUSION

6. {[19] *Briefly summarize the response.*}

PRAYER

7. For these reasons, {[20] *name of attorney*} asks the Court to allow {[21] *him/her*} to appear in this suit on behalf of {[22] *party*}.

SEE: Tex. R. Civ. P. 12
O'Connor's Texas Rules * Civil Trials (2019), "Attorney not authorized," ch. 1-H, §8.2.2(3), p. 72

ADD: STYLE OF THE CASE – FORM 1B:2
SIGNATURE BLOCK – FORM 1B:3
VERIFICATION – FORM 1B:7
CERTIFICATE OF SERVICE – FORM 1B:13

ATTACH: AFFIDAVIT – FORM 1B:8, if necessary
ORDER – FORM 1H:10

NOTE: At the hearing, the challenged attorney has the burden to show sufficient authority to prosecute or defend the suit on behalf of the party. Tex. R. Civ. P. 12; ***Boudreau v. Federal Trust Bank***, 115 S.W.3d 740, 741 (Tex.App.—Dallas 2003, pet. denied); ***City of San Antonio v. Aguilar***, 670 S.W.2d 681, 684 (Tex. App.—San Antonio 1984, writ dism'd).

ORDER ON {❶ *PARTY*}'S MOTION TO SHOW AUTHORITY TO ACT

After considering {❷ *party*} {❸ *name*}'s motion to show authority to act, the response, the evidence, and arguments of counsel, the Court

{*CHOOSE APPROPRIATE ORDER*}

DENIES the motion.

GRANTS the motion and orders that {❹ *name of attorney*} may no longer appear in this case on behalf of {❺ *adverse party*}. If no person who is authorized to act appears by __________, 20___, the Court will strike {❻ *adverse party*}'s pleadings.

SIGNED on ________________, 20___.

____
PRESIDING JUDGE

SEE: Tex. R. Civ. P. 12
O'Connor's Texas Rules * Civil Trials (2019), "Attorney not authorized," ch. 1-H, §8.2.2(3), p. 72

ADD: STYLE OF THE CASE – FORM 1B:2
CERTIFICATE OF SERVICE – FORM 1B:13, if proposed order served separately from motion or response

{❶ *PARTY*}'S MOTION TO DISQUALIFY
OPPOSING COUNSEL FOR {❷ *ADVERSE PARTY*}

{❸ *Party*}, {❹ *name*}, asks the Court to disqualify opposing counsel, {❺ *name of attorney or firm*}, from further representation of {❻ *adverse party*}, {❼ *name*}.

INTRODUCTION

1. Plaintiff, {❽ *name*}, sued defendant, {❾ *name*}, for {❿ *state basis of suit*}.

2. {⓫ *State other relevant facts about the suit.*}

BACKGROUND

3. {⓬ *State facts relevant to the motion.*}

ARGUMENT & AUTHORITIES

{*CHOOSE APPROPRIATE SECTIONS A-F*}

A. Disqualification of {⓭ *attorney/firm*} for conflict of interest.

4. An attorney must be disqualified if (1) she personally represented a former client, (2) she is now representing another client in a matter adverse to the former client, (3) she does not have the former client's consent to represent the other client, and (4) any of the following apply:

a. In the pending matter, the client questions the validity of the attorney's services or work performed for the former client. Tex. Disciplinary Rules Prof'l Conduct R. 1.09(a)(1).

b. In the pending matter, the attorney's representation of the client will in reasonable probability involve a violation of Texas Disciplinary Rule of Professional Conduct 1.05, governing the use of a client's confidential information. Tex. Disciplinary Rules Prof'l Conduct R. 1.09(a)(2).

c. The pending matter is the same as or substantially related to the earlier matter. Tex. Disciplinary Rules Prof'l Conduct R. 1.09(a)(3). A matter is "substantially related" when the facts of the earlier representation are so related to the facts in the pending litigation that there is a genuine threat that confidences revealed to former counsel will be divulged to a present adversary. *In re EPIC Holdings, Inc.*, 985 S.W.2d 41, 51 (Tex. 1998); *Metro. Life Ins. Co. v. Syntek Fin. Corp.*, 881 S.W.2d 319, 320-21 (Tex. 1994).

◄ *Continued on next page* ►

{*CHOOSE APPROPRIATE PARAGRAPH 5 IF DISQUALIFYING FIRM*}

5. A firm must be disqualified if a partner or associate of the firm would be disqualified from representing a client under Texas Disciplinary Rule of Professional Conduct 1.09(a). Tex. Disciplinary Rules Prof'l Conduct R. 1.09(b); *Texaco, Inc. v. Garcia*, 891 S.W.2d 255, 256-57 (Tex. 1995); *Henderson v. Floyd*, 891 S.W.2d 252, 253 (Tex. 1995); *see In re Columbia Valley Healthcare Sys., L.P.*, 320 S.W.3d 819, 824 (Tex. 2010).

5. The partners and associates of an attorney's former firm that were associated with the attorney when she left can be disqualified from representing a client if the attorney would be disqualified from representing that client under Texas Disciplinary Rule of Professional Conduct 1.09(a)(1) or (a)(2). Tex. Disciplinary Rules Prof'l Conduct R. 1.09(c) & cmts. 6 & 7; *In re Basco*, 221 S.W.3d 637, 638-39 (Tex. 2007).

{*CHOOSE APPROPRIATE PARAGRAPHS 6-8*}

6. Opposing counsel personally represented {[14] *party*} in an earlier matter and is currently representing {[15] *adverse party*} without {[16] *party*}'s consent. {[17] *State facts supporting grounds for disqualification under Rule 1.09(a), e.g., the earlier matter and the pending matter are substantially related. Specifically, both matters share similar liability issues and similar litigation strategies. Thus, there is a genuine threat that the party's former confidences will be divulged to the opposing party.*} Thus, the Court should disqualify opposing counsel from further representing {[18] *adverse party*} in this case.

7. {[19] *Name of attorney*} personally represented {[20] *party*} in an earlier matter before joining opposing counsel as {[21] *a partner/an associate*}. Opposing counsel is currently representing {[22] *adverse party*} without {[23] *party*}'s consent. {[24] *Name of attorney*} would be disqualified from doing so because {[25] *state facts supporting grounds for disqualification under Rule 1.09(a), e.g., the earlier matter and the pending matter are substantially related. Specifically, both matters share similar liability issues and similar litigation strategies. Thus, there is a genuine threat that party's former confidences will be divulged to adverse party*}. Thus, the Court should disqualify opposing counsel from further representing {[26] *adverse party*} in this case.

8. {[27] *Name of former attorney*} personally represented {[28] *party*} in an earlier matter while {[29] *a partner/an associate*} with opposing counsel. Opposing counsel is currently representing {[30] *adverse party*} without {[31] *party*}'s consent. {[32] *Name of former attorney*} would be disqualified from doing so because {[33] *state facts supporting grounds for disqualification under Rule 1.09(a)(1) or (a)(2)*}. Thus, the Court should disqualify opposing counsel from further representing {[34] *adverse party*} in this case.

B. Disqualification of attorney as participant to joint-defense agreement.

9. An attorney must be disqualified if (1) she participated in the joint defense of two or more parties, one of whom is adverse to the attorney's client in a current matter, (2) confidential information has been shared, and (3) the matter in which the information was shared is substantially related to the matter in which disqualification is sought. *See Nat'l Med. Enters., Inc. v. Godbey*, 924 S.W.2d 123, 129, 132 (Tex. 1996); *In re Skiles*, 102 S.W.3d 323, 327 (Tex. App.—Beaumont 2003, orig. proceeding); *Rio Hondo Implement Co. v. Euresti*, 903 S.W.2d 128, 132 (Tex. App.—Corpus Christi 1995, orig. proceeding). {*See* ***O'Connor's Texas Rules****, "Attorney assumed duty to preserve nonclient's confidences," ch. 1-H, §8.2.2(1), p. 71.*}

10. Opposing counsel personally represented {35 *name of person or entity*} in {36 *identify earlier matter*}. In that matter, opposing counsel was subject to a joint-defense agreement between {37 *name of person or entity*} and {38 *party*}. Under the joint-defense agreement, opposing counsel agreed to keep shared information confidential. {39 *Explain nature of counsel's duty of confidentiality.*} While representing {40 *name of person or entity*}, opposing counsel obtained confidential information from {41 *party*}'s counsel. The matter in which the information was shared is substantially related to the pending matter because {42 *explain how matters are substantially related*}. {43 *Party*} has not consented to the disclosure of that information; thus, opposing counsel should be disqualified. {44 *State any additional facts supporting disqualification.*}

C. Disqualification of attorney as witness.

11. An attorney is disqualified from acting as an attorney in the case if she becomes a witness. *Mauze v. Curry*, 861 S.W.2d 869, 870 (Tex. 1993). An attorney can be disqualified if

{*CHOOSE APPROPRIATE GROUND*}

A (1) her testimony is or may be necessary to establish an essential fact on behalf of her client, and (2) her role as both advocate and witness will cause actual prejudice to the party seeking disqualification. Tex. Disciplinary Rules Prof'l Conduct R. 3.08(a) & cmt. 4; *In re Sanders*, 153 S.W.3d 54, 56-57 (Tex. 2004); *Ayres v. Canales*, 790 S.W.2d 554, 557-58 (Tex. 1990); *In re Guidry*, 316 S.W.3d 729, 738 (Tex. App.—Houston [14th Dist.] 2010, orig. proceeding). An attorney's testimony is necessary on an essential fact when the essential fact cannot be established by other witnesses or other sources in the record. *See In re Sanders*, 153 S.W.3d at 57. {*See* ***O'Connor's Texas Rules****, "Rule 3.08 – attorney as witness," ch. 1-H, §8.2.1(3), p. 70.*}

Continued on next page

B (1) her testimony will be substantially adverse to her client, (2) she has not obtained consent from her client to testify, and (3) her role as both advocate and witness will cause actual prejudice to the party seeking disqualification. Tex. Disciplinary Rules Prof'l Conduct R. 3.08(b) & cmt. 4; *see In re Sanders*, 153 S.W.3d 54, 57 (Tex. 2004); *Ayres v. Canales*, 790 S.W.2d 554, 558 (Tex. 1990). {*See **O'Connor's Texas Rules**, "Rule 3.08 – attorney as witness," ch. 1-H, §8.2.1(3), p. 70.*}

{*CHOOSE APPROPRIATE PARAGRAPH 12*}

12. Opposing counsel has personal knowledge of the following essential facts: {45 *identify essential facts*}. Because there is no other source to establish these essential facts, opposing counsel's testimony is necessary in this case. {46 *Elaborate.*} Opposing counsel's role as both an advocate and a witness will cause {47 *party*} actual prejudice. {48 *Elaborate.*} Thus, the Court should disqualify opposing counsel from further representing {49 *adverse party*} in this case.

12. Opposing counsel may be called as a witness to provide testimony that is substantially adverse to {50 *adverse party*}, and opposing counsel has not obtained {51 *adverse party*}'s consent. Opposing counsel's role as both an advocate and a witness will cause {52 *party*} actual prejudice. {53 *Elaborate.*} Thus, the Court should disqualify opposing counsel from further representing {54 *adverse party*} in this case.

D. Disqualification of attorney in interest of justice for receiving privileged materials outside the normal discovery process.

13. An attorney should be disqualified in the interest of justice when she receives privileged material outside the normal discovery process. *In re Meador*, 968 S.W.2d 346, 351 (Tex. 1998). To determine whether the interest of justice requires disqualification, a court should consider the following factors: (1) whether the attorney knew or should have known the material was privileged, (2) the promptness with which the attorney notified opposing counsel, (3) the extent to which the attorney reviewed and digested the information, (4) the significance of the privileged information, (5) the extent to which the movant may be at fault, and (6) the extent to which the nonmovant will suffer prejudice from the disqualification. *Id.* at 351-52.

14. Opposing counsel obtained privileged material by {55 *explain how material was obtained outside the normal discovery process*}. Opposing counsel should be disqualified in the interest of justice because the factors support disqualification. {56 *Elaborate.*}

E. Disqualification of attorney in interest of justice for receiving privileged materials during the normal discovery process.

15. An attorney should be disqualified in the interest of justice when (1) she receives privileged material during the normal discovery process, (2) the attorney's review of the privileged material causes the opposing party actual harm, and (3) the attorney's disqualification is necessary because there are no lesser means to remedy the harm. *In re Nitla S.A. de C.V.*, 92 S.W.3d 419, 423 (Tex. 2002).

16. Opposing counsel obtained privileged material by {57 *explain how material was obtained during the normal discovery process*}. Opposing counsel should be disqualified in the interest of justice because {58 *his/her*} review of the privileged material has caused {59 *party*} actual harm and there are no lesser means to remedy the harm. {60 *Elaborate.*}

F. Disqualification of firm for employee's conflict of interest.

{*CHOOSE APPROPRIATE PARAGRAPHS 17-19*}

{*Rebuttable presumption of shared confidences*}

17. An attorney and her firm must be disqualified if one of the firm's nonattorney employees who is working on a pending matter previously worked for another firm and the employee (1) obtained confidential information about the same matter while working at the previous firm and (2) shared that confidential information with her current firm. *In re Turner*, 542 S.W.3d 553, 555-56 (Tex. 2017); *see In re Guar. Ins. Servs., Inc.*, 343 S.W.3d 130, 134-35 (Tex. 2011); *In re Am. Home Prods. Corp.*, 985 S.W.2d 68, 74 (Tex. 1998). If the employee actually worked on the same matter for the previous firm, there is a conclusive presumption that confidences about the matter were obtained during the course of the employee's earlier employment. *In re Turner*, 542 S.W.3d at 556; *see In re Guar. Ins.*, 343 S.W.3d at 134; *Phoenix Founders, Inc. v. Marshall*, 887 S.W.2d 831, 834 (Tex. 1994). There is also a presumption that the employee shared confidential information with her current firm, which can be rebutted only if the firm shows that (1) the employee was given a general instruction not to work on any matter that she worked on during her previous employment and (2) the firm took other reasonable steps to screen the employee from any contact with the matter in question. *In re Turner*, 542 S.W.3d at 556; *In re Guar. Ins.*, 343 S.W.3d at 134. {*See* ***O'Connor's Texas Rules****, "Rule 5.03 – responsibility for nonattorney employee," ch. 1-H, §8.2.1(2), p. 69.*}

18. {61 *Name of employee*} is an employee of opposing counsel and previously worked on this case for {62 *name of former firm*}. {63 *State facts of earlier employment and employee's previous contact with the case.*} Because {64 *name of employee*} actu-

Continued on next page

ally worked on the matter in question during {65 *his/her*} previous employment, there is a conclusive presumption that {66 *he/she*} obtained confidential information about the matter.

19. Because {67 *name of employee*} obtained confidential information about the matter in question during {68 *his/her*} previous employment, there is also a rebuttable presumption that {69 *he/she*} shared confidential information with {70 *his/her*} current firm. In this case, this presumption cannot be rebutted by opposing counsel; thus, the Court should disqualify opposing counsel from further representing {71 *adverse party*}. Specifically, opposing counsel cannot rebut this presumption for the following reasons:

{*CHOOSE APPROPRIATE REASONS*}

a. Opposing counsel did not instruct {72 *name of employee*} not to work on any matter that {73 *he/she*} worked on during {74 *his/her*} previous employment. {75 *Elaborate.*}

b. Opposing counsel did not take reasonable steps to screen {76 *name of employee*} from any contact with the matter in question. {77 *Elaborate.*}

{*Conclusive presumption of shared confidences*}

17. A firm must be disqualified if one of its nonattorney employees who is working on a pending matter previously worked for another firm and the employee (1) obtained confidential information about the same matter while working at the previous firm and (2) shared that confidential information with her current firm. *In re Turner*, 542 S.W.3d 553, 555-56 (Tex. 2017); *see In re Guar. Ins. Servs., Inc.*, 343 S.W.3d 130, 134-35 (Tex. 2011); *In re Am. Home Prods. Corp.*, 985 S.W.2d 68, 74 (Tex. 1998). If the employee actually worked on the same matter for the previous firm, there is a conclusive presumption that confidences about the matter were obtained during the course of the employee's earlier employment. *In re Turner*, 542 S.W.3d at 556; *see In re Guar. Ins.*, 343 S.W.3d at 134; *Phoenix Founders, Inc. v. Marshall*, 887 S.W.2d 831, 834 (Tex. 1994). There is also a presumption that the employee shared confidential information with her current firm, which becomes conclusive if the party seeking disqualification shows that (1) the employee did in fact share confidential information with her current firm, (2) the employee actually performed work, including clerical work, on the matter in question at an attorney's directive, and the attorney reasonably should have known about the conflict of interest, (3) screening the employee from the matter was or would be ineffective, or (4) the employee would necessarily be required to work on the matter in question. *In re Guar. Ins.*, 343 S.W.3d at 135; *In re Columbia Valley Healthcare Sys.*,

L.P., 320 S.W.3d 819, 828 (Tex. 2010); *see In re Turner*, 542 S.W.3d at 557 n.3; *Phoenix Founders*, 887 S.W.2d at 835. If the presumption of shared confidences is not shown to be conclusive, the firm can rebut it only by proving that (1) the employee was given a general instruction not to work on any matter that she worked on during her previous employment and (2) the firm took other reasonable steps to screen the employee from any contact with the matter in question. *In re Turner*, 542 S.W.3d at 556; *In re Guar. Ins.*, 343 S.W.3d at 134. {*See* ***O'Connor's Texas Rules***, *"Rule 5.03 – responsibility for nonattorney employee," ch. 1-H, §8.2.1(2), p. 69.*}

18. {78 *Name of employee*} is an employee of opposing counsel and previously worked on this case for {79 *name of former firm*}. {80 *State facts of earlier employment and employee's previous contact with the case.*} Because {81 *name of employee*} actually worked on the matter in question during {82 *his/her*} previous employment, there is a conclusive presumption that {83 *he/she*} obtained confidential information about the matter.

19. Because {84 *name of employee*} obtained confidential information about the matter in question during {85 *his/her*} previous employment, there is also a presumption that {86 *he/she*} shared confidential information with {87 *his/her*} current firm. In this case, this presumption is conclusive; thus, the Court should disqualify opposing counsel from further representing {88 *adverse party*} in this case. Specifically, this presumption is conclusive for the following reasons:

{*CHOOSE APPROPRIATE REASONS*}

a. {89 *Name of employee*} actually shared confidential information with opposing counsel. {90 *Elaborate.*}

b. {91 *Name of employee*} actually performed work on the matter in question at opposing counsel's directive, and opposing counsel reasonably should have known about the conflict of interest. {92 *Elaborate.*}

c. Screening {93 *name of employee*} from the matter in question {94 *was/would be*} ineffective. {95 *Elaborate.*}

d. {96 *Name of employee*} would necessarily be required to work on the matter in question. {97 *Elaborate.*}

Continued on next page

{ADD PARAGRAPH 20 IF ARGUING THAT PRESUMPTION IS CONCLUSIVE}

20. Even if the Court does not find that the presumption of shared confidences is conclusive, opposing counsel cannot rebut this presumption and thus should be disqualified from further representing {98 *adverse party*} in this case. Specifically, opposing counsel cannot rebut this presumption for the following reasons:

{CHOOSE APPROPRIATE REASONS}

a. Opposing counsel did not instruct {99 *name of employee*} not to work on any matter that {100 *he/she*} worked on during {101 *his/her*} previous employment. {102 *Elaborate.*}

b. Opposing counsel did not take reasonable steps to screen {103 *name of employee*} from any contact with the matter in question. {104 *Elaborate.*}

CONCLUSION

21. {105 *Briefly summarize the motion.*}

PRAYER

22. For these reasons, {106 *party*} asks the Court, after a hearing on the motion, to disqualify opposing counsel from further participation in this case.

SEE: Tex. Disc. R. Prof. Conduct 1.09, 1.10, 3.08
O'Connor's Texas Rules * Civil Trials (2019), "Disqualification," ch. 1-H, §8, p. 66

ADD: STYLE OF THE CASE – FORM 1B:2
SIGNATURE BLOCK – FORM 1B:3
VERIFICATION – FORM 1B:7
CERTIFICATE OF CONFERENCE – FORM 1B:12
CERTIFICATE OF SERVICE – FORM 1B:13

ATTACH: AFFIDAVIT – FORM 1B:8, if necessary
NOTICE OF HEARING OR SUBMISSION – FORM 1E:1
ORDER – FORM 1G:1

NOTE: Whether the standards and presumptions that apply to former nonattorney employees of opposing counsel (see §F, this form) also apply to former nonattorney employees of the opposing party depends on the following criteria: (1) whether the nonattorney employee was hired by her original employer specifically for litigation purposes and (2) whether the employee reported directly to the opposing party's attorneys. *See* ***In re RSR Corp.***, 475 S.W.3d 775, 782 (Tex.2015). In determining whether to apply these standards and presumptions, a court will look not only to the employee's former job title but also to her former duties. *See id.* at 780-81. See ***O'Connor's Texas Rules***, "Note," ch. 1-H, §8.2.1(2), p. 69.

When a party seeks to disqualify an attorney based on a violation of certain disciplinary rules, the party must show that the attorney's conduct caused it actual prejudice. *See* ***In re Sanders***, 153 S.W.3d 54, 57 (Tex.2004) (Tex. Disciplinary R. of Prof'l Conduct 3.08); ***In re Duke***, No. 09-16-00185-CV (Tex.App.—Beaumont 2016, orig. proceeding) (memo op.; 7-28-16) (Tex. Disciplinary R. of Prof'l Conduct 7.03); *see, e.g.*, ***Busby v. Harvey***, 551 S.W.3d 184, 187 (Tex.App.—Fort Worth 2017, no pet.) (court did not address whether attorney violated any disciplinary rules because fact that party did not show actual prejudice was dispositive); *see also* ***In re Nitla S.A. de C.V.***, 92 S.W.3d 419, 422 (Tex.2002) (although case did not involve violation of disciplinary rules, Court stated in dicta that, even if disciplinary rule is violated, party must still show actual prejudice). See ***O'Connor's Texas Rules***, "Rule 3.08 – attorney as witness," ch. 1-H, §8.2.1(3), p. 70. However, some courts have held that when an attorney violates Texas Disciplinary Rule of Professional Conduct 1.09, no specific showing of actual prejudice is required. *See* ***Cimarron Agric., Ltd. v. Guitar Holding Co.***, 209 S.W.3d 197, 203-04 (Tex.App.—El Paso 2006, no pet.); ***In re Innovation Res. Solution, LLC***, No. 12-15-00254-CV (Tex.App.—Tyler 2016, orig. proceeding) (memo op.; 3-31-16); *see, e.g.*, ***Hendricks v. Barker***, 523 S.W.3d 152, 159-60 (Tex.App.—Houston [14th Dist.] 2016, no pet.) (because party established violation of Tex. Disciplinary R. Prof'l Conduct 1.09(a)(3), no showing of actual prejudice was required).

{❶ *PARTY*}'S RESPONSE TO
{❷ *ADVERSE PARTY*}'S MOTION TO DISQUALIFY OPPOSING COUNSEL

{❸ *Party*}, {❹ *name*}, asks the Court to deny {❺ *adverse party*} {❻ *name*}'s motion to disqualify counsel, {❼ *name of attorney or firm*}, from further representation of {❽ *party*}.

INTRODUCTION

1. Plaintiff, {❾ *name*}, sued defendant, {❿ *name*}, for {⓫ *state basis of suit*}.

2. {⓬ *State other relevant facts about the suit.*}

BACKGROUND

3. On {⓭ *date*}, {⓮ *adverse party*} filed a motion to disqualify {⓯ *name of attorney or firm*} from further participation in this case.

4. {⓰ *State other facts relevant to the response.*}

ARGUMENT & AUTHORITIES

5. Disqualification of a party's counsel is a severe remedy. *In re Columbia Valley Healthcare Sys., L.P.*, 320 S.W.3d 819, 825 (Tex. 2010); *In re Nitla S.A. de C.V.*, 92 S.W.3d 419, 422 (Tex. 2002). When considering a motion to disqualify, a court must strictly adhere to an exacting standard to discourage a party from using the motion as a delay tactic. *In re Nitla*, 92 S.W.3d at 422.

{*CHOOSE APPROPRIATE SECTIONS A-F*}

A. Untimely motion.

6. If a party does not file a motion to disqualify opposing counsel in a timely manner, the party waives the complaint. *In re George*, 28 S.W.3d 511, 513 (Tex. 2000); *Grant v. Thirteenth Court of Appeals*, 888 S.W.2d 466, 468 (Tex. 1994); *Vaughan v. Walther*, 875 S.W.2d 690, 690 (Tex. 1994). To determine whether a party has waived the complaint, a court should consider the length of time between when the movant learned of the conflict and when she filed the motion to disqualify. *In re Kahn*, 533 S.W.3d 387, 391 (Tex. App.—Houston [14th Dist.] 2015, orig. proceeding); *Wasserman v. Black*, 910 S.W.2d 564, 568 (Tex. App.—Waco 1995, writ dism'd w.o.j.); *see Vaughan*, 875 S.W.2d at 690-91. The court can also consider whether the evidence indicates that the motion is being used as a dilatory trial tactic, whether there has been significant discovery in the case, and whether the delay in filing the motion has prejudiced the other party. *In re Kahn*, 533 S.W.3d at 391-92; *see Wasserman*, 910 S.W.2d at 568.

7. Counsel for {[17] *party*} should not be disqualified because {[18] *adverse party*} has waived the right to complain about the conflict. Specifically, counsel for {[19] *party*} should not be disqualified for the following reasons:

a. {[20] *Adverse party*} first became aware of the conflict on {[21] *date*}, when {[22] *state facts supporting knowledge of the conflict*}. Although the conflict was apparent to {[23] *adverse party*}, {[24] *he/she/it*} did not file a motion to disqualify until {[25] *date*}. Thus, {[26] *adverse party*} waited for {[27] *state length of time between knowledge of conflict and date of filing*} before filing the motion to disqualify.

{*CHOOSE APPROPRIATE PARAGRAPHS b-d*}

b. The evidence indicates that {[28] *adverse party*} is using the motion to disqualify as a dilatory trial tactic. Specifically, {[29] *explain*}.

c. There has been significant discovery in this case. Specifically, {[30] *explain*}.

d. {[31] *Adverse party*}'s delay in filing the motion to disqualify has prejudiced {[32] *party*}. Specifically, {[33] *explain*}.

B. {[34] *Attorney/Firm*} does not have conflict of interest.

8. If a party seeks to disqualify an attorney or her firm based on a violation of one or more disciplinary rules, the party must support its claim with specific evidence. *Spears v. Fourth Court of Appeals*, 797 S.W.2d 654, 656 (Tex. 1990). Mere allegations of unethical conduct or evidence showing a remote possibility of a disciplinary-rule violation will not suffice. *Id.*

9. An attorney should not be disqualified unless (1) she personally represented a former client, (2) she is now representing another client in a matter adverse to the former client, (3) she does not have the former client's consent to represent the other client, and (4) at least one of the following applies:

a. In the pending matter, the client questions the validity of the attorney's services or work performed for the former client. Tex. Disciplinary Rules Prof'l Conduct R. 1.09(a)(1).

b. In the pending matter, the attorney's representation of the client will in reasonable probability involve a violation of Texas Disciplinary Rule of Professional Conduct 1.05, governing the use of a client's confidential information. Tex. Disciplinary Rules Prof'l Conduct R. 1.09(a)(2).

◄ *Continued on next page* ►

c. The pending matter is the same as or substantially related to the earlier matter. Tex. Disciplinary Rules Prof'l Conduct R. 1.09(a)(3). A matter is "substantially related" when the facts of the earlier representation are so related to the facts in the pending litigation that there is a genuine threat that confidences revealed to former counsel will be divulged to a present adversary. *In re EPIC Holdings, Inc.*, 985 S.W.2d 41, 51 (Tex. 1998); *Metro. Life Ins. Co. v. Syntek Fin. Corp.*, 881 S.W.2d 319, 320-21 (Tex. 1994).

{*CHOOSE APPROPRIATE PARAGRAPH 10 IF MOTION SEEKS DISQUALIFICATION OF FIRM*}

10. A firm should not be disqualified unless a partner or associate of the firm would be disqualified from representing a client under Texas Disciplinary Rule of Professional Conduct 1.09(a). Tex. Disciplinary Rules Prof'l Conduct R. 1.09(b); *Texaco, Inc. v. Garcia*, 891 S.W.2d 255, 256-57 (Tex. 1995); *Henderson v. Floyd*, 891 S.W.2d 252, 254 (Tex. 1995); *see Nat'l Med. Enters., Inc. v. Godbey*, 924 S.W.2d 123, 128-29 (Tex. 1996).

10. The partners and associates of an attorney's former firm that were associated with the attorney when she left should not be disqualified from representing a client unless the attorney would be disqualified from representing that client under Texas Disciplinary Rule of Professional Conduct 1.09(a)(1) or (a)(2). Tex. Disciplinary Rules Prof'l Conduct R. 1.09(c) & cmt. 6 & 7; *In re Basco*, 221 S.W.3d 637, 638-39 (Tex. 2007).

11. Counsel for {㉟ *party*} should not be disqualified because {㊱ *explain why counsel should not be disqualified under Rule 1.09(a) if attorney, Rule 1.09(b) if attorney's current firm, or Rule 1.09(c) if attorney's former firm*}.

C. Attorney should not be disqualified for participating in joint-defense agreement.

12. If a party seeks to disqualify opposing counsel based on a claim that the attorney participated in a joint defense, the party must establish that (1) the attorney participated in the joint defense of two or more parties, one of whom is adverse to the attorney's client in a current matter, (2) confidential information has been shared, and (3) the matter in which the information was shared is substantially related to the matter in which disqualification is sought. *See Nat'l Med. Enters., Inc. v. Godbey*, 924 S.W.2d 123, 129, 132 (Tex. 1996); *In re Skiles*, 102 S.W.3d 323, 327 (Tex. App.—Beaumont 2003, orig. proceeding); *Rio Hondo Implement Co. v. Euresti*, 903 S.W.2d 128, 132 (Tex. App.—Corpus Christi 1995, orig. proceeding). {*See* ***O'Connor's Texas Rules***, *"Attorney assumed duty to preserve nonclient's confidences," ch. 1-H, §8.2.2(1), p. 71.*}

13. Counsel for {㊲ *party*} should not be disqualified because {㊳ *state facts demonstrating why counsel should not be disqualified, e.g., party was not a party to the joint-defense agreement in the earlier matter, counsel was subject to a joint-defense agreement but did not receive confidential information related to this matter*}.

D. Attorney should not be disqualified for being a potential witness.

14. If a party seeks to disqualify an attorney for her potential role as a witness in a matter, the party must support its claim with specific evidence. *Spears v. Fourth Court of Appeals*, 797 S.W.2d 654, 656 (Tex. 1990). Mere allegations of unethical conduct or evidence showing a remote possibility of a disciplinary-rule violation will not suffice. *Id.*

15. Under Texas Disciplinary Rule of Professional Conduct 3.08, an attorney can be disqualified as a potential witness in a matter only if

{*CHOOSE APPROPRIATE GROUND*}

Ⓐ (1) her testimony is or may be necessary to establish an essential fact on behalf of her client, and (2) her role as both advocate and witness will cause actual prejudice to the party seeking disqualification. Tex. Disciplinary Rules Prof'l Conduct R. 3.08(a) & cmt. 4; *In re Sanders*, 153 S.W.3d 54, 56-57 (Tex. 2004); *Ayres v. Canales*, 790 S.W.2d 554, 557-58 (Tex. 1990); *In re Guidry*, 316 S.W.3d 729, 738 (Tex. App.—Houston [14th Dist.] 2010, orig. proceeding). {*See **O'Connor's Texas Rules**, "Rule 3.08 – attorney as witness," ch. 1-H, §8.2.1(3), p. 70.*}

Ⓑ (1) her testimony will be substantially adverse to her client, (2) she has not obtained consent from her client to testify, and (3) her role as both advocate and witness will cause actual prejudice to the party seeking disqualification. Tex. Disciplinary Rules Prof'l Conduct R. 3.08(b) & cmt. 4; *In re Sanders*, 153 S.W.3d 54, 57 (Tex. 2004); *Ayres v. Canales*, 790 S.W.2d 554, 558 (Tex. 1990). {*See **O'Connor's Texas Rules**, "Rule 3.08 – attorney as witness," ch. 1-H, §8.2.1(3), p. 70.*}

{*CHOOSE APPROPRIATE PARAGRAPHS 16-21*}

16. Counsel for {㊴ *party*} should not be disqualified because her testimony falls within an exception under Texas Disciplinary Rule of Professional Conduct 3.08(a). Under Rule 3.08(a), an attorney can perform the dual role of attorney and witness if (1) her testimony is related to an uncontested issue, (2) the testimony relates solely to a matter of formality and there is no reason to believe that substantial opposing evidence

Continued on next page

will be offered, (3) the testimony relates to the nature and value of legal services rendered in the case, (4) the attorney is a party to the case and is appearing pro se, or (5) the attorney has promptly notified opposing counsel that the attorney expects to testify in the case and disqualification of the attorney will cause a substantial hardship for the client. Counsel's testimony in this case falls within {40 *describe applicable exception*}.

17. Counsel for {41 *party*} should not be disqualified because {42 *adverse party*} has not established that {43 *his/her*} testimony is necessary. An attorney's testimony is necessary on an essential fact only when the essential fact cannot be established by other witnesses or other sources in the record. *See In re Sanders*, 153 S.W.3d at 57. Thus, disqualification is inappropriate under Texas Disciplinary Rule of Professional Conduct 3.08(a) when a party merely announces an intention to call an attorney to testify without establishing a genuine need for the testimony. *In re Sandoval*, 308 S.W.3d 31, 34 (Tex. App.—San Antonio 2009, orig. proceeding). {44 *Elaborate.*}

18. Counsel for {45 *party*} should not be disqualified because {46 *adverse party*} has not established that {47 *his/her*} testimony concerns an essential fact. {48 *Elaborate.*}

19. Counsel for {49 *party*} should not be disqualified because {50 *adverse party*} has not established that {51 *his/her*} testimony will be substantially adverse to her client. {52 *Elaborate.*}

20. Counsel for {53 *party*} should not be disqualified because {54 *adverse party*} has not established that {55 *he/she*} has not obtained client's consent. {56 *Elaborate.*}

21. Counsel for {57 *party*} should not be disqualified because {58 *adverse party*} has not established that {59 *his/her*} role as both advocate and witness will cause actual prejudice. {60 *Elaborate.*}

E. Attorney should not be disqualified for receiving privileged material.

{*CHOOSE APPROPRIATE PARAGRAPHS 22-23*}

{*Privileged material received outside normal discovery process*}

22. If a party seeks to disqualify opposing counsel in the interest of justice for having received privileged material outside the normal discovery process, the party must show that counsel obtained the privileged material outside the normal discovery process and that the balance of the following factors supports disqualification: (1) whether the attorney knew or should have known the material was privileged, (2) the promptness with which the attorney notified opposing counsel, (3) the extent to which the attorney

reviewed and digested the information, (4) the significance of the privileged information, (5) the extent to which the movant may be at fault, and (6) the extent to which the nonmovant will suffer prejudice from the disqualification. *In re Meador*, 968 S.W.2d 346, 351-52 (Tex. 1998).

23. Counsel for {61 *party*} should not be disqualified because {62 *explain how counsel obtained the privileged information and why the balance of factors weighs against disqualification*}.

{*Privileged material received during normal discovery process*}

22. If a party seeks to disqualify opposing counsel in the interest of justice for having received privileged material during the normal discovery process, the party must show that (1) counsel received privileged material during the normal discovery process, (2) the attorney's review of the privileged material caused the opposing party actual harm, and (3) the attorney's disqualification is necessary because there are no lesser means to remedy the harm. *In re Nitla*, 92 S.W.3d at 423.

23. Counsel for {63 *party*} should not be disqualified because {64 *explain how counsel obtained the privileged information and show either why the attorney's review of the material did not cause harm or why there are lesser means to remedy any harm suffered*}.

F. {65 *Attorney/Firm*} should not be disqualified for employee's conflict of interest.

{*CHOOSE APPROPRIATE PARAGRAPHS 24-25*}

{*Adverse party argued rebuttable presumption of shared confidences*}

24. If a party seeks to disqualify opposing counsel and her firm based on a nonattorney employee's conflict of interest, the party must show that the employee who worked on the pending matter previously worked for another firm and the employee (1) obtained confidential information about the same matter while working at the previous firm and (2) shared that confidential information with her current firm. *See In re Turner*, 542 S.W.3d 553, 555-56 (Tex. 2017); *In re Am. Home Prods. Corp.*, 985 S.W.2d 68, 74 (Tex. 1998). If the employee actually worked on the same matter for the previous firm, there is a conclusive presumption that confidences about the matter were obtained during the course of the employee's earlier employment. *In re Turner*, 542 S.W.3d at 556; *see In re Guar. Ins. Servs., Inc.*, 343 S.W.3d 130, 134 (Tex. 2011); *Phoenix Founders, Inc. v. Marshall*, 887 S.W.2d 831, 834 (Tex. 1994). However, there is generally no conclusive presumption that the employee shared those confidences with her new firm. *In re Turner*, 542 S.W.3d at 556; *In re Guar. Ins.*, 343 S.W.3d at 134; *In re Columbia Val-*

Continued on next page

ley, 320 S.W.3d at 824. Thus, in most cases, the presumption of shared confidences is rebuttable and disqualification is not required if the firm (1) instructed the employee not to work on any matter that she worked on during her previous employment and (2) effectively screened the employee from any contact with the matter in question. *See In re Turner*, 542 S.W.3d at 556; *In re Guar. Ins.*, 343 S.W.3d at 134-35; *In re Columbia Valley*, 320 S.W.3d at 824. {*See* ***O'Connor's Texas Rules****, "Rule 5.03 – responsibility for nonattorney employee," ch. 1-H, §8.2.1(2), p. 69.*}

{*CHOOSE APPROPRIATE PARAGRAPH 25*}

25. Counsel for {66 *party*} should not be disqualified because {67 *name of employee*}, an employee of counsel for {68 *party*}, never worked on the current matter while employed by {69 *name of former firm*} and did not have access to confidential information related to this matter. {70 *Elaborate.*}

25. Although {71 *name of employee*}, an employee of counsel for {72 *party*}, {73 *previously worked on/obtained confidential information related to*} the current matter while employed by {74 *name of former firm*}, counsel for {75 *party*} should not be disqualified for the following reasons:

a. Counsel for {76 *party*} instructed {77 *name of employee*} not to work on any matter that {78 *he/she*} worked on during {79 *his/her*} previous employment. {80 *Describe the instruction and explain that it was given before the employee worked on any particular matter.*}

b. Counsel for {81 *party*} has screening procedures in place to ensure that {82 *name of employee*} has no contact with this case. {83 *Elaborate.*}

{*Adverse party argued conclusive presumption of shared confidences*}

24. If a party seeks to disqualify opposing counsel and her firm based on a nonattorney employee's conflict of interest, the party must show that the employee who worked on the pending matter previously worked for another firm and the employee (1) obtained confidential information about the same matter while working at the previous firm and (2) shared that confidential information with her current firm. *See In re Turner*, 542 S.W.3d 553, 555-56 (Tex. 2017); *In re Am. Home Prods. Corp.*, 985 S.W.2d 68, 74 (Tex. 1998). If the employee actually worked on the same matter for the previous firm, there is a conclusive presumption that confidences about the matter were obtained during the course of the employee's earlier employment. *In re Turner*, 542 S.W.3d at 556; *see In re Guar. Ins. Servs., Inc.*, 343 S.W.3d 130, 134 (Tex. 2011); *Phoenix Founders, Inc. v. Marshall*, 887 S.W.2d 831, 834 (Tex. 1994). There is also a presumption that the employee shared those confidences with her new firm, but this presumption is not conclusive unless the party seeking disqualification shows that (1) the employee did in fact

share confidential information with her current firm, (2) the employee actually performed work, including clerical work, on the matter in question at an attorney's directive, and the attorney reasonably should have known about the conflict of interest, (3) screening the employee from the matter was or would be ineffective, or (4) the employee would necessarily be required to work on the matter in question. *In re Guar. Ins.*, 343 S.W.3d at 135; *In re Columbia Valley*, 320 S.W.3d at 828; *see In re Turner*, 542 S.W.3d at 557 n.3; *Phoenix Founders*, 887 S.W.2d at 835. If this presumption is not conclusive, it can be rebutted and disqualification is not required if the firm (1) instructed the employee not to work on any matter that she worked on during her previous employment and (2) effectively screened the employee from any contact with the matter in question. *See In re Turner*, 542 S.W.3d at 556; *In re Guar. Ins.*, 343 S.W.3d at 134-35; *In re Columbia Valley*, 320 S.W.3d at 824. {*See* ***O'Connor's Texas Rules***, *"Rule 5.03 – responsibility for nonattorney employee," ch. 1-H, §8.2.1(2), p. 69.*}

{*CHOOSE APPROPRIATE PARAGRAPH 25*}

25. Counsel for {84 *party*} should not be disqualified because {85 *name of employee*}, an employee of counsel for {86 *party*}, never worked on the current matter while employed by {87 *name of former firm*} and did not have access to confidential information related to this matter. {88 *Elaborate.*}

25. Although {89 *name of employee*}, an employee of counsel for {90 *party*}, {91 *previously worked on/obtained confidential information related to*} the current matter while employed by {92 *name of former firm*}, counsel for {93 *party*} should not be disqualified. Contrary to {94 *adverse party*}'s assertion, there is no conclusive presumption that {95 *name of employee*} shared confidential information with counsel for {96 *party*}. Specifically, {97 *refute adverse party's allegations as to why presumption of shared confidences is conclusive*}.

{*ADD PARAGRAPH 26 IF ADVERSE PARTY ARGUED CONCLUSIVE PRESUMPTION*}

26. Because the presumption of shared confidences is not conclusive, counsel for {98 *party*} can rebut the presumption and should not be disqualified for the following reasons:

a. Counsel for {99 *party*} instructed {100 *name of employee*} not to work on any matter that {101 *he/she*} worked on during {102 *his/her*} previous employment. {103 *Describe the instruction and explain that it was given before the employee worked on any particular matter.*}

— *Continued on next page* —

b. Counsel for {104 *party*} has screening procedures in place to ensure that {105 *name of employee*} has no contact with this case. {106 *Elaborate.*}

CONCLUSION

27. {107 *Briefly summarize the response.*}

PRAYER

28. For these reasons, {108 *party*} asks the Court to deny {109 *adverse party*}'s motion to disqualify and allow counsel to continue participating in this case.

SEE: Tex. Disc. R. Prof. Conduct 1.09, 1.10, 3.08
O'Connor's Texas Rules * Civil Trials (2019), "Disqualification," ch. 1-H, §8, p. 66

ADD: STYLE OF THE CASE – FORM 1B:2
SIGNATURE BLOCK – FORM 1B:3
VERIFICATION – FORM 1B:7
CERTIFICATE OF CONFERENCE – FORM 1B:12
CERTIFICATE OF SERVICE – FORM 1B:13

ATTACH: AFFIDAVIT – FORM 1B:8, if necessary
ORDER – FORM 1G:1

RULE 11 AGREEMENT TO {❶ *IDENTIFY AGREEMENT*}

{❷ *Party*}, {❸ *name*}, and {❹ *adverse party*}, {❺ *name*}, file this agreement to {❻ *identify substance of agreement, e.g., extend the time to file discovery responses*}.

1. The parties agree as follows: {❼ *state details of agreement*}.

2. The {❽ *parties'/attorneys'*} signatures on this document are evidence of their intent that this document be a Rule 11 agreement, enforceable upon filing with the Court. Tex. R. Civ. P. 11.

SEE: Tex. R. Civ. P. 11, 191.1, 191.4(b)(3)
O'Connor's Texas Rules * Civil Trials (2019), "Agreements Between Attorneys – Rule 11," ch. 1-H, §9, p. 73

ADD: STYLE OF THE CASE – FORM 1B:2
SIGNATURE BLOCK FOR AGREED MOTIONS – FORM 1B:4
CERTIFICATE OF SERVICE – FORM 1B:13

NOTE: An e-filed document that must be sworn or notarized must include an electronic or scanned image of the necessary signatures. *See* Tex. R. Civ. P. 21(f)(7). For more information on e-filing requirements, see ***O'Connor's Texas Rules***, "E-filing," ch. 1-C, §4.1.1, p. 25.

Texas Rule of Civil Procedure 11 applies only to agreements about pending suits. See ***O'Connor's Texas Rules***, "Agreements before suit filed," ch. 1-H, §9.3, p. 74.

AFFIDAVIT OF {❶ *NAME OF ATTORNEY*}

STATE OF TEXAS §
{❷ ________} COUNTY §

Before me, the undersigned notary, on this day personally appeared {❸ *name of attorney*}, the affiant, whose identity is known to me. After I administered an oath, affiant testified as follows:

1. "My name is {❹ *name of attorney*}. I am over 18 years of age, of sound mind, and capable of making this affidavit. The facts stated in this affidavit are within my personal knowledge and are true and correct.

2. "I am an attorney licensed to practice in the State of Texas.

3. "{❺ *Party*} retained me to represent {❻ *him/her/it*} in this suit for {❼ *state basis of suit*}. I have personal knowledge of this case and the work performed.

4. "{❽ *Describe experience and expertise, e.g., I have over ten years of experience in civil litigation and over seven years of experience handling employment-discrimination claims.*}

5. "It was necessary for {❾ *party*} to retain an attorney {❿ *add if appropriate: with my level of skill and expertise*} in this case {⓫ *add if applicable: as well as paralegals and legal assistants to work on this case*}.

{*ADD PARAGRAPHS 6-7 IF APPLICABLE*}

6. "The paralegals and legal assistants assigned to this case (1) are qualified by education, experience, and training to perform the services required, (2) have knowledge of the legal system, principles, and procedures, (3) were supervised by an attorney, (4) performed tasks that are traditionally done by an attorney, and (5) performed services that were reasonable and necessary.

7. "{⓬ *Party*}'s retention of me on this case prevented me from accepting other employment. In particular, the following time limitations were imposed: {⓭ *describe limitations*}. Because of the {⓮ *identify factors making the case undesirable, e.g., uniqueness of the issues, difficulty or complexity of the case, unpopularity of the client*}, this case may be seen as undesirable by some attorneys, making the retention of an attorney difficult.

8. "{[15] *Party*} agreed to compensate me for my work based on {[16] *identify arrangement, e.g., an hourly fee, a contingency fee*}. {[17] *State details of the fee agreement.*} {[18] *Add if appropriate: This fee is equivalent to what is customarily charged in the locality for similar legal services.*}

{*CHOOSE APPROPRIATE PARAGRAPH 9*}

9. "I spent {[19] *state amount of time*} {[20] *prosecuting/defending*} this suit by (1) investigating claims, (2) drafting pleadings, questions, and responses, (3) engaging in discovery, (4) attending hearings, and (5) taking other necessary actions to perform my legal services properly. A detailed description of the hours and work performed in this case is attached as Exhibit A.

9. "The novelty and difficulty of the questions involved in this case required me to spend {[21] *state amount of time*} {[22] *prosecuting/defending*} this suit by (1) investigating claims, (2) drafting pleadings, questions, and responses, (3) engaging in discovery, (4) attending hearings, and (5) taking other necessary actions to perform my legal services properly. A detailed description of the hours and work performed in this case is attached as Exhibit A.

10. "Based on our fee agreement, {[23] *party*} incurred attorney {[24] *add if applicable: and paralegal*} fees in the amount of ${[25] *amount*}.

11. "In my opinion, the reasonable value of the attorney fees necessarily incurred by {[26] *party*} are as follows:

{*CHOOSE APPROPRIATE AMOUNTS*}

a. ${[27] *Amount*}, for representing {[28] *party*} in trial and through entry of judgment.

b. ${[29] *Amount*}, for representing {[30] *party*} on appeal to the {[31] *number*} Court of Appeals.

c. ${[32] *Amount*}, for representing {[33] *party*} on appeal to the Supreme Court of Texas.

12. "The attorney fees charged in this case were necessary, reasonable, and incurred in the {[34] *prosecution/defense*} of this suit. {[35] *Elaborate.*}

Continued on next page

{*CHOOSE APPROPRIATE PARAGRAPH 13*}

13. "The fees claimed in this affidavit were segregated from the fees incurred in the {㊱ *prosecution/defense*} of this suit {㊲ *on claims for which attorney fees are not recoverable/against other parties who are not liable for attorney fees*}. {㊳ *Elaborate.*} {*See* ***O'Connor's Texas Rules***, *"Segregation required," ch. 1-H, §10.5.4(1), p. 80.*}

13. "The fees claimed in this affidavit were not segregated because the discrete legal services advanced claims for which attorney fees are recoverable and claims for which they are not recoverable. *Tony Gullo Motors I, L.P. v. Chapa*, 212 S.W.3d 299, 313-14 (Tex. 2006). {㊴ *Elaborate.*} {*See* ***O'Connor's Texas Rules***, *"Inseparable legal services," ch. 1-H, §10.5.4(2)(b), p. 80.*}

{*CHOOSE APPROPRIATE PARAGRAPH 14*}

14. "Because the claim for attorney fees may be included in a suit for {㊵ *breach of an oral contract/breach of a written contract/sworn account/rendered services/performed labor/furnished materials/freight overcharges/lost or damaged freight/killed or injured stock*}, which is a claim listed in Texas Civil Practice & Remedies Code section 38.001, the Court can take judicial notice of the usual and customary attorney fees and the contents of the case file without receiving any further evidence. Tex. Civ. Prac. & Rem. Code §38.004."

14. "The fees I charged in this case are customarily charged in this area for the same or similar services for an attorney with my experience, reputation, and ability, considering {㊶ *add if applicable: the nature and length of my relationship with {party},*} the {㊷ *amount in/type of*} controversy, the time limitations imposed, and the results obtained."

____
{㊸ *Name of attorney*}

Sworn to and subscribed before me by {㊹ *name of affiant*} on __________, 20___.

____
Notary Public in and for
the State of Texas

SEE: Tex. Civ. Prac. & Rem. Code §§38.001-38.004
Tex. Disc. R. Prof. Conduct 1.04(b)
O'Connor's Texas Rules * Civil Trials (2019), "Attorney Fees from Adverse Party," ch. 1-H, §10, p. 74
O'Connor's Texas Causes of Action (2019), "Plaintiff incurred attorney fees," ch. 45-A, §2.6, p. 1468; "Attorney fees reasonable & necessary," ch. 45-A, §2.7, p. 1469

ADD: STYLE OF THE CASE – FORM 1B:2

ATTACH: Exhibit, detailing hours spent and work performed

NOTE: When a party is entitled to attorney fees from the adverse party on one claim but not another, the party seeking attorney fees must segregate the recoverable fees from the nonrecoverable fees. ***Kinsel v. Lindsey***, 526 S.W.3d 411, 427 (Tex.2017); ***Tony Gullo Motors I, L.P. v. Chapa***, 212 S.W.3d 299, 313 (Tex.2006). Segregation is not necessary if the legal services advanced all the claims in the suit. ***Tony Gullo Motors***, 212 S.W.3d at 313-14. See ***O'Connor's Texas Rules***, "Fees were segregated," ch. 1-H, §10.5.4, p. 80.

If an attorney expects to use the lodestar method to calculate a claim for attorney fees, she should be sure to document her time with detailed contemporaneous billing records or similar documentation recorded close to when her work was performed. See ***O'Connor's Texas Rules***, "Proving attorney fees," ch. 1-H, §10.6, p. 81; ***O'Connor's Texas COA***, "Lodestar method," ch. 45-A, §4.1.2(2)(a), p. 1476.

See notes under FORM 1B:8.

{❶ *PARTY*}'S MOTION FOR APPOINTMENT OF GUARDIAN AD LITEM

{❷ *Party*}, {❸ *name*}, asks the Court to appoint a guardian ad litem in this case, as authorized by Texas Rule of Civil Procedure 173.

INTRODUCTION

1. Plaintiff, {❹ *name*}, sued defendant, {❺ *name*}, for {❻ *state basis of suit*}.

2. {❼ *State other relevant facts about the suit.*}

BACKGROUND

3. {❽ *Name of incapacitated party*}, the {❾ *plaintiff/defendant/intervenor*} in this suit, is represented by {❿ *name of guardian or next friend*}, who is {⓫ *his/her*} {⓬ *guardian/next friend*}.

4. {⓭ *Identify any other incapacitated party and her guardian or next friend.*}

5. {⓮ *State other facts relevant to the motion.*}

ARGUMENT & AUTHORITIES

{*CHOOSE APPROPRIATE PARAGRAPHS 6-7*}

{*Adverse interest*}

6. A court must appoint a guardian ad litem when it appears that there is an adverse interest between a party and the party's guardian or next friend. Tex. R. Civ. P. 173.2(a)(1); *see Ford Motor Co. v. Stewart, Cox & Hatcher, P.C.*, 390 S.W.3d 294, 297 (Tex. 2013).

7. {⓯ *Party*} asks the Court to appoint a guardian ad litem in this case because it appears that {⓰ *name of incapacitated party*} has an interest adverse to {⓱ *name of incapacitated party*}'s {⓲ *guardian/next friend*}. Specifically, {⓳ *state facts establishing an adverse interest*}.

{*Agreement*}

6. A court must appoint a guardian ad litem for a party represented by a guardian or next friend when the parties agree to an appointment. Tex. R. Civ. P. 173.2(a)(2).

7. {⓴ *Party*} asks the Court to appoint a guardian ad litem in this case because the parties have agreed to an appointment.

{*ADD PARAGRAPHS 8-9 IF APPLICABLE*}

8. A court must appoint the same guardian ad litem for all similarly situated parties who are represented by a guardian or next friend. Tex. R. Civ. P. 173.2(b).

9. The Court should appoint the same guardian ad litem for {21 *name of incapacitated party*} and {22 *name of second incapacitated party*} to safeguard their interests because they are similarly situated in this case. {23 *Explain why parties are similarly situated.*}

CONCLUSION

10. {24 *Briefly summarize the motion.*}

PRAYER

11. For these reasons, {25 *party*} asks the Court to appoint a guardian ad litem for {26 *name of incapacitated party*}.

SEE: Tex. R. Civ. P. 173
O'Connor's Texas Rules * Civil Trials (2019), "Appointing a Guardian Ad Litem Under TRCP 173," ch. 1-I, §3, p. 87

ADD: STYLE OF THE CASE – FORM 1B:2
SIGNATURE BLOCK – FORM 1B:3
CERTIFICATE OF SERVICE – FORM 1B:13

ATTACH: AFFIDAVIT – FORM 1B:8, if necessary
NOTICE OF HEARING OR SUBMISSION – FORM 1E:1
ORDER – FORM 1I:3

NOTE: Texas Rule of Civil Procedure 173 refers to the party who needs a guardian ad litem as "a party who is represented by a next friend or guardian with an adverse interest." In this form, we use "incapacitated party" to refer to a person who needs a guardian ad litem.

Any party who believes that a guardian ad litem is necessary may file a motion for the court to appoint one. Tex. R. Civ. P. 173.3(a). The court may also appoint a guardian ad litem on its own initiative. *Id.*

A court located in a county with a population of 25,000 or more must select a guardian ad litem according to the process outlined in Texas Government Code §37.004. See ***O'Connor's Texas Rules***, "Selection," ch. 1-I, §3.3.2, p. 88.

Rule 173 does not apply to an appointment of a guardian ad litem governed by a statute, such as the Family Code or the Estates Code, or by other rules, such as the Parental Notification Rules. Tex. R. Civ. P. 173.1 & cmt. 2.

Continued on next page

Courts usually apply Rule 173 to adverse interests relating to the division of settlement proceeds. ***In re KC Greenhouse Patio Apts., LP***, 445 S.W.3d 168, 176 (Tex.App.—Houston [1st Dist.] 2012, orig. proceeding); *see* Tex. R. Civ. P. 173 cmt. 3. But a parent's obligation to provide for a child's medical care coupled with her desire to pay medical bills from the settlement proceeds does not, by itself, create a conflict of interest under Rule 173. *See* ***Ford Motor Co. v. Stewart, Cox & Hatcher, P.C.***, 390 S.W.3d 294, 298 (Tex.2013).

{1 *PARTY*}'S RESPONSE TO {2 *ADVERSE PARTY*}'S
MOTION FOR APPOINTMENT OF GUARDIAN AD LITEM

{3 *Party*}, {4 *name*}, asks the Court to deny {5 *adverse party*} {6 *name*}'s motion to appoint a guardian ad litem in this case.

INTRODUCTION

1. Plaintiff, {7 *name*}, sued defendant, {8 *name*}, for {9 *state basis of suit*}.

2. {10 *State other relevant facts about the suit.*}

BACKGROUND

3. {11 *Name of incapacitated party*}, the {12 *plaintiff/defendant/intervenor*} in this suit, is represented by {13 *name of guardian or next friend*}, who is {14 *his/her*} {15 *guardian/next friend*}.

4. {16 *Identify any other incapacitated party and her guardian or next friend.*}

5. {17 *State other facts relevant to the response.*}

ARGUMENT & AUTHORITIES

6. {18 *Party*} recognizes that a court must appoint a guardian ad litem to protect a party's interests when required by Texas Rule of Civil Procedure 173. However, Rule 173 does not require the appointment of a guardian ad litem in this case.

{*CHOOSE APPROPRIATE PARAGRAPHS 7-8*}

{*No adverse interest*}

7. The appointment of a guardian ad litem is not necessary when there is no adverse interest between a party and her guardian or next friend. *See* Tex. R. Civ. P. 173.2(a)(1); *see, e.g., Kennedy v. Mo. Pac. R.R. Co.*, 778 S.W.2d 552, 555 (Tex. App.—Beaumont 1989, writ denied) (trial court properly denied motion to appoint guardian ad litem; there was no indication that next friend sought to compromise minor's recovery for her own benefit).

8. {19 *Adverse party*} alleged that there was an adverse interest between {20 *name of incapacitated party*} and {21 *name of guardian or next friend*}, {22 *his/her*} {23 *guardian/next friend*}. But in fact there is no adverse interest between them. {24 *Elaborate.*} Thus, the Court should not appoint a guardian ad litem in this case.

◄ *Continued on next page* ►

{No agreement}

7. The appointment of a guardian ad litem is not necessary when the parties have not agreed to appoint a guardian ad litem. *See* Tex. R. Civ. P. 173.2(a)(2).

8. {㉕ *Adverse party*} alleged that there is an agreement to appoint a guardian ad litem for {㉖ *name of incapacitated party*}. But in fact the parties have not agreed to an appointment. {㉗ *Elaborate.*} Thus, the Court should not appoint a guardian ad litem in this case.

{ADD PARAGRAPHS 9-10 IF APPLICABLE}

9. Rule 173 requires the appointment of the same guardian ad litem for all similarly situated parties who are represented by a guardian or next friend, unless the court finds that the appointment of a different guardian ad litem is necessary. Tex. R. Civ. P. 173.2(b).

10. {㉘ *The parties are not similarly situated/Even though the parties are similarly situated, different guardians ad litem are necessary*} in this case because {㉙ *explain*}. Thus, if this Court grants {㉚ *adverse party*}'s motion to appoint a guardian ad litem, the Court should appoint different guardians ad litem for the parties.

CONCLUSION

11. {㉛ *Briefly summarize the response.*}

PRAYER

12. For these reasons, {㉜ *party*} asks the Court to deny the motion to appoint a guardian ad litem for {㉝ *name of incapacitated party*}. {㉞ *Add if appropriate: In the alternative, if the Court grants {adverse party}'s motion to appoint a guardian ad litem, {party} asks the Court to appoint different guardians ad litem for the incapacitated parties.*}

SEE: Tex. R. Civ. P. 44, 173
O'Connor's Texas Rules * Civil Trials (2019), "Appointing a Guardian Ad Litem Under TRCP 173," ch. 1-I, §3, p. 87

ADD: STYLE OF THE CASE – FORM 1B:2
SIGNATURE BLOCK – FORM 1B:3
CERTIFICATE OF SERVICE – FORM 1B:13

ATTACH: AFFIDAVIT – FORM 1B:8, if necessary
ORDER – FORM 1I:3

NOTE: Texas Rule of Civil Procedure 173 refers to the party who needs a guardian ad litem as "a party who is represented by a next friend or guardian with an adverse interest." In this form, we use "incapacitated party" to refer to a person who needs a guardian ad litem.

Any party can object to the appointment of a guardian ad litem. Tex. R. Civ. P. 173.3(c).

Once a person is appointed as a guardian ad litem, any party can object that the person is not qualified to serve in that capacity. See ***O'Connor's Texas Rules***, "Qualifications," ch. 1-I, §3.2, p. 88.

Courts usually apply Rule 173 to adverse interests relating to the division of settlement proceeds. ***In re KC Greenhouse Patio Apts., LP***, 445 S.W.3d 168, 176 (Tex.App.—Houston [1st Dist.] 2012, orig. proceeding); *see* Tex. R. Civ. P. 173 cmt. 3. But a parent's obligation to provide for a child's medical care coupled with her desire to pay medical bills from the settlement proceeds does not, by itself, create a conflict of interest under Rule 173. *See* ***Ford Motor Co. v. Stewart, Cox & Hatcher, P.C.***, 390 S.W.3d 294, 298 (Tex.2013).

ORDER ON MOTION FOR APPOINTMENT OF GUARDIAN AD LITEM

After considering {❶ *party*} {❷ *name*}'s motion to appoint a guardian ad litem for {❸ *name of incapacitated party*} {❹ *add if applicable: and {name of second incapacitated party}*}, the Court

{*CHOOSE APPROPRIATE ORDER*}

DENIES the motion.

GRANTS the motion and appoints the following {❺ *person/persons*} as {❻ *guardian/guardians*} ad litem for {❼ *name of incapacitated party*} {❽ *add if applicable: and {name of second incapacitated party}*}:

Name: ____
Address: ______________________________________
Telephone: _____________________________________
E-mail: ____

{❾ *Identify other guardian ad litem if more than one appointed.*}

SIGNED on _______________, 20___.

____
PRESIDING JUDGE

SEE: Tex. R. Civ. P. 173
O'Connor's Texas Rules * Civil Trials (2019), "Appointing a Guardian Ad Litem Under TRCP 173," ch. 1-I, §3, p. 87

ADD: STYLE OF THE CASE – FORM 1B:2
CERTIFICATE OF SERVICE – FORM 1B:13, if proposed order served separately from motion or response

NOTE: Texas Rule of Civil Procedure 173 refers to the party who needs a guardian ad litem as "a party who is represented by a next friend or guardian with an adverse interest." In this form, we use "incapacitated party" to refer to a person who needs a guardian ad litem.

Courts located in counties with populations of 25,000 or more are required to maintain a list of all attorneys and other persons who are qualified to serve as guardians ad litem and are registered with the court. *See* Tex. Gov't Code §§37.001(a), 37.003(a)(2). The court must annually post this list at the county courthouse where the court is located and on the court's website. *Id.* §37.005. The process for selecting a guardian ad litem from the list is outlined in Texas Government Code §37.004. See ***O'Connor's Texas Rules***, "Selection," ch. 1-I, §3.3.2, p. 88.

APPLICATION FOR GUARDIAN AD LITEM FEES

{❶ *Name of guardian ad litem*} asks the Court to award reasonable fees for {❷ *his/her*} services.

INTRODUCTION

1. Plaintiff, {❸ *name*}, sued defendant, {❹ *name*}, for {❺ *state basis of suit*}.

2. {❻ *State other relevant facts about the suit.*}

BACKGROUND

3. {❼ *Name of guardian ad litem*} was appointed as a guardian ad litem by written order on {❽ *date*}.

4. {❾ *Name of guardian ad litem*}'s appointment has ended because {❿ *explain, e.g., judgment has been rendered in the case, the conflict between plaintiff and incapacitated party has ended*}.

{*ADD PARAGRAPH 5 IF APPLICABLE*}

5. The parties agree to the application for guardian ad litem fees.

6. {⓫ *State other facts relevant to the application.*}

ARGUMENT & AUTHORITIES

7. A guardian ad litem may file an application requesting reimbursement for expenses and compensation for services performed at the conclusion of the guardian ad litem's appointment. Tex. R. Civ. P. 173.6(b).

{*CHOOSE APPROPRIATE PARAGRAPHS 8-15*}

{*For expenses incurred*}

8. The reasonable and necessary expenses incurred by {⓬ *name of guardian ad litem*} are as follows:

   a. ${⓭ *Amount*}, for {⓮ *expense incurred*}. {⓯ *Explain why the expense was reasonable and necessary.*}

{*Continue until all expenses are stated.*}

9. The total amount of expenses for reimbursement is ${⓰ *amount*}.

◄ *Continued on next page* ►

{For services performed by guardian ad litem}

10. The services performed as a guardian ad litem are as follows:

    a. {[17] *Identify service*}, which occurred on {[18] *date*} and required {[19] *number*} hours of {[20] *name of guardian ad litem*}'s time. {[21] *Explain why the service was reasonable and necessary.*}

{Continue until all services are stated.}

11. A reasonable hourly fee for {[22] *name of guardian ad litem*}'s services is ${[23] *amount*} per hour. {[24] *Explain why the hourly fee is reasonable.*}

12. The total amount claimed for services is ${[25] *amount*}.

{For services performed by person other than guardian ad litem}

13. {[26] *Identify person who performed services for guardian ad litem*} performed services necessary to fulfill the guardian ad litem's duties because {[27] *identify unusual circumstances that required the person's services*}. The services performed by {[28] *name of person*} are as follows:

    a. {[29] *Identify service*}, which occurred on {[30] *date*} and required {[31] *number*} hours of {[32] *name of person*}'s time. {[33] *Explain why the service was reasonable and necessary.*}

{Continue until all services are stated.}

14. A reasonable hourly fee for {[34] *name of person*}'s services is ${[35] *amount*} per hour. {[36] *Explain why the hourly fee is reasonable.*}

15. The total amount claimed for services is ${[37] *amount*}.

CONCLUSION

16. {[38] *Briefly summarize the application.*}

PRAYER

{CHOOSE APPROPRIATE PARAGRAPH 17}

17. Because the parties have agreed to the application, {[39] *name of guardian ad litem*} asks the Court to render judgment on the application and award the guardian ad litem fees.

17. Because the parties have not agreed to the application, {40 *name of guardian ad litem*} asks the Court to set the application fees for hearing and, after the hearing, to award the guardian ad litem fees.

SEE: Tex. R. Civ. P. 173.6
O'Connor's Texas Rules * Civil Trials (2019), "Application for fees," ch. 1-I, §6.1, p. 91; "Hearing on application," ch. 1-I, §6.3, p. 94

ADD: STYLE OF THE CASE – FORM 1B:2
SIGNATURE BLOCK – FORM 1B:3
VERIFICATION – FORM 1B:7

ATTACH: AFFIDAVIT – FORM 1B:8, if necessary

NOTE: A guardian ad litem may be compensated for services performed by a person other than the designated guardian ad litem. ***Ford Motor Co. v. Garcia***, 363 S.W.3d 573, 580 (Tex.2012). For example, a paralegal supervised by the guardian ad litem could perform tasks necessary to fulfill the guardian ad litem's appointed role, but at a lower rate, or an attorney familiar with the matter, rather than the guardian ad litem, could appear at a hearing because an emergency arose that kept the guardian from attending. *Id.* But the guardian ad litem should, if possible, get the trial court's authorization for using another person's services before any expenses are actually incurred. *Id.* at 580 n.5. See ***O'Connor's Texas Rules***, "For services of person other than guardian ad litem," ch. 1-I, §6.1.3(1)(b), p. 92.

Unless there are exceptional circumstances, a guardian ad litem is not entitled to be compensated for lost opportunity for other employment. *See **Land Rover U.K., Ltd. v. Hinojosa***, 210 S.W.3d 604, 608-09 (Tex.2006).

{❶ *PARTY*}'S OBJECTION TO GUARDIAN AD LITEM FEES

{❷ *Party*}, {❸ *name*}, objects to {❹ *name of guardian ad litem*}'s application for guardian ad litem fees.

INTRODUCTION

1. Plaintiff, {❺ *name*}, sued defendant, {❻ *name*}, for {❼ *state basis of suit*}.

2. The guardian ad litem is {❽ *name of guardian ad litem*}.

3. {❾ *State other relevant facts about the suit.*}

BACKGROUND

4. {❿ *Name of guardian ad litem*} filed an application for guardian ad litem fees on {⓫ *date*}.

5. {⓬ *State other facts relevant to the objection.*}

ARGUMENT & AUTHORITIES

6. At the conclusion of his or her appointment, a guardian ad litem can apply to the court for compensation. Tex. R. Civ. P. 173.6(b). The application must be verified and must detail the basis for the compensation requested. *Id.* If a guardian ad litem requests compensation, the guardian can only be reimbursed for reasonable and necessary expenses and paid a reasonable hourly fee for necessary services performed. Tex. R. Civ. P. 173.6(a). The guardian ad litem bears the burden to establish that the requested fees are reasonable and necessary. *Stewart Title Guar. Co. v. Sterling*, 822 S.W.2d 1, 10 (Tex. 1991), *modified on other grounds*, *Tony Gullo Motors I, L.P. v. Chapa*, 212 S.W.3d 299 (Tex. 2006); *Magna Donnelly Corp. v. DeLeon*, 267 S.W.3d 108, 113 (Tex. App.—San Antonio 2008, no pet.).

{*CHOOSE APPROPRIATE PARAGRAPHS 7-14*}

7. {⓭ *Party*} objects to the application for guardian ad litem fees because the application is not verified.

8. {⓮ *Party*} objects to the application because the guardian ad litem fees overbilled for expenses and services. *See* Tex. R. Civ. P. 173.6(b); *Jocson v. Crabb*, 133 S.W.3d 268, 270 (Tex. 2004); *Goodyear Dunlop Tires N. Am., Ltd. v. Gamez*, 151 S.W.3d 574, 588-89 (Tex. App.—San Antonio 2004, no pet.). {⓯ *Elaborate.*}

9. {[16] *Party*} objects to the application for guardian ad litem fees because the guardian ad litem's hourly rate is unreasonable. *See* Tex. R. Civ. P. 173.6(a); *Goodyear Dunlop Tires N. Am., Ltd. v. Gamez*, 151 S.W.3d 574, 590-91 (Tex. App.—San Antonio 2004, no pet.). {[17] *Elaborate.*}

10. {[18] *Party*} objects to the application for guardian ad litem fees because the amount of fees sought by {[19] *name of guardian ad litem*} exceeds the amount of the hours spent and the hourly fee supported by the evidence. *Land Rover U.K., Ltd. v. Hinojosa*, 210 S.W.3d 604, 608 (Tex. 2006). Because there are no exceptional circumstances in this case that would warrant a fee in excess of the hours spent, {[20] *name of guardian ad litem*} is not entitled to those additional fees. *Id.* at 609. {[21] *Elaborate.*}

11. {[22] *Party*} objects to the application for guardian ad litem fees because the guardian ad litem should not be compensated for work performed outside the scope of {[23] *his/her*} duties. *Ford Motor Co. v. Garcia*, 363 S.W.3d 573, 580 (Tex. 2012); *Land Rover U.K., Ltd. v. Hinojosa*, 210 S.W.3d 604, 607 (Tex. 2006); *see Ford Motor Co. v. Chacon*, 370 S.W.3d 359, 362-63 (Tex. 2012). {[24] *Elaborate.*}

12. {[25] *Party*} objects to the application for guardian ad litem fees because the guardian ad litem should not be compensated for work performed after it was determined that there was no conflict of interest. *Ford Motor Co. v. Stewart, Cox & Hatcher, P.C.*, 390 S.W.3d 294, 297-98 (Tex. 2013). {[26] *Elaborate.*}

13. {[27] *Party*} objects to the application for guardian ad litem fees because the guardian ad litem should not be compensated for work performed after the conflict of interest that necessitated the appointment has been resolved. *Brownsville-Valley Reg'l Med. Ctr., Inc. v. Gamez*, 894 S.W.2d 753, 757 (Tex. 1995). {[28] *Elaborate.*}

14. {[29] *Party*} objects to the application for guardian ad litem fees because the guardian ad litem should not be awarded a percentage of the {[30] *judgment/settlement*}. *See* Tex. R. Civ. P. 173.6(b). {[31] *Elaborate.*}

CONCLUSION

15. {[32] *Briefly summarize the objection.*}

PRAYER

16. For these reasons, {[33] *party*} objects to {[34] *name of guardian ad litem*}'s application for guardian ad litem fees and asks the Court to deny the application.

Continued on next page

Texas Civil Forms

Chapter 1. General Trial Forms

Form 11:5 Objection to Guardian Ad Litem Fees

SEE: Tex. R. Civ. P. 173.6
O'Connor's Texas Rules * Civil Trials (2019), "Objection to fees," ch. 1-I, §6.2, p. 93

ADD: STYLE OF THE CASE – FORM 1B:2
SIGNATURE BLOCK – FORM 1B:3

ATTACH: AFFIDAVIT – FORM 1B:8, if necessary

{❶ *PARTY*}'S MOTION FOR REFERRAL TO ASSOCIATE JUDGE

{❷ *Party*}, {❸ *name*}, asks the Court to refer the matters described below to the Associate Judge of the Court under the authority of Texas Government Code section 54A.107(a).

INTRODUCTION

1. Plaintiff, {❹ *name*}, sued defendant, {❺ *name*}, for {❻ *state basis of suit*}.

2. {❼ *State other relevant facts about the suit.*}

BACKGROUND

3. {❽ *State facts relevant to the motion.*}

ARGUMENT & AUTHORITIES

4. Under Texas Government Code section 54A.107(a), a case may be referred to an associate judge by an order of referral in a specific case. Unless specifically limited by the order of referral, an associate judge has the powers and duties listed under Texas Government Code section 54A.108.

{*CHOOSE APPROPRIATE PARAGRAPH 5*}

5. {❾ *Party*} asks the Court to refer all matters permitted under Texas Government Code section 54A.108 to the Associate Judge of the Court.

5. {❿ *Party*} asks the Court to refer the following matters to the Associate Judge of the Court: {⓫ *list matters to be referred*}.

CONCLUSION

6. {⓬ *Briefly summarize the motion.*}

PRAYER

7. For these reasons, {⓭ *party*} asks the Court to refer the matters described above to the Associate Judge of the Court.

◄ *Continued on next page* ►

TEXAS CIVIL FORMS

CHAPTER 1. GENERAL TRIAL FORMS

FORM 1J:1 MOTION FOR REFERRAL TO ASSOCIATE JUDGE

SEE: Tex. Gov't Code §§54A.106-54A.108
O'Connor's Texas Rules * Civil Trials (2019), "Associate Judge," ch. 1-J, p. 95

ADD: STYLE OF THE CASE – FORM 1B:2
SIGNATURE BLOCK – FORM 1B:3
CERTIFICATE OF CONFERENCE – FORM 1B:12, if necessary
CERTIFICATE OF SERVICE – FORM 1B:13

ATTACH: NOTICE OF HEARING OR SUBMISSION – FORM 1E:1
ORDER – FORM 1J:2

NOTE: Under Texas Government Code chapter 54A, subchapter B, a district court or statutory county court can appoint a full-time or part-time associate judge to perform certain duties if the creation of the associate judge position is authorized by the county commissioners court. Tex. Gov't Code §54A.102(a). If the creation of the position is authorized, the court can refer all or part of any civil case to an associate judge to resolve. *Id.* §54A.106(a). A case can be referred to an associate judge either by an order of referral in a specific case or by an omnibus order. *Id.* §54A.107(a). Unless limited by an order of referral, an associate judge will have the powers and duties listed under Texas Government Code section 54A.108.

ORDER ON {❶ *PARTY*}'S
MOTION FOR REFERRAL TO ASSOCIATE JUDGE

After considering {❷ *party*} {❸ *name*}'s motion for referral of an associate judge, the Court

{*CHOOSE APPROPRIATE ORDER*}

DENIES the motion.

GRANTS the motion, and refers the following to the Associate Judge of the Court: {❹ *list matters to be referred*}.

SIGNED on _______________, 20___.

____
PRESIDING JUDGE

SEE: Tex. Gov't Code §§54A.106-54A.108
O'Connor's Texas Rules * Civil Trials (2019), "Order of referral," ch. 1-J, §3.2, p. 96

ADD: STYLE OF THE CASE – FORM 1B:2
CERTIFICATE OF SERVICE – FORM 1B:13, if proposed order served separately from motion or response

NOTE: Under Texas Government Code chapter 54A, subchapter B, a district court or statutory county court can appoint a full-time or part-time associate judge to perform certain duties if the creation of the associate judge position is authorized by the county commissioners court. Tex. Gov't Code §54A.102(a). If the creation of the position is authorized, the court can refer all or part of any civil case to an associate judge to resolve. *Id.* §54A.106(a). A case can be referred to an associate judge either by an order of referral in a specific case or by an omnibus order. *Id.* §54A.107(a). Unless limited by an order of referral, an associate judge will have the powers and duties listed under Texas Government Code section 54A.108.

{❶ *PARTY*}'S OBJECTION TO REFERRAL TO ASSOCIATE JUDGE

{❷ *Party*}, {❸ *name*}, objects to the Associate Judge of the Court from {❹ *hearing the trial on the merits/presiding over the jury trial*} in this case.

INTRODUCTION

1. Plaintiff, {❺ *name*}, sued defendant, {❻ *name*}, for {❼ *state basis of suit*}.

2. {❽ *State other relevant facts about the suit.*}

BACKGROUND

3. On {❾ *date*}, the Court referred the trial in this case to the Associate Judge of the Court.

4. On {❿ *date*}, {⓫ *party*} received notice of the Court's order of referral.

5. {⓬ *State other facts relevant to the objection.*}

ARGUMENT & AUTHORITIES

6. Under Texas Government Code section 54A.106, a party may file a written objection to an associate judge hearing a trial on the merits or presiding over a jury trial. As long as the objection is filed within ten days after the party receives notice of the referral, the referring court, not the associate judge, must hear the trial on the merits or preside over the jury trial. Tex. Gov't Code §54A.106(c).

7. Because {⓭ *party*} timely filed {⓮ *his/her/its*} objection, {⓯ *party*} asks the Court to withdraw its order of referral and to {⓰ *hear the trial on the merits/preside over the jury trial*} in this case.

CONCLUSION

8. {⓱ *Briefly summarize the objection.*}

PRAYER

9. For these reasons, {⓲ *party*} asks the Court to withdraw its referral and {⓳ *hear the trial on the merits/preside over the jury trial*} in this case.

FORM 1J:3 OBJECTION TO REFERRAL TO ASSOCIATE JUDGE

SEE: Tex. Gov't Code §§54A.106-54A.108
O'Connor's Texas Rules * Civil Trials (2019), "Objection to referral," ch. 1-J, §3.3, p. 96

ADD: STYLE OF THE CASE – FORM 1B:2
SIGNATURE BLOCK – FORM 1B:3
CERTIFICATE OF CONFERENCE – FORM 1B:12, if necessary
CERTIFICATE OF SERVICE – FORM 1B:13

NOTE: Under Texas Government Code chapter 54A, subchapter B, a district court or statutory county court can appoint a full-time or part-time associate judge to perform certain duties if the creation of the associate judge position is authorized by the county commissioners court. Tex. Gov't Code §54A.102(a). If the creation of the position is authorized, the court can refer a full trial on the merits or a jury trial to an associate judge. *Id.* §54A.106(b). A party can prohibit the trial referral only if it files an objection within ten days after receiving notice of the referral. *Id.* §54A.106(c). Because the referring court is required to hear a full trial on the merits or preside over a jury trial if an objection is filed, the court does not need to issue an order on the objection.

{❶ *PARTY*}'S REQUEST FOR DE NOVO HEARING

{❷ *Party*}, {❸ *name*}, asks the Court for a de novo hearing on the Associate Judge's decision in this case.

INTRODUCTION

1. Plaintiff, {❹ *name*}, sued defendant, {❺ *name*}, for {❻ *state basis of suit*}.

2. {❼ *State other relevant facts about the suit.*}

BACKGROUND

3. On {❽ *date*}, the Associate Judge of the Court {❾ *describe hearing that resulted in appealable decision, e.g., heard plaintiff's motion to compel discovery*}.

4. On {❿ *date*}, the Associate Judge notified {⓫ *party*} of its decision. The Associate Judge {⓬ *describe judge's decision*}.

{*ADD PARAGRAPH 5 IF APPLICABLE*}

5. On {⓭ *date*}, {⓮ *plaintiff/defendant*} filed an initial request for a de novo hearing on the Associate Judge's decision.

6. {⓯ *State other facts relevant to the request.*}

ARGUMENT & AUTHORITIES

7. Under Texas Government Code section 54A.115(a), a party may ask the referring court to conduct a de novo hearing on an associate judge's decision. If the request is timely filed and the party has not previously waived its right to a de novo hearing, the referring court must conduct the de novo hearing on the issues specified in the request. *See* Tex. Gov't Code §§54A.113(b), 54A.115. The hearing must be conducted within 30 days after the initial request for a de novo hearing is filed. *Id.* §54A.115(e).

A. Request timely filed.

8. A request for a de novo hearing is timely if is filed either within seven working days after the party received notice of the associate judge's decision or within seven working days after another party made the initial request for a de novo hearing. Tex. Gov't Code §54A.115(a), (d).

9. {⓰ *Party*}'s request for a de novo hearing is timely because it was filed within seven working days {⓱ *after receiving notice of the Associate Judge's decision/after an initial request for a de novo hearing was made*}.

B. Hearing not waived.

10. A party may waive its right to a de novo hearing in writing or on the record before the start of a hearing with an associate judge. Tex. Gov't Code §54A.112(c).

11. {18 *Party*} has not waived its right to a de novo hearing in writing or on the record in this case.

C. Issues for hearing.

12. Because {19 *party*} has timely filed {20 *his/her/its*} request and has not waived {21 *his/her/its*} right to a de novo hearing, {22 *party*} asks the Court to conduct a de novo hearing on the following issues: {23 *list issues*}.

{*ADD SECTION D IF APPLICABLE*}

D. Jury demand.

13. {24 *Party*} also asks that the de novo hearing be conducted before a jury. A party can demand a jury in a de novo hearing as long as the associate judge's decision did not result from a jury trial. Because the Associate Judge's decision in this case did not result from a jury trial, {25 *party*}'s jury demand is proper.

CONCLUSION

14. {26 *Briefly summarize the motion.*}

PRAYER

15. For these reasons, {27 *party*} asks the Court to conduct a de novo hearing {28 *add if applicable: before a jury*} on the issues described above within 30 days after {29 *date*}.

SEE: Tex. Gov't Code §54A.115
O'Connor's Texas Rules * Civil Trials (2019), "To referring court – de novo hearing," ch. 1-J, §9.1, p. 98

ADD: STYLE OF THE CASE – FORM 1B:2
SIGNATURE BLOCK – FORM 1B:3
CERTIFICATE OF SERVICE – FORM 1B:13

NOTE: Under Texas Government Code chapter 54A, subchapter B, a district court or statutory county court can appoint a full-time or part-time associate judge to perform certain duties if the creation of the associate judge position is authorized by the county commissioners court. Tex. Gov't Code §54A.102(a). If the creation of the position is authorized, the court can refer all or part of any civil case to an associate judge to resolve. *Id.* §54A.106(a). A party can appeal an associate judge's decision by filing a request for a de novo hearing with the referring court. *Id.* §54A.111(b), (e). If a request for a de novo hearing is not timely filed as required by Texas Government Code section 54A.115(a), or if the party has waived the right to a de novo hearing, the party can still appeal or seek other relief from the court of appeals or the Supreme Court. *Id.* §54A.116(a).

{❶ *PARTY*}'S MOTION REQUESTING APPOINTMENT OF MASTER

{❷ *Party*}, {❸ *name*}, asks the Court to appoint a master in this case to {❹ *describe specific powers to assume, pending issues to decide, and acts to perform*}.

INTRODUCTION

1. Plaintiff, {❺ *name*}, sued defendant, {❻ *name*}, for {❼ *state basis of suit*}.

2. {❽ *State other relevant facts about the suit.*}

BACKGROUND

3. {❾ *State facts relevant to the motion.*}

ARGUMENT & AUTHORITIES

4. A court may appoint a master in exceptional cases when there is good cause. Tex. R. Civ. P. 171; *Simpson v. Canales*, 806 S.W.2d 802, 811 (Tex. 1991).

5. This case is exceptional, and there is good cause to appoint a master, because {❿ *state why the case is exceptional and why there is good cause to appoint a master, e.g., the number of parties, the amount of activity the case has generated, the problems that have arisen because of the size and complexity of the case, and the technical problems inherent in the evidence*}.

CONCLUSION

6. {⓫ *Briefly summarize the motion.*}

PRAYER

7. For these reasons, {⓬ *party*} asks the Court to appoint a master to {⓭ *describe specific powers to assume, pending issues to decide, and acts to perform*}.

SEE: Tex. R. Civ. P. 171
*O'Connor's Texas Rules * Civil Trials* (2019), "Motion for Referral to Master Under TRCP 171," ch. 1-K, §3, p. 100

ADD: STYLE OF THE CASE – FORM 1B:2
SIGNATURE BLOCK – FORM 1B:3
CERTIFICATE OF CONFERENCE – FORM 1B:12, if necessary
CERTIFICATE OF SERVICE – FORM 1B:13

ATTACH: AFFIDAVIT – FORM 1B:8, if necessary
NOTICE OF HEARING OR SUBMISSION – FORM 1E:1
ORDER – FORM 1K:3

{❶ *PARTY*}'S OBJECTION TO APPOINTMENT OF MASTER

{❷ *Party*}, {❸ *name*}, objects to

{*CHOOSE APPROPRIATE STATEMENT*}

Ⓐ {❹ *adverse party*}'s motion requesting the appointment of a master.

Ⓑ the Court's appointment of a master.

INTRODUCTION

1. Plaintiff, {❺ *name*}, sued defendant, {❻ *name*}, for {❼ *state basis of suit*}.

2. {❽ *State other relevant facts about the suit.*}

BACKGROUND

{*CHOOSE APPROPRIATE PARAGRAPH 3*}

3. On {❾ *date*}, {❿ *adverse party*} {⓫ *name*} filed a motion requesting the appointment of a master to {⓬ *describe the details of the requested appointment*}.

3. On {⓭ *date*}, the Court appointed {⓮ *name of master*} as master to {⓯ *describe the details of the appointment*}.

4. {⓰ *State other facts relevant to the objection.*}

ARGUMENT & AUTHORITIES

{*CHOOSE APPROPRIATE PARAGRAPHS 5-7*}

5. A court may appoint a master only in exceptional cases when there is good cause. Tex. R. Civ. P. 171; *Simpson v. Canales*, 806 S.W.2d 802, 811 (Tex. 1991). The requirements of "exceptional cases" and "good cause" are not met merely because a case is time-consuming or complicated or because the court is busy. *Simpson*, 806 S.W.2d at 811. This case is not exceptional, and there is no good cause to appoint a master. {⓱ *Specify why the case is not exceptional and why there is no good cause to appoint a master, e.g., although there have been numerous motions, none of them were particularly complex.*}

6. A court may appoint a master who is a citizen of Texas and who is not related to or representing one of the parties. Tex. R. Civ. P. 171. The Court's order referring this case to {⓲ *name of master*} violates Texas Rule of Civil Procedure 171 because {⓳ *name of master*} is not qualified to serve. Specifically, the master is {⓴ *not a citizen of Texas/related to one of the parties/an attorney for one of the parties*}.

Continued on next page

7. An order of referral to a master must clearly and specifically define the scope and limits of the master's authority and must refer only pending matters. *See* Tex. R. Civ. P. 171; *Owens-Corning Fiberglas Corp. v. Caldwell*, 830 S.W.2d 622, 626 (Tex. App.—Houston [1st Dist.] 1991, orig. proceeding). The Court's order referring this case to {21 *name of master*} violates Texas Rule of Civil Procedure 171 because {22 *specify how the referral order is too broad or nonspecific, e.g., it refers future issues, it confers powers of discovery production without the need for a request, it is a blanket order of referral*}.

CONCLUSION

8. {23 *Briefly summarize the objection.*}

PRAYER

9. For these reasons, {24 *party*} objects to

{*CHOOSE APPROPRIATE STATEMENT*}

[A] {25 *adverse party*}'s motion requesting the appointment of a master and asks the Court to deny the motion.

[B] the Court's appointment of a master and asks the Court to withdraw the appointment.

SEE: Tex. R. Civ. P. 171
*O'Connor's Texas Rules * Civil Trials* (2019), "Objection to Master's Appointment," ch. 1-K, §5, p. 101

ADD: STYLE OF THE CASE – FORM 1B:2
SIGNATURE BLOCK – FORM 1B:3
CERTIFICATE OF SERVICE – FORM 1B:13

ATTACH: AFFIDAVIT – FORM 1B:8, if necessary
ORDER – FORM 1K:3

ORDER ON {❶ *PARTY*}'S REQUEST FOR APPOINTMENT OF MASTER

After considering {❷ *party*} {❸ *name*}'s motion requesting appointment of a master and the objection, the Court

{*CHOOSE APPROPRIATE ORDER*}

DENIES the motion.

GRANTS the motion, finding that the case is exceptional because {❹ *state reasons*} and that there is good cause for the appointment because {❺ *state reasons*}. Thus, the Court orders the following:

1. The Court appoints ______________ as master for the following purposes: {❻ *specify master's powers and state specific, pending issues*}.

2. The master will hold hearings on the referred matters beginning on __________, 20___. The hearings will be held at {❼ *identify location*}. The master will file a report with the Court by __________, 20___.

3. The master will be allowed reasonable compensation, to be taxed as costs.

SIGNED on ________________, 20___.

____
PRESIDING JUDGE

SEE: Tex. R. Civ. P. 171
O'Connor's Texas Rules * Civil Trials (2019), "Order of Referral to Master," ch. 1-K, §4, p. 100

ADD: STYLE OF THE CASE – FORM 1B:2
CERTIFICATE OF SERVICE – FORM 1B:13, if proposed order served separately from motion or response

NOTE: If the parties agree to the appointment of a master, the order does not need to include findings about the exceptional nature of the case and good cause.

{❶ *PARTY*}'S REQUEST TO MASTER FOR A RECORD

{❷ *Party*}, {❸ *name*}, asks the master to provide a record of all proceedings before {❹ *him/her*}.

INTRODUCTION

1. Plaintiff, {❺ *name*}, sued defendant, {❻ *name*}, for {❼ *state basis of suit*}.

2. {❽ *State other relevant facts about the suit.*}

BACKGROUND

3. On {❾ *date*}, the Court appointed {❿ *name of master*} as master to {⓫ *describe the details of the appointment*}.

4. {⓬ *State other facts relevant to the request.*}

ARGUMENT & AUTHORITIES

5. When requested by a party, the master must make a record of the evidence offered and excluded in the same manner as a court sitting in the trial of a case. Tex. R. Civ. P. 171.

PRAYER

6. {⓭ *Party*} asks the master to make a record of all proceedings before {⓮ *him/her*}.

SEE: Tex. R. Civ. P. 171
O'Connor's Texas Rules * Civil Trials (2019), "Record of hearing," ch. 1-K, §6.1, p. 101

ADD: STYLE OF THE CASE – FORM 1B:2
SIGNATURE BLOCK – FORM 1B:3
CERTIFICATE OF SERVICE – FORM 1B:13

{❶ *PARTY*}'S OBJECTIONS TO MASTER'S REPORT

{❷ *Party*}, {❸ *name*}, objects to the master's report.

INTRODUCTION

1. Plaintiff, {❹ *name*}, sued defendant, {❺ *name*}, for {❻ *state basis of suit*}.

2. {❼ *State other relevant facts about the suit.*}

BACKGROUND

3. On {❽ *date*}, the Court appointed {❾ *name of master*} as a master to {❿ *describe the details of the appointment*}.

4. After a hearing, the master submitted a report to the Court.

5. {⓫ *State other facts relevant to the objection.*}

ARGUMENT & AUTHORITIES

6. A party has the right to present evidence on issues specified in objections to a master's report. *See Young v. Young*, 854 S.W.2d 698, 703 (Tex. App.—Dallas 1993, writ denied).

7. {⓬ *Party*} objects to the master's report. Specifically, {⓭ *state specific objections*}.

PRAYER

8. {⓮ *Party*} asks the Court to allow presentation of evidence before the {⓯ *Court/jury*} on the issues to which {⓰ *party*} has objected.

SEE: Tex. R. Civ. P. 171
O'Connor's Texas Rules * Civil Trials **(2019), "Objection to Master's Report," ch. 1-K, §8, p. 102**

ADD: STYLE OF THE CASE – FORM 1B:2
SIGNATURE BLOCK – FORM 1B:3
CERTIFICATE OF SERVICE – FORM 1B:13

THE STATE OF TEXAS

SUBPOENA FOR {❶ *TRIAL/HEARING/ DEPOSITION/PRODUCTION OF DOCUMENTS*}

To: Any sheriff or constable of the State of Texas or other person authorized to serve and execute subpoenas as provided in Texas Rule of Civil Procedure 176.5. {*See* ***O'Connor's Texas Rules***, *"Who may serve subpoenas," ch. 1-L, §3.4, p. 105.*}

You are commanded to summon {❷ *name of subpoenaed party*}, {❸ *add if appropriate: the custodian of records for {name of record holder},*} who may be found at {❹ *street address, city, county, state, zip code, phone number*}, to appear at {❺ *street address, city, county, state, zip code*}, on {❻ *date*}, at {❼ *time*},

{*CHOOSE APPROPRIATE DIRECTIONS*}

Ⓐ before {❽ *identify judge and court*}, to attend and give testimony at {❾ *trial/a hearing*} in this case on behalf of the {❿ *plaintiff/defendant*}, and to remain in attendance from day to day until lawfully discharged.

Ⓑ to attend and give testimony at a deposition in this case on behalf of the {⓫ *plaintiff/defendant*}, and to remain in attendance from day to day until lawfully discharged.

Ⓒ to attend and give testimony at a deposition in this case on behalf of the {⓬ *plaintiff/defendant*}, to produce and permit inspection and copying of documents or tangible things to be used as evidence in this case, and to remain in attendance from day to day until lawfully discharged. The following are the documents or tangible things that must be produced: {⓭ *list and number documents individually or by category and describe each item or category with reasonable particularity*}.

Ⓓ to produce and permit inspection and copying of the following documents or tangible things to be used as evidence in this case: {⓮ *list and number documents individually or by category and describe each item or category with reasonable particularity*}.

Duties of Person Served with Subpoena. You are advised that under Texas Rule of Civil Procedure 176, a person served with a subpoena has certain rights and obligations. Rule 176.6 provides the following:

(a) *Compliance required.* Except as provided in this subdivision, a person served with a subpoena must comply with the command stated therein unless discharged by the court or by the party summoning such witness. A person com-

manded to appear and give testimony must remain at the place of deposition, hearing, or trial from day to day until discharged by the court or by the party summoning the witness.

(b) *Organizations*. If a subpoena commanding testimony is directed to a corporation, partnership, association, governmental agency, or other organization, and the matters on which examination is requested are described with reasonable particularity, the organization must designate one or more persons to testify on its behalf as to matters known or reasonably available to the organization.

(c) *Production of documents or tangible things*. A person commanded to produce documents or tangible things need not appear in person at the time and place of production unless the person is also commanded to attend and give testimony, either in the same subpoena or a separate one. A person must produce documents as they are kept in the usual course of business or must organize and label them to correspond with the categories in the demand. A person may withhold material or information claimed to be privileged but must comply with Rule 193.3. A nonparty's production of a document authenticates the document for use against the nonparty to the same extent as a party's production of a document is authenticated for use against the party under Rule 193.7.

(d) *Objections*. A person commanded to produce and permit inspection or copying of designated documents and things may serve on the party requesting issuance of the subpoena—before the time specified for compliance—written objections to producing any or all of the designated materials. A person need not comply with the part of a subpoena to which objection is made as provided in this paragraph unless ordered to do so by the court. The party requesting the subpoena may move for such an order at any time after an objection is made.

(e) *Protective orders*. A person commanded to appear at a deposition, hearing, or trial, or to produce and permit inspection and copying of designated documents and things, and any other person affected by the subpoena, may move for a protective order under Rule 192.6(b)—before the time specified for compliance—either in the court in which the action is pending or in a district court in the county where the subpoena was served. The person must serve the motion on all parties in accordance with Rule 21a. A person need not comply with the part of a subpoena from which protection is sought under this paragraph unless ordered to do so by the court. The party requesting the subpoena may seek such an order at any time after the motion for protection is filed.

Continued on next page

(f) *Trial subpoenas.* A person commanded to attend and give testimony, or to produce documents or things, at a hearing or trial, may object or move for protective order before the court at the time and place specified for compliance, rather than under paragraphs (d) and (e).

Contempt. Failure by any person without adequate excuse to obey a subpoena served on that person may be deemed a contempt of the court from which the subpoena is issued or a district court in the county in which the subpoena is served, and may be punished by fine or confinement or both. Tex. R. Civ. P. 176.8(a).

DO NOT FAIL to return this writ to {15 *identify court in which case is pending*} with either the attached officer's return showing the manner of execution or the witness's signed memorandum showing that the witness accepted the subpoena.

This subpoena was issued at the request of {16 *party*}, {17 *name of party*}, whose attorney of record is {18 *name of party's attorney*}, {19 *street address, city, state, zip code, phone number*}. You may contact {20 *party*}'s attorney to arrange another time and date.

ISSUED on ______________, 20___.

{*CHOOSE APPROPRIATE SIGNATURE BLOCK*}

By:______________________
Deputy {21 *District/County*} Clerk
{22 *Name of clerk*}, {23 *District/County*} Clerk
{24 *County*}, Texas
{25 *Address, city, state, zip code*}

By:______________________
{26 *Name of attorney or deposition officer*}
{27 *Address, city, state, zip code*}

SEE: Tex. R. Civ. P. 176, 199.3, 205, 215.5
Tex. Civ. Prac. & Rem. Code §22.001
O'Connor's Texas Rules * Civil Trials (2019), "Formal Requirements for Subpoenas," ch. 1-L, §3, p. 104

ADD: STYLE OF THE CASE – FORM 1B:2
RETURN OR ACCEPTANCE OF SUBPOENA – FORM 1L:2

ATTACH: NOTICE OF ORAL DEPOSITION – FORM 6F:1, if applicable
NOTICE OF DEPOSITION ON WRITTEN QUESTIONS – FORM 6F:4, if applicable
Witness fee of $10.00, if applicable (i.e., if a nonparty is being subpoenaed to give testimony at a deposition, hearing, or trial)

NOTE: Attorneys may issue subpoenas. Tex. R. Civ. P. 176.4(b). Proof of service of the subpoena must be made by filing either of the following with the court: (1) a statement by the person who served the subpoena stating the date, time, and manner of service and the name of the person served, or (2) the witness's signed written memorandum. Tex. R. Civ. P. 176.5(b).

RETURN OF SERVICE OF SUBPOENA

I, ________________, delivered a copy of this subpoena to {❶ *name of witness*} in person at ____________________, in ________ County, Texas, on __________, 20___, at _____ o'clock __.m., and tendered to the witness a fee of $______ in cash.

I, ________________, was unable to deliver a copy of this subpoena to {❷ *name of witness*} for the following reasons: ____ ____ ____.

{*CHOOSE APPROPRIATE SIGNATURE BLOCK*}

By Deputy: ____________________
Sheriff/Constable ______________
____________________ County, Texas

By: ____________________
Person authorized by law or written order of the trial court who has no interest in the lawsuit and is at least 18 years old

By: ____________________
Person certified by order of the Supreme Court

ACCEPTANCE OF SERVICE OF SUBPOENA BY WITNESS UNDER TEXAS RULE OF CIVIL PROCEDURE 176

I accept service of this subpoena. {*See **O'Connor's Texas Rules**, "Proof of service," ch. 1-L, §3.9, p. 105.*}

____
Witness

____
Date

FEE FOR SERVICE OF SUBPOENA: $__________

FORM 1L:2 RETURN OR ACCEPTANCE OF SUBPOENA

SEE: Tex. R. Civ. P. 176.5(b)
Tex. Civ. Prac. & Rem. Code §22.001
O'Connor's Texas Rules * Civil Trials (2019), "Proof of service," ch. 1-L, §3.9, p. 105

NOTE: The witness fee is $10 per day. Tex. Civ. Prac. & Rem. Code §22.001(a).

Service of subpoenas is treated the same as service of process. *See* Tex. R. Civ. P. 103 (process includes citation and other notices, writs, orders, and papers issued by the court). See ***O'Connor's Texas Rules***, "Who May Serve Process," ch. 2-I, §3, p. 191. A person who is certified by order of the Supreme Court may serve process. Tex. R. Civ. P. 103. The Supreme Court has adopted guidelines in Judicial Branch Certification Commission Rule 8.0 for a person to be certified to serve process. *See* Tex.Sup.Ct. Order, Misc. Docket No. 18-9060 (eff. Apr. 12, 2018); *see also* Tex.Sup.Ct. Order, Misc. Docket No. 14-9186 (eff. Sept. 1, 2014) (person certified by Judicial Branch Certification Commission to serve process is certified by order of Supreme Court under Texas Rule of Civil Procedure 103). The Judicial Branch Certification Commission Rules and other information on process-server certification can be found on the Judicial Branch Certification Commission website at www.txcourts.gov/jbcc.

CHAPTER 2. PLAINTIFF'S LAWSUIT
TABLE OF CONTENTS

Statutory Notice

Plaintiff's Original Petition

Expedited Actions

Injunctive Relief

Declaratory Relief

TABLE OF CONTENTS

{*Letterhead*}

{❶ *Date*}

{❷ *Name of attorney, potential adverse party, or third party*}
{❸ *Address*}
{❹ *City, state, zip code*}

RE: Retention Notice for Documents, Electronic or Magnetic Data, and Tangible Things

Dear {❺ *name of attorney, potential adverse party, or third party*}:

{❻ *Name of attorney's client, potential adverse party, or third party*} must immediately suspend the normal retention and destruction policies for documents, electronic or magnetic data, and tangible things and must preserve and retain all documents, electronic or magnetic data, and tangible things relating to occurrences or transactions discussed in this letter. The failure to preserve and retain this information may constitute spoliation of evidence and subject {❼ *you/your client*} to legal claims for damages or monetary sanctions.

This letter is to inform you that my client, {❽ *name of client*}, believes that {❾ *you/your client/your company, corporation, organization, etc.*} may possess documents, electronic or magnetic data, and tangible things relating to {❿ *briefly describe occurrence or transaction at issue, e.g., corporation's termination of my client on July 1, 2006*}. Specifically, {⓫ *describe potential or current litigation in a manner that sufficiently informs attorney or party about the nature of the client's claim and the parties involved*}.

As part of my client's ongoing {⓬ *investigation/litigation*}, {⓭ *you/your client*} may be requested to produce responsive documents, electronic or magnetic data, and tangible things. Thus, {⓮ *you have/your client has*} an obligation to take reasonable steps to ensure that all relevant documents, electronic or magnetic data, and tangible things are safeguarded and preserved until the resolution of this legal matter.

DEFINITIONS

In this letter, the terms "document," "electronic or magnetic data," "occurrence or transaction," and "tangible thing" mean the following:

Document. The term "document" means all written, typed, or printed matter and all magnetic, electronic, or other records or documentation of any kind or description in your actual possession, custody, or control, including those in the possession, custody,

Continued on next page

or control of any and all present or former directors, officers, employees, consultants, accountants, attorneys, or other agents, whether or not prepared by you, that constitute or contain matters relevant to the subject matter of the action. "Document" includes, but is not limited to, the following: letters, reports, charts, diagrams, correspondence, telegrams, memoranda, notes, records, minutes, contracts, agreements, records or notations of telephone or personal conversations or conferences, interoffice communications, e-mail, microfilm, bulletins, circulars, pamphlets, photographs, faxes, invoices, tape recordings, computer printouts, drafts, résumés, logs, worksheets, {⓯ *continue listing examples as necessary*}.

Electronic or magnetic data. The term "electronic or magnetic data" means electronic information that is stored in a medium from which it can be retrieved and examined. The term refers to the original (or identical duplicate when the original is not available) and any other copies of the data that may have attached comments, notes, marks, or highlighting of any kind. Electronic or magnetic data includes, but is not limited to, the following: computer programs; operating systems; computer activity logs; programming notes or instructions; e-mail receipts, messages, or transmissions; output resulting from the use of any software program, including word-processing documents, spreadsheets, database files, charts, graphs, and outlines; metadata; PIF and PDF files; batch files; deleted files; temporary files; Internet- or web-browser-generated information stored in textual, graphical, or audio format, including history files, caches, and cookies; {⓰ *continue listing examples as necessary*}; and any miscellaneous files or file fragments. Electronic or magnetic data includes any items stored on magnetic, optical, digital, or other electronic-storage media, such as hard drives, floppy disks, CD-ROMs, DVDs, tapes, smart cards, integrated-circuit cards (e.g., SIM cards), removable media (e.g., Zip drives, Jaz cartridges), microfiche, punched cards, {⓱ *continue listing examples as necessary*}. Electronic or magnetic data also includes the file, folder, tabs, containers, and labels attached to or associated with any physical storage device with each original or copy.

Occurrence or transaction. The term "occurrence or transaction" means {⓲ *specifically describe the occurrence or transaction at issue, focusing on key dates, individuals, businesses, jurisdictions, etc.*}.

Tangible thing. The term "tangible thing" means a physical object that is not a document or electronic or magnetic data.

{*Continue listing definitions as necessary.*}

FORM 2A:1

PRESERVATION & RETENTION RESPONSIBILITIES

To preserve and retain documents, electronic or magnetic data, and tangible things {19 *you/your client*} must immediately suspend certain normal retention and destruction policies, including {20 *identify all procedures relating to documents and tangible things to be suspended, such as shredding, recycling, etc., and all procedures relating to electronic or magnetic data to be suspended, such as disk defragmentation, electronic data shredding, server backup tape rotation, recycling or destruction of computer systems or storage devices, etc.*}.

In addition to suspending the policies relating to documents, electronic or magnetic data, and tangible things, {21 *you/your client*} must immediately do the following:

1. Take affirmative steps to prevent anyone with access to documents, electronic or magnetic data, and tangible things relating to the occurrence or transaction from hiding, modifying, or destroying them.

2. Preserve and retain the following documents: {22 *identify any specific documents that should be preserved*}.

3. Preserve and retain the following electronic or magnetic data: {23 *identify any specific electronic or magnetic data that should be preserved*}.

4. Preserve and retain the following tangible things: {24 *identify any specific tangible things that should be preserved*}.

5. Preserve and retain all documents relating to the occurrence or transaction that either are in the possession of or were created, sent, or received by the following: {25 *list names of persons, companies, organizations, etc.*}.

6. Preserve and retain all electronic or magnetic data relating to the occurrence or transaction that either is in the possession of or was created, sent, or received by the following: {26 *list names of persons, companies, organizations, etc.*}.

7. Preserve and retain all documents, electronic or magnetic data, and computer hardware or software necessary to access, view, and reconstruct electronic or magnetic data relating to the occurrence or transaction.

8. Preserve and retain all tangible things relating to the occurrence or transaction that either are in the possession of or were created, sent, or received by the following: {27 *list names of persons, companies, organizations, etc.*}.

{*Continue listing responsibilities as appropriate.*}

Continued on next page

Because {㉘ *you/your client*} may also have to make relevant electronic or magnetic data available for litigation, {㉙ *you/your client*} should consider protecting that electronic or magnetic data by making a mirror image of it. A "mirror image" is a bit-by-bit copy of electronic or magnetic data (e.g., on a hard drive or flash drive) that ensures the computer system is not altered during the imaging process. The mirror image includes active, hidden, and deleted files, deleted file fragments, directories, and any other data contained on the drive. To alleviate any burden on {㉚ *you/your client*}, my client is prepared to hire a computer forensic expert to properly and noninvasively create mirror images of all media in {㉛ *your/your client's*} possession, custody, or control that may contain electronic or magnetic data related to the occurrence or transaction.

Please contact me if you have any questions about this letter. Thank you for your cooperation in this matter.

Sincerely,

____

{㉜ *Name of attorney*}

SEE: ***O'Connor's Texas Rules * Civil Trials*** (2019), "Preservation letter," ch. 6-C, §3.2.2(2), p. 594

{*Letterhead*}

{❶ *Date*}

{❷ *Name of defendant*}
{❸ *Address*}
{❹ *City, state, zip code*}

RE: {❺ *Description of claim*}

Dear {❻ *name of defendant*}:

I represent {❼ *name of client*}, who has retained me to assert a claim against you {❽ *identify claim, e.g., on a sworn account, for services rendered, for labor performed, for material furnished*}. {*Tex. Civ. Prac. & Rem. Code §38.001.*} This letter is notice of my client's claim and attempt to resolve this matter without litigation. {*See* ***O'Connor's Texas COA***, *"Plaintiff presented claim to defendant," ch. 45-B, §2.5, p. 1490.*} {❾ *Add if appropriate: Please forward this notice to your insurance carrier or bonding company.*}

On {❿ *date*}, my client

{*CHOOSE APPROPRIATE STATEMENT*}

[A] {⓫ *rendered services to/performed labor for/furnished material to*} you. {*Tex. Civ. Prac. & Rem. Code §38.001(1)-(3).*} Because you accepted the {⓬ *services/material*}, you became bound to pay my client for them. Attached is a copy of the account that accurately sets forth the quantities, prices, and dates of {⓭ *performance/delivery*} of the {⓮ *services/material*}, and all offsets, payments, and credits. At this time, the balance due to my client on the account is ${⓯ *amount*}. {*See* ***O'Connor's Texas COA***, *"Authorized claims," ch. 45-B, §2.2.2, p. 1488.*}

[B] provided {⓰ *goods/services*} to you on {⓱ *an open/a sworn*} account. {*Tex. Civ. Prac. & Rem. Code §38.001(7).*} Because you accepted the {⓲ *goods/services*}, you became bound to pay my client's charges, which were reasonable and customary for the {⓳ *goods/services*}. Attached is a copy of the account that accurately sets forth the quantities, prices, and dates of {⓴ *delivery/performance*} of the {㉑ *goods/services*}, and all offsets, payments, and credits. At this time, the balance due to my client on the account is ${㉒ *amount*}. {*See* ***O'Connor's Texas COA***, *"Sworn account," ch. 45-B, §2.2.2(7), p. 1488.*}

Continued on next page

[C] {㉓ *identify other claim listed in Texas Civil Practice & Remedies Code section 38.001 for which attorney fees are recoverable*}. {㉔ *Elaborate.*} At this time, my client's damages amount to ${㉕ *amount*}. {*See* ***O'Connor's Texas COA****, "Authorized claims," ch. 45-B, §2.2.2, p. 1488.*}

My client wishes to resolve this matter without filing suit. Therefore, we request that you remit payment in the amount of ${㉖ *amount*}. If this sum is not paid within 30 days of receipt of this notice, suit will be filed against you, and my client will seek recovery of reasonable attorney fees as allowed by Texas Civil Practice & Remedies Code section 38.001 et seq. {*See* ***O'Connor's Texas COA****, "Deadline," ch. 45-B, §2.6.2, p. 1491.*}

I look forward to hearing from you soon.

Sincerely,

____

{㉗ *Name of attorney*}

SEE: Tex. Civ. Prac. & Rem. Code ch. 38
O'Connor's Texas Rules * Civil Trials (2019), "Notices & Demands," ch. 2-A, §2, p. 113
O'Connor's Texas Causes of Action (2019), "Attorney Fees Under CPRC ch. 38," ch. 45-B, p. 1486

ATTACH: Documents that support the claim

NOTE: For the deadline for giving notice, see ***O'Connor's Texas COA***, "Deadline," ch. 45-B, §2.5.2, p. 1491.

For the notice letter for a breach-of-contract claim under Texas Civil Practice & Remedies Code chapter 38, see FORM 2A:3.

C enter into a separate written agreement to rescind the contract and remit payment in the amount of ${30 *amount*}, which includes my client's actual damages, attorney fees, and expenses. The agreement to rescind must include the following terms: {31 *specify terms*}. If you do not agree to rescind the contract and pay the sum within {32 *number of days, 30 or greater*} days of receipt of this notice, suit will be filed against you.

I look forward to hearing from you soon.

Sincerely,

____

{33 *Name of attorney*}

SEE: ***O'Connor's Texas Rules * Civil Trials*** (2019), "Notices & Demands," ch. 2-A, §2, p. 113
O'Connor's Texas Causes of Action (2019), "Breach of Contract," ch. 5-B, p. 69; "Attorney Fees," ch. 45, p. 1463

NOTE: If the plaintiff seeks attorney fees under Texas Civil Practice & Remedies Code chapter 38, the plaintiff must permit the defendant to settle the suit within 30 days. *See* Tex. Civ. Prac. & Rem. Code §38.002. If the plaintiff seeks attorney fees under a contractual provision, that provision may give the defendant more than 30 days to settle.

A plaintiff bringing a breach-of-contract claim relating to insurance claims for damage to or loss of real property caused by forces of nature must give written presuit notice of the plaintiff's claim under Texas Insurance Code chapter 542A. *See* Tex. Ins. Code §§542A.001(2), 542A.002(a)(1), 542A.003. For a discussion of presuit notice of a claim under chapter 542A, see ***O'Connor's Texas COA***, "Suits for real-property-related damage caused by forces of nature," ch. 13-C, §6.2, p. 370.

{*Letterhead*}

{❶ *Date*}

{❷ *Name of defendant*}
{❸ *Address*}
{❹ *City, state, zip code*}

RE: {❺ *Description of claim*}

Dear {❻ *name of defendant*}:

I represent {❼ *name of client*}, who has retained me to assert a claim against you for violations of the Texas Deceptive Trade Practices Act (DTPA), Texas Business & Commerce Code section 17.41 et seq. This letter is notice of my client's claim and attempt to resolve this matter without litigation. {*See **O'Connor's Texas COA**, "Plaintiff = consumer," ch. 8, §2.1, p. 210; "Consumer Status Under DTPA," chart 8-1, p. 214; "Presuit Notice of Claim," ch. 8, §6, p. 249.*} If this claim is covered by an insurance policy, please forward this letter to your insurance carrier to ensure that the carrier receives timely notice of the claim and will provide you with representation and coverage.

This claim arose from

{*CHOOSE APPROPRIATE STATEMENT*}

Ⓐ your engagement in false, misleading, or deceptive acts or practices that my client relied on to my client's detriment. Specifically, you {❽ *identify the deceptive acts and practices from the DTPA "laundry list," located in Tex. Bus. & Com. Code §17.46(b)*}. {❾ *Elaborate.*} {*See **O'Connor's Texas COA**, "False, misleading, or deceptive act or practice," ch. 8, §2.3.1, p. 227; "Detrimental reliance," ch. 8, §2.3.1(2), p. 233.*}

Ⓑ your breach of an {❿ *express/implied*} warranty. Specifically, you breached {⓫ *identify warranty that was breached*}. {⓬ *Elaborate.*} {*See **O'Connor's Texas COA**, "Breach of warranty," ch. 8, §2.3.2, p. 233.*}

Ⓒ your engagement in an unconscionable course of action that, to my client's detriment, took advantage of my client's lack of knowledge, ability, experience, or capacity to a grossly unfair degree. Specifically, you {⓭ *identify the unconscionable course of action*}. {⓮ *Elaborate.*} {*See **O'Connor's Texas COA**, "Unconscionable act," ch. 8, §2.3.3, p. 234.*}

D your use or employment of an act or practice in violation of Texas Insurance Code chapter 541. Specifically, you {15 *identify act or practice that violated chapter 541*}. {16 *Elaborate.*} {*See **O'Connor's Texas COA**, "Violation of chapter 541," ch. 8, §2.3.4, p. 235; "Deceptive Insurance Practices," ch. 13-C, p. 353.*}

E your engagement in false, misleading, or deceptive acts or practices that my client relied on to my client's detriment and that violated a "tie-in" consumer statute. Specifically, you {17 *identify the tie-in statute and the deceptive acts*}. {18 *Elaborate.*} {*See **O'Connor's Texas COA**, "Violation of tie-in statute," ch. 8, §2.3.5, p. 236.*}

Because of your violation of the DTPA, my client has incurred {19 *economic/actual*} damages of ${20 *amount*}. These damages represent {21 *specify damages incurred*}. In the event of litigation, these amounts will be adjusted upward to reflect any additional damages. {*See **O'Connor's Texas COA**, "Economic damages," ch. 8, §3.1.1, p. 239; "Actual damages," ch. 8, §3.1.3, p. 240.*}

{*IF CONDUCT WAS COMMITTED KNOWINGLY, ADD NEXT PARAGRAPH*}

In the event of litigation, my client will also seek recovery of mental-anguish damages in the amount of ${22 *amount*} and trebled {23 *economic/actual*} damages on the grounds that your conduct was committed knowingly. Specifically, {24 *describe facts that support allegation of knowing conduct*}. {*See **O'Connor's Texas COA**, "Mental-anguish damages," ch. 8, §3.1.2, p. 240; "Additional damages," ch. 8, §3.2, p. 241.*}

{*IF CONDUCT WAS COMMITTED INTENTIONALLY, ADD NEXT PARAGRAPH*}

In addition, because your conduct was intentional, my client will seek recovery of trebled mental-anguish damages. Specifically, {25 *describe facts that support allegation of intentional conduct*}. {*See **O'Connor's Texas COA**, "Mental-anguish damages," ch. 8, §3.1.2, p. 240; "Additional damages," ch. 8, §3.2, p. 241.*}

At this time, my client has incurred attorney fees in the amount of ${26 *amount*} and other related expenses in the amount of ${27 *amount*}. In the event of litigation, these amounts will be adjusted to reflect the additional time and expense incurred. {*See **O'Connor's Texas COA**, "Attorney fees," ch. 8, §3.7, p. 243.*}

Continued on next page

My client wishes to resolve this matter without filing suit. Therefore, we request that you remit payment in the amount of ${㉘ *amount*}. This sum includes my client's economic damages, {㉙ *add if appropriate: mental-anguish damages,*} attorney fees, and expenses. If this sum is not paid within 60 days of receipt of this notice, suit will be filed against you.

I look forward to hearing from you soon.

Sincerely,

____

{㉚ *Name of attorney*}

SEE: Tex. Bus. & Com. Code §§17.45, 17.46, 17.50, 17.505, 17.5052
O'Connor's Texas Rules * Civil Trials (2019), "Notices & Demands," ch. 2-A, §2, p. 113
O'Connor's Texas Causes of Action (2019), "Deceptive Trade Practices Act," ch. 8, p. 209
O'Connor's Texas Business & Commerce Code Plus (2018-19), "DTPA Consumer Status Chart," p. 999

NOTE: Under the DTPA, the plaintiff's recovery is generally limited to economic damages. But if the claim is based on a violation of a tie-in statute, the plaintiff can recover actual damages, which may be broader. See ***O'Connor's Texas COA***, "DTPA damages," ch. 8, §3.1, p. 239.

This form is for a DTPA claim for defective products. It can be modified if your client purchased defective services rather than products.

For the deadline for giving notice, see ***O'Connor's Texas COA***, "Deadline to give notice," ch. 8, §6.1.1, p. 249.

A plaintiff bringing a DTPA claim relating to insurance claims for damage to or loss of real property caused by forces of nature must give written presuit notice of the plaintiff's claim under Texas Insurance Code chapter 542A. *See* Tex. Ins. Code §§542A.001(2), 542A.002(a)(3)(C), 542A.003. For a discussion of presuit notice of a claim under chapter 542A, see ***O'Connor's Texas COA***, "Suits for real-property-related damage caused by forces of nature," ch. 13-C, §6.2, p. 370.

PLAINTIFF'S ORIGINAL PETITION
{❶ *STATE ADDITIONAL RELIEF REQUESTED*
IF APPROPRIATE, E.G., & REQUEST FOR DISCLOSURE}

Plaintiff, {❷ *name*}, files this original petition {❸ *state additional relief requested if appropriate, e.g., and request for disclosure*} against defendant, {❹ *name*}, and alleges as follows:

DISCOVERY-CONTROL PLAN

{*CHOOSE APPROPRIATE PARAGRAPH 1*}

1. Plaintiff intends to conduct discovery under Level 1 of Texas Rule of Civil Procedure 190.2 and affirmatively pleads that this suit is governed by the expedited-actions process in Texas Rule of Civil Procedure 169. {*See **O'Connor's Texas Rules**, "Discovery-Control Plans," ch. 2-B, §2, p. 115.*}

1. Plaintiff intends to conduct discovery under Level {❺ *2/3*} of Texas Rule of Civil Procedure {❻ *190.3/190.4*} and affirmatively pleads that this suit is not governed by the expedited-actions process in Texas Rule of Civil Procedure 169 because {❼ *explain, e.g., plaintiff requests injunctive relief, plaintiff seeks monetary relief over $100,000*}. {*See **O'Connor's Texas Rules**, "Discovery-Control Plans," ch. 2-B, §2, p. 115. For a motion to request a Level 3 discovery-control plan, see FORM 6A:6.*}

CLAIM FOR RELIEF

{*CHOOSE APPROPRIATE PARAGRAPH 2*}

2. Plaintiff seeks only monetary relief of $100,000 or less, including damages of any kind, penalties, court costs, expenses, prejudgment interest, and attorney fees. {*Tex. R. Civ. P. 47(c)(1).*}

2. Plaintiff seeks monetary relief of $100,000 or less and nonmonetary relief. {*Tex. R. Civ. P. 47(c)(2).*}

2. Plaintiff seeks monetary relief over $100,000 but not more than $200,000. {*Tex. R. Civ. P. 47(c)(3).*}

2. Plaintiff seeks monetary relief over $200,000 but not more than $1,000,000. {*Tex. R. Civ. P. 47(c)(4).*}

2. Plaintiff seeks monetary relief over $1,000,000. {*Tex. R. Civ. P. 47(c)(5).*}

Continued on next page

PARTIES

3. {*For plaintiff designation, see FORM 2B:9;* ***O'Connor's Texas Rules****, "Plaintiff," ch. 2-B, §4.4, p. 123.*}

4. {*For defendant designation, see FORMS 2B:10-19;* ***O'Connor's Texas Rules****, "Defendant," ch. 2-B, §4.5, p. 123.*}

JURISDICTION

5. {*For jurisdiction allegations, see FORM 2B:20. It is not necessary to plead jurisdiction for most suits. See* ***O'Connor's Texas Rules****, "Jurisdiction," ch. 2-B, §5, p. 125.*}

VENUE

6. {*For venue allegations, see FORM 2B:21. It is not necessary to plead venue, but pleading sufficient venue facts could avoid a motion to transfer venue. See* ***O'Connor's Texas Rules****, "Venue," ch. 2-B, §6, p. 127.*}

FACTS

7. On {❽ *date*}, at {❾ *identify location*}, {❿ ________} County, Texas, {⓫ *describe events that resulted in lawsuit*}.

8. {⓬ *State other relevant facts in separately numbered paragraphs.*} {*See* ***O'Connor's Texas Rules****, "Pleading a Cause of Action," ch. 2-B, §7, p. 127.*}

COUNT 1 – {⓭ *NAME OF FIRST CAUSE OF ACTION*}

9. {⓮ *In separately numbered paragraphs, identify elements and facts supporting a cause of action. For lists of elements for various causes of action, see* ***O'Connor's Texas COA****, "Causes of Action," Part 2, p. 7.*}

{*ADD APPROPRIATE PARAGRAPH 10*}

10. Plaintiff seeks unliquidated damages within the jurisdictional limits of this Court. {*See Tex. R. Civ. P. 47(b);* ***O'Connor's Texas Rules****, "Damages," ch. 2-B, §9, p. 130.*}

10. Plaintiff seeks liquidated damages in the amount of at least ${⓯ *amount*}, which is within the jurisdictional limits of this Court. {*See Tex. R. Civ. P. 47(b);* ***O'Connor's Texas Rules****, "Damages," ch. 2-B, §9, p. 130.*}

{ADD PARAGRAPHS 11-12 IF APPLICABLE}

11. Exemplary damages. Plaintiff's injury resulted from defendant's gross negligence, malice, or fraud, which entitles plaintiff to exemplary damages under Texas Civil Practice & Remedies Code section 41.003(a). {[16] *Elaborate.*} {*See* ***O'Connor's Texas COA****, "Exemplary Damages," ch. 42, p. 1419; "Types of Aggravated Conduct," ch. 42-B, §5, p. 1430;* ***O'Connor's Texas COA Pleadings****, FORMS 42.*}

12. Attorney fees. Plaintiff is entitled to recover reasonable and necessary attorney fees under {[17] *identify statute, contract provision, or equitable grounds permitting recovery of attorney fees*}. {[18] *Elaborate.*} {*See FORMS 2B:22-24;* ***O'Connor's Texas COA****, "Attorney Fees," ch. 45, p. 1463.*}

{ADD PARAGRAPHS 13-18 AS APPROPRIATE}

COUNT 2 – {[19] *NAME OF ANOTHER CAUSE OF ACTION*}

13. In {[20] *the alternative/addition*} to other counts, plaintiff sues defendant for {[21] *identify another cause of action*}. {[22] *In separately numbered paragraphs, identify elements and facts supporting the cause of action, add any claims for exemplary damages or attorney fees, and include a statement that damages are within the jurisdictional limits of the court. See ¶¶10-12, this form.*}

EQUITABLE RELIEF

14. Plaintiff seeks {[23] *identify equitable relief sought*}. {[24] *State facts supporting equitable relief.*} {*See FORM 2D:1;* ***O'Connor's Texas Rules****, "Injunctive Relief," ch. 2-D, p. 138.*}

JURY DEMAND

15. Plaintiff demands a jury trial and tenders the appropriate fee with this petition. {*See* ***O'Connor's Texas Rules****, "Request for Jury Trial," ch. 5-B, p. 400.*}

CONDITIONS PRECEDENT

16. All conditions precedent to plaintiff's claim for relief have been performed or have occurred. {*See* ***O'Connor's Texas Rules****, "Conditions Precedent," ch. 2-B, §12, p. 132.*}

REQUEST FOR DISCLOSURE

17. Under Texas Rule of Civil Procedure 194, plaintiff requests that defendant disclose, within 50 days of the service of this request, the information or material described in Rule 194.2. {*See* ***O'Connor's Texas Rules****, "Content of request," ch. 6-E, §3.2, p. 627.*}

Continued on next page

OBJECTION TO ASSOCIATE JUDGE

18. Plaintiff objects to the referral of this case to an associate judge for hearing a trial on the merits or presiding at a jury trial. {*See **O'Connor's Texas Rules**, "Objection to referral," ch. 1-J, §3.3, p. 96.*}

PRAYER

19. For these reasons, plaintiff asks that the Court issue citation for defendant to appear and answer, and that plaintiff be awarded a judgment against defendant for the following:

{*CHOOSE RELIEF SOUGHT*}

a. Actual damages. {*See **O'Connor's Texas COA**, "Pleading actual damages," ch. 41-A, §3.2, p. 1346.*}

b. {㉕ *Describe equitable relief.*}

c. Exemplary damages. {*See **O'Connor's Texas COA**, "Exemplary Damages," ch. 42, p. 1419.*}

d. Prejudgment and postjudgment interest. {*See **O'Connor's Texas COA**, "Interest," ch. 43, p. 1445.*}

e. Court costs. {*See **O'Connor's Texas COA**, "Court Costs," ch. 44, p. 1453.*}

f. Attorney fees. {*See **O'Connor's Texas COA**, "Attorney Fees," ch. 45, p. 1463.*}

g. All other relief to which plaintiff is entitled. {*See **O'Connor's Texas Rules**, "Prayer," ch. 2-B, §15, p. 132.*}

SEE: Tex. R. Civ. P. 45-59, 78-82, 169, 190, 194
Tex. Civ. Prac. & Rem. Code §41.003
O'Connor's Texas Rules * Civil Trials (2019), "Plaintiff's Original Petition," ch. 2-B, p. 115
O'Connor's Texas Causes of Action (2019), "Damages & Other Compensation," Part 4, p. 1343
O'Connor's Texas Causes of Action Pleadings (2019), FORMS 41-45

ADD: STYLE OF THE CASE – FORM 1B:2
SIGNATURE BLOCK – FORM 1B:3
VERIFICATION – FORM 1B:7, for injunctive relief

ATTACH: AFFIDAVIT – FORM 1B:8, if necessary to support facts for injunctive relief
NOTICE OF CURRENT/CHANGE OF ADDRESS – FORM 1B:14
Civil Process Request Form, if required by court clerk to issue citation
Exhibits, if necessary
Filing fees
Jury fee, if jury trial requested

NOTE: Many suits filed in district and county courts may be governed by the expedited-actions process outlined in Texas Rule of Civil Procedure 169. Tex.Sup.Ct. Order, Misc. Docket No. 13-9022 (eff. Mar. 1, 2013); *see* Tex. R. Civ. P. 169(a). See ***O'Connor's Texas Rules***, "Expedited Actions," ch. 2-C, p. 134. A plaintiff filing a suit that meets the requirements for an expedited action must conduct discovery under Level 1. *See* Tex. R. Civ. P. 169(d)(1), 190.2(a)(1). See ***O'Connor's Texas Rules***, "Level 1," ch. 6-A, §7.2, p. 520.

All original pleadings that set forth a claim for relief—whether an original petition, a counterclaim, a cross-claim, or a third-party claim—generally must contain a specific statement of the relief the party seeks. *See* Tex. R. Civ. P. 47(c). This requirement does not apply, however, to guardianship or probate proceedings, suits governed by the Family Code, or suits filed in justice court. See ***O'Connor's Texas Rules***, "Relief sought," ch. 1-B, §3.2.8, p. 9.

When one plaintiff asserts multiple claims against a single defendant, jurisdiction is determined by adding the amounts together. ***Texas City Tire Shop, Inc. v. Alexander***, 333 S.W.2d 690, 693 (Tex.App.—Houston 1960, no writ).

E-filing is mandatory for most courts in all counties. *See* Tex.Sup.Ct. Order, Misc. Docket No. 13-9164 (Dec. 9, 2013). See ***O'Connor's Texas Rules***, "E-filing," ch. 1-C, §4.1.1, p. 25.

Whether e-filing or not, a party may have to redact certain sensitive data from a document before filing. *See* Tex. R. Civ. P. 21c. See ***O'Connor's Texas Rules***, "Documents with sensitive data – privacy protection," ch. 1-C, §4.2, p. 29.

Before a court clerk will issue a citation for service, the plaintiff may be required to complete and file with its petition a Civil Process Request Form identifying the person to be served and the method of service. Check the court's website for specific requirements and to obtain a copy of the form.

PLAINTIFF'S ORIGINAL PETITION
{❶ *STATE ADDITIONAL RELIEF REQUESTED IF APPROPRIATE, E.G., & REQUEST FOR DISCLOSURE*}

Plaintiff, {❷ *name*}, files this original petition {❸ *state additional relief requested if appropriate, e.g., and request for disclosure*} against defendant, {❹ *name*}, and alleges as follows:

DISCOVERY-CONTROL PLAN

{*CHOOSE APPROPRIATE PARAGRAPH 1*}

1. Plaintiff intends to conduct discovery under Level 1 of Texas Rule of Civil Procedure 190.2 and affirmatively pleads that this suit is governed by the expedited-actions process in Texas Rule of Civil Procedure 169. {*See **O'Connor's Texas Rules**, "Discovery-Control Plans," ch. 2-B, §2, p. 115.*}

1. Plaintiff intends to conduct discovery under Level {❺ *2/3*} of Texas Rule of Civil Procedure {❻ *190.3/190.4*} and affirmatively pleads that this suit is not governed by the expedited-actions process in Texas Rule of Civil Procedure 169 because {❼ *explain, e.g., plaintiff requests injunctive relief, plaintiff seeks monetary relief over $100,000*}. {*See **O'Connor's Texas Rules**, "Discovery-Control Plans," ch. 2-B, §2, p. 115. For a motion to request a Level 3 discovery-control plan, see FORM 6A:6.*}

CLAIM FOR RELIEF

{*CHOOSE APPROPRIATE PARAGRAPH 2*}

2. Plaintiff seeks only monetary relief of $100,000 or less, including damages of any kind, penalties, court costs, expenses, prejudgment interest, and attorney fees. {*Tex. R. Civ. P. 47(c)(1).*}

2. Plaintiff seeks monetary relief of $100,000 or less and nonmonetary relief. {*Tex. R. Civ. P. 47(c)(2).*}

2. Plaintiff seeks monetary relief over $100,000 but not more than $200,000. {*Tex. R. Civ. P. 47(c)(3).*}

2. Plaintiff seeks monetary relief over $200,000 but not more than $1,000,000. {*Tex. R. Civ. P. 47(c)(4).*}

2. Plaintiff seeks monetary relief over $1,000,000. {*Tex. R. Civ. P. 47(c)(5).*}

PARTIES

3. {*For plaintiff designation, see FORM 2B:9;* ***O'Connor's Texas Rules****, "Plaintiff," ch. 2-B, §4.4, p. 123.*}

4. {*For defendant designation, see FORMS 2B:10-19;* ***O'Connor's Texas Rules****, "Defendant," ch. 2-B, §4.5, p. 123.*}

JURISDICTION

5. {*For jurisdiction allegations, see FORM 2B:20. It is not necessary to plead jurisdiction for most suits. See* ***O'Connor's Texas Rules****, "Jurisdiction," ch. 2-B, §5, p. 125.*}

VENUE

{*CHOOSE APPROPRIATE PARAGRAPH 6*}

6. Venue for this suit for breach of a written contract is permissive in {❽ _______} County under Texas Civil Practice & Remedies Code section 15.035(a) because this county {❾ *was identified as the place for an obligation under the contract to be performed/is where defendant is domiciled*}. {❿ *Elaborate.*} {*See* ***O'Connor's Texas COA****, "Written contract – contractual performance," ch. 5-B, §7.3.2, p. 112.*}

6. Venue for this suit for breach of a written contract is permissive in {⓫ _______} County under Texas Civil Practice & Remedies Code section 15.035(b) because this is a suit brought by a creditor on a written contract involving a consumer transaction for {⓬ *goods/services/loans/extensions of credit*} intended for {⓭ *personal/family/household/agricultural*} use, and this is the county where defendant {⓮ *signed the contract/resided when this suit was commenced*}. {⓯ *Elaborate.*} {*See* ***O'Connor's Texas COA****, "Written contract – consumer transaction," ch. 5-B, §7.3.3, p. 112.*}

6. Venue for this suit for breach of a written contract is mandatory in {⓰ _______} County under Texas Civil Practice & Remedies Code section 15.020(b) because this suit arises from a "major transaction" as defined by section 15.020(a), and this is the county designated in writing as the county for suit. {⓱ *Elaborate.*} {*See* ***O'Connor's Texas COA****, "Written contractual venue," ch. 5-B, §7.3.4, p. 112.*}

6. Venue for this suit for breach of {⓲ *an oral/a written*} contract is permissive in {⓳ *name of county and precinct*} Justice Court under Texas Civil Practice & Remedies Code section 15.092(b) because this is a suit on a contract for labor actually performed in this county and precinct. {⓴ *Elaborate.*} {*See* ***O'Connor's Texas COA****, "Oral contract," ch. 5-B, §7.3.1, p. 112.*}

◄ Continued on next page ►

6. Venue for this suit is permissive in {[21] _______} County under Texas Civil Practice & Remedies Code section 15.031 because defendant is the {[22] *executor/administrator/guardian*} of the estate of {[23] *name of decedent*}, the suit is brought to establish a money demand against the estate, and this is the county where the estate is administered. {[24] *Elaborate.*} {*See* ***O'Connor's Texas COA***, *"Estate administration," ch. 5-B, §7.3.5, p. 113.*}

6. {*For other venue allegations, see FORM 2B:21. It is not necessary to plead venue, but pleading sufficient venue facts could avoid a motion to transfer venue. See* ***O'Connor's Texas Rules***, *"Venue," ch. 2-B, §6, p. 127.*}

FACTS

7. On {[25] *date*}, at {[26] *identify location*}, {[27] _______} County, Texas, {[28] *describe events that resulted in lawsuit*}.

8. {[29] *State other relevant facts in separately numbered paragraphs.*} {*See* ***O'Connor's Texas Rules***, *"Alleging facts," ch. 2-B, §7.2.1, p. 128.*}

COUNT 1 – BREACH OF CONTRACT

{*CHOOSE APPROPRIATE PARAGRAPH 9*}

9. On {[30] *date*}, plaintiff and defendant executed a valid and enforceable written contract. Plaintiff attaches a copy of the contract as Exhibit {[31] *letter*} and incorporates it by reference. The contract provided that plaintiff would {[32] *list plaintiff's contractual obligations*}, and that defendant would {[33] *list defendant's contractual obligations*}. {*See* ***O'Connor's Texas COA***, *"Enforceable contract," ch. 5-B, §2.1, p. 71.*}

9. On {[34] *date*}, plaintiff and defendant entered into a valid and enforceable oral contract that was performable within one year. By this contract, the parties agreed that plaintiff would {[35] *list plaintiff's contractual obligations*}, and that defendant would {[36] *list defendant's contractual obligations*}. {*See* ***O'Connor's Texas COA***, *"Enforceable contract," ch. 5-B, §2.1, p. 71; "Statute of frauds," ch. 5-B, §5.1.12, p. 100.*}

9. On {[37] *date*}, defendant and {[38] *contracting party*} entered into a valid and enforceable contract. The contract provided that {[39] *contracting party*} would {[40] *list contracting party's contractual obligations*}, and that defendant would {[41] *list defendant's contractual obligations*}. Plaintiff has standing to enforce the contract executed by defendant and {[42] *contracting party*} because plaintiff is {[43] *an assignee of the contracting party's contractual rights/a third-party beneficiary of the contract*}. {*See* ***O'Connor's Texas COA***, *"Assignee," ch. 5-B, §2.2.2, p. 72; "Third-party beneficiary," ch. 5-B, §2.2.4, p. 73.*}

{*CHOOSE APPROPRIATE PARAGRAPH 10*}

10. Plaintiff {44 *fully performed/substantially performed/tendered performance of/was excused from performing*} plaintiff's contractual obligations. {45 *Elaborate.*} {*See* ***O'Connor's Texas COA***, *"Performance," ch. 5-B, §2.3, p. 73.*}

10. {46 *Contracting party*} {47 *fully performed/substantially performed/tendered performance of/was excused from performing*} {48 *his/her/its*} contractual obligations. {49 *Elaborate.*} {*See* ***O'Connor's Texas COA***, *"Performance," ch. 5-B, §2.3, p. 73.*}

11. Defendant breached the contract by {50 *describe nature of the breach*}. {*See* ***O'Connor's Texas COA***, *"Defendant breached contract," ch. 5-B, §2.4, p. 78.*}

12. Defendant's breach caused injury to plaintiff, which resulted in the following damages: {51 *identify damages*}. {*See* ***O'Connor's Texas COA***, *"Breach caused injury," ch. 5-B, §2.5, p. 81; "Remedies," ch. 5-B, §3, p. 82; "Damages that Must Be Specifically Pleaded," chart 41-1, p. 1348.*}

{*CHOOSE APPROPRIATE PARAGRAPH 13*}

13. Plaintiff seeks unliquidated damages within the jurisdictional limits of this Court. {*See Tex. R. Civ. P. 47(b);* ***O'Connor's Texas Rules***, *"Damages," ch. 2-B, §9, p. 130.*}

13. Plaintiff seeks liquidated damages in the amount of at least \${52 *amount*}, which is within the jurisdictional limits of this Court. {*See Tex. R. Civ. P. 47(b);* ***O'Connor's Texas Rules***, *"Damages," ch. 2-B, §9, p. 130.*}

13. Plaintiff seeks liquidated damages under an enforceable liquidated-damages clause in the contract in the amount of \${53 *amount*}, which is within the jurisdictional limits of this Court. {*See Tex. R. Civ. P. 47(b);* ***O'Connor's Texas Rules***, *"Damages," ch. 2-B, §9, p. 130.*} The parties agreed when they executed the contract that the harm caused by any breach was {54 *incapable of being estimated/difficult to estimate*} and that the amount of liquidated damages was a reasonable forecast of just compensation. {55 *Elaborate.*} {*See* ***O'Connor's Texas COA***, *"Liquidated damages," ch. 5-B, §3.2, p. 83.*}

{*CHOOSE APPROPRIATE PARAGRAPH 14*}

14. Attorney fees. Plaintiff is entitled to recover reasonable and necessary attorney fees under Texas Civil Practice & Remedies Code chapter 38 because this is a suit for breach of {56 *an oral/a written*} contract. Plaintiff retained counsel, who presented plaintiff's claim to {57 *defendant/defendant's duly authorized agent*}. Defendant did

Continued on next page

FORM 2B:2

not tender the amount owed within 30 days after the claim was presented. {58 *Elaborate.*} {*See* ***O'Connor's Texas COA****, "Defendant did not tender payment," ch. 45-B, §2.6, p. 1491.*}

14. Attorney fees. Plaintiff is entitled to recover reasonable and necessary attorney fees under the provisions of the written contract as set out in section {59 *number*}, which provides: {60 *quote relevant provisions of contract*}. Plaintiff has complied with all the requirements of this section. {61 *Elaborate.*} {*See* ***O'Connor's Texas COA****, "Plaintiff entitled to attorney fees," ch. 45-C, §2.6, p. 1500.*}

{*ADD PARAGRAPHS 15-23 AS APPROPRIATE*}

COUNT 2 – QUANTUM MERUIT

15. In the alternative to Count 1, defendant accepted {62 *services/materials*} from plaintiff without compensating plaintiff. {63 *In separately numbered paragraphs, identify elements and facts supporting quantum meruit, add any claim for attorney fees, and include a statement that damages are within the jurisdictional limits of the court. See ¶13, this form.*} {*See* ***O'Connor's Texas COA****, "Quantum Meruit," ch. 5-C, p. 114;* ***O'Connor's Texas COA Pleadings****, FORM 5C:1.*}

COUNT 3 – PROMISSORY ESTOPPEL

16. In the alternative to Count 1, defendant made a promise to plaintiff that defendant did not keep. {64 *In separately numbered paragraphs, identify elements and facts supporting promissory estoppel, add any claim for attorney fees, and include a statement that damages are within the jurisdictional limits of the court. See ¶13, this form.*} {*See* ***O'Connor's Texas COA****, "Promissory Estoppel as a Claim," ch. 5-D, p. 121;* ***O'Connor's Texas COA Pleadings****, FORM 5D:1.*}

COUNT 4 – {65 *NAME OF ANOTHER CAUSE OF ACTION*}

17. In {66 *the alternative/addition*} to other counts, plaintiff sues defendant for {67 *identify another cause of action*}. {68 *In separately numbered paragraphs, identify elements and facts supporting the cause of action, add any claims for exemplary damages, attorney fees, or equitable relief, and include a statement that damages are within the jurisdictional limits of the court. See ¶13, this form.*} {*For related claims, see* ***O'Connor's Texas COA****, "Related Causes of Action," ch. 5-B, §8, p. 113.*}

EQUITABLE RELIEF

18. In the alternative to monetary damages, plaintiff seeks the equitable relief of

{*CHOOSE ONE OF THE FOLLOWING*}

A specific performance of the contract. {69 *Elaborate.*} {*See* ***O'Connor's Texas COA****, "Specific performance," ch. 5-B, §3.5.1, p. 84.*}

- **B** rescission of the contract. {**70** *Elaborate.*} {*See **O'Connor's Texas COA**, "Rescission," ch. 5-B, §3.5.2, p. 86.*}

- **C** cancellation of the contract. {**71** *Elaborate.*} {*See **O'Connor's Texas COA**, "Rescission vs. cancellation," ch. 5-B, §3.5.2(3), p. 88.*}

- **D** reformation of the contract. {**72** *Elaborate.*} {*See **O'Connor's Texas COA**, "Reformation," ch. 5-B, §3.5.3, p. 89.*}

19. {**73** *Identify elements and facts supporting equitable relief.*} {*See FORM 2D:1; **O'Connor's Texas Rules**, "Injunctive Relief," ch. 2-D, p. 138; **O'Connor's Texas COA**, "Equitable remedies," ch. 5-B, §3.5, p. 84.*}

JURY DEMAND

20. Plaintiff demands a jury trial and tenders the appropriate fee with this petition. {*See **O'Connor's Texas Rules**, "Request for Jury Trial," ch. 5-B, p. 400.*}

CONDITIONS PRECEDENT

21. All conditions precedent to plaintiff's claim for relief have been performed or have occurred. {*See **O'Connor's Texas Rules**, "Conditions Precedent," ch. 2-B, §12, p. 132; **O'Connor's Texas COA**, "Conditions precedent," ch. 5-B, §2.3.4(1), p. 76.*}

REQUEST FOR DISCLOSURE

22. Under Texas Rule of Civil Procedure 194, plaintiff requests that defendant disclose, within 50 days of the service of this request, the information or material described in Rule 194.2. {*See **O'Connor's Texas Rules**, "Content of request," ch. 6-E, §3.2, p. 627.*}

OBJECTION TO ASSOCIATE JUDGE

23. Plaintiff objects to the referral of this case to an associate judge for hearing a trial on the merits or presiding at a jury trial. {*See **O'Connor's Texas Rules**, "Objection to referral," ch. 1-J, §3.3, p. 96.*}

PRAYER

24. For these reasons, plaintiff asks that the Court issue citation for defendant to appear and answer, and that plaintiff be awarded a judgment against defendant for the following:

Continued on next page

{*CHOOSE RELIEF SOUGHT*}

a. Actual damages. {*See* ***O'Connor's Texas COA***, *"Pleading actual damages," ch. 41-A, §3.2, p. 1346.*}

b. {⓻⓸ *Describe equitable relief.*}

c. Prejudgment and postjudgment interest. {*See* ***O'Connor's Texas COA***, *"Interest," ch. 43, p. 1445.*}

d. Court costs. {*See* ***O'Connor's Texas COA***, *"Court Costs," ch. 44, p. 1453.*}

e. Attorney fees. {*See* ***O'Connor's Texas COA***, *"Attorney Fees," ch. 45, p. 1463.*}

f. All other relief to which plaintiff is entitled. {*See* ***O'Connor's Texas Rules***, *"Prayer," ch. 2-B, §15, p. 132.*}

SEE: Tex. R. Civ. P. 45-59, 78-82, 169, 190, 194
O'Connor's Texas Rules * Civil Trials (2019), "Plaintiff's Original Petition," ch. 2-B, p. 115
O'Connor's Texas Causes of Action (2019), "Breach of Contract," ch. 5-B, p. 69; "Damages & Other Compensation," Part 4, p. 1343
O'Connor's Texas Causes of Action Pleadings (2019), FORMS 5C:1, 5D:1

ADD: STYLE OF THE CASE – FORM 1B:2
SIGNATURE BLOCK – FORM 1B:3
VERIFICATION – FORM 1B:7, for injunctive relief

ATTACH: AFFIDAVIT – FORM 1B:8, if necessary to support facts for injunctive relief
NOTICE OF CURRENT/CHANGE OF ADDRESS – FORM 1B:14
Civil Process Request Form, if required by court clerk to issue citation
Copy of contract
Filing fees
Jury fee, if jury trial requested
Other exhibits, if necessary

NOTE: A party may be able to bring a claim for breach of contract as an assignee, an agent, or a third-party beneficiary. See ***O'Connor's Texas COA***, "Proper party," ch. 5-B, §2.2, p. 71.

A plaintiff bringing a breach-of-contract claim relating to insurance claims for damage to or loss of real property caused by forces of nature must give written presuit notice of the plaintiff's claim under Texas Insurance Code chapter 542A. *See* Tex. Ins. Code §§542A.001(2), 542A.002(a)(1), 542A.003. For a discussion of presuit notice of a claim under chapter 542A, see ***O'Connor's Texas COA***, "Suits for real-property-related damage caused by forces of nature," ch. 13-C, §6.2, p. 370.

See notes under FORM 2B:1.

PLAINTIFF'S ORIGINAL PETITION
{❶ *STATE ADDITIONAL RELIEF REQUESTED IF APPROPRIATE, E.G., & REQUEST FOR DISCLOSURE*}

Plaintiff, {❷ *name*}, files this original petition {❸ *state additional relief requested if appropriate, e.g., and request for disclosure*} against defendant, {❹ *name*}, and alleges as follows:

DISCOVERY-CONTROL PLAN

{*CHOOSE APPROPRIATE PARAGRAPH 1*}

1. Plaintiff intends to conduct discovery under Level 1 of Texas Rule of Civil Procedure 190.2 and affirmatively pleads that this suit is governed by the expedited-actions process in Texas Rule of Civil Procedure 169. {*See **O'Connor's Texas Rules**, "Discovery-Control Plans," ch. 2-B, §2, p. 115.*}

1. Plaintiff intends to conduct discovery under Level {❺ *2/3*} of Texas Rule of Civil Procedure {❻ *190.3/190.4*} and affirmatively pleads that this suit is not governed by the expedited-actions process in Texas Rule of Civil Procedure 169 because {❼ *explain, e.g., plaintiff requests injunctive relief, plaintiff seeks monetary relief over $100,000*}. {*See **O'Connor's Texas Rules**, "Discovery-Control Plans," ch. 2-B, §2, p. 115. For a motion to request a Level 3 discovery-control plan, see FORM 6A:6.*}

CLAIM FOR RELIEF

{*CHOOSE APPROPRIATE PARAGRAPH 2*}

2. Plaintiff seeks only monetary relief of $100,000 or less, including damages of any kind, penalties, court costs, expenses, prejudgment interest, and attorney fees. {*Tex. R. Civ. P. 47(c)(1).*}

2. Plaintiff seeks monetary relief of $100,000 or less and nonmonetary relief. {*Tex. R. Civ. P. 47(c)(2).*}

2. Plaintiff seeks monetary relief over $100,000 but not more than $200,000. {*Tex. R. Civ. P. 47(c)(3).*}

2. Plaintiff seeks monetary relief over $200,000 but not more than $1,000,000. {*Tex. R. Civ. P. 47(c)(4).*}

2. Plaintiff seeks monetary relief over $1,000,000. {*Tex. R. Civ. P. 47(c)(5).*}

Continued on next page

PARTIES

3. {*For plaintiff designation, see FORM 2B:9;* ***O'Connor's Texas Rules****, "Plaintiff," ch. 2-B, §4.4, p. 123.*}

4. {*For defendant designation, see FORMS 2B:10-19;* ***O'Connor's Texas Rules****, "Defendant," ch. 2-B, §4.5, p. 123.*}

JURISDICTION

5. {*For jurisdiction allegations, see FORM 2B:20. It is not necessary to plead jurisdiction for most suits. See* ***O'Connor's Texas Rules****, "Jurisdiction," ch. 2-B, §5, p. 125.*}

VENUE

6. {*For venue allegations, see FORM 2B:21. It is not necessary to plead venue, but pleading sufficient venue facts could avoid a motion to transfer venue. See* ***O'Connor's Texas Rules****, "Venue," ch. 2-B, §6, p. 127.*}

FACTS

7. On {8 *date*}, at {9 *identify location*}, {10 _______} County, Texas, {11 *describe events that resulted in lawsuit*}.

8. {12 *State other relevant facts in separately numbered paragraphs.*} {*See* ***O'Connor's Texas Rules****, "Alleging facts," ch. 2-B, §7.2.1, p. 128.*}

COUNT 1 – SUIT ON SWORN ACCOUNT

9. Plaintiff provided {13 *goods/services*} to defendant on an open account. Defendant accepted the {14 *goods/services*} and became bound to pay plaintiff {15 *his/her/its*} designated charges, which were {16 *according to the terms of the parties' agreement/reasonable and customary for such {goods/services}*}. {*See* ***O'Connor's Texas COA****, "Plaintiff's Petition," ch. 5-E, §2, p. 126.*}

10. Plaintiff attaches a record of the account and the required affidavit as Exhibit {17 *letter*} and incorporates it by reference. The account accurately sets forth the {18 *goods/services*} plaintiff provided to defendant, the dates of {19 *delivery/performance*}, and the cost of the {20 *goods/services*} plaintiff provided. The account represents a record of the {21 *transaction/series of transactions*} that is similar to records plaintiff systematically keeps in the ordinary course of business. {*See* ***O'Connor's Texas COA****, "Systematic record," ch. 5-E, §2.3, p. 129.*}

{*CHOOSE APPROPRIATE PARAGRAPH 11*}

11. After the {22 *goods/services*} were {23 *delivered/performed*}, defendant made partial payments to plaintiff totaling ${24 *amount*}. The dates and amounts of defendant's payments are fully accounted for and credited to the account, as reflected in Exhibit {25 *letter*}. {*See* ***O'Connor's Texas COA****, "Offsets, payments & credits," ch. 5-E, §2.4, p. 129.*}

11. After the {26 *goods/services*} were {27 *delivered/performed*}, defendant did not make any payments to plaintiff.

12. This claim is just and true, it is due, and all just and lawful offsets, payments, and credits have been allowed. Plaintiff attaches an affidavit verifying these facts as Exhibit {28 *letter*} and incorporates it by reference. {*See* ***O'Connor's Texas COA****, "Plaintiff's Petition," ch. 5-E, §2, p. 126.*}

13. The principal balance due on the account is ${29 *amount*}.

14. Plaintiff seeks liquidated damages in the amount of at least ${30 *amount*}, which is within the jurisdictional limits of this Court. {*See Tex. R. Civ. P. 47(b);* ***O'Connor's Texas Rules****, "Damages," ch. 2-B, §9, p. 130;* ***O'Connor's Texas COA****, "Liquidated damages," ch. 5-E, §2.6, p. 129.*}

15. <u>Attorney fees.</u> Plaintiff is entitled to recover reasonable and necessary attorney fees under Texas Civil Practice & Remedies Code section 38.001(7) because this is a suit on a sworn account. Plaintiff retained counsel, who presented plaintiff's claim to {31 *defendant/defendant's duly authorized agent*}. Defendant did not tender the amount owed within 30 days after the claim was presented. {*See* ***O'Connor's Texas COA****, "Attorney fees," ch. 5-E, §3.4, p. 130.*}

{*ADD PARAGRAPHS 16-22 AS APPROPRIATE*}

COUNT 2 – BREACH OF CONTRACT

16. In the alternative to Count 1, defendant breached defendant's contract with plaintiff. {32 *In separately numbered paragraphs, identify elements and facts supporting breach of contract, add any claims for attorney fees or equitable relief, and include a statement that damages are within the jurisdictional limits of the court. See FORM 2B:2, ¶13.*} {*See* ***O'Connor's Texas COA****, "Breach of Contract," ch. 5-B, p. 69;* ***O'Connor's Texas COA Pleadings****, FORM 5B:2.*}

◄ *Continued on next page* ►

COUNT 3 – QUANTUM MERUIT

17. In the alternative to Count 1, defendant accepted {㉝ *services/materials*} from plaintiff without compensating plaintiff. {㉞ *In separately numbered paragraphs, identify elements and facts supporting quantum meruit, add any claim for attorney fees, and include a statement that damages are within the jurisdictional limits of the court. See FORM 2B:2, ¶13.*} {*See* ***O'Connor's Texas COA****, "Quantum Meruit," ch. 5-C, p. 114;* ***O'Connor's Texas COA Pleadings****, FORM 5C:1.*}

COUNT 4 – {㉟ *NAME OF ANOTHER CAUSE OF ACTION*}

18. In {㊱ *the alternative/addition*} to other counts, plaintiff sues defendant for {㊲ *identify another cause of action*}. {㊳ *In separately numbered paragraphs, identify elements and facts supporting the cause of action, add any claims for exemplary damages, attorney fees, or equitable relief, and include a statement that damages are within the jurisdictional limits of the court. See FORM 2B:2, ¶13.*} {*For related claims, see* ***O'Connor's Texas COA****, "Related Causes of Action," ch. 5-E, §7, p. 134.*}

JURY DEMAND

19. Plaintiff demands a jury trial and tenders the appropriate fee with this petition. {*See* ***O'Connor's Texas Rules****, "Request for Jury Trial," ch. 5-B, p. 400.*}

CONDITIONS PRECEDENT

20. All conditions precedent to plaintiff's claim for relief have been performed or have occurred. {*See* ***O'Connor's Texas Rules****, "Conditions Precedent," ch. 2-B, §12, p. 132;* ***O'Connor's Texas COA****, "Conditions precedent," ch. 5-B, §2.3.4(1), p. 76.*}

REQUEST FOR DISCLOSURE

21. Under Texas Rule of Civil Procedure 194, plaintiff requests that defendant disclose, within 50 days of the service of this request, the information or material described in Rule 194.2. {*See* ***O'Connor's Texas Rules****, "Content of request," ch. 6-E, §3.2, p. 627.*}

OBJECTION TO ASSOCIATE JUDGE

22. Plaintiff objects to the referral of this case to an associate judge for hearing a trial on the merits or presiding at a jury trial. {*See* ***O'Connor's Texas Rules****, "Objection to referral," ch. 1-J, §3.3, p. 96.*}

PRAYER

23. For these reasons, plaintiff asks that the Court issue citation for defendant to appear and answer, and that plaintiff be awarded a judgment against defendant for the following:

{*CHOOSE RELIEF SOUGHT*}

a. ${❸❾ *Amount*} as the amount due on the account.

b. Prejudgment and postjudgment interest. {*See* ***O'Connor's Texas COA****, "Interest," ch. 43, p. 1445.*}

c. Court costs. {*See* ***O'Connor's Texas COA****, "Court Costs," ch. 44, p. 1453.*}

d. Attorney fees. {*See* ***O'Connor's Texas COA****, "Attorney Fees Under CPRC ch. 38," ch. 45-B, p. 1486.*}

e. All other relief to which plaintiff is entitled. {*See* ***O'Connor's Texas Rules****, "Prayer," ch. 2-B, §15, p. 132.*}

SEE: Tex. R. Civ. P. 45-59, 78-82, 93, 169, 185, 190, 194
Tex. Civ. Prac. & Rem. Code §38.001(7)
O'Connor's Texas Rules * Civil Trials (2019), "Plaintiff's Original Petition," ch. 2-B, p. 115
O'Connor's Texas Causes of Action (2019), "Suit on Sworn Account," ch. 5-E, p. 126
O'Connor's Texas Causes of Action Pleadings (2019), FORMS 5B:2, 5C:1

ADD: STYLE OF THE CASE – FORM 1B:2
SIGNATURE BLOCK – FORM 1B:3

ATTACH: NOTICE OF CURRENT/CHANGE OF ADDRESS – FORM 1B:14
AFFIDAVIT – FORM 2B:4
Account record
Civil Process Request Form, if required by court clerk to issue citation
Filing fees
Jury fee, if jury trial requested
Other exhibits, if necessary

◄ *Continued on next page* ►

NOTE: Texas Rule of Civil Procedure 185 does not require that the petition include a systematic record of the goods or services sold unless the trial court sustains special exceptions. Because the courts of appeals have been inconsistent—sometimes within the same court—on whether summary judgment can be granted in a suit on a sworn account when the petition does not contain a systematic record, the best practice is to include a systematic record in the petition (see ¶10, above). *Compare* ***Southern Mgmt. Servs. v. SM Energy Co.***, 398 S.W.3d 350, 355 (Tex.App.—Houston [14th Dist.] 2013, no pet.) (no particularization or description of component parts of account required), ***Whiteside v. Ford Motor Credit Co.***, 220 S.W.3d 191, 194 (Tex.App.—Dallas 2007, no pet.) (same), *and* ***Enernational Corp. v. Exploitation Eng'rs, Inc.***, 705 S.W.2d 749, 750-51 (Tex.App.—Houston [1st Dist.] 1986, writ ref'd n.r.e.) (same), *with* ***Ellis v. Reliant Energy Retail Servs.***, 418 S.W.3d 235, 246 (Tex.App.—Houston [14th Dist.] 2013, no pet.) (petition must contain systematic, itemized statement), ***Panditi v. Apostle***, 180 S.W.3d 924, 926 (Tex.App.—Dallas 2006, no pet.) (same), *and* ***Mega Builders, Inc. v. American Door Prods.***, No. 01-12-00196-CV (Tex.App.—Houston [1st Dist.] 2013, no pet.) (memo op.; 3-19-13) (same).

See notes under FORM 2B:1.

AFFIDAVIT OF {❶ *NAME*}

STATE OF TEXAS §
{❷ ______} COUNTY §

Before me, the undersigned notary, on this day personally appeared {❸ *name of affiant*}, the affiant, whose identity is known to me. After I administered an oath, affiant testified as follows:

1. "My name is {❹ *name of affiant*}. I am over 18 years of age, of sound mind, and capable of making this affidavit.

2. "The facts stated in this affidavit are within my personal knowledge and are true and correct.

3. "I am {❺ *identify affiant's status, e.g., the plaintiff, an agent of the plaintiff*} in this case.

{*ADD PARAGRAPH 4 IF AFFIANT IS PLAINTIFF'S ATTORNEY OR AGENT*}

4. "I acquired personal knowledge of these facts by {❻ *state how personal knowledge was acquired*}.

5. "Plaintiff in this case is {❼ *name*}.

6. "Defendant in this case is {❽ *name*}.

{*CHOOSE APPROPRIATE PARAGRAPH 7*}

7. "This action is based on {❾ *an open account/a written contract/the business dealings between the parties/{identify other claim}*}, of which a systematic record was kept.

7. "This action is for {❿ *goods/services*} provided, of which a systematic record was kept.

8. "The principal balance of ${⓫ *amount*} is due on the account, which is attached to the petition as Exhibit {⓬ *letter*} and incorporated by reference. That amount is just and true, it is due, and all just and lawful offsets, payments, and credits have been allowed."

____
{⓭ *Name of affiant*}

◄ *Continued on next page* ►

Sworn to and subscribed before me by {⓮ *name of affiant*} on __________, 20___.

____
Notary Public in and for
the State of Texas

SEE: Tex. R. Civ. P. 185
O'Connor's Texas Rules * Civil Trials (2019), "Affidavits," ch. 1-B, §3.2.16, p. 12
O'Connor's Texas Causes of Action (2019), "Plaintiff's affidavit," ch. 5-E, §2.7, p. 130

ADD: STYLE OF THE CASE – FORM 1B:2

NOTE: See notes under FORM 1B:8.

PLAINTIFF'S ORIGINAL PETITION
{❶ *STATE ADDITIONAL RELIEF REQUESTED IF APPROPRIATE, E.G., & REQUEST FOR DISCLOSURE*}

Plaintiff, {❷ *name*}, files this original petition {❸ *state additional relief requested if appropriate, e.g., and request for disclosure*} against defendant, {❹ *name*}, and alleges as follows:

DISCOVERY-CONTROL PLAN

{*CHOOSE APPROPRIATE PARAGRAPH 1*}

1. Plaintiff intends to conduct discovery under Level 1 of Texas Rule of Civil Procedure 190.2 and affirmatively pleads that this suit is governed by the expedited-actions process in Texas Rule of Civil Procedure 169. {*See* ***O'Connor's Texas Rules****, "Discovery-Control Plans," ch. 2-B, §2, p. 115.*}

1. Plaintiff intends to conduct discovery under Level {❺ *2/3*} of Texas Rule of Civil Procedure {❻ *190.3/190.4*} and affirmatively pleads that this suit is not governed by the expedited-actions process in Texas Rule of Civil Procedure 169 because {❼ *explain, e.g., plaintiff requests injunctive relief, plaintiff seeks monetary relief over $100,000*}. {*See* ***O'Connor's Texas Rules****, "Discovery-Control Plans," ch. 2-B, §2, p. 115. For a motion to request a Level 3 discovery-control plan, see FORM 6A:6.*}

CLAIM FOR RELIEF

{*CHOOSE APPROPRIATE PARAGRAPH 2*}

2. Plaintiff seeks only monetary relief of $100,000 or less, including damages of any kind, penalties, court costs, expenses, prejudgment interest, and attorney fees. {*Tex. R. Civ. P. 47(c)(1).*}

2. Plaintiff seeks monetary relief of $100,000 or less and nonmonetary relief. {*Tex. R. Civ. P. 47(c)(2).*}

2. Plaintiff seeks monetary relief over $100,000 but not more than $200,000. {*Tex. R. Civ. P. 47(c)(3).*}

2. Plaintiff seeks monetary relief over $200,000 but not more than $1,000,000. {*Tex. R. Civ. P. 47(c)(4).*}

2. Plaintiff seeks monetary relief over $1,000,000. {*Tex. R. Civ. P. 47(c)(5).*}

◄ *Continued on next page* ►

PARTIES

3. {*For plaintiff designation, see FORM 2B:9;* ***O'Connor's Texas Rules****, "Plaintiff," ch. 2-B, §4.4, p. 123.*}

4. {*For defendant designation, see FORMS 2B:10-19;* ***O'Connor's Texas Rules****, "Defendant," ch. 2-B, §4.5, p. 123.*}

JURISDICTION

5. {*For jurisdiction allegations, see FORM 2B:20. It is not necessary to plead jurisdiction for most suits. See* ***O'Connor's Texas Rules****, "Jurisdiction," ch. 2-B, §5, p. 125.*}

VENUE

6. {*For venue allegations, see FORM 2B:21. It is not necessary to plead venue, but pleading sufficient venue facts could avoid a motion to transfer venue. See* ***O'Connor's Texas Rules****, "Venue," ch. 2-B, §6, p. 127.*}

FACTS

7. On {❽ *date*}, at {❾ *identify location*}, {❿ ________} County, Texas, {⓫ *describe events that resulted in lawsuit*}.

8. {⓬ *State other relevant facts in separately numbered paragraphs.*} {*See* ***O'Connor's Texas Rules****, "Alleging facts," ch. 2-B, §7.2.1, p. 128.*}

COUNT 1 – NEGLIGENCE

9. Defendant had a duty to exercise ordinary care and operate defendant's vehicle reasonably and prudently. {*See* ***O'Connor's Texas COA****, "Legal duty," ch. 21-A, §2.1, p. 719; "Ordinary care," ch. 21-A, §2.2.1, p. 731.*}

10. Defendant breached the duty of care in the following ways:

{*CHOOSE APPROPRIATE STATEMENTS*}

a. Failing to timely apply the brakes.

b. Failing to maintain a proper lookout.

c. Failing to maintain proper control of defendant's vehicle.

d. Failing to turn the vehicle to avoid the collision.

e. Failing to yield the right-of-way.

f. Failing to signal an intention to pass plaintiff's vehicle.

g. Failing to drive in a single lane.

h. {⓭ *Stopping/Slowing*} too suddenly.

i. Driving defendant's vehicle at a rate of speed greater than that at which an ordinarily prudent person would have driven under the same or similar circumstances.

j. Following plaintiff's vehicle more closely than an ordinarily prudent person would have under the same or similar circumstances.

11. Defendant's breach of duty proximately caused injury to plaintiff, which resulted in the following damages: {⓮ *identify damages*}. {*See* ***O'Connor's Texas COA****, "Proximate cause," ch. 21-A, §2.3, p. 734; "Remedies," ch. 21-A, §3, p. 735; "Damages that Must Be Specifically Pleaded," chart 41-1, p. 1348.*}

{*ADD APPROPRIATE PARAGRAPH 12*}

12. Plaintiff seeks unliquidated damages within the jurisdictional limits of this Court. {*See Tex. R. Civ. P. 47(b);* ***O'Connor's Texas Rules****, "Damages," ch. 2-B, §9, p. 130.*}

12. Plaintiff seeks liquidated damages in the amount of at least ${⓯ *amount*}, which is within the jurisdictional limits of this Court. {*See Tex. R. Civ. P. 47(b);* ***O'Connor's Texas Rules****, "Damages," ch. 2-B, §9, p. 130.*}

{*ADD PARAGRAPH 13 IF APPLICABLE*}

13. Exemplary damages. Plaintiff's injury resulted from defendant's gross negligence, which entitles plaintiff to exemplary damages under Texas Civil Practice & Remedies Code section 41.003(a)(3). {⓰ *Elaborate.*} {*See* ***O'Connor's Texas COA****, "Exemplary damages," ch. 21-A, §3.2, p. 735; "Gross negligence," ch. 42-B, §5.1, p. 1430.*}

{*ADD PARAGRAPHS 14-25 AS APPROPRIATE*}

COUNT 2 – NEGLIGENCE PER SE

14. In {⓱ *the alternative/addition*} to other counts, defendant's negligence described in Count 1 violated {⓲ *a statute/an ordinance/an administrative regulation*}. {*See* ***O'Connor's Texas COA****, "Negligence Per Se," ch. 21-B, p. 756.*}

◄ *Continued on next page* ►

15. Specifically, defendant violated

{CHOOSE APPROPRIATE STATEMENT}

[A] Texas Transportation Code section {[19] *identify specific section*}, which {[20] *requires/prohibits*} {[21] *describe duty imposed by Transportation Code*}. {*For a list of statutory duties in the Texas Transportation Code that impose tort liability related to operation of a motor vehicle, see* ***O'Connor's Texas COA***, *"Statutory & Rule-Based Duties," chart 21-2, p. 760.*}

[B] {[22] *identify other statute*}, which {[23] *requires/prohibits*} {[24] *describe duty imposed by statute*}.

[C] {[25] *identify ordinance*}, an ordinance of {[26] *name of city or county*}, which {[27] *requires/prohibits*} {[28] *describe duty imposed by ordinance*}. A copy of the ordinance is attached to this petition as Exhibit {[29] *letter*} and incorporated by reference.

[D] {[30] *identify administrative regulation*}, which {[31] *requires/prohibits*} {[32] *describe duty imposed by administrative regulation*}.

16. The {[33] *statute/ordinance/administrative regulation*} is designed to protect a class of persons to which plaintiff belongs against the type of injury suffered by plaintiff. {[34] *Elaborate.*} {*See* ***O'Connor's Texas COA***, *"Protected class & injury," ch. 21-B, §2.1, p. 757.*}

17. The {[35] *statute/ordinance/administrative regulation*} is of the type that imposes tort liability. {[36] *Elaborate.*} {*See* ***O'Connor's Texas COA***, *"Statute imposes tort liability," ch. 21-B, §2.2, p. 758; "Statutory & Rule-Based Duties," chart 21-2, p. 760.*}

18. Defendant's violation of the {[37] *statute/ordinance/administrative regulation*} was without a legal excuse. {[38] *Elaborate.*} {*See* ***O'Connor's Texas COA***, *"Unexcused violation of statute," ch. 21-B, §2.3, p. 763.*}

19. Defendant's breach of duty imposed by the {[39] *statute/ordinance/administrative regulation*} proximately caused injury to plaintiff, which resulted in the following damages: {[40] *identify damages*}. {*See* ***O'Connor's Texas COA***, *"Remedies," ch. 21-A, §3, p. 735; "Proximate cause," ch. 21-B, §2.4, p. 764; "Damages that Must Be Specifically Pleaded," chart 41-1, p. 1348.*}

{ADD APPROPRIATE PARAGRAPH 20}

20. Plaintiff seeks unliquidated damages within the jurisdictional limits of this Court. *{See Tex. R. Civ. P. 47(b); **O'Connor's Texas Rules**, "Damages," ch. 2-B, §9, p. 130.}*

20. Plaintiff seeks liquidated damages in the amount of at least ${❹❶ *amount*}, which is within the jurisdictional limits of this Court. *{See Tex. R. Civ. P. 47(b); **O'Connor's Texas Rules**, "Damages," ch. 2-B, §9, p. 130.}*

21. Exemplary damages. Plaintiff's injury resulted from defendant's gross negligence, which entitles plaintiff to exemplary damages under Texas Civil Practice & Remedies Code section 41.003(a)(3). {❹❷ *Elaborate.*} *{See **O'Connor's Texas COA**, "Exemplary damages," ch. 21-A, §3.2, p. 735; "Gross negligence," ch. 42-B, §5.1, p. 1430.}*

COUNT 3 – {❹❸ *NAME OF ANOTHER CAUSE OF ACTION*}

22. In {❹❹ *the alternative/addition*} to other counts, plaintiff sues defendant for {❹❺ *identify another cause of action*}. {❹❻ *In separately numbered paragraphs, identify elements and facts supporting the cause of action, add any claims for exemplary damages, attorney fees, or equitable relief, and include a statement that damages are within the jurisdictional limits of the court. See ¶12, this form.*} *{For related claims, see **O'Connor's Texas COA**, "Related Causes of Action," ch. 21-A, §8, p. 755.}*

JURY DEMAND

23. Plaintiff demands a jury trial and tenders the appropriate fee with this petition. *{See **O'Connor's Texas Rules**, "Request for Jury Trial," ch. 5-B, p. 400.}*

REQUEST FOR DISCLOSURE

24. Under Texas Rule of Civil Procedure 194, plaintiff requests that defendant disclose, within 50 days of the service of this request, the information or material described in Rule 194.2. *{See **O'Connor's Texas Rules**, "Content of request," ch. 6-E, §3.2, p. 627.}*

OBJECTION TO ASSOCIATE JUDGE

25. Plaintiff objects to the referral of this case to an associate judge for hearing a trial on the merits or presiding at a jury trial. *{See **O'Connor's Texas Rules**, "Objection to referral," ch. 1-J, §3.3, p. 96.}*

◄ *Continued on next page* ►

PRAYER

26. For these reasons, plaintiff asks that the Court issue citation for defendant to appear and answer, and that plaintiff be awarded a judgment against defendant for the following:

{*CHOOSE RELIEF SOUGHT*}

a. Actual damages. {*See **O'Connor's Texas COA**, "Pleading actual damages," ch. 41-A, §3.2, p. 1346.*}

b. Exemplary damages. {*See **O'Connor's Texas COA**, "Exemplary Damages," ch. 42, p. 1419.*}

c. Prejudgment and postjudgment interest. {*See **O'Connor's Texas COA**, "Interest," ch. 43, p. 1445.*}

d. Court costs. {*See **O'Connor's Texas COA**, "Court Costs," ch. 44, p. 1453.*}

e. All other relief to which plaintiff is entitled. {*See **O'Connor's Texas Rules**, "Prayer," ch. 2-B, §15, p. 132.*}

SEE: Tex. R. Civ. P. 45-59, 78-82, 169, 190, 194
Tex. Civ. Prac. & Rem. Code §41.003
O'Connor's Texas Rules * Civil Trials (2019), "Plaintiff's Original Petition," ch. 2-B, p. 115
O'Connor's Texas Causes of Action (2019), "Negligence," ch. 21-A, p. 719; "Damages & Other Compensation," Part 4, p. 1343

ADD: STYLE OF THE CASE – FORM 1B:2
SIGNATURE BLOCK – FORM 1B:3

ATTACH: NOTICE OF CURRENT/CHANGE OF ADDRESS – FORM 1B:14
Civil Process Request Form, if required by court clerk to issue citation
Exhibits, if necessary
Filing fees
Jury fee, if jury trial requested

NOTE: See notes under FORM 2B:1.

PLAINTIFF'S ORIGINAL PETITION
{❶ *STATE ADDITIONAL RELIEF REQUESTED IF APPROPRIATE, E.G., & REQUEST FOR DISCLOSURE*}

Plaintiff, {❷ *name*}, files this original petition {❸ *state additional relief requested if appropriate, e.g., and request for disclosure*} against defendant, {❹ *name*}, and alleges as follows:

DISCOVERY-CONTROL PLAN

{*CHOOSE APPROPRIATE PARAGRAPH 1*}

1. Plaintiff intends to conduct discovery under Level 1 of Texas Rule of Civil Procedure 190.2 and affirmatively pleads that this suit is governed by the expedited-actions process in Texas Rule of Civil Procedure 169. {*See* ***O'Connor's Texas Rules****, "Discovery-Control Plans," ch. 2-B, §2, p. 115.*}

1. Plaintiff intends to conduct discovery under Level {❺ *2/3*} of Texas Rule of Civil Procedure {❻ *190.3/190.4*} and affirmatively pleads that this suit is not governed by the expedited-actions process in Texas Rule of Civil Procedure 169 because {❼ *explain, e.g., plaintiff requests injunctive relief, plaintiff seeks monetary relief over $100,000*}. {*See* ***O'Connor's Texas Rules****, "Discovery-Control Plans," ch. 2-B, §2, p. 115. For a motion to request a Level 3 discovery-control plan, see FORM 6A:6.*}

CLAIM FOR RELIEF

{*CHOOSE APPROPRIATE PARAGRAPH 2*}

2. Plaintiff seeks only monetary relief of $100,000 or less, including damages of any kind, penalties, court costs, expenses, prejudgment interest, and attorney fees. {*Tex. R. Civ. P. 47(c)(1).*}

2. Plaintiff seeks monetary relief of $100,000 or less and nonmonetary relief. {*Tex. R. Civ. P. 47(c)(2).*}

2. Plaintiff seeks monetary relief over $100,000 but not more than $200,000. {*Tex. R. Civ. P. 47(c)(3).*}

2. Plaintiff seeks monetary relief over $200,000 but not more than $1,000,000. {*Tex. R. Civ. P. 47(c)(4).*}

2. Plaintiff seeks monetary relief over $1,000,000. {*Tex. R. Civ. P. 47(c)(5).*}

◄ Continued on next page ►

PARTIES

3. {*For plaintiff designation, see FORM 2B:9;* ***O'Connor's Texas Rules****, "Plaintiff," ch. 2-B, §4.4, p. 123.*}

4. {*For defendant designation, see FORMS 2B:10-19;* ***O'Connor's Texas Rules****, "Defendant," ch. 2-B, §4.5, p. 123.*}

JURISDICTION

5. {*For jurisdiction allegations, see FORM 2B:20. It is not necessary to plead jurisdiction for most suits. See* ***O'Connor's Texas Rules****, "Jurisdiction," ch. 2-B, §5, p. 125.*}

VENUE

6. {*For venue allegations, see FORM 2B:21. It is not necessary to plead venue, but pleading sufficient venue facts could avoid a motion to transfer venue. See* ***O'Connor's Texas Rules****, "Venue," ch. 2-B, §6, p. 127.*}

FACTS

7. On {❽ *date*}, at {❾ *identify location*}, {❿ ________} County, Texas, {⓫ *describe events that resulted in lawsuit*}.

8. {⓬ *State other relevant facts in separately numbered paragraphs.*} {*See* ***O'Connor's Texas Rules****, "Alleging facts," ch. 2-B, §7.2.1, p. 128.*}

COUNT 1 – PREMISES LIABILITY

9. Defendant was {⓭ *the owner/in possession*} of the premises at {⓮ *identify address or describe location of defendant's premises*} at the time plaintiff was injured. {*See* ***O'Connor's Texas COA****, "Defendant was possessor," ch. 23-B, §2.2, p. 832.*}

10. Plaintiff entered defendant's premises with defendant's knowledge and for their mutual benefit. {⓯ *Explain, e.g., plaintiff was a customer shopping at defendant's retail store.*} {*See* ***O'Connor's Texas COA****, "Plaintiff was invitee," ch. 23-B, §2.1, p. 829.*}

11. A condition on defendant's premises posed an unreasonable risk of harm. {⓰ *Describe dangerous condition.*} {*See* ***O'Connor's Texas COA****, "Condition posed unreasonable risk," ch. 23-B, §2.3, p. 836.*}

12. Defendant knew or reasonably should have known of the condition of the premises because

{*CHOOSE ONE OF THE FOLLOWING*}

[A] defendant, or its agent, servant, or employee, actually caused the substance to fall on the floor. {[17] *Elaborate.*} {*See **O'Connor's Texas COA**, "Slip & fall," ch. 23-B, §2.4.2(1), p. 842.*}

[B] customers notified defendant of the dangerous condition. {[18] *Elaborate.*} {*See **O'Connor's Texas COA**, "Slip & fall," ch. 23-B, §2.4.2(1), p. 842.*}

[C] the substance was on the floor for a long period of time. {[19] *Elaborate.*} {*See **O'Connor's Texas COA**, "Slip & fall," ch. 23-B, §2.4.2(1), p. 842.*}

13. Defendant had a duty to use ordinary care to ensure that the premises did not present a danger to plaintiff. This duty includes the duty to inspect and the duty to warn or to cure. Defendant breached the duty of ordinary care by {[20] *describe defendant's breach of duty*}. {*See **O'Connor's Texas COA**, "Breach of duty," ch. 23-B, §2.5, p. 842.*}

14. Defendant's breach of duty proximately caused injury to plaintiff, which resulted in the following damages: {[21] *identify damages*}. {*See **O'Connor's Texas COA**, "Proximate cause," ch. 23-B, §2.6, p. 844; "Remedies," ch. 23-B, §3, p. 844; "Damages that Must Be Specifically Pleaded," chart 41-1, p. 1348.*}

{*ADD APPROPRIATE PARAGRAPH 15*}

15. Plaintiff seeks unliquidated damages within the jurisdictional limits of this Court. {*See Tex. R. Civ. P. 47(b); **O'Connor's Texas Rules**, "Damages," ch. 2-B, §9, p. 130.*}

15. Plaintiff seeks liquidated damages in the amount of at least ${[22] *amount*}, which is within the jurisdictional limits of this Court. {*See Tex. R. Civ. P. 47(b); **O'Connor's Texas Rules**, "Damages," ch. 2-B, §9, p. 130.*}

{*ADD PARAGRAPH 16 IF APPLICABLE*}

16. Exemplary damages. Plaintiff's injury resulted from defendant's gross negligence, which entitles plaintiff to exemplary damages under Texas Civil Practice & Remedies Code section 41.003(a)(3). {[23] *Elaborate.*} {*See **O'Connor's Texas COA**, "Exemplary Damages," ch. 42, p. 1419; "Gross negligence," ch. 42-B, §5.1, p. 1430.*}

◄ *Continued on next page* ►

{*ADD PARAGRAPHS 17-20 AS APPROPRIATE*}

COUNT 2 – {㉔ *NAME OF ANOTHER CAUSE OF ACTION*}

17. In {㉕ *the alternative/addition*} to other counts, plaintiff sues defendant for {㉖ *identify another cause of action*}. {㉗ *In separately numbered paragraphs, identify elements and facts supporting the cause of action, add any claims for exemplary damages, attorney fees, or equitable relief, and include a statement that damages are within the jurisdictional limits of the court. See ¶15, this form.*} {*For related claims, see* ***O'Connor's Texas COA****, "Causes of Action Involving Injury on Real Property," ch. 23-A, §4, p. 825.*}

JURY DEMAND

18. Plaintiff demands a jury trial and tenders the appropriate fee with this petition. {*See* ***O'Connor's Texas Rules****, "Request for Jury Trial," ch. 5-B, p. 400.*}

REQUEST FOR DISCLOSURE

19. Under Texas Rule of Civil Procedure 194, plaintiff requests that defendant disclose, within 50 days of the service of this request, the information or material described in Rule 194.2. {*See* ***O'Connor's Texas Rules****, "Content of request," ch. 6-E, §3.2, p. 627.*}

OBJECTION TO ASSOCIATE JUDGE

20. Plaintiff objects to the referral of this case to an associate judge for hearing a trial on the merits or presiding at a jury trial. {*See* ***O'Connor's Texas Rules****, "Objection to referral," ch. 1-J, §3.3, p. 96.*}

PRAYER

21. For these reasons, plaintiff asks that the Court issue citation for defendant to appear and answer, and that plaintiff be awarded a judgment against defendant for the following:

{*CHOOSE RELIEF SOUGHT*}

a. Actual damages. {*See* ***O'Connor's Texas COA****, "Pleading actual damages," ch. 41-A, §3.2, p. 1346.*}

b. Exemplary damages. {*See* ***O'Connor's Texas COA****, "Exemplary Damages," ch. 42, p. 1419.*}

c. Prejudgment and postjudgment interest. {*See* ***O'Connor's Texas COA****, "Interest," ch. 43, p. 1445.*}

d. Court costs. {*See* ***O'Connor's Texas COA****, "Court Costs," ch. 44, p. 1453.*}

e. All other relief to which plaintiff is entitled. {*See* ***O'Connor's Texas Rules****, "Prayer," ch. 2-B, §15, p. 132.*}

SEE: Tex. R. Civ. P. 45-59, 78-82, 169, 190, 194
Tex. Civ. Prac. & Rem. Code §41.003
O'Connor's Texas Rules * Civil Trials (2019), "Plaintiff's Original Petition," ch. 2-B, p. 115
O'Connor's Texas Causes of Action (2019), "Liability to Invitees," ch. 23-B, p. 827; "Damages & Other Compensation," Part 4, p. 1343

ADD: STYLE OF THE CASE – FORM 1B:2
SIGNATURE BLOCK – FORM 1B:3

ATTACH: NOTICE OF CURRENT/CHANGE OF ADDRESS – FORM 1B:14
Civil Process Request Form, if required by court clerk to issue citation
Exhibits, if necessary
Filing fees
Jury fee, if jury trial requested

NOTE: See notes under FORM 2B:1.

PLAINTIFF'S ORIGINAL PETITION
{❶ *STATE ADDITIONAL RELIEF REQUESTED*
IF APPROPRIATE, E.G., & REQUEST FOR DISCLOSURE}

Plaintiff, {❷ *name*}, files this original petition {❸ *state additional relief requested if appropriate, e.g., and request for disclosure*} against defendant, {❹ *name*}, and alleges as follows:

DISCOVERY-CONTROL PLAN

{*CHOOSE APPROPRIATE PARAGRAPH 1*}

1. Plaintiff intends to conduct discovery under Level 1 of Texas Rule of Civil Procedure 190.2 and affirmatively pleads that this suit is governed by the expedited-actions process in Texas Rule of Civil Procedure 169. {*See* ***O'Connor's Texas Rules****, "Discovery-Control Plans," ch. 2-B, §2, p. 115.*}

1. Plaintiff intends to conduct discovery under Level {❺ *2/3*} of Texas Rule of Civil Procedure {❻ *190.3/190.4*} and affirmatively pleads that this suit is not governed by the expedited-actions process in Texas Rule of Civil Procedure 169 because {❼ *explain, e.g., plaintiff requests injunctive relief, plaintiff seeks monetary relief over $100,000*}. {*See* ***O'Connor's Texas Rules****, "Discovery-Control Plans," ch. 2-B, §2, p. 115. For a motion to request a Level 3 discovery-control plan, see FORM 6A:6.*}

CLAIM FOR RELIEF

{*CHOOSE APPROPRIATE PARAGRAPH 2*}

2. Plaintiff seeks only monetary relief of $100,000 or less, including damages of any kind, penalties, court costs, expenses, prejudgment interest, and attorney fees. {*Tex. R. Civ. P. 47(c)(1).*}

2. Plaintiff seeks monetary relief of $100,000 or less and nonmonetary relief. {*Tex. R. Civ. P. 47(c)(2).*}

2. Plaintiff seeks monetary relief over $100,000 but not more than $200,000. {*Tex. R. Civ. P. 47(c)(3).*}

2. Plaintiff seeks monetary relief over $200,000 but not more than $1,000,000. {*Tex. R. Civ. P. 47(c)(4).*}

2. Plaintiff seeks monetary relief over $1,000,000. {*Tex. R. Civ. P. 47(c)(5).*}

PARTIES

3. {*For plaintiff designation, see FORM 2B:9;* ***O'Connor's Texas Rules****, "Plaintiff," ch. 2-B, §4.4, p. 123.*}

4. {*For defendant designation, see FORMS 2B:10-19;* ***O'Connor's Texas Rules****, "Defendant," ch. 2-B, §4.5, p. 123.*}

JURISDICTION

5. {*For jurisdiction allegations, see FORM 2B:20. It is not necessary to plead jurisdiction for most suits. See* ***O'Connor's Texas Rules****, "Jurisdiction," ch. 2-B, §5, p. 125.*}

VENUE

{*CHOOSE APPROPRIATE PARAGRAPH 6*}

6. Venue for this suit under the Deceptive Trade Practices Act (DTPA) is proper in {❽ _______} County under Texas Business & Commerce Code section 17.56 and Texas Civil Practice & Remedies Code section {❾ *identify section in chapter 15*}. {❿ *Elaborate.*} {*See* ***O'Connor's Texas COA****, "Venue," ch. 8, §7.2, p. 250.*}

6. Venue for this suit under the Deceptive Trade Practices Act (DTPA) is proper in {⓫ _______} County under Texas Business & Commerce Code section 17.56 because this suit is filed in the county where {⓬ *defendant/defendant's authorized agent*} solicited the transaction underlying this suit. {⓭ *Elaborate.*} {*See* ***O'Connor's Texas COA****, "Venue," ch. 8, §7.2, p. 250.*}

6. {*For other venue allegations, see FORM 2B:21. It is not necessary to plead venue, but pleading sufficient venue facts could avoid a motion to transfer venue. See* ***O'Connor's Texas Rules****, "Venue," ch. 2-B, §6, p. 127.*}

FACTS

7. On {⓮ *date*}, at {⓯ *identify location*}, {⓰ _______} County, Texas, {⓱ *describe events that resulted in lawsuit*}.

8. {⓲ *State other relevant facts in separately numbered paragraphs.*} {*See* ***O'Connor's Texas Rules****, "Alleging facts," ch. 2-B, §7.2.1, p. 128.*}

◄ *Continued on next page* ►

FORM 2B:7

COUNT 1 – DTPA CLAIM

9. Plaintiff is a consumer under the DTPA because plaintiff is {[19] *an individual/a partnership/a corporation/the State of Texas/a subdivision or agency of the State of Texas*} who {[20] *sought/acquired*} {[21] *goods/services*} by {[22] *purchase/lease*}. {*See* ***O'Connor's Texas COA***, *"Plaintiff = consumer," ch. 8, §2.1, p. 210; "Consumer Status Under DTPA," chart 8-1, p. 214.*}

10. Defendant is {[23] *identify status, e.g., an individual, a corporation, an association*} that can be sued under the DTPA. {*See* ***O'Connor's Texas COA***, *"DTPA defendant," ch. 8, §2.2, p. 225.*}

{*CHOOSE APPROPRIATE PARAGRAPHS 11-15*}

11. Defendant violated the DTPA when defendant engaged in false, misleading, or deceptive acts or practices that plaintiff relied on to plaintiff's detriment. Specifically, defendant {[24] *identify the deceptive acts and practices from the DTPA "laundry list," located in Tex. Bus. & Com. Code §17.46(b)*}. {[25] *Elaborate.*} {*See* ***O'Connor's Texas COA***, *"False, misleading, or deceptive act or practice," ch. 8, §2.3.1, p. 227.*}

12. Defendant violated the DTPA when defendant breached an {[26] *express/implied*} warranty. Specifically, defendant breached {[27] *identify warranty that defendant breached*}. {[28] *Elaborate.*} {*See* ***O'Connor's Texas COA***, *"Breach of warranty," ch. 8, §2.3.2, p. 233.*}

13. Defendant violated the DTPA when defendant engaged in an unconscionable action or course of action that, to plaintiff's detriment, took advantage of plaintiff's lack of knowledge, ability, experience, or capacity to a grossly unfair degree. Specifically, defendant {[29] *identify the unconscionable action or course of action*}. {[30] *Elaborate.*} {*See* ***O'Connor's Texas COA***, *"Unconscionable act," ch. 8, §2.3.3, p. 234.*}

14. Defendant violated the DTPA when defendant used or employed an act or practice in violation of Texas Insurance Code chapter 541. Specifically, defendant {[31] *identify act or practice that violated chapter 541*}. {[32] *Elaborate.*} {*See* ***O'Connor's Texas COA***, *"Violation of chapter 541," ch. 8, §2.3.4, p. 235; "Deceptive Insurance Practices," ch. 13-C, p. 353.*}

15. Defendant violated the DTPA when defendant engaged in false, misleading, or deceptive acts or practices that plaintiff relied on to plaintiff's detriment and that violated a "tie-in" consumer statute. Specifically, defendant {[33] *identify the tie-in statute and the deceptive acts*}. {[34] *Elaborate.*} {*See* ***O'Connor's Texas COA***, *"Violation of tie-in statute," ch. 8, §2.3.5, p. 236; "DTPA Tie-In Statutes," chart 8-2, p. 236.*}

{CHOOSE APPROPRIATE PARAGRAPH 16}

16. Plaintiff gave defendant notice as required by Texas Business & Commerce Code section 17.505(a). *{See FORM 2A:4;* ***O'Connor's Texas COA****, "Presuit Notice of Claim," ch. 8, §6, p. 249.}* Attached as Exhibit {❸❺ *letter*} is a copy of the notice letter sent to defendant, which is incorporated by reference.

16. It was impracticable for plaintiff to give defendant written notice under Texas Business & Commerce Code section 17.505(a) because plaintiff needed to file this suit to prevent the expiration of the statute of limitations. Therefore, written notice was not required. {❸❻ *Elaborate.*} *{See* ***O'Connor's Texas COA****, "Deadline to give notice," ch. 8, §6.1.1, p. 249.}*

17. Defendant's wrongful conduct was a producing cause of plaintiff's injury, which resulted in the following damages: {❸❼ *identify damages, including economic or mental-anguish damages*}. *{See* ***O'Connor's Texas COA****, "Causation," ch. 8, §2.4, p. 238; "DTPA damages," ch. 8, §3.1, p. 239; "Damages that Must Be Specifically Pleaded," chart 41-1, p. 1348.}*

{ADD APPROPRIATE PARAGRAPH 18}

18. Plaintiff seeks unliquidated damages within the jurisdictional limits of this Court. *{See Tex. R. Civ. P. 47(b);* ***O'Connor's Texas Rules****, "Damages," ch. 2-B, §9, p. 130.}*

18. Plaintiff seeks liquidated damages in the amount of at least ${❸❽ *amount*}, which is within the jurisdictional limits of this Court. *{See Tex. R. Civ. P. 47(b);* ***O'Connor's Texas Rules****, "Damages," ch. 2-B, §9, p. 130.}*

{ADD PARAGRAPHS 19-23 AS APPROPRIATE}

19. Mental-anguish damages. Defendant acted {❸❾ *knowingly/intentionally*}, which entitles plaintiff to recover mental-anguish damages under Texas Business & Commerce Code section 17.50(b)(1). {❹⓿ *Elaborate.*} *{See* ***O'Connor's Texas COA****, "Mental-anguish damages," ch. 8, §3.1.2, p. 240.}*

20. Additional damages. Defendant acted knowingly, which entitles plaintiff to recover treble economic damages under Texas Business & Commerce Code section 17.50(b)(1). {❹❶ *Elaborate.*} *{See* ***O'Connor's Texas COA****, "Knowing violations," ch. 8, §3.2.1, p. 241.}*

Continued on next page

21. Additional damages. Defendant acted intentionally, which entitles plaintiff to recover treble economic {❹❷ *add if applicable: and mental-anguish*} damages under Texas Business & Commerce Code section 17.50(b)(1). {❹❸ *Elaborate.*} {*See* ***O'Connor's Texas COA****, "Intentional violations," ch. 8, §3.2.2, p. 242.*}

22. Attorney fees. Plaintiff is entitled to recover reasonable and necessary attorney fees for prosecuting this suit under Texas Business & Commerce Code section 17.50(d). {❹❹ *Elaborate.*} {*See* ***O'Connor's Texas COA****, "Attorney fees," ch. 8, §3.7, p. 243.*}

23. Tolling. Plaintiff is entitled to an extension of the limitations period of up to 180 days under Texas Business & Commerce Code section 17.565 because plaintiff's failure to timely commence {❹❺ *his/her/its*} action was caused by defendant knowingly engaging in conduct that was solely calculated to induce plaintiff to refrain from filing suit or postpone filing suit. {❹❻ *Elaborate.*} {*See* ***O'Connor's Texas COA****, "Tolling," ch. 8, §4.3, p. 244.*}

{*ADD PARAGRAPHS 24-29 AS APPROPRIATE*}

COUNT 2 – {❹❼ *NAME OF ANOTHER CAUSE OF ACTION*}

24. In {❹❽ *the alternative/addition*} to other counts, plaintiff sues defendant for {❹❾ *identify another cause of action*}. {❺⓪ *In separately numbered paragraphs, identify elements and facts supporting the cause of action, add any claims for exemplary damages, attorney fees, or equitable relief, and include a statement that damages are within the jurisdictional limits of the court. See ¶18, this form.*} {*For related claims, see* ***O'Connor's Texas COA****, "Related Causes of Action," ch. 8, §8, p. 251.*}

EQUITABLE RELIEF

25. Plaintiff seeks {❺❶ *identify equitable relief sought*}. {❺❷ *State facts supporting equitable relief.*} {*See FORM 2D:1;* ***O'Connor's Texas Rules****, "Injunctive Relief," ch. 2-D, p. 138;* ***O'Connor's Texas COA****, "Equitable relief," ch. 8, §3.4, p. 242.*}

JURY DEMAND

26. Plaintiff demands a jury trial and tenders the appropriate fee with this petition. {*See* ***O'Connor's Texas Rules****, "Request for Jury Trial," ch. 5-B, p. 400.*}

CONDITIONS PRECEDENT

27. All conditions precedent to plaintiff's claim for relief have been performed or have occurred. {*See* ***O'Connor's Texas Rules****, "Conditions Precedent," ch. 2-B, §12, p. 132.*}

REQUEST FOR DISCLOSURE

28. Under Texas Rule of Civil Procedure 194, plaintiff requests that defendant disclose, within 50 days of the service of this request, the information or material described in Rule 194.2. {*See **O'Connor's Texas Rules**, "Content of request," ch. 6-E, §3.2, p. 627.*}

OBJECTION TO ASSOCIATE JUDGE

29. Plaintiff objects to the referral of this case to an associate judge for hearing a trial on the merits or presiding at a jury trial. {*See **O'Connor's Texas Rules**, "Objection to referral," ch. 1-J, §3.3, p. 96.*}

PRAYER

30. For these reasons, plaintiff asks that the Court issue citation for defendant to appear and answer, and that plaintiff be awarded a judgment against defendant for the following:

{*CHOOSE RELIEF SOUGHT*}

a. {53 *Economic/Actual*} damages. {*See **O'Connor's Texas COA**, "DTPA damages," ch. 8, §3.1, p. 239; "Pleading actual damages," ch. 41-A, §3.2, p. 1346.*}

b. Treble damages. {*See **O'Connor's Texas COA**, "Additional damages," ch. 8, §3.2, p. 241.*}

c. {54 *Describe equitable relief.*}

d. Prejudgment and postjudgment interest. {*See **O'Connor's Texas COA**, "Interest," ch. 43, p. 1445.*}

e. Court costs. {*See **O'Connor's Texas COA**, "Court Costs," ch. 44, p. 1453.*}

f. Attorney fees. {*See **O'Connor's Texas COA**, "Attorney fees," ch. 8, §3.7, p. 243.*}

g. All other relief to which plaintiff is entitled. {*See **O'Connor's Texas Rules**, "Prayer," ch. 2-B, §15, p. 132.*}

Continued on next page

SEE: Tex. R. Civ. P. 45-59, 78-82, 169, 190, 194
Tex. Bus. & Com. Code §17.41 et seq.
Tex. Ins. Code ch. 541
O'Connor's Texas Rules * Civil Trials (2019), "Plaintiff's Original Petition," ch. 2-B, p. 115
O'Connor's Texas Causes of Action (2019), "Deceptive Trade Practices Act," ch. 8, p. 209; "Damages & Other Compensation," Part 4, p. 1343

ADD: STYLE OF THE CASE – FORM 1B:2
SIGNATURE BLOCK – FORM 1B:3
VERIFICATION – FORM 1B:7, for injunctive relief

ATTACH: AFFIDAVIT – FORM 1B:8, if necessary to support facts for injunctive relief
NOTICE OF CURRENT/CHANGE OF ADDRESS – FORM 1B:14
NOTICE UNDER THE DTPA – FORM 2A:4
Civil Process Request Form, if required by court clerk to issue citation
Exhibits, if necessary
Filing fees
Jury fee, if jury trial requested

NOTE: Under the DTPA, the plaintiff's recovery is generally limited to economic damages. But if the claim is based on a violation of a tie-in statute, the plaintiff can recover actual damages, which may be broader. See ***O'Connor's Texas COA***, "DTPA damages," ch. 8, §3.1, p. 239.

A plaintiff bringing a DTPA claim relating to insurance claims for damage to or loss of real property caused by forces of nature must give written presuit notice of the plaintiff's claim under Texas Insurance Code chapter 542A. *See* Tex. Ins. Code §§542A.001(2), 542A.002(a)(3)(C), 542A.003. For a discussion of presuit notice of a claim under chapter 542A, see ***O'Connor's Texas COA***, "Suits for real-property-related damage caused by forces of nature," ch. 13-C, §6.2, p. 370.

See notes under FORM 2B:1.

PLAINTIFF'S ORIGINAL PETITION FOR
BILL OF REVIEW {❶ *STATE ADDITIONAL RELIEF REQUESTED IF APPROPRIATE, E.G., & REQUEST FOR DISCLOSURE*}

Plaintiff, {❷ *name*}, files this original petition for bill of review {❸ *state additional relief requested if appropriate, e.g., and request for disclosure*} against defendant, {❹ *name*}, and alleges as follows:

DISCOVERY-CONTROL PLAN

1. Plaintiff intends to conduct discovery under Level {❺ *2/3*} of Texas Rule of Civil Procedure {❻ *190.3/190.4*} and affirmatively pleads that this suit is not governed by the expedited-actions process in Texas Rule of Civil Procedure 169 because {❼ *explain*}. {*See **O'Connor's Texas Rules**, "Discovery-Control Plans," ch. 2-B, §2, p. 115.*}

CLAIM FOR RELIEF

2. Plaintiff seeks monetary relief of $100,000 or less and nonmonetary relief. {*Tex. R. Civ. P. 47(c)(2).*}

PARTIES

3. {*For plaintiff designation, see FORM 2B:9; **O'Connor's Texas Rules**, "Plaintiff," ch. 2-B, §4.4, p. 123.*}

4. {*For defendant designation, see FORMS 2B:10-19; **O'Connor's Texas Rules**, "Defendant," ch. 2-B, §4.5, p. 123.*}

JURISDICTION

{*CHOOSE APPROPRIATE PARAGRAPH 5*}

{*If within the residual four-year statute of limitations*}

5. This bill of review is filed in the same court that rendered the judgment challenged by this bill of review, after the deadline for filing a motion for new trial, when a restricted appeal under Texas Rule of Appellate Procedure 30 is not available, and within the residual four-year statute of limitations. {*Tex. Civ. Prac. & Rem. Code §16.051.*} {*See **O'Connor's Texas Rules**, "Bill of review," ch. 7-A, §7.1.3, p. 717.*}

{*If after the residual four-year statute of limitations*}

5. This bill of review is filed, in the same court that rendered the judgment challenged by this bill of review, after the residual four-year statute of limitations because

Continued on next page

plaintiff was prevented by defendant's extrinsic fraud from filing earlier. Specifically, {❽ *explain how defendant engaged in wrongful conduct that prevented party from fully litigating rights within statute of limitations*}. {*See* ***O'Connor's Texas Rules****, "Extrinsic fraud," ch. 7-A, §7.1.3(1)(a)[2], p. 718.*}

FACTS

6. On {❾ *date*}, defendant (as plaintiff in the earlier suit) sued plaintiff (as defendant in the earlier suit) in this Court in cause number {❿ *number*}, {⓫ *style of case*}, for {⓬ *state basis of suit*}.

7. On {⓭ *date*}, a {⓮ *judgment/default judgment*} was rendered against plaintiff. A copy of the judgment is attached as Exhibit {⓯ *letter*} and incorporated by reference.

8. {⓰ *State other facts relevant to the petition.*}

BILL-OF-REVIEW STANDARD

9. To succeed on a bill of review, the plaintiff usually must plead and prove (1) a meritorious defense to the underlying cause of action, (2) which plaintiff was prevented from making by the opposing party's fraud, accident, or wrongful conduct or official mistake, (3) unmixed with any fault or negligence on plaintiff's own part. *Mabon Ltd. v. Afri-Carib Enters., Inc.*, 369 S.W.3d 809, 812 (Tex. 2012). When a bill-of-review plaintiff claims a due-process violation for no service or notice of the trial or default judgment, the plaintiff is relieved from proving the first two elements—a meritorious defense and wrongful conduct or official mistake—and must prove only the third element—no fault or negligence on the plaintiff's part contributed to the lack of service or notice. *Katy Venture, Ltd. v. Cremona Bistro Corp.*, 469 S.W.3d 160, 164 (Tex. 2015); *see Mabon Ltd.*, 369 S.W.3d at 812; *Caldwell v. Barnes*, 154 S.W.3d 93, 96-97 (Tex. 2004). {*See* ***O'Connor's Texas Rules****, "Sufficient cause," ch. 7-A, §7.1.3(1)(c), p. 718.*}

{*CHOOSE APPROPRIATE PARAGRAPH 10 IF DUE-PROCESS VIOLATION*}

{⓱ *NO SERVICE/NO NOTICE*}

10. Plaintiff was not served with citation and a copy of the petition. Specifically, {⓲ *state facts proving lack of service of process*}. Therefore, plaintiff's lack of service was not the result of any fault or negligence on plaintiff's part. In support, the affidavit of {⓳ *name of affiant*} is attached as Exhibit {⓴ *letter*} and incorporated by reference.

10. Plaintiff did not receive notice of the {[21] *hearing/trial*} held on {[22] *date*}, after which the Court rendered a default judgment against plaintiff. Specifically, {[23] *state facts proving lack of service of notice*}. Therefore, plaintiff's lack of notice was not the result of any fault or negligence on plaintiff's part. In support, the affidavit of {[24] *name of affiant*} is attached as Exhibit {[25] *letter*} and incorporated by reference.

{*ADD PARAGRAPHS 11-13 IF NO DUE-PROCESS VIOLATION*}

{[26] *FRAUD/ACCIDENT/WRONGFUL ACT/OFFICIAL MISTAKE*}

{*CHOOSE APPROPRIATE PARAGRAPH 11*}

11. The judgment in cause number {[27] *number*} was rendered against plaintiff as the result of {[28] *fraud/an accident/a wrongful act*} by defendant. Specifically, {[29] *identify specific act, e.g., fraudulent failure to serve party with process, failure to notify party of trial setting, and state how it prevented plaintiff from asserting its meritorious defense. See Lambert v. Coachmen Indus., Inc., 761 S.W.2d 82, 86-87 (Tex. App.—Houston [14th Dist.] 1988, writ denied)*}. In support, the affidavit of {[30] *name of affiant*} is attached as Exhibit {[31] *letter*} and incorporated by reference.

11. The judgment in cause number {[32] *number*} was rendered against plaintiff as the result of an official mistake. Specifically, {[33] *identify specific act, e.g., clerk's failure to send notice of a dismissal, misplacement of the original answer, clerk's failure to send notice of judgment, and state how it prevented plaintiff from asserting its meritorious defense. See Baker v. Goldsmith, 582 S.W.2d 404, 407 (Tex. 1979); K.B. Video & Elecs., Inc. v. Naylor, 847 S.W.2d 401, 405-06 (Tex. App.—Amarillo 1993, writ denied)*}. In support, the affidavit of {[34] *name of affiant*} is attached as Exhibit {[35] *letter*} and incorporated by reference.

12. Plaintiff's inability to prevent the entry of the {[36] *judgment/default judgment*} was not the result of any fault or negligence of plaintiff. {[37] *Explain in detail plaintiff's diligence in availing itself of all legal remedies, e.g., party exercised due diligence but did not learn of the judgment until the deadline for appeal and motion for new trial had passed.*} In support, the affidavit of {[38] *name of affiant*} is attached as Exhibit {[39] *letter*} and incorporated by reference.

13. Plaintiff has a meritorious defense to defendant's suit for {[40] *identify cause of action*}. {[41] *Identify defense and state facts establishing each element of the defense.*} In support, the affidavit of {[42] *name of affiant*} is attached as Exhibit {[43] *letter*} and incorporated by reference.

Continued on next page

{ADD PARAGRAPHS 14-15 IF APPROPRIATE}

REQUEST FOR DISCLOSURE

14. Under Texas Rule of Civil Procedure 194, plaintiff requests that defendant disclose, within 50 days of the service of this request, the information or material described in Rule 194.2. {*See **O'Connor's Texas Rules**, "Content of request," ch. 6-E, §3.2, p. 627.*}

OBJECTION TO ASSOCIATE JUDGE

15. Plaintiff objects to the referral of this case to an associate judge for hearing a trial on the merits or presiding at a jury trial. {*See **O'Connor's Texas Rules**, "Objection to referral," ch. 1-J, §3.3, p. 96.*}

PRAYER

16. For these reasons, plaintiff asks the Court to do the following:

{CHOOSE APPROPRIATE REMEDIES}

a. Vacate the judgment in cause number {44 *number*}, {45 *style of case*}.

b. Reopen cause number {46 *number*} and grant a new trial.

c. After a hearing, render a judgment in cause number {47 *number*} that defendant take nothing.

d. Assess costs against defendant.

e. Award plaintiff all other relief to which plaintiff is entitled. {*See **O'Connor's Texas Rules**, "Prayer," ch. 2-B, §15, p. 132.*}

SEE: Tex. R. Civ. P. 45-59, 78-82, 190, 194, 329b(f)
Tex. Civ. Prac. & Rem. Code §16.051
O'Connor's Texas Rules * Civil Trials (2019), "Plaintiff's Original Petition," ch. 2-B, p. 115; "Bill of review," ch. 7-A, §7.1.3, p. 717

ADD: STYLE OF THE CASE – FORM 1B:2
SIGNATURE BLOCK – FORM 1B:3
VERIFICATION – FORM 1B:7

ATTACH: AFFIDAVIT – FORM 1B:8
NOTICE OF CURRENT/CHANGE OF ADDRESS – FORM 1B:14
Civil Process Request Form, if required by court clerk to issue citation
Copy of judgment challenged by bill of review
Exhibits, as necessary
Filing fee

NOTE: A bill of review is a separate suit and should be given a separate docket number from the suit it challenges. In a bill-of-review proceeding, the bill-of-review plaintiff is the first suit's defendant, the party seeking to vacate the default judgment. The bill-of-review defendant is the first suit's plaintiff, the party that was granted the default judgment.

This form applies to equitable bills of review; however, in certain types of proceedings—generally probate and guardianship proceedings—a statutory bill of review may be available. See ***O'Connor's Texas Rules***, "Statutory bill of review," ch. 7-A, §7.1.3(2), p. 721.

When the party filing a bill of review does not claim there has been a due-process violation, she must make a prima facie showing of a meritorious defense as a preliminary matter. *See* ***Caldwell v. Barnes***, 154 S.W.3d 93, 97 (Tex.2004); ***State v. 1985 Chevrolet Pickup Truck***, 778 S.W.2d 463, 464 (Tex.1989). The court may require the party to make this showing at a pretrial hearing, sometimes referred to as a "***Baker*** hearing." *See* ***Beck v. Beck***, 771 S.W.2d 141, 142 (Tex.1989); ***Baker v. Goldsmith***, 582 S.W.2d 404, 409 (Tex.1979). If the party makes a prima facie showing, the court will conduct a trial on the remaining bill-of-review grounds. ***Beck***, 771 S.W.2d at 142; ***Baker***, 582 S.W.2d at 409. If the party does not make a prima facie showing, the court will deny the bill-of-review petition. ***Beck***, 771 S.W.2d at 142; ***Baker***, 582 S.W.2d at 409. See ***O'Connor's Texas Rules***, "Meritorious defense," ch. 7-A, §7.1.3(1)(c)[1][a], p. 718.

When the party filing a bill of review claims it has not received service of process, the party is not required to set up a meritorious defense or prove fraud, accident, wrongful conduct, or official mistake. ***Katy Venture, Ltd. v. Cremona Bistro Corp.***, 469 S.W.3d 160, 164 (Tex.2015). See ***O'Connor's Texas Rules***, "Due-process violation," ch. 7-A, §7.1.3(1)(c)[2], p. 719.

Because a bill of review is generally an equitable proceeding, discovery cannot be conducted under a Level 1 discovery-control plan. *See* Tex. R. Civ. P. 47(c), 190.2(a); *see also* ***PNS Stores v. Rivera***, 379 S.W.3d 267, 275 (Tex.2012) (bill of review is an equitable proceeding). A Level 1 discovery-control plan applies to expedited actions (i.e., civil actions in which only monetary relief is sought and the amount in controversy is no more than $100,000) or to suits for divorce not involving children where the value of the marital estate does not exceed $50,000. Tex. R. Civ. P. 169(d)(1), 190.2. See ***O'Connor's Texas Rules***, "Discovery-Control Plans," ch. 2-B, §2, p. 115.

See notes under FORM 2B:1.

PARTIES

{*CHOOSE APPROPRIATE DESIGNATION*}

1. Plaintiff, {[1] *name*}, is {[2] *identify capacity in which plaintiff brings suit, e.g., an individual, a corporation, a partnership*} {[3] *residing/doing business*} in {[4] _______} County at {[5] *address*}. {*See* ***O'Connor's Texas Rules****, "Parties," ch. 2-B, §4, p. 116.*}

2. Plaintiff, {[6] *name 1*}, is an individual doing business as {[7] *name 2*} in {[8] _______} County at {[9] *address*}. {*See* ***O'Connor's Texas Rules****, "Parties," ch. 2-B, §4, p. 116.*}

3. Plaintiff, {[10] *name 1*}, brings this suit {[11] *as next friend/individually and as next friend*} on behalf of {[12] *name 2*}, {[13] *a minor child/an incapacitated person*}. Plaintiff resides in {[14] _______} County at {[15] *address 1*}; {[16] *name 2*} resides in {[17] _______} County at {[18] *address 2*}. {*See Tex. Est. Code §1002.017; Tex. Fam. Code §102.003(a);* ***O'Connor's Texas Rules****, "Minor as P," ch. 2-B, §4.4.2, p. 123.*}

4. Plaintiff, {[19] *name 1*}, brings this suit as {[20] *identify representative capacity, e.g., guardian, guardian ad litem*} on behalf of {[21] *name 2*}, {[22] *a minor child/an incapacitated person*}. Plaintiff resides in {[23] _______} County at {[24] *address 1*}; {[25] *name 2*} resides in {[26] _______} County at {[27] *address 2*}. {*See Tex. Est. Code §§1002.017, 1151.101; Tex. Fam. Code §102.003(a);* ***O'Connor's Texas Rules****, "Minor as P," ch. 2-B, §4.4.2, p. 123.*}

5. Plaintiff, {[28] *name 1*}, brings this suit as the {[29] *executor/administrator*} on behalf of the estate of {[30] *name 2*}, decedent. Plaintiff resides in {[31] _______} County at {[32] *address 1*}; decedent, at the time of death, resided in {[33] _______} County at {[34] *address 2*}. {*See* ***O'Connor's Texas Rules****, "Estate," ch. 2-B, §4.3.2, p. 121.*}

6. Plaintiff, {[35] *name*}, brings this suit as the trustee on behalf of {[36] *name of trust*}. Plaintiff resides in {[37] _______} County at {[38] *address*}. {*See* ***O'Connor's Texas Rules****, "Trust," ch. 2-B, §4.3.3, p. 122.*}

{*ADD APPROPRIATE PARAGRAPH 7 IF APPLICABLE*}

7. The last three digits of plaintiff {[39] *name*}'s driver's license number are {[40] *digits of driver's license number*}. The last three digits of plaintiff's Social Security number are {[41] *digits of Social Security number*}. {*See Tex. Civ. Prac. & Rem. Code §30.014(a);* ***O'Connor's Texas Rules****, "ID number," ch. 1-B, §3.2.4(3), p. 8.*}

7. The last three digits of plaintiff {㊷ *name*}'s driver's license number are {㊸ *digits of driver's license number*}. Plaintiff has not been issued a Social Security number. {*See* Tex. Civ. Prac. & Rem. Code §30.014(a); ***O'Connor's Texas Rules***, "ID number," ch. 1-B, §3.2.4(3), p. 8.}

7. The last three digits of plaintiff {㊹ *name*}'s Social Security number are {㊺ *digits of Social Security number*}. Plaintiff has not been issued a driver's license number. {*See* Tex. Civ. Prac. & Rem. Code §30.014(a); ***O'Connor's Texas Rules***, "ID number," ch. 1-B, §3.2.4(3), p. 8.}

7. Plaintiff {㊻ *name*} has not been issued a driver's license number or a Social Security number. {*See* Tex. Civ. Prac. & Rem. Code §30.014(a); ***O'Connor's Texas Rules***, "ID number," ch. 1-B, §3.2.4(3), p. 8.}

SEE: Tex. R. Civ. P. 28-44, 79, 173
Tex. Civ. Prac. & Rem. Code §30.014
Tex. Est. Code §§1002.017, 1151.101
Tex. Fam. Code §102.003(a)
O'Connor's Texas Rules * Civil Trials (2019), "Plaintiff," ch. 2-B, §4.4, p. 123

NOTE: If the plaintiff is doing business under an assumed name, the style of the case should read, for example, "Plaintiff, {*name 1*}, d/b/a {*name 2*}." *See* Tex. Bus. & Com. Code §71.001 et seq.

PARTIES

{*CHOOSE APPROPRIATE DESIGNATION*}

1. Defendant, {1 *name*}, an individual, may be served with process at defendant's usual place of {2 *business/abode*} in {3 _______} County at {4 *address*}, or wherever defendant may be found. {*See Tex. R. Civ. P. 106;* ***O'Connor's Texas Rules****, "Defendant," ch. 2-B, §4.5, p. 123.*}

2. Defendant, {5 *name*}, a minor child, may be served with process in {6 _______} County at {7 *address*}, where defendant resides or wherever defendant may be found. {*See* ***O'Connor's Texas Rules****, "Minor as D," ch. 2-B, §4.5.4, p. 124.*}

3. Defendant, {8 *name 1*}, {9 *a minor child/an incapacitated person*}, may be served with process by serving defendant's court-appointed guardian of the estate, {10 *name 2*}, in {11 _______} County at {12 *address*}, where defendant's guardian {13 *resides/conducts business*}. {*See Tex. Est. Code ch. 51, §§1002.017, 1151.101;* ***O'Connor's Texas Rules****, "Guardian of estate," ch. 2-B, §4.5.4(1), p. 124.*}

4. Defendant, {14 *name 1*}, the {15 *executor/administrator*} of the estate of {16 *name 2*}, decedent, may be served with process at defendant's usual place of {17 *business/abode*} in {18 _______} County at {19 *address*}, or wherever defendant may be found. {*See* ***O'Connor's Texas Rules****, "Estate," ch. 2-B, §4.3.2, p. 121.*}

5. Defendant, {20 *name*}, the trustee of the {21 *name of trust*}, may be served with process at defendant's usual place of {22 *business/abode*} in {23 _______} County at {24 *address*}, or wherever defendant may be found. {*See* ***O'Connor's Texas Rules****, "Trust," ch. 2-B, §4.3.3, p. 122.*}

6. Defendant, {25 *name 1*}, an individual who maintains {26 *an office/a place of business/an agency*} in {27 _______} County at {28 *address*}, may be served with process by serving defendant's {29 *agent/clerk*}, {30 *name 2*}, at that address, because defendant is engaged in business in Texas, the lawsuit {31 *arises from/is connected with*} defendant's business in Texas, and defendant is not a resident of the county where the suit arose. {*Tex. Civ. Prac. & Rem. Code §17.021(a).*}

7. Defendant, {32 *name 1*}, an individual who maintains {33 *an office/a place of business/an agency*} in {34 _______} County at {35 *address*}, may be served with process by serving defendant's {36 *agent/clerk*}, {37 *name 2*}, at that address, because defendant is engaged in business in Texas, the lawsuit {38 *arises from/is connected with*} defendant's business in Texas, and defendant is a resident of the county where the suit arose, but after diligent search and inquiry, defendant could not be found. {*Tex. Civ. Prac. & Rem. Code §17.021(a), (b).*}

8. Defendant, {❸❾ *name 1*}, an individual doing business as {❹⓿ *name 2*}, {❹❶ *maintains business premises/maintains professional premises/regularly conducts business/regularly renders professional services*} at defendant's {❹❷ *office/place of business/agency*} located in {❹❸ _______} County at {❹❹ *address*}, and may be served with process by serving defendant's {❹❺ *agent/clerk*}, {❹❻ *name 3*}, at that address. {*See Tex. Bus. & Com. Code §§71.002(7)(A), 71.051;* ***O'Connor's Texas Rules****, "Assumed name," ch. 2-B, §4.3.5, p. 122.*}

9. Defendant, {❹❼ *name*}, an individual who is a resident of Texas and whose {❹❽ *home office/principal place of business*} is located in {❹❾ _______} County at {❺⓿ *address*}, may be served with process by serving the Texas Commissioner of Insurance at 333 Guadalupe Street, Austin, Texas 78701, because defendant is an unauthorized individual engaged in the practice of insurance business as provided by Texas Insurance Code section 101.051, and this suit is not being brought by the Texas Department of Insurance or the State of Texas. {*Tex. Ins. Code §804.107(b)(1).*}

10. Defendant, {❺❶ *name 1*}, an individual who is a resident of Texas and whose {❺❷ *home office/principal place of business*} is located in {❺❸ _______} County at {❺❹ *address*}, may be served with process by serving {❺❺ *name 2*}, in {❺❻ _______} County at {❺❼ *address*}, as the person who is conducting insurance business in Texas on behalf of defendant as provided by Texas Insurance Code section 101.051, because defendant is an unauthorized individual engaged in the practice of insurance business. {*Tex. Ins. Code §804.107(d).*}

11. Defendant, {❺❽ *name*}, an individual who is a resident of Texas and whose {❺❾ *home office/principal place of business*} is located in {❻⓿ _______} County at {❻❶ *address*}, may be served with process by serving the Texas Secretary of State, at 1019 Brazos Street, Austin, Texas 78701, as its agent for service, because this suit is being brought by the {❻❷ *Texas Department of Insurance/State of Texas*} against defendant, who is an unauthorized individual engaged in the practice of insurance business as provided by Texas Insurance Code section 101.051. {*See Tex. Ins. Code §804.107(b)(2), (c)(1);* ***O'Connor's Texas Rules****, "General rules," ch. 2-I, §5.1, p. 195.*}

12. Defendant, {❻❸ *name*}, an individual who is a patient confined in an inpatient mental health facility in {❻❹ _______} County at {❻❺ *address 1*}, may be served with process by serving the defendant's agent, {❻❻ *name of the facility administrator, superintendent, supervisor, or manager*}, at {❻❼ *address 2*}. {*Tex. Health & Safety Code §571.010.*}

Continued on next page

13. Defendant, {68 *name*}, is an individual whose usual place of {69 *business/abode*} is in {70 ________} County at {71 *address*}. Process should not be served on defendant at this time because it is believed that {72 *he/she*} will sign a waiver of service of process. If defendant does not sign a waiver, {73 *he/she*} may be served with process at {74 *his/her*} usual place of {75 *business/abode*} or wherever {76 *he/she*} may be found. {*See Tex. R. Civ. P. 106, 119; FORM 2I:1.*}

SEE: Tex. R. Civ. P. 28-44, 79, 106, 173
Tex. Civ. Prac. & Rem. Code §17.021
Tex. Est. Code ch. 51, §§1002.017, 1151.101
Tex. Fam. Code §102.009(a)
Tex. Health & Safety Code §571.010
Tex. Ins. Code §§101.051, 804.107
O'Connor's Texas Rules * Civil Trials (2019), "Defendant," ch. 2-B, §4.5, p. 123

NOTE: The petition does not need to include any statutory or rule citations for service.

If the defendant is doing business as an assumed name, the style of the case should read, for example, "Defendant, {*name 1*}, d/b/a {*name 2*}." *See* Tex. Bus. & Com. Code §71.001 et seq.

The party must mail a copy of the petition to the Attorney General for suits in which the Attorney General may represent an individual based on state liability for conduct of a public servant under Texas Civil Practice & Remedies Code chapter 104. Tex. Civ. Prac. & Rem. Code §30.004. The petition must be mailed to the Attorney General's office in Austin, Texas, by certified mail, return receipt requested. *Id.* §30.004(b). Mailing the petition does not relieve the party from serving process on any named party in the case. *Id.* §30.004(c). If the required notice to the Attorney General is not given, any default judgment in the case can be set aside without costs. *Id.* §30.004(d).

PARTIES

{*CHOOSE APPROPRIATE DESIGNATION*}

1. Defendant, {[1] *name 1*}, a Texas corporation whose registered office is located in {[2] _______} County at {[3] *address*}, may be served with process by serving

{*CHOOSE APPROPRIATE STATEMENT*}

[A] its {[4] *president/vice president*}, {[5] *name 2*}, at that address. {*See Tex. Bus. Orgs. Code §5.255(1).*}

[B] its registered agent for service of process, {[6] *name 2*}, in {[7] _______} County at {[8] *address*}. {*See Tex. Bus. Orgs. Code §5.201.*}

[C] the Texas Secretary of State at 1019 Brazos Street, Austin, Texas 78701, as its agent for service because defendant is required by Texas Business Organizations Code section 5.201 to appoint and maintain a registered agent in Texas but {[9] *defendant has not done so/defendant's registered agent cannot be found with reasonable diligence*}. {*See Tex. Bus. Orgs. Code §5.251(1);* ***O'Connor's Texas Rules****, "General rules," ch. 2-I, §5.1, p. 195.*}

2. Defendant, {[10] *name 1*}, a Texas nonprofit corporation whose registered office is located in {[11] _______} County at {[12] *address*}, may be served with process by serving

{*CHOOSE APPROPRIATE STATEMENT*}

[A] its {[13] *president/vice president*}, {[14] *name 2*}, at that address. {*See Tex. Bus. Orgs. Code §5.255(1).*}

[B] its registered agent for service of process, {[15] *name 2*}, in {[16] _______} County at {[17] *address*}. {*See Tex. Bus. Orgs. Code §5.201.*}

[C] {[18] *name 2*}, in {[19] _______} County at {[20] *address*}, because {[21] *name 2*} is a member of the committee authorized to perform the corporation's chief-executive function. {*See Tex. Bus. Orgs. Code §5.255(5).*}

[D] the Texas Secretary of State at 1019 Brazos Street, Austin, Texas 78701, as its agent for service because defendant is required by Texas Business Organizations Code section 5.201 to appoint and maintain a registered agent in Texas but {[22] *defendant has not done so/defendant's registered*

Continued on next page

agent cannot be found with reasonable diligence}. {*See Tex. Bus. Orgs. Code §5.251(1);* ***O'Connor's Texas Rules****, "General rules," ch. 2-I, §5.1, p. 195.*}

SEE: Tex. R. Civ. P. 28-44, 79
Tex. Bus. Orgs. Code §§5.200, 5.201, 5.251, 5.252, 5.255
O'Connor's Texas Rules * Civil Trials (2019), "Defendant," ch. 2-B, §4.5, p. 123; "General rules," ch. 2-I, §5.1, p. 195; "Who May Be Served," ch. 2-I, §6, p. 197

NOTE: The petition does not need to include any statutory or rule citations for service. However, when serving the Secretary of State or any other public official as agent for the defendant, cite the statute that authorizes the public official to accept service on behalf of the defendant. For other requirements for service on the Secretary of State as agent for the defendant, see ***O'Connor's Texas Rules***, "Service on Secretary of State," ch. 2-I, §5, p. 195.

The Citations Unit of the Texas Secretary of State is responsible for processing documents served on the Secretary of State as agent for process. Documents can be mailed to the following address:

Service of Process
Secretary of State
P.O. Box 12079
Austin, Texas 78711-2079

If the defendant is doing business as an assumed name, the style of the case should read, for example, "Defendant, {*name 1*}, d/b/a {*name 2*}." *See* Tex. Bus. & Com. Code §71.001 et seq.

For detailed charts for service on business entities, see ***O'Connor's Texas Rules***, "Service Through Secretary of State," chart 2-3, p. 195, and "Proper Person to Serve," chart 2-4, p. 197.

PARTIES

{*CHOOSE APPROPRIATE DESIGNATION*}

{*Partnership*}

1. Defendant, {[1] *name*}, is a partnership whose office is located in {[2] _______} County at {[3] *address*}. Defendant may be served with process by serving its partners as follows:

   a. {[4] *Name of partner*}, in {[5] _______} County at {[6] *address*}.

   b. {[7] *Continue to name partners until all are identified by name and address.*} {*See Tex. Civ. Prac. & Rem. Code §§17.022, 31.003;* ***O'Connor's Texas Rules****, "Partnership," ch. 2-I, §2.6.2, p. 191.*}

2. Defendant, {[8] *name 1*}, a partnership that maintains {[9] *an office/a place of business/an agency for transacting business in this state*} in {[10] _______} County at {[11] *address*}, may be served with process by serving its {[12] *agent/clerk*}, {[13] *name 2*}, who is employed in defendant's {[14] *office/place of business/agency*}, at that address, because this lawsuit {[15] *arises from/is connected with*} defendant's business transacted in Texas and defendant is not a resident of the county where the suit arose. {*Tex. Civ. Prac. & Rem. Code §17.021(a).*}

3. Defendant, {[16] *name 1*}, a partnership that maintains {[17] *an office/a place of business/an agency for transacting business in this state*} in {[18] _______} County at {[19] *address*}, may be served with process by serving its {[20] *agent/clerk*}, {[21] *name 2*}, who is employed in defendant's {[22] *office/place of business/agency*}, at that address, because this lawsuit {[23] *arises from/is connected with*} defendant's business transacted in Texas and defendant is a resident of the county where the suit arose, but after diligent search and inquiry, defendant could not be found. {*Tex. Civ. Prac. & Rem. Code §17.021(a), (b).*}

{*Unincorporated association*}

4. Defendant, {[24] *name 1*}, an unincorporated association that maintains {[25] *an office/a place of business/an agency for transacting business in this state*} in {[26] _______} County at {[27] *address*}, may be served with process by serving its {[28] *agent/clerk*}, {[29] *name 2*}, who is employed in defendant's {[30] *office/place of business/agency*}, at that address, because this lawsuit {[31] *arises from/is connected with*} defendant's business transacted in Texas and defendant is not a resident of the county where the suit arose. {*Tex. Civ. Prac. & Rem. Code §17.021(a).*}

Continued on next page

5. Defendant, {32 *name 1*}, an unincorporated association that maintains {33 *an office/a place of business/an agency for transacting business in this state*} in {34 _______} County at {35 *address*}, may be served with process by serving its {36 *agent/clerk*}, {37 *name 2*}, who is employed in defendant's {38 *office/place of business/agency*}, at that address, because this lawsuit {39 *arises from/is connected with*} defendant's business transacted in Texas and defendant is a resident of the county where the suit arose, but after diligent search and inquiry, defendant could not be found. {*Tex. Civ. Prac. & Rem. Code §17.021(a), (b).*}

{*Joint-stock association*}

6. Defendant, {40 *name 1*}, a joint-stock association, may be served with process by serving the {41 *president/vice president/secretary/treasurer/cashier/assistant cashier*}, {42 *name 2*}, in {43 _______} County at {44 *address*}. {*Tex. Civ. Prac. & Rem. Code §17.023(a)(1).*}

7. Defendant, {45 *name 1*}, a joint-stock association, may be served with process by serving its local agent in the county where suit is brought, {46 *name 2*}, in {47 _______} County at {48 *address*}. {*Tex. Civ. Prac. & Rem. Code §17.023(a)(2).*}

8. Defendant, {49 *name 1*}, a joint-stock association, whose principal business office is located in {50 _______} County at {51 *address*}, may be served with process by leaving a copy of the citation at that address during office hours. {*Tex. Civ. Prac. & Rem. Code §17.023(a)(3).*}

9. Defendant, {52 *name 1*}, a joint-stock association, may be served with process by serving {53 *name 2*}, an agent representing defendant in Texas, in {54 _______} County at {55 *address*}, because defendant does not have an agent in the county where the suit is brought and no officer of defendant on whom citation may be served resides in that county. {*Tex. Civ. Prac. & Rem. Code §17.023(b).*}

{*Unincorporated joint-stock company or association*}

10. Defendant, {56 *name 1*}, an unincorporated joint-stock {57 *company/association*} doing business in Texas, may be served with process by serving the {58 *president/secretary/treasurer/general agent*}, {59 *name 2*}, in {60 _______} County at {61 *address*}. {*Tex. Rev. Civ. Stat. arts. 6133, 6134.*}

SEE: Tex. R. Civ. P. 28-44, 79
Tex. Civ. Prac. & Rem. Code §§17.021-17.023, 31.003
Tex. Rev. Civ. Stat. arts. 6133, 6134, 6137
O'Connor's Texas Rules * Civil Trials (2019), "Defendant," ch. 2-B, §4.5, p. 123; "Who May Be Served," ch. 2-I, §6, p. 197

NOTE: To bring a claim against a partner in her individual capacity, direct the citation to the individual partner. See ***O'Connor's Texas Rules***, "Partnership," ch. 2-I, §2.6.2, p. 191.

If an individual stockholder or member of an unincorporated joint-stock company or association and the president, secretary, treasurer, or general agent are both served with process, judgment against the company or association will be binding on the individual property of that stockholder or member. Tex. Rev. Civ. Stat. art. 6137.

PARTIES

{*CHOOSE APPROPRIATE DESIGNATION*}

{*Domestic insurance carrier*}

1. Defendant, {❶ *name 1*}, a domestic insurance carrier authorized to conduct insurance business in Texas, whose {❷ *home office/principal place of business*} is located in {❸ _______} County at {❹ *address*}, may be served with process by serving {❺ *name 2*}, {❻ *the president/an active vice president/a secretary/its attorney-in-fact*}, at that address. {*Tex. Ins. Code §804.101(b)(1).*}

2. Defendant, {❼ *name*}, a domestic insurance carrier authorized to conduct insurance business in Texas, whose {❽ *home office/principal place of business*} is located in {❾ _______} County at {❿ *address*}, may be served with process by leaving a copy of the process at that address during regular business hours. {*Tex. Ins. Code §804.101(b)(2).*}

3. Defendant, {⓫ *name 1*}, a domestic insurance carrier that has moved its principal office outside Texas, may be served with process by serving its designated agent for service of process, {⓬ *name 2*}, in {⓭ _______} County at {⓮ *address*}. {*Tex. Ins. Code §804.102(b).*}

4. Defendant, {⓯ *name*}, a domestic insurance carrier that has moved its principal office outside Texas, may be served with process by serving the Texas Commissioner of Insurance at 333 Guadalupe Street, Austin, Texas 78701, because defendant is required by Texas Insurance Code section 804.102 to appoint and maintain an agent for service of process, but {⓰ *defendant has not done so/defendant's agent cannot be found with reasonable diligence*}. {*See Tex. Ins. Code §804.102(c).*}

{*Unauthorized insurer engaging in the practice of insurance business in Texas*}

5. Defendant, {⓱ *name*}, an insurer whose {⓲ *home office/principal place of business*} is located in {⓳ _______} County at {⓴ *address*}, may be served with process by serving the Texas Commissioner of Insurance at 333 Guadalupe Street, Austin, Texas 78701, because defendant is an unauthorized insurer engaged in the practice of insurance business in Texas as provided by Texas Insurance Code section 101.051, and this suit is not being brought by the Texas Department of Insurance or the State of Texas. {*See Tex. Ins. Code §804.107(b)(1).*}

6. Defendant, {[21] *name 1*}, an insurer whose {[22] *home office/principal place of business*} is located in {[23] _______} County at {[24] *address*}, may be served with process by serving {[25] *name 2*}, in {[26] _______} County at {[27] *address*}, as the person who is conducting insurance business in Texas on behalf of defendant as provided by Texas Insurance Code section 101.051, because defendant is an unauthorized insurer engaged in the practice of insurance business. {*Tex. Ins. Code §804.107(d).*}

7. Defendant, {[28] *name*}, an insurer whose {[29] *home office/principal place of business*} is located in {[30] _______} County at {[31] *address*}, may be served with process by serving the Texas Secretary of State at 1019 Brazos Street, Austin, Texas 78701, because this suit is being brought by the {[32] *Texas Department of Insurance/State of Texas*} against defendant, who is an unauthorized insurer engaged in the practice of insurance business as provided by Texas Insurance Code section 101.051. {*See Tex. Ins. Code §804.107(b)(2), (c)(1);* ***O'Connor's Texas Rules****, "General rules," ch. 2-I, §5.1, p. 195.*}

SEE: Tex. R. Civ. P. 28-44, 79
Tex. Ins. Code §§101.051, 804.101, 804.102, 804.107, 804.201 et seq., 804.301 et seq.
O'Connor's Texas Rules * Civil Trials (2019), "Defendant," ch. 2-B, §4.5, p. 123; "Service on Secretary of State," ch. 2-I, §5, p. 195; "Who May Be Served," ch. 2-I, §6, p. 197

NOTE: Texas Insurance Code §804.107 provides for service of process on unauthorized persons or insurers engaging in the practice of insurance business in Texas but does not apply to an entity that was an eligible surplus-lines insurer under Texas Insurance Code chapter 981 on the date the applicable coverage was issued. Tex. Ins. Code §804.107(f).

For service on the Secretary of State, see note under FORM 2B:11.

PARTIES

{*CHOOSE APPROPRIATE DESIGNATION*}

1. Defendant, {❶ *name*}, an individual who is a nonresident of Texas, whose usual place of {❷ *business/abode*} is located at {❸ *address, including city and state or country*}, may be served with process at that address.

2. Defendant, {❹ *name*}, an individual who is a nonresident of Texas, whose {❺ *home/home office*} is located at {❻ *address, including city and state or country*}, may be served with process by serving the Texas Secretary of State at 1019 Brazos Street, Austin, Texas 78701, as defendant's agent for service because

{*CHOOSE APPROPRIATE STATEMENT*}

Ⓐ defendant has not designated or maintained a resident agent for service of process in Texas as required by statute. {*See Tex. Civ. Prac. & Rem. Code §§17.044(a)(1), 17.045;* ***O'Connor's Texas Rules****, "General rules," ch. 2-I, §5.1, p. 195.*}

Ⓑ defendant has engaged in business in Texas but has not designated or maintained a resident agent for service of process in Texas. {*See Tex. Civ. Prac. & Rem. Code §§17.044(a)(1), 17.045;* ***O'Connor's Texas Rules****, "General rules," ch. 2-I, §5.1, p. 195.*}

Ⓒ defendant has one or more resident agents for service of process, and two unsuccessful attempts have been made on different business days to serve each agent. {*See Tex. Civ. Prac. & Rem. Code §§17.044(a)(2), 17.045;* ***O'Connor's Texas Rules****, "General rules," ch. 2-I, §5.1, p. 195.*}

Ⓓ defendant became a nonresident after this cause of action arose in Texas but before the cause matured by suit in a court of competent jurisdiction. {*See Tex. Civ. Prac. & Rem. Code §§17.044(a)(3), 17.045;* ***O'Connor's Texas Rules****, "General rules," ch. 2-I, §5.1, p. 195.*}

Ⓔ defendant engages in business in Texas but does not maintain a regular place of business in Texas or a designated agent for service of process, and this suit arose from defendant's business in this state. {*See Tex. Civ. Prac. & Rem. Code §§17.044(b), 17.045;* ***O'Connor's Texas Rules****, "General rules," ch. 2-I, §5.1, p. 195.*}

[F] this suit is being brought by the {[7] *Texas Department of Insurance/State of Texas*} against defendant, who is an unauthorized insurer engaged in the practice of insurance business as provided by Texas Insurance Code section 101.051. {*See Tex. Civ. Prac. & Rem. Code §17.045; Tex. Ins. Code §804.107(b)(2), (c)(1);* ***O'Connor's Texas Rules****, "General rules," ch. 2-I, §5.1, p. 195.*}

3. Defendant, {[8] *name 1*}, an individual who is a nonresident of Texas and whose {[9] *home/home office*} is located at {[10] *address, including city and state or country*}, may be served with process by serving defendant's {[11] *agent/clerk*}, {[12] *name 2*}, in {[13] ________} County at {[14] *address*}, because defendant engages in business in Texas and maintains {[15] *an office/a place of business/an agency*} in {[16] ________} County, Texas, and this lawsuit {[17] *arises from/is connected with*} defendant's business transacted in Texas. {*Tex. Civ. Prac. & Rem. Code §17.021(a).*}

4. Defendant, {[18] *name*}, an individual who is a nonresident of Texas and whose {[19] *home/home office*} is located at {[20] *address, including city and state or country*}, may be served with process by serving the Chairman of the Texas Transportation Commission at 125 E. 11th Street, Austin, Texas 78701, as defendant's agent for service because defendant was a party to a collision or accident while operating a motor vehicle in Texas. {*See Tex. Civ. Prac. & Rem. Code §§17.062(a), 17.063.*}

5. Defendant, {[21] *name*}, an individual who is a nonresident of Texas and whose {[22] *home/home office*} is located at {[23] *address, including city and state or country*}, may be served with process by serving the Chairman of the Texas Transportation Commission at 125 E. 11th Street, Austin, Texas 78701, as defendant's agent for service because defendant was a resident of Texas when defendant was involved in a collision or accident while operating a motor vehicle in Texas, but defendant has since moved outside Texas. {*See Tex. Civ. Prac. & Rem. Code §§17.062(b), 17.063.*}

6. Defendant, {[24] *name*}, an individual who is a nonresident of Texas and whose {[25] *home office/principal place of business*} is located at {[26] *address, including city and state or country*}, may be served with process by serving the Texas Commissioner of Insurance at 333 Guadalupe Street, Austin, Texas 78701, as defendant's agent for service because defendant is an unauthorized individual engaged in the practice of insurance business as provided by Texas Insurance Code section 101.051, and this suit is not being brought by the Texas Department of Insurance or the State of Texas. {*See Tex. Ins. Code §804.107(b)(1).*}

◄ *Continued on next page* ►

7. Defendant, {㉗ *name 1*}, an individual who is a nonresident of Texas and whose {㉘ *home office/principal place of business*} is located at {㉙ *address, including city and state or country*}, may be served with process by serving {㉚ *name 2*} in {㉛ ______} County at {㉜ *address*}, as the person who is conducting insurance business in Texas on behalf of defendant as provided by Texas Insurance Code section 101.051, because defendant is an unauthorized individual engaged in the practice of insurance business. {*Tex. Ins. Code §804.107(d).*}

SEE: Tex. R. Civ. P. 28-44, 79, 108, 108a
Tex. Civ. Prac. & Rem. Code §§17.021, 17.044, 17.045, 17.062, 17.063
Tex. Ins. Code §§101.051, 804.107
O'Connor's Texas Rules * Civil Trials (2019), "Defendant," ch. 2-B, §4.5, p. 123; "Service on Secretary of State," ch. 2-I, §5, p. 195, "Who May Be Served," ch. 2-I, §6, p. 197

NOTE: The petition does not need to include any statutory or rule citations for service. However, when serving the Secretary of State or any other public official as agent for the defendant, cite the statute that authorizes the public official to accept service on behalf of the defendant. For other requirements for service on the Secretary of State as agent for the defendant, see ***O'Connor's Texas Rules***, "Service on Secretary of State," ch. 2-I, §5, p. 195.

The Citations Unit of the Secretary of State is responsible for processing documents served on the Secretary of State as agent for process. Documents can be mailed to the following address:

Service of Process
Secretary of State
P.O. Box 12079
Austin, Texas 78711-2079

To support a no-answer default judgment against a nonresident defendant who was served under the long-arm statute, the plaintiff must allege facts in its petition that, if true, would make the defendant amenable to process under the long-arm statute and must also prove that the defendant was served in the manner required by statute. ***Whitney v. L&L Rlty. Corp.***, 500 S.W.2d 94, 95-96 (Tex.1973); ***Mobile-Vision Imaging Servs. v. LifeCare Hosps.***, 260 S.W.3d 561, 564 (Tex.App.—Dallas 2008, no pet.); *see* Tex. Civ. Prac. & Rem. Code §§17.041-17.045, 17.061-17.069.

PARTIES

{*CHOOSE APPROPRIATE DESIGNATION*}

1. Defendant, {❶ *name 1*}, a foreign corporation organized and existing under the laws of {❷ *name of state or country*}, whose principal office is located at {❸ *address, including city and state or country*}, is authorized to do business in Texas and may be served with process by serving its {❹ *president/vice president*}, {❺ *name 2*}, at that address. {*See Tex. Bus. Orgs. Code §5.255(1).*}

2. Defendant, {❻ *name 1*}, a foreign corporation organized and existing under the laws of {❼ *name of state or country*}, whose principal office is located at {❽ *address, including city and state or country*}, is authorized to do business in Texas and may be served with process by serving its registered agent for service of process, {❾ *name 2*}, in {❿ ________} County at {⓫ *address*}. {*Tex. Bus. Orgs. Code §5.201.*}

3. Defendant, {⓬ *name*}, a foreign corporation organized and existing under the laws of {⓭ *name of state or country*}, whose {⓮ *principal/home*} office is located at {⓯ *address, including city and state or country*}, may be served with process by serving the Texas Secretary of State at 1019 Brazos Street, Austin, Texas 78701, as its agent for service because

{*CHOOSE APPROPRIATE STATEMENT*}

Ⓐ defendant is required to register with the Secretary of State but has not appointed or maintained a registered agent for service of process in Texas. {*See Tex. Bus. Orgs. Code §5.251(1)(A);* ***O'Connor's Texas Rules****, "General rules," ch. 2-I, §5.1, p. 195.*}

Ⓑ defendant is required to register with the Secretary of State but defendant's registered agent cannot be found with reasonable diligence at defendant's registered office. {*See Tex. Bus. Orgs. Code §5.251(1)(B);* ***O'Connor's Texas Rules****, "General rules," ch. 2-I, §5.1, p. 195.*}

Ⓒ defendant is required to register with the Secretary of State but has not done so. {*See Tex. Bus. Orgs. Code §5.251(2)(B);* ***O'Connor's Texas Rules****, "General rules," ch. 2-I, §5.1, p. 195.*}

Ⓓ defendant registered with the Secretary of State but defendant's certificate of authority has since been revoked. {*See Tex. Bus. Orgs. Code §5.251(2)(A);* ***O'Connor's Texas Rules****, "General rules," ch. 2-I, §5.1, p. 195.*}

Continued on next page

E defendant has not designated or maintained a resident agent for service of process in Texas as required by statute. {*See Tex. Civ. Prac. & Rem. Code §§17.044(a)(1), 17.045;* ***O'Connor's Texas Rules****, "General rules," ch. 2-I, §5.1, p. 195.*}

F defendant engages in business in Texas but has not designated or maintained a resident agent for service of process in Texas. {*See Tex. Civ. Prac. & Rem. Code §§17.044(a)(1), 17.045;* ***O'Connor's Texas Rules****, "General rules," ch. 2-I, §5.1, p. 195.*}

G defendant has one or more resident agents for service of process, and two unsuccessful attempts have been made on different business days to serve each agent. {*See Tex. Civ. Prac. & Rem. Code §§17.044(a)(2), 17.045;* ***O'Connor's Texas Rules****, "General rules," ch. 2-I, §5.1, p. 195.*}

H defendant became a nonresident after this cause of action arose in Texas but before the cause matured by suit in a court of competent jurisdiction. {*See Tex. Civ. Prac. & Rem. Code §§17.044(a)(3), 17.045;* ***O'Connor's Texas Rules****, "General rules," ch. 2-I, §5.1, p. 195.*}

I defendant engages in business in Texas but does not maintain a regular place of business in Texas or a designated agent for service of process, and this suit arose from defendant's business in this state. {*See Tex. Civ. Prac. & Rem. Code §§17.044(b), 17.045;* ***O'Connor's Texas Rules****, "General rules," ch. 2-I, §5.1, p. 195.*}

SEE: Tex. R. Civ. P. 28-44, 79, 108, 108a
Tex. Bus. Orgs. Code §§5.200, 5.201, 5.251, 5.252, 5.255
Tex. Civ. Prac. & Rem. Code §§17.044, 17.045
O'Connor's Texas Rules * Civil Trials (2019), "Defendant," ch. 2-B, §4.5, p. 123; "Service on Secretary of State," ch. 2-I, §5, p. 195; "Who May Be Served," ch. 2-I, §6, p. 197

NOTE: For detailed charts for service on business entities, see ***O'Connor's Texas Rules***, "Service Through Secretary of State," chart 2-3, p. 195, and "Proper Person to Serve," chart 2-4, p. 197.

See notes under FORM 2B:14.

PARTIES

{*CHOOSE APPROPRIATE DESIGNATION*}

1. Defendant, {❶ *name 1*}, a foreign {❷ *partnership/unincorporated association*} organized and existing under the laws of {❸ *name of state or country*}, whose home office is located at {❹ *address, including city and state or country*}, may be served with process by serving its {❺ *agent/clerk*}, {❻ *name 2*}, at that address, because defendant engages in business in Texas, maintains {❼ *an office/a place of business/an agency*} in {❽ _______} County, Texas, and this lawsuit {❾ *arises from/is connected with*} defendant's business transacted in Texas. {*Tex. Civ. Prac. & Rem. Code §17.021(a).*}

2. Defendant, {❿ *name*}, a foreign {⓫ *partnership/unincorporated association*} organized and existing under the laws of {⓬ *name of state*}, whose home office is located at {⓭ *address, including city and state or country*}, may be served with process by serving the Texas Secretary of State at 1019 Brazos Street, Austin, Texas 78701, as its agent for service because

{*CHOOSE APPROPRIATE STATEMENT*}

Ⓐ defendant has not designated or maintained a resident agent for service of process in Texas as required by statute. {*See Tex. Civ. Prac. & Rem. Code §§17.044(a)(1), 17.045;* ***O'Connor's Texas Rules****, "General rules," ch. 2-I, §5.1, p. 195.*}

Ⓑ defendant engages in business in Texas but has not designated or maintained a resident agent for service of process in Texas. {*See Tex. Civ. Prac. & Rem. Code §§17.044(a)(1), 17.045;* ***O'Connor's Texas Rules****, "General rules," ch. 2-I, §5.1, p. 195.*}

Ⓒ defendant has one or more resident agents for service of process in Texas, and two unsuccessful attempts have been made on different business days to serve each agent. {*See Tex. Civ. Prac. & Rem. Code §§17.044(a)(2), 17.045;* ***O'Connor's Texas Rules****, "General rules," ch. 2-I, §5.1, p. 195.*}

Ⓓ defendant became a nonresident after this cause of action arose in Texas but before the cause matured by suit in a court of competent jurisdiction. {*See Tex. Civ. Prac. & Rem. Code §§17.044(a)(3), 17.045;* ***O'Connor's Texas Rules****, "General rules," ch. 2-I, §5.1, p. 195.*}

◄ *Continued on next page* ►

(E) defendant engages in business in Texas but does not maintain a regular place of business in Texas or a designated agent for service of process, and this suit arose from defendant's business in this state. {*See Tex. Civ. Prac. & Rem. Code §§17.044(b), 17.045;* ***O'Connor's Texas Rules***, *"General rules," ch. 2-I, §5.1, p. 195.*}

SEE: Tex. R. Civ. P. 28-44, 79, 108, 108a
Tex. Civ. Prac. & Rem. Code §§17.021, 17.022, 17.044, 17.045, 31.003
O'Connor's Texas Rules * Civil Trials (2019), "Defendant," ch. 2-B, §4.5, p. 123; "Service on Secretary of State," ch. 2-I, §5, p. 195; "Who May Be Served," ch. 2-I, §6, p. 197

NOTE: To bring a claim against a partner in her individual capacity, direct the citation to the individual partner. See ***O'Connor's Texas Rules***, "Partnership," ch. 2-I, §2.6.2, p. 191.

See notes under FORM 2B:14.

PARTIES

{*CHOOSE APPROPRIATE DESIGNATION*}

1. Defendant, {❶ *name 1*}, a foreign unincorporated joint-stock company doing business in Texas, whose home office is located at {❷ *address, including city and state or country*}, may be served with process by serving the {❸ *president/secretary/treasurer/general agent*}, {❹ *name 2*}, in {❺ _______} County at {❻ *address*}, because defendant engages in business in Texas. {*See Tex. Rev. Civ. Stat. arts. 6133, 6134.*}

2. Defendant, {❼ *name*}, a foreign unincorporated joint-stock company doing business in Texas, whose home office is located at {❽ *address, including city and state or country*}, may be served with process by serving the Texas Secretary of State at 1019 Brazos Street, Austin, Texas 78701, as its agent for service because

{*CHOOSE APPROPRIATE STATEMENT*}

Ⓐ defendant has not designated or maintained a resident agent for service of process in Texas as required by statute. {*See Tex. Civ. Prac. & Rem. Code §§17.044(a)(1), 17.045;* ***O'Connor's Texas Rules****, "General rules," ch. 2-I, §5.1, p. 195.*}

Ⓑ defendant engages in business in Texas but has not designated or maintained a resident agent for service of process in Texas. {*See Tex. Civ. Prac. & Rem. Code §§17.044(a)(1), 17.045;* ***O'Connor's Texas Rules****, "General rules," ch. 2-I, §5.1, p. 195.*}

Ⓒ defendant has one or more resident agents for service of process in Texas, and two unsuccessful attempts have been made on different business days to serve each agent. {*See Tex. Civ. Prac. & Rem. Code §§17.044(a)(2), 17.045;* ***O'Connor's Texas Rules****, "General rules," ch. 2-I, §5.1, p. 195.*}

Ⓓ defendant became a nonresident after this cause of action arose in Texas but before the cause matured by suit in a court of competent jurisdiction. {*See Tex. Civ. Prac. & Rem. Code §§17.044(a)(3), 17.045;* ***O'Connor's Texas Rules****, "General rules," ch. 2-I, §5.1, p. 195.*}

Ⓔ defendant engages in business in Texas but does not maintain a regular place of business in this state or a designated agent for service of process, and this suit arose from defendant's business in this state. {*See Tex. Civ. Prac. & Rem. Code §§17.044(b), 17.045;* ***O'Connor's Texas Rules****, "General rules," ch. 2-I, §5.1, p. 195.*}

Continued on next page

FORM 2B:17 PARTIES – DEFENDANT, NONRESIDENT JOINT-STOCK COMPANY

SEE: Tex. R. Civ. P. 28-44, 79, 108, 108a
Tex. Civ. Prac. & Rem. Code §§17.044, 17.045
Tex. Rev. Civ. Stat. arts. 6133, 6134, 6137
O'Connor's Texas Rules * Civil Trials (2019), "Defendant," ch. 2-B, §4.5, p. 123; "Service on Secretary of State," ch. 2-I, §5, p. 195; "Who May Be Served," ch. 2-I, §6, p. 197

NOTE: **If an individual stockholder or member of an unincorporated joint-stock company or association and the president, secretary, treasurer, or general agent are both served with process, judgment against the company or association will be binding on the individual property of that stockholder or member. Tex. Rev. Civ. Stat. art. 6137.**

See notes under FORM 2B:14.

PARTIES

{*CHOOSE APPROPRIATE DESIGNATION*}

{*Foreign or alien insurance carrier*}

1. Defendant, {❶ *name 1*}, {❷ *a foreign/an alien*} insurance carrier, organized and existing under the laws of {❸ *name of state or country*} and authorized to conduct business in Texas, may be served with process by serving its designated agent for service of process, {❹ *name 2*}, in {❺ ________} County at {❻ *address*}. {*See Tex. Ins. Code §§804.103(b), 982.001(2), (4).*}

2. Defendant, {❼ *name*}, {❽ *a foreign/an alien*} insurance carrier, organized and existing under the laws of {❾ *name of state or country*} and authorized to conduct business in Texas, whose {❿ *home office/principal place of business*} is located at {⓫ *address, including city and state or country*}, may be served with process by serving the Texas Commissioner of Insurance at 333 Guadalupe Street, Austin, Texas 78701, as its agent for service because

{*CHOOSE APPROPRIATE STATEMENT*}

Ⓐ defendant is required by Texas Insurance Code section 804.103(b) to appoint and maintain an agent for service of process but has not done so. {*See Tex. Ins. Code §§804.103(c)(1), 982.001(2), (4).*}

Ⓑ defendant is required by Texas Insurance Code section 804.103(b) to appoint and maintain an agent for service of process but defendant's agent for service cannot be found with reasonable diligence. {*See Tex. Ins. Code §§804.103(c)(2), 982.001(2), (4).*}

Ⓒ defendant's certificate of authority has been revoked. {*See Tex. Ins. Code §§804.103(c)(3), 982.001(2), (4).*}

◄ *Continued on next page* ►

{*Unauthorized insurer engaging in the practice of insurance business in Texas*}

3. Defendant, {⓬ *name 1*}, {⓭ *a foreign/an alien*} insurer organized and existing under the laws of {⓮ *name of state or country*}, whose {⓯ *home office/principal place of business*} is located at {⓰ *address, including city and state or country*}, may be served with process by serving

{*CHOOSE APPROPRIATE STATEMENT*}

Ⓐ the Texas Commissioner of Insurance at 333 Guadalupe Street, Austin, Texas 78701, as its agent for service because defendant is an unauthorized insurer engaged in the practice of insurance business as provided by Texas Insurance Code section 101.051, and this suit is not being brought by the Texas Department of Insurance or the State of Texas. {*See Tex. Ins. Code §§804.107(b)(1), 982.001(2), (4).*}

Ⓑ {⓱ *name 2*}, in {⓲ ________} County at {⓳ *address*}, as the person who is conducting insurance business in Texas on behalf of defendant as provided by Texas Insurance Code section 101.051, because defendant is an unauthorized insurer engaged in the practice of insurance business. {*See Tex. Ins. Code §§804.107(d), 982.001(2), (4).*}

Ⓒ the Texas Secretary of State at 1019 Brazos Street, Austin, Texas 78701, as its agent for service because this suit is being brought by the {⓴ *Texas Department of Insurance/State of Texas*} against defendant, who is an unauthorized insurer engaged in the practice of insurance business as provided by Texas Insurance Code section 101.051. {*See Tex. Civ. Prac. & Rem. Code §17.045; Tex. Ins. Code §§804.107(b)(2), (c)(1), 982.001(2), (4);* ***O'Connor's Texas Rules****, "General rules," ch. 2-I, §5.1, p. 195.*}

SEE: Tex. R. Civ. P. 28-44, 79, 108, 108a
Tex. Ins. Code §§101.051, 804.103, 804.107, 804.201 et seq., 804.301 et seq., 982.001
O'Connor's Texas Rules * Civil Trials (2019), "Defendant," ch. 2-B, §4.5, p. 123; "Service on Secretary of State," ch. 2-I, §5, p. 195; "Who May Be Served," ch. 2-I, §6, p. 197

NOTE: Texas Insurance Code §804.107 provides for service of process on unauthorized persons or insurers engaging in the practice of insurance business in Texas but does not apply to an entity that was an eligible surplus-lines insurer under Texas Insurance Code chapter 981 on the date the applicable coverage was issued. Tex. Ins. Code §804.107(f).

See notes under FORM 2B:14.

PARTIES

{*CHOOSE APPROPRIATE DESIGNATION*}

{*State*}

1. Defendant, the State of Texas, acting by and through the {[1] *name of governmental unit whose action forms the basis of the claim, e.g., Texas Department of Transportation*}, {[2] *identify unit of government, e.g., an agency, a department*} of the State of Texas, may be served with process by serving the {[3] *executive director/administrative head*} of {[4] *name of governmental unit*} in {[5] _______} County at {[6] *address*}. {*See* ***O'Connor's Texas COA****, "State of Texas," ch. 24-A, §3.1.1(1), p. 908.*}

{*County*}

2. Defendant, {[7] *corporate name of county*}, a county in Texas, may be served with process by serving the county judge, Honorable {[8] *name*}, at {[9] *address*}, under the authority of Texas Civil Practice & Remedies Code section 17.024(a). {*See* ***O'Connor's Texas COA****, "County," ch. 24-A, §3.1.1(2), p. 909.*}

{*City*}

3. Defendant, {[10] *corporate name of city*}, a city located in {[11] _______} County, Texas, may be served with process by serving the {[12] *mayor/clerk/secretary/treasurer*}, {[13] *name*}, at {[14] *address*}, under the authority of Texas Civil Practice & Remedies Code section 17.024(b). {*See* ***O'Connor's Texas COA****, "City," ch. 24-A, §3.1.1(3), p. 909.*}

{*School district*}

4. Defendant, {[15] *name of school district*}, a school district located in {[16] _______} County, Texas, may be served with process by serving the {[17] *president of the school board/superintendent*}, {[18] *name*}, at {[19] *address*}, under the authority of Texas Civil Practice & Remedies Code section 17.024(c). {*See* ***O'Connor's Texas COA****, "School district," ch. 24-A, §3.1.1(4), p. 909.*}

{*Special-purpose district or authority*}

5. Defendant, {[20] *name of special-purpose district or authority*}, a special-purpose {[21] *district/authority*} located in {[22] _______} County, Texas, may be served with process by serving its {[23] *executive director/administrative director/president/general manager/{identify other official}*}, {[24] *name*}, at {[25] *address*}.

Continued on next page

SEE: Tex. R. Civ. P. 28-44, 79

Tex. Civ. Prac. & Rem. Code §17.024

O'Connor's Texas Rules * Civil Trials (2019), "Defendant," ch. 2-B, §4.5, p. 123; "Who May Be Served," ch. 2-I, §6, p. 197

O'Connor's Texas Causes of Action (2019), "The Doctrines of Sovereign & Governmental Immunity," ch. 24-A, p. 878

NOTE: **Before suing a special-purpose district or authority, contact its attorney to identify its agent for service of process.**

The party must mail a copy of the petition to the Attorney General for suits in which (1) the State of Texas is named as a party, (2) an agency in the legislative or executive department is named as a party, or (3) the Attorney General may represent a party based on state liability for conduct of a public servant under Texas Civil Practice & Remedies Code chapter 104. Tex. Civ. Prac. & Rem. Code §30.004(a), (b). The petition must be mailed to the Attorney General's office in Austin, Texas, by certified mail, return receipt requested. *Id.* §30.004(b). Mailing the petition does not relieve the party from serving process on any named party in the case. *Id.* §30.004(c). If the required notice to the Attorney General is not given, any default judgment in the case can be set aside without costs. *Id.* §30.004(d).

To identify a governmental unit as a defendant in a suit under the Texas Tort Claims Act, see *O'Connor's Texas COA Pleadings*, FORM 1:16.

JURISDICTION

{*CHOOSE APPROPRIATE JURISDICTION ALLEGATION*}

{*Amount-in-controversy jurisdiction*}

1. The Court has subject-matter jurisdiction over the lawsuit because the amount in controversy exceeds this Court's minimum jurisdictional requirements. {*See* ***O'Connor's Texas Rules****, "Subject-matter jurisdiction," ch. 2-B, §5.2, p. 126.*}

{*If cause of action is statutory*}

2. The Court has subject-matter jurisdiction over the lawsuit under {❶ *identify statutory provision giving court jurisdiction, e.g., for wrongful-death action, Texas Civil Practice & Remedies Code section 71.002*}. {❷ *Explain why the statute gives the court jurisdiction over the lawsuit.*} {*See* ***O'Connor's Texas Rules****, "Statutory claims," ch. 2-B, §5.2.2, p. 126.*}

{*In TTCA suit*}

3. The Court has subject-matter jurisdiction over this claim against {❸ *identify governmental unit*} under the Texas Tort Claims Act (TTCA) because the Texas Legislature waived defendant's sovereign immunity for claims involving {❹ *personal injury/death/property damage*} caused by {❺ *describe act or omission causing injury*}. {*Tex. Civ. Prac. & Rem. Code §§101.021, 101.025.*} {❻ *Explain why the government's sovereign immunity was waived.*} {*See* ***O'Connor's Texas COA****, "Texas Tort Claims Act—Negligence," ch. 25, p. 939; "Texas Tort Claims Act—Premises Liability," ch. 26, p. 995;* ***O'Connor's Texas COA Pleadings****, FORMS 25, 26.*}

{*In other suits against government*}

4. The Court has subject-matter jurisdiction over the claim against {❼ *identify governmental unit*} under {❽ *identify statutory provision giving court jurisdiction*}. {❾ *Explain facts supporting waiver of sovereign or governmental immunity.*} {*See* ***O'Connor's Texas COA****, "Suits Against the Government," ch. 24, p. 877;* ***O'Connor's Texas COA Pleadings****, FORMS 24.*}

Continued on next page

{*For personal jurisdiction*}

5. The Court has personal jurisdiction over defendant, {10 *name*}, a nonresident, because defendant

{*CHOOSE APPROPRIATE STATEMENT*}

[A] engaged in business in Texas by contracting with a Texas resident. The contract was {11 *performed/to be performed*} in whole or in part in Texas by {12 *plaintiff/defendant/both parties*}. {13 *Explain, identifying date of contract, parties to contract, place of performance in Texas, and date of performance.*} {*See Tex. Civ. Prac. & Rem. Code §17.042(1);* ***O'Connor's Texas Rules****, "Over nonresident," ch. 2-B, §5.1.2, p. 126.*}

[B] committed a tort, which is the subject of this suit, in whole or in part in Texas. {14 *Explain, identifying type of tort, date, and place.*} {*See Tex. Civ. Prac. & Rem. Code §17.042(2);* ***O'Connor's Texas Rules****, "Over nonresident," ch. 2-B, §5.1.2, p. 126.*}

[C] recruited Texas residents {15 *directly/through an intermediary located in Texas*} for employment {16 *in/outside*} Texas. {17 *Explain, identifying actions that occurred in Texas and the dates and places of those actions.*} {*See Tex. Civ. Prac. & Rem. Code §17.042(3);* ***O'Connor's Texas Rules****, "Over nonresident," ch. 2-B, §5.1.2, p. 126.*}

[D] operated a motor vehicle in Texas that was involved in a collision or accident. {18 *Explain, identifying actions that occurred in Texas and the dates and places of those actions.*} {*See Tex. Civ. Prac. & Rem. Code §§17.042(2), 17.061-17.069;* ***O'Connor's Texas Rules****, "Over nonresident," ch. 2-B, §5.1.2, p. 126.*}

6. The Court has personal jurisdiction over defendant, {19 *name*}, a nonresident, because defendant purposefully availed {20 *himself/herself/itself*} of the privileges and benefits of conducting business in Texas by {21 *state allegations about defendant's acts that constitute doing business, that occurred in Texas, and that support either specific or general personal jurisdiction over defendant*}. {22 *Explain, identifying actions that occurred in Texas and the dates and places of those actions.*} {*See Tex. Civ. Prac. & Rem. Code §17.042;* ***O'Connor's Texas Rules****, "Over nonresident," ch. 2-B, §5.1.2, p. 126.*}

SEE: Tex. Const. art 5, §§1, 8, 16, 19
Tex. Civ. Prac. & Rem. Code §§17.042, 17.062, 101.021
Tex. Est. Code §§32.002-32.007, 1022.002-1022.006
Tex. Gov't Code chs. 24-27
Tex. Prop. Code §115.001
O'Connor's Texas Rules * Civil Trials (2019), "Jurisdiction," ch. 2-B, §5, p. 125; "Choosing the Court—Jurisdiction," ch. 2-G, p. 163
O'Connor's Federal Rules * Civil Trials (2019), "Prohibitions Against Removal," ch. 4-A, §6, p. 301
O'Connor's Texas Causes of Action (2019), "The Doctrines of Sovereign & Governmental Immunity," ch. 24-A, p. 878; "Texas Tort Claims Act—Negligence," ch. 25, p. 939; "Texas Tort Claims Act—Premises Liability," ch. 26, p. 995
O'Connor's Texas Causes of Action Pleadings (2019), FORMS 24-26

NOTE: The Texas rules of pleading do not require a plaintiff to make an allegation of jurisdiction in most cases or require the plaintiff, if it chooses to make an allegation of jurisdiction, to cite authority for that jurisdiction. However, the plaintiff must always plead enough facts to affirmatively demonstrate the trial court has jurisdiction to hear the case. See ***O'Connor's Texas Rules***, "Jurisdiction," ch. 2-B, §5, p. 125. The plaintiff should make allegations of jurisdiction (1) in a suit where the court's jurisdiction depends on a statute (e.g., the Texas Tort Claims Act), (2) in a suit that by statute is not removable to federal court (e.g., 28 U.S.C. §1445(a)), and (3) in a suit against a nonresident defendant to establish that the defendant is subject to personal jurisdiction in a Texas court.

To properly plead a claim against a nonresident defendant, the plaintiff must make factual allegations showing that the defendant "purposefully availed" itself of the privilege of conducting business in Texas, thus subjecting itself to the long-arm jurisdiction of Texas courts. See ***O'Connor's Texas Rules***, "Over nonresident," ch. 2-B, §5.1.2, p. 126.

VENUE

{*CHOOSE APPROPRIATE VENUE ALLEGATION*}

{*Mandatory-venue allegations*}

1. Venue is mandatory in {❶ ________} County under

{*CHOOSE APPROPRIATE STATEMENT*}

Ⓐ Texas Civil Practice & Remedies Code section 15.004 because plaintiff properly joined {❷ *number*} {❸ *claims/causes of action*} arising from the same {❹ *transaction/occurrence/series of transactions/series of occurrences*}, and one of the {❺ *claims/causes of action*} is governed by the mandatory-venue provision in {❻ *identify section in subchapter B*}. {❼ *Elaborate.*}

Ⓑ Texas Civil Practice & Remedies Code section 15.011 because this suit is for damages to real property, and this is the county where {❽ *all/part*} of the property is located. {❾ *Elaborate.*} {*See* ***O'Connor's Texas Rules****, "Land dispute," ch. 2-H, §4.1.1, p. 180;* ***O'Connor's Texas COA****, "Venue," ch. 22-A, §6.1, p. 804.*}

Ⓒ Texas Civil Practice & Remedies Code section 15.0115 because this suit is between a landlord and tenant arising under a lease, and this is the county where {❿ *all/part*} of the real property is located. {⓫ *Elaborate.*} {*See* ***O'Connor's Texas Rules****, "Landlord-tenant," ch. 2-H, §4.1.2, p. 181.*}

Ⓓ Texas Civil Practice & Remedies Code section 15.012 because this suit is to secure an injunction against another suit, and this is the county where the other suit is pending. {⓬ *Elaborate.*} {*See* ***O'Connor's Texas Rules****, "Injunction against suit," ch. 2-H, §4.1.3, p. 181.*}

Ⓔ Texas Civil Practice & Remedies Code section 15.013 because this suit is for an injunction against the execution of a {⓭ *judgment/writ*}, and this is the county where the judgment was rendered. {⓮ *Elaborate.*} {*See* ***O'Connor's Texas Rules****, "Injunction against execution of judgment," ch. 2-H, §4.1.4, p. 181.*}

F Texas Civil Practice & Remedies Code section 15.014 because this is a mandamus action against the head of a department of state government. {**15** *Elaborate.*} {*See* ***O'Connor's Texas Rules****, "Mandamus against State," ch. 2-H, §4.1.5, p. 181.*}

G Texas Civil Practice & Remedies Code section 15.015 because this is a suit against {**16** _______} County. {**17** *Elaborate.*} {*See* ***O'Connor's Texas Rules****, "Suit against county," ch. 2-H, §4.1.6, p. 181;* ***O'Connor's Texas COA****, "County," ch. 24-A, §3.2.3, p. 910.*}

H Texas Civil Practice & Remedies Code section 15.0151 because this is a suit against a {**18** *city/school district/junior-college district/hospital district/{identify other special-purpose district or authority}*} located in {**19** _______} County, which has a population of 100,000 or less. {**20** *Elaborate.*} {*See* ***O'Connor's Texas Rules****, "Suit against political subdivisions," ch. 2-H, §4.1.7, p. 181;* ***O'Connor's Texas COA****, "Small political subdivision," ch. 24-A, §3.2.4, p. 910.*}

I Texas Civil Practice & Remedies Code section 15.017 because this suit involves {**21** *libel/slander/invasion of privacy*}, and this is the county {**22** *where plaintiff resided when this claim accrued/where defendant resided when the suit was filed/of defendant's residence/of defendant's corporate domicile*}. {**23** *Elaborate.*} {*See* ***O'Connor's Texas Rules****, "Defamation or invasion of privacy," ch. 2-H, §4.1.8, p. 181;* ***O'Connor's Texas COA****, "Venue," ch. 15-A, §6.1, p. 431; "Venue," ch. 18-A, §6.4, p. 585.*}

J Texas Civil Practice & Remedies Code section 15.018 because this suit is brought under the Federal Employers' Liability Act, and this is the county where {**24** *all or a substantial part of the events or omissions giving rise to the claim occurred/defendant's principal Texas office is located/plaintiff resided when the claim accrued*}. {**25** *Elaborate.*} {*See* ***O'Connor's Texas Rules****, "FELA & Jones Act," ch. 2-H, §4.1.9, p. 181.*}

K Texas Civil Practice & Remedies Code section 15.0181 because this suit is brought under the Jones Act, and this is the county where {**26** *all or a substantial part of the events or omissions giving rise to the claim occurred/defendant's principal Texas office is located/plaintiff resided when the claim accrued*}. {**27** *Elaborate.*} {*See* ***O'Connor's Texas Rules****, "FELA & Jones Act," ch. 2-H, §4.1.9, p. 181.*}

Continued on next page

Ⓛ Texas Civil Practice & Remedies Code section 15.019 because this suit is filed by an inmate of {㉘ *name of TDCJ facility*}, a facility operated by Texas Department of Criminal Justice located in {㉙ ________} County. {㉚ *Elaborate.*} {*See **O'Connor's Texas Rules**, "Inmate litigation," ch. 2-H, §4.1.10, p. 182.*}

Ⓜ Texas Civil Practice & Remedies Code section 15.020(b) because this suit arises from a "major transaction" as defined by Texas Civil Practice & Remedies Code section 15.020(a), and this is the county designated in writing as the county for suit. {㉛ *Elaborate.*} {*See **O'Connor's Texas Rules**, "Contractual agreement for venue – major transaction," ch. 2-H, §4.1.11, p. 182; **O'Connor's Texas COA**, "Written contractual venue," ch. 5-B, §7.3.4, p. 112.*}

Ⓝ Texas Civil Practice & Remedies Code section 64.071 because this is a suit to appoint a receiver for a corporation with property in Texas, and this is the county where the principal office of the corporation is located. {㉜ *Elaborate.*}

Ⓞ Texas Civil Practice & Remedies Code section 65.023(a) because this is a suit in which the primary relief sought is an injunction against defendant, a resident of Texas, and this is the county where defendant is domiciled. {㉝ *Elaborate.*} {*See **O'Connor's Texas Rules**, "Venue generally," ch. 2-D, §3.2.2(1), p. 140; "Injunction suit against Texas resident," ch. 2-H, §4.2.1(3), p. 183.*}

Ⓟ Texas Civil Practice & Remedies Code section 65.023(b) because this is a suit in which the primary relief sought is an injunction to stay {㉞ *proceedings in a suit/execution of a judgment*}, the injunctive relief cannot be granted independently of the judgment, and this suit is filed in the Court where the {㉟ *suit is pending/judgment was rendered*}. {㊱ *Elaborate.*} {*See **O'Connor's Texas Rules**, "Venue for writ to stay proceeding or execution of judgment," ch. 2-D, §3.2.2(2), p. 140.*}

Ⓠ Texas Civil Practice & Remedies Code section 101.102(a) because this suit is brought under the Texas Tort Claims Act, and this is the county where {㊲ *all/part*} of the cause of action arose. {㊳ *Elaborate.*} {*See **O'Connor's Texas Rules**, "TTCA," ch. 2-H, §4.2.1(1), p. 183; **O'Connor's Texas COA**, "Venue," ch. 25-A, §5.1.2, p. 968.*}

Ⓡ Texas Health & Safety Code section 281.056(a) because this is a health-care-liability claim against the board of a hospital district established in this county, which has at least 190,000 inhabitants. {❸❾ *Elaborate.*}

Ⓢ {❹⓿ *identify statute, e.g., Texas Education Code section 106.38*} because this is a suit against {❹❶ *name of university*}, which has a mandatory-venue provision. {❹❷ *Elaborate.*} {*See* ***O'Connor's Texas COA****, "University," ch. 24-A, §3.2.5, p. 910.*}

Ⓣ Texas Finance Code title 4, subtitle A, section 305.006, because this is a suit for usury, and this is the county where {❹❸ *the transaction was entered into/the usurious interest was charged or received/defendant resided when the action was filed/defendant maintains its principal office/plaintiff resided when the claim accrued*}. {❹❹ *Elaborate.*} {*See* ***O'Connor's Texas COA****, "Subtitle A," ch. 31, §6.3.1, p. 1120.*}

Ⓤ Texas Finance Code title 4, subtitle B, section 349.401, because this is a suit for usury, and this is the county where {❹❺ *the transaction was entered into/defendant resided when the action was filed*}. {❹❻ *Elaborate.*} {*See* ***O'Connor's Texas COA****, "Subtitle B," ch. 31, §6.3.2, p. 1120.*}

Ⓥ {❹❼ *identify other mandatory-venue provision that applies, e.g., Texas Civil Practice & Remedies Code section 171.096(a) because this is an arbitration proceeding, and this is the county where defendant resides*}. {❹❽ *Elaborate.*} {*See* ***O'Connor's Texas Rules****, "Other mandatory-venue provisions," ch. 2-H, §4.2, p. 183.*}

{*Permissive-venue allegations*}

2. Venue is permissive in {❹❾ ________} County under

{*CHOOSE APPROPRIATE STATEMENT*}

Ⓐ Texas Civil Practice & Remedies Code section 15.031 because defendant is the {❺⓿ *executor/administrator/guardian*} of the estate of {❺❶ *name of person whose estate is being represented*}, this suit is brought to establish a money demand against the estate, and this is the county where the estate is administered. {❺❷ *Elaborate.*} {*See* ***O'Connor's Texas Rules****, "Debt of estate," ch. 2-H, §5.1.1(2), p. 186.*}

Ⓑ Texas Civil Practice & Remedies Code section 15.031 because defendant is the {❺❸ *executor/administrator/guardian*} of the estate of {❺❹ *name of*

◄ Continued on next page ►

person whose estate is being represented}, the suit is brought as a claim against {55 *name of person whose estate is being represented*} for {56 *his/her*} {57 *identify negligent act or omission*}, and this is the county where that {58 *negligent act or omission*} occurred. {59 *Elaborate.*} {*See* ***O'Connor's Texas Rules****, "Negligent act," ch. 2-H, §5.1.1(1), p. 186.*}

C Texas Civil Practice & Remedies Code section 15.032 because defendant is a {60 *fire/marine/inland*}-insurance company, and this is the county where the insured property is located. {61 *Elaborate.*} {*See* ***O'Connor's Texas Rules****, "Insurance contract," ch. 2-H, §5.1.5, p. 186.*}

D Texas Civil Practice & Remedies Code section 15.032 because defendant is a {62 *life/accident/health*}-insurance company, and this is the county where {63 *defendant's principal Texas office is located/the loss occurred/the policyholder who instituted suit resided when this cause of action accrued/the beneficiary who instituted suit resided when this cause of action accrued*}. {64 *Elaborate.*} {*See* ***O'Connor's Texas Rules****, "Insurance contract," ch. 2-H, §5.1.5, p. 186.*}

E Texas Civil Practice & Remedies Code section 15.033 because this is a suit for breach of warranty against a manufacturer of consumer goods, and this is the county where {65 *all or a substantial part of the events or omissions giving rise to the claim occurred/the manufacturer has its principal Texas office/plaintiff resided when this cause of action accrued*}. {66 *Elaborate.*} {*See* ***O'Connor's Texas Rules****, "Breach of warranty," ch. 2-H, §5.1.2, p. 186;* ***O'Connor's Texas COA****, "Venue for manufacturers," ch. 32-B, §6.5, p. 1150.*}

F Texas Civil Practice & Remedies Code section 15.035(a) because this is a suit for breach of a written contract, and this county {67 *was identified as the place for an obligation under the contract to be performed/is where defendant is domiciled*}. {68 *Elaborate.*} {*See* ***O'Connor's Texas Rules****, "County of performance," ch. 2-H, §5.1.3(1), p. 186;* ***O'Connor's Texas COA****, "Written contract – contractual performance," ch. 5-B, §7.3.2, p. 112.*}

G Texas Civil Practice & Remedies Code section 15.035(b) because this is a suit brought by a creditor on a written contract involving a consumer transaction for {69 *goods/services/loans/extensions of credit*} intended for {70 *personal/family/household/agricultural*} use, and this is the county where defendant {71 *signed the contract/resided when the suit*

was commenced}. {72 *Elaborate.*} {*See* ***O'Connor's Texas Rules****, "Contract in consumer transaction," ch. 2-H, §5.1.3(2), p. 186;* ***O'Connor's Texas COA****, "Written contract – consumer transaction," ch. 5-B, §7.3.3, p. 112.*}

H Texas Civil Practice & Remedies Code section 15.039 because defendant is a transient person, and this is the county where defendant can be found. {73 *Elaborate.*}

I Texas Civil Practice & Remedies Code section 15.092(b) because this is a suit on an oral contract for labor actually performed in this county and precinct. {74 *Elaborate.*} {*See* ***O'Connor's Texas COA****, "Oral contract," ch. 5-B, §7.3.1, p. 112.*}

J Texas Civil Practice & Remedies Code section 134.004 because this is a suit brought under the Texas Theft Liability Act, and this is the county where {75 *the theft occurred/defendant resides*}. {76 *Elaborate.*} {*See* ***O'Connor's Texas COA****, "Venue," ch. 27-A, §6.2, p. 1038.*}

K Texas Government Code section 554.007(a) because this suit is a Whistleblower Act claim brought by an employee of the State of Texas, and {77 *this is the county where the cause of action arose/suit may always be brought in Travis County*}. {78 *Elaborate.*} {*See* ***O'Connor's Texas Rules****, "State," ch. 2-H, §5.2.2(1), p. 187;* ***O'Connor's Texas COA****, "Venue," ch. 24-C, §6.1, p. 936.*}

L Texas Government Code section 554.007(b) because this suit is a Whistleblower Act claim brought by an employee of a local-government entity, and this is {79 *the county where the cause of action arose/a county that is in the same geographic area as the county where the cause of action arose and that has established a council of governments or regional planning commission with that county*}. {80 *Elaborate.*} {*See* ***O'Connor's Texas Rules****, "Local government," ch. 2-H, §5.2.2(2), p. 187;* ***O'Connor's Texas COA****, "Venue," ch. 24-C, §6.1, p. 936.*}

M Texas Business & Commerce Code section 17.56 because this suit is filed in the county where {81 *defendant/defendant's authorized agent*} solicited the transaction underlying this suit. {82 *Elaborate.*} {*See* ***O'Connor's Texas Rules****, "DTPA," ch. 2-H, §5.2.1, p. 187;* ***O'Connor's Texas COA****, "Venue," ch. 8, §7.2, p. 250.*}

N {83 *identify other permissive-venue provision that applies*}.

◄ *Continued on next page* ►

{*General venue allegations from venue statute*}

3. Venue is proper in {84 _______} County under Texas Civil Practice & Remedies Code section 15.002 because

{*CHOOSE APPROPRIATE STATEMENT*}

A all or a substantial part of the events or omissions giving rise to the claim occurred in {85 _______} County. {86 *Elaborate.*} {*See Tex. Civ. Prac. & Rem. Code §15.002(a)(1).*}

B defendant, {87 *name*}, a natural person, resides in {88 _______} County. {89 *Elaborate.*} {*See Tex. Civ. Prac. & Rem. Code §15.002(a)(2).*}

C defendant, {90 *name*}, a corporation, maintains its principal office in Texas in {91 _______} County. {92 *Elaborate.*} {*See Tex. Civ. Prac. & Rem. Code §15.002(a)(3).*}

D plaintiff resided in {93 _______} County when this cause of action accrued, and no other subdivision of Texas Civil Practice & Remedies Code section 15.002(a) applies. {94 *Elaborate.*} {*See Tex. Civ. Prac. & Rem. Code §15.002(a)(4).*}

SEE: Tex. R. Civ. P. 87
Tex. Civ. Prac. & Rem. Code §15.001 et seq.
O'Connor's Texas Rules * Civil Trials (2019), "Venue," ch. 2-B, §6, p. 127; "Choosing the Court—Venue," ch. 2-H, p. 179

NOTE: The Texas rules of pleading do not require the plaintiff to make an allegation of venue. The plaintiff should, however, state enough facts about the cause of action and the parties to establish venue in the particular county where the suit is filed. Pleading specific venue facts in the petition and citing the venue statute may prevent a defendant from pursuing a groundless motion to transfer venue.

Generally, when there are two counties of mandatory venue and both mandatory-venue provisions are under Texas Civil Practice & Remedies Code chapter 15, the plaintiff has the right to choose between the two provisions. *See **In re Fisher***, 433 S.W.3d 523, 533 (Tex.2014). For a discussion of other situations involving conflicting mandatory-venue provisions, see ***O'Connor's Texas Rules***, "Two counties of mandatory venue," ch. 2-H, §4.3.1, p. 184.

ATTORNEY FEES

1. Plaintiff is entitled to recover reasonable and necessary attorney fees under Texas Civil Practice & Remedies Code chapter 38 because this is a suit for

{*CHOOSE APPROPRIATE IDENTIFICATION OF CLAIM*}

Ⓐ services rendered by plaintiff.

Ⓑ labor performed by plaintiff.

Ⓒ material furnished by plaintiff.

Ⓓ overcharges for {❶ *freight/express*}.

Ⓔ {❷ *lost/damaged*} {❸ *freight/express*}.

Ⓕ {❹ *killed/injured*} livestock.

Ⓖ money owed on a sworn account.

Ⓗ breach of {❺ *an oral/a written*} contract.

2. Plaintiff retained counsel, who presented plaintiff's claim to {❻ *defendant/defendant's duly authorized agent*}. Defendant did not tender the amount owed within 30 days of when the claim was presented. {❼ *Elaborate.*} {*See* ***O'Connor's Texas COA****, "Plaintiff presented claim to defendant," ch. 45-B, §2.5, p. 1490; "Defendant did not tender payment," ch. 45-B, §2.6, p. 1491.*}

SEE: Tex. Civ. Prac. & Rem. Code ch. 38
O'Connor's Texas Rules * Civil Trials (2019), "CPRC ch. 38," ch. 1-H, §10.4.1(1), p. 75
O'Connor's Texas Causes of Action (2019), "Attorney Fees Under CPRC ch. 38," ch. 45-B, p. 1486

ATTACH: AFFIDAVIT FOR ATTORNEY FEES – FORM 1H:14

FORM 2B:22

ATTORNEY FEES

1. Plaintiff is entitled to recover reasonable and necessary attorney fees under the provisions of the written contract as set out in section {❶ *number*}, which provides: {❷ *quote relevant provisions of contract*}. Plaintiff has complied with all the requirements of this section of the contract. {❸ *Elaborate.*} {*See **O'Connor's Texas COA**, "Prerequisites for Recovery of Attorney Fees," ch. 45-C, §2, p. 1499.*}

SEE: ***O'Connor's Texas Rules * Civil Trials*** (2019), "Attorney Fees from Adverse Party," ch. 1-H, §10, p. 74
O'Connor's Texas Causes of Action (2019), "Attorney Fees Under Written Contract," ch. 45-C, p. 1498

ATTACH: AFFIDAVIT FOR ATTORNEY FEES – FORM 1H:14

NOTE: Contractual provisions for the recovery of attorney fees will trump the statutory provisions for the recovery of attorney fees in Texas Civil Practice & Remedies Code chapter 38. See ***O'Connor's Texas COA***, "Claims under contract vs. claims under CPRC ch. 38," ch. 45-C, §1.3, p. 1498.

ATTORNEY FEES

{*For recovery of fees under common-fund doctrine*}

1. Because of defendant's actions, plaintiff was required to retain an attorney and has incurred, and continues to incur, fees and expenses. Should plaintiff prevail, a common fund will be created that will substantially benefit others who have not borne the expenses of suit or incurred attorney fees. Plaintiff is entitled to recover payment for the reasonable and necessary expenses and fees for the services of legal counsel from the common fund. {*See **O'Connor's Texas COA**, "Common-fund doctrine," ch. 45-D, §2.2.1, p. 1504.*}

{*For recovery of fees incurred in earlier litigation brought about by defendant's wrongful acts*}

2. Defendant's actions resulted in {❶ *identify earlier suit*}, which plaintiff had to {❷ *prosecute/defend*} at plaintiff's own expense, including the payment of reasonable and necessary attorney fees. {❸ *Elaborate.*} Plaintiff is entitled to recover payment for the reasonable and necessary attorney fees and expenses of {❹ *state amount of fees and expenses*} incurred {❺ *prosecuting/defending*} {❻ *identify earlier suit*}. {*See **O'Connor's Texas COA**, "Attorney fees as damages," ch. 45-D, §2.2.2, p. 1505.*}

3. Defendant's wrongful actions during {❼ *identify plaintiff's earlier suit*} proximately and naturally caused plaintiff to incur additional attorney fees in that suit. {❽ *Elaborate.*} Plaintiff is entitled to recover payment for the reasonable and necessary additional attorney fees and expenses of {❾ *state amount of fees and expenses*} incurred. {*See **O'Connor's Texas COA**, "Defendant caused additional fees to be incurred," ch. 45-D, §2.2.2(4)(b), p. 1506.*}

SEE: ***O'Connor's Texas Rules * Civil Trials*** (2019), "Attorney Fees from Adverse Party," ch. 1-H, §10, p. 74
O'Connor's Texas Causes of Action (2019), "Attorney Fees Under Equity," ch. 45-D, p. 1503

ATTACH: AFFIDAVIT FOR ATTORNEY FEES – FORM 1H:14

Challenge to Constitutionality of a State Statute

This form must be completed by a party filing a petition, motion or other pleading **challenging the constitutionality of a state statute**. The completed form must be filed with the court in which the cause is pending as required by Section 402.010 (a-1), Texas Government Code.

Cause Number *(For Clerk Use Only):* ________ **Court** *(For Clerk Use Only):* ________

Styled: ____________________

(e.g., John Smith v. All American Insurance Co.; in re Mary Ann Jones; In the Matter of the Estate of George Jackson)

Contact information for party* challenging the constitutionality of a state statute. ***(*If party is not a person, provide contact information for party, party's representative or attorney.)***

Name: ____________ Telephone: ____________
Address: ____________ Fax: ____________
City/State/Zip: ____________ State Bar No. (if applicable): ____________
Email: ____________

Person completing this form is: ☐ Attorney for Party ☐ Unrepresented Party ☐ Other: ____________

Identify the type of pleading you have filed challenging the constitutionality of a state statute.

☐ Petition ☐ Answer ☐ Motion (Specify type): ____________
☐ Other: ____________

Is the Attorney General of the State of Texas a party to or counsel in this cause?

☐ Yes ☐ No

List the state statute(s) being challenged in your pleading and provide a summary of the basis for your challenge. (Additional pages may be attached if necessary.)

9/5/13

SEE: Tex. Gov't Code §402.010
O'Connor's Texas Rules * Civil Trials (2019), "Generally," ch. 1-B, §3.2.19(2)(a), p. 15

ATTACH: CERTIFICATE OF SERVICE – FORM 1B:13
Pleading

NOTE: If a party files a petition, motion, or other pleading challenging the constitutionality of a Texas statute, the party must also file a form in the court in which the suit is pending that identifies which pleading contains the constitutional challenge. *See* Tex. Gov't Code §402.010(a), (a-1). The Office of Court Administration has adopted this form as the proper one to use to notify the court of a constitutional challenge. *See id.* §402.010(a-1); www.txcourts.gov/rules-forms/forms. After receiving the pleading and the notice form, the court must then serve notice of the constitutional challenge and a copy of the pleading on the Attorney General, unless the Attorney General is a party to or counsel in the suit. Tex. Gov't Code §402.010(a). See ***O'Connor's Texas Rules***, "Suits involving constitutional challenge," ch. 1-B, §3.2.19(2), p. 15.

The Court of Criminal Appeals has held that Government Code §402.010(a) and (b) violate the separation-of-powers doctrine of the Texas Constitution. ***Ex parte Lo***, 424 S.W.3d 10, 28 (Tex.Crim.App.2014). In response to ***Ex parte Lo***, the Constitution was amended to allow the Legislature to require a court to provide notice to the Attorney General. *See* Tex. Const. art. 5, §32.

{❶ *PARTY*}'S MOTION TO
REMOVE SUIT FROM EXPEDITED-ACTIONS PROCESS

{❷ *Party*}, {❸ *name*}, asks the Court to remove this suit from the expedited-actions process in Texas Rule of Civil Procedure 169. {*See* ***O'Connor's Texas Rules****, "Removal by motion," ch. 2-C, §3.1, p. 134.*}

INTRODUCTION

1. Plaintiff, {❹ *name*}, sued defendant, {❺ *name*}, for {❻ *state basis of suit*}.

2. {❼ *State other relevant facts about the suit.*}

BACKGROUND

3. This suit qualifies as an expedited action under Texas Rule of Civil Procedure 169 because {❽ *explain*}. {*See* ***O'Connor's Texas Rules****, "Applicability," ch. 2-C, §2, p. 134.*}

4. {❾ *State other facts relevant to the motion.*}

ARGUMENT & AUTHORITIES

5. A court must remove a suit from the expedited-actions process if a party files a motion to remove and makes a showing of good cause. Tex. R. Civ. P. 169(c)(1)(A). When determining whether there is good cause to remove the suit from the expedited-actions process, the court should consider certain factors. *See* Tex. R. Civ. P. 169 cmt. 3.

{*CHOOSE APPROPRIATE PARAGRAPHS 6-11*}

6. There is good cause to remove this suit from the expedited-actions process because the total damages sought by multiple claimants against the same defendant exceed $100,000. *See* Tex. R. Civ. P. 169(a)(1) & cmt. 3. {❿ *Elaborate.*}

7. There is good cause to remove this suit from the expedited-actions process because a defendant has in good faith filed a compulsory counterclaim that seeks relief other than what is allowed under Texas Rule of Civil Procedure 169(a)(1). Tex. R. Civ. P. 169 cmt. 3. {⓫ *Elaborate.*}

8. There is good cause to remove this suit from the expedited-actions process because there is a large number of parties and witnesses. Tex. R. Civ. P. 169 cmt. 3. {⓬ *Elaborate.*}

9. There is good cause to remove this suit from the expedited-actions process because the legal and factual issues in the suit are complex. Tex. R. Civ. P. 169 cmt. 3. {⓭ *Elaborate.*}

10. There is good cause to remove this suit from the expedited-actions process because an interpreter is necessary. Tex. R. Civ. P. 169 cmt. 3. {⓮ *Elaborate.*}

11. There is good cause to remove this suit from the expedited-actions process because {⓯ *identify any other reason*}. *See* Tex. R. Civ. P. 169 cmt. 3. {⓰ *Elaborate.*}

12. If a suit is removed from the expedited-actions process, the court must reopen discovery under Texas Rule of Civil Procedure 190.2(c). Tex. R. Civ. P. 169(c)(3). {*See* ***O'Connor's Texas Rules****, "Period reopens," ch. 6-A, §8.1.1(2), p. 524.*} {⓱ *Add if appropriate: {Party} attaches a motion to reopen the discovery period to explain why the suit should be governed by a Level {2/3} discovery-control plan.*} {*See FORM 6A:8.*}

CONCLUSION

13. {⓲ *Briefly summarize the motion.*}

PRAYER

14. For these reasons, {⓳ *party*} asks the Court to remove this suit from the expedited-actions process in Texas Rule of Civil Procedure 169.

SEE: Tex. R. Civ. P. 169, 190.2
O'Connor's Texas Rules * Civil Trials (2019), "Removal from TRCP 169 Procedure," ch. 2-C, §3, p. 134

ADD: STYLE OF THE CASE – FORM 1B:2
SIGNATURE BLOCK – FORM 1B:3
CERTIFICATE OF SERVICE – FORM 1B:13

ATTACH: AFFIDAVIT – FORM 1B:8, if necessary
NOTICE OF HEARING OR SUBMISSION – FORM 1E:1
ORDER – FORM 1G:1
MOTION TO REOPEN DISCOVERY PERIOD – FORM 6A:8, if necessary

NOTE: Texas Rule of Civil Procedure 169 does not specify a deadline to file a motion to remove a suit from the expedited-actions process, but a party should file the motion as soon as practical.

FORM 2C:1

{❶ *PARTY*}'S MOTION TO EXTEND TIME LIMITS DURING TRIAL

{❷ *Party*}, {❸ *name*}, asks the Court to extend the time limits for certain procedures during trial under Texas Rule of Civil Procedure 169(d)(3). {*See* ***O'Connor's Texas Rules***, *"Motion for extension," ch. 2-C, §6.2.2, p. 136.*}

INTRODUCTION

1. Plaintiff, {❹ *name*}, sued defendant, {❺ *name*}, for {❻ *state basis of suit*}.

2. {❼ *State other relevant facts about the suit.*}

BACKGROUND

3. This suit qualifies as an expedited action under Texas Rule of Civil Procedure 169 because {❽ *explain*}. {*See* ***O'Connor's Texas Rules***, *"Applicability," ch. 2-C, §2, p. 134.*}

4. There are {❾ *number*} sides in this suit. "Side" refers to all the litigants with generally common interests in the litigation. *See* Tex. R. Civ. P. 233; *see also* Tex. R. Civ. P. 169(d)(3)(A) ("side" has same definition as that in Rule 233), Tex. R. Civ. P. 190 cmt. 6 (1999) (same). {❿ *Identify the parties on each side and elaborate if necessary, particularly for complex cases that have more than two sides.*}

5. {⓫ *State other facts relevant to the motion.*}

ARGUMENT & AUTHORITIES

6. A court may extend the time limits to complete jury selection, opening statements, presentation of the evidence, examination and cross-examination of witnesses, and closing arguments if a party files a motion to extend and makes a showing of good cause. Tex. R. Civ. P. 169(d)(3). When determining whether there is good cause to extend the time limits, the court should consider certain factors. *See* Tex. R. Civ. P. 169 cmt. 3.

{*CHOOSE APPROPRIATE PARAGRAPHS 7-11*}

7. There is good cause to extend the time limits because a defendant has in good faith filed a compulsory counterclaim that seeks relief other than what is allowed under Texas Rule of Civil Procedure 169(a)(1). Tex. R. Civ. P. 169 cmt. 3. {⓬ *Elaborate.*}

8. There is good cause to extend the time limits because there is a large number of parties and witnesses. Tex. R. Civ. P. 169 cmt. 3. {⓭ *Elaborate.*}

9. There is good cause to extend the time limits because the legal and factual issues in the suit are complex. Tex. R. Civ. P. 169 cmt. 3. {14 *Elaborate.*}

10. There is good cause to extend the time limits because an interpreter is necessary. Tex. R. Civ. P. 169 cmt. 3. {15 *Elaborate.*}

11. There is good cause to extend the time limits because {16 *identify any other reason*}. *See* Tex. R. Civ. P. 169 cmt. 3. {17 *Elaborate.*}

12. The time limit can be extended from 8 hours to no more than 12 hours per side. Tex. R. Civ. P. 169(d)(3). {18 *Party*} requests an extension of time to {19 *number*} hours for {20 *his/her/its*} side.

CONCLUSION

13. {21 *Briefly summarize the motion.*}

PRAYER

14. For these reasons, {22 *party*} asks the Court to extend the time limits during trial to {23 *number*} hours for {24 *his/her/its*} side.

SEE: Tex. R. Civ. P. 169
O'Connor's Texas Rules * Civil Trials (2019), "Time limits during trial," ch. 2-C, §6.2, p. 136

ADD: STYLE OF THE CASE – FORM 1B:2
SIGNATURE BLOCK – FORM 1B:3
CERTIFICATE OF SERVICE – FORM 1B:13

ATTACH: AFFIDAVIT – FORM 1B:8, if necessary
NOTICE OF HEARING OR SUBMISSION – FORM 1E:1
ORDER – FORM 1G:1

NOTE: Texas Rule of Civil Procedure 169 does not specify a deadline to file a motion to extend the time limits during trial, but a party should file the motion as soon as practical.

PLAINTIFF'S ORIGINAL PETITION & APPLICATION FOR TEMPORARY RESTRAINING ORDER {❶ *STATE ADDITIONAL RELIEF REQUESTED IF APPROPRIATE, E.G., & REQUEST FOR DISCLOSURE*}

Plaintiff, {❷ *name*}, files this original petition and application for temporary restraining order {❸ *state additional relief requested if appropriate, e.g., and request for disclosure*} against defendant, {❹ *name*}, and alleges as follows:

DISCOVERY-CONTROL PLAN

1. Plaintiff intends to conduct discovery under Level {❺ *2/3*} of Texas Rule of Civil Procedure {❻ *190.3/190.4*} and affirmatively pleads that this suit is not governed by the expedited-actions process in Texas Rule of Civil Procedure 169 because {❼ *he/she/it*} seeks injunctive relief. {*See* ***O'Connor's Texas Rules****, "Discovery-Control Plans," ch. 2-B, §2, p. 115. For a motion to request a Level 3 discovery-control plan, see FORM 6A:6.*}

CLAIM FOR RELIEF

{*CHOOSE APPROPRIATE PARAGRAPH 2*}

2. Plaintiff seeks monetary relief of $100,000 or less and nonmonetary relief. {*Tex. R. Civ. P. 47(c)(2).*}

2. Plaintiff seeks monetary relief over $100,000 but not more than $200,000. {*Tex. R. Civ. P. 47(c)(3).*}

2. Plaintiff seeks monetary relief over $200,000 but not more than $1,000,000. {*Tex. R. Civ. P. 47(c)(4).*}

2. Plaintiff seeks monetary relief over $1,000,000. {*Tex. R. Civ. P. 47(c)(5).*}

PARTIES

3. {*For plaintiff designation, see FORM 2B:9;* ***O'Connor's Texas Rules****, "Plaintiff," ch. 2-B, §4.4, p. 123.*}

4. {*For defendant designation, see FORMS 2B:10-19;* ***O'Connor's Texas Rules****, "Defendant," ch. 2-B, §4.5, p. 123.*}

JURISDICTION

5. {*For jurisdiction allegations, see FORM 2B:20. It is not necessary to plead jurisdiction for most suits. See* ***O'Connor's Texas Rules****, "Jurisdiction," ch. 2-B, §5, p. 125.*}

VENUE

6. {*For venue allegations, see FORM 2B:21. It is not necessary to plead venue, but pleading sufficient venue facts could avoid a motion to transfer venue. See* ***O'Connor's Texas Rules****, "Venue," ch. 2-B, §6, p. 127; "Venue," ch. 2-D, §3.2, p. 139.*}

FACTS

7. On {❽ *date*}, at {❾ *identify location*}, {❿ _______} County, Texas, {⓫ *describe events that resulted in lawsuit*}.

8. {⓬ *State other relevant facts in separately numbered paragraphs.*} {*See* ***O'Connor's Texas Rules****, "Pleading a Cause of Action," ch. 2-B, §7, p. 127.*}

9. Plaintiff attaches an affidavit as Exhibit {⓭ *letter*} that proves the allegations in this application for injunctive relief and incorporates it by reference.

COUNT 1 – {⓮ *NAME OF CAUSE OF ACTION*}

10. {⓯ *In separately numbered paragraphs, identify elements and facts supporting a cause of action. For lists of elements for various causes of action, see* ***O'Connor's Texas COA****, Part 2, p. 7.*}

11. {⓰ *Identify the damages sought and include a statement that the damages are within the jurisdictional limits of the court. See FORM 2B:1, ¶10.*} {*For types of damages available, see* ***O'Connor's Texas COA****, "Damages," ch. 41, p. 1345.*}

APPLICATION FOR TEMPORARY RESTRAINING ORDER

12. Plaintiff asks the Court to {⓱ *identify specific type of injunctive relief sought, e.g., prevent defendant from selling property, prevent defendant from coming within 100 feet of plaintiff*}. {*See* ***O'Connor's Texas Rules****, "Relief," ch. 2-D, §5.1.6, p. 143.*}

{*CHOOSE APPROPRIATE PARAGRAPHS 13-17*}

{*For injunctive relief under statute*}

13. Plaintiff's application for a temporary restraining order is authorized by {⓲ *identify statute authorizing injunctive relief, e.g., Tex. Civ. Prac. & Rem. Code §65.011(1)*}. {⓳ *Elaborate.*} {*See* ***O'Connor's Texas Rules****, "Grounds for injunctive relief," ch. 2-D, §4.1, p. 140.*}

◄ *Continued on next page* ►

{*For injunctive relief under common law*}

14. It is probable that plaintiff will recover from defendant after a trial on the merits because {[20] *state basis for probable recovery*}. {*See* ***O'Connor's Texas Rules****, "Probable right to relief," ch. 2-D, §4.2.2, p. 141.*}

15. If plaintiff's application is not granted, harm is imminent because {[21] *state harm that will result if temporary restraining order is not issued*}. {*See* ***O'Connor's Texas Rules****, "Imminent harm," ch. 2-D, §4.2.3(1), p. 142.*}

16. The harm that will result if the temporary restraining order is not issued is irreparable because {[22] *state reasons harm is irreparable, e.g., the estate will be depleted*}. {*See* ***O'Connor's Texas Rules****, "Irreparable injury," ch. 2-D, §4.2.3(2), p. 142.*}

17. Plaintiff has no adequate remedy at law because {[23] *state reason, e.g., damages are incalculable, defendant is insolvent*}. {*See* ***O'Connor's Texas Rules****, "Inadequate remedy," ch. 2-D, §4.2.3(3), p. 143.*}

{*IF REQUESTING EX PARTE RELIEF, ADD PARAGRAPH 18*}

18. There is not enough time to serve notice on defendant and to hold a hearing on this application. {[24] *Elaborate.*} {*See Tex. R. Civ. P. 680;* ***O'Connor's Texas Rules****, "Ex parte allegations," ch. 2-D, §5.1.4, p. 143.*}

REQUEST FOR TEMPORARY INJUNCTION

19. Plaintiff asks the Court to set {[25] *his/her/its*} application for temporary injunction for a hearing and, after the hearing, issue a temporary injunction against defendant. {*See* ***O'Connor's Texas Rules****, "Request for injunction," ch. 2-D, §5.1.3, p. 143; "Request for Temporary Injunction," ch. 2-D, §6, p. 145.*}

{*FOR A PERMANENT INJUNCTION, ADD PARAGRAPH 20*}

REQUEST FOR PERMANENT INJUNCTION

20. Plaintiff asks the Court to set {[26] *his/her/its*} request for a permanent injunction for a full trial on the merits and, after the trial, issue a permanent injunction against defendant. {*See* ***O'Connor's Texas Rules****, "Request for Permanent Injunction," ch. 2-D, §7, p. 147.*}

{ADD PARAGRAPHS 21-24 AS APPROPRIATE}

JURY DEMAND

21. Plaintiff demands a jury trial and tenders the appropriate fee with this petition. *{See **O'Connor's Texas Rules**, "Request for Jury Trial," ch. 5-B, p. 400.}*

CONDITIONS PRECEDENT

22. All conditions precedent to plaintiff's claim for relief have been performed or have occurred. *{See **O'Connor's Texas Rules**, "Conditions Precedent," ch. 2-B, §12, p. 132.}*

REQUEST FOR DISCLOSURE

23. Under Texas Rule of Civil Procedure 194, plaintiff requests that defendant disclose, within 50 days of the service of this request, the information or material described in Rule 194.2. *{See **O'Connor's Texas Rules**, "Content of request," ch. 6-E, §3.2, p. 627.}*

OBJECTION TO ASSOCIATE JUDGE

24. Plaintiff objects to the referral of this case to an associate judge for hearing a trial on the merits or presiding at a jury trial. *{See **O'Connor's Texas Rules**, "Objection to referral," ch. 1-J, §3.3, p. 96.}*

PRAYER

25. For these reasons, plaintiff asks that defendant be cited to appear and answer and, on final trial, that plaintiff be awarded a judgment against defendant for the following:

{CHOOSE RELIEF SOUGHT}

a. Temporary restraining order.

b. Temporary injunction.

c. Permanent injunction.

d. Actual damages. *{See **O'Connor's Texas COA**, "Pleading actual damages," ch. 41-A, §3.2, p. 1346.}*

e. Prejudgment and postjudgment interest. *{See **O'Connor's Texas COA**, "Interest," ch. 43, p. 1445.}*

Continued on next page

f. Court costs. {*See **O'Connor's Texas COA**, "Court Costs," ch. 44, p. 1453.*}

g. All other relief to which plaintiff is entitled. {*See **O'Connor's Texas Rules**, "Prayer," ch. 2-B, §15, p. 132.*}

SEE: Tex. R. Civ. P. 45-59, 78-82, 190, 194, 680-693a
Tex. Civ. Prac. & Rem. Code ch. 65
O'Connor's Texas Rules * Civil Trials (2019), "Plaintiff's Original Petition," ch. 2-B, p. 115; "Injunctive Relief," ch. 2-D, p. 138
O'Connor's Texas Causes of Action (2019), "Damages & Other Compensation," Part 4, p. 1343

ADD: STYLE OF THE CASE – FORM 1B:2
SIGNATURE BLOCK – FORM 1B:3
VERIFICATION – FORM 1B:7

ATTACH: AFFIDAVIT – FORM 1B:8
NOTICE OF CURRENT/CHANGE OF ADDRESS – FORM 1B:14
ORDER – FORM 2D:3
Civil Process Request Form, if required by court clerk to issue citation
Exhibits, if necessary
Filing fees
Jury fee, if jury trial requested

NOTE: An application for a temporary restraining order (TRO) must include a request for a temporary injunction. *See* Tex. R. Civ. P. 680. When the applicant seeks a temporary injunction without a TRO, its petition must meet all the pleading requirements for a TRO except the request for ex parte relief. See ***O'Connor's Texas Rules***, "Application," ch. 2-D, §6.2, p. 146.

A request for a permanent injunction can be included in the application for TRO. However, when the applicant seeks a permanent injunction without other injunctive relief, its petition must meet all of the requirements for a TRO except (1) a request for ex parte relief, (2) a statement of the willingness to post bond, and (3) verification or affidavits. See ***O'Connor's Texas Rules***, "Application," ch. 2-D, §7.1, p. 147.

A party should check the local rules to determine whether any additional written certificate is required and whether the application for TRO must be filed with the clerk or with the judge. See ***O'Connor's Texas Rules***, "Prepare petition & application," ch. 2-D, §2.1, p. 138; "File petition & application," ch. 2-D, §2.3, p. 139.

Discovery for suits for injunctive relief cannot be conducted under a Level 1 discovery-control plan. *See* Tex. R. Civ. P. 190 cmt. 2 (1999). A Level 1 discovery-control plan applies to expedited actions (i.e., civil actions in which only monetary relief is sought and the amount in controversy is no more than $100,000) or to suits for divorce not involving children where the value of the marital estate does not exceed $50,000. Tex. R. Civ. P. 169(d)(1), 190.2. See ***O'Connor's Texas Rules***, "Discovery-Control Plans," ch. 2-B, §2, p. 115.

If the applicant relies on a statute that defines the requirements for injunctive relief, the statutory requirements supersede the requirements for an injunction under common law. ***Sonwalkar v. St. Luke's Sugar Land Prtshp.***, 394 S.W.3d 186, 197 (Tex.App.—Houston [1st Dist.] 2012, no pet.); *see* ***Butnaru v. Ford Motor Co.***, 84 S.W.3d 198, 210 (Tex.2002).

Under Texas Rule of Civil Procedure 39, the applicant must join all parties who are indispensable in the injunction proceeding before the court can grant temporary injunctive relief. *See* ***Henry v. Cox***, 520 S.W.3d 28, 34 (Tex.2017). See ***O'Connor's Texas Rules***, "Parties," ch. 2-D, §6.1, p. 145.

See notes under FORM 2B:1.

DEFENDANT'S RESPONSE TO REQUEST FOR INJUNCTIVE RELIEF

Defendant, {❶ *name*}, asks the Court to deny plaintiff's request for {❷ *describe injunctive relief sought*}.

INTRODUCTION

1. Plaintiff, {❸ *name*}, sued defendant, {❹ *name*}, for {❺ *state basis of suit*}.

2. {❻ *State other relevant facts about the suit.*}

BACKGROUND

3. Plaintiff {❼ *name*} filed a request for {❽ *describe injunctive relief sought*} on {❾ *date*}.

4. {❿ *State other facts relevant to the response.*}

ARGUMENT & AUTHORITIES

{*CHOOSE APPROPRIATE PARAGRAPHS 5-12*}

5. Defendant objects to plaintiff's request for {⓫ *describe injunctive relief sought*} because plaintiff's application for injunctive relief does not show that plaintiff has a probable right to the relief on a final hearing of the case. {⓬ *Elaborate.*} {*See **O'Connor's Texas Rules**, "Probable right to relief," ch. 2-D, §4.2.2, p. 141.*}

6. Defendant objects to plaintiff's request for {⓭ *describe injunctive relief sought*} because plaintiff's application for injunctive relief does not show that harm to plaintiff is imminent. {⓮ *Elaborate.*} {*See **O'Connor's Texas Rules**, "Imminent harm," ch. 2-D, §4.2.3(1), p. 142.*}

7. Defendant objects to plaintiff's request for {⓯ *describe injunctive relief sought*} because plaintiff's application for injunctive relief does not show that plaintiff will sustain irreparable injury. {⓰ *Elaborate.*} {*See **O'Connor's Texas Rules**, "Irreparable injury," ch. 2-D, §4.2.3(2), p. 142.*}

8. Defendant objects to plaintiff's request for {⓱ *describe injunctive relief sought*} because plaintiff has an adequate remedy at law. {⓲ *Elaborate.*} {*See **O'Connor's Texas Rules**, "Inadequate remedy," ch. 2-D, §4.2.3(3), p. 143.*}

9. Defendant objects to plaintiff's request for temporary injunctive relief because granting the relief will accomplish the entire object of plaintiff's suit. {⓳ *Elaborate.*} A trial court cannot grant a temporary injunction that gives the plaintiff all the relief the plaintiff seeks without a trial on the merits. *See Tex. Foundries, Inc. v. Int'l Moulders & Foundry Workers' Union*, 248 S.W.2d 460, 464 (Tex. 1952).

10. Defendant objects to plaintiff's request for temporary injunctive relief because granting the relief will destroy, rather than preserve, the status quo. The status quo to be preserved by a temporary injunction is the last, actual, peaceable, noncontested status that preceded the controversy resulting in the suit. *Transp. Co. v. Robertson Transps., Inc.*, 261 S.W.2d 549, 553-54 (Tex. 1953). The status quo that should be preserved, but instead will be destroyed by the requested temporary injunction, is {20 *explain*}.

11. Defendant objects to plaintiff's request for {21 *describe injunctive relief sought*} because plaintiff is guilty of inequitable conduct and thus is not entitled to injunctive relief. *See San Miguel v. City of Windcrest*, 40 S.W.3d 104, 110-11 (Tex. App.—San Antonio 2000, no pet.); *Office Emps. Int'l Union Local No. 129 v. Hous. Lighting & Power Co.*, 314 S.W.2d 315, 325 (Tex. App.—Austin 1958, writ ref'd n.r.e.). {22 *Identify inequitable conduct, e.g., laches, unclean hands, and explain why relief is precluded.*}

12. Defendant objects to plaintiff's request for {23 *describe injunctive relief sought*} because plaintiff did not verify the application for injunction as required by Texas Rule of Civil Procedure 682. {24 *Elaborate.*}

CONCLUSION

13. {25 *Briefly summarize the response.*}

PRAYER

14. Defendant asks the Court to deny plaintiff's request for {26 *describe injunctive relief sought*}.

SEE: Tex. R. Civ. P. 682, 683, 690
O'Connor's Texas Rules * Civil Trials (2019), "Defenses to request for injunction," ch. 2-D, §8.1, p. 148

ADD: STYLE OF THE CASE – FORM 1B:2
SIGNATURE BLOCK – FORM 1B:3
VERIFICATION – FORM 1B:7
CERTIFICATE OF SERVICE – FORM 1B:13

ATTACH: AFFIDAVIT – FORM 1B:8, if necessary

NOTE: If the deadline to answer the suit has not passed, the defendant does not waive any objection to personal jurisdiction or venue by filing a response to the application for injunctive relief. See ***O'Connor's Texas Rules***, "Special appearance & venue," ch. 2-D, §8.3.1, p. 149.

The defendant should file an answer to the underlying suit. Once the deadline to file an answer has expired, the plaintiff can take a default judgment, even if the defendant appeared at the injunction hearing. *See* ***Borrego v. del Palacio***, 445 S.W.2d 620, 621 (Tex.App.—El Paso 1969, no writ).

TEMPORARY RESTRAINING ORDER & ORDER SETTING HEARING FOR TEMPORARY INJUNCTION

1. After considering plaintiff {❶ *name*}'s application for temporary restraining order, the pleadings, the affidavits, and arguments of counsel, the Court finds there is evidence that harm is imminent to plaintiff, and if the Court does not issue the temporary restraining order, plaintiff will be irreparably injured because {❷ *identify the injury that will result if temporary restraining order is not issued, state why the injury will be suffered, and describe why the injury is irreparable*}.

{*ADD PARAGRAPH 2 IF APPROPRIATE*}

2. An ex parte order, without notice to defendant, is necessary because there was not enough time to give notice to defendant, hold a hearing, and issue a restraining order before the irreparable injury, loss, or damage would occur. Specifically, {❸ *explain*}.

3. Therefore, by this order, the Court does the following:

   a. Restrains defendant, {❹ *name*}, from {❺ *identify specific act restrained, as requested in the application for temporary restraining order*}.

   b. Orders the clerk to issue notice to defendant, {❻ *name*}, that the hearing on plaintiff's application for temporary injunction is set for __________, 20___, at _____ a.m./p.m. The purpose of the hearing will be to determine whether this temporary restraining order should be made a temporary injunction pending a full trial on the merits.

   c. Sets bond at ${❼ *amount*}.

This order expires on ________________, 20___.

SIGNED on ________________, 20___, at _____ a.m./p.m.

____
PRESIDING JUDGE

SEE: Tex. R. Civ. P. 45-59, 78-82, 680-693a
Tex. Civ. Prac. & Rem. Code ch. 65
O'Connor's Texas Rules * Civil Trials (2019), "Form," ch. 2-D, §5.3.1, p. 144; "Bond," ch. 2-D, §5.4, p. 144

ADD: STYLE OF THE CASE – FORM 1B:2

NOTE: The court may grant a temporary restraining order for only 14 days. However, on motion and order finding good cause, the court may extend the order for an additional 14 days. If the parties agree, the order may be extended for more than 14 days. See ***O'Connor's Texas Rules***, "Extending the TRO," ch. 2-D, §5.3.2, p. 144.

For an order granting a temporary injunction, modify the last sentence of paragraph 3(b) of this order to include a setting for a trial on the merits. *See* Tex. R. Civ. P. 683. See ***O'Connor's Texas Rules***, "Order," ch. 2-D, §6.5, p. 147.

WRIT OF INJUNCTION

STATE OF TEXAS §
{❶ _______} COUNTY §

To: {❷ *Name of defendant*}

Plaintiff, {❸ *name*}, sued defendant, {❹ *name*}, for {❺ *state basis of suit*}. Plaintiff asked the Court to issue a {❻ *temporary restraining order/temporary injunction*}. After a hearing on the application, the Honorable {❼ *name of presiding judge*} ordered {❽ *specify actions ordered by court*}.

{❾ *Name of defendant*} will

{*CHOOSE APPROPRIATE RELIEF*}

Ⓐ desist and refrain from committing or continuing to {❿ *state acts being enjoined*}.

Ⓑ obey and execute the order signed by the Court. Specifically, {⓫ *state acts ordered to perform*}.

{*ADD PARAGRAPH IF WRIT ISSUED FOR TEMPORARY RESTRAINING ORDER*}

Plaintiff has requested that a temporary injunction be issued. A hearing on the temporary injunction will be held on __________, 20___, at _____ a.m./p.m., which is within 14 days of the signing of the temporary restraining order.

{*ADD PARAGRAPH IF WRIT ISSUED FOR TEMPORARY INJUNCTION*}

This writ of injunction is returnable at or before 10:00 a.m. of the first Monday after the expiration of 20 days from the date of service.

ISSUED under my hand and seal on _______________, 20___.

____
{⓬ *Name of clerk*}

SEE: Tex. R. Civ. P. 687
O'Connor's Texas Rules * Civil Trials (2019), "Writ," ch. 2-D, §5.5, p. 145

ADD: STYLE OF THE CASE – FORM 1B:2

NOTE: The writ of injunction must be served on the respondent by a sheriff or constable or by a person authorized by court order. *See* Tex. R. Civ. P. 103, 688, 689. The applicant should ensure that copies of the writ are also served on any other persons acting in concert with the respondent or the respondent's officers, agents, servants, employees, or attorneys. *See* Tex. R. Civ. P. 683. The officer or authorized person serving the writ of injunction must complete and file a return of service for the writ that meets the requirements of Texas Rule of Civil Procedure 107. *See* Tex. R. Civ. P. 689. The clerk must keep a copy of the temporary restraining order (or temporary injunction) in the court's file. Tex. R. Civ. P. 688.

PLAINTIFF'S MOTION REQUESTING RETURN OF POSTED BOND

Plaintiff, {❶ *name*}, asks the Court to order {❷ *name of appropriate officer*} to return the bond plaintiff posted.

INTRODUCTION

1. Plaintiff, {❸ *name*}, sued defendant, {❹ *name*}, for {❺ *state basis of suit*}.

2. As part of that suit, plaintiff asked the Court to issue a {❻ *temporary restraining order/temporary injunction*} to restrain defendant from {❼ *identify action restrained*}.

3. {❽ *State other relevant facts about the suit.*}

BACKGROUND

4. On {❾ *date*}, plaintiff executed and filed a bond for the issuance of a {❿ *temporary restraining order/temporary injunction*}, payable to defendant in the amount of ${⓫ *amount*}.

5. The conditions of the bond were that (1) plaintiff would abide by the Court's decision in the cause and (2) plaintiff would pay all sums of money and costs that may be adjudged against {⓬ *him/her/it*} if the restraining order or temporary injunction was dissolved in whole or in part.

6. On {⓭ *date*}, plaintiff fulfilled the conditions of the bond. Specifically, {⓮ *explain what action plaintiff took that satisfied the conditions*}.

7. {⓯ *State other facts relevant to the motion.*}

REQUEST

8. Because plaintiff has met the conditions of the bond, {⓰ *he/she/it*} asks the Court to order that the bond be returned to {⓱ *him/her/it*}.

CONCLUSION

9. {⓲ *Briefly summarize the motion.*}

PRAYER

10. For these reasons, plaintiff asks the Court to order {⓳ *name of appropriate officer*} to return to plaintiff the bond posted for the {⓴ *temporary restraining order/temporary injunction*}.

SEE: Tex. R. Civ. P. 680, 683, 684
O'Connor's Texas Rules * Civil Trials (2019), "Bond," ch. 2-D, §5.4, p. 144

ADD: STYLE OF THE CASE – FORM 1B:2
SIGNATURE BLOCK – FORM 1B:3
VERIFICATION – FORM 1B:7
CERTIFICATE OF SERVICE – FORM 1B:13

ATTACH: AFFIDAVIT – FORM 1B:8
NOTICE OF HEARING OR SUBMISSION – FORM 1E:1
ORDER – FORM 1G:1

PLAINTIFF'S ORIGINAL PETITION FOR
DECLARATORY JUDGMENT {❶ *STATE ADDITIONAL RELIEF REQUESTED IF APPROPRIATE, E.G., & REQUEST FOR DISCLOSURE*}

Plaintiff, {❷ *name*}, files this original petition for declaratory judgment {❸ *state additional relief requested if appropriate, e.g., and request for disclosure*} against defendant, {❹ *name*}, and alleges as follows:

DISCOVERY-CONTROL PLAN

1. Plaintiff intends to conduct discovery under Level {❺ *2/3*} of Texas Rule of Civil Procedure {❻ *190.3/190.4*} and affirmatively pleads that this suit is not governed by the expedited-actions process in Texas Rule of Civil Procedure 169 because {❼ *explain*}. {*See* ***O'Connor's Texas Rules****, "Discovery-Control Plans," ch. 2-B, §2, p. 115. For a motion to request a Level 3 discovery-control plan, see FORM 6A:6.*}

CLAIM FOR RELIEF

{*CHOOSE APPROPRIATE PARAGRAPH 2*}

2. Plaintiff seeks monetary relief of $100,000 or less and nonmonetary relief. {*Tex. R. Civ. P. 47(c)(2).*}

2. Plaintiff seeks monetary relief over $100,000 but not more than $200,000. {*Tex. R. Civ. P. 47(c)(3).*}

2. Plaintiff seeks monetary relief over $200,000 but not more than $1,000,000. {*Tex. R. Civ. P. 47(c)(4).*}

2. Plaintiff seeks monetary relief over $1,000,000. {*Tex. R. Civ. P. 47(c)(5).*}

PARTIES

3. {*For plaintiff designation, see FORM 2B:9;* ***O'Connor's Texas Rules****, "Plaintiff," ch. 2-B, §4.4, p. 123.*}

4. {*For defendant designation, see FORMS 2B:10-19;* ***O'Connor's Texas Rules****, "Defendant," ch. 2-B, §4.5, p. 123.*}

5. {❽ *List any person who may have a claim or interest that would be affected by the declaration. Tex. Civ. Prac. & Rem. Code §37.006(a).*} {*See* ***O'Connor's Texas Rules****, "Parties," ch. 2-E, §3.2, p. 155.*}

JURISDICTION

6. {*For jurisdiction allegations, see FORM 2B:20. It is not necessary to plead jurisdiction for most suits. See **O'Connor's Texas Rules**, "Jurisdiction," ch. 2-B, §5, p. 125.*}

VENUE

7. {*For venue allegations, see FORM 2B:21. It is not necessary to plead venue, but pleading sufficient venue facts could avoid a motion to transfer venue. See **O'Connor's Texas Rules**, "Venue," ch. 2-B, §6, p. 127.*}

FACTS

8. On {❾ *date*}, at {❿ *identify location*}, {⓫ _______} County, Texas, {⓬ *describe events that resulted in lawsuit*}.

9. {⓭ *State other relevant facts in separately numbered paragraphs.*} {*See **O'Connor's Texas Rules**, "Pleading a Cause of Action," ch. 2-B, §7, p. 127.*}

COUNT 1 – SUIT FOR DECLARATORY RELIEF

10. {⓮ *In separately numbered paragraphs, identify elements and facts supporting a cause of action and the request for declaratory relief.*} {*For lists of elements for various causes of action, see **O'Connor's Texas COA**, Part 2, p. 7.*}

11. Attorney Fees. Plaintiff is entitled to recover reasonable and necessary attorney fees that are equitable and just under Texas Civil Practice & Remedies Code section 37.009 because this is a suit for declaratory relief. {*See Tex. Civ. Prac. & Rem. Code §37.009; **O'Connor's Texas Rules**, "Costs & attorney fees," ch. 2-E, §3.8, p. 155.*}

{*ADD PARAGRAPHS 12-15 AS APPROPRIATE*}

JURY DEMAND

12. Plaintiff demands a jury trial and tenders the appropriate fee with this petition. {*See **O'Connor's Texas Rules**, "Request for Jury Trial," ch. 5-B, p. 400.*}

CONDITIONS PRECEDENT

13. All conditions precedent to plaintiff's claim for relief have been performed or have occurred. {*See **O'Connor's Texas Rules**, "Conditions Precedent," ch. 2-B, §12, p. 132.*}

Continued on next page

REQUEST FOR DISCLOSURE

14. Under Texas Rule of Civil Procedure 194, plaintiff requests that defendant disclose, within 50 days of the service of this request, the information or material described in Rule 194.2. {*See* ***O'Connor's Texas Rules****, "Content of request," ch. 6-E, §3.2, p. 627.*}

OBJECTION TO ASSOCIATE JUDGE

15. Plaintiff objects to the referral of this case to an associate judge for hearing a trial on the merits or presiding at a jury trial. {*See* ***O'Connor's Texas Rules****, "Objection to referral," ch. 1-J, §3.3, p. 96.*}

PRAYER

16. For these reasons, plaintiff asks that defendant be cited to appear and answer and that the Court declare {⓯ *state declaratory relief sought*}. In addition, plaintiff asks for the following damages:

{*CHOOSE RELIEF SOUGHT*}

a. Actual damages. {*See* ***O'Connor's Texas COA****, "Pleading actual damages," ch. 41-A, §3.2, p. 1346.*}

b. Prejudgment and postjudgment interest. {*See* ***O'Connor's Texas COA****, "Interest," ch. 43, p. 1445.*}

c. Court costs. {*See* ***O'Connor's Texas COA****, "Court Costs," ch. 44, p. 1453.*}

d. Attorney fees. {*See Tex. Civ. Prac. & Rem. Code §37.009;* ***O'Connor's Texas Rules****, "Costs & attorney fees," ch. 2-E, §3.8, p. 155.*}

e. All other relief to which plaintiff is entitled. {*See* ***O'Connor's Texas Rules****, "Prayer," ch. 2-B, §15, p. 132.*}

SEE: Tex. R. Civ. P. 45-49, 78-82, 190, 194
Tex. Civ. Prac. & Rem. Code §37.001 et seq.
O'Connor's Texas Rules * Civil Trials (2019), "Declaratory Judgment," ch. 2-E, p. 152
O'Connor's Texas Causes of Action (2019), "Damages & Other Compensation," Part 4, p. 1343

ADD: STYLE OF THE CASE – FORM 1B:2
SIGNATURE BLOCK – FORM 1B:3

ATTACH: NOTICE OF CURRENT/CHANGE OF ADDRESS – FORM 1B:14
Civil Process Request Form, if required by court clerk to issue citation
Exhibits, if necessary
Filing fees
Jury fee, if jury trial requested

NOTE: The purpose of a declaratory action is to establish existing rights, status, or other legal relationships. ***Republic Ins. v. Davis***, 856 S.W.2d 158, 164 (Tex.1993); *see* Tex. Civ. Prac. & Rem. Code §37.004(a); ***Bonham State Bank v. Beadle***, 907 S.W.2d 465, 467 (Tex.1995).

Discovery for a declaratory judgment cannot be conducted under a Level 1 discovery-control plan. A Level 1 discovery-control plan applies to expedited actions (i.e., civil actions in which only monetary relief is sought and the amount in controversy is no more than $100,000) or to suits for divorce not involving children where the value of the marital estate does not exceed $50,000. Tex. R. Civ. P. 169(d)(1), 190.2(a). See ***O'Connor's Texas Rules***, "Discovery-Control Plans," ch. 2-B, §2, p. 115.

If the suit challenges the validity of a municipal ordinance or franchise, the municipality must be made a party. Tex. Civ. Prac. & Rem. Code §37.006(b). If the suit challenges the constitutionality of a statute, ordinance, or franchise, the Attorney General must be served and is entitled to be heard. *Id.*

If a party seeks to join other persons in a declaratory-judgment action, the requirements of Texas Rule of Civil Procedure 39 must be satisfied. ***Crawford v. XTO Energy, Inc.***, 509 S.W.3d 906, 911 n.3 (Tex. 2017). See ***O'Connor's Texas Rules***, "Parties to be joined," ch. 2-F, §6.2, p. 161.

See notes under FORM 2B:1.

WAIVER OF CITATION

STATE OF TEXAS §
{❶ _______} COUNTY §

Before me, the undersigned notary, on this day personally appeared {❷ *name of defendant, authorized agent, or attorney*}, whose identity is known to me. After I administered an oath, {❸ *name of defendant, authorized agent, or attorney*} testified as follows:

"I, {❹ *name of defendant, authorized agent, or attorney*}, am the {❺ *defendant/authorized agent of defendant/attorney*} in this case. My mailing address is {❻ *address*}. Plaintiff has given me a copy of the original petition {❼ *he/she/it*} filed in this case. I waive the issuance of citation and service of process {❽ *add if appropriate: on behalf of the defendant*}."

____
{❾ *Name of defendant, authorized agent, or attorney*}

Sworn to and subscribed before me by {❿ *name of defendant, authorized agent, or attorney*} on __________, 20___.

____
Notary Public in and for
the State of Texas

SEE: Tex. R. Civ. P. 119
Tex. Civ. Prac. & Rem. Code §30.001
O'Connor's Texas Rules * Civil Trials (2019), "Written waiver," ch. 2-I, §8.2, p. 200

ADD: STYLE OF THE CASE – FORM 1B:2

NOTE: The waiver of citation must be (1) dated and signed after suit is filed, (2) notarized by someone other than an attorney in the case, and (3) filed with the papers of the case. *See* Tex. R. Civ. P. 119.

MOTION FOR SERVICE BY PRIVATE PROCESS SERVER

STATE OF TEXAS §
{❶ ______} COUNTY §

Before me, the undersigned notary, on this day personally appeared {❷ *name of private process server*}, whose identity is known to me. After I administered an oath to {❸ *him/her*}, upon {❹ *his/her*} oath {❺ *he/she*} said:

1. "My name is {❻ *name of private process server*}. {*See* ***O'Connor's Texas Rules****, "Trial-court order," ch. 2-I, §3.3.1, p. 192.*}

2. "I am not a party to, nor do I have any interest in the outcome of, this case.

3. "I am more than 18 years of age.

4. "I am familiar with the Texas Rules of Civil Procedure and other rules and statutes relating to service of citation.

5. "I ask the Court to authorize me to serve citation in this case."

____
{❼ *Name of private process server*}

Sworn to and subscribed before me by {❽ *name of private process server*} on __________, 20___.

____
Notary Public in and for
the State of Texas

Filed on ______________, 20___.

____
{❾ *Name of clerk*}

SEE: Tex. R. Civ. P. 103
O'Connor's Texas Rules * Civil Trials (2019), "Authorized by court order," ch. 2-I, §3.3, p. 192

ADD: STYLE OF THE CASE – FORM 1B:2

ATTACH: ORDER – FORM 2I:3

◄ *Continued on next page* ►

NOTE: The Supreme Court may authorize a person to serve process without a written motion. Tex. R. Civ. P. 103. The Supreme Court has adopted guidelines in Judicial Branch Certification Commission Rule 8.0 for a person to be certified to serve process. See ***O'Connor's Texas Rules***, "Supreme Court order," ch. 2-I, §3.3.2, p. 192.

ORDER AUTHORIZING PERSON TO SERVE CITATION UNDER TEXAS RULE OF CIVIL PROCEDURE 103

The Court finds that {❶ *name of private process server*} is more than 18 years of age, is not a party to this suit, and is not interested in the outcome of this suit. Therefore, the Court authorizes {❷ *name*} to serve citation on defendant, {❸ *name*}. {*See* ***O'Connor's Texas Rules***, *"Trial-court order," ch. 2-I, §3.3.1, p. 192.*}

SIGNED on ________________, 20___.

____
PRESIDING JUDGE

SEE: Tex. R. Civ. P. 103
O'Connor's Texas Rules * Civil Trials (2019), "Authorized by court order," ch. 2-I, §3.3, p. 192

ADD: STYLE OF THE CASE – FORM 1B:2

NOTE: The order authorizing a person to serve should accompany the citation. The court cannot impose a fee for issuing this order. Tex. R. Civ. P. 103.

PLAINTIFF'S MOTION FOR SUBSTITUTE SERVICE OF PROCESS

Plaintiff, {❶ *name*}, asks the Court to authorize substitute service on defendant, {❷ *name*}.

INTRODUCTION

1. Plaintiff, {❸ *name*}, sued defendant, {❹ *name*}, for {❺ *state basis of suit*}.

2. {❻ *State other relevant facts about the suit.*}

BACKGROUND

{*CHOOSE APPROPRIATE PARAGRAPHS 3-4*}

{*If requesting substituted service under TRCP 106*}

3. Defendant's {❼ *usual place of business/usual place of abode/probable location*} is {❽ *address*}.

4. Plaintiff attempted to serve defendant on {❾ *number*} occasions by {❿ *state methods of attempted service, e.g., personal delivery, registered mail, certified mail*} but has not been successful despite plaintiff's due diligence. {⓫ *Explain attempts to serve defendant and why each attempt was unsuccessful.*} {*See **O'Connor's Texas Rules**, "Motion & affidavit," ch. 2-I, §4.3.1(1), p. 193.*}

{*If requesting substituted service under TRCP 109 or 109a*}

3. Plaintiff has been unable to serve defendant by mail or personal delivery because

{*CHOOSE ONE OF THE FOLLOWING*}

Ⓐ defendant's {⓬ *residence/identity/residence and identity*} {⓭ *is/are*} unknown.

Ⓑ defendant is {⓮ *absent from/not a resident of*} Texas, and efforts to serve {⓯ *him/her*} outside Texas have been unsuccessful.

Ⓒ defendant is a transient person.

Ⓓ {⓰ *describe other impediments to service, e.g., defendant refuses to provide an address and is evading personal service*}. {*See Tex. R. Civ. P. 109.*}

4. Plaintiff has attempted to locate the defendant but has not been successful despite plaintiff's due diligence. {⓱ *Explain attempts to locate defendant and why each attempt was unsuccessful.*}

ARGUMENT & AUTHORITIES

5. Because plaintiff has not been able to serve defendant, plaintiff asks the Court to authorize plaintiff to serve defendant by

{*CHOOSE A OR B FOR SUBSTITUTED SERVICE UNDER TRCP 106*}

[A] leaving a true copy of the citation and the attached petition with anyone older than sixteen years of age at {⓲ *restate defendant's location*}. Tex. R. Civ. P. 106(b)(1).

[B] {⓳ *specify other manner of substitute service*}, which is reasonably effective to give defendant notice of the suit. Tex. R. Civ. P. 106(b)(2).

{*CHOOSE C OR D FOR SUBSTITUTED SERVICE UNDER TRCP 109 OR 109a*}

[C] publication in {⓴ *name of local newspaper*}. *See* Tex. R. Civ. P. 109, 116.

[D] {㉑ *specify other manner of service that would be as likely as publication to give actual notice, e.g., posting the citation at the courthouse door*}. {*See Tex. R. Civ. P. 109a, 648.*}

CONCLUSION

6. {㉒ *Briefly summarize the motion.*}

PRAYER

7. For these reasons, plaintiff asks the Court to authorize substitute service on defendant.

SEE: Tex. R. Civ. P. 106(b), 109, 109a
*O'Connor's Texas Rules * Civil Trials* (2019), "Substituted service," ch. 2-I, §4.3, p. 193

ADD: STYLE OF THE CASE – FORM 1B:2
SIGNATURE BLOCK – FORM 1B:3

ATTACH: AFFIDAVIT – FORM 2I:5
ORDER – FORM 2I:6

◄ *Continued on next page* ►

NOTE: A plaintiff should make multiple attempts at service before moving for substituted service; one attempt is insufficient. *See* ***Hubicki v. Festina***, 226 S.W.3d 405, 408 (Tex.2007).

For other situations in which service by publication may be authorized for an unknown party, see ***O'Connor's Texas Rules***, "Unknown defendant," ch. 2-I, §4.3.2(1)(a)[1], p. 194.

AFFIDAVIT OF {❶ *NAME*}

STATE OF TEXAS §
{❷ ________} COUNTY §

Before me, the undersigned notary, on this day personally appeared {❸ *name of affiant*}, the affiant, whose identity is known to me. After I administered an oath, affiant testified as follows:

1. "My name is {❹ *name of affiant*}. I am over 18 years of age, of sound mind, and capable of making this affidavit. The facts stated in this affidavit are within my personal knowledge and are true and correct.

{*CHOOSE APPROPRIATE PARAGRAPHS 2-3*}

{*If requesting service by method other than publication*}

2. "Defendant's {❺ *usual place of business/usual place of abode/probable location*} is {❻ *address*}.

3. "Plaintiff attempted to serve defendant on {❼ *number*} occasions by {❽ *state methods of attempted service, e.g., personal delivery, registered mail, certified mail*} but was unsuccessful despite plaintiff's due diligence. {❾ *Explain attempts to serve defendant and why each attempt was unsuccessful.*}"

{*If requesting service by publication*}

2. Plaintiff has been unable to serve defendant because

{*CHOOSE ONE OF THE FOLLOWING*}

Ⓐ defendant's {❿ *residence/identity/residence and identity*} {⓫ *is/are*} unknown.

Ⓑ defendant is {⓬ *absent from/not a resident of*} Texas, and efforts to serve {⓭ *him/her*} outside Texas have been unsuccessful.

Ⓒ defendant is a transient person.

Ⓓ {⓮ *describe other impediments to service, e.g., defendant refuses to provide an address and is evading personal service*}. {*See Tex. R. Civ. P. 109.*}

— *Continued on next page* —

3. "Plaintiff attempted to locate the defendant but has not been successful despite plaintiff's due diligence. {⓯ *Explain attempts to locate defendant and why each attempt was unsuccessful.*}"

____
{⓰ *Name of affiant*}

Sworn to and subscribed before me by {⓱ *name of affiant*} on __________, 20___.

____
Notary Public in and for
the State of Texas

SEE: Tex. R. Civ. P. 106(b), 109
O'Connor's Texas Rules * Civil Trials **(2019), "Substituted service," ch. 2-I, §4.3, p. 193**

ADD: STYLE OF THE CASE – FORM 1B:2

NOTE: See notes under FORM 1B:8.

ORDER ON PLAINTIFF'S MOTION FOR SUBSTITUTE SERVICE

After considering plaintiff {❶ *name*}'s Motion for Substitute Service and the supporting affidavit, the Court finds that plaintiff's attempts to {❷ *locate/serve*} defendant, {❸ *name*}, have been unsuccessful despite plaintiff's due diligence and that the substitute service requested in plaintiff's motion will be reasonably effective {❹ *add if applicable: and as likely as publication*} to give defendant notice of the suit.

Therefore, the Court GRANTS the motion and authorizes substitute service on defendant by {❺ *identify type of substitute service requested in motion*}.

SIGNED on ________________, 20___.

____
PRESIDING JUDGE

SEE: Tex. R. Civ. P. 106(b), 109, 109a
O'Connor's Texas Rules * Civil Trials (2019), "Substituted service," ch. 2-I, §4.3, p. 193

ADD: STYLE OF THE CASE – FORM 1B:2
CERTIFICATE OF SERVICE – FORM 1B:13, if proposed order served separately from motion

NOTE: The order must contain the specific method of service ordered or else it is defective. ***Steinke v. Mann***, 276 S.W.3d 608, 610 (Tex.App.—Waco 2008, no pet.); *see* Tex. R. Civ. P. 107(f) (when service is authorized under Rule 106, proof of service must be made in the manner ordered by the court).

NOTICE: THIS DOCUMENT CONTAINS SENSITIVE DATA

Cause Number: ______________________
(The Clerk's office will fill in the Cause Number when you file this form)

Plaintiff: ______________________
(Print first and last name of the person filing the lawsuit.)

And

Defendant: ______________________
(Print first and last name of the person being sued.)

In the ________ *(Court Number)* *(check one)*:
☐ District Court
☐ County Court / County Court at Law
☐ Justice Court

________ *(County)* Texas

Statement of Inability to Afford Payment of Court Costs or an Appeal Bond

1. Your Information

My full legal name is: ______________________ *(First Middle Last)* My date of birth is: ___/___/___ *(Month/Day/Year)*

My address is: *(Home)* ______________________

(Mailing) ______________________

My phone number: ____________ My email: ______________________

About my **dependents:** "The people who depend on me financially are listed below.

	Name	Age	Relationship to Me
1			
2			
3			
4			
5			
6			

2. Are you represented by Legal Aid?

☐ I am being represented in this case for free by an attorney who works for a legal aid provider or who received my case through a legal aid provider. I have attached the certificate the legal aid provider gave me as 'Exhibit: Legal Aid Certificate.

-or-

☐ I asked a legal-aid provider to represent me, and the provider determined that I am financially eligible for representation, but the provider could not take my case. I have attached documentation from legal aid stating this.

or-

☐ I am not represented by legal aid. I did not apply for representation by legal aid.

3. Do you receive public benefits?

☐ I do not receive needs-based public benefits. **- or -**

☐ I receive these **public benefits/government entitlements** that are based on indigency:
(Check ALL boxes that apply and attach proof to this form, such as a copy of an eligibility form or check.)

☐ Food stamps/SNAP ☐ TANF ☐ Medicaid ☐ CHIP ☐ SSI ☐ WIC ☐ AABD
☐ Public Housing or Section 8 Housing ☐ Low-Income Energy Assistance ☐ Emergency Assistance
☐ Telephone Lifeline ☐ Community Care via DADS ☐ LIS in Medicare ("Extra Help")
☐ Needs-based VA Pension ☐ Child Care Assistance under Child Care and Development Block Grant
☐ County Assistance, County Health Care, or General Assistance (GA)
☐ Other: ______________________

Statement of Inability to Afford Payment of Court Costs Page 1 of 2

4. What is your monthly income and income sources?

"I get this monthly income:

$________ in monthly wages. I work as a ________________ for ________________.
Your job title *Your employer*

$________ in monthly unemployment. I have been unemployed since *(date)* ________.

$________ in public benefits per month.

$________ from other people in my household each month: *(List only if other members contribute to your household income.)*

$________ from ☐ Retirement/Pension ☐ Tips, bonuses ☐ Disability ☐ Worker's Comp
☐ Social Security ☐ Military Housing ☐ Dividends, interest, royalties
☐ Child/spousal support
☐ My spouse's income or income from another member of my household *(If available)*

$________ from other jobs/sources of income. *(Describe)* ________________

$________ is my *total* **monthly** income.

5. What is the value of your property?

"My **property** includes: **Value***

Cash	$
Bank accounts, other financial assets	
	$
	$
	$
Vehicles (cars, boats) *(make and year)*	
	$
	$
	$
Other property (like jewelry, stocks, land, another house, etc.)	
	$
	$
	$
***Total* value of property →**	**$**

*The value is the amount the item would sell for less the amount you still owe on it, if anything.

6. What are your monthly expenses?

"My **monthly expenses** are: **Amount**

Rent/house payments/maintenance	$
Food and household supplies	$
Utilities and telephone	$
Clothing and laundry	$
Medical and dental expenses	$
Insurance (life, health, auto, etc.)	$
School and child care	$
Transportation, auto repair, gas	$
Child / spousal support	$
Wages withheld by court order	$
Debt payments paid to: *(List)*	$
	$
	$
***Total* Monthly Expenses →**	**$**

7. Are there debts or other facts explaining your financial situation?

"My **debts** include: *(List debt and amount owed)* ________________

________________"

(If you want the court to consider other facts, such as unusual medical expenses, family emergencies, etc., attach another page to this form labeled "Exhibit: Additional Supporting Facts.") ***Check here if you attach another page.*** ☐

8. Declaration

I declare under penalty of perjury that the foregoing is true and correct. I further swear:

☐ I cannot afford to pay court costs.

☐ I cannot furnish an appeal bond or pay a cash deposit to appeal a justice court decision.

My name is ________________. My date of birth is : ___/___/___.

My address is ________________
Street *City* *State* *Zip Code* *Country*

________________ signed on ___/___/___ in ________________ County, ________
Signature *Month/Day/Year* *county name* *State*

Statement of Inability to Afford Payment of Court Costs Page 2 of 2

◄ *Continued on next page* ►

FORM 2J:1 STATEMENT OF INABILITY TO AFFORD PAYMENT OF COURT COSTS

SEE: Tex. R. Civ. P. 145(b), 217
Tex. Civ. Prac. & Rem. Code §13.001 et seq., §132.001
O'Connor's Texas Rules * Civil Trials (2019), "Statement of Inability to Afford Payment of Costs," ch. 2-J, §3, p. 207

ADD: STYLE OF THE CASE – FORM 1B:2

ATTACH: INMATE'S DECLARATION – PREVIOUS FILINGS – FORM 2J:2, if appropriate
INMATE'S DECLARATION – GRIEVANCE-SYSTEM CLAIM – FORM 2J:3, if appropriate
Certificate from legal-aid provider, if appropriate
Exhibits, if appropriate

NOTE: A party claiming indigence must file a Statement of Inability to Afford Payment of Court Costs. *See* Tex. R. Civ. P. 145(a), (b). The party must use the form Statement provided by the Court or file a statement that includes all of the information in the Court-approved form. Tex. R. Civ. P. 145(b). An electronic version of the form Statement is available on the Office of Court Administration website at www.txcourts.gov/rules-forms/forms.

The Statement must be sworn to before a notary or made under penalty of perjury, as permitted by Texas Civil Practice & Remedies Code §132.001. Tex. R. Civ. P. 145(a) & cmt. (2016); *see* Tex. Civ. Prac. & Rem. Code §132.001.

The party must include in the Statement evidence of her inability to afford costs, attaching documentary evidence if applicable and available. *See* Tex. R. Civ. P. 145(e). See ***O'Connor's Texas Rules***, "Evidence," ch. 2-J, §3.3, p. 207.

PLAINTIFF'S DECLARATION RELATING TO PREVIOUS FILINGS

"My name is {❶ *full name of inmate*}, my date of birth is {❷ *date of birth*}, and {❸ *my inmate identifying number is _____/I do not have an inmate identifying number*}. I am presently incarcerated in {❹ *name of unit or county facility where incarcerated*} in {❺ *identify facility's city, county, state, and zip code*}. I am over 18 years of age, of sound mind, and capable of making this declaration.

I declare, under penalty of perjury, that the facts stated in this document are true and correct.

1. I am the plaintiff in this case.

2. I am unable to pay court costs in this case.

3. I have filed a Statement of Inability to Afford Payment of Court Costs in this case.

4. I have previously filed the following actions in which I was not represented by an attorney: {❻ *identify each suit, appeal, or original proceeding, excluding actions under the Texas Family Code, and for each action state the following: (1) the operative facts for which relief was sought, (2) the case name, cause number, and court in which the action was brought, (3) the identity of each party named in the action, and (4) the result of the action, including whether the action or a claim that was the basis of the action was dismissed as frivolous or malicious*}.

{*ADD PARAGRAPH 5 IF APPLICABLE*}

5. In cause number {❼ *number*}, which was dismissed as {❽ *frivolous/malicious*}, the final order affirming the dismissal was signed on {❾ *date*}.

{*CHOOSE APPROPRIATE PARAGRAPH 6*}

6. A certified copy of the trust-account statement required by Texas Civil Practice & Remedies Code section 14.006(f) is attached as Exhibit {❿ *letter*}."

6. I am unable to secure a certified copy of the trust-account statement as required by Texas Civil Practice & Remedies Code section 14.006(f) because {⓫ *state reason*}. I request that the Court require {⓬ *name of unit or county facility where incarcerated*} to provide the trust-account statement."

◄ *Continued on next page* ►

Executed on ________________, 20___.

____
{⓭ *Name of inmate*}

SEE: Tex. R. Civ. P. 145, 217
Tex. Civ. Prac. & Rem. Code §14.001 et seq., §132.001
O'Connor's Texas Rules * Civil Trials (2019), "Previous filings," ch. 2-J, §4.2.1, p. 208

ADD: STYLE OF THE CASE – FORM 1B:2

ATTACH: Certified copy of the trust-account statement

NOTE: This form can be modified to be an affidavit rather than an unsworn declaration. *See* Tex. Civ. Prac. & Rem. Code §14.004(a). For the general form for an affidavit, see FORM 1B:8.

PLAINTIFF'S DECLARATION RELATING TO GRIEVANCE-SYSTEM CLAIM

"My name is {❶ *full name of inmate*}, my date of birth is {❷ *date of birth*}, and {❸ *my inmate identifying number is ______/I do not have an inmate identifying number*}. I am presently incarcerated in {❹ *name of unit or county facility where incarcerated*} in {❺ *identify facility's city, county, state, and zip code*}. I am over 18 years of age, of sound mind, and capable of making this declaration.

I declare, under penalty of perjury, that the facts stated in this document are true and correct.

1. I am the plaintiff in this case.

2. I am unable to pay court costs in this case.

3. I have filed a Statement of Inability to Afford Payment of Court Costs in this case.

{*CHOOSE APPROPRIATE PARAGRAPH 4*}

4. On {❻ *date*}, I filed a grievance for the claim subject to this suit as required by Texas Government Code section 501.008(d). Tex. Civ. Prac. & Rem. Code §14.005(a). I received a copy of the written decision on {❼ *date*}. A copy of the decision is attached as Exhibit {❽ *letter*}."

4. On {❾ *date*}, I filed a grievance for the claim subject to this suit as required by Texas Government Code section 501.008(d). Tex. Civ. Prac. & Rem. Code §14.005(a). I have not received a copy of the written decision. {❿ *Elaborate.*}"

SEE: Tex. R. Civ. P. 145, 217
Tex. Civ. Prac. & Rem. Code §§14.005, 132.001
O'Connor's Texas Rules * Civil Trials (2019), "Grievance-system claims," ch. 2-J, §4.2.2, p. 209

ADD: STYLE OF THE CASE – FORM 1B:2

ATTACH: Copy of any grievance decision received

NOTE: This form can be modified to be an affidavit rather than an unsworn declaration. *See* Tex. Civ. Prac. & Rem. Code §14.004(a). For the general form for an affidavit, see FORM 1B:8.

An inmate must file a grievance-system claim in the court within 30 days after receiving the written grievance decision or, if a written decision has not been received, no earlier than 180 days after the grievance was filed. *See* Tex. Civ. Prac. & Rem. Code §14.005(b) (inmate must file claim "before the 31st day after the date" inmate receives written grievance decision); Tex. Gov't Code §501.008(d)(2) (if inmate has not received written grievance decision, claim must be filed no earlier than 180th day after

Continued on next page

grievance was filed). Although Texas Civil Practice & Remedies Code §14.005(b) says the claim must be filed "before the 31st day" after the inmate receives the written grievance decision, some courts have interpreted the deadline as "within 31 days." *See, e.g.*, ***Remsburg v. Marquez***, 542 S.W.3d 823, 828 (Tex.App.—Amarillo 2018, no pet.); ***Moreland v. Johnson***, 95 S.W.3d 392, 395 (Tex.App.—Houston [1st Dist.] 2002, no pet.); ***Retzlaff v. TDCJ***, 94 S.W.3d 650, 652 (Tex.App.—Houston [14th Dist.] 2002, pet. denied); ***Perez v. TDCJ***, No. 06-14-00065-CV (Tex.App.—Texarkana 2015, no pet.) (memo op.; 2-20-15). To avoid dismissal of a claim under Texas Civil Practice & Remedies Code §14.005, an inmate should follow the language of the statute and file before the 31st day—that is, within 30 days.

If no written decision has been provided, some courts have held that the inmate can satisfy the requirements of Texas Civil Practice & Remedies Code §14.005(a) by filing an affidavit or unsworn declaration that states the filing dates of her grievances and that specifically describes why she cannot give the date of the grievance decision or provide a copy of the decision. *See, e.g.*, ***Mahuron v. TDCJ***, 494 S.W.3d 377, 381-82 (Tex.App.—Waco 2015, no pet.). See ***O'Connor's Texas Rules***, "Requirements for affidavit or declaration," ch. 2-J, §4.2.2(1), p. 209.

DEFENDANT'S MOTION TO DISMISS INDIGENT PARTY'S SUIT

Defendant, {❶ *name*}, asks the Court to dismiss plaintiff's suit.

INTRODUCTION

1. Plaintiff, {❷ *name*}, sued defendant, {❸ *name*}, for {❹ *state basis of suit*}.

2. {❺ *State other relevant facts about the suit.*}

BACKGROUND

3. Plaintiff filed a Statement of Inability to Afford Payment of Court Costs under Texas Rule of Civil Procedure 145 to proceed as an indigent party and prosecute this suit without paying costs. {*See* ***O'Connor's Texas Rules****, "Statement of Inability to Afford Payment of Costs," ch. 2-J, §3, p. 207.*}

4. {❻ *State other facts relevant to the motion.*}

ARGUMENT & AUTHORITIES

{*CHOOSE APPROPRIATE PARAGRAPHS 5-13*}

{*Suit filed by indigent party who is not an inmate*}

5. A court has the authority to dismiss a suit filed by an indigent party if the allegation of poverty in the Statement of Inability to Afford Payment of Court Costs is false. *See* Tex. Civ. Prac. & Rem. Code §13.001(a)(1). {❼ *Elaborate.*} {*See* ***O'Connor's Texas Rules****, "Not indigent," ch. 2-J, §6.2.1(1), p. 210.*}

6. A court has the authority to dismiss a suit filed by an indigent party if the action is frivolous or malicious because the claim has no arguable basis in fact. Tex. Civ. Prac. & Rem. Code §13.001(a)(2), (b)(2). {❽ *Elaborate.*} {*See* ***O'Connor's Texas Rules****, "Action is frivolous or malicious," ch. 2-J, §6.2.1(2), p. 211.*}

7. A court has the authority to dismiss a suit filed by an indigent party if the action is frivolous or malicious because the claim has no arguable basis in law. Tex. Civ. Prac. & Rem. Code §13.001(a)(2), (b)(2). {❾ *Elaborate.*} {*See* ***O'Connor's Texas Rules****, "Action is frivolous or malicious," ch. 2-J, §6.2.1(2), p. 211.*} No hearing is necessary for the Court to determine this issue. {*See* ***O'Connor's Texas Rules****, "Hearing," ch. 2-J, §6.3, p. 212.*}

◄ *Continued on next page* ►

{*Suit filed by indigent party who is an inmate*}

8. A court has the authority to dismiss a suit filed by an inmate if the allegation of poverty in the Statement of Inability to Afford Payment of Court Costs is false. *See* Tex. Civ. Prac. & Rem. Code §14.003(a)(1). {⑩ *Elaborate.*} {*See* ***O'Connor's Texas Rules****, "Not indigent," ch. 2-J, §6.2.2(1), p. 211.*}

9. A court has the authority to dismiss a suit filed by an inmate if the action is frivolous or malicious because the claim has no arguable basis in fact. Tex. Civ. Prac. & Rem. Code §14.003(a)(2), (b)(2). {⑪ *Elaborate.*} {*See* ***O'Connor's Texas Rules****, "Claim is frivolous or malicious," ch. 2-J, §6.2.2(2)(b), p. 211.*}

10. A court has the authority to dismiss a suit filed by an inmate if the action is frivolous or malicious because the claim has no arguable basis in law. Tex. Civ. Prac. & Rem. Code §14.003(a)(2), (b)(2). {⑫ *Elaborate.*} {*See* ***O'Connor's Texas Rules****, "Claim is frivolous or malicious," ch. 2-J, §6.2.2(2)(b), p. 211.*} No hearing is necessary for the Court to determine this issue. {*See* ***O'Connor's Texas Rules****, "Hearing," ch. 2-J, §6.3, p. 212.*}

11. A court has the authority to dismiss a suit filed by an inmate if the inmate filed an {⑬ *affidavit/unsworn declaration*} relating to previous filings that the inmate knew was false. Tex. Civ. Prac. & Rem. Code §14.003(a)(3); *see id.* §14.004. {⑭ *Elaborate.*} {*See* ***O'Connor's Texas Rules****, "False filing," ch. 2-J, §6.2.2(3), p. 212.*}

12. A court has the authority to dismiss a suit filed by an inmate if the action is frivolous or malicious because the claim is substantially similar to and arises from the same operative facts as a previous claim filed by the inmate. Tex. Civ. Prac. & Rem. Code §14.003(a)(2), (b)(4). {⑮ *Elaborate.*} {*See* ***O'Connor's Texas Rules****, "Claim is frivolous or malicious," ch. 2-J, §6.2.2(2)(d), p. 211.*}

13. A court must dismiss a suit filed by an inmate if the action is filed more than 30 days after the date the inmate receives a written decision from the grievance system. Tex. Civ. Prac. & Rem. Code §14.005(b). {⑯ *Elaborate.*} {*See* ***O'Connor's Texas Rules****, "Deadline for filing with court," ch. 2-J, §4.2.2(2), p. 209.*}

CONCLUSION

14. {⑰ *Briefly summarize the motion.*}

PRAYER

{*CHOOSE APPROPRIATE PARAGRAPH 15*}

15. For these reasons, defendant asks the Court to set defendant's motion to dismiss for hearing and, after the hearing, dismiss plaintiff's suit. {*See **O'Connor's Texas Rules**, "Hearing," ch. 2-J, §6.3, p. 212.*}

15. Because the Court can determine from the pleadings that this case has no arguable basis in law, defendant asks the Court to dismiss the suit without a hearing. {*See **O'Connor's Texas Rules**, "Hearing," ch. 2-J, §6.3, p. 212.*}

SEE: Tex. R. Civ. P. 145
Tex. Civ. Prac. & Rem. Code §§13.001, 14.003, 14.005
O'Connor's Texas Rules * Civil Trials (2019), "Summary Dismissal," ch. 2-J, §6, p. 210

ADD: STYLE OF THE CASE – FORM 1B:2
SIGNATURE BLOCK – FORM 1B:3
CERTIFICATE OF CONFERENCE – FORM 1B:12, if necessary
CERTIFICATE OF SERVICE – FORM 1B:13

ATTACH: AFFIDAVIT – FORM 1B:8, if necessary
NOTICE OF HEARING OR SUBMISSION – FORM 1E:1
ORDER – FORM 2J:5

NOTE: A party claiming indigence must file a Statement of Inability to Afford Payment of Court Costs. *See* Tex. R. Civ. P. 145(a), (b). Texas Rule of Civil Procedure 145 no longer refers to the party filing the Statement as an "indigent"; instead, it uses the term "declarant." *See* Tex. R. Civ. P. 145(a). See FORM 2J:1. In this form, "indigent party" refers to the party filing the Statement.

Before or after service of process, any party, the clerk, or the court itself may move for a hearing to determine whether the court may dismiss a claim under Texas Civil Practice & Remedies Code §13.001 or §14.003. *See* Tex. Civ. Prac. & Rem. Code §§13.001(c), 14.003(c).

ORDER ON MOTION TO DISMISS INDIGENT PARTY'S SUIT

On __________, 20___, plaintiff, {❶ *name*}, filed this suit and a Statement of Inability to Afford Payment of Court Costs under Texas Rule of Civil Procedure 145 to proceed as an indigent party and prosecute this suit without paying costs. After considering the original petition, the Statement, defendant's motion to dismiss, and arguments of counsel, the Court

{*CHOOSE APPROPRIATE ORDER*}

DENIES the motion and retains plaintiff's suit on the Court's docket.

GRANTS the motion and dismisses plaintiff's suit {❷ *with/without*} prejudice because

{*CHOOSE APPROPRIATE FINDING*}

{*Suit filed by indigent party who is not an inmate*}

Ⓐ plaintiff's allegation of poverty in the Statement of Inability to Afford Payment of Court Costs is false.

Ⓑ plaintiff's claim is {❸ *frivolous/malicious/frivolous and malicious*}.

{*Suit filed by indigent party who is an inmate*}

Ⓒ plaintiff's allegation of poverty in the Statement of Inability to Afford Payment of Court Costs is false.

Ⓓ plaintiff's claim is {❹ *frivolous/malicious/frivolous and malicious*}.

Ⓔ plaintiff filed an {❺ *affidavit/unsworn declaration*} relating to previous filings that plaintiff knew was false.

Ⓕ plaintiff's claim is substantially similar to and based on the same operative facts as a previous claim filed by plaintiff.

Ⓖ plaintiff's claim was filed more than 30 days after the date that plaintiff received a written decision from the grievance system.

SIGNED on ______________, 20___.

____
PRESIDING JUDGE

FORM 2J:5 ORDER ON MOTION TO DISMISS INDIGENT PARTY'S SUIT

SEE: Tex. R. Civ. P. 145
Tex. Civ. Prac. & Rem. Code §§13.001, 14.003, 14.005
O'Connor's Texas Rules * Civil Trials (2019), "Order on summary dismissal," ch. 2-J, §6.6, p. 212

ADD: STYLE OF THE CASE – FORM 1B:2
CERTIFICATE OF SERVICE – FORM 1B:13, if proposed order served separately from motion

NOTE: See notes under FORM 2J:4.

DEFENDANT'S MOTION TO CHALLENGE PLAINTIFF'S CLAIM OF INABILITY TO AFFORD PAYMENT OF COSTS

Defendant, {❶ *name*}, asks the Court to order plaintiff, {❷ *name*}, to pay court costs, as defined by Texas Rule of Civil Procedure 145(c).

INTRODUCTION

1. Plaintiff, {❸ *name*}, sued defendant, {❹ *name*}, for {❺ *state basis of suit*}.

2. {❻ *State other relevant facts about the suit.*}

BACKGROUND

3. Plaintiff filed a Statement of Inability to Afford Payment of Court Costs under Texas Rule of Civil Procedure 145 to proceed as an indigent party and prosecute this suit without paying costs. {*See **O'Connor's Texas Rules**, "Statement of Inability to Afford Payment of Costs," ch. 2-J, §3, p. 207.*}

4. {❼ *State other facts relevant to the motion.*}

ARGUMENT & AUTHORITIES

5. A court has the authority to order a plaintiff who has filed a Statement of Inability to Afford Payment of Court Costs to pay costs if the Statement was materially false when made or, because of changed circumstances, is no longer true in material respects. Tex. R. Civ. P. 145(f)(1) & cmt. (2016). {*See **O'Connor's Texas Rules**, "False Statement or changed circumstances," ch. 2-J, §7.1.1, p. 213.*} Costs are defined as any fee charged by the court or an officer of the court that could be taxed in a bill of costs, including but not limited to, filing fees, fees for issuing service of process, fees for a court-appointed professional, and fees charged by the clerk or court reporter for preparing the appellate record. Tex. R. Civ. P. 145(c). {*See **O'Connor's Texas Rules**, "Costs," ch. 2-J, §2.2, p. 206.*}

{*CHOOSE APPROPRIATE PARAGRAPH 6*}

6. The Court should order plaintiff to pay costs because plaintiff's Statement of Inability to Afford Payment of Court Costs was materially false when made. {❽ *Elaborate.*}

6. The Court should order plaintiff to pay costs because, due to changed circumstances, plaintiff's Statement of Inability to Afford Payment of Court Costs is no longer true in material respects. {❾ *Elaborate.*}

CONCLUSION

7. {⑩ *Briefly summarize the motion.*}

PRAYER

8. For these reasons, defendant asks the Court to set defendant's motion for hearing and, after the hearing, order plaintiff to pay costs before proceeding with this suit. {*See* ***O'Connor's Texas Rules***, *"Hearing," ch. 2-J, §7.2, p. 213.*}

SEE: Tex. R. Civ. P. 145
O'Connor's Texas Rules * Civil Trials (2019), "Motion to challenge," ch. 2-J, §7.1, p. 212

ADD: STYLE OF THE CASE – FORM 1B:2
SIGNATURE BLOCK – FORM 1B:3
CERTIFICATE OF SERVICE – FORM 1B:13

ATTACH: NOTICE OF HEARING OR SUBMISSION – FORM 1E:1
ORDER – FORM 2J:7

NOTE: A defendant challenging a plaintiff's claim of inability to afford payment of costs must present sworn evidence that the claim was materially false when made or that there has been a change in the plaintiff's circumstances that makes the claim no longer true; a motion made on mere information or belief is insufficient. *See* Tex. R. Civ. P. 145(f)(1) & cmt. (2016).

The court must conduct an oral evidentiary hearing before it can require the plaintiff to pay costs. Tex. R. Civ. P. 145(f)(5). The plaintiff must be given ten days' notice of the hearing on the challenge to her claim of inability to afford payment of costs. *Id.*

Before the 2016 amendments to Texas Rule of Civil Procedure 145, if an affidavit of indigence was accompanied by an attorney's Interest on Lawyers' Trust Accounts (IOLTA) certificate confirming the party was screened by an IOLTA-funded program for income eligibility under IOLTA guidelines, then the affidavit could not be contested. *See* Tex. R. Civ. P. 145(c) (pre-9-1-16 version). Under the amended rule, a party can submit evidence that she is being represented through a legal-aid service provider, as defined in Rule 145(e)(2), to support her claim that she is unable to afford costs; however, such evidence does not prohibit a challenge of the claim, except in a suit filed in justice court. *See* Tex. R. Civ. P. 145(e)(2), (f), 502.3(c).

In certain circumstances, the court may require the plaintiff to prove her inability to afford costs. See ***O'Connor's Texas Rules***, "Evidence of ability to afford costs," ch. 2-J, §7.1.3, p. 213. The court reporter can also file a motion asking the plaintiff to prove her inability to afford costs when she requests preparation of a reporter's record but cannot pay for the record. Tex. R. Civ. P. 145(f)(3).

This form can be modified to be used by a court clerk or an attorney ad litem appointed to represent a parent under Texas Family Code §107.013. *See* Tex. R. Civ. P. 145(f)(1), (f)(2).

ORDER ON DEFENDANT'S MOTION TO CHALLENGE
PLAINTIFF'S CLAIM OF INABILITY TO AFFORD PAYMENT OF COSTS

After considering defendant's motion to challenge plaintiff's claim of inability to afford payment of costs, the evidence presented at the hearing, and the arguments of counsel, the Court

{*CHOOSE APPROPRIATE ORDER*}

DENIES the motion and orders that plaintiff be able to proceed with this suit without paying costs.

GRANTS the motion and finds that

{*CHOOSE APPROPRIATE FINDING*}

Ⓐ plaintiff's Statement of Inability to Afford Payment of Court Costs was materially false when made. {❶ *Explain how plaintiff can afford to pay costs.*}

Ⓑ because circumstances have changed, plaintiff's Statement of Inability to Afford Payment of Court Costs is no longer true in material respects. {❷ *Explain how plaintiff can afford to pay costs.*}

{*ADD SENTENCE BELOW IF MOTION GRANTED*}

The Court therefore ORDERS plaintiff to pay costs associated with this suit.

SIGNED on ______________, 20___.

____
PRESIDING JUDGE

SEE: Tex. R. Civ. P. 145
O'Connor's Texas Rules * Civil Trials (2019), "Order," ch. 2-J, §7.3, p. 214

ADD: STYLE OF THE CASE – FORM 1B:2
CERTIFICATE OF SERVICE – FORM 1B:13, if proposed order served separately from motion or response

NOTE: If the court finds that the declarant can afford only part of the costs, the court may order the declarant to make partial payment. Tex. R. Civ. P. 145(f)(7). The court may also order the declarant to pay costs in installments. *Id.*

Only the plaintiff can file a motion challenging the trial court's order issued under Texas Rule of Civil Procedure 145(f). Tex. R. Civ. P. 145(g)(1). See ***O'Connor's Texas Appeals***, FORM 2A:5. The motion must be filed in the court of appeals within 10 days after the trial court's order is signed; the court of appeals may extend the deadline, however, by 15 days for good cause. *See* Tex. R. Civ. P. 145(g)(1), (g)(2).

CHAPTER 3. DEFENDANT'S PLEADINGS

TABLE OF CONTENTS

TABLE OF CONTENTS

{*Letterhead*}

{❶ *Date*}

{❷ *Name of consumer's attorney*}
{❸ *Address 1*}
{❹ *Address 2*}
{❺ *City, state, zip code*}

RE: {❻ *Description of claim*}

Dear {❼ *name of consumer's attorney*}:

I represent {❽ *name of defendant*}, who has retained me to defend against the claim asserted by your client, {❾ *name of consumer*}, for violation of the Texas Deceptive Trade Practices Act (DTPA), Texas Business & Commerce Code section 17.41 et seq. This letter is notice of my client's request to inspect your client's {❿ *describe goods*} under Texas Business & Commerce Code section 17.505(a). {*See* ***O'Connor's Texas COA****, "Inspection," ch. 8, §6.1.5, p. 249.*}

On {⓫ *date*}, your client sent notice of a claim under the DTPA to my client. My client wishes to inspect the goods giving rise to this claim so that my client can evaluate the claim. My client requests that your client make the goods available for inspection {⓬ *describe time, place, and manner of inspection requested*}.

I look forward to hearing from you soon.

Sincerely,

____

{⓭ *Name of defendant's attorney*}

SEE: Tex. Bus. & Com. Code §17.505
O'Connor's Texas Causes of Action (2019), "Deceptive Trade Practices Act," ch. 8, p. 209

NOTE: During the 60-day period following the plaintiff's written notice of its claim, the defendant may make a written request to inspect the goods that are the subject of the plaintiff's claim. Tex. Bus. & Com. Code §17.505(a).

{*Letterhead*}

{❶ *Date*}

{❷ *Name of consumer's attorney*}
{❸ *Address 1*}
{❹ *Address 2*}
{❺ *City, state, zip code*}

RE: {❻ *Description of claim*}

Dear {❼ *name of consumer's attorney*}:

I represent {❽ *name of defendant*}, who has retained me to defend against the claim asserted by your client, {❾ *name of consumer*}, for violation of the Texas Deceptive Trade Practices Act (DTPA), Texas Business & Commerce Code section 17.41 et seq. On {❿ *date*}, my client received a demand letter from your client to settle this claim. This letter is notice of my client's agreement to the terms of that demand letter. {*See* ***O'Connor's Texas COA****, "Timing of offer," ch. 8, §7.1.2, p. 249.*}

To resolve this matter, my client requests that your client provide a full and final release of all claims against my client. In exchange, my client will tender the following to settle your client's claims: {*See* ***O'Connor's Texas COA****, "Form of offer," ch. 8, §7.1.1, p. 249.*}

{*CHOOSE APPROPRIATE PARAGRAPH 1*}

1. ${⓫ *Amount*}, which represents all monetary damages.

1. {⓬ *Identify other consideration*}, reduced to its cash value of ${⓭ *amount*}, which represents the cash value of all damages.

2. ${⓮ *Amount*}, which represents the attorney fees that were reasonably and necessarily incurred by your client, as of the date of this offer, in asserting the claim against my client.

This offer is made to avoid any further expenses and is not an admission of liability.

Please consult with your client about this settlement offer. This offer is valid until {⓯ *time*} on {⓰ *date*}.

I look forward to hearing from you within the next 30 days.

Sincerely,

____

{⓱ *Name of defendant's attorney*}

SEE: Tex. Bus. & Com. Code §§17.505, 17.5052, 17.506(d)
O'Connor's Texas Rules * Civil Trials (2019), "Offer to settle," ch. 3-A, §2.2, p. 219
O'Connor's Texas Causes of Action (2019), "Deceptive Trade Practices Act," ch. 8, p. 209

NOTE: The defendant can assert as a defense that it timely tendered an amount that satisfied the consumer's demand for economic damages, mental-anguish damages, and all expenses, including attorney fees. Tex. Bus. & Com. Code §17.506(d).

If a settlement offer is not accepted on or before the 30th day after it is made, the offer is deemed rejected. Tex. Bus. & Com. Code §17.5052(e).

{*Letterhead*}

{❶ *Date*}

{❷ *Name of consumer's attorney*}
{❸ *Address 1*}
{❹ *Address 2*}
{❺ *City, state, zip code*}

RE: {❻ *Description of claim*}

Dear {❼ *name of consumer's attorney*}:

I represent {❽ *name of defendant*}, who has retained me to defend against the claim asserted by your client, {❾ *name of consumer*}, for violation of the Texas Deceptive Trade Practices Act (DTPA), Texas Business & Commerce Code section 17.41 et seq. On {❿ *date*}, my client received a demand letter from your client. This letter is notice of my client's rejection of the terms of that demand letter and my client's counteroffer to settle on other terms.

My client cannot settle your client's claims for the amount demanded in your notice letter because my client disagrees with your assertions that {⓫ *list facts alleged in notice letter that are disputed*}.

However, in exchange for a full and final release of all claims against my client, my client will tender the following to settle your client's claims: {*See* ***O'Connor's Texas COA****, "Form of offer," ch. 8, §7.1.1, p. 249.*}

{*CHOOSE APPROPRIATE PARAGRAPH 1*}

1. ${⓬ *Amount*}, which represents all monetary damages.

1. {⓭ *Identify other consideration*}, reduced to its cash value of ${⓮ *amount*}, which represents the cash value of all damages.

2. ${⓯ *Amount*}, which represents the attorney fees that were reasonably and necessarily incurred by your client, as of the date of this offer, in asserting the claim against my client.

This offer is made to avoid any further expenses and is not an admission of liability.

Please consult with your client about this settlement offer. This offer is valid until {⓰ *time*} on {⓱ *date*}.

FORM 3A:3

I look forward to hearing from you within the next 30 days.

Sincerely,

____

{⓲ *Name of defendant's attorney*}

SEE: Tex. Bus. & Com. Code §§17.505, 17.5052
O'Connor's Texas Rules * Civil Trials (2019), "Offer to settle," ch. 3-A, §2.2, p. 219
O'Connor's Texas Causes of Action (2019), "Offers of settlement," ch. 8, §7.1, p. 249

NOTE: **If a settlement offer is not accepted on or before the 30th day after it is made, the offer is deemed rejected. Tex. Bus. & Com. Code §17.5052(e).**

{*Letterhead*}

{❶ *Date*}

{❷ *Name of consumer's attorney*}
{❸ *Address 1*}
{❹ *Address 2*}
{❺ *City, state, zip code*}

RE: {❻ *Description of claim*}

Dear {❼ *name of consumer's attorney*}:

I represent {❽ *name of defendant*}, who has retained me to defend against the claim asserted by your client, {❾ *name of consumer*}, for violation of the Texas Deceptive Trade Practices Act (DTPA), Texas Business & Commerce Code section 17.41 et seq. On {❿ *date*}, my client received a demand letter from your client. This letter is notice of my client's rejection of the terms of that demand letter.

I have reviewed your client's claims and have determined there is no evidence to substantiate them. First, my client did not violate the DTPA, as your letter alleges. {⓫ *Identify specific reasons and explain why there was no DTPA violation, e.g., my client's acts and practices were not false, misleading, or deceptive as defined by Texas Business & Commerce Code section 17.46(b).*} Second, my client specifically denies {⓬ *state disputed facts*}.

However, even if your client's allegations are true, the amount demanded for {⓭ *list damages contained in consumer's notice letter, e.g., actual damages, expenses, and attorney fees*} far exceeds a fair and equitable offer. {⓮ *Elaborate.*}

My client will defend this claim if your client decides to file suit. My client is aware of additional expenses that will be incurred by not settling this claim; however, my client will not agree to settle the disputed claim for the amount of money your client demands.

Please contact me with any additional information or questions you may have.

Sincerely,

____
{⓯ *Name of defendant's attorney*}

Form 3A:4 DTPA Rejection of Settlement Offer

SEE: Tex. Bus. & Com. Code §§17.46, 17.505
O'Connor's Texas Rules * Civil Trials (2019), "Offer to settle," ch. 3-A, §2.2, p. 219
O'Connor's Texas Causes of Action (2019), "Deceptive Trade Practices Act," ch. 8, p. 209

DEFENDANT'S AFFIDAVIT CERTIFYING REJECTION OF SETTLEMENT OFFER

STATE OF TEXAS §
{❶ ______} COUNTY §

Before me, the undersigned notary, on this day personally appeared {❷ *name of affiant*}, the affiant, whose identity is known to me. After I administered an oath, affiant testified as follows:

1. "My name is {❸ *name of affiant*}, and I am the attorney for defendant, {❹ *name*}, in this case. I am over 18 years of age, of sound mind, and capable of making this affidavit. The facts stated in this affidavit are within my personal knowledge and are true and correct.

2. "On {❺ *date*}, defendant, {❻ *name*}, received plaintiff {❼ *name of consumer*}'s notice of claim under the Texas Deceptive Trade Practices Act, Texas Business & Commerce Code section 17.505(a). I attach a copy of plaintiff's notice to this affidavit as Exhibit {❽ *letter*} and incorporate it by reference.

3. "On {❾ *date*}, defendant responded to plaintiff's notice of claim by making an offer of settlement, which complied with Texas Business & Commerce Code section 17.5052(a) and (d). I attach a copy of defendant's offer to this affidavit as Exhibit {❿ *letter*} and incorporate it by reference.

4. "I attach a copy of {⓫ *identify document showing proof of service of offer on plaintiff or plaintiff's attorney, e.g., the certified-mail receipt showing service of defendant's offer of settlement*} as Exhibit {⓬ *letter*}, as proof of service of the offer.

{*CHOOSE APPROPRIATE PARAGRAPH 5*}

5. "On {⓭ *date*}, plaintiff rejected defendant's offer. I attach a copy of plaintiff's letter of rejection as Exhibit {⓮ *letter*} and incorporate it by reference."

5. "Plaintiff did not accept defendant's {⓯ *tender/offer*}."

FORM 3A:5

____
{16 *Name of affiant*}
Texas Bar No. {17 _____}
{18 *Address 1*}
{19 *Address 2*}
{20 *City, state, zip code*}
Tel. {21 __________}
Fax {22 __________}
{23 *E-mail address*}

Sworn to and subscribed before me by {24 *name of affiant*} on __________, 20___.

____
Notary Public in and for
the State of Texas

SEE: Tex. Bus. & Com. Code §§17.505(a), 17.5052(a), (d), 17.506(d)
O'Connor's Texas Rules * Civil Trials (2019), "Offer to settle," ch. 3-A, §2.2, p. 219
O'Connor's Texas Causes of Action (2019), "Rejected offer," ch. 8, §7.1.4, p. 250

ADD: STYLE OF THE CASE – FORM 1B:2
CERTIFICATE OF SERVICE – FORM 1B:13

ATTACH: NOTICE UNDER THE DTPA – FORM 2A:4
DTPA OFFER OF SETTLEMENT – FORM 3A:2
Plaintiff's letter of rejection, if applicable

NOTE: If an offer is rejected, the defendant should file the offer with an affidavit certifying its rejection. *See* Tex. Bus. & Com. Code §17.5052(f).

See notes under FORM 1B:8.

DEFENDANT'S SPECIAL APPEARANCE

Defendant, {❶ *name*}, asks the Court to sustain {❷ *his/her/its*} special appearance and dismiss plaintiff {❸ *name*}'s suit.

INTRODUCTION

1. Plaintiff, {❹ *name*}, sued defendant, {❺ *name*}, for {❻ *state basis of suit*}.

2. {❼ *If special appearance is defendant's initial pleading, add appropriate identification for each defendant from FORM 3E:1.*}

3. {❽ *State other relevant facts about the suit.*}

BACKGROUND

4. Defendant is a nonresident of Texas and has had no purposeful contacts with this state. Defendant is {❾ *identify defendant's status and where defendant resides or does business, e.g., defendant is a corporation that has its principal place of business in Florida*}.

5. {❿ *State other facts relevant to the special appearance.*}

ARGUMENT & AUTHORITIES

6. Texas courts do not have jurisdiction over a nonresident defendant unless the defendant has purposefully established "minimum contacts" with Texas and the court's exercise of jurisdiction over the defendant comports with "fair play and substantial justice." *Burger King Corp. v. Rudzewicz*, 471 U.S. 462, 474-76 (1985); *Old Republic Nat'l Title Ins. Co. v. Bell*, 549 S.W.3d 550, 559 (Tex. 2018); *TV Azteca, S.A.B. de C.V. v. Ruiz*, 490 S.W.3d 29, 36-37 (Tex. 2016); *Moki Mac River Expeditions v. Drugg*, 221 S.W.3d 569, 575 (Tex. 2007).

A. No minimum contacts.

7. Texas courts must determine whether a nonresident defendant has purposefully established minimum contacts with Texas. *Moki Mac*, 221 S.W.3d at 575; *CSR Ltd. v. Link*, 925 S.W.2d 591, 594 (Tex. 1996); *Guardian Royal Exch. Assurance, Ltd. v. English China Clays, P.L.C.*, 815 S.W.2d 223, 226 (Tex. 1991). To prove it had no minimum contacts with Texas, the defendant must show that (1) it did not purposefully avail itself of the privilege of conducting activities within Texas, and (2) any contacts it may have had with Texas do not give rise to specific or general jurisdiction. *See M&F Worldwide Corp. v. Pepsi-Cola Metro. Bottling Co.*, 512 S.W.3d 878, 885-86 (Tex. 2017); *Moki Mac*, 221 S.W.3d at 575-76; *Commonwealth Gen. Corp. v. York*, 177 S.W.3d 923, 925

(Tex. 2005); *BMC Software Belg., N.V. v. Marchand*, 83 S.W.3d 789, 795-96 (Tex. 2002). {*See* ***O'Connor's Texas Rules****, "No minimum contacts," ch. 3-B, §2.4.2, p. 226.*}

8. For purposeful availment to be established, a defendant's acts must be purposeful rather than random, isolated, or fortuitous, and the defendant must have sought some benefit, advantage, or profit in availing itself of the Texas jurisdiction. *M&F Worldwide*, 512 S.W.3d at 886; *Searcy v. Parex Res., Inc.*, 496 S.W.3d 58, 67 (Tex. 2016); *TV Azteca*, 490 S.W.3d at 37-38; *Retamco Operating, Inc. v. Republic Drilling Co.*, 278 S.W.3d 333, 338-39 (Tex. 2009); *Moki Mac*, 221 S.W.3d at 575; *Michiana Easy Livin' Country, Inc. v. Holten*, 168 S.W.3d 777, 785 (Tex. 2005). Specifically, defendant did not purposefully avail {⓫ *himself/herself/itself*} of the privilege of conducting activities within Texas for the following reasons:

{*CHOOSE APPROPRIATE REASONS*}

a. When defendant put products in the stream of commerce, defendant did not know that some of them would reach Texas and did not engage in conduct indicating an intent to serve the Texas market. *See Spir Star AG v. Kimich*, 310 S.W.3d 868, 873 (Tex. 2010); *Moki Mac*, 221 S.W.3d at 576-77; *Michiana*, 168 S.W.3d at 786. {⓬ *Explain, e.g., defendant did not direct sales to Texas and did not design the product for Texas or advertise in Texas.*} {*See* ***O'Connor's Texas Rules****, "Analyzing contacts – stream of commerce," ch. 3-B, §2.4.2(1)(b), p. 227.*}

b. When defendant aired its broadcast, which originated outside Texas, defendant did not know that the broadcast could be viewed in Texas and did not intentionally target the Texas market with its broadcast. *See TV Azteca*, 490 S.W.3d at 46-47. {⓭ *Explain defendant's lack of knowledge about viewership in Texas and how defendant did not intentionally target the Texas market, e.g., the subject matter of the broadcast did not involve events in Texas, defendant did not rely on Texas sources to prepare the broadcast, defendant did not advertise in Texas or establish channels of regular communication with Texas customers.*} {⓮ *See* ***O'Connor's Texas Rules****, "Analyzing contacts – defamatory broadcasts," ch. 3-B, §2.4.2(1)(c), p. 228.*}

c. Defendant operates a passive website used only for {⓯ *providing contact information/advertising*}. *Riverside Exps., Inc. v. B.R. Crane & Equip., LLC*, 362 S.W.3d 649, 655 (Tex. App.—Houston [14th Dist.] 2011, pet. denied); *Waterman S.S. Corp. v. Ruiz*, 355 S.W.3d 387, 411-12 (Tex.

Continued on next page

FORM 3B:1

App.—Houston [1st Dist.] 2011, pet. denied); *Schexnayder v. Daniels*, 187 S.W.3d 238, 248-49 (Tex. App.—Texarkana 2006, pet. dism'd w.o.j.); *Exito Elecs., Co. v. Trejo*, 166 S.W.3d 839, 857-58 (Tex. App.—Corpus Christi 2005, no pet.). {⓰ *Elaborate.*} {*See* ***O'Connor's Texas Rules****, "Analyzing contacts – Internet activity," ch. 3-B, §2.4.2(1)(d), p. 228.*}

d. {⓱ *Identify other facts showing that defendant's acts were not purposeful.*} {*See* ***O'Connor's Texas Rules****, "No purposeful availment," ch. 3-B, §2.4.2(1), p. 226.*}

9. Texas courts cannot exercise specific jurisdiction over a nonresident defendant unless the plaintiff's litigation results from injuries that are alleged to arise from or relate to the defendant's contacts with Texas. *Moncrief Oil Int'l Inc. v. OAO Gazprom*, 414 S.W.3d 142, 156 (Tex. 2013); *Moki Mac*, 221 S.W.3d at 575; *BMC Software*, 83 S.W.3d at 796; *see Helicopteros Nacionales de Colom., S.A. v. Hall*, 466 U.S. 408, 414 & n.8 (1984); *M&F Worldwide*, 512 S.W.3d at 886; *TV Azteca*, 490 S.W.3d at 52. The defendant's acts must have a substantial connection with the operative facts of the litigation. *Old Republic Nat'l Title*, 549 S.W.3d at 559-60; *M&F Worldwide*, 512 S.W.3d at 890; *TV Azteca*, 490 S.W.3d at 52; *Spir Star AG v. Kimich*, 310 S.W.3d 868, 874 (Tex. 2010); *Retamco Operating*, 278 S.W.3d at 340. This Court does not have specific jurisdiction over defendant because plaintiff's cause of action does not arise from or relate to defendant's contacts with Texas. {⓲ *Explain how there is no substantial connection between the defendant's contacts and the operative facts of the litigation.*} {*See* ***O'Connor's Texas Rules****, "Specific jurisdiction," ch. 3-B, §2.4.2(2)(a), p. 230.*}

{*CHOOSE APPROPRIATE PARAGRAPH 10*}

{*For corporate defendant*}

10. Texas courts cannot exercise general jurisdiction over a nonresident defendant unless the defendant has affiliations with Texas that are so continuous and systematic as to render the defendant essentially "at home" in Texas. *See Daimler AG v. Bauman*, 571 U.S. 117, 138-39 (2014); *Searcy*, 496 S.W.3d at 72; *Booth v. Kontomitras*, 485 S.W.3d 461, 478 (Tex. App.—Beaumont 2016, no pet.); *Bautista v. Trinidad Drilling Ltd.*, 484 S.W.3d 491, 499 (Tex. App.—Houston [1st Dist.] 2016, no pet.). A corporation is considered at home where it is incorporated or where it has its principal place of business. *BNSF Ry. Co. v. Tyrrell*, ___ U.S. ___, 137 S. Ct. 1549, 1558 (2017); *see Daimler AG*, 571 U.S. at 137; *Bautista*, 484 S.W.3d at 500. A corporate defendant will be subject to general jurisdiction in a forum other than its place of incorporation or principal place of business only in an exceptional case in which its affiliations with that forum are so sub-

FORM 3B:1

stantial as to render it at home there. *BNSF Ry.*, ___ U.S. at ___, 137 S. Ct. at 1558; *see Daimler AG*, 571 U.S. at 139 n.19; *Searcy*, 496 S.W.3d at 72-73; *Booth*, 485 S.W.3d at 479-80. This Court does not have general jurisdiction over defendant because defendant is not incorporated in Texas and does not have its principal place of business in Texas, and this is not an exceptional case in which defendant's affiliations with Texas are so substantial as to render it at home in Texas. {19 *Elaborate.*} {*See* ***O'Connor's Texas Rules***, *"Corporate defendants," ch. 3-B, §2.4.2(2)(b)[1], p. 233.*}

{*For individual defendant*}

10. Texas courts cannot exercise general jurisdiction over a nonresident defendant unless the defendant has affiliations with Texas that are so continuous and systematic as to render the defendant essentially "at home" in Texas. *See Daimler AG v. Bauman*, 571 U.S. 117, 138-39 (2014); *Old Republic Nat'l Title*, 549 S.W.3d at 565; *Searcy*, 496 S.W.3d at 72; *Booth v. Kontomitras*, 485 S.W.3d 461, 478 (Tex. App.—Beaumont 2016, no pet.). An individual defendant is considered at home where she is domiciled. *See Daimler AG*, 571 U.S. at 137; *Henkel v. Emjo Invs., Ltd.*, 480 S.W.3d 1, 5 (Tex. App.—Houston [1st Dist.] 2015, no pet.). This Court does not have general jurisdiction over defendant because {20 *he/she*} is not domiciled in Texas. {21 *Elaborate.*} {*See* ***O'Connor's Texas Rules***, *"Individual defendants," ch. 3-B, §2.4.2(2)(b)[2], p. 233.*}

B. No fair play & substantial justice.

11. This Court's assertion of jurisdiction over defendant and {22 *his/her/its*} property will offend traditional notions of fair play and substantial justice and will be inconsistent with the constitutional requirements of due process; therefore, the Court should decline to exercise jurisdiction over defendant. *See Int'l Shoe Co. v. Washington*, 326 U.S. 310, 316 (1945); *TV Azteca*, 490 S.W.3d at 55; *Moncrief Oil*, 414 S.W.3d at 154-55; *Spir Star*, 310 S.W.3d at 878; *Guardian Royal*, 815 S.W.2d at 231. {23 *Explain how notions of fair play and substantial justice would be offended, analyzing each of the following factors: (1) the burden on defendant, (2) the interest of Texas in adjudicating the dispute, (3) plaintiff's interest in obtaining convenient and effective relief, (4) the interstate judicial system's interest (or the international interest) in obtaining the most efficient resolution of controversies, and (5) the shared interest of the states (or nations) in furthering fundamental social policies. Spir Star, 310 S.W.3d at 878; Guardian Royal, 815 S.W.2d at 231; Schexnayder v. Daniels, 187 S.W.3d 238, 246 (Tex. App.—Texarkana 2006, pet. dism'd w.o.j.).*} {*See* ***O'Connor's Texas Rules***, *"Exercise of jurisdiction unfair," ch. 3-B, §2.4.3, p. 234.*}

◄ *Continued on next page* ►

FORM 3B:1

CONCLUSION

12. Defendant does not have the minimum contacts with the State of Texas to justify a Texas court's assertion of jurisdiction. If this Court asserts jurisdiction over defendant, it will offend traditional notions of fair play and substantial justice.

PRAYER

13. For these reasons, defendant asks the Court to set {㉔ *his/her/its*} special appearance for hearing and, after the hearing, sustain defendant's special appearance and sign a final judgment dismissing plaintiff's cause of action. {*See* ***O'Connor's Texas Rules****, "Requesting hearing," ch. 3-B, §2.7, p. 235.*}

SEE: Tex. R. Civ. P. 120a
O'Connor's Texas Rules * Civil Trials (2019), "Grounds," ch. 3-B, §2.4, p. 225

ADD: STYLE OF THE CASE – FORM 1B:2
SIGNATURE BLOCK – FORM 1B:3
VERIFICATION – FORM 1B:7
CERTIFICATE OF SERVICE – FORM 1B:13

ATTACH: AFFIDAVIT – FORM 1B:8, with discovery excerpts or other evidence attached
NOTICE OF CURRENT/CHANGE OF ADDRESS – FORM 1B:14, if special appearance is defendant's initial pleading
NOTICE OF HEARING OR SUBMISSION – FORM 1E:1
ORDER – FORM 3B:4

NOTE: A special appearance must be heard and determined before a motion to transfer venue or any other pleading or motion. See ***O'Connor's Texas Rules***, "Due order of hearings," ch. 3-B, §2.3, p. 225.

In ***Daimler AG v. Bauman***, 571 U.S. 117 (2014), the U.S. Supreme Court changed the scope of the general-jurisdiction analysis. Specifically, the Court shifted the focus of the general-jurisdiction inquiry from whether the defendant had substantial, "continuous and systematic" contacts with the forum state to whether the defendant's affiliations (i.e., the defendant's contacts) are so continuous and systematic as to render it essentially "at home" in the forum state. ***Daimler AG***, 571 U.S. at 138-39 & n.20; *see* ***BNSF Ry. v. Tyrrell***, ___ U.S. ___, 137 S.Ct. 1549, 1558 (2017). An individual is considered at home where she is domiciled, and a corporation is considered at home where it is incorporated or where it has its principal place of business. *See* ***BNSF Ry.***, ___ U.S. at ___, 137 S.Ct. at 1558; ***Daimler AG***, 571 U.S. at 137. Although those forums are considered the model for exercising general jurisdiction, the Court suggested there could be an exceptional case in which a corporation's contacts are so substantial as to render it at home in a forum other than its place of incorporation or principal place of business. *See* ***Daimler AG***, 571 U.S. at 139 n.19 (suggesting that ***Perkins v. Benguet Consol. Mining Co.***, 342 U.S. 437 (1952), in which the Court found Ohio courts had general jurisdiction over D that was incorporated in the Philippines but temporarily moved its principal place of business to Ohio because of World War II, would qualify as "exceptional case"); ***Booth v. Kontomitras***, 485 S.W.3d 461, 479 (Tex.App.—Beaumont 2016, no pet.) (facts in ***Perkins*** illustrate type of continuous and systematic contacts by nonresident defendant that would suffice for general jurisdiction). The Court's opinion moves away from

previous opinions that allowed for general jurisdiction over a defendant "doing business" in the forum state. *See* ***Daimler AG***, 571 U.S. at 137-39 & n.20; *see, e.g.*, ***BNSF Ry.***, ___ U.S. at ___, 137 S.Ct. at 1559 (fact that D conducted in-state business in Montana was not sufficient to permit assertion of general jurisdiction over D for claims unrelated to that business; D must have been so heavily engaged in activity in Montana as to render it essentially at home there).

There is federal authority stating there may be exceptional cases in which an individual defendant may be considered "at home" in a forum outside her domicile. ***Reich v. Lopez***, 858 F.3d 55, 63 (2d Cir.2017); *see* ***Robatech Midwest, Inc. v. Leuthner***, No. 14-CV-1230-JPS (E.D.Wis.2015) (slip op.; 3-17-15). Texas authority, however, has been less clear on the issue. *See, e.g.*, ***Loya v. Taylor***, No. 01-14-01014-CV (Tex. App.—Houston [1st Dist.] 2016, pet. denied) (memo op.; 11-29-16) (D, who was domiciled in England, argued—and court agreed—that D's contacts with Texas were not continuous and systematic enough to render him at home there); *see also* ***Booth***, 485 S.W.3d at 479 n.8 (declining to address issue but questioning whether an individual's continuous and systematic contacts can be basis for general jurisdiction).

To determine whether contacts arising from Internet use are sufficient to establish personal jurisdiction, courts distinguish between three types of Internet activity: (1) websites used for transacting business (generally sufficient to establish minimum contacts), (2) passive websites used only to provide contact information or to advertise (generally insufficient to establish minimum contacts), and (3) interactive websites that allow for the exchange of information (personal jurisdiction determined by degree of interaction). See ***O'Connor's Texas Rules***, "Analyzing contacts – Internet activity," ch. 3-B, §2.4.2(1)(d), p. 228.

An agent's contacts can be attributed to its principal. In certain cases, a corporation's contacts can be attributed to its subsidiary corporation (or vice versa) or to its officers and employees. See ***O'Connor's Texas Rules***, "Analyzing contacts – attributed actions," ch. 3-B, §2.4.2(1)(e), p. 230.

In ***TV Azteca, S.A.B. de C.V. v. Ruiz***, 490 S.W.3d 29, 37-38 (Tex.2016), the Texas Supreme Court addressed purposeful availment in the context of allegedly defamatory television broadcasts. The Court held that the defendants, two Mexican broadcasting companies, had purposefully availed themselves of the Texas forum even though their broadcasts originated outside Texas and the subject matter of the broadcasts was unrelated to Texas. ***TV Azteca***, 490 S.W.3d at 47, 51-52. The Court likened its analysis to that used in stream-of-commerce cases and stated that a broadcaster's mere knowledge that its programs would be received in Texas is insufficient; there must be evidence of additional conduct establishing that the broadcaster had an intent or purpose to serve the Texas market. *E.g.*, *id.* at 46-47 (Ds "continuously and deliberately exploited" Texas market by physically entering Texas to produce and promote broadcasts, deriving substantial revenue by selling advertising to Texas businesses, and making substantial efforts to distribute programs and increase their popularity in Texas).

Under the "effects test" for determining personal jurisdiction based on a nonresident defendant's tortious conduct, there must be intentional conduct by the defendant that connects the defendant to the Texas forum itself—not merely to the resident plaintiff—for the court to have jurisdiction over the defendant. *See* ***Old Republic Nat'l Title Ins. v. Bell***, 549 S.W.3d 550, 564 (Tex.2018). Jurisdiction cannot turn on whether the defendant "directed a tort" at Texas or whether the plaintiff resided in Texas and felt the effects of the tort there. *See* ***Michiana Easy Livin' Country, Inc. v. Holten***, 168 S.W.3d 777, 791-92 (Tex.2005). See ***O'Connor's Texas Rules***, "Note," ch. 3-B, §2.4.2(1)(a), p. 227.

Continued on next page

In ***Daimler***, the U.S. Supreme Court suggested that the "fair play and substantial justice" analysis is not required in cases involving general jurisdiction. *See* ***Daimler AG***, 571 U.S. at 139 n.20. Until the issue is addressed by the Texas courts, the defendant should still argue that the court's assertion of jurisdiction over it will offend traditional notions of fair play and substantial justice.

When a presuit deposition is sought under Texas Rule of Civil Procedure 202, a potential defendant can file a special appearance if she does not have sufficient minimum contacts with Texas for the court to exercise personal jurisdiction over her. *See* ***In re Doe***, 444 S.W.3d 603, 604-05 (Tex.2014).

If the plaintiff files a response to the special appearance, the defendant can file a reply, supported by evidence, that refutes the allegations in the plaintiff's response. *See* ***Booth***, 485 S.W.3d at 474; ***Bautista v. Trinidad Drilling Ltd.***, 484 S.W.3d 491, 496 (Tex.App.—Houston [1st Dist.] 2016, no pet.).

DEFENDANT'S SPECIAL APPEARANCE

Defendant, {❶ *name*}, asks the Court to sustain {❷ *his/her/its*} special appearance and dismiss plaintiff {❸ *name*}'s suit.

INTRODUCTION

1. Plaintiff, {❹ *name*}, sued defendant, {❺ *name*}, for {❻ *state basis of suit*}.

2. {❼ *If special appearance is defendant's initial pleading, add appropriate identification for each defendant from FORM 3E:1.*}

3. {❽ *State other relevant facts about the suit.*}

BACKGROUND

4. Defendant is not a resident of the State of Texas. Defendant resides in {❾ *identify state*}.

5. Defendant attaches an affidavit to this special appearance to establish that {❿ *he/she/it*} is not a resident of Texas. The affidavit is attached as Exhibit {⓫ *letter*} and incorporated by reference into this motion.

ARGUMENT & AUTHORITIES

6. Texas courts do not have jurisdiction over a nonresident defendant unless the nonresident defendant purposefully established "minimum contacts" with Texas. *Burger King Corp. v. Rudzewicz*, 471 U.S. 462, 474-76 (1985); *TV Azteca, S.A.B. de C.V. v. Ruiz*, 490 S.W.3d 29, 36-37 (Tex. 2016); *Kelly v. Gen. Interior Constr., Inc.*, 301 S.W.3d 653, 657-58 (Tex. 2010); *Moki Mac River Expeditions v. Drugg*, 221 S.W.3d 569, 575-76 (Tex. 2007); *BMC Software Belg., N.V. v. Marchand*, 83 S.W.3d 789, 795 (Tex. 2002).

7. In {⓬ *his/her/its*} petition, plaintiff alleged that defendant is a nonresident of Texas, which is correct and is verified by defendant's affidavit, Exhibit {⓭ *letter*}. However, plaintiff did not plead any facts showing that defendant is subject to the jurisdiction of a Texas court.

8. When pleading a case against a nonresident, a plaintiff must allege facts that, if true, would make the nonresident defendant subject to personal jurisdiction in a Texas court. *See TV Azteca*, 490 S.W.3d at 35 n.2; *Paramount Pipe & Supply Co. v. Muhr*, 749 S.W.2d 491, 496 (Tex. 1988). The plaintiff has the initial burden of pleading sufficient allegations to bring a nonresident defendant within the provisions of the long-arm statute. *Kelly*, 301 S.W.3d at 658; *Retamco Operating, Inc. v. Republic Drilling Co.*, 278

◄ *Continued on next page* ►

S.W.3d 333, 337 (Tex. 2009); *Moki Mac*, 221 S.W.3d at 574; *Am. Type Culture Collection, Inc. v. Coleman*, 83 S.W.3d 801, 807 (Tex. 2002). When a plaintiff fails to plead jurisdictional allegations that a nonresident defendant committed an act in Texas or that the defendant's acts outside Texas had reasonably foreseeable consequences in Texas, the defendant can meet its burden to negate all potential bases of jurisdiction simply by presenting evidence that it is a nonresident. *Kelly*, 301 S.W.3d at 658-59; *see Siskind v. Villa Found. for Educ., Inc.*, 642 S.W.2d 434, 438 & n.5 (Tex. 1982); *Perna v. Hogan*, 162 S.W.3d 648, 653 (Tex. App.—Houston [14th Dist.] 2005, no pet.); *Frank A. Smith Sales, Inc. v. Atl. Aero, Inc.*, 31 S.W.3d 742, 746 (Tex. App.—Corpus Christi 2000, no pet.). {*See **O'Connor's Texas Rules**, "Not Texas resident," ch. 3-B, §2.4.1, p. 226.*}

9. Defendant has met {⓮ *his/her/its*} burden of negating all potential bases of jurisdiction by {⓯ *his/her/its*} affidavit, Exhibit {⓰ *letter*}, which establishes the fact that {⓱ *he/she/it*} is a nonresident of Texas.

PRAYER

10. For these reasons, defendant asks the Court to resolve the special appearance without a hearing, based on the pleadings and the affidavits and any discovery on file, to sustain defendant's special appearance, and to sign a final judgment dismissing plaintiff's suit.

SEE: Tex. R. Civ. P. 120a
*O'Connor's Texas Rules * Civil Trials* (2019), "Special Appearance," ch. 3-B, §2, p. 225

ADD: STYLE OF THE CASE – FORM 1B:2
SIGNATURE BLOCK – FORM 1B:3
VERIFICATION – FORM 1B:7
CERTIFICATE OF SERVICE – FORM 1B:13

ATTACH: AFFIDAVIT – FORM 1B:8, proving defendant is nonresident
NOTICE OF CURRENT/CHANGE OF ADDRESS – FORM 1B:14, if special appearance is defendant's initial pleading
NOTICE OF HEARING OR SUBMISSION – FORM 1E:1
ORDER – FORM 3B:4

NOTE: This form should be used only when the plaintiff did not allege any facts showing the defendant had contacts with Texas; in such a case, the defendant can prevail on a special appearance simply by proving it is a nonresident. The defendant should file a special appearance alleging—and an affidavit proving—it is a nonresident. *See **Frank A. Smith Sales, Inc. v. Atlantic Aero, Inc.***, 31 S.W.3d 742, 746-47 (Tex. App.—Corpus Christi 2000, no pet.).

PLAINTIFF'S RESPONSE TO DEFENDANT'S SPECIAL APPEARANCE

Plaintiff, {❶ *name*}, asks the Court to overrule defendant {❷ *name*}'s special appearance.

INTRODUCTION

1. Plaintiff, {❸ *name*}, sued defendant, {❹ *name*}, for {❺ *state basis of suit*}.

2. {❻ *State other relevant facts about the suit.*}

BACKGROUND

3. On {❼ *date*}, defendant filed a special appearance and asked the Court to dismiss plaintiff's suit for lack of personal jurisdiction over defendant.

4. {❽ *State other facts relevant to the response.*}

ARGUMENT & AUTHORITIES

{*CHOOSE APPROPRIATE PARAGRAPHS 5-10*}

5. The Court should overrule defendant's special appearance because defendant waived a special appearance by {❾ *explain how defendant waived special appearance, e.g., filing an answer before filing a special appearance*}. {*See **O'Connor's Texas Rules**, "Waiver," ch. 3-B, §3, p. 235.*}

6. The Court should overrule defendant's special appearance because it was not made by a sworn motion and no affidavits verified its contents. A special appearance must be presented by a sworn motion. Tex. R. Civ. P. 120a(1); *Exito Elecs. Co. v. Trejo*, 142 S.W.3d 302, 307 (Tex. 2004). {*See **O'Connor's Texas Rules**, "Verification," ch. 3-B, §2.5, p. 234.*}

7. The Court should overrule defendant's special appearance because defendant purposefully availed {❿ *himself/herself/itself*} of the privilege of conducting activities within Texas. *TV Azteca, S.A.B. de C.V. v. Ruiz*, 490 S.W.3d 29, 37-38 (Tex. 2016); *Spir Star AG v. Kimich*, 310 S.W.3d 868, 872-73 (Tex. 2010). Specifically, defendant purposefully availed {⓫ *himself/herself/itself*} of the privilege of conducting activities within Texas for the following reasons:

{*CHOOSE APPROPRIATE REASONS*}

a. Defendant put products in the stream of commerce knowing that some of them would reach Texas and engaged in additional conduct indicating an intent to serve the Texas market. *Spir Star*, 310 S.W.3d at 873; *Moki Mac*

◄ *Continued on next page* ►

River Expeditions v. Drugg, 221 S.W.3d 569, 576-77 (Tex. 2007); *see Michiana Easy Livin' Country, Inc. v. Holten*, 168 S.W.3d 777, 786 (Tex. 2005). {⓬ *Explain, e.g., defendant directed sales to Texas, designed the product for Texas, and advertised in Texas.*} {*See* ***O'Connor's Texas Rules****, "Analyzing contacts – stream of commerce," ch. 3-B, §2.4.2(1)(b), p. 227.*}

b. Defendant aired its broadcast, which originated outside of Texas, knowing that it could be viewed in Texas and intentionally targeting the Texas market. *TV Azteca*, 490 S.W.3d at 46-47. {⓭ *Explain defendant's knowledge about viewership in Texas and how defendant intentionally targeted the Texas market, e.g., the subject matter of the broadcast involved events in Texas, defendant relied on Texas sources to prepare the broadcast, defendant advertised in Texas and established channels of regular communication with Texas customers.*} {⓮ *See* ***O'Connor's Texas Rules****, "Analyzing contacts – defamatory broadcasts," ch. 3-B, §2.4.2(1)(c), p. 228.*}

c. Defendant operated a website that was clearly used for business transactions. *See Schexnayder v. Daniels*, 187 S.W.3d 238, 248 (Tex. App.—Texarkana 2006, pet. dism'd w.o.j.); *Exito Elecs., Co. v. Trejo*, 166 S.W.3d 839, 857-58 (Tex. App.—Corpus Christi 2005, no pet.). {⓯ *Elaborate.*} {*See* ***O'Connor's Texas Rules****, "Analyzing contacts – Internet activity," ch. 3-B, §2.4.2(1)(d), p. 228.*}

d. {⓰ *Refute any other ground raised by defendant.*} {*See* ***O'Connor's Texas Rules****, "Grounds," ch. 3-B, §2.4, p. 225.*}

8. The Court should overrule defendant's special appearance because plaintiff's suit arose from and was related to defendant's contacts with Texas. *TV Azteca, S.A.B. de C.V. v. Ruiz*, 490 S.W.3d 29, 52 (Tex. 2016); *Spir Star AG v. Kimich*, 310 S.W.3d 868, 874 (Tex. 2010); *Retamco Operating, Inc. v. Republic Drilling Co.*, 278 S.W.3d 333, 340-41 (Tex. 2009); *Schlobohm v. Schapiro*, 784 S.W.2d 355, 358 (Tex. 1990); *see M&F Worldwide Corp. v. Pepsi-Cola Metro. Bottling Co.*, 512 S.W.3d 878, 890 (Tex. 2017); *Moki Mac River Expeditions v. Drugg*, 221 S.W.3d 569, 575-76 (Tex. 2007). This suit involves {⓱ *explain*}. The incident giving rise to this suit was a result of defendant's {⓲ *list defendant's contacts and explain how there is a substantial connection between those contacts and the operative facts of the litigation*}. Therefore, the Court has specific jurisdiction over defendant.

9. The Court should overrule defendant's special appearance because defendant has affiliations with Texas that are so continuous and systematic as to render {⓳ *him/her/it*} "at home" in Texas; therefore, the Court has general jurisdiction over defendant. *See BNSF Ry. Co. v. Tyrrell*, ___ U.S. ___, 137 S. Ct. 1549, 1558 (2017); *Daimler AG v. Bauman*, 571 U.S. 117, 138-39 (2014); *Searcy v. Parex Res., Inc.*, 496 S.W.3d 58, 72 (Tex. 2016). Specifically,

{*CHOOSE ONE OF THE FOLLOWING*}

[A] defendant is an individual who is domiciled in Texas. *See Daimler AG*, 571 U.S. at 137; *Henkel v. Emjo Invs., Ltd.*, 480 S.W.3d 1, 5 (Tex. App.—Houston [1st Dist.] 2015, no pet.). {⓴ *Elaborate.*}

[B] defendant is incorporated in Texas. *See BNSF Ry.*, ___ U.S. at ___, 137 S. Ct. at 1558; *Daimler AG*, 571 U.S. at 137; *Bautista v. Trinidad Drilling Ltd.*, 484 S.W.3d 491, 500 (Tex. App.—Houston [1st Dist.] 2016, no pet.). {㉑ *Elaborate.*}

[C] defendant has its principal place of business in Texas. *See BNSF Ry.*, ___ U.S. at ___, 137 S. Ct. at 1558; *Daimler AG*, 571 U.S. at 137; *Bautista v. Trinidad Drilling Ltd.*, 484 S.W.3d 491, 500 (Tex. App.—Houston [1st Dist.] 2016, no pet.). {㉒ *Elaborate.*}

[D] even though defendant is not incorporated in Texas and does not have its principal place of business in Texas, this is an exceptional case in which defendant's contacts are so continuous and systematic that the assertion of general jurisdiction over defendant in Texas is warranted. *See BNSF Ry.*, ___ U.S. at ___, 137 S. Ct. at 1558; *Daimler AG*, 571 U.S. at 139 n.19; *Searcy*, 496 S.W.3d at 72; *Booth v. Kontomitras*, 485 S.W.3d 461, 479 (Tex. App.—Beaumont 2016, no pet.). {㉓ *Elaborate.*}

10. The Court's assertion of jurisdiction over defendant will not offend traditional notions of fair play and substantial justice and will be consistent with the constitutional requirement of due process. *Int'l Shoe Co. v. Washington*, 326 U.S. 310, 316 (1945); *TV Azteca, S.A.B. de C.V. v. Ruiz*, 490 S.W.3d 29, 55 (Tex. 2016); *Moncrief Oil Int'l Inc. v. OAO Gazprom*, 414 S.W.3d 142, 154-55 (Tex. 2013); *Spir Star AG v. Kimich*, 310 S.W.3d 868, 878 (Tex. 2010); *Retamco Operating, Inc. v. Republic Drilling Co.*, 278 S.W.3d 333, 341-42 (Tex. 2009); *see Guardian Royal Exch. Assurance, Ltd. v. English China Clays, P.L.C.*, 815 S.W.2d 223, 232 (Tex. 1991). Specifically, {㉔ *state why it is fair to assert jurisdiction over defendant, e.g., Texas has an inherent interest in protecting its citizens and providing remedies for alleged tortious injuries*}.

Continued on next page

{ADD SECTION BELOW IF DEFENDANT ALLEGED PLAINTIFF DID NOT PLEAD MINIMUM CONTACTS}

AMENDED PETITION

11. In its special appearance, defendant alleged that plaintiff did not meet {㉕ *his/her/its*} initial burden of pleading that defendant, a nonresident, purposefully established "minimum contacts" with the State of Texas. Plaintiff attaches an amended original petition as Exhibit {㉖ *letter*}. No leave is required because this amendment is filed more than seven days before trial. Tex. R. Civ. P. 63. In the amended original petition, plaintiff includes specific allegations that defendant, a nonresident, "purposefully availed" {㉗ *himself/herself/itself*} of the privilege of conducting activities in Texas, and defendant's contacts were sufficient to establish minimum contacts and give this Court personal jurisdiction over defendant. {㉘ *Elaborate, showing how, when, and where the nonresident made itself subject to the jurisdiction of Texas courts.*} *{See **O'Connor's Texas Rules**, "Amend petition," ch. 3-B, §5.1, p. 238.}*

CONCLUSION

12. {㉙ *Briefly summarize the response.*}

PRAYER

13. For these reasons, plaintiff asks the Court to overrule defendant's special appearance.

FORM 3B:3

SEE: Tex. R. Civ. P. 63, 120a
O'Connor's Texas Rules * Civil Trials (2019), "Response," ch. 3-B, §5, p. 238

ADD: STYLE OF THE CASE – FORM 1B:2
SIGNATURE BLOCK – FORM 1B:3
VERIFICATION – FORM 1B:7
CERTIFICATE OF SERVICE – FORM 1B:13

ATTACH: AFFIDAVIT – FORM 1B:8, if necessary
ORDER – FORM 3B:4
Amended petition, if necessary

NOTE: If the plaintiff did not allege facts in its petition to support personal jurisdiction over the defendant, the plaintiff should immediately amend its petition to add facts about the defendant's contacts with Texas. ***Kelly v. General Interior Constr., Inc.***, 301 S.W.3d 653, 659 & n.6 (Tex.2010).

See notes under FORM 3B:1.

ORDER ON DEFENDANT'S SPECIAL APPEARANCE

After considering defendant {❶ *name*}'s special appearance, the response, plaintiff's original petition, {❷ *add as appropriate: affidavits/stipulations/discovery on file/oral testimony,*} and arguments of counsel, the Court

{*CHOOSE APPROPRIATE ORDER*}

OVERRULES defendant's special appearance and retains plaintiff's suit on the Court's docket.

SUSTAINS the special appearance and dismisses plaintiff's suit for lack of personal jurisdiction.

SIGNED on _______________, 20___.

____
PRESIDING JUDGE

SEE: Tex. R. Civ. P. 120a
O'Connor's Texas Rules * Civil Trials (2019), "Ruling," ch. 3-B, §10, p. 241

ADD: STYLE OF THE CASE – FORM 1B:2
CERTIFICATE OF SERVICE – FORM 1B:13, if proposed order served separately from motion or response

NOTE: The party who receives an adverse ruling on the special appearance should request findings of fact. ***Goodenbour v. Goodenbour***, 64 S.W.3d 69, 75 (Tex.App.—Austin 2001, pet. denied); *see* Tex. R. Civ. P. 296; *see also* Tex. R. App. P. 28.1(c) (trial court may file findings of fact). However, the court is not required to file findings of fact on the special appearance. ***Niehaus v. Cedar Bridge, Inc.***, 208 S.W.3d 575, 579 n.5 (Tex.App.—Austin 2006, no pet.). See ***O'Connor's Texas Rules***, "Findings of Fact," ch. 3-B, §11, p. 241.

When sustaining a special appearance, the trial court should not rule on the merits of the claims. *E.g.*, ***Nguyen v. Desai***, 132 S.W.3d 115, 117 (Tex.App.—Houston [14th Dist.] 2004, no pet.) (in sustaining special appearance, court erred by ordering that Ps take nothing and by dismissing suit with prejudice).

PLAINTIFF'S MOTION FOR
CONTINUANCE TO CONDUCT JURISDICTIONAL DISCOVERY

Plaintiff, {❶ *name*}, asks the Court to continue the hearing on defendant {❷ *name*}'s special appearance until {❸ *date*} because additional time is needed to conduct jurisdictional discovery.

INTRODUCTION

1. Plaintiff, {❹ *name*}, sued defendant, {❺ *name*}, for {❻ *state basis of suit*}.

2. {❼ *State other relevant facts about the suit.*}

BACKGROUND

3. On {❽ *date*}, defendant filed a special appearance and asked the Court to dismiss plaintiff's suit for lack of personal jurisdiction over defendant.

4. The hearing on defendant's special appearance is set for {❾ *date*}.

5. {❿ *State other facts relevant to the motion.*}

ARGUMENT & AUTHORITIES

6. A court can continue a hearing on a special appearance to allow time for the plaintiff to conduct discovery if the plaintiff shows by affidavit that it cannot present facts essential to justify its opposition to the special appearance. Tex. R. Civ. P. 120a(3); *see Dawson-Austin v. Austin*, 968 S.W.2d 319, 323 (Tex. 1998). The plaintiff must show that (1) the information sought is material to establishing jurisdiction and (2) it acted diligently in trying to obtain the information sought. *See Lamar v. Poncon*, 305 S.W.3d 130, 139-40 (Tex. App.—Houston [1st Dist.] 2009, pet. denied); *Barron v. Vanier*, 190 S.W.3d 841, 849-51 (Tex. App.—Fort Worth 2006, no pet.).

7. Plaintiff asks the Court for a continuance to obtain the following discovery: {⓫ *identify discovery that plaintiff has yet to receive or request*}.

8. The information plaintiff seeks through this discovery is material to supporting {⓬ *his/her/its*} allegations of personal jurisdiction over the defendant. {⓭ *Elaborate.*}

9. Plaintiff has been unable to secure this information earlier despite {⓮ *his/her/its*} diligent efforts. {⓯ *Describe efforts to obtain discovery, including type of discovery requested, date of request, and response to request.*}

CONCLUSION

10. {⓰ *Briefly summarize the motion.*}

PRAYER

11. For these reasons, plaintiff asks the Court to continue the hearing on defendant's special appearance until {⓱ *date*}.

SEE: Tex. R. Civ. P. 120a(3)
O'Connor's Texas Rules * Civil Trials (2019), "Continuance," ch. 3-B, §8, p. 239

ADD: STYLE OF THE CASE – FORM 1B:2
SIGNATURE BLOCK – FORM 1B:3
CERTIFICATE OF SERVICE – FORM 1B:13

ATTACH: NOTICE OF HEARING OR SUBMISSION – FORM 1E:1
ORDER – FORM 3B:7
AFFIDAVIT FOR CONTINUANCE – FORM 5D:4, and modify to apply to continuance of a special appearance

DEFENDANT'S RESPONSE TO PLAINTIFF'S MOTION FOR CONTINUANCE TO CONDUCT JURISDICTIONAL DISCOVERY

Defendant, {❶ *name*}, asks the Court to deny plaintiff {❷ *name*}'s motion for continuance to conduct jurisdictional discovery.

INTRODUCTION

1. Plaintiff, {❸ *name*}, sued defendant, {❹ *name*}, for {❺ *state basis of suit*}.

2. {❻ *State other relevant facts about the suit.*}

BACKGROUND

3. On {❼ *date*}, defendant filed a special appearance and asked the Court to dismiss plaintiff's suit for lack of personal jurisdiction over defendant.

4. On {❽ *date*}, plaintiff filed a motion for a continuance under Texas Rule of Civil Procedure 120a(3).

5. {❾ *State other facts relevant to the response.*}

ARGUMENT & AUTHORITIES

6. A court can continue a hearing on a special appearance to allow time for the plaintiff to conduct discovery if the plaintiff shows by affidavit that it cannot present facts essential to justify its opposition to the special appearance. Tex. R. Civ. P. 120a(3); *see Dawson-Austin v. Austin*, 968 S.W.2d 319, 323 (Tex. 1998). Affidavits must be served at least seven days before the hearing, be made on personal knowledge, set forth specific facts that would be admissible in evidence, and affirmatively show that the affiant is competent to testify. Tex. R. Civ. P. 120a(3). To prevail on a motion to continue the hearing on a special appearance, the plaintiff must show that (1) the information sought is material to establishing jurisdiction and (2) it acted diligently in trying to obtain the information sought. *See Lamar v. Poncon*, 305 S.W.3d 130, 139-40 (Tex. App.—Houston [1st Dist.] 2009, pet. denied); *Barron v. Vanier*, 190 S.W.3d 841, 849-51 (Tex. App.—Fort Worth 2006, no pet.).

{*CHOOSE APPROPRIATE PARAGRAPHS 7-13*}

7. The Court should deny the motion for continuance because plaintiff's affidavit was not served at least seven days before the hearing. {❿ *Elaborate.*}

8. The Court should deny the motion for continuance because plaintiff's affidavit was not made on personal knowledge. {⓫ *Elaborate.*}

9. The Court should deny the motion for continuance because plaintiff's affidavit did not set forth specific facts that would be admissible in evidence. {⓬ *Elaborate.*}

10. The Court should deny the motion for continuance because plaintiff's affidavit did not affirmatively show that the affiant is competent to testify. {⓭ *Elaborate.*}

11. The Court should deny the motion for continuance because the information plaintiff seeks is not material to establishing jurisdiction. {⓮ *Elaborate.*}

12. The Court should deny the motion for continuance because plaintiff did not act diligently in trying to obtain the information sought. {⓯ *Elaborate.*}

13. The Court should deny the motion for continuance because {⓰ *identify any other defect justifying denial of the motion*}.

CONCLUSION

14. {⓱ *Briefly summarize the response.*}

PRAYER

15. For these reasons, defendant asks the Court to deny plaintiff's motion for continuance to conduct jurisdictional discovery.

SEE: Tex. R. Civ. P. 120a(3)
O'Connor's Texas Rules * Civil Trials (2019), "Continuance," ch. 3-B, §8, p. 239

ADD: STYLE OF THE CASE – FORM 1B:2
SIGNATURE BLOCK – FORM 1B:3
CERTIFICATE OF SERVICE – FORM 1B:13

ATTACH: AFFIDAVIT – FORM 1B:8, if necessary
ORDER – FORM 3B:7

ORDER ON MOTION FOR CONTINUANCE TO CONDUCT JURISDICTIONAL DISCOVERY

After considering plaintiff {❶ *name*}'s motion for continuance to conduct jurisdictional discovery under Texas Rule of Civil Procedure 120a(3), the response, the pleadings, and arguments of counsel, the Court

{*CHOOSE APPROPRIATE ORDER*}

DENIES the motion.

GRANTS the motion and continues the hearing on defendant {❷ *name*}'s special appearance until {❸ *date*} so that plaintiff can {❹ *specify scope of discovery*}.

SIGNED on ________________, 20___.

____
PRESIDING JUDGE

SEE: Tex. R. Civ. P. 120a(3)
O'Connor's Texas Rules * Civil Trials (2019), "Continuance," ch. 3-B, §8, p. 239

ADD: STYLE OF THE CASE – FORM 1B:2
CERTIFICATE OF SERVICE – FORM 1B:13, if proposed order served separately from motion or response

DEFENDANT'S MOTION TO TRANSFER VENUE

Defendant, {❶ *name*}, files this motion to transfer venue and asks the Court to transfer this case from {❷ *current*} County to {❸ *proposed*} County because {❹ *current*} County is not a proper county for venue. {*See* ***O'Connor's Texas Rules****, "Improper County or Convenience," ch. 3-C, §2, p. 243.*}

INTRODUCTION

1. Plaintiff, {❺ *name*}, sued defendant, {❻ *name*}, in {❼ *current*} County for {❽ *state basis of suit*}.

2. {❾ *If motion to transfer venue is defendant's initial pleading, add appropriate identification for each defendant from FORM 3E:1.*}

3. {❿ *State other relevant facts about the suit.*}

BACKGROUND

4. On {⓫ *date*}, plaintiff, {⓬ *name*}, filed an original petition in {⓭ *current*} County.

{*CHOOSE APPROPRIATE PARAGRAPH 5*}

5. In the petition, plaintiff did not plead any venue facts to show that {⓮ *current*} County is a proper county for venue.

5. In the petition, plaintiff pleaded the following venue facts: {⓯ *list each venue fact pleaded in plaintiff's petition*}.

{*ADD PARAGRAPH 6 IF APPLICABLE*}

6. Defendant specifically denies that {⓰ *state venue facts denied*}. {*See* ***O'Connor's Texas Rules****, "Denial of venue facts," ch. 3-C, §2.11.4(1), p. 250.*}

7. Defendant attaches affidavits to this motion as Exhibits {⓱ *letters*} to establish facts not apparent from the record and incorporates them by reference. {*See* ***O'Connor's Texas Rules****, "Affidavits," ch. 3-C, §2.3.5(2), p. 245.*}

{*ADD PARAGRAPH 8 IF SPECIAL APPEARANCE IS PENDING*}

8. The relief requested in this motion is subject to the Court's ruling on defendant's special appearance. {*See* ***O'Connor's Texas Rules****, "Due Order of Pleading," ch. 3-A, §3, p. 219.*}

◄ *Continued on next page* ►

FORM 3C:1

ARGUMENT & AUTHORITIES

A. Venue improper in {[18] *current*} County.

9. Venue for this case is improper in {[19] *current*} County because {[20] *explain, e.g., plaintiff's case is governed by Texas Civil Practice & Remedies Code section 15.011, a mandatory-venue provision*}. {[21] *Elaborate.*}

B. Venue proper in {[22] *proposed*} County.

{*CHOOSE APPROPRIATE PARAGRAPH 10*}

10. Because venue over this case is governed by {[23] *specify mandatory-venue provision, e.g., Texas Civil Practice & Remedies Code section 15.011*}, this case should be transferred to {[24] *proposed*} County. {[25] *Proposed*} County is a county of mandatory venue under {[26] *specify mandatory-venue provision*} because {[27] *specify reason, e.g., this suit involves the partition of real property in Lubbock County*}. {[28] *Elaborate.*} {*See* ***O'Connor's Texas Rules****, "Mandatory-Venue Provisions," ch. 2-H, §4, p. 180.*}

10. Because venue over this case is governed by {[29] *specify permissive-venue provision, e.g., Texas Civil Practice & Remedies Code section 15.031*}, this case should be transferred to {[30] *proposed*} County. {[31] *Proposed*} County is a county of permissive venue under {[32] *specify permissive-venue provision*} because {[33] *specify reason, e.g., this is a suit for a debt of an estate and the proposed county is the county where the estate is being administered*}. {[34] *Elaborate.*} {*See* ***O'Connor's Texas Rules****, "Permissive-Venue Provisions," ch. 2-H, §5, p. 185.*}

10. Because plaintiff's case is the same case filed earlier under cause number {[35] *number*}, in which plaintiff took a nonsuit after the Court granted defendant's motion to transfer venue, this case should be transferred to {[36] *proposed*} County. The earlier ruling on venue conclusively fixes venue in {[37] *proposed*} County. *Hendrick Med. Ctr. v. Howell*, 690 S.W.2d 42, 44 (Tex. App.—Dallas 1985, orig. proceeding); *see Hyman Farm Serv., Inc. v. Earth Oil & Gas Co.*, 920 S.W.2d 452, 456 (Tex. App.—Amarillo 1996, no writ).

10. Because the parties have signed a written consent to transfer this case to {[38] *proposed*} County, this case should be transferred to {[39] *proposed*} County, another county of proper venue. Tex. Civ. Prac. & Rem. Code §15.063(3); Tex. R. Civ. P. 255. {[40] *Elaborate.*} The signed agreement is attached as Exhibit {[41] *letter*}. {*See* ***O'Connor's Texas Rules****, "Consent of the Parties," ch. 3-C, §4, p. 254.*}

10. Because venue over this case is governed by the general venue rule in Texas Civil Practice & Remedies Code section 15.002(a), this case should be transferred to {㊷ *proposed*} County. {*See* ***O'Connor's Texas Rules****, "General Venue Rule," ch. 2-H, §6, p. 187.*}

{*CHOOSE APPROPRIATE PARAGRAPHS 11-14*
IF GENERAL VENUE RULE APPLIES}

11. {㊸ *Proposed*} County is a county of proper venue under the general venue rule because it {㊹ *is/was*} the county where all or a substantial part of the events or omissions giving rise to the claim occurred. Tex. Civ. Prac. & Rem. Code §15.002(a)(1). {㊺ *Elaborate.*}

12. {㊻ *Proposed*} County is a county of proper venue under the general venue rule because it {㊼ *is/was*} the county of defendant's residence at the time the cause of action accrued. Tex. Civ. Prac. & Rem. Code §15.002(a)(2). {㊽ *Elaborate.*}

13. {㊾ *Proposed*} County is a county of proper venue under the general venue rule because it {㊿ *is/was*} the county of defendant's principal office in this state. Tex. Civ. Prac. & Rem. Code §15.002(a)(3); *see In re Mo. Pac. R.R. Co.*, 998 S.W.2d 212, 216-17 (Tex. 1999) (FELA case). {51 *Elaborate.*}

14. {52 *Proposed*} County is a county of proper venue under the general venue rule because it {53 *is/was*} the county where plaintiff resided at the time the cause of action accrued. Tex. Civ. Prac. & Rem. Code §15.002(a)(4). {54 *Elaborate.*}

{*ADD SECTION BELOW IF APPLICABLE*}

TRANSFER FOR CONVENIENCE

15. Alternatively, defendant asks the Court to transfer the case to {55 *proposed*} County in the interest of justice and for the convenience of the parties and witnesses under the authority of Texas Civil Practice & Remedies Code section 15.002(b).

16. Maintaining this suit in {56 *current*} County will impose an economic and personal hardship on defendant. Tex. Civ. Prac. & Rem. Code §15.002(b)(1). Specifically, {57 *state why suit in current county will impose an economic and personal hardship and why suit in proposed county would not*}. {58 *Elaborate.*}

17. The balance of interests of all parties weighs in favor of the action being brought in {59 *proposed*} County. Tex. Civ. Prac. & Rem. Code §15.002(b)(2). Specifically, {60 *list factors that weigh in favor of proposed county*}. {61 *Elaborate.*}

Continued on next page

18. The transfer to {62 *proposed*} County will not cause a hardship or an injustice for any other party. Tex. Civ. Prac. & Rem. Code §15.002(b)(3). Specifically, {63 *state specific reasons why the move would not impose a hardship or injustice on plaintiff and any other parties*}. {64 *Elaborate.*}

19. {65 *Current*} County is not a county of mandatory venue, and {66 *proposed*} County is a county of proper venue. *See* Tex. Civ. Prac. & Rem. Code §15.002(b). {67 *Elaborate.*}

COSTS

20. Defendant asks the Court to tax against plaintiff all costs incurred before the case is transferred. *See* Tex. R. Civ. P. 89.

CONCLUSION

21. {68 *Briefly summarize the motion.*}

PRAYER

22. For these reasons, defendant asks the Court to set {69 *his/her/its*} motion to transfer venue for hearing and, after the hearing, grant defendant's motion and transfer this case to {70 *proposed*} County. {*See* ***O'Connor's Texas Rules****, "Request hearing," ch. 3-C, §2.2.5, p. 244.*}

SEE: Tex. R. Civ. P. 85-89, 255
Tex. Civ. Prac. & Rem. Code §15.001 et seq.
Tex. Const. art. 3, §45
O'Connor's Texas Rules * Civil Trials (2019), "Improper County or Convenience," ch. 3-C, §2, p. 243

ADD: STYLE OF THE CASE – FORM 1B:2
SIGNATURE BLOCK – FORM 1B:3
CERTIFICATE OF SERVICE – FORM 1B:13

ATTACH: AFFIDAVIT – FORM 1B:8, if necessary
NOTICE OF CURRENT/CHANGE OF ADDRESS – FORM 1B:14, if motion to transfer venue is defendant's initial pleading
NOTICE OF HEARING OR SUBMISSION – FORM 1E:1
ORDER – FORM 3C:11

NOTE: A defendant must file a motion to transfer venue based on an improper county or convenience before or along with all other pleadings or motions except a special appearance, which must be filed first. The defendant waives its objection to improper venue if it files a motion to transfer after it files an answer. See ***O'Connor's Texas Rules***, "Due Order of Pleading," ch. 3-A, §3, p. 219.

DEFENDANT'S MOTION TO SEVER & TRANSFER VENUE

Defendant, {❶ *name*}, files this motion to sever and transfer venue and asks the Court to sever the cause of action as to plaintiff, {❷ *name*}, and transfer that part of the case from {❸ *current*} County to {❹ *proposed*} County.

INTRODUCTION

1. Plaintiff, {❺ *name*}, sued defendant, {❻ *name*}, in {❼ *current*} County for {❽ *state basis of suit*}.

2. {❾ *If motion to transfer venue is defendant's initial pleading, add appropriate identification for each defendant from FORM 3E:1.*}

3. {❿ *State other relevant facts about the suit.*}

BACKGROUND

4. On {⓫ *date*}, plaintiff {⓬ *name*} filed an original petition in {⓭ *current*} County.

{*CHOOSE APPROPRIATE PARAGRAPH 5*}

5. In the petition, plaintiff did not plead any venue facts to show that {⓮ *current*} County is a proper county for venue.

5. In the petition, plaintiff pleaded the following venue facts: {⓯ *list each venue fact pleaded in plaintiff's petition*}.

{*ADD PARAGRAPH 6 IF APPLICABLE*}

6. Defendant specifically denies that {⓰ *state venue facts denied*}. {*See* ***O'Connor's Texas Rules****, "Denial of venue facts," ch. 3-C, §2.11.4(1), p. 250.*}

7. Defendant attaches affidavits to this motion as Exhibits {⓱ *letters*} to establish defendant's venue facts and incorporates them by reference. {*See* ***O'Connor's Texas Rules****, "Affidavits," ch. 3-C, §2.3.5(2), p. 245.*}

{*ADD PARAGRAPH 8 IF SPECIAL APPEARANCE IS PENDING*}

8. The relief requested in this motion is subject to the Court's ruling on defendant's special appearance. {*See* ***O'Connor's Texas Rules****, "Due Order of Pleading," ch. 3-A, §3, p. 219.*}

— Continued on next page —

ARGUMENT & AUTHORITIES

9. A plaintiff has the initial burden to establish, independently of every other plaintiff, that venue is proper as to the plaintiff in the county of suit. Tex. Civ. Prac. & Rem. Code §15.003(a). If the plaintiff is unable to establish proper venue, the plaintiff's portion of the suit must be transferred to a county of proper venue or dismissed unless the plaintiff can demonstrate that it was properly joined under Texas Civil Practice & Remedies Code section 15.003(a). *See Surgitek v. Abel*, 997 S.W.2d 598, 602 (Tex. 1999). To establish proper joinder, the plaintiff must prove each joinder element under section 15.003(a). *Surgitek*, 997 S.W.2d at 602-03. {*See* ***O'Connor's Texas Rules***, *"Venue or joinder proper in multiple-plaintiff case," ch. 3-C, §2.6.4, p. 247.*}

A. Venue improper in {18 *current*} County.

10. Plaintiff {19 *name*} cannot establish, independently of every other plaintiff, proper venue in {20 *current*} County.

11. Venue for this case is improper in {21 *current*} County because {22 *explain, e.g., plaintiff's suit for the recovery of real property is governed by a mandatory-venue provision*}.

B. Venue proper in {23 *proposed*} County.

{*CHOOSE APPROPRIATE PARAGRAPH 12*}

12. Because venue over plaintiff's portion of the suit is governed by {24 *specify mandatory-venue provision, e.g., Texas Civil Practice & Remedies Code section 15.011*}, plaintiff's case should be severed from the suit and transferred to {25 *proposed*} County. {26 *Proposed*} County is a county of mandatory venue under {27 *specify mandatory-venue provision*} because {28 *specify reason, e.g., this suit involves the partition of real property in Lubbock County*}. {29 *Elaborate.*} {*See* ***O'Connor's Texas Rules***, *"Mandatory-Venue Provisions," ch. 2-H, §4, p. 180.*}

12. Because venue over plaintiff's portion of the suit is governed by {30 *specify permissive-venue provision, e.g., Texas Civil Practice & Remedies Code section 15.031*}, plaintiff's case should be severed from the suit and transferred to {31 *proposed*} County. {32 *Proposed*} County is a county of permissive venue under {33 *specify permissive-venue provision*} because {34 *specify reason, e.g., this is a suit for a debt of an estate and the proposed county is the county where the estate is being administered*}. {35 *Elaborate.*} {*See* ***O'Connor's Texas Rules***, *"Permissive-Venue Provisions," ch. 2-H, §5, p. 185.*}

12. Because venue over this case is governed by the general venue rule in Texas Civil Practice & Remedies Code section 15.002(a), this case should be transferred to {㊱ *proposed*} County. {*See* ***O'Connor's Texas Rules****, "General Venue Rule," ch. 2-H, §6, p. 187.*}

{CHOOSE APPROPRIATE PARAGRAPHS 13-16
IF GENERAL VENUE RULE APPLIES}

13. {㊲ *Proposed*} County is a county of proper venue under the general venue rule because it {㊳ *is/was*} the county where all or a substantial part of the events or omissions giving rise to the claim occurred. Tex. Civ. Prac. & Rem. Code §15.002(a)(1). {㊴ *Elaborate.*}

14. {㊵ *Proposed*} County is a county of proper venue under the general venue rule because it {㊶ *is/was*} the county of defendant's residence at the time the cause of action accrued. Tex. Civ. Prac. & Rem. Code §15.002(a)(2). {㊷ *Elaborate.*}

15. {㊸ *Proposed*} County is a county of proper venue under the general venue rule because it {㊹ *is/was*} the county of defendant's principal office in this state. Tex. Civ. Prac. & Rem. Code §15.002(a)(3); *see In re Mo. Pac. R.R. Co.*, 998 S.W.2d 212, 216-17 (Tex. 1999) (FELA case). {㊺ *Elaborate.*}

16. {㊻ *Proposed*} County is a county of proper venue under the general venue rule because it {㊼ *is/was*} the county where plaintiff resided at the time the cause of action accrued. Tex. Civ. Prac. & Rem. Code §15.002(a)(4). {㊽ *Elaborate.*}

C. Improper joinder.

17. Plaintiff {㊾ *name*} cannot establish proper joinder under section 15.003(a) because {㊿ *explain*}. {*See* ***O'Connor's Texas Rules****, "Joinder proper," ch. 3-C, §2.6.4(2), p. 247.*}

{ADD SECTION BELOW IF APPLICABLE}

TRANSFER FOR CONVENIENCE

18. In the alternative, defendant asks the Court to transfer the case to {51 *proposed*} County in the interest of justice and for the convenience of the parties and witnesses under the authority of Texas Civil Practice & Remedies Code section 15.002(b).

Continued on next page

19. Maintaining this suit in {52 *current*} County will impose an economic and personal hardship on defendant. Tex. Civ. Prac. & Rem. Code §15.002(b)(1). Specifically, {53 *state why suit in current county will impose an economic and personal hardship and why suit in proposed county would not*}. {54 *Elaborate.*}

20. The balance of interests of all parties weighs in favor of the action being brought in {55 *proposed*} County. Tex. Civ. Prac. & Rem. Code §15.002(b)(2). Specifically, {56 *list factors that weigh in favor of proposed county*}. {57 *Elaborate.*}

21. The transfer to {58 *proposed*} County will not cause a hardship or an injustice for any other party. Tex. Civ. Prac. & Rem. Code §15.002(b)(3). Specifically, {59 *state specific reasons why the move would not impose a hardship or injustice on plaintiff and any other parties*}. {60 *Elaborate.*}

22. {61 *Current*} County is not a county of mandatory venue, and {62 *proposed*} County is a county of proper venue. *See* Tex. Civ. Prac. & Rem. Code §15.002(b). {63 *Elaborate.*}

COSTS

23. Defendant asks the Court to tax against plaintiff all costs incurred before the case is transferred. *See* Tex. R. Civ. P. 89.

CONCLUSION

24. {64 *Briefly summarize the motion.*}

PRAYER

25. For these reasons, defendant asks the Court to set {65 *his/her/its*} motion to sever and transfer venue for hearing and, after the hearing, grant defendant's motion and transfer plaintiff {66 *name*}'s case to {67 *proposed*} County. {*See* ***O'Connor's Texas Rules****, "Request hearing," ch. 3-C, §2.2.5, p. 244.*}

SEE: Tex. R. Civ. P. 85-89
Tex. Civ. Prac. & Rem. Code §15.001 et seq.
Tex. Const. art. 3, §45
O'Connor's Texas Rules * Civil Trials (2019), "Improper County or Convenience," ch. 3-C, §2, p. 243

ADD: STYLE OF THE CASE – FORM 1B:2
SIGNATURE BLOCK – FORM 1B:3
CERTIFICATE OF SERVICE – FORM 1B:13

FORM 3C:2

ATTACH: AFFIDAVIT – FORM 1B:8, if necessary
NOTICE OF CURRENT/CHANGE OF ADDRESS – FORM 1B:14, if motion to transfer venue is defendant's initial pleading
NOTICE OF HEARING OR SUBMISSION – FORM 1E:1
ORDER – FORM 3C:11

NOTE: This form is designed for use in a suit with multiple plaintiffs when one of the plaintiffs cannot independently establish proper venue or proper joinder under Texas Civil Practice & Remedies Code §15.003(a). If a defendant in a suit with multiple defendants wants to sever and transfer the claims against it based on other grounds (e.g., a mandatory-venue provision requires transfer), it should use FORM 5I:1 (a more general motion-to-sever form) with an appropriate transfer motion from this chapter.

DEFENDANT'S MOTION TO TRANSFER FOR CONVENIENCE

Defendant, {❶ *name*}, files this motion to transfer venue and asks the Court to transfer the case from {❷ *current*} County to {❸ *proposed*} County in the interest of justice and for the convenience of the parties and witnesses. {*See **O'Connor's Texas Rules**, "Venue convenient elsewhere," ch. 3-C, §2.3.5, p. 245.*}

INTRODUCTION

1. Plaintiff, {❹ *name*}, sued defendant, {❺ *name*}, in {❻ *current*} County for {❼ *state basis of suit*}.

2. {❽ *If motion to transfer venue is defendant's initial pleading, add appropriate identification for each defendant from FORM 3E:1.*}

3. {❾ *State other relevant facts about the suit.*}

BACKGROUND

4. {❿ *State facts relevant to the motion.*}

ARGUMENT & AUTHORITIES

5. Defendant asks that the Court transfer this case to {⓫ *proposed*} County in the interest of justice and for the convenience of the parties and witnesses under the authority of Texas Civil Practice & Remedies Code section 15.002(b).

6. Maintaining this suit in {⓬ *current*} County will impose an economic and personal hardship on defendant. Tex. Civ. Prac. & Rem. Code §15.002(b)(1). Specifically, {⓭ *state why suit in current county will impose an economic and personal hardship and why suit in proposed county would not*}.

7. The balance of interests of all the parties weighs in favor of the action being brought in {⓮ *proposed*} County. Tex. Civ. Prac. & Rem. Code §15.002(b)(2). Specifically, {⓯ *list factors that weigh in favor of proposed county*}.

8. The transfer to {⓰ *proposed*} County will not cause a hardship or an injustice for any other party. Tex. Civ. Prac. & Rem. Code §15.002(b)(3). Specifically, {⓱ *state specific reasons why the transfer would not impose a hardship or injustice on plaintiff and any other parties*}.

9. {⓲ *Current*} County is not a county of mandatory venue, and {⓳ *proposed*} County is a county of proper venue. *See* Tex. Civ. Prac. & Rem. Code §15.002(b). {⓴ *Elaborate.*}

CONCLUSION

10. Because venue is more convenient in {21 *proposed*} County, a county of proper venue, the Court should transfer this case to {22 *proposed*} County.

PRAYER

11. For these reasons, defendant asks the Court to set {23 *his/her/its*} motion to transfer venue for hearing and, after the hearing, grant defendant's motion and transfer this case to {24 *proposed*} County. {*See* ***O'Connor's Texas Rules****, "Request hearing," ch. 3-C, §2.2.5, p. 244.*}

SEE: Tex. R. Civ. P. 85-89
Tex. Civ. Prac. & Rem. Code §15.002(b)
Tex. Const. art. 3, §45
O'Connor's Texas Rules * Civil Trials (2019), "Improper County or Convenience," ch. 3-C, §2, p. 243

ADD: STYLE OF THE CASE – FORM 1B:2
SIGNATURE BLOCK – FORM 1B:3
CERTIFICATE OF SERVICE – FORM 1B:13

ATTACH: AFFIDAVIT – FORM 1B:8
NOTICE OF CURRENT/CHANGE OF ADDRESS – FORM 1B:14, if motion to transfer venue is defendant's initial pleading
NOTICE OF HEARING OR SUBMISSION – FORM 1E:1
ORDER – FORM 3C:11

{[1] *PARTY*}'S MOTION TO CHANGE VENUE

{[2] *Party*}, {[3] *name*}, asks the Court to transfer this case from {[4] *current*} County to {[5] *proposed*} County because of local prejudice, as authorized by Texas Rules of Civil Procedure 257-259. {*See* ***O'Connor's Texas Rules****, "Local Prejudice," ch. 3-C, §3, p. 252.*}

INTRODUCTION

1. Plaintiff, {[6] *name*}, sued defendant, {[7] *name*}, in {[8] *current*} County for {[9] *state basis of suit*}.

2. {[10] *If motion to change venue is defendant's initial pleading, add appropriate identification for each defendant from FORM 3E:1.*}

3. {[11] *State other relevant facts about the suit.*}

BACKGROUND

4. This motion was filed as soon as the local prejudice became known. {[12] *Elaborate, stating dates.*} {*See* ***O'Connor's Texas Rules****, "Deadline to file," ch. 3-C, §3.4, p. 253.*}

5. {[13] *State other facts relevant to the motion.*}

6. {[14] *Party*} attaches {[15] *his/her/its*} affidavit and the affidavits of {[16] *identify number, at least three*} credible residents of this county to this motion as Exhibits {[17] *letters*} to support the facts stated in the motion. These exhibits are incorporated into the motion by reference. {*See* ***O'Connor's Texas Rules****, "Affidavits," ch. 3-C, §3.5, p. 253.*}

ARGUMENT & AUTHORITIES

{*CHOOSE APPROPRIATE PARAGRAPHS 7-10*}

7. The Court should transfer this case to another county because the prejudice in this county is so great that {[18] *party*} cannot obtain a fair and impartial trial. Tex. R. Civ. P. 257(a); *see Dorchester Gas Producing Co. v. Harlow Corp.*, 743 S.W.2d 243, 253 & n.6 (Tex. App.—Amarillo 1987, no writ). A trial in this county will deprive {[19] *party*} of {[20] *his/her/its*} due-process rights to a fair trial under both United States Constitution amendment 14 and Texas Constitution article 1, section 19. {[21] *Elaborate.*}

8. The Court should transfer this case to another county because there is a combination against {[22] *party*} instigated by influential persons in this county that will prevent a fair and impartial trial. Tex. R. Civ. P. 257(b). {[23] *Elaborate.*}

9. The Court should transfer this case to another county because an impartial trial cannot be had here. Tex. R. Civ. P. 257(c); *see In re E. Tex. Med. Ctr. Athens*, 154 S.W.3d 933, 935 (Tex. App.—Tyler 2005, orig. proceeding). A trial in this county will deprive {[24] *party*} of {[25] *his/her/its*} due-process rights to a fair trial under both United States Constitution amendment 14 and Texas Constitution article 1, section 19. {[26] *Elaborate.*}

10. The Court should transfer this case to another county because {[27] *assert any other relevant reasons*}. Tex. R. Civ. P. 257(d). {[28] *Elaborate.*}

CONCLUSION

11. Because {[29] *party*} cannot obtain a fair and impartial trial in {[30] *current*} County, the Court should transfer this case to {[31] *proposed*} County, which is

{*CHOOSE ONE OF THE FOLLOWING*}

[A] a county of proper venue in {[32] *this/an adjoining*} district. Tex. R. Civ. P. 259(a). {*See* ***O'Connor's Texas Rules****, "Ruling," ch. 3-C, §3.11, p. 254.*}

[B] {[33] *an adjoining/a*} county of proper venue. {[34] *Tex. R. Civ. P. 259(b)/ Tex. R. Civ. P. 259(c).*} {*See* ***O'Connor's Texas Rules****, "Ruling," ch. 3-C, §3.11, p. 254.*}

[C] a county in {[35] *this/an adjoining*} district. Tex. R. Civ. P. 259(d)(1). {*See* ***O'Connor's Texas Rules****, "Ruling," ch. 3-C, §3.11, p. 254.*}

[D] an adjoining county. Tex. R. Civ. P. 259(d)(2). {*See* ***O'Connor's Texas Rules****, "Ruling," ch. 3-C, §3.11, p. 254.*}

[E] any district where an impartial trial can be had. Tex. R. Civ. P. 259(d). {*See* ***O'Connor's Texas Rules****, "Ruling," ch. 3-C, §3.11, p. 254.*}

[F] a county to which the parties agree to transfer the case. Tex. R. Civ. P. 259. {*See* ***O'Connor's Texas Rules****, "Ruling," ch. 3-C, §3.11, p. 254.*}

PRAYER

12. For these reasons, {[36] *party*} asks the Court to set {[37] *his/her/its*} motion to change venue for a hearing to receive evidence and, after the hearing, grant {[38] *his/her/its*} motion and transfer the case to {[39] *proposed*} County.

Continued on next page

Form 3C:4 Venue – Motion to Change, Local Prejudice

SEE: Tex. R. Civ. P. 85-89, 257-259
Tex. Civ. Prac. & Rem. Code §15.063
U.S. Const. 14th amend.
Tex. Const. art. 1, §19; art. 3, §45
O'Connor's Texas Rules * Civil Trials (2019), "Local Prejudice," ch. 3-C, §3, p. 252

ADD: STYLE OF THE CASE – FORM 1B:2
SIGNATURE BLOCK – FORM 1B:3
CERTIFICATE OF SERVICE – FORM 1B:13

ATTACH: AFFIDAVIT – FORM 1B:8
NOTICE OF CURRENT/CHANGE OF ADDRESS – FORM 1B:14, if motion to change venue is defendant's initial pleading
NOTICE OF HEARING OR SUBMISSION – FORM 1E:1
ORDER – FORM 3C:11

NOTE: Either party, plaintiff or defendant, can file a motion to change venue based on local prejudice.

PLAINTIFF'S RESPONSE TO
DEFENDANT'S MOTION TO TRANSFER VENUE

Plaintiff, {❶ *name*}, files this response to defendant {❷ *name*}'s motion to transfer venue and asks the Court to deny defendant's motion and retain the case on the Court's docket in {❸ *current*} County.

INTRODUCTION

1. Plaintiff, {❹ *name*}, sued defendant, {❺ *name*}, in {❻ *current*} County for {❼ *state basis of suit*}.

2. {❽ *State other relevant facts about the suit.*}

BACKGROUND

3. On {❾ *date*}, defendant filed a motion to transfer venue to {❿ *proposed*} County.

{*CHOOSE APPROPRIATE PARAGRAPHS 4-7*}

4. In defendant's motion, defendant did not specifically deny that {⓫ *identify plaintiff's venue facts that were not denied, e.g., a substantial part of the events giving rise to this suit occurred in this county, defendant has its principal office in this county*}. Because these venue facts were not specifically denied, they must be taken as true. {*See* ***O'Connor's Texas Rules****, "Denial of venue facts," ch. 3-C, §2.11.4(1), p. 250.*}

5. In defendant's motion, defendant globally denied that {⓬ *identify plaintiff's venue facts that were not properly contested, e.g., a substantial part of the events giving rise to this suit occurred in this county, defendant has its principal office in this county*}. Because these venue facts were not specifically denied, they must be taken as true. {*See* ***O'Connor's Texas Rules****, "Denial of venue facts," ch. 3-C, §2.11.4(1), p. 250.*}

6. In defendant's motion, defendant specifically denied that {⓭ *identify plaintiff's venue facts that defendant specifically denied*}. Contrary to defendant's specific denial, {⓮ *state venue facts from the petition that support venue*}. {*See* ***O'Connor's Texas Rules****, "Proof of denied venue facts," ch. 3-C, §2.7.1, p. 248.*}

7. In defendant's motion, defendant pleaded that {⓯ *identify defendant's venue facts*}. Plaintiff specifically denies that {⓰ *identify defendant's venue facts that are being denied*}. {*See* ***O'Connor's Texas Rules****, "Deny defendant's venue facts," ch. 3-C, §2.6.6, p. 248.*}

◄ *Continued on next page* ►

{*ADD PARAGRAPH 8 IF APPLICABLE*}

8. On {17 *date*}, plaintiff filed an amended petition to {18 *add/delete*} the following claims: {19 *identify claims added or deleted*}. {*See* ***O'Connor's Texas Rules****, "Amend petition," ch. 3-C, §2.8.1, p. 248.*}

9. Plaintiff attaches affidavits to this response as Exhibits {20 *letters*} and incorporates them by reference. By these affidavits, plaintiff makes a prima facie case of {21 *his/her/its*} venue facts. {*See* ***O'Connor's Texas Rules****, "Plaintiff's proof," ch. 3-C, §2.7, p. 248; "Prima facie proof," ch. 3-C, §2.11.4(2), p. 250.*}

ARGUMENT & AUTHORITIES

10. Under Texas law, the plaintiff is given the first choice of where to file suit. *Wilson v. Tex. Parks & Wildlife Dep't*, 886 S.W.2d 259, 260 (Tex. 1994). Only when the plaintiff's choice of venue is properly challenged by the defendant does the plaintiff have the burden to present prima facie proof that venue is proper in the venue of choice. *See id.* If the plaintiff presents prima facie proof supporting venue, the court must accept those facts as true; the plaintiff's proof cannot be rebutted, cross-examined, impeached, or disproved. *Ruiz v. Conoco, Inc.*, 868 S.W.2d 752, 757 (Tex. 1993). If the plaintiff's proof establishes that venue is proper in the county of suit, the court cannot transfer venue to another county—even to one that would have been proper—unless the defendant establishes that an impartial trial cannot be held in that county. *See Wilson*, 886 S.W.2d at 260-61 & n.2.

{*CHOOSE APPROPRIATE SECTIONS A-C*}

A. Venue waived.

11. Defendant did not properly challenge venue in this suit because defendant's motion was filed after the deadline required by both Texas Rule of Civil Procedure 86(1) and Texas Civil Practice & Remedies Code section 15.063. {22 *Elaborate.*} Because defendant's motion was not timely filed, defendant waived {23 *his/her/its*} right to challenge venue. {*See* ***O'Connor's Texas Rules****, "Allege waiver," ch. 3-C, §2.6.7, p. 248.*}

B. Venue proper in {㉔ *current*} County.

{*CHOOSE APPROPRIATE PARAGRAPHS 12-17*}

{*Venue facts not specifically denied*}

12. Defendant did not specifically deny {㉕ *identify plaintiff's venue facts that defendant did not specifically deny, e.g., that a substantial part of the events giving rise to this suit occurred in this county*}. Because plaintiff's venue facts were properly pleaded and are unchallenged, they must be taken as true. Tex. R. Civ. P. 87(3)(a); *Sanes v. Clark*, 25 S.W.3d 800, 803 (Tex. App.—Waco 2000, pet. denied). Taken as true, these facts establish that venue is proper in {㉖ *current*} County under {㉗ *identify venue statute that the facts support*}. {㉘ *Elaborate.*} {*See **O'Connor's Texas Rules**, "Denial of venue facts," ch. 3-C, §2.11.4(1), p. 250.*}

{*Venue facts globally denied*}

13. Defendant made a global denial of plaintiff's venue facts by stating "{㉙ *quote defendant's denial*}." Because a global denial does not satisfy the requirements of Texas Rule of Civil Procedure 87(3)(a), plaintiff's venue facts must be taken as true. *See Bleeker v. Villarreal*, 941 S.W.2d 163, 175-76 (Tex. App.—Corpus Christi 1996, writ dism'd) (denying "the fact that venue is proper" is not a specific denial); *Maranatha Temple, Inc. v. Enter. Prods. Co.*, 833 S.W.2d 736, 740 (Tex. App.—Houston [1st Dist.] 1992, writ denied) (same). Taken as true, these facts establish that venue is proper in {㉚ *current*} County under {㉛ *identify venue statute that the facts support*}. {㉜ *Elaborate.*} {*See **O'Connor's Texas Rules**, "Denial of venue facts," ch. 3-C, §2.11.4(1), p. 250.*}

{*Mandatory venue*}

14. Contrary to defendant's motion, venue is proper in this county because {㉝ *current*} County is a county of mandatory venue under {㉞ *identify statute prescribing mandatory venue, e.g., Texas Civil Practice & Remedies Code section 15.011*}. {㉟ *Current*} County is a county of mandatory venue under {㊱ *identify statute, e.g., section 15.011*} because {㊲ *state facts supporting mandatory venue under the statute*}. Because this suit is filed in the county of mandatory venue, the suit cannot be transferred to another county. *See* Tex. Civ. Prac. & Rem. Code §15.001(b)(1). {*See **O'Connor's Texas Rules**, "Mandatory-Venue Provisions," ch. 2-H, §4, p. 180.*}

◄ *Continued on next page* ►

{*Permissive venue*}

15. Contrary to defendant's motion, venue is proper in this county because {❸❽ *current*} County is a county of permissive venue under {❸❾ *identify statute providing permissive venue, e.g., Texas Civil Practice & Remedies Code section 15.031*}. {❹⓿ *Current*} County is a county of permissive venue under {❹❶ *identify statute, e.g., section 15.031*} because {❹❷ *state facts supporting permissive venue under the statute*}. Because this suit is filed in a county of permissive venue and no mandatory-venue provision applies, this suit cannot be transferred to another county. {*See* ***O'Connor's Texas Rules****, "Permissive-Venue Provisions," ch. 2-H, §5, p. 185.*}

{*General venue*}

16. Contrary to defendant's motion, venue is proper in this county because {❹❸ *current*} County is a county of proper venue under the general venue rule, as provided in Texas Civil Practice & Remedies Code section 15.002(a). {❹❹ *Current*} County is a county of proper venue under section 15.002(a) because {❹❺ *state facts supporting general venue under the statute*}. Because this suit is filed in a county of general venue and no mandatory-venue provision applies, this suit cannot be transferred to another county. {*See* ***O'Connor's Texas Rules****, "General Venue Rule," ch. 2-H, §6, p. 187; "Venue proper under general rule," ch. 3-C, §2.6.2, p. 246.*}

{*Venue proper as to one defendant*}

17. Contrary to defendant's motion, plaintiff's choice of venue complies with the requirements of Texas Civil Practice & Remedies Code section 15.005 because this suit involves multiple defendants. Venue is proper against defendant {❹❻ *name of defendant as to whom venue is proper*} in {❹❼ *current*} County because {❹❽ *state venue facts showing venue is proper against that defendant, e.g., defendant is a corporation with its principal office in this county*}. Venue is therefore proper against {❹❾ *names of additional defendants*} because all of plaintiff's claims against {❺⓿ *names of additional defendants*} arose from the same transaction, occurrence, or series of transactions or occurrences. {❺❶ *Explain how claims arose from same transaction, occurrence, or series of transactions or occurrences.*} {*See* ***O'Connor's Texas Rules****, "Multiple defendants," ch. 2-H, §7.3, p. 188.*}

C. Venue improper in {52 *proposed*} County.

18. Regardless of whether {53 *current*} County is a county of proper venue, defendant has not met {54 *his/her/its*} burden to prove that {55 *proposed*} County is a county of proper venue. Contrary to defendant's motion, this case should not be transferred to {56 *proposed*} County because that county is not, as defendant alleges,

{*CHOOSE ONE OF THE FOLLOWING*}

A a county of mandatory venue under {57 *specify mandatory-venue provision, e.g., Texas Civil Practice & Remedies Code section 15.011*}. {58 *State why the mandatory-venue provision does not apply.*}

B a proper county under a permissive-venue provision. Venue is not permissive in {59 *proposed*} County under {60 *identify statute cited by defendant, e.g., Texas Civil Practice & Remedies Code section 15.031*} because {61 *specify reason, e.g., this is a suit for a debt of an estate and the proposed county is not the county where the estate is being administered*}.

C a proper county under the general venue rule, Texas Civil Practice & Remedies Code section 15.002(a). {62 *State why proposed county is not a proper county under Tex. Civ. Prac. & Rem. Code §15.002(a).*}

{*ADD SECTION BELOW IF APPLICABLE*}

TRANSFER FOR CONVENIENCE

19. In the alternative, defendant asked the Court to transfer the suit to {63 *proposed*} County in the interest of justice and for the convenience of the parties and witnesses under the authority of Texas Civil Practice & Remedies Code section 15.002(b).

20. {64 *Insert responses from FORM 3C:7.*} {*See* ***O'Connor's Texas Rules****, "Venue not convenient elsewhere," ch. 3-C, §2.6.5, p. 247.*}

CONCLUSION

21. Because plaintiff properly pleaded and proved that venue is proper in {65 *current*} County, this suit must be maintained in this county. *See Wilson*, 886 S.W.2d at 261.

PRAYER

22. For these reasons, plaintiff asks the Court to deny defendant's motion to transfer venue and retain this case on the Court's docket in {66 *current*} County.

◄ *Continued on next page* ►

SEE: Tex. R. Civ. P. 85-89, 252
Tex. Civ. Prac. & Rem. Code §15.001 et seq., §15.063
Tex. Const. art. 3, §45
O'Connor's Texas Rules * Civil Trials (2019), "Improper County or Convenience," ch. 3-C, §2, p. 243

ADD: STYLE OF THE CASE – FORM 1B:2
SIGNATURE BLOCK – FORM 1B:3
CERTIFICATE OF SERVICE – FORM 1B:13

ATTACH: AFFIDAVIT – FORM 1B:8, with discovery excerpts or other evidence attached, if necessary
ORDER – FORM 3C:11

NOTE: When a party specifically denies a venue fact, the party pleading the venue fact must make prima facie proof of that fact. Tex. R. Civ. P. 87(2)(b); ***GeoChem Tech v. Verseckes***, 962 S.W.2d 541, 543 (Tex.1998). Prima facie proof is made when the venue facts are properly pleaded and are supported by proper affidavit proof. Tex. R. Civ. P. 87(3)(a). See ***O'Connor's Texas Rules***, "Prima facie proof," ch. 3-C, §2.11.4(2), p. 250.

The deadline to file a response to the motion to transfer is 30 days before the venue hearing, unless the plaintiff gets permission to file it later. Tex. R. Civ. P. 87(1).

If a plaintiff needs time to conduct discovery before opposing a motion to transfer venue, the plaintiff can file a motion to continue the hearing on the motion to transfer venue before filing a response. See FORM 5D:1.

PLAINTIFF'S RESPONSE TO
DEFENDANT'S MOTION TO SEVER & TRANSFER

Plaintiff, {❶ *name*}, asks the Court to deny defendant {❷ *name*}'s motion to sever and transfer plaintiff's portion of the suit to {❸ *proposed*} County.

INTRODUCTION

1. Plaintiff, {❹ *name*}, sued defendant, {❺ *name*}, in {❻ *current*} County for {❼ *state basis of suit*}.

2. {❽ *State other relevant facts about the suit.*}

BACKGROUND

3. On {❾ *date*}, defendant filed a motion to sever and transfer plaintiff's portion of the suit to {❿ *proposed*} County.

{*CHOOSE APPROPRIATE PARAGRAPHS 4-7*}

4. In defendant's motion, defendant did not specifically deny that {⓫ *identify plaintiff's venue facts that were not denied, e.g., a substantial part of the events giving rise to this suit occurred in this county, defendant has its principal office in this county*}. Because these venue facts were not specifically denied, they must be taken as true. {*See* ***O'Connor's Texas Rules***, *"Denial of venue facts," ch. 3-C, §2.11.4(1), p. 250.*}

5. In defendant's motion, defendant globally denied that {⓬ *identify plaintiff's venue facts that were not properly contested, e.g., a substantial part of the events giving rise to this suit occurred in this county, defendant has its principal office in this county*}. Because these venue facts were not specifically denied, they must be taken as true. {*See* ***O'Connor's Texas Rules***, *"Denial of venue facts," ch. 3-C, §2.11.4(1), p. 250.*}

6. In defendant's motion, defendant specifically denied that {⓭ *identify plaintiff's venue facts that defendant specifically denied*}. Contrary to defendant's specific denial, {⓮ *state venue facts from the petition that support venue*}. {*See* ***O'Connor's Texas Rules***, *"Proof of denied venue facts," ch. 3-C, §2.7.1, p. 248.*}

7. In defendant's motion, defendant pleaded that {⓯ *identify defendant's venue facts*}. Plaintiff specifically denies that {⓰ *identify defendant's venue facts that are being denied*}. {*See* ***O'Connor's Texas Rules***, *"Deny defendant's venue facts," ch. 3-C, §2.6.6, p. 248.*}

Continued on next page

FORM 3C:6

{*ADD PARAGRAPH 8 IF APPLICABLE*}

8. On {17 *date*}, plaintiff filed an amended petition to {18 *add/delete*} the following claims: {19 *identify claims added or deleted*}. {*See* ***O'Connor's Texas Rules****, "Amend petition," ch. 3-C, §2.8.1, p. 248.*}

9. Plaintiff attaches affidavits to this response as Exhibits {20 *letters*} and incorporates them by reference. By these affidavits, plaintiff makes a prima facie case of {21 *his/her/its*} {22 *proper venue/proper joinder/proper venue and proper joinder*}. {*See* ***O'Connor's Texas Rules****, "Plaintiff's proof," ch. 3-C, §2.7, p. 248; "Prima facie proof," ch. 3-C, §2.11.4(2), p. 250.*}

ARGUMENT & AUTHORITIES

10. A plaintiff has the initial burden to establish, independently of every other plaintiff, that venue is proper as to the plaintiff in the county of suit. Tex. Civ. Prac. & Rem. Code §15.003(a). If the plaintiff is unable to establish proper venue, the plaintiff's portion of the suit must be transferred to a county of proper venue or dismissed unless the plaintiff can demonstrate that it was properly joined under Texas Civil Practice & Remedies Code section 15.003(a). *See Surgitek v. Abel*, 997 S.W.2d 598, 602 (Tex. 1999). {*See* ***O'Connor's Texas Rules****, "Venue or joinder proper in multiple-plaintiff case," ch. 3-C, §2.6.4, p. 247.*}

{*CHOOSE APPROPRIATE PARAGRAPHS 11-12*}

11. On the issue of venue, plaintiff can establish proper venue by offering prima facie proof that venue is proper in the county of suit. If the plaintiff presents prima facie proof supporting venue, the court must accept those facts as true; the plaintiff's proof cannot be rebutted, cross-examined, impeached, or disproved. *Ruiz v. Conoco, Inc.*, 868 S.W.2d 752, 757 (Tex. 1993). If the plaintiff's proof establishes that venue is proper in the county of suit, the court cannot transfer venue to another county—even to one that would have been proper—unless the defendant establishes that an impartial trial cannot be held in that county. *See Wilson v. Tex. Parks & Wildlife Dep't*, 886 S.W.2d 259, 260-61 & n.2 (Tex. 1994).

12. On the issue of joinder, plaintiff can establish proper joinder by offering prima facie proof of the four joinder elements listed in section 15.003(a). *Surgitek*, 997 S.W.2d at 602-03. If the defendant does not offer evidence to rebut plaintiff's prima facie proof, then joinder is proper as a matter of law. *See id.* at 603.

FORM 3C:6

{*CHOOSE APPROPRIATE SECTIONS A-D*}

A. Venue waived.

13. Defendant did not properly challenge venue in this suit because defendant's motion was filed after the deadline required by both Texas Rule of Civil Procedure 86(1) and Texas Civil Practice & Remedies Code section 15.063. {23 *Elaborate.*} Because defendant's motion was not timely filed, defendant waived {24 *his/her/its*} right to challenge venue. {*See* ***O'Connor's Texas Rules****, "Allege waiver," ch. 3-C, §2.6.7, p. 248.*}

B. Venue proper in {25 *current*} County.

{*CHOOSE APPROPRIATE PARAGRAPHS 14-18*}

{*Venue facts not specifically denied*}

14. Defendant did not specifically deny {26 *identify plaintiff's venue facts that defendant did not specifically deny, e.g., that a substantial part of the events giving rise to this suit occurred in this county*}. Because plaintiff's venue facts were properly pleaded and are unchallenged, they must be taken as true. Tex. R. Civ. P. 87(3)(a); *Sanes v. Clark*, 25 S.W.3d 800, 803 (Tex. App.—Waco 2000, pet. denied). Taken as true, these facts establish that venue is proper in {27 *current*} County under {28 *identify venue statute that the facts support*}. {29 *Elaborate.*} {*See* ***O'Connor's Texas Rules****, "Denial of venue facts," ch. 3-C, §2.11.4(1), p. 250.*}

{*Venue facts globally denied*}

15. Defendant made a global denial of plaintiff's venue facts by stating "{30 *quote defendant's denial*}." Because a global denial does not satisfy the requirements of Texas Rule of Civil Procedure 87(3)(a), plaintiff's venue facts must be taken as true. *See Bleeker v. Villarreal*, 941 S.W.2d 163, 175-76 (Tex. App.—Corpus Christi 1996, writ dism'd) (denying "the fact that venue is proper" is not a specific denial); *Maranatha Temple, Inc. v. Enter. Prods. Co.*, 833 S.W.2d 736, 740 (Tex. App.—Houston [1st Dist.] 1992, writ denied) (same). Taken as true, these facts establish that venue is proper in {31 *current*} County under {32 *identify venue statute that the facts support*}. {33 *Elaborate.*} {*See* ***O'Connor's Texas Rules****, "Denial of venue facts," ch. 3-C, §2.11.4(1), p. 250.*}

{*Mandatory venue*}

16. Contrary to defendant's motion, venue is proper in this county because {34 *current*} County is a county of mandatory venue under {35 *identify statute prescribing mandatory venue, e.g., Texas Civil Practice & Remedies Code section*

Continued on next page

FORM 3C:6

15.011}. {36 *Current*} County is a county of mandatory venue under {37 *identify statute, e.g., section 15.011*} because {38 *state facts supporting mandatory venue under the statute*}. Because this suit is filed in the county of mandatory venue, the suit cannot be transferred to another county. *See* Tex. Civ. Prac. & Rem. Code §15.001(b)(1). {*See **O'Connor's Texas Rules**, "Mandatory-Venue Provisions," ch. 2-H, §4, p. 180.*}

{*Permissive venue*}

17. Contrary to defendant's motion, venue is proper in this county because {39 *current*} County is a county of permissive venue under {40 *identify statute providing permissive venue, e.g., Texas Civil Practice & Remedies Code section 15.031*}. {41 *Current*} County is a county of permissive venue under {42 *identify statute, e.g., section 15.031*} because {43 *state facts supporting permissive venue under the statute*}. Because this suit is filed in a county of permissive venue and no mandatory-venue provision applies, this suit cannot be transferred to another county. {*See **O'Connor's Texas Rules**, "Permissive-Venue Provisions," ch. 2-H, §5, p. 185.*}

{*General venue*}

18. Contrary to defendant's motion, venue is proper in this county because {44 *current*} County is a county of proper venue under the general venue rule, as provided in Texas Civil Practice & Remedies Code section 15.002(a). {45 *Current*} County is a county of proper venue under section 15.002(a) because {46 *state facts supporting general venue under the statute*}. Because this suit is filed in a county of general venue and no mandatory-venue provision applies, this suit cannot be transferred to another county. {*See **O'Connor's Texas Rules**, "General Venue Rule," ch. 2-H, §6, p. 187; "Venue proper under general rule," ch. 3-C, §2.6.2, p. 246.*}

C. Venue improper in {47 *proposed*} County.

19. Regardless of whether {48 *current*} County is a county of proper venue, defendant has not met {49 *his/her/its*} burden to prove that {50 *proposed*} County is a county of proper venue. Contrary to defendant's motion, this case should not be transferred to {51 *proposed*} County because that county is not, as defendant alleges,

{*CHOOSE ONE OF THE FOLLOWING*}

A a county of mandatory venue under {52 *specify mandatory-venue provision, e.g., Texas Civil Practice & Remedies Code section 15.011*}. {53 *State why the mandatory-venue provision does not apply.*}

FORM 3C:6

B a proper county under a permissive-venue provision. Venue is not permissive in {54 *proposed*} County under {55 *identify statute cited by defendant, e.g., Texas Civil Practice & Remedies Code section 15.031*} because {56 *specify reason, e.g., this is a suit for a debt of an estate and the proposed county is not the county where the estate is being administered*}.

C a proper county under the general venue rule, Texas Civil Practice & Remedies Code section 15.002(a). {57 *State why proposed county is not a proper county under Tex. Civ. Prac. & Rem. Code §15.002(a).*}

D. Proper joinder.

20. Regardless of whether {58 *current*} County is a county of proper venue, plaintiff {59 *name*} can defeat defendant's motion by establishing, independently of every other plaintiff, proper joinder under Texas Civil Practice & Remedies Code section 15.003(a). {*See* ***O'Connor's Texas Rules****, "Joinder proper," ch. 3-C, §2.6.4(2), p. 247.*} {60 *Elaborate.*}

21. Plaintiff's joinder in this suit is proper under the Texas Rules of Civil Procedure. Tex. Civ. Prac. & Rem. Code §15.003(a)(1). {61 *Elaborate.*}

22. Maintaining venue in {62 *current*} County will not unfairly prejudice any other party. Tex. Civ. Prac. & Rem. Code §15.003(a)(2). {63 *Elaborate.*}

23. There is an essential need to have the claims of plaintiff's suit tried in {64 *current*} County. Tex. Civ. Prac. & Rem. Code §15.003(a)(3); *see Surgitek*, 997 S.W.2d at 604. {65 *Elaborate.*}

24. {66 *Current*} County is a fair and convenient venue for plaintiff {67 *name*} and all defendants. Tex. Civ. Prac. & Rem. Code §15.003(a)(4). {68 *Elaborate.*}

{*ADD SECTION BELOW IF APPLICABLE*}

TRANSFER FOR CONVENIENCE

25. In the alternative, defendant asked the Court to transfer the suit to {69 *proposed*} County in the interest of justice and for the convenience of the parties and witnesses under the authority of Texas Civil Practice & Remedies Code section 15.002(b).

26. {70 *Insert responses from FORM 3C:7.*} {*See* ***O'Connor's Texas Rules****, "Venue not convenient elsewhere," ch. 3-C, §2.6.5, p. 247.*}

◄ *Continued on next page* ►

CONCLUSION

27. {(71) *Briefly summarize the response.*}

PRAYER

28. For these reasons, plaintiff {(72) *name*} asks the Court to deny defendant's motion to sever and transfer venue.

SEE: Tex. R. Civ. P. 85-89, 252
Tex. Civ. Prac. & Rem. Code §§15.003, 15.063
Tex. Const. art. 3, §45
O'Connor's Texas Rules * Civil Trials (2019), "Improper County or Convenience," ch. 3-C, §2, p. 243

ADD: STYLE OF THE CASE – FORM 1B:2
SIGNATURE BLOCK – FORM 1B:3
CERTIFICATE OF SERVICE – FORM 1B:13

ATTACH: AFFIDAVIT – FORM 1B:8, with discovery excerpts or other evidence attached, if necessary
ORDER – FORM 3C:11

NOTE: A person cannot intervene or join a pending suit as a plaintiff unless the person, independently of every other plaintiff, can establish venue is proper in the current county or can satisfy the requirements listed in paragraphs 21-24 of this form. *See* Tex. Civ. Prac. & Rem. Code §15.003. See FORM 5J:3 for additional grounds to deny objections to intervention.

When a party specifically denies a venue fact, the party pleading the venue fact must make prima facie proof of that fact. Tex. R. Civ. P. 87(2)(b); ***GeoChem Tech v. Verseckes***, 962 S.W.2d 541, 543 (Tex.1998). Similarly, a plaintiff who is establishing venue based on joinder must offer prima facie proof of each of the four joinder elements of Texas Civil Practice & Remedies Code §15.003(a). Prima facie proof is made when the venue facts are properly pleaded and are supported by proper affidavit proof. Tex. R. Civ. P. 87(3)(a). See ***O'Connor's Texas Rules***, "Prima facie proof," ch. 3-C, §2.11.4(2), p. 250.

The deadline to file a response to the motion to transfer is 30 days before the venue hearing, unless the plaintiff gets permission to file it later. Tex. R. Civ. P. 87(1).

If a plaintiff needs time to conduct discovery before opposing a motion to transfer venue, the plaintiff can file a motion to continue the hearing on the motion to transfer venue before filing a response. See FORM 5D:1.

PLAINTIFF'S RESPONSE TO DEFENDANT'S MOTION TO TRANSFER FOR CONVENIENCE

Plaintiff, {❶ *name*}, files this response to defendant {❷ *name*}'s motion to transfer venue and asks the Court to deny the motion and retain the case on the Court's docket because the parties and witnesses will not be inconvenienced by having this case tried in {❸ *current*} County. {*See* ***O'Connor's Texas Rules****, "Venue not convenient elsewhere," ch. 3-C, §2.6.5, p. 247.*}

INTRODUCTION

1. Plaintiff, {❹ *name*}, sued defendant, {❺ *name*}, in {❻ *current*} County for {❼ *state basis of suit*}.

2. {❽ *State other relevant facts about the suit.*}

BACKGROUND

3. On {❾ *date*}, defendant filed a motion to transfer venue to {❿ *proposed*} County in the interest of justice and for the convenience of the parties and witnesses under the authority of Texas Civil Practice & Remedies Code section 15.002(b).

4. In defendant's motion, defendant argued that {⓫ *state defendant's arguments*}.

5. {⓬ *State other facts relevant to the response.*}

6. Plaintiff attaches affidavits to this response as Exhibits {⓭ *letters*} to establish facts not apparent from the record and incorporates them by reference. {*See* ***O'Connor's Texas Rules****, "Proof of convenience issues," ch. 3-C, §2.7.3, p. 248.*}

ARGUMENT & AUTHORITIES

{*CHOOSE APPROPRIATE PARAGRAPHS 7-12*}

7. Defendant waived {⓮ *his/her/its*} right to challenge venue for convenience by making the request after the deadline required by both Texas Rule of Civil Procedure 86(1) and Texas Civil Practice & Remedies Code section 15.063. {⓯ *Elaborate.*} {*See* ***O'Connor's Texas Rules****, "Due order of pleading," ch. 3-C, §2.2.2, p. 243.*}

8. Contrary to defendant's motion, venue is proper in this county because {⓰ *current*} County is a county of mandatory venue, so this suit cannot be transferred for convenience. {⓱ *Identify mandatory-venue provision and state facts showing mandatory venue in this county.*} {*See* ***O'Connor's Texas Rules****, "Mandatory-Venue Provisions," ch. 2-H, §4, p. 180.*}

— Continued on next page —

FORM 3C:7

9. Contrary to defendant's motion, maintaining this suit in {[18] *current*} County will not impose a hardship on defendant. Tex. Civ. Prac. & Rem. Code §15.002(b)(1). Specifically, {[19] *state why suit in current county will not be inconvenient to defendant, identify names of deposition witnesses who will not be inconvenienced, state why suit in the proposed county would be inconvenient, and specifically deny any of defendant's venue facts related to this issue*}.

10. Contrary to defendant's motion, the balance of interests of all the parties weighs in favor of the action being maintained in {[20] *current*} County. Tex. Civ. Prac. & Rem. Code §15.002(b)(2). Specifically, {[21] *list factors that weigh in favor of keeping case in current county and specifically deny any of defendant's venue facts related to this issue*}.

11. Contrary to defendant's motion, the transfer will cause an injustice or hardship for the plaintiff or other parties. Tex. Civ. Prac. & Rem. Code §15.002(b)(3). Specifically, {[22] *state specific reasons why the transfer will impose a hardship on the plaintiff, its witnesses, and any other parties*}.

12. Regardless of whether maintaining this suit in {[23] *current*} County would be inconvenient for the parties and witnesses, this suit cannot be transferred to {[24] *proposed*} County because it is not a county of proper venue. Tex. Civ. Prac. & Rem. Code §15.002(b). {[25] *Elaborate.*}

CONCLUSION

13. {[26] *Briefly summarize the response.*}

PRAYER

14. For these reasons, plaintiff asks the Court to deny defendant's motion to transfer venue.

SEE: Tex. R. Civ. P. 85-89, 252
Tex. Civ. Prac. & Rem. Code §§15.002(b), 15.063
Tex. Const. art. 3, §45
O'Connor's Texas Rules * Civil Trials (2019), "Improper County or Convenience," ch. 3-C, §2, p. 243

ADD: STYLE OF THE CASE – FORM 1B:2
SIGNATURE BLOCK – FORM 1B:3
CERTIFICATE OF SERVICE – FORM 1B:13

ATTACH: AFFIDAVIT – FORM 1B:8, with discovery excerpts or other evidence attached, if necessary
ORDER – FORM 3C:11

NOTE: The deadline to file a response to the motion to transfer is 30 days before the venue hearing, unless the plaintiff gets permission to file it later. Tex. R. Civ. P. 87(1).

If a plaintiff needs time to conduct discovery before opposing a motion to transfer venue, the plaintiff can file a motion to continue the hearing on the motion to transfer venue before filing a response. See FORM 5D:1.

{[1] *PARTY*}'S RESPONSE TO
{[2] *ADVERSE PARTY*}'S MOTION TO CHANGE VENUE

{[3] *Party*}, {[4] *name*}, files this response to {[5] *adverse party*}'s motion to change venue under Texas Rules of Civil Procedure 257-259 and asks the Court to deny the motion and retain the case on the Court's docket in {[6] *current*} County because {[7] *adverse party*}, {[8] *name*}, can obtain a fair and impartial trial in {[9] *current*} County.

INTRODUCTION

1. Plaintiff, {[10] *name*}, sued defendant, {[11] *name*}, for {[12] *state basis of suit*}.

2. {[13] *State other relevant facts about the suit.*}

BACKGROUND

3. On {[14] *date*}, {[15] *adverse party*} filed a motion to change venue to {[16] *proposed*} County because of local prejudice.

4. In {[17] *adverse party*}'s motion, {[18] *adverse party*} argued that {[19] *state arguments*}.

5. {[20] *State other facts relevant to the response.*}

6. {[21] *Party*} attaches the affidavits of {[22] *list affiants*} to this response as Exhibits {[23] *letters*} to establish facts not apparent from the record and incorporates them by reference. {*See **O'Connor's Texas Rules**, "Response," ch. 3-C, §3.7, p. 253.*}

ARGUMENT & AUTHORITIES

{*CHOOSE APPROPRIATE PARAGRAPHS 7-13*}

7. The Court should deny {[24] *adverse party*}'s motion because the motion was untimely filed. In {[25] *his/her/its*} motion, {[26] *adverse party*} claimed to have filed the motion as soon as the local prejudice became known, on {[27] *date*}. However, {[28] *state facts showing that adverse party knew about prejudice earlier*}. {[29] *Elaborate.*} {*See **O'Connor's Texas Rules**, "Deadline to file," ch. 3-C, §3.4, p. 253.*}

8. The Court should deny {[30] *adverse party*}'s motion because {[31] *adverse party*}'s affidavits are made by persons who are not residents of this county and therefore do not comply with Texas Rule of Civil Procedure 257. {[32] *Elaborate.*} {*See **O'Connor's Texas Rules**, "Affidavits," ch. 3-C, §3.5, p. 253.*}

9. The Court should deny {33 *adverse party*}'s motion because {34 *adverse party*}'s affidavits are made by persons who {35 *are not credible/are not truthful/do not have any means of knowing about local prejudice*}. *See* Tex. R. Civ. P. 258. {36 *Elaborate.*}

10. Contrary to {37 *adverse party*}'s motion, there is no prejudice in this county that will deprive {38 *him/her/it*} of a fair and impartial trial. *See* Tex. R. Civ. P. 257(a). {39 *Elaborate.*}

11. Contrary to {40 *adverse party*}'s motion, there is no combination against {41 *him/her/it*} instigated by influential persons in this county that would prevent a fair and impartial trial. *See* Tex. R. Civ. P. 257(b). {42 *Elaborate.*}

12. Contrary to {43 *adverse party*}'s motion, an impartial trial can be had in {44 *current*} County. *See* Tex. Civ. Prac. & Rem. Code §15.063(2); Tex. R. Civ. P. 257(c). A trial in this county will not deprive {45 *adverse party*} of {46 *his/her/its*} due-process rights to a fair trial. {47 *Elaborate.*} {*See* ***O'Connor's Texas Rules****, "No impartial trial," ch. 3-C, §3.3.3, p. 253.*}

13. In the alternative, if the Court decides to grant {48 *adverse party*}'s motion, the Court should not transfer the case to {49 *proposed*} County because {50 *state reasons why adverse party's proposed county is not a county of proper venue*}. Instead of {51 *proposed*} County, the Court should transfer the case to {52 *alternative*} County, a county of proper venue under {53 *identify statute*}. {54 *Elaborate.*} {*See* ***O'Connor's Texas Rules****, "Ruling," ch. 3-C, §3.11, p. 254.*}

CONCLUSION

14. {55 *Briefly summarize the response.*}

PRAYER

15. For these reasons, {56 *party*} asks the Court to deny {57 *adverse party*}'s motion to change venue and retain this case on the Court's docket in {58 *current*} County. If the Court decides to grant {59 *adverse party*}'s motion, {60 *party*} asks the Court to transfer the case to {61 *alternative*} County.

SEE: Tex. R. Civ. P. 88, 252, 257-259
Tex. Civ. Prac. & Rem. Code §15.063
U.S. Const. 14th amend.
Tex. Const. art. 1, §19; art. 3, §45
O'Connor's Texas Rules * Civil Trials (2019), "Local Prejudice," ch. 3-C, §3, p. 252

◄ *Continued on next page* ►

ADD: STYLE OF THE CASE – FORM 1B:2
SIGNATURE BLOCK – FORM 1B:3
CERTIFICATE OF SERVICE – FORM 1B:13

ATTACH: AFFIDAVIT – FORM 1B:8, with discovery excerpts or other evidence attached, if necessary
ORDER – FORM 3C:11

NOTE: If the plaintiff does not file affidavits controverting the claim of local prejudice, the court must transfer the case. *See* ***City of Abilene v. Downs***, 367 S.W.2d 153, 155 (Tex.1963).

If a plaintiff needs time to conduct discovery before opposing a motion to change venue, the plaintiff can file a motion to continue the hearing on the motion to change venue before filing a response. See FORM 5D:1.

DEFENDANT'S REPLY TO PLAINTIFF'S RESPONSE TO MOTION TO TRANSFER VENUE

Defendant, {❶ *name*}, files this reply to plaintiff's response to defendant's motion to transfer venue.

INTRODUCTION

1. Plaintiff, {❷ *name*}, sued defendant, {❸ *name*}, in {❹ *current*} County for {❺ *state basis of suit*}.

2. {❻ *State other relevant facts about the suit.*}

BACKGROUND

3. On {❼ *date*}, defendant filed a motion to transfer venue to {❽ *proposed*} County.

4. On {❾ *date*}, plaintiff {❿ *name*} filed a response to defendant's motion.

5. In plaintiff's response, plaintiff argued {⓫ *state plaintiff's argument*}.

{*CHOOSE APPROPRIATE PARAGRAPHS 6-8*}

6. Defendant specifically denies {⓬ *specifically deny any new venue facts pleaded in plaintiff's response or in an amended petition*}.

7. Defendant specifically pleads {⓭ *plead venue facts supporting transfer to county of proper venue*}.

8. Defendant objects to {⓮ *the affidavits attached to plaintiff's response/the attachments to plaintiff's affidavits*} because {⓯ *state basis of objection, e.g., the statements in the affidavits are hearsay*}.

9. Defendant attaches affidavits to this reply as Exhibits {⓰ *letters*} to establish {⓱ *defendant's venue facts that were specifically denied by plaintiff/rebuttal facts on the issue of joinder*} and incorporates them by reference. {*See* ***O'Connor's Texas Rules***, *"Affidavits & attachments," ch. 3-C, §2.9.2, p. 249.*}

ARGUMENT & AUTHORITIES

{*CHOOSE APPROPRIATE PARAGRAPHS 10-12*}

10. Contrary to plaintiff's response, defendant's motion was timely filed and thus defendant has not waived {⓲ *his/her/its*} right to challenge venue. {⓳ *Elaborate.*}

◄ *Continued on next page* ►

11. Contrary to plaintiff's response, plaintiff has not met {[20] *his/her/its*} burden of pleading and proving that venue is proper in {[21] *current*} County. {[22] *Elaborate.*}

12. Contrary to plaintiff's response, venue is proper in {[23] *proposed*} County because

{*CHOOSE APPROPRIATE STATEMENT*}

[A] defendant specifically pleaded {[24] *state venue facts specifically pleaded in motion to transfer venue*}, and plaintiff has not denied defendant's venue facts. Therefore, the venue facts pleaded by defendant are taken as true. Tex. R. Civ. P. 87(3)(a); *Acker v. Denton Publ'g Co.*, 937 S.W.2d 111, 115 (Tex. App.—Fort Worth 1996, no writ). {[25] *Elaborate.*}

[B] , as shown by the attached affidavits and their attachments, {[26] *state facts proved by affidavits and attachments*}. {[27] *Elaborate.*}

CONCLUSION

13. {[28] *Briefly summarize the reply.*}

PRAYER

14. For these reasons, defendant asks the Court to grant {[29] *his/her/its*} motion to transfer venue and transfer this case to {[30] *proposed*} County.

SEE: Tex. R. Civ. P. 85-89
Tex. Civ. Prac. & Rem. Code §15.001 et seq.
Tex. Const. art. 3, §45
O'Connor's Texas Rules * Civil Trials (2019), "Procedure for defendant's reply," ch. 3-C, §2.9, p. 248

ADD: STYLE OF THE CASE – FORM 1B:2
SIGNATURE BLOCK – FORM 1B:3
CERTIFICATE OF SERVICE – FORM 1B:13

ATTACH: AFFIDAVIT – FORM 1B:8, with discovery excerpts or other evidence attached, if necessary

NOTE: When a party specifically denies a venue fact, the party pleading the venue fact must make prima facie proof. Tex. R. Civ. P. 87(3)(a). Prima facie proof is made when the venue facts are properly pleaded and an affidavit that fully and specifically sets forth the facts supporting the pleading is filed, along with any duly proved attachments to the affidavit. *Id.*

The deadline to file a reply to the plaintiff's response is seven days before the venue hearing, unless the defendant gets permission to file it later. Tex. R. Civ. P. 87(1).

AGREED MOTION TO TRANSFER VENUE

{❶ *Party*}, {❷ *name*}, and {❸ *adverse party*}, {❹ *name*}, ask the Court to transfer this case to {❺ *proposed*} County.

INTRODUCTION

1. Plaintiff, {❻ *name*}, sued defendant, {❼ *name*}, in {❽ *current*} County for {❾ *state basis of suit*}.

2. {❿ *State other relevant facts about the suit.*}

BACKGROUND

3. {⓫ *State facts relevant to the motion.*}

ARGUMENT & AUTHORITIES

4. Under the authority of Texas Civil Practice & Remedies Code section 15.063(3), {⓬ *party*} and {⓭ *adverse party*} have agreed to transfer this case to {⓮ *proposed*} County.

5. Venue is proper in {⓯ *proposed*} County because {⓰ *state why venue is proper*}.

CONCLUSION

6. {⓱ *Briefly summarize the motion.*}

PRAYER

7. For these reasons, {⓲ *party*} and {⓳ *adverse party*} ask the Court to grant their agreed motion to transfer venue and transfer this case to {⓴ *proposed*} County.

SEE: Tex. R. Civ. P. 86, 255
Tex. Civ. Prac. & Rem. Code §15.063(3)
Tex. Const. art. 3, §45
O'Connor's Texas Rules * Civil Trials (2019), "Consent of the Parties," ch. 3-C, §4, p. 254

ADD: STYLE OF THE CASE – FORM 1B:2
SIGNATURE BLOCK FOR AGREED MOTIONS – FORM 1B:4

ATTACH: ORDER – FORM 3C:11

ORDER ON {❶ *PARTY*}'S MOTION TO {❷ *CHANGE/TRANSFER*} VENUE

{*CHOOSE APPROPRIATE INTRODUCTORY PARAGRAPH*}

After considering {❸ *party*} {❹ *name*}'s motion to {❺ *change/transfer*} venue, the response, the pleadings, {❻ *add if appropriate: the affidavits/the discovery on file/the oral testimony,*} and arguments of counsel, the Court

After considering the parties' agreed motion to transfer venue, the pleadings, {❼ *add if appropriate: the affidavits/the discovery on file/the oral testimony,*} and arguments of counsel, the Court

{*CHOOSE APPROPRIATE ORDER*}

DENIES the motion and retains the case on the Court's docket.

DENIES the motion to sever and transfer plaintiff {❽ *name*}'s case to {❾ *proposed*} County.

DENIES the motion to transfer the case to {❿ *proposed*} County for the convenience of the parties and witnesses under Texas Civil Practice & Remedies Code section 15.002(b).

GRANTS the motion, transfers the case to {⓫ *proposed*} County, and orders plaintiff to pay court costs in the amount of ${⓬ *amount*}.

GRANTS the motion to sever and transfers plaintiff {⓭ *name*}'s case to {⓮ *proposed*} County.

GRANTS the motion and transfers the case to {⓯ *proposed*} County for the convenience of the parties and the witnesses under Texas Civil Practice & Remedies Code section 15.002(b).

SIGNED on ________________, 20___.

____
PRESIDING JUDGE

FORM 3C:11 VENUE – ORDER ON MOTION TO CHANGE OR TRANSFER

SEE: Tex. R. Civ. P. 86-89
Tex. Civ. Prac. & Rem. Code §§15.002(b), 15.064(a)
O'Connor's Texas Rules * Civil Trials (2019), "Ruling," ch. 3-C, §3.11, p. 254

ADD: STYLE OF THE CASE – FORM 1B:2
CERTIFICATE OF SERVICE – FORM 1B:13, if proposed order served separately from motion or response

NOTE: If the court grants a motion to transfer venue that includes a request to transfer for convenience, the order does not need to state whether the case was transferred for the convenience of the parties under Texas Civil Practice & Remedies Code §15.002(b). *See Garza v. Garcia*, 137 S.W.3d 36, 39 (Tex.2004). Although the order does not need to expressly state whether the case was transferred on convenience grounds, a party should still include such a statement when drafting the order. A transfer order based on convenience is not subject to review by appeal or mandamus. See ***O'Connor's Texas Rules***, "No appeal of convenience transfer," ch. 3-C, §5.1, p. 254.

FORM 3C:11

DEFENDANT'S MOTION TO
{❶ *DISMISS/STAY*} SUIT FOR FORUM NON CONVENIENS

Defendant, {❷ *name*}, asks the Court to {❸ *dismiss/stay*} this suit on grounds of forum non conveniens, as authorized by Texas Civil Practice & Remedies Code section 71.051.

INTRODUCTION

1. Plaintiff, {❹ *name*}, sued defendant, {❺ *name*}, for {❻ *personal injury/wrongful death*}.

2. {❼ *If motion to dismiss or stay is defendant's initial pleading, add appropriate identification for each defendant from FORM 3E:1.*}

3. {❽ *State other relevant facts about the suit.*}

BACKGROUND

4. {❾ *State facts relevant to the motion.*}

ARGUMENT & AUTHORITIES

5. Under Texas Civil Practice & Remedies Code section 71.051, a court must decline to exercise jurisdiction and dismiss or stay a claim or an action for personal injury or wrongful death if, on a written motion, the court finds that (1) the plaintiff is not a "plaintiff" as defined in section 71.051(h)(2) or the plaintiff is not a legal resident of Texas or a derivative claimant of a legal resident of Texas and (2) in the interest of justice and for the convenience of the parties, the claim or action would be more properly heard in a forum outside Texas. *See* Tex. Civ. Prac. & Rem. Code §71.051(b), (e), (h), (i); *In re Bridgestone Ams. Tire Operations, LLC*, 459 S.W.3d 565, 568-69 (Tex. 2015); *In re Gen. Elec. Co.*, 271 S.W.3d 681, 685-86 (Tex. 2008).

6. In determining whether, in the interest of justice and for the convenience of the parties, the claim or action would be more properly heard in a forum outside Texas, the court must consider the following: (1) whether an alternate forum exists in which the action may be tried, (2) whether the alternate forum provides an adequate remedy, (3) whether keeping the action in Texas would work a substantial injustice to the moving party, (4) whether the alternate forum can exercise jurisdiction over all the defendants properly joined, (5) whether the balance of the private interests of the parties and the public interest of the state predominate in favor of the action being brought in an alternate forum, and (6) whether the dismissal or stay would not result in unreasonable duplication or proliferation of litigation. Tex. Civ. Prac. & Rem. Code §71.051(b); *In re Bridgestone Ams.*, 459 S.W.3d at 575; *In re Gen. Elec.*, 271 S.W.3d at 685-86.

{*CHOOSE APPROPRIATE SECTIONS A-B*}

A. Plaintiff is not a "plaintiff" as defined in Texas Civil Practice & Remedies Code section 71.051.

7. A {⓾ *dismissal/stay*} is proper in this case because plaintiff is not a "plaintiff" as defined in Texas Civil Practice & Remedies Code section 71.051(h)(2), and therefore {⓫ *his/her*} Texas residency does not prohibit the court from {⓬ *dismissing/staying*} {⓭ *his/her*} claim. *See* Tex. Civ. Prac. & Rem. Code §71.051(e), (h)(2). A plaintiff, for purposes of the statute, is a party seeking to recover damages for personal injury or wrongful death, which can include an intervenor seeking affirmative relief. *See id.* §71.051(h)(2); *In re Mahindra, USA Inc.*, 549 S.W.3d 541, 546 (Tex. 2018); *In re Ford Motor Co.*, 442 S.W.3d 265, 275 (Tex. 2014). The following persons are not considered a plaintiff under the statute: (1) a defendant or a party characterized as a defendant that files a counterclaim, cross-claim, or third-party claim, (2) a person who is assigned a cause of action for personal injury, (3) an intervenor that is properly characterized as a defendant, or (4) a representative, administrator, guardian, or next friend who is not otherwise a derivative claimant of a Texas resident. *See* Tex. Civ. Prac. & Rem. Code §71.051(h)(2); *In re Bridgestone Ams.*, 459 S.W.3d at 572-73; *In re Ford Motor*, 442 S.W.3d at 270, 274-75. {*See* ***O'Connor's Texas Rules****, "Not a 'plaintiff' under CPRC §71.051," ch. 3-D, §3.1.4(1)(a), p. 259.*}

8. Plaintiff is not a "plaintiff" as defined in Texas Civil Practice & Remedies Code section 71.051(h)(2) because {⓮ *explain*}.

B. Plaintiff is not a {⓯ *legal resident/derivative claimant of a legal resident/legal resident or a derivative claimant of a legal resident*} of Texas.

{*CHOOSE APPROPRIATE PARAGRAPHS 9-10*}

9. A {⓰ *dismissal/stay*} is proper in this case because plaintiff is not a legal resident of Texas. *See* Tex. Civ. Prac. & Rem. Code §71.051(e). Plaintiff is not a legal resident of Texas because {⓱ *explain*}. {*See* ***O'Connor's Texas Rules****, "Not a legal resident or derivative claimant of legal resident," ch. 3-D, §3.1.4(1)(b), p. 259.*}

10. A {⓲ *dismissal/stay*} is proper in this case because plaintiff is not a derivative claimant of a legal resident of Texas. *See* Tex. Civ. Prac. & Rem. Code §71.051(e). A derivative claimant is a person whose damages were caused by the personal injury to or wrongful death of another person. *Id.* §71.051(h)(1). When a plaintiff brings claims as a derivative claimant and the plaintiff herself is not a Texas resident, the residency of the person whose injury or death the plaintiff's claims are based on controls for the purpose of determining whether a dismissal or stay is proper. *See id.* §71.051(e). Plaintiff is not

Continued on next page

a derivative claimant of a legal resident of Texas because {[19] *explain*}. {*See* ***O'Connor's Texas Rules****, "Not a legal resident or derivative claimant of legal resident," ch. 3-D, §3.1.4(1)(b), p. 259.*}

C. {[20] *Alternate forum*} is an available forum.

11. A {[21] *dismissal/stay*} is proper in this case because an alternate forum is available to hear plaintiff's suit. *See* Tex. Civ. Prac. & Rem. Code §71.051(b)(1). An alternate forum is available where the defendant is amenable to process. *In re ENSCO Offshore Int'l Co.*, 311 S.W.3d 921, 924 (Tex. 2010). A defendant is amenable to process when either it has minimum contacts sufficient for a court to exercise jurisdiction over it or it agrees to submit to the court's jurisdiction. *Direct Color Servs., Inc. v. Eastman Kodak Co.*, 929 S.W.2d 558, 564 (Tex. App.—Tyler 1996, writ denied).

12. {[22] *Alternate forum*} is an available forum because the defendant {[23] *has sufficient minimum contacts with/has agreed to submit to the jurisdiction of*} {[24] *alternate forum*}. {[25] *Elaborate.*}

D. {[26] *Alternate forum*} provides adequate remedy.

13. A {[27] *dismissal/stay*} is proper in this case because {[28] *alternate forum*} offers an adequate remedy for plaintiff's suit. *See* Tex. Civ. Prac. & Rem. Code §71.051(b)(2). An alternate forum provides an adequate remedy if the parties will not be deprived of all remedies or treated unfairly, even though they may not enjoy the same benefits as they might receive in the current forum. *In re Pirelli Tire, L.L.C.*, 247 S.W.3d 670, 678 (Tex. 2007). Thus, the fact that the substantive law of the alternate forum may be less favorable to the plaintiff is entitled to little, if any, weight. *Id.*

14. The courts of {[29] *alternate forum*} offer an adequate remedy for plaintiff's suit because {[30] *explain*}.

E. Maintaining suit in Texas would cause defendant substantial injustice.

15. A {[31] *dismissal/stay*} is proper in this case because maintaining this suit in Texas would cause a substantial injustice to defendant. *See* Tex. Civ. Prac. & Rem. Code §71.051(b)(3). {[32] *Elaborate.*}

F. {[33] *Alternate forum*} can exercise jurisdiction over all properly joined defendants.

16. A {[34] *dismissal/stay*} is proper in this case because the courts of {[35] *alternate forum*} can exercise jurisdiction over all the defendants properly joined in plaintiff's suit. *See* Tex. Civ. Prac. & Rem. Code §71.051(b)(4). {[36] *Identify properly joined de-*

FORM 3D:1

fendants and show why alternate forum can exercise jurisdiction over each. If necessary, file a stipulation agreeing to the exercise of personal jurisdiction by that forum.}

G. Dismissal will not result in unreasonable duplication or proliferation of litigation.

17. A {㊲ *dismissal/stay*} is proper in this case because it will not result in unreasonable duplication or proliferation of litigation. *See* Tex. Civ. Prac. & Rem. Code §71.051(b)(6). {㊳ *Elaborate.*}

H. Private-interest factors favor {㊴ *alternate forum*}.

18. A {㊵ *dismissal/stay*} is proper in this case because the private-interest factors favor this suit being heard in {㊶ *alternate forum*}. *See* Tex. Civ. Prac. & Rem. Code §71.051(b)(5). The private-interest factors the court can weigh against the plaintiff's choice of forum are (1) the relative ease of access to sources of proof, (2) the availability of compulsory process for attendance of unwilling witnesses, (3) the cost of obtaining the attendance of willing witnesses, (4) the possibility to view the premises if appropriate, (5) the enforceability of a judgment if one is obtained, and (6) all other practical issues that make trial of a case easy, expeditious, and inexpensive. *In re Omega Protein, Inc.*, 288 S.W.3d 17, 20-21 (Tex. App.—Houston [1st Dist.] 2009, orig. proceeding); *see In re Gen. Elec.*, 271 S.W.3d at 691.

19. As discussed below, these private-interest factors weigh in favor of this case being heard in {㊷ *alternate forum*} rather than in Texas.

{*INCLUDE ALL RELEVANT FACTORS BELOW*}

a. Access to sources of proof will be easier in {㊸ *alternate forum*} than in Texas. {㊹ *Elaborate.*}

b. Compulsory process for the attendance of unwilling witnesses is available in {㊺ *alternate forum*}. {㊻ *Elaborate.*}

c. The cost of securing the presence of willing witnesses will be lower in {㊼ *alternate forum*} than in Texas. {㊽ *Elaborate.*}

d. Viewing the relevant premises is possible in {㊾ *alternate forum*}. {㊿ *Elaborate.*}

e. The enforcement of a judgment is easier in {51 *alternate forum*} than in Texas. {52 *Elaborate.*}

Continued on next page

f. {53 *Describe any other practical issues that would make trial easier, more expeditious, and less expensive in the alternate forum, e.g., the cost, time, and scheduling difficulties necessary to obtain evidence and present witness testimony would be far less in {alternate forum} than in Texas.*}

I. Public-interest factors favor {54 *alternate forum*}.

20. A {55 *dismissal/stay*} is proper in this case because the public-interest factors favor this suit being heard in {56 *alternate forum*}. *See* Tex. Civ. Prac. & Rem. Code §71.051(b)(5). The public-interest factors the court can weigh against the plaintiff's choice of forum are (1) the burden imposed on the citizens of a community that have no relation to the litigation, (2) the administrative burden on the courts, (3) the general interest in having localized controversies decided locally, and (4) the interest in having a diversity case tried in a forum that is familiar with the law that must govern the action. *In re Gen. Elec.*, 271 S.W.3d at 691.

21. As discussed below, these public-interest factors weigh in favor of this case being heard in {57 *alternate forum*} rather than in Texas.

{*INCLUDE ALL RELEVANT FACTORS BELOW*}

a. The burden of jury duty is more appropriately placed on {58 *alternate forum*} citizens than on Texas citizens. {59 *Elaborate.*}

b. The administrative burden on the {60 *alternate forum*} court is less than on this Court. Specifically, {61 *explain, e.g., there is a congested docket in the Texas court*}.

c. {62 *Alternate forum*} has an interest in adjudicating this case, and Texas does not. {63 *Elaborate.*}

d. {64 *Alternate forum*}'s law will control the disposition of this case. {65 *Elaborate.*}

22. When balancing the private interests of the parties and the public interest of Texas, a court must also consider the extent to which the injury or death resulted from acts or omissions that occurred in Texas. Tex. Civ. Prac. & Rem. Code §71.051(b)(5); *In re ENSCO*, 311 S.W.3d at 926. The {66 *act/omission*} that plaintiff alleges resulted in {67 *personal injury/wrongful death*} occurred in {68 *alternate forum*}. {69 *Elaborate.*}

FORM 3D:1

CONCLUSION

23. {70 *Briefly summarize the motion.*}

PRAYER

24. For these reasons, defendant asks the Court to set this motion for hearing and, after the hearing, grant this motion and sign an order {71 *dismissing/staying*} plaintiff's suit.

SEE: Tex. Civ. Prac. & Rem. Code §71.051
O'Connor's Texas Rules * Civil Trials (2019), "Code FNC Motion," ch. 3-D, §3, p. 258

ADD: STYLE OF THE CASE – FORM 1B:2
SIGNATURE BLOCK – FORM 1B:3
CERTIFICATE OF SERVICE – FORM 1B:13

ATTACH: AFFIDAVIT – FORM 1B:8, if necessary
NOTICE OF CURRENT/CHANGE OF ADDRESS – FORM 1B:14, if motion to dismiss or stay is defendant's initial pleading
NOTICE OF HEARING OR SUBMISSION – FORM 1E:1
ORDER – FORM 3D:6

NOTE: For a Code FNC motion to be applicable, the plaintiff must have asserted a claim for personal injury or wrongful death. Tex. Civ. Prac. & Rem. Code §71.051(i). Although Texas Civil Practice & Remedies Code §71.051 does not define the term "personal injury," at least one court of appeals has interpreted the statute as covering only claims involving bodily injury and excluding claims for other torts. *See, e.g.*, ***Gottwald v. de Cano***, 568 S.W.3d 241, 247-48 (Tex.App.—El Paso 2019, no pet.) (because claim for intentional infliction of emotional distress does not require manifestation of physical injury, it is not personal-injury claim under Tex. Civ. Prac. & Rem. Code §71.051).

A Code FNC motion filed in a personal-injury or wrongful-death action must be filed within 180 days after the deadline for filing a motion to transfer venue. Tex. Civ. Prac. & Rem. Code §71.051(d). Because the deadline to file a motion to transfer venue is the same as the deadline to file an answer, the deadline to file a Code FNC motion is approximately 200 days after the date the lawsuit is served. See ***O'Connor's Texas Rules***, "Deadline to file," ch. 3-D, §3.1.3, p. 258.

The parties must have at least 21 days' notice of the hearing, and the hearing must be set at least 30 days before trial. Tex. Civ. Prac. & Rem. Code §71.051(d). See ***O'Connor's Texas Rules***, "Hearing," ch. 3-D, §3.6, p. 264.

Continued on next page

In many cases, the person bringing suit will be considered both a plaintiff and a derivative claimant under Texas Civil Practice & Remedies Code §71.051. *See* ***In re Mahindra, USA Inc.***, 549 S.W.3d 541, 546-47 (Tex.2018). In such a case, if the plaintiff herself is a Texas resident, she can rely on this fact to prevent dismissal of her claim. *See id.* at 548 (Texas-resident exception is not merely Texas-decedent exception). Whether the person whose injury or death her claims are based on is a Texas resident would then be irrelevant. *See id.*; *see also* ***In re Ford Motor Co.***, 442 S.W.3d 265, 280 (Tex.2014) (wrongful-death beneficiaries and decedent are distinct Ps under statute). If the plaintiff is not a Texas resident, however, she will have to rely on her status as a derivative claimant and can prevent dismissal of her claims under the Texas-resident exception only if the injured or deceased person is a Texas resident. *See* ***In re Mahindra, USA***, 549 S.W.3d at 548. Thus, to dismiss a case on Code FNC grounds when the plaintiff is a derivative claimant, the defendant should show that both the plaintiff and the injured or deceased person are not Texas residents.

When arguing a Code FNC motion, the defendant does not need to prove or present evidence on each of the factors under Texas Civil Practice & Remedies Code §71.051(b). ***In re General Elec. Co.***, 271 S.W.3d 681, 687 (Tex.2008). At the very least, however, a defendant should argue that another forum is both available and adequate. The U.S. Supreme Court has considered both factors to be a prerequisite to dismissing a case for FNC. *See* ***Piper Aircraft Co. v. Reyno***, 454 U.S. 235, 254 n.22 (1981) (not discussing Tex. Civ. Prac. & Rem. Code §71.051).

Because most of the defendant's factual allegations are outside the record, the defendant should probably verify the motion; however, nothing in Texas Civil Practice & Remedies Code §71.051 requires verification.

DEFENDANT'S MOTION TO
{❶ *DISMISS/STAY*} SUIT FOR FORUM NON CONVENIENS

Defendant, {❷ *name*}, asks the Court to {❸ *dismiss/stay*} this suit on grounds of forum non conveniens, as allowed by Texas common law.

INTRODUCTION

1. Plaintiff, {❹ *name*}, sued defendant, {❺ *name*}, for {❻ *state basis of suit*}.

2. {❼ *If motion to dismiss or stay is defendant's initial pleading, add appropriate identification for each defendant from FORM 3E:1.*}

3. {❽ *State other relevant facts about the suit.*}

BACKGROUND

4. {❾ *State facts relevant to the motion.*}

{*ADD PARAGRAPH 5 IF APPLICABLE*}

5. Defendant attaches as Exhibit {❿ *letter*} a signed stipulation that it agrees to be sued in {⓫ *alternate forum*}.

ARGUMENT & AUTHORITIES

6. Under Texas common law, a court can decline to exercise jurisdiction over a case under the doctrine of forum non conveniens if there is another, more appropriate forum available to hear the dispute. *See Van Winkle-Hooker Co. v. Rice*, 448 S.W.2d 824, 826 (Tex. App.—Dallas 1969, no writ). Forum non conveniens is an equitable doctrine designed to protect nonresident defendants from having to litigate in distant and inconvenient forums. *See Sarieddine v. Moussa*, 820 S.W.2d 837, 839 (Tex. App.—Dallas 1991, writ denied). A court will dismiss a case under forum non conveniens if it determines that, in the interest of justice and for the convenience of the parties and witnesses, the action should be heard in another forum. *Id.*

7. To obtain a dismissal under forum non conveniens, the defendant has the initial burden to establish that an alternate forum is available. *See Vinmar Trade Fin., Ltd. v. Util. Trailers de Mex., S.A. de C.V.*, 336 S.W.3d 664, 672 (Tex. App.—Houston [1st Dist.] 2010, no pet.); *RSR Corp. v. Siegmund*, 309 S.W.3d 686, 710 (Tex. App.—Dallas 2010, no pet.). If the defendant meets its burden, the burden shifts to the plaintiff to prove that the alternate forum is inadequate. *RSR Corp.*, 309 S.W.3d at 710. If the alternate forum is both available and adequate, the defendant then has the burden to establish that the alternate forum is the more appropriate forum to hear the case. *See id.* at 710-11.

◄ *Continued on next page* ►

FORM 3D:2

A. {[12] *Alternate forum*} is an available forum.

8. A {[13] *dismissal/stay*} is proper in this case because an alternate forum is available to hear plaintiff's suit. An alternate forum is available when the entire case and all the parties can come within the jurisdiction of that forum. *Gottwald v. de Cano*, 568 S.W.3d 241, 249 (Tex. App.—El Paso 2019, no pet.); *Vinmar Trade Fin.*, 336 S.W.3d at 674; *Direct Color Servs., Inc. v. Eastman Kodak Co.*, 929 S.W.2d 558, 564 (Tex. App.—Tyler 1996, writ denied). This requirement is satisfied if the defendant establishes that it is amenable to process in the alternate forum. *Gottwald*, 568 S.W.3d at 249; *Direct Color*, 929 S.W.2d at 564. A defendant is amenable to process when either it has minimum contacts sufficient for a court to exercise jurisdiction over it or it agrees to submit to the court's jurisdiction. *Direct Color*, 929 S.W.2d at 564. {*See* ***O'Connor's Texas Rules***, *"Alternate forum available & adequate," ch. 3-D, §4.1.3(1), p. 265.*}

9. {[14] *Alternate forum*} is an available forum because the defendant {[15] *has sufficient minimum contacts with/has agreed to submit to the jurisdiction of*} {[16] *alternate forum*}. {[17] *Elaborate.*}

B. {[18] *Alternate forum*} is the more appropriate forum.

10. A {[19] *dismissal/stay*} is proper in this case because {[20] *alternate forum*} is the more appropriate forum to hear plaintiff's suit. To determine whether one forum is more appropriate than another, the court must weigh certain private-interest and public-interest factors against the relevant deference given to the plaintiff's choice of forum. *See Quixtar Inc. v. Signature Mgmt. Team, LLC*, 315 S.W.3d 28, 31-33 (Tex. 2010); *Vinmar Trade Fin.*, 336 S.W.3d at 676, 678. The extent of deference given to the plaintiff's choice of forum depends on the plaintiff's status. *See Quixtar Inc.*, 315 S.W.3d at 31. If the plaintiff is a resident of Texas, the plaintiff's choice of forum is given deference and the defendant must show that the balance of private and public interests strongly favors dismissal. *See id.* at 32-33 & n.2. If the plaintiff is a nonresident of Texas or a Texas corporation doing extensive foreign business, the plaintiff's choice of forum is given substantially less deference. *See id.* at 32-33; *Vinmar Trade Fin.*, 336 S.W.3d at 678.

11. A {[21] *dismissal/stay*} is proper in this case because the private-interest factors favor this suit being heard in {[22] *alternate forum*}. The private-interest factors the court can weigh against the plaintiff's choice of forum are (1) the relative ease of access to sources of proof, (2) the availability of compulsory process for attendance of unwilling witnesses, (3) the cost of obtaining the attendance of willing witnesses, (4) the possibility to view the premises if appropriate, (5) the enforceability of a judgment if one is obtained, and (6) all other practical issues that make trial of a case easy, expeditious, and inexpensive. *Quixtar Inc.*, 315 S.W.3d at 33.

{*CHOOSE APPROPRIATE PARAGRAPH 12*}

12. Considering the private-interest factors below and the little deference that should be given to plaintiff's choice of forum because of {23 *his/her/its*} {24 *status as a nonresident of Texas/extensive foreign business*}, a {25 *dismissal/stay*} is favored in this case.

12. Although deference should be given to the plaintiff's choice of forum because of {26 *his/her/its*} status as a resident of Texas, the private-interest factors below strongly favor a {27 *dismissal/stay*} in this case.

{*INCLUDE ALL RELEVANT FACTORS BELOW*}

a. Access to sources of proof will be easier in {28 *alternate forum*} than in Texas. {29 *Elaborate.*}

b. Compulsory process for the attendance of unwilling witnesses is available in {30 *alternate forum*}. {31 *Elaborate.*}

c. The cost of securing the presence of willing witnesses will be lower in {32 *alternate forum*} than in Texas. {33 *Elaborate.*}

d. Viewing the relevant premises is possible in {34 *alternate forum*}. {35 *Elaborate.*}

e. The enforcement of a judgment is easier in {36 *alternate forum*} than in Texas. {37 *Elaborate.*}

f. {38 *Describe any other practical issues that would make trial easier, more expeditious, and less expensive in the alternate forum.*}

13. A {39 *dismissal/stay*} is proper in this case because the public-interest factors favor this suit being heard in {40 *alternate forum*}. The public-interest factors the court can weigh against the plaintiff's choice of forum are (1) the burden imposed on the citizens of a community that have no relation to the litigation, (2) the administrative burden on the courts, (3) the general interest in having localized controversies decided locally, and (4) the interest in having a diversity case tried in a forum that is familiar with the law that must govern the action. *See Quixtar Inc.*, 315 S.W.3d at 33-34.

Continued on next page

{*CHOOSE APPROPRIATE PARAGRAPH 14*}

14. Considering the public-interest factors below and the little deference that should be given to plaintiff's choice of forum, a {㊶ *dismissal/stay*} is favored in this case.

14. Considering the public-interest factors below, a {㊷ *dismissal/stay*} is strongly favored in this case.

{*INCLUDE ALL RELEVANT FACTORS BELOW*}

a. The burden of jury duty is more appropriately placed on {㊸ *alternate forum*} citizens than on Texas citizens. {㊹ *Elaborate.*}

b. The administrative burden on the {㊺ *alternate forum*} court is less than on this Court. Specifically, {㊻ *explain, e.g., there is a congested docket in the Texas court*}.

c. {㊼ *Alternate forum*} has an interest in adjudicating this case, and Texas does not. {㊽ *Elaborate.*}

d. {㊾ *Alternate forum*}'s law will control the disposition of this case. {㊿ *Elaborate.*}

CONCLUSION

15. Because plaintiff's suit can be properly heard in {(51) *alternate forum*} and because the private and public interests would be better served if plaintiff's case were heard in {(52) *alternate forum*}, the Court should grant defendant's motion.

PRAYER

16. For these reasons, defendant asks the Court to set this motion for hearing and, after the hearing, grant defendant's motion and sign an order {(53) *dismissing/staying*} plaintiff's suit.

SEE: ***O'Connor's Texas Rules * Civil Trials*** (2019), "Common-Law FNC Motion," ch. 3-D, §4, p. 265

ADD: STYLE OF THE CASE – FORM 1B:2
SIGNATURE BLOCK – FORM 1B:3
CERTIFICATE OF SERVICE – FORM 1B:13

ATTACH: AFFIDAVIT – FORM 1B:8, if necessary
NOTICE OF CURRENT/CHANGE OF ADDRESS – FORM 1B:14, if motion to dismiss or stay is defendant's initial pleading
NOTICE OF HEARING OR SUBMISSION – FORM 1E:1
ORDER – FORM 3D:6
Stipulation agreeing to be sued in alternate forum, if applicable

NOTE: A common-law FNC motion should be filed only for claims not involving personal injury or wrongful death. If a claim involves personal injury or wrongful death, an FNC motion must be filed under Texas Civil Practice & Remedies Code §71.051 instead.

There is no deadline for filing the motion for common-law FNC; however, the motion should be brought before trial. *See* ***Direct Color Servs. v. Eastman Kodak Co.***, 929 S.W.2d 558, 567 (Tex.App.—Tyler 1996, writ denied).

Under Code FNC analysis, whether an alternate forum is available and adequate is one of several factors the court considers in making its determination. ***Gottwald v. de Cano***, 568 S.W.3d 241, 249 (Tex. App.—El Paso 2019, no pet.); *see* Tex. Civ. Prac. & Rem. Code §71.051(b). See ***O'Connor's Texas Rules***, "Action should be heard in alternate forum," ch. 3-D, §3.1.4(2), p. 260. But under common-law FNC analysis, whether the alternate forum is both available and adequate is a threshold question that the court must answer before it weighs the private- and public-interest factors. ***Gottwald***, 568 S.W.3d at 249.

PLAINTIFF'S RESPONSE TO DEFENDANT'S MOTION
TO {❶ *DISMISS/STAY*} SUIT FOR FORUM NON CONVENIENS

Plaintiff, {❷ *name*}, asks the Court to deny defendant {❸ *name*}'s motion to {❹ *dismiss/stay*} this suit on grounds of forum non conveniens.

INTRODUCTION

1. Plaintiff, {❺ *name*}, sued defendant, {❻ *name*}, for {❼ *state basis of suit*}.

2. {❽ *State other relevant facts about the suit.*}

BACKGROUND

3. On {❾ *date*}, defendant filed a motion to {❿ *dismiss/stay*} plaintiff's suit on the grounds of forum non conveniens under Texas Civil Practice & Remedies Code section 71.051.

4. {⓫ *State other facts relevant to the response.*}

ARGUMENT & AUTHORITIES

5. Under Texas Civil Practice & Remedies Code section 71.051, a court can decline to exercise jurisdiction and dismiss or stay a claim or an action for personal injury or wrongful death only if the court finds that (1) the motion was properly brought, (2) the plaintiff whose claim or action is being dismissed is a not a "plaintiff" as defined in Texas Civil Practice & Remedies Code section 71.051(h)(2) or the plaintiff is not a legal resident of Texas or a derivative claimant of a legal resident of Texas, and (3) in the interest of justice and for the convenience of the parties, the claim or action would be more properly heard in a forum outside Texas. *See* Tex. Civ. Prac. & Rem. Code §71.051(b), (e), (h), (i); *In re Bridgestone Ams. Tire Operations, LLC*, 459 S.W.3d 565, 568-69 (Tex. 2015); *In re Gen. Elec. Co.*, 271 S.W.3d 681, 685-86 (Tex. 2008).

6. In determining whether, in the interest of justice and for the convenience of the parties, the claim or action would be more properly heard in a forum outside Texas, the court must consider the following: (1) whether an alternate forum exists in which the action may be tried, (2) whether the alternate forum provides an adequate remedy, (3) whether keeping the action in Texas would work a substantial injustice to the moving party, (4) whether the alternate forum can exercise jurisdiction over all the defendants properly joined, (5) whether the balance of the private interests of the parties and the public interest of the state predominate in favor of the action being brought in an alternate forum, and (6) whether the dismissal or stay would not result in unreasonable duplication or proliferation of litigation. Tex. Civ. Prac. & Rem. Code §71.051(b); *In re Gen. Elec.*, 271 S.W.3d at 685-86.

{*CHOOSE APPROPRIATE SECTIONS A-D*}

A. The motion is defective.

{*CHOOSE APPROPRIATE PARAGRAPHS 7-9*}

7. The Court should deny defendant's motion because defendant did not timely file the motion. A motion to dismiss or stay for forum non conveniens based on Texas Civil Practice & Remedies Code section 71.051 must be filed no later than 180 days after the deadline to file a motion to transfer venue. Tex. Civ. Prac. & Rem. Code §71.051(d). The deadline for defendant to file a motion to transfer venue in this case was {⓬ *date*}; 180 days from that date was {⓭ *date*}. Defendant filed {⓮ *his/her/its*} motion on {⓯ *date*}, which was {⓰ *number*} days after the deadline to file a motion to transfer venue. Under section 71.051(d), defendant waived the right to contest the forum for this lawsuit. {*See* ***O'Connor's Texas Rules****, "Waiver," ch. 3-D, §3.2.2(5), p. 263.*}

8. The Court should deny defendant's motion because defendant did not give proper notice of the hearing on the motion. A defendant must give at least 21 days' notice of the hearing. *See* Tex. Civ. Prac. & Rem. Code §71.051(d). Defendant did not give 21 days' notice. {⓱ *Elaborate.*} {*See* ***O'Connor's Texas Rules****, "Improper notice of hearing," ch. 3-D, §3.2.2(4), p. 263.*}

9. The Court should deny defendant's motion because defendant set the hearing too close to trial. A motion to dismiss or stay for forum non conveniens based on Texas Civil Practice & Remedies Code section 71.051 must be heard at least 30 days before trial. Defendant set {⓲ *his/her/its*} motion for hearing on a date less than 30 days before trial. {⓳ *Elaborate.*} {*See* ***O'Connor's Texas Rules****, "Improper notice of hearing," ch. 3-D, §3.2.2(4), p. 263.*}

B. Plaintiff is a "plaintiff" as defined in Texas Civil Practice & Remedies Code section 71.051.

10. The Court should deny defendant's motion because, contrary to defendant's allegations, plaintiff is a "plaintiff" as defined in Texas Civil Practice & Remedies Code section 71.051(h)(2). *See* Tex. Civ. Prac. & Rem. Code §71.051(e), (h)(2). A plaintiff, for purposes of the statute, is a party seeking to recover damages for personal injury or wrongful death, which can include an intervenor seeking affirmative relief. *See id.* §71.051(h)(2); *In re Mahindra, USA Inc.*, 549 S.W.3d 541, 546 (Tex. 2018); *In re Ford Motor Co.*, 442 S.W.3d 265, 275 (Tex. 2014). The following persons are not considered a plaintiff under the statute: (1) a defendant or a party characterized as a defendant that files a counterclaim, cross-claim, or third-party claim, (2) a person who is assigned a cause of action for personal injury, (3) an intervenor that is properly characterized as a

Continued on next page

defendant, or (4) a representative, administrator, guardian, or next friend who is not otherwise a derivative claimant of a legal resident of Texas. *See* Tex. Civ. Prac. & Rem. Code §71.051(h)(2); *In re Bridgestone Ams.*, 459 S.W.3d at 572-73; *In re Ford Motor*, 442 S.W.3d at 270, 274-75. {*See* ***O'Connor's Texas Rules***, *"Not a 'plaintiff' under CPRC §71.051," ch. 3-D, §3.1.4(1)(a), p. 259.*}

11. Plaintiff is a "plaintiff" as defined by Texas Civil Practice & Remedies Code section 71.051(h)(2) because {[20] *explain*}.

C. Plaintiff is a {[21] *legal resident/derivative claimant of a legal resident*} of Texas.

{*CHOOSE APPROPRIATE PARAGRAPH 12*}

12. The Court should deny defendant's motion because, contrary to defendant's allegations, plaintiff is a legal resident of Texas. *See* Tex. Civ. Prac. & Rem. Code §71.051(e). {*See* ***O'Connor's Texas Rules***, *"Not a legal resident or derivative claimant of legal resident," ch. 3-D, §3.1.4(1)(b), p. 259.*}

12. The Court should deny defendant's motion because, contrary to defendant's allegations, plaintiff is a derivative claimant of a legal resident of Texas. *See* Tex. Civ. Prac. & Rem. Code §71.051(e). A derivative claimant is a person whose damages were caused by the personal injury to or wrongful death of another person. *Id.* §71.051(h)(1). When a plaintiff brings suit as a derivative claimant and the plaintiff herself is not a Texas resident, the residency of the person whose injury or death the plaintiff's claims are based on controls for the purpose of determining whether a dismissal or stay is proper. *See id.* §71.051(e). {*See* ***O'Connor's Texas Rules***, *"Not a legal resident or derivative claimant of legal resident," ch. 3-D, §3.1.4(1)(b), p. 259.*}

13. Plaintiff is a {[22] *legal resident/derivative claimant of a legal resident*} of Texas because {[23] *explain*}.

D. The interest of justice & convenience of parties favors Texas.

14. The Court should deny defendant's motion because the factors under Texas Civil Practice & Remedies Code section 71.051(b) do not weigh in favor of having the case heard outside Texas.

{*CHOOSE APPROPRIATE PARAGRAPHS 15-22*}

15. Defendant did not identify an available alternate forum to decide plaintiff's cause of action. *See* Tex. Civ. Prac. & Rem. Code §71.051(b)(1). {[24] *Elaborate.*}

16. The courts of {㉕ *alternate forum*} do not offer an adequate remedy for plaintiff's cause of action. *See* Tex. Civ. Prac. & Rem. Code §71.051(b)(2). {㉖ *Elaborate.*}

17. Maintaining this suit in Texas would not cause a substantial injustice for defendant. *See* Tex. Civ. Prac. & Rem. Code §71.051(b)(3). {㉗ *Elaborate.*}

18. The courts of {㉘ *alternate forum*} cannot exercise jurisdiction over all defendants properly joined in plaintiff's suit. *See* Tex. Civ. Prac. & Rem. Code §71.051(b)(4). {㉙ *Identify properly joined defendants and show that alternate forum cannot exercise jurisdiction over one or more of them.*} {㉚ *Defendant has not/Not all the defendants have*} filed {㉛ *identify document, e.g., a stipulation*} agreeing to the exercise of personal jurisdiction in this case by {㉜ *alternate forum*}.

19. Granting the motion would result in unreasonable duplication or proliferation of litigation. *See* Tex. Civ. Prac. & Rem. Code §71.051(b)(6). {㉝ *Elaborate.*}

20. The private-interest factors favor keeping the action in Texas. *See* Tex. Civ. Prac. & Rem. Code §71.051(b)(5).

{*INCLUDE ALL RELEVANT FACTORS BELOW*}

a. Access to proof will be easier in Texas than in {㉞ *alternate forum*}. *See In re Gen. Elec.*, 271 S.W.3d at 691. {㉟ *Elaborate.*}

b. Compulsory process for the attendance of unwilling witnesses is available in Texas. *See In re Gen. Elec.*, 271 S.W.3d at 691. {㊱ *Elaborate.*}

c. The cost of securing the presence of willing witnesses will be lower in Texas than in {㊲ *alternate forum*}. *See In re Gen. Elec.*, 271 S.W.3d at 691; *In re Omega Protein, Inc.*, 288 S.W.3d 17, 20-21 (Tex. App.—Houston [1st Dist.] 2009, orig. proceeding). {㊳ *Elaborate.*}

d. Viewing the relevant premises is possible in Texas. *See In re Gen. Elec.*, 271 S.W.3d at 691. {㊴ *Elaborate.*}

e. The enforcement of a judgment is easier in Texas than in {㊵ *alternate forum*}. *See In re Omega Protein, Inc.*, 288 S.W.3d 17, 20-21 (Tex. App.—Houston [1st Dist.] 2009, orig. proceeding). {㊶ *Elaborate.*}

f. {㊷ *Describe any other practical issues that would make trial easier, more expeditious, and less expensive in Texas, e.g., the cost, time, and scheduling difficulties necessary to obtain evidence and present witness testimony would be far less in Texas than in {alternate forum}.*}

Continued on next page

21. The public-interest factors favor keeping the action in Texas. *See* Tex. Civ. Prac. & Rem. Code §71.051(b)(5).

{*INCLUDE ALL RELEVANT FACTORS BELOW*}

a. The burden of jury duty is more appropriately placed on Texas citizens than on {43 *alternate forum*} citizens. *See In re Gen. Elec.*, 271 S.W.3d at 691. {44 *Elaborate.*}

b. The administrative burden on the Texas court is less than the burden on the {45 *alternate forum*} court. *See In re Gen. Elec.*, 271 S.W.3d at 691. {46 *Elaborate.*}

c. Texas has an interest in adjudicating this case, and {47 *alternate forum*} does not. *See In re Gen. Elec.*, 271 S.W.3d at 691. {48 *Elaborate.*}

d. Texas law will control the disposition of this case. *See In re Gen. Elec.*, 271 S.W.3d at 691. {49 *Elaborate.*}

22. The act or omission that resulted in plaintiff's claim for {50 *injury/death*} occurred in Texas. *See* Tex. Civ. Prac. & Rem. Code §71.051(b)(5). {51 *Elaborate.*}

{*CHOOSE APPROPRIATE PARAGRAPHS 23-24 IF APPLICABLE*}

ALTERNATIVE ARGUMENT

23. If this Court grants defendant's motion, plaintiff asks the Court to stay, not dismiss, this suit because {52 *state reasons court should stay instead of dismiss*}. {*See* ***O'Connor's Texas Rules****, "Code FNC," ch. 3-D, §5.1, p. 268.*}

24. If this Court grants defendant's motion, plaintiff asks the Court to sign an order that imposes the following conditions: {53 *list conditions*}. {*See* ***O'Connor's Texas Rules****, "Code FNC," ch. 3-D, §5.1, p. 268.*}

CONCLUSION

25. {54 *Briefly summarize the response.*}

PRAYER

26. For these reasons, plaintiff asks the Court to deny defendant's motion to {55 *dismiss/stay*} this suit for forum non conveniens {56 *add if appropriate: or, in the alternative, to {dismiss/stay} this suit and impose the following conditions: {list conditions}*}.

SEE: Tex. Civ. Prac. & Rem. Code §71.051
*O'Connor's Texas Rules * Civil Trials* (2019), "Response," ch. 3-D, §3.2, p. 262

ADD: STYLE OF THE CASE – FORM 1B:2
SIGNATURE BLOCK – FORM 1B:3
CERTIFICATE OF SERVICE – FORM 1B:13

ATTACH: AFFIDAVIT – FORM 1B:8, if necessary
ORDER – FORM 3D:6

NOTE: In addition to negating the defendant's allegations, the plaintiff should address any conditions that it would like for the court to include in the order should the court grant the defendant's FNC motion. *See* Tex. Civ. Prac. & Rem. Code §71.051(c). See ***O'Connor's Texas Rules***, "Practice Tip," ch. 3-D, §3.2.2, p. 262.

See notes under FORM 3D:1.

PLAINTIFF'S RESPONSE TO DEFENDANT'S MOTION
TO {❶ *DISMISS/STAY*} SUIT FOR FORUM NON CONVENIENS

Plaintiff, {❷ *name*}, asks the Court to deny defendant {❸ *name*}'s motion to {❹ *dismiss/stay*} this suit on grounds of forum non conveniens.

INTRODUCTION

1. Plaintiff, {❺ *name*}, sued defendant, {❻ *name*}, for {❼ *state basis of suit*}.

2. {❽ *State other relevant facts about the suit.*}

BACKGROUND

3. On {❾ *date*}, defendant filed a motion to {❿ *dismiss/stay*} plaintiff's suit under the common-law doctrine of forum non conveniens.

4. {⓫ *State other facts relevant to the response.*}

ARGUMENT & AUTHORITIES

5. Under Texas common law, a court can decline to exercise jurisdiction over a case under the doctrine of forum non conveniens if there is another, more appropriate forum available to hear the dispute. *See RSR Corp. v. Siegmund*, 309 S.W.3d 686, 710 (Tex. App.—Dallas 2010, no pet.). The doctrine should, however, be applied with caution, exceptionally, and only for good reasons. *Id.* at 711. The defendant has the initial burden to establish that an alternate forum is available. *See Vinmar Trade Fin., Ltd. v. Util. Trailers de Mex., S.A. de C.V.*, 336 S.W.3d 664, 672 (Tex. App.—Houston [1st Dist.] 2010, no pet.); *RSR Corp.*, 309 S.W.3d at 710. If the defendant meets its burden, the burden shifts to the plaintiff to prove that the alternate forum is inadequate. *RSR Corp.*, 309 S.W.3d at 710. If the alternate forum is both available and adequate, the defendant then has the burden to establish that the alternate forum is the more appropriate forum to hear the case. *See id.* at 710-11. The defendant's burden is especially high when a plaintiff has chosen its home forum. *See Quixtar Inc. v. Signature Mgmt. Team, LLC*, 315 S.W.3d 28, 32-33 (Tex. 2010). Unless the balance weighs strongly in favor of the defendant, a court should rarely disturb the plaintiff's choice of forum. *See id.* at 33.

{*CHOOSE APPROPRIATE PARAGRAPHS 6-10*}

6. The Court should deny defendant's forum non conveniens motion because this is a {⓬ *personal-injury/wrongful-death*} action. For personal-injury and wrongful-death cases, forum non conveniens motions must be made under Texas Civil Practice & Remedies Code section 71.051. Tex. Civ. Prac. & Rem. Code §71.051(i).

FORM 3D:4

7. The Court should deny defendant's forum non conveniens motion because, contrary to defendant's assertions, {13 *alternate forum*} is not available. *See Gottwald v. de Cano*, 568 S.W.3d 241, 249 (Tex. App.—El Paso 2019, no pet.); *Vinmar Trade Fin.*, 336 S.W.3d at 674. {14 *Elaborate.*}

8. The Court should deny defendant's forum non conveniens motion because {15 *alternate forum*} is not adequate. *See Gottwald v. de Cano*, 568 S.W.3d 241, 249 (Tex. App.—El Paso 2019, no pet.); *Vinmar Trade Fin.*, 336 S.W.3d at 674. A forum is not adequate if the parties will be deprived of remedies or be treated unfairly. *See Vinmar Trade Fin.*, 336 S.W.3d at 674. Specifically, {16 *alternate forum*} is not adequate because {17 *explain*}.

9. The Court should deny defendant's forum non conveniens motion because the private-interest factors do not favor a {18 *dismissal/stay*}. The private interests of the litigants will be better served in Texas than in {19 *alternate forum*} for the following reasons:

{*INCLUDE ALL RELEVANT FACTORS BELOW*}

a. Access to sources of proof will be easier in Texas than in {20 *alternate forum*}. *RSR Corp.*, 309 S.W.3d at 710; *see Quixtar Inc.*, 315 S.W.3d at 33. {21 *Elaborate.*}

b. Compulsory process for the attendance of unwilling witnesses is available in Texas. *RSR Corp.*, 309 S.W.3d at 710; *see Quixtar Inc.*, 315 S.W.3d at 33. {22 *Elaborate.*}

c. The cost of securing the presence of willing witnesses will be lower in Texas than in {23 *alternate forum*}. *RSR Corp.*, 309 S.W.3d at 710; *see Quixtar Inc.*, 315 S.W.3d at 33. {24 *Elaborate.*}

d. Viewing of the premises is possible in Texas. *See Quixtar Inc.*, 315 S.W.3d at 33. {25 *Elaborate.*}

e. The enforcement of a judgment is easier in Texas than in {26 *alternate forum*}. *RSR Corp.*, 309 S.W.3d at 710; *see Quixtar Inc.*, 315 S.W.3d at 33. {27 *Elaborate.*}

f. {28 *Describe any other practical issues that would make trial easier, more expeditious, and less expensive in Texas. RSR Corp., 309 S.W.3d at 710; see Quixtar Inc., 315 S.W.3d at 33.*}

Continued on next page

FORM 3D:4

10. The Court should deny defendant's forum non conveniens motion because the public-interest factors do not favor a {㉙ *dismissal/stay*}. The public interest will be better served in Texas than in {㉚ *alternate forum*} for the following reasons:

{*INCLUDE ALL RELEVANT FACTORS BELOW*}

a. The burden of jury duty is more appropriately placed on Texas citizens than on {㉛ *alternate forum*} citizens. *RSR Corp.*, 309 S.W.3d at 710; *see Quixtar Inc.*, 315 S.W.3d at 33-34. {㉜ *Elaborate.*}

b. The administrative burden on the Texas court is less than on the {㉝ *alternate forum*} court. *RSR Corp.*, 309 S.W.3d at 710; *see Quixtar Inc.*, 315 S.W.3d at 33-34. Specifically, {㉞ *explain, e.g., there is a congested docket in the {alternate forum} court*}.

c. Texas has an interest in adjudicating this case, and {㉟ *alternate forum*} does not. *RSR Corp.*, 309 S.W.3d at 710; *see Quixtar Inc.*, 315 S.W.3d at 33-34. {㊱ *Elaborate.*}

d. Texas law will control the disposition of this case. *See Quixtar Inc.*, 315 S.W.3d at 33-34; *RSR Corp.*, 309 S.W.3d at 710. {㊲ *Elaborate.*}

CONCLUSION

11. {㊳ *Briefly summarize the response.*}

PRAYER

12. For these reasons, plaintiff asks the Court to deny defendant's motion to {㊴ *dismiss/stay*} this suit for forum non conveniens.

SEE: ***O'Connor's Texas Rules * Civil Trials*** (2019), "Response," ch. 3-D, §4.2, p. 267

ADD: STYLE OF THE CASE – FORM 1B:2
SIGNATURE BLOCK – FORM 1B:3
CERTIFICATE OF SERVICE – FORM 1B:13

ATTACH: AFFIDAVIT – FORM 1B:8, if necessary
ORDER – FORM 3D:6

NOTE: Although there is no deadline for filing the response, the plaintiff should file (and serve) it far enough in advance of the hearing for the court to consider the arguments and evidence.
See notes under FORM 3D:2.

DEFENDANT'S REPLY TO PLAINTIFF'S RESPONSE TO
MOTION TO {1 *DISMISS/STAY*} SUIT FOR FORUM NON CONVENIENS

Defendant, {2 *name*}, asks the Court to {3 *dismiss/stay*} plaintiff {4 *name*}'s suit on grounds of forum non conveniens, as authorized by Texas Civil Practice & Remedies Code section 71.051.

INTRODUCTION

1. Plaintiff, {5 *name*}, sued defendant, {6 *name*}, for {7 *state basis of suit*}.

2. {8 *State other relevant facts about the suit.*}

BACKGROUND

3. On {9 *date*}, defendant filed a motion to {10 *dismiss/stay*} plaintiff's suit on the grounds of forum non conveniens under Texas Civil Practice & Remedies Code section 71.051.

4. On {11 *date*}, plaintiff filed a response to defendant's motion to {12 *dismiss/stay*} for forum non conveniens.

5. {13 *State other facts relevant to the reply.*}

ARGUMENT & AUTHORITIES

{*CHOOSE APPROPRIATE PARAGRAPHS 6-15*}

6. Plaintiff alleges that {14 *he/she*} is a "plaintiff" as defined in Texas Civil Practice & Remedies Code section 71.051(h)(2) and therefore that {15 *his/her*} Texas residency prohibits the court from {16 *dismissing/staying*} {17 *his/her*} claim. *See* Tex. Civ. Prac. & Rem. Code §71.051(e). This is not correct. {18 *Refute plaintiff's allegations and refer to evidence attached to the reply.*} {*See* ***O'Connor's Texas Rules****, "Not a 'plaintiff' under CPRC §71.051," ch. 3-D, §3.1.4(1)(a), p. 259.*}

7. Plaintiff alleges that {19 *he/she*} is a {20 *legal resident/derivative claimant of a legal resident*} of Texas. *See* Tex. Civ. Prac. & Rem. Code §71.051(e). This is not correct. {21 *Refute plaintiff's allegations and refer to evidence attached to the reply.*} {*See* ***O'Connor's Texas Rules****, "Not a legal resident or derivative claimant of legal resident," ch. 3-D, §3.1.4(1)(b), p. 259.*}

◄ *Continued on next page* ►

8. Plaintiff alleges that defendant did not identify an available alternate forum to decide plaintiff's cause of action. *See* Tex. Civ. Prac. & Rem. Code §71.051(b)(1). This is not correct. {22 *Refute plaintiff's allegations and refer to evidence attached to the reply.*} {*See* ***O'Connor's Texas Rules***, *"Alternate forum available," ch. 3-D, §3.1.4(2)(a), p. 260.*}

9. Plaintiff alleges that the courts of {23 *alternate forum*} do not offer an adequate remedy for plaintiff's cause of action because {24 *repeat plaintiff's allegations*}. *See* Tex. Civ. Prac. & Rem. Code §71.051(b)(2). This is not correct. {25 *Refute plaintiff's allegations and refer to evidence attached to the reply.*} {*See* ***O'Connor's Texas Rules***, *"Alternate forum adequate," ch. 3-D, §3.1.4(2)(b), p. 260.*}

10. Plaintiff alleges that maintaining this suit in Texas will not cause a substantial injustice for defendant because {26 *repeat plaintiff's allegations*}. *See* Tex. Civ. Prac. & Rem. Code §71.051(b)(3). This is not correct. {27 *Refute plaintiff's allegations and refer to evidence attached to the reply.*} {*See* ***O'Connor's Texas Rules***, *"Substantial injustice imposed," ch. 3-D, §3.1.4(2)(c), p. 261.*}

11. Plaintiff alleges that the courts of {28 *alternate forum*} cannot exercise jurisdiction over all the defendants properly joined in plaintiff's suit. *See* Tex. Civ. Prac. & Rem. Code §71.051(b)(4). This is not correct. {29 *Identify properly joined defendants and show that alternate forum can exercise jurisdiction over each and refer to evidence attached to the reply. If necessary, file a stipulation agreeing to the exercise of personal jurisdiction by that forum.*} {*See* ***O'Connor's Texas Rules***, *"Alternate forum can exercise jurisdiction," ch. 3-D, §3.1.4(2)(d), p. 261.*}

12. Plaintiff alleges that this Court's {30 *dismissal/stay*} of plaintiff's suit based on forum non conveniens will result in unreasonable duplication and proliferation of litigation. *See* Tex. Civ. Prac. & Rem. Code §71.051(b)(6). This is not correct. {31 *Refute plaintiff's allegations and refer to evidence attached to the reply.*} {*See* ***O'Connor's Texas Rules***, *"No duplication or proliferation of litigation," ch. 3-D, §3.1.4(2)(f), p. 262.*}

13. Plaintiff alleges that the private interests of the litigants will be better served in Texas than in {32 *alternate forum*} because {33 *repeat plaintiff's private-interest arguments*}. This is not correct. {34 *Refute each of plaintiff's arguments.*} {*See* ***O'Connor's Texas Rules***, *"Private interests," ch. 3-D, §3.1.4(2)(e)[1], p. 261.*}

14. Plaintiff alleges that the public interest will be better served in Texas than in {35 *alternate forum*} because {36 *repeat plaintiff's public-interest arguments*}. This is not correct. {37 *Refute each of plaintiff's arguments.*} {*See* ***O'Connor's Texas Rules***, *"Public interests," ch. 3-D, §3.1.4(2)(e)[2], p. 261.*}

15. Plaintiff alleges that the act or omission that resulted in {38 *his/her*} claim for {39 *personal injury/wrongful death*} occurred in Texas. *See* Tex. Civ. Prac. & Rem. Code §71.051(b)(5). This is not correct. {40 *Refute plaintiff's allegations and refer to evidence attached to the reply.*} {*See* ***O'Connor's Texas Rules****, "No act or omission in Texas," ch. 3-D, §3.1.4(2)(e)[3], p. 262.*}

{*CHOOSE APPROPRIATE PARAGRAPHS 16-17 IF APPLICABLE*}

ALTERNATIVE ARGUMENT

16. Plaintiff made the alternative argument that if the Court grants defendant's motion, the Court should merely stay the lawsuit, not dismiss it. *See* Tex. Civ. Prac. & Rem. Code §71.051(b), (c). The Court should deny plaintiff's request because {41 *state reasons court should dismiss instead of stay*}. {*See* ***O'Connor's Texas Rules****, "Code FNC," ch. 3-D, §5.1, p. 268.*}

17. Plaintiff made the alternative argument that if the Court grants defendant's motion, the Court should set terms and conditions for the order dismissing or staying the lawsuit. *See* Tex. Civ. Prac. & Rem. Code §71.051(c). Plaintiff listed the terms and conditions that {42 *he/she*} asked the Court to impose. The Court should deny plaintiff's request because {43 *state why terms and conditions are not appropriate*}. {*See* ***O'Connor's Texas Rules****, "Code FNC," ch. 3-D, §5.1, p. 268.*}

CONCLUSION

18. {44 *Briefly summarize the reply.*}

PRAYER

19. For these reasons, defendant asks the Court to {45 *dismiss/stay*} plaintiff's suit for forum non conveniens.

SEE: Tex. Civ. Prac. & Rem. Code §71.051
O'Connor's Texas Rules * Civil Trials (2019), "Code FNC Motion," ch. 3-D, §3, p. 258

ADD: STYLE OF THE CASE – FORM 1B:2
SIGNATURE BLOCK – FORM 1B:3
CERTIFICATE OF SERVICE – FORM 1B:13

ATTACH: AFFIDAVIT – FORM 1B:8, if necessary

NOTE: If the plaintiff provides evidence to negate the defendant's allegations, the defendant should respond by supplying verified evidence to support its motion. See ***O'Connor's Texas Rules***, "Verified," ch. 3-D, §3.1.5, p. 262.

See notes under FORM 3D:1.

ORDER ON DEFENDANT'S MOTION TO
{❶ *DISMISS/STAY*} SUIT FOR FORUM NON CONVENIENS

After considering defendant {❷ *name*}'s motion to {❸ *dismiss/stay*} this suit on grounds of forum non conveniens, the response, the pleadings, {❹ *add if appropriate: the affidavits/the stipulations/the discovery on file/the oral testimony,*} and arguments of counsel, the Court

{*CHOOSE APPROPRIATE ORDER*}

DENIES defendant's motion and retains plaintiff's suit on the Court's docket.

GRANTS defendant's motion and {❺ *dismisses/stays*} plaintiff's suit. {❻ *Add for Code FNC order: The Court makes the following findings and conclusions: {state the specific findings of fact and conclusions of law}.*}

GRANTS defendant's motion and {❼ *dismisses/stays*} plaintiff's suit on the following terms and conditions: {❽ *specify the terms and conditions on which the dismissal or stay is granted, e.g., all properly joined defendants agree to waive any defense based on the statute of limitations*}. If any defendant violates the terms and conditions of this order, the Court will withdraw this order to {❾ *dismiss/stay*} the suit. {❿ *Add for Code FNC order: The Court makes the following findings and conclusions: {state the specific findings of fact and conclusions of law}.*}

SIGNED on _______________, 20___.

____
PRESIDING JUDGE

SEE: Tex. Civ. Prac. & Rem. Code §71.051(b), (c), (f)
O'Connor's Texas Rules * Civil Trials (2019), "Order," ch. 3-D, §5, p. 268

ADD: STYLE OF THE CASE – FORM 1B:2
CERTIFICATE OF SERVICE – FORM 1B:13, if proposed order served separately from motion or response

NOTE: Generally, a court must determine whether it has jurisdiction over a defendant before ruling on an FNC motion. *See* ***Exxon Corp. v. Choo***, 881 S.W.2d 301, 302 n.2 (Tex.1994). A court may, however, take the less burdensome approach and resolve an FNC motion before a jurisdictional challenge if the jurisdictional challenge would be more difficult to resolve and the FNC considerations weigh heavily in favor of dismissal. ***Sinochem Int'l Co. v. Malaysia Int'l Shipping Corp.***, 549 U.S. 422, 436 (2007); *see, e.g.*, ***Schippers v. Mazak Props., Inc.***, 350 S.W.3d 294, 296 (Tex.App.—San Antonio 2011, pet. denied) (court addressed FNC motion before special appearance; Code FNC); ***Vinmar Trade Fin., Ltd. v. Utility Trailers de Mex., S.A. de C.V.***, 336 S.W.3d 664, 671-72 (Tex.App.—Houston [1st Dist.] 2010, no pet.) (same; common-law FNC). See ***O'Connor's Texas Rules***, "Timing," ch. 3-D, §3.7.2, p. 264.

The court must set forth specific findings of fact and conclusions of law when it grants a Code FNC motion. Tex. Civ. Prac. & Rem. Code §71.051(f).

DEFENDANT'S MOTION TO DISMISS SUIT

Defendant, {❶ *name*}, asks the Court to dismiss plaintiff {❷ *name*}'s suit because a forum-selection clause identifies another state as the proper forum.

INTRODUCTION

1. Plaintiff, {❸ *name*}, sued defendant, {❹ *name*}, for {❺ *state basis of suit*}.

2. {❻ *If motion to dismiss is defendant's initial pleading, add appropriate identification for each defendant from FORM 3E:1.*}

3. {❼ *State other relevant facts about the suit.*}

BACKGROUND

4. On {❽ *date*}, defendant and plaintiff entered into a contract that includes a forum-selection clause. The contract is attached as Exhibit {❾ *letter*}.

5. In the contract, the parties specified {❿ *identify state*} as the proper forum for suit.

6. {⓫ *State other facts relevant to the motion.*}

ARGUMENT & AUTHORITIES

7. Forum-selection clauses are presumed valid and enforceable in Texas. *In re Laibe Corp.*, 307 S.W.3d 314, 316 (Tex. 2010); *see Pinto Tech. Ventures, L.P. v. Sheldon*, 526 S.W.3d 428, 436 (Tex. 2017); *In re Int'l Profit Assocs., Inc.*, 274 S.W.3d 672, 675 (Tex. 2009). {*See* ***O'Connor's Texas Rules****, "Enforcement," ch. 3-D, §6.1, p. 268.*}

8. The forum-selection clause is mandatory. *See Phoenix Network Techs. (Eur.) Ltd. v. Neon Sys., Inc.*, 177 S.W.3d 605, 615 (Tex. App.—Houston [1st Dist.] 2005, no pet.); *Mabon Ltd. v. Afri-Carib Enters., Inc.*, 29 S.W.3d 291, 297 (Tex. App.—Houston [14th Dist.] 2000, no pet.). {⓬ *Elaborate.*} {*See* ***O'Connor's Texas Rules****, "Mandatory vs. permissive," ch. 3-D, §6.1.2, p. 269.*}

9. Plaintiff's claims for {⓭ *identify claims*} fall within the scope of the forum-selection clause. *See Pinto Tech.*, 526 S.W.3d at 441-42; *In re Lisa Laser USA, Inc.*, 310 S.W.3d 880, 884-85 (Tex. 2010). {⓮ *Elaborate.*} {*See* ***O'Connor's Texas Rules****, "Within scope," ch. 3-D, §6.1.3, p. 270.*}

◄ *Continued on next page* ►

10. The Court should enforce the forum-selection clause because (1) the clause is valid and not the result of fraud or overreaching, (2) enforcement of the clause would not be unreasonable or unjust, (3) enforcement of the clause would not contravene a strong Texas public policy, (4) the selected forum would not be seriously inconvenient for trial, and (5) defendant did not waive the right to rely on the forum-selection clause. *See In re Nationwide Ins. Co. of Am.*, 494 S.W.3d 708, 712 (Tex. 2016); *In re Laibe Corp.*, 307 S.W.3d at 316; *In re ADM Inv'r Servs., Inc.*, 304 S.W.3d 371, 374-75 (Tex. 2010); *In re AIU Ins. Co.*, 148 S.W.3d 109, 112, 121 (Tex. 2004). {⓯ *Elaborate.*} {*See* ***O'Connor's Texas Rules****, "No exception or waiver," ch. 3-D, §6.1.4, p. 271.*}

CONCLUSION

11. {⓰ *Briefly summarize the motion.*}

PRAYER

12. For these reasons, defendant asks the Court to set defendant's motion to dismiss for hearing, and, after the hearing, grant defendant's motion and sign an order dismissing plaintiff's suit.

SEE: ***O'Connor's Texas Rules * Civil Trials*** (2019), "Forum-Selection Clause," ch. 3-D, §6, p. 268

ADD: STYLE OF THE CASE – FORM 1B:2
SIGNATURE BLOCK – FORM 1B:3
CERTIFICATE OF SERVICE – FORM 1B:13

ATTACH: AFFIDAVIT – FORM 1B:8, if necessary
NOTICE OF CURRENT/CHANGE OF ADDRESS – FORM 1B:14, if motion to dismiss is defendant's initial pleading
NOTICE OF HEARING OR SUBMISSION – FORM 1E:1
ORDER – FORM 3D:9
Contract

PLAINTIFF'S RESPONSE TO DEFENDANT'S MOTION TO DISMISS SUIT

Plaintiff, {❶ *name*}, asks the Court to deny defendant {❷ *name*}'s motion to dismiss this suit.

INTRODUCTION

1. Plaintiff, {❸ *name*}, sued defendant, {❹ *name*}, for {❺ *state basis of suit*}.

2. {❻ *State other relevant facts about the suit.*}

BACKGROUND

3. On {❼ *date*}, plaintiff and defendant entered into a contract that includes a forum-selection clause. The contract is attached as Exhibit {❽ *letter*}.

4. {❾ *State other facts relevant to the response.*}

ARGUMENT & AUTHORITIES

5. Although forum-selection clauses are enforceable in Texas, the Court should not enforce the forum-selection clause in this case.

{*CHOOSE APPROPRIATE PARAGRAPHS 6-13*}

6. The forum-selection clause should not be enforced because the clause is permissive. *See Pinto Tech. Ventures, L.P. v. Sheldon*, 526 S.W.3d 428, 437-38 (Tex. 2017); *Phoenix Network Techs. (Eur.) Ltd. v. Neon Sys., Inc.*, 177 S.W.3d 605, 615 (Tex. App.—Houston [1st Dist.] 2005, no pet.); *Mabon Ltd. v. Afri-Carib Enters., Inc.*, 29 S.W.3d 291, 297 (Tex. App.—Houston [14th Dist.] 2000, no pet.). {❿ *Elaborate.*} {*See* ***O'Connor's Texas Rules****, "Mandatory vs. permissive," ch. 3-D, §6.1.2, p. 269.*}

7. The forum-selection clause should not be enforced because plaintiff's claims for {⓫ *identify claims*} do not fall within the scope of the forum-selection clause. *See In re Lisa Laser USA, Inc.*, 310 S.W.3d 880, 884-85 (Tex. 2010). {⓬ *Elaborate.*} {*See* ***O'Connor's Texas Rules****, "Within scope," ch. 3-D, §6.1.3, p. 270.*}

8. The forum-selection clause should not be enforced because it is not valid—it is the result of fraud. *See In re Lyon Fin. Servs., Inc.*, 257 S.W.3d 228, 231-32 (Tex. 2008). {⓭ *In separately numbered paragraphs, identify elements and facts supporting fraud.*} {*See* ***O'Connor's Texas Rules****, "Fraud or overreaching," ch. 3-D, §6.1.4(1)(b), p. 271;* ***O'Connor's Texas COA****, "Plaintiff's Elements," ch. 12-A, §2, p. 299.*}

◄ *Continued on next page* ►

9. The forum-selection clause should not be enforced because it is not valid—it is the result of overreaching. *See In re Lyon Fin. Servs., Inc.*, 257 S.W.3d 228, 231 (Tex. 2008). The forum-selection clause resulted in unfair surprise and oppression to plaintiff. *See In re Int'l Profit Assocs., Inc.*, 274 S.W.3d 672, 678 (Tex. 2009). {[14] *Elaborate.*} {*See* ***O'Connor's Texas Rules****, "Fraud or overreaching," ch. 3-D, §6.1.4(1)(b), p. 271.*}

10. The forum-selection clause should not be enforced because it would be unreasonable and unjust to do so. *See In re Laibe Corp.*, 307 S.W.3d 314, 316 (Tex. 2010); *In re ADM Inv'r Servs., Inc.*, 304 S.W.3d 371, 375 (Tex. 2010); *In re Int'l Profit Assocs., Inc.*, 274 S.W.3d 672, 675 (Tex. 2009). {[15] *Explain any extreme or exceptional circumstances that would make enforcement of the forum-selection clause unreasonable and unjust.*} {*See* ***O'Connor's Texas Rules****, "Unreasonable & unjust," ch. 3-D, §6.1.4(1)(a), p. 271.*}

11. The forum-selection clause should not be enforced because it would contravene strong Texas public policy. *See In re Laibe Corp.*, 307 S.W.3d 314, 316 (Tex. 2010); *In re Int'l Profit Assocs., Inc.*, 274 S.W.3d 672, 675 (Tex. 2009). {[16] *Elaborate.*} {*See* ***O'Connor's Texas Rules****, "Against public policy," ch. 3-D, §6.1.4(1)(c), p. 271.*}

12. The forum-selection clause should not be enforced because {[17] *identify forum*} would be seriously inconvenient for trial and thus would deprive plaintiff of {[18] *his/her/its*} day in court. *See In re Laibe Corp.*, 307 S.W.3d 314, 316-17 (Tex. 2010); *In re Int'l Profit Assocs., Inc.*, 274 S.W.3d 672, 675 (Tex. 2009). Special and unusual circumstances have developed that would make litigation in {[19] *identify forum*} difficult and inconvenient. *See In re Int'l Profit*, 274 S.W.3d at 680. {[20] *Elaborate.*} {*See* ***O'Connor's Texas Rules****, "Seriously inconvenient," ch. 3-D, §6.1.4(1)(d), p. 271.*}

13. The forum-selection clause should not be enforced because defendant waived {[21] *his/her/its*} right to rely on the forum-selection clause. *See In re Nationwide Ins. Co. of Am.*, 494 S.W.3d 708, 712 (Tex. 2016); *In re ADM Inv'r Servs., Inc.*, 304 S.W.3d 371, 374 (Tex. 2010); *In re AIU Ins. Co.*, 148 S.W.3d 109, 121 (Tex. 2004). {[22] *Explain, e.g., defendant indicated a desire to resolve the case in the forum where plaintiff filed suit.*} {*See* ***O'Connor's Texas Rules****, "Waiver," ch. 3-D, §6.1.4(2), p. 272.*}

CONCLUSION

14. {[23] *Briefly summarize the response.*}

PRAYER

15. For these reasons, plaintiff asks the Court to deny defendant's motion to dismiss this suit.

FORM 3D:8

FORM 3D:8 PLAINTIFF'S RESPONSE TO MOTION TO DISMISS – FORUM-SELECTION CLAUSE

SEE: ***O'Connor's Texas Rules * Civil Trials*** (2019), "Forum-Selection Clause," ch. 3-D, §6, p. 268
O'Connor's Texas Causes of Action (2019), "Plaintiff's Elements," ch. 12-A, §2, p. 299

ADD: STYLE OF THE CASE – FORM 1B:2
SIGNATURE BLOCK – FORM 1B:3
CERTIFICATE OF SERVICE – FORM 1B:13

ATTACH: AFFIDAVIT – FORM 1B:8, if necessary
ORDER – FORM 3D:9
Contract

ORDER ON DEFENDANT'S MOTION TO DISMISS SUIT

After considering defendant {❶ *name*}'s motion to dismiss this suit, the response, the pleadings, {❷ *add if appropriate: the affidavits/the stipulations/the discovery on file/the oral testimony,*} and arguments of counsel, the Court

{*CHOOSE APPROPRIATE ORDER*}

DENIES defendant's motion and retains plaintiff's suit on the Court's docket.

GRANTS defendant's motion and dismisses plaintiff's suit.

SIGNED on _______________, 20___.

____
PRESIDING JUDGE

SEE: *O'Connor's Texas Rules * Civil Trials* (2019), "Forum-Selection Clause," ch. 3-D, §6, p. 268

ADD: STYLE OF THE CASE – FORM 1B:2
CERTIFICATE OF SERVICE – FORM 1B:13, if proposed order served separately from motion or response

DEFENDANT'S ORIGINAL ANSWER
{❶ *STATE ADDITIONAL RELIEF REQUESTED IF APPROPRIATE, E.G., & PLEA TO THE JURISDICTION*}

Defendant, {❷ *name*}, files this original answer {❸ *state additional relief requested if appropriate, e.g., and plea to the jurisdiction*} to plaintiff {❹ *name*}'s original petition.

{*CHOOSE ONE OF THE FOLLOWING IF DEFENDANT IS AN INDIVIDUAL*}

Ⓐ The last three digits of defendant's driver's license number are {❺ *digits of driver's license number*}. The last three digits of defendant's Social Security number are {❻ *digits of Social Security number*}. {*See Tex. Civ. Prac. & Rem. Code §30.014(a);* ***O'Connor's Texas Rules****, "ID number," ch. 1-B, §3.2.4(3), p. 8.*}

Ⓑ The last three digits of defendant's driver's license number are {❼ *digits of driver's license number*}. Defendant has not been issued a Social Security number. {*See Tex. Civ. Prac. & Rem. Code §30.014(a);* ***O'Connor's Texas Rules****, "ID number," ch. 1-B, §3.2.4(3), p. 8.*}

Ⓒ The last three digits of defendant's Social Security number are {❽ *digits of Social Security number*}. Defendant has not been issued a driver's license number. {*See Tex. Civ. Prac. & Rem. Code §30.014(a);* ***O'Connor's Texas Rules****, "ID number," ch. 1-B, §3.2.4(3), p. 8.*}

Ⓓ Defendant has not been issued a driver's license number or a Social Security number. {*See Tex. Civ. Prac. & Rem. Code §30.014(a);* ***O'Connor's Texas Rules****, "ID number," ch. 1-B, §3.2.4(3), p. 8.*}

GENERAL DENIAL

1. Defendant generally denies the allegations in plaintiff's original petition. {*See* ***O'Connor's Texas Rules****, "General Denial," ch. 3-E, §3, p. 274.*}

{*ADD SECTIONS BELOW AS APPROPRIATE*}

PLEA TO THE JURISDICTION

2. Defendant asks the Court to dismiss plaintiff's suit because of lack of jurisdiction. {❾ *Elaborate.*} {*See FORM 3F:1;* ***O'Connor's Texas Rules****, "Plea to the Jurisdiction—Challenging the Court," ch. 3-F, p. 287.*}

◄ *Continued on next page* ►

VERIFIED PLEAS

3. {*For verified pleas, see FORM 3E:10;* ***O'Connor's Texas Rules****, "Verified Pleas," ch. 3-E, §4, p. 275.*}

OTHER DEFENSES

4. {*For affirmative defenses, see FORM 3E:11;* ***O'Connor's Texas Rules****, "Affirmative Defenses," ch. 3-E, §5, p. 277.*}

COUNTERCLAIM – {⑩ *NAME OF COUNTERCLAIM*}

5. {***⑪ Identify cause of action against plaintiff, e.g., plaintiff breached its fiduciary duty to defendant. In separately numbered paragraphs, identify elements and facts supporting the counterclaim, add any claims for exemplary damages, attorney fees, or equitable relief, and include a statement that damages are within the jurisdictional limits of the court. See FORM 2B:1, ¶10.***} {*See* ***O'Connor's Texas Rules****, "Counterclaims," ch. 3-E, §7.1, p. 282.*}

CROSS-CLAIM

6. Codefendant, {⑫ *name*}, is liable to defendant, {⑬ *name*}, for {⑭ *identify cause of action against codefendant*}. {***⑮ In separately numbered paragraphs, identify elements and facts supporting the cross-claim and include a statement that damages are within the jurisdictional limits of the court. See FORM 2B:1, ¶10.***} {*See* ***O'Connor's Texas Rules****, "Cross-claims," ch. 3-E, §7.2, p. 283.*}

{*ADD SECTION BELOW IF INCLUDING COUNTERCLAIM OR CROSS-CLAIM*}

CLAIM FOR RELIEF

{*CHOOSE APPROPRIATE PARAGRAPH 7*}

7. Defendant seeks only monetary relief of $100,000 or less, including damages of any kind, penalties, court costs, expenses, prejudgment interest, and attorney fees. {*Tex. R. Civ. P. 47(c)(1).*}

7. Defendant seeks monetary relief of $100,000 or less and nonmonetary relief. {*Tex. R. Civ. P. 47(c)(2).*}

7. Defendant seeks monetary relief over $100,000 but not more than $200,000. {*Tex. R. Civ. P. 47(c)(3).*}

7. Defendant seeks monetary relief over $200,000 but not more than $1,000,000. {*Tex. R. Civ. P. 47(c)(4).*}

7. Defendant seeks monetary relief over $1,000,000. {*Tex. R. Civ. P. 47(c)(5).*}

EXEMPLARY-DAMAGES CAP

8. If defendant is found liable for exemplary damages, those damages must be capped under the Texas Damages Act, the Due Process Clause of the United States Constitution, and the Due Course of Law provisions of the Texas Constitution. {*See* ***O'Connor's Texas COA****, "Capping Exemplary Damages," ch. 42-B, §7, p. 1434.*}

{*For designation of unknown person as responsible third party in amended answer*}

PROPORTIONATE RESPONSIBILITY OF UNKNOWN PERSON

9. Defendant designates an unknown person as a responsible third party within the meaning of Texas Civil Practice & Remedies Code section 33.004(j). {*See* ***O'Connor's Texas Rules****, "Amended answer – RTP is unknown criminal," ch. 3-E, §7.4.2(1), p. 284.*} The unknown person, {[16] *John Doe/Jane Doe*}, is a responsible third party for the following reasons:

a. {[17] *John Doe/Jane Doe*} committed an act that caused the loss or injury that is the subject of the lawsuit. {[18] *Elaborate.*} {*Tex. Civ. Prac. & Rem. Code §33.004(j).*}

b. The act committed by {[19] *John Doe/Jane Doe*} was criminal. {[20] *State facts showing a reasonable probability that the act was criminal.*} {*Tex. Civ. Prac. & Rem. Code §33.004(j)(1).*}

c. At this time, defendant is {[21] *unaware/aware*} of {[22] *any/certain*} identifying characteristics of {[23] *John Doe/Jane Doe*}. {[24] *State all identifying characteristics known when the answer is filed.*} {*Tex. Civ. Prac. & Rem. Code §33.004(j)(2).*}

d. {[25] *John Doe/Jane Doe*} is responsible for the criminal act because {[26] *state facts about unknown person's responsibility to satisfy the pleading requirements of the Texas Rules of Civil Procedure*}. {*Tex. Civ. Prac. & Rem. Code §33.004(j)(3).*}

Continued on next page

ATTORNEY FEES

10. Defendant is entitled to recover reasonable and necessary attorney fees under {㉗ *identify code, statute, or contract permitting recovery of attorney fees*}. {㉘ *Elaborate.*} {*See FORMS 2B:22-24;* ***O'Connor's Texas COA****, "Attorney Fees," ch. 45, p. 1463.*}

JURY DEMAND

11. Defendant demands a jury trial and tenders the appropriate fee with this answer. {*See* ***O'Connor's Texas Rules****, "Request for Jury Trial," ch. 5-B, p. 400.*}

SPECIAL EXCEPTIONS

12. Defendant specially excepts to plaintiff's original petition, paragraph {㉙ *number*} regarding the relief sought, and asks the Court to require plaintiff to specify the maximum amount that plaintiff claims. {*See* ***O'Connor's Texas Rules****, "Claims for relief," ch. 3-G, §2.2.5, p. 300.*}

13. {*For other special exceptions, see FORM 3G:1.*}

REQUEST FOR DISCLOSURE

14. Under Texas Rule of Civil Procedure 194, defendant requests that plaintiff disclose, within 30 days of the service of this request, the information or material described in Rule 194.2. {*See* ***O'Connor's Texas Rules****, "Content of request," ch. 6-E, §3.2, p. 627.*}

OBJECTION TO ASSOCIATE JUDGE

15. Defendant objects to the referral of this case to an associate judge for hearing a trial on the merits or presiding at a jury trial. {*See* ***O'Connor's Texas Rules****, "Objection to referral," ch. 1-J, §3.3, p. 96.*}

PRAYER

16. For these reasons, defendant asks the Court to {㉚ *state all relief requested, e.g., dismiss this suit, render judgment that plaintiff take nothing, award reasonable and necessary attorney fees to defendant*}, assess costs against plaintiff, and award defendant all other relief to which defendant is entitled. {*See* ***O'Connor's Texas Rules****, "Prayer," ch. 2-B, §15, p. 132.*} {*If defendant asserts claims for affirmative relief, include a request for rendition of judgment on those claims. See FORM 2B:1, ¶19.*}

SEE: Tex. R. Civ. P. 54, 92-94, 194
O'Connor's Texas Rules * Civil Trials (2019), "The Answer—Denying Liability," ch. 3-E, p. 273
O'Connor's Texas Causes of Action (2019), "Capping Exemplary Damages," ch. 42-B, §7, p. 1434; "Attorney Fees," ch. 45, p. 1463

ADD: STYLE OF THE CASE – FORM 1B:2
SIGNATURE BLOCK – FORM 1B:3
VERIFICATION – FORM 1B:7, for other verified pleas
CERTIFICATE OF SERVICE – FORM 1B:13

ATTACH: AFFIDAVIT – FORM 1B:8, if necessary to support plea to the jurisdiction
NOTICE OF CURRENT/CHANGE OF ADDRESS – FORM 1B:14, if answer is defendant's initial pleading
MOTION TO DISMISS FOR LACK OF JURISDICTION – FORM 3F:1, if necessary
ORDER ON SPECIAL EXCEPTIONS – FORM 3G:2, if necessary
Exhibits, if necessary
Filing fee, if counterclaim or cross-claim asserted
Jury fee, if jury trial requested

NOTE: Before filing an answer, the defendant should consider the need for pre-answer pleadings such as a special appearance or a motion to transfer venue. See ***O'Connor's Texas Rules***, "Due Order of Pleading," ch. 3-A, §3, p. 219. If the defendant chooses to include the pre-answer pleadings in its original answer, the special appearance should be the first numbered paragraph in the answer and the motion to transfer venue should be the second. See ***O'Connor's Texas Rules***, "Inclusive answer + some motions," ch. 3-A, §4.2, p. 221.

The defendant must file its answer by 10:00 a.m. on the first Monday after the expiration of 20 days from the date the defendant was served with citation. Tex. R. Civ. P. 99(b). See ***O'Connor's Texas Rules***, "Deadline to Answer," ch. 3-E, §2, p. 273.

All original pleadings that set forth a claim for relief—whether an original petition, a counterclaim, a cross-claim, or a third-party claim—generally must contain a specific statement of the relief the party seeks. *See* Tex. R. Civ. P. 47(c). This requirement does not apply, however, to guardianship or probate proceedings, suits governed by the Family Code, or suits filed in justice court. See ***O'Connor's Texas Rules***, "Relief sought," ch. 1-B, §3.2.8, p. 9.

If a defendant wants to rely on an affirmative defense, it must specifically raise the defense in its pretrial pleadings. ***MAN Engines & Components, Inc. v. Shows***, 434 S.W.3d 132, 137 (Tex.2014); *see* Tex. R. Civ. P. 94. If an affirmative defense is not timely raised in the trial court, it is waived and cannot be argued on appeal. *See* ***MAN Engines & Components***, 434 S.W.3d at 137.

The defendant may file a motion for leave to designate a person as a responsible third party. Tex. Civ. Prac. & Rem. Code §33.004(a). See FORM 3E:14. If the responsible third party is an unknown person alleged to have committed a criminal act, the defendant must designate that person in an amended answer before filing a motion for leave to designate the person as a responsible third party. *See* Tex. Civ. Prac. & Rem. Code §33.004(j). The responsible third party must be designated in an amended answer no later than 60 days after the defendant filed its original answer. *See id.*; ***Arango v. Davila***, No. 13-09-00470-CV (Tex.App.—Corpus Christi 2011, pet. denied) (memo op.; 5-19-11), *disapproved on other grounds*, ***Haygood v. De Escabedo***, 356 S.W.3d 390 (Tex.2011).

Continued on next page

Relevant evidence of a plaintiff's preoccurrence, injury-causing conduct that causes or contributes in any way to the plaintiff's damages (e.g., nonuse of a seat belt) may be considered when assessing each party's percentage of responsibility. ***Nabors Well Servs. v. Romero***, 456 S.W.3d 553, 562-63 (Tex.2015); *see* Tex. Civ. Prac. & Rem. Code §33.003(a). A jury question seeking percentage-of-responsibility findings can be submitted only if the pleadings and evidence raise the issue of a party's liability. See ***O'Connor's Texas COA***, "Evidence supporting submission," ch. 51, §4.3, p. 1598.

Under Texas Government Code chapter 54A, subchapter B, a district court or statutory county court can appoint a full-time or part-time associate judge to perform certain duties if the creation of the associate-judge position is authorized by the county commissioners court. Tex. Gov't Code §54A.102(a). If the creation of the position is authorized, the court can refer a full trial on the merits or a jury trial to an associate judge. *See id.* §54A.106. A case can be referred to an associate judge either by an order of referral in a specific case or by an omnibus order. *Id.* §54A.107(a). A party can prohibit the trial referral only if it files an objection within ten days after receiving notice of the referral. *Id.* §54A.106(c). See ***O'Connor's Texas Rules***, "Associate Judge," ch. 1-J, p. 95.

DEFENDANT'S ORIGINAL ANSWER
{❶ *STATE ADDITIONAL RELIEF REQUESTED IF APPROPRIATE, E.G., & PLEA TO THE JURISDICTION*}

Defendant, {❷ *name*}, files this original answer {❸ *state additional relief requested if appropriate, e.g., and plea to the jurisdiction*} to plaintiff {❹ *name*}'s original petition.

{*CHOOSE ONE OF THE FOLLOWING IF DEFENDANT IS AN INDIVIDUAL*}

Ⓐ The last three digits of defendant's driver's license number are {❺ *digits of driver's license number*}. The last three digits of defendant's Social Security number are {❻ *digits of Social Security number*}. {*See Tex. Civ. Prac. & Rem. Code §30.014(a); **O'Connor's Texas Rules**, "ID number," ch. 1-B, §3.2.4(3), p. 8.*}

Ⓑ The last three digits of defendant's driver's license number are {❼ *digits of driver's license number*}. Defendant has not been issued a Social Security number. {*See Tex. Civ. Prac. & Rem. Code §30.014(a); **O'Connor's Texas Rules**, "ID number," ch. 1-B, §3.2.4(3), p. 8.*}

Ⓒ The last three digits of defendant's Social Security number are {❽ *digits of Social Security number*}. Defendant has not been issued a driver's license number. {*See Tex. Civ. Prac. & Rem. Code §30.014(a); **O'Connor's Texas Rules**, "ID number," ch. 1-B, §3.2.4(3), p. 8.*}

Ⓓ Defendant has not been issued a driver's license number or a Social Security number. {*See Tex. Civ. Prac. & Rem. Code §30.014(a); **O'Connor's Texas Rules**, "ID number," ch. 1-B, §3.2.4(3), p. 8.*}

GENERAL DENIAL

1. Defendant generally denies the allegations in plaintiff's original petition. {*See **O'Connor's Texas Rules**, "General Denial," ch. 3-E, §3, p. 274.*}

{*ADD SECTIONS BELOW AS APPROPRIATE*}

PLEA TO THE JURISDICTION

2. Defendant asks the Court to dismiss plaintiff's suit because of lack of jurisdiction. {❾ *Elaborate.*} {*See FORM 3F:1; **O'Connor's Texas Rules**, "Plea to the Jurisdiction—Challenging the Court," ch. 3-F, p. 287.*}

Continued on next page

VERIFIED PLEAS

{*CHOOSE APPROPRIATE PARAGRAPHS 3-8*}

3. Defendant denies that defendant executed the agreement as plaintiff claims. {⓾ *Elaborate.*} {*See* ***O'Connor's Texas Rules****, "Verified pleas in TRCP 93," ch. 3-E, §4.1.7, p. 276.*}

4. Defendant denies that defendant is liable on the agreement because the agreement was made without consideration. {⓫ *Elaborate.*} {*See* ***O'Connor's Texas Rules****, "Verified pleas in TRCP 93," ch. 3-E, §4.1.9, p. 276;* ***O'Connor's Texas COA****, "Consideration," ch. 5-A, §2.5, p. 63; "Lack of consideration," ch. 5-B, §5.1.9(2), p. 97.*}

5. Defendant denies that defendant is liable on the agreement because the consideration for the agreement failed in whole or in part. {⓬ *Elaborate.*} {*See* ***O'Connor's Texas Rules****, "Verified pleas in TRCP 93," ch. 3-E, §4.1.9, p. 276;* ***O'Connor's Texas COA****, "Consideration," ch. 5-A, §2.5, p. 63; "Failure of consideration," ch. 5-B, §5.1.9(1), p. 96.*}

6. Defendant denies plaintiff's allegation that plaintiff gave notice and proof of claim as required by the agreement. Specifically, {⓭ *describe deficiencies in notice with particularity*}. {*See* ***O'Connor's Texas Rules****, "Verified pleas in TRCP 93," ch. 3-E, §4.1.12, p. 277.*}

7. Defendant denies plaintiff's allegation that all conditions precedent have been performed or have occurred. {⓮ *Identify specific conditions precedent that have not been performed or have not occurred.*} {*See* ***O'Connor's Texas Rules****, "Denial of conditions precedent," ch. 3-E, §6.1, p. 281;* ***O'Connor's Texas COA****, "Failure to perform conditions precedent," ch. 5-B, §5.1.13, p. 100.*}

8. {*For other verified pleas, see FORM 3E:10;* ***O'Connor's Texas Rules****, "Verified Pleas," ch. 3-E, §4, p. 275.*}

OTHER DEFENSES

{*CHOOSE APPROPRIATE PARAGRAPHS 9-37*}

9. Defendant is not liable to plaintiff because plaintiff's claim for breach of contract is barred by the four-year statute of limitations in Texas Civil Practice & Remedies Code section {⓯ *16.004(a)/16.051*}. Plaintiff's claim accrued on {⓰ *date*}; plaintiff filed suit on {⓱ *date*}. {⓲ *Elaborate.*} {*See* ***O'Connor's Texas COA****, "Limitations," ch. 5-B, §4, p. 90.*}

10. Defendant is not liable to plaintiff because plaintiff's claim for breach of contract is barred by the limitations period agreed on in the contract, which is {[19] *state limitations period*}. {[20] *Elaborate.*} {*See* ***O'Connor's Texas COA***, *"Contractual period," ch. 5-B, §4.1.2, p. 90.*}

11. Defendant is not liable to plaintiff because plaintiff lacks standing to sue. {[21] *Elaborate.*} {*See* ***O'Connor's Texas COA***, *"Standing," ch. 5-B, §5.1.2, p. 91.*}

12. Defendant is not liable to plaintiff because plaintiff repudiated the agreement when, without excuse, plaintiff indicated that {[22] *he/she/it*} would not perform the agreement. Thus, defendant's obligations under the agreement were discharged. {[23] *Elaborate.*} {*See* ***O'Connor's Texas COA***, *"Plaintiff repudiated contract," ch. 5-B, §5.1.3(1), p. 92.*}

13. Defendant is not liable to plaintiff because defendant timely retracted {[24] *his/her/its*} repudiation of the agreement. {[25] *Elaborate.*} {*See* ***O'Connor's Texas COA***, *"Defendant timely retracted repudiation," ch. 5-B, §5.1.3(2), p. 92.*}

14. Defendant is not liable to plaintiff because defendant revoked the offer before plaintiff accepted it. {[26] *Elaborate.*} {*See* ***O'Connor's Texas COA***, *"Revocation," ch. 5-B, §5.1.4, p. 92.*}

15. Defendant is not liable to plaintiff because defendant lacked the capacity to enter into the agreement. {[27] *Explain, describing basis of incapacity.*} {*See* ***O'Connor's Texas COA***, *"Lack of capacity," ch. 5-B, §5.1.5, p. 93.*}

16. Defendant is not liable to plaintiff because the agreement is illegal. {[28] *Elaborate.*} {*See* ***O'Connor's Texas COA***, *"Illegality," ch. 5-B, §5.1.6, p. 94.*}

17. Defendant is not liable to plaintiff because the agreement is void as against public policy. {[29] *Elaborate.*} {*See* ***O'Connor's Texas COA***, *"Void as against public policy," ch. 5-B, §5.1.7, p. 95.*}

18. Defendant is not liable to plaintiff because the agreement was the product of fraud. {[30] *Elaborate.*} {*See* ***O'Connor's Texas COA***, *"Fraud," ch. 12, p. 297.*}

19. Defendant is not liable to plaintiff because the agreement was the product of duress. {[31] *Elaborate.*} {*See* ***O'Connor's Texas COA***, *"Duress," ch. 5-B, §5.1.10, p. 97.*}

20. Defendant is not liable to plaintiff because of a {[32] *unilateral/mutual*} mistake of fact. {[33] *Elaborate.*} {*See* ***O'Connor's Texas COA***, *"Mistake," ch. 5-B, §5.1.11, p. 99.*}

Continued on next page

21. Defendant is not liable to plaintiff because the agreement does not comply with the requirements of the statute of frauds. {34 *Elaborate.*} {*See* ***O'Connor's Texas COA****, "Statute of frauds," ch. 5-B, §5.1.12, p. 100; "Statute of Frauds," ch. 50, p. 1575.*}

22. Defendant is not liable to plaintiff because defendant's performance was excused due to {35 *impossibility/impracticability*} of performance. {36 *Elaborate.*} {*See* ***O'Connor's Texas COA****, "Impossibility or impracticability of performance," ch. 5-B, §5.1.14, p. 100.*}

23. Defendant is not liable to plaintiff because the agreement was discharged by an accord and satisfaction {37 *add if defendant tendered a check or other negotiable instrument as an accord and satisfaction: under Texas Business & Commerce Code section 3.311*}. {38 *Elaborate.*} {*See* ***O'Connor's Texas COA****, "Accord & satisfaction," ch. 5-B, §5.1.15, p. 102.*}

24. Defendant is not liable to plaintiff because the contract was discharged by a novation. {39 *Elaborate.*} {*See* ***O'Connor's Texas COA****, "Novation," ch. 5-B, §5.1.16, p. 103.*}

25. Defendant is not liable to plaintiff because enforcement of the agreement would be unconscionable. {40 *Elaborate.*} {*See* ***O'Connor's Texas COA****, "Unconscionability," ch. 5-B, §5.1.17, p. 103.*}

26. Defendant is not liable to plaintiff because the original contract was modified and defendant complied with the terms of the modification. {41 *Elaborate.*} {*See* ***O'Connor's Texas COA****, "Modification," ch. 5-B, §5.1.18, p. 104.*}

27. Defendant is not liable to plaintiff because plaintiff ratified defendant's acts. {42 *Elaborate.*} {*See* ***O'Connor's Texas COA****, "Ratification," ch. 5-B, §5.1.19, p. 105.*}

28. Defendant is not liable to plaintiff because plaintiff waived defendant's {43 *performance/breach*} by {44 *state facts that establish plaintiff's waiver*}. {*See* ***O'Connor's Texas COA****, "Waiver," ch. 5-B, §5.1.20, p. 106.*}

29. Defendant is not liable to plaintiff for the amount of damages claimed because plaintiff did not mitigate damages. {45 *Elaborate.*} {*See* ***O'Connor's Texas COA****, "Mitigation of damages," ch. 5-B, §5.1.21, p. 106.*}

30. Defendant is not liable to plaintiff for the amount of damages claimed because defendant is entitled to an offset. {46 *Elaborate.*} {*See* ***O'Connor's Texas COA****, "Offset," ch. 5-B, §5.1.22, p. 106.*}

31. Defendant is not liable to plaintiff for the amount of damages claimed because the liquidated-damages provision of the agreement amounts to a penalty. {47 *Elaborate.*} {*See **O'Connor's Texas COA**, "Penalty," ch. 5-B, §5.1.23, p. 107.*}

32. Defendant is not liable to plaintiff for the amount of damages claimed because plaintiff's damages are limited by the provisions of the agreement. {48 *Quote contract provisions limiting liability.*} {*See **O'Connor's Texas COA**, "Limitation-of-liability provisions," ch. 5-B, §5.1.24, p. 107.*}

33. Defendant is not liable to plaintiff because defendant is immune from liability under {49 *identify type of immunity*} immunity. {50 *Elaborate.*} {*See **O'Connor's Texas COA**, "Immunity," ch. 5-B, §5.1.25, p. 107; "Defenses," Part 5, p. 1509.*}

34. Defendant is not liable to plaintiff because plaintiff's {51 *material breach/repudiation*} of the agreement discharged defendant's obligations. {52 *Elaborate.*} {*See **O'Connor's Texas COA**, "Discharge – plaintiff's repudiation or material breach," ch. 5-B, §5.1.26, p. 107.*}

35. Defendant is not liable to plaintiff because the contract was executed by an unauthorized agent. {53 *Elaborate.*} {*See **O'Connor's Texas COA**, "Unauthorized agent," ch. 5-B, §5.1.27, p. 108.*}

36. Defendant is not liable to plaintiff because a condition subsequent listed in the contract occurred and excused defendant from the contract. {54 *Elaborate.*} {*See **O'Connor's Texas COA**, "Condition subsequent," ch. 5-B, §5.1.28, p. 108.*}

37. {*For other defenses, see FORM 3E:11.*}

COUNTERCLAIM

COUNT 1 – BREACH OF CONTRACT

38. Plaintiff is liable to defendant because plaintiff breached the contract by {55 *repudiating/improperly terminating/refusing to perform plaintiff's obligations under*} the contract. {56 *Elaborate.*} {*See **O'Connor's Texas COA**, "Types of breach," ch. 5-B, §2.4.2, p. 79.*}

39. The breach was material because plaintiff did not substantially perform a material obligation required under the contract. {57 *Elaborate.*} {*See **O'Connor's Texas COA**, "Materiality of breach," ch. 5-B, §2.4.1, p. 78.*}

Continued on next page

FORM 3E:2

40. Defendant's injury was a natural, probable, and foreseeable consequence of plaintiff's breach. {58 *Elaborate.*} {*See **O'Connor's Texas COA**, "Breach caused injury," ch. 5-B, §2.5, p. 81.*}

41. {59 *Include a statement that damages are within the jurisdictional limits of the court. See FORM 2B:2, ¶13.*}

{*ADD SECTION BELOW IF INCLUDING COUNTERCLAIM*}

CLAIM FOR RELIEF

{*CHOOSE APPROPRIATE PARAGRAPH 42*}

42. Defendant seeks only monetary relief of $100,000 or less, including damages of any kind, penalties, court costs, expenses, prejudgment interest, and attorney fees. {*Tex. R. Civ. P. 47(c)(1).*}

42. Defendant seeks monetary relief of $100,000 or less and nonmonetary relief. {*Tex. R. Civ. P. 47(c)(2).*}

42. Defendant seeks monetary relief over $100,000 but not more than $200,000. {*Tex. R. Civ. P. 47(c)(3).*}

42. Defendant seeks monetary relief over $200,000 but not more than $1,000,000. {*Tex. R. Civ. P. 47(c)(4).*}

42. Defendant seeks monetary relief over $1,000,000. {*Tex. R. Civ. P. 47(c)(5).*}

ATTORNEY FEES

{*CHOOSE APPROPRIATE PARAGRAPH 43*}

43. Defendant is entitled to recover reasonable and necessary attorney fees under the provisions of the written contract as set out in paragraph {60 *number*}, which provides: {61 *quote relevant contract provisions*}. By that agreement, defendant is entitled to attorney fees as the prevailing party in this suit. {*See **O'Connor's Texas COA**, "Prevailing defendant," ch. 45-C, §2.6.2(2), p. 1500.*}

43. Defendant is entitled to recover reasonable and necessary attorney fees on {62 *his/her/its*} counterclaim for breach of contract under Texas Civil Practice & Remedies Code chapter 38. Defendant retained counsel, who presented defendant's claim to {63 *plaintiff/plaintiff's duly authorized agent*}. Plaintiff did not tender the amount owed within 30 days after the claim was presented. {*See **O'Connor's Texas COA**, "Attorney Fees Under CPRC ch. 38," ch. 45-B, p. 1486.*}

EQUITABLE RELIEF

44. Defendant seeks {❻❹ *identify equitable relief sought*}. {❻❺ *Identify elements and facts supporting equitable relief.*} {❻❻ *See FORMS 2B:2, ¶18, 2D:1;* ***O'Connor's Texas Rules****, "Injunctive Relief," ch. 2-D, p. 138;* ***O'Connor's Texas COA****, "Equitable remedies," ch. 5-B, §3.5, p. 84.*}

JURY DEMAND

45. Defendant demands a jury trial and tenders the appropriate fee with this answer. {*See* ***O'Connor's Texas Rules****, "Request for Jury Trial," ch. 5-B, p. 400.*}

SPECIAL EXCEPTIONS

46. Defendant specially excepts to plaintiff's original petition, paragraph {❻❼ *number*} regarding the relief sought, and asks the Court to require plaintiff to specify the maximum amount that plaintiff claims. {*See* ***O'Connor's Texas Rules****, "Claims for relief," ch. 3-G, §2.2.5, p. 300.*}

47. {*For other special exceptions, see FORM 3G:1.*}

REQUEST FOR DISCLOSURE

48. Under Texas Rule of Civil Procedure 194, defendant requests that plaintiff disclose, within 30 days of the service of this request, the information or material described in Rule 194.2. {*See* ***O'Connor's Texas Rules****, "Content of request," ch. 6-E, §3.2, p. 627.*}

OBJECTION TO ASSOCIATE JUDGE

49. Defendant objects to the referral of this case to an associate judge for hearing a trial on the merits or presiding at a jury trial. {*See* ***O'Connor's Texas Rules****, "Objection to referral," ch. 1-J, §3.3, p. 96.*}

PRAYER

50. For these reasons, defendant asks the Court to {❻❽ *state all relief requested, e.g., dismiss this suit, render judgment that plaintiff take nothing, award reasonable and necessary attorney fees to defendant*}, assess costs against plaintiff, and award defendant all other relief to which defendant is entitled. {*See* ***O'Connor's Texas Rules****, "Prayer," ch. 2-B, §15, p. 132.*} {*If defendant asserts claims for affirmative relief, include a request for rendition of judgment on those claims. See FORM 2B:1, ¶19.*}

◄ *Continued on next page* ►

FORM 3E:2 ANSWER – BREACH OF CONTRACT

SEE: Tex. R. Civ. P. 54, 92-94, 194
*O'Connor's Texas Rules * Civil Trials* (2019), "The Answer—Denying Liability," ch. 3-E, p. 273
O'Connor's Texas Causes of Action (2019), "Breach of Contract," ch. 5-B, p. 69; "Attorney Fees," ch. 45, p. 1463

ADD: STYLE OF THE CASE – FORM 1B:2
SIGNATURE BLOCK – FORM 1B:3
VERIFICATION – FORM 1B:7, for verified pleas
CERTIFICATE OF SERVICE – FORM 1B:13

ATTACH: AFFIDAVIT – FORM 1B:8, if necessary to support plea to the jurisdiction
NOTICE OF CURRENT/CHANGE OF ADDRESS – FORM 1B:14, if answer is defendant's initial pleading
MOTION TO DISMISS FOR LACK OF JURISDICTION – FORM 3F:1, if necessary
ORDER ON SPECIAL EXCEPTIONS – FORM 3G:2, if necessary
Exhibits, if necessary
Filing fee, if counterclaim asserted
Jury fee, if jury trial requested

NOTE: See notes under FORM 3E:1.

DEFENDANT'S ORIGINAL ANSWER
{❶ *STATE ADDITIONAL RELIEF REQUESTED*
IF APPROPRIATE, E.G., & PLEA TO THE JURISDICTION}

Defendant, {❷ *name*}, files this original answer {❸ *state additional relief requested if appropriate, e.g., and plea to the jurisdiction*} to plaintiff {❹ *name*}'s original petition.

{*CHOOSE ONE OF THE FOLLOWING IF DEFENDANT IS AN INDIVIDUAL*}

Ⓐ The last three digits of defendant's driver's license number are {❺ *digits of driver's license number*}. The last three digits of defendant's Social Security number are {❻ *digits of Social Security number*}. {*See Tex. Civ. Prac. & Rem. Code §30.014(a);* ***O'Connor's Texas Rules****, "ID number," ch. 1-B, §3.2.4(3), p. 8.*}

Ⓑ The last three digits of defendant's driver's license number are {❼ *digits of driver's license number*}. Defendant has not been issued a Social Security number. {*See Tex. Civ. Prac. & Rem. Code §30.014(a);* ***O'Connor's Texas Rules****, "ID number," ch. 1-B, §3.2.4(3), p. 8.*}

Ⓒ The last three digits of defendant's Social Security number are {❽ *digits of Social Security number*}. Defendant has not been issued a driver's license number. {*See Tex. Civ. Prac. & Rem. Code §30.014(a);* ***O'Connor's Texas Rules****, "ID number," ch. 1-B, §3.2.4(3), p. 8.*}

Ⓓ Defendant has not been issued a driver's license number or a Social Security number. {*See Tex. Civ. Prac. & Rem. Code §30.014(a);* ***O'Connor's Texas Rules****, "ID number," ch. 1-B, §3.2.4(3), p. 8.*}

GENERAL DENIAL

1. Defendant generally denies the allegations in plaintiff's original petition. {*See* ***O'Connor's Texas Rules****, "General Denial," ch. 3-E, §3, p. 274.*}

{*ADD SECTIONS BELOW AS APPROPRIATE*}

PLEA TO THE JURISDICTION

2. Defendant asks the Court to dismiss plaintiff's suit because of lack of jurisdiction. {❾ *Elaborate.*} {*See FORM 3F:1;* ***O'Connor's Texas Rules****, "Plea to the Jurisdiction—Challenging the Court," ch. 3-F, p. 287.*}

◄ *Continued on next page* ►

VERIFIED PLEAS

{CHOOSE APPROPRIATE PARAGRAPHS 3-12}

3. Defendant denies the account on which plaintiff files suit because not every item of the account is just or true. {⑩ *List each item that is not just or true and explain.*} {*See* ***O'Connor's Texas COA****, "Not just & true," ch. 5-E, §5.2.2(1), p. 132.*}

4. Defendant denies the account on which plaintiff files suit because the claim is not due. {⑪ *Elaborate.*} {*See* ***O'Connor's Texas COA****, "Not due," ch. 5-E, §5.2.2(2), p. 132.*}

5. Defendant denies the account on which plaintiff files suit because plaintiff has not credited defendant's account with all just and lawful offsets, payments, and other credits. {⑫ *Elaborate.*} {*See* ***O'Connor's Texas COA****, "Not credited," ch. 5-E, §5.2.2(3), p. 132.*}

6. Defendant denies the account on which plaintiff files suit because the amount plaintiff claims is due is incorrect. {⑬ *Elaborate.*} {*See* ***O'Connor's Texas COA****, "Not just & true," ch. 5-E, §5.2.2(1), p. 132.*}

7. Defendant denies the account on which plaintiff files suit because plaintiff charged defendant prices for the {⑭ *goods/services/goods and services*} that are not in accordance with the parties' agreement and are unreasonable. {⑮ *Elaborate.*} {*See* ***O'Connor's Texas COA****, "Contents," ch. 5-E, §5.2.2, p. 132.*}

8. Defendant denies the account on which plaintiff files suit because no systematic record was kept of amounts due on the account. {⑯ *Elaborate.*} {*See* ***O'Connor's Texas COA****, "Systematic record," ch. 5-E, §2.3, p. 129.*}

9. Defendant denies the account on which plaintiff files suit because defendant has never had an open account with plaintiff, a written or oral contract with plaintiff for goods or services, or any business dealings with plaintiff on which an account could be founded. {⑰ *Explain, e.g., defendant had only one business transaction with plaintiff, and defendant paid plaintiff in full at the time of that transaction.*} {*See* ***O'Connor's Texas COA****, "Response to properly pleaded claim," ch. 5-E, §5.2, p. 131.*}

10. Defendant denies the account on which plaintiff files suit because {[18] *state any other reason that defendant is not liable to plaintiff as alleged in plaintiff's suit*}. {[19] *Elaborate.*} {*See* ***O'Connor's Texas COA****, "Response to properly pleaded claim," ch. 5-E, §5.2, p. 131.*}

11. Defendant denies plaintiff's allegation that all conditions precedent have been performed or have occurred. {[20] *Identify specific conditions precedent that have not been performed or have not occurred.*} {*See* ***O'Connor's Texas Rules****, "Denial of conditions precedent," ch. 3-E, §6.1, p. 281;* ***O'Connor's Texas COA****, "Failure to perform conditions precedent," ch. 5-B, §5.1.13, p. 100.*}

12. {*For other verified pleas, see FORM 3E:10;* ***O'Connor's Texas Rules****, "Verified Pleas," ch. 3-E, §4, p. 275.*}

OTHER DEFENSES

{*CHOOSE APPROPRIATE PARAGRAPHS 13-16*}

13. Defendant is not liable to plaintiff because plaintiff's claim is barred by the four-year statute of limitations in Texas Civil Practice & Remedies Code section 16.004(c). Plaintiff's claim accrued on {[21] *date*}; plaintiff filed suit on {[22] *date*}. {[23] *Elaborate.*} {*See* ***O'Connor's Texas COA****, "Limitations," ch. 5-E, §4, p. 131.*}

14. Defendant is not liable to plaintiff because plaintiff was not a party to the original transaction. {*See* ***O'Connor's Texas COA****, "Not third parties," ch. 5-E, §2.1.1(2), p. 127.*}

15. Defendant is not liable to plaintiff because there was no transfer of goods or services. {*See* ***O'Connor's Texas COA****, "Goods or services," ch. 5-E, §2.1.2, p. 127.*}

16. {*For other defenses, see FORM 3E:11.*}

COUNTERCLAIM – {[24] *NAME OF COUNTERCLAIM*}

17. {[25] *Identify cause of action against plaintiff, e.g., breach of contract. In separately numbered paragraphs, identify elements and facts supporting the counterclaim, add any claims for exemplary damages, attorney fees, or equitable relief, and include a statement that damages are within the jurisdictional limits of the court. See FORM 2B:1, ¶10.*} {*See* ***O'Connor's Texas Rules****, "Counterclaims," ch. 3-E, §7.1, p. 282;* ***O'Connor's Texas COA****, "Counterclaims," ch. 5-E, §5.4, p. 133.*}

Continued on next page

{ADD SECTION BELOW IF INCLUDING COUNTERCLAIM}

CLAIM FOR RELIEF

{CHOOSE APPROPRIATE PARAGRAPH 18}

18. Defendant seeks only monetary relief of $100,000 or less, including damages of any kind, penalties, court costs, expenses, prejudgment interest, and attorney fees. {*Tex. R. Civ. P. 47(c)(1).*}

18. Defendant seeks monetary relief of $100,000 or less and nonmonetary relief. {*Tex. R. Civ. P. 47(c)(2).*}

18. Defendant seeks monetary relief over $100,000 but not more than $200,000. {*Tex. R. Civ. P. 47(c)(3).*}

18. Defendant seeks monetary relief over $200,000 but not more than $1,000,000. {*Tex. R. Civ. P. 47(c)(4).*}

18. Defendant seeks monetary relief over $1,000,000. {*Tex. R. Civ. P. 47(c)(5).*}

JURY DEMAND

19. Defendant demands a jury trial and tenders the appropriate fee with this answer. {*See **O'Connor's Texas Rules**, "Request for Jury Trial," ch. 5-B, p. 400.*}

SPECIAL EXCEPTIONS

{CHOOSE APPROPRIATE PARAGRAPHS 20-22}

20. Defendant specially excepts to plaintiff's petition because this claim is not properly brought as a suit on a sworn account. This is a suit for {㉖ *describe cause of action, e.g., breach of a lease*}. {㉗ *Explain, e.g., a suit involving a breach of a lease agreement is not a valid suit on a sworn account.*} {*See **O'Connor's Texas COA**, "Not included," ch. 5-E, §2.1.2(3), p. 128.*}

21. Defendant specially excepts to plaintiff's petition because the petition does not adequately specify the {㉘ *account/amount due*}. {㉙ *Elaborate.*} {*See **O'Connor's Texas COA**, "Defects in petition," ch. 5-E, §6.1.1, p. 133.*}

22. {*For other special exceptions, see FORM 3G:1.*}

REQUEST FOR DISCLOSURE

23. Under Texas Rule of Civil Procedure 194, defendant requests that plaintiff disclose, within 30 days of the service of this request, the information or material described in Rule 194.2. {*See **O'Connor's Texas Rules**, "Content of request," ch. 6-E, §3.2, p. 627.*}

OBJECTION TO ASSOCIATE JUDGE

24. Defendant objects to the referral of this case to an associate judge for hearing a trial on the merits or presiding at a jury trial. {*See **O'Connor's Texas Rules**, "Objection to referral," ch. 1-J, §3.3, p. 96.*}

PRAYER

25. For these reasons, defendant asks the Court to {30 *state all relief requested, e.g., dismiss this suit, render judgment that plaintiff take nothing*}, assess costs against plaintiff, and award defendant all other relief to which defendant is entitled. {*If defendant asserts claims for affirmative relief, include a request for rendition of judgment on those claims. See FORM 2B:1, ¶19.*}

SEE: Tex. R. Civ. P. 54, 92-94, 185, 194
O'Connor's Texas Rules * Civil Trials (2019), "The Answer—Denying Liability," ch. 3-E, p. 273
O'Connor's Texas Causes of Action (2019), "Suit on Sworn Account," ch. 5-E, p. 126

ADD: STYLE OF THE CASE – FORM 1B:2
SIGNATURE BLOCK – FORM 1B:3
VERIFICATION – FORM 1B:7, for verified pleas
CERTIFICATE OF SERVICE – FORM 1B:13

ATTACH: AFFIDAVIT – FORM 1B:8, if necessary to support plea to the jurisdiction
NOTICE OF CURRENT/CHANGE OF ADDRESS – FORM 1B:14, if answer is defendant's initial pleading
AFFIDAVIT DENYING SWORN ACCOUNT – FORM 3E:4
MOTION TO DISMISS FOR LACK OF JURISDICTION – FORM 3F:1, if necessary
ORDER ON SPECIAL EXCEPTIONS – FORM 3G:2, if necessary
Exhibits, if necessary
Filing fee, if counterclaim asserted
Jury fee, if jury trial requested

NOTE: The defendant's answer must be sworn and must make specific statements denying the claim and giving notice of the fact issues in the plaintiff's affidavit that the defendant intends to rebut. See FORM 3E:4; ***O'Connor's Texas COA***, "Contents," ch. 5-E, §5.2.2, p. 132.

See notes under FORM 3E:1.

AFFIDAVIT OF {❶ *NAME*}

STATE OF TEXAS §
{❷ ________} COUNTY §

Before me, the undersigned notary, on this day personally appeared {❸ *name of affiant*}, the affiant, whose identity is known to me. After I administered an oath, affiant testified as follows:

1. "My name is {❹ *name of affiant*}. I am over 18 years of age, of sound mind, and capable of making this affidavit. The facts stated in this affidavit are within my personal knowledge and are true and correct.

2. "I am {❺ *identify affiant's status, e.g., the defendant, an agent of the defendant*} in this case.

{*ADD PARAGRAPH 3 IF AFFIANT IS DEFENDANT'S ATTORNEY OR AGENT*}

3. "I acquired personal knowledge of these facts by {❻ *state how personal knowledge was acquired*}.

4. "I have read defendant's original answer, and the facts stated in it are within my personal knowledge and are true and correct.

{*CHOOSE APPROPRIATE PARAGRAPHS 5-8*}

5. "Not every item of the account that forms the basis of plaintiff's suit is just or true. {❼ *List each item that is not just or true, and explain.*}

6. "The claim is not due. {❽ *Elaborate.*}

7. "All just and lawful offsets, payments, and credits have not been allowed. {❾ *Elaborate.*}

8. "{❿ *Support any other matters included in the verified pleas in the answer, FORM 3E:3.*}"

____
{⓫ *Name of affiant*}

Sworn to and subscribed before me by {⓬ *name of affiant*} on __________, 20___.

____
Notary Public in and for
the State of Texas

SEE: Tex. R. Civ. P. 93, 185
O'Connor's Texas Rules * Civil Trials (2019), "Affidavits," ch. 1-B, §3.2.16, p. 12
O'Connor's Texas Causes of Action (2019), "Defendant's affidavit," ch. 5-E, §5.2.3, p. 132

ADD: STYLE OF THE CASE – FORM 1B:2

NOTE: See notes under FORM 1B:8.

DEFENDANT'S ORIGINAL ANSWER
{❶ *STATE ADDITIONAL RELIEF REQUESTED IF APPROPRIATE, E.G., & PLEA TO THE JURISDICTION*}

Defendant, {❷ *name*}, files this original answer {❸ *state additional relief requested if appropriate, e.g., and plea to the jurisdiction*} to plaintiff {❹ *name*}'s original petition.

{*CHOOSE ONE OF THE FOLLOWING IF DEFENDANT IS AN INDIVIDUAL*}

Ⓐ The last three digits of defendant's driver's license number are {❺ *digits of driver's license number*}. The last three digits of defendant's Social Security number are {❻ *digits of Social Security number*}. {*See Tex. Civ. Prac. & Rem. Code §30.014(a);* ***O'Connor's Texas Rules****, "ID number," ch. 1-B, §3.2.4(3), p. 8.*}

Ⓑ The last three digits of defendant's driver's license number are {❼ *digits of driver's license number*}. Defendant has not been issued a Social Security number. {*See Tex. Civ. Prac. & Rem. Code §30.014(a);* ***O'Connor's Texas Rules****, "ID number," ch. 1-B, §3.2.4(3), p. 8.*}

Ⓒ The last three digits of defendant's Social Security number are {❽ *digits of Social Security number*}. Defendant has not been issued a driver's license number. {*See Tex. Civ. Prac. & Rem. Code §30.014(a);* ***O'Connor's Texas Rules****, "ID number," ch. 1-B, §3.2.4(3), p. 8.*}

Ⓓ Defendant has not been issued a driver's license number or a Social Security number. {*See Tex. Civ. Prac. & Rem. Code §30.014(a);* ***O'Connor's Texas Rules****, "ID number," ch. 1-B, §3.2.4(3), p. 8.*}

GENERAL DENIAL

1. Defendant generally denies the allegations in plaintiff's original petition. {*See* ***O'Connor's Texas Rules****, "General Denial," ch. 3-E, §3, p. 274.*}

{*ADD SECTIONS BELOW AS APPROPRIATE*}

PLEA TO THE JURISDICTION

2. Defendant asks the Court to dismiss plaintiff's suit because of lack of jurisdiction. {❾ *Elaborate.*} {*See FORM 3F:1;* ***O'Connor's Texas Rules****, "Plea to the Jurisdiction—Challenging the Court," ch. 3-F, p. 287.*}

VERIFIED PLEAS

3. {*For verified pleas, see FORM 3E:10;* ***O'Connor's Texas Rules****, "Verified Pleas," ch. 3-E, §4, p. 275.*}

OTHER DEFENSES

{*CHOOSE APPROPRIATE PARAGRAPHS 4-14*}

4. Defendant is not liable to plaintiff because plaintiff's claim for negligence is barred by the two-year statute of limitations in Texas Civil Practice & Remedies Code section 16.003(a). Plaintiff's claim accrued on {⑩ *date*}; plaintiff filed suit on {⑪ *date*}. {⑫ *Elaborate.*} {*See* ***O'Connor's Texas COA****, "Limitations," ch. 21-A, §4, p. 736.*}

5. Defendant is not liable to plaintiff because defendant is immune from liability under {⑬ *identify type of immunity*} immunity. {⑭ *Elaborate.*} {*See* ***O'Connor's Texas COA****, "Defenses," Part 5, p. 1509.*}

6. Defendant is not liable to plaintiff because plaintiff's own acts or omissions proximately caused or contributed to plaintiff's injury. {⑮ *Elaborate.*} {*See* ***O'Connor's Texas COA****, "Plaintiff's fault," ch. 21-A, §5.3, p. 736.*}

7. Defendant is not liable to plaintiff for the amount of damages claimed because plaintiff's nonuse of the vehicle's seat belt caused or contributed to plaintiff's damages. {*See Tex. Civ. Prac. & Rem. Code §33.003(a); Nabors Well Servs., Ltd. v. Romero, 456 S.W.3d 553, 562-63 (Tex. 2015)*}. {⑯ *Elaborate.*}

8. Defendant is not liable to plaintiff because plaintiff released this claim against defendant. {⑰ *Elaborate.*} {*See* ***O'Connor's Texas COA****, "Release agreements," ch. 21-A, §5.4, p. 737.*}

9. Defendant is not liable to plaintiff because plaintiff's injury was sustained in the commission of a felony or misdemeanor for which plaintiff was convicted. {⑱ *Elaborate.*} {*See* ***O'Connor's Texas COA****, "Plaintiff's conviction," ch. 21-A, §5.6, p. 741.*}

10. Defendant is not liable to plaintiff because {⑲ *name of tortfeasor*}, an independent contractor for whom defendant is not liable, caused plaintiff's injury. {⑳ *Elaborate.*} {*See* ***O'Connor's Texas COA****, "Independent-contractor defense," ch. 21-A, §5.8, p. 742.*}

◄ *Continued on next page* ►

11. Defendant is not liable to plaintiff for the amount of damages claimed because plaintiff did not mitigate damages. {[21] *Elaborate.*} {*See* ***O'Connor's Texas COA***, *"Mitigating Damages," ch. 41-A, §7, p. 1354.*}

12. Defendant is not liable to plaintiff because defendant's unforeseeable loss of consciousness caused the accident. {[22] *Elaborate.*} {*See* ***O'Connor's Texas COA***, *"Unforeseeable incapacity," ch. 21-A, §5.11, p. 744.*}

13. If defendant is found liable for damages, defendant intends to seek a reduction of damages under the proportionate-responsibility statute. {[23] *Elaborate.*} {*See* ***O'Connor's Texas COA***, *"Proportionate Responsibility & Contribution," ch. 51, p. 1589.*}

14. {*For other defenses, see FORM 3E:11.*}

INFERENTIAL-REBUTTAL DEFENSES

15. When this case is submitted to the jury, defendant asks the Court to submit as instructions the following inferential-rebuttal defenses raised by the evidence:

{*CHOOSE APPROPRIATE STATEMENTS*}

a. The collision with plaintiff's vehicle was the result of a new and independent cause. {[24] *Elaborate.*} {*See* ***O'Connor's Texas COA***, *"New & independent cause," ch. 21-A, §5.12.1, p. 744.*}

b. The collision with plaintiff's vehicle was caused solely by the {[25] *acts/omissions*} of {[26] *name of tortfeasor*}, for whom defendant is not liable. {[27] *Elaborate.*} {*See* ***O'Connor's Texas COA***, *"Sole proximate cause," ch. 21-A, §5.12.2, p. 745.*}

c. The collision with plaintiff's vehicle was an unavoidable accident. {[28] *Elaborate.*} {*See* ***O'Connor's Texas COA***, *"Unavoidable accident," ch. 21-A, §5.12.3, p. 745.*}

d. The collision with plaintiff's vehicle was the result of defendant's response to a sudden emergency. {[29] *Elaborate.*} {*See* ***O'Connor's Texas COA***, *"Sudden emergency," ch. 21-A, §5.12.4, p. 745.*}

e. The collision with plaintiff's vehicle was the result of an act of God. {[30] *Elaborate.*} {*See* ***O'Connor's Texas COA***, *"Act of God," ch. 21-A, §5.12.5, p. 746.*}

EXEMPLARY-DAMAGES CAP

16. If defendant is found liable for exemplary damages, those damages must be capped under the Texas Damages Act, the Due Process Clause of the United States Constitution, and the Due Course of Law provisions of the Texas Constitution. {*See **O'Connor's Texas COA**, "Capping Exemplary Damages," ch. 42-B, §7, p. 1434.*}

{*For designation of unknown person as responsible third party in amended answer*}

PROPORTIONATE RESPONSIBILITY OF UNKNOWN PERSON

17. Defendant designates an unknown person as a responsible third party within the meaning of Texas Civil Practice & Remedies Code section 33.004(j). {*See **O'Connor's Texas Rules**, "Amended answer – RTP is unknown criminal," ch. 3-E, §7.4.2(1), p. 284.*} The unknown person, {❸❶ *John Doe/Jane Doe*}, is a responsible third party for the following reasons:

a. {❸❷ *John Doe/Jane Doe*} committed an act that caused the loss or injury that is the subject of this lawsuit. {❸❸ *Elaborate.*} {*Tex. Civ. Prac. & Rem. Code §33.004(j).*}

b. The act committed by {❸❹ *John Doe/Jane Doe*} was criminal. {❸❺ *State facts showing a reasonable probability that the act was criminal.*} {*Tex. Civ. Prac. & Rem. Code §33.004(j)(1).*}

c. At this time, defendant is {❸❻ *unaware/aware*} of {❸❼ *any/certain*} identifying characteristics of {❸❽ *John Doe/Jane Doe*}. {❸❾ *State all identifying characteristics known when the answer is filed.*} {*Tex. Civ. Prac. & Rem. Code §33.004(j)(2).*}

d. {❹⓿ *John Doe/Jane Doe*} is responsible for the criminal act because {❹❶ *state facts about unknown person's responsibility to satisfy the pleading requirements of the Texas Rules of Civil Procedure*}. {*Tex. Civ. Prac. & Rem. Code §33.004(j)(3).*}

JURY DEMAND

18. Defendant demands a jury trial and tenders the appropriate fee with this answer. {*See **O'Connor's Texas Rules**, "Request for Jury Trial," ch. 5-B, p. 400.*}

◄ *Continued on next page* ►

SPECIAL EXCEPTIONS

19. Defendant specially excepts to plaintiff's original petition, paragraph {❹❷ *number*} regarding the relief sought, and asks the Court to require plaintiff to specify the maximum amount that plaintiff claims. {*See* ***O'Connor's Texas Rules****, "Claims for relief," ch. 3-G, §2.2.5, p. 300.*}

20. {*For other special exceptions, see FORM 3G:1.*}

REQUEST FOR DISCLOSURE

21. Under Texas Rule of Civil Procedure 194, defendant requests that plaintiff disclose, within 30 days of the service of this request, the information or material described in Rule 194.2. {*See* ***O'Connor's Texas Rules****, "Content of request," ch. 6-E, §3.2, p. 627.*}

OBJECTION TO ASSOCIATE JUDGE

22. Defendant objects to the referral of this case to an associate judge for hearing a trial on the merits or presiding at a jury trial. {*See* ***O'Connor's Texas Rules****, "Objection to referral," ch. 1-J, §3.3, p. 96.*}

PRAYER

23. For these reasons, defendant asks the Court to {❹❸ *state all relief requested, e.g., dismiss this suit, render judgment that plaintiff take nothing*}, assess costs against plaintiff, and award defendant all other relief to which defendant is entitled.

SEE: Tex. R. Civ. P. 92-94, 194
O'Connor's Texas Rules * Civil Trials (2019), "The Answer—Denying Liability," ch. 3-E, p. 273
O'Connor's Texas Causes of Action (2019), "Negligence," ch. 21-A, p. 719

ADD: STYLE OF THE CASE – FORM 1B:2
SIGNATURE BLOCK – FORM 1B:3
VERIFICATION – FORM 1B:7, for verified pleas
CERTIFICATE OF SERVICE – FORM 1B:13

ATTACH: AFFIDAVIT – FORM 1B:8, if necessary to support plea to the jurisdiction
NOTICE OF CURRENT/CHANGE OF ADDRESS – FORM 1B:14, if answer is defendant's initial pleading
MOTION TO DISMISS FOR LACK OF JURISDICTION – FORM 3F:1, if necessary
ORDER ON SPECIAL EXCEPTIONS – FORM 3G:2, if necessary
Exhibits, if necessary
Jury fee, if jury trial requested

NOTE: If the defendant asserts claims for affirmative relief, include (1) a separate section with a specific statement of the relief sought and (2) a request in the prayer for rendition of judgment on those claims for relief. See FORM 2B:1, ¶19; FORM 3E:1, ¶¶5-7.

See notes under FORM 3E:1.

DEFENDANT'S ORIGINAL ANSWER
{❶ *STATE ADDITIONAL RELIEF REQUESTED*
IF APPROPRIATE, E.G., & PLEA TO THE JURISDICTION}

Defendant, {❷ *name*}, files this original answer {❸ *state additional relief requested if appropriate, e.g., and plea to the jurisdiction*} to plaintiff {❹ *name*}'s original petition.

{*CHOOSE ONE OF THE FOLLOWING IF DEFENDANT IS AN INDIVIDUAL*}

Ⓐ The last three digits of defendant's driver's license number are {❺ *digits of driver's license number*}. The last three digits of defendant's Social Security number are {❻ *digits of Social Security number*}. {*See Tex. Civ. Prac. & Rem. Code §30.014(a); **O'Connor's Texas Rules**, "ID number," ch. 1-B, §3.2.4(3), p. 8.*}

Ⓑ The last three digits of defendant's driver's license number are {❼ *digits of driver's license number*}. Defendant has not been issued a Social Security number. {*See Tex. Civ. Prac. & Rem. Code §30.014(a); **O'Connor's Texas Rules**, "ID number," ch. 1-B, §3.2.4(3), p. 8.*}

Ⓒ The last three digits of defendant's Social Security number are {❽ *digits of Social Security number*}. Defendant has not been issued a driver's license number. {*See Tex. Civ. Prac. & Rem. Code §30.014(a); **O'Connor's Texas Rules**, "ID number," ch. 1-B, §3.2.4(3), p. 8.*}

Ⓓ Defendant has not been issued a driver's license number or a Social Security number. {*See Tex. Civ. Prac. & Rem. Code §30.014(a); **O'Connor's Texas Rules**, "ID number," ch. 1-B, §3.2.4(3), p. 8.*}

GENERAL DENIAL

1. Defendant generally denies the allegations in plaintiff's original petition. {*See **O'Connor's Texas Rules**, "General Denial," ch. 3-E, §3, p. 274.*}

{*ADD SECTIONS BELOW AS APPROPRIATE*}

PLEA TO THE JURISDICTION

2. Defendant asks the Court to dismiss plaintiff's suit because of lack of jurisdiction. {❾ *Elaborate.*} {*See FORM 3F:1; **O'Connor's Texas Rules**, "Plea to the Jurisdiction—Challenging the Court," ch. 3-F, p. 287.*}

◄ *Continued on next page* ►

VERIFIED PLEAS

3. {*For verified pleas, see FORM 3E:10;* ***O'Connor's Texas Rules****, "Verified Pleas," ch. 3-E, §4, p. 275.*}

OTHER DEFENSES

{*CHOOSE APPROPRIATE PARAGRAPHS 4-6*}

4. Defendant is not liable to plaintiff because plaintiff's claim for negligence is barred by the two-year statute of limitations in Texas Civil Practice & Remedies Code section 16.003(a). Plaintiff's claim accrued on {❿ *date*}; plaintiff filed suit on {⓫ *date*}. {⓬ *Elaborate.*} {*See* ***O'Connor's Texas COA****, "Two-year statute," ch. 21-A, §4.1, p. 736.*}

5. Defendant is not liable to plaintiff because plaintiff's own acts or omissions proximately caused or contributed to plaintiff's injury. {⓭ *Elaborate.*} {*See* ***O'Connor's Texas COA****, "Plaintiff's fault," ch. 21-A, §5.3, p. 736.*}

6. {*For other defenses, see FORM 3E:11;* ***O'Connor's Texas COA****, "Defenses," ch. 23-B, §5.1, p. 845.*}

INFERENTIAL-REBUTTAL DEFENSES

7. When this case is submitted to the jury, defendant asks the Court to submit as instructions the following inferential-rebuttal defenses raised by the evidence:

a. Plaintiff's accident was caused solely by the {⓮ *acts/omissions*} of {⓯ *name of tortfeasor*}, for whom defendant is not liable. {⓰ *Elaborate.*} {*See* ***O'Connor's Texas COA****, "Sole proximate cause," ch. 21-A, §5.12.2, p. 745.*}

b. {*For other inferential-rebuttal defenses, see* ***O'Connor's Texas COA****, "Inferential rebuttals," ch. 21-A, §5.12, p. 744.*}

EXEMPLARY-DAMAGES CAP

8. If defendant is found liable for exemplary damages, those damages must be capped under the Texas Damages Act, the Due Process Clause of the United States Constitution, and the Due Course of Law provisions of the Texas Constitution. {*See* ***O'Connor's Texas COA****, "Capping Exemplary Damages," ch. 42-B, §7, p. 1434.*}

FORM 3E:6

JURY DEMAND

9. Defendant demands a jury trial and tenders the appropriate fee with this answer. {*See **O'Connor's Texas Rules**, "Request for Jury Trial," ch. 5-B, p. 400.*}

SPECIAL EXCEPTIONS

10. Defendant specially excepts to plaintiff's original petition, paragraph {⓱ *number*} regarding the relief sought, and asks the Court to require plaintiff to specify the maximum amount that plaintiff claims. {*See **O'Connor's Texas Rules**, "Claims for relief," ch. 3-G, §2.2.5, p. 300.*}

11. {*For other special exceptions, see FORM 3G:1.*}

REQUEST FOR DISCLOSURE

12. Under Texas Rule of Civil Procedure 194, defendant requests that plaintiff disclose, within 30 days of the service of this request, the information or material described in Rule 194.2. {*See **O'Connor's Texas Rules**, "Content of request," ch. 6-E, §3.2, p. 627.*}

OBJECTION TO ASSOCIATE JUDGE

13. Defendant objects to the referral of this case to an associate judge for hearing a trial on the merits or presiding at a jury trial. {*See **O'Connor's Texas Rules**, "Objection to referral," ch. 1-J, §3.3, p. 96.*}

PRAYER

14. For these reasons, defendant asks the Court to {⓲ *state all relief requested, e.g., dismiss this suit, render judgment that plaintiff take nothing*}, assess costs against plaintiff, and award defendant all other relief to which defendant is entitled.

SEE: Tex. R. Civ. P. 92-94, 194
O'Connor's Texas Rules * Civil Trials (2019), "The Answer—Denying Liability," ch. 3-E, p. 273
O'Connor's Texas Causes of Action (2019), "Negligence," ch. 21-A, p. 719; "General Concepts," ch. 23-A, p. 815

ADD: STYLE OF THE CASE – FORM 1B:2
SIGNATURE BLOCK – FORM 1B:3
VERIFICATION – FORM 1B:7, for verified pleas
CERTIFICATE OF SERVICE – FORM 1B:13

◄ *Continued on next page* ►

ATTACH: AFFIDAVIT – FORM 1B:8, if necessary to support plea to the jurisdiction
NOTICE OF CURRENT/CHANGE OF ADDRESS – FORM 1B:14, if answer is defendant's initial pleading
MOTION TO DISMISS FOR LACK OF JURISDICTION – FORM 3F:1, if necessary
ORDER ON SPECIAL EXCEPTIONS – FORM 3G:2, if necessary
Exhibits, if necessary
Jury fee, if jury trial requested

NOTE: If the defendant asserts claims for affirmative relief, include (1) a separate section with a specific statement of the relief sought and (2) a request in the prayer for rendition of judgment on those claims for relief. See FORM 2B:1, ¶19; FORM 3E:1, ¶¶5-7.

See notes under FORM 3E:1.

DEFENDANT'S ORIGINAL ANSWER
{❶ *STATE ADDITIONAL RELIEF REQUESTED IF APPROPRIATE, E.G., & PLEA TO THE JURISDICTION*}

Defendant, {❷ *name*}, files this original answer {❸ *state additional relief requested if appropriate, e.g., and plea to the jurisdiction*} to plaintiff {❹ *name*}'s original petition.

{*CHOOSE ONE OF THE FOLLOWING IF DEFENDANT IS AN INDIVIDUAL*}

Ⓐ The last three digits of defendant's driver's license number are {❺ *digits of driver's license number*}. The last three digits of defendant's Social Security number are {❻ *digits of Social Security number*}. {*See Tex. Civ. Prac. & Rem. Code §30.014(a);* ***O'Connor's Texas Rules****, "ID number," ch. 1-B, §3.2.4(3), p. 8.*}

Ⓑ The last three digits of defendant's driver's license number are {❼ *digits of driver's license number*}. Defendant has not been issued a Social Security number. {*See Tex. Civ. Prac. & Rem. Code §30.014(a);* ***O'Connor's Texas Rules****, "ID number," ch. 1-B, §3.2.4(3), p. 8.*}

Ⓒ The last three digits of defendant's Social Security number are {❽ *digits of Social Security number*}. Defendant has not been issued a driver's license number. {*See Tex. Civ. Prac. & Rem. Code §30.014(a);* ***O'Connor's Texas Rules****, "ID number," ch. 1-B, §3.2.4(3), p. 8.*}

Ⓓ Defendant has not been issued a driver's license number or a Social Security number. {*See Tex. Civ. Prac. & Rem. Code §30.014(a);* ***O'Connor's Texas Rules****, "ID number," ch. 1-B, §3.2.4(3), p. 8.*}

GENERAL DENIAL

1. Defendant generally denies the allegations in plaintiff's original petition. {*See* ***O'Connor's Texas Rules****, "General Denial," ch. 3-E, §3, p. 274.*}

{*ADD SECTIONS BELOW AS APPROPRIATE*}

PLEA TO THE JURISDICTION

{*CHOOSE APPROPRIATE PARAGRAPHS 2-4*}

2. Defendant asks the Court to dismiss plaintiff's suit because of lack of jurisdiction. Plaintiff's suit is preempted by {❾ *cite state or federal law that preempts action*}. {❿ *Elaborate.*} {*See* ***O'Connor's Texas Rules****, "Grounds," ch. 3-F, §3, p. 289;* ***O'Connor's Texas COA****, "Preemption," ch. 8, §5.14, p. 248.*}

◄ *Continued on next page* ►

3. Defendant asks the Court to dismiss plaintiff's suit because of lack of jurisdiction. Plaintiff does not have standing to sue under the Texas Deceptive Trade Practices Act (DTPA). Plaintiff is a business consumer {⓫ *with assets/owned by a company with assets/controlled by a company with assets*} of $25 million or more. {⓬ *Elaborate.*} {***O'Connor's Texas COA**, "Standing," ch. 8, §5.4, p. 244.*}

4. {*For other challenges to jurisdiction, see FORM 3F:1; **O'Connor's Texas Rules**, "Plea to the Jurisdiction—Challenging the Court," ch. 3-F, p. 287.*}

VERIFIED PLEAS

5. Defendant denies plaintiff's allegation that all conditions precedent have been performed or have occurred. Specifically, plaintiff did not give defendant the notice required under the DTPA. {⓭ *Elaborate.*} Defendant requests that the suit be abated until proper notice is given. During the period of abatement, defendant requests the right to inspect the goods subject to the suit. {*See **O'Connor's Texas Rules**, "Motion to Abate—Challenging the Suit," ch. 3-I, p. 314; **O'Connor's Texas COA**, "Abatement," ch. 8, §6.1.4, p. 249; "Inspection," ch. 8, §6.1.5, p. 249.*}

6. {*For other verified pleas, see FORM 3E:10; **O'Connor's Texas Rules**, "Verified Pleas," ch. 3-E, §4, p. 275.*}

OTHER DEFENSES

{*CHOOSE APPROPRIATE PARAGRAPHS 7-21*}

7. Defendant is not liable to plaintiff because plaintiff's DTPA claim is barred by the two-year statute of limitations in Texas Business & Commerce Code section 17.565. Plaintiff's claim accrued on {⓮ *date*}; plaintiff filed suit on {⓯ *date*}. {⓰ *Elaborate.*} {*See **O'Connor's Texas COA**, "Limitations," ch. 8, §4, p. 244.*}

8. Defendant is not liable to plaintiff because defendant is immune from DTPA liability under {⓱ *identify type of immunity*} immunity. {⓲ *Elaborate.*} {*See **O'Connor's Texas COA**, "Defenses," Part 5, p. 1509.*}

9. Defendant is not liable to plaintiff because plaintiff's own acts or omissions proximately caused or contributed to plaintiff's injury. {⓳ *Elaborate.*} {*See **O'Connor's Texas COA**, "Plaintiff's fault," ch. 8, §5.3, p. 244.*}

10. Defendant is not liable to plaintiff because defendant is exempt from liability under the DTPA. {⓴ *Elaborate.*} {*See **O'Connor's Texas COA**, "Exempt defendants," ch. 8, §5.5.1, p. 245.*}

11. Defendant is not liable to plaintiff because {21 *defendant's claim/the transaction between defendant and plaintiff*} is subject to an exemption from liability under the DTPA. {22 *Elaborate.*} {*See* ***O'Connor's Texas COA***, *"Exempt claims – acts regulated by FTC," ch. 8, §5.5.2, p. 245; "Exempt transactions," ch. 8, §5.5.3, p. 245.*}

12. Plaintiff's claim for {23 *personal injury/death/mental anguish*} is not actionable under the DTPA. {24 *Elaborate.*} {*See* ***O'Connor's Texas COA***, *"Claims for personal injury, death, or mental anguish," ch. 8, §5.6, p. 245.*}

13. Defendant is not liable to plaintiff because within 30 days after receiving notice of the claim, defendant tendered to plaintiff the amount of damages claimed and the expenses reasonably incurred. {25 *Elaborate.*} {*See* ***O'Connor's Texas COA***, *"Response to settlement demand," ch. 8, §5.7, p. 246.*}

14. Defendant is not liable to plaintiff because the information that plaintiff alleges was the producing cause of injury was provided to defendant in writing by {26 *identify source of information*}, and defendant did not know and could not reasonably have known of the {27 *falsity/inaccuracy*} of the information. {28 *Elaborate.*} {*See* ***O'Connor's Texas COA***, *"Reliance on information from other sources," ch. 8, §5.8, p. 246.*}

15. Defendant is not liable to plaintiff because plaintiff purchased the {29 *describe goods*} on an "as is" basis, which bars plaintiff's claim as a matter of law. {30 *Elaborate.*} {*See* ***O'Connor's Texas COA***, *"'As is' contract," ch. 8, §5.9, p. 246.*}

16. Defendant is not liable to plaintiff because plaintiff waived the claim. {31 *Elaborate.*} {*See* ***O'Connor's Texas COA***, *"Waiver of warranties," ch. 8, §5.10, p. 247; "Waiver of DTPA remedies," ch. 8, §5.11, p. 247.*}

17. Plaintiff complains of statements that do not rise above the level of {32 *puffing/opinion*} and are not actionable under the DTPA. {33 *Elaborate.*} {*See* ***O'Connor's Texas COA***, *"Puffing or opinion," ch. 8, §5.12, p. 247.*}

18. Defendant is not liable to plaintiff because plaintiff purchased the {34 *describe product*} from {35 *name of intermediary*}, to whom defendant, the manufacturer, provided all necessary information to assess any risk that the {36 *describe product*} might pose to an ultimate user. {37 *Elaborate.*} {*See* ***O'Connor's Texas COA***, *"Learned intermediary," ch. 8, §5.13, p. 247.*}

19. Plaintiff's claim is merely for breach of contract and is not actionable under the DTPA. {38 *Elaborate.*} {*See* ***O'Connor's Texas COA***, *"Mere breach of contract," ch. 8, §5.15, p. 248.*}

◄ *Continued on next page* ►

FORM 3E:7

20. If defendant is found liable for damages, defendant intends to seek a reduction of damages under the proportionate-responsibility statute. {㊴ *Elaborate.*} {*See* ***O'Connor's Texas COA****, "Proportionate Responsibility & Contribution," ch. 51, p. 1589.*}

21. {*For other defenses, see FORM 3E:11.*}

ADDITIONAL DAMAGES

22. Defendant is not liable to plaintiff for treble damages. {㊵ *Elaborate.*} {*See* ***O'Connor's Texas COA****, "Additional damages," ch. 8, §3.2, p. 241.*}

DAMAGES CAP

23. Defendant is not liable to plaintiff for the amount of damages claimed because defendant timely responded to plaintiff's demand letter with an offer to settle for damages plus reasonable and necessary attorney fees incurred as of the date of the offer. {㊶ *Elaborate.*} Attached to this answer is defendant's offer to settle, Exhibit {㊷ *letter*}, and an affidavit certifying rejection of the offer, Exhibit {㊸ *letter*}. If the damages awarded to plaintiff are substantially the same as defendant's offer, the offer caps defendant's liability for damages and attorney fees. {*See* ***O'Connor's Texas COA****, "Response to settlement demand," ch. 8, §5.7, p. 246; "Offers of settlement," ch. 8, §7.1, p. 249.*}

ATTORNEY FEES

24. Plaintiff's suit is {㊹ *groundless in fact or law/brought in bad faith/brought for the purpose of harassment*}. {㊺ *Elaborate.*} Defendant seeks recovery of defendant's reasonable and necessary attorney fees under Texas Business & Commerce Code section 17.50(c). {*See* ***O'Connor's Texas COA****, "For the defendant," ch. 8, §3.7.2, p. 243.*}

JURY DEMAND

25. Defendant demands a jury trial and tenders the appropriate fee with this answer. {*See* ***O'Connor's Texas Rules****, "Request for Jury Trial," ch. 5-B, p. 400.*}

SPECIAL EXCEPTIONS

26. Defendant specially excepts to plaintiff's original petition, paragraph {㊻ *number*} regarding the relief sought, and asks the Court to require plaintiff to specify the maximum amount that plaintiff claims. {*See* ***O'Connor's Texas Rules****, "Claims for relief," ch. 3-G, §2.2.5, p. 300.*}

27. {*For other special exceptions, see FORM 3G:1.*}

REQUEST FOR DISCLOSURE

28. Under Texas Rule of Civil Procedure 194, defendant requests that plaintiff disclose, within 30 days of the service of this request, the information or material described in Rule 194.2. {*See **O'Connor's Texas Rules**, "Content of request," ch. 6-E, §3.2, p. 627.*}

OBJECTION TO ASSOCIATE JUDGE

29. Defendant objects to the referral of this case to an associate judge for hearing a trial on the merits or presiding at a jury trial. {*See **O'Connor's Texas Rules**, "Objection to referral," ch. 1-J, §3.3, p. 96.*}

PRAYER

30. For these reasons, defendant asks the Court to {47 *state all relief requested, e.g., dismiss this suit, render judgment that plaintiff take nothing, award reasonable and necessary attorney fees to defendant*}, assess costs against plaintiff, and award defendant all other relief to which defendant is entitled.

SEE: Tex. R. Civ. P. 54, 92-94, 194
O'Connor's Texas Rules * Civil Trials (2019), "The Answer—Denying Liability," ch. 3-E, p. 273
O'Connor's Texas Causes of Action (2019), "Deceptive Trade Practices Act," ch. 8, p. 209

ADD: STYLE OF THE CASE – FORM 1B:2
SIGNATURE BLOCK – FORM 1B:3
VERIFICATION – FORM 1B:7, for verified pleas
CERTIFICATE OF SERVICE – FORM 1B:13

ATTACH: AFFIDAVIT – FORM 1B:8, if necessary to support plea to the jurisdiction
NOTICE OF CURRENT/CHANGE OF ADDRESS – FORM 1B:14, if answer is defendant's initial pleading
DTPA OFFER OF SETTLEMENT – FORM 3A:2, if necessary
DTPA AFFIDAVIT CERTIFYING REJECTION OF SETTLEMENT OFFER – FORM 3A:5, if necessary
MOTION TO DISMISS FOR LACK OF JURISDICTION – FORM 3F:1, if necessary
ORDER ON SPECIAL EXCEPTIONS – FORM 3G:2, if necessary
ORDER TO COMPEL DTPA MEDIATION – FORM 4B:3, if necessary
Exhibits, if necessary
Jury fee, if jury trial requested

NOTE: In most cases under the Deceptive Trade Practices Act, a defendant can compel mediation by filing a motion to compel within 90 days of service. See ***O'Connor's Texas Rules***, "DTPA claims," ch. 4-B, §3.1, p. 353; ***O'Connor's Texas COA***, "Compelled mediation," ch. 8, §7.3, p. 250.

If the defendant asserts claims for affirmative relief, include (1) a separate section with a specific statement of the relief sought and (2) a request in the prayer for rendition of judgment on those claims for relief. See FORM 2B:1, ¶19; FORM 3E:1, ¶¶5-7.

See notes under FORM 3E:1.

DEFENDANT'S ORIGINAL ANSWER
{❶ *STATE ADDITIONAL RELIEF REQUESTED IF APPROPRIATE, E.G., & PLEA TO THE JURISDICTION*}

Defendant, {❷ *name*}, files this original answer {❸ *state additional relief requested if appropriate, e.g., and plea to the jurisdiction*} to plaintiff {❹ *name*}'s original petition for bill of review.

{*CHOOSE ONE OF THE FOLLOWING IF DEFENDANT IS AN INDIVIDUAL*}

Ⓐ The last three digits of defendant's driver's license number are {❺ *digits of driver's license number*}. The last three digits of defendant {❻ *name*}'s Social Security number are {❼ *digits of Social Security number*}. {*See Tex. Civ. Prac. & Rem. Code §30.014(a);* ***O'Connor's Texas Rules****, "ID number," ch. 1-B, §3.2.4(3), p. 8.*}

Ⓑ The last three digits of defendant's driver's license number are {❽ *digits of driver's license number*}. Defendant has not been issued a Social Security number. {*See Tex. Civ. Prac. & Rem. Code §30.014(a);* ***O'Connor's Texas Rules****, "ID number," ch. 1-B, §3.2.4(3), p. 8.*}

Ⓒ The last three digits of defendant's Social Security number are {❾ *digits of Social Security number*}. Defendant has not been issued a driver's license number. {*See Tex. Civ. Prac. & Rem. Code §30.014(a);* ***O'Connor's Texas Rules****, "ID number," ch. 1-B, §3.2.4(3), p. 8.*}

Ⓓ Defendant has not been issued a driver's license number or a Social Security number. {*See Tex. Civ. Prac. & Rem. Code §30.014(a);* ***O'Connor's Texas Rules****, "ID number," ch. 1-B, §3.2.4(3), p. 8.*}

GENERAL DENIAL

1. Defendant generally denies the allegations in plaintiff's original petition for bill of review. {*See* ***O'Connor's Texas Rules****, "General Denial," ch. 3-E, §3, p. 274.*}

{*ADD SECTIONS BELOW AS APPROPRIATE*}

PLEA TO THE JURISDICTION

2. Defendant asks the Court to dismiss plaintiff's petition for bill of review because of lack of jurisdiction. {❿ *Elaborate.*} {*See FORM 3F:1;* ***O'Connor's Texas Rules****, "Plea to the Jurisdiction—Challenging the Court," ch. 3-F, p. 287.*}

VERIFIED PLEAS

3. Plaintiff is not entitled to challenge the judgment in cause number {[11] *number*} by bill of review because {[12] *explain, e.g., plaintiff was not a party to the earlier judgment*}.

4. {*For other verified pleas, see FORM 3E:10;* ***O'Connor's Texas Rules****, "Verified Pleas," ch. 3-E, §4, p. 275.*}

OTHER DEFENSES

{*CHOOSE APPROPRIATE PARAGRAPHS 5-8*}

5. Plaintiff permitted the judgment in this case to become final by failing to appeal it and thus is not entitled to bill-of-review relief. {*See French v. Brown, 424 S.W.2d 893, 895 (Tex. 1967).*} Relief by bill of review is available only if a party has exercised due diligence in pursuing all available legal remedies against a former judgment. {*Wembley Inv. Co. v. Herrera, 11 S.W.3d 924, 927 (Tex. 1999).*} When a party ignores available remedies, relief by equitable bill of review is not available. {*Id.*}

6. Plaintiff prosecuted an appeal of this judgment, and that appeal affirmed the judgment. For the appeal, see {[13] *case name*}, cause number {[14] *number*}, {[15] *date*}. A bill of review cannot be used as an additional remedy by a litigant who has made a timely but unsuccessful appeal. {*Rizk v. Mayad, 603 S.W.2d 773, 776 (Tex. 1980).*}

7. Defendant is not liable to plaintiff because plaintiff's bill of review is barred by the four-year statute of limitations in Texas Civil Practice & Remedies Code section 16.051. {*Caldwell v. Barnes, 975 S.W.2d 535, 538 (Tex. 1998).*} Plaintiff's claim accrued on {[16] *date*}; plaintiff filed suit on {[17] *date*}. {[18] *Elaborate.*}

8. {*For other defenses, see FORM 3E:11.*}

ATTORNEY FEES

{*CHOOSE APPROPRIATE PARAGRAPH 9*}

9. Defendant is entitled to recover reasonable and necessary attorney fees because {[19] *he/she/it*} was entitled to attorney fees on the underlying claim that plaintiff is challenging by the bill of review. The underlying claim was for {[20] *identify claim*}, which entitles defendant to attorney fees under Texas Civil Practice & Remedies Code section 38.001. Defendant retained counsel, who presented defendant's claim to {[21] *plaintiff/plaintiff's duly authorized agent*}. Plaintiff did not tender the amount owed within 30 days after the claim was presented. {*See* ***O'Connor's Texas COA****, "Attorney Fees Under CPRC ch. 38," ch. 45-B, p. 1486.*}

Continued on next page

9. Defendant is entitled to recover reasonable and necessary attorney fees under the provisions of the written contract, as set out in paragraph {❷❷ *number*}. By that contract, defendant is entitled to attorney fees as the prevailing party on this bill of review. {*See **O'Connor's Texas COA**, "Attorney Fees Under Written Contract," ch. 45-C, p. 1498.*}

SPECIAL EXCEPTIONS

10. Defendant specially excepts to plaintiff's petition for bill of review, paragraph {❷❸ *number*} regarding the relief sought, and asks the Court to require plaintiff to specify the maximum amount that plaintiff claims. {*See **O'Connor's Texas Rules**, "Claims for relief," ch. 3-G, §2.2.5, p. 300.*}

11. {*For other special exceptions, see FORM 3G:1.*}

REQUEST FOR DISCLOSURE

12. Under Texas Rule of Civil Procedure 194, defendant requests that plaintiff disclose, within 30 days of the service of this request, the information or material described in Rule 194.2. {*See **O'Connor's Texas Rules**, "Content of request," ch. 6-E, §3.2, p. 627.*}

OBJECTION TO ASSOCIATE JUDGE

13. Defendant objects to the referral of this case to an associate judge for hearing a trial on the merits or presiding at a jury trial. {*See **O'Connor's Texas Rules**, "Objection to referral," ch. 1-J, §3.3, p. 96.*}

PRAYER

14. For these reasons, defendant asks the Court to {❷❹ *state all relief requested, e.g., dismiss this suit, render judgment that plaintiff take nothing, award reasonable and necessary attorney fees to defendant*}, assess costs against plaintiff, and award defendant all other relief to which defendant is entitled. {*See **O'Connor's Texas Rules**, "Prayer," ch. 2-B, §15, p. 132.*}

FORM 3E:8

SEE: Tex. R. Civ. P. 92-94, 194, 329b(f)
Tex. Civ. Prac. & Rem. Code §§16.051, 38.001
O'Connor's Texas Rules * Civil Trials (2019), "The Answer—Denying Liability," ch. 3-E, p. 273; "Bill of review," ch. 7-A, §7.1.3, p. 717
O'Connor's Texas Causes of Action (2019), "Attorney Fees," ch. 45, p. 1463

ADD: STYLE OF THE CASE – FORM 1B:2
SIGNATURE BLOCK – FORM 1B:3
VERIFICATION – FORM 1B:7, for verified pleas
CERTIFICATE OF SERVICE – FORM 1B:13

ATTACH: AFFIDAVIT – FORM 1B:8, if necessary to support plea to the jurisdiction
NOTICE OF CURRENT/CHANGE OF ADDRESS – FORM 1B:14, if answer is defendant's initial pleading
MOTION TO DISMISS FOR LACK OF JURISDICTION – FORM 3F:1, if necessary
ORDER ON SPECIAL EXCEPTIONS – FORM 3G:2, if necessary
Exhibits, if necessary
Jury fee, if jury trial requested

NOTE: In this form, the "defendant" is the original plaintiff in the suit; the "plaintiff" is the original defendant who filed the petition for bill of review.

This form applies to equitable bills of review; however, in certain types of proceedings—generally probate and guardianship proceedings—a statutory bill of review may be available. See ***O'Connor's Texas Rules***, "Statutory bill of review," ch. 7-A, §7.1.3(2), p. 721.

Attorney fees are available to the successful party in a bill-of-review action if there is a legal basis for awarding them in the underlying cause of action. ***Palomin v. Zarsky Lumber Co.***, 26 S.W.3d 690, 696 (Tex.App.—Corpus Christi 2000, pet. denied); ***Lowe v. Farm Credit Bank***, 2 S.W.3d 293, 299 (Tex. App.—San Antonio 1999, pet. denied).

The defendant must file its answer by 10:00 a.m. on the first Monday after the expiration of 20 days from the date the defendant was served with citation. Tex. R. Civ. P. 99(b). See ***O'Connor's Texas Rules***, "Deadline to Answer," ch. 3-E, §2, p. 273.

Under Texas Government Code chapter 54A, subchapter B, a district court or statutory county court can appoint a full-time or part-time associate judge to perform certain duties if the creation of the associate-judge position is authorized by the county commissioners court. Tex. Gov't Code §54A.102(a). If the creation of the position is authorized, the court can refer a full trial on the merits or a jury trial to an associate judge. *See id.* §54A.106. A case can be referred to an associate judge either by an order of referral in a specific case or by an omnibus order. *Id.* §54A.107(a). A party can prohibit the trial referral only if it files an objection within ten days after receiving notice of the referral. *Id.* §54A.106(c). See ***O'Connor's Texas Rules***, "Associate Judge," ch. 1-J, p. 95.

FORM 3E:8

DEFENDANT'S ORIGINAL ANSWER
{❶ *STATE ADDITIONAL RELIEF REQUESTED IF APPROPRIATE, E.G., & PLEA TO THE JURISDICTION*}

Defendant, {❷ *name*}, files this original answer {❸ *state additional relief requested if appropriate, e.g., and plea to the jurisdiction*} to plaintiff {❹ *name*}'s original petition.

{*CHOOSE ONE OF THE FOLLOWING IF DEFENDANT IS AN INDIVIDUAL*}

Ⓐ The last three digits of defendant's driver's license number are {❺ *digits of driver's license number*}. The last three digits of defendant's Social Security number are {❻ *digits of Social Security number*}. {*See Tex. Civ. Prac. & Rem. Code §30.014(a);* ***O'Connor's Texas Rules****, "ID number," ch. 1-B, §3.2.4(3), p. 8.*}

Ⓑ The last three digits of defendant's driver's license number are {❼ *digits of driver's license number*}. Defendant has not been issued a Social Security number. {*See Tex. Civ. Prac. & Rem. Code §30.014(a);* ***O'Connor's Texas Rules****, "ID number," ch. 1-B, §3.2.4(3), p. 8.*}

Ⓒ The last three digits of defendant's Social Security number are {❽ *digits of Social Security number*}. Defendant has not been issued a driver's license number. {*See Tex. Civ. Prac. & Rem. Code §30.014(a);* ***O'Connor's Texas Rules****, "ID number," ch. 1-B, §3.2.4(3), p. 8.*}

Ⓓ Defendant has not been issued a driver's license number or a Social Security number. {*See Tex. Civ. Prac. & Rem. Code §30.014(a);* ***O'Connor's Texas Rules****, "ID number," ch. 1-B, §3.2.4(3), p. 8.*}

GENERAL DENIAL

1. Defendant generally denies the allegations in plaintiff's original petition. {*See* ***O'Connor's Texas Rules****, "General Denial," ch. 3-E, §3, p. 274.*}

{*ADD SECTIONS BELOW AS APPROPRIATE*}

PLEA TO THE JURISDICTION

2. Defendant asks the Court to dismiss plaintiff's suit because of lack of jurisdiction. {❾ *Elaborate.*} {*See FORM 3F:1;* ***O'Connor's Texas Rules****, "Plea to the Jurisdiction—Challenging the Court," ch. 3-F, p. 287.*}

VERIFIED PLEAS

3. {*For verified pleas, see FORM 3E:10;* ***O'Connor's Texas Rules****, "Verified Pleas," ch. 3-E, §4, p. 275.*}

OTHER DEFENSES

4. {*For affirmative defenses, see FORM 3E:11;* ***O'Connor's Texas Rules****, "Affirmative Defenses," ch. 3-E, §5, p. 277.*}

ATTORNEY FEES

5. Defendant is entitled to recover reasonable and necessary attorney fees under {⑩ *identify code, statute, or contract permitting recovery of attorney fees*}. {⑪ *Elaborate.*} {*See Tex. Civ. Prac. & Rem. Code §37.009; FORMS 2B:22-24;* ***O'Connor's Texas Rules****, "Costs & attorney fees," ch. 2-E, §3.8, p. 155;* ***O'Connor's Texas COA****, "Attorney Fees," ch. 45, p. 1463.*}

JURY DEMAND

6. Defendant demands a jury trial and tenders the appropriate fee with this answer. {*See* ***O'Connor's Texas Rules****, "Request for Jury Trial," ch. 5-B, p. 400.*}

SPECIAL EXCEPTIONS

{*CHOOSE APPROPRIATE PARAGRAPHS 7-16*}

7. Defendant specially excepts to plaintiff's original petition, paragraph {⑫ *number*} regarding the relief sought, and asks the Court to require plaintiff to specify the maximum amount that plaintiff claims. {*See* ***O'Connor's Texas Rules****, "Claims for relief," ch. 3-G, §2.2.5, p. 300.*}

8. Defendant specially excepts to paragraph {⑬ *number*} because a declaratory judgment is not available when there is no justiciable conflict. *See Bonham State Bank v. Beadle*, 907 S.W.2d 465, 467 (Tex. 1995); *Di Portanova v. Monroe*, 229 S.W.3d 324, 329 (Tex. App.—Houston [1st Dist.] 2006, pet. denied). There is no justiciable conflict in this case. {⑭ *Elaborate.*} {*See* ***O'Connor's Texas Rules****, "No justiciable conflict," ch. 2-E, §2.2.1, p. 153.*}

9. Defendant specially excepts to paragraph {⑮ *number*} because a declaratory judgment is not available to resolve issues that are not yet mature and are subject to change. *See Cal. Prods., Inc. v. Puretex Lemon Juice, Inc.*, 334 S.W.2d 780, 782-83 (Tex. 1960). The issues in this case are not yet mature and are subject to change. {⑯ *Elaborate.*} {*See* ***O'Connor's Texas Rules****, "Future controversy," ch. 2-E, §2.2.3, p. 154.*}

◄ *Continued on next page* ►

FORM 3E:9

10. Defendant specially excepts to paragraph {17 *number*} because a declaratory judgment is not available to resolve an issue when another action is pending that will adjudicate the same issue between the same parties. *Tex. Liquor Control Bd. v. Canyon Creek Land Corp.*, 456 S.W.2d 891, 895 (Tex. 1970). The issues in this case are the same as the issues in {18 *identify the cause number, style, and court of the other case*}. {*See* ***O'Connor's Texas Rules****, "In another court," ch. 2-E, §2.2.4, p. 154.*}

11. Defendant specially excepts to paragraph {19 *number*} because a declaratory judgment is not available to resolve issues that are already pending before the same court. *BHP Petroleum Co. v. Millard*, 800 S.W.2d 838, 841 (Tex. 1990). The issues in this case are already the subject of a lawsuit pending in this Court under cause number {20 *number*}, in the case styled {21 *identify case*}. {*See* ***O'Connor's Texas Rules****, "In same suit," ch. 2-E, §2.2.5, p. 154.*}

12. Defendant specially excepts to paragraph {22 *number*} because a declaratory judgment is not available if a court does not have jurisdiction over the underlying cause of action. *Chenault v. Phillips*, 914 S.W.2d 140, 141 (Tex. 1996); *see Sw. Airlines Co. v. Tex. High-Speed Rail Auth.*, 863 S.W.2d 123, 125-26 (Tex. App.—Austin 1993, writ denied). The Court does not have jurisdiction over the underlying cause of action because {23 *explain*}. {*See* ***O'Connor's Texas Rules****, "No jurisdiction over underlying dispute," ch. 2-E, §2.2.6, p. 154.*}

13. Defendant specially excepts to paragraph {24 *number*} because a declaratory judgment is not available to seek a judicial interpretation of an earlier judgment. *Martin v. Dosohs I, Ltd., Inc.*, 2 S.W.3d 350, 353 (Tex. App.—San Antonio 1999, pet. denied). Plaintiff seeks a judicial interpretation of {25 *identify earlier judgment*}. {26 *Elaborate.*} {*See* ***O'Connor's Texas Rules****, "Earlier judgment," ch. 2-E, §2.2.7, p. 154.*}

14. Defendant specially excepts to paragraph {27 *number*} because a declaratory judgment is not available to determine the rights, status, or other legal relationships arising under a penal statute. *State v. Morales*, 869 S.W.2d 941, 947 (Tex. 1994). Plaintiff seeks to determine the rights, status, or other legal relationships arising under {28 *identify penal statute*}. {29 *Elaborate.*} {*See* ***O'Connor's Texas Rules****, "Criminal issue," ch. 2-E, §2.2.8, p. 154.*}

15. Defendant specially excepts to paragraph {30 *number*} because a declaratory judgment cannot be used against the government or a government official to establish the validity of a contract, enforce the performance of a contract, or impose contractual liability. *Tex. Nat. Res. Conservation Comm'n v. IT-Davy*, 74 S.W.3d 849, 855-56 (Tex. 2002) (plurality op.); *Tex. S. Univ. v. State St. Bank & Tr. Co.*, 212 S.W.3d 893, 903 (Tex. App.—Houston [1st Dist.] 2007, pet. denied). Plaintiff seeks to circumvent

FORM 3E:9

{❸❶ *identify governmental unit or official*}'s sovereign immunity by mischaracterizing this suit, which seeks to impose liability, as a suit to determine rights. {❸❷ *Elaborate.*} {*See **O'Connor's Texas COA**, "Declaratory judgment & immunity," ch. 24-B, §6.1, p. 925.*}

16. Defendant specially excepts to paragraph {❸❸ *number*} because a declaratory judgment cannot be used to determine the rights of the parties under a contract when a contractual dispute with the government must be submitted to an administrative procedure. *See Tex. Dep't of Transp. v. Jones Bros. Dirt & Paving Contractors, Inc.*, 92 S.W.3d 477, 484-85 (Tex. 2002). Plaintiff seeks to determine the rights of {❸❹ *identify parties to contract*} under {❸❺ *identify contract*}. {❸❻ *Elaborate.*} {*See **O'Connor's Texas Rules**, "Suit against the government," ch. 2-E, §2.2.9, p. 154.*}

REQUEST FOR DISCLOSURE

17. Under Texas Rule of Civil Procedure 194, defendant requests that plaintiff disclose, within 30 days of the service of this request, the information or material described in Rule 194.2. {*See **O'Connor's Texas Rules**, "Content of request," ch. 6-E, §3.2, p. 627.*}

OBJECTION TO ASSOCIATE JUDGE

18. Defendant objects to the referral of this case to an associate judge for hearing a trial on the merits or presiding at a jury trial. {*See **O'Connor's Texas Rules**, "Objection to referral," ch. 1-J, §3.3, p. 96.*}

PRAYER

19. For these reasons, defendant asks the Court to {❸❼ *state all relief requested, e.g., dismiss this suit, render judgment that plaintiff take nothing, award reasonable and necessary attorney fees to defendant*}, assess costs against plaintiff, and award defendant all other relief to which defendant is entitled. {*See **O'Connor's Texas Rules**, "Prayer," ch. 2-B, §15, p. 132.*}

SEE: Tex. R. Civ. P. 54, 92-94, 194
O'Connor's Texas Rules * Civil Trials (2019), "Declaratory Judgment," ch. 2-E, p. 152; "The Answer—Denying Liability," ch. 3-E, p. 273
O'Connor's Texas Causes of Action (2019), "Declaratory judgment & immunity," ch. 24-B, §6.1, p. 925

ADD: STYLE OF THE CASE – FORM 1B:2
SIGNATURE BLOCK – FORM 1B:3
VERIFICATION – FORM 1B:7, for verified pleas
CERTIFICATE OF SERVICE – FORM 1B:13

◄ *Continued on next page* ►

ATTACH: AFFIDAVIT – FORM 1B:8, if necessary to support plea to the jurisdiction
NOTICE OF CURRENT/CHANGE OF ADDRESS – FORM 1B:14, if answer is defendant's initial pleading
MOTION TO DISMISS FOR LACK OF JURISDICTION – FORM 3F:1, if necessary
ORDER ON SPECIAL EXCEPTIONS – FORM 3G:2, if necessary
Exhibits, if necessary
Jury fee, if jury trial requested

NOTE: Although generally filed by the defendant, special exceptions filed in response to a declaratory-judgment action may also be filed by a plaintiff. Rather than filing the special exceptions in an answer as a defendant might, the plaintiff may file special exceptions separately. See FORM 3G:1.

If the defendant asserts claims for affirmative relief, include (1) a separate section with a specific statement of the relief sought and (2) a request in the prayer for rendition of judgment on those claims for relief. See FORM 2B:1, ¶19; FORM 3E:1, ¶¶5-7.

See notes under FORM 3E:1.

VERIFIED PLEAS

{*CHOOSE APPROPRIATE PARAGRAPHS*}

1. Defendant denies plaintiff's allegation that all conditions precedent have been performed or have occurred. {❶ *Identify specific conditions precedent that have not been performed or have not occurred.*} {*See* ***O'Connor's Texas Rules****, "Denial of conditions precedent," ch. 3-E, §6.1, p. 281.*}

2. Defendant denies that {❷ *plaintiff has the legal capacity to sue/defendant has the legal capacity to be sued*} because {❸ *state reason*}. {*See* ***O'Connor's Texas Rules****, "Verified pleas in TRCP 93," ch. 3-E, §4.1.1, p. 275.*}

3. Defendant denies that {❹ *plaintiff is entitled to recover in the capacity in which plaintiff sues/defendant is liable in the capacity in which defendant is sued*} because {❺ *state reason*}. {*See* ***O'Connor's Texas Rules****, "Verified pleas in TRCP 93," ch. 3-E, §4.1.2, p. 275.*}

4. Defendant denies plaintiff's allegation that {❻ *defendant/plaintiff*} is a partnership. {*See* ***O'Connor's Texas Rules****, "Verified pleas in TRCP 93," ch. 3-E, §4.1.5, p. 276.*}

5. Defendant denies plaintiff's allegation that {❼ *defendant/plaintiff*} is a corporation. {*See* ***O'Connor's Texas Rules****, "Verified pleas in TRCP 93," ch. 3-E, §4.1.6, p. 276.*}

6. Defendant denies plaintiff's allegation that {❽ *defendant/plaintiff*} is doing business as {❾ *name*}. {*See* ***O'Connor's Texas Rules****, "Verified pleas in TRCP 93," ch. 3-E, §4.1.14, p. 277.*}

7. There is a defect of the parties. Specifically, {❿ *state other defects of parties*}. {*See* ***O'Connor's Texas Rules****, "Verified pleas in TRCP 93," ch. 3-E, §4.1.4, p. 275.*}

8. Another suit involving the same parties and the same claim is pending in another Texas court. {⓫ *Identify the cause number, style, and court of the other suit.*} {*See* ***O'Connor's Texas Rules****, "Verified pleas in TRCP 93," ch. 3-E, §4.1.3, p. 275.*}

9. Defendant denies plaintiff's allegation that defendant executed the {⓬ *identify document*}. {*See* ***O'Connor's Texas Rules****, "Verified pleas in TRCP 93," ch. 3-E, §4.1.7, p. 276.*}

FORM 3E:10

◄ *Continued on next page* ►

10. Defendant has reason to believe that {[13] *identify document*} was not executed {[14] *by/under the authority of*} {[15] *name of decedent*}, a person who is now deceased. {*See* ***O'Connor's Texas Rules****, "Verified pleas in TRCP 93," ch. 3-E, §4.1.7, p. 276.*}

11. Defendant has reason to believe that the {[16] *indorsement/assignment*} of {[17] *identify document*} is not genuine. {*See* ***O'Connor's Texas Rules****, "Verified pleas in TRCP 93," ch. 3-E, §4.1.8, p. 276.*}

12. The {[18] *identify document*} {[19] *is without consideration/required consideration that failed in whole or in part*}. {*See* ***O'Connor's Texas Rules****, "Verified pleas in TRCP 93," ch. 3-E, §4.1.9, p. 276.*}

13. Defendant denies the account on which plaintiff files suit because {[20] *state reason for denial*}. {*See FORM 3E:3;* ***O'Connor's Texas Rules****, "Verified pleas in TRCP 93," ch. 3-E, §4.1.10, p. 276.*}

14. The contract on which plaintiff sues is usurious. {*See* ***O'Connor's Texas Rules****, "Verified pleas in TRCP 93," ch. 3-E, §4.1.11, p. 277.*}

15. Defendant denies plaintiff's allegation that plaintiff gave notice and proof of plaintiff's claim. Specifically, {[21] *describe deficiencies in notice and proof of loss with particularity*}. {*See* ***O'Connor's Texas Rules****, "Verified pleas in TRCP 93," ch. 3-E, §4.1.12, p. 277.*}

16. Defendant has reason to believe that {[22] *identify matters listed in Tex. R. Civ. P. 93(13) regarding an appeal from the Division of Workers' Compensation, Texas Department of Insurance*}. {*See* ***O'Connor's Texas Rules****, "Verified pleas in TRCP 93," ch. 3-E, §4.1.13, p. 277.*}

17. Defendant is an automobile-insurance company that is being sued by its insured under the provisions of an insurance policy that provides protection against uninsured motorists. In plaintiff's petition, plaintiff alleged that plaintiff complied with all the terms of the policy as a condition precedent to bringing the suit. Defendant denies that plaintiff complied with the following terms of the policy, which are conditions precedent to bringing this suit: {[23] *quote specific terms with which plaintiff did not comply*}. {*See* ***O'Connor's Texas Rules****, "Verified pleas in TRCP 93," ch. 3-E, §4.1.15, p. 277.*}

18. As required by {[24] *identify statute*}, defendant denies {[25] *state matter that must be denied by statute*}. {*See* ***O'Connor's Texas Rules****, "Verified pleas in TRCP 93," ch. 3-E, §4.1.16, p. 277.*}

SEE: Tex. R. Civ. P. 54, 93
O'Connor's Texas Rules * Civil Trials (2019), "Verified Pleas," ch. 3-E, §4, p. 275

NOTE: The defendant should always check Texas Rule of Civil Procedure 93 to determine whether a defense must be verified. When in doubt, the defendant should verify. The defendant can deny matters in Texas Rule of Civil Procedure 93(7), (8), (13)(a), (13)(g), and (15) on information and belief. See the wording of each subsection for the exact language.

Other matters that must be verified include the following: a confession of judgment, Tex. R. Civ. P. 314; a writ of certiorari to a county court, Tex. R. Civ. P. 506.4(a), (b); the answer of a garnishee, Tex. R. Civ. P. 665; a complaint seeking an injunction, Tex. R. Civ. P. 680, 682; a request to dissolve an injunction before a final hearing, Tex. R. Civ. P. 690; a claimant's oath by a third party to reclaim personal property that has been levied, Tex. R. Civ. P. 717; and a claim of right of property, Tex. R. Civ. P. 717.

FORM 3E:10

OTHER DEFENSES

{*CHOOSE APPROPRIATE AFFIRMATIVE DEFENSES*}

{*General affirmative defenses*}

1. Defendant is not liable to plaintiff because of an arbitration and award. {[1] *Elaborate.*}

2. Defendant is not liable to plaintiff because defendant was discharged in bankruptcy. {[2] *Elaborate.*}

3. Defendant is not liable to plaintiff because of estoppel. {[3] *Elaborate.*}

4. Defendant is not liable to plaintiff because of fraud. {[4] *Elaborate.*}

5. Defendant is not liable to plaintiff because of laches. {[5] *Elaborate.*}

6. Defendant is not liable to plaintiff because of absence of license. {[6] *Elaborate.*}

7. Defendant is not liable to plaintiff because of release. {[7] *Elaborate.*}

8. Defendant is not liable to plaintiff because of res judicata. {[8] *Elaborate.*}

9. Defendant is not liable to plaintiff because plaintiff's claim for {[9] *state cause of action*} is barred by the {[10] *number*}-year statute of limitations in Texas Civil Practice & Remedies Code section {[11] *number*}. Plaintiff's claim accrued on {[12] *date*}; plaintiff filed suit on {[13] *date*}. {[14] *Elaborate.*}

10. Defendant is not liable to plaintiff because of waiver. {[15] *Elaborate.*}

11. Defendant is not liable to plaintiff because of consent. {[16] *Elaborate.*}

12. Defendant is not liable to plaintiff because of justification. {[17] *Elaborate.*}

13. Defendant is not liable to plaintiff because of privilege. {[18] *Elaborate.*}

14. Defendant is not liable to plaintiff because plaintiff did not mitigate damages. {[19] *Elaborate.*}

15. Defendant is not liable to plaintiff because defendant is immune from liability under {[20] *identify type of immunity*} immunity. {[21] *Elaborate.*}

16. Defendant is not liable to plaintiff because plaintiff's claim is preempted by {[22] *cite federal law that preempts action*}. {[23] *Elaborate.*}

17. Defendant is not liable to plaintiff because plaintiff's claim for {㉔ *state cause of action*} is barred by a statute of repose. {㉕ *Elaborate.*}

18. Defendant is not liable to plaintiff because {㉖ *identify other general affirmative defense*}. {㉗ *Elaborate.*} {*For other affirmative defenses, see* ***O'Connor's Texas Rules****, "Other avoidances or affirmative defenses," ch. 3-E, §5.3, p. 280.*}

{*Contract-related affirmative defenses*}

19. Defendant is not liable to plaintiff because of an accord and satisfaction. {㉘ *Elaborate.*}

20. Defendant is not liable to plaintiff because of duress. {㉙ *Elaborate.*}

21. Defendant is not liable to plaintiff because of failure of consideration. {㉚ *Elaborate.*}

22. Defendant is not liable to plaintiff because of illegality. {㉛ *Elaborate.*}

23. Defendant is not liable to plaintiff because of payment. {㉜ *Describe payment with enough specificity to give plaintiff full notice of the nature of the payment.*}

24. Defendant is not liable to plaintiff because of the statute of frauds. {㉝ *Elaborate.*}

25. Defendant is not liable to plaintiff because plaintiff's loss falls within a specific exception to general liability. {㉞ *Elaborate.*}

26. Defendant is not liable to plaintiff because of ambiguity. {㉟ *Elaborate.*}

27. Defendant is not liable to plaintiff because of mistake. {㊱ *Elaborate.*}

28. Defendant is not liable to plaintiff because defendant is entitled to offset. {㊲ *Elaborate.*}

29. Defendant is not liable to plaintiff because of penalty. {㊳ *Elaborate.*}

30. Defendant is not liable to plaintiff because of ratification. {㊴ *Elaborate.*}

31. Defendant is not liable to plaintiff because of rescission. {㊵ *Elaborate.*}

32. Defendant is not liable to plaintiff because {㊶ *identify other contract-related affirmative defense*}. {㊷ *Elaborate.*}

◄ *Continued on next page* ►

{*Tort-related affirmative defenses*}

33. Defendant is not liable to plaintiff because plaintiff assumed the risk. {43 *Elaborate.*}

34. Defendant is not liable to plaintiff because plaintiff's own acts or omissions proximately caused or contributed to plaintiff's injuries. If defendant is found liable for damages, defendant intends to seek a reduction of damages under the proportionate-responsibility statute. {44 *Elaborate.*}

35. Defendant is not liable to plaintiff because of injury by a fellow servant. {45 *Elaborate.*}

36. Defendant is not liable to plaintiff because the injury was the result of the criminal act of {46 *plaintiff/a third person*}. {47 *Elaborate.*}

37. Defendant is not liable to plaintiff because {48 *identify other tort-related affirmative defense*}. {49 *Elaborate.*}

SEE: Tex. R. Civ. P. 94, 95
O'Connor's Texas Rules * Civil Trials (2019), "Affirmative Defenses," ch. 3-E, §5, p. 277

NOTE: Any other matter constituting an avoidance or affirmative defense not listed in Texas Rule of Civil Procedure 94 must be specifically raised in the defendant's pretrial pleadings. *See* Tex. R. Civ. P. 94. For a particular matter to constitute an avoidance or affirmative defense that must be specifically pleaded under Rule 94, the defendant must have the burden of proof to present sufficient evidence to establish the defense and obtain the requisite jury findings. *See, e.g.*, ***Zorrilla v. Aypco Constr. II, LLC***, 469 S.W.3d 143, 156-57 (Tex.2015) (exemplary-damages cap under CPRC §41.008(b) is not avoidance or affirmative defense because cap applies automatically and does not place burden of proof on D).

{❶ *NAME*}'S THIRD-PARTY PLAINTIFF'S
ORIGINAL PETITION {❷ *STATE ADDITIONAL RELIEF REQUESTED IF APPROPRIATE, E.G., & REQUEST FOR DISCLOSURE*}

Third-party plaintiff, {❸ *name*}, defendant in the above-styled case, files this third-party petition {❹ *state additional relief requested if appropriate, e.g., and request for disclosure*} against third-party defendant, {❺ *name*}, and alleges as follows:

DISCOVERY-CONTROL PLAN

{*CHOOSE APPROPRIATE PARAGRAPH 1*}

1. Third-party plaintiff intends to conduct discovery under Level 1 of Texas Rule of Civil Procedure 190.2 and affirmatively pleads that this suit is governed by the expedited-actions process in Texas Rule of Civil Procedure 169. {*See* ***O'Connor's Texas Rules****, "Discovery-Control Plans," ch. 2-B, §2, p. 115.*}

1. Third-party plaintiff intends to conduct discovery under Level {❻ *2/3*} of Texas Rule of Civil Procedure {❼ *190.3/190.4*} and affirmatively pleads that this suit is not governed by the expedited-actions process in Texas Rule of Civil Procedure 169 because {❽ *explain, e.g., third-party plaintiff requests injunctive relief, third-party plaintiff seeks monetary relief over $100,000*}. {*See* ***O'Connor's Texas Rules****, "Discovery-Control Plans," ch. 2-B, §2, p. 115.*}

CLAIM FOR RELIEF

{*CHOOSE APPROPRIATE PARAGRAPH 2*}

2. Third-party plaintiff seeks only monetary relief of $100,000 or less, including damages of any kind, penalties, court costs, expenses, prejudgment interest, and attorney fees. {*Tex. R. Civ. P. 47(c)(1).*}

2. Third-party plaintiff seeks monetary relief of $100,000 or less and nonmonetary relief. {*Tex. R. Civ. P. 47(c)(2).*}

2. Third-party plaintiff seeks monetary relief over $100,000 but not more than $200,000. {*Tex. R. Civ. P. 47(c)(3).*}

2. Third-party plaintiff seeks monetary relief over $200,000 but not more than $1,000,000. {*Tex. R. Civ. P. 47(c)(4).*}

2. Third-party plaintiff seeks monetary relief over $1,000,000. {*Tex. R. Civ. P. 47(c)(5).*}

Continued on next page

PARTIES

3. Third-party plaintiff, {9 *name*}, {10 *identify third-party plaintiff, e.g., is an individual residing in Harris County, Texas*}. {*For third-party plaintiff's designation, see FORM 2B:9 and modify as necessary;* ***O'Connor's Texas Rules****, "Plaintiff," ch. 2-B, §4.4, p. 123.*}

4. Third-party defendant, {11 *name*}, {12 *identify third-party defendant for purposes of service*}. {*For third-party defendant's designation, see FORMS 2B:10-19 and modify as necessary;* ***O'Connor's Texas Rules****, "Defendant," ch. 2-B, §4.5, p. 123.*}

{*ADD SECTION BELOW IF APPLICABLE*}

PERSONAL JURISDICTION

5. {*For allegations of personal jurisdiction, see FORM 2B:20.*}

FACTS

6. On {13 *date*}, plaintiff, {14 *name*}, filed suit against third-party plaintiff in {15 _______} County, Texas, for {16 *state basis of suit*}.

7. {17 *State other relevant facts in separately numbered paragraphs.*} {*See* ***O'Connor's Texas Rules****, "Pleading a Cause of Action," ch. 2-B, §7, p. 127.*}

COUNT 1 – {18 *NAME OF CAUSE OF ACTION*}

8. Third-party defendant is liable to {19 *plaintiff/third-party plaintiff*} for all or part of plaintiff's claim for {20 *state cause of action*} against third-party plaintiff because {21 *state reason third-party defendant is liable*}. {*See* ***O'Connor's Texas Rules****, "Third-party petitions," ch. 3-E, §7.3, p. 283.*}

{*CHOOSE APPROPRIATE PARAGRAPH 9*}

9. Third-party plaintiff seeks unliquidated damages within the jurisdictional limits of this Court. {*See Tex. R. Civ. P. 47(b);* ***O'Connor's Texas Rules****, "Damages," ch. 2-B, §9, p. 130.*}

9. Third-party plaintiff seeks liquidated damages in the amount of at least ${22 *amount*}, which is within the jurisdictional limits of this Court. {*See Tex. R. Civ. P. 47(b);* ***O'Connor's Texas Rules****, "Damages," ch. 2-B, §9, p. 130.*}

{ADD SECTIONS BELOW AS APPROPRIATE}

ATTORNEY FEES

10. Third-party plaintiff is entitled to recover reasonable and necessary attorney fees under {㉓ *identify code, statute, or contract permitting recovery of attorney fees*}. {㉔ *Elaborate.*} {*See FORMS 2B:22-24;* ***O'Connor's Texas COA****, "Attorney Fees," ch. 45, p. 1463.*}

JURY DEMAND

11. Third-party plaintiff demands a jury trial and tenders the appropriate fee with this petition. {*See* ***O'Connor's Texas Rules****, "Jury Demand," ch. 2-B, §13, p. 132.*}

CONDITIONS PRECEDENT

12. All conditions precedent to third-party plaintiff's claim for relief have been performed or have occurred. {*See* ***O'Connor's Texas Rules****, "Conditions Precedent," ch. 2-B, §12, p. 132.*}

REQUEST FOR DISCLOSURE

13. Under Texas Rule of Civil Procedure 194, third-party plaintiff requests that third-party defendant disclose, within 50 days of the service of this request, the information or material described in Rule 194.2. {*See* ***O'Connor's Texas Rules****, "Content of request," ch. 6-E, §3.2, p. 627.*}

PRAYER

14. For these reasons, third-party plaintiff asks that the Court issue citation for third-party defendant to appear and answer, and that third-party plaintiff be awarded a judgment against third-party defendant for {㉕ *specify relief sought*} and for all other relief to which third-party plaintiff is entitled.

SEE: Tex. R. Civ. P. 38, 169, 190
O'Connor's Texas Rules * Civil Trials (2019), "Discovery-Control Plans," ch. 2-B, §2, p. 115; "Damages," ch. 2-B, §9, p. 130; "Third-party petitions," ch. 3-E, §7.3, p. 283
O'Connor's Texas Causes of Action (2019), "Attorney Fees," ch. 45, p. 1463

ADD: STYLE OF THE CASE – FORM 1B:2
SIGNATURE BLOCK – FORM 1B:3

Continued on next page

ATTACH: MOTION FOR LEAVE TO FILE THIRD-PARTY PETITION – FORM 3E:13, if petition filed more than 30 days after answer
Exhibits, as necessary
Filing fee
Jury fee, if requested

NOTE: A defendant, as a third-party plaintiff, may bring into the suit any third party who is or may be liable to it or to the plaintiff for all or part of the plaintiff's claim. Tex. R. Civ. P. 38(a); *see* ***Bennett v. Grant***, 525 S.W.3d 642, 653 (Tex.2017).

Before a court clerk will issue a citation for service, the plaintiff may be required to complete and file with its petition a Civil Process Request Form identifying the person to be served and the method of service. Check the court's website for specific requirements and to obtain a copy of the form.

For information on the procedures for expedited actions and for making a specific claim for relief, see the notes under FORM 2B:1.

DEFENDANT'S MOTION FOR LEAVE TO FILE THIRD-PARTY PETITION

Defendant, {❶ *name*}, files this motion for leave to file a third-party petition against third-party defendant.

INTRODUCTION

1. Plaintiff, {❷ *name*}, sued defendant, {❸ *name*}, for {❹ *state basis of suit*}.

2. Defendant {❺ *name*}, the third-party plaintiff, is seeking leave to sue {❻ *name*}, the third-party defendant, for {❼ *contribution/indemnity/contribution and indemnity*}.

3. {❽ *State other relevant facts about the suit.*}

BACKGROUND

4. {❾ *State facts relevant to the motion.*}

5. Defendant attaches {❿ *his/her/its*} third-party petition to this motion as Exhibit {⓫ *letter*} and incorporates it by reference.

ARGUMENT & AUTHORITIES

6. Third-party defendant is liable to {⓬ *plaintiff/defendant*} for all or part of plaintiff's claim for {⓭ *state cause of action*} against defendant because {⓮ *state reason third-party defendant is liable*}.

7. Defendant did not file {⓯ *his/her/its*} third-party petition within 30 days after filing {⓰ *his/her/its*} answer because {⓱ *state reason, e.g., defendant did not discover third-party defendant's liability until after it conducted a diligent investigation, which occurred more than 30 days after the answer was filed*}. {*See* ***O'Connor's Texas Rules****, "Leave of court," ch. 3-E, §7.3.1, p. 283.*}

8. Filing the third-party petition will not cause a delay and will not inconvenience the parties because {⓲ *explain, e.g., the case is not set for trial and no discovery has been conducted*}.

CONCLUSION

9. {⓳ *Briefly summarize the motion.*}

PRAYER

10. For these reasons, defendant asks the Court to grant {⓴ *his/her/its*} motion for leave to file a third-party petition against third-party defendant.

Continued on next page

FORM 3E:13

SEE: Tex. R. Civ. P. 38, 97
O'Connor's Texas Rules * Civil Trials (2019), "Third-party petitions," ch. 3-E, §7.3, p. 283

ADD: STYLE OF THE CASE – FORM 1B:2
SIGNATURE BLOCK – FORM 1B:3
CERTIFICATE OF CONFERENCE – FORM 1B:12, if necessary
CERTIFICATE OF SERVICE – FORM 1B:13

ATTACH: AFFIDAVIT – FORM 1B:8, if necessary
NOTICE OF HEARING OR SUBMISSION – FORM 1E:1
ORDER – FORM 1G:1
PETITION – THIRD PARTY – FORM 3E:12

DEFENDANT'S MOTION FOR LEAVE
TO DESIGNATE RESPONSIBLE THIRD PARTY

Defendant, {❶ *name*}, files this motion for leave to designate a responsible third party. {*See* ***O'Connor's Texas Rules****, "Motion for leave to designate," ch. 3-E, §7.4.2(2), p. 284.*}

INTRODUCTION

1. Plaintiff, {❷ *name*}, sued defendant, {❸ *name*}, for {❹ *state basis of suit*}.

{*CHOOSE APPROPRIATE PARAGRAPH* 2}

2. The responsible third party is {❺ *name*}.

2. The responsible third party is an unknown person.

3. This case is set for trial on {❻ *date*}.

4. {❼ *State other relevant facts about the suit.*}

BACKGROUND

5. {❽ *State facts relevant to the motion.*}

{*ADD PARAGRAPH 6 IF APPLICABLE*}

6. Defendant attaches {❾ *his/her/its*} amended answer to this motion as Exhibit {❿ *letter*} to plead the foregoing facts and incorporates it by reference.

ARGUMENT & AUTHORITIES

{*CHOOSE APPROPRIATE PARAGRAPH 7*}

{*If third party is known*}

7. Under Texas Civil Practice & Remedies Code section 33.004(a), a defendant can move for leave to designate a person as a responsible third party. A responsible third party is a person who is alleged to have caused or contributed to causing in any way the harm for which recovery of damages is sought, whether by negligent act or omission, by any defective or unreasonably dangerous product, or by other conduct or activity that violates an applicable legal standard. Tex. Civ. Prac. & Rem. Code §33.011(6). In this case, {⓫ *name*} is a responsible third party because {⓬ *he/she/it*} caused or contributed to the harm for which recovery of damages is sought {⓭ *through a negligent act or omission/with a defective or unreasonably dangerous product/{identify other*

— *Continued on next page* —

FORM 3E:14

conduct or activity that violates an applicable legal standard}}. {⓮ *State facts demonstrating the responsible third party's fault that are sufficient to satisfy the pleading requirements of the Texas Rules of Civil Procedure.*} {*See* ***O'Connor's Texas Rules****, "Who is an RTP," ch. 3-E, §7.4.1(1), p. 283.*}

{*If third party is unknown criminal*}

7. Under Texas Civil Practice & Remedies Code section 33.004(j), a defendant can move for leave to designate an unknown person as a responsible third party if (1) the defendant alleges in an answer filed with the court that an unknown person committed a criminal act that was a cause of the loss or injury, (2) the court determines that the defendant has pleaded facts sufficient for the court to determine that there is a reasonable probability that the act of the unknown person was criminal, (3) the defendant has stated in the answer all identifying characteristics of the unknown person, known at the time of the answer, and (4) the allegation satisfies the pleading requirements of the Texas Rules of Civil Procedure. {*See* ***O'Connor's Texas Rules****, "Amended answer – RTP is unknown criminal," ch. 3-E, §7.4.2(1), p. 284.*} The Court should grant this motion for leave to designate a responsible third party for the following reasons:

a. Defendant alleged in {⓯ *his/her/its*} answer that an unknown person committed a criminal act that was a cause of the {⓰ *loss/injury*} that is the subject of this suit. Plaintiff's injuries were caused by the criminal act of {⓱ *John Doe/Jane Doe*}, whose true identity is unknown to defendant. {⓲ *Elaborate.*}

b. There is a reasonable probability that the act of {⓳ *John Doe/Jane Doe*} was criminal. {⓴ *State sufficient facts to show reasonable probability the act was criminal.*}

c. Defendant provided in {㉑ *his/her/its*} answer all identifying characteristics of {㉒ *John Doe/Jane Doe*} known to defendant at the time of the answer. At this time, defendant is {㉓ *unaware/aware*} of {㉔ *any/certain*} identifying characteristics of {㉕ *John Doe/Jane Doe*}. {㉖ *State all identifying characteristics known to defendant.*}

d. Defendant's allegations satisfy the pleading requirements of the Texas Rules of Civil Procedure. {㉗ *State sufficient facts about Doe's responsibility to satisfy the pleading requirements of the Texas Rules of Civil Procedure.*}

{*ADD SECTION BELOW IF APPLICABLE*}

TIMELINESS

{*CHOOSE APPROPRIATE PARAGRAPH 8*}

8. Although the applicable limitations period against the responsible third party has expired, defendant can still file this motion because defendant timely disclosed {㉘ *his/her/its*} intent to designate the responsible third party. *See* Tex. Civ. Prac. & Rem. Code §33.004(d). {㉙ *Elaborate.*} {*See **O'Connor's Texas Rules**, "Limitations period has expired," ch. 3-E, §7.4.2(2)(a)[2], p. 285.*}

8. A court can allow a late motion for leave to designate a person as a responsible third party on a showing of good cause. Tex. Civ. Prac. & Rem. Code §33.004(a). Defendant files this motion on {㉚ *date*}, {㉛ *number*} days before the date set for trial, which is {㉜ *date*}. Although {㉝ *date*} is less than 60 days before the trial date, defendant can show good cause for the late filing. {㉞ *Elaborate.*} {*See **O'Connor's Texas Rules**, "Limitations period has not expired," ch. 3-E, §7.4.2(2)(a)[1], p. 284.*}

CONCLUSION

9. {㉟ *Briefly summarize the motion.*}

PRAYER

10. For these reasons, defendant asks the Court to grant {㊱ *his/her/its*} motion for leave to designate the responsible third party.

SEE: Tex. R. Civ. P. 38
Tex. Civ. Prac. & Rem. Code §§33.004, 33.011(6)
O'Connor's Texas Rules * Civil Trials (2019), "RTP," ch. 3-E, §7.4, p. 283

ADD: STYLE OF THE CASE – FORM 1B:2
SIGNATURE BLOCK – FORM 1B:3
CERTIFICATE OF CONFERENCE – FORM 1B:12, if necessary
CERTIFICATE OF SERVICE – FORM 1B:13

ATTACH: AFFIDAVIT – FORM 1B:8, if necessary
NOTICE OF HEARING OR SUBMISSION – FORM 1E:1
ORDER – FORM 1G:1
Amended answer, if necessary

◄ *Continued on next page* ►

NOTE: If the responsible third party is an unknown person alleged to have committed a criminal act, the defendant must designate that person in an amended answer (no later than 60 days after the original answer was filed) before filing a motion for leave to designate the person as a responsible third party. *See* Tex. Civ. Prac. & Rem. Code §33.004(j); ***Arango v. Davila***, No. 13-09-00470-CV (Tex.App.—Corpus Christi 2011, pet. denied) (memo op.; 5-19-11), *disapproved on other grounds*, ***Haygood v. De Escabedo***, 356 S.W.3d 390 (Tex.2011). See FORM 3E:1; ***O'Connor's Texas Rules***, "Amended answer – RTP is unknown criminal," ch. 3-E, §7.4.2(1), p. 284.

If the trial date is reset, the motion must be filed at least 60 days before the new trial date. ***See In re Coppola***, 535 S.W.3d 506, 507-08 (Tex.2017). See ***O'Connor's Texas Rules***, "Deadline to file," ch. 3-E, §7.4.2(2)(a), p. 284.

PLAINTIFF'S OBJECTION TO DEFENDANT'S MOTION FOR LEAVE TO DESIGNATE RESPONSIBLE THIRD PARTY

Plaintiff, {❶ *name*}, files this objection to defendant {❷ *name*}'s motion for leave to designate a responsible third party. {*See* ***O'Connor's Texas Rules****, "Objection," ch. 3-E, §7.4.2(2)(d), p. 285.*}

INTRODUCTION

1. Plaintiff, {❸ *name*}, sued defendant, {❹ *name*}, for {❺ *state basis of suit*}.

2. {❻ *State other relevant facts about the suit.*}

BACKGROUND

{*CHOOSE APPROPRIATE PARAGRAPH 3*}

3. On {❼ *date*}, defendant filed a motion for leave to designate {❽ *name*} as a responsible third party.

3. On {❾ *date*}, defendant filed a motion for leave to designate an unknown person as a responsible third party.

4. {❿ *State other facts relevant to the objection.*}

ARGUMENT & AUTHORITIES

{*CHOOSE APPROPRIATE SECTIONS A-C*}

A. Motion untimely.

{*CHOOSE APPROPRIATE PARAGRAPHS 5-7*}

5. The Court should deny defendant's motion for leave to designate a responsible third party because the motion was filed less than 60 days before the {⓫ *original/new*} trial date. *See* Tex. Civ. Prac. & Rem. Code §33.004(a); *In re Coppola*, 535 S.W.3d 506, 507-08 (Tex. 2017). Defendant did not show good cause for filing the motion at this late date. {⓬ *Elaborate.*} {*See* ***O'Connor's Texas Rules****, "Limitations period has not expired," ch. 3-E, §7.4.2(2)(a)[1], p. 284.*}

6. The Court should deny defendant's motion for leave to designate a responsible third party because the motion was filed after the limitations period expired against {⓭ *name of allegedly responsible third party*}, and defendant did not timely disclose that this person may be designated as a responsible third party. *In re Dawson*, 550

Continued on next page

S.W.3d 625, 629-30 (Tex. 2018); *see* Tex. Civ. Prac. & Rem. Code §33.004(d). {14 *Elaborate.*} {*See* ***O'Connor's Texas Rules****, "Limitations period has expired," ch. 3-E, §7.4.2(2)(a)[2], p. 285.*}

7. The Court should deny defendant's motion for leave to designate a responsible third party because an amended answer designating an unknown person as a responsible third party was {15 *not filed/filed more than 60 days after defendant's original answer was filed*}. *See* Tex. Civ. Prac. & Rem. Code §33.004(j); *Arango v. Davila*, No. 13-09-00470-CV (Tex. App.—Corpus Christi 2011, pet. denied) (memo op.; 5-19-11), *disapproved on other grounds, Haygood v. De Escabedo*, 356 S.W.3d 390 (Tex. 2011). {16 *Elaborate.*} {*See* ***O'Connor's Texas Rules****, "Amended answer – RTP is unknown criminal," ch. 3-E, §7.4.2(1), p. 284.*}

B. Defendant did not plead sufficient facts.

8. The Court should deny defendant's motion for leave to designate a responsible third party because defendant {17 *add if applicable: , after given an opportunity to replead,*} has not pleaded sufficient facts to satisfy the pleading requirements of the Texas Rules of Civil Procedure. Tex. Civ. Prac. & Rem. Code §33.004(g). {*See* ***O'Connor's Texas Rules****, "Insufficient facts pleaded," ch. 3-E, §7.4.2(2)(e)[2][a], p. 286.*} Specifically, defendant has not satisfied the pleading requirements for the following reasons:

{*CHOOSE APPROPRIATE REASONS*}

a. Defendant did not plead sufficient facts about the alleged responsibility of the third party. Tex. Civ. Prac. & Rem. Code §33.004(g)(1). {18 *Elaborate.*}

b. Defendant did not plead facts sufficient to show a reasonable probability that the unknown person committed a criminal act. Tex. Civ. Prac. & Rem. Code §33.004(j)(1). {19 *Elaborate.*}

c. Defendant did not plead all identifying characteristics of the unknown person when defendant filed defendant's amended answer. Tex. Civ. Prac. & Rem. Code §33.004(j)(2). {20 *Elaborate.*}

C. Not a proper responsible third party.

9. The Court should deny defendant's motion because {21 *name*} is not a proper responsible third party under Texas Civil Practice & Remedies Code section 33.011(6); {22 *name*} is a seller eligible for indemnity in a products-liability action under Texas Civil Practice & Remedies Code section 82.002. Tex. Civ. Prac. & Rem. Code §33.011(6). {23 *Elaborate.*} {*See* ***O'Connor's Texas Rules****, "Identifying an RTP," ch. 3-E, §7.4.1, p. 283.*}

FORM 3E:15

CONCLUSION

10. {㉔ *Briefly summarize the objection.*}

PRAYER

11. For these reasons, plaintiff asks the Court to deny defendant's motion for leave to designate a responsible third party.

SEE: Tex. Civ. Prac. & Rem. Code §§33.004, 33.011(6), 82.002
O'Connor's Texas Rules * Civil Trials (2019), "Objection," ch. 3-E, §7.4.2(2)(d), p. 285

ADD: STYLE OF THE CASE – FORM 1B:2
SIGNATURE BLOCK – FORM 1B:3
CERTIFICATE OF SERVICE – FORM 1B:13

ATTACH: AFFIDAVIT – FORM 1B:8, if necessary
ORDER – FORM 1G:1

NOTE: A party must file an objection to a motion for leave to designate a responsible third party within 15 days after the motion is served. Tex. Civ. Prac. & Rem. Code §33.004(f). If there is no timely objection to the motion for leave, the court must grant leave to designate the named person as a responsible third party. *Id.*; *e.g.*, ***In re Brokers Logistics, Ltd.***, 320 S.W.3d 402, 406 & n.4 (Tex.App.—El Paso 2010, orig. proceeding) (court granted motion because P filed objection after 15-day deadline).

If the trial court sustains the initial objection, it must give the defendant an opportunity to replead. *See* Tex. Civ. Prac. & Rem. Code §33.004(g)(2); ***In re Coppola***, 535 S.W.3d 506, 508 (Tex.2017); ***In re Oncor Elec. Delivery Co.***, 355 S.W.3d 304, 306 (Tex.App.—Dallas 2011, orig. proceeding). After the defendant has had an opportunity to replead, the objecting party must establish that the defendant still did not satisfy the pleading requirements of the Texas Rules of Civil Procedure. *See* Tex. Civ. Prac. & Rem. Code §33.004(g)(2). Only then can the court deny the motion for leave. *See id.*; ***In re Oncor Elec.***, 355 S.W.3d at 306.

If the court grants the motion for leave, a party may move to strike the designation of a named person as a responsible third party after an adequate time for discovery has passed. Tex. Civ. Prac. & Rem. Code §33.004(*l*). See FORM 3E:17.

If the trial date is reset, the motion for leave to designate must be filed at least 60 days before the new trial date. *See* ***In re Coppola***, 535 S.W.3d at 507-08.

PLAINTIFF'S MOTION TO JOIN RESPONSIBLE THIRD PARTY

Plaintiff, {❶ *name*}, asks the Court to join {❷ *{name of responsible third party}/ John Doe/Jane Doe*}, the responsible third party, as a defendant under Texas Civil Practice & Remedies Code section 33.004.

INTRODUCTION

1. Plaintiff, {❸ *name*}, sued defendant, {❹ *name*}, for {❺ *state basis of suit*}.

2. {❻ *State other relevant facts about the suit.*}

BACKGROUND

3. On {❼ *date*}, {❽ *{name of responsible third party}/John Doe/Jane Doe*} was designated as a responsible third party.

4. {❾ *State other facts relevant to the motion.*}

ARGUMENT & AUTHORITIES

5. A plaintiff may seek to join a responsible third party if the limitations period has not expired against the responsible third party and the request is made before the deadline for joinder set by the trial court. *See* Tex. R. Civ. P. 40(a). {*See* ***O'Connor's Texas Rules****, "Deadline," ch. 3-E, §7.4.2(4)(a), p. 286.*}

6. Joinder is proper in this case because the limitations period has not expired against {❿ *{name of responsible third party}/John Doe/Jane Doe*} and the deadline for joinder has not passed. {⓫ *Elaborate.*}

CONCLUSION

7. {⓬ *Briefly summarize the motion.*}

PRAYER

8. For these reasons, plaintiff asks the Court to grant plaintiff's motion to join the responsible third party as a defendant.

SEE: Tex. Civ. Prac. & Rem. Code §33.004
O'Connor's Texas Rules * Civil Trials (2019), "Plaintiff's joinder," ch. 3-E, §7.4.2(4), p. 286

ADD: STYLE OF THE CASE – FORM 1B:2
SIGNATURE BLOCK – FORM 1B:3
CERTIFICATE OF CONFERENCE – FORM 1B:12, if necessary
CERTIFICATE OF SERVICE – FORM 1B:13

ATTACH: AFFIDAVIT – FORM 1B:8, if necessary
NOTICE OF HEARING OR SUBMISSION – FORM 1E:1
ORDER – FORM 1G:1

NOTE: To properly join a defendant, a plaintiff must also file an amended petition adding the responsible third party as a defendant. *See* ***Valverde v. Biela's Glass & Aluminum Prods.***, 293 S.W.3d 751, 755 (Tex. App.—San Antonio 2009, pet. denied); ***Dilthey v. Ballenger Constr. Co.***, No. 13-09-00564-CV (Tex. App.—Corpus Christi 2011, no pet.) (memo op.; 2-10-11). It is unclear whether an amended petition must also be filed within the 60-day deadline when a timely motion to join the responsible third party has already been filed. To be safe, the plaintiff should file the amended petition within the 60-day deadline as well.

A plaintiff must join a responsible third party before the statute of limitations for the underlying cause of action expires; if the limitations period has expired, the plaintiff cannot join the responsible third party as a defendant. See ***O'Connor's Texas Rules***, "Deadline," ch. 3-E, §7.4.2(4)(a), p. 286.

PLAINTIFF'S MOTION TO STRIKE
THE DESIGNATION OF RESPONSIBLE THIRD PARTY

Plaintiff, {❶ *name*}, asks the Court to strike the designation of {❷ *{name of responsible third party}/John Doe/Jane Doe*} as a responsible third party under Texas Civil Practice & Remedies Code section 33.004.

INTRODUCTION

1. Plaintiff, {❸ *name*}, sued defendant, {❹ *name*}, for {❺ *state basis of suit*}.

2. {❻ *State other relevant facts about the suit.*}

BACKGROUND

3. On {❼ *date*}, defendant's motion for leave to designate {❽ *{name of responsible third party}/John Doe/Jane Doe*} a responsible third party was granted.

4. {❾ *State other facts relevant to the motion.*}

ARGUMENT & AUTHORITIES

5. A party may move to strike the designation of a responsible third party after an adequate time for discovery has passed if there is no evidence that the designated person is responsible for any part of plaintiff's injury or damage. Tex. Civ. Prac. & Rem. Code §33.004(*l*); *In re Coppola*, 535 S.W.3d 506, 508 (Tex. 2017). {*See* ***O'Connor's Texas Rules***, *"Motion to strike designation," ch. 3-E, §7.4.2(3), p. 286.*}

6. An adequate time for discovery has passed because {❿ *explain*}.

7. There is no evidence that {⓫ *{name of responsible third party}/John Doe/Jane Doe*} is responsible for any part of plaintiff's injury or damage.

{*CHOOSE APPROPRIATE PARAGRAPH 8*}

8. {⓬ *Name of responsible third party*} did not cause or contribute to the harm for which recovery of damages is sought by

{*CHOOSE APPROPRIATE REASON*}

Ⓐ a negligent act or omission. Tex. Civ. Prac. & Rem. Code §33.011(6). {⓭ *Elaborate.*}

Ⓑ a defective or unreasonably dangerous product. Tex. Civ. Prac. & Rem. Code §33.011(6). {⓮ *Elaborate.*}

Ⓒ {⓯ *identify other conduct or activity that defendant alleged violates an applicable legal standard*}. Tex. Civ. Prac. & Rem. Code §33.011(6). {⓰ *Elaborate.*}

8. {⓱ *John Doe/Jane Doe*} did not commit a criminal act that caused the loss or injury that is the subject of the lawsuit. Tex. Civ. Prac. & Rem. Code §33.004(j). {⓲ *Elaborate.*}

CONCLUSION

9. {⓳ *Briefly summarize the motion.*}

PRAYER

10. For these reasons, plaintiff asks the Court to strike the designation of the responsible third party.

SEE: Tex. Civ. Prac. & Rem. Code §33.004(*l*)
O'Connor's Texas Rules * Civil Trials (2019), "Motion to strike designation," ch. 3-E, §7.4.2(3), p. 286

ADD: STYLE OF THE CASE – FORM 1B:2
SIGNATURE BLOCK – FORM 1B:3
CERTIFICATE OF CONFERENCE – FORM 1B:12, if necessary
CERTIFICATE OF SERVICE – FORM 1B:13

ATTACH: AFFIDAVIT – FORM 1B:8, if necessary
NOTICE OF HEARING OR SUBMISSION – FORM 1E:1
ORDER – FORM 1G:1

DEFENDANT'S MOTION TO DISMISS FOR LACK OF JURISDICTION

Defendant, {❶ *name*}, asks the Court to dismiss plaintiff's suit for lack of jurisdiction.

INTRODUCTION

1. Plaintiff, {❷ *name*}, sued defendant, {❸ *name*}, for {❹ *state basis of suit*}.

2. {❺ *State other relevant facts about the suit.*}

BACKGROUND

3. Plaintiff {❻ *name*}'s petition alleges {❼ *state factual allegations relevant to jurisdiction*}.

4. {❽ *State other facts relevant to jurisdiction.*}

ARGUMENT & AUTHORITIES

5. The purpose of a plea to the jurisdiction is to dismiss a cause of action without regard to whether the claim has merit. *Bland Indep. Sch. Dist. v. Blue*, 34 S.W.3d 547, 554 (Tex. 2000).

6. The Court must decide whether plaintiff has affirmatively demonstrated this Court's jurisdiction to hear this suit, based on the facts alleged by plaintiff and, when necessary to resolve jurisdictional facts, on evidence submitted by the parties. *See Alamo Heights Indep. Sch. Dist. v. Clark*, 544 S.W.3d 755, 770-71 (Tex. 2018); *State v. Holland*, 221 S.W.3d 639, 642-43 (Tex. 2007); *Tex. Dep't of Parks & Wildlife v. Miranda*, 133 S.W.3d 217, 226-27 (Tex. 2004); *Bland Indep. Sch. Dist.*, 34 S.W.3d at 555; *see, e.g., State v. Sledge*, 36 S.W.3d 152, 155 (Tex. App.—Houston [1st Dist.] 2000, pet. denied) (trial court conducted hearing and received oral testimony, affidavits, exhibits, and a stipulation).

{*CHOOSE APPROPRIATE PARAGRAPHS 7-22*}

7. This Court does not have jurisdiction over this suit because there are no justiciable issues that the Court can resolve. Plaintiff's petition does not allege a real controversy between the parties that could be resolved by the judicial relief plaintiff seeks. *See, e.g., In re Nolo Press/Folk Law, Inc.*, 991 S.W.2d 768, 778 (Tex. 1999) (district court did not have authority to modify order of Supreme Court on the basis of policy reasons); *State Bar v. Gomez*, 891 S.W.2d 243, 245-46 (Tex. 1994) (district court did not have authority to compel State Bar or Supreme Court to implement mandatory pro bono program). {❾ *Elaborate.*} {*See* ***O'Connor's Texas Rules***, *"No justiciable issue," ch. 3-F, §3.1, p. 289.*}

FORM 3F:1

8. This Court does not have jurisdiction over this suit because plaintiff has no standing to bring the suit. *M.D. Anderson Cancer Ctr. v. Novak*, 52 S.W.3d 704, 710-11 (Tex. 2001); *see Vernco Constr., Inc. v. Nelson*, 460 S.W.3d 145, 149 (Tex. 2015). Because standing is a component of subject-matter jurisdiction, plaintiff's lack of standing deprives the Court of jurisdiction over the claims asserted in plaintiff's petition. *See Tex. Ass'n of Bus. v. Tex. Air Control Bd.*, 852 S.W.2d 440, 443 (Tex. 1993). {❿ *Elaborate.*} {*See **O'Connor's Texas Rules**, "No standing," ch. 3-F, §3.2, p. 289.*}

9. This Court does not have jurisdiction over this suit because the cause of action asserted by plaintiff is not ripe. A case is not ripe when a determination of whether the plaintiff has a concrete injury depends on contingent or hypothetical facts or on events that have not yet happened. *Waco Indep. Sch. Dist. v. Gibson*, 22 S.W.3d 849, 852 (Tex. 2000). {⓫ *Elaborate.*} {*See **O'Connor's Texas Rules**, "Not ripe," ch. 3-F, §3.3, p. 289.*}

10. This Court does not have jurisdiction over this suit because the cause of action asserted by plaintiff has become moot. *See Heckman v. Williamson Cty.*, 369 S.W.3d 137, 162 (Tex. 2012); *Hansen v. JP Morgan Chase Bank*, 346 S.W.3d 769, 773 (Tex. App.—Dallas 2011, no pet.). A case becomes moot if (1) a party seeks a judgment based on a controversy that no longer exists (i.e., the controversy is not "live") or (2) the parties have no legally cognizable interest in the outcome. *State v. Harper*, 562 S.W.3d 1, 6 (Tex. 2018); *Heckman*, 369 S.W.3d at 162. {⓬ *Explain why the case has become moot and negate any exceptions that would allow the court to decide the case even though it is moot.*} {*See **O'Connor's Texas Rules**, "Mootness," ch. 3-F, §3.4, p. 289.*}

11. This Court does not have jurisdiction over this suit because another court has exclusive jurisdiction over the suit. *See Jansen v. Fitzpatrick*, 14 S.W.3d 426, 430-31 (Tex. App.—Houston [14th Dist.] 2000, no pet.); *see, e.g., Geary v. Peavy*, 878 S.W.2d 602, 604-05 (Tex. 1994) (Minnesota court had jurisdiction over child-custody case). {⓭ *Elaborate.*} {*See **O'Connor's Texas Rules**, "Another court has exclusive jurisdiction," ch. 3-F, §3.5, p. 290.*}

12. This Court does not have jurisdiction over this suit because an administrative agency has exclusive jurisdiction over the dispute. *Oncor Elec. Delivery Co. v. Chaparral Energy, LLC*, 546 S.W.3d 133, 138 (Tex. 2018); *City of Hous. v. Rhule*, 417 S.W.3d 440, 442 (Tex. 2013); *In re Entergy Corp.*, 142 S.W.3d 316, 321-22 (Tex. 2004). When an agency's jurisdiction is exclusive, a plaintiff must exhaust all administrative remedies before seeking judicial review of a decision; until the plaintiff exhausts those remedies, a court lacks subject-matter jurisdiction, and a dismissal is mandatory. *Forest Oil Corp. v. El Rucio Land & Cattle Co.*, 518 S.W.3d 422, 428 (Tex. 2017); *Clint Indep. Sch. Dist. v. Marquez*, 487 S.W.3d 538, 544 (Tex. 2016); *Thomas v. Long*, 207 S.W.3d

◄ *Continued on next page* ►

334, 340 (Tex. 2006). {⓮ *Elaborate.*} {*See* ***O'Connor's Texas Rules****, "Administrative agency has exclusive jurisdiction," ch. 3-F, §3.6, p. 290.*}

13. This Court does not have jurisdiction over this suit because plaintiff has not demonstrated and cannot affirmatively demonstrate that this Court has jurisdiction to hear the suit under the Texas Tort Claims Act or any other statute waiving the government's immunity from suit. *See Sampson v. Univ. of Tex. at Austin*, 500 S.W.3d 380, 384 (Tex. 2016); *Suarez v. City of Tex. City*, 465 S.W.3d 623, 632-33 (Tex. 2015); *Tex. Dep't of Criminal Justice v. Miller*, 51 S.W.3d 583, 587 (Tex. 2001). Simply put, the Texas Legislature has not waived defendant's immunity from suit for this claim. Plaintiff's suit involves a claim against the {⓯ *identify governmental unit, e.g., State of Texas*} for damages arising from {⓰ *identify basis for suit*}. A governmental unit cannot be sued for damages unless the Legislature has waived that unit's immunity from suit for that specific claim. *Tex. Dep't of Transp. v. Jones*, 8 S.W.3d 636, 638 (Tex. 1999); *Fed. Sign v. Tex. S. Univ.*, 951 S.W.2d 401, 405 (Tex. 1997). Nothing in the Texas Tort Claims Act or any other statute or act of the Texas Legislature gives plaintiff the authority to file this suit against defendant. {⓱ *Elaborate.*} {*See* ***O'Connor's Texas Rules****, "Governmental immunity from suit," ch. 3-F, §3.7, p. 291;* ***O'Connor's Texas COA****, "Government immune from suit," ch. 24-A, §3.3.1(1), p. 911.*}

14. This Court does not have jurisdiction over this suit because plaintiff has not complied with the jurisdictional requirements in the statute on which the cause of action is based. *See City of DeSoto v. White*, 288 S.W.3d 389, 393 (Tex. 2009); *Sierra Club v. Tex. Nat. Res. Conservation Comm'n*, 26 S.W.3d 684, 688 (Tex. App.—Austin 2000), *aff'd*, 70 S.W.3d 809 (Tex. 2002). Statutory requirements are jurisdictional if the statute clearly identifies them as such or if the Legislature intended them to be so. *See Tex. Dep't of Protective & Regulatory Servs. v. Mega Child Care, Inc.*, 145 S.W.3d 170, 176-77 (Tex. 2004); *Subaru of Am., Inc. v. David McDavid Nissan, Inc.*, 84 S.W.3d 212, 220-21 (Tex. 2002); *Sierra Club*, 26 S.W.3d at 688. {⓲ *Elaborate.*} {*See* ***O'Connor's Texas Rules****, "Suits generally," ch. 3-F, §3.8.1, p. 291.*}

15. This Court does not have jurisdiction over this suit against {⓳ *identify governmental entity*} because plaintiff has not complied with the jurisdictional prerequisites in the statute on which the cause of action is based. *See* Tex. Gov't Code §311.034; *Prairie View A&M Univ. v. Chatha*, 381 S.W.3d 500, 511 (Tex. 2012). To be a statutory prerequisite and thus a jurisdictional requirement, the prerequisite must (1) appear in the statutory language, (2) be mandatory, and (3) have to be accomplished before suit is filed. *Prairie View A&M*, 381 S.W.3d at 511-12; *see* Tex. Gov't Code §311.034. {⓴ *Elaborate.*} {*See* ***O'Connor's Texas Rules****, "Statutory prerequisites," ch. 3-F, §3.8.2(1), p. 292.*}

FORM 3F:1

16. This Court does not have jurisdiction over this suit against {21 *identify governmental entity*} because the statutory elements of the cause of action asserted by plaintiff are jurisdictional and plaintiff has not complied with those elements. *See Mission Consol. Indep. Sch. Dist. v. Garcia*, 372 S.W.3d 629, 637 (Tex. 2012); *State v. Lueck*, 290 S.W.3d 876, 883-84 (Tex. 2009). {22 *Elaborate.*} {*See* ***O'Connor's Texas Rules****, "Statutory elements of a cause of action," ch. 3-F, §3.8.2(2), p. 292.*}

17. This Court does not have jurisdiction over this suit because the suit is preempted by federal law, requiring that the claim be tried in federal court. *See Southland Life Ins. Co. v. Estate of Small*, 806 S.W.2d 800, 801 (Tex. 1991) (ERISA). {23 *Elaborate.*} {*See* ***O'Connor's Texas Rules****, "Federal preemption," ch. 3-F, §3.9, p. 292.*}

18. This Court does not have jurisdiction over this suit because the cause of action alleged by plaintiff was extinguished by the death of {24 *name of decedent*}. *See, e.g., Whatley v. Bacon*, 649 S.W.2d 297, 299 (Tex. 1983) (when party to divorce suit dies before judgment is rendered, the suit should be dismissed); *Orr v. Int'l Bank of Commerce*, 649 S.W.2d 769, 772 (Tex. App.—San Antonio 1983, no writ) (suit for usury does not survive death of either party). {25 *Elaborate.*} {*See* ***O'Connor's Texas Rules****, "Death," ch. 3-F, §3.10, p. 292.*}

19. This Court does not have jurisdiction over this suit because plaintiff has fabricated jurisdiction by fraudulently alleging an amount in controversy to make it appear that the Court has jurisdiction. *See Miranda*, 133 S.W.3d at 224 & n.4; *Delk v. City of Dall.*, 560 S.W.2d 519, 520 (Tex. App.—Texarkana 1977, no writ). {26 *Elaborate.*} {*See* ***O'Connor's Texas Rules****, "Fabricated jurisdiction," ch. 3-F, §3.11, p. 293.*}

20. This Court does not have jurisdiction over this suit because plaintiff has asserted a controversy that clearly involves a religious or ecclesiastical matter. *See Westbrook v. Penley*, 231 S.W.3d 389, 394-95 (Tex. 2007); *Thiagarajan v. Tadepalli*, 430 S.W.3d 589, 593-94 (Tex. App.—Houston [14th Dist.] 2014, pet. denied); *Green v. United Pentecostal Church Int'l*, 899 S.W.2d 28, 30-31 (Tex. App.—Austin 1995, writ denied). Secular courts do not have jurisdiction over theological controversies and cannot constitutionally determine the truth or falsity of religious matters. *See Serbian E. Orthodox Diocese v. Milivojevich*, 426 U.S. 696, 713 (1976); *Masterson v. Diocese of Nw. Tex.*, 422 S.W.3d 594, 605-06 (Tex. 2013); *Tilton v. Marshall*, 925 S.W.2d 672, 678 (Tex. 1996). {27 *Elaborate.*} {*See* ***O'Connor's Texas Rules****, "Religious matters," ch. 3-F, §3.12, p. 293.*}

21. This Court does not have jurisdiction over this suit because plaintiff named an estate as the defendant without any reference to the personal representative. *See Henson v. Estate of Crow*, 734 S.W.2d 648, 649 (Tex. 1987); *Miller v. Estate of Self*, 113 S.W.3d

Continued on next page

FORM 3F:1

554, 556 (Tex. App.—Texarkana 2003, no pet.). The Court does not have jurisdiction if the personal representative has not been served with citation and has not participated in the suit. *See Miller*, 113 S.W.3d at 557. {㉘ *Elaborate.*} {*See **O'Connor's Texas Rules**, "Estate as defendant," ch. 3-F, §3.13, p. 293.*}

22. This Court does not have jurisdiction over this suit because plaintiff cannot establish a viable takings claim. *See Harris Cty. Flood Control Dist. v. Kerr*, 499 S.W.3d 793, 807 (Tex. 2016); *City of Hous. v. Carlson*, 451 S.W.3d 828, 830 (Tex. 2014). {㉙ *Elaborate.*} {*See **O'Connor's Texas Rules**, "No viable takings claim," ch. 3-F, §3.14, p. 293.*}

CONCLUSION

23. Because it is clear from plaintiff's pleadings and the evidence submitted with this motion that the Court does not have jurisdiction to hear plaintiff's cause of action, the Court should dismiss plaintiff's suit.

PRAYER

24. For these reasons, defendant asks the Court {㉚ *add if appropriate: to set this motion for a hearing and, after a hearing,*} to grant defendant's motion and dismiss plaintiff's suit for lack of subject-matter jurisdiction.

SEE: Tex. R. Civ. P. 85, 120a
O'Connor's Texas Rules * Civil Trials (2019), "Grounds," ch. 3-F, §3, p. 289
O'Connor's Texas Causes of Action (2019), "Government immune from suit," ch. 24-A, §3.3.1(1), p. 911

ADD: STYLE OF THE CASE – FORM 1B:2
SIGNATURE BLOCK – FORM 1B:3
CERTIFICATE OF SERVICE – FORM 1B:13

ATTACH: AFFIDAVIT – FORM 1B:8, if necessary
NOTICE OF HEARING OR SUBMISSION – FORM 1E:1
ORDER – FORM 1G:1

NOTE: A defendant may include an objection to jurisdiction in its original answer. If so, it should be labeled "Plea to the Jurisdiction." A plea to the jurisdiction filed as a separate motion is captioned "Motion to Dismiss for Lack of Jurisdiction." Subject-matter jurisdiction can also be challenged in another procedural instrument, such as a traditional motion for summary judgment. ***State v. Lueck***, 290 S.W.3d 876, 884 (Tex.2009); ***Bland ISD v. Blue***, 34 S.W.3d 547, 554 (Tex.2000); *see, e.g.*, ***City of Dallas v. Sanchez***, 494 S.W.3d 722, 725 (Tex.2016) (subject-matter jurisdiction challenged in motion to dismiss under Texas Rule of Civil Procedure 91a). See ***O'Connor's Texas Rules***, "Note," ch. 3-F, §2.1, p. 288.

If evidence is necessary to establish jurisdictional facts to show lack of jurisdiction, the defendant should attach affidavits and discovery and, if necessary, ask for a hearing to provide oral testimony. See ***O'Connor's Texas Rules***, "Necessary," ch. 3-F, §2.2.2, p. 288.

If the court lacks subject-matter jurisdiction over a claim, a defendant may be able to use a Texas Rule of Civil Procedure 91a motion, rather than a plea to the jurisdiction, to argue that the claim has no basis in law and thus should be dismissed. See FORM 3H:1; ***O'Connor's Texas Rules***, "Note," ch. 3-H, §2.4.3(1), p. 308.

PLAINTIFF'S RESPONSE TO DEFENDANT'S MOTION TO DISMISS FOR LACK OF JURISDICTION

Plaintiff, {❶ *name*}, asks the Court to deny defendant's motion to dismiss for lack of jurisdiction and retain plaintiff's suit on the Court's docket.

INTRODUCTION

1. Plaintiff, {❷ *name*}, sued defendant, {❸ *name*}, for {❹ *state basis of suit*}.

2. {❺ *State other relevant facts about the suit.*}

BACKGROUND

3. {❻ *State facts relevant to the response.*}

ARGUMENT & AUTHORITIES

4. When a defendant asks a court to dismiss a suit, the court must overrule the motion unless the pleadings and the parties' evidence clearly demonstrate that the court lacks jurisdiction. *See Sw. Bell Tel., L.P. v. Emmett*, 459 S.W.3d 578, 587-88 (Tex. 2015); *Heckman v. Williamson Cty.*, 369 S.W.3d 137, 150 (Tex. 2012); *Bland Indep. Sch. Dist. v. Blue*, 34 S.W.3d 547, 555 (Tex. 2000). In ruling on the motion, a court is required to construe the pleadings in the plaintiff's favor. *See Heckman*, 369 S.W.3d at 150; *Tex. Ass'n of Bus. v. Tex. Air Control Bd.*, 852 S.W.2d 440, 446 (Tex. 1993).

5. Defendant alleged in {❼ *his/her/its*} motion to dismiss that this Court did not have jurisdiction over this suit because {❽ *repeat defendant's allegations*}.

6. Defendant's arguments and factual allegations disputing jurisdiction are untrue. {❾ *State factual allegations controverting the arguments and facts alleged by defendant.*}

CONCLUSION

7. Because plaintiff's pleadings establish the Court's jurisdiction and defendant's factual allegations disputing jurisdiction are untrue, the Court should retain plaintiff's suit on the Court's docket.

PRAYER

8. For these reasons, plaintiff asks the Court to deny defendant's motion to dismiss for lack of jurisdiction and retain plaintiff's suit on the Court's docket.

SEE: ***O'Connor's Texas Rules * Civil Trials*** (2019), "Response," ch. 3-F, §4, p. 293

ADD: STYLE OF THE CASE – FORM 1B:2
SIGNATURE BLOCK – FORM 1B:3
CERTIFICATE OF SERVICE – FORM 1B:13

ATTACH: AFFIDAVIT – FORM 1B:8, if defendant attached affidavits to the motion to dismiss
ORDER – FORM 1G:1

NOTE: If the defendant's objection to jurisdiction is valid, the plaintiff should not oppose it. Instead, the plaintiff should take whatever steps are necessary to correct the jurisdictional defect. For example, the plaintiff should nonsuit the case and refile it in the proper court. If the jurisdictional defect can be cured by an amendment, the court will permit the plaintiff to amend. *See* ***Westbrook v. Penley***, 231 S.W.3d 389, 395 (Tex.2007). See ***O'Connor's Texas Rules***, "Opportunity to amend," ch. 3-F, §6.1.1, p. 295. For a discussion of refiling suit and tolling limitations, see ***O'Connor's Texas Rules***, "Dismissal & limitations," ch. 3-F, §6.2, p. 296.

If the plaintiff needs additional time to conduct discovery and gather evidence that supports the court's jurisdiction, the plaintiff should file a motion for continuance. *See* ***Patten v. Johnson***, 429 S.W.3d 767, 775 (Tex.App.—Dallas 2014, pet. denied). See FORM 5D:1; ***O'Connor's Texas Rules***, "Continuance for Additional Discovery," ch. 5-D, §8, p. 420.

{[1] *PARTY*}'S SPECIAL EXCEPTIONS TO
{[2] *ADVERSE PARTY*}'S {[3] *NAME OF PLEADING*}

{[4] *Party*}, {[5] *name*}, specially excepts to {[6] *adverse party*} {[7] *name*}'s {[8] *name of pleading*} and asks the Court to order {[9] *adverse party*} to replead and cure {[10] *his/her/its*} pleading defects.

SPECIAL EXCEPTIONS

{*CHOOSE APPROPRIATE PARAGRAPHS 1-23*}

1. Defendant specially excepts to plaintiff's original petition because plaintiff did not plead the discovery level for the case, as required by Texas Rule of Civil Procedure 190.1. {*See* ***O'Connor's Texas Rules****, "Failure to plead discovery level," ch. 3-G, §2.1.2, p. 299.*}

2. {[11] *Party*} specially excepts to paragraph {[12] *number*} because {[13] *adverse party*}'s pleading does not give fair notice of {[14] *adverse party*}'s {[15] *claim/defense*}. {[16] *Elaborate.*} {*See* ***O'Connor's Texas Rules****, "General allegations," ch. 3-G, §2.2.1, p. 299.*}

3. {[17] *Party*} specially excepts to paragraph {[18] *number*} because {[19] *adverse party*} did not plead all elements of {[20] *his/her/its*} {[21] *cause of action/defense*}. Specifically, the pleading for {[22] *identify claim or defense pleaded, e.g., fraud*} did not include the element of {[23] *identify omitted element*}. {*See* ***O'Connor's Texas Rules****, "Inadequate allegations," ch. 3-G, §2.2.2, p. 299.*}

4. {[24] *Party*} specially excepts to {[25] *adverse party*}'s pleading because {[26] *adverse party*} did not verify it. {*See* ***O'Connor's Texas Rules****, "Lack of verification," ch. 3-G, §2.1.1, p. 299.*}

5. {[27] *Party*} specially excepts to paragraph {[28] *number*} regarding the relief sought. {[29] *Party*} asks the Court to require {[30] *adverse party*} to specify the maximum amount that {[31] *adverse party*} claims. *See* Tex. R. Civ. P. 47. {*See* ***O'Connor's Texas Rules****, "Claims for relief," ch. 3-G, §2.2.5, p. 300.*}

6. {[32] *Party*} specially excepts to paragraph {[33] *number*} because {[34] *adverse party*}'s pleading did not state that {[35] *adverse party*} gave proper notice as required by {[36] *specify notice provision relied on, e.g., the DTPA*}.

7. {[37] *Party*} specially excepts to paragraph {[38] *number*} because {[39] *adverse party*}'s suit is precluded by law. {[40] *Explain, e.g., parents do not have a cause of action for negligence for injury to a fetus.*} {*See* ***O'Connor's Texas Rules****, "No viable cause of action," ch. 3-G, §2.2.3, p. 299.*}

8. {41 *Party*} specially excepts to paragraph {42 *number*} because the pleading incorporates by reference {43 *identify document or exhibit*}, which is prohibited by Texas Rule of Civil Procedure 59.

9. {44 *Party*} specially excepts to paragraph {45 *number*} because the pleading incorporates by reference {46 *identify document or exhibit*} from an earlier, superseded pleading. {47 *Elaborate.*} {*See* ***O'Connor's Texas Rules***, *"Improper incorporation by reference," ch. 3-G, §2.1.3, p. 299.*}

10. {48 *Party*} specially excepts to paragraph {49 *number*} because the pleading asks for attorney fees in a general allegation but does not specify which statute makes them available in this type of suit.

11. {50 *Party*} specially excepts to paragraph {51 *number*} because the Damages Act does not apply to suits brought under {52 *identify statute, e.g., the DTPA*}. {*See* ***O'Connor's Texas COA***, *"Damages Act does not apply," ch. 42-B, §3.2, p. 1429.*}

12. {53 *Party*} specially excepts to paragraph {54 *number*} because {55 *adverse party*}'s suit for {56 *identify type of suit, e.g., breach of contract*} does not provide a basis for exemplary damages. {*See* ***O'Connor's Texas COA***, *"Exemplary damages prohibited," ch. 42-A, §2.2, p. 1421.*}

13. {57 *Party*} specially excepts to paragraph {58 *number*} because a declaratory-judgment action seeking declaration of nonliability of a potential defendant is not a proper function of the Declaratory Judgments Act. *In re Houston Specialty Ins. Co.*, 569 S.W.3d 138, 140-41 (Tex. 2019); *Abor v. Black*, 695 S.W.2d 564, 566 (Tex. 1985), *overruled on other grounds*, *In re J.B. Hunt Transp., Inc.*, 492 S.W.3d 287 (Tex. 2016); *see also* Tex. Civ. Prac. & Rem. Code §37.001 et seq. (Declaratory Judgments Act). {59 *Adverse party*} filed a declaratory-judgment action asking the Court to declare that {60 *he/she/it*} is not liable for {61 *his/her/its*} past conduct. {62 *Elaborate.*} {*See* ***O'Connor's Texas Rules***, *"Potential tort liability," ch. 2-E, §2.2.2, p. 154.*}

14. {63 *Party*} specially excepts to paragraph {64 *number*} because a declaratory judgment is not available when there is no justiciable conflict. *Bonham State Bank v. Beadle*, 907 S.W.2d 465, 467 (Tex. 1995); *Di Portanova v. Monroe*, 229 S.W.3d 324, 329 (Tex. App.—Houston [1st Dist.] 2006, pet. denied). There is no justiciable conflict in this case. {65 *Elaborate.*} {*See* ***O'Connor's Texas Rules***, *"No justiciable conflict," ch. 2-E, §2.2.1, p. 153.*}

Continued on next page

15. {66 *Party*} specially excepts to paragraph {67 *number*} because a declaratory judgment is not available to resolve issues that are not yet mature and are subject to change. *Cal. Prods., Inc. v. Puretex Lemon Juice, Inc.*, 334 S.W.2d 780, 782-83 (Tex. 1960). The issues in this case are not yet mature and are subject to change. {68 *Elaborate.*} {*See **O'Connor's Texas Rules**, "Future controversy," ch. 2-E, §2.2.3, p. 154.*}

16. {69 *Party*} specially excepts to paragraph {70 *number*} because a declaratory judgment is not available to resolve an issue when another action is pending that will adjudicate the same issue between the same parties. *Tex. Liquor Control Bd. v. Canyon Creek Land Corp.*, 456 S.W.2d 891, 895 (Tex. 1970). The issues in this case are the same as the issues in {71 *identify the cause number, style, and court of the other case*}. {*See **O'Connor's Texas Rules**, "In another court," ch. 2-E, §2.2.4, p. 154.*}

17. {72 *Party*} specially excepts to paragraph {73 *number*} because a declaratory judgment is not available to resolve issues that are already pending before the same court. *BHP Petroleum Co. v. Millard*, 800 S.W.2d 838, 841 (Tex. 1990). The issues in this case are already the subject of a lawsuit pending in this Court under cause number {74 *number*}, in the case styled {75 *identify case*}. {*See **O'Connor's Texas Rules**, "In same suit," ch. 2-E, §2.2.5, p. 154.*}

18. {76 *Party*} specially excepts to paragraph {77 *number*} because a declaratory judgment is not available if a court does not have jurisdiction over the underlying cause of action. *Chenault v. Phillips*, 914 S.W.2d 140, 141 (Tex. 1996); *see Sw. Airlines Co. v. Tex. High-Speed Rail Auth.*, 863 S.W.2d 123, 125-26 (Tex. App.—Austin 1993, writ denied). The Court does not have jurisdiction over the underlying cause of action because {78 *explain*}. {*See **O'Connor's Texas Rules**, "No jurisdiction over underlying dispute," ch. 2-E, §2.2.6, p. 154.*}

19. {79 *Party*} specially excepts to paragraph {80 *number*} because a declaratory judgment is not available to seek a judicial interpretation of an earlier judgment. *Martin v. Dosohs I, Ltd., Inc.*, 2 S.W.3d 350, 353 (Tex. App.—San Antonio 1999, pet. denied). {81 *Adverse party*} seeks a judicial interpretation of {82 *identify earlier judgment*}. {83 *Elaborate.*} {*See **O'Connor's Texas Rules**, "Earlier judgment," ch. 2-E, §2.2.7, p. 154.*}

20. {84 *Party*} specially excepts to paragraph {85 *number*} because a declaratory judgment is not available to determine the rights, status, or other legal relationships arising under a penal statute. *See State v. Morales*, 869 S.W.2d 941, 947 (Tex. 1994). {86 *Adverse party*} seeks to determine the rights, status, or other legal relationships arising under {87 *identify penal statute*}. {88 *Elaborate.*} {*See **O'Connor's Texas Rules**, "Criminal issue," ch. 2-E, §2.2.8, p. 154.*}

21. {89 *Party*} specially excepts to paragraph {90 *number*} because a declaratory judgment cannot be used against the government or a government official to establish the validity of a contract, enforce the performance of a contract, or impose contractual liability. *Tex. Nat. Res. Conservation Comm'n v. IT-Davy*, 74 S.W.3d 849, 855-56 (Tex. 2002) (plurality op.); *Tex. S. Univ. v. State St. Bank & Tr. Co.*, 212 S.W.3d 893, 903 (Tex. App.—Houston [1st Dist.] 2007, pet. denied). {91 *Adverse party*} seeks to circumvent {92 *identify governmental unit or official*}'s sovereign immunity by mischaracterizing this suit, which seeks to impose liability, as a suit to determine rights. {93 *Elaborate.*} {*See **O'Connor's Texas COA**, "Declaratory judgment & immunity," ch. 24-B, §6.1, p. 925.*}

22. {94 *Party*} specially excepts to paragraph {95 *number*} because a declaratory judgment cannot be used to determine the rights of the parties under a contract when a contractual dispute with the government must be submitted to an administrative procedure. *See Tex. Dep't of Transp. v. Jones Bros. Dirt & Paving Contractors, Inc.*, 92 S.W.3d 477, 484-85 (Tex. 2002). {96 *Adverse party*} seeks to determine the rights of {97 *identify parties to contract*} under {98 *identify contract*}. {99 *Elaborate.*} {*See **O'Connor's Texas Rules**, "Suit against the government," ch. 2-E, §2.2.9, p. 154.*}

23. {100 *Party*} specially excepts to paragraph {101 *number*} because {102 *adverse party*} did not {103 *identify defect in form or substance of pleading*}. {*See **O'Connor's Texas Rules**, "Types of Pleading Defects to Challenge by Special Exceptions," ch. 3-G, §2, p. 299.*}

PRAYER

24. For these reasons, {104 *party*} asks the Court to set {105 *his/her/its*} special exceptions for hearing and, after the hearing, sustain {106 *his/her/its*} special exceptions and order {107 *adverse party*} to replead and cure {108 *his/her/its*} pleading defects and, if {109 *adverse party*} does not cure {110 *his/her/its*} defects, strike the defective portions of {111 *adverse party*}'s pleading.

SEE: Tex. R. Civ. P. 47, 90, 91
O'Connor's Texas Rules * Civil Trials (2019), "When not available," ch. 2-E, §2.2, p. 153; "Special Exceptions—Challenging the Pleadings," ch. 3-G, p. 298
O'Connor's Texas Causes of Action (2019), "Damages Act does not apply," ch. 42-B, §3.2, p. 1429

ADD: STYLE OF THE CASE – FORM 1B:2
SIGNATURE BLOCK – FORM 1B:3
CERTIFICATE OF SERVICE – FORM 1B:13

◄ *Continued on next page* ►

ATTACH: NOTICE OF HEARING OR SUBMISSION – FORM 1E:1
ORDER – FORM 3G:2

NOTE: If the special exceptions are valid, the party whose pleadings were challenged should agree to replead to cure the defects. If the special exceptions are not valid, the party should file a response stating why the exceptions should be denied.

Special exceptions may be filed by either party but are generally filed by the defendant. See ***O'Connor's Texas Rules***, "Grounds," ch. 3-G, §5, p. 301.

ORDER ON {❶ *PARTY*}'S SPECIAL EXCEPTIONS

After considering {❷ *party*} {❸ *name*}'s special exceptions to {❹ *name of pleading*}, the response, the pleadings, and arguments of counsel, the Court makes the following rulings on exceptions that have not been agreed to by the parties:

1. {❺ *Party*} specially excepts to paragraph {❻ *number*} because {❼ *repeat text of special exception*}.

____________ SUSTAINED   ____________ OVERRULED

2. {❽ *Party*} specially excepts to paragraph {❾ *number*} because {❿ *repeat text of special exception*}.

____________ SUSTAINED   ____________ OVERRULED

{*Continue until all special exceptions are covered.*}

The Court orders {⓫ *adverse party*} to replead and cure the defects identified by the special exceptions that were sustained. If {⓬ *adverse party*} does not replead and cure the defects by __________, 20___, the Court will strike each defective paragraph.

SIGNED on _______________, 20___.

____
PRESIDING JUDGE

SEE: Tex. R. Civ. P. 47, 90, 91
***O'Connor's Texas Rules * Civil Trials* (2019), "Ruling," ch. 3-G, §9, p. 303**

ADD: **STYLE OF THE CASE – FORM 1B:2**
CERTIFICATE OF SERVICE – FORM 1B:13, if proposed order served separately from motion or response

DEFENDANT'S MOTION TO DISMISS BASELESS CAUSE OF ACTION

Defendant, {❶ *name*}, asks the Court to dismiss plaintiff {❷ *name*}'s cause of action that has no basis in {❸ *law/fact/law or fact*}. {*See* ***O'Connor's Texas Rules****, "Motion to Dismiss—Baseless Cause of Action," ch. 3-H, p. 307.*}

INTRODUCTION

1. Plaintiff, {❹ *name*}, sued defendant, {❺ *name*}, for {❻ *state basis of suit*}.

2. {❼ *State other relevant facts about the suit.*}

BACKGROUND

3. On {❽ *date*}, plaintiff served defendant with {❾ *identify pleading, e.g., an original petition*} containing a cause of action for {❿ *identify cause of action*}.

4. {⓫ *State other facts relevant to the motion.*}

ARGUMENT & AUTHORITIES

5. Defendant files this motion to dismiss plaintiff's cause of action under the authority of Texas Rule of Civil Procedure 91a. Tex. R. Civ. P. 91a.1, 91a.2. Under Rule 91a, the Court can dismiss a cause of action that has no basis in law or fact. Tex. R. Civ. P. 91a.1.

{*CHOOSE APPROPRIATE PARAGRAPHS 6-7*}

6. The Court should dismiss plaintiff's cause of action because it has no basis in law. Tex. R. Civ. P. 91a.1, 91a.2. A cause of action has no basis in law if the allegations, taken as true, together with inferences reasonably drawn from them, do not entitle the plaintiff to the relief sought. Tex. R. Civ. P. 91a.1; *Stallworth v. Ayers*, 510 S.W.3d 187, 189-90 (Tex. App.—Houston [1st Dist.] 2016, no pet.); *see In re Essex Ins. Co.*, 450 S.W.3d 524, 527-28 (Tex. 2014). Plaintiff's suit for {⓬ *identify cause of action*} has no basis in law because {⓭ *explain*}.

7. The Court should dismiss plaintiff's cause of action because it has no basis in fact. Tex. R. Civ. P. 91a.1, 91a.2. A cause of action has no basis in fact if no reasonable person could believe the facts pleaded. Tex. R. Civ. P. 91a.1. Plaintiff's suit for {⓮ *identify cause of action*} has no basis in fact because {⓯ *explain*}.

{*ADD PARAGRAPHS 8-9 IF APPLICABLE*}

ATTORNEY FEES & COSTS

8. Under Rule 91a, the prevailing party on a motion to dismiss must be awarded reasonable and necessary attorney fees and all costs incurred as a result of plaintiff's

FORM 3H:1

cause of action. *See* Tex. R. Civ. P. 91a.7. Therefore, if the Court grants defendant's motion to dismiss, either in whole or in part, defendant asks the Court to award defendant reasonable and necessary attorney fees and all costs incurred as a result of {⑯ *explain, e.g., preparing this motion to dismiss*}. *See id.* {*See* ***O'Connor's Texas Rules****, "Award of attorney fees & costs," ch. 3-H, §7.2, p. 311.*}

9. The reasonable and necessary attorney fees and all costs incurred are ${⑰ *amount*}, which are established by the affidavit of {⑱ *name of attorney*}, attached as Exhibit {⑲ *letter*}.

CONCLUSION

10. {⑳ *Briefly summarize the motion.*}

PRAYER

11. For these reasons, defendant asks the Court to set this motion for hearing and, after the hearing, grant this motion and sign an order dismissing the challenged cause of action and awarding defendant reasonable and necessary attorney fees and all costs.

SEE: Tex. R. Civ. P. 91a
O'Connor's Texas Rules * Civil Trials (2019), "Motion," ch. 3-H, §2, p. 307

ADD: STYLE OF THE CASE – FORM 1B:2
SIGNATURE BLOCK – FORM 1B:3
CERTIFICATE OF SERVICE – FORM 1B:13

ATTACH: AFFIDAVIT – FORM 1B:8, if necessary
NOTICE OF HEARING OR SUBMISSION – FORM 1E:1
AFFIDAVIT FOR ATTORNEY FEES – FORM 1H:14, if necessary
ORDER – FORM 3H:4

NOTE: A motion to dismiss a baseless cause of action must be filed within 60 days after the defendant is served with the first pleading containing the challenged cause of action. Tex. R. Civ. P. 91a.3(a).

The court must conduct a hearing on the motion to dismiss. Tex. R. Civ. P. 91a.6 & cmt. The court can hold an oral hearing or base its ruling on the written submission from the parties. *See* Tex. R. Civ. P. 91a.6 & cmt.; ***In re Butt***, 495 S.W.3d 455, 461 (Tex.App.—Corpus Christi 2016, orig. proceeding); ***Wooley v. Schaffer***, 447 S.W.3d 71, 74 (Tex.App.—Houston [14th Dist.] 2014, pet. denied). The defendant should request that the motion to dismiss be set for hearing or submission as early as possible, but the motion cannot be set for hearing or submission any earlier than 21 days after it is filed. *See* Tex. R. Civ. P. 91a.3(b), (c). The parties must receive notice of the hearing at least 14 days before the hearing date. Tex. R. Civ. P. 91a.6.

Continued on next page

The defendant should not attach any affidavits, evidence, or other extrinsic materials to the motion, except to support a request for attorney fees and costs. *See* Tex. R. Civ. P. 91a.6, 91a.7; ***In re Butt***, 495 S.W.3d at 461; ***Drake v. Chase Bank***, No. 02-13-00340-CV (Tex.App.—Fort Worth 2014, no pet.) (memo op.; 11-20-14).

Reasonable and necessary attorney fees and all costs must be awarded to the prevailing party on the motion to dismiss. Tex. Civ. Prac. & Rem. Code §30.021; Tex. R. Civ. P. 91a.7. When a plaintiff timely nonsuits its claims, the defendant who filed the motion to dismiss is not considered a prevailing party and is not entitled to an award of attorney fees and costs. ***Thuesen v. Amerisure Ins.***, 487 S.W.3d 291, 301 (Tex.App.—Houston [14th Dist.] 2016, no pet.). See ***O'Connor's Texas Rules***, "Award of attorney fees & costs," ch. 3-H, §7.2, p. 311.

Attorney fees and costs cannot be awarded if the action was brought by or against the State, a governmental entity, or a public official acting in her official capacity or under color of law. Tex. Civ. Prac. & Rem. Code §30.021; Tex. R. Civ. P. 91a.7.

A motion to dismiss a cause of action that has no basis in law or fact cannot be brought in a suit under the Family Code or a suit governed by Texas Civil Practice & Remedies Code chapter 14. Tex. R. Civ. P. 91a.1.

PLAINTIFF'S RESPONSE TO DEFENDANT'S
MOTION TO DISMISS BASELESS CAUSE OF ACTION

Plaintiff, {❶ *name*}, asks the Court to deny defendant {❷ *name*}'s motion to dismiss plaintiff's cause of action.

INTRODUCTION

1. Plaintiff, {❸ *name*}, sued defendant, {❹ *name*}, for {❺ *state basis of suit*}.

2. {❻ *State other relevant facts about the suit.*}

BACKGROUND

3. On {❼ *date*}, plaintiff served defendant with {❽ *identify pleading, e.g., an original petition*} containing a cause of action for {❾ *identify cause of action*}.

4. On {❿ *date*}, defendant filed a motion to dismiss plaintiff's cause of action for having no basis in {⓫ *law/fact/law or fact*}.

5. The motion to dismiss will be heard on {⓬ *date*}.

6. {⓭ *State other facts relevant to the response.*}

ARGUMENT & AUTHORITIES

7. Under Texas Rule of Civil Procedure 91a, the Court can dismiss a cause of action that has no basis in law or fact; however, this is not a case in which the Court should do so. *See* Tex. R. Civ. P. 91a.1, 91a.2.

{*CHOOSE APPROPRIATE SECTIONS A-B*}

A. Motion untimely.

8. A motion to dismiss a cause of action that has no basis in law or fact must be filed within 60 days after the defendant is served with the first pleading containing the challenged cause of action. Tex. R. Civ. P. 91a.3(a). In this case, defendant was served on {⓮ *date*}, and the motion to dismiss was filed on {⓯ *date*}. Defendant's motion was not timely filed and therefore should be denied.

◄ *Continued on next page* ►

B. Basis in law or fact.

9. Under Rule 91a, the Court can dismiss a cause of action if it has no basis in law or fact. Tex. R. Civ. P. 91a.1. A cause of action has no basis in law if the allegations, taken as true, together with inferences reasonably drawn from them, do not entitle the plaintiff to the relief sought. *Id.* A cause of action has no basis in fact if no reasonable person could believe the facts pleaded. *Id.*

10. The Court should not dismiss plaintiff's suit for {[16] *identify cause of action*} because it has a valid basis in law. {[17] *Elaborate.*}

11. The Court should not dismiss plaintiff's suit for {[18] *identify cause of action*} because it has a valid basis in fact. {[19] *Elaborate.*}

{*ADD PARAGRAPHS 12-13 IF APPLICABLE*}

ATTORNEY FEES & COSTS

12. Under Rule 91a, the prevailing party on a motion to dismiss must be awarded reasonable and necessary attorney fees and all costs incurred as a result of defendant's motion to dismiss. *See* Tex. R. Civ. P. 91a.7. Therefore, if the Court denies defendant's motion to dismiss, either in whole or in part, the Court must award plaintiff reasonable and necessary attorney fees and all costs incurred as a result of {[20] *explain, e.g., responding to the motion to dismiss*}. *See id.* {*See* ***O'Connor's Texas Rules****, "Award of attorney fees & costs," ch. 3-H, §7.2, p. 311.*}

13. The reasonable and necessary attorney fees and all costs incurred are ${[21] *amount*}, which are established by the affidavit of {[22] *name of attorney*}, attached as Exhibit {[23] *letter*}.

CONCLUSION

14. {[24] *Briefly summarize the response.*}

PRAYER

15. For these reasons, plaintiff asks the Court to deny defendant's motion to dismiss and award plaintiff reasonable and necessary attorney fees and all costs.

FORM 3H:2 RESPONSE TO MOTION TO DISMISS BASELESS CAUSE OF ACTION

SEE: Tex. R. Civ. P. 91a
*O'Connor's Texas Rules * Civil Trials* (2019), "Response," ch. 3-H, §3, p. 309

ADD: STYLE OF THE CASE – FORM 1B:2
SIGNATURE BLOCK – FORM 1B:3
CERTIFICATE OF SERVICE – FORM 1B:13

ATTACH: AFFIDAVIT – FORM 1B:8, if necessary
AFFIDAVIT FOR ATTORNEY FEES – FORM 1H:14, if necessary
ORDER – FORM 3H:4

NOTE: If the plaintiff chooses to respond to the motion to dismiss, the response must be filed at least seven days before the hearing date. Tex. R. Civ. P. 91a.4.

The plaintiff can file an amended pleading in addition to or instead of a response. *See* Tex. R. Civ. P. 91a.5(b); ***In re Estate of Savana***, 529 S.W.3d 587, 592 (Tex.App.—Houston [14th Dist.] 2017, no pet.). See ***O'Connor's Texas Rules***, "Amend pleading," ch. 3-H, §3.2, p. 309. The plaintiff can also nonsuit the challenged cause of action. ***In re Estate of Savana***, 529 S.W.3d at 592; *see* Tex. R. Civ. P. 91a.5(a). See ***O'Connor's Texas Rules***, "Take nonsuit," ch. 3-H, §3.3, p. 310.

Reasonable and necessary attorney fees and all costs must be awarded to the prevailing party on the motion to dismiss. Tex. Civ. Prac. & Rem. Code §30.021; Tex. R. Civ. P. 91a.7. When a plaintiff timely nonsuits its claims, the defendant who filed the motion to dismiss is not considered a prevailing party and is not entitled to an award of attorney fees and costs. ***Thuesen v. Amerisure Ins.***, 487 S.W.3d 291, 301 (Tex.App.—Houston [14th Dist.] 2016, no pet.). See ***O'Connor's Texas Rules***, "Award of attorney fees & costs," ch. 3-H, §7.2, p. 311.

Attorney fees and costs cannot be awarded if the action was brought by or against the State, a governmental entity, or a public official acting in her official capacity or under color of law. Tex. Civ. Prac. & Rem. Code §30.021; Tex. R. Civ. P. 91a.7.

A motion to dismiss a cause of action that has no basis in law or fact cannot be brought in a suit under the Family Code or governed by Texas Civil Practice & Remedies Code chapter 14. Tex. R. Civ. P. 91a.1.

{[1] *DEFENDANT'S/AGREED*} MOTION TO WITHDRAW
DEFENDANT'S MOTION TO DISMISS BASELESS CAUSE OF ACTION

{*CHOOSE APPROPRIATE INTRODUCTORY PARAGRAPH*}

Defendant, {[2] *name*}, asks the Court to withdraw {[3] *his/her/its*} motion to dismiss plaintiff's cause of action.

Plaintiff, {[4] *name*}, and defendant, {[5] *name*}, ask the Court to withdraw defendant's motion to dismiss plaintiff's cause of action.

INTRODUCTION

1. Plaintiff, {[6] *name*}, sued defendant, {[7] *name*} for {[8] *state basis of suit*}.

2. {[9] *State other relevant facts about the suit.*}

BACKGROUND

3. On {[10] *date*}, plaintiff served defendant with {[11] *identify pleading, e.g., an original petition*} containing a cause of action for {[12] *identify cause of action*}.

4. On {[13] *date*}, defendant filed a motion to dismiss plaintiff's cause of action for having no basis in {[14] *law/fact/law or fact*}. The motion is attached as Exhibit {[15] *letter*}.

{*CHOOSE APPROPRIATE PARAGRAPHS 5-6*}

5. On {[16] *date*}, plaintiff filed a response to defendant's motion to dismiss.

6. On {[17] *date*}, plaintiff filed an amended pleading in response to defendant's motion to dismiss. In the amended pleading, plaintiff alleged {[18] *identify changes to cause of action from original pleading*}.

7. The motion to dismiss will be heard on {[19] *date*}.

8. {[20] *State other facts relevant to the motion.*}

{*ADD SECTION BELOW IF MOTION IS AGREED*}

AGREEMENT

9. The parties agree to the withdrawal of defendant's motion to dismiss plaintiff's suit for {[21] *identify cause of action*}. *See* Tex. R. Civ. P. 91a.5(c).

10. Attorneys for all parties agree to the withdrawal and have signed the agreed motion.

{*ADD SECTION BELOW IF MOTION IS NOT AGREED*}

ARGUMENT & AUTHORITIES

{*CHOOSE APPROPRIATE PARAGRAPHS 11-12*}

{*No amended pleading filed*}

11. A defendant can withdraw a motion to dismiss if {❷❷ *he/she/it*} does so at least three days before the hearing date. Tex. R. Civ. P. 91a.5(a).

12. Defendant withdraws this motion to dismiss on {❷❸ *date*}, which is at least three days before the hearing date. {❷❹ *Elaborate.*}

{*Amended pleading filed*}

11. A defendant can withdraw a motion to dismiss anytime before the hearing date if the plaintiff amends the challenged cause of action. Tex. R. Civ. P. 91a.5(b).

12. Defendant withdraws this motion on {❷❺ *date*}, which is before the hearing date. {❷❻ *Elaborate.*}

CONCLUSION

13. {❷❼ *Briefly summarize the motion.*}

PRAYER

14. For these reasons, {❷❽ *defendant/the parties*} {❷❾ *asks/ask*} the Court to grant this motion to withdraw defendant's motion to dismiss plaintiff's cause of action.

SEE: Tex. R. Civ. P. 91a
O'Connor's Texas Rules * Civil Trials (2019), "Reply," ch. 3-H, §4, p. 310

ADD: STYLE OF THE CASE – FORM 1B:2
SIGNATURE BLOCK – FORM 1B:3, if motion is not agreed
SIGNATURE BLOCK FOR AGREED MOTIONS – FORM 1B:4, if motion is agreed
CERTIFICATE OF SERVICE – FORM 1B:13

ATTACH: ORDER – FORM 1G:1
MOTION TO DISMISS BASELESS CAUSE OF ACTION – FORM 3H:1

Continued on next page

NOTE: If the plaintiff filed a response to the motion but did not file an amended pleading, the defendant can either withdraw the motion or let the court rule on it. *See* Tex. R. Civ. P. 91a.3(c), 91a.5(a), (c). The motion to withdraw must be filed at least three days before the hearing date. Tex. R. Civ. P. 91a.5(a). See ***O'Connor's Texas Rules***, "No amended pleading," ch. 3-H, §4.1, p. 310.

If the plaintiff amends the challenged cause of action, the defendant can (1) withdraw the motion to dismiss, (2) let the court rule on it, or (3) amend the motion. *See* Tex. R. Civ. P. 91a.5(b); ***Drake v. Walker***, No. 05-14-00355-CV (Tex.App.—Dallas 2015, no pet.) (memo op.; 5-8-15). The motion can be withdrawn anytime before the hearing date. Tex. R. Civ. P. 91a.5(b). If the defendant amends the motion, all time periods in Texas Rule of Civil Procedure 91a are reset. Tex. R. Civ. P. 91a.5(d). See ***O'Connor's Texas Rules***, "Amended pleading," ch. 3-H, §4.2, p. 310.

ORDER ON DEFENDANT'S MOTION
TO DISMISS BASELESS CAUSE OF ACTION

After considering defendant {❶ *name*}'s motion to dismiss under Texas Rule of Civil Procedure 91a, the response, and arguments of counsel, the Court

{*CHOOSE APPROPRIATE ORDER*}

DENIES the motion and orders that plaintiff's suit for {❷ *identify cause of action*} is retained on the Court's docket.

GRANTS the motion and orders that plaintiff's suit for {❸ *identify cause of action*} is dismissed {❹ *in whole/in part*}. {❺ *Elaborate.*}

{*ADD PARAGRAPH BELOW IF APPROPRIATE*}

Accordingly, the Court orders that {❻ *plaintiff/defendant*} is awarded the following reasonable and necessary attorney fees and costs: {❼ *list attorney fees and costs*}.

SIGNED on ____________, 20___.

____
PRESIDING JUDGE

SEE: Tex. R. Civ. P. 91a
O'Connor's Texas Rules * Civil Trials (2019), "Order," ch. 3-H, §7, p. 311

ADD: STYLE OF THE CASE – FORM 1B:2
CERTIFICATE OF SERVICE – FORM 1B:13, if proposed order served separately from motion or response

NOTE: The court must issue a ruling within 45 days after the motion is filed. Gov't Code §22.004(g); Tex. R. Civ. P. 91a.3(c) & cmt. There is not, however, any statutory consequence (e.g., denial by operation of law) for noncompliance with the deadline, and the court is not divested of its jurisdiction to issue a ruling after the deadline passes. See ***O'Connor's Texas Rules***, "Deadline – generally," ch. 3-H, §6.2.1, p. 311. In making a ruling, the court cannot consider any extrinsic evidence except when determining the amount of attorney fees and costs. *See* Tex. R. Civ. P. 91a.6, 91a.7. See ***O'Connor's Texas Rules***, "Matter considered," ch. 3-H, §6.1, p. 310.

Reasonable and necessary attorney fees and all costs must be awarded to the prevailing party on the motion to dismiss. Tex. Civ. Prac. & Rem. Code §30.021; Tex. R. Civ. P. 91a.7. When a plaintiff timely nonsuits its claims, the defendant who filed the motion to dismiss is not considered a prevailing party and is not entitled to an award of attorney fees and costs. ***Thuesen v. Amerisure Ins.***, 487 S.W.3d 291, 301 (Tex.App.—Houston [14th Dist.] 2016, no pet.). See ***O'Connor's Texas Rules***, "Award of attorney fees & costs," ch. 3-H, §7.2, p. 311.

Attorney fees and costs cannot be awarded if the action was brought by or against the State, a governmental entity, or a public official acting in her official capacity or under color of law. Tex. Civ. Prac. & Rem. Code §30.021; Tex. R. Civ. P. 91a.7.

FORM 3H:4

DEFENDANT'S PLEA IN ABATEMENT

Defendant, {❶ *name*}, asks the Court to abate these proceedings.

INTRODUCTION

1. Plaintiff, {❷ *name*}, sued defendant, {❸ *name*}, for {❹ *state basis of suit*}.

2. {❺ *State other relevant facts about the suit.*}

BACKGROUND

3. {❻ *State facts relevant to the motion.*}

ARGUMENT & AUTHORITIES

{*CHOOSE APPROPRIATE PARAGRAPHS 4-15*}

4. Plaintiff {❼ *name*}, who is {❽ *age*}, is a minor whose disability has not been removed. As a minor, plaintiff {❾ *name*} cannot bring this action on {❿ *his/her*} own behalf. *See Sax v. Votteler*, 648 S.W.2d 661, 666 (Tex. 1983). {⓫ *Elaborate.*} {*See* ***O'Connor's Texas Rules****, "Minor or incapacitated person," ch. 3-I, §3.1.1(1), p. 315.*}

5. Plaintiff {⓬ *name*} is not the proper party to represent the estate of the decedent on whose behalf {⓭ *he/she/it*} sues. The estate's legal representative is the only proper party who may represent the estate. *Glover v. Landes*, 530 S.W.2d 910, 911 (Tex. App.—Houston [1st Dist.] 1975, writ ref'd n.r.e.); *see Coakley v. Reising*, 436 S.W.2d 315, 317 (Tex. 1968). Plaintiff is not the legal representative of decedent's estate and therefore cannot represent the estate. {*See* ***O'Connor's Texas Rules****, "Estate of decedent," ch. 3-I, §3.1.1(2), p. 315.*}

6. Plaintiff {⓮ *name*} does not have standing to prosecute this suit under the Texas Survival Statute. Plaintiff is not the heir or legal representative of the estate of the decedent. *See* Tex. Civ. Prac. & Rem. Code §71.021(b). {⓯ *Elaborate.*} {*See* ***O'Connor's Texas Rules****, "Death-action beneficiary," ch. 3-I, §3.1.1(3), p. 315;* ***O'Connor's Texas COA****, "Legal representative of estate," ch. 7-A, §2.1.2, p. 187.*}

7. Plaintiff {⓰ *name*} does not have standing to prosecute this suit under the Texas Wrongful Death Act. Plaintiff is not the surviving spouse, parent, or child of the decedent or the executor or administrator of the estate of the decedent. *See* Tex. Civ. Prac. & Rem. Code §71.004. {⓱ *Elaborate.*} {*See* ***O'Connor's Texas Rules****, "Death-action beneficiary," ch. 3-I, §3.1.1(3), p. 315;* ***O'Connor's Texas COA****, "Executor or administrator," ch. 7-B, §2.1.3, p. 198.*}

FORM 31:1

8. Plaintiff {[18] *name*} lacks standing to sue because {[19] *state reason for lack of standing, e.g., plaintiff is a stockholder suing for damages to a corporation*}. {[20] *Elaborate.*} {*See* ***O'Connor's Texas Rules****, "Wrong representative of corporation," ch. 3-I, §3.1.1(4), p. 315.*}

9. Plaintiff {[21] *name*} is not a {[22] *corporation/partnership*} as plaintiff alleged. {[23] *Elaborate.*} *See* Tex. R. Civ. P. 52, 93(5), 93(6); *Lighthouse Church of Cloverleaf v. Tex. Bank*, 889 S.W.2d 595, 600 (Tex. App.—Houston [14th Dist.] 1994, writ denied). {*See* ***O'Connor's Texas Rules****, "Not corporation or partnership," ch. 3-I, §3.1.1(5), p. 315.*}

10. Plaintiff {[24] *name*} is a foreign corporation doing business in Texas but has not registered with the Secretary of State. Therefore, plaintiff cannot maintain an action for affirmative relief. *See* Tex. Bus. Orgs. Code §9.051; *Jay-Lor Textiles, Inc. v. Pac. Compress Warehouse Co.*, 547 S.W.2d 738, 741 (Tex. App.—Corpus Christi 1977, writ ref'd n.r.e.). {[25] *Elaborate.*} {*See* ***O'Connor's Texas Rules****, "Unauthorized foreign corporation," ch. 3-I, §3.1.1(6), p. 315.*}

11. Plaintiff {[26] *name*} sued under an assumed name but does not have an assumed-name certificate on file with the county clerk. Therefore, {[27] *he/she/it*} does not have capacity to bring suit. *See* Tex. Bus. & Com. Code §§71.051-71.054, 71.201; Tex. R. Civ. P. 93(1), (2); *Sixth RMA Partners, L.P. v. Sibley*, 111 S.W.3d 46, 55 (Tex. 2003). {[28] *Elaborate.*} {*See* ***O'Connor's Texas Rules****, "No assumed-name certificate," ch. 3-I, §3.1.1(7), p. 316.*}

12. A party necessary to the adjudication of this suit is absent. {[29] *Elaborate.*} Therefore, this suit cannot continue without the absent party. *See Allison v. Nat'l Union Fire Ins. Co.*, 703 S.W.2d 637, 638 (Tex. 1986). {*See* ***O'Connor's Texas Rules****, "Necessary party absent," ch. 3-I, §3.1.1(8), p. 316.*}

13. Plaintiff {[30] *name*} sued defendant in the wrong name. Defendant was sued as {[31] *name*}, but defendant's correct name is {[32] *name*}. {*See* ***O'Connor's Texas Rules****, "Misnomer of defendant," ch. 3-I, §3.1.1(9), p. 316.*}

14. Plaintiff {[33] *name*} did not give defendant proper notice of suit as required by {[34] *state notice provision relied on, e.g., the DTPA, Texas Civil Practice & Remedies Code section 74.051*}. *See De Checa v. Diagnostic Ctr. Hosp., Inc.*, 852 S.W.2d 935, 939 (Tex. 1993). {[35] *Elaborate.*} {*See* ***O'Connor's Texas Rules****, "Lack of notice," ch. 3-I, §3.1.2(1), p. 316.*}

Continued on next page

15. Plaintiff {㊱ *name*} did not satisfy the residency requirements of {㊲ *state provision with residency requirements, e.g., Texas Family Code section 6.301(2)*}. *See Reynolds v. Reynolds*, 86 S.W.3d 272, 277 (Tex. App.—Austin 2002, no pet.). {㊳ *Elaborate.*} {*See **O'Connor's Texas Rules**, "Lack of residency," ch. 3-I, §3.1.2(2), p. 316.*}

CONCLUSION

16. Because {㊴ *restate reasons for abatement*}, the Court should abate plaintiff's suit until the defect is corrected.

REQUEST FOR HEARING

17. Defendant asks the Court to set this plea for an evidentiary hearing at the earliest practical time. {*See **O'Connor's Texas Rules**, "Hearing," ch. 3-I, §6, p. 320.*}

PRAYER

18. For these reasons, defendant asks the Court to set {㊵ *his/her/its*} plea in abatement for hearing and, after the hearing, grant defendant's plea in abatement, order plaintiff to cure {㊶ *his/her/its*} pleading defect, and, if plaintiff does not, strike plaintiff's petition.

SEE: Tex. R. Civ. P. 150-156, 158-160, 175
O'Connor's Texas Rules * Civil Trials (2019), "Abate – defect in pleadings," ch. 3-I, §3.1, p. 315

ADD: STYLE OF THE CASE – FORM 1B:2
SIGNATURE BLOCK – FORM 1B:3
VERIFICATION – FORM 1B:7
CERTIFICATE OF CONFERENCE – FORM 1B:12, if necessary
CERTIFICATE OF SERVICE – FORM 1B:13

ATTACH: AFFIDAVIT – FORM 1B:8, if necessary
NOTICE OF HEARING OR SUBMISSION – FORM 1E:1
ORDER – FORM 1G:1

NOTE: A defendant should look at the verified pleas in its original answer to determine whether to file a plea in abatement. Many of the matters the defendant is required to deny under oath, listed in Texas Rule of Civil Procedure 93, are also matters that should be made the subject of a verified plea in abatement. See FORM 3E:10.

DEFENDANT'S {1 *PLEA IN ABATEMENT/MOTION TO STAY*}

Defendant, {2 *name*}, asks the Court to {3 *abate/stay*} the proceedings pending in {4 *current*} County because the dispute is already pending in another forum.

INTRODUCTION

1. Plaintiff, {5 *name*}, sued defendant, {6 *name*}, for {7 *state basis of suit*}.

2. {8 *State other relevant facts about the suit.*}

BACKGROUND

{*CHOOSE APPROPRIATE PARAGRAPH 3*}

3. A suit was filed in {9 *identify other forum*} on {10 *date*}, styled {11 *identify cause number*}. Attached as Exhibit {12 *letter*} is a copy of the petition in that suit. That suit and this suit involve the same parties and the same issues. {13 *Elaborate.*}

3. An administrative proceeding was begun in {14 *identify other forum*}, by {15 *name of administrative agency*}, on {16 *date*}, under {17 *identify statute under which administrative proceeding was commenced*}, and designated as {18 *identify proceeding number*}. Attached as Exhibit {19 *letter*} is a copy of the {20 *identify document from agency, e.g., complaint, request, notice*}. The administrative proceeding and this suit involve the same parties and the same issues. {21 *Elaborate.*} The dispute before the {22 *name of administrative agency*} involves the resolution of issues within that agency's special competence.

4. Thus, this dispute is already pending in {23 *another county/federal court/another state's court/an administrative proceeding*}.

5. {24 *State other facts relevant to the plea or motion.*}

ARGUMENT & AUTHORITIES

{*CHOOSE APPROPRIATE PARAGRAPH 6*}

6. The Court should abate this suit because another suit involving the same parties and issues was first commenced in {25 *other*} County, giving that court dominant jurisdiction. Dominant jurisdiction belongs to the first court in which suit is properly filed. *In re J.B. Hunt Transp., Inc.*, 492 S.W.3d 287, 294 (Tex. 2016); *In re Puig*, 351 S.W.3d 301, 305 (Tex. 2011). To have a suit abated, a party must show that the suit in the other county (1) was commenced first and citation was timely served, (2) was filed in a county of proper venue, (3) is still pending, (4) involves the same parties, and (5) in-

◄ Continued on next page ►

FORM 31:2

volves the same controversies. *See In re Red Dot Bldg. Sys., Inc.*, 504 S.W.3d 320, 322 (Tex. 2016); *In re King*, 478 S.W.3d 930, 933 (Tex. App.—Dallas 2015, orig. proceeding); *In re Sims*, 88 S.W.3d 297, 303 (Tex. App.—San Antonio 2002, orig. proceeding). When the subject matter of two suits is inherently interrelated, the court where the second suit was filed must grant a plea in abatement. *In re J.B. Hunt*, 492 S.W.3d at 294; *Curtis v. Gibbs*, 511 S.W.2d 263, 267 (Tex. 1974); *Sweezy Constr., Inc. v. Murray*, 915 S.W.2d 527, 531 (Tex. App.—Corpus Christi 1995, orig. proceeding); *see In re Puig*, 351 S.W.3d at 305-06. It is not necessary that the exact issues and all the parties be included in the first suit before the second is filed, as long as the claim in the first suit may be amended to bring in all necessary and proper issues and parties. *Wyatt v. Shaw Plumbing Co.*, 760 S.W.2d 245, 247 (Tex. 1988), *overruled on other grounds*, *In re J.B. Hunt Transp., Inc.*, 492 S.W.3d 287 (Tex. 2016). {*See* ***O'Connor's Texas Rules***, *"Abate – same dispute in another Texas court," ch. 3-I, §3.2, p. 316.*}

6. The Court should stay this suit because a suit involving the same parties and issues was first filed in federal court. Although the mere pendency of a suit in federal court involving the same parties and issues is not a reason to abate the later-filed state-court suit, a court should grant a motion to stay the state-court suit when the subject matter of the two suits is inherently interrelated. *See Taiwan Shrimp Farm Vill. Ass'n v. U.S.A. Shrimp Farm Dev., Inc.*, 915 S.W.2d 61, 68 (Tex. App.—Corpus Christi 1996, writ denied); *Space Master Int'l, Inc. v. Porta-Kamp Mfg. Co.*, 794 S.W.2d 944, 946 (Tex. App.—Houston [1st Dist.] 1990, no writ); *Williamson v. Tucker*, 615 S.W.2d 881, 885-86 (Tex. App.—Dallas 1981, writ ref'd n.r.e.). Because the federal suit was filed first and the subject matter of the two suits is inherently interrelated, the Court should stay this suit until the federal suit is resolved. {*See* ***O'Connor's Texas Rules***, *"Stay – same dispute in federal court," ch. 3-I, §4.3, p. 319.*}

6. The Court should stay this suit because a suit involving the same parties and issues was first filed in the State of {㉖ *other state*}. Although the mere pendency of a suit in another state's court involving the same parties and subject matter is not a reason to abate the later-filed state-court suit, a court should grant a motion to stay the later-filed suit when the subject matter of the two suits is inherently interrelated. *See Wyatt v. Shaw Plumbing Co.*, 760 S.W.2d 245, 247 (Tex. 1988), *overruled on other grounds*, *In re J.B. Hunt Transp., Inc.*, 492 S.W.3d 287 (Tex. 2016); *Space Master Int'l, Inc. v. Porta-Kamp Mfg. Co.*, 794 S.W.2d 944, 946 (Tex. App.—Houston [1st Dist.] 1990, no writ); *see also VE Corp. v. Ernst & Young*, 860 S.W.2d 83, 84 (Tex. 1993) (principles of comity generally require the second suit to be abated). Because plaintiff first sued defendant in {㉗ *other state*} and the subject matter of the two suits is inherently interrelated, the Court should stay this suit until the {㉘ *other state*} suit is resolved. {*See* ***O'Connor's Texas Rules***, *"Stay – same dispute in another state's court," ch. 3-I, §4.2, p. 319.*}

6. The Court should abate this suit because the same dispute is pending in an administrative hearing before {㉙ *name of administrative agency*}. Under {㉚ *identify statute*}, the {㉛ *name of administrative agency*} has concurrent jurisdiction with the courts over this dispute. The doctrine of primary jurisdiction requires this Court to abate this suit until the {㉜ *name of administrative agency*} hears the dispute or makes specific findings. *Forest Oil Corp. v. El Rucio Land & Cattle Co.*, 518 S.W.3d 422, 430 (Tex. 2017); *Subaru of Am., Inc. v. David McDavid Nissan, Inc.*, 84 S.W.3d 212, 221 (Tex. 2002); *see O'Neal v. Ector Cty. Indep. Sch. Dist.*, 251 S.W.3d 50, 51-52 (Tex. 2008); *In re Sw. Bell Tel. Co., L.P.*, 226 S.W.3d 400, 404 (Tex. 2007). Only after the agency has heard the dispute may it be submitted to the courts. *See Thomas v. Long*, 207 S.W.3d 334, 340 (Tex. 2006); *Subaru of Am.*, 84 S.W.3d at 221; *Meekey v. Rick's Cabaret Int'l, Inc.*, 171 S.W.3d 394, 399 (Tex. App.—Houston [14th Dist.] 2005, pet. denied). This Court should defer to {㉝ *name of administrative agency*} because (1) the agency is adjudicating a dispute that requires resolving issues within its special competence and (2) great benefit is derived from the agency's uniform interpretation of its laws and regulations. *See Forest Oil*, 518 S.W.3d at 429-30; *Subaru of Am.*, 84 S.W.3d at 221. {*See **O'Connor's Texas Rules**, "Abate – administrative agency has primary jurisdiction," ch. 3-I, §3.4, p. 318.*}

7. {㉞ *Elaborate on argument, applying the facts to the law.*}

CONCLUSION

8. {㉟ *Briefly summarize the plea or motion.*}

REQUEST FOR HEARING

9. Defendant asks the Court to set this {㊱ *plea/motion*} for an evidentiary hearing at the earliest practical time. {*See **O'Connor's Texas Rules**, "Hearing," ch. 3-I, §6, p. 320.*}

PRAYER

10. For these reasons, defendant asks the Court to set this {㊲ *plea in abatement/motion to stay*} for hearing and, after the hearing, grant defendant's {㊳ *plea/motion*}.

SEE: Tex. R. Civ. P. 150-156, 158-160, 175
O'Connor's Texas Rules * Civil Trials (2019), "Types of Motions to Abate," ch. 3-I, §3, p. 315; "Motion to Stay," ch. 3-I, §4, p. 319

◄ *Continued on next page* ►

ADD: STYLE OF THE CASE – FORM 1B:2
SIGNATURE BLOCK – FORM 1B:3
VERIFICATION – FORM 1B:7
CERTIFICATE OF CONFERENCE – FORM 1B:12, if necessary
CERTIFICATE OF SERVICE – FORM 1B:13

ATTACH: AFFIDAVIT – FORM 1B:8, if necessary
NOTICE OF HEARING OR SUBMISSION – FORM 1E:1
ORDER – FORM 1G:1
Administrative document, if necessary
Petition in other suit, if necessary

NOTE: When the same case is pending in another state's court or in federal court, a defendant should, instead of filing a plea in abatement, file a motion to stay that requests a suspension of the suit. *See* ***Crown Leasing Corp. v. Sims***, 92 S.W.3d 924, 927 (Tex.App.—Texarkana 2002, no pet.). See ***O'Connor's Texas Rules***, "Motion to stay vs. motion to abate," ch. 3-I, §4.1, p. 319.

When breach-of-contract and bad-faith claims (i.e., contractual and extracontractual claims) are brought in the same suit, an insurer can seek to sever the claims and abate the bad-faith claim until liability on the insurance contract is determined. *See* ***Liberty Nat'l Fire Ins. v. Akin***, 927 S.W.2d 627, 630 (Tex.1996); ***In re Progressive Cty. Mut. Ins.***, 439 S.W.3d 422, 425 (Tex.App.—Houston [1st Dist.] 2014, orig. proceeding). See ***O'Connor's Texas COA***, "Severing claims," ch. 13-B, §7.2, p. 351.

When the dispute should have been submitted to arbitration, a defendant may file a plea in abatement that requests a suspension of the suit. See FORM 4C:1; ***O'Connor's Texas Rules***, "Motion to Compel ADR Arbitration," ch. 4-C, §2, p. 355.

When the same case is filed in a Texas court and another state's court, a defendant may be able to file an application for an antisuit injunction in the Texas court to enjoin the plaintiff from proceeding with the suit in the other state's court. *See* ***Golden Rule Ins. v. Harper***, 925 S.W.2d 649, 651 (Tex.1996). See ***O'Connor's Texas Rules***, "CPRC §65.011," ch. 2-D, §4.1.1(2)(b), p. 141.

PLAINTIFF'S RESPONSE TO
DEFENDANT'S {❶ *PLEA IN ABATEMENT/MOTION TO STAY*}

Plaintiff, {❷ *name*}, asks the Court to deny defendant {❸ *name*}'s {❹ *plea in abatement/motion to stay*}.

INTRODUCTION

1. Plaintiff, {❺ *name*}, sued defendant, {❻ *name*}, for {❼ *state basis of suit*}.

2. {❽ *State other relevant facts about the suit.*}

BACKGROUND

3. On {❾ *date*}, defendant {❿ *name*} moved to {⓫ *abate/stay*} and alleged {⓬ *restate defendant's allegation*}.

4. {⓭ *State other facts relevant to the response.*}

ARGUMENT & AUTHORITIES

{*CHOOSE APPROPRIATE PARAGRAPHS 5-20*}

{*Waiver*}

5. The Court should not abate plaintiff's suit because defendant waived abatement by not filing the plea in abatement in a timely manner. *See Wyatt v. Shaw Plumbing Co.*, 760 S.W.2d 245, 248 (Tex. 1988), *overruled on other grounds, In re J.B. Hunt Transp., Inc.*, 492 S.W.3d 287 (Tex. 2016); *Bluebonnet Farms, Inc. v. Gibraltar Sav. Ass'n*, 618 S.W.2d 81, 83-84 (Tex. App.—Houston [1st Dist.] 1980, writ ref'd n.r.e.). {⓮ *Elaborate.*} {*See* ***O'Connor's Texas Rules****, "Deadline to file," ch. 3-I, §2.4, p. 314.*}

6. The Court should not abate plaintiff's suit because defendant waived abatement by not having the plea in abatement set for hearing before {⓯ *trial/a hearing on the merits*}. *See* Tex. R. Civ. P. 175; *Mekeel v. U.S. Bank Nat'l Ass'n*, 355 S.W.3d 349, 353 (Tex. App.—El Paso 2011, pet. dism'd). {⓰ *Elaborate.*} {*See* ***O'Connor's Texas Rules****, "Waiver," ch. 3-I, §6.3, p. 320.*}

{*Defective pleadings*}

7. The Court should not abate plaintiff's suit because plaintiff's pleadings are not defective. Specifically, {⓱ *state reason defendant's allegation of pleading defect is inaccurate, e.g., plaintiff is not a minor, plaintiff has standing*}.

◄ *Continued on next page* ►

{*Same dispute in another Texas court*}

8. The Court should not abate plaintiff's suit because the other suit in {[18] *identify other Texas court*} was not commenced first. {[19] *Elaborate.*} {*See **O'Connor's Texas Rules**, "Commenced," ch. 3-I, §3.2.1(1), p. 317.*}

9. The Court should not abate plaintiff's suit because the other suit in {[20] *identify other Texas court*} was not filed in a county of proper venue. {[21] *Elaborate.*} {*See **O'Connor's Texas Rules**, "Venue proper," ch. 3-I, §3.2.1(2), p. 317.*}

10. The Court should not abate plaintiff's suit because the other suit in {[22] *identify other Texas court*} is not pending. {[23] *Elaborate.*} {*See **O'Connor's Texas Rules**, "Pending," ch. 3-I, §3.2.1(3), p. 317.*}

11. The Court should not abate plaintiff's suit because the other suit in {[24] *identify other Texas court*} does not involve the same parties. {[25] *Elaborate.*} {*See **O'Connor's Texas Rules**, "Same parties & dispute," ch. 3-I, §3.2.1(4), p. 317.*}

12. The Court should not abate plaintiff's suit because the other suit in {[26] *identify other Texas court*} does not involve the same controversy. {[27] *Elaborate.*} {*See **O'Connor's Texas Rules**, "Same parties & dispute," ch. 3-I, §3.2.1(4), p. 317.*}

13. Defendant is estopped from asserting that the other court has dominant jurisdiction because defendant engaged in inequitable conduct and plaintiff was prejudiced by the inequitable conduct. *See In re J.B. Hunt Transp., Inc.*, 492 S.W.3d 287, 294-95 (Tex. 2016). {[28] *Elaborate.*} {*See **O'Connor's Texas Rules**, "Estoppel," ch. 3-I, §3.2.2(1), p. 317.*}

14. Defendant has no intention of prosecuting the other suit. *Mission Res., Inc. v. Garza Energy Tr.*, 166 S.W.3d 301, 328 (Tex. App.—Corpus Christi 2005), *rev'd in part on other grounds sub nom. Coastal Oil & Gas Corp. v. Garza Energy Tr.*, 268 S.W.3d 1 (Tex. 2008); *see In re J.B. Hunt Transp., Inc.*, 492 S.W.3d 287, 295-96 (Tex. 2016). {[29] *Elaborate.*} {*See **O'Connor's Texas Rules**, "Lack of intent to prosecute," ch. 3-I, §3.2.2(2), p. 318.*}

15. All parties necessary to this suit are not parties in the other suit, and joinder is infeasible or impossible in the other suit. *See Perry v. Del Rio*, 66 S.W.3d 239, 252 (Tex. 2001); *Wyatt v. Shaw Plumbing Co.*, 760 S.W.2d 245, 248 (Tex. 1988), *overruled on other grounds, In re J.B. Hunt Transp., Inc.*, 492 S.W.3d 287 (Tex. 2016). {[30] *Elaborate.*} {*See **O'Connor's Texas Rules**, "Lack of necessary parties," ch. 3-I, §3.2.2(3), p. 318.*}

{*Same dispute in administrative agency*}

16. Under {㉛ *identify statute*}, the {㉜ *name of administrative agency*} has concurrent jurisdiction with this Court over this suit. Under the doctrine of primary jurisdiction, the courts should defer to an administrative agency when (1) it is adjudicating a claim that requires resolving issues within that agency's special competence and (2) great benefit is derived from the agency's uniform interpretation of laws, rules, and regulations within its purview. *Forest Oil Corp. v. El Rucio Land & Cattle Co.*, 518 S.W.3d 422, 429-30 (Tex. 2017); *Subaru of Am., Inc. v. David McDavid Nissan, Inc.*, 84 S.W.3d 212, 221 (Tex. 2002). However, the {㉝ *name of administrative agency*} does not have special competence to resolve the issues in this dispute. {㉞ *Elaborate.*} {*See* ***O'Connor's Texas Rules**, "Abate – administrative agency has primary jurisdiction," ch. 3-I, §3.4, p. 318.*}

{*Same dispute in federal court*}

17. The Court should not stay plaintiff's suit because the other suit in the {㉟ *identify federal court*} was not filed first. {㊱ *Elaborate.*} {*See* ***O'Connor's Texas Rules**, "Stay – same dispute in federal court," ch. 3-I, §4.3, p. 319.*}

18. The Court should not stay plaintiff's suit because the other suit in the {㊲ *identify federal court*} is not inherently interrelated with the subject matter of this suit. *Taiwan Shrimp Farm Vill. Ass'n v. U.S.A. Shrimp Farm Dev., Inc.*, 915 S.W.2d 61, 68 (Tex. App.—Corpus Christi 1996, writ denied). {㊳ *Elaborate.*} {*See* ***O'Connor's Texas Rules**, "Stay – same dispute in federal court," ch. 3-I, §4.3, p. 319.*}

{*Same dispute in other state's court*}

19. The Court should not stay plaintiff's suit because the other suit in {㊴ *identify other state's court*} was not filed first. {㊵ *Elaborate.*} {*See* ***O'Connor's Texas Rules**, "Stay – same dispute in another state's court," ch. 3-I, §4.2, p. 319.*}

20. The Court should not stay plaintiff's suit because the other suit in {㊶ *identify other state's court*} is not inherently interrelated with the subject matter of this suit. *See Wyatt v. Shaw Plumbing Co.*, 760 S.W.2d 245, 247-48 (Tex. 1988), *overruled on other grounds*, *In re J.B. Hunt Transp., Inc.*, 492 S.W.3d 287 (Tex. 2016); *Space Master Int'l, Inc. v. Porta-Kamp Mfg. Co.*, 794 S.W.2d 944, 946 (Tex. App.—Houston [1st Dist.] 1990, no writ). {㊷ *Elaborate.*} {*See* ***O'Connor's Texas Rules**, "Stay – same dispute in another state's court," ch. 3-I, §4.2, p. 319.*}

FORM 31:3

Continued on next page

CONCLUSION

21. Because {㊸ *restate reasons to deny plea in abatement or motion to stay*}, the Court should deny defendant's {㊹ *plea in abatement/motion to stay plaintiff's suit*}.

PRAYER

22. For these reasons, plaintiff asks the Court to deny defendant's {㊺ *plea in abatement/motion to stay*}.

SEE: Tex. R. Civ. P. 150-156, 158-160, 175
O'Connor's Texas Rules * Civil Trials (2019), "Response," ch. 3-I, §5, p. 320

ADD: STYLE OF THE CASE – FORM 1B:2
SIGNATURE BLOCK – FORM 1B:3
VERIFICATION – FORM 1B:7
CERTIFICATE OF SERVICE – FORM 1B:13

ATTACH: AFFIDAVIT – FORM 1B:8, if necessary
ORDER – FORM 1G:1

DEFENDANT'S MOTION TO DISMISS UNDER TEXAS CITIZENS PARTICIPATION ACT

Defendant, {❶ *name*}, asks the Court to dismiss plaintiff {❷ *name*}'s {❸ *describe legal action being dismissed, e.g., claim for defamation, petition, complaint*} under the Texas Citizens Participation Act (codified in Texas Civil Practice & Remedies Code chapter 27).

INTRODUCTION

1. Plaintiff, {❹ *name*}, sued defendant, {❺ *name*}, for {❻ *state basis of suit*}.

2. {❼ *State other relevant facts about the suit.*}

BACKGROUND

3. {❽ *State facts relevant to the motion.*}

4. Defendant attaches affidavits to this motion as Exhibits {❾ *letters*} to establish facts not apparent from the record and incorporates them by reference.

ARGUMENT & AUTHORITIES

5. The Texas Legislature enacted the Texas Citizens Participation Act (TCPA) to encourage and safeguard the constitutional rights of a defendant to speak freely, petition, associate freely, and otherwise participate in government to the maximum extent provided by law. Tex. Civ. Prac. & Rem. Code §27.002.

6. To safeguard these constitutional rights expeditiously and by cost-effective means, the TCPA gives defendants the power to resolve at an early stage whether a legal action impinging on such rights has merit by filing a motion to dismiss (commonly referred to as an "anti-SLAPP motion"). *See* Tex. Civ. Prac. & Rem. Code §27.003(a), (b). Once the motion is filed, all discovery is stayed in the legal action until the court rules on the motion, which must occur within 60 days after the motion is served. *See id.* §§27.003(c), 27.004, 27.005. If the defendant is successful in dismissing the legal action, the defendant is entitled to court costs, attorney fees, and other expenses incurred in defending against the action as justice and equity may require. *Id.* §27.009(a)(1). The court must also impose sanctions sufficient to deter the plaintiff from bringing a similar action in the future. *Id.* §§27.007(a), 27.009(a)(2).

7. To succeed on a motion to dismiss under the TCPA, the defendant must show by a preponderance of the evidence that the plaintiff's legal action is based on, related to, or in response to the defendant's exercise of (1) the right of free speech, (2) the right to petition, or (3) the right of association. Tex. Civ. Prac. & Rem. Code §27.005(b);

◄ *Continued on next page* ►

FORM 3K:1

ExxonMobil Pipeline Co. v. Coleman, 512 S.W.3d 895, 898 (Tex. 2017); *In re Lipsky*, 460 S.W.3d 579, 586 (Tex. 2015). If the defendant meets its burden, the court must dismiss the plaintiff's action unless the plaintiff can either (1) establish that the challenged claim is exempt from the TCPA, or (2) establish by clear and specific evidence a prima facie case for each essential element of the challenged claim. *See* Tex. Civ. Prac. & Rem. Code §§27.005(c), 27.010; *D Magazine Partners, L.P. v. Rosenthal*, 529 S.W.3d 429, 434 (Tex. 2017); *Bedford v. Spassoff*, 520 S.W.3d 901, 904 (Tex. 2017); *In re Lipsky*, 460 S.W.3d at 587. Even if the plaintiff meets its prima facie burden, the court must dismiss the legal action if the defendant can establish by a preponderance of the evidence each essential element of a valid defense to the plaintiff's claim. Tex. Civ. Prac. & Rem. Code §27.005(d); *Youngkin v. Hines*, 546 S.W.3d 675, 681 (Tex. 2018); *see D Magazine*, 529 S.W.3d at 434. In evaluating a motion to dismiss, the court must construe the TCPA liberally to fully effectuate its purpose and intent to encourage and safeguard a defendant's constitutional rights. *See* Tex. Civ. Prac. & Rem. Code §§27.002, 27.011(b).

A. Plaintiff's legal action impinges on defendant's constitutional rights under the TCPA.

{*ADD PARAGRAPHS 8-10 IF ACTION IMPINGES ON RIGHT OF FREE SPEECH*}

8. Plaintiff's {⓾ *describe legal action, e.g., claim for defamation, petition, complaint*} should be dismissed because it is based on, related to, or in response to defendant's exercise of {⓫ *his/her*} right of free speech. Under the TCPA, a defendant exercises her right of free speech when she makes a communication in connection with a matter of public concern. Tex. Civ. Prac. & Rem. Code §27.001(3); *Adams v. Starside Custom Builders, LLC*, 547 S.W.3d 890, 894 (Tex. 2018); *Coleman*, 512 S.W.3d at 898; *Lippincott v. Whisenhunt*, 462 S.W.3d 507, 509 (Tex. 2015). The TCPA does not require more than a tangential relationship between the communication and the matter of public concern. *Coleman*, 512 S.W.3d at 900. A communication includes the making or submitting of a statement or document in any form or medium, including oral, visual, written, audiovisual, or electronic, regardless of whether the communication is made or submitted publicly or privately. *Coleman*, 512 S.W.3d at 898-99; *Lippincott*, 462 S.W.3d at 509; *see* Tex. Civ. Prac. & Rem. Code §27.001(1). A matter of public concern includes an issue related to (1) health or safety, (2) environmental, economic, or community well-being, (3) the government, (4) a public official or public figure, or (5) a good, product, or service in the marketplace. Tex. Civ. Prac. & Rem. Code §27.001(7); *Coleman*, 512 S.W.3d at 899; *see Adams*, 547 S.W.3d at 894; *Lippincott*, 462 S.W.3d at 509-10. {*See* ***O'Connor's Texas Rules***, *"Right of free speech," ch. 3-K, §2.3.1, p. 327.*}

FORM 3K:1

9. In {12 *his/her/its*} {13 *describe pleading, e.g., petition, complaint*}, plaintiff alleged the following in support of {14 *his/her/its*} {15 *describe claim, e.g., claim for defamation*} against defendant: {16 *describe allegations that are based on, related to, or in response to defendant's exercise of free speech*}.

10. In construing the TCPA liberally, these allegations clearly fall within the scope of the TCPA because they are based on, related to, or in response to a communication made by defendant on a matter of public concern. {17 *Explain and provide evidentiary support.*}

{ADD PARAGRAPHS 11-13 IF ACTION IMPINGES ON RIGHT TO PETITION}

11. Plaintiff's {18 *describe legal action, e.g., claim for defamation, petition, complaint*} should be dismissed because it is based on, related to, or in response to defendant's exercise of {19 *his/her*} right to petition. Under the TCPA, a defendant exercises her right to petition when she makes (1) a communication in or pertaining to a judicial proceeding or one of the other proceedings described in Texas Civil Practice & Remedies Code section 27.001(4)(A), (2) a communication in connection with an issue under consideration or review by a legislative, executive, judicial, or other governmental body or in another governmental or official proceeding, (3) a communication that is reasonably likely to encourage consideration or review of an issue by a legislative, executive, judicial, or other governmental body or in another governmental or official proceeding, (4) a communication reasonably likely to enlist public participation in an effort to effect consideration of an issue by a legislative, executive, judicial, or other governmental body or in another governmental or official proceeding, or (5) any other communication that falls within the protection of the right to petition government under the U.S. Constitution or the Texas Constitution. Tex. Civ. Prac. & Rem. Code §27.001(4); *see Youngkin*, 546 S.W.3d at 680. A communication includes the making or submitting of a statement or document in any form or medium, including oral, visual, written, audiovisual, or electronic, regardless of whether the communication is made or submitted publicly or privately. *Coleman*, 512 S.W.3d at 898-99; *Lippincott v. Whisenhunt*, 462 S.W.3d 507, 509 (Tex. 2015); *see* Tex. Civ. Prac. & Rem. Code §27.001(1); *Johnson-Todd v. Morgan*, 480 S.W.3d 605, 609 (Tex. App.—Beaumont 2015, pet. denied). {*See **O'Connor's Texas Rules**, "Right to petition," ch. 3-K, §2.3.2, p. 328.*}

12. In {20 *his/her/its*} {21 *describe pleading, e.g., petition, complaint*}, plaintiff alleged the following in support of {22 *his/her/its*} {23 *describe claim, e.g., claim for defamation*} against defendant: {24 *describe allegations that are based on, related to, or in response to defendant's right to petition*}.

Continued on next page

13. In construing the TCPA liberally, these allegations clearly fall within the scope of the TCPA because they are based on, related to, or in response to a communication made by defendant in exercising {㉕ *his/her*} right to petition. {㉖ *Explain and provide evidentiary support.*}

{*ADD PARAGRAPHS 14-16 IF ACTION IMPINGES ON RIGHT OF ASSOCIATION*}

14. Plaintiff's {㉗ *describe legal action, e.g., claim for defamation, petition, complaint*} should be dismissed because it is based on, related to, or in response to defendant's exercise of {㉘ *his/her*} right of association. Under the TCPA, a defendant exercises her right of association when she communicates with individuals who are joined together to collectively express, promote, pursue, or defend common interests. Tex. Civ. Prac. & Rem. Code §27.001(2); *see Levatino v. Apple Tree Café Touring, Inc.*, 486 S.W.3d 724, 727 (Tex. App.—Dallas 2016, pet. denied); *Backes v. Misko*, 486 S.W.3d 7, 20-21 (Tex. App.—Dallas 2015, pet. denied), *overruled on other grounds*, *Castleman v. Internet Money Ltd.*, 546 S.W.3d 684 (Tex. 2018). A communication includes the making or submitting of a statement or document in any form or medium, including oral, visual, written, audiovisual, or electronic, regardless of whether the communication is made or submitted publicly or privately. *Coleman*, 512 S.W.3d at 898-99; *Lippincott v. Whisenhunt*, 462 S.W.3d 507, 509 (Tex. 2015); *see* Tex. Civ. Prac. & Rem. Code §27.001(1); *Fawcett v. Rogers*, 492 S.W.3d 18, 24-25 (Tex. App.—Houston [1st Dist.] 2016, no pet.). {*See* ***O'Connor's Texas Rules***, *"Right of association," ch. 3-K, §2.3.3, p. 330.*}

15. In {㉙ *his/her/its*} {㉚ *describe pleading, e.g., petition, complaint*}, plaintiff alleged the following in support of {㉛ *his/her/its*} {㉜ *describe claim, e.g., claim for defamation*} against defendant: {㉝ *describe allegations that are based on, related to, or in response to defendant's right of association*}.

16. In construing the TCPA liberally, these allegations clearly fall within the scope of the TCPA because they are based on, related to, or in response to a communication made by defendant in exercising {㉞ *his/her*} right of association. {㉟ *Explain and provide evidentiary support.*}

B. Plaintiff cannot establish prima facie case for each element of {㊱ *his/her/its*} claim.

17. Because defendant has established by a preponderance of the evidence that plaintiff's {㊲ *describe legal action, e.g., claim for defamation, petition, complaint*} is based on, related to, or in response to defendant's protected rights under the TCPA, the

FORM 3K:1

burden shifts to the plaintiff to establish by clear and specific evidence a prima facie case for each essential element of {38 *his/her/its*} claim. To maintain an action for {39 *describe claim, e.g., defamation*}, plaintiff must prove the following elements: {40 *list elements*}. As discussed below, plaintiff cannot meet {41 *his/her/its*} burden on each element. {42 *Discuss each element of plaintiff's claim that cannot be established by clear and specific evidence. See In re Lipsky, 460 S.W.3d at 590-91.*}

{*ADD SECTION C IF APPLICABLE*}

C. Defendant can establish each essential element of a valid defense to plaintiff's claim.

18. Even if plaintiff has met {43 *his/her/its*} burden by establishing a prima facie case for each essential element of {44 *describe challenged claim*}, the court must dismiss the legal action if defendant can establish by a preponderance of the evidence each essential element of a valid defense to plaintiff's claim. Specifically, defendant asserts the defense of {45 *identify defense*}, the essential elements of which are the following: {46 *list elements*}. {47 *Explain and provide support for each essential element of defense.*} {*See* ***O'Connor's Texas Rules****, "Valid defenses to liability," ch. 3-K, §3.4.3, p. 332.*}

ATTORNEY FEES & COSTS

19. Under the TCPA, when a legal action is dismissed, the court must award the defendant court costs, reasonable attorney fees, and other expenses incurred in defending the legal action as justice and equity may require. Tex. Civ. Prac. & Rem. Code §27.009(a)(1); *Sullivan v. Abraham*, 488 S.W.3d 294, 296 (Tex. 2016); *see D Magazine*, 529 S.W.3d at 441. Therefore, if the Court grants defendant's motion to dismiss, defendant asks the Court to award {48 *his/her*} court costs, reasonable attorney fees, and other expenses incurred in defending the action. *See* Tex. Civ. Prac. & Rem. Code §27.009(a)(1). {*See* ***O'Connor's Texas Rules****, "Costs, attorney fees & other expenses," ch. 3-K, §8.2.2(1), p. 339.*}

20. The costs, reasonable attorney fees, and other expenses incurred total ${49 *amount*} and are established by the affidavit of {50 *name of attorney*}, attached as Exhibit {51 *letter*}.

SANCTIONS

21. Under the TCPA, when a legal action is dismissed, the court must sanction the plaintiff to deter the plaintiff from bringing similar actions and must award the defendant those sanctions in addition to costs, reasonable attorney fees, and other ex-

Continued on next page

FORM 3K:1

penses. Tex. Civ. Prac. & Rem. Code §27.009(a); *Cox Media Grp., LLC v. Joselevitz*, 524 S.W.3d 850, 864 (Tex. App.—Houston [14th Dist.] 2017, no pet.); *Serafine v. Blunt*, 466 S.W.3d 352, 364 (Tex. App.—Austin 2015, no pet.). Therefore, if the Court grants defendant's motion to dismiss, defendant asks the Court to sanction plaintiff and award those sanctions to defendant. *See* Tex. Civ. Prac. & Rem. Code §27.009(a)(2). {52 *Elaborate.*} {*See* ***O'Connor's Texas Rules****, "Sanctions," ch. 3-K, §8.2.2(2), p. 340.*}

CONCLUSION

22. {53 *Briefly summarize the motion.*}

PRAYER

23. For these reasons, defendant asks the Court to set {54 *his/her*} motion to dismiss plaintiff's {55 *describe legal action being dismissed*} for a hearing, and, after the hearing, grant defendant's motion; dismiss plaintiff's {56 *describe legal action being dismissed*} with prejudice; award defendant {57 *his/her*} court costs, reasonable attorney fees, and other expenses incurred in defending against plaintiff's legal action as justice and equity may require; and impose sanctions that the Court determines are sufficient to deter plaintiff from bringing similar actions in the future.

SEE: Tex. Civ. Prac. & Rem. Code §27.001 et seq.
O'Connor's Texas Rules * Civil Trials (2019), "Motion to Dismiss—Anti-SLAPP Motion," ch. 3-K, p. 325

ADD: STYLE OF THE CASE – FORM 1B:2
SIGNATURE BLOCK – FORM 1B:3
CERTIFICATE OF SERVICE – FORM 1B:13

ATTACH: AFFIDAVIT – FORM 1B:8
NOTICE OF HEARING OR SUBMISSION – FORM 1E:1
AFFIDAVIT FOR ATTORNEY FEES – FORM 1H:14
ORDER – FORM 3K:5

NOTE: If a party brings a legal action that is based on, related to, or in response to a person's protected rights under the Texas Citizens Participation Act (TCPA), that person can file a motion to dismiss the legal action (commonly known as an anti-SLAPP motion). Tex. Civ. Prac. & Rem. Code §27.003(a). See ***O'Connor's Texas Rules***, "D's exercise of protected right," ch. 3-K, §2.2.3, p. 327. A "legal action" includes any of the following: (1) a lawsuit, (2) a cause of action, (3) a petition, (4) a complaint, (5) a cross-claim, (6) a counterclaim, or (7) any other judicial pleading or filing that requests legal or equitable relief. Tex. Civ. Prac. & Rem. Code §27.001(6); *see* ***In re Elliott***, 504 S.W.3d 455, 465-66 (Tex.App.—Austin 2016, orig. proceeding) (Texas Rule of Civil Procedure 202 petition for presuit deposition is a legal action under TCPA). Thus, although the motion will most often apply to claims asserted by a plaintiff, the motion can be filed against any party who asserts an affirmative or equitable claim for relief (e.g., cross-claimant, counterclaimant). *See* Tex. Civ. Prac. & Rem. Code §27.001(6).

The basis of a legal action is determined by the plaintiff's allegations, not by the defendant's admissions or denials. ***Hersh v. Tatum***, 526 S.W.3d 462, 467 (Tex.2017). Thus, even if the defendant asserts an actual-innocence defense—claiming it did not do the act that formed the basis of the legal action—it can still rely on the TCPA to obtain an order of dismissal. *Id.* at 463.

One court has held that an anti-SLAPP motion is not itself a legal action and, thus, a plaintiff cannot bring a countermotion under the TCPA to dismiss a defendant's anti-SLAPP motion. ***Paulsen v. Yarrell***, 537 S.W.3d 224, 233-34 (Tex.App.—Houston [1st Dist.] 2017, pet. denied).

An anti-SLAPP motion generally must be filed within 60 days after service of the legal action, but the filing of an amended legal action (e.g., an amended counterclaim) may extend the deadline for filing the anti-SLAPP motion if the amendment adds new parties or claims. *See* Tex. Civ. Prac. & Rem. Code §27.003(b); ***In re Estate of Check***, 438 S.W.3d 829, 837 (Tex.App.—San Antonio 2014, no pet.). When an amendment adds new parties or claims, the deadline for filing an anti-SLAPP motion is reset for those claims and runs from the date the amended legal action was served. ***In re Estate of Check***, 438 S.W.3d at 837. If a defendant voluntarily appears by filing an answer before receiving service of the legal action, the 60-day period will begin to run on the date she appears. ***Jordan v. Hall***, 510 S.W.3d 194, 198 (Tex.App.—Houston [1st Dist.] 2016, no pet.).

Generally, a hearing on an anti-SLAPP motion must be set within 60 days after service of the motion, but, under certain circumstances, the hearing must be set within either 90 or 120 days after service of the motion instead. *See* Tex. Civ. Prac. & Rem. Code §27.004. See ***O'Connor's Texas Rules***, "Deadline," ch. 3-K, §6.1, p. 337.

When requesting attorney fees and costs for bringing the anti-SLAPP motion, the defendant should support its request with sufficient evidence establishing the amount of attorney fees and costs incurred in defending the legal action by either attaching documents to its motion or presenting affidavits at the hearing on the motion. *See* ***Fawcett v. Grosu***, 498 S.W.3d 650, 665 (Tex.App.—Houston [14th Dist.] 2016, pet. denied). See ***O'Connor's Texas Rules***, "Proving attorney fees," ch. 1-H, §10.6, p. 81.

PLAINTIFF'S MOTION FOR LIMITED DISCOVERY TO OPPOSE MOTION TO DISMISS UNDER TEXAS CITIZENS PARTICIPATION ACT

Plaintiff, {❶ *name*}, asks the Court to allow plaintiff to conduct certain discovery to oppose defendant's motion to dismiss under the Texas Citizens Participation Act (codified in Texas Civil Practice & Remedies Code chapter 27).

INTRODUCTION

1. Plaintiff, {❷ *name*}, sued defendant, {❸ *name*}, for {❹ *state basis of suit*}.

2. {❺ *State other relevant facts about the suit.*}

BACKGROUND

3. On {❻ *date*}, defendant, {❼ *name*}, moved to dismiss plaintiff's suit under the Texas Citizens Participation Act (TCPA).

4. {❽ *State other facts relevant to the motion.*}

ARGUMENT & AUTHORITIES

5. Under the TCPA, when a defendant files a motion to dismiss, all discovery in the action is suspended until the court rules on the motion. Tex. Civ. Prac. & Rem. Code §27.003(c); *Greer v. Abraham*, 489 S.W.3d 440, 443 (Tex. 2016). However, the court may allow specified and limited discovery relevant to the motion on a showing of good cause. Tex. Civ. Prac. & Rem. Code §27.006(b); *Greer*, 489 S.W.3d at 443.

6. Plaintiff asks the Court to grant {❾ *him/her/it*} permission to {❿ *describe discovery sought*} because (1) this discovery is relevant to the motion to dismiss and (2) there is good cause for the discovery. {⓫ *Elaborate.*}

CONCLUSION

7. {⓬ *Briefly summarize the motion.*}

PRAYER

8. For these reasons, plaintiff asks the Court to lift the stay on discovery and allow plaintiff to {⓭ *describe discovery sought*}.

FORM 3K:2

SEE: Tex. Civ. Prac. & Rem. Code §27.001 et seq.
See ***O'Connor's Texas Rules * Civil Trials*** (2019), "Motion to conduct discovery," ch. 3-K, §4.1, p. 332

ADD: STYLE OF THE CASE – FORM 1B:2
SIGNATURE BLOCK – FORM 1B:3
CERTIFICATE OF SERVICE – FORM 1B:13

ATTACH: AFFIDAVIT – FORM 1B:8, if necessary
NOTICE OF HEARING OR SUBMISSION – FORM 1E:1
ORDER – FORM 1G:1

NOTE: The Texas Citizens Participation Act does not specify when to file and serve a motion for limited discovery to oppose an anti-SLAPP motion. Because the hearing on an anti-SLAPP motion must be set within 60 days after service of the motion, the plaintiff should file and serve the motion to conduct discovery as soon as possible after the anti-SLAPP motion is served. *See* Tex. Civ. Prac. & Rem. Code §27.004(a); ***Whisenhunt v. Lippincott***, 474 S.W.3d 30, 41 (Tex.App.—Texarkana 2015, no pet.), *overruled on other grounds*, ***Castleman v. Internet Money Ltd.***, 546 S.W.3d 684 (Tex.2018).

PLAINTIFF'S RESPONSE TO DEFENDANT'S MOTION TO DISMISS UNDER TEXAS CITIZENS PARTICIPATION ACT

Plaintiff, {❶ *name*}, asks the Court to deny defendant {❷ *name*}'s motion to dismiss under the Texas Citizens Participation Act (codified in Texas Civil Practice & Remedies Code chapter 27).

INTRODUCTION

1. Plaintiff, {❸ *name*}, sued defendant, {❹ *name*}, for {❺ *state basis of suit*}.

2. {❻ *State other relevant facts about the suit.*}

BACKGROUND

3. On {❼ *date*}, defendant moved to dismiss plaintiff's suit under the Texas Citizens Participation Act (TCPA).

4. {❽ *State other facts relevant to the response.*}

5. Plaintiff attaches affidavits to this motion as Exhibits {❾ *letters*} to establish facts not apparent from the record and incorporates them by reference.

ARGUMENT & AUTHORITIES

{*CHOOSE APPROPRIATE SECTIONS A-E*}

A. Motion untimely.

6. To properly bring a motion to dismiss under the TCPA, the motion must be filed within 60 days after the defendant is served with plaintiff's legal action unless the defendant obtains an extension from the court for good cause. Tex. Civ. Prac. & Rem. Code §27.003(b).

7. Defendant was served on {❿ *date*} and filed {⓫ *his/her*} motion to dismiss on {⓬ *date*}, which is more than 60 days after the date of service. {⓭ *Elaborate.*} Because defendant's motion was untimely filed and defendant did not obtain an extension from the Court for good cause, defendant's motion should be denied.

B. Plaintiff's legal action against defendant is exempt from the TCPA.

8. Under the TCPA, not all legal actions brought by a plaintiff are subject to a motion to dismiss. The TCPA expressly excludes the following legal actions from its scope: (1) an enforcement action by the State that is brought by the attorney general, a district attorney, a criminal district attorney, or a county attorney, (2) a legal action

brought against a person primarily engaged in the business of selling or leasing goods or services, if the statement or conduct arises from the sale or lease of goods, services, or an insurance product, from insurance services, or from a commercial transaction in which the intended audience is an actual or potential buyer or customer, (3) a legal action seeking recovery for bodily injury, wrongful death, or survival, (4) a legal action brought under the Insurance Code or arising out of an insurance contract, and (5) a legal action brought under Texas Civil Practice & Remedies Code ch. 129A involving the cyberbullying of a child. Tex. Civ. Prac. & Rem. Code §27.010 (#1-4), §129A.004(b) (#5); *State v. Harper*, 562 S.W.3d 1, 11 (Tex. 2018) (#1); *Castleman v. Internet Money Ltd.*, 546 S.W.3d 684, 690 (Tex. 2018) (#2). {*See* ***O'Connor's Texas Rules***, *"Legal action is exempt from TCPA," ch. 3-K, §4.2.2(1)(c), p. 334.*}

9. Plaintiff's legal action against the defendant for {⓮ *describe challenged claim, e.g., defamation*} is clearly exempt from the scope of the TCPA. {⓯ *Elaborate.*} Because the plaintiff's legal action is exempt from the TCPA, defendant's motion to dismiss should be denied.

C. Defendant has not met {⓰ *his/her*} burden under the TCPA.

10. To prevail on a motion to dismiss under the TCPA, a defendant must show by a preponderance of the evidence that the plaintiff's legal action is based on, related to, or in response to the defendant's exercise of (1) the right of free speech, (2) the right to petition, or (3) the right of association. Tex. Civ. Prac. & Rem. Code §27.005(b); *ExxonMobil Pipeline Co. v. Coleman*, 512 S.W.3d 895, 898 (Tex. 2017); *In re Lipsky*, 460 S.W.3d 579, 586 (Tex. 2015). Only after the defendant has met its burden does the burden shift to the plaintiff to establish by clear and specific evidence a prima facie case for each essential element of its claim. Tex. Civ. Prac. & Rem. Code §27.005(c); *Coleman*, 512 S.W.3d at 899; *In re Lipsky*, 460 S.W.3d at 587.

11. The Court should deny defendant's motion because defendant has not shown by a preponderance of the evidence that plaintiff's {⓱ *describe challenged claim, e.g., claim for defamation*} is based on, related to, or in response to the defendant's exercise of a protected right.

{*ADD PARAGRAPHS 12-14 IF ACTION DOES NOT IMPINGE ON RIGHT OF FREE SPEECH*}

12. In {⓲ *his/her*} motion to dismiss, defendant argued that plaintiff's {⓳ *describe challenged claim, e.g., claim for defamation*} should be dismissed because it is based on, related to, or in response to defendant's exercise of {⓴ *his/her*} right of free speech. Under the TCPA, a defendant exercises her right of free speech when she makes a

◄ *Continued on next page* ►

communication in connection with a matter of public concern. Tex. Civ. Prac. & Rem. Code §27.001(3); *Coleman*, 512 S.W.3d at 898; *Lippincott v. Whisenhunt*, 462 S.W.3d 507, 509 (Tex. 2015). There must be at least a tangential relationship between the communication and the matter of public concern. *Coleman*, 512 S.W.3d at 900. A communication includes the making or submitting of a statement or document in any form or medium, including oral, visual, written, audiovisual, or electronic, regardless of whether the communication is made or submitted publicly or privately. *Id.* at 898-99; *Lippincott*, 462 S.W.3d at 509; *see* Tex. Civ. Prac. & Rem. Code §27.001(1). A matter of public concern includes an issue related to (1) health or safety, (2) environmental, economic, or community well-being, (3) the government, (4) a public official or public figure, or (5) a good, product, or service in the marketplace. Tex. Civ. Prac. & Rem. Code §27.001(7); *Coleman*, 512 S.W.3d at 899; *see Lippincott*, 462 S.W.3d at 509-10 (issue of medical services provided by health-care professional is matter of public concern). {*See **O'Connor's Texas Rules**, "Right of free speech," ch. 3-K, §2.3.1, p. 327.*}

13. In support of plaintiff's claim against the defendant for {21 *describe challenged claim, e.g., defamation*}, plaintiff alleged the following: {22 *describe allegations in support of claim*}.

14. These allegations clearly do not fall within the scope of the TCPA because they are not based on, related to, or in response to a communication made by the defendant on a matter of public concern. {23 *Explain and provide evidentiary support.*}

{*ADD PARAGRAPHS 15-17 IF ACTION DOES NOT IMPINGE ON RIGHT TO PETITION*}

15. In {24 *his/her*} motion to dismiss, defendant argued that plaintiff's {25 *describe challenged claim, e.g., claim for defamation*} should be dismissed because it is based on, related to, or in response to defendant's exercise of {26 *his/her*} right to petition. Under the TCPA, a defendant exercises her right to petition when she makes (1) a communication in or pertaining to a judicial proceeding or one of the other proceedings described in Texas Civil Practice & Remedies Code section 27.001(4)(A), (2) a communication in connection with an issue under consideration or review by a legislative, executive, judicial, or other governmental body or in another governmental or official proceeding, (3) a communication that is reasonably likely to encourage consideration or review of an issue by a legislative, executive, judicial, or other governmental body or in another governmental or official proceeding, (4) a communication reasonably likely to enlist public participation in an effort to effect consideration of an issue by a legislative, executive, judicial, or other governmental body or in another governmental or official proceeding, or (5) any other communication that falls within the protection of the right to petition government under the U.S. Constitution or the Texas

Constitution. Tex. Civ. Prac. & Rem. Code §27.001(4). A communication includes the making or submitting of a statement or document in any form or medium, including oral, visual, written, audiovisual, or electronic, regardless of whether the communication is made or submitted publicly or privately. *Coleman*, 512 S.W.3d at 898-99; *Lippincott v. Whisenhunt*, 462 S.W.3d 507, 509 (Tex. 2015); *see* Tex. Civ. Prac. & Rem. Code §27.001(1). {*See* ***O'Connor's Texas Rules****, "Right to petition," ch. 3-K, §2.3.2, p. 328.*}

16. In support of plaintiff's claim against the defendant for {㉗ *describe challenged claim, e.g., defamation*}, plaintiff alleged the following: {㉘ *describe allegations in support of claim*}.

17. These allegations clearly do not fall within the scope of the TCPA because they are not based on, related to, or in response to a communication made by the defendant in the exercise of {㉙ *his/her*} right to petition. {㉚ *Explain and provide evidentiary support.*}

{ADD PARAGRAPHS 18-20 IF ACTION DOES NOT IMPINGE ON RIGHT OF ASSOCIATION}

18. In {㉛ *his/her*} motion to dismiss, defendant argued that plaintiff's {㉜ *describe challenged claim, e.g., claim for defamation*} should be dismissed because it is based on, related to, or in response to defendant's exercise of {㉝ *his/her*} right of association. Under the TCPA, a defendant exercises her right of association when she communicates with individuals who are joined together to collectively express, promote, pursue, or defend common interests. Tex. Civ. Prac. & Rem. Code §27.001(2); *see Backes v. Misko*, 486 S.W.3d 7, 20-21 (Tex. App.—Dallas 2015, pet. denied), *overruled on other grounds*, *Castleman v. Internet Money Ltd.*, 546 S.W.3d 684 (Tex. 2018). A communication includes the making or submitting of a statement or document in any form or medium, including oral, visual, written, audiovisual, or electronic, regardless of whether the communication is made or submitted publicly or privately. *Coleman*, 512 S.W.3d at 898-99; *Lippincott v. Whisenhunt*, 462 S.W.3d 507, 509 (Tex. 2015); *see* Tex. Civ. Prac. & Rem. Code §27.001(1); *Fawcett v. Rogers*, 492 S.W.3d 18, 24-25 (Tex. App.—Houston [1st Dist.] 2016, no pet.). {*See* ***O'Connor's Texas Rules****, "Right of association," ch. 3-K, §2.3.3, p. 330.*}

19. In support of plaintiff's claim against defendant for {㉞ *describe challenged claim, e.g., defamation*}, plaintiff alleged the following: {㉟ *describe allegations in support of claim*}.

Continued on next page

FORM 3K:3

20. These allegations clearly do not fall within the scope of the TCPA because they are not based on, related to, or in response to a communication made by the defendant in exercising {㊱ *his/her*} right of association. {㊲ *Explain and provide evidentiary support.*}

D. Plaintiff can establish prima facie evidence of {㊳ *describe challenged claim, e.g., defamation*}.

21. Even assuming defendant has met {㊴ *his/her*} burden by establishing that plaintiff's suit is based on, related to, or in response to defendant's exercise of a protected right under the TCPA, the Court can deny defendant's motion if the plaintiff can establish by clear and specific evidence a prima facie case for each essential element of {㊵ *his/her/its*} claim. Tex. Civ. Prac. & Rem. Code §27.005(c); *Bedford v. Spassoff*, 520 S.W.3d 901, 904 (Tex. 2017); *In re Lipsky*, 460 S.W.3d 579, 587 (Tex. 2015). Prima facie evidence is the minimum amount of evidence necessary to support a rational inference that a factual allegation is true. *In re Lipsky*, 460 S.W.3d at 590; *Tex. Campaign for the Env't v. Partners Dewatering Int'l, LLC*, 485 S.W.3d 184, 191-92 (Tex. App.—Corpus Christi 2016, no pet.).

22. Plaintiff can establish by clear and specific evidence a prima facie case for each essential element of {㊶ *describe challenged claim, e.g., defamation*}. The essential elements of {㊷ *describe challenged claim, e.g., defamation*} are the following: {㊸ *list elements*}. Plaintiff has prima facie evidence for each element. {㊹ *Explain and provide detailed support using direct or circumstantial evidence for each essential element of challenged claim. See In re Lipsky, 460 S.W.3d at 590-91.*}

E. Defendant has not met {㊺ *his/her*} burden to establish each essential element of a valid defense.

23. Even if a plaintiff has met its burden by establishing a prima facie case for each essential element of its claim, the court must dismiss the legal action if the defendant can establish by a preponderance of the evidence each essential element of a valid defense to plaintiff's claim. Tex. Civ. Prac. & Rem. Code §27.005(d); *see D Magazine Partners, L.P. v. Rosenthal*, 529 S.W.3d 429, 434 (Tex. 2017). Defendant has not, however, met this burden. {*See* ***O'Connor's Texas Rules****, "Valid defenses to liability," ch. 3-K, §3.4.3, p. 332.*}

{*CHOOSE APPROPRIATE PARAGRAPH 24*}

24. In its motion, defendant raised the defense of {㊻ *identify defense*} but did not establish by a preponderance of the evidence each essential element of that defense. {㊼ *Elaborate.*} Specifically, the essential elements of {㊽ *identify defense*} are the following: {㊾ *list elements*}. {㊿ *Explain and provide support to refute at least one essential element of the defense.*}

24. In its motion, defendant raised the defense of {51 *identify defense*}. This is not a valid defense to plaintiff's claim. {52 *Elaborate.*}

{*ADD SECTION BELOW IF APPLICABLE*}

COSTS & ATTORNEY FEES

25. Under the TCPA, if a court finds that a motion to dismiss is frivolous or solely intended to cause delay, the court can award court costs and attorney fees to the plaintiff. Tex. Civ. Prac. & Rem. Code §27.009(b).

26. Plaintiff asks the Court to award {53 *his/her/its*} costs and attorney fees because defendant's motion is frivolous and solely intended to cause delay. {54 *Elaborate.*}

CONCLUSION

27. {55 *Briefly summarize the response.*}

PRAYER

28. For these reasons, plaintiff asks the Court to deny defendant's motion to dismiss under the TCPA {56 *add if appropriate: and award plaintiff {his/her/its} costs and attorney fees*}.

SEE: Tex. Civ. Prac. & Rem. Code §27.001 et seq.
O'Connor's Texas Rules * Civil Trials (2019), "Motion to Dismiss—Anti-SLAPP Motion," ch. 3-K, p. 325

ADD: STYLE OF THE CASE – FORM 1B:2
SIGNATURE BLOCK – FORM 1B:3
CERTIFICATE OF SERVICE – FORM 1B:13

ATTACH: AFFIDAVIT – FORM 1B:8
AFFIDAVIT FOR ATTORNEY FEES – FORM 1H:14
ORDER – FORM 3K:5

◄ *Continued on next page* ►

FORM 3K:3

NOTE: Because the hearing on a motion to dismiss under the Texas Citizens Participation Act (commonly known as an anti-SLAPP motion) generally must be within 60 days after service of the motion, the plaintiff should file and serve the response as soon as possible after the anti-SLAPP motion is served. *See* Tex. Civ. Prac. & Rem. Code §27.004(a).

Although the TCPA requires more information about the underlying claim than the fair-notice pleading standard under Texas Rules of Civil Procedure 45(b) and 47(a), the Texas Supreme Court has disapproved of cases interpreting "clear and specific evidence" as a heightened evidentiary standard and held that the TCPA does not categorically reject the use of circumstantial evidence. *See* ***In re Lipsky***, 460 S.W.3d 579, 590-91 (Tex.2015).

Some courts of appeals have used a four-part test based on the California anti-SLAPP statute to determine whether the TCPA's commercial-speech exemption applies. ***Castleman v. Internet Money Ltd.***, 546 S.W.3d 684, 686 (Tex.2018). The Texas Supreme Court recently rejected relying on the California four-part test in construing the TCPA and set out its own test for determining application of the exemption. *Id.* at 687-88. Although the Court refused to rely on courts' construction of the California commercial-speech exemption, the Court determined that the exemption under the TCPA carries the same meaning. *Id.* at 687. See ***O'Connor's Texas Rules***, "Commercial-speech actions," ch. 3-K, §4.2.2(1)(c)[2], p. 334.

See notes under FORM 3K:1.

DEFENDANT'S REPLY TO PLAINTIFF'S RESPONSE TO
MOTION TO DISMISS UNDER TEXAS CITIZENS PARTICIPATION ACT

Defendant, {❶ *name*}, asks the Court to dismiss plaintiff {❷ *name*}'s {❸ *describe legal action being dismissed, e.g., claim for defamation, petition, complaint*} under the Texas Citizens Participation Act (codified in Texas Civil Practice & Remedies Code chapter 27) because defendant can establish by a preponderance of the evidence each essential element of a valid defense to {❹ *describe legal action*}.

INTRODUCTION

1. Plaintiff, {❺ *name*}, sued defendant, {❻ *name*}, for {❼ *state basis of suit*}.

2. {❽ *State other relevant facts about the suit.*}

BACKGROUND

3. On {❾ *date*}, defendant filed a motion to dismiss plaintiff's suit under the Texas Citizens Participation Act (TCPA).

4. On {❿ *date*}, plaintiff filed a response to defendant's motion to dismiss under the TCPA.

5. {⓫ *State other facts relevant to the reply.*}

ARGUMENT & AUTHORITIES

6. Under the TCPA, a defendant can file a motion to dismiss to resolve whether a legal action impinges on certain constitutional rights of the defendant. *See* Tex. Civ. Prac. & Rem. Code §§27.002, 27.003(a). To succeed on a motion to dismiss under the TCPA, a defendant must show by a preponderance of the evidence that the plaintiff's legal action is based on, related to, or in response to the defendant's exercise of the right of free speech, the right to petition, or the right of association. *Id.* §27.005(b). Once the defendant has filed the motion to dismiss, the plaintiff can file a response in which the plaintiff has the burden to establish by clear and specific evidence a prima facie case for each essential element of its claim. *Id.* §27.005(c). Even if the plaintiff meets its burden, the court must dismiss the legal action if the defendant can establish by a preponderance of the evidence each essential element of a valid defense to the plaintiff's claim. *Id.* §27.005(d); *see D Magazine Partners, L.P. v. Rosenthal*, 529 S.W.3d 429, 434 (Tex. 2017); *Johnson-Todd v. Morgan*, 480 S.W.3d 605, 610 (Tex. App.—Beaumont 2015, pet. denied).

Continued on next page

7. In {⓬ *his/her/its*} motion, defendant established that plaintiff's {⓭ *describe legal action*} should be dismissed because it is based on, related to, or in response to defendant's exercise of {⓮ *his/her/its*} right {⓯ *of free speech/to petition/of association*}. {⓰ *Elaborate.*}

{*CHOOSE APPROPRIATE PARAGRAPHS 8-9*}

8. In {⓱ *his/her/its*} response, plaintiff alleged a prima facie case for each essential element of {⓲ *describe challenged claim, e.g., defamation*} against defendant. Specifically, {⓳ *list elements of plaintiff's claim and describe plaintiff's support for each element*}. Plaintiff has not met {⓴ *his/her/its*} burden to establish a prima facie case for each essential element of {㉑ *describe challenged claim*} against defendant because {㉒ *explain*}.

9. In {㉓ *his/her/its*} response, plaintiff alleged that defendant did not meet {㉔ *his/her*} burden to establish by a preponderance of the evidence each essential element of a valid defense to plaintiff's claim. Specifically, {㉕ *describe plaintiff's argument*}. Defendant has, however, met {㉖ *his/her*} burden because {㉗ *refute plaintiff's argument and explain why defendant can establish a valid defense to plaintiff's claim*}. {*See* ***O'Connor's Texas Rules****, "Valid defenses," ch. 3-K, §5.2.2, p. 337.*}

CONCLUSION

10. {㉘ *Briefly summarize the reply.*}

PRAYER

11. For these reasons, defendant asks the Court to dismiss plaintiff's {㉙ *describe legal action*}.

FORM 3K:4

SEE: Tex. Civ. Prac. & Rem. Code §27.001 et seq.
O'Connor's Texas Rules * Civil Trials (2019), "Reply," ch. 3-K, §5, p. 337

ADD: STYLE OF THE CASE – FORM 1B:2
SIGNATURE BLOCK – FORM 1B:3
CERTIFICATE OF SERVICE – FORM 1B:13

ATTACH: AFFIDAVIT – FORM 1B:8

NOTE: Because the hearing on a motion to dismiss under the Texas Citizens Participation Act (commonly known as an anti-SLAPP motion) generally must be within 60 days after service of the motion, a defendant choosing to file a reply should file and serve the reply as soon as possible after the plaintiff's response is served. *See* Tex. Civ. Prac. & Rem. Code §27.004(a).

If additional attorney fees and expenses have been incurred since the anti-SLAPP motion was filed, or if new evidence has developed that strengthens the case for the amount of sanctions sought, the defendant should attach supplemental evidence on attorney fees and sanctions to the reply. See ***O'Connor's Texas Rules***, "Request for attorney fees & costs," ch. 3-K, §3.4.4, p. 332.

ORDER ON DEFENDANT'S MOTION TO DISMISS SUIT

After considering defendant {❶ *name*}'s motion to dismiss this suit under the Texas Citizens Participation Act, the response, the pleadings, the evidence, and arguments of counsel, the Court

{*CHOOSE APPROPRIATE ORDER*}

DENIES defendant's motion and retains plaintiff's suit on the Court's docket. {❷ *Add if appropriate: Because the Court finds that the motion was frivolous and intended solely to cause delay, the Court awards the following attorney fees and court costs to plaintiff: {list attorney fees and court costs}.*}

GRANTS defendant's motion and orders the following:

a. Plaintiff's {❸ *describe legal action being dismissed, e.g., claim for defamation, petition, complaint*} is dismissed with prejudice.

b. Defendant is awarded court costs, reasonable attorney fees, and other expenses incurred in defending against plaintiff's legal action in the amount of ${❹ *amount*}.

c. To deter plaintiff from bringing similar actions in the future, plaintiff is ordered to pay sanctions in the amount of ${❺ *amount*}.

SIGNED on _______________, 20___.

____
PRESIDING JUDGE

SEE: Tex. Civ. Prac. & Rem. Code §27.001 et seq.
O'Connor's Texas Rules * Civil Trials (2019), "Order," ch. 3-K, §8, p. 339

ADD: STYLE OF THE CASE – FORM 1B:2
CERTIFICATE OF SERVICE – FORM 1B:13, if proposed order served separately from motion or response

NOTE: If a court does not rule on a motion to dismiss under the Texas Citizens Participation Act (TCPA) within 30 days after the hearing, the motion is considered to have been denied by operation of law and the defendant may appeal. Tex. Civ. Prac. & Rem. Code §27.008(a); ***Inwood Forest Cmty. Imprv. Ass'n v. Arce***, 485 S.W.3d 65, 69-70 (Tex.App.—Houston [14th Dist.] 2015, pet. denied). For the methods for appellate review of an order on a motion to dismiss under the TCPA, see ***O'Connor's Texas Rules***, "Appellate Review," ch. 3-K, §10, p. 341.

◄ *Continued on next page* ►

When a court grants the defendant's motion and dismisses the legal action, it must award the defendant court costs, reasonable attorney fees, and other expenses incurred in defending the legal action as justice and equity may require. Tex. Civ. Prac. & Rem. Code §27.009(a)(1); ***Sullivan v. Abraham***, 488 S.W.3d 294, 296 (Tex.2016); *see* ***D Mag. Partners v. Rosenthal***, 529 S.W.3d 429, 441 (Tex.2017). Although the court must award costs and reasonable attorney fees, it has discretion to determine the amount of reasonable attorney fees; however, it may not adjust what is reasonable based on consideration of what justice and equity may require. *See* ***Sullivan***, 488 S.W.3d at 299. The court may consider justice and equity only when determining whether to award "other expenses" incurred in defending the legal action. *See* Tex. Civ. Prac. & Rem. Code §27.009(a)(1); ***Sullivan***, 488 S.W.3d at 298-99.

If a case includes multiple claims that each constitute a legal action and the court dismisses some but not all of them, the defendant can still recover attorney fees based on the partial dismissal. *E.g.*, ***D Mag.***, 529 S.W.3d at 441-42 (D was entitled to attorney fees when court dismissed statutory claims even though defamation claim was not dismissed).

As with costs, attorney fees, and expenses, the court must impose sanctions on the plaintiff if it grants the defendant's motion to dismiss under the TCPA; however, it has discretion to determine what sanction is appropriate to deter the plaintiff from bringing similar future actions. ***Rauhauser v. McGibney***, 508 S.W.3d 377, 389 (Tex.App.—Fort Worth 2014, no pet.), *disapproved on other grounds*, ***Hersh v. Tatum***, 526 S.W.3d 462 (Tex.2017). At least two courts have held that the trial court has discretion to award a nominal sanction if it determines that the plaintiff does not need to be deterred from bringing a similar action. *E.g.*, ***Tatum v. Hersh***, 559 S.W.3d 581, 588 (Tex.App.—Dallas 2018, no pet.); *see, e.g.*, ***Rich v. Range Res.***, 535 S.W.3d 610, 612-13 (Tex.App.—Fort Worth 2017, pet. denied). The court cannot, however, award nonmonetary sanctions. ***McGibney v. Rauhauser***, 549 S.W.3d 816, 835 (Tex.App.—Fort Worth 2018, pet. denied).

CHAPTER 4. ALTERNATIVE DISPUTE RESOLUTION

TABLE OF CONTENTS

TEXAS CIVIL FORMS
CHAPTER 4. ALTERNATIVE DISPUTE RESOLUTION

CHAPTER 4

{❶ *PARTY*}'S MOTION TO REFER
CASE TO ALTERNATIVE DISPUTE RESOLUTION

{❷ *Party*}, {❸ *name*}, asks the Court to refer this case to alternative dispute resolution (ADR) under the authority of Texas Civil Practice & Remedies Code section 154.021. {*See* ***O'Connor's Texas Rules***, *"Procedure for proposing ADR," ch. 4-A, §3.1, p. 347.*}

INTRODUCTION

1. Plaintiff, {❹ *name*}, sued defendant, {❺ *name*}, for {❻ *state basis of suit*}.

2. Discovery in this suit is governed by a Level {❼ *1/2/3*} discovery-control plan. The discovery period {❽ *will end/ended*} on {❾ *date*}. {*See* ***O'Connor's Texas Rules***, *"Discovery-Control Plans," ch. 6-A, §7, p. 520.*}

3. {❿ *All/Most/A significant part/No significant part/None*} of the discovery has been completed.

4. {⓫ *State other relevant facts about the suit.*}

BACKGROUND

5. {⓬ *State facts relevant to the motion.*}

ARGUMENT & AUTHORITIES

6. {⓭ *Party*} asks the Court to refer this case

{*CHOOSE APPROPRIATE FORM OF ADR*}

Ⓐ to mediation under Texas Civil Practice & Remedies Code section 154.023. {*See* ***O'Connor's Texas Rules***, *"Mediation," ch. 4-A, §2.1.1, p. 345.*}

Ⓑ to a moderated settlement conference under Texas Civil Practice & Remedies Code section 154.025. {*See* ***O'Connor's Texas Rules***, *"Moderated settlement conference," ch. 4-A, §2.1.2, p. 345.*}

Ⓒ to a summary jury trial so that the parties may make an early evaluation of the case and engage in realistic settlement negotiations. Tex. Civ. Prac. & Rem. Code §154.026. {*See* ***O'Connor's Texas Rules***, *"Summary jury trial," ch. 4-A, §2.1.4, p. 346.*}

Continued on next page

D to {⓮ *binding/nonbinding*} arbitration under Texas Civil Practice & Remedies Code section 154.027. {*See* ***O'Connor's Texas Rules****, "Arbitration," ch. 4-A, §2.1.5, p. 346.*}

E to {⓯ *identify other form of ADR*}.

7. This case is appropriate for referral to ADR because {⓰ *state reasons ADR is appropriate, e.g., it will promote the peaceable resolution of a dispute, the cost and length of trial will be significantly greater than that of ADR*}. {*See* ***O'Connor's Texas Rules****, "Considerations for referral," ch. 4-A, §3.2.1, p. 347.*}

CONCLUSION

8. {⓱ *Briefly summarize the motion.*}

PRAYER

9. For these reasons, {⓲ *party*} asks the Court to refer this case to {⓳ *identify ADR procedure requested*}.

SEE: Tex. Civ. Prac. & Rem. Code §152.001 et seq., §§154.021, 154.023, 154.025-154.027, 154.051
O'Connor's Texas Rules * Civil Trials (2019), "The ADR System," ch. 4-A, p. 345

ADD: STYLE OF THE CASE – FORM 1B:2
SIGNATURE BLOCK – FORM 1B:3
CERTIFICATE OF CONFERENCE – FORM 1B:12, if necessary
CERTIFICATE OF SERVICE – FORM 1B:13

ATTACH: AFFIDAVIT – FORM 1B:8, if necessary
NOTICE OF HEARING OR SUBMISSION – FORM 1E:1
ORDER – FORMS 4A:4-7

NOTE: The court may order alternative dispute resolution (ADR) at the request of either party or on its own motion. Tex. Civ. Prac. & Rem. Code §154.021(a). When the court decides that a case should go to ADR, the court must give the parties at least ten days' notice that it intends to send the case to ADR. See ***O'Connor's Texas Rules***, "Notice of intent to refer," ch. 4-A, §3.2.3, p. 347. The court may refer the parties to one of several types of ADR providers, including a county-sponsored ADR center, a dispute-resolution organization, an impartial third party, or any other ADR provider deemed appropriate. See ***O'Connor's Texas Rules***, "ADR providers," ch. 4-A, §5.3, p. 348. Although the court may order ADR at any point during the trial process, the court should consider whether the parties have completed enough discovery to properly evaluate the case. The court cannot order mediation in an action that is subject to the Federal Arbitration Act unless the parties agree. Tex. Civ. Prac. & Rem. Code §154.021(c).

Unless the parties agree, the court cannot refer the parties to a minitrial, a special-judge trial, an expert panel, a jury-determined settlement, or a collaborative-law procedure. See ***O'Connor's Texas Rules***, "By agreement only," ch. 4-A, §2.2, p. 346. For an agreed motion for a minitrial, see FORM 4A:8. For an agreed motion to refer to a special judge, see FORM 4D:1.

{❶ *PARTY*}'S OBJECTION TO {❷ *ADVERSE PARTY*}'S
MOTION TO REFER CASE TO ALTERNATIVE DISPUTE RESOLUTION

{❸ *Party*}, {❹ *name*}, objects to {❺ *adverse party*} {❻ *name*}'s motion to refer this case to alternative dispute resolution (ADR).

INTRODUCTION

1. Plaintiff, {❼ *name*}, sued defendant, {❽ *name*}, for {❾ *state basis of suit*}.

2. {❿ *State other relevant facts about the suit.*}

BACKGROUND

3. {⓫ *State facts relevant to the objection.*}

ARGUMENT & AUTHORITIES

{*CHOOSE APPROPRIATE PARAGRAPH 4*}

4. {⓬ *Party*} objects to the referral of this case to ADR because {⓭ *state reasons ADR is inappropriate, e.g., the cost and length of trial will be no greater than that of ADR, not enough discovery has been completed for the case to be properly evaluated*}. {*See* ***O'Connor's Texas Rules****, "Considerations for referral," ch. 4-A, §3.2.1, p. 347.*}

4. {⓮ *Party*} objects to the referral of this case to {⓯ *specify type of ADR requested by opposing party*}. Instead, {⓰ *party*} requests that the Court refer this case to {⓱ *specify different type of ADR requested*}. {⓲ *Elaborate.*}

CONCLUSION

5. {⓳ *Briefly summarize the objection.*}

PRAYER

6. For these reasons, {⓴ *party*} asks the Court to deny {㉑ *adverse party*}'s motion to refer this case to ADR.

FORM 4A:2

SEE: U.S. Const. amends. 5, 14, §1
Tex. Const. art. 1, §§13, 15
O'Connor's Texas Rules * Civil Trials (2019), "Considerations for referral," ch. 4-A, §3.2.1, p. 347

ADD: STYLE OF THE CASE – FORM 1B:2
SIGNATURE BLOCK – FORM 1B:3
CERTIFICATE OF SERVICE – FORM 1B:13

ATTACH: AFFIDAVIT – FORM 1B:8, if necessary
ORDER – FORMS 4A:4-7

{❶ *PARTY*}'S OBJECTION TO COURT'S
REFERRAL OF CASE TO ALTERNATIVE DISPUTE RESOLUTION

{❷ *Party*}, {❸ *name*}, objects to the referral of this case to alternative dispute resolution (ADR).

INTRODUCTION

1. Plaintiff, {❹ *name*}, sued defendant, {❺ *name*}, for {❻ *state basis of suit*}.

2. {❼ *State other relevant facts about the suit.*}

BACKGROUND

3. {❽ *State facts relevant to the objection.*}

ARGUMENT & AUTHORITIES

{*CHOOSE APPROPRIATE PARAGRAPHS 4-9*}

4. The Court should not have referred this case to ADR because the Court did not confer with the parties before doing so. Tex. Civ. Prac. & Rem. Code §154.021(b). {❾ *Elaborate.*} {*See* ***O'Connor's Texas Rules****, "No conference with parties," ch. 4-A, §4.3.2, p. 348.*}

5. The Court should not have referred this case to ADR because the case is subject to the Federal Arbitration Act and the Court ordered mediation without the parties' agreement. Tex. Civ. Prac. & Rem. Code §154.021(c). {❿ *Elaborate.*} {*See* ***O'Connor's Texas Rules****, "Mediation order in FAA case," ch. 4-A, §4.3.6, p. 348.*}

6. The Court should not have referred this case to ADR because the Court gave the parties less than ten days' notice of the referral. *See* Tex. Civ. Prac. & Rem. Code §154.022(b); *Keene Corp. v. Gardner*, 837 S.W.2d 224, 232 (Tex. App.—Dallas 1992, writ denied). {⓫ *Elaborate.*} {*See* ***O'Connor's Texas Rules****, "Less than 10 days' notice," ch. 4-A, §4.3.3, p. 348.*}

7. The Court should not have referred this case to ADR because the Court's order referring this case to ADR is overbroad. *See In re Acceptance Ins. Co.*, 33 S.W.3d 443, 451-52 (Tex. App.—Fort Worth 2000, orig. proceeding); *Decker v. Lindsay*, 824 S.W.2d 247, 251-52 (Tex. App.—Houston [1st Dist.] 1992, orig. proceeding). Specifically, {⓬ *state how order is overbroad, e.g., it orders parties to negotiate in good faith*}. {*See* ***O'Connor's Texas Rules****, "Too broad," ch. 4-A, §4.3.1, p. 348.*}

8. The Court should not have referred this case to ADR because the case has previously been submitted to ADR. Specifically, {⓭ *explain*}. {*See* ***O'Connor's Texas Rules***, *"Multiple referrals in same case," ch. 4-A, §4.3.7, p. 348.*}

9. The Court should not have referred this case to ADR because {⓮ *state reasons ADR is inappropriate, e.g., the cost and length of trial will be no greater than that of ADR, not enough discovery has been completed for the case to be properly evaluated*}. {*See* ***O'Connor's Texas Rules***, *"Case not appropriate," ch. 4-A, §4.3.4, p. 348.*}

CONCLUSION

10. {⓯ *Briefly summarize the objection.*}

PRAYER

11. For these reasons, {⓰ *party*} asks the Court to set aside the order referring this case to alternative dispute resolution.

SEE: Tex. Civ. Prac. & Rem. Code §§154.021, 154.022
O'Connor's Texas Rules * Civil Trials (2019), "Objecting to ADR," ch. 4-A, §4, p. 348

ADD: STYLE OF THE CASE – FORM 1B:2
SIGNATURE BLOCK – FORM 1B:3
CERTIFICATE OF SERVICE – FORM 1B:13

ATTACH: AFFIDAVIT – FORM 1B:8, if necessary

ORDER ON {❶ *PARTY*}'S MOTION TO
REFER CASE TO ALTERNATIVE DISPUTE RESOLUTION

After considering {❷ *party*} {❸ *name*}'s motion to refer this case to alternative dispute resolution (ADR) {❹ *add if appropriate: , and the objection,*} and after conferring with the parties, the Court

{*CHOOSE APPROPRIATE ORDER*}

DENIES the motion.

GRANTS the motion and orders as follows:

1. This case is referred for mediation under Texas Civil Practice & Remedies Code section 154.023. {*See **O'Connor's Texas Rules**, "Order for ADR," ch. 4-A, §5, p. 348; "Mediation," ch. 4-B, p. 352.*}

2. {❺ *Name of impartial third party*} is appointed to assist the parties in the resolution of this case.

3. All counsel will contact {❻ *name of impartial third party*} within ___ business days to schedule the mediation.

4. The mediation will be completed by _____________, 20___.

5. The following parties and their counsel will attend the mediation and remain present until its completion: {❼ *list parties and their attorneys*}.

6. All statements made during mediation sessions and all materials prepared for the mediation are confidential. No party will attempt to compel {❽ *name of impartial third party*}'s testimony, to compel {❾ *name of impartial third party*} to produce any documents provided by any party, or to compel any party to testify about statements made in the mediation sessions, unless the oral communications or written materials are admissible or discoverable independent of the ADR procedure. {*See **O'Connor's Texas Rules**, "Confidentiality," ch. 4-A, §7, p. 350.*}

7. {❿ *Name of impartial third party*} will not disclose confidential information provided during the mediation, testify on behalf of any party, or submit any report to the Court in connection with this suit, other than to state whether the parties have reached a settlement. {*See **O'Connor's Texas Rules**, "Confidentiality," ch. 4-A, §7, p. 350.*}

8. The mediation will be confidential, privileged from discovery, and otherwise conducted in accordance with Texas Civil Practice & Remedies Code section 154.073. {*See **O'Connor's Texas Rules**, "Confidentiality," ch. 4-A, §7, p. 350.*}

{*CHOOSE APPROPRIATE PARAGRAPH 9*}

9. The Court sets the fee for the services of the mediator at {⓫ *state reasonable fee*}. Because the parties did not agree to a method of payment, the fees of the mediator will be taxed as costs. {*See* ***O'Connor's Texas Rules****, "Fees," ch. 4-A, §6.3, p. 350.*}

9. The Court sets the fee for the services of the mediator at {⓬ *state reasonable fee*}. The parties will pay the fee for the services of the mediator by {⓭ *identify method of payment*}, according to their agreement, which provides that they will share the cost of the mediator {⓮ *equally/in the following proportions: {state agreed proportions}*}. {*See* ***O'Connor's Texas Rules****, "Fees," ch. 4-A, §6.3, p. 350.*}

SIGNED on ________________, 20____.

____
PRESIDING JUDGE

SEE: Tex. Civ. Prac. & Rem. Code §§154.023, 154.073
O'Connor's Texas Rules * Civil Trials (2019), "The ADR System," ch. 4-A, p. 345

ADD: STYLE OF THE CASE – FORM 1B:2
CERTIFICATE OF SERVICE – FORM 1B:13, if proposed order served separately from motion or objection

NOTE: Unless the parties agree to a method of payment, the court must tax the fee for the services of the impartial third party as other costs of suit. Tex. Civ. Prac. & Rem. Code §154.054(b). See ***O'Connor's Texas Rules***, "Fees," ch. 4-A, §6.3, p. 350.

ORDER ON {❶ *PARTY*}'S MOTION TO
REFER CASE TO ALTERNATIVE DISPUTE RESOLUTION

After considering {❷ *party*} {❸ *name*}'s motion to refer this case to alternative dispute resolution (ADR) {❹ *add if appropriate: , and the objection,*} and after conferring with the parties, the Court

{*CHOOSE APPROPRIATE ORDER*}

DENIES the motion.

GRANTS the motion and orders as follows:

1. This case is referred to a moderated settlement conference under Texas Civil Practice & Remedies Code section 154.025. {*See **O'Connor's Texas Rules**, "Moderated settlement conference," ch. 4-A, §2.1.2, p. 345; "Order for ADR," ch. 4-A, §5, p. 348.*}

2. {❺ *Names of impartial third parties*} are appointed to assist the parties in the resolution of this case.

3. All counsel will contact {❻ *names of impartial third parties*} within ___ business days to schedule the moderated settlement conference.

4. The moderated settlement conference will be completed by __________, 20___.

5. The following parties and their counsel will attend the moderated settlement conference and remain present until its completion: {❼ *list parties and their attorneys*}.

6. All statements made during the moderated settlement conference sessions and all materials prepared for the conference are confidential. No party will attempt to compel the moderators' testimony, to compel the moderators to produce any documents provided by any party, or to compel any party to testify about statements made in the moderated settlement conference, unless the oral communications or written materials are admissible or discoverable independent of the ADR procedure. {*See **O'Connor's Texas Rules**, "Confidentiality," ch. 4-A, §7, p. 350.*}

7. The moderators will not disclose confidential information provided during the moderated settlement conference, testify on behalf of any party, or submit any report to the Court in connection with this suit, other than to state whether the parties reached a settlement. {*See **O'Connor's Texas Rules**, "Confidentiality," ch. 4-A, §7, p. 350.*}

8. The moderated settlement conference will be confidential, privileged from discovery, and otherwise conducted in accordance with Texas Civil Practice & Remedies Code section 154.073. {*See* ***O'Connor's Texas Rules***, *"Confidentiality," ch. 4-A, §7, p. 350.*}

{*CHOOSE APPROPRIATE PARAGRAPH 9*}

9. The Court sets the fee for the services of the moderators at {❽ *state reasonable fee*}. Because the parties did not agree to a method of payment, the fees of the moderators will be taxed as costs. {*See* ***O'Connor's Texas Rules***, *"Fees," ch. 4-A, §6.3, p. 350.*}

9. The Court sets the fee for the services of the moderators at {❾ *state reasonable fee*}. The parties will pay the fee for the services of the moderators by {❿ *identify method of payment*}, according to their agreement, which provides that they will share the cost of the moderators {⓫ *equally/in the following proportions: {state agreed proportions}*}. {*See* ***O'Connor's Texas Rules***, *"Fees," ch. 4-A, §6.3, p. 350.*}

SIGNED on __________, 20___.

____
PRESIDING JUDGE

SEE: Tex. Civ. Prac. & Rem. Code §§154.025, 154.073
O'Connor's Texas Rules * Civil Trials (2019), "The ADR System," ch. 4-A, p. 345

ADD: STYLE OF THE CASE – FORM 1B:2
CERTIFICATE OF SERVICE – FORM 1B:13, if proposed order served separately from motion or objection

NOTE: Unless the parties agree to a method of payment, the court must tax the fee for the services of the impartial third parties as other costs of suit. Tex. Civ. Prac. & Rem. Code §154.054(b). See ***O'Connor's Texas Rules***, "Fees," ch. 4-A, §6.3, p. 350.

ORDER ON {❶ *PARTY*}'S MOTION TO
REFER CASE TO ALTERNATIVE DISPUTE RESOLUTION

After considering {❷ *party*} {❸ *name*}'s motion to refer this case to alternative dispute resolution (ADR) {❹ *add if appropriate: , and the objection,*} and after conferring with the parties, the Court

{*CHOOSE APPROPRIATE ORDER*}

DENIES the motion.

GRANTS the motion and orders as follows:

1. This case is referred to a summary jury trial under Texas Civil Practice & Remedies Code section 154.026. {*See* ***O'Connor's Texas Rules****, "Summary jury trial," ch. 4-A, §2.1.4, p. 346; "Order for ADR," ch. 4-A, §5, p. 348.*}

2. The summary jury trial will be completed by ______________, 20___.

3. Each party will be allowed {❺ *time*} for voir dire, {❻ *time*} for an opening statement, {❼ *time*} for summary of admissible evidence, and {❽ *time*} for a closing argument.

4. After the jury returns its verdict, the parties will be allowed {❾ *time*} for final discussions with the jury.

5. The following parties and their counsel will attend the summary jury trial and remain present until its completion: {❿ *list parties and their attorneys*}.

6. All statements made during the summary jury trial and all materials prepared for the summary jury trial are confidential. Any record made during the summary jury trial is confidential. No party will attempt to compel any party to testify about statements made in the summary jury trial or to compel any party to produce any documents provided by any party during the summary jury trial, unless the oral communications or written materials are admissible or discoverable independent of the ADR procedure. {*See* ***O'Connor's Texas Rules****, "Confidentiality," ch. 4-A, §7, p. 350.*}

7. The summary jury trial will be confidential, privileged from discovery, and otherwise conducted in accordance with Texas Civil Practice & Remedies Code section 154.073. {*See **O'Connor's Texas Rules**, "Confidentiality," ch. 4-A, §7, p. 350.*}

SIGNED on ______________, 20___.

____
PRESIDING JUDGE

SEE: Tex. Civ. Prac. & Rem. Code §§154.026, 154.073
O'Connor's Texas Rules * Civil Trials (2019), "The ADR System," ch. 4-A, p. 345

ADD: STYLE OF THE CASE – FORM 1B:2
CERTIFICATE OF SERVICE – FORM 1B:13, if proposed order served separately from motion or objection

ORDER ON {❶ *PARTY*}'S MOTION TO
REFER CASE TO ALTERNATIVE DISPUTE RESOLUTION

After considering {❷ *party*} {❸ *name*}'s motion to refer this case to alternative dispute resolution (ADR) {❹ *add if appropriate: , and the objection,*} and after conferring with the parties, the Court

{*CHOOSE APPROPRIATE ORDER*}

DENIES the motion.

GRANTS the motion and orders as follows:

1. This case is referred to {❺ *binding/nonbinding*} arbitration under Texas Civil Practice & Remedies Code section 154.027. {*See **O'Connor's Texas Rules**, "Order for ADR," ch. 4-A, §5, p. 348; "Arbitration," ch. 4-C, p. 355.*}

2. {❻ *Name of impartial third party*} is appointed to assist the parties in the resolution of this case.

3. All counsel will contact {❼ *name of impartial third party*} within ___ business days to schedule the arbitration.

4. The arbitration will be completed by _______________, 20___.

5. The following parties and their counsel will attend the arbitration and remain present until its completion: {❽ *list parties and their attorneys*}.

6. All statements made during the arbitration and all materials prepared for the arbitration are confidential. No party will attempt to compel {❾ *name of impartial third party*}'s testimony, to compel {❿ *name of impartial third party*} to produce any documents provided by any party, or to compel any party to testify about statements made in the arbitration, unless the oral communications or written materials are admissible or discoverable independent of the ADR procedure. {*See **O'Connor's Texas Rules**, "Confidentiality," ch. 4-A, §7, p. 350.*}

7. {⓫ *Name of impartial third party*} will not disclose confidential information provided during the arbitration, testify on behalf of any party, or submit any report to the Court in connection with this suit, other than to state whether the parties have reached a settlement. {*See **O'Connor's Texas Rules**, "Confidentiality," ch. 4-A, §7, p. 350.*}

8. The arbitration will be confidential, privileged from discovery, and otherwise conducted in accordance with Texas Civil Practice & Remedies Code section 154.073. {*See **O'Connor's Texas Rules**, "Confidentiality," ch. 4-A, §7, p. 350.*}

{*CHOOSE APPROPRIATE PARAGRAPH 9*}

9. The Court sets the fee for the services of the arbitrator at {⓬ *state reasonable fee*}. Because the parties did not agree to a method of payment, the fees of the arbitrator will be taxed as costs. {*See **O'Connor's Texas Rules**, "Fees," ch. 4-A, §6.3, p. 350.*}

9. The Court sets the fee for the services of the arbitrator at {⓭ *state reasonable fee*}. The parties will pay the fee for the services of the arbitrator by {⓮ *identify method of payment*}, according to their agreement, which provides that they will share the cost of the arbitrator {⓯ *equally/in the following proportions: {state agreed proportions}*}. {*See **O'Connor's Texas Rules**, "Fees," ch. 4-A, §6.3, p. 350.*}

SIGNED on ________________, 20___.

____
PRESIDING JUDGE

SEE: Tex. Civ. Prac. & Rem. Code §§154.027, 154.073
O'Connor's Texas Rules * Civil Trials (2019), "The ADR System," ch. 4-A, p. 345

ADD: STYLE OF THE CASE – FORM 1B:2
CERTIFICATE OF SERVICE – FORM 1B:13, if proposed order served separately from motion or objection

NOTE: Unless the parties agree to a method of payment, the court must tax the fee for the services of an impartial third party as other costs of suit. Tex. Civ. Prac. & Rem. Code §154.054(b). See ***O'Connor's Texas Rules***, "Fees," ch. 4-A, §6.3, p. 350.

AGREED MOTION FOR REFERRAL OF CASE TO MINITRIAL

{❶ *Party*}, {❷ *name*}, and {❸ *adverse party*}, {❹ *name*}, ask the Court to refer this case to a minitrial, as permitted by Texas Civil Practice & Remedies Code section 154.024. {*See* ***O'Connor's Texas Rules****, "Minitrial," ch. 4-A, §2.2.1, p. 346.*}

INTRODUCTION

1. Plaintiff, {❺ *name*}, sued defendant, {❻ *name*}, for {❼ *state basis of suit*}.

2. {❽ *State other relevant facts about the suit.*}

BACKGROUND

3. {❾ *State facts relevant to the motion.*}

AGREEMENT

4. The parties agree to the following:

a. This case should be referred to a minitrial to be conducted before

{*CHOOSE ONE OF THE FOLLOWING*}

Ⓐ selected representatives for each party.

Ⓑ an impartial third party. The parties ask the Court to appoint {❿ *name*} to act as the impartial third party.

Ⓒ selected representatives for each party and an impartial third party. The parties ask the Court to appoint {⓫ *name*} to act as the impartial third party.

b. The opinion from the minitrial will be binding only if the parties enter into a written settlement agreement.

{*IF IMPARTIAL THIRD PARTY APPOINTED, ADD PARAGRAPHS 5-6*}

5. The parties ask the Court to set a reasonable fee for the services of the impartial third party. Tex. Civ. Prac. & Rem. Code §154.054(a). The parties suggest that a reasonable fee for the services of the impartial third party is {⓬ *state reasonable fee*}. {*See* ***O'Connor's Texas Rules****, "Fees," ch. 4-A, §6.3, p. 350.*}

{*CHOOSE APPROPRIATE PARAGRAPH 6*}

6. The parties agree to pay the impartial third party by {⓭ *identify method of payment*}. The parties agree to share the cost of the impartial third party {⓮ *equally/in the following proportions: {state agreed proportions}*}. {*See* ***O'Connor's Texas Rules****, "Fees," ch. 4-A, §6.3, p. 350.*}

6. Because the parties have not agreed to a method of payment for the impartial third party, the parties ask the Court to tax the fees for the services of the impartial third party as costs. Tex. Civ. Prac. & Rem. Code §154.054(b). {*See* ***O'Connor's Texas Rules****, "Fees," ch. 4-A, §6.3, p. 350.*}

CONCLUSION

7. {⓯ *Briefly summarize the motion.*}

PRAYER

8. For these reasons, the parties ask the Court to grant their agreed motion to refer this case to a minitrial.

SEE: Tex. Civ. Prac. & Rem. Code §§154.024, 154.054
O'Connor's Texas Rules * Civil Trials (2019), "The ADR System," ch. 4-A, p. 345

ADD: STYLE OF THE CASE – FORM 1B:2
SIGNATURE BLOCK FOR AGREED MOTIONS – FORM 1B:4
CERTIFICATE OF SERVICE – FORM 1B:13

ATTACH: ORDER – FORM 4A:9

ORDER ON AGREED MOTION TO REFER CASE TO MINITRIAL

After considering the parties' agreed motion to refer the case to a minitrial under Texas Civil Practice & Remedies Code section 154.024, the Court

GRANTS the agreed motion and orders as follows:

1. This case is referred to a minitrial under Texas Civil Practice & Remedies Code section 154.024. {*See **O'Connor's Texas Rules**, "Minitrial," ch. 4-A, §2.2.1, p. 346; "Order for ADR," ch. 4-A, §5, p. 348.*}

2. The proceedings in this case will be stayed pending the outcome of the minitrial.

3. The parties will conduct the minitrial before

{*CHOOSE ONE OF THE FOLLOWING*}

Ⓐ selected representatives for each party. The parties must select their representatives and submit the names to the Court by {❶ *date*}.

Ⓑ {❷ *name of impartial third party*}, who is the impartial third party selected by the parties.

Ⓒ {❸ *name of impartial third party*}, who is the impartial third party selected by the parties, and selected representatives for each party. The parties must select their representatives and submit the names to the Court by {❹ *date*}.

4. The {❺ *selected representatives/impartial third party/selected representatives and impartial third party*} will assist the parties in defining the issues and developing a basis for realistic settlement negotiations.

5. The minitrial will be conducted according to the following terms and conditions: {❻ *state the date, time, and place for the minitrial*}. All proceedings related to the minitrial must be concluded by {❼ *date*}.

6. The following parties and their counsel will attend the minitrial and remain present until its completion: {❽ *list parties and their attorneys*}.

7. All statements made during minitrial sessions and all materials prepared for the minitrial are confidential. Any record made during the minitrial is confidential. No party will attempt to compel any party to testify about statements made in the minitrial or to compel any party to produce any documents provided by any party during the minitrial, unless the oral communication or written materials are admissible or discoverable independent of the alternative-dispute-resolution procedure. {*See **O'Connor's Texas Rules**, "Confidentiality," ch. 4-A, §7, p. 350.*}

8. The minitrial will be confidential, privileged from discovery, and conducted in accordance with Texas Civil Practice & Remedies Code section 154.073. {*See* ***O'Connor's Texas Rules****, "Confidentiality," ch. 4-A, §7, p. 350.*}

9. If the parties enter into a written settlement agreement following the minitrial, the agreement will be binding.

{IF TRIAL CONDUCTED BY IMPARTIAL THIRD PARTY, ADD PARAGRAPHS 10-14}

10. No party will attempt to compel {❾ *name of impartial third party*}'s testimony, to compel {❿ *name of impartial third party*} to produce any documents provided by any party, or to compel any party to testify about statements made during the minitrial. {*See* ***O'Connor's Texas Rules****, "Confidentiality," ch. 4-A, §7, p. 350.*}

11. {⓫ *Name of impartial third party*} will not disclose confidential information provided during the minitrial, testify on behalf of any party, or submit any report to the Court in connection with this suit, other than to state whether the parties have reached a settlement. {*See* ***O'Connor's Texas Rules****, "Confidentiality," ch. 4-A, §7, p. 350.*}

12. {⓬ *Name of impartial third party*} may issue a nonbinding advisory opinion about the merits of the case.

13. The reasonable fee for the services of {⓭ *name of impartial third party*} will be set at {⓮ *identify fee*}.

{CHOOSE APPROPRIATE PARAGRAPH 14}

14. Because the parties did not agree to a method of payment, the fees of the impartial third party will be taxed as costs. {*See* ***O'Connor's Texas Rules****, "Fees," ch. 4-A, §6.3, p. 350.*}

14. The parties will pay the fee for the services of {⓯ *name of impartial third party*} by {⓰ *identify method of payment*}, according to their agreement, which provides that they will share the cost of {⓱ *name of impartial third party*} {⓲ *equally/in the following proportions: {state agreed proportions}*}. {*See* ***O'Connor's Texas Rules****, "Fees," ch. 4-A, §6.3, p. 350.*}

SIGNED on _______________, 20___.

____
PRESIDING JUDGE

Continued on next page

SEE: Tex. Civ. Prac. & Rem. Code §§154.024, 154.054, 154.073
O'Connor's Texas Rules * Civil Trials (2019), "The ADR System," ch. 4-A, p. 345

ADD: STYLE OF THE CASE – FORM 1B:2
CERTIFICATE OF SERVICE – FORM 1B:13, if proposed order served separately from motion

{❶ *PARTY*}'S MOTION TO COMPEL MEDIATION OF DTPA CLAIM

{❷ *Party*}, {❸ *name*}, asks the Court to compel mediation of the parties' dispute as allowed by Texas Business & Commerce Code section 17.5051. {*See **O'Connor's Texas Rules**, "DTPA claims," ch. 4-B, §3.1, p. 353.*}

INTRODUCTION

1. Plaintiff, {❹ *name*}, sued defendant, {❺ *name*}, for {❻ *state basis of suit*}.

2. {❼ *State other relevant facts about the suit.*}

BACKGROUND

3. {❽ *Party*} files this motion within 90 days after the original petition was served on defendant.

4. {❾ *State other facts relevant to the motion.*}

REQUEST

5. {❿ *Party*} asks the Court to appoint an impartial third party as mediator.

{*ADD PARAGRAPH 6 IF APPROPRIATE*}

6. Because the amount of economic damages claimed is less than $15,000, {⓫ *party*} agrees to pay the costs of the mediation. Tex. Bus. & Com. Code §17.5051(f).

CONCLUSION

7. {⓬ *Briefly summarize the motion.*}

PRAYER

8. For these reasons, {⓭ *party*} asks the Court to compel mediation and appoint an impartial third party to mediate this dispute.

FORM 4B:1

SEE: Tex. Civ. Prac. & Rem. Code §154.023
Tex. Bus. & Com. Code §17.5051
O'Connor's Texas Rules * Civil Trials (2019), "DTPA claims," ch. 4-B, §3.1, p. 353
O'Connor's Texas Causes of Action (2019), "Deceptive Trade Practices Act," ch. 8, p. 209

◄ *Continued on next page* ►

ADD: STYLE OF THE CASE – FORM 1B:2
SIGNATURE BLOCK – FORM 1B:3
CERTIFICATE OF CONFERENCE – FORM 1B:12, if necessary
CERTIFICATE OF SERVICE – FORM 1B:13

ATTACH: NOTICE OF HEARING OR SUBMISSION – FORM 1E:1
ORDER – FORM 4B:3

NOTE: A party can compel mediation by filing a motion within 90 days after service of a pleading requesting relief under the Deceptive Trade Practices Act. Tex. Bus. & Com. Code §17.5051(a). See ***O'Connor's Texas Rules***, "DTPA claims," ch. 4-B, §3.1, p. 353.

{❶ *PARTY*}'S OBJECTION TO MOTION
TO COMPEL MEDIATION OF DTPA CLAIM

{❷ *Party*}, {❸ *name*}, objects to {❹ *adverse party*}'s motion to compel a Deceptive Trade Practices Act (DTPA) mediation under Texas Business & Commerce Code section 17.5051. {*See* ***O'Connor's Texas Rules****, "DTPA claims," ch. 4-B, §3.1, p. 353.*}

INTRODUCTION

1. Plaintiff, {❺ *name*}, sued defendant, {❻ *name*}, for {❼ *state basis of suit*}.

2. {❽ *State other relevant facts about the suit.*}

BACKGROUND

3. {❾ *State facts relevant to the objection.*}

OBJECTION

{*CHOOSE APPROPRIATE PARAGRAPH 4*}

4. A motion to compel a DTPA mediation must be filed within 90 days after service of a pleading requesting relief under the DTPA. Tex. Bus. & Com. Code §17.5051(a). This case should not be sent to a mediation under Texas Business & Commerce Code section 17.5051 because {❿ *adverse party*} did not file the motion before this deadline. {⓫ *Elaborate.*}

4. This case should not be sent to a mediation under Texas Business & Commerce Code section 17.5051 because {⓬ *elaborate*}.

CONCLUSION

5. {⓭ *Briefly summarize the objection.*}

PRAYER

6. For these reasons, {⓮ *party*} asks the Court to deny {⓯ *adverse party*}'s motion to compel a DTPA mediation.

FORM 4B:2

Continued on next page

SEE: Tex. Bus. & Com. Code §17.5051
O'Connor's Texas Rules * Civil Trials (2019), "DTPA claims," ch. 4-B, §3.1, p. 353
O'Connor's Texas Causes of Action (2019), "Deceptive Trade Practices Act," ch. 8, p. 209

ADD: STYLE OF THE CASE – FORM 1B:2
SIGNATURE BLOCK – FORM 1B:3
CERTIFICATE OF SERVICE – FORM 1B:13

ATTACH: AFFIDAVIT – FORM 1B:8, if necessary
ORDER – FORM 4B:3

ORDER ON {❶ *PARTY*}'S MOTION
TO COMPEL MEDIATION OF DTPA CLAIM

After considering {❷ *party*} {❸ *name*}'s motion to compel mediation {❹ *add if appropriate: and the objection*}, the Court

{*CHOOSE APPROPRIATE ORDER*}

DENIES the motion.

GRANTS the motion and orders as follows:

1. {❺ *Name of mediator*} is appointed to assist the parties in the resolution of this case.

2. The mediation is set for _______________, 20___.

3. The following parties and their counsel will attend the mediation at {❻ *identify place of mediation*} and remain present until its completion: {❼ *list parties and their attorneys*}.

4. All statements made during mediation sessions and all materials prepared for the mediation are confidential. No party will attempt to compel {❽ *name of mediator*}'s testimony, to compel {❾ *name of mediator*} to produce any documents provided by any party, or to compel any party to testify about statements made in the mediation sessions, unless the oral communications or written materials are admissible or discoverable independent of the alternative-dispute-resolution procedure. {*See **O'Connor's Texas Rules**, "Confidentiality," ch. 4-A, §7, p. 350.*}

5. {❿ *Name of mediator*} will not disclose confidential information provided during the mediation on behalf of any party, testify on behalf of any party, or submit any type of report to the Court in connection with this suit, other than to state whether the parties reached a settlement. {*See **O'Connor's Texas Rules**, "Confidentiality," ch. 4-A, §7, p. 350.*}

6. The mediation will be confidential, privileged from discovery, and otherwise conducted in accordance with Texas Civil Practice & Remedies Code section 154.073. {*See **O'Connor's Texas Rules**, "Confidentiality," ch. 4-A, §7, p. 350.*}

{*CHOOSE APPROPRIATE PARAGRAPH 7*}

7. The parties will share all fees associated with the mediation {⓫ *equally/in the following proportions: {state agreed proportions}*} and will pay the fees directly to {⓬ *name of mediator*}. {*See **O'Connor's Texas Rules**, "Fees," ch. 4-B, §3.1.2, p. 353.*}

Continued on next page

7. Because the amount of economic damages claimed is less than $15,000, {⓭ *party*} will pay all fees associated with the mediation. The fees will be paid directly to {⓮ *name of mediator*}. {*See **O'Connor's Texas Rules**, "DTPA claims," ch. 4-B, §3.1, p. 353.*}

SIGNED on ______________, 20___.

____
PRESIDING JUDGE

SEE: Tex. Civ. Prac. & Rem. Code §§154.023, 154.073
Tex. Bus. & Com. Code §17.5051
O'Connor's Texas Rules * Civil Trials (2019), "DTPA claims," ch. 4-B, §3.1, p. 353
O'Connor's Texas Causes of Action (2019), "Deceptive Trade Practices Act," ch. 8, p. 209

ADD: STYLE OF THE CASE – FORM 1B:2
CERTIFICATE OF SERVICE – FORM 1B:13, if proposed order served separately from motion or objection

NOTE: Within 30 days after the motion is filed, the court must sign an order setting the time and place of the mediation. Tex. Bus. & Com. Code §17.5051(b). The mediation must be held within 30 days after the order is signed unless the parties agree otherwise or the court determines that additional time (up to 30 more days) is warranted. *Id.* §17.5051(d).

Unless the parties agree otherwise, the parties must share the mediation fee. Tex. Bus. & Com. Code §17.5051(e). If the amount of economic damages claimed is less than $15,000, the party seeking to compel mediation must agree to pay the costs of the mediation. *Id.* §17.5051(f).

{❶ *PARTY*}'S MEDIATION MEMORANDUM

* * PRIVILEGED & CONFIDENTIAL * *

{❷ *Party*}, {❸ *name*}, provides this confidential mediation memorandum for use only in this mediation. The mediator will not disclose any information in this memorandum to any party. All information in this memorandum is privileged and confidential and cannot be disclosed without {❹ *party*}'s consent.

1. Plaintiffs. {❺ *State the names, addresses, and telephone numbers of plaintiffs; identify authorized representatives, if known, and attorneys of record.*}

2. Defendants. {❻ *State the names, addresses, and telephone numbers of defendants; identify authorized representatives, if known, and attorneys of record.*}

3. Other Parties. {❼ *State the names, addresses, and telephone numbers of other parties, e.g., intervenors; identify authorized representatives, if known, and attorneys of record.*}

4. Plaintiff's Claims. {❽ *State the nature of plaintiff's claims.*}

5. Defendant's Defenses. {❾ *State the nature of defendant's defenses, counterclaims, cross-claims, and third-party claims.*}

6. Relief. {❿ *State the relief sought by the parties.*}

7. Disputed Facts. {⓫ *List and summarize the disputed issues of fact.*}

8. Disputed Issues of Law. {⓬ *List and summarize the disputed issues of law.*}

9. Discovery Status. {⓭ *State the status of discovery, e.g., complete, substantially complete.*}

10. Settlement. {⓮ *State whether you have sufficient information to form a realistic settlement position. If not, describe the information you need to establish a position.*}

11. Offers to Settle. {⓯ *State the last offers of the parties.*}

SEE: Tex. Civ. Prac. & Rem. Code §§154.023, 154.073
O'Connor's Texas Rules * Civil Trials (2019), "Mediation," ch. 4-B, p. 352

ADD: STYLE OF THE CASE – FORM 1B:2
SIGNATURE BLOCK – FORM 1B:3

{❶ *PARTY*}'S MOTION TO COMPEL ARBITRATION & STAY PROCEEDINGS

{❷ *Party*}, {❸ *name*}, asks the Court to order arbitration and stay this {❹ *lawsuit/dispute*}.

INTRODUCTION

1. Plaintiff, {❺ *name*}, sued defendant, {❻ *name*}, for {❼ *state basis of suit*}.

2. {❽ *State other relevant facts about the suit.*}

BACKGROUND

3. On {❾ *date*}, plaintiff filed this suit, invoking the Court's jurisdiction over the dispute subject to the arbitration agreement.

4. On {❿ *date*}, the parties signed a contract to {⓫ *describe purpose of contract*}. Attached to this motion as Exhibit {⓬ *letter*} is a copy of the contract, which is incorporated by reference. That contract contained a requirement that

{*CHOOSE ONE OF THE FOLLOWING*}

Ⓐ all disputes be submitted to arbitration.

Ⓑ the following disputes be submitted to arbitration: {⓭ *specify disputes subject to arbitration*}.

5. The arbitration agreement, as part of the contract, was made in consideration of {⓮ *describe consideration*}. {⓯ *Party*} fully performed all of {⓰ *his/her/its*} duties under the contract.

{*CHOOSE APPROPRIATE PARAGRAPH 6*}

6. The arbitration agreement provides for arbitration under {⓱ *the Federal Arbitration Act (FAA)/the Texas Arbitration Act (TAA)/both the Federal Arbitration Act (FAA) and the Texas Arbitration Act (TAA)*}.

6. The arbitration agreement does not specify whether the arbitration agreement is governed by the Federal Arbitration Act (FAA) or the Texas Arbitration Act (TAA).

7. On {⓲ *date*}, a dispute arose between the parties relating to the subject of the contract.

8. {⓳ *State other facts relevant to the motion.*}

ARGUMENT & AUTHORITIES

9. Although the parties contractually agreed to arbitrate, {[20] *adverse party*} refuses to arbitrate.

10. Once a party seeking to compel arbitration establishes that (1) there is a valid agreement to arbitrate, (2) the claims raised are within the agreement's scope, and (3) the claims are arbitrable, the trial court must compel arbitration. *See* 9 U.S.C. §§2, 4 (FAA); Tex. Civ. Prac. & Rem. Code §§171.001, 171.002, 171.021 (TAA); *Henry v. Cash Biz, LP*, 551 S.W.3d 111, 115 (Tex. 2018) (FAA); *G.T. Leach Builders, LLC v. Sapphire V.P., LP*, 458 S.W.3d 502, 524 (Tex. 2015) (TAA); *Rachal v. Reitz*, 403 S.W.3d 840, 843 (Tex. 2013) (TAA); *In re Rubiola*, 334 S.W.3d 220, 223 (Tex. 2011) (FAA). {*See* ***O'Connor's Texas Rules****, "Motion to compel arbitration under FAA," ch. 4-C, §5.2, p. 361; "Motion to compel arbitration under TAA," ch. 4-C, §6.2, p. 363.*}

11. The arbitration agreement is valid because {[21] *explain*}. {*See* ***O'Connor's Texas Rules****, "Valid arbitration agreement," ch. 4-C, §5.2.1(1), p. 361; "Valid arbitration agreement," ch. 4-C, §6.2.1(1), p. 364.*}

12. {[22] *Party*}'s claims for {[23] *identify claims*} are within the scope of the agreement because {[24] *explain*}. {*See* ***O'Connor's Texas Rules****, "Claim within scope," ch. 4-C, §5.2.1(2), p. 362; "Claim within scope," ch. 4-C, §6.2.1(2), p. 365.*}

13. The claim is arbitrable because {[25] *explain, e.g., no federal statute shows clear congressional intent to preclude application of the FAA*}. {*See* ***O'Connor's Texas Rules****, "Arbitrable claim," ch. 4-C, §5.2.2, p. 363; "Arbitrable claim," ch. 4-C, §6.2.2, p. 365.*}

{*CHOOSE APPROPRIATE PARAGRAPH 14*}

{*For arbitration under the FAA*}

14. The parties agreed to arbitrate under the FAA. *Henry*, 551 S.W.3d at 115; *In re Rubiola*, 334 S.W.3d at 223; *In re Kellogg Brown & Root*, 80 S.W.3d 611, 617 (Tex. App.—Houston [1st Dist.] 2002, orig. proceeding); *see* 9 U.S.C. §2. See Exhibit {[26] *letter*}, page {[27] *number*}, paragraph {[28] *number*}. {[29] *Elaborate.*} {*See* ***O'Connor's Texas Rules****, "Agreement specifies FAA," ch. 4-C, §4.1, p. 356.*}

FORM 4C:1

Continued on next page

{*For arbitration under the TAA*}

14. The parties agreed to arbitrate under the TAA. *See* Tex. Civ. Prac. & Rem. Code §171.021(a)(1); *G.T. Leach Builders*, 458 S.W.3d at 519 n.14; *In re Olshan Found. Repair Co.*, 328 S.W.3d 883, 890-91 (Tex. 2010). See Exhibit {❸⓪ *letter*}, page {❸① *number*}, paragraph {❸② *number*}. {❸③ *Elaborate.*} {*See* ***O'Connor's Texas Rules****, "Agreement specifies TAA," ch. 4-C, §4.2, p. 356.*}

14. The parties did not specify arbitration under either the FAA or the TAA, the transaction does not involve interstate commerce, and the agreement does not contain a general "law of the place" provision; thus, the TAA applies. *See In re D. Wilson Constr. Co.*, 196 S.W.3d 774, 778-79 (Tex. 2006); *In re L & L Kempwood Assocs., L.P.*, 9 S.W.3d 125, 127-28 (Tex. 1999). See Exhibit {❸④ *letter*}, page {❸⑤ *number*}, paragraph {❸⑥ *number*}. {❸⑦ *Elaborate.*} {*See* ***O'Connor's Texas Rules****, "No interstate commerce or law-of-the-place provision," ch. 4-C, §4.4.3, p. 357.*}

14. The parties did not specify arbitration under either the FAA or the TAA, but the agreement contains a "law of the place" provision that specifically excludes application of the FAA; thus, the TAA applies. *See In re Olshan Found. Repair Co.*, 328 S.W.3d 883, 890 (Tex. 2010). See Exhibit {❸⑧ *letter*}, page {❸⑨ *number*}, paragraph {❹⓪ *number*}. {❹① *Elaborate.*} {*See* ***O'Connor's Texas Rules****, "Law of the place," ch. 4-C, §4.4.2, p. 357.*}

{*For arbitration under both the FAA & the TAA*}

14. The parties agreed to arbitrate under both the FAA and the TAA. See Exhibit {❹② *letter*}, page {❹③ *number*}, paragraph {❹④ *number*}. {❹⑤ *Elaborate.*} Thus, both Acts apply unless the FAA preempts the TAA. *See In re D. Wilson Constr. Co.*, 196 S.W.3d 774, 779-80 (Tex. 2006). {*See* ***O'Connor's Texas Rules****, "Agreement specifies FAA & TAA," ch. 4-C, §4.3, p. 357; "FAA preemption of TAA," ch. 4-C, §4.5, p. 357.*}

14. The parties did not specify arbitration under either the FAA or the TAA, but the transaction involves interstate commerce. *In re D. Wilson Constr. Co.*, 196 S.W.3d 774, 778-79 (Tex. 2006). See Exhibit {❹⑥ *letter*}, page {❹⑦ *number*}, paragraph {❹⑧ *number*}. {❹⑨ *Elaborate.*} Thus, both Acts apply unless the FAA preempts the TAA. *See id.* at 779. {*See* ***O'Connor's Texas Rules****, "Interstate commerce," ch. 4-C, §4.4.1, p. 357; "FAA preemption of TAA," ch. 4-C, §4.5, p. 357.*}

14. The parties did not specify arbitration under either the FAA or the TAA, but the agreement contains a general "law of the place" provision. *In re Olshan Found. Repair Co.*, 328 S.W.3d 883, 890 (Tex. 2010); *In re D. Wilson Constr. Co.*, 196 S.W.3d 774, 778-79 (Tex. 2006); *In re L & L Kempwood Assocs., L.P.*, 9 S.W.3d 125, 127-28 (Tex.

FORM 4C:1

1999). See Exhibit {50 *letter*}, page {51 *number*}, paragraph {52 *number*}. {53 *Elaborate.*} Thus, both Acts apply unless the FAA preempts the TAA. *See In re D. Wilson Constr.*, 196 S.W.3d at 779. {*See **O'Connor's Texas Rules**, "Law of the place," ch. 4-C, §4.4.2, p. 357; "FAA preemption of TAA," ch. 4-C, §4.5, p. 357.*}

15. When a court orders the parties to arbitration, it must stay the proceedings pending the outcome of the arbitration. *See* {54 *9 U.S.C. §3/Tex. Civ. Prac. & Rem. Code §171.025*}. {*See **O'Connor's Texas Rules**, "Stay proceedings," ch. 4-C, §8.2.3(1)(b), p. 375.*}

CONCLUSION

16. {55 *Briefly summarize the motion.*}

PRAYER

17. For these reasons, {56 *party*} asks this Court to set {57 *his/her/its*} motion to compel arbitration for a hearing, grant {58 *party*}'s motion to compel, order the parties to arbitrate, and stay this {59 *lawsuit/dispute*} pending the outcome of the arbitration.

SEE: 9 U.S.C. §§2-4
Tex. Civ. Prac. & Rem. Code §171.001 et seq.
O'Connor's Texas Rules * Civil Trials (2019), "Arbitration," ch. 4-C, p. 355

ADD: STYLE OF THE CASE – FORM 1B:2
SIGNATURE BLOCK – FORM 1B:3
VERIFICATION – FORM 1B:7
CERTIFICATE OF CONFERENCE – FORM 1B:12, if necessary
CERTIFICATE OF SERVICE – FORM 1B:13

ATTACH: AFFIDAVIT – FORM 1B:8, if necessary
NOTICE OF HEARING OR SUBMISSION – FORM 1E:1
ORDER – FORM 4C:3
Copy of contract

NOTE: Persons who are not parties to the arbitration agreement can sometimes be subject to or may sometimes enforce an arbitration clause. ***G.T. Leach Builders, LLC v. Sapphire V.P., LP***, 458 S.W.3d 502, 524 (Tex.2015) (TAA); *see* ***In re Labatt Food Serv.***, 279 S.W.3d 640, 643 (Tex.2009) (FAA); *see, e.g.*, ***In re Rubiola***, 334 S.W.3d 220, 226 (Tex.2011) (FAA) (because arbitration agreement expressly provided that certain nonsignatories were considered parties, those parties could compel arbitration). Whether a nonsignatory is bound by the arbitration agreement is a matter for the courts to determine unless the parties clearly and unmistakably provide otherwise. ***In re Labatt Food***, 279 S.W.3d at 643; *see* ***Jody James Farms, JV v. Altman Grp.***, 547 S.W.3d 624, 629 (Tex.2018); ***G.T. Leach Builders***, 458 S.W.3d at 524. See ***O'Connor's Texas Rules***, "Nonsignatory," ch. 4-C, §5.1.2, p. 359; "Nonsignatory," ch. 4-C, §6.1.2, p. 363.

◄ *Continued on next page* ►

Factors used to determine whether a transaction involves or affects interstate commerce include: (1) the location of headquarters in another state, (2) transportation of materials across state lines, (3) manufacture of parts in another state, (4) preparation of invoices in another state, and (5) interstate mail and phone calls showing a contract. ***In re Big 8 Food Stores***, 166 S.W.3d 869, 879 (Tex. App.—El Paso 2005, orig. proceeding) (FAA); ***Service Corp. v. Lopez***, 162 S.W.3d 801, 807 (Tex.App.—Corpus Christi 2005, no pet.) (FAA).

A claim can be submitted to arbitration as long as a statute does not show clear congressional or legislative intent to preclude the application of the Federal Arbitration Act (FAA) or Texas Arbitration Act (TAA). See ***O'Connor's Texas Rules***, "Arbitrable claim," ch. 4-C, §5.2.2, p. 363; "Arbitrable claim," ch. 4-C, §6.2.2, p. 365.

If an agreement refers to both the FAA and the TAA, or if it does not refer to either act, both acts may apply, raising the issue of preemption. *See* ***In re D. Wilson Constr. Co.***, 196 S.W.3d 774, 778-79 (Tex.2006) (FAA and TAA). The FAA preempts the TAA to the extent that they conflict if the following occur: (1) the agreement is in writing, (2) the agreement involves interstate commerce, (3) the agreement can withstand scrutiny under traditional state-law contract defenses, and (4) Texas law adversely affects the enforceability of the agreement because the TAA expressly exempts the agreement from coverage or imposes a requirement for enforceability not found in the FAA. ***Nafta Traders, Inc. v. Quinn***, 339 S.W.3d 84, 98 (Tex.2011) (TAA); ***In re D. Wilson Constr.***, 196 S.W.3d at 780; *see* ***In re Nexion Health at Humble, Inc.***, 173 S.W.3d 67, 69 (Tex.2005) (FAA). The FAA may also preempt Texas law other than the TAA if an FAA-enforceable agreement is unenforceable under Texas law because the Texas law imposes a requirement for enforceability not found in the FAA. *See, e.g.*, ***Fredericksburg Care Co. v. Perez***, 461 S.W.3d 513, 518 (Tex.2015) (Tex. Civ. Prac. & Rem. Code §74.451 affected enforceability because it required arbitration agreement for health-care-liability claim to include bold and conspicuous warning of patient's right to consult attorney). See ***O'Connor's Texas Rules***, "FAA preemption of TAA," ch. 4-C, §4.5, p. 357.

A law-of-the-place provision may include language that the arbitration is under "the arbitration laws in your state" or that the arbitration "shall be governed by the law of the place where the Project is located." *See* ***In re Olshan Found. Repair Co.***, 328 S.W.3d 883, 890 (Tex.2010) (FAA and TAA); ***In re D. Wilson Constr.***, 196 S.W.3d at 778-79; ***In re L&L Kempwood Assocs.***, 9 S.W.3d 125, 127-28 (Tex. 1999) (FAA). The Texas Supreme Court has interpreted a law-of-the-place provision to include both federal and state laws. ***In re L&L Kempwood***, 9 S.W.3d at 127-28; *see* ***In re Olshan Found.***, 328 S.W.3d at 890 (FAA is part of "arbitration laws of Texas").

{❶ *PARTY*}'S RESPONSE TO {❷ *ADVERSE PARTY*}'S
MOTION TO COMPEL ARBITRATION & STAY PROCEEDINGS

{❸ *Party*}, {❹ *name*}, asks the Court to deny {❺ *adverse party*} {❻ *name*}'s motion to compel arbitration and stay proceedings. {*See* ***O'Connor's Texas Rules***, *"Objections to Arbitration," ch. 4-C, §7, p. 366.*}

INTRODUCTION

1. Plaintiff, {❼ *name*}, sued defendant, {❽ *name*}, for {❾ *state basis of suit*}.

2. {❿ *State other relevant facts about the suit.*}

BACKGROUND

3. On {⓫ *date*}, {⓬ *adverse party*} filed a motion to compel arbitration and alleged that the parties agreed to arbitrate {⓭ *all disputes/{identify specific disputes alleged to be subject to arbitration}*} between them.

{*CHOOSE APPROPRIATE PARAGRAPH 4*}

4. {⓮ *Adverse party*} argued that the arbitration agreement provides for arbitration under {⓯ *the Federal Arbitration Act (FAA)/the Texas Arbitration Act (TAA)/both the Federal Arbitration Act (FAA) and the Texas Arbitration Act (TAA)*}.

4. {⓰ *Adverse party*} argued that the arbitration agreement does not specify whether the arbitration agreement is governed by the Federal Arbitration Act (FAA) or the Texas Arbitration Act (TAA).

5. {⓱ *State other facts relevant to the response.*}

ARGUMENT & AUTHORITIES

6. A court can compel arbitration only after a party seeking to compel arbitration establishes that (1) there is a valid agreement to arbitrate, (2) the claims raised are within the agreement's scope, and (3) the claims are arbitrable. *See* 9 U.S.C. §§2, 4 (FAA); Tex. Civ. Prac. & Rem. Code §§171.001, 171.002, 171.021 (TAA); *Henry v. Cash Biz, LP*, 551 S.W.3d 111, 115 (Tex. 2018) (FAA); *G.T. Leach Builders, LLC v. Sapphire V.P., LP*, 458 S.W.3d 502, 524 (Tex. 2015) (TAA); *Rachal v. Reitz*, 403 S.W.3d 840, 843 (Tex. 2013) (TAA); *In re Rubiola*, 334 S.W.3d 220, 223 (Tex. 2011) (FAA). {*See* ***O'Connor's Texas Rules***, *"Motion to compel arbitration under FAA," ch. 4-C, §5.2, p. 361; "Motion to compel arbitration under TAA," ch. 4-C, §6.2, p. 363.*}

◄ Continued on next page ►

FORM 4C:2

{*CHOOSE APPROPRIATE PARAGRAPHS 7-21*}

7. The Court should deny {18 *adverse party*}'s motion to compel arbitration because there was no agreement to arbitrate this dispute. Tex. Civ. Prac. & Rem. Code §171.021(b) (TAA); *see In re Morgan Stanley & Co.*, 293 S.W.3d 182, 187 (Tex. 2009) (FAA). {19 *Elaborate.*} {*See* ***O'Connor's Texas Rules****, "No agreement," ch. 4-C, §7.1, p. 366.*}

8. The Court should deny {20 *adverse party*}'s motion to compel arbitration because the dispute is outside the scope of the agreement to arbitrate. *See Henry*, 551 S.W.3d at 115-16 (FAA); *In re FirstMerit Bank, N.A.*, 52 S.W.3d 749, 754-55 (Tex. 2001) (FAA). {21 *Elaborate.*} {*See* ***O'Connor's Texas Rules****, "Claim outside scope of agreement," ch. 4-C, §7.3, p. 370.*}

9. The Court should deny {22 *adverse party*}'s motion to compel arbitration because the agreement to arbitrate was fraudulently induced. *See Forest Oil Corp. v. McAllen*, 268 S.W.3d 51, 56 (Tex. 2008) (TAA); *In re U.S. Home Corp.*, 236 S.W.3d 761, 764 (Tex. 2007) (FAA); *In re FirstMerit Bank, N.A.*, 52 S.W.3d 749, 756 (Tex. 2001) (FAA). {23 *Elaborate.*} {*See* ***O'Connor's Texas Rules****, "Fraud," ch. 4-C, §7.2.1, p. 367.*}

10. The Court should deny {24 *adverse party*}'s motion to compel arbitration because the arbitration agreement in the contract that {25 *adverse party*} alleges is subject to arbitration was unconscionable at the time it was made. Tex. Civ. Prac. & Rem. Code §171.022. Specifically, the agreement is procedurally unconscionable because {26 *explain how the circumstances surrounding the actual making of the arbitration agreement were unconscionable, e.g., party did not have the means to understand the agreement and misrepresentations were made about what was being signed*}. *See In re Palm Harbor Homes, Inc.*, 195 S.W.3d 672, 677 (Tex. 2006) (FAA); *In re McKinney*, 167 S.W.3d 833, 835 (Tex. 2005) (FAA). {*See* ***O'Connor's Texas Rules****, "Procedural unconscionability," ch. 4-C, §7.2.2(1), p. 367.*}

11. The Court should deny {27 *adverse party*}'s motion to compel arbitration because the arbitration agreement in the contract that {28 *adverse party*} alleges is subject to arbitration was unconscionable at the time it was made. Tex. Civ. Prac. & Rem. Code §171.022. Specifically, the arbitration agreement is substantively unconscionable because {29 *explain how, given the parties' commercial backgrounds and the commercial demands of the particular trade or case, the arbitration agreement is so grossly one-sided that it was unconscionable under the circumstances at the time the contract was signed*}. *See Royston, Rayzor, Vickery & Williams, LLP v. Lopez*, 467 S.W.3d 494, 499 (Tex. 2015) (TAA); *In re Olshan Found. Repair Co.*, 328 S.W.3d 883, 892 (Tex. 2010)

(FAA and TAA); *In re Palm Harbor Homes, Inc.*, 195 S.W.3d 672, 677 (Tex. 2006) (FAA). {*See **O'Connor's Texas Rules**, "Substantive unconscionability," ch. 4-C, §7.2.2(2), p. 368.*}

12. The Court should deny {❸⓪ *adverse party*}'s motion to compel arbitration because the arbitration agreement in the contract that {❸① *adverse party*} alleges is subject to arbitration was unconscionable at the time it was made. Tex. Civ. Prac. & Rem. Code §171.022. Specifically, the arbitration agreement is substantively unconscionable because the costs imposed by the arbitration agreement are excessive and effectively prevent {❸② *party*} from asserting {❸③ *his/her/its*} rights in an arbitration proceeding. *See In re Olshan Found. Repair Co.*, 328 S.W.3d 883, 892-93 (Tex. 2010) (FAA and TAA). The costs are excessive for the following reasons: (1) {❸④ *party*} is unable to pay the arbitration fees and costs, (2) the actual amount of the fees compared to the amount of the underlying claim is excessive, and (3) the expected cost differential between arbitration and litigation is so substantial that {❸⑤ *party*} is deterred from asserting {❸⑥ *his/her/its*} rights in the arbitration proceeding. *See id.* at 893-94; *see, e.g., Olshan Found. Repair Co. v. Ayala*, 180 S.W.3d 212, 215-16 (Tex. App.—San Antonio 2005, pet. denied) (arbitration with American Arbitration Association; cost of arbitration was more than three times the amount of underlying claim; agreement was unconscionable). {❸⑦ *Elaborate.*} {*See **O'Connor's Texas Rules**, "Excessive costs," ch. 4-C, §7.2.2(2)(b), p. 368.*}

13. The Court should deny {❸⑧ *adverse party*}'s motion to compel arbitration because the arbitration agreement in the contract that {❸⑨ *adverse party*} alleges is subject to arbitration was unconscionable at the time it was made. Tex. Civ. Prac. & Rem. Code §171.022. Specifically, the arbitration agreement is substantively unconscionable because {❹⓪ *party*} was forced to give up {❹① *his/her/its*} substantive rights and remedies under {❹② *identify statute*}. *In re Poly-Am., L.P.*, 262 S.W.3d 337, 349-50 (Tex. 2008) (FAA; arbitration provision that substantially limited employer's liability for wrongful retaliation by eliminating key remedies under Workers' Compensation Act's antiretaliation provisions was unconscionable). {❹③ *Elaborate.*} {*See **O'Connor's Texas Rules**, "Waiver of statutory rights & remedies," ch. 4-C, §7.2.2(2)(c), p. 369.*}

14. The Court should deny {❹④ *adverse party*}'s motion to compel arbitration because {❹⑤ *party*} was under duress to agree to the arbitration clause. *See In re RLS Legal Sols., L.L.C.*, 221 S.W.3d 629, 630 (Tex. 2007) (FAA). {❹⑥ *Elaborate.*} {*See **O'Connor's Texas Rules**, "Duress," ch. 4-C, §7.2.3, p. 369.*}

15. The Court should deny {❹⑦ *adverse party*}'s motion to compel arbitration because the arbitration clause is illusory. Specifically, {❹⑧ *adverse party*} has the unilateral and unrestricted right to amend or terminate the arbitration agreement and avoid

◄ *Continued on next page* ►

{㊾ *his/her/its*} promise to arbitrate. *See Royston, Rayzor, Vickery & Williams, LLP v. Lopez*, 467 S.W.3d 494, 505 (Tex. 2015) (TAA); *In re 24R, Inc.*, 324 S.W.3d 564, 567 (Tex. 2010) (FAA); *In re Odyssey Healthcare, Inc.*, 310 S.W.3d 419, 424 (Tex. 2010) (FAA). {㊿ *Elaborate.*} {*See* ***O'Connor's Texas Rules***, *"Illusory agreement," ch. 4-C, §7.2.4, p. 369.*}

16. The court should deny {51 *adverse party*}'s motion to compel arbitration because {52 *{party}/the person on whose behalf the suit was filed, {identify person},*} was a minor at the time the arbitration agreement was entered into and {53 *he/she*} subsequently voided the agreement. *See Pak Foods Houston, LLC v. Garcia*, 433 S.W.3d 171, 176 (Tex. App.—Houston [14th Dist.] 2014, pet. dism'd) (FAA). {54 *Elaborate.*} {*See* ***O'Connor's Texas Rules***, *"Minority," ch. 4-C, §7.2.5, p. 370.*}

17. The Court should deny {55 *adverse party*}'s motion to compel arbitration because {56 *adverse party*} expressly waived {57 *his/her/its*} right to arbitration. *See G.T. Leach Builders*, 458 S.W.3d at 511 (TAA); *In re Citigroup Glob. Mkts., Inc.*, 258 S.W.3d 623, 625-26 (Tex. 2008) (FAA). {58 *Elaborate.*} {*See* ***O'Connor's Texas Rules***, *"Express waiver," ch. 4-C, §7.5.1, p. 370.*}

18. The Court should deny {59 *adverse party*}'s motion to compel arbitration because {60 *adverse party*} impliedly waived {61 *his/her/its*} right to arbitration. *Perry Homes v. Cull*, 258 S.W.3d 580, 593 (Tex. 2008) (FAA). Specifically, {62 *adverse party*} took action that substantially invoked the judicial process and that action was prejudicial to {63 *party*}. *Id.* at 589-90 (FAA); *see G.T. Leach Builders*, 458 S.W.3d at 511-12 (TAA); *Richmont Holdings, Inc. v. Superior Recharge Sys., L.L.C.*, 455 S.W.3d 573, 574-75 (Tex. 2014) (TAA); *In re Fleetwood Homes of Tex., L.P.*, 257 S.W.3d 692, 694 (Tex. 2008) (FAA). {64 *Elaborate.*} {*See* ***O'Connor's Texas Rules***, *"Implied waiver," ch. 4-C, §7.5.2, p. 370.*}

19. The Court should deny {65 *adverse party*}'s motion to compel arbitration because

{*CHOOSE APPROPRIATE STATEMENT*}

Ⓐ the dispute involves a collective-bargaining agreement between an employer and a labor union and therefore is not arbitrable under the Texas Arbitration Act. Tex. Civ. Prac. & Rem. Code §171.002(a)(1). {66 *Elaborate.*} {*See* ***O'Connor's Texas Rules***, *"Arbitrable claim," ch. 4-C, §6.2.2(2), p. 365.*}

B the dispute involves an agreement for an individual to purchase real property, services, money, or credit in which the total consideration paid does not exceed $50,000, and there is no written agreement to arbitrate signed by {67 *party*} and {68 *party*}'s attorney. Therefore, the dispute is not arbitrable under the Texas Arbitration Act. Tex. Civ. Prac. & Rem. Code §171.002(a)(2), (b). {69 *Elaborate.*} {*See **O'Connor's Texas Rules**, "Arbitrable claim," ch. 4-C, §6.2.2(3), p. 365.*}

C the dispute involves a claim for personal injury, {70 *party*} did not consult with counsel before signing an agreement to arbitrate, and the written agreement is not signed by {71 *party*} and {72 *party*}'s attorney. Therefore, the dispute is not arbitrable under the Texas Arbitration Act. Tex. Civ. Prac. & Rem. Code §171.002(a)(3), (c). {73 *Elaborate.*} {*See **O'Connor's Texas Rules**, "Arbitrable claim," ch. 4-C, §6.2.2(4), p. 365.*}

D the dispute involves a claim for workers' compensation benefits and therefore is not arbitrable under the Texas Arbitration Act. Tex. Civ. Prac. & Rem. Code §171.002(a)(4). {74 *Elaborate.*} {*See **O'Connor's Texas Rules**, "Arbitrable claim," ch. 4-C, §6.2.2(5), p. 365.*}

E the dispute involves an agreement made before January 1, 1966, and therefore is not arbitrable under the Texas Arbitration Act. Tex. Civ. Prac. & Rem. Code §171.002(a)(5). {75 *Elaborate.*} {*See **O'Connor's Texas Rules**, "Arbitrable claim," ch. 4-C, §6.2.2(6), p. 365.*}

20. The Court should deny {76 *adverse party*}'s motion to compel arbitration because the dispute involves a matter for which a federal statute precludes the application of the Federal Arbitration Act. *In re American Homestar of Lancaster, Inc.*, 50 S.W.3d 480, 485 (Tex. 2001). {77 *Elaborate.*} {*See **O'Connor's Texas Rules**, "Conflicting federal statute," ch. 4-C, §5.2.2(1), p. 363.*}

21. The Court should deny {78 *adverse party*}'s motion to compel arbitration because {79 *refute any other ground from the motion to compel arbitration*}. {*See **O'Connor's Texas Rules**, "Motion to Compel Contractual Arbitration—FAA or TAA?," ch. 4-C, §4, p. 356; "Motion to Compel Contractual Arbitration Under FAA," ch. 4-C, §5, p. 358; "Motion to Compel Contractual Arbitration Under TAA," ch. 4-C, §6, p. 363.*}

CONCLUSION

22. {80 *Briefly summarize the response.*}

◄ *Continued on next page* ►

PRAYER

23. For these reasons, {81 *party*} asks the Court to deny {82 *adverse party*}'s motion to compel arbitration and stay proceedings.

SEE: 9 U.S.C. §§2, 4
Tex. Civ. Prac. & Rem. Code §171.001 et seq.
O'Connor's Texas Rules * Civil Trials (2019), "Objections to Arbitration," ch. 4-C, §7, p. 366

ADD: STYLE OF THE CASE – FORM 1B:2
SIGNATURE BLOCK – FORM 1B:3
VERIFICATION – FORM 1B:7
CERTIFICATE OF CONFERENCE – FORM 1B:12, if necessary
CERTIFICATE OF SERVICE – FORM 1B:13

ATTACH: AFFIDAVIT – FORM 1B:8, if necessary
ORDER – FORM 4C:3

NOTE: Defenses to arbitration that relate to the substantive arbitrability of the agreement itself (i.e., the existence, enforceability, and scope of the agreement) are decided by the court unless the parties clearly and unmistakably agree otherwise. *See* ***Howsam v. Dean Witter Reynolds, Inc.***, 537 U.S. 79, 83-85 (2002) (FAA); ***G.T. Leach Builders, LLC v. Sapphire V.P., LP***, 458 S.W.3d 502, 520-21 (Tex.2015) (TAA); ***Saxa Inc. v. DFD Architecture Inc.***, 312 S.W.3d 224, 229 (Tex.App.—Dallas 2010, pet. denied) (TAA). But the arbitrator, not the court, generally must decide defenses to arbitration that relate to procedural arbitrability (i.e., the meaning and application of all procedural prerequisites to an obligation to arbitrate, such as whether time limits and notice requirements have been met). *See* ***Howsam***, 537 U.S. at 84-85; ***G.T. Leach Builders***, 458 S.W.3d at 520-21; ***Perry Homes v. Cull***, 258 S.W.3d 580, 588-89 (Tex. 2008) (FAA). See ***O'Connor's Texas Rules***, "Objections to Arbitration," ch. 4-C, §7, p. 366; "Questions of arbitrability," ch. 4-C, §8.2.2, p. 373.

In determining whether an agreement is procedurally unconscionable, the court will focus on the factors surrounding the bargaining process, which include (1) the parties' bargaining ability, (2) the viable alternatives available to the parties, (3) whether the contract is illegal or against public policy, and (4) whether the contract is oppressive or unreasonable or results in unfair surprise. *See* ***In re Palm Harbor Homes, Inc.***, 195 S.W.3d 672, 679 (Tex.2006) (FAA); ***Whataburger Rests. LLC v. Cardwell***, 545 S.W.3d 73, 80 (Tex.App.—El Paso 2017, no pet.) (FAA).

The party opposing arbitration has the burden to show that the costs of arbitration would be prohibitively expensive such that the arbitration agreement is unconscionable. ***In re Olshan Found. Repair Co.***, 328 S.W.3d 883, 893 (Tex.2010) (FAA and TAA); *see* ***In re Odyssey Healthcare, Inc.***, 310 S.W.3d 419, 422 (Tex.2010) (FAA). The party opposing arbitration must submit specific evidence showing the likelihood of incurring excessive costs for her particular arbitration. ***In re Olshan Found.***, 328 S.W.3d at 893-94 & n.5. The party can submit invoices, expert testimony, cost estimates, or other comparable evidence. *Id.* at 895. Once the party has met her burden, the other party must show contradictory evidence that arbitration costs will not be excessive. *See id.* See ***O'Connor's Texas Rules***, "Burden to prove excessive costs," ch. 4-C, §7.2.2(2)(b)[1], p. 368.

In considering whether a party impliedly waived its right to arbitrate, a court will apply a totality-of-the-circumstances test to determine whether the judicial process was substantially invoked. ***RSL Funding, LLC v. Pippins***, 499 S.W.3d 423, 430 (Tex.2016) (FAA); ***G.T. Leach Builders***, 458 S.W.3d at 511-12; ***Richmont Holdings, Inc. v. Superior Recharge Sys.***, 455 S.W.3d 573, 574-75 (Tex.2014) (TAA). For a list of factors courts can consider when determining whether the judicial process has been invoked, see ***O'Connor's Texas Rules***, "Test," ch. 4-C, §7.5.2(1)(a), p. 371. The presumption against waiver is so strong, however, that the Texas Supreme Court has only once held that a party waived arbitration by substantially invoking the judicial process. ***Perry Homes***, 258 S.W.3d at 589-90; *see* ***Henry v. Cash Biz, LP***, 551 S.W.3d 111, 116 (Tex.2018) (FAA; court will find that right to arbitration has been waived in only "most unequivocal of circumstances").

If a state statute conflicts with the FAA, the FAA controls as long as the claim is subject to a valid arbitration clause. *See* ***Nitro-Lift Techs. v. Howard***, 568 U.S. 17, 21-22 (2012).

FORM 4C:2

ORDER ON {❶ *PARTY*}'S MOTION
TO COMPEL ARBITRATION & STAY PROCEEDINGS

After considering {❷ *party*} {❸ *name*}'s motion to compel arbitration and stay proceedings, the response, and arguments of counsel, and after a hearing on the motion, the Court

{*CHOOSE APPROPRIATE ORDER*}

DENIES the motion.

GRANTS the motion and orders the parties to arbitrate the following disputes: {❹ *identify disputes subject to arbitration*}. The Court stays the proceedings pending the outcome of the arbitration.

GRANTS the motion and orders the parties to arbitrate the following disputes: {❺ *identify disputes subject to arbitration*}. Because these disputes are severable from the rest of the proceedings, the Court stays the proceedings for only these disputes pending the outcome of the arbitration.

SIGNED on _______________, 20___.

____
PRESIDING JUDGE

SEE: Tex. Civ. Prac. & Rem. Code §171.001 et seq.
O'Connor's Texas Rules * Civil Trials (2019), "Order," ch. 4-C, §8.2.3, p. 375

ADD: STYLE OF THE CASE – FORM 1B:2
CERTIFICATE OF SERVICE – FORM 1B:13, if proposed order served separately from motion or response

{❶ *PARTY*}'S MOTION TO CONFIRM ARBITRATION AWARD

{❷ *Party*}, {❸ *name*}, asks the Court to confirm the arbitration award in this case. {*See* ***O'Connor's Texas Rules****, "Motion to confirm award," ch. 4-C, §9.5.1, p. 379.*}

INTRODUCTION

1. Plaintiff, {❹ *name*}, sued defendant, {❺ *name*}, for {❻ *state basis of suit*}.

2. {❼ *State other relevant facts about the suit.*}

BACKGROUND

3. On {❽ *date*}, plaintiff filed this suit, invoking the Court's jurisdiction over the dispute subject to the arbitration agreement.

4. The parties submitted the dispute to arbitration. On {❾ *date*}, an arbitration hearing was held in {❿ *identify city and state*}. On {⓫ *date*}, the {⓬ *arbitrator/arbitration panel*} issued an award in favor of {⓭ *identify prevailing party*} and granted {⓮ *identify relief awarded*}.

5. {⓯ *State other facts relevant to the motion.*}

ARGUMENT & AUTHORITIES

6. A court's review of the arbitration process is severely limited. *United Paperworkers Int'l Union v. Misco, Inc.*, 484 U.S. 29, 36-37 (1987); *see CVN Grp., Inc. v. Delgado*, 95 S.W.3d 234, 238 (Tex. 2002). A court should indulge all reasonable presumptions in favor of the arbitration award. *CVN Grp.*, 95 S.W.3d at 238.

{*CHOOSE APPROPRIATE PARAGRAPHS 7-14*}

{*Under FAA*}

7. On a timely filed motion to confirm an arbitration award with the proper attachments, the award must be confirmed unless there are grounds to modify, correct, or vacate the award. *See* 9 U.S.C. §§9, 13.

{*CHOOSE APPROPRIATE PARAGRAPH 8*}

8. A motion to confirm an arbitration award must be filed within one year after the award is made. 9 U.S.C. §9. In this case, the award was issued on {⓰ *date*}, and {⓱ *party*} filed this motion on {⓲ *date*}. Therefore, this motion was timely filed.

Continued on next page

8. A motion to confirm an arbitration award must be filed within one year after the award is made. 9 U.S.C. §9. A motion to modify, correct, or vacate an arbitration award must be made within three months after the award is filed or delivered. *Id.* §12. In this case, the award was issued on {[19] *date*}, {[20] *party*} filed this motion on {[21] *date*}, and {[22] *adverse party*} has not filed a motion to modify, correct, or vacate the award. Therefore, this motion was timely filed, and any future motions to modify, correct, or vacate the arbitration award would be untimely.

{*CHOOSE APPROPRIATE PARAGRAPH 9*}

9. An arbitration award must be confirmed when the parties have provided in the arbitration agreement that a judgment will be entered on the arbitration award. 9 U.S.C. §9. In this case, the parties entered into an arbitration agreement on {[23] *date*}. A copy of the arbitration agreement is attached, and paragraph {[24] *number*} provides that a judgment will be entered on the arbitration award. An award was issued on {[25] *date*} and granted {[26] *identify relief awarded*}.

9. An arbitration award must be confirmed when the parties have provided in the arbitration agreement that a judgment will be entered on the arbitration award. 9 U.S.C. §9. In this case, the parties entered into an arbitration agreement on {[27] *date*}. A copy of the arbitration agreement is attached. An award was issued on {[28] *date*} and granted {[29] *identify relief awarded*}. Although there is no specific paragraph providing that a judgment will be entered on the arbitration award, the agreement sufficiently confers authority on the Court to confirm the award. {[30] *Explain, e.g., the language of the agreement or the parties' participation in the arbitration is sufficient to give the Court authority to confirm even though there is no explicit language on judicial enforcement.*}

10. There are no grounds for modifying, correcting, or vacating the award in this case, and the {[31] *arbitrator/arbitration panel*}'s decision and award are correct. *See* 9 U.S.C. §9. {[32] *Elaborate.*}

11. Because this motion, proposed order, and proper attachments have been filed and because there are no grounds for modifying, correcting, or vacating the award, the Court must confirm the arbitration award in this case. *See* 9 U.S.C. §§9, 13. {[33] *Elaborate.*}

{*Under TAA*}

12. The arbitration award must be confirmed unless there are grounds for modifying, correcting, or vacating the award. Tex. Civ. Prac. & Rem. Code §171.087; *Nafta Traders, Inc. v. Quinn*, 339 S.W.3d 84, 89-90 (Tex. 2011); *City of Baytown v. C.L. Winter, Inc.*, 886 S.W.2d 515, 520 (Tex. App.—Houston [1st Dist.] 1994, writ denied).

13. There are no grounds for modifying, correcting, or vacating the award in this case, and the {㉞ *arbitrator/arbitration panel*}'s decision and award are correct. *See* Tex. Civ. Prac. & Rem. Code §171.087. {㉟ *Elaborate.*}

14. Because this motion, proposed order, and proper attachments have been filed and because there are no grounds for modifying, correcting, or vacating the award, the Court must confirm the arbitration award in this case. *See* Tex. Civ. Prac. & Rem. Code §171.087. {㊱ *Elaborate.*}

ATTACHMENTS

15. In support of this motion to confirm, {㊲ *party*} includes documents in the attached appendix, which is incorporated by reference. {㊳ *Party*} requests that the Court include the attached documents with its order confirming the arbitration award.

CONCLUSION

16. {㊴ *Briefly summarize the motion.*}

PRAYER

17. For these reasons, {㊵ *party*} asks the Court to confirm the arbitration award and enter judgment in accordance with the award.

SEE: 9 U.S.C. §§9-13
Tex. Civ. Prac. & Rem. Code §§171.087, 171.088, 171.091
O'Connor's Texas Rules * Civil Trials (2019), "Motion to confirm award," ch. 4-C, §9.5.1, p. 379
O'Connor's Federal Rules * Civil Trials (2019), "Confirming Arbitration Award," ch. 7-E, §4, p. 772

ADD: STYLE OF THE CASE – FORM 1B:2
SIGNATURE BLOCK – FORM 1B:3
CERTIFICATE OF CONFERENCE – FORM 1B:12, if necessary
CERTIFICATE OF SERVICE – FORM 1B:13

ATTACH: AFFIDAVIT – FORM 1B:8, if necessary
NOTICE OF HEARING OR SUBMISSION – FORM 1E:1
ORDER – FORM 4C:6
APPENDIX – FORM 4C:13

NOTE: A party may file a motion for summary judgment to confirm the award, but by filing a motion for summary judgment, the party assumes the additional burdens and procedural requirements of summary-judgment practice. ***Baker Hughes Oilfield Opers., Inc. v. Hennig Prod. Co.***, 164 S.W.3d 438, 442-43 (Tex.App.—Houston [14th Dist.] 2005, no pet.) (TAA). See ***O'Connor's Texas Rules***, "Motion to confirm award," ch. 4-C, §9.5.1, p. 379.

Although only the Federal Arbitration Act requires an appendix, the movant should also attach the appropriate documents in Texas Arbitration Act cases.

{[1] *PARTY*}'S RESPONSE TO
{[2] *ADVERSE PARTY*}'S MOTION TO CONFIRM ARBITRATION AWARD

{[3] *Party*}, {[4] *name*}, asks the Court to deny {[5] *adverse party*} {[6] *name*}'s motion to confirm the arbitration award in this case.

INTRODUCTION

1. Plaintiff, {[7] *name*}, sued defendant, {[8] *name*}, for {[9] *state basis of suit*}.

2. {[10] *State other relevant facts about the suit.*}

BACKGROUND

3. The parties submitted the dispute to arbitration. On {[11] *date*}, an arbitration hearing was held. On {[12] *date*}, the {[13] *arbitrator/arbitration panel*} issued an award in favor of {[14] *identify prevailing party*} and granted {[15] *identify relief awarded*}.

4. {[16] *State other facts relevant to the response.*}

ARGUMENT & AUTHORITIES

5. A court's review of the arbitration process is severely limited. *United Paperworkers Int'l Union v. Misco, Inc.*, 484 U.S. 29, 36-37 (1987); *see CVN Grp., Inc. v. Delgado*, 95 S.W.3d 234, 238 (Tex. 2002). However, in this case, judicial confirmation is not proper.

{*CHOOSE APPROPRIATE PARAGRAPHS 6-9*}

{*Under FAA*}

6. A motion to confirm an arbitration award must be filed within one year after the award is made. 9 U.S.C. §9. In this case, the award was made on {[17] *date*}, and {[18] *adverse party*} filed {[19] *his/her/its*} motion on {[20] *date*}. {[21] *Adverse party*}'s motion was untimely. {[22] *Elaborate.*} Thus, {[23] *adverse party*}'s motion to confirm should be denied.

7. An arbitration award may be confirmed only when the parties have provided in the arbitration agreement that a judgment will be entered on the arbitration award. *See* 9 U.S.C. §9. In this case, the parties entered into an arbitration agreement on {[24] *date*}. A copy of the arbitration agreement is attached. The agreement does not provide that a judgment will be entered on the arbitration agreement, and neither the language of the agreement nor the parties' actions sufficiently confer authority on the Court to confirm the award. *See id.* {[25] *Explain how the agreement and the parties' participation are insufficient.*}

{*Under FAA or TAA*}

8. A motion to confirm an arbitration award must be denied when the award should be modified or corrected. *See* {㉖ *9 U.S.C. §9/Tex. Civ. Prac. & Rem. Code §171.087*}. {㉗ *Explain and provide grounds for modifying or correcting the award. See FORM 4C:7.*}

9. A motion to confirm an arbitration award must be denied when the award should be vacated. *See* {㉘ *9 U.S.C. §9/Tex. Civ. Prac. & Rem. Code §171.087*}. {㉙ *Explain and provide grounds for vacating the award. See FORM 4C:10.*}

CONCLUSION

10. {㉚ *Briefly summarize the response.*}

PRAYER

11. For these reasons, {㉛ *party*} asks the Court to deny {㉜ *adverse party*}'s motion to confirm the arbitration award.

SEE: 9 U.S.C. §§9-13
Tex. Civ. Prac. & Rem. Code §§171.087, 171.088, 171.091
O'Connor's Texas Rules * Civil Trials (2019), "Motion to confirm award," ch. 4-C, §9.5.1, p. 379
O'Connor's Federal Rules * Civil Trials (2019), "Confirming Arbitration Award," ch. 7-E, §4, p. 772

ADD: STYLE OF THE CASE – FORM 1B:2
SIGNATURE BLOCK – FORM 1B:3
CERTIFICATE OF CONFERENCE – FORM 1B:12, if necessary
CERTIFICATE OF SERVICE – FORM 1B:13

ATTACH: AFFIDAVIT – FORM 1B:8, if necessary
ORDER – FORM 4C:6

ORDER ON {❶ *PARTY*}'S MOTION TO CONFIRM ARBITRATION AWARD

After considering {❷ *party*} {❸ *name*}'s motion to confirm the arbitration award, the response, and arguments of counsel, and after a hearing on the motion, the Court

{*CHOOSE APPROPRIATE ORDER*}

DENIES the motion.

GRANTS the motion and enters judgment in accordance with the arbitration award.

SIGNED on _______________, 20___.

____
PRESIDING JUDGE

SEE: 9 U.S.C. §§9-13
Tex. Civ. Prac. & Rem. Code §§171.087, 171.092
O'Connor's Texas Rules * Civil Trials (2019), "Motion to confirm award," ch. 4-C, §9.5.1, p. 379
O'Connor's Federal Rules * Civil Trials (2019), "Confirming Arbitration Award," ch. 7-E, §4, p. 772

ADD: STYLE OF THE CASE – FORM 1B:2
CERTIFICATE OF SERVICE – FORM 1B:13, if proposed order served separately from motion or response

{[1] *PARTY*}'S MOTION TO MODIFY ARBITRATION AWARD

{[2] *Party*}, {[3] *name*}, asks the Court to modify the arbitration award in this case. {*See **O'Connor's Texas Rules**, "Motion to modify or correct award," ch. 4-C, §9.5.2, p. 379.*}

INTRODUCTION

1. Plaintiff, {[4] *name*}, sued defendant, {[5] *name*}, for {[6] *state basis of suit*}.

2. {[7] *State other relevant facts about the suit.*}

BACKGROUND

3. On {[8] *date*}, plaintiff filed this suit, invoking the Court's jurisdiction over the dispute subject to the arbitration agreement.

4. The parties submitted the dispute to arbitration. On {[9] *date*}, an arbitration hearing was held. On {[10] *date*}, the {[11] *arbitrator/arbitration panel*} issued an award in favor of {[12] *identify prevailing party*} and granted {[13] *identify relief awarded*}.

5. {[14] *State other facts relevant to the motion.*}

ARGUMENT & AUTHORITIES

{*CHOOSE APPROPRIATE PARAGRAPH 6*}

{*Under FAA*}

6. A motion to modify an arbitration award must be served within three months after the award is filed or delivered. 9 U.S.C. §12. In this case, the award was {[15] *filed/delivered*} on {[16] *date*}, and {[17] *party*} served this motion on {[18] *date*}. Therefore, this motion was timely served.

{*Under TAA*}

6. A motion to modify an arbitration award must be filed within 90 days after the party receives a copy of the award. Tex. Civ. Prac. & Rem. Code §171.091(b). In this case, {[19] *party*} received the copy on {[20] *date*}, and {[21] *party*} filed this motion on {[22] *date*}. Therefore, this motion was timely filed.

Continued on next page

{*CHOOSE APPROPRIATE PARAGRAPHS 7-9*}

7. The arbitration award should be modified because there was {[23] *an evident miscalculation of numbers/a mistake in the description of a person, thing, or property referred to in the award*}. {[24] *9 U.S.C. §11(a)/Tex. Civ. Prac. & Rem. Code §171.091(a)(1)*}. {[25] *Elaborate.*} {*See* ***O'Connor's Texas Rules****, "Grounds," ch. 4-C, §9.5.2(2), p. 379.*}

8. The arbitration award should be modified because the award was based on a matter not submitted to the {[26] *arbitrator/arbitration panel*}. {[27] *9 U.S.C. §11(b)/Tex. Civ. Prac. & Rem. Code §171.091(a)(2); Sydow v. Verner, Liipfert, Bernhard, McPherson & Hand, 218 S.W.3d 162, 168 (Tex. App.—Houston [14th Dist.] 2007, no pet.)*}. {[28] *Elaborate.*} {*See* ***O'Connor's Texas Rules****, "Grounds," ch. 4-C, §9.5.2(2), p. 379.*}

9. The arbitration award should be modified because there was an error in the form of the award, on a matter not affecting the merits of the controversy. {[29] *9 U.S.C. §11(c)/Tex. Civ. Prac. & Rem. Code §171.091(a)(3)*}. {[30] *Explain, e.g., the error in the award is clerical.*} {*See* ***O'Connor's Texas Rules****, "Grounds," ch. 4-C, §9.5.2(2), p. 379.*}

ATTACHMENTS

10. In support of this motion to modify, {[31] *party*} includes documents in the attached appendix, which is incorporated by reference. {[32] *Party*} requests that the Court include the attached documents with its order modifying the arbitration award.

CONCLUSION

11. {[33] *Briefly summarize the motion.*}

PRAYER

12. For these reasons, {[34] *party*} asks the Court to modify the arbitration award.

SEE: 9 U.S.C. §§11-13
Tex. Civ. Prac. & Rem. Code §171.091
O'Connor's Texas Rules * Civil Trials (2019), "Motion to modify or correct award," ch. 4-C, §9.5.2, p. 379
O'Connor's Federal Rules * Civil Trials (2019), "Modifying – grounds," ch. 7-E, §3.1.4, p. 768

ADD: STYLE OF THE CASE – FORM 1B:2
SIGNATURE BLOCK – FORM 1B:3
CERTIFICATE OF CONFERENCE – FORM 1B:12, if necessary
CERTIFICATE OF SERVICE – FORM 1B:13

ATTACH: AFFIDAVIT – FORM 1B:8, if necessary
NOTICE OF HEARING OR SUBMISSION – FORM 1E:1
ORDER – FORM 4C:9
APPENDIX – FORM 4C:13

NOTE: Under both the Federal Arbitration Act (FAA) and the Texas Arbitration Act (TAA), a party may apply to "modify or correct" an arbitration award. *See* 9 U.S.C. §11; Tex. Civ. Prac. & Rem. Code §171.091(a). For simplicity, this form uses only the term "modify."

Although only the FAA requires an appendix, the movant should also attach the appropriate documents in TAA cases. *See* 9 U.S.C. §13.

The exclusive grounds for modifying an arbitration award authorized under the FAA are provided by 9 U.S.C. §11. ***Hall St. Assocs. v. Mattel, Inc.***, 552 U.S. 576, 584 (2008). Therefore, when seeking to modify an arbitration award under the FAA, parties must limit the grounds to those listed in 9 U.S.C. §11 and not argue common-law grounds.

Under the TAA, a motion to modify an arbitration award can be joined in the alternative with a motion to vacate the award. Tex. Civ. Prac. & Rem. Code §171.091(d). See FORM 4C:10.

{[1] *PARTY*}'S RESPONSE TO
{[2] *ADVERSE PARTY*}'S MOTION TO MODIFY ARBITRATION AWARD

{[3] *Party*}, {[4] *name*}, asks the Court to deny {[5] *adverse party*} {[6] *name*}'s motion to modify the arbitration award in this case.

INTRODUCTION

1. Plaintiff, {[7] *name*}, sued defendant, {[8] *name*}, for {[9] *state basis of suit*}.

2. {[10] *State other relevant facts about the suit.*}

BACKGROUND

3. The parties submitted the dispute to arbitration. On {[11] *date*}, an arbitration hearing was held. On {[12] *date*}, the {[13] *arbitrator/arbitration panel*} issued an award in favor of {[14] *identify prevailing party*} and granted {[15] *identify relief awarded*}.

4. {[16] *State other facts relevant to the response.*}

ARGUMENT & AUTHORITIES

{*CHOOSE APPROPRIATE PARAGRAPHS 5-9*}

5. A motion to modify an arbitration award must be served within three months after the award is filed or delivered. 9 U.S.C. §12. In this case, the award was {[17] *filed/delivered*} on {[18] *date*}, and {[19] *adverse party*} served {[20] *his/her/its*} motion on {[21] *date*}. {[22] *Adverse party*}'s motion was not timely served and therefore should be denied.

6. A motion to modify an arbitration award must be filed within 90 days after the party receives a copy of the award. Tex. Civ. Prac. & Rem. Code §171.091(b). In this case, {[23] *adverse party*} received the copy on {[24] *date*}, and {[25] *adverse party*} filed {[26] *his/her/its*} motion on {[27] *date*}. {[28] *Adverse party*}'s motion was not timely filed and therefore should be denied.

7. The arbitration award should not be modified because there was no {[29] *evident miscalculation of numbers/mistake in the description of a person, thing, or property referred to in the award*}. {[30] *9 U.S.C. §11(a)/Tex. Civ. Prac. & Rem. Code §171.091(a)(1)*}. {[31] *Elaborate.*} {*See* ***O'Connor's Texas Rules****, "Grounds," ch. 4-C, §9.5.2(2), p. 379.*}

8. The arbitration award should not be modified because the award was based on a matter submitted to the {㉜ *arbitrator/arbitration panel*}. {㉝ *9 U.S.C. §11(b)/Tex. Civ. Prac. & Rem. Code §171.091(a)(2); Sydow v. Verner, Liipfert, Bernhard, McPherson & Hand, 218 S.W.3d 162, 168 (Tex. App.—Houston [14th Dist.] 2007, no pet.)*}. {㉞ *Elaborate.*} {*See* ***O'Connor's Texas Rules****, "Grounds," ch. 4-C, §9.5.2(2), p. 379.*}

9. The arbitration award should not be modified because there was no error in the form of the award. {㉟ *9 U.S.C. §11(c)/Tex. Civ. Prac. & Rem. Code §171.091(a)(3)*}. {㊱ *Adverse party*}'s requested modification would impermissibly affect the merits of the controversy. {㊲ *Elaborate.*} {*See* ***O'Connor's Texas Rules****, "Grounds," ch. 4-C, §9.5.2(2), p. 379.*}

CONCLUSION

10. {㊳ *Briefly summarize the response.*}

PRAYER

11. For these reasons, {㊴ *party*} asks the Court to deny {㊵ *adverse party*}'s motion to modify the arbitration award.

SEE: 9 U.S.C. §§11-13
Tex. Civ. Prac. & Rem. Code §171.091
O'Connor's Texas Rules * Civil Trials (2019), "Motion to modify or correct award," ch. 4-C, §9.5.2, p. 379
O'Connor's Federal Rules * Civil Trials (2019), "Modifying – grounds," ch. 7-E, §3.1.4, p. 768

ADD: STYLE OF THE CASE – FORM 1B:2
SIGNATURE BLOCK – FORM 1B:3
CERTIFICATE OF CONFERENCE – FORM 1B:12, if necessary
CERTIFICATE OF SERVICE – FORM 1B:13

ATTACH: AFFIDAVIT – FORM 1B:8, if necessary
ORDER – FORM 4C:9

NOTE: Under both the Federal Arbitration Act (FAA) and the Texas Arbitration Act (TAA), a party may apply to "modify or correct" an arbitration award. *See* 9 U.S.C. §11; Tex. Civ. Prac. & Rem. Code §171.091(a). For simplicity, this form uses only the term "modify."

The exclusive grounds for modifying an arbitration award authorized under the FAA are provided by 9 U.S.C. §11. ***Hall St. Assocs. v. Mattel, Inc.***, 552 U.S. 576, 584 (2008). Therefore, when seeking to modify an arbitration award under the FAA, parties must limit the grounds to those listed in 9 U.S.C. §11 and not argue common-law grounds.

ORDER ON {❶ *PARTY*}'S MOTION TO MODIFY ARBITRATION AWARD

After considering {❷ *party*} {❸ *name*}'s motion to modify the arbitration award, the response, and arguments of counsel, and after a hearing on the motion, the Court

{*CHOOSE APPROPRIATE ORDER*}

DENIES the motion.

GRANTS the motion and modifies the arbitration award as follows: {❹ *describe modification*}.

{*IF ARBITRATION UNDER TAA, ADD THE FOLLOWING PARAGRAPH*}

The Court awards the following costs to {❺ *party*}: {❻ *list costs*}.

SIGNED on _______________, 20___.

____
PRESIDING JUDGE

SEE: 9 U.S.C. §§11-13
Tex. Civ. Prac. & Rem. Code §§171.091, 171.092
O'Connor's Texas Rules * Civil Trials (2019), "Motion to modify or correct award," ch. 4-C, §9.5.2, p. 379
O'Connor's Federal Rules * Civil Trials (2019), "Modifying – grounds," ch. 7-E, §3.1.4, p. 768

ADD: STYLE OF THE CASE – FORM 1B:2
CERTIFICATE OF SERVICE – FORM 1B:13, if proposed order served separately from motion or response

{❶ *PARTY*}'S MOTION TO VACATE ARBITRATION AWARD

{❷ *Party*}, {❸ *name*}, asks the Court to vacate the arbitration award in this case. {*See **O'Connor's Texas Rules**, "Motion to vacate award," ch. 4-C, §9.5.3, p. 380.*}

INTRODUCTION

1. Plaintiff, {❹ *name*}, sued defendant, {❺ *name*}, for {❻ *state basis of suit*}.

2. {❼ *State other relevant facts about the suit.*}

BACKGROUND

3. On {❽ *date*}, plaintiff filed this suit, invoking the Court's jurisdiction over the dispute subject to the arbitration agreement.

4. The parties submitted the dispute to arbitration. On {❾ *date*}, an arbitration hearing was held. On {❿ *date*}, the {⓫ *arbitrator/arbitration panel*} issued an award in favor of {⓬ *identify prevailing party*} and granted {⓭ *identify relief awarded*}.

5. {⓮ *State other facts relevant to the motion.*}

ARGUMENT & AUTHORITIES

{*CHOOSE APPROPRIATE PARAGRAPH 6*}

{*Under FAA*}

6. A motion to vacate an arbitration award must be served within three months after the award is filed or delivered. 9 U.S.C. §12. In this case, the award was {⓯ *filed/delivered*} on {⓰ *date*}, and {⓱ *party*} served this motion on {⓲ *date*}. Therefore, this motion was timely served. {*See **O'Connor's Texas Rules**, "Under FAA," ch. 4-C, §9.5.3(1)(a), p. 380.*}

{*Under TAA*}

6. A motion to vacate an arbitration award must be filed within 90 days after the party receives a copy of the award. Tex. Civ. Prac. & Rem. Code §171.088(b). In this case, {⓳ *party*} received a copy of the award on {⓴ *date*}, and {㉑ *party*} filed this motion on {㉒ *date*}. Therefore, this motion was timely filed. {*See **O'Connor's Texas Rules**, "Under TAA," ch. 4-C, §9.5.3(1)(b), p. 380.*}

◄ *Continued on next page* ►

6. A motion to vacate an arbitration award must be filed within 90 days after the party learned or should have learned that the award was procured by corruption, fraud, or other undue means. Tex. Civ. Prac. & Rem. Code §171.088(a)(1), (b). In this case, {㉓ *party*} {㉔ *learned/should have learned*} that the award was procured by {㉕ *corruption/fraud/{identify other undue means}*} on {㉖ *date*}, and {㉗ *party*} filed this motion on {㉘ *date*}. {㉙ *Elaborate.*} Therefore, this motion was timely filed. {*See* ***O'Connor's Texas Rules****, "Under TAA," ch. 4-C, §9.5.3(1)(b), p. 380.*}

{*CHOOSE APPROPRIATE PARAGRAPHS 7-19*}

{*Under FAA*}

7. The arbitration award should be vacated because the award was procured by corruption, fraud, or undue means. 9 U.S.C. §10(a)(1). {㉚ *Elaborate.*} {*See* ***O'Connor's Texas Rules****, "Corruption, fraud, or undue means," ch. 4-C, §9.5.3(2)(a)[1], p. 381.*}

8. The arbitration award should be vacated because there is evidence of partiality or corruption by the {㉛ *arbitrator/arbitration panel*}. 9 U.S.C. §10(a)(2); *see, e.g., Tenaska Energy, Inc. v. Ponderosa Pine Energy, LLC*, 437 S.W.3d 518, 524-25 (Tex. 2014) (evident partiality when arbitrator did not fully disclose extent of business contacts with plaintiff's law firm, which had recommended him as arbitrator). {㉜ *Elaborate.*} {*See* ***O'Connor's Texas Rules****, "Arbitrator's evident partiality or corruption," ch. 4-C, §9.5.3(2)(a)[2], p. 381.*}

9. The arbitration award should be vacated because the {㉝ *arbitrator/arbitration panel*} was guilty of misconduct or misbehavior that prejudiced the rights of {㉞ *party*}. 9 U.S.C. §10(a)(3); *see SSP Holdings Ltd. P'ship v. Lopez*, 432 S.W.3d 487, 496-97 (Tex. App.—San Antonio 2014, pet. denied). {㉟ *Explain, e.g., the arbitrator refused to postpone the hearing, the arbitrator excluded material evidence.*} {*See* ***O'Connor's Texas Rules****, "Procedural misconduct," ch. 4-C, §9.5.3(2)(a)[3], p. 382.*}

10. The arbitration award should be vacated because the {㊱ *arbitrator/arbitration panel*} exceeded {㊲ *his/her/its*} powers or executed those powers so imperfectly that there was no mutual, final, and definite award. 9 U.S.C. §10(a)(4). {㊳ *Explain, e.g., the arbitrator issued an award that had no connection to the parties' agreement, the arbitrator was appointed in violation of the terms of the arbitration agreement. See Oxford Health Plans LLC v. Sutter, 569 U.S. 564, 569 (2013); Americo Life, Inc. v. Myer, 440 S.W.3d 18, 24-25 (Tex. 2014).*} {*See* ***O'Connor's Texas Rules****, "Arbitrator exceeded powers," ch. 4-C, §9.5.3(2)(a)[4], p. 382.*}

{*Under TAA*}

11. The arbitration award should be vacated because the award was procured by corruption, fraud, or undue means. Tex. Civ. Prac. & Rem. Code §171.088(a)(1). {39 *Elaborate.*} {*See **O'Connor's Texas Rules**, "Corruption, fraud, or undue means," ch. 4-C, §9.5.3(2)(b)[1], p. 383.*}

12. The arbitration award should be vacated because of the {40 *arbitrator/arbitration panel*}'s evident partiality that prejudiced the rights of {41 *party*}. Tex. Civ. Prac. & Rem. Code §171.088(a)(2)(A); *Burlington N. R.R. v. TUCO, Inc.*, 960 S.W.2d 629, 636 (Tex. 1997). {42 *Elaborate.*} {*See **O'Connor's Texas Rules**, "Evident partiality," ch. 4-C, §9.5.3(2)(b)[2], p. 383.*}

13. The arbitration award should be vacated because of the {43 *arbitrator/arbitration panel*}'s corruption that prejudiced the rights of {44 *party*}. Tex. Civ. Prac. & Rem. Code §171.088(a)(2)(B). {45 *Elaborate.*} {*See **O'Connor's Texas Rules**, "Arbitrator's corruption or misconduct," ch. 4-C, §9.5.3(2)(b)[3], p. 384.*}

14. The arbitration award should be vacated because of the {46 *arbitrator/arbitration panel*}'s misconduct or willful misbehavior that prejudiced the rights of {47 *party*}. Tex. Civ. Prac. & Rem. Code §171.088(a)(2)(C). {48 *Explain how the misconduct deprived the party of a fair hearing.*} {*See **O'Connor's Texas Rules**, "Arbitrator's corruption or misconduct," ch. 4-C, §9.5.3(2)(b)[3], p. 384.*}

15. The arbitration award should be vacated because the {49 *arbitrator/arbitration panel*} exceeded {50 *his/her/its*} power by deciding a matter outside of the scope of {51 *his/her/its*} authority. Tex. Civ. Prac. & Rem. Code §171.088(a)(3)(A). An arbitrator's authority comes from the arbitration agreement and is limited to the matters submitted to arbitration, whether expressly or by necessary implication. *City of Pasadena v. Smith*, 292 S.W.3d 14, 20 & n.41 (Tex. 2009). Specifically, the arbitration award should be vacated because {52 *explain, e.g., the arbitrator decided matters that the parties did not agree to submit to arbitration, the arbitration award cannot be rationally inferred from the parties' agreement*}. {*See **O'Connor's Texas Rules**, "Arbitrator exceeded powers," ch. 4-C, §9.5.3(2)(b)[4], p. 384.*}

16. The arbitration award should be vacated because the {53 *arbitrator/arbitration panel*} refused to postpone the hearing after a showing of sufficient cause for the postponement. Tex. Civ. Prac. & Rem. Code §171.088(a)(3)(B). {54 *Elaborate.*} {*See **O'Connor's Texas Rules**, "Procedural misconduct," ch. 4-C, §9.5.3(2)(b)[5], p. 385.*}

Continued on next page

17. The arbitration award should be vacated because the {55 *arbitrator/arbitration panel*} refused to hear evidence material to the controversy. Tex. Civ. Prac. & Rem. Code §171.088(a)(3)(C). {56 *Elaborate.*} {*See **O'Connor's Texas Rules**, "Procedural misconduct," ch. 4-C, §9.5.3(2)(b)[5], p. 385.*}

18. The arbitration award should be vacated because the {57 *arbitrator/arbitration panel*} conducted the hearing in a manner that substantially prejudiced the rights of {58 *party*}. Tex. Civ. Prac. & Rem. Code §171.088(a)(3)(D). {59 *Elaborate.*} {*See **O'Connor's Texas Rules**, "Procedural misconduct," ch. 4-C, §9.5.3(2)(b)[5], p. 385.*}

19. The arbitration award should be vacated because there was no agreement to arbitrate, the issue was not adversely determined in proceedings to compel arbitration, and {60 *party*} objected at the arbitration proceeding. Tex. Civ. Prac. & Rem. Code §171.088(a)(4); *see Women's Reg'l Healthcare, P.A. v. FemPartners of N. Tex., Inc.*, 175 S.W.3d 365, 368-69 (Tex. App.—Houston [1st Dist.] 2005, no pet.). {61 *Elaborate.*} {*See **O'Connor's Texas Rules**, "No arbitration agreement," ch. 4-C, §9.5.3(2)(b)[6], p. 385.*}

ATTACHMENTS

20. In support of this motion to vacate, {62 *party*} includes documents in the attached appendix, which is incorporated by reference. {63 *Party*} requests that the Court include the attached documents with its order vacating the arbitration award.

CONCLUSION

21. {64 *Briefly summarize the motion.*}

PRAYER

22. For these reasons, {65 *party*} asks the Court to vacate the arbitration award.

FORM 4C:10

SEE: 9 U.S.C. §§10, 12
Tex. Civ. Prac. & Rem. Code §171.088
O'Connor's Texas Rules * Civil Trials (2019), "Motion to vacate award," ch. 4-C, §9.5.3, p. 380
O'Connor's Federal Rules * Civil Trials (2019), "Vacating – grounds," ch. 7-E, §3.1.5, p. 769

ADD: STYLE OF THE CASE – FORM 1B:2
SIGNATURE BLOCK – FORM 1B:3
CERTIFICATE OF CONFERENCE – FORM 1B:12, if necessary
CERTIFICATE OF SERVICE – FORM 1B:13

ATTACH: AFFIDAVIT – FORM 1B:8, if necessary
NOTICE OF HEARING OR SUBMISSION – FORM 1E:1
ORDER – FORM 4C:12
APPENDIX – FORM 4C:13

NOTE: Although only the Federal Arbitration Act (FAA) requires an appendix, the movant should also attach the appropriate documents in Texas Arbitration Act (TAA) cases.

Although there is a limitations period for filing the motion under the TAA, the motion does not need to include every ground the party will raise for vacating the arbitration award. ***Black v. Shor***, 443 S.W.3d 154, 163 (Tex.App.—Corpus Christi 2013, pet. denied). Thus, if a motion to vacate has been timely filed, the party can raise additional grounds for vacating the award after the 90-day deadline as long as the grounds are raised before the court confirms the award. *See id.* at 163-64.

The challenging party may not have a full 90 days to file a motion to vacate. ***Hamm v. Millennium Income Fund, L.L.C.***, 178 S.W.3d 256, 264 (Tex.App.—Houston [1st Dist.] 2005, pet. denied) (FAA and TAA). If the other party files a motion to confirm the award, the challenging party should immediately move to vacate. *Id.*; *see* ***Human Biostar, Inc. v. Celltex Therapeutics Corp.***, 514 S.W.3d 844, 851 (Tex. App.—Houston [14th Dist.] 2017, pet. denied). Once an award has been confirmed, a party cannot file a motion to vacate. *See* ***Human Biostar***, 514 S.W.3d at 851; ***Black***, 443 S.W.3d at 163-64.

The exclusive grounds for vacating an arbitration award authorized under the FAA are provided by 9 U.S.C. §10. ***Hall St. Assocs. v. Mattel, Inc.***, 552 U.S. 576, 584 (2008). Therefore, when seeking to vacate an arbitration award under the FAA, parties must limit the grounds to those listed in 9 U.S.C. §10(a) and not argue common-law grounds. See ***O'Connor's Texas Rules***, "Under FAA," ch. 4-C, §9.5.3(2)(a), p. 381. The Texas Supreme Court has similarly held that Texas Civil Practice & Remedies Code §171.088 provides the exclusive grounds for vacating an arbitration award under the TAA; thus, a party seeking to vacate an arbitration award under the TAA cannot argue common-law grounds (e.g., manifest disregard of the law). ***Hoskins v. Hoskins***, 497 S.W.3d 490, 494-95 (Tex.2016). See ***O'Connor's Texas Rules***, "Under TAA," ch. 4-C, §9.5.3(2)(b), p. 383.

One court has held that nothing in the FAA or TAA prevents parties from agreeing to narrow the review of an arbitration award to a specific subset of the statutory grounds for vacating an award. *E.g.*, ***Denbury Onshore, LLC v. TexCal Energy S. Tex., L.P.***, 513 S.W.3d 511, 519 (Tex.App.—Houston [14th Dist.] 2016, no pet.) (parties agreed to restrict grounds for vacating award to fraud and corruption).

The TAA does not preclude an agreement limiting an arbitrator's power to that of a judge and providing for judicial review of an arbitration award for reversible error. ***Nafta Traders, Inc. v. Quinn***, 339 S.W.3d 84, 97 (Tex.2011). See ***O'Connor's Texas Rules***, "Expanded scope of judicial review," ch. 4-C, §9.5.3(2)(b)[4][b], p. 384.

Under the TAA, a motion to modify an arbitration award can be joined in the alternative with a motion to vacate the award. Tex. Civ. Prac. & Rem. Code §171.091(d). See FORM 4C:7.

{1 *PARTY*}'S RESPONSE TO
{2 *ADVERSE PARTY*}'S MOTION TO VACATE ARBITRATION AWARD

{3 *Party*}, {4 *name*}, asks the Court to deny {5 *adverse party*} {6 *name*}'s motion to vacate the arbitration award in this case.

INTRODUCTION

1. Plaintiff, {7 *name*}, sued defendant, {8 *name*}, for {9 *state basis of suit*}.

2. {10 *State other relevant facts about the suit.*}

BACKGROUND

3. The parties submitted the dispute to arbitration. On {11 *date*}, an arbitration hearing was held. On {12 *date*}, the {13 *arbitrator/arbitration panel*} issued an award in favor of {14 *identify prevailing party*} and granted {15 *identify relief awarded*}.

4. {16 *State other facts relevant to the response.*}

ARGUMENT & AUTHORITIES

{*CHOOSE APPROPRIATE PARAGRAPHS 5-22*}

{*Under FAA*}

5. A motion to vacate an arbitration award must be served within three months after the award is filed or delivered. 9 U.S.C. §12. In this case, the award was {17 *filed/delivered*} on {18 *date*}, and {19 *adverse party*} served {20 *his/her/its*} motion on {21 *date*}. {22 *Adverse party*}'s motion was not timely served and therefore should be denied. {*See* ***O'Connor's Texas Rules****, "Under FAA," ch. 4-C, §9.5.3(1)(a), p. 380.*}

6. The arbitration award should not be vacated because the award was not procured by corruption, fraud, or undue means. 9 U.S.C. §10(a)(1); *Perry Homes v. Cull*, 173 S.W.3d 565, 570 (Tex. App.—Fort Worth 2005), *rev'd on other grounds*, 258 S.W.3d 580 (Tex. 2008). {23 *Elaborate.*} {*See* ***O'Connor's Texas Rules****, "Corruption, fraud, or undue means," ch. 4-C, §9.5.3(2)(a)[1], p. 381.*}

7. The arbitration award should not be vacated because there is no evidence of partiality or corruption by the {24 *arbitrator/arbitration panel*}. 9 U.S.C. §10(a)(2); *see Tenaska Energy, Inc. v. Ponderosa Pine Energy, LLC*, 437 S.W.3d 518, 524-25 (Tex. 2014). {25 *Elaborate.*} {*See* ***O'Connor's Texas Rules****, "Arbitrator's evident partiality or corruption," ch. 4-C, §9.5.3(2)(a)[2], p. 381.*}

8. The arbitration award should not be vacated because the {㉖ *arbitrator/arbitration panel*} was not guilty of misconduct or misbehavior that prejudiced the rights of {㉗ *adverse party*}. 9 U.S.C. §10(a)(3); *SSP Holdings Ltd. P'ship v. Lopez*, 432 S.W.3d 487, 496-97 (Tex. App.—San Antonio 2014, pet. denied). {㉘ *Explain, e.g., the arbitrator did not refuse to postpone the hearing, the arbitrator did not exclude pertinent or material evidence.*} {*See* ***O'Connor's Texas Rules****, "Procedural misconduct," ch. 4-C, §9.5.3(2)(a)[3], p. 382.*}

9. The arbitration award should not be vacated because the {㉙ *arbitrator/arbitration panel*} did not exceed {㉚ *his/her/its*} powers or execute those powers so imperfectly that there was no mutual, final, and definite award. 9 U.S.C. §10(a)(4). {㉛ *Explain, e.g., the arbitrator issued an award that was properly connected to the parties' agreement, the arbitrator was appointed in accord with the terms of the arbitration agreement.*} {*See* ***O'Connor's Texas Rules****, "Arbitrator exceeded powers," ch. 4-C, §9.5.3(2)(a)[4], p. 382.*}

{*Under TAA*}

10. A motion to vacate an arbitration award must be filed within 90 days after the party receives a copy of the award. Tex. Civ. Prac. & Rem. Code §171.088(b). In this case, {㉜ *adverse party*} received a copy of the award on {㉝ *date*}, and {㉞ *adverse party*} filed {㉟ *his/her/its*} motion on {㊱ *date*}. {㊲ *Adverse party*}'s motion was not timely filed and therefore should be denied. {*See* ***O'Connor's Texas Rules****, "Under TAA," ch. 4-C, §9.5.3(1)(b), p. 380.*}

11. A motion to vacate an arbitration award must be filed within 90 days after the party learned or should have learned that the award was procured by corruption, fraud, or other undue means. Tex. Civ. Prac. & Rem. Code §171.088(a)(1), (b). In this case, {㊳ *adverse party*} alleges that {㊴ *he/she/it*} learned the award was procured by corruption, fraud, or other undue means on {㊵ *date*}. Even assuming the allegations to be true, {㊶ *adverse party*}'s motion was not filed timely because {㊷ *he/she/it*} filed the motion on {㊸ *date*}, which is more than 90 days after {㊹ *he/she/it*} learned of the alleged corruption, fraud, or undue means. {*See* ***O'Connor's Texas Rules****, "Under TAA," ch. 4-C, §9.5.3(1)(b), p. 380.*}

12. A motion to vacate an arbitration award must be filed within 90 days after the party learned or should have learned that the award was procured by corruption, fraud, or other undue means. Tex. Civ. Prac. & Rem. Code §171.088(a)(1), (b). In this case, {㊺ *adverse party*} alleges {㊻ *he/she/it*} learned the award was procured by corruption, fraud, or other undue means on {㊼ *date*}. But the award was not procured by corruption, fraud, or undue means, and thus {㊽ *adverse party*}'s motion is untimely be-

Continued on next page

cause {㊾ *he/she/it*} filed the motion on {㊿ *date*}, which is more than 90 days after {51 *he/she/it*} received a copy of the award on {52 *date*}. {53 *Elaborate.*} {*See* ***O'Connor's Texas Rules***, *"Under TAA," ch. 4-C, §9.5.3(1)(b), p. 380.*}

13. The arbitration award should not be vacated because the award was not procured by corruption, fraud, or undue means. Tex. Civ. Prac. & Rem. Code §171.088(a)(1). {54 *Elaborate.*} {*See* ***O'Connor's Texas Rules***, *"Corruption, fraud, or undue means," ch. 4-C, §9.5.3(2)(b)[1], p. 383.*}

14. The arbitration award should not be vacated because there was no evident partiality by the {55 *arbitrator/arbitration panel*} that prejudiced {56 *adverse party*}. Tex. Civ. Prac. & Rem. Code §171.088(a)(2)(A); *Forest Oil Corp. v. El Rucio Land & Cattle Co.*, 518 S.W.3d 422, 431 (Tex. 2017); *see Burlington N. R.R. v. TUCO, Inc.*, 960 S.W.2d 629, 636 (Tex. 1997). {57 *Elaborate.*} {*See* ***O'Connor's Texas Rules***, *"Evident partiality," ch. 4-C, §9.5.3(2)(b)[2], p. 383.*}

15. The arbitration award should not be vacated because there was no corruption by the {58 *arbitrator/arbitration panel*} that prejudiced {59 *adverse party*}. Tex. Civ. Prac. & Rem. Code §171.088(a)(2)(B). {60 *Elaborate.*} {*See* ***O'Connor's Texas Rules***, *"Arbitrator's corruption or misconduct," ch. 4-C, §9.5.3(2)(b)[3], p. 384.*}

16. The arbitration award should not be vacated because there was no misconduct or willful misbehavior by the {61 *arbitrator/arbitration panel*} that prejudiced {62 *adverse party*}. Tex. Civ. Prac. & Rem. Code §171.088(a)(2)(C). {63 *Elaborate.*} {*See* ***O'Connor's Texas Rules***, *"Arbitrator's corruption or misconduct," ch. 4-C, §9.5.3(2)(b)[3], p. 384.*}

17. The arbitration award should not be vacated because the {64 *arbitrator/arbitration panel*} did not exceed {65 *his/her/its*} power. Tex. Civ. Prac. & Rem. Code §171.088(a)(3)(A); *see Forest Oil Corp. v. El Rucio Land & Cattle Co.*, 518 S.W.3d 422, 431-32 (Tex. 2017). The award must be limited to matters submitted to arbitration or rationally inferable from the parties' agreement. *See City of Pasadena v. Smith*, 292 S.W.3d 14, 20 & n.41 (Tex. 2009). Specifically, the arbitration award should not be vacated because {66 *explain*}. {*See* ***O'Connor's Texas Rules***, *"Arbitrator exceeded powers," ch. 4-C, §9.5.3(2)(b)[4], p. 384.*}

18. The arbitration award should not be vacated because the {67 *arbitrator/arbitration panel*} did not refuse to postpone the hearing after a showing of sufficient cause for the postponement. Tex. Civ. Prac. & Rem. Code §171.088(a)(3)(B). {68 *Elaborate.*} {*See* ***O'Connor's Texas Rules***, *"Procedural misconduct," ch. 4-C, §9.5.3(2)(b)[5], p. 385.*}

19. The arbitration award should not be vacated because the {69 *arbitrator/arbitration panel*} did not refuse to hear evidence material to the controversy. Tex. Civ. Prac. & Rem. Code §171.088(a)(3)(C). {70 *Elaborate.*} {*See* ***O'Connor's Texas Rules****, "Procedural misconduct," ch. 4-C, §9.5.3(2)(b)[5], p. 385.*}

20. The arbitration award should not be vacated because the {71 *arbitrator/arbitration panel*} did not conduct the hearing in a manner that substantially prejudiced the rights of {72 *adverse party*}. Tex. Civ. Prac. & Rem. Code §171.088(a)(3)(D); *Hoskins v. Hoskins*, 497 S.W.3d 490, 494 (Tex. 2016). {73 *Elaborate.*} {*See* ***O'Connor's Texas Rules****, "Procedural misconduct," ch. 4-C, §9.5.3(2)(b)[5], p. 385.*}

21. The arbitration award should not be vacated because there was an agreement to arbitrate, the issue was not adversely determined in proceedings to compel arbitration, and {74 *adverse party*} did not object at the arbitration. Tex. Civ. Prac. & Rem. Code §171.088(a)(4); *see Women's Reg'l Healthcare, P.A. v. FemPartners of N. Tex., Inc.*, 175 S.W.3d 365, 368-69 (Tex. App.—Houston [1st Dist.] 2005, no pet.). {75 *Elaborate.*} {*See* ***O'Connor's Texas Rules****, "No arbitration agreement," ch. 4-C, §9.5.3(2)(b)[6], p. 385.*}

{*Under FAA or TAA – waiver of objection to evident partiality*}

22. The arbitration award should not be vacated because {76 *adverse party*} waived any objection to the arbitrator's evident partiality. During the arbitration proceeding, {77 *adverse party*} did not object to known factors showing the arbitrator's evident partiality before the arbitration award was issued. *Kendall Builders, Inc. v. Chesson*, 149 S.W.3d 796, 806 (Tex. App.—Austin 2004, pet. denied); *see Burlington N. R.R. v. TUCO, Inc.*, 960 S.W.2d 629, 637 n.9 (Tex. 1997). {78 *Elaborate.*}

CONCLUSION

23. {79 *Briefly summarize the response.*}

PRAYER

24. For these reasons, {80 *party*} asks the Court to deny {81 *adverse party*}'s motion to vacate the arbitration award.

SEE: 9 U.S.C. §§10, 12
Tex. Civ. Prac. & Rem. Code §171.088
O'Connor's Texas Rules * Civil Trials (2019), "Motion to vacate award," ch. 4-C, §9.5.3, p. 380
O'Connor's Federal Rules * Civil Trials (2019), "Vacating – grounds," ch. 7-E, §3.1.5, p. 769

Continued on next page

ADD: STYLE OF THE CASE – FORM 1B:2
SIGNATURE BLOCK – FORM 1B:3
CERTIFICATE OF CONFERENCE – FORM 1B:12, if necessary
CERTIFICATE OF SERVICE – FORM 1B:13

ATTACH: AFFIDAVIT – FORM 1B:8, if necessary
ORDER – FORM 4C:12

NOTE: The exclusive grounds for vacating an arbitration award authorized under the Federal Arbitration Act (FAA) are provided by 9 U.S.C. §10. ***Hall St. Assocs. v. Mattel, Inc.***, 552 U.S. 576, 584 (2008). Therefore, when seeking to vacate an arbitration award under the FAA, parties must limit the grounds to those listed in 9 U.S.C. §10(a) and not argue common-law grounds. See ***O'Connor's Texas Rules***, "Under FAA," ch. 4-C, §9.5.3(2)(a), p. 381. The Texas Supreme Court has similarly held that Texas Civil Practice & Remedies Code §171.088 provides the exclusive grounds for vacating an arbitration award under the Texas Arbitration Act (TAA); thus, a party seeking to vacate an arbitration award under the TAA cannot argue common-law grounds (e.g., manifest disregard of the law). ***Hoskins v. Hoskins***, 497 S.W.3d 490, 494-95 (Tex.2016). See ***O'Connor's Texas Rules***, "Under TAA," ch. 4-C, §9.5.3(2)(b), p. 383.

One court has held that nothing in the FAA or TAA prevents parties from agreeing to narrow the review of an arbitration award to a specific subset of the statutory grounds for vacating an award. *E.g.*, ***Denbury Onshore, LLC v. TexCal Energy S. Tex., L.P.***, 513 S.W.3d 511, 519 (Tex.App.—Houston [14th Dist.] 2016, no pet.) (parties agreed to restrict grounds for vacating award to fraud and corruption).

The TAA does not preclude an agreement limiting an arbitrator's power to that of a judge and providing for judicial review of an arbitration award for reversible error. ***Nafta Traders, Inc. v. Quinn***, 339 S.W.3d 84, 97 (Tex.2011).

FORM 4C:11

ORDER ON {❶ *PARTY*}'S MOTION TO VACATE ARBITRATION AWARD

After considering {❷ *party*} {❸ *name*}'s motion to vacate the arbitration award, the response, and arguments of counsel, and after a hearing on the motion, the Court

{*CHOOSE APPROPRIATE ORDER*}

DENIES the motion.

GRANTS the motion and vacates the arbitration award.

SIGNED on ________________, 20___.

____
PRESIDING JUDGE

SEE: 9 U.S.C. §§10, 12
Tex. Civ. Prac. & Rem. Code §171.088
O'Connor's Texas Rules * Civil Trials (2019), "Motion to vacate award," ch. 4-C, §9.5.3, p. 380
O'Connor's Federal Rules * Civil Trials (2019), "Vacating – grounds," ch. 7-E, §3.1.5, p. 769

ADD: STYLE OF THE CASE – FORM 1B:2
CERTIFICATE OF SERVICE – FORM 1B:13, if proposed order served separately from motion or response

FORM 4C:12

APPENDIX

{❶ *Party*}, {❷ *name*}, files this appendix of evidence in support of {❸ *his/her/its*} motion to {❹ *confirm/modify/vacate*} the arbitration award and incorporates the evidence into the motion by reference.

1. Arbitration agreement..Tab A
2. Arbitration award..Tab B

{*ADD IF APPLICABLE*}

3. Parties' selection of additional arbitrator..Tab C
4. Order appointing additional arbitrator..Tab D
5. Written extension of time to make arbitration award..Tab E
6. Affidavit of {❺ *name*} in support of motion..Tab F
7. {❻ *Other evidence in support of motion*}..Tab G

{*Continue with list until all evidence is identified.*}

SEE: 9 U.S.C. §13

ATTACH: Documents listed in the appendix

FORM 4C:13

AGREED MOTION TO REFER CASE TO A SPECIAL JUDGE

{❶ *Party*}, {❷ *name*}, and {❸ *adverse party*}, {❹ *name*}, ask the Court to refer this case to a special judge, as authorized by Texas Civil Practice & Remedies Code section 151.001. {*See **O'Connor's Texas Rules**, "Types of Cases for Referral to Special Judge," ch. 4-D, §2, p. 386.*}

INTRODUCTION

1. Plaintiff, {❺ *name*}, sued defendant, {❻ *name*}, for {❼ *state basis of suit*}.

2. {❽ *State other relevant facts about the suit.*}

BACKGROUND

3. {❾ *State facts relevant to the motion.*}

AGREEMENT

4. This case is appropriate for referral to a special judge because {❿ *summarize reasons why referral is appropriate*}.

5. The parties agree to the following:

a. The parties waive their right to a jury trial.

b. The parties request that the Court refer the following issues to a special judge: {⓫ *list issues to be referred*}.

c. The parties ask the Court to appoint Judge {⓬ *name of special judge*} to act as the special judge. Judge {⓭ *name of special judge*} has agreed to hear the case.

d. The parties request that the Court set the agreed trial for {⓮ *date*}, at {⓯ *time*}, at {⓰ *place*}.

e. The agreed fee for Judge {⓱ *name of special judge*} is ${⓲ *amount*}.

{*CHOOSE APPROPRIATE PARAGRAPH f*}

f. The parties agree to share equally the cost of the special judge and all administrative costs related to the trial. {*See **O'Connor's Texas Rules**, "Costs & fees," ch. 4-D, §6.5, p. 388.*}

f. The parties agree to share the cost of the special judge and all administrative costs related to the trial as follows: {⓳ *outline agreement on costs*}.

◄ *Continued on next page* ►

FORM 4D:1

PRAYER

6. For these reasons, the parties ask the Court to grant their agreed motion to refer this case to Judge {⑳ *name of special judge*} as special judge.

SEE: Tex. Civ. Prac. & Rem. Code §§151.001-151.003, 151.009
O'Connor's Texas Rules * Civil Trials (2019), "Special Judge," ch. 4-D, p. 386

ADD: STYLE OF THE CASE – FORM 1B:2
SIGNATURE BLOCK FOR AGREED MOTIONS – FORM 1B:4
CERTIFICATE OF SERVICE – FORM 1B:13

ATTACH: ORDER – FORM 4D:2

NOTE: One way to locate a special judge is to search the Internet for "private trials." Then verify with the Texas Center for the Judiciary that the judge has fulfilled the CLE requirements for the calendar year. See ***O'Connor's Texas Rules***, "Practice Tip," ch. 4-D, §4.5, p. 387.

If the issues that were submitted to the special judge involved private or confidential matters, the parties should consider asking the judge to seal the record. See FORM 5L:1; ***O'Connor's Texas Rules***, "Motion to seal records," ch. 4-D, §7.2, p. 388; "Motion to Seal Court Records," ch. 5-L, p. 482.

ORDER ON AGREED MOTION TO REFER CASE TO A SPECIAL JUDGE

After considering the parties' agreed motion to refer this case to a special judge, the Court finds that the parties have waived their right to a jury and have asked the Court to refer the case to a special judge. {*See* ***O'Connor's Texas Rules***, *"Order of Referral," ch. 4-D, §5, p. 387.*} Therefore, the Court

GRANTS the agreed motion and orders as follows:

1. The proceedings in this case will be stayed pending the outcome of the trial before a special judge.

2. The special judge will hear the following issues: {❶ *list the issues the parties agreed to refer*}.

3. {❷ *Name of special judge*} is appointed as the special judge to hear the referred issues.

4. The hearing before Judge {❸ *name of special judge*} will take place on {❹ *date*}, at {❺ *time*}, at {❻ *place*}.

5. After hearing the issues, Judge {❼ *name of special judge*} will submit a copy of the verdict to the Court {❽ *by/within*} {❾ *identify specific date or number of days from date of adjournment*}.

6. The agreed fee for Judge {❿ *name of special judge*} is ${⓫ *amount*}.

7. The parties agree to share the cost of the special judge and all administrative costs related to the trial as follows: {⓬ *outline agreement on costs*}.

SIGNED on ______________, 20___.

____
PRESIDING JUDGE

SEE: Tex. Civ. Prac. & Rem. Code §§151.001-151.006, 151.009
O'Connor's Texas Rules * Civil Trials (2019), "Order of Referral," ch. 4-D, §5, p. 387

ADD: STYLE OF THE CASE – FORM 1B:2
CERTIFICATE OF SERVICE – FORM 1B:13, if proposed order served separately from motion

NOTE: If one of the parties disagrees with the verdict, that party can file a motion for new trial with the special judge. See FORM 10B:2.

★

{[1] *PARTY*}'S MOTION FOR NEW TRIAL

{[2] *Party*}, {[3] *name*}, asks the Court to grant a new trial under Texas Civil Practice & Remedies Code section 151.012. {*See* ***O'Connor's Texas Rules****, "Motion for new trial," ch. 4-D, §7.3, p. 389.*}

INTRODUCTION

1. Plaintiff, {[4] *name*}, sued defendant, {[5] *name*}, for {[6] *state basis of suit*}.

2. {[7] *State other relevant facts about the suit.*}

BACKGROUND

3. On {[8] *date*}, the Court referred this case to Judge {[9] *name of special judge*} as special judge, as authorized by Texas Civil Practice & Remedies Code section 151.001.

{*CHOOSE APPROPRIATE PARAGRAPH 4*}

4. The order of referral specified that Judge {[10] *name of special judge*} was required to submit the verdict to the Court {[11] *by/within*} {[12] *identify specific date or number of days from date of adjournment*}.

4. The order of referral did not specify a deadline for Judge {[13] *name of special judge*} to submit the verdict to the Court.

5. On {[14] *date*}, Judge {[15] *name of special judge*} heard this case, which adjourned on {[16] *date*}.

6. {[17] *State other facts relevant to the motion.*}

ARGUMENT & AUTHORITIES

{*CHOOSE APPROPRIATE PARAGRAPH 7*}

7. Judge {[18] *name of special judge*} did not submit the verdict to the Court {[19] *by/within*} {[20] *identify specific date or number of days from date of adjournment*}. Because Judge {[21] *name of special judge*} did not submit a verdict by the deadline set in the order, {[22] *party*} asks the Court to grant a new trial. Tex. Civ. Prac. & Rem. Code §151.012.

7. Unless otherwise specified in the order, a special judge must submit the verdict no later than 60 days after the trial adjourns. Tex. Civ. Prac. & Rem. Code §151.011. Because Judge {[23] *name of special judge*} did not submit a verdict within the statutory time period, {[24] *party*} asks the Court to grant a new trial. *Id.* §151.012.

HEARING

8. {㉕ *Party*} asks the Court to hold a hearing on this motion, as required by Texas Civil Practice & Remedies Code section 151.012(3).

PRAYER

9. For these reasons, {㉖ *party*} asks the Court to set this motion for a hearing and, after the hearing, grant a new trial.

SEE: Tex. Civ. Prac. & Rem. Code §§151.011, 151.012
O'Connor's Texas Rules * Civil Trials (2019), "Motion for new trial," ch. 4-D, §7.3, p. 389

ADD: STYLE OF THE CASE – FORM 1B:2
SIGNATURE BLOCK – FORM 1B:3
CERTIFICATE OF SERVICE – FORM 1B:13

ATTACH: AFFIDAVIT – FORM 1B:8, if necessary
NOTICE OF HEARING OR SUBMISSION – FORM 1E:1
ORDER – FORM 4D:4

NOTE: A court may grant a new trial under Texas Civil Practice & Remedies Code §151.012 if notice of the hearing on the motion is given to all parties and the hearing is held.

ORDER ON {❶ *PARTY*}'S MOTION FOR NEW TRIAL

After considering {❷ *party*} {❸ *name*}'s motion for new trial and arguments of counsel, the Court finds:

1. On {❹ *date*}, the Court appointed Judge {❺ *name of special judge*} as special judge to hear this case.

2. On {❻ *date*}, Judge {❼ *name of special judge*} heard this case, which adjourned on {❽ *date*}.

3. Judge {❾ *name of special judge*} did not submit a verdict {❿ *by/within*} {⓫ *identify specific date or number of days from date of adjournment*}.

Because Judge {⓬ *name of special judge*} did not submit a verdict by the deadline, the Court

GRANTS {⓭ *party*}'s motion for new trial and sets this case for trial on {⓮ *date*}.

SIGNED on ________________, 20___.

____
PRESIDING JUDGE

SEE: Tex. Civ. Prac. & Rem. Code §§151.011, 151.012
O'Connor's Texas Rules * Civil Trials (2019), "Motion for new trial," ch. 4-D, §7.3, p. 389

ADD: STYLE OF THE CASE – FORM 1B:2
CERTIFICATE OF SERVICE – FORM 1B:13, if proposed order served separately from motion

TEXAS CIVIL FORMS
CHAPTER 5. PRETRIAL MOTIONS
TABLE OF CONTENTS

TABLE OF CONTENTS

CHAPTER 5. PRETRIAL MOTIONS

TABLE OF CONTENTS

Exclude Expert Testimony

JOINT PRETRIAL ORDER

{*CHOOSE APPROPRIATE SECTIONS BELOW*}

APPEARANCE OF COUNSEL

1. Plaintiff. {❶ *List in separate paragraphs the names of the plaintiff and the plaintiff's attorneys and their addresses, telephone numbers, and fax numbers.*}

2. Defendant. {❷ *List in separate paragraphs the names of the defendant and the defendant's attorneys and their addresses, telephone numbers, and fax numbers.*}

STATEMENT OF THE CASE

3. {❸ *Briefly explain the nature of the dispute and the history of the lawsuit.*}

DISCOVERY

4. Discovery in this suit is governed by a Level {❹ *1/2/3*} discovery-control plan. The discovery period {❺ *will end/ended*} on {❻ *date*}. {*See **O'Connor's Texas Rules**, "Discovery-Control Plans," ch. 6-A, §7, p. 520.*}

{*CHOOSE APPROPRIATE PARAGRAPH 5*}

5. All discovery is complete.

5. Discovery is not complete. The following discovery requests remain unanswered: {❼ *list pending discovery requests*}. {❽ *Party*} intends to serve the following discovery requests on {❾ *adverse party*}: {❿ *list discovery requests party intends to serve*}.

5. Discovery is not complete. {⓫ *Party*} intends to serve the following discovery requests on {⓬ *adverse party*}: {⓭ *list discovery requests party intends to serve*}.

MOTIONS

6. {⓮ *List pending motions.*}

PLEADING AMENDMENTS

7. {⓯ *List the pleadings that can be amended and the deadline to amend.*}

CONTENTIONS OF THE PARTIES

8. {⓰ *In separate paragraphs, provide a brief statement of the parties' contentions.*}

◄ *Continued on next page* ►

ADMISSIONS OF FACT

9. {[17] *List all the facts the parties have admitted and stipulated.*}

CONTESTED ISSUES OF FACT

10. {[18] *List the disputed fact issues and the resolutions necessary to the disposition of the case.*}

AGREED APPLICABLE PROPOSITIONS OF LAW

11. {[19] *List the agreed propositions of law.*}

CONTESTED PROPOSITIONS OF LAW

12. {[20] *List the disputed propositions of law.*}

EXHIBITS

13. Attached are lists of each party's trial exhibits. {[21] *Attach lists of the parties' trial exhibits. All exhibits should be provided to the other party so the parties can make objections to authenticity before trial.*}

WITNESSES

14. Attached are lists of each party's trial witnesses. {[22] *List the names, addresses, and telephone numbers of witnesses who will or may be used at trial, with a short statement of the anticipated testimony.*}

SETTLEMENT

15. All settlement efforts have been exhausted, and the case cannot be settled and must be tried.

TRIAL

16. {[23] *State whether the trial will be jury or nonjury, the probable length of trial, and the availability of witnesses, including out-of-state witnesses.*}

ATTACHMENTS

17. {㉔ *Identify the attachments, including exhibits, jury instructions, definitions, and questions.*}

SIGNED on ______________, 20___.

____
PRESIDING JUDGE

SEE: Tex. R. Civ. P. 166
O'Connor's Texas Rules * Civil Trials **(2019), "Scope of Pretrial Conference," ch. 5-A, §3, p. 395; "Pretrial Order," ch. 5-A, §5, p. 398**

ADD: STYLE OF THE CASE – FORM 1B:2
SIGNATURE BLOCK FOR AGREED MOTIONS – FORM 1B:4

ATTACH: Exhibits, if necessary
Witness lists, if necessary

{❶ *PARTY*}'S DEMAND FOR JURY TRIAL

1. {❷ *Party*}, {❸ *name*}, asserts {❹ *his/her/its*} right to a trial by jury under Texas Constitution article 1, section 15, and makes this demand for a jury trial.

{*CHOOSE APPROPRIATE PARAGRAPH 2*}

2. Because {❺ *party*} is making this demand at least 30 days before the {❻ *date*} trial setting, the demand is presumed to have been made a reasonable time before trial under Texas Rule of Civil Procedure 216. *Halsell v. Dehoyos*, 810 S.W.2d 371, 371 (Tex. 1991). {*See* ***O'Connor's Texas Rules***, *"30 days – presumed reasonable," ch. 5-B, §4.1.2(1), p. 402.*}

2. Although {❼ *party*} is making this demand less than 30 days before the {❽ *date*} trial setting, a court may still permit a jury trial. *See Monroe v. Alts. in Motion*, 234 S.W.3d 56, 69-70 (Tex. App.—Houston [1st Dist.] 2007, no pet.). {❾ *Party*} attaches a motion to strike this case from the nonjury docket to explain why the Court should permit a jury trial despite the short notice. {*See* ***O'Connor's Texas Rules***, *"Less than 30 days – no presumption," ch. 5-B, §4.1.2(2), p. 402.*}

{*CHOOSE APPROPRIATE PARAGRAPH 3*}

3. {❿ *Party*} tenders the jury fee of $40 for {⓫ *county/district*} court, as required by Texas Government Code section 51.604(a). {*See* ***O'Connor's Texas Rules***, *"Amount," ch. 5-B, §3.2.1, p. 402.*}

3. Under Texas Rule of Civil Procedure 217, {⓬ *party*} files the attached affidavit of indigence with this demand to establish that {⓭ *party*} is unable to tender the jury fee in this case. {*See* ***O'Connor's Texas Rules***, *"Indigent," ch. 5-B, §3.2.2, p. 402.*}

SEE: Tex. R. Civ. P. 216-220, 245
Tex. Const. art. 1, §15
Tex. Gov't Code §51.604
O'Connor's Texas Rules * Civil Trials (2019), "Requirements," ch. 5-B, §3, p. 401

ADD: STYLE OF THE CASE – FORM 1B:2
SIGNATURE BLOCK – FORM 1B:3
CERTIFICATE OF SERVICE – FORM 1B:13

ATTACH: AFFIDAVIT/DECLARATION OF INDIGENCE – FORM 2J:1, if necessary
MOTION TO STRIKE FROM NONJURY DOCKET – FORM 5B:2, if necessary

NOTE: The demand for a jury trial may be in the petition, the answer, or a separate motion.

If the trial court does not give the parties 45 days' notice of the first trial setting, as required by Texas Rule of Civil Procedure 245, a late request for a jury trial is deemed timely. ***In re J.C.***, 108 S.W.3d 914, 916-17 (Tex.App.—Texarkana 2003, no pet.); ***In re V.R.W.***, 41 S.W.3d 183, 195 (Tex.App.—Houston [14th Dist.] 2001, no pet.), *disapproved on other grounds*, ***In re J.F.C.***, 96 S.W.3d 256 (Tex.2002).

The jury fee paid under Texas Government Code §51.604 includes the jury fee paid under Texas Rule of Civil Procedure 216. Tex. Gov't Code §51.604(c). Specifically, the portion of the jury fee due under Rule 216—$10 in district court or $5 in county court—must be paid 30 days before trial and the remainder of the jury fee due under §51.604—$30 in district court or $35 in county court—must be paid 10 days before trial. *See* ***In re I.M.B.***, 148 S.W.3d 653, 656 (Tex.App.—Beaumont 2004, no pet.) (applying former version of §51.604); ***Universal Printing Co. v. Premier Victorian Homes, Inc.***, 73 S.W.3d 283, 292 (Tex.App.—Houston [1st Dist.] 2001, pet. denied) (same). To be safe, however, pay both fees when you make your request, which should be at least 30 days before the date the case is set for trial.

{❶ *PARTY*}'S MOTION TO STRIKE CASE FROM NONJURY DOCKET {❷ *ADD IF APPROPRIATE: & MOTION FOR CONTINUANCE*}

{❸ *Party*}, {❹ *name*}, asks the Court to strike this case from the nonjury docket {❺ *add if appropriate: and continue the trial until a jury panel becomes available*}. {*See* ***O'Connor's Texas Rules****, "For untimely request," ch. 5-B, §3.1.2(2), p. 401.*}

INTRODUCTION

1. Plaintiff, {❻ *name*}, sued defendant, {❼ *name*}, for {❽ *state basis of suit*}.

2. {❾ *State other relevant facts about the suit.*}

BACKGROUND

3. This case is set for a nonjury trial on {❿ *date*}.

4. On {⓫ *date*}, {⓬ *party*} filed {⓭ *his/her/its*} demand for a jury trial and {⓮ *tendered the appropriate jury fee/filed an affidavit of indigence*}.

5. {⓯ *State other facts relevant to the motion.*}

ARGUMENT & AUTHORITIES

6. The Texas Constitution guarantees a trial by jury. Tex. Const. art. 1, §15. To obtain a jury trial, a party must usually (1) file a written request for a jury trial and pay an initial $10 jury fee (district court) or $5 jury fee (county court) to the court clerk at least 30 days before the date set for trial on the nonjury docket and (2) pay the remainder of the jury fee at least 10 days before the date set for jury trial. *See* Tex. Gov't Code §51.604(b); Tex. R. Civ. P. 216; *Universal Printing Co. v. Premier Victorian Homes, Inc.*, 73 S.W.3d 283, 292 (Tex. App.—Houston [1st Dist.] 2001, pet. denied). {*See* ***O'Connor's Texas Rules****, "Right to Jury Trial," ch. 5-B, §2, p. 400; "Requirements," ch. 5-B, §3, p. 401.*}

7. If the request is untimely, the right to a jury trial can be denied, but only if a jury trial would (1) interfere with the court's docket, (2) delay the trial, or (3) injure the opposing party. *See Gen. Motors Corp. v. Gayle*, 951 S.W.2d 469, 476 (Tex. 1997); *Monroe v. Alts. in Motion*, 234 S.W.3d 56, 69-70 (Tex. App.—Houston [1st Dist.] 2007, no pet.). {*See* ***O'Connor's Texas Rules****, "For untimely request," ch. 5-B, §3.1.2(2), p. 401.*}

8. The Court should grant {16 *party*}'s motion to strike this case from the nonjury docket because {17 *explain how a jury trial will not interfere with the court's docket, delay the trial, or injure the opposing party*}. {18 *Party*} did not request a jury trial earlier because {19 *state reasons*}.

9. This case is appropriate for a jury trial because it involves disputed fact issues. *See Halsell v. Dehoyos*, 810 S.W.2d 371, 372 (Tex. 1991). Specifically, {20 *identify disputed fact issues*}.

{*CHOOSE APPROPRIATE PARAGRAPH 10*}

10. A jury is available to hear this case. Attached to this motion as Exhibit {21 *letter*} is an affidavit of the clerk stating that a jury panel is available for the week of {22 *identify week*}.

10. A jury is not available to hear this case. Attached to this motion as Exhibit {23 *letter*} is an affidavit of the clerk stating that no jury panel is available for the week of {24 *identify week*}. But {25 *party*} is ready, willing, and able to try this case before a jury and asks the Court to continue the trial in this case until a jury panel becomes available. *See McCrann v. Tandy Comput. Leasing*, 737 S.W.2d 10, 11 (Tex. App.—Corpus Christi 1987, no writ).

CONCLUSION

11. {26 *Briefly summarize the motion.*}

PRAYER

12. For these reasons, {27 *party*} asks the Court to strike this case from the nonjury docket {28 *add if appropriate: and continue the trial until a jury panel becomes available*}.

SEE: Tex. R. Civ. P. 216-220, 245
Tex. Const. art. 1, §15
Tex. Gov't Code §51.604
O'Connor's Texas Rules * Civil Trials (2019), "For untimely request," ch. 5-B, §3.1.2(2), p. 401

ADD: STYLE OF THE CASE – FORM 1B:2
SIGNATURE BLOCK – FORM 1B:3
VERIFICATION – FORM 1B:7
CERTIFICATE OF SERVICE – FORM 1B:13

Continued on next page

ATTACH: AFFIDAVIT – FORM 1B:8
NOTICE OF HEARING OR SUBMISSION – FORM 1E:1
ORDER – FORM 1G:1

NOTE: The jury fee paid under Texas Government Code §51.604 includes the jury fee paid under Texas Rule of Civil Procedure 216. Tex. Gov't Code §51.604(c). Specifically, the portion of the jury fee due under Rule 216—$10 in district court or $5 in county court—must be paid 30 days before trial and the remainder of the jury fee due under §51.604—$30 in district court or $35 in county court—must be paid 10 days before trial. *See* ***In re I.M.B.***, 148 S.W.3d 653, 656 (Tex.App.—Beaumont 2004, no pet.) (applying former version of §51.604); ***Universal Printing Co. v. Premier Victorian Homes, Inc.***, 73 S.W.3d 283, 292 (Tex.App.—Houston [1st Dist.] 2001, pet. denied) (same).

{❶ *PARTY*}'S RESPONSE TO
{❷ *ADVERSE PARTY*}'S DEMAND FOR JURY TRIAL

{❸ *Party*}, {❹ *name*}, asks the Court to deny {❺ *adverse party*} {❻ *name*}'s demand for a jury trial. {*See* ***O'Connor's Texas Rules****, "Response," ch. 5-B, §5, p. 403.*}

INTRODUCTION

1. Plaintiff, {❼ *name*}, sued defendant, {❽ *name*}, for {❾ *state basis of suit*}.

2. {❿ *State other relevant facts about the suit.*}

BACKGROUND

3. On {⓫ *date*}, {⓬ *adverse party*} filed {⓭ *his/her/its*} demand for a jury trial.

4. {⓮ *State other facts relevant to the response.*}

ARGUMENT & AUTHORITIES

{*CHOOSE APPROPRIATE PARAGRAPHS 5-6*}

{*If demand timely but unreasonable*}

5. A request for a trial by jury made at least 30 days before the date set for trial is presumed to have been made a reasonable time before trial. *Halsell v. Dehoyos*, 810 S.W.2d 371, 371 (Tex. 1991). This presumption, however, can be rebutted by a showing that a jury trial would (1) injure the adverse party, (2) disrupt the court's docket, or (3) impede the ordinary handling of the court's business. *Id.*; *In re J.N.F.*, 116 S.W.3d 426, 436 (Tex. App.—Houston [14th Dist.] 2003, no pet.).

6. The Court should deny {⓯ *adverse party*}'s demand for a jury trial because {⓰ *explain how a jury trial will interfere with the court's docket, delay the trial, or injure the opposing party*}.

{*If demand or jury fee payment untimely*}

5. A party is not guaranteed a right to a jury trial when (1) the request is made less than 30 days before the date set for trial, (2) the jury fee under Texas Rule of Civil Procedure 216 is paid less than 30 days before the date set for trial, or (3) the jury fee under Texas Government Code section 51.604 is paid less than 10 days before the date set for trial. *Universal Printing Co. v. Premier Victorian Homes, Inc.*, 73 S.W.3d 283, 292 (Tex. App.—Houston [1st Dist.] 2001, pet. denied); *see Gen. Motors Corp. v. Gayle*, 951 S.W.2d 469, 476 (Tex. 1997); *In re I.M.B.*, 148 S.W.3d 653, 656 (Tex. App.—Beaumont 2004, no pet.). A trial court should deny an untimely request unless the re-

◄ *Continued on next page* ►

questing party establishes that a jury trial would not (1) interfere with the court's docket, (2) delay the trial, or (3) injure the adverse party. *See Gen. Motors*, 951 S.W.2d at 476; *Monroe v. Alts. in Motion*, 234 S.W.3d 56, 69-70 (Tex. App.—Houston [1st Dist.] 2007, no pet.). {*See* ***O'Connor's Texas Rules****, "Deadline to pay jury fee," ch. 5-B, §4.2, p. 403; "Request filed less than 30 days before trial," ch. 5-B, §5.2, p. 403.*}

6. The Court should deny {[17] *adverse party*}'s demand for a jury trial because {[18] *adverse party*} {[19] *demanded a jury/paid the jury fee*} less than {[20] *30/10*} days before the date set for trial and did not show how a jury trial could be granted without interfering with the court's docket, delaying the trial, or injuring the adverse party. *See Gen. Motors*, 951 S.W.2d at 476; *Wright v. Brooks*, 773 S.W.2d 649, 651 (Tex. App.—San Antonio 1989, writ denied). {[21] *Elaborate.*}

CONCLUSION

7. {[22] *Briefly summarize the response.*}

PRAYER

8. For these reasons, {[23] *party*} asks the Court to deny {[24] *adverse party*}'s demand for a jury trial.

SEE: Tex. R. Civ. P. 216-220, 245
Tex. Const. art. 1, §15
Tex. Gov't Code §51.604
O'Connor's Texas Rules * Civil Trials (2019), "Response," ch. 5-B, §5, p. 403

ADD: STYLE OF THE CASE – FORM 1B:2
SIGNATURE BLOCK – FORM 1B:3
CERTIFICATE OF SERVICE – FORM 1B:13

ATTACH: AFFIDAVIT – FORM 1B:8, if necessary
ORDER – FORM 1G:1

NOTE: Parties can contractually agree to waive their right to a jury trial, but if a party does not timely assert the waiver, it can be lost. See ***O'Connor's Texas Rules***, "Waiver by contract," ch. 5-B, §7.4, p. 405.

See notes under FORM 5B:1.

{[1] *PARTY*}'S RESPONSE TO {[2] *ADVERSE PARTY*}'S
MOTION TO STRIKE CASE FROM NONJURY DOCKET

{[3] *Party*}, {[4] *name*}, asks the Court to deny {[5] *adverse party*} {[6] *name*}'s motion to strike this case from the nonjury docket. {*See **O'Connor's Texas Rules**, "Response," ch. 5-B, §5, p. 403.*}

INTRODUCTION

1. Plaintiff, {[7] *name*}, sued defendant, {[8] *name*}, for {[9] *state basis of suit*}.

2. {[10] *State other relevant facts about the suit.*}

BACKGROUND

3. On {[11] *date*}, {[12] *adverse party*} filed {[13] *his/her/its*} demand for a jury trial.

4. On {[14] *date*}, {[15] *adverse party*} filed {[16] *his/her/its*} motion to strike the case from the nonjury docket.

5. {[17] *State other facts relevant to the response.*}

ARGUMENT & AUTHORITIES

6. A party is not guaranteed a right to a jury trial when (1) the request is made less than 30 days before the date set for trial, (2) the jury fee under Texas Rule of Civil Procedure 216 is paid less than 30 days before the date set for trial, or (3) the jury fee under Texas Government Code section 51.604 is paid less than 10 days before the date set for trial. *In re I.M.B.*, 148 S.W.3d 653, 656 (Tex. App.—Beaumont 2004, no pet.); *Universal Printing Co. v. Premier Victorian Homes, Inc.*, 73 S.W.3d 283, 292 (Tex. App.—Houston [1st Dist.] 2001, pet. denied); *see Gen. Motors Corp. v. Gayle*, 951 S.W.2d 469, 476 (Tex. 1997). A trial court should deny an untimely request unless the requesting party establishes that a jury trial would not (1) interfere with the court's docket, (2) delay the trial, or (3) injure the adverse party. *See Gen. Motors*, 951 S.W.2d at 476; *Monroe v. Alts. in Motion*, 234 S.W.3d 56, 69-70 (Tex. App.—Houston [1st Dist.] 2007, no pet.). {*See **O'Connor's Texas Rules**, "Deadline to pay jury fee," ch. 5-B, §4.2, p. 403; "Request filed less than 30 days before trial," ch. 5-B, §5.2, p. 403.*}

7. The Court should deny {[18] *adverse party*}'s motion to strike the case from the nonjury docket because {[19] *adverse party*} {[20] *demanded a jury/paid the jury fee*} less than {[21] *30/10*} days before the date set for trial and did not show how a jury trial could be granted without interfering with the court's docket, delaying the trial, or injuring the adverse party. *See Gen. Motors*, 951 S.W.2d at 476; *Wright v. Brooks*, 773 S.W.2d 649, 651 (Tex. App.—San Antonio 1989, writ denied). {[22] *Elaborate.*}

Continued on next page

CONCLUSION

8. {23 *Briefly summarize the response.*}

PRAYER

9. For these reasons, {24 *party*} asks the Court to deny {25 *adverse party*}'s motion to strike this case from the nonjury docket.

SEE: Tex. R. Civ. P. 216-220, 245
Tex. Const. art. 1, §15
Tex. Gov't Code §51.604
O'Connor's Texas Rules * Civil Trials (2019), "Response," ch. 5-B, §5, p. 403

ADD: STYLE OF THE CASE – FORM 1B:2
SIGNATURE BLOCK – FORM 1B:3
CERTIFICATE OF SERVICE – FORM 1B:13

ATTACH: AFFIDAVIT – FORM 1B:8
ORDER – FORM 1G:1

NOTE: Parties can contractually agree to waive their right to a jury trial, but if a party does not timely assert the waiver, it can be lost. See ***O'Connor's Texas Rules***, "Waiver by contract," ch. 5-B, §7.4, p. 405.

See notes under FORM 5B:2.

{❶ *PARTY*}'S MOTION TO WITHDRAW CASE FROM JURY DOCKET

{❷ *Party*}, {❸ *name*}, asks the Court to withdraw this case from the jury docket. {*See* ***O'Connor's Texas Rules***, *"Withdrawing request for jury," ch. 5-B, §6.3, p. 404.*}

INTRODUCTION

1. Plaintiff, {❹ *name*}, sued defendant, {❺ *name*}, for {❻ *state basis of suit*}.

2. {❼ *State other relevant facts about the suit.*}

REQUEST

3. This case is set for trial on {❽ *date*}.

4. {❾ *Party*} timely demanded a jury trial and paid the jury fee.

5. {❿ *Party*} now wishes to withdraw {⓫ *his/her/its*} demand and have this case placed on the nonjury docket.

{*ADD PARAGRAPH 6 IF APPLICABLE*}

6. {⓬ *Adverse party*} does not object to this request.

PRAYER

7. For these reasons, {⓭ *party*} asks the Court to withdraw {⓮ *his/her/its*} case from the jury docket and place it on the nonjury docket.

SEE: Tex. R. Civ. P. 220
O'Connor's Texas Rules * Civil Trials (2019), "Withdrawing request for jury," ch. 5-B, §6.3, p. 404

ADD: STYLE OF THE CASE – FORM 1B:2
SIGNATURE BLOCK – FORM 1B:3
CERTIFICATE OF SERVICE – FORM 1B:13

NOTE: If the court permits withdrawal of the case from the jury docket, the party may also be able to withdraw the jury fee deposit. Tex. R. Civ. P. 220.

{❶ *PARTY*}'S OBJECTION TO {❷ *ADVERSE PARTY*}'S MOTION TO WITHDRAW CASE FROM JURY DOCKET

{❸ *Party*}, {❹ *name*}, objects to {❺ *adverse party*} {❻ *name*}'s motion to withdraw this case from the jury docket. {*See* ***O'Connor's Texas Rules****, "Withdrawing request for jury," ch. 5-B, §6.3, p. 404.*}

INTRODUCTION

1. Plaintiff, {❼ *name*}, sued defendant, {❽ *name*}, for {❾ *state basis of suit*}.

2. {❿ *State other relevant facts about the suit.*}

BACKGROUND

3. This case is set for jury trial on {⓫ *date*}.

4. On {⓬ *date*}, {⓭ *adverse party*} filed a motion to withdraw the case from the jury docket.

ARGUMENT & AUTHORITIES

5. A trial court cannot withdraw a case from the jury docket over the objection of any party, even if that party did not originally request a jury or pay the jury fee. *See* Tex. R. Civ. P. 220; *In re J.N.F.*, 116 S.W.3d 426, 434 (Tex. App.—Houston [14th Dist.] 2003, no pet.).

6. Because {⓮ *party*} objects to removing this case from the jury docket, this case must be tried before a jury.

PRAYER

7. For these reasons, {⓯ *party*} asks the Court to deny {⓰ *adverse party*}'s motion to withdraw the case from the jury docket.

SEE: Tex. R. Civ. P. 220
O'Connor's Texas Rules* * *Civil Trials (2019), "Withdrawing request for jury," ch. 5-B, §6.3, p. 404

ADD: STYLE OF THE CASE – FORM 1B:2
SIGNATURE BLOCK – FORM 1B:3
CERTIFICATE OF SERVICE – FORM 1B:13

{1 *PARTY*}'S OBJECTION TO ASSIGNED JUDGE

{2 *Party*}, {3 *name*}, files an objection to the judge assigned to hear this case. Because this objection is timely, and because the basis for it is valid, the assigned judge's removal from the case is mandatory and automatic. {*See* ***O'Connor's Texas Rules***, *"Objection to Assigned Judge," ch. 5-C, §3, p. 407.*}

INTRODUCTION

1. Plaintiff, {4 *name*}, sued defendant, {5 *name*}, for {6 *state basis of suit*}.

2. {7 *State other relevant facts about the suit.*}

BACKGROUND

3. Judge {8 *name*} was assigned to preside over this case on {9 *date*}.

4. Judge {10 *name*} is a {11 *former judge/retired judge/senior judge/judge who was defeated in the last primary or general election in which the judge was seeking reelection*}. {12 *Elaborate, if necessary, to explain judge's status.*} {*See* ***O'Connor's Texas Rules***, *"Who may be assigned," ch. 5-C, §3.2, p. 407.*}

{*CHOOSE APPROPRIATE PARAGRAPH 5*}

5. The {13 *first hearing/trial*} that Judge {14 *name*} will preside over is set for {15 *date*}, which is {16 *number*} days after this objection was filed. {*See* ***O'Connor's Texas Rules***, *"Deadline to object," ch. 5-C, §3.4, p. 408.*}

5. {17 *Party*} received actual notice of Judge {18 *name*}'s assignment on {19 *date*}, which is no more than seven days before this objection was filed. {*See* ***O'Connor's Texas Rules***, *"Deadline to object," ch. 5-C, §3.4, p. 408.*}

6. {20 *State other facts relevant to the objection.*}

ARGUMENT & AUTHORITIES

{*CHOOSE APPROPRIATE PARAGRAPH 7*}

7. This is {21 *party*}'s first objection to a judge assigned to preside over this case. Because {22 *party*}'s objection is timely, Judge {23 *name*}'s removal from the case is mandatory and automatic. Tex. Gov't Code §74.053(b); *In re Canales*, 52 S.W.3d 698, 701 (Tex. 2001); *Flores v. Banner*, 932 S.W.2d 500, 501 (Tex. 1996). {*See* ***O'Connor's Texas Rules***, *"Single challenge," ch. 5-C, §3.5.2(1), p. 409.*}

Continued on next page

7. This is {㉔ *party*}'s {㉕ *identify number, e.g., second*} objection to a judge assigned to preside over this case. {㉖ *Party*} is entitled to this objection because Judge {㉗ *name*} was defeated in the last {㉘ *primary/general*} election in which Judge {㉙ *name*} was seeking reelection. Tex. Gov't Code §74.053(d). Because {㉚ *party*}'s objection is timely, Judge {㉛ *name*}'s removal from the case is mandatory and automatic. *Id.* §74.053(b); *In re Canales*, 52 S.W.3d 698, 701 (Tex. 2001); *Flores v. Banner*, 932 S.W.2d 500, 501 (Tex. 1996). {*See **O'Connor's Texas Rules**, "Unlimited challenges," ch. 5-C, §3.5.2(2), p. 409.*}

PRAYER

8. For these reasons, {㉜ *party*} asks Judge {㉝ *name*} to remove {㉞ *himself/herself*} from this case and requests that the regional presiding judge assign another judge.

SEE: Tex. Gov't Code §74.053
O'Connor's Texas Rules * Civil Trials (2019), "Objection to Assigned Judge," ch. 5-C, §3, p. 407

ADD: STYLE OF THE CASE – FORM 1B:2
SIGNATURE BLOCK – FORM 1B:3
CERTIFICATE OF SERVICE – FORM 1B:13

ATTACH: ORDER – FORM 5C:7

NOTE: There is no statutory requirement that an objection to an assigned judge be verified. ***O'Connor v. Lykos***, 960 S.W.2d 96, 99 (Tex.App.—Houston [1st Dist.] 1997, orig. proceeding). The standard objection does not need to be verified because a party does not need to assert any facts in an objection to an assigned judge. *Id.* See ***O'Connor's Texas Rules***, "Verification," ch. 5-C, §3.7.5, p. 410.

An objection to an assigned judge may be filed by e-mail. Tex. Gov't Code §74.053(f).

A party must object to any procedural errors in the assignment or it waives the error. See ***O'Connor's Texas Rules***, "Objections to procedural errors in assignment," ch. 5-C, §3.7.3(2), p. 409.

When a party has exhausted its objections to assigned judges, the party can assert any available recusal or disqualification challenges. See FORMS 5C:3, 5.

{[1] *PARTY*}'S RESPONSE TO {[2] *ADVERSE PARTY*}'S OBJECTION TO ASSIGNED JUDGE

{[3] *Party*}, {[4] *name*}, asks the Court to overrule {[5] *adverse party*} {[6] *name*}'s objection to the judge assigned to hear this case. {*See **O'Connor's Texas Rules**, "Objection to Assigned Judge," ch. 5-C, §3, p. 407.*}

INTRODUCTION

1. Plaintiff, {[7] *name*}, sued defendant, {[8] *name*}, for {[9] *state basis of suit*}.

2. {[10] *State other relevant facts about the suit.*}

BACKGROUND

3. {[11] *Adverse party*} filed an objection to the assignment of Judge {[12] *name*} on {[13] *date*}, arguing that Judge {[14] *name*} should be removed from this case because {[15] *state grounds for objection*}.

4. {[16] *State other facts relevant to the response.*}

ARGUMENT & AUTHORITIES

{*CHOOSE APPROPRIATE PARAGRAPHS 5-11*}

{*Objection untimely*}

5. A party seeking to remove a judge assigned to a trial court must file an objection to the assignment no later than seven days after the party received actual notice of the assignment, or before the commencement of the first hearing or trial that the assigned judge will preside over, whichever occurs first. Tex. Gov't Code §74.053(c). If an objection is filed after the assigned judge makes any ruling in the case, regardless of whether the court allowed oral argument on the matter, the objection is untimely. *See In re S.N.Z.*, 421 S.W.3d 899, 907 (Tex. App.—Dallas 2014, pet. denied). When the objection is untimely, the challenge is waived. *In re Canales*, 52 S.W.3d 698, 704 (Tex. 2001). {*See **O'Connor's Texas Rules**, "Deadline to object," ch. 5-C, §3.4, p. 408.*}

6. Judge {[17] *name*} should deny the objection to the assignment and refuse to remove {[18] *himself/herself*} from this case because the objection was untimely. Specifically, {[19] *adverse party*} filed the objection on {[20] *date*}, which was {[21] *number*} days after {[22] *actual notice of the assignment was received/the Court commenced the first hearing or trial of this case*}. {[23] *Elaborate if necessary.*} Because {[24] *adverse party*}'s objection was untimely, the challenge to Judge {[25] *name*} was waived.

— *Continued on next page* —

{Judge is an active judge}

7. A party seeking to remove a judge assigned to a trial court can file an objection to the assigned judge if the judge is a former, retired, or senior judge. Tex. Gov't Code §74.053. But a party cannot object to an active judge—that is, one who is a current judicial officeholder. *Id.* §§74.053(e), 74.041(4). *{See **O'Connor's Texas Rules**, "Active judge," ch. 5-C, §3.2.1, p. 407; "Active judge – no challenge," ch. 5-C, §3.5.1, p. 408.}*

8. Judge {㉖ *name*} should deny the objection to the assignment and refuse to remove {㉗ *himself/herself*} from this case because Judge {㉘ *name*} is an active judge not subject to an objection.

{Previous objection filed}

9. A party seeking to remove a judge assigned to a trial court is entitled to only one objection to the assignment of a former, retired, or senior judge unless the assigned judge was defeated in the last primary or general election in which the judge was seeking reelection. *See* Tex. Gov't Code §74.053(b), (d).

10. Judge {㉙ *name*} should deny the objection to the assignment and refuse to remove {㉚ *himself/herself*} from this case because {㉛ *adverse party*} previously filed an objection to another {㉜ *former/retired/senior*} judge assigned to hear this case. {㉝ *Describe earlier objection to another assigned judge.*}

11. Judge {㉞ *name*} was not defeated in the last primary or general election in which the judge was seeking reelection. Thus, {㉟ *adverse party*} has exhausted {㊱ *his/her/its*} right to object to an assigned judge who is a {㊲ *former/retired/senior*} judge.

CONCLUSION

12. {㊳ *Briefly summarize the response.*}

PRAYER

13. For these reasons, {㊴ *party*} asks the Court to overrule the objection to the assigned judge.

FORM 5C:2 RESPONSE TO OBJECTION TO ASSIGNED JUDGE

SEE: Tex. Gov't Code §74.053
*O'Connor's Texas Rules * Civil Trials* (2019), "Objection to Assigned Judge," ch. 5-C, §3, p. 407

ADD: STYLE OF THE CASE – FORM 1B:2
SIGNATURE BLOCK – FORM 1B:3
VERIFICATION – FORM 1B:7
CERTIFICATE OF SERVICE – FORM 1B:13

ATTACH: AFFIDAVIT – FORM 1B:8, if necessary
ORDER – FORM 5C:7

{❶ *PARTY*}'S MOTION TO DISQUALIFY

{❷ *Party*}, {❸ *name*}, asks the judge of the Court to disqualify {❹ *himself/herself*} from hearing this case. {*See* ***O'Connor's Texas Rules****, "Motion to Disqualify or Recuse," ch. 5-C, §4, p. 410.*}

INTRODUCTION

1. Plaintiff, {❺ *name*}, sued defendant, {❻ *name*}, for {❼ *state basis of suit*}.

2. {❽ *State other relevant facts about the suit.*}

BACKGROUND

3. {❾ *State facts relevant to the motion.*}

ARGUMENT & AUTHORITIES

4. Texas Constitution article 5, section 11, and Texas Rule of Civil Procedure 18b(a) govern the disqualification of judges. If the grounds for disqualification are established, disqualification of a judge is mandatory. *See Tesco Am., Inc. v. Strong Indus., Inc.*, 221 S.W.3d 550, 553 (Tex. 2006). {*See* ***O'Connor's Texas Appeals****, "Grounds for Disqualification," ch. 3-I, §3, p. 136.*}

{*CHOOSE APPROPRIATE SECTIONS A-D*}

A. Judge served as an attorney in the matter in controversy.

5. Under Texas Constitution article 5, section 11, and Texas Rule of Civil Procedure 18b(a), a judge is disqualified when the judge served as an attorney in the matter in controversy. Tex. Const. art. 5, §11; Tex. R. Civ. P. 18b(a)(1); *Slaven v. Wheeler*, 58 Tex. 23, 26 (1882); *Williams v. Kirven*, 532 S.W.2d 159, 160 (Tex. App.—Austin 1976, writ ref'd n.r.e.); *see Zarate v. Sun Operating Ltd., Inc.*, 40 S.W.3d 617, 621-22 (Tex. App.—San Antonio 2001, pet. denied).

6. Judge {❿ *name*} should be disqualified because {⓫ *explain how the judge served as an attorney in the matter in controversy*}.

B. Judge practiced law with an attorney in the matter in controversy.

7. Under Texas Constitution article 5, section 11, and Texas Rule of Civil Procedure 18b(a), a judge is disqualified when an attorney who previously practiced law with the judge served, during that association, as an attorney in the matter in controversy. Tex. R. Civ. P. 18b(a)(1); *Tesco Am., Inc.*, 221 S.W.3d at 554; *In re O'Connor*, 92 S.W.3d 446, 449 (Tex. 2002); *see* Tex. Const. art. 5, §11.

8. Judge {[12] *name*} should be disqualified because {[13] *elaborate on the judge's association with the attorney who served in the matter in controversy*}.

C. Judge has an interest in the matter in controversy.

9. Under Texas Constitution article 5, section 11, and Texas Rule of Civil Procedure 18b(a), a judge is disqualified when the judge has a direct financial or property interest in the subject matter in controversy, either individually or as a fiduciary. *See* Tex. Const. art. 5, §11; Tex. R. Civ. P. 18b(a)(2); *Cameron v. Greenhill*, 582 S.W.2d 775, 776 (Tex. 1979); *Bank of Tex., N.A. v. Mexia*, 135 S.W.3d 356, 361 (Tex. App.—Dallas 2004, pet. denied); *Gulf Mar. Warehouse Co. v. Towers*, 858 S.W.2d 556, 558 (Tex. App.—Beaumont 1993, writ denied). {[14] *Add if appropriate: A judge who is married to an attorney with a financial interest in the case has a direct financial interest in the case through the community estate. See Tex. Const. art. 5, §11; see also Tex. Gov't Code §82.066 (attorney cannot appear before judge if related within first degree).*} Once an interest is established, the judge is disqualified no matter how slight the interest is. *Gulf Mar.*, 858 S.W.2d at 558.

10. Judge {[15] *name*} should be disqualified because {[16] *explain the judge's interest in the subject matter in controversy*}.

D. Judge is related to {[17] *adverse party*}.

11. Under Texas Constitution article 5, section 11, and Texas Rule of Civil Procedure 18b(a), a judge is disqualified when the judge is related to a party in the suit within the third degree of affinity or consanguinity. Texas Rule of Civil Procedure 18b(a)(3); *see* Tex. Const. art. 5, §11.

12. Judge {[18] *name*} should be disqualified because {[19] *explain how the judge is related to a party within the third degree of affinity or consanguinity*}.

CONCLUSION

13. {[20] *Briefly summarize the motion.*}

PRAYER

14. For these reasons, {[21] *party*} asks the Judge to disqualify {[22] *himself/herself*} and requests that the presiding judge of this administrative judicial district transfer this case to another court or assign another judge to this case. In the alternative, {[23] *party*} asks the Judge to refer this motion to the presiding judge of this administrative judicial district for a hearing on the motion.

◄ *Continued on next page* ►

SEE: Tex. R. Civ. P. 18a, 18b
Tex. Const. art. 5, §11
Tex. Gov't Code §§573.021-573.025
O'Connor's Texas Rules * Civil Trials (2019), "Motion to Disqualify or Recuse," ch. 5-C, §4, p. 410
O'Connor's Texas Civil Appeals (2019), "Grounds for Disqualification," ch. 3-I, §3, p. 136

ADD: STYLE OF THE CASE – FORM 1B:2
SIGNATURE BLOCK – FORM 1B:3
VERIFICATION – FORM 1B:7
CERTIFICATE OF SERVICE – FORM 1B:13

ATTACH: AFFIDAVIT – FORM 1B:8
ORDER – FORM 5C:7

NOTE: The terms "disqualification" and "recusal" are distinct. ***Kuykendall v. State***, 335 S.W.3d 429, 433 (Tex. App.—Beaumont 2011, pet. ref'd) (criminal case). Motions to disqualify are based on constitutional grounds and can be filed at any time, unlike motions to recuse, but should be filed as soon as possible after the movant learns of the grounds for disqualification. *See* Tex. Const. art. 5, §11; Tex. R. Civ. P. 18b(a); ***Buckholts ISD v. Glaser***, 632 S.W.2d 146, 148 (Tex.1982); ***McElwee v. McElwee***, 911 S.W.2d 182, 186 (Tex.App.—Houston [1st Dist.] 1995, writ denied). See ***O'Connor's Texas Rules***, "Deadline to file," ch. 5-C, §4.1.6, p. 412.

The party filing the motion must serve copies on all other parties by the same method used for filing, if possible. Tex. R. Civ. P. 18a(d). Texas Rule of Civil Procedure 18a(d) does not specify when to serve a motion to disqualify. Because the challenged judge must either grant the motion or refer it within three business days after it is filed, the party should probably serve the motion at the same time it is filed. *See* Tex. R. Civ. P. 18a(f)(1).

For the procedure for filing a tertiary motion to disqualify, see ***O'Connor's Texas Rules***, "Tertiary Motion to Disqualify or Recuse," ch. 5-C, §5, p. 415.

{❶ *PARTY*}'S RESPONSE TO
{❷ *ADVERSE PARTY*}'S MOTION TO DISQUALIFY

{❸ *Party*}, {❹ *name*}, asks the Court to deny {❺ *adverse party*} {❻ *name*}'s motion to disqualify. {*See **O'Connor's Texas Rules**, "Response by other party," ch. 5-C, §4.2, p. 413.*}

INTRODUCTION

1. Plaintiff, {❼ *name*}, sued defendant, {❽ *name*}, for {❾ *state basis of suit*}.

2. {❿ *State other relevant facts about the suit.*}

BACKGROUND

3. On {⓫ *date*}, {⓬ *adverse party*} filed a motion to disqualify Judge {⓭ *name*}.

4. {⓮ *State other facts relevant to the response.*}

ARGUMENT & AUTHORITIES

5. A judge is disqualified only if the grounds under Texas Constitution article 5, section 11, and Texas Rule of Civil Procedure 18b(a) are stated with particularity in a motion to disqualify. *See* Tex. R. Civ. P. 18a(a)(2), (a)(4). Under section 11 and Rule 18b(a), a judge is disqualified when the judge (1) served as an attorney in the matter in controversy, (2) was associated with an attorney who at the time of the association served as an attorney in the matter in controversy, (3) has a financial or property interest in the subject matter in controversy, or (4) is related to a party in the case. *See* Tex. Const. art. 5, §11; Tex. R. Civ. P. 18b(a). {*See **O'Connor's Texas Appeals**, "Grounds for Disqualification," ch. 3-I, §3, p. 136; "Relationships that do not require recusal," ch. 3-I, §4.4, p. 142.*}

6. {⓯ *Adverse party*} argues that Judge {⓰ *name*} should be disqualified because {⓱ *state grounds for disqualification identified in motion to disqualify*}. The Court should deny the motion to disqualify because {⓲ *explain, e.g., adverse party did not state with particularity why the judge should be disqualified*}.

{*ADD PARAGRAPH 7 IF APPLICABLE*}

SANCTIONS

7. A party can be sanctioned if {⓳ *his/her/its*} motion to disqualify was (1) groundless and filed in bad faith or for the purpose of harassment or (2) clearly brought for unnecessary delay and without sufficient cause. Tex. R. Civ. P. 18a(h).

◄ *Continued on next page* ►

{[20] *Adverse party*}'s motion to disqualify was {[21] *explain*}. Thus, {[22] *party*} requests that the Court sanction {[23] *adverse party*}, as authorized by Texas Rule of Civil Procedure 18a(h).

CONCLUSION

8. {[24] *Briefly summarize the response.*}

PRAYER

9. For these reasons, {[25] *party*} asks that the judge hearing the motion to disqualify deny the motion {[26] *add if applicable: and impose sanctions under Texas Rule of Civil Procedure 18a(h)*}.

SEE: Tex. R. Civ. P. 18a, 18b
Tex. Const. art. 5, §11
O'Connor's Texas Rules * Civil Trials (2019), "Motion to Disqualify or Recuse," ch. 5-C, §4, p. 410

ADD: STYLE OF THE CASE – FORM 1B:2
SIGNATURE BLOCK – FORM 1B:3
VERIFICATION – FORM 1B:7
CERTIFICATE OF SERVICE – FORM 1B:13

ATTACH: AFFIDAVIT – FORM 1B:8, if necessary
ORDER – FORM 5C:7

NOTE: The party filing the response must serve copies on all other parties by the same method used for filing, if possible. Tex. R. Civ. P. 18a(d). Although Texas Rule of Civil Procedure 18a(d) does not specify when to serve a response to a motion to disqualify, the party should probably serve the response at the same time it is filed.

{❶ *PARTY*}'S MOTION TO RECUSE

{❷ *Party*}, {❸ *name*}, asks the judge of the Court to recuse {❹ *himself/herself*} from this case. {*See* ***O'Connor's Texas Rules****, "Motion to Disqualify or Recuse," ch. 5-C, §4, p. 410.*}

INTRODUCTION

1. Plaintiff, {❺ *name*}, sued defendant, {❻ *name*}, for {❼ *state basis of suit*}.

2. {❽ *State other relevant facts about the suit.*}

BACKGROUND

{*ADD APPROPRIATE PARAGRAPH 3 IF FILING AFTER DEADLINE*}

3. On {❾ *date*}, {❿ *party*} learned {⓫ *state facts indicating need to file motion for recusal and explain that party did not know and should not have reasonably known of the reason for recusal before the deadline*}. Immediately after learning of these facts, {⓬ *party*} filed this motion for recusal, which is being made less than ten days before this case is set for {⓭ *trial/{identify other proceeding}*}.

3. On {⓮ *date*}, this case was reversed by {⓯ *identify appellate court*} for retrial and remanded for further proceedings. Following the order of remand, {⓰ *party*} filed this motion for recusal, which is being made less than ten days before this case is set for {⓱ *trial/{identify other proceeding}*}.

4. {⓲ *State other facts relevant to the motion.*}

ARGUMENT & AUTHORITIES

5. The right to a fair and impartial tribunal is guaranteed by both the Texas and United States Constitutions. *See Marshall v. Jerrico, Inc.*, 446 U.S. 238, 242 (1980); *Rymer v. Lewis*, 206 S.W.3d 732, 736 (Tex. App.—Dallas 2006, no pet.); *Metzger v. Sebek*, 892 S.W.2d 20, 37-38 (Tex. App.—Houston [1st Dist.] 1994, writ denied). This right is codified in Texas Rule of Civil Procedure 18b, which sets out the grounds for recusal. A judge must recuse {⓳ *himself/herself*} when a valid motion is timely filed. *See* Tex. R. Civ. P. 18a(b)(1), 18b(b).

{*CHOOSE APPROPRIATE SECTIONS A-L*}

A. Judge's impartiality might reasonably be questioned.

6. A judge must recuse {⓴ *himself/herself*} if the judge's impartiality might reasonably be questioned. Tex. R. Civ. P. 18b(b)(1); *see In re Fifty-One Gambling Devices*,

◄ *Continued on next page* ►

298 S.W.3d 768, 775 (Tex. App.—Amarillo 2009, pet. denied); *Woodruff v. Wright*, 51 S.W.3d 727, 735-36 (Tex. App.—Texarkana 2001, pet. denied). The court must ask whether a reasonable member of the public, knowing all the facts in the public domain, would have a reasonable doubt that the judge is actually impartial. *In re Fifty-One Gambling*, 298 S.W.3d at 775; *Ex parte Ellis*, 275 S.W.3d 109, 115-16 (Tex. App.—Austin 2008, no pet.); *Sears v. Olivarez*, 28 S.W.3d 611, 613 (Tex. App.—Corpus Christi 2000, no pet.); *see Woodruff*, 51 S.W.3d at 736 (reasonable-person standard). {*See **O'Connor's Texas Appeals**, "Impartiality might be questioned," ch. 3-I, §4.1.1, p. 140.*}

7. Judge {㉑ *name*} must recuse {㉒ *himself/herself*} because {㉓ *explain how the judge's impartiality might reasonably be questioned*}.

B. Judge has a bias or prejudice.

8. A judge must recuse {㉔ *himself/herself*} if the judge has a personal bias or prejudice against {㉕ *the subject matter of the case/a party*}. Tex. R. Civ. P. 18b(b)(2); *see Wright v. Wright*, 867 S.W.2d 807, 811 (Tex. App.—El Paso 1993, writ denied); *see, e.g., Aetna Life Ins. Co. v. Lavoie*, 475 U.S. 813, 823-25 (1986) (judge was biased because success of judge's own suit in lower court depended on ruling in case before judge). {*See **O'Connor's Texas Appeals**, "Bias or prejudice," ch. 3-I, §4.1.2, p. 140.*}

9. Judge {㉖ *name*} must recuse {㉗ *himself/herself*} because {㉘ *explain judge's bias or prejudice*}.

C. Judge has personal knowledge of a disputed fact.

10. A judge must recuse {㉙ *himself/herself*} if the judge has personal knowledge of a disputed evidentiary fact in the suit. Tex. R. Civ. P. 18b(b)(3). {*See **O'Connor's Texas Appeals**, "Judge has personal knowledge," ch. 3-I, §4.1.3, p. 141.*}

11. Judge {㉚ *name*} must recuse {㉛ *himself/herself*} because {㉜ *explain judge's personal knowledge of a disputed fact in the suit*}.

D. Judge {㉝ *has been/is likely to be*} a material witness.

12. A judge must recuse {㉞ *himself/herself*} if the judge has been or is likely to be a material witness in the proceeding. Tex. R. Civ. P. 18b(b)(4), (b)(7)(C). {*See **O'Connor's Texas Appeals**, "Material witness," ch. 3-I, §4.1.4, p. 141.*}

13. Judge {㉟ *name*} must recuse {㊱ *himself/herself*} because {㊲ *explain judge's role as witness*}.

E. Judge has practiced with an attorney who has been a material witness.

14. A judge must recuse {㊳ *himself/herself*} if an attorney with whom the judge previously practiced law has been a material witness in the proceeding. Tex. R. Civ. P. 18b(b)(4).

15. Judge {㊴ *name*} must recuse {㊵ *himself/herself*} because {㊶ *identify attorney and proceeding and explain role as witness*}.

F. Judge participated in the matter while in government service.

16. A judge must recuse {㊷ *himself/herself*} if the judge has, while acting as an attorney in government service, participated as {㊸ *counsel/an adviser/a material witness*} in the matter in controversy or expressed an opinion about the merits of the controversy. Tex. R. Civ. P. 18b(b)(5). {*See* ***O'Connor's Texas Appeals****, "Judge expressed opinion," ch. 3-I, §4.1.5, p. 141.*}

17. Judge {㊹ *name*} must recuse {㊺ *himself/herself*} because {㊻ *explain judge's role in or opinion about the matter while in government service*}.

G. Judge has an interest in the matter.

18. A judge must recuse {㊼ *himself/herself*} if the judge has {㊽ *an interest/a financial interest in the subject matter in controversy/a financial interest in a party to the proceeding*} that could be substantially affected by the outcome of the proceeding. Tex. R. Civ. P. 18b(b)(6), (b)(7)(B). {㊾ *Add if appropriate: The interest can be based on the judge's role as a fiduciary. Tex. R. Civ. P. 18b(b)(6).*} {*See* ***O'Connor's Texas Appeals****, "Fiduciary interest," ch. 3-I, §4.1.6, p. 141; "Financial or other interest," ch. 3-I, §4.1.7, p. 141.*}

19. Judge {㊿ *name*} must recuse {51 *himself/herself*} because {52 *explain judge's interest*}.

H. Judge's {53 *spouse/child*} has an interest in the matter.

20. A judge must recuse {54 *himself/herself*} if {55 *the judge's spouse/a minor child residing in the judge's household*} has {56 *an interest/a financial interest in the subject matter in controversy/a financial interest in a party to the proceeding*} that could be substantially affected by the outcome of the proceeding. Tex. R. Civ. P. 18b(b)(6), (b)(7)(B). {*See* ***O'Connor's Texas Appeals****, "Fiduciary interest," ch. 3-I, §4.1.6, p. 141; "Financial or other interest," ch. 3-I, §4.1.7, p. 141.*}

— *Continued on next page* —

21. Judge {57 *name*} must recuse {58 *himself/herself*} because {59 *explain spouse's or child's interest*}.

I. Judge's relative has an interest in the matter.

22. A judge must recuse {60 *himself/herself*} if {61 *a person related to the judge within the third degree/a person related to the judge's spouse within the third degree/the spouse of a person related to the judge within the third degree/the spouse of a person related to the judge's spouse within the third degree*} is known by the judge to have an interest that could be substantially affected by the outcome of the proceeding. Tex. R. Civ. P. 18b(b)(7)(B).

23. Judge {62 *name*} must recuse {63 *himself/herself*} because {64 *explain relative's interest*}.

J. {65 *Judge/Judge's relative*} {66 *is a party/is an officer, director, or trustee of a party*}.

24. A judge must recuse {67 *himself/herself*} if {68 *the judge/the judge's spouse/a person related to the judge within the third degree/a person related to the judge's spouse within the third degree/the spouse of a person related to the judge within the third degree/the spouse of a person related to the judge's spouse within the third degree*} {69 *is a party to the proceeding/is an officer, director, or trustee of a party*}. Tex. R. Civ. P. 18b(b)(7)(A).

25. Judge {70 *name*} must recuse {71 *himself/herself*} because {72 *explain*}.

K. Judge's {73 *relative/spouse*} is likely to be a material witness.

26. A judge must recuse {74 *himself/herself*} if {75 *the judge's spouse/a person related to the judge within the third degree/a person related to the judge's spouse within the third degree/the spouse of a person related to the judge within the third degree/the spouse of a person related to the judge's spouse within the third degree*} is likely to be a material witness in the proceeding. Tex. R. Civ. P. 18b(b)(7)(C).

27. Judge {76 *name*} must recuse {77 *himself/herself*} because {78 *explain how the relative is likely to be a material witness*}.

L. {79 *Judge/Judge's relative*} is acting as an attorney in the proceeding.

28. A judge must recuse {80 *himself/herself*} if {81 *the judge/the judge's spouse/a person related to the judge within the first degree/a person related to the judge's spouse within the first degree/the spouse of a person related to the judge within the first degree/the spouse of a person related to the judge's spouse within the first degree*} is acting as

an attorney in this proceeding. Tex. R. Civ. P. 18b(b)(8); *see also* Tex. Gov't Code §82.066 (attorney cannot appear before judge in civil case if attorney is related to judge within first degree). {*See **O'Connor's Texas Appeals**, "Acting as attorney," ch. 3-I, §4.1.9, p. 141.*}

29. Judge {82 *name*} must recuse {83 *himself/herself*} because {84 *explain*}.

CONCLUSION

30. {85 *Briefly summarize the motion.*}

PRAYER

31. For these reasons, {86 *party*} asks the Judge to recuse {87 *himself/herself*} and request that the presiding judge of this administrative judicial district transfer this case to another court or assign another judge to this case. In the alternative, {88 *party*} asks the Judge to refer this motion to the presiding judge of this administrative judicial district for a hearing on the motion.

SEE: Tex. R. Civ. P. 18a, 18b
Tex. Const. art. 5, §11
Tex. Code of Judicial Conduct Canons 2B, 3B, 3C, 4D, 4E
Tex. Gov't Code §82.066, §573.021 et seq.
O'Connor's Texas Rules * Civil Trials (2019), "Motion to Disqualify or Recuse," ch. 5-C, §4, p. 410
O'Connor's Texas Civil Appeals (2019), "Grounds for Recusal," ch. 3-I, §4, p. 140

ADD: STYLE OF THE CASE – FORM 1B:2
SIGNATURE BLOCK – FORM 1B:3
VERIFICATION – FORM 1B:7
CERTIFICATE OF SERVICE – FORM 1B:13

ATTACH: AFFIDAVIT – FORM 1B:8
ORDER – FORM 5C:7

NOTE: The terms "recusal" and "disqualification" are distinct. ***Kuykendall v. State***, 335 S.W.3d 429, 433 (Tex. App.—Beaumont 2011, pet. ref'd) (criminal case). Motions to disqualify are based on constitutional grounds and can be filed at any time but should be filed as soon as possible after the movant learns of the grounds for disqualification. *See* Tex. Const. art. 5, §11; Tex. R. Civ. P. 18b(a); ***Buckholts ISD v. Glaser***, 632 S.W.2d 146, 148 (Tex.1982); ***McElwee v. McElwee***, 911 S.W.2d 182, 186 (Tex.App.—Houston [1st Dist.] 1995, writ denied). Motions to recuse, however, must be filed (1) as soon as possible after the party learns of the reason for recusal and (2) at least ten days before the date set for the trial or other hearing. Tex. R. Civ. P. 18a(b)(1). A motion to recuse may be filed after the ten-day deadline if the party did not know and should not have reasonably known (1) that the judge it seeks to recuse would preside at the trial or hearing or (2) of the reason for recusal until after the deadline. Tex. R. Civ. P. 18a(b)(1)(B). See ***O'Connor's Texas Rules***, "Motion to recuse," ch. 5-C, §4.1.6(2), p. 412.

Continued on next page

Removing a judge based on a direct financial or property interest should be done through a motion to disqualify. See FORM 5C:3. Disqualification is always mandatory and cannot be denied based on procedural error. Tex. R. Civ. P. 18a(f)(1), (g)(3)(B). If the movant is not sure if the interest is direct enough, it can file a "motion to disqualify or recuse." *See* ***Gulf Maritime Whs. Co. v. Towers***, 858 S.W.2d 556, 560 (Tex.App.—Beaumont 1993, writ denied).

The party filing the motion must serve copies on all other parties by the same method used for filing, if possible. Tex. R. Civ. P. 18a(d). Texas Rule of Civil Procedure 18a(d) does not specify when to serve a motion to recuse. Because the challenged judge must either grant the motion or refer it within three business days after it is filed, the party should probably serve the motion at the same time it is filed. *See* Tex. R. Civ. P. 18a(f)(1).

For the procedure for filing a tertiary motion to recuse, see ***O'Connor's Texas Rules***, "Tertiary Motion to Disqualify or Recuse," ch. 5-C, §5, p. 415.

{1 *PARTY*}'S RESPONSE TO
{2 *ADVERSE PARTY*}'S MOTION TO RECUSE

{3 *Party*}, {4 *name*}, asks the Court to deny {5 *adverse party*} {6 *name*}'s motion to recuse. {*See* ***O'Connor's Texas Rules****, "Response by other party," ch. 5-C, §4.2, p. 413.*}

INTRODUCTION

1. Plaintiff, {7 *name*}, sued defendant, {8 *name*}, for {9 *state basis of suit*}.

2. {10 *State other relevant facts about the suit.*}

BACKGROUND

3. On {11 *date*}, {12 *adverse party*} filed a motion to recuse Judge {13 *name*}.

4. {14 *State other facts relevant to the response.*}

ARGUMENT & AUTHORITIES

{*CHOOSE APPROPRIATE SECTIONS A-D*}

A. {15 *Adverse party*} did not timely file the motion.

5. A motion to recuse must be filed (1) as soon as possible after the party learns of the reason for recusal and (2) at least ten days before the date set for the trial or other hearing. Tex. R. Civ. P. 18a(b)(1); *see Waste-Water, Inc. v. Alpha Finishing & Developing Corp.*, 874 S.W.2d 940, 944 (Tex. App.—Houston [14th Dist.] 1994, no writ). A motion can be filed after the ten-day deadline if the party did not know and should not have reasonably known (1) that the judge it seeks to recuse would preside at the trial or hearing or (2) of the reason for recusal until after that deadline. Tex. R. Civ. P. 18a(b)(1)(B).

{*CHOOSE APPROPRIATE PARAGRAPHS 6-7*}

6. The motion to recuse should be denied because the motion was not filed at least ten days before the case was set for {16 *trial/{identify other proceeding}*}. The reason for recusal was discovered on {17 *date*}, giving {18 *adverse party*} time to file the motion before the ten-day deadline, which was on {19 *date*}. Instead, the motion was filed on {20 *date*}. {21 *Elaborate.*} Because the motion was not timely filed, the grounds for recusal are waived.

Continued on next page

7. The motion to recuse should be denied because {[22] *adverse party*} did not immediately file the motion after learning of the reason for recusal. The reason for recusal was discovered on or about {[23] *date*}. {[24] *Adverse party*} did not file the motion until {[25] *date*}. Because the motion was not timely filed, the grounds for recusal are waived.

B. {[26] *Adverse party*} has not shown that recusal is appropriate.

8. A judge can recuse {[27] *himself/herself*} under Texas Rule of Civil Procedure 18b(b), but the party seeking recusal has a high evidentiary threshold to meet. *Ex parte Ellis*, 275 S.W.3d 109, 115-16 (Tex. App.—Austin 2008, no pet.). In the motion to recuse, {[28] *adverse party*} argues that Judge {[29] *name*} should recuse {[30] *himself/herself*} because {[31] *state grounds for recusal*}. To determine whether recusal is required, the Court must find {[32] *identify each of the legal criteria that must be met to justify recusal and refute the adverse party's assertions*}. {*See* ***O'Connor's Texas Rules****, "Motion to Disqualify or Recuse," ch. 5-C, §4, p. 410.*}

C. {[33] *Adverse party*} did not verify the motion.

9. A motion to recuse must be verified. Tex. R. Civ. P. 18a(a)(1); *McElwee v. McElwee*, 911 S.W.2d 182, 186 (Tex. App.—Houston [1st Dist.] 1995, writ denied). The Court should deny {[34] *adverse party*}'s motion to recuse because it includes facts outside the record that are not verified. {[35] *Elaborate.*}

D. {[36] *Adverse party*} based the motion on a defective {[37] *affidavit/declaration*}.

10. A motion to recuse must set out facts that would be admissible in evidence and be based on personal knowledge or on information and belief if the basis of the belief is specifically stated. Tex. R. Civ. P. 18a(a)(4)(A), (a)(4)(B). The Court should deny {[38] *adverse party*}'s motion to recuse because the {[39] *affidavit/declaration*} attached to the motion is defective and thus does not support the motion. {[40] *Elaborate.*}

{*ADD PARAGRAPH 11 IF APPLICABLE*}

SANCTIONS

11. A party can be sanctioned if {[41] *his/her/its*} motion to recuse was (1) groundless and filed in bad faith or for the purpose of harassment or (2) clearly brought for unnecessary delay and without sufficient cause. Tex. R. Civ. P. 18a(h). {[42] *Adverse party*}'s motion to disqualify was {[43] *explain*}. Thus, {[44] *party*} requests that the Court sanction {[45] *adverse party*}, as authorized by Texas Rule of Civil Procedure 18a(h).

CONCLUSION

12. {46 *Briefly summarize the response.*}

PRAYER

13. For these reasons, {47 *party*} asks that the judge hearing the motion to recuse deny the motion {48 *add if applicable: and impose sanctions under Texas Rule of Civil Procedure 18a(h)*}.

SEE: Tex. R. Civ. P. 18a, 18b
Tex. Const. art. 5, §11
Tex. Code of Judicial Conduct Canons 2B, 3B, 3C, 4D, 4E
Tex. Gov't Code §573.021 et seq.
O'Connor's Texas Rules * Civil Trials (2019), "Motion to Disqualify or Recuse," ch. 5-C, §4, p. 410

ADD: STYLE OF THE CASE – FORM 1B:2
SIGNATURE BLOCK – FORM 1B:3
VERIFICATION – FORM 1B:7
CERTIFICATE OF SERVICE – FORM 1B:13

ATTACH: AFFIDAVIT – FORM 1B:8, if necessary
ORDER – FORM 5C:7

NOTE: The party filing the response must serve copies on all other parties by the same method used for filing, if possible. Tex. R. Civ. P. 18a(d). Although Texas Rule of Civil Procedure 18a(d) does not specify when to serve a response to a motion to recuse, the party should probably serve the response at the same time it is filed.

ORDER ON {❶ *PARTY*}'S {❷ *MOTION TO DISQUALIFY/MOTION TO RECUSE/OBJECTION TO ASSIGNED JUDGE*}

After considering {❸ *party*} {❹ *name*}'s {❺ *motion to disqualify/motion to recuse/ objection to an assigned judge*}, the response, the pleadings, {❻ *add, if any: the affidavits,*} and arguments of counsel, I

{*CHOOSE APPROPRIATE ORDER*}

AGREE to {❼ *disqualify/recuse/remove*} myself and request that the regional presiding judge transfer this case to another court or assign another judge to preside over the case.

DECLINE to {❽ *disqualify/recuse/remove*} myself and refer this {❾ *motion/objection*} to the regional presiding judge.

SIGNED on _______________, 20___.

____
PRESIDING JUDGE

SEE: Tex. R. Civ. P. 18a, 18b
Tex. Const. art. 5, §11
Tex. Code of Judicial Conduct Canons 2B, 3B, 3C, 4D, 4E
Tex. Gov't Code §74.053, §573.021 et seq.
O'Connor's Texas Rules * Civil Trials (2019), "Objection to Assigned Judge," ch. 5-C, §3, p. 407; "Motion to Disqualify or Recuse," ch. 5-C, §4, p. 410

ADD: STYLE OF THE CASE – FORM 1B:2
CERTIFICATE OF SERVICE – FORM 1B:13, if proposed order served separately from motion or response

{[1] *PARTY*}'S MOTION FOR
CONTINUANCE TO OBTAIN ADDITIONAL DISCOVERY

{*CHOOSE APPROPRIATE OPENING PARAGRAPH*}

{[2] *Party*}, {[3] *name*}, asks the Court to continue the hearing on {[4] *identify subject of hearing, e.g., Plaintiff's Motion to Exclude Experts*} until {[5] *date*} because additional time is needed to obtain discovery.

{[6] *Party*} asks the Court to continue the trial in this case for {[7] *number*} days because additional time is needed to obtain discovery. {*See* ***O'Connor's Texas Rules****, "Continuance for Additional Discovery," ch. 5-D, §8, p. 420.*}

INTRODUCTION

1. Plaintiff, {[8] *name*}, sued defendant, {[9] *name*}, for {[10] *state basis of suit*}.

2. {[11] *State other relevant facts about the suit.*}

BACKGROUND

{*CHOOSE APPROPRIATE PARAGRAPH 3*}

3. This case is set for hearing on {[12] *date*} on {[13] *identify subject of hearing, e.g., Plaintiff's Motion to Exclude Experts*}.

3. This case is set for trial on {[14] *date*}. {[15] *Party*} {[16] *has/has not*} made an unconditional announcement of ready for trial.

4. Discovery in this suit {[17] *is/was*} governed by a Level {[18] *1/2/3*} discovery-control plan. The discovery period {[19] *will end/ended*} on {[20] *date*}. {*See* ***O'Connor's Texas Rules****, "Discovery-Control Plans," ch. 6-A, §7, p. 520.*}

5. {[21] *All/Most/A significant part/No significant part/None*} of the discovery has been completed.

6. This is {[22] *party*}'s {[23] *identify number, e.g., first*} motion for continuance to obtain additional discovery.

7. {[24] *State other facts relevant to the motion.*}

ARGUMENT & AUTHORITIES

8. A court may continue a hearing or trial so that a party may obtain additional discovery when the party (1) describes the discovery sought, (2) explains how the discov-

Continued on next page

FORM 5D:1

ery is material, (3) shows that due diligence was used to obtain the discovery, (4) explains why the discovery was not obtained earlier, and (5) states that the continuance is not sought for delay but so that justice may be done. *See* Tex. R. Civ. P. 252; *see, e.g., State v. Wood Oil Distrib., Inc.*, 751 S.W.2d 863, 865 (Tex. 1988) (depositions); *In re Guardianship of Villarreal*, 330 S.W.3d 11, 27 (Tex. App.—Corpus Christi 2010, no pet.) (testimony); *Wal-Mart Stores Tex., LP v. Crosby*, 295 S.W.3d 346, 356 (Tex. App.—Dallas 2009, pet. denied) (additional discovery); *Tri-Steel Structures, Inc. v. Baptist Found.*, 166 S.W.3d 443, 447-48 (Tex. App.—Fort Worth 2005, pet. denied) (testimony); *Verkin v. Sw. Ctr. One, Ltd.*, 784 S.W.2d 92, 94-95 (Tex. App.—Houston [1st Dist.] 1989, writ denied) (additional discovery). {*See* ***O'Connor's Texas Rules***, *"Continuance for Additional Discovery," ch. 5-D, §8, p. 420.*}

9. {㉕ *Party*} needs additional time to obtain {㉖ *testimony/evidence*} on {㉗ *describe the testimony or other evidence needed*}.

10. The {㉘ *testimony/evidence*} is material to {㉙ *party*}'s {㉚ *claim/defense*} of {㉛ *identify claim or defense*} because {㉜ *state facts showing materiality of evidence*}.

11. {㉝ *Party*} was unable to obtain this {㉞ *testimony/evidence*} earlier even though {㉟ *he/she/it*} diligently used the discovery process. {㊱ *Summarize discovery attempts demonstrating diligence. If known, state why discovery attempts did not obtain evidence.*}

{*CHOOSE APPROPRIATE PARAGRAPHS 12-15*}

{*If continuance based on need for testimony*}

12. This testimony can be obtained by the deposition of {㊲ *name of witness*}, who resides at {㊳ *street address, county, state*}.

13. This witness has been unavailable for deposition because {㊴ *state facts showing unavailability*}.

14. {㊵ *Party*} sent a notice of intent to take the deposition of {㊶ *name of witness*}. The notice is attached as Exhibit {㊷ *letter*}.

{*If continuance based on need for other evidence*}

15. To obtain this evidence, {㊸ *party*} needs additional time to {㊹ *describe type of discovery needed, e.g., request production of documents, and identify person from whom discovery will be sought*}. Attached to this motion as Exhibit {㊺ *letter*} is the {㊻ *describe discovery request, e.g., request for production of documents*}.

{ADD PARAGRAPH 16 IF SECOND OR LATER MOTION}

16. {❹❼ *Party*} cannot obtain the {❹❽ *testimony/evidence*} from any other source. Tex. R. Civ. P. 252. {❹❾ *State facts that demonstrate inability to obtain testimony elsewhere.*} {*See* ***O'Connor's Texas Rules****, "Not otherwise available," ch. 5-D, §8.1.6, p. 421.*}

17. {❺⓪ *Party*} is not seeking a continuance for purposes of delay, but so that justice may be done.

{ADD PARAGRAPH 18 IF UNCONDITIONAL ANNOUNCEMENT OF READY FOR TRIAL WAS MADE}

18. Although {❺❶ *party*} made an unconditional announcement of ready for trial, {❺❷ *party*} has not waived the right to seek a continuance. At the time of the announcement, {❺❸ *party*} did not know and could not with diligence have known of the facts giving rise to the motion. After the announcement, {❺❹ *party*} learned of these facts, which were unforeseeable and arose through no fault of {❺❺ *party*}. *See Reyna v. Reyna*, 738 S.W.2d 772, 775 (Tex. App.—Austin 1987, no writ). {❺❻ *Elaborate.*}

CONCLUSION

19. {❺❼ *Briefly summarize the motion.*}

PRAYER

20. For these reasons, {❺❽ *party*} asks the Court to continue the {❺❾ *hearing/trial*} in this case for at least {❻⓪ *number*} days until {❻❶ *date*}.

SEE: Tex. R. Civ. P. 251, 252
O'Connor's Texas Rules * Civil Trials (2019), "Continuance for Additional Discovery," ch. 5-D, §8, p. 420

ADD: STYLE OF THE CASE – FORM 1B:2
SIGNATURE BLOCK – FORM 1B:3
VERIFICATION – FORM 1B:7
CERTIFICATE OF SERVICE – FORM 1B:13

ATTACH: NOTICE OF HEARING OR SUBMISSION – FORM 1E:1
ORDER – FORM 1G:1
AFFIDAVIT FOR CONTINUANCE – FORM 5D:4
Discovery request, if necessary
Notice of intent to take deposition, if necessary

◄ Continued on next page ►

NOTE: The purpose of a motion for continuance is to delay the setting for a trial or hearing. To extend the time to file a pleading, see FORM 1C:1.

The facts in a motion for continuance must be verified or supported by an affidavit. ***Hawthorne v. Guenther***, 917 S.W.2d 924, 929 (Tex.App.—Beaumont 1996, writ denied); *see* Tex. R. Civ. P. 251; ***Taherzadeh v. Ghaleh-Assadi***, 108 S.W.3d 927, 928 (Tex.App.—Dallas 2003, pet. denied).

Parties should consult the court's local rules for additional requirements for a motion for continuance. *See, e.g.*, Dallas Cty. Loc. R. 3.01.b (client must personally approve motion for continuance in writing when case is more than one year old).

If the court refuses to grant a motion for continuance, the party should ask the court to make a ruling to preserve error. See ***O'Connor's Texas Rules***, "Obtain a ruling," ch. 5-D, §5.1, p. 419.

{1 *PARTY*}'S MOTION FOR CONTINUANCE

{*CHOOSE APPROPRIATE OPENING PARAGRAPH*}

{2 *Party*}, {3 *name*}, asks the Court to continue the hearing on {4 *identify subject of hearing, e.g., Plaintiff's Motion to Exclude Experts*} until {5 *date*} because {6 *identify reason*}.

{7 *Party*} asks the Court to continue the trial in this case until {8 *date*} because additional time is needed to {9 *identify reason*}. {*See* ***O'Connor's Texas Rules***, *"Motion," ch. 5-D, §2, p. 417.*}

INTRODUCTION

1. Plaintiff, {10 *name*}, sued defendant, {11 *name*}, for {12 *state basis of suit*}.

2. {13 *State other relevant facts about the suit.*}

BACKGROUND

{*CHOOSE APPROPRIATE PARAGRAPH 3*}

3. This case is set for hearing on {14 *date*} on {15 *identify subject of hearing, e.g., Plaintiff's Motion to Exclude Experts*}.

3. This case is set for trial on {16 *date*}. {17 *Party*} {18 *has/has not*} made an unconditional announcement of ready for trial.

4. {19 *State other facts relevant to the motion.*}

{*CHOOSE APPROPRIATE ARGUMENTS*}

INSUFFICIENT NOTICE OF TRIAL

5. A court must give the parties at least 45 days' notice of the first trial setting. Tex. R. Civ. P. 245; *In re K.M.L.*, 443 S.W.3d 101, 118 (Tex. 2014); *Smith v. Lippmann*, 826 S.W.2d 137, 138 n.1 (Tex. 1992). If a court gives a party less than 45 days' notice of a trial setting and that party objects, the Court must continue the setting. *Hardin v. Hardin*, 932 S.W.2d 566, 567 (Tex. App.—Tyler 1995, no writ). {*See* ***O'Connor's Texas Rules***, *"Motion," ch. 5-D, §7.2, p. 419.*}

6. {20 *Party*} received notice of the first trial setting on {21 *date*}, which is less than 45 days before trial.

◄ *Continued on next page* ►

7. Only {[22] *number*} days' notice of the trial date does not give {[23] *party*} adequate time to prepare for trial. {[24] *Elaborate.*}

8. Only {[25] *number*} days' notice of the trial date violates {[26] *party*}'s right of due process and the mandate in Rule 245. *Hardin*, 932 S.W.2d at 567.

{[27] *PARTY/WITNESS*} UNAVAILABLE

9. A court may continue a hearing or trial when a party or witness is unavailable to testify if the party requesting the continuance (1) provides the name and residence of the person testifying, (2) describes the testimony needed, (3) explains how the testimony is material and that proceeding without the testimony will prejudice the party requesting the continuance, (4) explains why the person is not available to testify, (5) shows that due diligence was used to obtain the testimony, (6) explains why the testimony was not obtained earlier, and (7) states that the continuance is not sought for delay but so that justice may be done. *See* Tex. R. Civ. P. 252; *Richards v. Schion*, 969 S.W.2d 131, 132-33 (Tex. App.—Houston [1st Dist.] 1998, no pet.); *Hawthorne v. Guenther*, 917 S.W.2d 924, 929-30 (Tex. App.—Beaumont 1996, writ denied); *Humphrey v. Ahlschlager*, 778 S.W.2d 480, 483-84 (Tex. App.—Dallas 1989, no writ); *Burke v. Scott*, 410 S.W.2d 826, 828-29 (Tex. App.—Austin 1967, writ ref'd n.r.e.). {*See* ***O'Connor's Texas Rules***, *"Continuance – Party or Witness Unavailable for Trial," ch. 5-D, §10, p. 423.*}

10. {[28] *Name of party or witness*}, who resides at {[29] *street address, county, state*}, is unavailable to testify at the {[30] *hearing/trial*} because {[31] *state reasons*}.

11. {[32] *Party*} expects {[33] *name of party or witness*} to provide the following testimony: {[34] *describe expected testimony*}.

12. {[35] *Party*} expects that the testimony will prove the following facts: {[36] *describe facts*}.

13. The testimony is material because {[37] *describe materiality*}.

14. {[38] *Party*} will be prejudiced if the court proceeds without {[39] *name of party or witness*}'s testimony because {[40] *explain*}.

15. {[41] *Party*} has been diligent in attempting to obtain the testimony of {[42] *name of party or witness*}. {[43] *Name of party or witness*} resides within 100 miles of the courthouse where the suit is pending. {[44] *Party*} subpoenaed {[45] *name of party or witness*} for the {[46] *hearing/trial*}, but {[47] *name of party or witness*} will not be able to attend because {[48] *state reasons, e.g., she is hospitalized due to an illness*}. {[49] *Party*} could not have anticipated that {[50] *name of party or witness*} would not be able to ap-

pear at the {51 *hearing/trial*}. {52 *Explain why absence was unexpected and why deposition was not previously taken or why deposition testimony would be insufficient.*} {*See **O'Connor's Texas Rules**, "Witness within 100-mile range," ch. 5-D, §10.5.1, p. 424.*}

{*ADD PARAGRAPH 16 IF PARTY OR WITNESS IS ILL*}

16. {53 *Party*} attaches as Exhibit {54 *letter*} the affidavit of Dr. {55 *name of physician*}, {56 *name of party or witness*}'s physician, and incorporates it by reference. In that affidavit, Dr. {57 *name of physician*} states that {58 *name of party or witness*} is suffering from {59 *identify nature and severity of illness*} and is too ill to attend the {60 *hearing/trial*}. In Dr. {61 *name of physician*}'s opinion, {62 *name of party or witness*}'s health will be jeopardized if forced to attend the {63 *hearing/trial*}. {64 *Name of party or witness*}'s prognosis for recovery is {65 *explain prognosis and identify when person is expected to be able to testify*}. {*See **O'Connor's Texas Rules**, "Medical-excuse affidavit," ch. 5-D, §10.6, p. 424.*}

{*ADD PARAGRAPH 17 IF SECOND OR LATER MOTION*}

17. {66 *Party*} cannot obtain the {67 *testimony/evidence*} from any other source. Tex. R. Civ. P. 252. {68 *State facts that demonstrate inability to obtain testimony elsewhere.*} {*See **O'Connor's Texas Rules**, "Not otherwise available," ch. 5-D, §8.1.6, p. 421.*}

18. {69 *Party*} is not seeking a continuance for purposes of delay, but so that justice may be done.

ATTORNEY UNAVAILABLE

{*CHOOSE APPROPRIATE PARAGRAPHS 19-24*}

{*Attorney on vacation*}

19. A court must continue a trial if a local rule mandates that the lead attorney is entitled to a continuance when a case is set for trial within the period designated by the attorney in a vacation letter, regardless of when the order setting the case for trial was signed. *See In re N. Am. Refractories Co.*, 71 S.W.3d 391, 394 (Tex. App.—Beaumont 2001, orig. proceeding). {*See **O'Connor's Texas Rules**, "Attorney's vacation letter," ch. 5-D, §11.1, p. 425.*}

20. {70 *Identify local rule governing attorney vacation letters and show how rule protects an attorney from trials during vacation weeks.*}

Continued on next page

21. {71 *Party*}'s lead attorney, {72 *name of attorney*}, filed a vacation letter on {73 *date*} and designated the following weeks as vacation: {74 *specify designated weeks*}. This case is set for trial on {75 *date*}, which is during {76 *name of attorney*}'s vacation. Thus, the Court must continue the trial of this case until {77 *name of attorney*}'s vacation is completed.

{*Attorney otherwise unavailable*}

22. A court has discretion to continue a case when a party's attorney is unavailable for a hearing or trial if the motion for continuance shows proof of good cause. Tex. R. Civ. P. 253. To establish good cause, the party should (1) state that the attorney's presence is necessary for the proper representation of the case and explain why, (2) state the reasons for the attorney's unavailability, (3) if another attorney is available, explain why that attorney cannot handle the matter, and (4) state that the continuance is not sought for delay but so that justice may be done. *See Rehab. Facility at Austin, Inc. v. Cooper*, 962 S.W.2d 151, 155-56 (Tex. App.—Austin 1998, no pet.); *Rabe v. Guar. Nat'l Ins. Co.*, 787 S.W.2d 575, 579 (Tex. App.—Houston [1st Dist.] 1990, writ denied). {*See* ***O'Connor's Texas Rules***, *"Attorney not available," ch. 5-D, §11.2, p. 425.*}

23. The presence of {78 *party*}'s attorney, {79 *name of attorney*}, is necessary for the proper representation of the case. {80 *Elaborate.*} {*See* ***O'Connor's Texas Rules***, *"Attorney is necessary," ch. 5-D, §11.2.1, p. 425.*}

24. {81 *Name of attorney*}, is unavailable for {82 *hearing/trial*} on the date it has been set because {83 *state reason and show good cause, e.g., attorney is in another trial that has a preferential setting; provide details, e.g., name other case, identify other court, and if absence is due to scheduling conflict, show how attorney tried to avoid it*}. {*See* ***O'Connor's Texas Rules***, *"Reason attorney unavailable," ch. 5-D, §11.2.2, p. 425.*}

{*CHOOSE APPROPRIATE PARAGRAPH 25*}

25. No other attorney with {84 *name of attorney*}'s firm can handle the matter because {85 *state reasons*}. {*See* ***O'Connor's Texas Rules***, *"No substitute possible," ch. 5-D, §11.2.3, p. 426.*}

25. {86 *Party*}'s attorney is a sole practitioner and has no other attorney to substitute at the {87 *hearing/trial*}. {*See* ***O'Connor's Texas Rules***, *"No substitute possible," ch. 5-D, §11.2.3, p. 426.*}

26. {88 *Party*} is not seeking a continuance for purposes of delay but so that justice may be done.

PARTY NOT REPRESENTED

27. A court has discretion to continue a case when a party's attorney withdraws before trial and the party's lack of representation is not due to the party's own fault or negligence. *See* Tex. R. Civ. P. 253; *see, e.g., Villegas v. Carter*, 711 S.W.2d 624, 626 (Tex. 1986) (attorneys voluntarily withdrew); *State v. Crank*, 666 S.W.2d 91, 94 (Tex. 1984) (party asked attorney to withdraw). When a court allows an attorney to voluntarily withdraw, it must give the party time to secure a new attorney and time for that attorney to investigate the case and prepare for trial. *Villegas*, 711 S.W.2d at 626. {*See* ***O'Connor's Texas Rules****, "Party not represented," ch. 5-D, §11.3, p. 426.*}

28. {89 *Party*}'s attorney, {90 *name of attorney*}, withdrew on {91 *date*}, which is {92 *number*} days before this case is set for trial.

29. {93 *Party*}'s lack of representation is not the result of {94 *his/her/its*} own fault or negligence. {95 *Elaborate.*}

LEGISLATIVE CONTINUANCE

{*CHOOSE APPROPRIATE PARAGRAPH 30*}

{*Party is member or member-elect of Legislature*}

30. While the Legislature is in session or within 30 days of a date when the Legislature is to be in session, a court must continue a case when a party is unavailable for a hearing or trial because the party is a member or member-elect of the Legislature and is or will be attending a legislative session. Tex. Civ. Prac. & Rem. Code §30.003(b); Tex. R. Civ. P. 254. {*See* ***O'Connor's Texas Rules****, "Ruling," ch. 5-D, §12.4, p. 428.*} When a party makes a proper motion for legislative continuance, a continuance until 30 days after the Legislature adjourns is mandatory, unless the other party can show irreparable harm by the delay. *See* Tex. Civ. Prac. & Rem. Code §30.003(b); Tex. R. Civ. P. 254; *In re Ford Motor Co.*, 165 S.W.3d 315, 319 (Tex. 2005); *Waites v. Sondock*, 561 S.W.2d 772, 776 (Tex. 1977); *In re Starr Produce Co.*, 988 S.W.2d 808, 811 (Tex. App.—San Antonio 1999, orig. proceeding). {*See* ***O'Connor's Texas Rules****, "Continuance for Legislator," ch. 5-D, §12, p. 426.*}

{*Party's attorney is member or member-elect of Legislature, hired more than 30 days before trial date*}

30. While the Legislature is in session or within 30 days of a date when the Legislature is to be in session, a court must continue a case when a party's attorney (1) is unavailable for a hearing or trial because the attorney is a member or member-elect of the Legislature and is or will be attending a legislative session and (2) was employed more

Continued on next page

than 30 days before the trial date. Tex. Civ. Prac. & Rem. Code §30.003(b); Tex. R. Civ. P. 254. {*See **O'Connor's Texas Rules**, "Ruling," ch. 5-D, §12.4, p. 428.*} When a party makes a proper motion for legislative continuance, a continuance until 30 days after the Legislature adjourns is mandatory, unless the other party can show irreparable harm by the delay. *See* Tex. Civ. Prac. & Rem. Code §30.003(b); Tex. R. Civ. P. 254; *In re Ford Motor Co.*, 165 S.W.3d 315, 319 (Tex. 2005); *Waites v. Sondock*, 561 S.W.2d 772, 776 (Tex. 1977); *In re Starr Produce Co.*, 988 S.W.2d 808, 811 (Tex. App.—San Antonio 1999, orig. proceeding). {*See **O'Connor's Texas Rules**, "Continuance for Legislator," ch. 5-D, §12, p. 426.*}

{*Party's attorney is member or member-elect of Legislature, hired within 30 days of the trial date*}

30. While the Legislature is in session or within 30 days of a date when the Legislature is to be in session, a court may continue a case when a party's attorney (1) is unavailable for a hearing or trial because the attorney is a member or member-elect of the Legislature and is or will be attending a legislative session and (2) was employed within 30 days of the trial date. Tex. Civ. Prac. & Rem. Code §30.003(b); Tex. R. Civ. P. 254. {*See **O'Connor's Texas Rules**, "Ruling," ch. 5-D, §12.4, p. 428.*} If a continuance is granted, it should be until 30 days after the Legislature adjourns. *See* Tex. Civ. Prac. & Rem. Code §30.003(b), (c); Tex. R. Civ. P. 254. {*See **O'Connor's Texas Rules**, "Continuance for Legislator," ch. 5-D, §12, p. 426.*}

31. {96 *{Party}/{name of attorney}*} is a {97 *member/member-elect*} of the Texas Legislature and {98 *is/will be*} in attendance in the Legislature from {99 *state dates of attendance*}.

{*ADD PARAGRAPHS 32-34 IF ATTORNEY IS LEGISLATOR*}

{*CHOOSE APPROPRIATE PARAGRAPH 32*}

32. {100 *Party*} employed {101 *name of attorney*} as {102 *his/her/its*} attorney more than 30 days before trial. Trial is set for {103 *date*}. {104 *Name of attorney*} was employed on {105 *date*}. {*See **O'Connor's Texas Rules**, "Mandatory," ch. 5-D, §12.1.1(3)(a), p. 427.*}

32. {106 *Party*} employed {107 *name of attorney*} as {108 *his/her/its*} attorney within 30 days of the trial date. Trial is set for {109 *date*}. {110 *Name of attorney*} was employed on {111 *date*}. {*See **O'Connor's Texas Rules**, "Discretionary," ch. 5-D, §12.1.1(3)(b), p. 427.*}

33. {112 *Name of attorney*} intends to participate actively in the {113 *preparation/presentation/preparation and presentation*} of the case. Tex. Civ. Prac. & Rem. Code §30.003(e); Tex. R. Civ. P. 254. Attached to this motion as Exhibit {114 *letter*} is the affidavit of {115 *name of attorney*} confirming {116 *his/her*} participation in the case. {*See* ***O'Connor's Texas Rules***, *"Legislator statements," ch. 5-D, §12.1.1(2)(a), p. 427.*}

34. {117 *Name of attorney*} was not hired for the purpose of supporting a motion for continuance. Tex. Civ. Prac. & Rem. Code §30.003(e). Attached to this motion as Exhibit {118 *letter*} is the affidavit of {119 *name of attorney*} confirming that {120 *he/she*} was not hired for the purpose of supporting a motion for continuance. {*See* ***O'Connor's Texas Rules***, *"Legislator statements," ch. 5-D, §12.1.1(2)(b), p. 427.*}

35. The {121 *hearing/trial*} is scheduled to begin while {122 *{party}/{name of attorney}*} is in attendance in the Legislature. Thus, the Court {123 *must/may*} continue this matter until 30 days after the Legislature adjourns.

RELIGIOUS CONTINUANCE

36. A court should grant a continuance when a party or party's attorney is required to appear at a court proceeding on a religious holy day observed by the party or party's attorney. Tex. Civ. Prac. & Rem. Code §30.005(b). A "religious holy day" is a day on which the tenets of a religious organization, as determined under Texas Tax Code section 11.20, prohibit its members from participating in secular activities. Tex. Civ. Prac. & Rem. Code §30.005(a)(2). {*See* ***O'Connor's Texas Rules***, *"Continuance for Religious Holy Day," ch. 5-D, §13, p. 428.*}

{*ADD PARAGRAPH 37 IF APPROPRIATE*}

37. {124 *Party*} is represented in this matter by {125 *name of attorney*}.

38. {126 *{Party}/{Name of attorney}*} is a member of an organization that qualifies as a religious organization under Texas Tax Code section 11.20(c). {127 *Elaborate, identifying the religious organization.*}

39. As a member of that religious organization, {128 *{party}/{name of attorney}*} holds religious beliefs that prohibit {129 *him/her*} from taking part in court proceedings on {130 *date*}, the day {131 *he/she*} is required to appear in court. *See* Tex. Civ. Prac. & Rem. Code §30.005(c). {132 *Elaborate, identifying name of religious holy day.*}

◄ Continued on next page ►

{ADD SECTION BELOW IF UNCONDITIONAL ANNOUNCEMENT OF READY FOR TRIAL WAS MADE}

NO WAIVER

40. Although {133 *party*} made an unconditional announcement of ready for trial, {134 *party*} has not waived the right to seek a continuance. At the time of the announcement, {135 *party*} did not know and could not with diligence have known of the facts giving rise to the motion. After the announcement, {136 *party*} learned of these facts, which were unforeseeable and arose through no fault of {137 *party*}. *See Reyna v. Reyna*, 738 S.W.2d 772, 775 (Tex. App.—Austin 1987, no writ). {138 *Elaborate.*}

CONCLUSION

41. {139 *Briefly summarize the motion.*}

PRAYER

42. For these reasons, {140 *party*} asks the Court to continue this case for at least {141 *number*} days until {142 *date*}.

SEE: Tex. R. Civ. P. 251-254, 330(d)
Tex. Civ. Prac. & Rem. Code §§30.003, 30.005
Tex. Tax Code §11.20
O'Connor's Texas Rules * Civil Trials (2019), "Motion for Continuance," ch. 5-D, p. 417

ADD: STYLE OF THE CASE – FORM 1B:2
SIGNATURE BLOCK – FORM 1B:3
VERIFICATION – FORM 1B:7
CERTIFICATE OF SERVICE – FORM 1B:13

ATTACH: AFFIDAVIT – FORM 1B:8, if necessary because party or witness is ill
NOTICE OF HEARING OR SUBMISSION – FORM 1E:1
ORDER – FORM 1G:1
AFFIDAVIT FOR CONTINUANCE – FORM 5D:4
Vacation letter, if appropriate

NOTE: The purpose of a motion for continuance is to delay the setting for a trial or hearing. To extend the time to file a pleading, see FORM 1C:1.

The facts in a motion for continuance must be verified or supported by an affidavit. ***Hawthorne v. Guenther***, 917 S.W.2d 924, 929 (Tex.App.—Beaumont 1996, writ denied); *see* Tex. R. Civ. P. 251; ***Taherzadeh v. Ghaleh-Assadi***, 108 S.W.3d 927, 928 (Tex.App.—Dallas 2003, pet. denied).

To continue a summary-judgment hearing, see FORMS 7B:2 and 7B:5.

An attorney may waive her right to rely on a vacation letter by acting in a manner that is inconsistent with reliance on the letter. *See* ***In re North Am. Refractories Co.***, 71 S.W.3d 391, 394 (Tex.App.—Beaumont 2001, orig. proceeding); *see, e.g.*, ***Siegler v. Williams***, 658 S.W.2d 236, 239 (Tex.App.—Houston [1st Dist.] 1983, no writ) (member of attorney's firm agreed to preferential trial setting to take place during week covered by attorney's vacation letter; attorney's right to rely on letter was waived); ***Bennett v. Coghlan***, No. 01-04-00104-CV (Tex.App.—Houston [1st Dist.] 2007, pet. denied) (memo op.; 8-16-07) (three months after filing vacation letter, attorney agreed to preferential trial setting to take place during week covered by letter; attorney waived right to rely on letter).

If an attorney for a party seeking a legislative continuance is a member or member-elect of the Legislature, the attorney must file a copy of the motion with the Texas Ethics Commission no later than three business days after the motion is filed with the court. Tex. Civ. Prac. & Rem. Code §30.003(g).

A party is not entitled to a legislative continuance of a hearing on a temporary restraining order. Tex. Civ. Prac. & Rem. Code §30.003(a); Tex. R. Civ. P. 254.

{❶ *PARTY*}'S RESPONSE TO
{❷ *ADVERSE PARTY*}'S MOTION FOR CONTINUANCE

{❸ *Party*}, {❹ *name*}, asks the Court to deny {❺ *adverse party*} {❻ *name*}'s motion for continuance because {❼ *adverse party*} has not shown sufficient cause for a continuance.

INTRODUCTION

1. Plaintiff, {❽ *name*}, sued defendant, {❾ *name*}, for {❿ *state basis of suit*}.

2. {⓫ *State other relevant facts about the suit.*}

BACKGROUND

3. On {⓬ *date*}, {⓭ *adverse party*} filed a motion for continuance.

{*CHOOSE APPROPRIATE PARAGRAPH 4*}

4. This case is set for hearing on {⓮ *date*} on {⓯ *identify subject of hearing, e.g., Plaintiff's Motion to Exclude Experts*}.

4. This case is set for trial on {⓰ *date*}. {⓱ *Party*} {⓲ *has/has not*} made an unconditional announcement of ready for trial.

5. {⓳ *State other facts relevant to the response.*}

{*CHOOSE APPROPRIATE ARGUMENTS*}

TECHNICAL DEFECTS IN MOTION

{*CHOOSE APPROPRIATE SECTIONS A-B*}

A. Motion {⓴ *not verified or supported by affidavit/supported by defective affidavit*}.

6. A court should deny a motion for continuance when the motion is not verified or supported by an affidavit or when the affidavit is defective. *See* Tex. R. Civ. P. 251; *Villegas v. Carter*, 711 S.W.2d 624, 626 (Tex. 1986); *Taherzadeh v. Ghaleh-Assadi*, 108 S.W.3d 927, 928 (Tex. App.—Dallas 2003, pet. denied); *Hawthorne v. Guenther*, 917 S.W.2d 924, 929 (Tex. App.—Beaumont 1996, writ denied). {*See* ***O'Connor's Texas Rules***, *"Verification & affidavits," ch. 5-D, §2.3, p. 418.*}

{*CHOOSE APPROPRIATE PARAGRAPH 7*}

7. The Court should deny {㉑ *adverse party*}'s motion for continuance because the motion was not verified or supported by an affidavit.

7. The Court should deny {[22] *adverse party*}'s motion for continuance because the affidavit attached to the motion is defective.

{*CHOOSE APPROPRIATE PARAGRAPHS 8-12*}

8. The affidavit of {[23] *name of affiant*} is not an "affidavit" because it is not signed. *See Hawthorne*, 917 S.W.2d at 929. Thus, the entire affidavit should be struck.

9. The affidavit of {[24] *name of affiant*} is not an "affidavit" because it is not properly sworn or certified, as required by law. Texas Government Code section 312.011(1) defines an affidavit as "a statement in writing of a fact or facts signed by the party making it, sworn to before an officer authorized to administer oaths, and officially certified to by the officer under his seal of office." The affidavit of {[25] *name of affiant*} is defective because {[26] *describe the defect in the affidavit*}. Thus, the entire affidavit should be struck.

10. The affidavit is defective because {[27] *name of affiant*} is not a competent witness. *See* Tex. R. Evid. 601. {[28] *State why the person is not competent to testify about the statements in the affidavit.*} Because the affiant is not competent to testify, the entire affidavit should be struck. {*See **O'Connor's Texas Rules**, "Competency of witness," ch. 1-B, §3.2.16(2), p. 13.*}

11. The affidavit is defective because it contains statements that are not based on personal knowledge. Tex. R. Evid. 602; *Humphreys v. Caldwell*, 888 S.W.2d 469, 470 (Tex. 1994); *see Southtex 66 Pipeline Co. v. Spoor*, 238 S.W.3d 538, 544-45 (Tex. App.—Houston [14th Dist.] 2007, pet. denied). {[29] *Identify statements and state why the person does not have personal knowledge.*} Because the affiant has not shown how the statements are based on personal knowledge, those statements should be struck. {*See **O'Connor's Texas Rules**, "Personal knowledge," ch. 1-B, §3.2.16(3)(a), p. 13.*}

12. The affidavit is defective because it is based only on the affiant's knowledge and belief. An affidavit cannot be based on "knowledge and belief" unless it is authorized by statute or rule. *See Burke v. Satterfield*, 525 S.W.2d 950, 955 (Tex. 1975); *Hawthorne*, 917 S.W.2d at 930; *Int'l Turbine Serv., Inc. v. Lovitt*, 881 S.W.2d 805, 808 (Tex. App.—Fort Worth 1994, writ denied). {[30] *Adverse party*} sought a continuance under {[31] *specify rule or statute, e.g., Texas Rule of Civil Procedure 252*}, which does not allow an affidavit to be based on knowledge and belief. Because the affiant based the affidavit on knowledge and belief, the entire affidavit should be struck. {*See **O'Connor's Texas Rules**, "Knowledge & belief," ch. 1-B, §3.2.16(3)(b), p. 13.*}

Continued on next page

B. {㉜ *Adverse party*} made an unconditional announcement of ready for trial.

13. A court should deny a motion for continuance of a trial when the party seeking the continuance has made an unconditional announcement of ready for trial, and at the time of the announcement knew or could have with diligence known of the facts giving rise to the motion. *Reyna v. Reyna*, 738 S.W.2d 772, 775 (Tex. App.—Austin 1987, no writ). {*See* ***O'Connor's Texas Rules****, "Before announcement of ready," ch. 5-D, §3.1, p. 418.*}

14. On {㉝ *date*}, {㉞ *adverse party*} made an unconditional announcement of ready for trial. At the time of the announcement, {㉟ *adverse party*} knew or could have with diligence known of the facts giving rise to the motion. These facts {㊱ *were foreseeable by/arose because of*} {㊲ *adverse party*}. {㊳ *Elaborate.*}

CONTINUANCE FOR ADDITIONAL DISCOVERY

15. A court should not continue a hearing or trial so that a party may obtain additional discovery unless the party requesting the continuance (1) describes the discovery sought, (2) explains how the discovery is material, (3) shows that due diligence was used to obtain the discovery, (4) explains why the discovery was not obtained earlier, and (5) states that the continuance is not sought for delay but so that justice may be done. *See* Tex. R. Civ. P. 252; *see, e.g., State v. Wood Oil Distrib., Inc.*, 751 S.W.2d 863, 865 (Tex. 1988) (depositions); *In re Guardianship of Villarreal*, 330 S.W.3d 11, 27 (Tex. App.—Corpus Christi 2010, no pet.) (testimony); *Wal-Mart Stores Tex., LP v. Crosby*, 295 S.W.3d 346, 356 (Tex. App.—Dallas 2009, pet. denied) (additional discovery); *Tri-Steel Structures, Inc. v. Baptist Found.*, 166 S.W.3d 443, 447-48 (Tex. App.—Fort Worth 2005, pet. denied) (testimony); *Verkin v. Sw. Ctr. One, Ltd.*, 784 S.W.2d 92, 94-95 (Tex. App.—Houston [1st Dist.] 1989, writ denied) (additional discovery). {*See* ***O'Connor's Texas Rules****, "Continuance for Additional Discovery," ch. 5-D, §8, p. 420.*}

{*CHOOSE APPROPRIATE PARAGRAPHS 16-22*}

16. The Court should deny the motion for continuance because the motion did not describe the {㊴ *evidence/testimony*} {㊵ *adverse party*} expects to obtain through discovery.

17. The Court should deny the motion for continuance because the motion did not {㊶ *state/adequately show*} why the {㊷ *evidence/testimony*} sought is material to {㊸ *adverse party*}'s {㊹ *claim/defense*}. {㊺ *Elaborate.*}

FORM 5D:3

18. The Court should deny the motion for continuance because the motion did not {46 *state/adequately show*} that {47 *adverse party*} was unable to obtain this {48 *evidence/testimony*} earlier through diligent use of the discovery process.

19. The Court should deny the motion for continuance because the discovery attempts {49 *adverse party*} identified in the motion for continuance were undertaken only {50 *number*} days before the {51 *trial/hearing*}. A last-minute attempt at discovery is not sufficient to show due diligence. *Hatteberg v. Hatteberg*, 933 S.W.2d 522, 526-27 (Tex. App.—Houston [1st Dist.] 1994, no writ).

20. The motion for continuance is {52 *adverse party*}'s {53 *identify number, e.g., second*} motion for continuance; thus, {54 *adverse party*} was required to show that {55 *he/she/it*} could not obtain the necessary {56 *evidence/testimony*} from any other source. Tex. R. Civ. P. 252. The Court should deny the motion for continuance because the motion did not show that {57 *adverse party*} could not obtain the necessary {58 *evidence/testimony*} from any other source. {59 *Elaborate.*} {*See* ***O'Connor's Texas Rules***, *"Not otherwise available," ch. 5-D, §8.1.6, p. 421.*}

21. {60 *Party*} controverts, by {61 *his/her/its*} affidavit attached as Exhibit {62 *letter*}, the facts {63 *adverse party*} asserts in {64 *his/her/its*} affidavit to prove {65 *identify what adverse party is trying to prove, e.g., the materiality of the evidence, the diligence in obtaining the evidence*}. {66 *Elaborate.*} {*See* ***O'Connor's Texas Rules***, *"Response," ch. 5-D, §4, p. 419.*}

22. The Court should deny the motion for continuance because {67 *identify any other defect justifying denial of the motion*}.

{68 *PARTY/WITNESS*} UNAVAILABLE

23. A court should not continue a hearing or trial when a party or witness is unavailable to testify unless the party requesting the continuance (1) provides the name and residence of the person testifying, (2) describes the testimony needed, (3) explains how the testimony is material and that proceeding without the testimony will prejudice the party requesting the continuance, (4) explains why the person is not available to testify, (5) shows that due diligence was used to obtain the testimony, (6) explains why the testimony was not obtained earlier, and (7) states that the continuance is not sought for delay but so that justice may be done. *See* Tex. R. Civ. P. 252; *Richards v. Schion*, 969 S.W.2d 131, 132-33 (Tex. App.—Houston [1st Dist.] 1998, no pet.); *Hawthorne v. Guenther*, 917 S.W.2d 924, 929-30 (Tex. App.—Beaumont 1996, writ denied); *Humphrey v. Ahlschlager*, 778 S.W.2d 480, 483-84 (Tex. App.—Dallas 1989, no writ);

Continued on next page

Echols v. Brewer, 524 S.W.2d 731, 734 (Tex. App.—Houston [14th Dist.] 1975, no writ). {*See* ***O'Connor's Texas Rules***, *"Continuance – Party or Witness Unavailable for Trial," ch. 5-D, §10, p. 423.*}

{*CHOOSE APPROPRIATE PARAGRAPHS 24-35*}

24. The Court should deny the motion for continuance because the motion did not identify the name of the {69 *party/witness*} who {70 *adverse party*} alleges is unavailable to testify.

25. The Court should deny the motion for continuance because the motion did not identify the residence of the {71 *party/witness*} who {72 *adverse party*} alleges is unavailable to testify.

26. The Court should deny the motion for continuance because the motion did not explain why {73 *name of party or witness*}, who {74 *adverse party*} alleges is unavailable for the {75 *trial/hearing*}, is not available to testify.

27. The Court should deny the motion for continuance because the motion did not {76 *state/adequately show*} why the testimony of {77 *name of party or witness*} is material to {78 *adverse party*}'s {79 *claim/defense*}. {80 *Elaborate.*}

28. The Court should deny the motion for continuance because the motion did not {81 *state/adequately show*} why {82 *adverse party*} would be prejudiced if the Court proceeds without {83 *name of party or witness*}'s testimony.

29. The Court should deny the motion for continuance because the motion did not {84 *state/adequately show*} that {85 *adverse party*} was unable to obtain the testimony of {86 *name of party or witness*} earlier through diligent use of the discovery process. {87 *Elaborate.*}

30. The Court should deny the motion for continuance because {88 *name of party or witness*}, who {89 *adverse party*} alleges is unavailable for the {90 *trial/hearing*}, resides within 100 miles of the courthouse where the suit is pending, and {91 *adverse party*} did not subpoena the {92 *party/witness*} for the {93 *trial/hearing*}. {94 *Elaborate.*} {*See* ***O'Connor's Texas Rules***, *"Witness within 100-mile range," ch. 5-D, §10.5.1, p. 424.*}

31. The Court should deny the motion for continuance because {95 *name of party or witness*}, who {96 *adverse party*} alleges is unavailable for the {97 *trial/hearing*}, resides within 100 miles of the courthouse where the suit is pending, and {98 *adverse party*} could have anticipated that {99 *name of party or witness*} would not be able to attend the {100 *trial/hearing*} because {101 *of age/of infirmity/of sickness/of official duty/the witness is about to leave the state or county of suit/the witness has left the state*

or county of suit} and should have taken the {102 *party/witness*}'s deposition. {103 *Elaborate.*} {*See* ***O'Connor's Texas Rules****, "Witness within 100-mile range," ch. 5-D, §10.5.1, p. 424.*}

32. The Court should deny the motion for continuance because {104 *name of party or witness*}, who {105 *adverse party*} alleges is unavailable for the {106 *trial/hearing*}, resides more than 100 miles from the courthouse where the suit is pending and thus should have been deposed for the {107 *trial/hearing*}. {108 *Elaborate.*} {*See* ***O'Connor's Texas Rules****, "Witness outside 100-mile range," ch. 5-D, §10.5.2, p. 424.*}

33. The Court should deny the motion for continuance, which alleged that a {109 *party/witness*} was too ill to appear at the {110 *trial/hearing*}, because the motion did not include the affidavit of a doctor stating {111 *explain, e.g., that the party's health would be jeopardized if forced to attend trial*}. {*See* ***O'Connor's Texas Rules****, "Medical-excuse affidavit," ch. 5-D, §10.6, p. 424.*}

34. The motion for continuance is {112 *adverse party*}'s {113 *identify number, e.g., second*} motion for continuance; thus, {114 *adverse party*} was required to show that {115 *he/she/it*} could not obtain the necessary {116 *evidence/testimony*} from any other source. Tex. R. Civ. P. 252. The Court should deny the motion for continuance because the motion did not show that {117 *adverse party*} could not obtain the necessary {118 *evidence/testimony*} from any other source. {119 *Elaborate.*} {*See* ***O'Connor's Texas Rules****, "Not otherwise available," ch. 5-D, §8.1.6, p. 421.*}

35. The Court should deny the motion for continuance because {120 *adverse party*} is seeking the continuance merely for delay. {121 *Elaborate.*}

ATTORNEY UNAVAILABLE

36. A court should not continue a case when a party's attorney is unavailable for a hearing or trial unless the motion for continuance shows proof of good cause. Tex. R. Civ. P. 253. To establish good cause, the party seeking the continuance should (1) state that the attorney's presence is necessary for the proper representation of the case and explain why, (2) state the reasons for the attorney's unavailability, (3) if another attorney is available, explain why that attorney cannot handle the matter, and (4) state that the continuance is not sought for delay but so that justice may be done. *See Rehab. Facility at Austin, Inc. v. Cooper*, 962 S.W.2d 151, 155-56 (Tex. App.—Austin 1998, no pet.); *Rabe v. Guar. Nat'l Ins. Co.*, 787 S.W.2d 575, 579 (Tex. App.—Houston [1st Dist.] 1990, writ denied). {*See* ***O'Connor's Texas Rules****, "Attorney not available," ch. 5-D, §11.2, p. 425.*}

◄ Continued on next page ►

{CHOOSE APPROPRIATE PARAGRAPHS 37-40}

37. The Court should deny the motion for continuance because {122 *adverse party*} did not adequately show that {123 *his/her/its*} attorney's presence at the {124 *hearing/trial*} was necessary for the proper representation of the case. {125 *Elaborate.*}

38. The Court should deny the motion for continuance because {126 *adverse party*}'s attorney, {127 *attorney's name*}, did not give any reasons for being unavailable for the {128 *trial/hearing*}. {129 *Elaborate.*}

39. The Court should deny the motion for continuance because {130 *adverse party*}'s attorney, {131 *attorney's name*}, did not {132 *state/adequately show*} why another attorney in the firm could not handle the matter. {133 *Elaborate.*}

40. The Court should deny the motion for continuance because {134 *adverse party*} is seeking the continuance merely for delay. {135 *Elaborate.*}

PARTY NOT REPRESENTED

41. A court should not continue a case when a party's attorney has withdrawn before trial unless the motion for continuance shows that the party's lack of representation is not a result of the party's own fault or negligence. *See* Tex. R. Civ. P. 253; *see, e.g., Villegas v. Carter*, 711 S.W.2d 624, 626 (Tex. 1986) (attorneys voluntarily withdrew); *State v. Crank*, 666 S.W.2d 91, 94 (Tex. 1984) (party asked attorney to withdraw). {*See* ***O'Connor's Texas Rules****, "Party not represented," ch. 5-D, §11.3, p. 426.*}

42. The Court should deny the motion for continuance because {136 *adverse party*}'s lack of representation is a result of {137 *his/her/its*} own fault or negligence. {138 *Explain, e.g., adverse party fired its attorney just before the hearing.*}

LEGISLATIVE CONTINUANCE

{CHOOSE APPROPRIATE PARAGRAPH 43}

{Party is member or member-elect of Legislature}

43. While the Legislature is in session or within 30 days of a date when the Legislature is to be in session, a court is usually required to continue a case when the party is unavailable for a hearing or trial because the party is a member or member-elect of the Legislature and is or will be attending a legislative session. Tex. Civ. Prac. & Rem. Code §30.003(b); Tex. R. Civ. P. 254. {*See* ***O'Connor's Texas Rules****, "Ruling," ch. 5-D, §12.4, p. 428.*} However, the court should deny the motion when a party opposing the continuance shows that irreparable harm will be caused by the delay. *See In*

re Ford Motor Co., 165 S.W.3d 315, 319 (Tex. 2005); *Waites v. Sondock*, 561 S.W.2d 772, 776 (Tex. 1977); *In re Starr Produce Co.*, 988 S.W.2d 808, 811 (Tex. App.—San Antonio 1999, orig. proceeding). When a party claims irreparable harm, the court is required to hold a hearing on the legislative continuance. *In re Ford Motor Co.*, 165 S.W.3d at 319; *Waites*, 561 S.W.2d at 776. {*See* ***O'Connor's Texas Rules***, *"Continuance for Legislator," ch. 5-D, §12, p. 426.*}

{*Party's attorney is member or member-elect of Legislature, hired more than 30 days before trial date*}

43. While the Legislature is in session or within 30 days of a date when the Legislature is to be in session, a court is usually required to continue a case when the party's attorney (1) is unavailable for a hearing or trial because the attorney is a member or member-elect of the Legislature and is or will be attending a legislative session and (2) was employed more than 30 days before the trial date. Tex. Civ. Prac. & Rem. Code §30.003(b); Tex. R. Civ. P. 254. {*See* ***O'Connor's Texas Rules***, *"Ruling," ch. 5-D, §12.4, p. 428.*} However, the court should deny the motion when a party opposing the continuance shows that irreparable harm will be caused by the delay. *See In re Ford Motor Co.*, 165 S.W.3d 315, 319 (Tex. 2005); *Waites v. Sondock*, 561 S.W.2d 772, 776 (Tex. 1977); *In re Starr Produce Co.*, 988 S.W.2d 808, 811 (Tex. App.—San Antonio 1999, orig. proceeding). When a party claims irreparable harm, the court is required to hold a hearing on the legislative continuance. *In re Ford Motor Co.*, 165 S.W.3d at 319; *Waites*, 561 S.W.2d at 776. {*See* ***O'Connor's Texas Rules***, *"Continuance for Legislator," ch. 5-D, §12, p. 426.*}

{*Party's attorney is member or member-elect of Legislature, hired within 30 days of the trial date*}

43. While the Legislature is in session or within 30 days of a date when the Legislature is to be in session, a court can deny a motion to continue a case when the party's attorney (1) is unavailable for a hearing or trial because the attorney is a member or member-elect of the Legislature and is or will be attending a legislative session and (2) was employed within 30 days of the trial date. Tex. Civ. Prac. & Rem. Code §30.003(b); Tex. R. Civ. P. 254. {*See* ***O'Connor's Texas Rules***, *"Ruling," ch. 5-D, §12.4, p. 428.*}

{*CHOOSE APPROPRIATE PARAGRAPHS 44-50*}

44. The Court should deny the motion for continuance because {139 *adverse party*} will not be attending a legislative session. {140 *Elaborate.*}

45. The Court should deny the motion for continuance because {141 *name of attorney*} will not be attending a legislative session. {142 *Elaborate.*}

Continued on next page

46. The Court should deny the motion for continuance because the delay will cause {143 *party*} irreparable harm. {144 *Elaborate.*}

47. The Court should deny the motion for continuance because {145 *adverse party*} employed {146 *name of attorney*} within 30 days of trial. {147 *Identify date for trial and date attorney was hired.*}

48. The Court should deny the motion for continuance because {148 *name of attorney*} has not participated in the preparation or the presentation of the case and has no intention of doing so. *See* Tex. Civ. Prac. & Rem. Code §30.003(e); Tex. R. Civ. P. 254. {149 *Elaborate.*}

49. The Court should deny the motion for continuance because {150 *adverse party*} employed {151 *name of attorney*} for the purpose of getting a continuance. *See* Tex. Civ. Prac. & Rem. Code §30.003(e). {152 *Elaborate.*}

50. The Court should deny the motion for continuance because the setting is for a temporary restraining order. Tex. Civ. Prac. & Rem. Code §30.003(a); Tex. R. Civ. P. 254. {153 *Elaborate.*}

RELIGIOUS CONTINUANCE

51. A court should not continue a hearing or trial to observe a religious holy day unless a party or party's attorney files an affidavit showing that (1) {154 *he/she*} is a member of an organization that qualifies as a religious organization under Texas Tax Code section 11.20(c), and (2) the organization's tenets prohibit its members from participating in secular activities on the day the hearing or trial is scheduled. *See* Tex. Civ. Prac. & Rem. Code §30.005(a), (c).

{*CHOOSE APPROPRIATE PARAGRAPHS 52-55*}

52. The Court should deny the motion for continuance because {155 *adverse party*} is not a member of an organization that qualifies as a religious organization under Texas Tax Code section 11.20(c). {156 *Elaborate.*}

53. The Court should deny the motion for continuance because {157 *name of attorney*} is not a member of an organization that qualifies as a religious organization under Texas Tax Code section 11.20(c). {158 *Elaborate.*}

54. The Court should deny the motion for continuance because {159 *name of religious organization*} does not prohibit {160 *adverse party*} from participating in secular activities on {161 *date*}, the day {162 *adverse party*} is required to appear in court. {163 *Elaborate.*}

55. The Court should deny the motion for continuance because {164 *name of religious organization*} does not prohibit {165 *name of attorney*} from participating in secular activities on {166 *date*}, the day {167 *name of attorney*} is required to appear in court. {168 *Elaborate.*}

{169 *PROVIDE HEADING FOR OTHER GROUNDS*}

56. The Court should deny the motion for continuance because {170 *identify any other grounds justifying denial of the motion*}.

CONCLUSION

57. {171 *Briefly summarize the response.*}

PRAYER

58. For these reasons, {172 *party*} asks the Court to deny {173 *adverse party*}'s motion for continuance.

SEE: Tex. R. Civ. P. 251-254, 330(d)
Tex. Const. art. 1, §13
Tex. Civ. Prac. & Rem. Code §§30.003, 30.005
O'Connor's Texas Rules * Civil Trials (2019), "Motion for Continuance," ch. 5-D, p. 417

ADD: STYLE OF THE CASE – FORM 1B:2
SIGNATURE BLOCK – FORM 1B:3
VERIFICATION – FORM 1B:7
CERTIFICATE OF SERVICE – FORM 1B:13

ATTACH: AFFIDAVIT – FORM 1B:8, if necessary
ORDER – FORM 1G:1

NOTE: Uncontroverted statements in a sworn motion for continuance will be accepted as true. See ***O'Connor's Texas Rules***, "Uncontested motion," ch. 5-D, §5.3, p. 419.

{❶ *PARTY*}'S AFFIDAVIT IN
SUPPORT OF MOTION FOR CONTINUANCE

STATE OF TEXAS §
{❷ _______} COUNTY §

{❸ *Party*}, {❹ *name*}, submits this affidavit supporting the allegations in {❺ *his/her/its*} motion for continuance.

Before me, the undersigned notary, on this day personally appeared {❻ *name of affiant*}, the affiant, whose identity is known to me. After I administered an oath, affiant testified as follows:

1. "My name is {❼ *name of affiant*}. I am over 18 years of age, of sound mind, and capable of making this affidavit. The facts stated in this affidavit are within my personal knowledge and are true and correct.

2. "{❽ *Insert from the motion for continuance the basis for the continuance, and support each element with sworn proof.*}

{*CHOOSE APPROPRIATE PARAGRAPH 3*}

3. "This is {❾ *party*}'s first motion for continuance. {❿ *Party*} cannot obtain this testimony from any other source. Tex. R. Civ. P. 252.

3. "This is {⓫ *party*}'s {⓬ *identify number, e.g., second*} motion for continuance. {⓭ *Party*} cannot obtain this testimony from any other source. Tex. R. Civ. P. 252. {⓮ *State facts that demonstrate the inability to obtain the testimony elsewhere.*}

4. "This request for continuance is not for delay only, but so that justice may be done."

____
{⓯ *Name of affiant*}

Sworn to and subscribed before me by {⓰ *name of affiant*} on __________, 20___.

____
Notary Public in and for
the State of Texas

FORM 5D:4 AFFIDAVIT FOR CONTINUANCE

SEE: Tex. R. Civ. P. 252
*O'Connor's Texas Rules * Civil Trials* (2019), "Verification & affidavits," ch. 5-D, §2.3, p. 418

ADD: STYLE OF THE CASE – FORM 1B:2

NOTE: See notes under FORM 1B:8.

{❶ *PARTY*}'S MOTION IN LIMINE

Before the voir dire examination of the jury panel, and outside the presence and hearing of the jury panel, {❷ *party*}, {❸ *name*}, makes this motion in limine. {❹ *Party*} seeks to exclude matters that are inadmissible, irrelevant, or prejudicial in this case. If {❺ *adverse party*}, {❻ *name*}, injects these matters into the trial of this case through a party, an attorney, or a witness, it will cause irreparable harm to {❼ *party*}'s case, which no jury instruction could cure. If any of these matters are brought to the attention of the jury, directly or indirectly, {❽ *party*} will be compelled to move for a mistrial. In an effort to avoid prejudice and a mistrial, {❾ *party*} urges this motion in limine. {*See* ***O'Connor's Texas Rules**, "Motion," ch. 5-E, §2, p. 429.*}

{❿ *Party*} asks the Court to instruct {⓫ *adverse party*} and all counsel not to mention, refer to, interrogate about, or attempt to convey to the jury in any manner, either directly or indirectly, any of the matters listed below without first obtaining a ruling from the Court outside the presence and hearing of the jury, and to instruct {⓬ *adverse party*} and all counsel to warn and caution each witness to follow the same instructions.

GROUNDS

{*CHOOSE APPROPRIATE PARAGRAPHS BELOW*}

{*Grounds for either party*}

1. Any witness {⓭ *adverse party*} did not name in response to requests for disclosures or interrogatories, or any evidence requested by {⓮ *party*} but not produced by {⓯ *adverse party*}. *See Gee v. Liberty Mut. Fire Ins. Co.*, 765 S.W.2d 394, 395 (Tex. 1989).

2. Any testimony or argument that contradicts {⓰ *adverse party*}'s deemed admissions. *See Marshall v. Vise*, 767 S.W.2d 699, 700 (Tex. 1989).

3. Any testimony or argument suggesting that {⓱ *party*} asserted claims of privilege during discovery. Claims of privilege are not admissible as evidence. *See* Tex. R. Evid. 513(a), (b).

4. Any attempt to elicit testimony from {⓲ *party*} about communications with {⓳ *his/her/its*} attorneys. Such communications are privileged. Tex. R. Evid. 503.

5. Any attempt in the presence of the jury to ask {⓴ *party*}'s attorneys to produce documents, stipulate to any fact, or make any agreement.

6. Any testimony by {㉑ *adverse party*}'s expert about {㉒ *his/her*} discussions with another expert. *See* Tex. R. Evid. 801, 802; *Birchfield v. Texarkana Mem'l Hosp.*, 747 S.W.2d 361, 365 (Tex. 1987).

7. Any evidence that {㉓ *party*}'s expert was represented by {㉔ *party*}'s counsel in a past lawsuit. Such evidence is not admissible for impeachment purposes. *Stam v. Mack*, 984 S.W.2d 747, 751 (Tex. App.—Texarkana 1999, no pet.).

8. Any mention that {㉕ *party*} is an atheist. Evidence of a witness's religious beliefs is not admissible to enhance or impair credibility. Tex. R. Evid. 610.

9. Any mention that any party or witness goes to church every Sunday and tithes or does not go to church or does not tithe. Evidence of a witness's religious beliefs is not admissible to enhance or impair credibility. Tex. R. Evid. 610.

10. Any mention that {㉖ *party*} often {㉗ *describe conduct*}. Even though evidence of a habit may be admissible to prove that a party's conduct on a particular occasion conformed with the habit or routine practice, evidence of past conduct that does not rise to the level of habit is inadmissible. *See* Tex. R. Evid. 406, 608(b); *Magro v. Ragsdale Bros.*, 721 S.W.2d 832, 834 (Tex. 1986).

11. Any mention that {㉘ *party*} drinks or spends excessively on the purchase of alcoholic beverages. Intoxication is not an issue in this trial, and this evidence would unduly prejudice the jury against {㉙ *party*}. *See McCarty v. Gappelberg*, 273 S.W.2d 943, 947-48 (Tex. App.—Fort Worth 1954, writ ref'd n.r.e.).

12. Any mention that {㉚ *party*} received a dishonorable discharge from the military.

13. Any mention that {㉛ *party*} has not filed income-tax returns. *See Wilkins v. Royal Indem. Co.*, 592 S.W.2d 64, 67-68 (Tex. App.—Tyler 1979, no writ).

14. Any mention that any party or witness is rich or poor, which is irrelevant and prejudicial. *See Wilmoth v. Limestone Prods. Co.*, 255 S.W.2d 532, 534 (Tex. App.—Waco 1953, writ ref'd n.r.e.).

15. Any mention of the value of {㉜ *party*}'s assets, which can be an indicator of wealth; such evidence is irrelevant and prejudicial. *See First Nat'l Bank v. Beavers*, 619 S.W.2d 288, 289-90 (Tex. App.—Texarkana 1981, writ ref'd n.r.e.).

16. Any mention that {㉝ *party*} {㉞ *did not receive/received/paid*} a traffic ticket. *See Isaacs v. Plains Transp. Co.*, 367 S.W.2d 152, 153 (Tex. 1963); *Condra Funeral Home v. Rollin*, 314 S.W.2d 277, 282 (Tex. 1958).

Continued on next page

17. Any mention that {❸❺ *party*} was convicted of misdemeanor DWI. Evidence of criminal convictions is admissible for impeachment only if the crime was a felony or involved moral turpitude and the court rules that the probative value outweighs the prejudicial effect. Tex. R. Evid. 609(a); *see Theus v. State*, 845 S.W.2d 874, 879-81 (Tex. Crim. App. 1992); *Ortiz v. Furr's Supermarkets*, 26 S.W.3d 646, 655 (Tex. App.—El Paso 2000, no pet.). A conviction for misdemeanor DWI does not involve moral turpitude. *Shipman v. State*, 604 S.W.2d 182, 184 (Tex. Crim. App. 1980).

18. Any mention of a statement made by {❸❻ *party*} during plea negotiations that did not result in a guilty plea, or resulted in a guilty plea that was later withdrawn. Tex. R. Evid. 410(a)(4).

19. Any mention that {❸❼ *adverse party*} received a Purple Heart from the military.

20. Any mention that {❸❽ *party*}'s witness is a resident alien and is about to be deported. *See Plyler v. Doe*, 457 U.S. 202, 215 (1982) (illegal aliens are covered by the 14th Amendment and must be treated equally with citizens).

21. Any mention, by reference to title or otherwise, that the witness, {❸❾ *name*}, who will be called by {❹⓿ *adverse party*}, {❹❶ *is/was*} a judge. The jury should not be influenced by {❹❷ *name*}'s {❹❸ *present/former*} status as a judge, which would increase the probative value of {❹❹ *name*}'s testimony and unfairly prejudice the jury in {❹❺ *adverse party*}'s favor. *See Weiss v. Comm'n for Lawyer Discipline*, 981 S.W.2d 8, 22 (Tex. App.—San Antonio 1998, pet. denied).

22. Any mention of the probable testimony of a witness who is absent, unavailable, or not called or allowed to testify in this case.

23. Any testimony in violation of the Dead Man's Rule. Tex. R. Evid. 601(b).

24. Any comment by {❹❻ *adverse party*}'s attorney that informs the jury of the effect of its answers to the questions in the charge. *See Magic Chef, Inc. v. Sibley*, 546 S.W.2d 851, 857 (Tex. App.—San Antonio 1977, writ ref'd n.r.e.).

25. Before the Court rules on the law applicable to this case, any statement of the law other than that regarding the burden of proof and the basic legal definitions that counsel believes to be applicable.

26. Any mention of the letter from {❹❼ *adverse party*}'s attorneys advising that {❹❽ *party*}'s claim was a certain {❹❾ *winner/loser*}. *See Beacon Nat'l Ins. Co. v. Reynolds*, 799 S.W.2d 390, 397 (Tex. App.—Fort Worth 1990, writ denied). Self-serving evidence generated by a party is inadmissible.

27. Any mention of a regulatory measure, which is not admissible without a showing of both its application to the situation in question and a clear violation of the regulation. *See Mottu v. Navistar Int'l Transp. Corp.*, 804 S.W.2d 144, 146-47 (Tex. App.—Houston [14th Dist.] 1990, writ denied).

28. Any mention that the parties engaged in settlement negotiations. *See* Tex. R. Evid. 408(a)(1); *Birchfield v. Texarkana Mem'l Hosp.*, 747 S.W.2d 361, 365 (Tex. 1987).

29. Any mention of any statement made by {➉ *party*} during settlement negotiations. Tex. R. Evid. 408(a)(2); *see Ochs v. Martinez*, 789 S.W.2d 949, 959-60 (Tex. App.—San Antonio 1990, writ denied).

30. Any mention that {51 *party*} {52 *is/was*} involved in other suits. *See Birchfield v. Texarkana Mem'l Hosp.*, 747 S.W.2d 361, 365 (Tex. 1987).

31. Any comment that an award of damages will affect insurance premiums, the price of any goods or services, or the level of taxation.

32. Any comment that the jurors should put themselves in the position of {53 *adverse party*}. *MAPCO, Inc. v. Farrington*, 476 S.W.2d 50, 53-54 (Tex. App.—Amarillo 1971, writ ref'd n.r.e.).

33. Any comment from {54 *adverse party*}'s attorney regarding {55 *his/her*} personal opinion about the credibility of any witness. *See Menefee v. State*, 614 S.W.2d 167, 168 (Tex. Crim. App. 1981).

{*Grounds for plaintiff*}

34. Any attempt to elicit testimony or introduce records from plaintiff's {56 *physician/psychologist*} concerning plaintiff's mental or emotional health. Such communications are privileged because plaintiff's mental and emotional health do not relate in a significant way to {57 *his/her*} claim. *See* Tex. R. Evid. 509, 510; *R.K. v. Ramirez*, 887 S.W.2d 836, 842-43 (Tex. 1994).

35. Any testimony or argument suggesting that plaintiff's attorney has a contingency fee in the suit. *See Azar Nut Co. v. Caille*, 720 S.W.2d 685, 688 (Tex. App.—El Paso 1986), *aff'd*, 734 S.W.2d 667 (Tex. 1987).

36. Any photographs of plaintiff exercising strenuously after the accident, which were obtained by defendant's investigator in violation of Texas Disciplinary Rule of Professional Conduct 4.02. *See Barham v. Turner Constr. Co.*, 803 S.W.2d 731, 739 (Tex. App.—Dallas 1990, writ denied). Plaintiff contends that defendant's attorney in-

◄ Continued on next page ►

structed {58 *his/her*} investigator, in violation of the Texas Disciplinary Rules of Professional Conduct, to contact plaintiff, befriend {59 *him/her*}, and invite {60 *him/her*} to exercise strenuously. If the Court overrules this matter, plaintiff asks for the opportunity to make a record on this issue and examine defendant's attorney and {61 *his/her/its*} investigator.

37. Any mention that plaintiff received benefits under the provisions of {62 *his/her*} uninsured-motorist policy. *See Allen v. Avery*, 537 S.W.2d 789, 791 (Tex. App.—Texarkana 1976, no writ).

38. Any mention that plaintiff received health, accident, or disability insurance. *See Lee-Wright, Inc. v. Hall*, 840 S.W.2d 572, 581-82 (Tex. App.—Houston [1st Dist.] 1992, no writ).

39. Any mention that plaintiff received retirement benefits. *See Azar Nut Co. v. Caille*, 720 S.W.2d 685, 688 (Tex. App.—El Paso 1986), *aff'd*, 734 S.W.2d 667 (Tex. 1987).

40. Any mention that plaintiff received unemployment benefits. *See Century Papers, Inc. v. Perrino*, 551 S.W.2d 507, 511 (Tex. App.—Texarkana 1977, writ ref'd n.r.e.).

41. Any mention that plaintiff received Social Security disability payments. *See Traders & Gen. Ins. Co. v. Reed*, 376 S.W.2d 591, 593 (Tex. App.—Corpus Christi 1964, writ ref'd n.r.e.).

42. Any mention that plaintiff received veteran's benefits. *See Montandon v. Colehour*, 469 S.W.2d 222, 229-30 (Tex. App.—Fort Worth 1971, no writ).

43. Any mention that plaintiff received free medical care. *See City of Fort Worth v. Barlow*, 313 S.W.2d 906, 911 (Tex. App.—Fort Worth 1958, writ ref'd n.r.e.).

44. Any mention that plaintiff received contributions from family, friends, or {63 *his/her*} employer.

45. Any mention that plaintiff received benefits from sick leave or vacation time.

46. Any mention that plaintiff, the surviving spouse in a death case, {64 *had an extramarital relationship/is married under the common law/is engaged to be married*}. Tex. Civ. Prac. & Rem. Code §71.005; *see Exxon Corp. v. Brecheen*, 526 S.W.2d 519, 525 (Tex. 1975).

47. Any mention of the financial consequences of plaintiff's remarriage. *See Richardson v. Holmes*, 525 S.W.2d 293, 299 (Tex. App.—Beaumont 1975, writ ref'd n.r.e.).

48. Any mention that plaintiff's recovery will not be subject to taxation. *See Turner v. Gen. Motors Corp.*, 584 S.W.2d 844, 853 (Tex. 1979).

49. Any testimony or argument suggesting that plaintiff {65 *should have pursued/did not pursue*} any remedy authorized by the Texas Workers' Compensation Act. *See Brown v. Hopkins*, 921 S.W.2d 306, 318 (Tex. App.—Corpus Christi 1996, no writ).

50. Any reference to collateral sources, including group health-insurance benefits. *See Kendrix v. S. Pac. Transp. Co.*, 907 S.W.2d 111, 112 (Tex. App.—Beaumont 1995, writ denied); *Dove v. Dir., State Emps. Workers' Comp. Div.*, 857 S.W.2d 577, 578-79 (Tex. App.—Houston [1st Dist.] 1993, writ denied).

51. Any mention of plaintiff's claim against {66 *name*}. Evidence of another claim to show that plaintiff is a "professional litigant" is improper. *See Emp'rs Cas. Co. v. Peterson*, 609 S.W.2d 579, 585 (Tex. App.—Dallas 1980, no writ).

52. Any mention that an insurance company owns a portion of plaintiff's claim.

53. Any testimony or evidence regarding injuries plaintiff suffered before the injuries that are the subject of this suit. *See McClintock v. Travelers Ins. Co.*, 393 S.W.2d 421, 424 (Tex. App.—Amarillo 1965, writ ref'd n.r.e.).

{*Grounds for defendant*}

54. Any reference to minutes of a hospital section meeting, which are privileged under Texas Health & Safety Code sections 161.031-161.033. *See Birchfield v. Texarkana Mem'l Hosp.*, 747 S.W.2d 361, 365-66 (Tex. 1987).

55. Any comment that attempts to impose liability on or create prejudice against defendant simply because it is a corporation.

56. Any comment or reference to defendant corporation as "foreign" or "alien" or any similar comment that may draw on the jury's prejudices toward defendant corporation's home country. Such evidence is irrelevant, and its probative value is substantially outweighed by the danger of unfair prejudice.

57. Any comment to the jury that the Court can reduce the amount of the jury's award.

Continued on next page

58. Any comment regarding who pays the damages, or whether defendant will pay the damages.

59. Any mention that defendant is or is not covered by liability insurance on issues of fault. Tex. R. Evid. 411; *see Rojas v. Vuocolo*, 177 S.W.2d 962, 964 (Tex. 1944); *Atchison, Topeka & Santa Fe Ry. v. Acosta*, 435 S.W.2d 539, 549 (Tex. App.—Houston [1st Dist.] 1968, writ ref'd n.r.e.). Referring to a witness as an "adjuster" introduces insurance into the case. *See Acosta*, 435 S.W.2d at 549.

60. Any mention that plaintiff's collateral compensation was reduced. For example, the loss of Social Security benefits by a widow and child is not admissible as evidence that they are entitled to a larger damages award. *See McLemore v. Broussard*, 670 S.W.2d 301, 303 (Tex. App.—Houston [1st Dist.] 1983, no writ).

61. Any mention of postaccident changes. Evidence of postaccident changes is not admissible to prove negligence, culpable conduct, a defect in a product or its design, or a need for a warning or instruction. Tex. R. Evid. 407(a).

62. Any comment on or reference to other criminal activity that took place at defendant's other {67 *identify premises, e.g., apartment buildings, stores*}. Merely because crimes have occurred at {68 *identify premises, e.g., an apartment building, a store*} in a high-crime area does not make it more likely that crimes will occur at another {69 *identify premises, e.g., apartment building, store*} in another area. For a risk to be foreseeable, there must be evidence of criminal activity within the specific area at issue, either in close proximity to or on the landowner's property. *Timberwalk Apartments, Partners, Inc. v. Cain*, 972 S.W.2d 749, 757 (Tex. 1998). The factors of proximity, recency, frequency, similarity, and publicity must be considered in determining whether criminal conduct was foreseeable. *Id.* at 759. These factors are not present in this case.

63. Any comment on or reference to unreported criminal activity at defendant's other {70 *identify premises, e.g., apartment buildings, stores*}. *See Timberwalk Apartments, Partners, Inc. v. Cain*, 972 S.W.2d 749, 758-59 (Tex. 1998). Unreported criminal activity on the premises is not evidence of foreseeability. Previous similar incidents cannot make future crime foreseeable if no one knew or should have known that those incidents occurred. *Id.* at 759.

64. Any mention that defendant paid or made offers to pay any of plaintiff's medical expenses. Tex. R. Evid. 409; *see* Tex. R. Evid. 408(a).

PRAYER

65. For these reasons, {71 *party*} asks the Court to instruct {72 *adverse party*} and {73 *his/her/its*} counsel and witnesses not to mention, refer to, interrogate about, or attempt to convey to the jury in any manner, either directly or indirectly, any of the matters listed above without first obtaining a ruling from the Court outside the presence and hearing of the jury.

SEE: Tex. R. Civ. P. 166(g)
Tex. R. Evid. 103(a)(1), (b), 401-610
O'Connor's Texas Rules * Civil Trials (2019), "Motion in Limine," ch. 5-E, p. 429

ADD: STYLE OF THE CASE – FORM 1B:2
SIGNATURE BLOCK – FORM 1B:3
CERTIFICATE OF SERVICE – FORM 1B:13

ATTACH: NOTICE OF HEARING OR SUBMISSION – FORM 1E:1
ORDER – FORM 5E:2

ORDER IN LIMINE

After considering {❶ *party*} {❷ *name*}'s motion in limine, the Court orders {❸ *adverse party*}, {❹ *name*}, counsel for {❺ *adverse party*}, and all witnesses called on behalf of {❻ *adverse party*} to refrain from any mention or interrogation, directly or indirectly, including offering documentary evidence, about any of the following matters without first requesting and obtaining a ruling from the Court outside the presence and hearing of all prospective and impaneled jurors:

{*CHOOSE APPROPRIATE PARAGRAPHS FROM FORM 5E:1, FOR EXAMPLE*}

1. Any mention that {❼ *party*} has not filed income-tax returns.

________ AGREED	________ GRANTED	________ DENIED

2. Any mention that {❽ *adverse party*} goes to church every Sunday and tithes.

________ AGREED	________ GRANTED	________ DENIED

{*Repeat other paragraphs from FORM 5E:1 as needed.*}

SIGNED on _______________, 20___.

____
PRESIDING JUDGE

SEE: Tex. R. Civ. P. 166(g)
Tex. R. Evid. 103(a)(1), (b), 401-610
O'Connor's Texas Rules * Civil Trials (2019), "Motion in Limine," ch. 5-E, p. 429

ADD: STYLE OF THE CASE – FORM 1B:2
CERTIFICATE OF SERVICE – FORM 1B:13, if proposed order served separately from motion or response

{[1] *PARTY*}'S MOTION FOR LEAVE TO FILE AMENDED PLEADING

{[2] *Party*}, {[3] *name*}, asks the Court for leave to file the attached {[4] *identify amended pleading*}. {*See **O'Connor's Texas Rules**, "Motion for Leave to Amend Pleadings Before Trial," ch. 5-F, §4, p. 434.*}

INTRODUCTION

1. Plaintiff, {[5] *name*}, sued defendant, {[6] *name*}, for {[7] *state basis of suit*}.

2. {[8] *State other relevant facts about the suit.*}

BACKGROUND

3. On {[9] *date*}, {[10] *party*} filed {[11] *his/her/its*} {[12] *identify last live pleading, e.g., Second Amended Petition*}.

4. {[13] *Party*} now seeks leave to file {[14] *identify amended pleading, e.g., Third Amended Petition*}. {[15] *Party*} files the amended pleading simultaneously with this motion.

{*CHOOSE APPROPRIATE PARAGRAPHS 5-8*}

5. The purpose of {[16] *party*}'s amendment is to correct a procedural defect in the pleadings. Specifically, the amended pleading corrects {[17] *describe correction of procedural defect*}. {*See **O'Connor's Texas Rules**, "Procedural change," ch. 5-F, §3.2.3(1), p. 433.*}

6. The purpose of {[18] *party*}'s amendment is to correct a substantive defect in the pleadings by {[19] *adding/deleting*} allegations that {[20] *explain the allegations*}.

7. The purpose of {[21] *party*}'s amendment is to add a new {[22] *claim/defense*} of {[23] *identify claim or defense*}.

8. The purpose of {[24] *party*}'s amendment is to {[25] *state other purpose, e.g., join a new party*}.

9. This case is set for trial on {[26] *date*}.

10. {[27] *State other facts relevant to the motion.*}

ARGUMENT & AUTHORITIES

11. A court should grant leave to amend a pleading after the filing deadline unless (1) the opposing party presents evidence of surprise, (2) the opposing party establishes the amendment is prejudicial on its face, or (3) the amendment removes the suit from the expedited-actions process in Texas Rule of Civil Procedure 169 and the party pre-

Continued on next page

senting the amendment does not show that good cause for filing the amendment outweighs any prejudice to the opposing party. *See* Tex. R. Civ. P. 63, 169(c)(2); *see also Greenhalgh v. Serv. Lloyds Ins. Co.*, 787 S.W.2d 938, 939 (Tex. 1990) (burden to show surprise or prejudice is on party opposing amendment).

A. {㉘ *Adverse party*} cannot show surprise.

12. No court has defined "surprise" for purposes of Rule 63, but courts have considered certain factors when determining whether a party opposing an amendment was surprised. To establish surprise, the opposing party should address these factors, which include (1) how long the suit has been pending before the amendment was filed, (2) how soon before trial the amendment was made, and (3) whether the amendment presents a new claim. *Dunnagan v. Watson*, 204 S.W.3d 30, 38 (Tex. App.—Fort Worth 2006, pet. denied); *see Stevenson v. Koutzarov*, 795 S.W.2d 313, 321 (Tex. App.—Houston [1st Dist.] 1990, writ denied). If the amendment presents a new claim, the opposing party should also address whether the claim is based on recently discovered matters and indicate whether the opposing party is prepared to try the new claim. *See Dunnagan*, 204 S.W.3d at 38; *Stevenson*, 795 S.W.2d at 321.

13. The Court should grant leave to file the amended pleading because {㉙ *adverse party*} cannot claim to be surprised by the amendment. {㉚ *Elaborate and show how the amendment was made as soon as possible.*}

B. {㉛ *Adverse party*} cannot show prejudice.

14. To establish prejudice on the face of an amendment, the opposing party should show that the amendment (1) asserts a new substantive matter that reshapes the nature of the suit, (2) could not have been anticipated by the opposing party, and (3) will detrimentally affect the opposing party's ability to present its case. *Hardin v. Hardin*, 597 S.W.2d 347, 349-50 (Tex. 1980); *Halmos v. Bombardier Aerospace Corp.*, 314 S.W.3d 606, 623 (Tex. App.—Dallas 2010, no pet.). {*See* ***O'Connor's Texas Rules****, "Prejudice," ch. 5-F, §5.2.2, p. 435.*}

15. The Court should grant leave to file the amended pleading because {㉜ *adverse party*} cannot claim to be prejudiced by the amendment. {㉝ *Elaborate.*}

{*CHOOSE APPROPRIATE SECTION C*}

C. Suit is not an expedited action.

16. The Court should grant leave to file the amended pleading because this suit is not an expedited action under Texas Rule of Civil Procedure 169. {㉞ *Elaborate.*}

C. {㉟ *Party*}'s proposed amendment will not remove suit from expedited-actions process.

16. The Court should grant leave to file the amended pleading because the amendment will not remove the suit from the expedited-actions process in Texas Rule of Civil Procedure 169. {㊱ *Elaborate.*}

C. Good cause for amendment outweighs any possible prejudice.

16. Although the amended pleading will remove the suit from the expedited-actions process in Texas Rule of Civil Procedure 169, the Court should grant leave to file the amended pleading because good cause for the amendment outweighs any prejudice to {㊲ *adverse party*}. {㊳ *Elaborate.*}

CONCLUSION

17. {㊴ *Briefly summarize the motion.*}

PRAYER

18. For these reasons, {㊵ *party*} asks the Court to grant leave to file the amended pleading.

SEE: Tex. R. Civ. P. 62-65, 70, 166(b), 169, 190.2 (pre-March 1, 2013, version)
O'Connor's Texas Rules * Civil Trials (2019), "Motion to Amend Pleadings—Pretrial," ch. 5-F, p. 432

ADD: STYLE OF THE CASE – FORM 1B:2
SIGNATURE BLOCK – FORM 1B:3
CERTIFICATE OF SERVICE – FORM 1B:13

ATTACH: AFFIDAVIT – FORM 1B:8, if necessary
NOTICE OF HEARING OR SUBMISSION – FORM 1E:1
ORDER – FORM 1G:1
Amended pleading

NOTE: A court's permission to file an amended pleading is required only when (1) the pleading is filed less than seven days before trial, (2) the pleading is filed after a deadline in a pretrial order, or (3) the amendment removes the suit from the expedited-actions process in Texas Rule of Civil Procedure 169 and is filed more than 30 days after the discovery period closed or less than 30 days before trial, whichever is earlier. *See* Tex. R. Civ. P. 63, 169(c)(2); ***Chapin & Chapin, Inc. v. Texas Sand & Gravel Co.***, 844 S.W.2d 664, 665 (Tex.1992); ***Hart v. Moore***, 952 S.W.2d 90, 95 (Tex.App.—Amarillo 1997, pet. denied). See ***O'Connor's Texas Rules***, "Leave to amend required," ch. 5-F, §3.2, p. 433.

Any claimant, other than a counterclaimant, can file an amended pleading that removes a suit from the expedited-actions process in Texas Rule of Civil Procedure 169. *See* Tex. R. Civ. P. 169(c)(1)(B). See ***O'Connor's Texas Rules***, "Removal by pleading," ch. 2-C, §3.2, p. 135.

{❶ *PARTY*}'S RESPONSE TO {❷ *ADVERSE PARTY*}'S MOTION FOR LEAVE TO FILE AMENDED PLEADING

{❸ *Party*}, {❹ *name*}, asks the Court to deny {❺ *adverse party*} {❻ *name*}'s motion for leave to file {❼ *his/her/its*} {❽ *identify amended pleading*}. {*See* ***O'Connor's Texas Rules****, "Response to Motion for Pretrial Amendment," ch. 5-F, §5, p. 434.*}

INTRODUCTION

1. Plaintiff, {❾ *name*}, sued defendant, {❿ *name*}, for {⓫ *state basis of suit*}.

2. {⓬ *State other relevant facts about the suit.*}

BACKGROUND

3. On {⓭ *date*}, {⓮ *adverse party*} filed {⓯ *his/her/its*} {⓰ *identify last live pleading, e.g., Second Amended Petition*}.

4. On {⓱ *date*}, {⓲ *adverse party*} sought leave to file {⓳ *his/her/its*} {⓴ *identify amended pleading, e.g., Third Amended Petition*}, which {㉑ *describe nature of amendment, e.g., adds a new claim for fraud*}.

5. {㉒ *State other facts relevant to the response.*}

ARGUMENT & AUTHORITIES

{*CHOOSE APPROPRIATE PARAGRAPHS 6-7*}

6. The court may deny a motion for leave to file a late amendment to a pleading when the party opposing the motion shows that (1) it was surprised by the amendment or (2) the amendment is prejudicial on its face. *See* Tex. R. Civ. P. 63; *see also Greenhalgh v. Serv. Lloyds Ins. Co.*, 787 S.W.2d 938, 939 (Tex. 1990) (burden to show surprise or prejudice is on party opposing amendment).

7. The court may deny a motion for leave to file a late amendment to a pleading when the amendment removes the suit from the expedited-actions process in Texas Rule of Civil Procedure 169 and the party presenting the amendment does not show that good cause for filing the amendment outweighs any prejudice to the opposing party. Tex. R. Civ. P. 169(c)(2).

{*CHOOSE APPROPRIATE SECTIONS A-C*}

A. {23 *Party*} was surprised by amendment.

8. To determine whether a party has been "surprised" by a late amendment, courts have considered certain factors, such as (1) how long the suit has been pending before the amendment was filed, (2) how soon before trial the amendment was made, and (3) whether the amendment presents a new claim. *Dunnagan v. Watson*, 204 S.W.3d 30, 38 (Tex. App.—Fort Worth 2006, pet. denied); *Stevenson v. Koutzarov*, 795 S.W.2d 313, 321 (Tex. App.—Houston [1st Dist.] 1990, writ denied); *see Taiwan Shrimp Farm Vill. Ass'n v. U.S.A. Shrimp Farm Dev., Inc.*, 915 S.W.2d 61, 70 (Tex. App.—Corpus Christi 1996, writ denied); *AmSav Grp., Inc. v. Am. Sav. & Loan Ass'n*, 796 S.W.2d 482, 490 (Tex. App.—Houston [14th Dist.] 1990, writ denied). When an amendment presents a new claim, courts have also considered whether the claim is based on recently discovered matters and whether the party opposing the motion is prepared to try the new claim. *See Dunnagan*, 204 S.W.3d at 38; *Stevenson*, 795 S.W.2d at 321.

9. The Court should deny leave to file the amended pleading because the amendment is a surprise to {24 *party*}. {25 *Elaborate, and if possible, show how adverse party was not diligent in trying to make the amendment.*}

B. {26 *Party*} was prejudiced by amendment.

10. To determine whether a party has been "prejudiced" by a late amendment, courts consider whether the amendment (1) asserts a new substantive matter that reshapes the nature of the suit, (2) could not have been anticipated by the opposing party, and (3) will detrimentally affect the opposing party's ability to present its case. *Hardin v. Hardin*, 597 S.W.2d 347, 349-50 (Tex. 1980); *Halmos v. Bombardier Aerospace Corp.*, 314 S.W.3d 606, 623 (Tex. App.—Dallas 2010, no pet.). {*See* ***O'Connor's Texas Rules***, *"Prejudice," ch. 5-F, §5.2.2, p. 435.*}

11. The Court should deny leave to file the amended pleading because the amendment is prejudicial on its face. {27 *Elaborate.*}

C. {28 *Party*} will be prejudiced by removal of the suit from the expedited-actions process.

12. {29 *Adverse party*}'s amendment will remove the suit from the expedited-actions process in Texas Rule of Civil Procedure 169.

Continued on next page

13. The Court should deny {㉚ *adverse party*}'s motion for leave to file an amended pleading because there is no good cause for the amendment, and even if there were, the good cause would not outweigh the prejudice to {㉛ *party*}. Tex. R. Civ. P. 169(c)(2). {㉜ *Elaborate.*}

CONCLUSION

14. {㉝ *Briefly summarize the response.*}

PRAYER

15. For these reasons, {㉞ *party*} asks the Court to deny {㉟ *adverse party*}'s motion for leave to file {㊱ *identify amended pleading*}.

SEE: Tex. R. Civ. P. 62-65, 70, 166(b), 169, 190.2 (pre-March 1, 2013, version)
O'Connor's Texas Rules * Civil Trials (2019), "Motion to Amend Pleadings—Pretrial," ch. 5-F, p. 432

ADD: STYLE OF THE CASE – FORM 1B:2
SIGNATURE BLOCK – FORM 1B:3
CERTIFICATE OF SERVICE – FORM 1B:13

ATTACH: AFFIDAVIT – FORM 1B:8, if necessary
ORDER – FORM 1G:1
Amended pleading

NOTE: Any claimant, other than a counterclaimant, can file an amended pleading that removes a suit from the expedited-actions process in Texas Rule of Civil Procedure 169. *See* Tex. R. Civ. P. 169(c)(1)(B). See ***O'Connor's Texas Rules***, "Removal by pleading," ch. 2-C, §3.2, p. 135.

A response to a motion for leave to file an amended pleading is used to object to an amended pleading before it is filed. A motion to strike an amended pleading is used to object to an amended pleading that was filed without leave of court. *See, e.g.*, ***Stevenson v. Koutzarov***, 795 S.W.2d 313, 321 (Tex.App.—Houston [1st Dist.] 1990, writ denied) (motion to strike timely filed amended petition); ***Singleton v. Northwest Tex. Healthcare Sys.***, No. 07-03-0552-CV (Tex.App.—Amarillo 2006, no pet.) (memo op.; 2-28-06) (motion to strike untimely amended petition filed without leave of court). The response should contain the same allegations as the motion to strike. See FORM 5F:3.

Although Texas Rule of Civil Procedure 63 does not require a showing of lack of diligence of the party offering the amendment, some courts of appeals require it. However, lack of diligence has never been recognized by the Supreme Court as a factor in pretrial amendments, and one court of appeals has specifically held that it is not a proper factor. See ***O'Connor's Texas Rules***, "Practice Tip," ch. 5-F, §5.2, p. 434.

{❶ *PARTY*}'S MOTION TO STRIKE
{❷ *ADVERSE PARTY*}'S AMENDED PLEADING

{❸ *Party*}, {❹ *name*}, asks the Court to strike {❺ *adverse party*} {❻ *name*}'s {❼ *identify amended pleading*}. {*See **O'Connor's Texas Rules**, "Response to Motion for Pretrial Amendment," ch. 5-F, §5, p. 434.*}

INTRODUCTION

1. Plaintiff, {❽ *name*}, sued defendant, {❾ *name*}, for {❿ *state basis of suit*}.
2. {⓫ *State other relevant facts about the suit.*}

BACKGROUND

3. On {⓬ *date*}, {⓭ *adverse party*} filed {⓮ *his/her/its*} {⓯ *identify amended pleading*}.

{*CHOOSE APPROPRIATE PARAGRAPH 4 IF APPLICABLE*}

{*Less than seven days before trial*}

4. This case is set for trial on {⓰ *date*}. The amended pleading was filed less than seven days before the date set for trial.

{*After deadline in pretrial order*}

4. The pretrial order in this case required the parties to file all amended pleadings by {⓱ *date*}. The amended pleading was filed after that date.

{*After deadline for expedited action*}

4. {⓲ *The discovery period for this case closed/This case is set for trial*} on {⓳ *date*}. The amended pleading was filed {⓴ *choose whichever is earlier: more than 30 days after the discovery period closed/less than 30 days before trial*}.

5. {㉑ *State other facts relevant to the motion.*}

ARGUMENT & AUTHORITIES

{*ADD PARAGRAPH 6 IF AMENDMENT UNTIMELY*}

6. A court's permission to file an amended pleading is required when (1) the pleading is filed less than seven days before trial, (2) the pleading is filed after a deadline in a pretrial order, or (3) the amendment removes the suit from the expedited-actions process in Texas Rule of Civil Procedure 169 and is filed more than 30 days after the discovery period closed or less than 30 days before trial, whichever is earlier. *See* Tex. R.

Continued on next page

Civ. P. 63, 169(c)(2); *Chapin & Chapin, Inc. v. Tex. Sand & Gravel Co.*, 844 S.W.2d 664, 665 (Tex. 1992); *Hart v. Moore*, 952 S.W.2d 90, 95 (Tex. App.—Amarillo 1997, pet. denied). {*See* ***O'Connor's Texas Rules****, "Leave to amend required," ch. 5-F, §3.2, p. 433.*}

{*CHOOSE APPROPRIATE PARAGRAPHS 7-8*}

7. A court may strike {❷❷ *an amended pleading/a late amended pleading*} when the party opposing the amendment shows that (1) it was surprised by the amendment or (2) the amendment is prejudicial on its face. *See* Tex. R. Civ. P. 63; *see also Greenhalgh v. Serv. Lloyds Ins. Co.*, 787 S.W.2d 938, 939 (Tex. 1990) (burden to show surprise or prejudice is on party opposing amendment). {*See* ***O'Connor's Texas Rules****, "Leave to amend required," ch. 5-F, §3.2, p. 433.*}

8. The court may strike a late amended pleading when the amendment removes the suit from the expedited-actions process in Texas Rule of Civil Procedure 169 and the party presenting the amendment does not show that good cause for filing the amendment outweighs any prejudice to the opposing party. *See* Tex. R. Civ. P. 169(c)(2). {*See* ***O'Connor's Texas Rules****, "After deadline for expedited actions," ch. 5-F, §3.2.2, p. 433.*}

{*ADD SECTION A IF APPLICABLE*}

A. Leave of court was not obtained.

9. The Court should strike the amended pleading because {❷❸ *adverse party*} did not obtain leave to file a late amended pleading and {❷❹ *party*} can show that {❷❺ *he/she/it*} was surprised or prejudiced by the late amendment. *See* Tex. R. Civ. P. 63, 169(c)(2); *Goswami v. Metro. Sav. & Loan Ass'n*, 751 S.W.2d 487, 490 (Tex. 1988).

{*CHOOSE APPROPRIATE SECTIONS B-D*}

B. {❷❻ *Party*} was surprised by amendment.

10. To determine whether a party has been "surprised" by an amendment, courts have considered certain factors, such as (1) how long the suit has been pending before the amendment was filed, (2) how soon before trial the amendment was made, and (3) whether the amendment presents a new claim. *Dunnagan v. Watson*, 204 S.W.3d 30, 38 (Tex. App.—Fort Worth 2006, pet. denied); *Stevenson v. Koutzarov*, 795 S.W.2d 313, 321 (Tex. App.—Houston [1st Dist.] 1990, writ denied); *see Taiwan Shrimp Farm Vill. Ass'n v. U.S.A. Shrimp Farm Dev., Inc.*, 915 S.W.2d 61, 70 (Tex. App.—Corpus Christi 1996, writ denied); *AmSav Grp., Inc. v. Am. Sav. & Loan Ass'n*, 796 S.W.2d 482, 490

(Tex. App.—Houston [14th Dist.] 1990, writ denied). When an amendment adds a new claim, courts have also considered whether the claim is based on recently discovered matters and whether the party opposing the motion is prepared to try the new claim. *See Dunnagan*, 204 S.W.3d at 38; *Stevenson*, 795 S.W.2d at 321.

11. The Court should strike the amended pleading because the amendment is a surprise to {㉗ *party*}. {㉘ *Elaborate, and if possible, show how adverse party was not diligent in trying to make the amendment.*}

C. {㉙ *Party*} was prejudiced by amendment.

12. To determine whether a party has been "prejudiced" by an amendment, courts consider whether the amendment (1) asserts a new substantive matter that reshapes the nature of the suit, (2) could not have been anticipated by the opposing party, and (3) will detrimentally affect the opposing party's ability to present its case. *Hardin v. Hardin*, 597 S.W.2d 347, 349-50 (Tex. 1980); *Halmos v. Bombardier Aerospace Corp.*, 314 S.W.3d 606, 623 (Tex. App.—Dallas 2010, no pet.). {*See* ***O'Connor's Texas Rules****, "Prejudice," ch. 5-F, §5.2.2, p. 435.*}

13. The Court should strike the amended pleading because the amendment is prejudicial on its face. {㉚ *Elaborate.*}

D. {㉛ *Party*} will be prejudiced by removal of the suit from the expedited-actions process.

14. {㉜ *Adverse party*}'s amendment will remove the suit from the expedited-actions process in Texas Rule of Civil Procedure 169.

15. The Court should strike the amended pleading because {㉝ *adverse party*} did not obtain leave to file a late amended pleading and there is no good cause for the amendment; even if there were good cause, it would not outweigh the prejudice to {㉞ *party*}. *See* Tex. R. Civ. P. 169(c)(2). {㉟ *Elaborate.*}

CONTINUANCE

{*CHOOSE APPROPRIATE PARAGRAPH 16*}

16. In the alternative, if the Court denies {㊱ *party*}'s motion to strike, {㊲ *party*} files a motion for continuance and asks that the Court assess costs related to the continuance against {㊳ *adverse party*}. In the motion for continuance, {㊴ *party*} describes the additional discovery needed to respond to the amended pleadings. {*See FORM 5D:1;* ***O'Connor's Texas Rules****, "Motion for continuance," ch. 5-F, §6.2.3, p. 435.*}

Continued on next page

16. In the alternative, if the Court denies {40 *party*}'s motion to strike, {41 *party*} asks the Court to continue the trial date until {42 *date*} to allow {43 *party*} additional time to complete discovery because the discovery-control plan has changed from Level 1 to Level {44 *2/3*}. *See* Tex. R. Civ. P. 190.2(c).

{ADD PARAGRAPH 17 IF APPLICABLE}

REOPEN DISCOVERY PERIOD

17. In the alternative, if the Court denies {45 *party*}'s motion to strike, {46 *party*} files a motion to reopen the discovery period. In the motion, {47 *party*} describes the reasons why the discovery period should be reopened. {*See FORM 6A:8; **O'Connor's Texas Rules**, "Period reopens," ch. 6-A, §8.1.1(2), p. 524.*}

CONCLUSION

18. {48 *Briefly summarize the motion.*}

PRAYER

19. For these reasons, {49 *party*} asks the Court to strike {50 *identify amended pleading*}. If the Court denies the motion, {51 *party*} asks the Court to grant {52 *his/her/its*} {53 *motion for continuance/motion to reopen discovery*}.

SEE: Tex. R. Civ. P. 62-65, 70, 166(b), 169, 190.2
O'Connor's Texas Rules * Civil Trials (2019), "Motion to Amend Pleadings—Pretrial," ch. 5-F, p. 432

ADD: STYLE OF THE CASE – FORM 1B:2
SIGNATURE BLOCK – FORM 1B:3
CERTIFICATE OF SERVICE – FORM 1B:13

ATTACH: AFFIDAVIT – FORM 1B:8, if necessary
NOTICE OF HEARING OR SUBMISSION – FORM 1E:1
ORDER – FORM 1G:1
MOTION FOR CONTINUANCE – FORM 5D:1, if necessary
MOTION TO REOPEN DISCOVERY PERIOD – FORM 6A:8, if necessary

NOTE: Any claimant, other than a counterclaimant, can file an amended pleading that removes a suit from the expedited-actions process in Texas Rule of Civil Procedure 169. *See* Tex. R. Civ. P. 169(c)(1)(B). See ***O'Connor's Texas Rules***, "Removal by pleading," ch. 2-C, §3.2, p. 135.

A motion to strike an amended pleading is used to object to an amended pleading that was filed without leave of court. *See, e.g.*, ***Stevenson v. Koutzarov***, 795 S.W.2d 313, 321 (Tex.App.—Houston [1st Dist.] 1990, writ denied) (motion to strike timely filed amended petition); ***Singleton v. Northwest Tex. Healthcare Sys.***, No. 07-03-0552-CV (Tex.App.—Amarillo 2006, no pet.) (memo op.; 2-28-06) (motion to strike untimely amended petition filed without leave of court). A response to a motion for leave to file an amended pleading is used to object to an amended pleading before it is filed. The motion to strike should contain the same allegations as the response. See FORM 5F:2.

Although Texas Rule of Civil Procedure 63 does not require a showing of lack of diligence of the party offering the amendment, some courts of appeals require it. However, lack of diligence has never been recognized by the Supreme Court as a factor in pretrial amendments, and one court of appeals has specifically held that it is not a proper factor. See ***O'Connor's Texas Rules***, "Practice Tip," ch. 5-F, §5.2, p. 434.

{❶ *PARTY*}'S RESPONSE TO
{❷ *ADVERSE PARTY*}'S MOTION TO STRIKE AMENDED PLEADING

{❸ *Party*}, {❹ *name*}, asks the Court to deny {❺ *adverse party*} {❻ *name*}'s motion to strike {❼ *party*}'s {❽ *identify amended pleading*}. {*See* ***O'Connor's Texas Rules***, *"Response to Motion for Pretrial Amendment," ch. 5-F, §5, p. 434.*}

INTRODUCTION

1. Plaintiff, {❾ *name*}, sued defendant, {❿ *name*}, for {⓫ *state basis of suit*}.

2. {⓬ *State other relevant facts about the suit.*}

BACKGROUND

3. On {⓭ *date*}, {⓮ *party*} filed {⓯ *his/her/its*} {⓰ *identify amended pleading*}.

{*CHOOSE APPROPRIATE PARAGRAPH 4*
IF AMENDMENT UNTIMELY}

{*Less than seven days before trial*}

4. This case is set for trial on {⓱ *date*}. The amended pleading was filed less than seven days before the date set for trial.

{*After deadline in pretrial order*}

4. The pretrial order in this case required the parties to file all amended pleadings by {⓲ *date*}. The amended pleading was filed after that date.

{*After deadline for expedited actions*}

4. {⓳ *The discovery period for this case closed/This case is set for trial*} on {⓴ *date*}. The amended pleading was filed {㉑ *choose whichever is earlier: more than 30 days after the discovery period closed/less than 30 days before trial*}.

5. {㉒ *State other facts relevant to the response.*}

ARGUMENT & AUTHORITIES

{*ADD PARAGRAPH 6 IF APPLICABLE*}

6. A court has discretion to consider a late amendment that was filed without leave of court if the party opposing the amendment has not made a sufficient showing of surprise or prejudice. *Goswami v. Metro. Sav. & Loan Ass'n*, 751 S.W.2d 487, 490 (Tex. 1988). {㉓ *Elaborate.*}

{*CHOOSE APPROPRIATE PARAGRAPHS 7-8*}

7. The court may strike {㉔ *an amended pleading/a late amended pleading*} only when the party opposing the amendment shows that (1) it was surprised by the amendment or (2) the amendment is prejudicial on its face. *See* Tex. R. Civ. P. 63; *see also Greenhalgh v. Serv. Lloyds Ins. Co.*, 787 S.W.2d 938, 939 (Tex. 1990) (burden to show surprise or prejudice is on party opposing amendment). {*See* ***O'Connor's Texas Rules***, *"Leave to amend required," ch. 5-F, §3.2, p. 433.*}

8. The court may strike a late amended pleading when the amendment removes the suit from the expedited-actions process in Texas Rule of Civil Procedure 169 and the party presenting the amendment does not show that good cause for filing the amendment outweighs any prejudice to the opposing party. Tex. R. Civ. P. 169(c)(2). {*See* ***O'Connor's Texas Rules***, *"After deadline for expedited actions," ch. 5-F, §3.2.2, p. 433.*}

{*CHOOSE APPROPRIATE SECTIONS A-C*}

A. {㉕ *Adverse party*} was not surprised by amendment.

9. To determine whether a party has been "surprised" by an amendment, courts have considered certain factors, such as (1) how long the suit has been pending before the amendment was filed, (2) how soon before trial the amendment was made, and (3) whether the amendment presents a new claim. *Dunnagan v. Watson*, 204 S.W.3d 30, 38 (Tex. App.—Fort Worth 2006, pet. denied); *Stevenson v. Koutzarov*, 795 S.W.2d 313, 321 (Tex. App.—Houston [1st Dist.] 1990, writ denied); *see Taiwan Shrimp Farm Vill. Ass'n v. U.S.A. Shrimp Farm Dev., Inc.*, 915 S.W.2d 61, 70 (Tex. App.—Corpus Christi 1996, writ denied); *AmSav Grp., Inc. v. Am. Sav. & Loan Ass'n*, 796 S.W.2d 482, 490 (Tex. App.—Houston [14th Dist.] 1990, writ denied). When an amendment adds a new claim, courts have also considered whether the claim is based on recently discovered matters and whether the party opposing the motion is prepared to try the new claim. *See Dunnagan*, 204 S.W.3d at 38; *Stevenson*, 795 S.W.2d at 321.

10. The Court should deny the motion to strike the amended pleading because the amendment is not a surprise to {㉖ *adverse party*}. {㉗ *Elaborate, and if possible, show how the amendment was made as soon as possible.*}

B. No prejudice from amendment.

11. To determine whether a party has been "prejudiced" by an amendment, courts consider whether the amendment (1) asserts a new substantive matter that reshapes the nature of the suit, (2) could not have been anticipated by the opposing party, and (3) will

Continued on next page

detrimentally affect the opposing party's ability to present its case. *Hardin v. Hardin*, 597 S.W.2d 347, 349-50 (Tex. 1980); *Halmos v. Bombardier Aerospace Corp.*, 314 S.W.3d 606, 623 (Tex. App.—Dallas 2010, no pet.). {*See* ***O'Connor's Texas Rules***, *"Prejudice," ch. 5-F, §5.2.2, p. 435.*}

12. The Court should deny the motion to strike the amended pleading because the amendment is not prejudicial on its face. {㉘ *Elaborate.*}

C. No prejudice from removal of suit from expedited-actions process.

13. {㉙ *Party*}'s amendment will remove the suit from the expedited-actions process in Texas Rule of Civil Procedure 169.

14. The Court should deny the motion to strike the late amended pleading because the good cause for the amendment outweighs the prejudice to {㉚ *adverse party*}. Tex. R. Civ. P. 169(c)(2). {㉛ *Elaborate.*}

CONCLUSION

15. {㉜ *Briefly summarize the response.*}

PRAYER

16. For these reasons, {㉝ *party*} asks the Court to deny {㉞ *adverse party*}'s motion to strike {㉟ *party*}'s {㊱ *identify amended pleading*}.

SEE: Tex. R. Civ. P. 62-65, 70, 166(b), 169, 190.2 (pre-March 1, 2013, version)
O'Connor's Texas Rules * Civil Trials (2019), "Motion to Amend Pleadings—Pretrial," ch. 5-F, p. 432

ADD: STYLE OF THE CASE – FORM 1B:2
SIGNATURE BLOCK – FORM 1B:3
CERTIFICATE OF SERVICE – FORM 1B:13

ATTACH: AFFIDAVIT – FORM 1B:8, if necessary
ORDER – FORM 1G:1

NOTE: Any claimant, other than a counterclaimant, can file an amended pleading that removes a suit from the expedited-actions process in Texas Rule of Civil Procedure 169. *See* Tex. R. Civ. P. 169(c)(1)(B). See ***O'Connor's Texas Rules***, "Removal by pleading," ch. 2-C, §3.2, p. 135.

Although Texas Rule of Civil Procedure 63 does not require a showing of lack of diligence of the party offering the amendment, some courts of appeals require it. However, lack of diligence has never been recognized by the Supreme Court as a factor in pretrial amendments, and one court of appeals has specifically held that it is not a proper factor. See ***O'Connor's Texas Rules***, "Practice Tip," ch. 5-F, §5.2, p. 434.

☆

No. {❶ *docket number*}

In re {❷ *name of litigation*}	§	JUDICIAL PANEL ON
	§	MULTIDISTRICT LITIGATION
	§	

{❸ *PARTY*}'S MOTION TO TRANSFER
TO MULTIDISTRICT LITIGATION PRETRIAL COURT

{❹ *Party*}, {❺ *name*}, asks the Multidistrict Litigation (MDL) Panel to transfer this case and {❻ *identify style and cause number of related case*} to the {❼ ______} District Court in {❽ ________} County, Texas, to decide all pretrial matters. {*See* ***O'Connor's Texas Rules****, "Motion to Transfer to Pretrial Court," ch. 5-G, §3, p. 437.*}

INTRODUCTION

1. Plaintiff, {❾ *name*}, sued defendant, {❿ *name*}, for {⓫ *state basis of suit*}.

2. {⓬ *State other relevant facts about the suit.*}

BACKGROUND

3. All parties {⓭ *agree/do not agree*} to this motion to transfer to multidistrict litigation pretrial court. Tex. R. Jud. Admin. 13.3(a)(3). {⓮ *Identify any parties that object to the request for pretrial consolidation.*}

4. {⓯ *State other facts relevant to the motion.*}

ARGUMENT & AUTHORITIES

5. Under Texas Rule of Judicial Administration 13 and Texas Government Code section 74.162, the MDL Panel may transfer related cases pending in different counties to a single court that decides all pretrial matters. To be related, the cases should involve one or more common questions of fact. Tex. R. Jud. Admin. 13.2(f); *see* Tex. Gov't Code §74.162; Tex. R. Jud. Admin. 13.3(a)(1); *In re Ad Valorem Tax Litig.*, 287 S.W.3d 517, 519-20 (Tex. J.P.M.L. 2007). The transfer of related cases to a single court is appropriate when the transfer would be for the convenience of the parties and witnesses and would promote the just and efficient conduct of the cases. Tex. Gov't Code §74.162; *see* Tex. R. Jud. Admin. 13.3(a)(2).

6. The MDL Panel should transfer this case with the related case because these cases involve one or more common questions of fact. {⓰ *Elaborate.*}

Continued on next page

7. The MDL Panel should transfer this case with the related case because the assignment of a single pretrial judge to these cases would be convenient for the parties and witnesses and would promote the just and efficient conduct of the cases. {[17] *Elaborate.*}

CONCLUSION

8. Because the cases involve common questions of fact, and because the assignment of a pretrial judge would be convenient for the parties and witnesses and would promote the just and efficient conduct of the cases, the MDL Panel should transfer these cases and assign a pretrial judge to conduct all pretrial proceedings and decide all pretrial matters.

PRAYER

9. For these reasons, {[18] *party*} asks the MDL Panel, after a hearing, to transfer this case with {[19] *identify style and cause number of related case*} for pretrial purposes and assign a pretrial judge in {[20] ________} District Court in {[21] ________} County, Texas.

SEE: Tex. Gov't Code §74.162
Tex. R. Jud. Admin. 13
O'Connor's Texas Rules * Civil Trials (2019), "Motion to Transfer to Multidistrict Litigation Pretrial Court," ch. 5-G, p. 436

ADD: SIGNATURE BLOCK – FORM 1B:3
CERTIFICATE OF CONFERENCE – FORM 1B:12
CERTIFICATE OF SERVICE – FORM 1B:13, served on all parties to the cases

ATTACH: AFFIDAVIT – FORM 1B:8, if necessary
NOTICE OF HEARING OR SUBMISSION – FORM 1E:1
APPENDIX – FORM 5G:2
NOTICE TO TRANSFER – FORM 5G:3
ORDER – FORM 5G:5
Brief in support, if necessary
Filing fee

NOTE: A motion to transfer to the MDL pretrial court must be electronically filed (e-filed) with the MDL Panel Clerk. www.txcourts.gov/about-texas-courts/multi-district-litigation-panel; *see* Tex. R. Jud. Admin. 13.3(f). The motion must be filed using the e-filing manager established by the Office of Court Administration. *See* Tex. R. App. P. 9.2(c)(2); www.txcourts.gov/about-texas-courts/multi-district-litigation-panel. All accepted documents e-filed with the MDL Panel Clerk will be sent to the MDL Panel by the MDL staff. www.txcourts.gov/about-texas-courts/multi-district-litigation-panel. The MDL Panel Clerk no longer requires paper copies. *Id.* All papers filed under Texas Rule of Judicial Administration 13.3 must be served on all parties to the cases. Tex. R. Jud. Admin. 13.3(h).

The motion must be in writing and must conform with Texas Rule of Appellate Procedure 9.4. Tex. R. Jud. Admin. 13.3(a), (e).

The motion must contain an appendix that lists the cause number, style, and trial court of the related cases, along with a list of all parties in those cases, and the names, addresses, telephone numbers, fax numbers, and e-mail addresses of all counsel. Tex. R. Jud. Admin. 13.3(a)(4).

The fee for filing a motion to transfer to the MDL pretrial court is $275. Tex.Sup.Ct. Order, Misc. Docket No. 15-9158 (eff. Sept. 1, 2015).

APPENDIX A

As required by Texas Rule of Judicial Administration 13, the following is the information on the related {❶ *case/cases*}:

{❷ *Style, cause number, court, and county of related case*}

{*REPEAT THE FOLLOWING FOR EACH PARTY*}

{❸ *Party name*}

{❹ *Attorney for party*}

{❺ *Attorney's address*}

{❻ *Attorney's telephone number*}

{❼ *Attorney's fax number*}

{❽ *Attorney's e-mail address*}

{*Continue until all related cases are listed*}

SEE: Tex. R. Jud. Admin. 13.3(a)(4)
O'Connor's Texas Rules * Civil Trials (2019), "Appendix," ch. 5-G, §3.2.5, p. 437

{❶ *PARTY*}'S NOTICE TO
COURT OF FILING OF MOTION TO TRANSFER
UNDER TEXAS RULE OF JUDICIAL ADMINISTRATION 13

To the Honorable Court:

As required by Texas Rule of Judicial Administration 13.3(i), this notice is to inform the Court that on {❷ *date motion to transfer was filed*}, {❸ *party*}, {❹ *name*}, filed a motion to transfer to a multidistrict litigation pretrial court under Texas Rule of Judicial Administration 13 in this case and related cases.

The motion to transfer was filed with the Judicial Panel on Multidistrict Litigation, Docket No. {❺ *number*}, styled {❻ *case name*}.

Texas Rule of Judicial Administration 13.4 discusses the effect of the motion to transfer on the trial court.

SEE: Tex. R. Jud. Admin. 13.3(i)
O'Connor's Texas Rules * Civil Trials (2019), "Notice," ch. 5-G, §3.4, p. 437

ADD: STYLE OF THE CASE – FORM 1B:2
CERTIFICATE OF SERVICE – FORM 1B:13

NOTE: The motion to transfer under Texas Rule of Judicial Administration 13 must be filed with the Multi-district Litigation (MDL) Panel Clerk. See ***O'Connor's Texas Rules***, "Filing," ch. 5-G, §5.1, p. 438. The notice of the motion, however, must be filed in the trial court. Tex. R. Jud. Admin. 13.3(i).

☆

No. {❶ *docket number*}

In re {❷ *name of litigation*}	§	JUDICIAL PANEL ON
	§	MULTIDISTRICT LITIGATION
	§	

{❸ *PARTY*}'S RESPONSE TO
{❹ *ADVERSE PARTY*}'S MOTION TO TRANSFER
TO MULTIDISTRICT LITIGATION PRETRIAL COURT

{❺ *Party*}, {❻ *name*}, asks the Multidistrict Litigation (MDL) Panel to deny {❼ *adverse party*} {❽ *name*}'s motion to transfer this case and {❾ *identify style and cause number of related case*} for pretrial purposes. {*See **O'Connor's Texas Rules**, "Response," ch. 5-G, §4, p. 438.*}

INTRODUCTION

1. Plaintiff, {❿ *name*}, sued defendant, {⓫ *name*}, for {⓬ *state basis of suit*}.

2. The case that {⓭ *adverse party*} claims is related to this case for pretrial consolidation is {⓮ *identify style and cause number of related case*}. {*See **O'Connor's Texas Rules**, "Related cases," ch. 5-G, §3.2.5(1), p. 437.*}

3. {⓯ *State other relevant facts about the suit.*}

BACKGROUND

4. On {⓰ *date*}, {⓱ *adverse party*} filed a motion to transfer under Texas Rule of Judicial Administration 13.

5. {⓲ *State other facts relevant to the response.*}

ARGUMENT & AUTHORITIES

6. Under Texas Rule of Judicial Administration 13 and Texas Government Code section 74.162, transfer of cases to a single court for pretrial consolidation is appropriate only if (1) the cases are related and (2) the transfer would be for the convenience of the parties and witnesses and would promote the just and efficient conduct of the cases.

{*CHOOSE APPROPRIATE PARAGRAPHS 7-8*}

7. To be related, cases should involve one or more common questions of fact. Tex. R. Jud. Admin. 13.2(f); *see* Tex. Gov't Code §74.162; Tex. R. Jud. Admin. 13.3(a)(1); *In re Ad Valorem Tax Litig.*, 287 S.W.3d 517, 519-20 (Tex. J.P.M.L. 2007). The MDL Panel should deny the motion to transfer because this case is not related to {⓳ *identify case adverse party claims is related and explain why the cases are not related, e.g., they involve different plaintiffs, defendants, and subject matter*}.

8. The MDL Panel should deny the motion to transfer because the assignment of a pretrial judge would not be for the convenience of the parties and witnesses and would hinder the just and efficient conduct of the cases. *See* Tex. Gov't Code §74.162; Tex. R. Jud. Admin. 13.3(a)(2). {20 *Elaborate.*}

CONCLUSION

9. {21 *Briefly summarize the response.*}

PRAYER

10. For these reasons, {22 *party*} asks the MDL Panel to deny {23 *adverse party*}'s motion to transfer this case with {24 *identify style and cause number of related case*} for pretrial purposes.

SEE: Tex. Gov't Code §74.162
Tex. R. Jud. Admin. 13
O'Connor's Texas Rules * Civil Trials (2019), "Motion to Transfer to Multidistrict Litigation Pretrial Court," ch. 5-G, p. 436

ADD: SIGNATURE BLOCK – FORM 1B:3
CERTIFICATE OF SERVICE – FORM 1B:13, served on all parties to the cases

ATTACH: AFFIDAVIT – FORM 1B:8, if necessary
ORDER – FORM 5G:5
Brief in support, if necessary

NOTE: A response to a motion to transfer to the MDL pretrial court must be electronically filed (e-filed) with the MDL Panel Clerk. www.txcourts.gov/about-texas-courts/multi-district-litigation-panel; *see* Tex. R. Jud. Admin. 13.3(f). The response must be filed using the e-filing manager established by the Office of Court Administration. *See* Tex. R. App. P. 9.2(c)(2); www.txcourts.gov/about-texas-courts/multi-district-litigation-panel. All accepted documents e-filed with the MDL Panel Clerk will be sent to the MDL Panel by the MDL staff. www.txcourts.gov/about-texas-courts/multi-district-litigation-panel. The MDL Panel Clerk no longer requires paper copies. *Id.* All papers filed under Texas Rule of Judicial Administration 13.3 must be served on all parties to the cases. Tex. R. Jud. Admin. 13.3(h).

The response must be in writing and must conform with Texas Rule of Appellate Procedure 9.4. Tex. R. Jud. Admin. 13.3(e).

A response to a motion to transfer for pretrial consolidation must be filed within 20 days after the motion is served. Tex. R. Jud. Admin. 13.3(d)(1).

The fee for filing a response to a motion to transfer to the MDL pretrial court is $50. *See* Tex.Sup.Ct. Order, Misc. Docket No. 15-9158 (eff. Sept. 1, 2015).

No. {❶ *docket number*}

In re {❷ *name of litigation*}	§	JUDICIAL PANEL ON
	§	MULTIDISTRICT LITIGATION
	§	

ORDER ON MOTION TO TRANSFER TO MULTIDISTRICT LITIGATION PRETRIAL COURT

After considering {❸ *party*} {❹ *name*}'s motion to transfer under Texas Rule of Judicial Administration 13, the response, the pleadings, and arguments of counsel, a majority of the Multidistrict Litigation Panel

{*CHOOSE APPROPRIATE ORDER*}

DENIES the motion.

GRANTS the motion and finds that the following cases involve one or more common questions of fact and the transfer of these cases will be for the convenience of the parties and witnesses and will promote the just and efficient conduct of the cases: {❺ *identify all cases by style, cause number, court, and county in which they are pending*}. The panel assigns Judge {❻ *name*} of {❼ ______} Court in {❽ ________} County, Texas, to preside over all pretrial proceedings and decide all pretrial matters for the consolidated case.

The concurring panel members are ________________________________.

SIGNED on ____________, 20____.

____
MULTIDISTRICT LITIGATION PANEL
{❾ *CHAIR/CLERK*}

SEE: Tex. R. Jud. Admin. 13
O'Connor's Texas Rules * Civil Trials (2019), "Order," ch. 5-G, §7, p. 439

ADD: CERTIFICATE OF SERVICE – FORM 1B:13, if proposed order served separately from motion or response

{❶ *{PARTY}'S/AGREED*} MOTION FOR ADDITIONAL RESOURCES

{*CHOOSE APPROPRIATE OPENING PARAGRAPH*}

{❷ *Party*}, {❸ *name*}, asks the Court to determine that additional resources are necessary in this case and to submit a request for additional resources to {❹ *name of presiding judge*}, the presiding judge of the administrative judicial region in which this case is filed. {*See* ***O'Connor's Texas Rules****, "Motion for Additional Resources," ch. 5-H, §4, p. 442.*}

{❺ *Party*}, {❻ *name*}, and {❼ *adverse party*}, {❽ *name*}, ask the Court to determine that additional resources are necessary in this case and to submit a request for additional resources to {❾ *name of presiding judge*}, the presiding judge of the administrative judicial region in which this case is filed. {*See* ***O'Connor's Texas Rules****, "Motion for Additional Resources," ch. 5-H, §4, p. 442.*}

INTRODUCTION

1. Plaintiff, {❿ *name*}, sued defendant, {⓫ *name*}, for {⓬ *state basis of suit*}.

2. {⓭ *State other relevant facts about the suit.*}

BACKGROUND

3. All parties {⓮ *agree/do not agree*} to this motion for additional resources. Tex. R. Jud. Admin. 16.6(a)(4). {⓯ *Identify any parties that do not agree to the motion.*}

4. {⓰ *State other facts relevant to the motion.*}

ARGUMENT & AUTHORITIES

5. Under Texas Rule of Judicial Administration 16 and Texas Government Code section 74.253, any party can file a motion for additional judicial resources in a large or complex civil case to promote the just and efficient resolution of the case. If the trial court determines that additional resources are necessary, the court must submit a request for additional resources to the presiding judge of the administrative judicial region in which the case is filed. Tex. R. Jud. Admin. 16.6(c); *see* Tex. Gov't Code §74.253(b).

6. For a court to determine that additional resources are necessary, a party must show that the case involves or is likely to involve certain considerations that justify additional resources. *See* Tex. R. Jud. Admin. 16.6(a)(1). {*See* ***O'Connor's Texas Rules****, "Factors to consider," ch. 5-H, §6.1.1, p. 443.*} Specifically, additional resources are necessary in this case for the following reasons:

◄ *Continued on next page* ►

{*CHOOSE APPROPRIATE REASONS*}

a. This case {[17] *involves/is likely to involve*} a large number of parties separately represented by counsel. Tex. Gov't Code §74.252(b)(1); Tex. R. Jud. Admin. 16.4(a). {[18] *Elaborate.*}

b. This case {[19] *involves/is likely to involve*} coordination with related actions pending in one or more courts in other Texas counties or one or more U.S. district courts. Tex. Gov't Code §74.252(b)(2); Tex. R. Jud. Admin. 16.4(b). {[20] *Elaborate.*}

c. This case {[21] *involves/is likely to involve*} numerous pretrial motions that present difficult or novel legal issues that will be time-consuming to resolve. Tex. Gov't Code §74.252(b)(3); Tex. R. Jud. Admin. 16.4(c). {[22] *Elaborate.*}

d. This case {[23] *involves/is likely to involve*} a large number of witnesses. Tex. Gov't Code §74.252(b)(4); Tex. R. Jud. Admin. 16.4(d). {[24] *Elaborate.*}

e. This case {[25] *involves/is likely to involve*} substantial documentary evidence. Tex. Gov't Code §74.252(b)(4); Tex. R. Jud. Admin. 16.4(d). {[26] *Elaborate.*}

f. This case {[27] *involves/is likely to involve*} substantial postjudgment supervision. Tex. Gov't Code §74.252(b)(5); Tex. R. Jud. Admin. 16.4(e). {[28] *Elaborate.*}

g. This case {[29] *involves/is likely to involve*} a trial that will last more than four weeks. Tex. Gov't Code §74.252(b)(6); Tex. R. Jud. Admin. 16.4(f). {[30] *Elaborate.*}

h. This case {[31] *involves/is likely to involve*} a substantial additional burden on the trial court's docket and the resources available to hear the case. Tex. Gov't Code §74.252(b)(7); Tex. R. Jud. Admin. 16.4(g). {[32] *Elaborate.*}

7. To promote the just and efficient resolution of this case, certain additional resources are necessary. *See* Tex. R. Jud. Admin. 16.6(a)(2). {*See **O'Connor's Texas Rules**, "Available resources," ch. 5-H, §4.3, p. 442.*} Specifically, {[33] *{party}/the parties*} {[34] *requests/request*} the following additional resources:

{*CHOOSE APPROPRIATE RESOURCES*}

a. The assignment of an active or retired judge, as long as the Court consents to the assignment. Tex. Gov't Code §74.254(d)(1); Tex. R. Jud. Admin. 16.5(a). {35 *Elaborate.*}

b. Additional legal, administrative, or clerical personnel. Tex. Gov't Code §74.254(d)(2); Tex. R. Jud. Admin. 16.5(b). {36 *Elaborate.*}

c. Information and communication technology. Tex. Gov't Code §74.254(d)(3); Tex. R. Jud. Admin. 16.5(c). {37 *Elaborate, e.g., video teleconferencing, software to help show evidence to the jury.*}

d. Specialized continuing legal education. Tex. Gov't Code §74.254(d)(4); Tex. R. Jud. Admin. 16.5(d). {38 *Elaborate.*}

e. Referral of the case to an associate judge. *See* Tex. Gov't Code §74.254(d)(5); Tex. R. Jud. Admin. 16.5(e). {39 *Elaborate.*}

f. Special accommodations or furnishings for the parties. Tex. Gov't Code §74.254(d)(6); Tex. R. Jud. Admin. 16.5(f). {40 *Elaborate.*}

g. {41 *Specify any other services or items necessary to try the case.*} *See* Tex. Gov't Code §74.254(d)(7); Tex. R. Jud. Admin. 16.5(g). {42 *Elaborate.*}

h. {43 *Identify any other appropriate resources.*} *See* Tex. Gov't Code §74.254(d)(8); Tex. R. Jud. Admin. 16.5(h). {44 *Elaborate.*}

8. These additional resources are needed by {45 *specify time by which additional resources are needed*}. Tex. R. Jud. Admin. 16.6(a)(3). {46 *Elaborate.*}

CONCLUSION

9. {47 *Briefly summarize the motion.*}

PRAYER

10. For these reasons, {48 *{party}/the parties*} {49 *asks/ask*} the Court to grant the motion for additional resources and to file a request with {50 *name of presiding judge*}, the presiding judge of the judicial administrative region in which the case is filed.

Continued on next page

FORM 5H:1 MOTION FOR ADDITIONAL RESOURCES

SEE: Tex. Gov't Code §§74.251-74.257
Tex. R. Jud. Admin. 16
O'Connor's Texas Rules * Civil Trials (2019), "Motion for Additional Resources," ch. 5-H, p. 441

ADD: STYLE OF THE CASE – FORM 1B:2
SIGNATURE BLOCK – FORM 1B:3
CERTIFICATE OF SERVICE – FORM 1B:13

ATTACH: AFFIDAVIT – FORM 1B:8, if necessary
NOTICE OF HEARING OR SUBMISSION – FORM 1E:1
ORDER – FORM 5H:2

NOTE: A party can file a motion for additional resources only in civil cases in a constitutional county court, county court at law, probate court, or district court. Tex. R. Jud. Admin. 16.1(b). A motion for additional resources is not available in criminal matters, cases involving grants for local court improvement under Texas Government Code §72.029, cases where a party seeks judicial review of a state-agency decision under Texas Government Code §§2001.171-2001.178, and cases that have been transferred to a district court for consolidated pretrial proceedings under Texas Government Code §§74.161-74.164. Tex. R. Jud. Admin. 16.1(c); *see* Tex. Gov't Code §74.251.

Texas Rule of Judicial Administration 16.6(a) does not provide a deadline for filing a motion for additional resources. A party should, however, file the motion as soon as possible after learning that the case is likely to involve considerations that justify additional resources.

If the presiding judge of the judicial administrative region receives a request for additional resources from the trial court, the presiding judge can (1) use previously allotted resources to fulfill the request if there are sufficient resources at the presiding judge's disposal, (2) submit a request to the Judicial Committee for Additional Resources (JCAR) asking for additional resources if there are insufficient resources at the presiding judge's disposal, or (3) deny the request. See ***O'Connor's Texas Rules***, "Review of request by presiding judge," ch. 5-H, §6.2, p. 444. If the presiding judge sends a request to JCAR for additional resources, JCAR must independently determine whether the case requires additional resources. See ***O'Connor's Texas Rules***, "Review of request by JCAR," ch. 5-H, §6.3, p. 444.

ORDER ON {❶ *{PARTY}'S/AGREED*}
MOTION FOR ADDITIONAL RESOURCES

{*CHOOSE APPROPRIATE INTRODUCTORY PARAGRAPH*}

After considering {❷ *party*} {❸ *name*}'s motion for additional resources {❹ *add if applicable: and the arguments of the parties at the hearing*}, the Court

After considering the parties' agreed motion for additional resources {❺ *add if applicable: and the arguments of the parties at the hearing*}, the Court

{*CHOOSE APPROPRIATE ORDER*}

DENIES the motion.

GRANTS the motion for the following reasons: {❻ *explain why additional resources are necessary*}. The Court will file a request with {❼ *name of presiding judge*}, the presiding judge of the judicial administrative region, for the following additional resources:

{*CHOOSE APPROPRIATE PARAGRAPHS 1-8*}

1. The assignment of an active or retired judge. {❽ *Elaborate.*}

2. Additional legal, administrative, or clerical personnel. {❾ *Elaborate.*}

3. Information and communication technology. {❿ *Elaborate.*}

4. Specialized continuing legal education. {⓫ *Elaborate.*}

5. Referral of the case to an associate judge. {⓬ *Elaborate.*}

6. Special accommodations or furnishings for the parties. {⓭ *Elaborate.*}

7. {⓮ *Specify any other services or items necessary to try the case.*} {⓯ *Elaborate.*}

8. {⓰ *Identify any other appropriate resources.*} {⓱ *Elaborate.*}

SIGNED on ______________, 20___.

____
PRESIDING JUDGE

◄ *Continued on next page* ►

FORM 5H:2 ORDER ON MOTION FOR ADDITIONAL RESOURCES

SEE: Tex. Gov't Code §§74.251-74.257
Tex. R. Jud. Admin. 16
O'Connor's Texas Rules * Civil Trials (2019), "Motion for Additional Resources," ch. 5-H, p. 441

ADD: STYLE OF THE CASE – FORM 1B:2
CERTIFICATE OF SERVICE – FORM 1B:13, if proposed order served separately from motion.

NOTE: If the presiding judge of the judicial administrative region receives a request for additional resources from the trial court, the presiding judge can (1) use previously allotted resources to fulfill the request if there are sufficient resources at the presiding judge's disposal, (2) submit a request to the Judicial Committee for Additional Resources (JCAR) asking for additional resources if there are insufficient resources at the presiding judge's disposal, or (3) deny the request. See ***O'Connor's Texas Rules***, "Review of request by presiding judge," ch. 5-H, §6.2, p. 444. If the presiding judge sends a request to JCAR for additional resources, JCAR must independently determine whether the case requires additional resources. See ***O'Connor's Texas Rules***, "Review of request by JCAR," ch. 5-H, §6.3, p. 444.

{❶ *PARTY*}'S MOTION TO SEVER

{❷ *Party*}, {❸ *name*}, asks the Court to sever this case into separate proceedings. {*See **O'Connor's Texas Rules**, "Motion for Severance," ch. 5-I, §3, p. 446.*}

INTRODUCTION

1. Plaintiff, {❹ *name*}, sued defendant, {❺ *name*}, for {❻ *state basis of suit*}.

2. {❼ *State other relevant facts about the suit.*}

3. The discovery period {❽ *will end/ended*} on {❾ *date*}.

4. This case is set for trial on {❿ *date*}.

BACKGROUND

5. {⓫ *State facts relevant to the motion.*}

ARGUMENT & AUTHORITIES

6. {⓬ *Party*} asks the Court to sever {⓭ *identify claim to be severed*} from the rest of this suit and assign it a new cause number.

7. A court may sever part of a case before the case is submitted to the trier of fact. Tex. R. Civ. P. 41; *State Dep't of Highways & Pub. Transp. v. Cotner*, 845 S.W.2d 818, 819 (Tex. 1993); *Christopher Columbus St. Mkt. LLC v. Zoning Bd. of Adjustments*, 302 S.W.3d 408, 414 (Tex. App.—Houston [14th Dist.] 2009, no pet.). This case has not been submitted to the trier of fact. {*See **O'Connor's Texas Rules**, "Deadline for motion to sever," ch. 5-I, §3.5, p. 448.*}

8. A lawsuit may be severed into two suits if (1) it involves more than one distinct and separate cause of action, (2) the severed cause could have been independently asserted in a separate lawsuit, and (3) the severed cause is not so interwoven with the remaining action that they involve the same facts and issues. *State v. Morello*, 547 S.W.3d 881, 889 (Tex. 2018); *In re State*, 355 S.W.3d 611, 614 (Tex. 2011); *F.F.P. Operating Partners, L.P. v. Duenez*, 237 S.W.3d 680, 693 (Tex. 2007). When considering whether a cause of action should be severed, the court's discretion is guided by the following controlling reasons: to do justice, avoid prejudice, and further the convenience of the parties and the court. *In re State*, 355 S.W.3d at 613; *F.F.P. Operating Partners*, 237 S.W.3d at 693; *Guar. Fed. Sav. Bank v. Horseshoe Operating Co.*, 793 S.W.2d 652, 658 (Tex. 1990); *Owens v. Owens*, 228 S.W.3d 721, 726 (Tex. App.—Houston [14th Dist.] 2006, pet. dism'd).

Continued on next page

9. This case involves the following distinct and separate causes of action: {[14] *identify distinct and separate causes of action*}.

10. This case can be severed because the cause of action to be severed could have been independently asserted. {[15] *Elaborate.*}

11. This case can be severed because the cause of action to be severed is not so interwoven with the remaining action that they involve the same facts and issues. {[16] *Elaborate.*}

12. The Court should grant a severance in this case because the severance would work to avoid prejudice, do justice, and further the convenience of the parties and the Court. {[17] *Elaborate.*}

MOTION FOR SEPARATE TRIALS

13. In the alternative, if the Court denies this motion to sever, {[18] *party*} asks the Court to order separate trials for {[19] *specify claims or issues to be tried separately*}. A court may order a separate trial of any claim, cross-claim, counterclaim, third-party claim, or issue to further convenience or to avoid prejudice. Tex. R. Civ. P. 174(b). {*See FORM 51:4.*}

14. The Court should grant {[20] *party*}'s motion for separate trials because {[21] *state facts showing inconvenience or risk of prejudice from trying the claims or issues together*}.

CONCLUSION

15. {[22] *Briefly summarize the motion.*}

PRAYER

16. For these reasons, {[23] *party*} asks the Court to sever the {[24] *specify cause*} from the other causes of action in this case and order the clerk of the Court to assign a new number to the severed cause. In the alternative, {[25] *party*} asks the Court to grant {[26] *his/her/its*} motion for separate trials.

SEE: Tex. R. Civ. P. 41, 174(b)
O'Connor's Texas Rules * Civil Trials (2019), "Motion for Severance," ch. 5-I, §3, p. 446

ADD: STYLE OF THE CASE – FORM 1B:2
SIGNATURE BLOCK – FORM 1B:3
CERTIFICATE OF CONFERENCE – FORM 1B:12
CERTIFICATE OF SERVICE – FORM 1B:13

ATTACH: AFFIDAVIT – FORM 1B:8, if necessary
NOTICE OF HEARING OR SUBMISSION – FORM 1E:1
ORDER – FORM 5I:3

NOTE: It is uncertain whether a movant should support a motion to sever with evidence. See ***O'Connor's Texas Rules***, "Hearing & evidence," ch. 5-I, §3.3, p. 447.

Severance or bifurcation may be required when evidence is admissible for one claim but prejudicial to another. *See* ***Liberty Nat'l Fire Ins. v. Akin***, 927 S.W.2d 627, 630 (Tex.1996). See ***O'Connor's Texas Rules***, "Severance required," ch. 5-I, §3.7, p. 449.

{[1] *PARTY*}'S RESPONSE TO
{[2] *ADVERSE PARTY*}'S MOTION TO SEVER

{[3] *Party*}, {[4] *name*}, asks the Court to deny {[5] *adverse party*} {[6] *name*}'s motion to sever.

INTRODUCTION

1. Plaintiff, {[7] *name*}, sued defendant, {[8] *name*}, for {[9] *state basis of suit*}.

2. {[10] *State other relevant facts about the suit.*}

3. The discovery period {[11] *will end/ended*} on {[12] *date*}.

4. This case is set for trial on {[13] *date*}.

BACKGROUND

5. On {[14] *date*}, {[15] *adverse party*} filed a motion to sever, asking the Court to sever {[16] *identify claim to be severed*} from the rest of this suit.

6. {[17] *State other facts relevant to the response.*}

ARGUMENT & AUTHORITIES

{*CHOOSE APPROPRIATE SECTIONS A-H*}

A. The motion is untimely.

7. A court should deny a motion to sever when the motion is made after the case has been submitted to the trier of fact. *State Dep't of Highways & Pub. Transp. v. Cotner*, 845 S.W.2d 818, 819 (Tex. 1993); *see* Tex. R. Civ. P. 41.

8. The Court should deny {[18] *adverse party*}'s motion to sever because the motion was made on {[19] *date*}, which was after the case was submitted to the {[20] *jury/Court*}. {[21] *Elaborate.*}

B. The lawsuit does not involve more than one distinct and separate cause of action.

9. A court should deny a motion to sever if the lawsuit does not involve more than one distinct and separate cause of action. *F.F.P. Operating Partners, L.P. v. Duenez*, 237 S.W.3d 680, 693 (Tex. 2007); *Liberty Nat'l Fire Ins. Co. v. Akin*, 927 S.W.2d 627, 629 (Tex. 1996). A court cannot sever a single cause of action into multiple claims. *Pierce v. Reynolds*, 329 S.W.2d 76, 78 (Tex. 1959); *Duncan v. Calhoun Cty. Navigation Dist.*, 28

S.W.3d 707, 710 (Tex. App.—Corpus Christi 2000, pet. denied); *Ryland Grp., Inc. v. White*, 723 S.W.2d 160, 161 (Tex. App.—Houston [1st Dist.] 1986, orig. proceeding).

10. The Court should deny {22 *adverse party*}'s motion to sever because this case does not involve distinct and separate causes of action; rather, it involves {23 *describe case and explain why claims are not distinct*}.

C. The claim is not a proper subject of a separate lawsuit.

11. A court should deny a motion to sever if the claim to be severed could not have been independently asserted in a separate lawsuit. *In re State*, 355 S.W.3d 611, 614 (Tex. 2011); *F.F.P. Operating Partners, L.P. v. Duenez*, 237 S.W.3d 680, 693 (Tex. 2007); *Liberty Nat'l Fire Ins. Co. v. Akin*, 927 S.W.2d 627, 629 (Tex. 1996).

12. The Court should deny {24 *adverse party*}'s motion to sever because the claim to be severed is not the proper subject of a separate lawsuit. {25 *Elaborate.*}

D. The claim involves the same facts and issues.

13. A court should deny the motion to sever if the claim to be severed is so interwoven with the remaining action that it involves the same facts and issues. *In re State*, 355 S.W.3d 611, 614 (Tex. 2011); *F.F.P. Operating Partners, L.P. v. Duenez*, 237 S.W.3d 680, 693 (Tex. 2007); *Liberty Nat'l Fire Ins. Co. v. Akin*, 927 S.W.2d 627, 629 (Tex. 1996); *see Guar. Fed. Sav. Bank v. Horseshoe Operating Co.*, 793 S.W.2d 652, 658 (Tex. 1990).

14. The Court should deny {26 *adverse party*}'s motion to sever because {27 *explain how the claim involves the same facts and issues*}.

E. Injustice, prejudice, and inconvenience.

15. A court should deny a motion to sever if granting the motion will not do justice, avoid prejudice, or further the convenience of the parties or the court. *In re State*, 355 S.W.3d 611, 613 (Tex. 2011); *F.F.P. Operating Partners, L.P. v. Duenez*, 237 S.W.3d 680, 693 (Tex. 2007); *Owens v. Owens*, 228 S.W.3d 721, 726 (Tex. App.—Houston [14th Dist.] 2006, pet. dism'd).

16. The Court should deny {28 *adverse party*}'s motion to sever because granting the motion will not do justice, avoid prejudice, or further the convenience of the parties or the Court. {29 *Elaborate, describing injustice, prejudice, and inconvenience that will result from severance.*}

Continued on next page

F. The defendants have the same liability.

17. A court should deny a motion to sever a cause of action against one defendant from a cause of action against another defendant if the defendants are alleged to have the same liability. *See, e.g., McRoberts v. Tesoro Sav. & Loan Ass'n*, 781 S.W.2d 705, 706 (Tex. App.—San Antonio 1989, writ denied) (trial court could not sever cause of action against maker of note—the partnership—from cause of action against guarantors—the individual partners).

18. The Court should deny {㉚ *adverse party*}'s motion to sever because it asks the Court to sever the cause of action against defendant {㉛ *name*} from the cause of action against defendant {㉜ *name*}, and {㉝ *adverse party*} alleges the same liability against both defendants. Specifically, {㉞ *identify liability and describe similarities*}.

G. The injury is indivisible.

19. A court should deny a motion to sever claims against multiple defendants if the injury is indivisible. *See Landers v. E. Tex. Salt Water Disposal Co.*, 248 S.W.2d 731, 734 (Tex. 1952). When the torts of two or more parties cause an indivisible injury, the claims should be tried together. *See id.*

20. The Court should deny {㉟ *adverse party*}'s motion to sever because {㊱ *explain how defendants are liable for indivisible injury*}.

H. A compulsory counterclaim cannot be severed.

21. A court should deny a motion to sever a compulsory counterclaim that arises from the same transaction as the issue in the main suit. *Rucker v. Bank One Tex., N.A.*, 36 S.W.3d 649, 651-52 (Tex. App.—Waco 2000, pet. denied); *Fuentes v. McFadden*, 825 S.W.2d 772, 779-80 (Tex. App.—El Paso 1992, no writ); *Mathis v. Bill De La Garza & Assocs., P.C.*, 778 S.W.2d 105, 106-07 (Tex. App.—Texarkana 1989, no writ).

22. The Court should deny {㊲ *adverse party*}'s motion to sever because it asks the Court to sever a compulsory counterclaim for {㊳ *identify compulsory counterclaim*}.

CONCLUSION

23. {㊴ *Briefly summarize the response.*}

PRAYER

24. For these reasons, {㊵ *party*} asks the Court to deny {㊶ *adverse party*}'s motion to sever.

SEE: Tex. R. Civ. P. 41, 174(b)
O'Connor's Texas Rules * Civil Trials (2019), "Motion for Severance," ch. 5-I, §3, p. 446

ADD: STYLE OF THE CASE – FORM 1B:2
SIGNATURE BLOCK – FORM 1B:3
CERTIFICATE OF SERVICE – FORM 1B:13

ATTACH: AFFIDAVIT – FORM 1B:8, if necessary
ORDER – FORM 5I:3

NOTE: Some courts of appeals have held that a court cannot sever a compulsory counterclaim and that doing so is an abuse of discretion. *E.g.*, ***Rucker v. Bank One Tex.***, 36 S.W.3d 649, 651-52 (Tex.App.—Waco 2000, pet. denied); ***Fuentes v. McFadden***, 825 S.W.2d 772, 779 (Tex.App.—El Paso 1992, no writ); ***Mathis v. Bill De La Garza & Assocs.***, 778 S.W.2d 105, 106 (Tex.App.—Texarkana 1989, no writ). But the Supreme Court has held—without determining whether the particular counterclaims at issue were in fact compulsory—that a trial court has discretion to sever any claim as long as the court applies the criteria under Texas Rule of Civil Procedure 41. ***McGuire v. Commercial Un. Ins.***, 431 S.W.2d 347, 351 (Tex. 1968).

ORDER ON {❶ *PARTY*}'S MOTION TO SEVER

After considering {❷ *party*} {❸ *name*}'s motion to sever, the response, the pleadings, and arguments of counsel, the Court

{*CHOOSE APPROPRIATE ORDER*}

DENIES the motion.

GRANTS the motion to sever, severs {❹ *identify claims or parties being severed*}, and orders the court clerk to assign the severed action the separate cause number of {❺ *docket number*}, copy the following documents, and include them in that file:

1. {❻ *Identify all live pleadings and dates filed.*}

{*CHOOSE APPROPRIATE PARAGRAPHS 2-7*}

2. The following discovery on file in this case: {❼ *in subparts, identify discovery on file to be copied for the severed cause by type of discovery, name of party filing the discovery, and date the discovery was filed*}.

3. The following motions and responses filed in this case: {❽ *in subparts, identify motions and responses to be copied for the severed cause by name of motion or response, name of party filing the motion or response, and date the motion or response was filed*}.

4. The following notices sent by the Court to the parties: {❾ *in subparts, identify type of notice and date the notice was sent*}.

5. The following signed orders: {❿ *in subparts, identify signed orders to be copied for the severed cause by name of order and date the judge signed the order*}.

6. The {⓫ *summary/default/final/partial*} judgment signed on {⓬ *date*}.

7. {⓭ *Any other relevant matter from the original file.*}

8. A copy of the docket sheet.

9. A copy of this order.

SIGNED on _______________, 20___.

____
PRESIDING JUDGE

SEE: Tex. R. Civ. P. 41, 174(b)
O'Connor's Texas Rules * Civil Trials (2019), "Order on motion to sever," ch. 5-I, §3.4, p. 447

ADD: STYLE OF THE CASE – FORM 1B:2
CERTIFICATE OF SERVICE – FORM 1B:13, if proposed order served separately from motion or response

{❶ *PARTY*}'S MOTION FOR SEPARATE TRIALS

{❷ *Party*}, {❸ *name*}, asks the Court to order separate trials in this case. {*See* ***O'Connor's Texas Rules****, "Motion for Separate (Bifurcated) Trial," ch. 5-I, §4, p. 449.*}

INTRODUCTION

1. Plaintiff, {❹ *name*}, sued defendant, {❺ *name*}, for {❻ *state basis of suit*}.

2. {❼ *State other relevant facts about the suit.*}

3. This case is set for trial on {❽ *date*}.

BACKGROUND

4. {❾ *State facts relevant to the motion.*}

ARGUMENT & AUTHORITIES

5. The purpose of a motion for separate trials is to further convenience, avoid prejudice, and promote the ends of justice. *In re Ethyl Corp.*, 975 S.W.2d 606, 610 (Tex. 1998); *Womack v. Berry*, 291 S.W.2d 677, 683 (Tex. 1956).

6. A court may order separate trials of any claim, cross-claim, counterclaim, third-party claim, or separate issue to avoid prejudice or to further convenience. Tex. R. Civ. P. 174(b).

7. The Court should order separate trials for {❿ *specify claims or issues to be tried separately*} to avoid prejudice, further convenience, and promote the ends of justice. {⓫ *Elaborate.*}

CONCLUSION

8. {⓬ *Briefly summarize the motion.*}

PRAYER

9. For these reasons, {⓭ *party*} asks the Court to order separate trials for {⓮ *specify claims or issues to be tried separately*}.

FORM 5I:4 MOTION FOR SEPARATE TRIALS

SEE: Tex. R. Civ. P. 174(b)
O'Connor's Texas Rules * Civil Trials (2019), "Motion for Separate (Bifurcated) Trial," ch. 5-I, §4, p. 449

ADD: STYLE OF THE CASE – FORM 1B:2
SIGNATURE BLOCK – FORM 1B:3
CERTIFICATE OF CONFERENCE – FORM 1B:12
CERTIFICATE OF SERVICE – FORM 1B:13

ATTACH: AFFIDAVIT – FORM 1B:8, if necessary
NOTICE OF HEARING OR SUBMISSION – FORM 1E:1
ORDER – FORM 1G:1

NOTE: When seeking a separate trial on exemplary damages, use FORM 5I:6.

Additional grounds for determining whether separate trials are proper may apply in mass-tort litigation (e.g., asbestos litigation). See ***O'Connor's Texas Rules***, "Grounds in mass torts," ch. 5-I, §4.1.2, p. 450.

{❶ *PARTY*}'S RESPONSE TO
{❷ *ADVERSE PARTY*}'S MOTION FOR SEPARATE TRIALS

{❸ *Party*}, {❹ *name*}, asks the Court to deny {❺ *adverse party*} {❻ *name*}'s motion for separate trials.

INTRODUCTION

1. Plaintiff, {❼ *name*}, sued defendant, {❽ *name*}, for {❾ *state basis of suit*}.

2. {❿ *State other relevant facts about the suit.*}

3. This case is set for trial on {⓫ *date*}.

BACKGROUND

4. {⓬ *State facts relevant to the response.*}

ARGUMENT & AUTHORITIES

{*CHOOSE APPROPRIATE SECTIONS A-E*}

A. No furtherance of convenience.

5. A court should deny a motion for separate trials when a bifurcated trial will not further the convenience of the parties or the court. *See* Tex. R. Civ. P. 174(b); *Kaiser Found. Health Plan v. Bridewell*, 946 S.W.2d 642, 645 (Tex. App.—Waco 1997, orig. proceeding).

6. The Court should deny {⓭ *adverse party*}'s motion for separate trials because bifurcating the trial will not further the convenience of the parties or the Court. {⓮ *Elaborate, describing inconvenience that will result from bifurcation, if applicable.*}

B. No avoidance of prejudice.

7. A court should deny a motion for separate trials when a bifurcated trial will not avoid prejudice. *See* Tex. R. Civ. P. 174(b); *Kaiser Found. Health Plan v. Bridewell*, 946 S.W.2d 642, 645 (Tex. App.—Waco 1997, orig. proceeding).

8. The Court should deny {⓯ *adverse party*}'s motion for separate trials because bifurcating the trial will not avoid prejudice. {⓰ *Explain how prejudice will not result from a single trial or how a bifurcated trial will not avoid prejudice. Describe prejudice that will result from bifurcation, if applicable.*}

C. No promotion of justice.

9. A court should deny a motion for separate trials when a bifurcated trial will not promote the ends of justice. *See In re Ethyl Corp.*, 975 S.W.2d 606, 610 (Tex. 1998); *Womack v. Berry*, 291 S.W.2d 677, 683 (Tex. 1956).

10. The Court should deny {17 *adverse party*}'s motion for separate trials because bifurcating the trial will not promote the ends of justice. {18 *Explain, e.g., describing injustice that will result from bifurcation.*}

D. Avoidance of piecemeal litigation.

11. Courts disfavor piecemeal trials. *Iley v. Hughes*, 311 S.W.2d 648, 651 (Tex. 1958); *see Transp. Ins. Co. v. Moriel*, 879 S.W.2d 10, 30 n.29 (Tex. 1994). The public interest, the interests of litigants, and the administration of justice are better served by rules of trial that avoid a multiplicity of suits. *Iley*, 311 S.W.2d at 651.

12. The Court should deny {19 *adverse party*}'s motion for separate trials to avoid piecemeal trials and an unnecessary multiplicity of suits. {20 *Explain how separate trials would amount to an unnecessary multiplicity of suits.*}

E. Indivisible cause of action.

13. When liability and damages are elements of an indivisible cause of action, they cannot be tried separately. *See Iley v. Hughes*, 311 S.W.2d 648, 651 (Tex. 1958); *Waples-Platter Co. v. Commercial Standard Ins. Co.*, 294 S.W.2d 375, 377 (Tex. 1956).

14. The Court should deny {21 *adverse party*}'s motion for separate trials because in this case liability and damages are elements of an indivisible cause of action. {22 *Elaborate.*}

CONCLUSION

15. {23 *Briefly summarize the response.*}

PRAYER

16. For these reasons, {24 *party*} asks the Court to deny {25 *adverse party*}'s motion for separate trials.

Continued on next page

SEE: Tex. R. Civ. P. 174(b)
O'Connor's Texas Rules * Civil Trials (2019), "Response," ch. 5-I, §4.2, p. 450

ADD: STYLE OF THE CASE – FORM 1B:2
SIGNATURE BLOCK – FORM 1B:3
CERTIFICATE OF SERVICE – FORM 1B:13

ATTACH: AFFIDAVIT – FORM 1B:8, if necessary
ORDER – FORM 1G:1

DEFENDANT'S MOTION FOR SEPARATE TRIAL ON EXEMPLARY DAMAGES

Defendant, {❶ *name*}, asks the Court to order a separate trial on the amount of exemplary damages, as provided by Texas Civil Practice & Remedies Code section 41.009(a).

INTRODUCTION

1. Plaintiff, {❷ *name*}, sued defendant, {❸ *name*}, for {❹ *state basis of suit*}.

2. {❺ *State other relevant facts about the suit.*}

3. This case is set for trial on {❻ *date*}.

BACKGROUND

4. In {❼ *his/her/its*} petition, plaintiff requested exemplary damages from defendant.

5. {❽ *State other facts relevant to the motion.*}

ARGUMENT & AUTHORITIES

6. On a defendant's timely request, a court must provide a bifurcated trial separating the issue of the amount of exemplary damages from all other issues in the case. *See* Tex. Civ. Prac. & Rem. Code §41.009(a). A motion for a separate trial on exemplary damages is timely if it is made before the voir dire examination of the jury or at the time specified in a pretrial court order. *Id.*

7. The Court must order a separate trial on the amount of exemplary damages because this motion is filed {❾ *before the voir dire examination of the jury/at the time specified by the pretrial order in this case*} and therefore is timely.

CONCLUSION

8. {❿ *Briefly summarize the motion.*}

PRAYER

9. For these reasons, defendant asks the Court to order a separate trial on the amount of exemplary damages.

Continued on next page

FORM 51:6 MOTION FOR SEPARATE TRIAL ON EXEMPLARY DAMAGES

SEE: Tex. Civ. Prac. & Rem. Code §41.009
O'Connor's Texas Rules * Civil Trials (2019), "Motion to Bifurcate Exemplary Damages," ch. 5-I, §5, p. 451
O'Connor's Texas Causes of Action (2019), "Bifurcated Trial on Exemplary Damages," ch. 42-B, §9, p. 1441

ADD: STYLE OF THE CASE – FORM 1B:2
SIGNATURE BLOCK – FORM 1B:3
CERTIFICATE OF CONFERENCE – FORM 1B:12
CERTIFICATE OF SERVICE – FORM 1B:13

ATTACH: NOTICE OF HEARING OR SUBMISSION – FORM 1E:1
ORDER – FORM 51:7

NOTE: If the defendant makes a timely request under Texas Civil Practice & Remedies Code §41.009, the court must grant the motion. The only ground for objecting is that the defendant's motion is untimely. *See* Tex. Civ. Prac. & Rem. Code §41.009(a).

ORDER ON DEFENDANT'S MOTION FOR
SEPARATE TRIAL ON EXEMPLARY DAMAGES

After considering defendant {❶ *name*}'s motion for separate trial on the amount of exemplary damages, the response, and arguments of counsel, the Court

{*CHOOSE APPROPRIATE ORDER*}

DENIES the motion.

GRANTS the motion. Therefore, the Court orders the following:

In the first phase of this trial, the trier of fact must determine (1) liability for compensatory and exemplary damages, if any, and (2) the amount of compensatory damages, if any.

In the second phase of this trial, if liability for exemplary damages is established during the first phase, the trier of fact must determine the amount of exemplary damages to be awarded, if any.

SIGNED on ________________, 20___.

____
PRESIDING JUDGE

SEE: Tex. Civ. Prac. & Rem. Code §41.009
O'Connor's Texas Rules * Civil Trials (2019), "Motion to Bifurcate Exemplary Damages," ch. 5-I, §5, p. 451
O'Connor's Texas Causes of Action (2019), "Bifurcated Trial on Exemplary Damages," ch. 42-B, §9, p. 1441

ADD: STYLE OF THE CASE – FORM 1B:2
CERTIFICATE OF SERVICE – FORM 1B:13, if proposed order served separately from motion or response

FORM 51:7

{❶ *NAME*}'S ORIGINAL PETITION
IN INTERVENTION {❷ *STATE ADDITIONAL RELIEF REQUESTED IF APPROPRIATE, E.G., & REQUEST FOR DISCLOSURE*}

Intervenor, {❸ *name*}, files this petition in intervention {❹ *state additional relief requested if appropriate, e.g., and request for disclosure*} as a party-{❺ *plaintiff/defendant*} and alleges as follows: {*See* ***O'Connor's Texas Rules****, "Petition in Intervention," ch. 5-J, §2, p. 453.*}

PARTIES

1. Intervenor is {❻ *identify capacity in which the intervenor joins, e.g., an individual, a corporation, a partnership*} {❼ *who/that*} {❽ *resides/conducts business*} in {❾ ________} County at {❿ *address*}.

{*CHOOSE ONE OF THE FOLLOWING IF INTERVENOR IS AN INDIVIDUAL*}

Ⓐ The last three digits of intervenor's driver's license number are {⓫ *digits of driver's license number*}. The last three digits of intervenor's Social Security number are {⓬ *digits of Social Security number*}. {*See Tex. Civ. Prac. & Rem. Code §30.014(a);* ***O'Connor's Texas Rules****, "ID number," ch. 1-B, §3.2.4(3), p. 8.*}

Ⓑ The last three digits of intervenor's driver's license number are {⓭ *digits of driver's license number*}. Intervenor has not been issued a Social Security number. {*See Tex. Civ. Prac. & Rem. Code §30.014(a);* ***O'Connor's Texas Rules****, "ID number," ch. 1-B, §3.2.4(3), p. 8.*}

Ⓒ The last three digits of intervenor's Social Security number are {⓮ *digits of Social Security number*}. Intervenor has not been issued a driver's license number. {*See Tex. Civ. Prac. & Rem. Code §30.014(a);* ***O'Connor's Texas Rules****, "ID number," ch. 1-B, §3.2.4(3), p. 8.*}

Ⓓ Intervenor has not been issued a driver's license number or a Social Security number. {*See Tex. Civ. Prac. & Rem. Code §30.014(a);* ***O'Connor's Texas Rules****, "ID number," ch. 1-B, §3.2.4(3), p. 8.*}

2. Plaintiff, {⓯ *name*}, is {⓰ *identify capacity in which plaintiff sued defendant, e.g., an individual, a corporation, a partnership*} whose address is {⓱ *address*}. A copy of this petition will be forwarded to {⓲ *name of attorney*}, attorney of record for plaintiff, at {⓳ *address*}.

3. Defendant, {[20] *name*}, {[21] *identify capacity in which defendant was sued, e.g., an individual, a corporation, a partnership*}, has appeared and answered. A copy of this petition will be forwarded to {[22] *name of attorney*}, attorney of record for defendant, at {[23] *address*}.

4. {*If movant is an intervening plaintiff, see FORM 2B:20 for proper jurisdiction allegations. It is not necessary to plead jurisdiction for most suits. See **O'Connor's Texas Rules**, "Jurisdiction," ch. 2-B, §5, p. 125.*}

VENUE

5. {*If movant is an intervening plaintiff, plead proper venue allegations. See Tex. Civ. Prac. & Rem. Code §15.003(a). For venue allegations, see FORM 2B:21. It is not necessary to plead venue, but pleading sufficient venue facts could avoid a motion to transfer venue. See **O'Connor's Texas Rules**, "Venue," ch. 2-B, §6, p. 127.*}

THE ORIGINAL LAWSUIT

6. On {[24] *date*}, plaintiff sued defendant for {[25] *state basis of suit*}.

7. On {[26] *date*}, defendant filed an answer asserting {[27] *identify defenses*}.

8. {[28] *State other relevant facts about the original lawsuit.*}

{*ADD SECTION BELOW IF PETITION IS BEING FILED AFTER JUDGMENT*}

TIMELINESS

9. Intervenor is entitled to file this petition after judgment because {[29] *he/she/it*}

{*CHOOSE APPROPRIATE STATEMENT*}

[A] is not attacking the judgment but instead seeks protection of property interests under Texas Civil Practice & Remedies Code section 31.002. {[30] *Elaborate.*} {*Breazeale v. Casteel, 4 S.W.3d 434, 436 (Tex. App.—Austin 1999, pet. denied).*}

[B] is a subrogee whose interest was at first adequately represented by {[31] *other party*} but was later abandoned, and intervention will not cause unnecessary delay or prejudice to the existing parties. {[32] *Elaborate.*} {*Tex. Mut. Ins. Co. v. Ledbetter, 251 S.W.3d 31, 36 (Tex. 2008).*}

Continued on next page

INTERVENOR'S INTEREST IN LAWSUIT

10. {㉝ *State facts relevant to the petition.*}

11. A party has a justiciable interest in a lawsuit when its interests will be affected by the litigation. {*In re Union Carbide Corp., 273 S.W.3d 152, 155 (Tex. 2008); Law Offices of Windle Turley, P.C. v. Ghiasinejad, 109 S.W.3d 68, 70 (Tex. App.—Fort Worth 2003, no pet.).*} A party may intervene in a suit if it

{*CHOOSE APPROPRIATE STATEMENT*}

Ⓐ could have brought all or part of the same suit in its own name. {*Nghiem v. Sajib, 567 S.W.3d 718, 721 n.16 (Tex. 2019); In re Union Carbide, 273 S.W.3d at 155; Guar. Fed. Sav. Bank v. Horseshoe Operating Co., 793 S.W.2d 652, 657 (Tex. 1990).*}

Ⓑ would have been able to defeat all or part of the recovery if the suit had been filed against it. {*Guar. Fed. Sav. Bank v. Horseshoe Operating Co., 793 S.W.2d 652, 657 (Tex. 1990); Metromedia Long Distance, Inc. v. Hughes, 810 S.W.2d 494, 497 (Tex. App.—San Antonio 1991, writ denied).*}

12. {㉞ *Demonstrate how facts support intervenor's justiciable interest in the lawsuit.*}

INTERVENOR'S {㉟ *CAUSES OF ACTION/DEFENSES*}

13. {㊱ *In separately numbered paragraphs, identify elements and facts supporting a cause of action or defense. For lists of elements for various causes of action, see* ***O'Connor's Texas COA****, Part 2, p. 7.*}

{*ADD PARAGRAPHS 14-20 AS APPROPRIATE*}

DAMAGES

14. {㊲ *Identify the damages sought, and state that they are within the jurisdictional limits of the Court.*}

EQUITABLE RELIEF

15. Intervenor seeks {㊳ *identify equitable relief sought*}. {㊴ *State facts supporting equitable relief.*} {*See FORM 2D:1;* ***O'Connor's Texas Rules****, "Injunctive Relief," ch. 2-D, p. 138.*}

ATTORNEY FEES

16. Intervenor is entitled to recover reasonable and necessary attorney fees under {❹⓪ *identify statute or contract permitting recovery of attorney fees*}. {❹① *Elaborate.*} {*See* ***O'Connor's Texas COA***, *"Attorney Fees," ch. 45, p. 1463.*}

JURY DEMAND

17. Intervenor demands a jury trial and tenders the appropriate fee with this petition. {*See* ***O'Connor's Texas Rules***, *"Request for Jury Trial," ch. 5-B, p. 400.*}

CONDITIONS PRECEDENT

18. All conditions precedent to intervenor's claim for relief have been performed or have occurred. {*See* ***O'Connor's Texas Rules***, *"Conditions Precedent," ch. 2-B, §12, p. 132.*}

REQUEST FOR DISCLOSURE

19. Under Texas Rule of Civil Procedure 194, intervenor requests that plaintiff and defendant disclose, within 30 days after service of this request, the information or material described in Rule 194.2. {*See* ***O'Connor's Texas Rules***, *"Content of request," ch. 6-E, §3.2, p. 627.*}

OBJECTION TO ASSOCIATE JUDGE

20. Intervenor objects to the referral of this case to an associate judge for hearing a trial on the merits or presiding at a jury trial. {*See* ***O'Connor's Texas Rules***, *"Objection to referral," ch. 1-J, §3.3, p. 96.*}

PRAYER

{*CHOOSE APPROPRIATE PARAGRAPH 21*}

21. For these reasons, intervenor asks the Court to render judgment for intervenor that plaintiff take nothing against {❹② *him/her/it*} and award intervenor {❹③ *identify relief sought, e.g., attorney fees, interest, court costs*}.

21. For these reasons, intervenor asks that, after trial, intervenor be awarded a judgment against defendant for the following damages: {❹④ *identify damages, attorney fees, interest, court costs, and any other relief sought*}.

◄ Continued on next page ►

SEE: Tex. R. Civ. P. 60, 61
O'Connor's Texas Rules * Civil Trials (2019), "Petition in Intervention," ch. 5-J, §2, p. 453
O'Connor's Texas Causes of Action (2019), "Attorney Fees," ch. 45, p. 1463

ADD: STYLE OF THE CASE – FORM 1B:2
SIGNATURE BLOCK – FORM 1B:3
CERTIFICATE OF SERVICE – FORM 1B:13, for all attorneys of record

NOTE: The intervenor is not required to serve citation on the parties that are before the court. However, the intervenor is required to serve citation on any defendant that has not appeared, on any third-party defendant that it brings into the suit, and on the plaintiff if the intervenor's claim is against the plaintiff and the plaintiff makes no further appearance after the intervention. ***Baker v. Monsanto Co.***, 111 S.W.3d 158, 160 (Tex.2003).

Before a court clerk will issue a citation for service, the plaintiff may be required to complete and file with its petition a Civil Process Request Form identifying the person to be served and the method of service. Check the court's website for specific requirements and to obtain a copy of the form.

Each intervening plaintiff must, independently of every other plaintiff, establish proper venue or proper joinder. Tex. Civ. Prac. & Rem. Code §15.003(a). See ***O'Connor's Texas Rules***, "Venue or joinder proper in multiple-plaintiff case," ch. 3-C, §2.6.4, p. 247.

There is no deadline for intervention in the Texas Rules of Civil Procedure. ***Texas Mut. Ins. v. Ledbetter***, 251 S.W.3d 31, 36 (Tex.2008). Generally, a party cannot intervene after final judgment, but under certain circumstances it can. *Id.* See ***O'Connor's Texas Rules***, "After judgment," ch. 5-J, §2.2.2, p. 455.

A person or entity not named as a party may attempt to intervene after judgment through the virtual-representation doctrine; however, to do so, the prospective intervenor must first show that it has standing under the virtual-representation doctrine and then meet certain equitable considerations. *See* ***State v. Naylor***, 466 S.W.3d 783, 791 (Tex.2015). See ***O'Connor's Texas Rules***, "Note," ch. 5-J, §2.2.2(1), p. 455.

Under Texas Government Code chapter 54A, subchapter B, a district court or statutory county court can appoint a full-time or part-time associate judge to perform certain duties if the creation of the associate-judge position is authorized by the county commissioners court. Tex. Gov't Code §54A.102(a). If the creation of the position is authorized, the court can refer a full trial on the merits or a jury trial to an associate judge. *See id.* §54A.106. A case can be referred to an associate judge either by an order of referral in a specific case or by an omnibus order. *Id.* §54A.107(a). A party can prohibit the trial referral only if it files an objection within ten days after receiving notice of the referral. *Id.* §54A.106(c). See ***O'Connor's Texas Rules***, "Associate Judge," ch. 1-J, p. 95.

{❶ *PARTY*}'S MOTION TO STRIKE PETITION IN INTERVENTION

{❷ *Party*}, {❸ *name*}, asks the Court to strike {❹ *name of intervenor*}'s petition in intervention. {*See* ***O'Connor's Texas Rules***, *"Petition in Intervention," ch. 5-J, §2, p. 453.*}

INTRODUCTION

1. On {❺ *date original petition was filed*}, plaintiff, {❻ *name*}, sued defendant, {❼ *name*}, for {❽ *state basis of suit*}.

2. {❾ *State other relevant facts about the suit.*}

BACKGROUND

3. On {❿ *date*}, {⓫ *name*}, filed a petition in intervention that {⓬ *describe nature of the intervention*}.

4. {⓭ *State other facts relevant to the motion.*}

ARGUMENT & AUTHORITIES

{*CHOOSE APPROPRIATE SECTIONS A-E*}

A. The petition was not timely filed.

5. A court should strike a petition in intervention if it was not timely filed. *See Armstrong v. Tidelands Life Ins. Co.*, 466 S.W.2d 407, 412 (Tex. App.—Corpus Christi 1971, no writ).

6. The petition in intervention was not timely because {⓮ *state facts showing untimeliness*}.

B. The petition was filed after judgment was rendered.

7. A court should strike a petition in intervention if it was filed after judgment was rendered and the judgment has not been set aside. *First Alief Bank v. White*, 682 S.W.2d 251, 252 (Tex. 1984); *Gore v. Peck*, 191 S.W.3d 927, 928 (Tex. App.—Dallas 2006, no pet.). {*See* ***O'Connor's Texas Rules***, *"After judgment," ch. 5-J, §2.2.2, p. 455.*}

8. The petition in intervention was filed after judgment was rendered, and the judgment has not been set aside. {⓯ *Elaborate.*}

Continued on next page

C. Intervenor has no justiciable interest in the suit.

9. A court should strike a petition in intervention if the intervenor has no justiciable interest in the suit. *See In re Union Carbide Corp.*, 273 S.W.3d 152, 154-55 (Tex. 2008); *Law Offices of Windle Turley, P.C. v. Ghiasinejad*, 109 S.W.3d 68, 70 (Tex. App.—Fort Worth 2003, no pet.). A party has a justiciable interest in a suit only when the intervenor (1) could have brought all or part of the same suit in its own name or (2) would have been able to defeat all or part of the recovery if the suit had been filed against it. *See In re Union Carbide*, 273 S.W.3d at 155; *Guar. Fed. Sav. Bank v. Horseshoe Operating Co.*, 793 S.W.2d 652, 657 (Tex. 1990).

10. {[16] *Name of intervenor*} has no justiciable interest in this suit because {[17] *explain*}.

D. Intervention is not essential to protect intervenor's interest.

11. A court should strike a petition in intervention if the intervention is not essential to protect the intervenor's interest. *See Guar. Fed. Sav. Bank v. Horseshoe Operating Co.*, 793 S.W.2d 652, 657 (Tex. 1990); *Law Offices of Windle Turley, P.C. v. Ghiasinejad*, 109 S.W.3d 68, 70 (Tex. App.—Fort Worth 2003, no pet.).

12. Intervention in this suit is not essential because {[18] *name of intervenor*} may protect {[19] *his/her/its*} interest by {[20] *explain how intervenor can protect interest*}.

E. Intervention will complicate the case by an excessive multiplication of issues.

13. A court should strike a petition in intervention if the intervention will complicate the case by an excessive multiplication of the issues. *See Nghiem v. Sajib*, 567 S.W.3d 718, 721 n.17 (Tex. 2019); *Guar. Fed. Sav. Bank v. Horseshoe Operating Co.*, 793 S.W.2d 652, 657 (Tex. 1990); *Law Offices of Windle Turley, P.C. v. Ghiasinejad*, 109 S.W.3d 68, 70 (Tex. App.—Fort Worth 2003, no pet.).

14. Intervention will complicate this case by an excessive multiplication of issues because {[21] *explain*}.

CONCLUSION

15. {[22] *Briefly summarize the motion.*}

PRAYER

16. For these reasons, {[23] *party*} asks the Court to set this motion for a hearing and, after the hearing, strike the petition in intervention.

FORM 5J:2 MOTION TO STRIKE PETITION IN INTERVENTION

SEE: Tex. R. Civ. P. 40, 60, 61
*O'Connor's Texas Rules * Civil Trials* (2019), "Motion to strike," ch. 5-J, §2.4, p. 456

ADD: STYLE OF THE CASE – FORM 1B:2
SIGNATURE BLOCK – FORM 1B:3
CERTIFICATE OF SERVICE – FORM 1B:13

ATTACH: NOTICE OF HEARING OR SUBMISSION – FORM 1E:1
ORDER – FORM 1G:1

NOTE: **If an intervening plaintiff has not established proper venue, the defendant should file a motion to sever the intervening plaintiff's claims and transfer venue. See FORM 3C:2.**

If an intervening plaintiff has not alleged facts demonstrating the court's subject-matter jurisdiction over its claims for relief, the defendant should file a motion to dismiss for lack of jurisdiction. See FORM 3F:1.

INTERVENOR'S RESPONSE TO
{❶ *ADVERSE PARTY*}'S MOTION TO STRIKE PETITION IN INTERVENTION

Intervenor, {❷ *name*}, asks the Court to deny {❸ *adverse party*} {❹ *name*}'s motion to strike the petition in intervention.

INTRODUCTION

1. On {❺ *date*}, plaintiff, {❻ *name*}, sued defendant, {❼ *name*}, for {❽ *state basis of suit*}.

2. {❾ *State other relevant facts about the suit.*}

BACKGROUND

3. On {❿ *date*}, intervenor filed a petition in intervention that {⓫ *describe nature of the intervention*}.

4. On {⓬ *date*}, {⓭ *adverse party*} filed a motion to strike the petition in intervention.

5. {⓮ *State other facts relevant to the response.*}

ARGUMENT & AUTHORITIES

6. A court should deny a motion to strike a petition in intervention when (1) the intervenor has a justiciable interest in the suit, (2) the intervention is essential to protect the intervenor's interest, and (3) the intervention will not complicate the case by an excessive multiplication of the issues. *Guar. Fed. Sav. Bank v. Horseshoe Operating Co.*, 793 S.W.2d 652, 657 (Tex. 1990).

{*CHOOSE APPROPRIATE SECTIONS A-C*}

A. Intervenor has justiciable interest in the suit.

7. A party can intervene in a suit as a matter of right when it has a justiciable interest in the suit. *Nghiem v. Sajib*, 567 S.W.3d 718, 721 (Tex. 2019); *In re Union Carbide Corp.*, 273 S.W.3d 152, 155 (Tex. 2008); *Intermarque Auto. Prods., Inc. v. Feldman*, 21 S.W.3d 544, 549 (Tex. App.—Texarkana 2000, no pet.).

{*CHOOSE APPROPRIATE PARAGRAPH 8*}

8. A party has a justiciable interest as a plaintiff when it could have brought all or part of the suit in its own name. *Nghiem*, 567 S.W.3d at 721 n.16; *In re Union Carbide*,

273 S.W.3d at 155; *Guar. Fed.*, 793 S.W.2d at 657. {*See **O'Connor's Texas Rules**, "Justiciable interest," ch. 5-J, §2.1.3(3), p. 454; "Burden on intervenor," ch. 5-J, §2.5.2, p. 456.*}

8. A party has a justiciable interest as a defendant when it could have defeated all or part of the recovery if the suit had been filed against it. *Guar. Fed.*, 793 S.W.2d at 657; *Metromedia Long Distance, Inc. v. Hughes*, 810 S.W.2d 494, 497 (Tex. App.—San Antonio 1991, writ denied). {*See **O'Connor's Texas Rules**, "Justiciable interest," ch. 5-J, §2.1.3(3), p. 454; "Burden on intervenor," ch. 5-J, §2.5.2, p. 456.*}

9. Intervenor has a justiciable interest in the suit because {15 *describe the interest and how it either entitles the intervenor to some recovery or allows the intervenor to defeat some recovery*}. Thus, the Court should deny {16 *adverse party*}'s motion to strike.

B. Intervention is essential to protect interest.

10. A party can intervene when the intervention is essential to protect the intervenor's interest. *Guar. Fed.*, 793 S.W.2d at 657; *Law Offices of Windle Turley, P.C. v. Ghiasinejad*, 109 S.W.3d 68, 70 (Tex. App.—Fort Worth 2003, no pet.). The asserted interest can be legal or equitable. *Guar. Fed.*, 793 S.W.2d at 657.

11. If the Court strikes the petition in intervention, intervenor will not be able to protect {17 *his/her/its*} interest because {18 *explain*}. Thus, the Court should deny {19 *adverse party*}'s motion to strike.

C. Intervention will not complicate the case.

12. A party can intervene when the intervention will not complicate the case by an excessive multiplication of the issues. *Guar. Fed.*, 793 S.W.2d at 657; *Law Offices of Windle Turley, P.C. v. Ghiasinejad*, 109 S.W.3d 68, 70 (Tex. App.—Fort Worth 2003, no pet.).

13. The intervention will not complicate the case because {20 *explain*}. Thus, the Court should deny {21 *adverse party*}'s motion to strike.

CONCLUSION

14. {22 *Briefly summarize the response.*}

PRAYER

15. For these reasons, intervenor asks the Court to deny {23 *adverse party*}'s motion to strike the petition in intervention.

Continued on next page

SEE: Tex. R. Civ. P. 40, 60, 61
O'Connor's Texas Rules * Civil Trials (2019), "Motion to strike," ch. 5-J, §2.4, p. 456

ADD: STYLE OF THE CASE – FORM 1B:2
SIGNATURE BLOCK – FORM 1B:3
CERTIFICATE OF SERVICE – FORM 1B:13

ATTACH: AFFIDAVIT – FORM 1B:8, if necessary
ORDER – FORM 1G:1

NOTE: The issue of whether the intervenor has a justiciable interest in the suit may be resolved by reference to the petition in intervention. ***Potash Corp. v. Mancias***, 942 S.W.2d 61, 64 (Tex.App.—Corpus Christi 1997, orig. proceeding).

{❶ *NAME*}'S ORIGINAL PETITION IN INTERPLEADER

Interpleader-plaintiff, {❷ *name*} ("plaintiff"), files this petition in interpleader, under Texas Rule of Civil Procedure 43, against {❸ *names of adverse parties*} and alleges as follows: {*See* ***O'Connor's Texas Rules****, "Interpleader Suit," ch. 5-J, §3, p. 457.*}

DISCOVERY-CONTROL PLAN

{*CHOOSE APPROPRIATE PARAGRAPH 1*}

1. Plaintiff intends to conduct discovery under Level 1 of Texas Rule of Civil Procedure 190.2 and affirmatively pleads that this suit is governed by the expedited-actions process of Texas Rule of Civil Procedure 169. {*See* ***O'Connor's Texas Rules****, "Discovery-Control Plans," ch. 2-B, §2, p. 115.*}

1. Plaintiff intends to conduct discovery under Level {❹ *2/3*} of Texas Rule of Civil Procedure {❺ *190.3/190.4*} and affirmatively pleads that this suit is not governed by the expedited-actions process of Texas Rule of Civil Procedure 169 because {❻ *explain*}. {*See* ***O'Connor's Texas Rules****, "Discovery-Control Plans," ch. 2-B, §2, p. 115.*}

PARTIES

2. {*For plaintiff designation, see FORM 2B:9;* ***O'Connor's Texas Rules****, "Plaintiff," ch. 2-B, §4.4, p. 123.*}

3. {*For defendant designation, see FORMS 2B:10-19;* ***O'Connor's Texas Rules****, "Defendant," ch. 2-B, §4.5, p. 123.*}

JURISDICTION

4. {*For jurisdiction allegations, see FORM 2B:20. It is not necessary to plead jurisdiction for most suits. See* ***O'Connor's Texas Rules****, "Jurisdiction," ch. 2-B, §5, p. 125.*}

VENUE

5. {*For venue allegations, see FORM 2B:21. It is not necessary to plead venue, but pleading sufficient venue facts could avoid a motion to transfer venue. See* ***O'Connor's Texas Rules****, "Venue," ch. 2-B, §6, p. 127.*}

Continued on next page

FACTS

6. Plaintiff is an innocent stakeholder holding {❼ *describe the disputed property*}.

7. There {❽ *are/may be*} rival claimants to this property. {❾ *Identify rival claimants, describe each claimant's interest in the property, and state why the interests are adverse.*}

8. {❿ *State other facts relevant to the petition.*}

PROPERTY SUBJECT TO MULTIPLE CLAIMS

9. Plaintiff {⓫ *is subject to/has reasonable grounds to anticipate*} rival claims to the same property by {⓬ *identify rival claimants*}. There is reasonable doubt about which claim is valid. {⓭ *Elaborate.*} {*See Tri-State Pipe & Equip., Inc. v. S. Cty. Mut. Ins. Co., 8 S.W.3d 394, 402 (Tex. App.—Texarkana 1999, no pet.); Olmos v. Pecan Grove Mun. Util. Dist., 857 S.W.2d 734, 741 (Tex. App.—Houston [14th Dist.] 1993, no writ);* ***O'Connor's Texas Rules****, "Rival claims," ch. 5-J, §3.2.2, p. 458.*}

10. Plaintiff makes an unconditional tender of the disputed property into the Court's registry. Attached to this petition is a copy of a receipt for the property provided by the court clerk. {*See* ***O'Connor's Texas Rules****, "Unconditional tender," ch. 5-J, §3.2.3, p. 458.*}

{*ADD SECTION BELOW IF APPLICABLE*}

ATTORNEY FEES

11. Plaintiff is an innocent, disinterested stakeholder and should be awarded reasonable attorney fees for the following reasons:

a. Plaintiff needed to hire {⓮ *name of attorney*} to prepare this petition.

b. Plaintiff did not unreasonably delay in filing this petition. {⓯ *Elaborate.*}

c. Plaintiff is not responsible for the conflicting claims to the property. {⓰ *Elaborate.*}

12. The reasonable and necessary attorney fees incurred in filing this petition are ${⓱ *amount*}, which are established by the affidavit of {⓲ *name of attorney*}, attached as Exhibit {⓳ *letter*}. {*See* ***O'Connor's Texas Rules****, "Attorney fees," ch. 5-J, §3.2.5, p. 458.*}

PRAYER

13. For these reasons, plaintiff asks the Court to set this petition in interpleader for a hearing, and after the hearing, sign an order that discharges plaintiff from this suit and awards plaintiff {⓴ *add if appropriate: attorney fees and*} court costs.

SEE: Tex. R. Civ. P. 43
O'Connor's Texas Rules * Civil Trials (2019), "Interpleader Suit," ch. 5-J, §3, p. 457

ADD: STYLE OF THE CASE – FORM 1B:2
SIGNATURE BLOCK – FORM 1B:3
CERTIFICATE OF SERVICE – FORM 1B:13

ATTACH: AFFIDAVIT – FORM 1B:8, if necessary
NOTICE OF HEARING OR SUBMISSION – FORM 1E:1
AFFIDAVIT FOR ATTORNEY FEES – FORM 1H:14, if necessary
ORDER – FORM 5J:6
Copy of interpleader's receipt for funds or property

NOTE: Before a court clerk will issue a citation for service, the plaintiff may be required to complete and file with its petition a Civil Process Request Form identifying the person to be served and the method of service. Check the court's website for specific requirements and to obtain a copy of the form.

Although many courts have applied a timeliness requirement to interpleader suits, the Supreme Court has clarified that the only requirement for bringing an interpleader suit is conflicting claims. ***State Farm Life Ins. v. Martinez***, 216 S.W.3d 799, 807 (Tex.2007). Unreasonable delay does not make interpleader improper, but it may bar the stakeholder from recovering attorney fees or may subject the stakeholder to any applicable statutory penalties. *Id.*

For information on the procedures for expedited actions and e-filing requirements, see the notes under FORM 2B:1.

{❶ *PARTY*}'S MOTION TO STRIKE PETITION IN INTERPLEADER

{❷ *Party*}, {❸ *name*}, asks the Court to strike {❹ *name of interpleader*}'s petition in interpleader. {*See* ***O'Connor's Texas Rules***, *"Response," ch. 5-J, §3.3, p. 458.*}

INTRODUCTION

1. On {❺ *date*}, interpleader-plaintiff, {❻ *name of interpleader*}, filed a petition in interpleader against claimant-defendants {❼ *name of party*} and {❽ *names of other claimant-defendants*} to interplead {❾ *identify the interpleaded property*}.

2. {❿ *State other relevant facts about the suit.*}

BACKGROUND

3. {⓫ *State facts relevant to the motion.*}

ARGUMENT & AUTHORITIES

4. A party who anticipates or has received multiple claims to property in its possession can join all the claimants in a single suit and obtain a discharge when a reasonable doubt exists in law or fact about which claim is valid and when the party unconditionally tenders the property into the court's registry. *See* Tex. R. Civ. P. 43; *Young v. Gumfory*, 322 S.W.3d 731, 743 (Tex. App.—Dallas 2010, no pet.); *Clayton v. Mony Life Ins. Co.*, 284 S.W.3d 398, 402 (Tex. App.—Beaumont 2009, no pet.).

{*CHOOSE APPROPRIATE SECTIONS A-F*}

A. The property is not subject to rival claims.

5. A court should deny a petition in interpleader if the interpleader-plaintiff is not subject to and has no reasonable grounds to anticipate rival claims to the same property. *See Davis v. E. Tex. S&L Ass'n*, 354 S.W.2d 926, 930 (Tex. 1962); *Young*, 322 S.W.3d at 743-44; *Clayton*, 284 S.W.3d at 402. {*See* ***O'Connor's Texas Rules***, *"No rival claims," ch. 5-J, §3.3.1, p. 458.*}

6. Interpleader-plaintiff is not subject to and has no reasonable grounds to anticipate rival claims to the same property. {⓬ *Elaborate.*} Thus, the Court should strike the petition in interpleader.

B. There is no reasonable doubt about which claim is valid.

7. A court should deny a petition in interpleader if there is no reasonable doubt about which rival claim is valid. *See Young*, 322 S.W.3d at 744; *Clayton*, 284 S.W.3d at 402.

8. {⓭ *Party*} is the only claimant-defendant with a valid claim to the property. {⓮ *Name of other claimant-defendant*}'s claim is invalid on its face and does not raise a reasonable doubt about which claimant is entitled to the property. {⓯ *Elaborate.*} Thus, the Court should strike the petition in interpleader.

C. Interpleader-plaintiff has not tendered the disputed property.

9. A court should deny a petition in interpleader if the interpleader-plaintiff has not unconditionally tendered the disputed property into the court's registry. *See Fort Worth Transp. Auth. v. Rodriguez*, 547 S.W.3d 830, 850-51 (Tex. 2018); *Rapp v. Mandell & Wright, P.C.*, 127 S.W.3d 888, 895 (Tex. App.—Corpus Christi 2004, pet. denied); *Tri-State Pipe & Equip., Inc. v. S. Cty. Mut. Ins. Co.*, 8 S.W.3d 394, 402-03 (Tex. App.—Texarkana 1999, no pet.).

10. Interpleader-plaintiff has not unconditionally tendered the disputed property into the Court's registry. {⓰ *Elaborate.*} Thus, the Court should strike the petition in interpleader.

D. Interpleader-plaintiff has an interest in the property.

11. A court cannot award attorney fees if the interpleader-plaintiff has an interest in the property. *See Fort Worth Transp. Auth. v. Rodriguez*, 547 S.W.3d 830, 851-52 (Tex. 2018); *FinServ Cas. Corp. v. Transamerica Life Ins. Co.*, 523 S.W.3d 129, 141 (Tex. App.—Houston [14th Dist.] 2016, pet. denied); *Brown v. Getty Reserve Oil, Inc.*, 626 S.W.2d 810, 815 (Tex. App.—Amarillo 1981, writ dism'd w.o.j.).

12. The Court should deny interpleader-plaintiff's request for attorney fees because interpleader-plaintiff is not a disinterested stakeholder but instead has an interest in the property. {⓱ *Elaborate.*}

E. Interpleader-plaintiff caused the conflicting claims.

13. A court cannot award attorney fees if the interpleader-plaintiff is responsible for causing the conflicting claims. *See Fort Worth Transp. Auth. v. Rodriguez*, 547 S.W.3d 830, 851 (Tex. 2018); *Olmos v. Pecan Grove Mun. Util. Dist.*, 857 S.W.2d 734, 742 (Tex. App.—Houston [14th Dist.] 1993, no writ); *Brown v. Getty Reserve Oil, Inc.*, 626 S.W.2d 810, 815 (Tex. App.—Amarillo 1981, writ dism'd w.o.j.).

14. The Court should deny interpleader-plaintiff's request for attorney fees because interpleader-plaintiff is responsible for the conflicting claims to the property. {⓲ *Elaborate.*}

◄ *Continued on next page* ►

F. Interpleader-plaintiff did not timely file the petition.

15. A court should not award attorney fees if the interpleader-plaintiff did not timely file the petition. *See State Farm Life Ins. Co. v. Martinez*, 216 S.W.3d 799, 807 (Tex. 2007).

16. The Court should deny interpleader-plaintiff's request for attorney fees because interpleader-plaintiff unreasonably delayed the filing of the petition. {⓳ *Elaborate.*}

CONCLUSION

17. {⓴ *Briefly summarize the motion.*}

PRAYER

18. For these reasons, {㉑ *party*} asks the Court to strike the petition in interpleader.

SEE: Tex. R. Civ. P. 43
O'Connor's Texas Rules * Civil Trials (2019), "Response," ch. 5-J, §3.3, p. 458

ADD: STYLE OF THE CASE – FORM 1B:2
SIGNATURE BLOCK – FORM 1B:3
CERTIFICATE OF SERVICE – FORM 1B:13

ATTACH: AFFIDAVIT – FORM 1B:8, if necessary
ORDER – FORM 5J:6

NOTE: Although many courts have applied a timeliness requirement to interpleader suits, the Supreme Court has clarified that the only requirement for bringing an interpleader suit is conflicting claims. ***State Farm Life Ins. v. Martinez***, 216 S.W.3d 799, 807 (Tex.2007). Unreasonable delay does not make interpleader improper, but it may bar the stakeholder from recovering attorney fees or may subject the stakeholder to any applicable statutory penalties. *Id.*

ORDER ON PETITION IN INTERPLEADER

After considering interpleader-plaintiff {❶ *name of interpleader*}'s petition in interpleader, the motion to strike, and arguments of counsel, the Court

{*CHOOSE APPROPRIATE ORDER*}

STRIKES the petition in interpleader {❷ *add if appropriate: and orders the interpleaded property to be returned to the interpleader-plaintiff*}. {*See* ***O'Connor's Texas Rules****, "Interpleader not appropriate," ch. 5-J, §3.5.2, p. 459.*}

GRANTS the petition in interpleader. {*See* ***O'Connor's Texas Rules****, "Interpleader appropriate," ch. 5-J, §3.5.1, p. 459.*}

1. The Court orders interpleader-plaintiff to deposit the following property into the registry of the Court. {❸ *Describe the property or state the amount of funds.*}

2. The Court orders interpleader-plaintiff discharged from this suit.

{*ADD PARAGRAPH 3 IF APPLICABLE*}

3. The Court orders {❹ *names of rival claimants*}, jointly and severally, to pay court costs of ${❺ *amount*} and attorney fees of ${❻ *amount*} to interpleader-plaintiff.
4. This case will continue on the merits between {❼ *names of rival claimants*} to determine their respective rights to the property.

SIGNED on _______________, 20___.

____
PRESIDING JUDGE

SEE: Tex. R. Civ. P. 43
O'Connor's Texas Rules * Civil Trials (2019), "Order on interpleader," ch. 5-J, §3.5, p. 459

ADD: STYLE OF THE CASE – FORM 1B:2
CERTIFICATE OF SERVICE – FORM 1B:13, if proposed order served separately from motion or response

{[1] *PARTY*}'S MOTION TO CONSOLIDATE

{[2] *Party*}, {[3] *name*}, asks the Court to consolidate this case with {[4] *identify style and cause number of other case*}, in {[5] _______} Court in {[6] _______} County, Texas. {*See* ***O'Connor's Texas Rules****, "Motion to Consolidate," ch. 5-J, §4, p. 459.*}

INTRODUCTION

1. Plaintiff, {[7] *name*}, sued defendant, {[8] *name*}, for {[9] *state basis of suit*}.

2. {[10] *State other relevant facts about the suit.*}

BACKGROUND

3. This case relates to and shares common questions of law or fact with {[11] *identify style and cause number of other case*}, in {[12] _______} Court in {[13] _______} County, Texas. {[14] *Identify parties in related case and state basis of suit.*}

4. {[15] *State other facts relevant to the motion.*}

ARGUMENT & AUTHORITIES

5. Consolidation of cases is appropriate if (1) the cases relate to substantially the same subject matter, transaction, or occurrence and involve common questions of law or fact, (2) the same evidence is material, relevant, and admissible in both cases, (3) consolidation promotes judicial economy and convenience, and (4) consolidation will not result in an unfair trial. *See* Tex. R. Civ. P. 174(a); *In re Van Waters & Rogers, Inc.*, 145 S.W.3d 203, 207 (Tex. 2004); *Lone Star Ford, Inc. v. McCormick*, 838 S.W.2d 734, 737-38 (Tex. App.—Houston [1st Dist.] 1992, writ denied).

6. The Court should consolidate this case with {[16] *identify style and cause number of other case*}, in {[17] _______} Court in {[18] _______} County, Texas, because the cases arose from the same {[19] *subject matter/transaction/occurrence*} and involve common questions of {[20] *law/fact/law and fact*}. {[21] *Elaborate.*}

7. In a consolidated trial of these cases, the evidence presented will be material, relevant, and admissible in each case. {[22] *Elaborate.*} {*See* ***O'Connor's Texas Rules****, "Standards to apply," ch. 5-J, §4.1.1, p. 460.*}

8. The consolidation of these cases promotes judicial economy and convenience. {[23] *Elaborate with facts on promoting judicial economy and convenience such as preventing inconsistent adjudications of factual and legal issues, avoiding unnecessary costs, preventing undue delay, shortening the time necessary for multiple trials by having one trial, witness availability, and availability of judicial resources.*}

9. Consolidation will not result in an unfair trial. {㉔ *Elaborate with facts showing that a consolidated trial will not result in delay, jury confusion, or prejudice to the parties.*}

CONCLUSION

10. {㉕ *Briefly summarize the motion.*}

PRAYER

11. For these reasons, {㉖ *party*} asks the Court, after a hearing, to consolidate this case with {㉗ *identify style and cause number of other case*} in {㉘ _______} Court in {㉙ _______} County, Texas.

SEE: Tex. R. Civ. P. 41, 174(a)
O'Connor's Texas Rules * Civil Trials (2019), "Motion to Consolidate," ch. 5-J, §4, p. 459

ADD: STYLE OF THE CASE – FORM 1B:2
SIGNATURE BLOCK – FORM 1B:3
CERTIFICATE OF CONFERENCE – FORM 1B:12
CERTIFICATE OF SERVICE – FORM 1B:13

ATTACH: AFFIDAVIT – FORM 1B:8, if necessary
NOTICE OF HEARING OR SUBMISSION – FORM 1E:1
ORDER – FORM 5J:9

NOTE: Some local rules require that the motion to consolidate be filed in the court where the first-filed case is pending. *E.g.*, ***Waterman S.S. Corp. v. Ruiz***, 355 S.W.3d 387, 399 n.4 (Tex.App.—Houston [1st Dist.] 2011, pet. denied) (Harris County Local Rule 3.2.3(a)); *see, e.g.*, ***Starnes v. Holloway***, 779 S.W.2d 86, 96 (Tex.App.—Dallas 1989, writ denied) (Dallas County Local Rule 1.1(e), now 1.04). However, a consolidation order based on a motion filed in the court of the later-filed case is not necessarily void. *See* ***Starnes***, 779 S.W.2d at 96.

{1 *PARTY*}'S RESPONSE TO
{2 *ADVERSE PARTY*}'S MOTION TO CONSOLIDATE

{3 *Party*}, {4 *name*}, asks the Court to deny {5 *adverse party*} {6 *name*}'s motion to consolidate this case with {7 *identify style and cause number of other case*}, in {8 _______} Court in {9 _______} County, Texas. {*See* ***O'Connor's Texas Rules***, *"Objection," ch. 5-J, §4.2, p. 460.*}

INTRODUCTION

1. Plaintiff, {10 *name*}, sued defendant, {11 *name*}, for {12 *state basis of suit*}.

2. {13 *State other relevant facts about the suit.*}

BACKGROUND

3. {14 *Identify style and cause number of other case*} is currently pending in {15 _______} Court in {16 _______} County, Texas. {17 *Identify parties in related case and state basis of suit.*}

4. {18 *State other facts relevant to the response.*}

ARGUMENT & AUTHORITIES

5. To be consolidated, cases should relate to substantially the same subject matter, involve common questions of law or fact, and require the same evidence. *Owens-Corning Fiberglas Corp. v. Martin*, 942 S.W.2d 712, 716 (Tex. App.—Dallas 1997, no writ); *Lone Star Ford, Inc. v. McCormick*, 838 S.W.2d 734, 737 (Tex. App.—Houston [1st Dist.] 1992, writ denied); *see* Tex. R. Civ. P. 41. If consolidation would result in prejudice, delay, or confusion, a court should deny consolidation. *In re Van Waters & Rogers, Inc.*, 145 S.W.3d 203, 207 (Tex. 2004) (prejudice or confusion); *In re Shell Oil Co.*, 202 S.W.3d 286, 290 (Tex. App.—Beaumont 2006, orig. proceeding) (prejudice, delay, or confusion); *Dal-Briar Corp. v. Baskette*, 833 S.W.2d 612, 615 (Tex. App.—El Paso 1992, orig. proceeding) (same).

6. The Court should not consolidate this case with {19 *identify style and cause number of other case*} because {20 *state facts demonstrating that consolidation will result in delay, confusion, or prejudice, or that the cases do not actually arise from the same transaction or occurrence, or that the same evidence is not material, relevant, or admissible in each case*}.

CONCLUSION

7. {21 *Briefly summarize the response.*}

PRAYER

8. For these reasons, {22 *party*} asks the Court to deny {23 *adverse party*}'s motion to consolidate this case with {24 *identify style and cause number of other case*} in {25 _______} Court in {26 _______} County, Texas.

SEE: Tex. R. Civ. P. 41, 174(a)
O'Connor's Texas Rules * Civil Trials (2019), "Motion to Consolidate," ch. 5-J, §4, p. 459

ADD: STYLE OF THE CASE – FORM 1B:2
SIGNATURE BLOCK – FORM 1B:3
CERTIFICATE OF SERVICE – FORM 1B:13

ATTACH: AFFIDAVIT – FORM 1B:8, if necessary
ORDER – FORM 5J:9

ORDER ON MOTION TO CONSOLIDATE

After considering {❶ *party*} {❷ *name*}'s motion to consolidate, the response, and arguments of counsel, the Court

{*CHOOSE APPROPRIATE ORDER*}

DENIES the motion to consolidate.

GRANTS the motion to consolidate, orders that {❸ *style of case*}, cause number {❹ *cause number*}, be consolidated with {❺ *style of case*}, cause number {❻ *cause number*}, and orders the clerk to note on the docket sheets in both cases that the cases were consolidated under cause number {❼ *cause number*}.

SIGNED on _______________, 20___.

____
PRESIDING JUDGE

SEE: Tex. R. Civ. P. 174(a)
O'Connor's Texas Rules * Civil Trials (2019), "Order," ch. 5-J, §4.3, p. 460

ADD: STYLE OF THE CASE – FORM 1B:2
CERTIFICATE OF SERVICE – FORM 1B:13, if proposed order served separately from motion or response

{❶ *PARTY*}'S MOTION FOR SANCTIONS

{❷ *Party*}, {❸ *name*}, asks the Court to impose appropriate sanctions against {❹ *identify person or persons to be sanctioned, e.g., plaintiff, plaintiff's attorney, both plaintiff and plaintiff's attorney*} for filing a groundless {❺ *pleading/motion/paper*}.

INTRODUCTION

1. Plaintiff, {❻ *name*}, sued defendant, {❼ *name*}, for {❽ *state basis of suit*}.

2. {❾ *State other relevant facts about the suit.*}

BACKGROUND

3. On {❿ *date*}, {⓫ *adverse party*} filed {⓬ *identify groundless pleading, motion, or other paper*}.

4. {⓭ *State other facts relevant to the motion.*}

ARGUMENT & AUTHORITIES

{*CHOOSE APPROPRIATE SECTIONS A-C*}

A. The {⓮ *identify pleading, motion, or other paper filed by adverse party*} is groundless under Tex. R. Civ. P. 13.

5. A court must impose sanctions against an attorney or party who signs a pleading, motion, or other paper if it (1) is groundless and (2) was brought in bad faith or for the purpose of harassment. Tex. R. Civ. P. 13. A party can be sanctioned for its attorney's conduct if the party is implicated in the conduct apart from having entrusted the legal representation to the attorney. *TransAmerican Nat. Gas Corp. v. Powell*, 811 S.W.2d 913, 917 (Tex. 1991); *Loeffler v. Lytle Indep. Sch. Dist.*, 211 S.W.3d 331, 349-50 (Tex. App.—San Antonio 2006, pet. denied).

6. A paper is groundless when it has no basis in law or fact and is not warranted by a good-faith argument for the extension, modification, or reversal of existing law. Tex. R. Civ. P. 13; *see, e.g.*, *Robson v. Gilbreath*, 267 S.W.3d 401, 406 (Tex. App.—Austin 2008, pet. denied) (groundless pleading); *In re A.C.B.*, 103 S.W.3d 570, 576 (Tex. App.—San Antonio 2003, no pet.) (groundless paper). The standard for reviewing whether a paper is groundless is objective: did the party and the attorney make a reasonable inquiry into the legal and factual basis of the claim? The reasonableness of the inquiry is judged by the facts available and the circumstances present when the party filed the paper. *See Tarrant Cty. v. Chancey*, 942 S.W.2d 151, 155 (Tex. App.—Fort Worth 1997, no writ).

Continued on next page

7. A paper is brought in bad faith when the signer consciously acted with a dishonest, discriminatory, or malicious purpose. *Parker v. Walton*, 233 S.W.3d 535, 540 (Tex. App.—Houston [14th Dist.] 2007, no pet.); *Campos v. Ysleta Gen. Hosp., Inc.*, 879 S.W.2d 67, 71 (Tex. App.—El Paso 1994, writ denied). A pleading, motion, or other paper is brought to harass when the signer means to annoy, alarm, and abuse another person. *Parker*, 233 S.W.3d at 540. {*See* ***O'Connor's Texas Rules***, *"TRCP 13," ch. 5-K, §5.2.2, p. 468.*}

8. {[15] *Adverse party*}'s {[16] *pleading/motion/paper*} is groundless and was brought {[17] *in bad faith/for the purpose of harassment*}. Specifically, the {[18] *pleading/motion/paper*} {[19] *explain why document is groundless and describe acts that constitute bad faith or harassment*}. {[20] *Name of signing person*} signed the {[21] *pleading/motion/paper*}, so {[22] *he/she*} is subject to sanctions.

{*ADD PARAGRAPH 9 IF APPROPRIATE*}

9. {[23] *Adverse party*} is also subject to sanctions because {[24] *he/she/it*} is implicated in the sanctionable conduct apart from having entrusted the legal representation to the attorney. {[25] *Elaborate.*}

B. The {[26] *identify pleading or motion filed by adverse party*} was signed in violation of Tex. Civ. Prac. & Rem. Code §10.001.

10. A court can impose sanctions on a person who signs a pleading or motion in violation of Texas Civil Practice & Remedies Code section 10.001, a party represented by the signing person, or both. Tex. Civ. Prac. & Rem. Code §10.004(a). A party can be sanctioned for its attorney's conduct if the party is implicated in the conduct apart from having entrusted the legal representation to the attorney. *TransAmerican Nat. Gas Corp. v. Powell*, 811 S.W.2d 913, 917 (Tex. 1991); *Loeffler v. Lytle Indep. Sch. Dist.*, 211 S.W.3d 331, 349-50 (Tex. App.—San Antonio 2006, pet. denied). {*See* ***O'Connor's Texas Rules***, *"CPRC ch. 10," ch. 5-K, §5.2.1, p. 468.*}

{*CHOOSE APPROPRIATE PARAGRAPHS 11-14*}

11. A pleading or motion is signed in violation of section 10.001 if it is presented for an improper purpose, such as to harass, cause unnecessary delay, or needlessly increase the cost of litigation. Tex. Civ. Prac. & Rem. Code §10.001(1).

12. A pleading or motion is signed in violation of section 10.001 if its claims, defenses, or other legal contentions are unsupported by existing law or by a nonfrivolous argument for the extension, modification, or reversal of existing law or the establishment of new law. Tex. Civ. Prac. & Rem. Code §10.001(2).

13. A pleading or motion is signed in violation of section 10.001 if its allegations or factual contentions lack evidentiary support or if a specifically identified allegation or factual contention is unlikely to have evidentiary support after a reasonable opportunity for further investigation or discovery. Tex. Civ. Prac. & Rem. Code §10.001(3).

14. A pleading or motion is signed in violation of section 10.001 if each denial of a factual contention is unwarranted by the evidence or if a specifically identified denial is not reasonably based on a lack of information or belief. Tex. Civ. Prac. & Rem. Code §10.001(4).

15. {㉗ *Adverse party*}'s {㉘ *pleading/motion*} was signed in violation of section 10.001 because {㉙ *demonstrate how pleading or motion violates the statute*}. {㉚ *Name of signing person*} signed the {㉛ *pleading/motion*}, so {㉜ *he/she*} is subject to sanctions.

{*ADD PARAGRAPH 16 IF APPROPRIATE*}

16. {㉝ *Adverse party*} is also subject to sanctions because {㉞ *he/she/it*} is implicated in the sanctionable conduct apart from having entrusted the legal representation to the attorney. {㉟ *Elaborate.*}

C. The {㊱ *identify pleading or motion filed by adverse party*} is groundless under Tex. Civ. Prac. & Rem. Code §9.011.

17. A court must impose sanctions on a person who signs a pleading or motion in violation of Texas Civil Practice & Remedies Code section 9.011, a party represented by the signing person, or both. Tex. Civ. Prac. & Rem. Code §9.012(c). A party can be sanctioned for its attorney's conduct if the party is implicated in the conduct apart from having entrusted the legal representation to the attorney. *TransAmerican Nat. Gas Corp. v. Powell*, 811 S.W.2d 913, 917 (Tex. 1991); *Loeffler v. Lytle Indep. Sch. Dist.*, 211 S.W.3d 331, 349-50 (Tex. App.—San Antonio 2006, pet. denied). {*See* ***O'Connor's Texas Rules***, *"CPRC ch. 9," ch. 5-K, §5.2.3, p. 469.*}

18. A pleading or motion is signed in violation of section 9.011 if it is both groundless and brought in bad faith, to harass, or for any improper purpose (e.g., to cause delay or needless increase in the cost of litigation). *Elkins v. Stotts-Brown*, 103 S.W.3d 664, 668 (Tex. App.—Dallas 2003, no pet.); *Herrmann & Andreas Ins. Agency, Inc. v. Appling*, 800 S.W.2d 312, 320 (Tex. App.—Corpus Christi 1990, no writ); *see* Tex. Civ. Prac. & Rem. Code §9.011. {*See* ***O'Connor's Texas Rules***, *"CPRC ch. 9," ch. 5-K, §5.2.3, p. 469.*}

Continued on next page

19. {㊲ *Adverse party*}'s {㊳ *pleading/motion*} was signed in violation of section 9.011 because {㊴ *demonstrate how pleading or motion violates the statute*}. {㊵ *Name of signing person*} signed the {㊶ *pleading/motion*}, so {㊷ *he/she*} is subject to sanctions.

{*ADD PARAGRAPH 20 IF APPROPRIATE*}

20. {㊸ *Adverse party*} is also subject to sanctions because {㊹ *he/she/it*} is implicated in the sanctionable conduct apart from having entrusted the legal representation to the attorney. {㊺ *Elaborate.*}

REQUEST FOR SANCTIONS

21. Sanctions are just if they have a direct relationship to the offensive conduct and are not excessive. *Nath v. Tex. Children's Hosp.*, 446 S.W.3d 355, 363 (Tex. 2014); *Am. Flood Research, Inc. v. Jones*, 192 S.W.3d 581, 583 (Tex. 2006); *Spohn Hosp. v. Mayer*, 104 S.W.3d 878, 882 (Tex. 2003). {*See* ***O'Connor's Texas Rules***, *"Request sanction," ch. 5-K, §8.2.3, p. 476.*}

{*ADD APPROPRIATE PARAGRAPH 22 IF APPLICABLE*}

22. Death-penalty sanctions are appropriate when (1) the court has already used a lesser sanction to attempt to secure {㊻ *adverse party*}'s compliance and (2) the party's conduct justifies the presumption that {㊼ *his/her/its*} {㊽ *claims/defenses*} lack merit. *Chrysler Corp. v. Blackmon*, 841 S.W.2d 844, 849-50 (Tex. 1992).

22. Death-penalty sanctions are appropriate when (1) a party has committed egregious misconduct, (2) the Court has considered lesser sanctions, and (3) the party's conduct justifies the presumption that {㊾ *his/her/its*} {㊿ *claims/defenses*} lack merit. *Cire v. Cummings*, 134 S.W.3d 835, 841-42 (Tex. 2004). {*See* ***O'Connor's Texas Rules***, *"Egregious misconduct," ch. 5-K, §3.2.3(2), p. 465; "No merit," ch. 5-K, §3.2.4, p. 465.*}

23. {51 *Party*} asks the Court to impose the following sanctions on {52 *identify person or persons to be sanctioned*}.

{*CHOOSE APPROPRIATE SANCTIONS*}

{*For violation of Rule 13*}

a. An order designating certain matters as established against {53 *adverse party*}. Tex. R. Civ. P. 215.2(b)(3); *see* Tex. R. Civ. P. 13. {54 *Elaborate.*}

b. An order prohibiting {55 *adverse party*} from {56 *supporting/opposing*} certain {57 *claims/defenses*}. Tex. R. Civ. P. 215.2(b)(4); *see* Tex. R. Civ. P. 13. {58 *Elaborate.*}

c. An order striking all or part of {59 *adverse party*}'s pleadings. Tex. R. Civ. P. 215.2(b)(5); *see* Tex. R. Civ. P. 13. {60 *Elaborate.*}

d. An order dismissing {61 *adverse party*}'s suit with prejudice. Tex. R. Civ. P. 215.2(b)(5); *see* Tex. R. Civ. P. 13. {62 *Elaborate.*}

e. An order {63 *identify other appropriate sanctions from Tex. R. Civ. P. 215.2(b)*}. {64 *Elaborate.*}

{*For violation of Tex. Civ. Prac. & Rem. Code §10.001*}

f. An order directing {65 *identify person or persons to be sanctioned*} to {66 *perform/refrain from performing*} {67 *identify act*}. Tex. Civ. Prac. & Rem. Code §10.004(c)(1). {68 *Elaborate.*}

g. An order imposing a penalty to be paid to the Court. Tex. Civ. Prac. & Rem. Code §10.004(c)(2). {69 *Elaborate.*}

{*For violation of Tex. Civ. Prac. & Rem. Code §9.011*}

h. An order striking all or part of {70 *adverse party*}'s pleadings. Tex. Civ. Prac. & Rem. Code §9.012(e)(1). {71 *Elaborate.*}

i. An order dismissing {72 *party*} from the suit. Tex. Civ. Prac. & Rem. Code §9.012(e)(2). {73 *Elaborate.*}

24. The sanction of {74 *identify sanction requested*} has a direct relationship to the offensive conduct and is not excessive. {75 *Elaborate.*}

{*ADD APPROPRIATE PARAGRAPH 25 IF APPLICABLE*}

25. Death-penalty sanctions are appropriate in this case because the Court has already used a lesser sanction to attempt to secure {76 *adverse party*}'s compliance with {77 *Texas Rule of Civil Procedure 13/Texas Civil Practice & Remedies Code section 10.001/Texas Civil Practice & Remedies Code section 9.011*}. {78 *Describe earlier sanctions and show how they were not effective.*} {79 *Adverse party*}'s conduct justifies the presumption that {80 *his/her/its*} {81 *claims/defenses*} lack merit. {82 *Elaborate.*}

◄ Continued on next page ►

25. Death-penalty sanctions are appropriate in this case because {83 *adverse party*} has committed egregious misconduct. {84 *Describe misconduct.*} Even though the Court has not used a lesser sanction to attempt to secure {85 *adverse party's*} compliance with {86 *Texas Rule of Civil Procedure 13/Texas Civil Practice & Remedies Code section 10.001/Texas Civil Practice & Remedies Code section 9.011*}, it has considered lesser sanctions, and {87 *adverse party*}'s conduct justifies the presumption that {88 *his/her/its*} {89 *claims/defenses*} lack merit. {90 *Explain how the record reflects the court's consideration of lesser sanctions and how they would not have been effective.*}

{*ADD APPROPRIATE PARAGRAPHS 26-28 IF APPLICABLE*}

REQUEST FOR ATTORNEY FEES & EXPENSES

26. As a sanction under {91 *Texas Rule of Civil Procedure 215.2(b)(8)/Texas Civil Practice & Remedies Code section 10.004(c)(3)/Texas Civil Practice & Remedies Code section 9.012(e)(3)*}, a court can award to a party the reasonable expenses incurred because of the filing of an improper {92 *pleading/motion/paper*}. {93 *Party*} has incurred reasonable expenses, including attorney fees, because of {94 *adverse party*}'s {95 *pleading/motion/paper*}. Attached to this motion as Exhibit {96 *letter*} is the affidavit of {97 *party*}'s attorney detailing these expenses. {98 *Party*} asks the Court to award {99 *party*} attorney fees in the amount of ${100 *amount*} and other expenses in the amount of ${101 *amount*}.

27. A court can award to a party who prevails on a motion for sanctions under Texas Civil Practice & Remedies Code section 10.002 the reasonable expenses and attorney fees incurred in presenting the motion. Tex. Civ. Prac. & Rem. Code §10.002(c). {102 *Party*} has incurred reasonable expenses, including attorney fees, in presenting this motion. Attached to this motion as Exhibit {103 *letter*} is the affidavit of {104 *party*}'s attorney detailing these expenses. If the Court grants this motion, {105 *party*} asks the Court to award {106 *party*} attorney fees in the amount of ${107 *amount*} and other expenses in the amount of ${108 *amount*}.

28. A court can award to a party who prevails on a motion for sanctions under Texas Civil Practice & Remedies Code section 10.002 all costs for inconvenience, harassment, and out-of-pocket expenses incurred or caused by the underlying litigation if the party to be sanctioned has not shown due diligence. Tex. Civ. Prac. & Rem. Code §10.002(c). {109 *Party*} has incurred expenses from the litigation, and {110 *adverse party*} did not exercise due diligence. Specifically, {111 *describe acts showing lack of diligence as evidenced by the groundless pleading or motion, e.g., adverse party denied a fact based on lack of information when, with due diligence, it could have reasonably*

gained the information, and if adverse party had done so, it could not have made the denial}. Attached to this motion as Exhibit {112 *letter*} is the affidavit of {113 *party*}'s attorney detailing these costs. If the Court grants this motion, {114 *party*} asks the Court to award {115 *party*} costs in the amount of ${116 *amount*}.

CONCLUSION

29. {117 *Briefly summarize the motion.*}

PRAYER

30. For these reasons, {118 *party*} asks the Court, after a hearing, to {119 *state appropriate sanction*}. {120 *Request attorney fees, expenses, and costs as appropriate.*}

SEE: Tex. R. Civ. P. 13, 215
Tex. Civ. Prac. & Rem. Code §§9.011, 9.012, §10.001 et seq.
O'Connor's Texas Rules * Civil Trials (2019), "Motion for Sanctions," ch. 5-K, p. 461

ADD: STYLE OF THE CASE – FORM 1B:2
SIGNATURE BLOCK – FORM 1B:3
VERIFICATION – FORM 1B:7, if necessary
CERTIFICATE OF CONFERENCE – FORM 1B:12, if necessary
CERTIFICATE OF SERVICE – FORM 1B:13

ATTACH: AFFIDAVIT – FORM 1B:8, if necessary
NOTICE OF HEARING OR SUBMISSION – FORM 1E:1
AFFIDAVIT FOR ATTORNEY FEES – FORM 1H:14, if necessary
ORDER – FORM 5K:5

NOTE: Sanctions are available under Texas Civil Practice & Remedies Code §9.012 only if they are not available under either Texas Rule of Civil Procedure 13 or Texas Civil Practice & Remedies Code §10.004. Tex. Civ. Prac. & Rem. Code §9.012(h); *see also* ***Nath v. Texas Children's Hosp.***, 446 S.W.3d 355, 362 n.6 (Tex.2014) (Texas Civil Practice & Remedies Code ch. 9 has largely been supplanted by Rule 13 and Texas Civil Practice & Remedies Code ch. 10).

The court also has inherent power to impose sanctions for an abuse of the judicial process that is not covered by a rule or statute. ***Liles v. Contreras***, 547 S.W.3d 280, 290 (Tex.App.—San Antonio 2018, pet. denied); *see* ***In re Bennett***, 960 S.W.2d 35, 40 (Tex.1997). See ***O'Connor's Texas Rules***, "Inherent power," ch. 5-K, §2.2, p. 462. The standards for imposing sanctions under the court's inherent power are the same as those for imposing sanctions under a rule or statute. *See* ***Altesse Healthcare Solutions, Inc. v. Wilson***, 540 S.W.3d 570, 574-75 (Tex.2018). See ***O'Connor's Texas Rules***, "Standards for Imposing Sanctions," ch. 5-K, §3, p. 462.

The court is not required to hold an oral hearing; sanctions can be resolved by a hearing on submission. See ***O'Connor's Texas Rules***, "Hearing by submission," ch. 5-K, §10.1.2, p. 477.

Continued on next page

A party can bring a motion for sanctions before or after a nonsuit, as long as the motion is filed while the court retains plenary power. ***Crites v. Collins***, 284 S.W.3d 839, 843 (Tex.2009). See ***O'Connor's Texas Rules***, "Effect on sanctions," ch. 7-F, §6.8, p. 778; "Finality for purposes of changing the judgment," ch. 9-C, §6.4, p. 913.

If the moving party is requesting monetary sanctions, the court can consider certain factors in assessing whether the sanction amount is excessive, including the degree to which the moving party's behavior contributed to the expenses incurred. *See **Bennett v. Grant***, 525 S.W.3d 642, 654-55 (Tex.2017); ***Nath***, 446 S.W.3d at 371-72 & n.29.

If a party is requesting attorney fees as sanctions, she must, in the affidavit for attorney fees, show evidence that attorney fees were incurred and how those fees were caused by or resulted from the sanctionable conduct. *See **CHRISTUS Health Gulf Coast v. Carswell***, 505 S.W.3d 528, 540 (Tex.2016).

{❶ *PARTY*}'S RESPONSE TO
{❷ *ADVERSE PARTY*}'S MOTION FOR SANCTIONS

{❸ *Party*}, {❹ *name*}, asks the Court to deny {❺ *adverse party*} {❻ *name*}'s motion for sanctions. {*See* ***O'Connor's Texas Rules****, "Response," ch. 5-K, §9, p. 477.*}

INTRODUCTION

1. Plaintiff, {❼ *name*}, sued defendant, {❽ *name*}, for {❾ *state basis of suit*}.

2. {❿ *State other relevant facts about the suit.*}

BACKGROUND

3. On {⓫ *date*}, {⓬ *party*} filed {⓭ *identify the pleading, motion, or other paper that adverse party is attacking*}.

4. On {⓮ *date*}, {⓯ *adverse party*} filed a motion seeking sanctions against {⓰ *identify person or person against whom sanctions are being sought*} for {⓱ *summarize grounds for sanctions request*}.

5. {⓲ *State other facts relevant to the response.*}

ARGUMENT & AUTHORITIES

{*CHOOSE APPROPRIATE SECTIONS A-G*}

A. The {⓳ *identify pleading, motion, or other paper that adverse party is attacking*} is not groundless under Tex. R. Civ. P. 13.

6. A court should not impose sanctions against an attorney or party who signs a pleading, motion, or other paper unless it (1) is groundless and (2) was brought in bad faith or for the purpose of harassment. Tex. R. Civ. P. 13. A party cannot be sanctioned for its attorney's conduct unless the party is implicated in the conduct apart from having entrusted the legal representation to the attorney. *TransAmerican Nat. Gas Corp. v. Powell*, 811 S.W.2d 913, 917 (Tex. 1991); *Loeffler v. Lytle Indep. Sch. Dist.*, 211 S.W.3d 331, 349-50 (Tex. App.—San Antonio 2006, pet. denied).

7. A paper is considered groundless only if it has no basis in law or fact and is not warranted by a good-faith argument for the extension, modification, or reversal of existing law. Tex. R. Civ. P. 13; *see, e.g.*, *Robson v. Gilbreath*, 267 S.W.3d 401, 406 (Tex. App.—Austin 2008, pet. denied) (groundless pleading); *In re A.C.B.*, 103 S.W.3d 570, 576 (Tex. App.—San Antonio 2003, no pet.) (groundless paper). The standard for reviewing whether a paper is groundless is objective: did the party and the attorney make

◄ *Continued on next page* ►

a reasonable inquiry into the legal and factual basis of the claim? The reasonableness of the inquiry is judged by the facts available and the circumstances present when the party filed the paper. *Tarrant Cty. v. Chancey*, 942 S.W.2d 151, 155 (Tex. App.—Fort Worth 1997, no writ).

8. A paper is considered to be brought in bad faith only when the signer consciously acted with a dishonest, discriminatory, or malicious purpose. *Parker v. Walton*, 233 S.W.3d 535, 540 (Tex. App.—Houston [14th Dist.] 2007, no pet.); *Campos v. Ysleta Gen. Hosp., Inc.*, 879 S.W.2d 67, 71 (Tex. App.—El Paso 1994, writ denied). A paper is brought to harass when the signer means to annoy, alarm, and abuse another person. *Parker*, 233 S.W.3d at 540. {*See* ***O'Connor's Texas Rules****, "TRCP 13," ch. 5-K, §5.2.2, p. 468.*}

9. In determining whether a paper violates Rule 13, the court must start with the presumption that the party and the attorney filed the paper in good faith. *See* Tex. R. Civ. P. 13; *GTE Commc'ns Sys. Corp. v. Tanner*, 856 S.W.2d 725, 731 (Tex. 1993); *Emmons v. Purser*, 973 S.W.2d 696, 700 (Tex. App.—Austin 1998, no pet.). The party seeking sanctions must overcome this presumption and show that the acts or omissions of the party or attorney—not the legal merits of the paper—support a finding of good cause for imposing sanctions. *See Emmons*, 973 S.W.2d at 700. For example, an opposing party is not entitled to Rule 13 sanctions simply because the party filed a motion that the court later denies. *Id.*

10. {[20] *Party*} did not file a groundless {[21] *pleading/motion/paper*} in bad faith or for the purpose of harassment. {[22] *Elaborate.*} {[23] *Adverse party*} has not proved that {[24] *party*} or {[25] *his/her/its*} attorney did not make a reasonable inquiry into the legal and factual basis of the claim. {[26] *Elaborate.*} Thus, the Court should deny {[27] *adverse party*}'s motion for sanctions.

{*ADD APPROPRIATE PARAGRAPHS 11-12 IF APPLICABLE*}

11. {[28] *Adverse party*} seeks sanctions based on {[29] *party*}'s filing of a general denial, which does not constitute a violation of Texas Rule of Civil Procedure 13. {[30] *Elaborate.*} Thus, the Court should deny {[31] *adverse party*}'s motion for sanctions.

12. {[32] *Adverse party*} seeks sanctions based on the amount of money {[33] *party*} requested as damages, which does not constitute a violation of Texas Rule of Civil Procedure 13. {[34] *Elaborate.*} Thus, the Court should deny {[35] *adverse party*}'s motion for sanctions.

B. The {36 *identify pleading or motion that adverse party is attacking*} was not signed in violation of Tex. Civ. Prac. & Rem. Code §10.001.

13. A court should not impose sanctions on a person who signs a pleading or motion unless the person signs in violation of Texas Civil Practice & Remedies Code section 10.001. Tex. Civ. Prac. & Rem. Code §10.004(a). A party should not be sanctioned for its attorney's conduct unless the party is implicated in the conduct apart from having entrusted the legal representation to the attorney. *TransAmerican Nat. Gas Corp. v. Powell*, 811 S.W.2d 913, 917 (Tex. 1991); *Loeffler v. Lytle Indep. Sch. Dist.*, 211 S.W.3d 331, 349-50 (Tex. App.—San Antonio 2006, pet. denied). {*See* ***O'Connor's Texas Rules***, *"CPRC ch. 10," ch. 5-K, §5.2.1, p. 468.*}

{*CHOOSE APPROPRIATE PARAGRAPHS 14-19*}

14. A pleading or motion is not signed in violation of section 10.001 if it was presented for a proper purpose and was not filed to harass, cause unnecessary delay, or needlessly increase the cost of litigation. Tex. Civ. Prac. & Rem. Code §10.001(1). {37 *Party*}'s {38 *pleading/motion*} was not signed in violation of section 10.001 because {39 *explain why the pleading or motion is not intended to harass or cause unnecessary delay or expense*}. Thus, the Court should deny {40 *adverse party*}'s motion for sanctions.

15. A pleading or motion is not signed in violation of section 10.001 if each claim, defense, or other legal contention is warranted by existing law or by a nonfrivolous argument for the extension, modification, or reversal of existing law or the establishment of new law. Tex. Civ. Prac. & Rem. Code §10.001(2). {41 *Party*}'s {42 *pleading/motion*} was not signed in violation of section 10.001 because {43 *explain why the challenged claim, defense, or contention is warranted by existing law or is a nonfrivolous argument for the extension, modification, or reversal of existing law or the establishment of new law*}. Thus, the Court should deny {44 *adverse party*}'s motion for sanctions.

16. A pleading or motion is not signed in violation of section 10.001 if each allegation or factual contention has evidentiary support or is likely to have evidentiary support after a reasonable opportunity for further investigation or discovery. Tex. Civ. Prac. & Rem. Code §10.001(3). {45 *Party*}'s {46 *pleading/motion*} was not signed in violation of section 10.001 because {47 *explain why the challenged allegation or factual contention has evidentiary support or is likely to have evidentiary support*}. Thus, the Court should deny {48 *adverse party*}'s motion for sanctions.

Continued on next page

17. A pleading or motion is not signed in violation of section 10.001 if each denial of a factual contention is warranted by the evidence or if a specifically identified denial is reasonably based on a lack of information or belief. Tex. Civ. Prac. & Rem. Code §10.001(4). {㊾ *Party*}'s {㊿ *pleading/motion*} was not signed in violation of section 10.001 because {51 *explain why the challenged denial is warranted by the evidence or reasonably based on lack of information or belief*}. Thus, the Court should deny {52 *adverse party*}'s motion for sanctions.

18. {53 *Adverse party*} seeks sanctions based on {54 *party*}'s filing of a general denial, which does not constitute a violation of Texas Civil Practice & Remedies Code section 10.001. Tex. Civ. Prac. & Rem. Code §10.004(f). {55 *Elaborate.*}

19. {56 *Adverse party*} seeks monetary sanctions against {57 *party*} based on a violation of section 10.001(2), but {58 *party*} is represented by an attorney, {59 *name*}. A court cannot award monetary sanctions against a represented party for a violation of Texas Civil Practice & Remedies Code section 10.001(2). Tex. Civ. Prac. & Rem. Code §10.004(d). {60 *Elaborate.*} Thus, the Court should deny {61 *adverse party*}'s motion for sanctions.

C. The {62 *identify pleading or motion that adverse party is attacking*} is not groundless under Tex. Civ. Prac. & Rem. Code §9.011.

20. A court should not impose sanctions on a person who signs a pleading unless the signing person does so in violation of Texas Civil Practice & Remedies Code section 9.011. Tex. Civ. Prac. & Rem. Code §9.012(c). A party should not be sanctioned for its attorney's conduct unless the party is implicated in the conduct apart from having entrusted the legal representation to the attorney. *TransAmerican Nat. Gas Corp. v. Powell*, 811 S.W.2d 913, 917 (Tex. 1991); *Loeffler v. Lytle Indep. Sch. Dist.*, 211 S.W.3d 331, 349-50 (Tex. App.—San Antonio 2006, pet. denied). {*See **O'Connor's Texas Rules**, "CPRC ch. 9," ch. 5-K, §5.2.3, p. 469.*}

21. A pleading is signed in violation of section 9.011 only when it is both groundless and brought in bad faith, to harass, or for any improper purpose (e.g., to cause delay or needless increase in the cost of litigation). *Elkins v. Stotts-Brown*, 103 S.W.3d 664, 668 (Tex. App.—Dallas 2003, no pet.); *Herrmann & Andreas Ins. Agency, Inc. v. Appling*, 800 S.W.2d 312, 320 (Tex. App.—Corpus Christi 1990, no writ); *see* Tex. Civ. Prac. & Rem. Code §9.011. {*See **O'Connor's Texas Rules**, "CPRC ch. 9," ch. 5-K, §5.2.3, p. 469.*}

22. {63 *Party*}'s {64 *identify pleading or motion*} is not groundless and was not brought {65 *in bad faith/to harass/for an improper purpose*}, as alleged by {66 *adverse party*}. {67 *Elaborate.*} Thus, the Court should deny {68 *adverse party*}'s motion for sanctions.

D. {69 *Adverse party*} did not give reasonable notice of the requested sanctions.

23. {70 *Texas Rule of Civil Procedure 13/Texas Civil Practice & Remedies Code section 10.003/Texas Civil Practice & Remedies Code section 9.012(a)*} requires that reasonable notice be given for a hearing on sanctions.

24. The Court should deny the motion for sanctions because reasonable notice was not given. {71 *Elaborate.*}

E. {72 *Adverse party*} is not entitled to the requested sanctions.

25. Even if a court finds that the {73 *pleading/motion/paper*} is sanctionable, the court should deny the motion for sanctions if the requested sanctions are unjust. Sanctions are unjust if there is no direct relationship between the alleged offensive conduct and the sanctions or if the sanctions are excessive. *Nath v. Tex. Children's Hosp.*, 446 S.W.3d 355, 363 (Tex. 2014); *Spohn Hosp. v. Mayer*, 104 S.W.3d 878, 882 (Tex. 2003). If the attorney was responsible for the sanctionable conduct and the party was unaware of it, the court should sanction the attorney and not the party. *Am. Flood Research, Inc. v. Jones*, 192 S.W.3d 581, 584 (Tex. 2006); *see Jones v. Andrews*, 873 S.W.2d 102, 106 (Tex. App.—Dallas 1994, no writ). {*See* ***O'Connor's Texas Rules****, "Standards for Imposing Sanctions," ch. 5-K, §3, p. 462; "Attorney," ch. 5-K, §4.2, p. 466.*}

{*ADD APPROPRIATE PARAGRAPH 26 IF APPLICABLE*}

26. Death-penalty sanctions are appropriate only in exceptional cases when (1) the court has already used a lesser sanction to attempt to secure a party's compliance and (2) the party's conduct justifies the presumption that {74 *his/her/its*} {75 *claims/defenses*} lack merit. *Chrysler Corp. v. Blackmon*, 841 S.W.2d 844, 849-50 (Tex. 1992). {*See* ***O'Connor's Texas Rules****, "Typical misconduct," ch. 5-K, §3.2.3(1), p. 464; "No merit," ch. 5-K, §3.2.4, p. 465.*}

26. Death-penalty sanctions are appropriate only in exceptional cases when (1) a party has committed egregious misconduct, (2) the court has considered lesser sanctions, and (3) the party's conduct justifies the presumption that {76 *his/her/its*} {77 *claims/defenses*} lack merit. *Cire v. Cummings*, 134 S.W.3d 835, 841-42 (Tex. 2004). {*See* ***O'Connor's Texas Rules****, "Egregious misconduct," ch. 5-K, §3.2.3(2), p. 465; "No merit," ch. 5-K, §3.2.4, p. 465.*}

Continued on next page

27. {78 *Adverse party*} has requested that the Court sign an order {79 *identify sanctions requested*}.

{*CHOOSE APPROPRIATE PARAGRAPHS 28-34*}

28. The Court should deny the motion for sanctions because the sanctions are unjust. Specifically, they have no direct relationship to {80 *identify alleged sanctionable conduct*}. {81 *Elaborate.*}

29. The Court should deny the motion for sanctions because the sanctions are unjust. Specifically, they are excessive—that is, they are more severe than necessary to promote full compliance with {82 *identify rule or statute*}. {83 *Elaborate.*}

30. The Court should deny the motion for sanctions because {84 *party*}'s attorney, {85 *name*}, was responsible for the sanctionable conduct, and {86 *party*} was unaware of it. {87 *Elaborate.*}

31. The Court should deny the motion for sanctions because the sanctions {88 *adverse party*} requested, {89 *identify sanctions requested*}, are not authorized by {90 *Texas Rule of Civil Procedure 13/Texas Civil Practice & Remedies Code section 10.004(c)/Texas Civil Practice & Remedies Code section 9.012(e)*}.

32. The Court should deny {91 *adverse party*}'s request for death-penalty sanctions because the motion is {92 *adverse party*}'s first request for sanctions, and the Court must first use a lesser sanction before imposing death-penalty sanctions. {93 *Elaborate.*}

33. The Court should deny {94 *adverse party*}'s request for death-penalty sanctions because {95 *party*}'s conduct is not so egregious that the Court cannot impose lesser sanctions first. {96 *Describe conduct and explain how lesser sanctions would be effective.*}

34. The Court should deny {97 *adverse party*}'s request for death-penalty sanctions because {98 *party*}'s conduct does not justify the presumption that {99 *his/her/its*} {100 *claims/defenses*} lack merit. {101 *Elaborate.*}

F. {102 *Adverse party*} is not entitled to expenses or attorney fees.

{*CHOOSE APPROPRIATE PARAGRAPHS 35-37*}

35. As a sanction under {103 *Texas Rule of Civil Procedure 215.2(b)(8)/Texas Civil Practice & Remedies Code section 10.004(c)(3)/Texas Civil Practice & Remedies Code section 9.012(e)(3)*}, a court can award to a party the reasonable expenses, including attorney fees, incurred because of the filing of an improper {104 *pleading/motion/pa-*

per}. In the motion for sanctions, {105 *adverse party*} requested {106 *describe expenses and attorney fees requested*}. The Court should deny {107 *adverse party*}'s request because the expenses and attorney fees requested are not reasonable. {108 *Elaborate.*}

36. A court can award to a party who prevails on a motion for sanctions under Texas Civil Practice & Remedies Code section 10.002 the reasonable expenses and attorney fees incurred in presenting the motion. Tex. Civ. Prac. & Rem. Code §10.002(c). In the motion for sanctions, {109 *adverse party*} requested {110 *describe expenses and attorney fees requested*}. If the Court grants {111 *adverse party*}'s motion, it should deny {112 *adverse party*}'s request because the expenses and attorney fees requested are not reasonable. {113 *Elaborate.*}

37. A court can award to a party who prevails on a motion for sanctions under Texas Civil Practice & Remedies Code section 10.002 all costs for inconvenience, harassment, and out-of-pocket expenses incurred or caused by the underlying litigation if the party to be sanctioned has not shown due diligence. Tex. Civ. Prac. & Rem. Code §10.002(c). In the motion for sanctions, {114 *adverse party*} requested {115 *describe costs requested*}. The Court should deny {116 *adverse party*}'s request because {117 *party*} can show that it exercised due diligence before filing its {118 *pleading/motion*}. {119 *Elaborate.*}

G. {120 *Party*} is entitled to attorney fees & expenses.

38. A court can award to a party who prevails on a motion for sanctions under Texas Civil Practice & Remedies Code section 10.002 the reasonable expenses and attorney fees incurred in opposing the motion and all costs for inconvenience, harassment, and out-of-pocket expenses incurred or caused by the underlying litigation if the party bringing the motion has not shown diligence. Tex. Civ. Prac. & Rem. Code §10.002(c).

39. {121 *Party*} has incurred reasonable expenses in opposing this motion, including attorney fees. Attached to this response as Exhibit {122 *letter*} is the affidavit of {123 *party*}'s attorney detailing these expenses. If the Court denies the motion for sanctions, {124 *party*} asks the Court to award {125 *party*} attorney fees in the amount of ${126 *amount*} and other expenses in the amount of ${127 *amount*}.

40. {128 *Party*} has incurred expenses because of the underlying litigation, and {129 *adverse party*} did not exercise due diligence. Specifically, {130 *describe acts showing lack of diligence*}. Attached to this response as Exhibit {131 *letter*} is the affidavit of {132 *party*}'s attorney detailing these expenses. If the Court denies the motion for sanctions, {133 *party*} asks the Court to award {134 *party*} expenses in the amount of ${135 *amount*}.

Continued on next page

CONCLUSION

41. {136 *Briefly summarize the response.*}

PRAYER

42. For these reasons, {137 *party*} asks the Court, after a hearing, to deny {138 *adverse party*}'s motion for sanctions. {139 *Request attorney fees and costs as appropriate.*}

SEE: Tex. R. Civ. P. 13, 215
Tex. Civ. Prac. & Rem. Code §§9.011, 9.012, §10.001 et seq.
O'Connor's Texas Rules * Civil Trials (2019), "Response," ch. 5-K, §9, p. 477

ADD: STYLE OF THE CASE – FORM 1B:2
SIGNATURE BLOCK – FORM 1B:3
CERTIFICATE OF SERVICE – FORM 1B:13

ATTACH: AFFIDAVIT – FORM 1B:8, if necessary
AFFIDAVIT FOR ATTORNEY FEES – FORM 1H:14, if necessary
ORDER – FORM 5K:5

NOTE: The court begins with the presumption that all pleadings, motions, or other papers are filed in good faith, under Texas Rule of Civil Procedure 13. ***GTE Comms. Sys. v. Tanner***, 856 S.W.2d 725, 731 (Tex. 1993). Courts have extended the good-faith presumption to sanctions claims under Texas Civil Practice & Remedies Code §10.001 as well. ***Low v. Henry***, 221 S.W.3d 609, 614 (Tex.2007).

The court is not required to hold an oral hearing; sanctions can be resolved by a hearing on submission. See ***O'Connor's Texas Rules***, "Hearing by submission," ch. 5-K, §10.1.2, p. 477.

{❶ *PARTY*}'S MOTION FOR SANCTIONS

{❷ *Party*}, {❸ *name*}, asks the Court to impose appropriate sanctions against {❹ *identify person or persons to be sanctioned, e.g., plaintiff, plaintiff's attorney, both plaintiff and plaintiff's attorney*} for failure to serve, as authorized by Texas Rule of Civil Procedure 21b.

INTRODUCTION

1. Plaintiff, {❺ *name*}, sued defendant, {❻ *name*}, for {❼ *state basis of suit*}.

2. {❽ *State other relevant facts about the suit.*}

BACKGROUND

3. On {❾ *date*}, {❿ *adverse party*} filed {⓫ *describe the pleading, plea, motion, or other application for order that adverse party filed but did not serve*}.

4. {⓬ *Adverse party*} did not serve a copy of {⓭ *name of document*} on {⓮ *party*} in accordance with Texas Rules of Civil Procedure 21 and 21a.

5. {⓯ *State other facts relevant to the motion.*}

ARGUMENT & AUTHORITIES

6. When a party does not serve on or deliver to the other party a copy of any pleading, plea, motion, or other application for an order, in accordance with Rules 21 and 21a, the court may impose sanctions under Texas Rule of Civil Procedure 215.2(b). Tex. R. Civ. P. 21b; *see Union City Body Co. v. Ramirez*, 911 S.W.2d 196, 200 (Tex. App.—San Antonio 1995, orig. proceeding). {*See* ***O'Connor's Texas Rules****, "Failure to serve – TRCP 21b," ch. 5-K, §5.3, p. 469.*}

7. Because {⓰ *adverse party*} did not serve a copy of {⓱ *name of document*} on {⓲ *party*} in accordance with Rules 21 and 21a, the Court should sanction {⓳ *identify person or persons to be sanctioned*}.

REQUEST FOR SANCTIONS

8. Sanctions are just if they have a direct relationship to the offensive conduct and are not excessive. *Nath v. Tex. Children's Hosp.*, 446 S.W.3d 355, 363 (Tex. 2014); *Am. Flood Research, Inc. v. Jones*, 192 S.W.3d 581, 583 (Tex. 2006); *Spohn Hosp. v. Mayer*, 104 S.W.3d 878, 882 (Tex. 2003). {*See* ***O'Connor's Texas Rules****, "Request sanction," ch. 5-K, §8.2.3, p. 476.*}

◄ *Continued on next page* ►

{*ADD APPROPRIATE PARAGRAPH 9 IF APPLICABLE*}

9. Death-penalty sanctions are appropriate if (1) the court has already used a lesser sanction to attempt to secure {[20] *adverse party*}'s compliance and (2) the party's conduct justifies the presumption that {[21] *his/her/its*} {[22] *claims/defenses*} lack merit. *Chrysler Corp. v. Blackmon*, 841 S.W.2d 844, 849-50 (Tex. 1992). {*See* ***O'Connor's Texas Rules****, "Typical misconduct," ch. 5-K, §3.2.3(1), p. 464; "No merit," ch. 5-K, §3.2.4, p. 465.*}

9. Death-penalty sanctions are appropriate if (1) a party has committed egregious misconduct, (2) the court has considered lesser sanctions, and (3) the party's conduct justifies the presumption that {[23] *his/her/its*} {[24] *claims/defenses*} lack merit. *Cire v. Cummings*, 134 S.W.3d 835, 839-40 (Tex. 2004). {*See* ***O'Connor's Texas Rules****, "Egregious misconduct," ch. 5-K, §3.2.3(2), p. 465; "No merit," ch. 5-K, §3.2.4, p. 465.*}

10. {[25] *Party*} asks the Court to impose the following sanctions on {[26] *identify person or persons to be sanctioned*}.

{*CHOOSE APPROPRIATE SANCTIONS*}

a. An order designating certain matters as established against {[27] *adverse party*}. Tex. R. Civ. P. 215.2(b)(3). {[28] *Elaborate.*}

b. An order prohibiting {[29] *adverse party*} from {[30] *supporting/opposing*} certain {[31] *claims/defenses*}. Tex. R. Civ. P. 215.2(b)(4). {[32] *Elaborate.*}

c. An order striking all or part of {[33] *adverse party*}'s pleadings. Tex. R. Civ. P. 215.2(b)(5). {[34] *Elaborate.*}

d. An order dismissing {[35] *adverse party*}'s suit with prejudice. Tex. R. Civ. P. 215.2(b)(5). {[36] *Elaborate.*}

e. {[37] *Identify other sanctions from Tex. R. Civ. P. 215.2(b).*} {[38] *Elaborate.*}

11. The sanction of {[39] *identify sanction requested*} has a direct relationship to the offensive conduct and is not excessive. {[40] *Elaborate.*}

{*ADD APPROPRIATE PARAGRAPH 12 IF APPLICABLE*}

12. Death-penalty sanctions are appropriate in this case because the Court has already used a lesser sanction to attempt to secure {[41] *adverse party*}'s compliance with

Rules 21 and 21a. {42 *Describe earlier sanctions and show how they were not effective.*} {43 *Adverse party*}'s conduct justifies the presumption that {44 *claims/defenses*} lack merit. {45 *Elaborate.*}

12. Death-penalty sanctions are appropriate in this case because {46 *adverse party*} has committed egregious misconduct. {47 *Describe misconduct.*} Even though the Court has not used a lesser sanction to attempt to secure {48 *adverse party*}'s compliance with Rules 21 and 21a, it has considered lesser sanctions, and {49 *adverse party*}'s conduct justifies the presumption that {50 *his/her/its*} lack merit. {51 *Explain how the record reflects the court's consideration of lesser sanctions and how those sanctions would not have been effective.*}

{*ADD PARAGRAPH 13 IF APPLICABLE*}

REQUEST FOR ATTORNEY FEES & EXPENSES

13. As a sanction for failure to serve in accordance with Rules 21 and 21a, a court can award a party the reasonable expenses incurred because of the failure to serve. *See* Tex. R. Civ. P. 21b, 215.2(b)(8). {52 *Party*} has incurred reasonable expenses, including attorney fees, because of {53 *adverse party*}'s failure to serve a copy of {54 *name of document*}. Attached to this motion as Exhibit {55 *letter*} is the affidavit of {56 *party*}'s attorney detailing these expenses. {57 *Party*} asks the Court to award {58 *party*} attorney fees in the amount of ${59 *amount*} and other expenses in the amount of ${60 *amount*}.

CONCLUSION

14. {61 *Briefly summarize the motion.*}

PRAYER

15. For these reasons, {62 *party*} asks the Court, after a hearing, to {63 *state appropriate sanction*}. {64 *Request attorney fees and expenses as appropriate.*}

SEE: Tex. R. Civ. P. 21, 21a, 21b, 215.2
O'Connor's Texas Rules * Civil Trials (2019), "Failure to serve – TRCP 21b," ch. 5-K, §5.3, p. 469

ADD: STYLE OF THE CASE – FORM 1B:2
SIGNATURE BLOCK – FORM 1B:3
VERIFICATION – FORM 1B:7, if necessary
CERTIFICATE OF CONFERENCE – FORM 1B:12, if necessary
CERTIFICATE OF SERVICE – FORM 1B:13

Continued on next page

ATTACH: AFFIDAVIT – FORM 1B:8, if necessary
NOTICE OF HEARING OR SUBMISSION – FORM 1E:1
AFFIDAVIT FOR ATTORNEY FEES – FORM 1H:14, if necessary
ORDER – FORM 5K:5

NOTE: The court is not required to hold an oral hearing; sanctions can be resolved by a hearing on submission. See ***O'Connor's Texas Rules***, "Hearing by submission," ch. 5-K, §10.1.2, p. 477.

{[1] *PARTY*}'S RESPONSE TO
{[2] *ADVERSE PARTY*}'S MOTION FOR SANCTIONS

{[3] *Party*}, {[4] *name*}, asks the Court to deny {[5] *adverse party*} {[6] *name*}'s motion for sanctions for failure to serve, made under Texas Rule of Civil Procedure 21b. {*See* ***O'Connor's Texas Rules**, "Failure to serve – TRCP 21b," ch. 5-K, §5.3, p. 469.*}

INTRODUCTION

1. Plaintiff, {[7] *name*}, sued defendant, {[8] *name*}, for {[9] *state basis of suit*}.

2. {[10] *State other relevant facts about the suit.*}

BACKGROUND

3. On {[11] *date*}, {[12] *party*} filed {[13] *identify document adverse party claims was not served*}. {[14] *Adverse party*} claims in {[15] *his/her/its*} motion for sanctions that {[16] *he/she/it*} was not served with the document.

{*CHOOSE APPROPRIATE PARAGRAPH 4*}

4. {[17] *Party*} properly served {[18] *identify document*} by {[19] *state method of service*} on {[20] *date*}. The attached affidavit of {[21] *party*}'s attorney, {[22] *name*}, which is incorporated by reference, establishes the date and method of service.

4. Although the {[23] *identify document*} was not properly served, {[24] *party*}'s failure to serve was not intentional. The attached affidavit of {[25] *party*}'s attorney, {[26] *name*}, which is incorporated by reference, explains the failure to serve.

5. {[27] *State other facts relevant to the response.*}

ARGUMENT & AUTHORITIES

6. The purpose of sanctions is to secure compliance with the rules and to deter future violations of the rules. *Chrysler Corp. v. Blackmon*, 841 S.W.2d 844, 849 (Tex. 1992). If a party can demonstrate good cause for its failure to comply with discovery rules, a court should not impose sanctions. *See* Tex. R. Civ. P. 193.6(a) (party who does not timely respond to discovery request cannot introduce material into evidence unless there is good cause or no unfair surprise or prejudice to other parties). That same reasoning should apply to imposing sanctions under Rule 21b. There must be a direct relationship between the alleged offensive conduct and the sanctions, and the sanctions must not be excessive. *See Nath v. Tex. Children's Hosp.*, 446 S.W.3d 355, 363 (Tex. 2014); *Am. Flood Research, Inc. v. Jones*, 192 S.W.3d 581, 583 (Tex. 2006).

Continued on next page

{*ADD APPROPRIATE PARAGRAPH 7 IF APPLICABLE*}

7. Death-penalty sanctions are appropriate only in exceptional cases when (1) the court has already used a lesser sanction to attempt to secure a party's compliance and (2) the party's conduct justifies the presumption that {㉘ *his/her/its*} {㉙ *claims/defenses*} lack merit. *Chrysler Corp.*, 841 S.W.2d at 849-50. {*See **O'Connor's Texas Rules**, "Typical misconduct," ch. 5-K, §3.2.3(1), p. 464; "No merit," ch. 5-K, §3.2.4, p. 465.*}

7. Death-penalty sanctions are appropriate only in exceptional cases when (1) a party has committed egregious misconduct, (2) the court has considered lesser sanctions, and (3) the party's conduct justifies the presumption that {㉚ *his/her/its*} {㉛ *claims/defenses*} lack merit. *Cire v. Cummings*, 134 S.W.3d 835, 839-40 (Tex. 2004). {*See **O'Connor's Texas Rules**, "Egregious misconduct," ch. 5-K, §3.2.3(2), p. 465; "No merit," ch. 5-K, §3.2.4, p. 465.*}

{*CHOOSE APPROPRIATE PARAGRAPH 8*}

8. The Court should deny the motion for sanctions because {㉜ *party*} served {㉝ *adverse party*} with the {㉞ *identify document*} in accordance with Texas Rule of Civil Procedure 21a. {㉟ *Elaborate.*}

8. The Court should deny the motion for sanctions because even though {㊱ *party*} did not properly serve {㊲ *adverse party*} with the {㊳ *identify document*}, the failure was not intentional, there was good cause for not complying with the rules, and sanctioning {㊴ *party*} would not further the purposes of sanctions—deterrence and punishment. {㊵ *Elaborate.*}

{*CHOOSE APPROPRIATE PARAGRAPHS 9-14*}

9. The Court should deny the motion for sanctions because the sanctions {㊶ *adverse party*} requested, {㊷ *identify sanctions requested*}, are unjust. Specifically, they have no direct relationship to the failure to serve. {㊸ *Elaborate.*}

10. The Court should deny the motion for sanctions because the sanctions {㊹ *adverse party*} requested, {㊺ *identify sanctions requested*}, are unjust. Specifically, they are excessive—that is, they are more severe than necessary to promote full compliance with Texas Rule of Civil Procedure 21b. {㊻ *Elaborate.*}

11. The Court should deny the motion for sanctions because the sanctions {㊼ *adverse party*} requested, {㊽ *identify sanctions requested*}, are not authorized by Texas Rule of Civil Procedure 215.2(b). *See* Tex. R. Civ. P. 21b.

12. The Court should deny the motion for sanctions, in which {㊾ *adverse party*} asks for death-penalty sanctions, because the motion is {㊿ *adverse party*}'s first request for sanctions, and the Court must first use a lesser sanction before imposing death-penalty sanctions. {51 *Elaborate.*}

13. The Court should deny the motion for sanctions, in which {52 *adverse party*} asks for death-penalty sanctions, because {53 *party*}'s conduct is not so egregious that the Court can choose not to use a lesser sanction first. {54 *Describe conduct and explain how lesser sanctions would be effective.*}

14. The Court should deny the motion for sanctions, in which {55 *adverse party*} asks for death-penalty sanctions, because {56 *party*}'s conduct does not justify the presumption that {57 *his/her/its*} {58 *claims/defenses*} lack merit. {59 *Elaborate.*}

CONCLUSION

15. {60 *Briefly summarize the response.*}

PRAYER

16. For these reasons, {61 *party*} asks the Court, after a hearing, to deny {62 *adverse party*}'s motion for sanctions.

SEE: Tex. R. Civ. P. 21, 21a, 21b, 193.6, 215.2
O'Connor's Texas Rules * Civil Trials (2019), "Failure to serve – TRCP 21b," ch. 5-K, §5.3, p. 469

ADD: STYLE OF THE CASE – FORM 1B:2
SIGNATURE BLOCK – FORM 1B:3
CERTIFICATE OF SERVICE – FORM 1B:13

ATTACH: AFFIDAVIT – FORM 1B:8, if necessary
ORDER – FORM 5K:5

NOTE: The court is not required to hold an oral hearing; sanctions can be resolved by a hearing on submission. See ***O'Connor's Texas Rules***, "Hearing by submission," ch. 5-K, §10.1.2, p. 477.

ORDER ON MOTION FOR SANCTIONS

After considering {❶ *party*} {❷ *name*}'s motion for sanctions, the response, the evidence, and arguments of counsel, the Court

{*CHOOSE APPROPRIATE ORDER*}

DENIES the motion and refuses to impose sanctions.

GRANTS the motion for sanctions.

{*CHOOSE APPROPRIATE PROVISIONS*}

1. The Court imposes the following sanctions on {❸ *adverse party*}, {❹ *name*}: {❺ *list sanctions*}.

2. The Court imposes the following sanctions on {❻ *name*}, the attorney for {❼ *adverse party*}: {❽ *list sanctions*}.

3. The Court awards the following attorney fees and {❾ *court costs/expenses*} to {❿ *party*}: {⓫ *list attorney fees and court costs or expenses*}.

{*ADD FINDINGS IF APPLICABLE*}

FINDINGS IN SUPPORT OF SANCTIONS UNDER
{⓬ *IDENTIFY RULE, STATUTE, OR BOTH*}

The Court makes the following findings in support of the sanctions imposed under {⓭ *identify rule, statute, or both*}:

a. The {⓮ *identify paper*} was signed in violation of {⓯ *Rule 13/section 9.011/section 10.001*}. {⓰ *Explain.*}

b. {⓱ *Describe the specific acts or omissions for which sanctions are imposed.*}

c. There is a direct relationship between the sanction and the offensive conduct. {⓲ *Elaborate.*}

d. This sanction is no more severe than necessary to promote full compliance. {⓳ *Elaborate.*}

{*ADD PARAGRAPH e IF IMPOSING SANCTIONS UNDER RULE 13*}

e. There is good cause to support the imposition of sanctions because {20 *explain*}.

{*ADD PARAGRAPH f IF SANCTIONS IMPOSED ON PARTY*}

f. {21 *State why sanctions are imposed on the party and not just the attorney.*}

{*ADD PARAGRAPHS g-h IF IMPOSING DEATH-PENALTY SANCTIONS*}

{*CHOOSE APPROPRIATE PARAGRAPH g*}

g. This Court imposed an earlier sanction on {22 *adverse party*}. {23 *Identify earlier conduct and sanction.*} That sanction was not sufficient to deter similar conduct.

g. A lesser sanction was not imposed because {24 *adverse party*} committed egregious misconduct. {25 *Describe misconduct.*} The Court considered lesser sanctions, but they would not have been effective. {26 *Explain.*} {*See* ***O'Connor's Texas Rules****, "Egregious misconduct," ch. 5-K, §3.2.3(2), p. 465; "Explanation," ch. 5-K, §11.1.3, p. 478.*}

h. {27 *Adverse party*}'s conduct justifies the presumption that {28 *his/her/its*} {29 *claims/defenses*} lack merit. {30 *Elaborate.*}

SIGNED on _______________, 20___.

____
PRESIDING JUDGE

SEE: Tex. R. Civ. P. 13, 21b, 215
Tex. Civ. Prac. & Rem. Code §9.011 et seq., §10.001 et seq.
O'Connor's Texas Rules * Civil Trials (2019), "Order for Sanctions," ch. 5-K, §11, p. 478

ADD: STYLE OF THE CASE – FORM 1B:2
CERTIFICATE OF SERVICE – FORM 1B:13, if proposed order served separately from motion or response

NOTE: When a court imposes sanctions for violation of Texas Civil Practice & Remedies Code §10.001, it must include in the order a description of the conduct that violated the section and explain the basis for the sanctions imposed. Tex. Civ. Prac. & Rem. Code §10.005. When imposing a monetary penalty, the court should explain how it determined the amount of sanctions, particularly when those sanctions are severe. ***Low v. Henry***, 221 S.W.3d 609, 620-21 (Tex.2007); *see* ***Nath v. Texas Children's Hosp.***, 446 S.W.3d 355, 372 (Tex.2014).

Continued on next page

When a court imposes sanctions under Texas Rule of Civil Procedure 13, it must include in the order a statement of good cause to support the imposition of sanctions. *See* Tex. R. Civ. P. 13 ("[n]o sanctions … may be imposed except for good cause … stated in the sanction order").

Before a court imposes sanctions for violation of Texas Civil Practice & Remedies Code §9.011, it must give the attorney or party 90 days to withdraw or amend the offending pleading or motion. Tex. Civ. Prac. & Rem. Code §9.012(c), (d).

{❶ *{PARTY}/INTERVENOR*}'S MOTION TO SEAL COURT RECORDS {❷ *ADD IF APPROPRIATE: & CLOSE COURTROOM*}

{*CHOOSE APPROPRIATE OPENING PARAGRAPH*}

{*If temporary and permanent orders are requested*}

{❸ *{Party}/Intervenor*}, {❹ *name*}, asks the Court to (1) immediately sign a temporary order under Texas Rule of Civil Procedure 76a(5) sealing the following court records and (2) after notice and a hearing, sign an order under Texas Rule of Civil Procedure 76a sealing the records permanently: {❺ *identify each record to be sealed*}. {*See* ***O'Connor's Texas Rules****, "Motion for temporary sealing order," ch. 5-L, §3.2, p. 484.*}

{*If temporary and permanent orders are requested with motion to close courtroom*}

{❻ *{Party}/Intervenor*} asks the Court to (1) immediately sign a temporary order under Texas Rule of Civil Procedure 76a(5) sealing the following court records, (2) after notice and a hearing, sign an order under Texas Rule of Civil Procedure 76a sealing the records permanently, and (3) order the courtroom closed when the records are presented in court: {❼ *identify each record to be sealed*}. {*See* ***O'Connor's Texas Rules****, "Motion for temporary sealing order," ch. 5-L, §3.2, p. 484.*}

{*If permanent order is requested with motion to close courtroom*}

{❽ *{Party}/Intervenor*} asks the Court to (1) sign an order under Texas Rule of Civil Procedure 76a sealing the following court records permanently and (2) order the courtroom closed when the records are presented in court: {❾ *identify each record to be sealed*}.

{*If only permanent order is requested*}

{❿ *{Party}/Intervenor*} asks the Court to sign an order under Texas Rule of Civil Procedure 76a sealing the following court records permanently: {⓫ *identify each record to be sealed*}.

INTRODUCTION

1. Plaintiff, {⓬ *name*}, sued defendant, {⓭ *name*}, for {⓮ *state basis of suit*}.
2. {⓯ *State other relevant facts about the suit.*}

◄ ***Continued on next page*** ►

BACKGROUND

{ADD APPROPRIATE PARAGRAPHS 3-5 IF APPLICABLE}

3. Intervenor, {16 *name*}, is entitled to intervene in this suit to ask the Court to seal court records. Tex. R. Civ. P. 76a(7).

4. {17 *{Party}/Intervenor*} posted notice of this motion on {18 *date*} at {19 *location*}, and a verified copy of the notice is attached to this motion as Exhibit A. {*See* ***O'Connor's Texas Rules***, *"Public notice," ch. 5-L, §4.1, p. 485.*}

5. {20 *{Party}/Intervenor*} filed a verified copy of the notice with the clerk of the Texas Supreme Court on {21 *date*}. Tex. R. Civ. P. 76a(3). {*See* ***O'Connor's Texas Rules***, *"Filed with two clerks," ch. 5-L, §4.2, p. 486.*}

6. {22 *State other facts relevant to the motion.*}

PERMANENT SEALING ORDER

7. Under Texas Rule of Civil Procedure 76a, court records are presumed to be open to the general public. Tex. R. Civ. P. 76a(1). The presumption of openness can be overcome, however, if the party seeking to seal the records establishes that (1) it has a specific, serious, and substantial interest in sealing the records that clearly outweighs the presumption of openness and any probable adverse effect on the general public health or safety and (2) no less restrictive means than sealing will adequately and effectively protect that interest. *Id.*; *Fox v. Doe*, 869 S.W.2d 507, 511 (Tex. App.—San Antonio 1993, writ denied). In determining whether court records should be sealed, the court should balance the public's interest in open court proceedings against a party's personal or proprietary interest in privacy. *Gen. Tire, Inc. v. Kepple*, 970 S.W.2d 520, 526 (Tex. 1998). {*See* ***O'Connor's Texas Rules***, *"Grounds," ch. 5-L, §3.1.2, p. 484.*}

8. {23 *{Party}/Intervenor*} has a specific, serious, and substantial interest in preventing the public disclosure of {24 *identify court record*} because the record contains {25 *identify contents that establish a serious and substantial interest, e.g., party's trade secrets, party's personal financial information*}. This interest clearly outweighs the presumption of openness and any probable adverse effect the sealing would have on the general public health or safety because {26 *explain, e.g., a party's personal financial information has no bearing on the general public health or safety*}.

9. There are no less restrictive means than sealing the records that will adequately and effectively protect {27 *{party}/intervenor*}'s interest. {28 *State facts demonstrating that less restrictive means (e.g., redaction) will not protect movant's interest, referring to attached affidavits if necessary.*}

{ADD SECTION BELOW IF APPROPRIATE}

TEMPORARY SEALING ORDER

10. Under Texas Rule of Civil Procedure 76a(5), a court can issue an order temporarily sealing court records until a hearing on a motion to permanently seal records can be held. Specifically, Rule 76a permits a court to temporarily seal court records if a party can show a compelling need from specific facts shown by affidavit or verified petition that immediate and irreparable injury will result to a specific interest of a party before a hearing is held on a motion to permanently seal. Tex. R. Civ. P. 76a(5).

11. {❷❾ *{Party}/Intervenor*}'s {❸⓿ *verified petition on file with the court/attached affidavit*} establishes that {❸❶ *{party}/intervenor*} will suffer an immediate and irreparable injury to {❸❷ *his/her/its*} {❸❸ *identify interest that will suffer, e.g., privacy interest, financial interest*} if the Court does not immediately seal the records listed above. The records contain {❸❹ *identify contents that establish a protectable interest, e.g., party's trade secrets, party's personal financial information*}. Once the information is made available to the public, the injury will be immediate and irreparable because {❸❺ *state how public access to the information will result in immediate and irreparable injury, e.g., party's business competitors will have access to party's trade secrets*}.

{ADD SECTION BELOW IF APPROPRIATE}

MOTION TO CLOSE COURTROOM

12. In addition to sealing the court records, {❸❻ *{party}/intervenor*} asks the Court to close the courtroom to the public when the records are presented in court. Although the public's right to attend civil proceedings is recognized under Texas law and grounded in the First Amendment, this right is not absolute. *See Richmond Newspapers, Inc. v. Virginia*, 448 U.S. 555, 600 & n.5 (1980) (Stewart, J., concurring); *Dall. Morning News v. Fifth Court of Appeals*, 842 S.W.2d 655, 657 (Tex. 1992); *Doe v. Santa Fe Indep. Sch. Dist.*, 933 F. Supp. 647, 650-51 (S.D. Tex. 1996); *In re Samsung Telecomms. of Am., Inc.*, No. 05-99-01960-CV (Tex. App.—Dallas 1999, orig. proceeding) (no pub.; 12-2-99). A trial court may close its courtroom to protect the dissemination of certain sensitive information to the public. *See, e.g., Brown & Williamson Tobacco Corp. v. Fed. Trade Comm'n*, 710 F.2d 1165, 1179 (6th Cir. 1983) (civil courtroom can be closed to protect disclosure of documents implicating certain privacy rights of participants or third parties, trade secrets, or issues involving national security); *In re Samsung Telecomms. of Am., Inc.*, No. 05-99-01960-CV (no pub.) (civil courtroom can be closed to protect trade secrets). In this case, the courtroom should be closed to the public because {❸❼ *explain*}.

Continued on next page

CONCLUSION

13. {❸❽ *Briefly summarize the motion.*}

PRAYER

14. For these reasons, {❸❾ *party*} asks the Court to do the following:

{*CHOOSE APPROPRIATE PARAGRAPHS a-f*}

a. Immediately sign a temporary order sealing the records described above.

b. Set the time and place for a hearing on {❹⓿ *{party}/intervenor*}'s motion for a permanent sealing order.

c. After the hearing, seal the records described above permanently.

d. When the sealed records are presented at {❹❶ *specify proceeding, e.g., trial, the temporary injunction hearing*} {❹❷ *state relief, e.g., (1) close the courtroom to the public or, in the alternative, require any public spectators to sign a confidentiality agreement, (2) prohibit the jurors from taking notes, (3) give the jury a cautionary instruction on the sealed documents, and (4) seal any portion of the court's transcript on the sealed documents*}.

e. To the extent that the Court denies {❹❸ *{party}/intervenor*}'s request to seal, {❹❹ *{party}/intervenor*} asks the Court to stay the order until it is considered on appeal.

f. Grant other relief as the Court may find in the interest of justice.

FORM 5L:1 MOTION TO SEAL COURT RECORDS

SEE: Tex. R. Civ. P. 76a
O'Connor's Texas Rules * Civil Trials (2019), "Sealing Court Records," ch. 5-L, §3, p. 484; "Public Notice," ch. 5-L, §4, p. 485

ADD: STYLE OF THE CASE – FORM 1B:2
SIGNATURE BLOCK – FORM 1B:3
CERTIFICATE OF CONFERENCE – FORM 1B:12
CERTIFICATE OF SERVICE – FORM 1B:13

ATTACH: AFFIDAVIT – FORM 1B:8, if necessary
PUBLIC NOTICE OF MOTION TO SEAL COURT RECORDS – FORM 5L:2, if public notice has already been posted
VERIFICATION OF NOTICE TO SEAL COURT RECORDS – FORM 5L:3
ORDER ON MOTION TO PERMANENTLY SEAL COURT RECORDS – FORM 5L:5
TEMPORARY ORDER TO SEAL COURT RECORDS – FORM 5L:6, if necessary

NOTE: If a party wants to seal or restrict the disclosure of documents obtained through discovery, the party should file a motion for a protective order under Texas Rule of Civil Procedure 192.6(a). See FORM 6A:10; ***O'Connor's Texas Rules***, "Motion for protective order," ch. 5-L, §8.1, p. 487. If the list of documents to be sealed is long, consider putting the list in an attached exhibit rather than listing all the documents in the motion's introduction.

PUBLIC NOTICE OF MOTION TO SEAL COURT RECORDS

1. As required by Texas Rule of Civil Procedure 76a(3), {❶ *{party}/intervenor*}, {❷ *name*}, posts this notice to seal court records. {*See* ***O'Connor's Texas Rules****, "Public notice," ch. 5-L, §4.1, p. 485.*}

2. Plaintiff, {❸ *name*}, sued defendant, {❹ *name*}, for {❺ *provide a brief but specific description of the nature of the suit*}.

3. In this case, {❻ *{party}/intervenor*} has filed a motion to seal the following court records: {❼ *provide a brief but specific description of the records to be sealed, e.g., Plaintiff's Original Petition*}.

4. The motion to seal court records will be heard on {❽ *date*}, at {❾ *time*}, in the {❿ ________} Court in {⓫ ________} County, at {⓬ *address*}.

5. The hearing on the motion to seal court records will be held in open court.

6. Any person may intervene and be heard on the sealing of court records.

SEE: Tex. R. Civ. P. 76a(3)
O'Connor's Texas Rules * Civil Trials (2019), "Public Notice," ch. 5-L, §4, p. 485

ADD: STYLE OF THE CASE – FORM 1B:2
SIGNATURE BLOCK – FORM 1B:3

NOTE: After posting the notice, the movant must immediately file the notice and verification (FORM 5L:3) with both the clerk of the court in which the case is pending and the clerk of the Texas Supreme Court. Tex. R. Civ. P. 76a(3).

★

VERIFICATION OF PUBLIC NOTICE OF MOTION TO SEAL COURT RECORDS

STATE OF TEXAS §
{❶ ______} COUNTY §

Before me, the undersigned notary, on this day personally appeared {❷ *name of affiant*}, the affiant, whose identity is known to me. After I administered an oath, affiant testified as follows:

"My name is {❸ *name of affiant*}. I am capable of making this verification. I certify that the Public Notice of Motion to Seal Court Records attached as Exhibit {❹ *letter*} was posted at the place where notices for meetings of county governmental bodies are required to be posted for {❺ ________} County, Texas, on {❻ *date*}. The facts stated in the Public Notice are within my personal knowledge and are true and correct."

____
{❼ *Name of affiant*}

Sworn to and subscribed before me by {❽ *name of affiant*} on __________, 20___.

____
Notary Public in and for
the State of Texas

SEE: Tex. R. Civ. P. 76a(3)
O'Connor's Texas Rules * Civil Trials **(2019), "Public Notice," ch. 5-L, §4, p. 485**

ADD: STYLE OF THE CASE – FORM 1B:2

NOTE: The movant must file the notice (FORM 5L:2) and verification with both the clerk of the court in which the case is pending and the clerk of the Texas Supreme Court. Tex. R. Civ. P. 76a(3).

See notes under FORM 1B:7.

{❶ *{PARTY}/INTERVENOR*}'S RESPONSE
TO {❷ *ADVERSE PARTY*}'S MOTION TO SEAL COURT
RECORDS {❸ *ADD IF APPROPRIATE: & CLOSE COURTROOM*}

{❹ *{Party}/Intervenor*}, {❺ *name*}, asks the Court to deny {❻ *adverse party*} {❼ *name*}'s motion to seal the following court records under Texas Rule of Civil Procedure 76a {❽ *add if appropriate: and to close the courtroom when they are presented in court*}: {❾ *identify each record being opposed*}.

INTRODUCTION

1. Plaintiff sued defendant for {❿ *state basis of suit*}.

{*ADD PARAGRAPH 2 IF APPLICABLE*}

2. Intervenor, {⓫ *name*}, is entitled to intervene in this suit as a matter of right. Tex. R. Civ. P. 76a(7).

3. {⓬ *State other relevant facts about the suit.*}

BACKGROUND

4. On {⓭ *date*}, {⓮ *adverse party*} asked the Court to seal the court records listed above {⓯ *add if appropriate: and to close the courtroom during their presentation in court*}.

5. {⓰ *State other facts relevant to the response.*}

MOTION TO SEAL

6. Under Texas Rule of Civil Procedure 76a, court records are presumed to be open to the general public and can be sealed only if both the procedural and the substantive requirements of Rule 76a are met. *See Davenport v. Garcia*, 834 S.W.2d 4, 24 (Tex. 1992) (sealing of record must meet procedural prerequisites in Rule 76a); *McAfee, Inc. v. Weiss*, 336 S.W.3d 840, 844 (Tex. App.—Dallas 2011, pet. denied) (party seeking sealing order has burden to establish substantive requirements under Rule 76a(1)); *see, e.g., Clear Channel Commc'ns, Inc. v. United Servs. Auto. Ass'n*, 195 S.W.3d 129, 136-37 (Tex. App.—San Antonio 2006, no pet.) (court committed reversible error by sealing court records before procedural requirements in Rule 76a were met).

{*CHOOSE APPROPRIATE SECTIONS A-B*}

A. Procedural error.

7. To meet the procedural requirements of Rule 76a, the party seeking to seal court records must file a written motion, post public notice at least 14 days before the hearing, and file a verified copy of the posted notice with the clerk of the court in which the case is pending and the clerk of the Texas Supreme Court. *See* Tex. R. Civ. P. 76a(3), (4). The public notice must (1) state that a hearing will be held in open court and that any person may intervene and be heard, (2) state the time and place of the hearing, (3) state the style and number of the case and the identity of the movant, (4) contain a brief but specific description of the nature of the case and the records sought to be sealed, and (5) be posted at the place where notices for meetings of county governmental bodies are required to be posted. Tex. R. Civ. P. 76a(3). {*See **O'Connor's Texas Rules**, "Public Notice," ch. 5-L, §4, p. 485.*}

8. {17 *Adverse party*} did not comply with the procedural requirements of Rule 76a because {18 *explain*}.

B. Substantive error.

9. To meet the substantive requirements of Rule 76a, the party seeking to seal court records must establish that (1) it has a specific, serious, and substantial interest in sealing the records that clearly outweighs the presumption of openness and any probable adverse effect on the general public health or safety and (2) no less restrictive means than sealing will adequately and effectively protect that interest. Tex. R. Civ. P. 76a(1); *Fox v. Doe*, 869 S.W.2d 507, 511 (Tex. App.—San Antonio 1993, writ denied). {*See **O'Connor's Texas Rules**, "Grounds," ch. 5-L, §3.1.2, p. 484.*}

10. {19 *Adverse party*} has not established a specific, serious, and substantial interest in sealing the records that clearly outweighs the presumption of openness and any probable adverse effect on the general public health and safety. {20 *Explain, e.g., the public has an interest in open records generally and these records in particular.*} {*See **O'Connor's Texas Rules**, "Burden," ch. 5-L, §5.4, p. 486.*}

11. {21 *Adverse party*} has not established that there are no less restrictive means than sealing that will adequately and effectively protect {22 *his/her/its*} interest. {23 *Describe alternatives to sealing the records (e.g., redaction) that will protect adverse party's interest, referring to attached affidavits if necessary.*} {*See **O'Connor's Texas Rules**, "Burden," ch. 5-L, §5.4, p. 486.*}

Continued on next page

{*ADD SECTION BELOW IF APPROPRIATE*}

MOTION TO CLOSE COURTROOM

12. In addition to denying {㉔ *adverse party*}'s motion to seal the records under Texas Rule of Civil Procedure 76a, the Court should deny {㉕ *adverse party*}'s request to close the courtroom. The public's right to attend civil proceedings is recognized under Texas law and grounded in the First Amendment. *Dall. Morning News v. Fifth Court of Appeals*, 842 S.W.2d 655, 657 (Tex. 1992); *Doe v. Santa Fe Indep. Sch. Dist.*, 933 F. Supp. 647, 650 (S.D. Tex. 1996); *see Richmond Newspapers, Inc. v. Virginia*, 448 U.S. 555, 580 n.17 (1980) (plurality opinion) (dicta; "historically both civil and criminal trials have been presumptively open"); *id.* at 599 (Stewart, J., concurring) ("the First and Fourteenth Amendments clearly give the press and the public a right of access to trials themselves, civil as well as criminal"). The public's right to attend serves to promote trustworthiness of the judicial process, to curb judicial abuses, and to give the public a more complete understanding of the judicial system. *Littlejohn v. Bic Corp.*, 851 F.2d 673, 682 (3d Cir. 1988). Although the public's right to attend civil proceedings is not absolute, the Court should exercise its discretion to close a courtroom only when the standards set out in Texas Rule of Civil Procedure 76a are met—that is, when there is a specific and substantial interest that clearly outweighs the presumption of openness and when there is no less restrictive means of protecting that interest. *See Doe*, 933 F. Supp. at 650-51 (under First Amendment, must show that closure is essential to preserve an overriding interest and is narrowly tailored to preserve that interest); *see also Publicker Indus., Inc. v. Cohen*, 733 F.2d 1059, 1070 (3d Cir. 1984) ("[T]he right of access to civil trials is … a First Amendment right … to be accorded the due process protection that other fundamental rights enjoy").

{*CHOOSE APPROPRIATE PARAGRAPHS 13-14*}

13. {㉖ *Adverse party*} has not established a specific, serious, and substantial interest that clearly outweighs the presumption that the courtroom should remain open to the public. {㉗ *Elaborate.*}

14. {㉘ *Adverse party*} has not established that there are no less restrictive means than closing the courtroom that will adequately and effectively protect {㉙ *his/her/its*} interest. {㉚ *Explain, e.g., plaintiff's request to close the courtroom during the entire proceeding is too broad, requiring the Court to repeatedly determine whether certain testimony will discuss a protected interest and then forcing the Court to clear the courtroom during that testimony will result in significant disruption and delay and alter defendant's trial strategy to minimize disruption.*}

CONCLUSION

15. {㉛ *Briefly summarize the response.*}

PRAYER

16. For these reasons, {㉜ *{party}/intervenor*} asks the Court to deny {㉝ *adverse party*}'s motion to seal the court records listed above {㉞ *add if appropriate: and close the courtroom*}.

SEE: Tex. R. Civ. P. 76a
O'Connor's Texas Rules * Civil Trials **(2019), "Sealing Court Records," ch. 5-L, §3, p. 484; "Public Notice," ch. 5-L, §4, p. 485**

ADD: STYLE OF THE CASE – FORM 1B:2
SIGNATURE BLOCK – FORM 1B:3
CERTIFICATE OF SERVICE – FORM 1B:13

ATTACH: AFFIDAVIT – FORM 1B:8, if necessary
ORDER – FORM 5L:5

ORDER ON MOTION TO PERMANENTLY SEAL COURT RECORDS

After considering {❶ *{party}/intervenor*} {❷ *name*}'s motion to seal court records, the response, {❸ *add if appropriate: stipulations of the parties/pleadings/affidavits/ oral testimony/discovery,*} and arguments of counsel, the Court

{*CHOOSE APPROPRIATE ORDER*}

DENIES the motion, and makes the following findings and conclusions:

{*CHOOSE APPROPRIATE PARAGRAPHS 1-3*}

1. {❹ *{Party}/Intervenor*} did not demonstrate a specific, serious, and substantial interest that clearly outweighs the presumption of openness and any probable adverse effect on the general public health or safety. {❺ *Specify reasons for making this finding and conclusion.*}

2. {❻ *{Party}/Intervenor*} did not demonstrate that there are no less restrictive means than sealing the documents that will adequately and effectively protect {❼ *{party}/intervenor*}'s interest. {❽ *Specify reasons for making this finding and conclusion.*}

3. {❾ *{Party}/Intervenor*} did not comply with the procedural requirements of Texas Rule of Civil Procedure 76a(3) because {❿ *explain procedural defect*}.

GRANTS the motion, and makes the following findings and conclusions:

1. {⓫ *{Party}/Intervenor*} demonstrated a specific, serious, and substantial interest that clearly outweighs the presumption of openness and any probable adverse effect on the general public health and safety. {⓬ *Specify reasons for making this finding and conclusion.*}

2. {⓭ *{Party}/Intervenor*} demonstrated that there are no less restrictive means than sealing the documents that will adequately and effectively protect {⓮ *{party}/intervenor*}'s interest. {⓯ *Specify reasons for making this finding and conclusion.*}

Therefore, the Court orders that the following court records be permanently sealed under Texas Rule of Civil Procedure 76a: {⓰ *list records or specific parts of records to be sealed*}.

The records listed above will not become public or be disclosed by any person, will not be included in the public records of this case, and will not be otherwise disclosed or permitted to come into the possession, control, or knowledge of any persons other than the attorneys of record for the parties in this case, the regular staff of the parties' attorneys, certified court reporters and their staffs, and the personnel of the court.

Further, the Court orders that all persons who gain possession of records sealed under this order will not disclose, transfer, or in any way allow the sealed documents to come into the possession of any other person at any time. Nothing in this order will be construed as a limitation or restriction on {⓱ *{party}/intervenor*} {⓲ *name*}, or {⓳ *his/her/its*} employees, officers, agents, authorized representatives, or attorneys, concerning the use, possession, control, or disclosure of the sealed documents.

Further, the Court orders the court clerk to take notice of this order and to institute procedures to ensure that court personnel comply with the terms of this order, including marking the court records sealed by this order as being under seal of the Court and subject to this order.

{*ADD PARAGRAPH BELOW IF COURTROOM CLOSURE WAS GRANTED*}

Further, the Court orders {⓴ *specify conditions of courtroom closure, e.g., the courtroom will be closed to the public during the presentation of the sealed records, any public spectators must sign a confidentiality agreement, the jurors must not take notes during the presentation of the sealed records, any portion of the court's transcript concerning the sealed records must be sealed*}.

The Court will retain jurisdiction, as provided by law, to enforce, alter, or vacate this order before or after judgment in this case.

Any violation of this order will be a contempt of court.

SIGNED on ______________, 20___.

____
PRESIDING JUDGE

SEE: Tex. R. Civ. P. 76a(6)
O'Connor's Texas Rules * Civil Trials (2019), "Sealing order," ch. 5-L, §6.2, p. 486

ADD: STYLE OF THE CASE – FORM 1B:2
CERTIFICATE OF SERVICE – FORM 1B:13, if proposed order served separately from motion or response

◄ *Continued on next page* ►

NOTE: Any party or intervenor who participated in the hearing preceding an order may seek review by appeal because any order sealing or unsealing court records is deemed to be severed from the case and is a final judgment. Tex. R. Civ. P. 76a(8). Mandamus is generally not available, but it may be appropriate (1) when a trial court refuses to hold a hearing and render a decision on a motion under Texas Rule of Civil Procedure 76a or (2) to challenge an interim order that causes harm that cannot be remedied by appeal. See ***O'Connor's Texas Rules***, "Exceptions," ch. 5-L, §10.1.2(2), p. 488. For an appellate court to review an error in a sealing order, the appellant (or relator) must file a reporter's record from the hearing. See ***O'Connor's Texas Rules***, "Record," ch. 5-L, §10.1.3, p. 489.

TEMPORARY SEALING ORDER

{❶ *{Party}/Intervenor*}, {❷ *name*}, filed a motion for a temporary sealing order under Texas Rule of Civil Procedure 76a(5) and supported the motion with a verification. As required by Texas Rules of Civil Procedure 21 and 21a(a), {❸ *{party}/intervenor*} gave notice of the motion to all parties who filed pleadings in the case. {❹ *By affidavit evidence/At a hearing on the motion*}, {❺ *{party}/intervenor*} proved a compelling need for a temporary sealing order and demonstrated that delay in sealing would result in immediate and irreparable harm to a specific interest.

Therefore, the Court orders that the following court records in this case be temporarily sealed until the Court hears the motion to place the records under permanent seal: {❻ *list records*}.

Further, the Court orders that {❼ *{party}/intervenor*}'s motion to permanently seal court records be heard in open court on __________, 20___, at _____ o'clock a.m./p.m., in the {❽ _______} Court in {❾ _______} County, Texas.

Further, the Court orders that {❿ *{party}/intervenor*} immediately give the public notice, as required by Rule 76a(3), of {⓫ *his/her/its*} request to place the records under permanent seal.

SIGNED on _______________, 20___, at _____ o'clock a.m./p.m.

____
PRESIDING JUDGE

SEE: Tex. R. Civ. P. 76a(5)
O'Connor's Texas Rules * Civil Trials (2019), "Temporary order," ch. 5-L, §6.1, p. 486

ADD: STYLE OF THE CASE – FORM 1B:2
CERTIFICATE OF SERVICE – FORM 1B:13, if proposed order served separately from motion

{❶ *{PARTY}/INTERVENOR*}'S MOTION TO
{❷ *MODIFY/WITHDRAW*} TEMPORARY SEALING ORDER

{❸ *{Party}/Intervenor*}, {❹ *name*}, asks the Court to unseal certain court records that are under a temporary sealing order. The records to be unsealed are the following: {❺ *identify each record*}.

INTRODUCTION

1. Plaintiff, {❻ *name*}, sued defendant, {❼ *name*}, for {❽ *state basis of suit*}.

{*ADD PARAGRAPH 2 IF APPLICABLE*}

2. Intervenor, {❾ *name*}, intervenes in this suit to {❿ *modify/withdraw*} the temporary order sealing the court records.

3. {⓫ *State other relevant facts about the suit.*}

BACKGROUND

4. On {⓬ *date*}, {⓭ *adverse party*} filed a motion for temporary order to seal court records asking the Court to temporarily seal the records listed above.

5. On {⓮ *date*}, the Court granted the motion and temporarily sealed those records.

6. {⓯ *State other facts relevant to the motion.*}

ARGUMENT & AUTHORITIES

7. The Texas Constitution guarantees public access to court records. Tex. Const. art. 1, §8; *see* U.S. Const. amend. 1. The common law recognizes an indisputable public right of access to judicial proceedings and judicial records. *See Nixon v. Warner Commc'ns, Inc.*, 435 U.S. 589, 597 (1978). The presumption of open records is based on the need to preserve the public's right to monitor its judicial system. *Wilson v. Am. Motors Corp.*, 759 F.2d 1568, 1570 (11th Cir. 1985); *In re Cont'l Ill. Sec. Litig.*, 732 F.2d 1302, 1308 (7th Cir. 1984). To overcome the presumption of openness, the court must find a compelling need to protect a greater interest. *See Wilson*, 759 F.2d at 1570-71.

8. The court can temporarily seal court records only if the movant shows a compelling need that immediate and irreparable injury will result to a specific interest of the movant before notice can be posted and a hearing held. Tex. R. Civ. P. 76a(5). If a temporary sealing order is entered, Texas Rule of Civil Procedure 76a(5) allows the court to modify or withdraw the order.

{*CHOOSE APPROPRIATE PARAGRAPHS 9-12*}

{*If unsealing all records*}

9. The Court should withdraw the temporary sealing order because the documents are not "court records" under Rule 76a(2). {16 *Elaborate.*}

10. The Court should withdraw the temporary sealing order because {17 *adverse party*} failed to show a compelling need that immediate and irreparable injury will result to a specific interest before notice can be posted and a hearing held. {18 *Elaborate.*}

{*If unsealing only some of the court records*}

11. The Court should modify the temporary sealing order by removing the documents listed above from the order because the documents are not "court records" under Rule 76a(2). {19 *Elaborate.*}

12. The Court should modify the temporary sealing order by removing the documents listed above from the order because public review of those documents will not result in an immediate and irreparable injury to {20 *adverse party*}.

CONCLUSION

13. {21 *Briefly summarize the motion.*}

PRAYER

14. For these reasons, {22 *{party}/intervenor*} asks the Court to set this motion for a hearing and, after notice and the hearing, grant this motion to unseal records, vacate its sealing order, and make the records identified in this motion open to the public.

SEE: Tex. R. Civ. P. 76a
U.S. Const. amend. 1
Tex. Const. art. 1, §8
O'Connor's Texas Rules * Civil Trials (2019), "Motion to Seal Court Records," ch. 5-L, p. 482

ADD: STYLE OF THE CASE – FORM 1B:2
SIGNATURE BLOCK – FORM 1B:3
CERTIFICATE OF SERVICE – FORM 1B:13

ATTACH: AFFIDAVIT – FORM 1B:8, if necessary
NOTICE OF HEARING OR SUBMISSION – FORM 1E:1
ORDER – FORM 1G:1

INTERVENOR'S PLEA IN INTERVENTION TO UNSEAL COURT RECORDS

Intervenor, {❶ *name*}, files this plea in intervention under Texas Rule of Civil Procedure 76a and asks the Court to unseal the following court records: {❷ *identify each record*}.

INTRODUCTION

1. Plaintiff, {❸ *name*}, sued defendant, {❹ *name*}, for {❺ *state basis of suit*}.

2. {❻ *State other relevant facts about the suit.*}

{*CHOOSE APPROPRIATE PARAGRAPH 3*}

{*If documents were sealed under a discovery protective order*}

3. Intervenor is entitled to intervene in this suit and ask the Court to unseal the records. *See* Tex. R. Civ. P. 76a(7) (any person may intervene as a matter of right at any time to unseal court records); *Gen. Tire, Inc. v. Kepple*, 970 S.W.2d 520, 525 (Tex. 1998) (person's right to intervene under Rule 76a applies to protective orders).

{*If documents were sealed under TRCP 76a*}

3. Intervenor did not have actual notice of the hearing on {❼ *adverse party*}'s motion to seal and is entitled to intervene and ask the Court to unseal the records. Tex. R. Civ. P. 76a(7).

BACKGROUND

4. On {❽ *date*}, the Court granted {❾ *adverse party*} {❿ *name*}'s {⓫ *motion to seal/motion for protective order*} and ordered the records listed above sealed.

5. {⓬ *State other facts relevant to the plea.*}

{*CHOOSE APPROPRIATE ARGUMENT & AUTHORITIES SECTION*}

{*If documents were sealed under a discovery protective order*}

ARGUMENT & AUTHORITIES

6. A court may order the results of discovery sealed subject to the provisions of Rule 76a. Tex. R. Civ. P. 192.6(b)(5). Under Rule 76a, court records are presumed to be open to the general public. However, a court is not required to determine whether unfiled discovery or other unfiled documents constitute court records until requested to do

so by a party or an intervenor. *Gen. Tire, Inc. v. Kepple*, 970 S.W.2d 520, 525 (Tex. 1998). Once a party or an intervenor claims that documents sealed under a protective order are court records, the court must make a threshold determination on whether the documents are court records. *Id.* If the court finds that the documents are court records, the documents are presumed to be open to the general public and the party seeking to keep those records sealed must meet the procedural and substantive requirements of Rule 76a. *See Upjohn Co. v. Freeman*, 906 S.W.2d 92, 96 (Tex. App.—Dallas 1995, no writ); *see, e.g., Clear Channel Commc'ns, Inc. v. United Servs. Auto. Ass'n*, 195 S.W.3d 129, 137 (Tex. App.—San Antonio 2006, no pet.) (court's protective order reversed because it was entered without complying with procedural requirements of Rule 76a). {*See* ***O'Connor's Texas Rules***, *"What Documents Are 'Court Records'," ch. 5-L, §2, p. 482.*}

{*CHOOSE APPROPRIATE PARAGRAPHS 7-9*}

7. The documents the Court sealed under {⓭ *adverse party*}'s protective order are court records as defined by Rule 76a(2) because the documents were filed with the Court in connection with the litigation between plaintiff and defendant. Tex. R. Civ. P. 76a(2)(a). A document is filed when it is delivered or tendered to, or otherwise put under the custody or control of, the court clerk. *Jamar v. Patterson*, 868 S.W.2d 318, 319 (Tex. 1993). This is true regardless of whether the document is file-stamped. *Biffle v. Morton Rubber Indus., Inc.*, 785 S.W.2d 143, 144 (Tex. 1990).

8. The documents the Court sealed under {⓮ *adverse party*}'s protective order are court records as defined by Rule 76a(2) because the documents are unfiled settlement agreements concerning matters that have a probable adverse effect on {⓯ *the general public health or safety/the administration of public office/the operation of government*}. Tex. R. Civ. P. 76a(2)(b). The documents have this probable adverse effect because {⓰ *explain*}.

9. The documents the Court sealed under {⓱ *adverse party*}'s protective order are court records as defined by Rule 76a(2) because the documents are unfiled discovery concerning matters that have a probable adverse effect on {⓲ *the general public health or safety/the administration of public office/the operation of government*}. Tex. R. Civ. P. 76a(2)(c). The documents have this probable adverse effect because {⓳ *explain*}.

{*If documents were sealed under TRCP 76a*}

ARGUMENT & AUTHORITIES

10. Under Texas Rule of Civil Procedure 76a, court records are presumed to be open to the general public and can be sealed only if both the procedural and the substantive

Continued on next page

requirements of Rule 76a are met. *See Davenport v. Garcia*, 834 S.W.2d 4, 24 (Tex. 1992) (sealing of record must meet procedural prerequisites in Rule 76a); *McAfee, Inc. v. Weiss*, 336 S.W.3d 840, 844 (Tex. App.—Dallas 2011, pet. denied) (party seeking sealing order has burden to establish substantive requirements under Rule 76a(1)); *see, e.g., Clear Channel Commc'ns, Inc. v. United Servs. Auto. Ass'n*, 195 S.W.3d 129, 137 (Tex. App.—San Antonio 2006, no pet.) (court committed reversible error by sealing court records before procedural requirements were met).

{*CHOOSE APPROPRIATE SECTIONS A-B*}

A. Procedural error.

11. To meet the procedural requirements of Rule 76a, the party seeking to seal court records must file a written motion, post public notice at least 14 days before the hearing, and file a verified copy of the posted notice with the clerk of the court in which the case is pending and the clerk of the Texas Supreme Court. *See* Tex. R. Civ. P. 76a(3), (4). The public notice must (1) state that a hearing will be held in open court and that any person may intervene and be heard, (2) state the time and place of the hearing, (3) state the style and number of the case and the identity of the movant, (4) contain a brief but specific description of the nature of the case and the records sought to be sealed, and (5) be posted at the place where notices for meetings of county governmental bodies are required to be posted. Tex. R. Civ. P. 76a(3). {*See* ***O'Connor's Texas Rules****, "Public Notice," ch. 5-L, §4, p. 485.*}

12. {❿20 *Adverse party*} did not comply with the procedural requirements of Rule 76a because {21 *explain*}.

B. Substantive error.

13. To meet the substantive requirements of Rule 76a, the party seeking to seal court records must establish that (1) it has a specific, serious, and substantial interest in sealing the records that clearly outweighs the presumption of openness and any probable adverse effect on the general public health or safety and (2) no less restrictive means than sealing will adequately and effectively protect that interest. Tex. R. Civ. P. 76a(1); *Fox v. Doe*, 869 S.W.2d 507, 511 (Tex. App.—San Antonio 1993, writ denied). {*See* ***O'Connor's Texas Rules****, "Grounds," ch. 5-L, §3.1.2, p. 484.*}

{*CHOOSE APPROPRIATE PARAGRAPHS 14-15*}

14. {22 *Adverse party*} did not establish a specific, serious, and substantial interest in sealing the records that clearly outweighs the presumption of openness and any probable adverse effect on the general public health and safety. {23 *Explain, e.g., the public*

has an interest in open records generally and these records in particular.} {*See* ***O'Connor's Texas Rules***, *"Burden," ch. 5-L, §5.4, p. 486.*}

15. {㉔ *Adverse party*} did not establish that there are no less restrictive means than sealing that will adequately and effectively protect {㉕ *his/her/its*} interest. {㉖ *Describe alternatives to sealing the records (e.g., redaction) that will protect adverse party's interests, referring to attached affidavits if necessary.*} {*See* ***O'Connor's Texas Rules***, *"Burden," ch. 5-L, §5.4, p. 486.*}

CONCLUSION

16. {㉗ *Briefly summarize the plea.*}

PRAYER

17. For these reasons, intervenor asks the Court to set this plea in intervention for a hearing and, after notice and the hearing, grant this plea in intervention to unseal records, vacate the Court's sealing order, and make the records identified in this plea in intervention open to the public.

SEE: Tex. R. Civ. P. 76a
U.S. Const. amend. 1
Tex. Const. art. 1, §8
O'Connor's Texas Rules * Civil Trials (2019), "Motion to Seal Court Records," ch. 5-L, p. 482

ADD: STYLE OF THE CASE – FORM 1B:2
SIGNATURE BLOCK – FORM 1B:3
CERTIFICATE OF SERVICE – FORM 1B:13

ATTACH: AFFIDAVIT – FORM 1B:8, if necessary
NOTICE OF HEARING OR SUBMISSION – FORM 1E:1
ORDER – FORM 1G:1

NOTE: The burden to prove that the documents are court records is on the party claiming that the documents are open to the public. ***Upjohn Co. v. Freeman***, 906 S.W.2d 92, 96 (Tex.App.—Dallas 1995, no writ).

{❶ *PARTY*}'S MOTION FOR GAG ORDER

{❷ *Party*}, {❸ *name*}, asks the Court to issue a gag order in this case. {*See **O'Connor's Texas Rules**, "Gag Order," ch. 5-L, §9, p. 487.*}

INTRODUCTION

1. Plaintiff, {❹ *name*}, sued defendant, {❺ *name*}, for {❻ *state basis of suit*}.

2. {❼ *State other relevant facts about the suit.*}

BACKGROUND

3. {❽ *State facts relevant to the motion.*}

ARGUMENT & AUTHORITIES

4. A court may issue a gag order if, after a hearing to receive evidence, it finds that (1) an imminent and irreparable harm to the judicial process will deprive litigants of a just resolution of their dispute, and (2) judicial action represents the least-restrictive means to prevent that harm. *Grigsby v. Coker*, 904 S.W.2d 619, 620 (Tex. 1995); *Davenport v. Garcia*, 834 S.W.2d 4, 10 (Tex. 1992).

5. The gag order requested by this motion asks the Court to restrain {❾ *identify persons to be restrained by the order and state the limits of the restraint*}.

6. The Court should issue a gag order because an imminent and irreparable harm to the judicial process will deprive the litigants of a just resolution in this case. {❿ *Elaborate.*}

7. The Court should issue a gag order because a gag order represents the least-restrictive means to prevent imminent and irreparable harm to the judicial process. {⓫ *Elaborate.*}

CONCLUSION

8. {⓬ *Briefly summarize the motion.*}

PRAYER

9. For these reasons, {⓭ *party*} asks the Court, after a hearing, to issue a gag order preventing {⓮ *identify scope of requested order*}.

SEE: *O'Connor's Texas Rules * Civil Trials* (2019), "Gag Order," ch. 5-L, §9, p. 487

ADD: STYLE OF THE CASE – FORM 1B:2
SIGNATURE BLOCK – FORM 1B:3
CERTIFICATE OF CONFERENCE – FORM 1B:12, if necessary
CERTIFICATE OF SERVICE – FORM 1B:13

ATTACH: AFFIDAVIT – FORM 1B:8, if necessary
NOTICE OF HEARING OR SUBMISSION – FORM 1E:1
ORDER – FORM 5L:11

{❶ *PARTY*}'S RESPONSE TO {❷ *ADVERSE PARTY*}'S MOTION FOR GAG ORDER

{❸ *Party*}, {❹ *name*}, asks the Court to deny {❺ *adverse party*} {❻ *name*}'s motion for a gag order. {*See **O'Connor's Texas Rules**, "Gag Order," ch. 5-L, §9, p. 487.*}

INTRODUCTION

1. Plaintiff, {❼ *name*}, sued defendant, {❽ *name*}, for {❾ *state basis of suit*}.

2. {❿ *State other relevant facts about the suit.*}

BACKGROUND

3. {⓫ *State facts relevant to the response.*}

ARGUMENT & AUTHORITIES

4. Texas has a strong and long-standing commitment to free speech. *Davenport v. Garcia*, 834 S.W.2d 4, 7 (Tex. 1992). Throughout this state's history, freedom of expression has been a priority. *Id.* The scope of Texas Constitution article 1, section 8, is broader than that of the First Amendment to the United States Constitution. *See Davenport*, 834 S.W.2d at 8-9. The presumption in all cases under article 1, section 8, is that pre-speech sanctions, or "prior restraints," are unconstitutional. *Davenport*, 834 S.W.2d at 9; *see Ex parte Price*, 741 S.W.2d 366, 369 (Tex. 1987) (Gonzalez, J., concurring) ("Prior restraints … are subject to judicial scrutiny with a heavy presumption against their constitutional validity.").

5. A court may issue a gag order only if, after a hearing to receive evidence, it finds that (1) an imminent and irreparable harm to the judicial process will deprive litigants of a just resolution of their dispute, and (2) judicial action represents the least-restrictive means to prevent that harm. *Grigsby v. Coker*, 904 S.W.2d 619, 620 (Tex. 1995); *Davenport*, 834 S.W.2d at 10.

6. The Court should not issue a gag order because {⓬ *adverse party*} cannot establish that an imminent and irreparable harm to the judicial process will deprive the litigants of a just resolution in this case. {⓭ *Elaborate.*}

7. The Court should not issue a gag order because {⓮ *adverse party*} cannot establish that a gag order represents the least-restrictive means to prevent imminent and irreparable harm to the judicial process. {⓯ *Elaborate, identifying a less restrictive means of preventing harm.*}

{ADD PARAGRAPH 8 IF APPLICABLE}

8. A court should not grant a gag order that is overly broad. *See Grigsby*, 904 S.W.2d at 620. The Court should deny {⑯ *adverse party*}'s motion for a gag order because the scope of the requested order is overly broad. Specifically, {⑰ *explain how order is too broad*}.

CONCLUSION

9. {⑱ *Briefly summarize the response.*}

PRAYER

10. For these reasons, {⑲ *party*} asks the Court to deny {⑳ *adverse party*}'s motion for a gag order.

SEE: ***O'Connor's Texas Rules * Civil Trials*** (2019), "Gag Order," ch. 5-L, §9, p. 487

ADD: STYLE OF THE CASE – FORM 1B:2
SIGNATURE BLOCK – FORM 1B:3
CERTIFICATE OF SERVICE – FORM 1B:13

ATTACH: AFFIDAVIT – FORM 1B:8, if necessary
ORDER – FORM 5L:11

GAG ORDER

After considering {❶ *party*} {❷ *name*}'s motion for a gag order, the response, {❸ *add if appropriate: stipulations of the parties/pleadings/affidavits/oral testimony/{specify discovery document},*} and arguments of counsel, the Court

{*CHOOSE APPROPRIATE ORDER*}

DENIES the motion.

GRANTS the motion.

The Court makes the following findings and conclusions:

1. The following persons are to be restrained by the gag order: {❹ *list persons*}.

2. The exact limits of the restraint are {❺ *state the limits of the restraint*}.

3. {❻ *Party*} demonstrated that an imminent and irreparable harm to the judicial process will deprive the litigants of a just resolution of their dispute.

4. {❼ *Party*} demonstrated that a gag order represents the least-restrictive means to prevent an imminent or irreparable harm to the judicial process.

The Court makes these findings and conclusions based on {❽ *describe the specific facts the movant proved to establish findings and conclusions 1-4*}.

The Court will retain jurisdiction, as provided by law, to enforce, alter, or vacate this order before or after judgment in this case.

Any violation of this order will be a contempt of court.

SIGNED on ______________________, 20___.

____
PRESIDING JUDGE

SEE: ***O'Connor's Texas Rules * Civil Trials*** (2019), "Gag Order," ch. 5-L, §9, p. 487

ADD: STYLE OF THE CASE – FORM 1B:2
CERTIFICATE OF SERVICE – FORM 1B:13, if proposed order served separately from motion or response

NOTE: A party may challenge a gag order by mandamus. *See* ***Grigsby v. Coker***, 904 S.W.2d 619, 621 (Tex.1995). For an appellate court to review an error in a gag order, the relator must file a reporter's record from the hearing. *See* Tex. R. App. P. 52.7(a).

{❶ *PARTY*}'S MOTION TO TAKE JUDICIAL NOTICE

{❷ *Party*}, {❸ *name*}, asks the Court to take judicial notice of {❹ *identify material to be judicially noticed*}. {*See* ***O'Connor's Texas Rules****, "Motion for Judicial Notice," ch. 5-M, §3, p. 491.*}

INTRODUCTION

1. Plaintiff, {❺ *name*}, sued defendant, {❻ *name*}, for {❼ *state basis of suit*}.

2. {❽ *State other relevant facts about the suit.*}

BACKGROUND

3. {❾ *State facts relevant to the motion.*}

{*CHOOSE APPROPRIATE ARGUMENTS*}

NOTORIOUS FACTS

4. Under Texas Rule of Evidence 201, a court may take judicial notice of notorious facts if properly requested by a party. *See* Tex. R. Evid. 201(b)(1). A notorious fact is a fact that everyone of average intelligence and knowledge can be presumed to know within the court's territorial jurisdiction. *See id.*; *City of Garland v. Louton*, 683 S.W.2d 725, 726 (Tex. App.—Dallas 1984), *rev'd on other grounds*, 691 S.W.2d 603 (Tex. 1985); *see, e.g.*, *Barber v. Intercoast Jobbers & Brokers*, 417 S.W.2d 154, 158 (Tex. 1967) (Odessa is in Ector County); *Choice Auto Brokers, Inc. v. Dawson*, 274 S.W.3d 172, 174 n.1 (Tex. App.—Houston [1st Dist.] 2008, no pet.) (eBay auction process); *Apostolic Church v. Am. Honda Motor Co.*, 833 S.W.2d 553, 555-56 (Tex. App.—Tyler 1992, writ denied) (Highway 96 is known as Tenaha Highway); *McCulloch v. State*, 740 S.W.2d 74, 76 (Tex. App.—Fort Worth 1987, pet. ref'd) (explosive nature of gasoline). A fact can be generally known even if it has to be processed with commonly possessed mental skills. *E.g.*, *Drake v. Holstead*, 757 S.W.2d 909, 910 (Tex. App.—Beaumont 1988, no writ) (court erred in not taking judicial notice of party's mathematical computation). Because notorious facts are well known, the court can take judicial notice of them without any extrinsic support. *Tranter v. Duemling*, 129 S.W.3d 257, 262 (Tex. App.—El Paso 2004, no pet.); *Drake*, 757 S.W.2d at 911. {*See* ***O'Connor's Texas Rules****, "Notorious fact," ch. 5-M, §4.1.1(1), p. 492; Brown & Rondon,* ***Evidence Handbook****, p. 114.*}

5. {❿ *Party*} asks the Court to take judicial notice of {⓫ *identify fact*} because it is generally known within the Court's territorial jurisdiction. {⓬ *Elaborate.*}

◄ *Continued on next page* ►

VERIFIABLE FACTS

6. Under Texas Rule of Evidence 201, a court must take judicial notice of a verifiable fact if a party makes a proper request and supplies the court with the necessary information. *See* Tex. R. Evid. 201(b)(2), (c)(2). A verifiable fact is a fact that is capable of accurate and ready determination by resorting to sources whose accuracy cannot reasonably be questioned. *See* Tex. R. Evid. 201(b)(2); *see, e.g., City of Hous. v. Todd*, 41 S.W.3d 289, 301 & n.16 (Tex. App.—Houston [1st Dist.] 2001, pet. denied) (railroads supplied transportation to all developed sections of Texas by 1900, verified by consulting history sources); *Tex. Dep't of Pub. Safety v. Ackerman*, 31 S.W.3d 672, 676 (Tex. App.—Waco 2000, pet. denied) (Dallas County's population was over 1,800,000 in 1990, verified by consulting federal census). {*See* ***O'Connor's Texas Rules****, "Verifiable fact," ch. 5-M, §4.1.1(2), p. 492; Brown & Rondon,* ***Evidence Handbook****, p. 116.*}

7. {[13] *Party*} asks the Court to take judicial notice of {[14] *identify fact*}. This fact is verified by {[15] *identify verifying source*}, a source whose accuracy cannot reasonably be questioned. {[16] *Elaborate.*} A verified copy of {[17] *identify source*} is attached to this motion as Exhibit {[18] *number*}.

TEXAS ORDINANCE

8. Under Texas Rule of Evidence 204, a court must take judicial notice of the ordinances of municipalities and counties of Texas if the party requesting judicial notice supplies the court with the necessary information. Tex. R. Evid. 204(a), (b)(2); *see Hollingsworth v. King*, 810 S.W.2d 772, 774 (Tex. App.—Amarillo 1991), *writ denied*, 816 S.W.2d 340 (Tex. 1991).

9. {[19] *Party*} asks the Court to take judicial notice of {[20] *identify and explain ordinance*}. A verified copy of the {[21] *identify ordinance*} is attached to this motion as Exhibit {[22] *number*}.

CONCLUSION

10. {[23] *Briefly summarize the motion.*}

PRAYER

11. For these reasons, {[24] *party*} asks the Court to take judicial notice of {[25] *identify material to be judicially noticed*}.

FORM 5M:1 JUDICIAL NOTICE OF FACTS OR TEXAS ORDINANCE

SEE: Tex. R. Evid. 201, 204
*O'Connor's Texas Rules * Civil Trials* (2019), "Motion for Judicial Notice," ch. 5-M, §3, p. 491; "Grounds for Judicial Notice," ch. 5-M, §4, p. 492
Brown & Rondon, *Texas Rules of Evidence Handbook* (2019), pp. 106, 145

ADD: STYLE OF THE CASE – FORM 1B:2
SIGNATURE BLOCK – FORM 1B:3
CERTIFICATE OF SERVICE – FORM 1B:13

ATTACH: AFFIDAVIT – FORM 1B:8, if necessary
NOTICE OF HEARING OR SUBMISSION – FORM 1E:1
ORDER – FORM 5M:8
Necessary information to support judicial notice
Verified copies of sources relied on in support of verifiable fact or Texas ordinance

NOTE: Some appellate courts require that copies of municipal ordinances be verified. *See, e.g.*, ***City of Houston v. Southwest Concrete Constr., Inc.***, 835 S.W.2d 728, 733 n.5 (Tex.App.—Houston [14th Dist.] 1992, writ denied) (court refused to take judicial notice because ordinance was not verified). See ***O'Connor's Texas Rules***, "Texas city & county ordinances," ch. 5-M, §4.3, p. 494.

FORM 5M:1

{❶ *PARTY*}'S MOTION TO JUDICIALLY NOTICE AND APPLY {❷ *SISTER STATE*} LAW

{❸ *Party*}, {❹ *name*}, asks the Court to judicially notice and apply {❺ *sister state*} law to {❻ *identify dispute, e.g., plaintiff's claim for breach of contract*}. {*See* ***O'Connor's Texas Rules****, "Laws of sister state," ch. 5-M, §4.5, p. 495.*}

INTRODUCTION

1. Plaintiff, {❼ *name*}, sued defendant, {❽ *name*}, for {❾ *state basis of suit*}.

2. {❿ *State other relevant facts about the suit.*}

BACKGROUND

3. {⓫ *State facts relevant to the motion.*}

JUDICIAL NOTICE

4. Under Texas Rule of Evidence 202, a court must take judicial notice of the constitutions, public statutes, rules, regulations, ordinances, court decisions, and common law of every other state, territory, or jurisdiction of the United States if the party requesting judicial notice supplies the court with the necessary information. Tex. R. Evid. 202(a), (b)(2); *see Daugherty v. S. Pac. Transp. Co.*, 772 S.W.2d 81, 82 (Tex. 1989).

5. {⓬ *Party*} asks the Court to take judicial notice of {⓭ *identify sister state's law, e.g., California Civil Code §48a*}. A copy of {⓮ *sister state*}'s law is attached to this motion as Exhibit {⓯ *number*} and verified by {⓰ *explain method of verification, e.g., affidavit, deposition*}.

CHOICE OF LAW

6. Texas courts can apply the law of a sister state to a dispute when the substantive laws of that state differ from Texas on one or more points in issue and the party requesting its application can demonstrate that the sister state's law would apply. *Weatherly v. Deloitte & Touche*, 905 S.W.2d 642, 650 (Tex. App.—Houston [14th Dist.] 1995, writ dism'd w.o.j.), *abrogated on other grounds*, *Tracker Marine, L.P. v. Ogle*, 108 S.W.3d 349 (Tex. App.—Houston [14th Dist.] 2003, no pet.); *see Greenberg Traurig of N.Y., P.C. v. Moody*, 161 S.W.3d 56, 69 (Tex. App.—Houston [14th Dist.] 2004, no pet.) (court must make conflicts-of-laws decision only when case is connected to more than one state and the laws of the states differ on a point in issue); *PennWell Corp. v. Ken Assocs., Inc.*, 123 S.W.3d 756, 764 (Tex. App.—Houston [14th Dist.] 2003, pet. denied) (conflicts in procedural law are not subject to a conflict-of-law analysis).

A. Conflict between Texas and {17 *sister state*}.

7. On {18 *identify dispute*}, {19 *sister state*} law is substantively different from Texas law because {20 *identify substantive differences*}.

B. Applicability of {21 *sister state*} law.

{*ADD PARAGRAPHS 8-12 FOR MOST SIGNIFICANT RELATIONSHIP – TORTS*}

8. To determine whose law applies in conflict cases involving a tort, Texas courts apply the "most significant relationship" test as set forth in the Restatement (Second) of Conflict of Laws sections 6 and 145. *Torrington Co. v. Stutzman*, 46 S.W.3d 829, 848 (Tex. 2000). Under section 145, the law of the state that has the most significant relationship to the occurrence and the parties under the principles stated in section 6 will govern the rights of litigants in a tort suit.

9. Section 145 lists the contacts that should be considered when determining whose law applies to a suit involving a tort. These contacts include the following:

a. the place where the injury occurred,

b. the place where the conduct causing the injury occurred,

c. the domicile, residence, nationality, place of incorporation, and place of business of the parties, and

d. the place where the relationship, if any, between the parties is centered. *Torrington Co.*, 46 S.W.3d at 848; Restatement (Second) of Conflict of Laws §145 (1971).

{*ADD PARAGRAPH 10 IF APPLICABLE*}

10. In addition to the contacts listed above, for {22 *identify specific tort action, e.g., torts involving fraud or misrepresentation*}, the following contacts under {23 *identify applicable Restatement section, e.g., section 148*} should also be considered: {24 *list contacts*}.

11. In determining whose law should apply, the number of contacts is not determinative. *Torrington Co.*, 46 S.W.3d at 848; *Duncan v. Cessna Aircraft Co.*, 665 S.W.2d 414, 421 (Tex. 1984). Some contacts are more important than others because they implicate state policies underlying the particular substantive issue. *Duncan*, 665 S.W.2d at

Continued on next page

421; *see Torrington Co.*, 46 S.W.3d at 848-49. Thus, selecting the applicable law depends on the qualitative nature of the particular contacts as affected by the following policy factors:

a. the needs of the interstate and international systems,

b. the relevant policies of the forum,

c. the relevant policies of other interested states and the relative interests of those states in the determination of the particular issue,

d. the protection of justified expectations,

e. the basic policies underlying the particular field of law,

f. certainty, predictability, and uniformity of result, and

g. ease in the determination and application of the law to be applied. Restatement (Second) of Conflict of Laws §6; *see Torrington Co.*, 46 S.W.3d at 848.

12. {㉕ *Identify law*} is applicable to {㉖ *identify tort action*} because {㉗ *sister state*} has the most significant relationship to this dispute. {㉘ *Explain how the contacts and factors under the Restatement (Second) of Conflict of Laws demonstrate that the other state's law has the most significant relationship to the particular substantive issue to be resolved. Hughes Wood Prods., Inc. v. Wagner, 18 S.W.3d 202, 205 (Tex. 2000).*}

{ADD PARAGRAPHS 13-17 FOR MOST SIGNIFICANT RELATIONSHIP – CONTRACTS}

13. To determine whose law applies in conflict cases involving a contract dispute, Texas courts apply the "most significant relationship" test as set forth in Restatement (Second) of Conflict of Laws sections 6 and 188. *See Maxus Expl. Co. v. Moran Bros.*, 817 S.W.2d 50, 53 (Tex. 1991). Under section 188(1), the local law of the state that has the most significant relationship to the transaction and the parties under the principles stated in section 6 will govern the rights and duties of the parties with respect to an issue in contract.

14. Section 188(2) lists the contacts that should be considered when determining whose law applies to an issue in contract. *Maxus Expl.*, 817 S.W.2d at 53. These contacts include the following:

a. the place of contracting,

b. the place of negotiation of the contract,

c. the place of performance,

d. the location of the subject matter of the contract, and

e. the domicile, residence, nationality, place of incorporation, and place of business of the parties. *Maxus Expl.*, 817 S.W.2d at 53; Restatement (Second) of Conflict of Laws §188(2) (1971).

{*ADD PARAGRAPH 15 IF APPLICABLE*}

15. In addition to the contacts listed above, for {㉙ *identify specific contract action, e.g., disputes involving a personal-services contract*}, the following contacts under {㉚ *identify Restatement section, e.g., section 196*} should also be considered: {㉛ *list contacts*}.

16. In determining whose law should apply, the number of contacts is not determinative. *Duncan v. Cessna Aircraft Co.*, 665 S.W.2d 414, 421 (Tex. 1984). Some contacts are more important than others because they implicate state policies underlying the particular substantive issue. *Id.* Thus, selection of the applicable law depends on the qualitative nature of the particular contacts as affected by the following policy factors:

a. the needs of the interstate and international systems,

b. the relevant policies of the forum,

c. the relevant policies of other interested states and the relative interests of those states in the determination of the particular issue,

d. the protection of justified expectations,

e. the basic policies underlying the particular field of law,

f. certainty, predictability, and uniformity of result, and

g. ease in the determination and application of the law to be applied. Restatement (Second) of Conflict of Laws §6.

17. {㉜ *Identify law*} is applicable to {㉝ *identify contract dispute*} because {㉞ *sister state*} has the most significant relationship to this dispute. {㉟ *Explain how the applicable contacts and factors under the Restatement (Second) of Conflict of Laws dem-*

Continued on next page

onstrate that the other state's law has the most significant relationship to the particular substantive issue to be resolved. Hughes Wood Prods., Inc. v. Wagner, 18 S.W.3d 202, 205 (Tex. 2000).}

{*ADD PARAGRAPHS 18-20 FOR CONTRACTUAL CHOICE-OF-LAW PROVISION – ISSUE CAN BE RESOLVED BY AGREEMENT*}

18. To determine whose law applies in conflict cases involving a contractual choice-of-law provision, Texas courts apply Restatement (Second) of Conflict of Laws section 187. *DeSantis v. Wackenhut Corp.*, 793 S.W.2d 670, 677 (Tex. 1990). Under section 187(1), the law of the state chosen by the parties to govern their contractual rights and duties will be applied if the particular issue is one that the parties could have resolved by an explicit provision in their agreement. *In re J.D. Edwards World Sols. Co.*, 87 S.W.3d 546, 549 (Tex. 2002); *see Nexen Inc. v. Gulf Interstate Eng'g Co.*, 224 S.W.3d 412, 419 (Tex. App.—Houston [1st Dist.] 2006, no pet.) (if section 187(1) applies, then parties' contractual choice of law will govern).

19. Contractual issues that parties can resolve by an explicit provision in their agreement include issues of construction, conditions precedent and subsequent, and performance. *See* Restatement (Second) of Conflict of Laws §187 cmt. c (1971).

20. {36 *Identify issue subject to choice-of-law provision*} is an issue the parties can resolve by an explicit provision in their agreement. {37 *Elaborate.*}

{*ADD PARAGRAPHS 21-25 FOR CONTRACTUAL CHOICE-OF-LAW PROVISION – ISSUE CANNOT BE RESOLVED BY AGREEMENT*}

21. To determine whose law applies in conflict cases involving a contractual choice-of-law provision, Texas courts apply Restatement (Second) of Conflict of Laws section 187. *DeSantis v. Wackenhut Corp.*, 793 S.W.2d 670, 677 (Tex. 1990). Under section 187(2), the law of the state chosen by the parties to govern their contractual rights and duties will be applied to an issue that cannot be resolved by an explicit provision in their agreement if (1) the parties' chosen state has a substantial relationship to the parties or the transaction, and (2) applying the law of the chosen state would not be contrary to a fundamental policy of a state with a materially greater interest. *DeSantis*, 793 S.W.2d at 678; *Nexen Inc. v. Gulf Interstate Eng'g Co.*, 224 S.W.3d 412, 419-20 (Tex. App.—Houston [1st Dist.] 2006, no pet.).

22. {38 *Identify issue that cannot be resolved by agreement, e.g., the enforceability of the parties' agreement*} is an issue the parties cannot resolve by an explicit provision in their agreement. {39 *Elaborate.*}

23. {40 *Sister state*} has a substantial relationship with the parties and the transaction. {41 *Elaborate.*}

24. Texas does not have a materially greater interest in this dispute than {42 *sister state*}. {43 *Elaborate.*}

25. Enforcing the parties' choice-of-law provision would not be contrary to a fundamental policy of Texas. {44 *Elaborate.*}

CONCLUSION

26. {45 *Briefly summarize the motion.*}

PRAYER

27. For these reasons, {46 *party*} asks the Court to judicially notice and apply {47 *identify law*} to {48 *identify dispute*}.

SEE: Tex. R. Evid. 202
Restatement (2d) of Conflict of Laws §§6, 145, 187, 188 (1971)
O'Connor's Texas Rules * Civil Trials (2019), "Laws of sister state," ch. 5-M, §4.5, p. 495
Brown & Rondon, ***Texas Rules of Evidence Handbook*** (2019), p. 137

ADD: STYLE OF THE CASE – FORM 1B:2
SIGNATURE BLOCK – FORM 1B:3
CERTIFICATE OF SERVICE – FORM 1B:13

ATTACH: AFFIDAVIT – FORM 1B:8, if necessary
NOTICE OF HEARING OR SUBMISSION – FORM 1E:1
ORDER – FORM 5M:9
Copy of the law of United States or other state or territory, if necessary

NOTE: When evaluating the contacts for a particular tort or contract action, check the Restatement (Second) of Conflict of Laws to see if there are any additional contacts that should be evaluated for that particular cause of action. *See, e.g.*, Restatement (2d) of Conflict of Laws §196 (contracts for personal service), §221 (unjust enrichment) (1971).

{❶ *PARTY*}'S MOTION TO JUDICIALLY
NOTICE & APPLY THE LAW OF {❷ *FOREIGN COUNTRY*}

{❸ *Party*}, {❹ *name*}, asks the Court to judicially notice and apply the law of {❺ *foreign country*} to {❻ *identify dispute, e.g., plaintiff's claim for breach of contract*}. {*See* ***O'Connor's Texas Rules****, "Foreign laws," ch. 5-M, §4.7, p. 495.*}

INTRODUCTION

1. Plaintiff, {❼ *name*}, sued defendant, {❽ *name*}, for {❾ *state basis of suit*}.

2. {❿ *State other relevant facts about the suit.*}

BACKGROUND

3. {⓫ *State facts relevant to the motion.*}

JUDICIAL NOTICE

4. Under Texas Rule of Evidence 203, a court can take judicial notice of the law of a foreign country if the party requesting judicial notice (1) gives reasonable, written notice of its intent to use foreign law and (2) provides copies of any written materials or sources that the party intends to use as proof of foreign law at least 30 days before the date of trial. *See* Tex. R. Evid. 203(a). Proof of the foreign law can come from any material or source, including affidavits or deposition testimony. *See* Tex. R. Evid. 203(c); *see, e.g., Reading & Bates Constr. Co. v. Baker Energy Res. Corp.*, 976 S.W.2d 702, 707 (Tex. App.—Houston [1st Dist.] 1998, pet. denied) (parties provided affidavits from law professors explaining Canadian law). {*See* ***O'Connor's Texas Rules****, "Foreign laws," ch. 5-M, §4.7, p. 495.*}

{*ADD PARAGRAPH 5 IF APPLICABLE*}

5. If the foreign laws or the material explaining the foreign laws are in a language other than English, the party must also provide the following information to the court and all other parties at least 45 days before trial: (1) a copy of the foreign-language text, (2) a copy of the English translation, and (3) an affidavit or unsworn declaration from a qualified translator that states the translator's qualifications and certifies that the translation is accurate. *See* Tex. R. Evid. 203(b), 1009(a); *In re Estates of Garcia-Chapa*, 33 S.W.3d 859, 862 (Tex. App.—Corpus Christi 2000, no pet.).

6. {⓬ *Party*} asks the Court to take judicial notice of the law of {⓭ *foreign country*} relating to {⓮ *identify law, e.g., contracts*}.

7. A copy of {⓯ *foreign country*}'s law is attached to this motion as Exhibit {⓰ *number*} and verified by {⓱ *explain method of verification, e.g., affidavit, deposition*}.

{*ADD PARAGRAPH 8 IF APPLICABLE*}

8. In addition to providing a copy of the law, {⓲ *party*} has attached the following documents {⓳ *he/she/it*} intends to use as proof of the foreign law:

{*CHOOSE APPROPRIATE PARAGRAPHS a-e*}

a. A treatise on the law of {⓴ *foreign country*}, {㉑ *name of treatise*}, attached as Exhibit {㉒ *letter*}.

b. An affidavit by {㉓ *name*}, the legal adviser to Ambassador {㉔ *name*} from {㉕ *foreign country*}, attached as Exhibit {㉖ *letter*}.

c. A brief by {㉗ *name*}, who is an expert on the law of {㉘ *foreign country*}, attached as Exhibit {㉙ *letter*}.

d. A deposition by {㉚ *name*}, who is an expert on the law of {㉛ *foreign country*}, attached as Exhibit {㉜ *letter*}.

e. {㉝ *Identify any other material or source to be used as proof of the foreign law.*}

{*ADD PARAGRAPH 9 IF APPLICABLE*}

9. Because {㉞ *the law/the material explaining the law*} of {㉟ *foreign country*} is written in {㊱ *identify language other than English*}, {㊲ *party*} attaches to this request as Exhibits {㊳ *letters*} the following: (1) a copy of the law of {㊴ *foreign country*}, (2) a copy of an English translation, and (3) an {㊵ *affidavit/unsworn declaration*} from {㊶ *name of qualified translator*} stating {㊷ *his/her*} qualifications and certifying that the translation is accurate.

CHOICE OF LAW

10. Texas courts can apply the law of a foreign country to a dispute when the substantive laws of that foreign country differ from Texas on one or more points in issue and the party requesting its application can demonstrate that the foreign country's law would apply. *See Nexen Inc. v. Gulf Interstate Eng'g Co.*, 224 S.W.3d 412, 415-16 (Tex. App.—Houston [1st Dist.] 2006, no pet.); *PennWell Corp. v. Ken Assocs., Inc.*, 123 S.W.3d 756, 763-64 (Tex. App.—Houston [14th Dist.] 2003, pet. denied).

Continued on next page

A. Conflict between Texas and {㊸ *foreign country*}.

11. On {㊹ *identify dispute*}, {㊺ *foreign country*} law is substantively different from Texas law because {㊻ *identify substantive differences*}.

B. Applicability of {㊼ *foreign country*} law.

{ADD PARAGRAPHS 12-16 FOR MOST SIGNIFICANT RELATIONSHIP – TORTS}

12. To determine whose law applies in conflict cases involving a tort, Texas courts apply the "most significant relationship" test as set forth in the Restatement (Second) of Conflict of Laws sections 6 and 145. *Torrington Co. v. Stutzman*, 46 S.W.3d 829, 848 (Tex. 2000); *Gutierrez v. Collins*, 583 S.W.2d 312, 318 (Tex. 1979); *Bridas Corp. v. Unocal Corp.*, 16 S.W.3d 893, 897 (Tex. App.—Houston [14th Dist.] 2000, pet. denied); *CPS Int'l, Inc. v. Dresser Indus., Inc.*, 911 S.W.2d 18, 28-29 (Tex. App.—El Paso 1995, writ denied). Under section 145, the law of the country that has the most significant relationship to the occurrence and the parties under the principles stated in section 6 will govern the rights of litigants in a tort suit.

13. Section 145 lists the contacts that should be considered when determining whose law applies to a suit involving a tort. These contacts include the following:

a. the place where the injury occurred,

b. the place where the conduct causing the injury occurred,

c. the domicile, residence, nationality, place of incorporation, and place of business of the parties, and

d. the place where the relationship, if any, between the parties is centered. *Torrington Co.*, 46 S.W.3d at 848; Restatement (Second) of Conflict of Laws §145 (1971).

{ADD PARAGRAPH 14 IF APPLICABLE}

14. In addition to the contacts listed above, for {㊽ *identify specific tort action, e.g., torts involving fraud or misrepresentation*}, the following contacts under {㊾ *identify applicable Restatement section, e.g., section 148*} should also be considered: {㊿ *list contacts*}.

15. In determining whose law should apply, the number of contacts is not determinative. *Torrington Co.*, 46 S.W.3d at 848; *Duncan v. Cessna Aircraft Co.*, 665 S.W.2d 414, 421 (Tex. 1984). Some contacts are more important than others because they implicate state policies underlying the particular substantive issue. *Duncan*, 665 S.W.2d at 421; *see Torrington Co.*, 46 S.W.3d at 848-49. Thus, selecting the applicable law depends on the qualitative nature of the particular contacts as affected by the following policy factors:

a. the needs of the interstate and international systems,

b. the relevant policies of the forum,

c. the relevant policies of other interested states and the relative interests of those states in the determination of the particular issue,

d. the protection of justified expectations,

e. the basic policies underlying the particular field of law,

f. certainty, predictability, and uniformity of result, and

g. ease in the determination and application of the law to be applied. *Gutierrez*, 583 S.W.2d at 318-19; Restatement (Second) of Conflict of Laws §6; *see Torrington Co.*, 46 S.W.3d at 848; *Bridas Corp.*, 16 S.W.3d at 899-900.

16. {51 *Identify law*} is applicable to {52 *identify tort action*} because {53 *foreign country*} has the most significant relationship to this dispute. {54 *Explain how the contacts and factors under the Restatement (Second) of Conflict of Laws demonstrate that the foreign country's law has the most significant relationship to the particular substantive issue to be resolved. Hughes Wood Prods., Inc. v. Wagner, 18 S.W.3d 202, 205 (Tex. 2000).*}

{*ADD PARAGRAPHS 17-21 FOR MOST SIGNIFICANT RELATIONSHIP – CONTRACTS*}

17. To determine whose law applies in conflict cases involving a contract dispute, Texas courts apply the "most significant relationship" test as set forth in Restatement (Second) of Conflict of Laws sections 6 and 188. *See Maxus Expl. Co. v. Moran Bros.*, 817 S.W.2d 50, 53 (Tex. 1991). Under section 188(1), the local law of the place that has the most significant relationship to the transaction and the parties under the principles stated in section 6 will govern the rights and duties of the parties with respect to an issue in contract.

◄ *Continued on next page* ►

18. Section 188(2) lists the contacts that should be considered when determining whose law applies to an issue in contract. *Maxus Expl.*, 817 S.W.2d at 53. These contacts include the following:

a. the place of contracting,

b. the place of negotiation of the contract,

c. the place of performance,

d. the location of the subject matter of the contract, and

e. the domicile, residence, nationality, place of incorporation, and place of business of the parties. *Id.*; Restatement (Second) of Conflict of Laws §188(2) (1971).

{*ADD PARAGRAPH 19 IF APPLICABLE*}

19. In addition to the contacts listed above, for {55 *identify specific contract action, e.g., disputes involving a personal-services contract*}, the following contacts under {56 *identify Restatement section, e.g., section 196*} should also be considered: {57 *list contacts*}.

20. In determining whose law should apply, the number of contacts is not determinative. *Duncan v. Cessna Aircraft Co.*, 665 S.W.2d 414, 421 (Tex. 1984). Some contacts are more important than others because they implicate state policies underlying the particular substantive issue. *Id.* Thus, selection of the applicable law depends on the qualitative nature of the particular contacts as affected by the following policy factors:

a. the needs of the interstate and international systems,

b. the relevant policies of the forum,

c. the relevant policies of other interested states and the relative interests of those states in the determination of the particular issue,

d. the protection of justified expectations,

e. the basic policies underlying the particular field of law,

f. certainty, predictability, and uniformity of result, and

g. ease in the determination and application of the law to be applied. Restatement (Second) of Conflict of Laws §6.

21. {58 *Identify law*} is applicable to {59 *identify contract dispute*} because {60 *foreign country*} has the most significant relationship to this dispute. {61 *Explain how the applicable contacts and factors under the Restatement (Second) of Conflict of Laws demonstrate that the other country's law has the most significant relationship to the particular substantive issue to be resolved. Hughes Wood Prods., Inc. v. Wagner, 18 S.W.3d 202, 205 (Tex. 2000).*}

{ADD PARAGRAPHS 22-24 FOR CONTRACTUAL CHOICE-OF-LAW PROVISION – ISSUE CAN BE RESOLVED BY AGREEMENT}

22. To determine whose law applies in conflict cases involving a contractual choice-of-law provision, Texas courts apply Restatement (Second) of Conflict of Laws section 187. *DeSantis v. Wackenhut Corp.*, 793 S.W.2d 670, 677 (Tex. 1990); *CPS Int'l, Inc. v. Dresser Indus., Inc.*, 911 S.W.2d 18, 23-24 (Tex. App.—El Paso 1995, writ denied). Under section 187(1), the law of the place chosen by the parties to govern their contractual rights and duties will be applied if the particular issue is one that the parties could have resolved by an explicit provision in their agreement. *In re J.D. Edwards World Sols. Co.*, 87 S.W.3d 546, 549 (Tex. 2002); *see Nexen Inc.*, 224 S.W.3d at 419 (if section 187(1) applies, then parties' contractual choice of law will govern).

23. Contractual issues that parties can resolve by an explicit provision in their agreement include issues of construction, conditions precedent and subsequent, and performance. *See* Restatement (Second) of Conflict of Laws §187 cmt. c (1971).

24. {62 *Identify issue subject to choice-of-law provision*} is an issue the parties can resolve by an explicit provision in their agreement. {63 *Elaborate.*}

{ADD PARAGRAPHS 25-29 FOR CONTRACTUAL CHOICE-OF-LAW PROVISION – ISSUE CANNOT BE RESOLVED BY AGREEMENT}

25. To determine whose law applies in conflict cases involving a contractual choice-of-law provision, Texas courts apply Restatement (Second) of Conflict of Laws section 187. *DeSantis v. Wackenhut Corp.*, 793 S.W.2d 670, 677 (Tex. 1990). Under section 187(2), the law of the place chosen by the parties to govern their contractual rights and duties will be applied to an issue that cannot be resolved by an explicit provision in their agreement if (1) the parties' chosen place has a substantial relationship to the parties or the transaction, and (2) applying the law of the chosen place would not be contrary to a fundamental policy of a state with a materially greater interest. *See DeSantis*, 793 S.W.2d at 678; *Nexen Inc.*, 224 S.W.3d at 419-20.

Continued on next page

26. {64 *Identify issue that cannot be resolved by agreement, e.g., the enforceability of the parties' agreement*} is an issue the parties cannot resolve by an explicit provision in their agreement. {65 *Elaborate.*}

27. {66 *Name of foreign country*} has a substantial relationship with the parties and the transaction. {67 *Elaborate.*}

28. Texas does not have a materially greater interest in this dispute than {68 *foreign country*}. {69 *Elaborate.*}

29. Enforcing the parties' choice-of-law provision would not be contrary to a fundamental policy of Texas. {70 *Elaborate.*}

CONCLUSION

30. {71 *Briefly summarize the motion.*}

PRAYER

31. For these reasons, {72 *party*} asks the Court to judicially notice of the law of {73 *foreign country*}.

SEE: Tex. R. Evid. 203, 1009(a)
Restatement (2d) of Conflict of Laws §§6, 145, 187, 188 (1971)
O'Connor's Texas Rules * Civil Trials (2019), "Foreign laws," ch. 5-M, §4.7, p. 495
Brown & Rondon, ***Texas Rules of Evidence Handbook*** (2019), pp. 141, 1059

ADD: STYLE OF THE CASE – FORM 1B:2
SIGNATURE BLOCK – FORM 1B:3
VERIFICATION – FORM 1B:7, if necessary
CERTIFICATE OF SERVICE – FORM 1B:13

ATTACH: AFFIDAVIT – FORM 1B:8, if necessary
NOTICE OF HEARING OR SUBMISSION – FORM 1E:1
ORDER – FORM 5M:9
Affidavit or unsworn declaration of qualified translator, if necessary
Affidavits of experts, if necessary
Briefs by experts, if necessary
Copy of the law of foreign country
Depositions of experts, if necessary
English translation of law of foreign country, if necessary
Treatises on law of foreign country, if necessary

NOTE: Texas Rule of Evidence 203(b) requires a party to provide a copy of the foreign-language text and an English translation at least 30 days before trial; however, Texas Rule of Evidence 1009(a) requires the party to provide the text and translation, along with the translator's affidavit or unsworn declaration, at least 45 days before trial for the translation to be admissible as evidence. Therefore, a party should comply with the deadline and procedures in Rule 1009(a) if it wants to dispense with the need for live testimony of the translation of the foreign-language document. *See* Tex. R. Evid. 1009(a), (e).

For good cause, a party can ask to shorten the 45-day deadline for providing an English translation of a foreign-language text. Tex. R. Evid. 1009(f).

If the court considers any material or source not submitted by a party, it must give all parties notice and a reasonable opportunity to comment and submit additional materials. Tex. R. Evid. 203(c).

Texas Rule of Civil Procedure 308b provides procedures for determining the recognition or enforcement of a judgment or an arbitration award based on foreign law in suits involving a marriage relationship or parent-child relationship under the Texas Family Code. *See* Tex. R. Civ. P. 308b. The requirements for raising a foreign-law issue under Texas Rule of Evidence 203(a) and (b) do not apply to actions covered by Rule 308b. *See* Tex. R. Civ. P. 308b(c)(2); Tex. R. Evid. 203(e). Rule 308b provides its own deadlines and procedures for notice, pretrial conferences, hearings, and orders.

{1 *PARTY*}'S RESPONSE TO
{2 *ADVERSE PARTY*}'S MOTION TO TAKE JUDICIAL NOTICE

{3 *Party*}, {4 *name*}, asks the Court to deny {5 *adverse party*} {6 *name*}'s motion to take judicial notice of {7 *identify material to be judicially noticed*}. {*See* ***O'Connor's Texas Rules****, "Response," ch. 5-M, §5, p. 497.*}

INTRODUCTION

1. Plaintiff, {8 *name*}, sued defendant, {9 *name*}, for {10 *state basis of suit*}.

2. {11 *State other relevant facts about the suit.*}

BACKGROUND

3. On {12 *date*}, {13 *adverse party*} filed a motion asking the Court to take judicial notice of {14 *state facts sought to be judicially noticed*}.

4. {15 *State other facts relevant to the response.*}

{*CHOOSE APPROPRIATE ARGUMENTS*}

NOTORIOUS FACTS

5. A court should deny a request to take judicial notice of an allegedly notorious fact if the fact is reasonably disputable or not generally known within the court's territorial jurisdiction. *See* Tex. R. Evid. 201(b)(1). If facts are based on the personal knowledge of the parties or the judge or commonly known only among a specially informed class of persons, the facts are not generally known. *See Eagle Trucking Co. v. Tex. Bitulithic Co.*, 612 S.W.2d 503, 506 (Tex. 1981); *Haden Co. v. Mixers, Inc.*, 667 S.W.2d 316, 317 (Tex. App.—Dallas 1984, no writ). {*See* ***O'Connor's Texas Rules****, "Notorious fact," ch. 5-M, §4.1.1(1), p. 492; Brown & Rondon,* ***Evidence Handbook****, p. 114.*}

{*CHOOSE APPROPRIATE PARAGRAPHS 6-7*}

6. The Court should deny {16 *adverse party*}'s motion to take judicial notice of {17 *identify facts*} because the facts are reasonably disputable. {18 *Elaborate.*}

7. The Court should deny {19 *adverse party*}'s motion to take judicial notice of {20 *identify facts*} because the facts are not common knowledge within the Court's territorial jurisdiction. {21 *Explain, e.g., facts are based on the judge's personal knowledge or commonly known only among a specially informed class of persons.*} {*See* ***O'Connor's Texas Rules****, "Objections," ch. 5-M, §5.2, p. 497.*}

VERIFIABLE FACTS

8. A court should deny a request to take judicial notice of an allegedly verifiable fact if the fact is reasonably disputable, the movant does not provide the court with necessary information, or the accuracy of the information the movant provides can be reasonably questioned. *See* Tex. R. Evid. 201(b)(2), (c)(2). {*See Brown & Rondon,* ***Evidence Handbook****, p. 116.*}

{*CHOOSE APPROPRIATE PARAGRAPHS 9-11*}

9. The Court should deny {[22] *adverse party*}'s motion to take judicial notice of {[23] *identify facts*} because the facts are reasonably disputable. {[24] *Elaborate.*}

10. The Court should deny {[25] *adverse party*}'s motion to take judicial notice of {[26] *identify facts*} because {[27] *adverse party*} did not provide the Court with the necessary information. {[28] *Elaborate.*}

11. The Court should deny {[29] *adverse party*}'s motion to take judicial notice of {[30] *identify facts*} because the accuracy of the support that {[31] *adverse party*} provided the Court can be reasonably questioned. {[32] *Elaborate.*}

TEXAS ORDINANCE

12. A court should deny a request to take judicial notice of a Texas ordinance if the party does not (1) supply the court with the necessary information or (2) give all parties reasonable notice to prepare to respond to the party's request if such notice is required by the court. *See* Tex. R. Evid. 204(a), (b)(2), (c)(1); *Hollingsworth v. King*, 810 S.W.2d 772, 774 (Tex. App.—Amarillo 1991), *writ denied*, 816 S.W.2d 340 (Tex. 1991).

{*CHOOSE APPROPRIATE PARAGRAPHS 13-14*}

13. The Court should deny {[33] *adverse party*}'s motion to take judicial notice of the {[34] *identify city or county*} ordinance because {[35] *adverse party*} did not supply the Court with the necessary information. {[36] *State facts challenging the sufficiency or accuracy of information provided by adverse party.*}

14. The Court should deny {[37] *adverse party*}'s motion to take judicial notice of the {[38] *identify city or county*} ordinance because {[39] *adverse party*} did not give {[40] *party*} reasonable notice to prepare to respond to the request. {[41] *Elaborate.*}

Continued on next page

REQUEST FOR HEARING

15. On timely request, a party is entitled to an opportunity to be heard on the propriety of taking judicial notice and the nature of the matter noticed. {42 *Tex. R. Evid. 201(e)/Tex. R. Evid. 204(c)(2)*}. {43 *Party*} asks the Court to hold a hearing to give {44 *party*} the opportunity to respond.

CONCLUSION

16. {45 *Briefly summarize the response.*}

PRAYER

17. For these reasons, {46 *party*} asks the Court to deny {47 *adverse party*}'s motion for judicial notice of {48 *identify material to be judicially noticed*}.

SEE: Tex. R. Evid. 201, 204
O'Connor's Texas Rules * Civil Trials (2019), "Response," ch. 5-M, §5, p. 497
Brown & Rondon, ***Texas Rules of Evidence Handbook*** (2019), pp. 106, 145

ADD: STYLE OF THE CASE – FORM 1B:2
SIGNATURE BLOCK – FORM 1B:3
CERTIFICATE OF SERVICE – FORM 1B:13

ATTACH: AFFIDAVIT – FORM 1B:8, if necessary
ORDER – FORM 5M:8

{❶ *PARTY*}'S RESPONSE TO
{❷ *ADVERSE PARTY*}'S MOTION TO JUDICIALLY
NOTICE & APPLY THE LAW OF {❸ *SISTER STATE*}

{❹ *Party*}, {❺ *name*}, asks the Court to deny {❻ *adverse party*} {❼ *name*}'s motion to judicially notice and apply the law of {❽ *sister state*} to {❾ *identify dispute, e.g., plaintiff's claim for breach of contract*}.

INTRODUCTION

1. Plaintiff, {❿ *name*}, sued defendant, {⓫ *name*}, for {⓬ *state basis of suit*}.

2. {⓭ *State other relevant facts about the suit.*}

BACKGROUND

3. On {⓮ *date*}, {⓯ *adverse party*} filed a motion asking the Court to judicially notice and apply the law of {⓰ *sister state*} to {⓱ *identify dispute*}.

4. {⓲ *State other facts relevant to the response.*}

JUDICIAL NOTICE

5. A court should deny a request to take judicial notice of the constitutions, public statutes, rules, regulations, ordinances, court decisions, or common law of another state, territory, or jurisdiction of the United States if (1) the request is untimely made, (2) the party does not supply the court with the necessary information, or (3) the party does not give all parties reasonable notice to prepare to respond to the party's request, if such notice is required by the court. *See* Tex. R. Evid. 202(a), (b)(2), (c)(1); *Colvin v. Colvin*, 291 S.W.3d 508, 513-14 (Tex. App.—Tyler 2009, no pet.). When a request is untimely made or a party does not submit sufficient proof, the court should presume that the laws of the other jurisdiction are the same as the laws of Texas. *Colvin*, 291 S.W.3d at 514; *see Coca-Cola Co. v. Harmar Bottling Co.*, 218 S.W.3d 671, 684-85 (Tex. 2006); *Gerdes v. Kennamer*, 155 S.W.3d 541, 548 (Tex. App.—Corpus Christi 2004, no pet.); *Burns v. Resolution Tr. Corp.*, 880 S.W.2d 149, 151 (Tex. App.—Houston [14th Dist.] 1994, no writ). {*See* ***O'Connor's Texas Rules****, "No request," ch. 5-M, §4.5.2, p. 495; "Lack of sufficient information," ch. 5-M, §5.2.3, p. 497.*}

Continued on next page

{*CHOOSE APPROPRIATE PARAGRAPHS 6-9*}

{*Motion untimely*}

6. The Court should deny {[19] *adverse party*}'s motion to take judicial notice of {[20] *sister state*} law because {[21] *adverse party*} did not request judicial notice in a timely manner. {[22] *Elaborate.*}

{*Insufficient information*}

7. The Court should deny {[23] *adverse party*}'s motion to take judicial notice of {[24] *sister state*} law because {[25] *adverse party*} did not supply the Court with the necessary information. {[26] *Elaborate.*}

{*No notice*}

8. The court should deny {[27] *adverse party*}'s motion to take judicial notice of {[28] *sister state*} law because {[29] *adverse party*} did not give {[30] *party*} reasonable notice to prepare to respond to the request. {[31] *Elaborate.*}

{*Private act or order not proper basis for judicial notice*}

9. The Court should deny {[32] *adverse party*}'s motion to take judicial notice of {[33] *identify private act or order*} because it is a {[34] *private act/private order*}. Under Texas Rule of Evidence 202, a court is not permitted to take judicial notice of private acts or orders. *See Centex Corp. v. Dalton*, 810 S.W.2d 812, 824 (Tex. App.—San Antonio 1991), *rev'd on other grounds*, 840 S.W.2d 952 (Tex. 1992). Rule 202 only permits the court to take judicial notice of public acts. *See* Tex. R. Evid. 202(a) (court may take judicial notice of constitutions, public statutes, rules, regulations, ordinances, court decisions, and common law).

CHOICE OF LAW

10. Texas courts cannot apply a sister state's law to a dispute unless the party requesting the application establishes that the sister state's substantive laws differ from Texas's and the sister state's law would apply to the dispute. *Weatherly v. Deloitte & Touche*, 905 S.W.2d 642, 650 (Tex. App.—Houston [14th Dist.] 1995, writ dism'd w.o.j.), *abrogated on other grounds*, *Tracker Marine, L.P. v. Ogle*, 108 S.W.3d 349 (Tex. App.—Houston [14th Dist.] 2003, no pet.); *see Greenberg Traurig of N.Y., P.C. v. Moody*, 161 S.W.3d 56, 69 (Tex. App.—Houston [14th Dist.] 2004, no pet.) (court must make conflicts-of-laws decision only when case is connected to more than one state and the laws of the states differ on a point in issue); *PennWell Corp. v. Ken Assocs., Inc.*, 123 S.W.3d 756, 764 (Tex. App.—Houston [14th Dist.] 2003, pet. denied) (conflicts in procedural law are not subject to a conflict-of-law analysis).

A. No conflict between Texas and {㉟ *sister state*} law.

{*CHOOSE APPROPRIATE PARAGRAPHS 11-13*}

{*No proof of conflict*}

11. {㊱ *Adverse party*} did not offer any proof that the substantive law of {㊲ *sister state*} conflicts with Texas law on {㊳ *identify dispute*}. Because {㊴ *adverse party*} has not offered any proof of a conflict, Texas law must apply to resolve this dispute.

{*No conflict*}

12. Contrary to {㊵ *adverse party*}'s motion, the substantive law of {㊶ *sister state*} does not conflict with Texas law on {㊷ *identify dispute*}. {㊸ *Elaborate.*}

{*Conflict is procedural*}

13. Contrary to {㊹ *adverse party*}'s motion, the conflict {㊺ *he/she/it*} identified between {㊻ *sister state*} law and Texas law is a conflict in procedural law, not substantive law. Generally, whether a legal issue is a matter of substance or procedure is determined by the law of the forum state according to its own laws. *PennWell Corp.*, 123 S.W.3d at 764. Under Texas law, {㊼ *identify legal issue to be resolved*} is a matter of procedure. {㊽ *Elaborate.*}

B. {㊾ *Sister state*} law is not applicable.

{*ADD PARAGRAPHS 14-21 TO RESPOND TO MOST SIGNIFICANT RELATIONSHIP – TORTS*}

14. To determine whose law applies in conflict cases involving a tort, Texas courts apply the "most significant relationship" test as set forth in the Restatement (Second) of Conflict of Laws sections 6 and 145. *Torrington Co. v. Stutzman*, 46 S.W.3d 829, 848 (Tex. 2000). Under section 145, the law of the state that has the most significant relationship to the occurrence and the parties under the principles stated in section 6 will govern the rights of litigants in a tort suit.

15. Section 145 lists the contacts that should be considered when determining whose law applies to a suit involving a tort. These contacts include the following:

a. the place where the injury occurred,

b. the place where the conduct causing the injury occurred,

◄ Continued on next page ►

c. the domicile, residence, nationality, place of incorporation, and place of business of the parties, and

d. the place where the relationship, if any, between the parties is centered. *Torrington Co.*, 46 S.W.3d at 848; Restatement (Second) of Conflict of Laws §145 (1971).

{*ADD PARAGRAPH 16 IF APPLICABLE*}

16. In addition to the contacts listed above, for {㊿ *identify specific tort action, e.g., torts involving fraud or misrepresentation*}, the following contacts under {51 *identify applicable Restatement section, e.g., section 148*} should also be considered: {52 *list contacts*}.

17. In determining whose law should apply, the number of contacts is not determinative. *Torrington Co.*, 46 S.W.3d at 848; *Duncan v. Cessna Aircraft Co.*, 665 S.W.2d 414, 421 (Tex. 1984). Some contacts are more important than others because they implicate state policies underlying the particular substantive issue. *Duncan*, 665 S.W.2d at 421; *see Torrington Co.*, 46 S.W.3d at 848-49. Thus, selecting the applicable law depends on the qualitative nature of the particular contacts as affected by the following policy factors:

a. the needs of the interstate and international systems,

b. the relevant policies of the forum,

c. the relevant policies of other interested states and the relative interests of those states in the determination of the particular issue,

d. the protection of justified expectations,

e. the basic policies underlying the particular field of law,

f. certainty, predictability, and uniformity of result, and

g. ease in the determination and application of the law to be applied. Restatement (Second) of Conflict of Laws §6; *see Torrington Co.*, 46 S.W.3d at 848.

{*CHOOSE APPROPRIATE PARAGRAPHS 18-21*}

{*Texas has most significant relationship*}

18. Contrary to {53 *adverse party*}'s motion, Texas has the most significant relationship to this dispute. {54 *Elaborate.*}

{*Contractual choice-of-law provision governs*}

19. Contrary to {55 *adverse party*}'s motion, {56 *sister state*} law does not apply to {57 *identify dispute*} because the parties have contractually agreed to have this dispute governed by Texas law. When applicable, a court should enforce a contractual choice-of-law provision. *See DeSantis v. Wackenhut Corp.*, 793 S.W.2d 670, 677 (Tex. 1990). {58 *Elaborate.*}

{*Statutory choice-of-law directive governs*}

20. Contrary to {59 *adverse party*}'s motion, {60 *sister state*} law does not apply to {61 *identify dispute*} because this dispute is governed by a statutory choice-of-law directive that requires the Court to apply Texas law. When applicable, a court must follow a statutory choice-of-law directive. *Satterfield v. Crown Cork & Seal Co.*, 268 S.W.3d 190, 199 (Tex. App.—Austin 2008, no pet.); *Am. Home Assurance Co. v. Safway Steel Prods. Co.*, 743 S.W.2d 693, 697 (Tex. App.—Austin 1987, writ denied); Restatement (Second) of Conflict of Laws §6(1). Under {62 *identify statutory choice-of-law directive*}, the parties' dispute must be resolved under Texas law. {63 *Elaborate.*}

{*Sister state law violates Texas public policy*}

21. Contrary to {64 *adverse party*}'s motion, {65 *sister state*} law should not apply to {66 *identify dispute*} because it is contrary to Texas public policy in that it is {67 *against good morals and natural justice/prejudicial to the general interests of Texas citizens*}. A court should not enforce a sister state's law that violates Texas public policy. *Larchmont Farms, Inc. v. Parra*, 941 S.W.2d 93, 95 (Tex. 1997). {68 *Elaborate.*}

{*ADD PARAGRAPHS 22-29 TO RESPOND TO MOST SIGNIFICANT RELATIONSHIP – CONTRACTS*}

22. To determine whose law applies in conflict cases involving a contract dispute, Texas courts apply the "most significant relationship" test as set forth in Restatement (Second) of Conflict of Laws sections 6 and 188. *See Maxus Expl. Co. v. Moran Bros.*, 817 S.W.2d 50, 53 (Tex. 1991). Under section 188(1), the local law of the state that has the most significant relationship to the transaction and the parties under the principles stated in section 6 will govern the rights and duties of the parties with respect to an issue in contract.

23. Section 188(2) lists the contacts that should be considered when determining whose law applies to an issue in contract. *Maxus Expl.*, 817 S.W.2d at 53. These contacts include the following:

Continued on next page

a. the place of contracting,

b. the place of negotiation of the contract,

c. the place of performance,

d. the location of the subject matter of the contract, and

e. the domicile, residence, nationality, place of incorporation, and place of business of the parties. *Maxus Expl.*, 817 S.W.2d at 53; Restatement (Second) of Conflict of Laws §188(2) (1971).

{*ADD PARAGRAPH 24 IF APPLICABLE*}

24. In addition to the contacts listed above, for {➏➒ *identify specific contract action, e.g., disputes involving a personal-services contract*}, the following contacts under {➐⓪ *identify Restatement section, e.g., section 196*} should also be considered: {➐➊ *list contacts*}.

25. In determining whose law should apply, the number of contacts is not determinative. *Duncan v. Cessna Aircraft Co.*, 665 S.W.2d 414, 421 (Tex. 1984). Some contacts are more important than others because they implicate state policies underlying the particular substantive issue. *Id.* Thus, selection of the applicable law depends on the qualitative nature of the particular contacts as affected by the following policy factors:

a. the needs of the interstate and international systems,

b. the relevant policies of the forum,

c. the relevant policies of other interested states and the relative interests of those states in the determination of the particular issue,

d. the protection of justified expectations,

e. the basic policies underlying the particular field of law,

f. certainty, predictability, and uniformity of result, and

g. ease in the determination and application of the law to be applied. Restatement (Second) of Conflict of Laws §6.

{*CHOOSE APPROPRIATE PARAGRAPHS 26-29*}

{*Texas has most significant relationship*}

26. Contrary to {➐➋ *adverse party*}'s motion, Texas has the most significant relationship to this dispute. {➐➌ *Elaborate.*}

{Contractual choice-of-law provision governs}

27. Contrary to {74 *adverse party*}'s motion, {75 *sister state*} law does not apply to {76 *identify dispute*} because the parties have contractually agreed to have this dispute governed by Texas law. When applicable, a court should enforce a contractual choice-of-law provision. *See DeSantis v. Wackenhut Corp.*, 793 S.W.2d 670, 677 (Tex. 1990). {77 *Elaborate.*}

{Statutory choice-of-law directive governs}

28. Contrary to {78 *adverse party*}'s motion, {79 *sister state*} law does not apply to {80 *identify dispute*} because this dispute is governed by a statutory choice-of-law directive that requires the Court to apply Texas law. When applicable, a court must follow a statutory choice-of-law directive. *Satterfield v. Crown Cork & Seal Co.*, 268 S.W.3d 190, 199 (Tex. App.—Austin 2008, no pet.); *Am. Home Assurance Co. v. Safway Steel Prods. Co.*, 743 S.W.2d 693, 697 (Tex. App.—Austin 1987, writ denied); Restatement (Second) of Conflict of Laws §6(1). Under {81 *identify statutory choice-of-law directive*}, the parties' dispute must be resolved under Texas law. {82 *Elaborate.*}

{Sister state law violates Texas public policy}

29. Contrary to {83 *adverse party*}'s motion, {84 *sister state*} law should not apply to {85 *identify dispute*} because it is contrary to Texas public policy in that it is {86 *against good morals and natural justice/prejudicial to the general interests of Texas citizens*}. A court should not enforce a sister state's law that violates Texas public policy. *Larchmont Farms, Inc. v. Parra*, 941 S.W.2d 93, 95 (Tex. 1997). {87 *Elaborate.*}

{CHOOSE APPROPRIATE PARAGRAPHS 30-33 TO RESPOND TO CONTRACTUAL CHOICE-OF-LAW PROVISION}

{Contractual provision does not cover dispute}

30. Contrary to {88 *adverse party*}'s motion, the parties' contractual choice-of-law provision does not cover {89 *identify dispute*}. {90 *Elaborate.*}

{Contractual provision obtained by improper means}

31. Contrary to {91 *adverse party*}'s motion, the Court should not enforce the parties' contractual choice-of-law provision because it was obtained by improper means. Courts should not give effect to a choice-of-law provision if a party's consent to its inclusion was obtained by improper means, such as by misrepresentation, duress, undue influence, or mistake. Restatement (Second) of Conflict of Laws §187 cmt. b. {92 *Elaborate.*}

Continued on next page

{*Contractual provision has no substantial relationship with chosen state*}

32. Contrary to {93 *adverse party*}'s motion, the Court should not enforce the parties' contractual choice-of-law provision because {94 *sister state*} does not have a substantial relationship to the parties or the transaction. A court can decline to enforce a contractual choice-of-law provision if the parties' chosen state does not have a substantial relationship to the parties or the transaction and there is no other reasonable basis for the parties' choice. *DeSantis v. Wackenhut Corp.*, 793 S.W.2d 670, 678 (Tex. 1990); Restatement (Second) of Conflict of Laws §187(2)(a). {95 *Elaborate.*}

{*Texas has materially greater interest in dispute*}

33. Contrary to {96 *adverse party*}'s motion, the Court should not enforce the parties' contractual choice-of-law provision because Texas has a materially greater interest in this dispute than {97 *sister state*}, and {98 *sister state*} law is contrary to the fundamental policy interest in Texas. A court can decline to enforce a contractual choice-of-law provision if (1) Texas has a materially greater interest in the dispute than the sister state and (2) the sister state's law is contrary to the fundamental policy interest in Texas. *DeSantis v. Wackenhut Corp.*, 793 S.W.2d 670, 678 (Tex. 1990); Restatement (Second) of Conflict of Laws §187(2)(b). {99 *Elaborate.*}

REQUEST FOR HEARING

34. On timely request, a party is entitled to an opportunity to be heard on the propriety of taking judicial notice and the nature of the matter noticed. Tex. R. Evid. 202(c)(2). {100 *Party*} asks the Court to hold a hearing to give {101 *party*} the opportunity to respond.

CONCLUSION

35. {102 *Briefly summarize the response.*}

PRAYER

36. For these reasons, {103 *party*} asks the Court to deny {104 *adverse party*}'s motion to judicially notice and apply the law of {105 *sister state*}.

FORM 5M:5 RESPONSE – JUDICIAL NOTICE & APPLICATION OF SISTER STATE LAW

SEE: Tex. R. Evid. 202
Restatement (2d) of Conflict of Laws §§6, 145, 187, 188 (1971)
O'Connor's Texas Rules * Civil Trials (2019), "Response," ch. 5-M, §5, p. 497
Brown & Rondon, ***Texas Rules of Evidence Handbook*** (2019), p. 137

ADD: STYLE OF THE CASE – FORM 1B:2
SIGNATURE BLOCK – FORM 1B:3
CERTIFICATE OF SERVICE – FORM 1B:13

ATTACH: AFFIDAVIT – FORM 1B:8, if necessary
ORDER – FORM 5M:9

{❶ *PARTY*}'S RESPONSE TO
{❷ *ADVERSE PARTY*}'S MOTION TO JUDICIALLY
NOTICE & APPLY THE LAW OF {❸ *FOREIGN COUNTRY*}

{❹ *Party*}, {❺ *name*}, asks the Court to deny {❻ *adverse party*} {❼ *name*}'s motion to judicially notice and apply the law of {❽ *foreign country*}.

INTRODUCTION

1. Plaintiff, {❾ *name*}, sued defendant, {❿ *name*}, for {⓫ *state basis of suit*}.

2. {⓬ *State other relevant facts about the suit.*}

BACKGROUND

3. On {⓭ *date*}, {⓮ *adverse party*} filed a motion asking the Court to judicially notice and apply the law of {⓯ *foreign country*} to {⓰ *identify dispute*}.

4. {⓱ *State other facts relevant to the response.*}

JUDICIAL NOTICE

5. A court should deny a request to take judicial notice of the law of another country if the party requesting judicial notice does not comply with the requirements under Texas Rule of Evidence 203. A party must (1) give reasonable, written notice of its intent to use foreign law and (2) provide copies of any written materials or sources that the party intends to use as proof of foreign law at least 30 days before the date of trial. Tex. R. Evid. 203(a). If a party does not comply with these requirements, the court should presume that the laws of the other jurisdiction are the same as the laws of Texas and apply Texas law. *PennWell Corp. v. Ken Assocs., Inc.*, 123 S.W.3d 756, 761 (Tex. App.—Houston [14th Dist.] 2003, pet. denied); *cf. Pittsburgh Corning Corp. v. Walters*, 1 S.W.3d 759, 769 (Tex. App.—Corpus Christi 1999, pet. denied) (applying Tex. R. Evid. 202). If the law to be judicially noticed is in a language other than English, the party making the request must provide to the court and all parties at least 45 days before trial (1) a copy of the foreign-language text, (2) a copy of the English translation, and (3) an affidavit or unsworn declaration from a qualified translator that states the translator's qualifications and certifies that the translation is accurate. *See* Tex. R. Evid. 203(b), 1009(a); *In re Estates of Garcia-Chapa*, 33 S.W.3d 859, 862 (Tex. App.—Corpus Christi 2000, no pet.). {*See* ***O'Connor's Texas Rules****, "Foreign laws," ch. 5-M, §4.7, p. 495.*}

{*CHOOSE APPROPRIATE PARAGRAPHS 6-10*}

6. The Court should deny {[18] *adverse party*}'s motion to take judicial notice of {[19] *foreign country*} law because {[20] *adverse party*} did not request judicial notice in a timely manner.

7. The Court should deny {[21] *adverse party*}'s motion to take judicial notice of {[22] *foreign country*} law because {[23] *adverse party*} did not give reasonable, written notice of its intent to use foreign law. {[24] *Elaborate.*}

8. The Court should deny {[25] *adverse party*}'s motion to take judicial notice of {[26] *foreign country*} law because {[27] *adverse party*} did not provide copies of any written materials or sources that the party intended to use as proof of foreign law at least 30 days before the date of trial. {[28] *Elaborate.*}

9. The Court should deny {[29] *adverse party*}'s motion to take judicial notice of {[30] *foreign country*} law because {[31] *adverse party*} provided laws or material explaining the foreign law in a language other than English and did not provide {[32] *a copy of the English translation/an affidavit or unsworn declaration from a qualified translator that states the translator's qualifications and certifies that the translation is accurate*}. {[33] *Elaborate.*}

10. The Court should deny {[34] *adverse party*}'s motion to take judicial notice of {[35] *foreign country*} law because {[36] *adverse party*} did not provide copies of the English translation and the affidavit or unsworn declaration from the translator at least 45 days before trial. {[37] *Elaborate.*}

CHOICE OF LAW

11. Texas courts cannot apply a foreign country's law to a dispute unless the party requesting the application establishes that the foreign country's substantive laws differ from Texas's and the foreign country's law would apply to the dispute. *See Nexen Inc. v. Gulf Interstate Eng'g Co.*, 224 S.W.3d 412, 415-16 (Tex. App.—Houston [1st Dist.] 2006, no pet.); *PennWell Corp.*, 123 S.W.3d at 763-64.

A. No conflict between Texas and {[38] *foreign country*} law.

{*CHOOSE APPROPRIATE PARAGRAPHS 12-14*}

{*No proof of conflict*}

12. {[39] *Adverse party*} did not offer any proof that the substantive law of {[40] *foreign country*} conflicts with Texas law on {[41] *identify dispute*}. Because {[42] *adverse party*} has not offered any proof of a conflict, Texas law must apply to resolve this dispute.

Continued on next page

{No conflict}

13. Contrary to {㊸ *adverse party*}'s motion, the substantive law of {㊹ *foreign country*} does not conflict with Texas law on {㊺ *identify dispute to be resolved by foreign country law*}. {㊻ *Elaborate.*}

{Conflict is procedural}

14. Contrary to {㊼ *adverse party*}'s motion, the conflict {㊽ *he/she/it*} identified between {㊾ *foreign country*} law and Texas law is a conflict in procedural law, not substantive law. Generally, whether a legal issue is a matter of substance or procedure is determined by the law of the forum state according to its own laws. *PennWell Corp.*, 123 S.W.3d at 764. Under Texas law, {㊿ *identify legal issue to be resolved*} is a matter of procedure. {51 *Elaborate.*}

B. {52 *Foreign country*} law is not applicable.

{ADD PARAGRAPHS 15-22 TO RESPOND TO MOST SIGNIFICANT RELATIONSHIP – TORTS}

15. To determine whose law applies in conflict cases involving a tort, Texas courts apply the "most significant relationship" test as set forth in the Restatement (Second) of Conflict of Laws sections 6 and 145. *Torrington Co. v. Stutzman*, 46 S.W.3d 829, 848 (Tex. 2000); *Gutierrez v. Collins*, 583 S.W.2d 312, 318 (Tex. 1979); *Bridas Corp. v. Unocal Corp.*, 16 S.W.3d 893, 897 (Tex. App.—Houston [14th Dist.] 2000, pet. denied); *CPS Int'l, Inc. v. Dresser Indus., Inc.*, 911 S.W.2d 18, 28-29 (Tex. App.—El Paso 1995, writ denied). Under section 145, the law of the country that has the most significant relationship to the occurrence and the parties under the principles stated in section 6 will govern the rights of litigants in a tort suit.

16. Section 145 lists the contacts that should be considered when determining whose law applies to a suit involving a tort. These contacts include the following:

a. the place where the injury occurred,

b. the place where the conduct causing the injury occurred,

c. the domicile, residence, nationality, place of incorporation, and place of business of the parties, and

d. the place where the relationship, if any, between the parties is centered. *Torrington Co.*, 46 S.W.3d at 848; Restatement (Second) of Conflict of Laws §145 (1971).

{*ADD PARAGRAPH 17 IF APPLICABLE*}

17. In addition to the contacts listed above, for {53 *identify specific tort action, e.g., torts involving fraud or misrepresentation*}, the following contacts under {54 *identify applicable Restatement section, e.g., section 148*} should also be considered: {55 *list contacts*}.

18. In determining whose law should apply, the number of contacts is not determinative. *Torrington Co.*, 46 S.W.3d at 848; *Duncan v. Cessna Aircraft Co.*, 665 S.W.2d 414, 421 (Tex. 1984). Some contacts are more important than others because they implicate state policies underlying the particular substantive issue. *Duncan*, 665 S.W.2d at 421; *see Torrington Co.*, 46 S.W.3d at 848-49. Thus, selecting the applicable law depends on the qualitative nature of the particular contacts as affected by the following policy factors:

a. the needs of the interstate and international systems,

b. the relevant policies of the forum,

c. the relevant policies of other interested states and the relative interests of those states in the determination of the particular issue,

d. the protection of justified expectations,

e. the basic policies underlying the particular field of law,

f. certainty, predictability, and uniformity of result, and

g. ease in the determination and application of the law to be applied. *Gutierrez*, 583 S.W.2d at 318-19; Restatement (Second) of Conflict of Laws §6; *see Torrington Co.*, 46 S.W.3d at 848; *Bridas Corp.*, 16 S.W.3d at 899-900.

{*CHOOSE APPROPRIATE PARAGRAPHS 19-22*}

{*Texas has most significant relationship*}

19. Contrary to {56 *adverse party*}'s motion, Texas has the most significant relationship to this dispute. {57 *Elaborate.*}

{*Contractual choice-of-law provision governs*}

20. Contrary to {58 *adverse party*}'s motion, {59 *foreign country*} law does not apply to {60 *identify dispute*} because the parties have contractually agreed to have this

◄ *Continued on next page* ►

dispute governed by Texas law. When applicable, a court should enforce a contractual choice-of-law provision. *See DeSantis v. Wackenhut Corp.*, 793 S.W.2d 670, 677 (Tex. 1990). {61 *Elaborate.*}

{*Statutory choice-of-law directive governs*}

21. Contrary to {62 *adverse party*}'s motion, {63 *foreign country*} law does not apply to {64 *identify dispute*} because this dispute is governed by a statutory choice-of-law directive that requires the Court to apply Texas law. When applicable, a court must follow a statutory choice-of-law directive. *Satterfield v. Crown Cork & Seal Co.*, 268 S.W.3d 190, 199 (Tex. App.—Austin 2008, no pet.); *Am. Home Assurance Co. v. Safway Steel Prods. Co.*, 743 S.W.2d 693, 697 (Tex. App.—Austin 1987, writ denied); Restatement (Second) of Conflict of Laws §6(1) (1971). Under {65 *identify statutory choice-of-law directive*}, the parties' dispute must be resolved under Texas law. {66 *Elaborate.*}

{*Foreign law violates Texas public policy*}

22. Contrary to {67 *adverse party*}'s motion, {68 *foreign country*} law should not apply to {69 *identify dispute*} because it is contrary to Texas public policy in that it is {70 *against good morals and natural justice/prejudicial to the general interests of Texas citizens*}. A court should not enforce a foreign law that violates Texas public policy. *Gutierrez*, 583 S.W.2d at 321. {71 *Elaborate.*}

{*ADD PARAGRAPHS 23-30 TO RESPOND TO MOST SIGNIFICANT RELATIONSHIP – CONTRACTS*}

23. To determine whose law applies in conflict cases involving a contract dispute, Texas courts apply the "most significant relationship" test as set forth in Restatement (Second) of Conflict of Laws sections 6 and 188. *See Maxus Expl. Co. v. Moran Bros.*, 817 S.W.2d 50, 53 (Tex. 1991). Under section 188(1), the local law of the place that has the most significant relationship to the transaction and the parties under the principles stated in section 6 will govern the rights and duties of the parties with respect to an issue in contract.

24. Section 188(2) lists the contacts that should be considered when determining whose law applies to an issue in contract. *Maxus Expl.*, 817 S.W.2d at 53. These contacts include the following:

a. the place of contracting,

b. the place of negotiation of the contract,

c. the place of performance,

d. the location of the subject matter of the contract, and

e. the domicile, residence, nationality, place of incorporation, and place of business of the parties. *Id.*; Restatement (Second) of Conflict of Laws §188(2) (1971).

{*ADD PARAGRAPH 25 IF APPLICABLE*}

25. In addition to the contacts listed above, for {❼❷ *identify specific contract action, e.g., disputes involving a personal-services contract*}, the following contacts under {❼❸ *identify Restatement section, e.g., section 196*} should also be considered: {❼❹ *list contacts*}.

26. In determining whose law should apply, the number of contacts is not determinative. *Duncan v. Cessna Aircraft Co.*, 665 S.W.2d 414, 421 (Tex. 1984). Some contacts are more important than others because they implicate state policies underlying the particular substantive issue. *Id.* Thus, selection of the applicable law depends on the qualitative nature of the particular contacts as affected by the following policy factors:

a. the needs of the interstate and international systems,

b. the relevant policies of the forum,

c. the relevant policies of other interested states and the relative interests of those states in the determination of the particular issue,

d. the protection of justified expectations,

e. the basic policies underlying the particular field of law,

f. certainty, predictability, and uniformity of result, and

g. ease in the determination and application of the law to be applied. Restatement (Second) of Conflict of Laws §6.

{*CHOOSE APPROPRIATE PARAGRAPHS 27-30*}

{*Texas has most significant relationship*}

27. Contrary to {❼❺ *adverse party*}'s motion, Texas has the most significant relationship to this dispute. {❼❻ *Elaborate.*}

◄ *Continued on next page* ►

{*Contractual choice-of-law provision governs*}

28. Contrary to {⓱77 *adverse party*}'s motion, {78 *foreign country*} law does not apply to {79 *identify dispute*} because the parties have contractually agreed to have this dispute governed by Texas law. When applicable, a court should enforce a contractual choice-of-law provision. *See DeSantis v. Wackenhut Corp.*, 793 S.W.2d 670, 677 (Tex. 1990). {80 *Elaborate.*}

{*Statutory choice-of-law directive governs*}

29. Contrary to {81 *adverse party*}'s motion, {82 *foreign country*} law does not apply to {83 *identify dispute*} because this dispute is governed by a statutory choice-of-law directive that requires the Court to apply Texas law. When applicable, a court must follow a statutory choice-of-law directive. *Satterfield v. Crown Cork & Seal Co.*, 268 S.W.3d 190, 199 (Tex. App.—Austin 2008, no pet.); *Am. Home Assurance Co. v. Safway Steel Prods. Co.*, 743 S.W.2d 693, 697 (Tex. App.—Austin 1987, writ denied); Restatement (Second) of Conflict of Laws §6(1). Under {84 *identify statutory choice-of-law directive*}, the parties' dispute must be resolved under Texas law. {85 *Elaborate.*}

{*Foreign law violates Texas public policy*}

30. Contrary to {86 *adverse party*}'s motion, {87 *foreign country*} law should not apply to {88 *identify dispute*} because it is contrary to Texas public policy in that it is {89 *against good morals and natural justice/prejudicial to the general interests of Texas citizens*}. A court should not enforce a foreign law that violates Texas public policy. *Gutierrez v. Collins*, 583 S.W.2d 312, 321 (Tex. 1979). {90 *Elaborate.*}

{*CHOOSE APPROPRIATE PARAGRAPHS 31-34 TO RESPOND TO CONTRACTUAL CHOICE-OF-LAW PROVISION*}

{*Contractual provision does not cover dispute*}

31. Contrary to {91 *adverse party*}'s motion, the parties' contractual choice-of-law provision does not cover {92 *identify dispute*}. {93 *Elaborate.*}

{*Contractual provision obtained by improper means*}

32. Contrary to {94 *adverse party*}'s motion, the Court should not enforce the parties' contractual choice-of-law provision because it was obtained by improper means. Courts should not give effect to a choice-of-law provision if a party's consent to its inclusion was obtained by improper means, such as by misrepresentation, duress, undue influence, or mistake. Restatement (Second) of Conflict of Laws §187 cmt. b. {95 *Elaborate.*}

{*Contractual provision has no substantial relationship with chosen country*}

33. Contrary to {96 *adverse party*}'s motion, the Court should not enforce the parties' contractual choice-of-law provision because {97 *foreign country*} does not have a substantial relationship to the parties or the transaction and there is no other reasonable basis for the parties' choice. A court can decline to enforce a contractual choice-of-law provision if the parties' chosen law does not have a substantial relationship to the parties or the transaction and there is no other reasonable basis for the parties' choice. *DeSantis v. Wackenhut Corp.*, 793 S.W.2d 670, 678 (Tex. 1990); Restatement (Second) of Conflict of Laws §187(2)(a). {98 *Elaborate.*}

{*Texas has materially greater interest in dispute*}

34. Contrary to {99 *adverse party*}'s motion, the Court should not enforce the parties' contractual choice-of-law provision because Texas has a materially greater interest in this dispute than {100 *foreign country*}, and {101 *foreign country*} law is contrary to the fundamental policy interest in Texas. A court can decline to enforce a contractual choice-of-law provision if (1) Texas has a materially greater interest in the dispute than the chosen foreign country and (2) the foreign country's law is contrary to the fundamental policy interest in Texas. *DeSantis v. Wackenhut Corp.*, 793 S.W.2d 670, 678 (Tex. 1990); Restatement (Second) of Conflict of Laws §187(2)(b). {102 *Elaborate.*}

CONCLUSION

35. {103 *Briefly summarize the response.*}

PRAYER

36. For these reasons, {104 *party*} asks the Court to deny {105 *adverse party*}'s motion to judicially notice and apply the law of {106 *foreign country*}.

SEE: Tex. R. Evid. 203, 1009
Restatement (2d) of Conflict of Laws §§6, 145, 187, 188 (1971)
O'Connor's Texas Rules * Civil Trials (2019), "Foreign law," ch. 5-M, §5.2.4, p. 497
Brown & Rondon, ***Texas Rules of Evidence Handbook*** (2019), pp. 141, 1059

ADD: STYLE OF THE CASE – FORM 1B:2
SIGNATURE BLOCK – FORM 1B:3
CERTIFICATE OF SERVICE – FORM 1B:13

Continued on next page

ATTACH: AFFIDAVIT – FORM 1B:8, if necessary
ORDER – FORM 5M:9
Affidavits of experts, if necessary
Briefs by experts, if necessary
Copy of the law of foreign country, if necessary
Depositions of experts, if necessary
English translation of law of foreign country, if necessary
Treatises on law of foreign country, if necessary

NOTE: If the court considers any material or source not submitted by a party, it must give all parties notice and a reasonable opportunity to comment and submit additional materials. Tex. R. Evid. 203(c).

Texas Rule of Civil Procedure 308b provides procedures for determining the recognition or enforcement of a judgment or an arbitration award based on foreign law in suits involving a marriage relationship or parent-child relationship under the Texas Family Code. *See* Tex. R. Civ. P. 308b. The requirements for raising a foreign-law issue under Texas Rule of Evidence 203(a) and (b) do not apply to actions covered by Rule 308b. *See* Tex. R. Civ. P. 308b(c)(2); Tex. R. Evid. 203(e). Rule 308b provides its own deadlines and procedures for notice, pretrial conferences, hearings, and orders.

☆

{1 *PARTY*}'S OBJECTION TO
{2 *ADVERSE PARTY*}'S TRANSLATION OF {3 *FOREIGN COUNTRY*} LAW

{4 *Party*}, {5 *name*}, files this objection to {6 *adverse party*} {7 *name*}'s English translation of {8 *foreign country*}'s law.

INTRODUCTION

1. Plaintiff, {9 *name*}, sued defendant, {10 *name*}, for {11 *state basis of suit*}.

2. {12 *State other relevant facts about the suit.*}

BACKGROUND

3. On {13 *date*}, {14 *adverse party*} filed a request asking the Court to judicially notice and apply the law of {15 *foreign country*} to {16 *identify dispute*}.

4. In support of {17 *his/her/its*} request for judicial notice, {18 *adverse party*} submitted an English translation of {19 *identify foreign law*}.

5. {20 *State other facts relevant to the objection.*}

ARGUMENT & AUTHORITIES

6. Under Texas Rule of Evidence 1009, a party may object to the accuracy of another party's English translation of foreign law. Tex. R. Evid. 1009(b). The objecting party should point out the specific inaccuracies of the translation and offer an accurate translation. *Id.*

7. {21 *Party*} asks the Court to disregard {22 *adverse party*}'s English translation of {23 *foreign country*}'s law because it is inaccurate. The following is a list of the inaccuracies in {24 *adverse party*}'s English translation and the correct translation that should apply: {25 *list the inaccuracies and the correct translation*}.

{*ADD PARAGRAPH 8 IF APPLICABLE*}

8. {26 *Party*} attaches to this objection, as Exhibit {27 *letter*}, an {28 *affidavit/unsworn declaration*} from a qualified translator that states the translator's qualifications and certifies that {29 *party*}'s translation above is accurate.

CONCLUSION

9. {30 *Briefly summarize the objection.*}

— *Continued on next page* —

PRAYER

10. For these reasons, {㉛ *party*} asks the Court to determine that there is a genuine issue regarding the accuracy of a material part of {㉜ *adverse party*}'s English translation of {㉝ *foreign country*}'s law, and that the decision of which translation is accurate should be resolved by the trier of fact.

SEE: Tex. R. Evid. 203, 1009
O'Connor's Texas Rules * Civil Trials (2019), "Challenging translation – 15 days before trial," ch. 5-M, §4.7.4, p. 496
Brown & Rondon, ***Texas Rules of Evidence Handbook*** (2019), pp. 141, 1059

ADD: STYLE OF THE CASE – FORM 1B:2
SIGNATURE BLOCK – FORM 1B:3
CERTIFICATE OF SERVICE – FORM 1B:13

ATTACH: AFFIDAVIT – FORM 1B:8, if necessary
Affidavit or unsworn declaration of qualified translator, if necessary

NOTE: To challenge the accuracy of the translation of a foreign law, a party must serve objections to the translation at least 15 days before trial. Tex. R. Evid. 1009(b). The 15-day period can be altered on a motion showing good cause. Tex. R. Evid. 1009(f). The objecting party should identify specific inaccuracies of the translation and offer an accurate translation. Tex. R. Evid. 1009(b). Unlike the original translation offered under Rule 1009(a), the objecting party's translation does not need to be accompanied by an affidavit or unsworn declaration from a qualified translator certifying that the translation is accurate. *See* Tex. R. Evid. 1009(b).

ORDER ON MOTION FOR JUDICIAL NOTICE

After considering {❶ *party*}'s motion for judicial notice of {❷ *identify material to be judicially noticed*}, the response, and arguments of counsel, the Court

{*CHOOSE APPROPRIATE ORDER*}

DENIES the motion for judicial notice of {❸ *identify material to be judicially noticed*}.

GRANTS the motion for judicial notice of {❹ *identify material to be judicially noticed*} and, at trial, will {❺ *accept/instruct the jury to accept*} this {❻ *identify material to be judicially noticed*} as conclusive.

SIGNED on _______________, 20___.

____
PRESIDING JUDGE

SEE: Tex. R. Evid. 201, 204
O'Connor's Texas Rules * Civil Trials (2019), "Order," ch. 5-M, §7.1, p. 498
Brown & Rondon, ***Texas Rules of Evidence Handbook*** (2019), pp. 106, 145

ADD: STYLE OF THE CASE – FORM 1B:2
CERTIFICATE OF SERVICE – FORM 1B:13, if proposed order served separately from motion or response

ORDER ON MOTION FOR
JUDICIAL NOTICE & APPLICATION OF
{❶ *NAME OF LAW TO BE APPLIED, E.G., CALIFORNIA, MEXICO*} LAW

After considering {❷ *party*}'s motion for judicial notice and application of {❸ *name of law to be applied, e.g., California, Mexico*} law, the response, and arguments of counsel, the Court

{*CHOOSE APPROPRIATE ORDER*}

DENIES the motion for judicial notice and application of {❹ *name of law to be applied, e.g., California, Mexico*} law.

GRANTS the motion for judicial notice and application of {❺ *name of law to be applied, e.g., California, Mexico*} law, and orders that the substantive law of {❻ *name of law to be applied, e.g., California, Mexico*} be applied {❼ *specify scope of application, e.g., in this case, to plaintiff's claim for breach of contract*}.

SIGNED on _______________, 20___.

____
PRESIDING JUDGE

SEE: Tex. R. Evid. 202, 203
O'Connor's Texas Rules * Civil Trials (2019), "Order," ch. 5-M, §7.1, p. 498
Brown & Rondon, ***Texas Rules of Evidence Handbook*** (2019), pp. 137, 141

ADD: STYLE OF THE CASE – FORM 1B:2
CERTIFICATE OF SERVICE – FORM 1B:13, if proposed order served separately from motion or response

{❶ *PARTY*}'S MOTION TO EXCLUDE
TESTIMONY OF {❷ *ADVERSE PARTY*}'S EXPERT

{❸ *Party*}, {❹ *name*}, asks the Court to exclude the testimony of {❺ *name of expert*}, {❻ *adverse party*} {❼ *name*}'s expert.

INTRODUCTION

1. Plaintiff, {❽ *name*}, sued defendant, {❾ *name*}, for {❿ *state basis of suit*}.

2. {⓫ *State other relevant facts about the suit.*}

BACKGROUND

3. This case is set for {⓬ *trial/summary-judgment hearing*} on {⓭ *date*}.

4. {⓮ *Adverse party*} identified {⓯ *name of expert*} as an expert in this case to provide opinion testimony about the following matters: {⓰ *identify subject of proposed testimony*}.

5. {⓱ *State other facts relevant to the motion.*}

ARGUMENT & AUTHORITIES

6. If a motion to exclude expert testimony is filed, the party offering the expert testimony bears the burden of showing that the testimony is admissible. *E.I. du Pont de Nemours & Co. v. Robinson*, 923 S.W.2d 549, 557 (Tex. 1995).

7. An expert may testify about scientific, technical, or other specialized knowledge only if (1) the expert is qualified, (2) the probative value of the testimony is not outweighed by the prejudice, and (3) the opinion is relevant and based on a reliable foundation. *See* Tex. R. Evid. 401-403, 702; *Transcon. Ins. Co. v. Crump*, 330 S.W.3d 211, 215 (Tex. 2010).

{*CHOOSE APPROPRIATE SECTIONS A-F*}

A. Expert is not qualified.

8. A court must exclude the opinion testimony of an expert witness who is not qualified to give an opinion by knowledge, skill, experience, training, or education. *See* Tex. R. Evid. 702; *Broders v. Heise*, 924 S.W.2d 148, 153-54 (Tex. 1996). An expert must have a higher degree of knowledge, skill, experience, training, or education about the subject of the testimony than an ordinary person has. *See* Tex. R. Evid. 702; *Roberts v. Williamson*, 111 S.W.3d 113, 121 (Tex. 2003); *Broders*, 924 S.W.2d at 153. {*See* ***O'Connor's Texas Rules**, "Qualifications test," ch. 5-N, §2.1, p. 499.*}

Continued on next page

9. The Court should exclude the testimony of {[18] *adverse party*}'s expert on {[19] *identify subject*} because the expert is not qualified. {[20] *Elaborate.*}

B. Subject of opinion is not specialized knowledge.

10. A court must exclude the opinion testimony of an expert witness whose testimony does not involve "scientific, technical, or other specialized knowledge." *See* Tex. R. Evid. 702; *see, e.g., GTE Sw., Inc. v. Bruce*, 998 S.W.2d 605, 619-20 (Tex. 1999) (in suit for emotional distress, expert could not testify that certain conduct was extreme and outrageous; issue did not involve specialized knowledge). {*See* ***O'Connor's Texas Rules***, *"Knowledge test," ch. 5-N, §2.2, p. 500.*}

11. The Court should exclude the testimony of {[21] *adverse party*}'s expert on {[22] *identify subject*} because that subject involves only general knowledge and does not involve scientific, technical, or other specialized knowledge. {[23] *Elaborate.*}

C. Probative value substantially outweighed by prejudice.

12. A court must exclude the opinion testimony of an expert if its probative value is substantially outweighed by (1) the danger of unfair prejudice, confusion of the issues, or misleading the jury, (2) undue delay, or (3) needless presentation of cumulative evidence. *See* Tex. R. Evid. 403; *Robinson*, 923 S.W.2d at 557. {*See* ***O'Connor's Texas Rules***, *"Allegations," ch. 5-N, §3.2.1(6), p. 504.*}

13. The Court should exclude the testimony of {[24] *adverse party*}'s expert on {[25] *identify subject*} because {[26] *explain why probative value is outweighed by prejudice or other factors*}.

D. Opinion does not have sufficient basis.

14. A court must exclude the opinion testimony of an expert if it is not based on sufficient underlying facts or data, as required by Texas Rules of Evidence 702 and 703. Tex. R. Evid. 705(c); *see Merrell Dow Pharms., Inc. v. Havner*, 953 S.W.2d 706, 714 (Tex. 1997). {*See* ***O'Connor's Texas Rules***, *"Foundation test," ch. 5-N, §2.4, p. 503.*}

15. The Court should exclude the testimony of {[27] *adverse party*}'s expert on {[28] *identify subject*} because {[29] *explain lack of sufficient basis*}.

E. Opinion is not relevant.

16. A court must exclude the opinion testimony of an expert if it is not relevant. *See* Tex. R. Evid. 401, 402. To be relevant, opinion testimony must be "sufficiently tied to the facts of the case that it will aid the jury in resolving a factual dispute." *Robinson*, 923 S.W.2d at 556. {*See* ***O'Connor's Texas Rules***, *"Relevance of opinion," ch. 5-N, §2.3.2, p. 503.*}

17. The Court should exclude the testimony of {30 *adverse party*}'s expert on {31 *identify subject*} because it is not relevant. The opinion of {32 *adverse party*}'s expert has no relationship to any of the issues in the case. {33 *Explain why the testimony is irrelevant.*}

F. Opinion is not reliable.

18. A court must exclude the opinion testimony of an expert if it is not reliable. *Whirlpool Corp. v. Camacho*, 298 S.W.3d 631, 637 (Tex. 2009); *Robinson*, 923 S.W.2d at 557. Unreliable evidence does not assist the trier of fact and is therefore inadmissible under Texas Rule of Evidence 702. *Cooper Tire & Rubber Co. v. Mendez*, 204 S.W.3d 797, 801 (Tex. 2006); *Robinson*, 923 S.W.2d at 557. In determining whether expert testimony is reliable, a court should consider the *Daubert-Robinson* factors and whether the analytical gap between the expert's methodology and the opinion offered is too great. *Transcon.*, 330 S.W.3d at 215-16; *see Daubert v. Merrell Dow Pharms., Inc.*, 509 U.S. 579, 593-94 (1993); *Gharda USA, Inc. v. Control Sols., Inc.*, 464 S.W.3d 338, 349 (Tex. 2015); *Gammill v. Jack Williams Chevrolet, Inc.*, 972 S.W.2d 713, 727 (Tex. 1998); *Robinson*, 923 S.W.2d at 557. {*See* ***O'Connor's Texas Rules****, "Reliability of opinion," ch. 5-N, §2.3.1, p. 501.*}

{*For Daubert-Robinson factors*}

19. The *Daubert-Robinson* factors include the following: (1) the extent to which the expert's theory has been or can be tested, (2) the technique's potential rate of error, (3) whether the theory has been subjected to peer review or publication, (4) whether the underlying theory or technique has been generally accepted as valid by the relevant scientific community, (5) the extent to which the technique relies on the expert's subjective interpretation, and (6) the nonjudicial uses of the theory or technique. *See Daubert*, 509 U.S. at 593-94; *Robinson*, 923 S.W.2d at 557. These factors are nonexclusive and may not apply to all expert testimony. *Cooper Tire*, 204 S.W.3d at 801; *Gammill*, 972 S.W.2d at 726.

{*CHOOSE APPROPRIATE FACTORS*}

20. The expert's opinion on {34 *identify subject*} is not reliable because it does not lend itself to verification by the scientific method through testing. {35 *Explain why the opinion cannot be tested, e.g., the opinion was formed under circumstances not easily duplicated.*}

{*ADD APPROPRIATE PARAGRAPH 21 IF APPLICABLE*}

21. The expert's opinion on {36 *identify subject*} is not reliable because it has not been evaluated in light of the potential rate of error for the scientific methodology. {37 *Explain why the evaluation of the rate of error is insufficient.*}

◄ Continued on next page ►

21. The expert's opinion on {38 *identify subject*} is not reliable because it is based on a scientific method that has a high rate of error. {39 *Elaborate.*}

22. The expert's opinion on {40 *identify subject*} is not reliable because it has not been subjected to {41 *peer review/publication*}. {42 *Elaborate.*}

23. The expert's opinion on {43 *identify subject*} is not reliable because it is not consistent with the generally accepted methods used for gathering the relevant scientific evidence in the expert's discipline. {44 *Elaborate.*}

24. The expert's opinion on {45 *identify subject*} is not reliable because it is based on a technique that relies on subjective interpretation. {46 *Elaborate.*}

25. The expert's opinion on {47 *identify subject*} is not reliable because it was generated solely for this litigation. {48 *Elaborate.*}

{*For analytical gap*}

26. The expert's opinion on {49 *identify subject*} is not reliable because the "analytical gap" between the data relied on by the expert and the testimony offered is too great. In assessing the analytical gap, the court should consider whether (1) the expert's field of expertise is legitimate, (2) the subject matter of the testimony is within the scope of the expert's field of expertise, (3) the testimony properly relies on principles involved in the expert's field of expertise, and (4) the expert showed a connection between the data relied on and the opinion offered. *See Sw. Energy Prod. Co. v. Berry-Helfand*, 491 S.W.3d 699, 717 (Tex. 2016); *Volkswagen of Am., Inc. v. Ramirez*, 159 S.W.3d 897, 906 (Tex. 2004); *In re J.R.*, 501 S.W.3d 738, 748 (Tex. App.—Waco 2016, pet. denied); *Coastal Tankships, U.S.A., Inc. v. Anderson*, 87 S.W.3d 591, 601 (Tex. App.—Houston [1st Dist.] 2002, pet. denied); *see, e.g., Gammill*, 972 S.W.2d at 727-28 (opinion testimony was unreliable when expert failed to show how his observations supported conclusion that plaintiff was wearing seat belt or that seat belt was defective). {*See **O'Connor's Texas Rules**, "Gammill 'analytical gap' analysis," ch. 5-N, §2.3.1(2), p. 502.*}

27. The analytical gap is too great because {50 *explain why the gap is too great and address each factor above*}.

CONCLUSION

28. {51 *Briefly summarize the motion.*}

PRAYER

29. For these reasons, {52 *party*} asks the Court to set this motion for a hearing, require {53 *adverse party*} to meet {54 *his/her/its*} burden of proof, and, after the hearing, exclude the testimony of {55 *adverse party*}'s expert, {56 *name of expert*}.

SEE: Tex. R. Evid. 104, 401-403, 702, 703, 705
O'Connor's Texas Rules * Civil Trials (2019), "*Daubert-Robinson* Test for Expert Testimony," ch. 5-N, §2, p. 499; "Gatekeeper Hearing on Qualifications & Opinions of Experts," ch. 5-N, §3, p. 504
Brown & Rondon, ***Texas Rules of Evidence Handbook*** (2019), pp. 226, 694, 736, 755

ADD: STYLE OF THE CASE – FORM 1B:2
SIGNATURE BLOCK – FORM 1B:3
CERTIFICATE OF SERVICE – FORM 1B:13

ATTACH: AFFIDAVIT – FORM 1B:8, if necessary
NOTICE OF HEARING OR SUBMISSION – FORM 1E:1
ORDER – FORM 1G:1

NOTE: The party who moves to exclude an expert has no burden of proof; thus, it is not necessary to include in this motion any citations to authority or to attach affidavits.

{[1] *PARTY*}'S RESPONSE TO {[2] *ADVERSE PARTY*}'S MOTION TO EXCLUDE EXPERT TESTIMONY

{[3] *Party*}, {[4] *name*}, asks the Court to deny {[5] *adverse party*} {[6] *name*}'s motion to exclude the testimony of {[7] *name of expert*}, {[8] *party*}'s expert.

INTRODUCTION

1. Plaintiff, {[9] *name*}, sued defendant, {[10] *name*}, for {[11] *state basis of suit*}.

2. {[12] *State other relevant facts about the suit.*}

BACKGROUND

3. This case is set for {[13] *trial/summary-judgment hearing*} on {[14] *date*}.

4. {[15] *Party*} identified {[16] *name of expert*} as an expert in this case to testify about the following matters: {[17] *identify subject of proposed testimony*}.

5. {[18] *Adverse party*} filed a motion to exclude the testimony of {[19] *name of expert*} on {[20] *identify subject*} on the grounds that {[21] *the expert is not qualified/the testimony is not reliable/the testimony is not relevant/{identify other reason}*}.

6. {[22] *State other facts relevant to the response.*}

ARGUMENT & AUTHORITIES

{*CHOOSE APPROPRIATE SECTIONS A-F*}

A. Expert is qualified.

7. A court should allow the opinion testimony of an expert if the expert is qualified to give an opinion by knowledge, skill, experience, training, or education. Tex. R. Evid. 702. An expert must have a higher degree of knowledge, skill, experience, training, or education about the subject of the testimony than an ordinary person has. *See id.*; *Roberts v. Williamson*, 111 S.W.3d 113, 121 (Tex. 2003); *Broders v. Heise*, 924 S.W.2d 148, 153 (Tex. 1996). {*See* ***O'Connor's Texas Rules***, *"Qualifications test," ch. 5-N, §2.1, p. 499.*}

8. {[23] *Name of expert*} is qualified to offer an expert opinion on {[24] *identify subject*}. Specifically, {[25] *explain why the expert is qualified, e.g., list education, practical experience, publications*}.

B. Subject of opinion is specialized knowledge.

9. A court should allow the opinion testimony of an expert if the subject about which {㉖ *party*} proposes to offer the expert's testimony involves "scientific, technical, or other specialized knowledge" under Texas Rule of Evidence 702. {*See* ***O'Connor's Texas Rules****, "Knowledge test," ch. 5-N, §2.2, p. 500.*}

10. {㉗ *Name of expert*} should be allowed to testify because {㉘ *his/her*} testimony on {㉙ *identify subject*} involves scientific, technical, or other specialized knowledge. {㉚ *Elaborate.*}

C. Probative value is not substantially outweighed by prejudice.

11. A court should allow the opinion of an expert if the probative value of the opinion is not substantially outweighed by (1) the danger of unfair prejudice, confusion of the issues, or misleading the jury, (2) undue delay, or (3) needless presentation of cumulative evidence. Tex. R. Evid. 403; *see E.I. du Pont de Nemours & Co. v. Robinson*, 923 S.W.2d 549, 557 (Tex. 1995). {*See* ***O'Connor's Texas Rules****, "Allegations," ch. 5-N, §3.3.1(6), p. 505.*}

12. {㉛ *Name of expert*} should be allowed to testify because the probative value of {㉜ *his/her*} testimony is not substantially outweighed by the danger of unfair prejudice, undue delay, or needless presentation of cumulative evidence. {㉝ *Elaborate.*}

D. Opinion has sufficient basis.

13. A court should allow the opinion testimony of an expert if the expert's opinion is based on sufficient facts or data, as required by Texas Rules of Evidence 702 and 703. Tex. R. Evid. 705(c). {*See* ***O'Connor's Texas Rules****, "Foundation test," ch. 5-N, §2.4, p. 503.*}

14. {㉞ *Name of expert*} should be allowed to testify because {㉟ *his/her*} testimony is based on sufficient {㊱ *facts/data*}. {㊲ *Elaborate.*}

E. Opinion is relevant.

15. A court should allow the opinion testimony of an expert if it is relevant. *See* Tex. R. Evid. 401, 402; *JLG Trucking, LLC v. Garza*, 466 S.W.3d 157, 161 (Tex. 2015). To be relevant, the testimony must be "sufficiently tied to the facts of the case that it will aid the jury in resolving a factual dispute." *E.I. du Pont de Nemours & Co. v. Robinson*, 923 S.W.2d 549, 556 (Tex. 1995). {*See* ***O'Connor's Texas Rules****, "Relevance of opinion," ch. 5-N, §2.3.2, p. 503.*}

◄ *Continued on next page* ►

16. {38 *Name of expert*} should be allowed to testify because {39 *his/her*} opinion testimony is relevant. The testimony is directly related to material issues in the case and will therefore assist the jury. {40 *Elaborate.*}

F. Opinion is reliable.

17. A court should allow the opinion testimony of an expert if each part of the expert's opinion is reliable. *Whirlpool Corp. v. Camacho*, 298 S.W.3d 631, 637 (Tex. 2009). In determining whether expert testimony is reliable, a court should consider the *Daubert-Robinson* factors and whether the analytical gap between the expert's methodology and the opinion offered is too great. *See Daubert v. Merrell Dow Pharms., Inc.*, 509 U.S. 579, 593-94 (1993); *Transcon. Ins. Co. v. Crump*, 330 S.W.3d 211, 215-16 (Tex. 2010); *Gammill v. Jack Williams Chevrolet, Inc.*, 972 S.W.2d 713, 727 (Tex. 1998); *E.I. du Pont de Nemours & Co. v. Robinson*, 923 S.W.2d 549, 557 (Tex. 1995). {*See* ***O'Connor's Texas Rules***, *"Reliability of opinion," ch. 5-N, §2.3.1, p. 501.*}

{*For Daubert-Robinson factors*}

18. The *Daubert-Robinson* factors include the following: (1) the extent to which the expert's theory has been or can be tested, (2) the technique's potential rate of error, (3) whether the theory has been subjected to peer review or publication, (4) whether the underlying theory or technique has been generally accepted as valid by the relevant scientific community, (5) the extent to which the technique relies on the expert's subjective interpretation, and (6) the nonjudicial uses of the theory or technique. *See Daubert*, 509 U.S. at 593-94; *Robinson*, 923 S.W.2d at 557. These factors are nonexclusive and may not apply to all expert testimony. *Cooper Tire & Rubber Co. v. Mendez*, 204 S.W.3d 797, 801 (Tex. 2006); *Gammill*, 972 S.W.2d at 726.

{*CHOOSE APPROPRIATE FACTORS*}

19. The expert's opinion on {41 *identify subject*} is reliable because it lends itself to verification by the scientific method through testing. The expert's opinion has been subjected to extensive testing. {42 *Elaborate.*}

20. The expert's opinion on {43 *identify subject*} is reliable because it was properly evaluated in light of the potential rate of error for the scientific methodology and the potential rate of error is low. {44 *Explain why the opinion has been properly evaluated considering the low rate of error.*}

21. Publication is a significant indicator of the reliability of scientific evidence when the expert's testimony is in an area in which peer review or publication would not be uncommon. *Merrell Dow Pharms., Inc. v. Havner*, 953 S.W.2d 706, 726 (Tex. 1997);

see Robinson, 923 S.W.2d at 557. Publication in reputable, established scientific journals and other forms of peer review increases the likelihood that substantive flaws in methodology will be detected. *Havner*, 953 S.W.2d at 726-27.

22. The expert's opinion on {㊺ *identify subject*} is reliable because it is based on a theory that has been the subject of numerous articles published in reputable professional journals. {㊻ *Elaborate, providing names and dates of the journals.*}

23. The expert's opinion on {㊼ *identify subject*} is reliable because it was subjected to peer review. The reviews have been favorable to the theory underlying the expert's opinion. {㊽ *Elaborate.*}

24. The expert's opinion on {㊾ *identify subject*} is reliable because the {㊿ *theory/technique*} underlying the expert's opinion has been generally accepted as valid by the relevant scientific community. {51 *Elaborate, identifying the relevant scientific community and its acceptance of the underlying theory or technique.*}

25. The expert's opinion on {52 *identify subject*} is reliable because the expert based {53 *his/her*} opinion on a technique that relies on {54 *his/her*} objective interpretation. {55 *Elaborate.*}

26. The expert's opinion on {56 *identify subject*} is reliable because it was not generated solely for this litigation. {57 *Elaborate.*} The expert's opinion was developed through research conducted independently of the litigation, which provides important, objective proof that the research comports with the dictates of good science. {58 *Elaborate.*}

{*For analytical gap*}

27. The expert's opinion on {59 *identify subject*} is reliable because the analytical gap between the expert's methodology and the opinion offered is not too great. In assessing the analytical gap, the court should consider whether (1) the expert's field of expertise is legitimate, (2) the subject matter of the testimony is within the scope of the expert's field of expertise, (3) the testimony properly relies on principles involved in the expert's field of expertise, and (4) the expert showed a connection between the data relied on and the opinion offered. *See Sw. Energy Prod. Co. v. Berry-Helfand*, 491 S.W.3d 699, 717 (Tex. 2016); *Volkswagen of Am., Inc. v. Ramirez*, 159 S.W.3d 897, 906 (Tex. 2004); *In re J.R.*, 501 S.W.3d 738, 748 (Tex. App.—Waco 2016, pet. denied); *Coastal Tankships, U.S.A., Inc. v. Anderson*, 87 S.W.3d 591, 601 (Tex. App.—Houston [1st Dist.] 2002, pet. denied); *see, e.g., Kia Motors Corp. v. Ruiz*, 432 S.W.3d 865, 877-78 (Tex. 2014) (expert's testimony on structural defects in airbag system was specific enough that there was no analytical gap between data and opinion that those defects

◄ *Continued on next page* ►

prevented air bag from deploying); *Transcon.*, 330 S.W.3d at 219-20 (treating physician's opinion on cause of plaintiff's death based on differential diagnosis was reliable); *Gammill*, 972 S.W.2d at 726 (beekeeper could testify that bees take off into the wind based on beekeeper's own observations). {*See* ***O'Connor's Texas Rules****, "Gammill 'analytical gap' analysis," ch. 5-N, §2.3.1(2), p. 502.*}

28. The analytical gap is not too great because {60 *explain why the gap is not too great and address each factor above*}.

{*ADD PARAGRAPH 29 IF APPLICABLE*}

29. If the Court rules that {61 *party*}'s expert will not be permitted to give an opinion, {62 *party*} requests a continuance of the {63 *trial/summary-judgment hearing*} to secure another expert.

CONCLUSION

30. {64 *Briefly summarize the response.*}

PRAYER

31. For these reasons, {65 *party*} asks the Court to set this motion for a hearing and, after the hearing, deny the motion to exclude the testimony of {66 *party*}'s expert.

SEE: Tex. R. Evid. 104, 401-403, 702, 703, 705
O'Connor's Texas Rules * Civil Trials (2019), "*Daubert-Robinson* Test for Expert Testimony," ch. 5-N, §2, p. 499; "Gatekeeper Hearing on Qualifications & Opinions of Experts," ch. 5-N, §3, p. 504
Brown & Rondon, ***Texas Rules of Evidence Handbook*** (2019), pp. 226, 694, 736, 755

ADD: STYLE OF THE CASE – FORM 1B:2
SIGNATURE BLOCK – FORM 1B:3
CERTIFICATE OF SERVICE – FORM 1B:13

ATTACH: AFFIDAVIT – FORM 1B:8, if necessary
NOTICE OF HEARING OR SUBMISSION – FORM 1E:1
ORDER – FORM 1G:1
Exhibits, if necessary

NOTE: Once a party opposing the expert objects, the sponsor of the expert bears the burden of demonstrating the admissibility of the opinion. See ***O'Connor's Texas Rules***, "Sponsor's response to objection," ch. 5-N, §3.3, p. 505.

{1 *PARTY*}'S OBJECTION TO
TESTIMONY OF {2 *ADVERSE PARTY*}'S EXPERT

{3 *Party*}, {4 *name*}, objects to the opinion testimony of Dr. {5 *name of expert*}, {6 *adverse party*} {7 *name*}'s expert. {*See* ***O'Connor's Texas COA****, "Objecting to experts," ch. 20-A, §8.5, p. 696.*}

INTRODUCTION

1. Plaintiff, {8 *name*}, sued defendant, {9 *name*}, for {10 *state basis of suit*}.

2. {11 *State other relevant facts about the suit.*}

BACKGROUND

3. {12 *Adverse party*} identified Dr. {13 *name of expert*} to testify as an expert in this case on the issue of whether defendant, Dr. {14 *name of defendant-physician*}, {15 *departed from accepted standards of medical care/caused the plaintiff's injury*}.

{*ADD PARAGRAPH 4 IF APPLICABLE*}

4. An objection to an expert's testimony made after the 21-day deadline to object is still timely if (1) the basis for the objection arose after the deadline expired, (2) the basis for the objection could not reasonably have been anticipated before the deadline expired, (3) the objection was not made earlier, (4) the objection is made in good faith, and (5) the objection is made as soon as possible. Tex. Civ. Prac. & Rem. Code §74.401(e). {16 *Party*}'s objection is timely because {17 *explain*}. {*See* ***O'Connor's Texas COA****, "Deadline," ch. 20-A, §8.5.1, p. 696.*}

5. {18 *State other facts relevant to the objection.*}

OBJECTION TO PHYSICIAN'S TESTIMONY

6. If an objection is made to an expert's testimony, the party offering the expert testimony bears the burden of showing that the testimony is admissible. *E.I. du Pont de Nemours & Co. v. Robinson*, 923 S.W.2d 549, 557 (Tex. 1995); *Halim v. Ramchandani*, 203 S.W.3d 482, 489 (Tex. App.—Houston [14th Dist.] 2006, no pet.).

{*CHOOSE APPROPRIATE SECTIONS A-B*}

A. Expert is not qualified to testify about accepted standards of medical care.

7. The Court should exclude the testimony of Dr. {19 *name of expert*} because {20 *adverse party*} cannot demonstrate that Dr. {21 *name of expert*} is qualified to give

Continued on next page

opinion testimony on whether the defendant departed from accepted standards of medical care. {*See* ***O'Connor's Texas COA***, *"General qualifications," ch. 20-A, §8.5.2(1), p. 697.*}

{*CHOOSE APPROPRIATE PARAGRAPHS 8-10*}

8. Dr. {22 *name of expert*} is not qualified because {23 *he/she*} was not practicing medicine at the time {24 *the incident occurred/{he/she} made the affidavit*}, as the term "practicing medicine" is defined in section 74.401(b). Tex. Civ. Prac. & Rem. Code §74.401(a)(1).

9. Dr. {25 *name of expert*} is not qualified because {26 *he/she*} does not have knowledge of accepted standards of medical care for the diagnosis, care, or treatment of the illness, injury, or condition involved in this suit. Tex. Civ. Prac. & Rem. Code §74.401(a)(2).

10. Dr. {27 *name of expert*} is not qualified because {28 *he/she*} does not have the training or experience to offer an expert opinion about accepted standards of medical care. Tex. Civ. Prac. & Rem. Code §74.401(a)(3).

B. Expert is not qualified to testify about causation.

11. The Court should exclude the testimony of Dr. {29 *name of expert*} because {30 *adverse party*} cannot demonstrate that Dr. {31 *name of expert*} is qualified to give opinion testimony on the causal relationship between the departure from accepted standards of care and the injury, harm, or damages claimed in this suit. Tex. Civ. Prac. & Rem. Code §74.403(a). {*See* ***O'Connor's Texas COA***, *"Causation," ch. 20-A, §8.5.2(2), p. 697.*}

{*CHOOSE APPROPRIATE PARAGRAPHS 12-16*}

12. Dr. {32 *name of expert*} is not qualified because {33 *he/she*} does not have the education, training, specialized knowledge, skill, or experience to provide an opinion on causation. {34 *Elaborate.*} {*See* ***O'Connor's Texas Rules***, *"Qualifications test," ch. 5-N, §2.1, p. 499.*}

13. Dr. {35 *name of expert*} is not qualified because {36 *his/her*} opinion is not reliable. {37 *Elaborate.*} {*See* ***O'Connor's Texas Rules***, *"Reliability of opinion," ch. 5-N, §2.3.1, p. 501.*}

14. Dr. {㊳ *name of expert*} is not qualified because {㊴ *his/her*} opinion is not based on sufficient underlying facts or data. Tex. R. Evid. 705(c). {㊵ *Elaborate.*} {*See* ***O'Connor's Texas Rules****, "Foundation test," ch. 5-N, §2.4, p. 503.*}

15. Dr. {㊶ *name of expert*} is not qualified because {㊷ *his/her*} opinion is not relevant. {㊸ *Elaborate.*} {*See* ***O'Connor's Texas Rules****, "Relevance of opinion," ch. 5-N, §2.3.2, p. 503.*}

16. Dr. {㊹ *name of expert*} is not qualified because the probative value of {㊺ *his/her*} opinion is substantially outweighed by the danger of unfair prejudice, confusing the issues, misleading the jury, undue delay, or needlessly presenting cumulative evidence. Tex. R. Evid. 403. {㊻ *Elaborate.*} {*See* ***O'Connor's Texas Rules****, "Allegations," ch. 5-N, §3.2.1(6), p. 504.*}

REQUEST FOR HEARING

17. {㊼ *Party*} requests that the Court set this objection for a hearing at the earliest opportunity before {㊽ *date*}, which is the date set for the {㊾ *trial/summary-judgment hearing*}.

PRAYER

18. For these reasons, {㊿ *party*} asks the Court to set this objection for a hearing, require {51 *adverse party*} to meet its burden of proof, and exclude the testimony of Dr. {52 *name of expert*} as an expert witness for {53 *adverse party*}.

SEE: Tex. Civ. Prac. & Rem. Code §§74.401-74.403
Tex. R. Evid. 403, 702, 705
O'Connor's Texas Rules * Civil Trials (2019), "Motion to Exclude Expert," ch. 5-N, p. 499
O'Connor's Texas Causes of Action (2019), "Expert Testimony," ch. 20-A, §8, p. 690
Brown & Rondon, ***Texas Rules of Evidence Handbook*** (2019), pp. 202, 694, 755

ADD: STYLE OF THE CASE – FORM 1B:2
SIGNATURE BLOCK – FORM 1B:3
CERTIFICATE OF CONFERENCE – FORM 1B:12, if necessary
CERTIFICATE OF SERVICE – FORM 1B:13

ATTACH: AFFIDAVIT – FORM 1B:8, if necessary
NOTICE OF HEARING OR SUBMISSION – FORM 1E:1
ORDER – FORM 1G:1

Continued on next page

NOTE: The court may depart from the criteria under Texas Civil Practice & Remedies Code §74.401(a) if the court determines there is a good reason to admit the expert's testimony. Tex. Civ. Prac. & Rem. Code §74.401(d). If the court departs from the criteria, the court must state on the record the reason for admitting the testimony. *Id.*

The party who objects to an expert has no burden of proof; thus, it is not necessary to include in this objection any citations to authority or to attach affidavits.

This form can be modified for a suit against a health-care provider (e.g., a hospital). *See* Tex. Civ. Prac. & Rem. Code §74.402. See ***O'Connor's Texas COA***, "For claims against health-care providers," ch. 20-A, §8.3.1(2), p. 694.

{1 *PARTY*}'S RESPONSE TO
{2 *ADVERSE PARTY*}'S OBJECTION TO EXPERT TESTIMONY

{3 *Party*}, {4 *name*}, asks the Court to overrule {5 *adverse party*} {6 *name*}'s objection to the opinion testimony of {7 *party*}'s expert, Dr. {8 *name of expert*}.

INTRODUCTION

1. Plaintiff, {9 *name*}, sued defendant, {10 *name*}, for {11 *state basis of suit*}.

2. {12 *State other relevant facts about the suit.*}

BACKGROUND

3. This case is set for {13 *trial/summary-judgment hearing*} on {14 *date*}.

4. {15 *Party*} identified Dr. {16 *name of expert*} to testify as an expert in this case on the issue of whether defendant, Dr. {17 *name of defendant-physician*}, {18 *departed from accepted standards of medical care/caused plaintiff's injury*}.

5. On {19 *date*}, {20 *adverse party*} filed an objection to the opinion testimony of Dr. {21 *name of expert*} on the grounds that {22 *identify reasons*}.

6. {23 *State other facts relevant to the response.*}

ARGUMENT & AUTHORITIES

{*CHOOSE APPROPRIATE SECTIONS A-C*}

A. Objection is untimely.

7. An objection to expert testimony is timely only if it is made no later than 21 days after (1) a party received a copy of the expert's curriculum vitae or (2) the expert's deposition. Tex. Civ. Prac. & Rem. Code §74.401(e). When the objection is not timely, it should be allowed only if (1) the basis for the objection arose after the deadline expired, (2) the basis for the objection could not reasonably have been anticipated before the deadline expired, (3) the objection was not made earlier, (4) the objection is made in good faith, and (5) the objection is made as soon as possible. *Id.* {*See* ***O'Connor's Texas COA****, "Deadline," ch. 20-A, §8.5.1, p. 696.*}

8. The Court should overrule the objection because it is untimely and {24 *adverse party*} has waived the right to object. {25 *Identify specific dates to demonstrate untimeliness.*} {26 *Adverse party*} has not established sufficient grounds for making an untimely objection. {27 *Elaborate, rebutting adverse party's arguments.*} {*See* ***O'Connor's Texas COA****, "Response to untimely objections," ch. 20-A, §8.5.3(1), p. 697.*}

◄ *Continued on next page* ►

B. Expert is qualified to testify about accepted standards of medical care.

9. An expert is qualified to give opinion testimony on whether the defendant departed from the accepted standards of medical care if the expert (1) is a physician practicing medicine when her testimony is given or when the claim arose, (2) has knowledge of accepted standards of medical care for the diagnosis, care, or treatment of the illness, injury, or condition involved in the suit, and (3) has the training or experience to offer an expert opinion about accepted standards of medical care. Tex. Civ. Prac. & Rem. Code §74.401(a). {*See* ***O'Connor's Texas COA***, *"General rule," ch. 20-A, §8.3.1(1)(a), p. 692.*}

10. The Court can depart from the qualification requirements of Texas Civil Practice & Remedies Code section 74.401(a) if, under the circumstances, the Court determines there is good reason to admit the testimony. Tex. Civ. Prac. & Rem. Code §74.401(d). {*See* ***O'Connor's Texas COA***, *"Exception," ch. 20-A, §8.3.1(1)(b), p. 693.*}

{*CHOOSE APPROPRIATE PARAGRAPH 11*}

11. The Court should overrule the objection because Dr. {㉘ *name of expert*} meets the requirements of section 74.401(a) to testify as an expert. {㉙ *Elaborate.*}

11. Even though Dr. {㉚ *name of expert*} does not meet the requirements of Texas Civil Practice & Remedies Code section 74.401(a), the Court should overrule the objection because, under the circumstances, there is "good reason" to admit the testimony. Tex. Civ. Prac. & Rem. Code §74.401(d). {㉛ *Show why the court should permit expert to testify even though expert does not qualify under §74.401(a).*}

C. Expert is qualified to testify about causation.

12. An expert is qualified to give opinion testimony on the causal relationship between the departure from accepted standards of care and the plaintiff's injury, harm, or damages if the expert is a physician and is otherwise qualified under the Texas Rules of Evidence. Tex. Civ. Prac. & Rem. Code §74.403(a). {*See* ***O'Connor's Texas COA***, *"Expert testimony on causation," ch. 20-A, §8.3.2, p. 695.*}

13. The Court should overrule the objection because Dr. {㉜ *name of expert*} is a physician qualified to testify as an expert under the Texas Rules of Evidence. {*See* ***O'Connor's Texas COA***, *"Response to causation objections," ch. 20-A, §8.5.3(3), p. 697.*}

{*CHOOSE APPROPRIATE PARAGRAPHS 14-17*}

14. Dr. {㉝ *name of expert*} is qualified to offer an expert opinion. An expert must have a higher degree of knowledge, skill, experience, training, or education about the subject of the testimony than an ordinary person has. *See* Tex. R. Evid. 702; *Roberts v. Williamson*, 111 S.W.3d 113, 121 (Tex. 2003); *Broders v. Heise*, 924 S.W.2d 148, 153 (Tex. 1996). {㉞ *Party*}'s expert is well qualified. Specifically, the Court should allow the testimony because {㉟ *explain why expert is qualified, e.g., list education, practical experience, publications*}. {*See* ***O'Connor's Texas Rules***, *"Qualifications test," ch. 5-N, §2.1, p. 499.*}

15. The opinion testimony of Dr. {㊱ *name of expert*} is relevant. To be relevant, the testimony must be "sufficiently tied to the facts of the case that it will aid the jury in resolving a factual dispute." *See E.I. du Pont de Nemours & Co. v. Robinson*, 923 S.W.2d 549, 556 (Tex. 1995). Specifically, the Court should allow the testimony because {㊲ *explain why testimony is relevant*}. {*See* ***O'Connor's Texas Rules***, *"Relevance of opinion," ch. 5-N, §2.3.2, p. 503.*}

16. The probative value of Dr. {㊳ *name of expert*}'s opinion testimony is not substantially outweighed by (1) the danger of unfair prejudice, confusion of the issues, or misleading the jury, (2) undue delay, or (3) needless presentation of cumulative evidence. *See* Tex. R. Evid. 403; *E.I. du Pont de Nemours & Co. v. Robinson*, 923 S.W.2d 549, 557 (Tex. 1995). {㊴ *Specify probative value of testimony and why it is not misleading, confusing, prejudicial, or cumulative and why it will not cause undue delay.*} {*See* ***O'Connor's Texas Rules***, *"Allegations," ch. 5-N, §3.3.1(6), p. 505.*}

17. The opinion testimony of Dr. {㊵ *name of expert*} is reliable. *See E.I. du Pont de Nemours & Co. v. Robinson*, 923 S.W.2d 549, 557 (Tex. 1995). A court should allow the opinion testimony of an expert if each part of the expert's opinion is reliable. *Whirlpool Corp. v. Camacho*, 298 S.W.3d 631, 637 (Tex. 2009). In determining whether expert testimony is reliable, a court should consider the *Daubert-Robinson* factors and whether the analytical gap between the expert's methodology and the opinion offered is too great. *Transcon. Ins. Co. v. Crump*, 330 S.W.3d 211, 215-16 (Tex. 2010); *see Daubert v. Merrell Dow Pharms., Inc.*, 509 U.S. 579, 593-94 (1993); *Gammill v. Jack Williams Chevrolet, Inc.*, 972 S.W.2d 713, 727 (Tex. 1998); *Robinson*, 923 S.W.2d at 557. {*See* ***O'Connor's Texas Rules***, *"Reliability of opinion," ch. 5-N, §2.3.1, p. 501.*}

{*ADD PARAGRAPHS 18-20 IF ARGUING THAT TESTIMONY IS RELIABLE*}

18. The *Daubert-Robinson* factors include the following: (1) the extent to which the expert's theory has been or can be tested, (2) the technique's potential rate of error,

Continued on next page

(3) whether the theory has been subjected to peer review or publication, (4) whether the underlying theory or technique has been generally accepted as valid by the relevant scientific community, (5) the extent to which the technique relies on the expert's subjective interpretation, and (6) the nonjudicial uses of the theory or technique. *See Daubert v. Merrell Dow Pharms., Inc.*, 509 U.S. 579, 593-94 (1993); *E.I. du Pont de Nemours & Co. v. Robinson*, 923 S.W.2d 549, 557 (Tex. 1995). These factors are nonexclusive and may not apply to all expert testimony. *Cooper Tire & Rubber Co. v. Mendez*, 204 S.W.3d 797, 801 (Tex. 2006); *Gammill v. Jack Williams Chevrolet, Inc.*, 972 S.W.2d 713, 726 (Tex. 1998).

19. In assessing the analytical gap, the court should consider whether (1) the expert's field of expertise is legitimate, (2) the subject matter of the testimony is within the scope of the expert's field of expertise, (3) the testimony properly relies on principles involved in the expert's field of expertise, and (4) the expert showed a connection between the data relied on and the opinion offered. *See Volkswagen of Am., Inc. v. Ramirez*, 159 S.W.3d 897, 906 (Tex. 2004); *Coastal Tankships, U.S.A., Inc. v. Anderson*, 87 S.W.3d 591, 601 (Tex. App.—Houston [1st Dist.] 2002, pet. denied); *see, e.g., Transcon. Ins. Co. v. Crump*, 330 S.W.3d 211, 219-20 (Tex. 2010) (treating physician's opinion on cause of plaintiff's death based on differential diagnosis was reliable); *Gammill*, 972 S.W.2d at 726 (beekeeper could testify that bees take off into the wind based on beekeeper's own observations).

20. The opinion testimony of Dr. {41 *name of expert*} is reliable because {42 *establish reliability using the Daubert-Robinson factors and the Gammill factors*}.

{*ADD FOLLOWING SECTION IF APPLICABLE*}

CONTINUANCE

21. If the Court rules that {43 *party*}'s expert will not be permitted to give an opinion, {44 *party*} requests a continuance of the {45 *trial/summary-judgment hearing*} to secure another expert.

CONCLUSION

22. {46 *Briefly summarize the response.*}

PRAYER

23. For these reasons, {47 *party*} asks the Court to set the objection for a hearing and, after the hearing, overrule {48 *adverse party*}'s objection to Dr. {49 *name of expert*} as an expert witness for {50 *party*}.

FORM 5N:4 RESPONSE TO OBJECTION TO PHYSICIAN'S TESTIMONY

SEE: Tex. Civ. Prac. & Rem. Code §§74.401-74.403
Tex. R. Evid. 104, 403, 702
O'Connor's Texas Rules * Civil Trials (2019), "Motion to Exclude Expert," ch. 5-N, p. 499
O'Connor's Texas Causes of Action (2019), "Expert Testimony," ch. 20-A, §8, p. 690
Brown & Rondon, ***Texas Rules of Evidence Handbook*** (2019), p. 694

ADD: STYLE OF THE CASE – FORM 1B:2
SIGNATURE BLOCK – FORM 1B:3
CERTIFICATE OF SERVICE – FORM 1B:13

ATTACH: AFFIDAVIT – FORM 1B:8, if necessary
NOTICE OF HEARING OR SUBMISSION – FORM 1E:1
ORDER – FORM 1G:1
Exhibits, if necessary

NOTE: The court may depart from the criteria under Texas Civil Practice & Remedies Code §74.401(a) if the court determines there is a good reason to admit the expert's testimony. Tex. Civ. Prac. & Rem. Code §74.401(d). If the court departs from the criteria, the court must state on the record the reason for admitting the testimony. *Id.*

This form can be modified for a suit against a health-care provider (e.g., a hospital). *See* Tex. Civ. Prac. & Rem. Code §74.402. See ***O'Connor's Texas COA***, "For claims against health-care providers," ch. 20-A, §8.3.1(2), p. 694.

Texas Civil Forms

Chapter 6. Discovery

Table of Contents

Discovery Motions

Discovery Sanctions

Spoliation Sanctions

Amend/Supplement Discovery

Person's Statement

Expert Discovery

TEXAS CIVIL FORMS
CHAPTER 6. DISCOVERY
TABLE OF CONTENTS

Request for Disclosure

Oral Deposition

Deposition on Written Questions

Deposition Outside Discovery Period

Deposition Before Suit

Interrogatories

Request for Admissions

TABLE OF CONTENTS

RULE 11 AGREED PRESERVATION PLAN

{❶ *Party*} and {❷ *adverse party*} file this agreement, made under Texas Rules of Civil Procedure 11 and 191.1, regarding the preservation of documents, electronically stored information, and other tangible things. {*See* ***O'Connor's Texas Rules***, *"Modifying discovery by agreement," ch. 6-A, §6.1, p. 519.*} The parties recognize that they must take steps to preserve materials that are relevant to the claims and defenses asserted in this case or that may lead to the discovery of admissible information. Although efforts aimed at preserving discoverable material can become unduly burdensome and unreasonably costly, the parties believe that these concerns can be addressed with a plan that (1) clearly targets materials reasonably likely to be relevant or to lead to the discovery of admissible information and (2) takes into account the unique issues associated with the discoverable material, including electronic or magnetic data. Thus, the parties agree that this plan adequately defines the scope of their preservation obligations for the purposes of this litigation.

DEFINITIONS

1. The following definitions apply to this preservation plan:

   a. Material. The term "material" means all documents, electronically stored information, or tangible things. The term is synonymous with and equal in scope to the terms "documents," "electronic or magnetic data," or "tangible things" in Texas Rules of Civil Procedure 196.1 and 196.4. A draft or nonidentical copy of a document, electronically stored information, or a tangible thing is a separate item within the meaning of this term.

      (1) Document. The term "document" means all written, typed, or printed matter and all magnetic, electronic, or other records or documentation of any kind or description in your actual possession, custody, or control, including those in the possession, custody, or control of any and all present or former directors, officers, employees, consultants, accountants, attorneys, or other agents, whether or not prepared by you, that constitute or contain matters relevant to the subject matter of the action. "Document" includes, but is not limited to, the following: letters, reports, charts, diagrams, correspondence, telegrams, memoranda, notes, records, minutes, contracts, agreements, records or notations of telephone or personal conversations or conferences, interoffice communications, e-mail, microfilm, bulletins, circulars, pamphlets, photographs, faxes, invoices, tape recordings, computer printouts, drafts, résumés, logs, worksheets, {❸ *continue listing examples as necessary*}.

Continued on next page

(2) Electronic or magnetic data. The term "electronic or magnetic data" means electronic information that is stored in a medium from which it can be retrieved and examined. The term refers to the original (or identical duplicate when the original is not available) and any other copies of the data that may have attached comments, notes, marks, or highlighting of any kind. Electronic or magnetic data includes, but is not limited to, the following: computer programs; operating systems; computer activity logs; programming notes or instructions; e-mail receipts, messages, or transmissions; output resulting from the use of any software program, including word-processing documents, spreadsheets, database files, charts, graphs, and outlines; metadata; PIF and PDF files; batch files; deleted files; temporary files; Internet- or web-browser-generated information stored in textual, graphical, or audio format, including history files, caches, and cookies; {❹ *continue listing examples as necessary*}; and any miscellaneous files or file fragments. Electronic or magnetic data includes any items stored on magnetic, optical, digital, or other electronic-storage media, such as hard drives, floppy disks, CD-ROMs, DVDs, tapes, smart cards, integrated-circuit cards (e.g., SIM cards), removable media (e.g., Zip drives, Jaz cartridges), microfiche, punched cards, {❺ *continue listing examples as necessary*}. Electronic or magnetic data also includes the file, folder, tabs, containers, and labels attached to or associated with any physical storage device with each original or copy.

(3) Tangible thing. The term "tangible thing" means a physical object that is not a document or electronic or magnetic data.

b. Parties. The term "parties" means the plaintiff and the defendant. The term "plaintiff" or "defendant," as well as a party's full or abbreviated name or a pronoun referring to a party, means the party and, when applicable, the party's agents, representatives, officers, directors, employees, partners, corporate parent, subsidiaries, or affiliates. This definition is not intended to impose an obligation on any person who is not a party to the litigation.

c. Preservation. The term "preservation" means maintaining the integrity of all documents, electronic or magnetic data, and tangible things reasonably anticipated to be subject to discovery under the Texas Rules of Civil Procedure in this case. Preservation includes, but is not limited to, taking reasonable steps to prevent partial or full destruction, alteration, deletion, shredding, incineration, wiping, relocation, migration, theft, removal,

concealment, or other disposal of the documents, electronic or magnetic data, and tangible things. Preservation also includes taking reasonable steps to prevent negligent or intentional handling that would make the material incomplete or inaccessible.

{*Continue listing definitions as necessary.*}

PRESERVATION PLAN

2. The parties agree that they will take reasonable steps to preserve all materials containing information that is relevant to the allegations and defenses in this case or that may lead to the discovery of admissible evidence in this case, including, but not limited to, materials related to the following: {❻ *explain and identify areas of information that are relevant to the case*}.

3. The parties agree that the preservation obligation applies for the following time period: {❼ *state time period, including a start date and an end date*}.

4. The parties agree to the following protocol for preserving relevant materials: {❽ *explain and describe the necessary steps to preserve materials*}.

5. {❾ *Identify any additional provisions of the agreement.*}

6. The {❿ *parties/attorneys*}' signatures are evidence of their intent that this document be a Rule 11 agreement, enforceable upon filing with the Court. Tex. R. Civ. P. 11.

SEE: Tex. R. Civ. P. 11, 191.1
O'Connor's Texas Rules * Civil Trials (2019), "Preservation of Evidence," ch. 6-A, §3, p. 516; "Preservation," ch. 6-C, §3.2, p. 593
O'Connor's Federal Rules * Civil Trials (2019), "Preservation plan," ch. 6-A, §4.4.4, p. 489

ADD: STYLE OF THE CASE – FORM 1B:2
SIGNATURE BLOCK FOR AGREED MOTIONS – FORM 1B:4
CERTIFICATE OF SERVICE – FORM 1B:13, if other parties not included in the agreement

NOTE: The Texas Rules of Civil Procedure use the term "electronic or magnetic data," and the Federal Rules of Civil Procedure use the term "electronically stored information." *See* Tex. R. Civ. P. 196.4; Fed. R. Civ. P. 26(b)(2)(B). There is no substantive difference between these terms, and they are used interchangeably.

Unless specifically prohibited, the parties can agree to modify discovery procedures. Tex. R. Civ. P. 191.1 & cmt. 1; ***In re BP Prods. N. Am., Inc.***, 244 S.W.3d 840, 845 (Tex.2008). The agreement to modify a discovery rule must comply with Texas Rule of Civil Procedure 11. Tex. R. Civ. P. 191.1. See ***O'Connor's Texas Rules***, "Modifying discovery by agreement," ch. 6-A, §6.1, p. 519.

Before using this form, see the notes accompanying the general form for a Rule 11 agreement (FORM 1H:13).

{[1] *PARTY*}'S MOTION TO EXTEND TIME TO RESPOND TO {[2] *ADVERSE PARTY*}'S {[3] *IDENTIFY DISCOVERY*}

{[4] *Party*}, {[5] *name*}, asks the Court to grant additional time to object and respond to {[6] *adverse party*} {[7] *name*}'s {[8] *specify request, e.g., requests for production*}. {*See **O'Connor's Texas Rules**, "Court order to extend," ch. 6-A, §15.2, p. 528.*}

INTRODUCTION

1. Plaintiff, {[9] *name*}, sued defendant, {[10] *name*}, for {[11] *state basis of suit*}.

2. Discovery in this suit is governed by a Level {[12] *1/2/3*} discovery-control plan. The discovery period {[13] *will end/ended*} on {[14] *date*}. {*See **O'Connor's Texas Rules**, "Discovery-Control Plans," ch. 6-A, §7, p. 520.*}

3. This case is set for trial on {[15] *date*}.

4. {[16] *State other relevant facts about the suit.*}

BACKGROUND

5. On {[17] *date*}, {[18] *adverse party*} served the attached {[19] *identify type of discovery*}.

6. {[20] *Party*}'s objections and responses {[21] *are/were*} due on {[22] *date*}.

7. {[23] *State other facts relevant to the motion.*}

ARGUMENT & AUTHORITIES

8. {[24] *Party*} asks the Court to grant additional time to {[25] *object/respond/object and respond*} to {[26] *identify discovery*}.

9. When a party files a motion to extend the deadline to respond to discovery, Texas Rule of Civil Procedure 191.1 permits a court to enlarge the period to respond to discovery based on a showing of "good cause." {*See **O'Connor's Texas Rules**, "Court order to extend," ch. 6-A, §15.2, p. 528.*}

10. {[27] *Party*} requests additional time for good cause. Tex. R. Civ. P. 5, 191.1. Specifically, {[28] *party*} needs additional time because {[29] *state specific facts showing good cause for extension of time*}.

11. {[30] *Party*} asks the Court to extend the time by {[31] *number*} days, to {[32] *date*}.

CONCLUSION

12. {㉝ *Briefly summarize the motion.*}

PRAYER

13. For these reasons, {㉞ *party*} asks the Court to set this motion for hearing and, after the hearing, grant the motion to extend time to object and respond to {㉟ *identify discovery*} and extend the deadline to {㊱ *date*}.

SEE: Tex. R. Civ. P. 5, 191.1, 193.2(e)
O'Connor's Texas Rules * Civil Trials (2019), "Court order to extend," ch. 6-A, §15.2, p. 528

ADD: STYLE OF THE CASE – FORM 1B:2
SIGNATURE BLOCK – FORM 1B:3
CERTIFICATE OF CONFERENCE – FORM 1B:12
CERTIFICATE OF SERVICE – FORM 1B:13

ATTACH: AFFIDAVIT – FORM 1B:8, if necessary
NOTICE OF HEARING OR SUBMISSION – FORM 1E:1
ORDER – FORM 1G:1
Discovery request subject to the motion

RULE 11 AGREEMENT TO EXTEND
TIME TO OBJECT & RESPOND TO DISCOVERY

{❶ *Party*}, {❷ *name*}, and {❸ *adverse party*}, {❹ *name*}, file this agreement, made under Texas Rules of Civil Procedure 11 and 191.1, to extend time to object and respond to discovery. {*See **O'Connor's Texas Rules**, "Modifying discovery by agreement," ch. 6-A, §6.1, p. 519.*}

1. On {❺ *date*}, {❻ *party*} {❼ *filed/served*} {❽ *his/her/its*} {❾ *identify type of discovery*}.

2. {❿ *Adverse party*}'s objections and responses {⓫ *are/were*} due on {⓬ *date*}.

3. The parties agree to extend the time for objecting and responding to {⓭ *identify type of discovery*} to {⓮ *date*}.

4. The extended deadline is within the discovery period for this suit.

5. The {⓯ *parties/attorneys*}' signatures are evidence of their intent that this document be a Rule 11 agreement, enforceable upon filing with the Court. Tex. R. Civ. P. 11.

SEE: Tex. R. Civ. P. 11, 191.1
O'Connor's Texas Rules * Civil Trials (2019), "Modifying discovery by agreement," ch. 6-A, §6.1, p. 519

ADD: STYLE OF THE CASE – FORM 1B:2
SIGNATURE BLOCK FOR AGREED MOTIONS – FORM 1B:4
CERTIFICATE OF SERVICE – FORM 1B:13, if other parties not included in the agreement

NOTE: Unless specifically prohibited, parties can agree to modify discovery procedures. Tex. R. Civ. P. 191.1 & cmt. 1; ***In re BP Prods. N. Am., Inc.***, 244 S.W.3d 840, 845 (Tex.2008). The agreement to modify a discovery rule must comply with Texas Rule of Civil Procedure 11. Tex. R. Civ. P. 191.1.

{[1] *PARTY*}'S MOTION FOR EXPEDITED DISCOVERY

{[2] *Party*}, {[3] *name*}, asks the Court to grant expedited discovery under Texas Rule of Civil Procedure 191.1. {*See* ***O'Connor's Texas Rules****, "Modifying discovery by court order," ch. 6-A, §6.2, p. 519.*}

INTRODUCTION

1. Plaintiff, {[4] *name*}, sued defendant, {[5] *name*}, for {[6] *state basis of suit*}.

2. Discovery in this suit is governed by a Level {[7] *1/2/3*} discovery-control plan. The discovery period {[8] *will end/ended*} on {[9] *date*}. {*See* ***O'Connor's Texas Rules****, "Discovery-Control Plans," ch. 6-A, §7, p. 520.*}

3. This case is set for trial on {[10] *date*}.

4. {[11] *State other relevant facts about the suit.*}

BACKGROUND

5. {[12] *State facts relevant to the motion.*}

ARGUMENT & AUTHORITIES

6. Texas Rule of Civil Procedure 191.1 permits a court to shorten the period to respond to discovery based on a showing of "good cause." Tex. R. Civ. P. 191.1.

7. For good cause, {[13] *party*} asks the Court to shorten {[14] *adverse party*}'s time to respond to {[15] *party*}'s {[16] *identify discovery requests*}. Tex. R. Civ. P. 191.1. Specifically, {[17] *party*} needs expedited discovery because {[18] *state specific facts showing good cause, e.g., it needs to adequately prepare for the hearing on its application for temporary injunction scheduled to take place within 14 days*}.

PRAYER

8. For these reasons, {[19] *party*} asks the Court to grant this motion and order {[20] *adverse party*} to respond to {[21] *identify discovery requests*} by {[22] *date*}.

Continued on next page

TEXAS CIVIL FORMS

CHAPTER 6. DISCOVERY

FORM 6A:4 MOTION FOR EXPEDITED DISCOVERY

SEE: Tex. R. Civ. P. 191.1
*O'Connor's Texas Rules * Civil Trials* (2019), "Modifying discovery by court order," ch. 6-A, §6.2, p. 519

ADD: STYLE OF THE CASE – FORM 1B:2
SIGNATURE BLOCK – FORM 1B:3
CERTIFICATE OF CONFERENCE – FORM 1B:12
CERTIFICATE OF SERVICE – FORM 1B:13

ATTACH: AFFIDAVIT – FORM 1B:8, if necessary
NOTICE OF HEARING OR SUBMISSION – FORM 1E:1
ORDER – FORM 1G:1
Discovery request subject to the motion

{❶ *PARTY*}'S CERTIFICATE OF WRITTEN DISCOVERY

{❷ *Party*}, {❸ *name*}, certifies under {❹ *specify local rule*} that the following documents were served on {❺ *adverse party*}, {❻ *name*}, on {❼ *date*}:

{*CHOOSE APPROPRIATE STATEMENTS*}

a. {❽ *Party*}'s {❾ *identify discovery, e.g., first set of interrogatories*} to {❿ *adverse party*}.

b. {⓫ *Party*}'s response to {⓬ *adverse party*}'s {⓭ *identify discovery, e.g., first set of interrogatories*}.

c. Documents accompanying {⓮ *party*}'s responses to {⓯ *adverse party*}'s request for production.

d. A copy of the deposition of {⓰ *name of deponent*}.

e. {⓱ *Identify other material.*}

SEE: ***O'Connor's Texas Rules * Civil Trials*** (2019), "Certificate of written discovery," ch. 6-A, §4.3, p. 518

ADD: STYLE OF THE CASE – FORM 1B:2
SIGNATURE BLOCK – FORM 1B:3
CERTIFICATE OF SERVICE – FORM 1B:13

NOTE: The Texas Rules of Civil Procedure do not require parties to file a certificate of written discovery. A certificate is necessary only if required by local rule.

{❶ *{PARTY}'S/AGREED*} MOTION FOR
ENTRY OF LEVEL 3 DISCOVERY-CONTROL PLAN

{❷ *{Party} asks/Plaintiff and defendant ask*} the Court to order that discovery be conducted according to a Level 3 discovery-control plan tailored to the circumstances of the suit, as authorized by Texas Rule of Civil Procedure 190.4. {*See **O'Connor's Texas Rules**, "Level 3," ch. 6-A, §7.4, p. 523.*}

INTRODUCTION

1. Plaintiff, {❸ *name*}, sued defendant, {❹ *name*}, for {❺ *state basis of suit*}.

2. {❻ *State other relevant facts about the suit.*}

BACKGROUND

3. {❼ *State facts supporting entry of proposed discovery-control plan*}.

{*ADD SECTION BELOW IF MOTION IS AGREED*}

AGREEMENT

4. The parties attach a proposed discovery-control plan as Exhibit A.

5. Attorneys for all parties agree to the proposed discovery-control plan and have signed this agreed motion.

{*ADD SECTION BELOW IF MOTION IS NOT AGREED*}

ARGUMENT & AUTHORITIES

4. A court must, on a party's motion (and may, on its own initiative), order that discovery be conducted as a Level 3 case with a discovery-control plan tailored to the specific suit. Tex. R. Civ. P. 190.4(a).

5. {❽ *Party*} attaches a proposed discovery-control plan as Exhibit A.

PRAYER

6. For these reasons, {❾ *{party} asks/plaintiff and defendant ask*} the Court to approve the proposed discovery-control plan.

SEE: Tex. R. Civ. P. 166, 190.4
*O'Connor's Texas Rules * Civil Trials* (2019), "Level 3," ch. 6-A, §7.4, p. 523

ADD: STYLE OF THE CASE – FORM 1B:2
SIGNATURE BLOCK – FORM 1B:3, if motion is not agreed
SIGNATURE BLOCK FOR AGREED MOTIONS – FORM 1B:4, if motion is agreed
CERTIFICATE OF CONFERENCE – FORM 1B:12, if motion is not agreed
CERTIFICATE OF SERVICE – FORM 1B:13, if motion is not agreed

ATTACH: NOTICE OF HEARING OR SUBMISSION – FORM 1E:1, if motion is not agreed
ORDER – FORM 1G:1
PROPOSED LEVEL 3 DISCOVERY-CONTROL PLAN – FORM 6A:7

LEVEL 3 DISCOVERY-CONTROL PLAN

It is ORDERED that discovery in this case will be conducted according to this discovery-control plan and that the parties will meet and adhere to the following deadlines:

{*CHOOSE APPROPRIATE PARAGRAPH 1*}

1. Trial. Trial is set for __________, 20___, at _____ o'clock a.m./p.m.

1. Trial. A pretrial conference to determine the trial setting is set for __________, 20___, at _____ o'clock a.m./p.m.

2. End of discovery period. All discovery {❶ *must be conducted/requests must be sent*} by {❷ *date*}, for the {❸ *entire case/{identify phase of case}*}.

3. Limits on discovery.

   a. Oral depositions. The total time for oral depositions will be {❹ *number*} hours per side. "Side" refers to all the litigants with generally common interests in the litigation. Tex. R. Civ. P. 190.3(b)(2); *see* Tex. R. Civ. P. 169(d)(3)(A), 190 cmt. 6 (1999). {❺ *Identify the parties on each side and elaborate if necessary, particularly for complex cases that have more than two sides.*}

   b. Interrogatories. The total number of interrogatories that any party may serve on any other party is {❻ *number*}, excluding interrogatories asking a party only to identify or authenticate specified documents.

   c. {❼ *Identify limits for other type of discovery.*}

4. Deadline to add parties. All new parties must be added no later than {❽ *date*}.

5. Deadline for amending or supplementing pleadings. The deadline to amend or supplement pleadings is {❾ *date*}.

6. Deadline to designate testifying expert witnesses. An expert not designated before the following deadlines will not be permitted to testify unless good cause is shown for late designation:

   a. Plaintiff's experts. By {❿ *date*}, plaintiff must designate testifying expert witnesses and provide both the information requested in Texas Rule of Civil Procedure 194.2(f) and a written report prepared by the expert setting forth the substance of the expert's opinions.

b. Defendant's experts. By {⓫ *date*}, defendant must designate testifying expert witnesses and provide both the information requested in Texas Rule of Civil Procedure 194.2(f) and a written report prepared by the expert setting forth the substance of the expert's opinions.

7. Pretrial conference. The pretrial conference will take place on ________, 20___, at _____ o'clock a.m./p.m. Before the pretrial conference, the parties must exchange the following:

{*CHOOSE APPROPRIATE STATEMENTS*}

a. Proposed jury instructions and questions.

b. Proposed findings of fact and law.

c. Motions in limine.

d. Exhibit lists.

e. Labeled and numbered exhibits. Before the pretrial conference, the parties must exchange all exhibits they intend to introduce at trial and make good-faith efforts to reach an agreement on the admissibility of each exhibit. At the pretrial conference, the parties should be prepared to discuss objections to exhibits that they do not agree are admissible.

f. Witness lists stating each witness's name, address, and phone number, and whether the witness is a party, a fact witness, or an expert witness. At the pretrial conference, the parties should be prepared to discuss any scheduling problems relating to witnesses and any objections to improperly designated experts or fact witnesses.

{*ADD PARAGRAPH 8 IF APPROPRIATE*}

8. Mediation.

a. Deadline. The parties must attend mediation on or before {⓬ *date*}.

b. Objections to mediation. The parties must file any objections to mediation within 30 days of the date of this order.

c. Designation of mediator. The parties must submit to the Court within 30 days of the date of this discovery-control plan an agreed order naming a mediator. At least 30 days before the mediation deadline, the parties must agree with the mediator on a specific date to conduct mediation.

Continued on next page

d. Failure to designate mediator. If the parties do not submit an order designating a mediator and if no objection to mediation is filed, the Court will appoint the following person to serve as mediator in this case:

Name: ______________________________
Address: ____________________________
Phone: ______________________________
Fax: ________________________________

SIGNED on _______________, 20___.

____
PRESIDING JUDGE

SEE: Tex. R. Civ. P. 190.4
O'Connor's Texas Rules * Civil Trials (2019), "Level 3," ch. 6-A, §7.4, p. 523

ADD: STYLE OF THE CASE – FORM 1B:2

NOTE: A court cannot order a Level 3 discovery-control plan for an expedited action; for a Level 1 case, the court can order a Level 3 discovery-control plan only for certain suits for divorce. *See* Tex. R. Civ. P. 169 cmt. 2, 190.2(a)(2). See ***O'Connor's Texas Rules***, "Expedited Actions," ch. 2-C, p. 134; "Court order," ch. 6-A, §7.2.1(2)(b)[2], p. 521.

{1 *PARTY*}'S MOTION TO REOPEN DISCOVERY PERIOD

{2 *Party*}, {3 *name*}, asks the Court to reopen the discovery period and allow discovery to be completed under Level {4 *1/2/3*}. {*See* ***O'Connor's Texas Rules***, *"Period reopens," ch. 6-A, §8.1.1(2), p. 524; "Modification of discovery periods," ch. 6-A, §8.2, p. 524.*}

INTRODUCTION

1. Plaintiff, {5 *name*}, sued defendant, {6 *name*}, for {7 *state basis of suit*}.

2. Discovery in this suit is governed by a Level {8 *1/2/3*} discovery-control plan. The discovery period {9 *will end/ended*} on {10 *date*}. {*See* ***O'Connor's Texas Rules***, *"Discovery-Control Plans," ch. 6-A, §7, p. 520.*}

3. The discovery-control plan provides the following limitations on discovery: {11 *specify discovery limitations, e.g., for Level 1 cases, six hours to examine and cross-examine all witnesses in oral depositions*}.

4. This case is set for trial on {12 *date*}.

5. {13 *State other relevant facts about the suit.*}

BACKGROUND

{*CHOOSE APPROPRIATE PARAGRAPH 6*}

{*Level 1 inapplicable – suit removed from expedited-actions process by motion*}

6. On {14 *date*}, {15 *party/adverse party, {name}*}, filed a motion to remove this suit from the expedited-actions process in Texas Rule of Civil Procedure 169. {16 *Elaborate.*} On {17 *date*}, the Court granted the motion and removed the suit from the expedited-actions process. {*See* ***O'Connor's Texas Rules***, *"Removal from TRCP 169 Procedure," ch. 2-C, §3, p. 134.*}

{*Level 1 inapplicable – suit removed from expedited-actions process by pleading*}

6. On {18 *date*}, {19 *adverse party*}, {20 *name*}, filed {21 *a pleading/an amended pleading/a supplemental pleading*} {22 *alleging/disclosing*} that {23 *state facts pleaded or disclosed that make the expedited-actions process under Level 1 discovery inapplicable, e.g., adverse party seeks relief other than nonmonetary relief of $100,000 or less*}. {24 *Adverse party*}'s {25 *pleading/amended pleading/supplemental pleading*} removes the suit from the expedited-actions process in Texas Rule of Civil Procedure 169. {*See* ***O'Connor's Texas Rules***, *"Removal from TRCP 169 Procedure," ch. 2-C, §3, p. 134.*}

Continued on next page

{*Level 1 inapplicable – pleading filed in divorce suit*}

6. On {㉖ *date*}, {㉗ *adverse party*}, {㉘ *name*}, filed {㉙ *a pleading/an amended pleading/a supplemental pleading*} {㉚ *alleging/disclosing*} that {㉛ *state facts pleaded or disclosed that make Level 1 discovery inapplicable to the divorce suit, e.g., the amount in controversy in the divorce suit is more than $50,000*}.

{*Request for additional discovery – any action*}

6. On {㉜ *date*}, {㉝ *adverse party*}, {㉞ *name*}, filed {㉟ *a pleading/an amended pleading/a supplemental pleading/a discovery request*} {㊱ *alleging/disclosing*} that {㊲ *state facts pleaded or disclosed that require further discovery*}.

7. {㊳ *State other facts relevant to the motion.*}

ARGUMENT & AUTHORITIES

8. The Court should reopen the discovery period and allow {㊴ *add if appropriate: additional*} discovery to be completed under Level {㊵ *1/2/3*} because {㊶ *state facts supporting change of discovery plan or need for additional discovery*}.

{*CHOOSE APPROPRIATE PARAGRAPHS 9-13*}

{*Level 1 inapplicable – suit removed from expedited-actions process*}

9. When a suit is removed from the expedited-actions process in Texas Rule of Civil Procedure 169, a court must reopen the discovery period to allow discovery to be completed under a Level 2 or 3 discovery-control plan, whichever is applicable. Tex. R. Civ. P. 190.2(c); *see* Tex. R. Civ. P. 190.2(a)(1). Under Texas Rule of Civil Procedure 190.2(c), any person previously deposed may be redeposed, and a court, on a party's motion, should continue the trial date if necessary to allow completion of discovery. {㊷ *Elaborate.*}

{*Level 1 inapplicable – pleading filed in divorce suit*}

10. When a party to a divorce suit files a pleading or an amended or supplemental pleading that makes a Level 1 discovery-control plan inapplicable, a court must reopen the discovery period to allow discovery to be completed under a Level 2 or 3 discovery-control plan, whichever is applicable. Tex. R. Civ. P. 190.2(c); *see* Tex. R. Civ. P. 190.2(a)(2). Under Texas Rule of Civil Procedure 190.2(c), any person previously deposed may be redeposed, and a court, on a party's motion, should continue the trial date if necessary to allow completion of discovery. {㊸ *Elaborate.*}

{*Additional discovery – any action other than expedited action*}

11. When a party files a new pleading or an amended or supplemental pleading, or new information is disclosed in a discovery response or in an amended or supplemental response, a court must allow additional discovery if (1) the pleadings or responses were made after the deadline for completion of discovery or so close to that deadline that an adverse party would not have an adequate opportunity to conduct discovery related to the new matters, and (2) the adverse party would be unfairly prejudiced without the additional discovery. Tex. R. Civ. P. 190.5(a). {44 *Elaborate.*}

12. When matters change materially after the discovery cutoff and the trial date is more than three months after the end of the discovery period, a court must allow additional discovery. Tex. R. Civ. P. 190.5(b). {45 *Elaborate.*}

{*Additional discovery – expedited action*}

13. When a party files a new pleading or an amended or supplemental pleading, or when new information is disclosed in a discovery response or in an amended or supplemental response, a court may allow additional discovery if (1) the pleadings or responses were made after the deadline for completion of discovery or so close to that deadline that an adverse party would not have an adequate opportunity to conduct discovery related to the new matters, and (2) the adverse party would be unfairly prejudiced without the additional discovery. Tex. R. Civ. P. 190.5(a) & cmt. (2013). {46 *Elaborate.*}

{*ADD PARAGRAPH 14 IF NECESSARY*}

14. The Court should continue the trial date to allow the parties to complete all necessary discovery. {47 *Elaborate.*}

CONCLUSION

15. {48 *Briefly summarize the motion.*}

PRAYER

16. For these reasons, {49 *party*} asks the Court to reopen the discovery period and allow {50 *add if appropriate: additional*} discovery to be completed under Level {51 *1/2/3*}.

Continued on next page

TEXAS CIVIL FORMS

CHAPTER 6. DISCOVERY

FORM 6A:8 MOTION TO REOPEN DISCOVERY PERIOD

SEE: Tex. R. Civ. P. 190.2(c), 190.3, 190.4, 190.5
*O'Connor's Texas Rules * Civil Trials* (2019), "Period reopens," ch. 6-A, §8.1.1(2), p. 524; "Modification of discovery periods," ch. 6-A, §8.2, p. 524

ADD: STYLE OF THE CASE – FORM 1B:2
SIGNATURE BLOCK – FORM 1B:3
CERTIFICATE OF CONFERENCE – FORM 1B:12
CERTIFICATE OF SERVICE – FORM 1B:13

ATTACH: AFFIDAVIT – FORM 1B:8, if necessary
NOTICE OF HEARING OR SUBMISSION – FORM 1E:1
ORDER – FORM 1G:1
REMOVAL FROM EXPEDITED ACTION – FORM 2C:1, if necessary

NOTE: The discovery period in a Level 1 case reopens if (1) a suit is removed from the expedited-actions process in Texas Rule of Civil Procedure 169 or (2) in a suit for divorce not involving children, the court permits an amendment that would make the amount in controversy more than $50,000. *See* Tex. R. Civ. P. 190.2(a)(2), (c). See ***O'Connor's Texas Rules***, "Removal from TRCP 169 Procedure," ch. 2-C, §3, p. 134. The court must also allow for additional discovery under a modified discovery-control plan when the conditions of either Texas Rule of Civil Procedure 190.5(a) or Rule 190.5(b) are met. *See* Tex. R. Civ. P. 190.5. Expedited actions, however, are not subject to mandatory additional discovery, but the court may still allow additional discovery if the conditions of Rule 190.5(a) are met. Tex. R. Civ. P. 190.5 & cmt. (2013).

{[1] *PARTY*}'S OBJECTIONS TO
{[2] *ADVERSE PARTY*}'S {[3] *IDENTIFY DISCOVERY REQUEST*}

To: {[4] *Adverse party*}, {[5] *name*}, by and through {[6] *his/her/its*} attorney of record, {[7] *name*}, {[8] *address*}.

{[9] *Party*}, {[10] *name*}, serves these objections to {[11] *adverse party*}'s {[12] *identify discovery request, e.g., interrogatories*}.

1. {[13] *Identify discovery request, e.g., INTERROGATORY 1*}: {[14] *Restate discovery request.*}

{*CHOOSE APPROPRIATE OBJECTION*}

WITHHOLDING STATEMENT: Material or information responsive to this discovery request is withheld under the {[15] *identify privilege*}. Tex. R. Civ. P. 193.3(a). {*See* ***O'Connor's Texas Rules****, "Withholding statement," ch. 6-A, §2.8, p. 516.*}

OBJECTION: {[16] *Party*} objects to {[17] *identify discovery request*} because the deadline to comply with the discovery request falls outside the discovery period. Tex. R. Civ. P. 190 cmt. 4 (1999). The discovery period in this case ends on {[18] *date*}; the deadline to comply with the request is {[19] *date*}. {[20] *Elaborate.*} {*See* ***O'Connor's Texas Rules****, "Discovery periods," ch. 6-A, §8.1, p. 523.*}

OBJECTION: {[21] *Party*} objects to this discovery request because {[22] *state ground for objection*}. {[23] *Party*} refuses to provide

{*CHOOSE APPROPRIATE STATEMENT*}

[A] some of the information requested by {[24] *identify discovery request*}. However, {[25] *party*} will provide the part of the information requested that is not subject to this objection. That is, {[26] *party*} will provide {[27] *identify limit of compliance*}. {*See* ***O'Connor's Texas Rules****, "Partial compliance necessary," ch. 6-A, §18.10.1, p. 538.*}

[B] any of the information requested by {[28] *identify discovery request*} because it is unreasonable to do so before obtaining a ruling on the objection. {[29] *Explain why it is unreasonable, e.g., the request requires a search of thousands of records.*} If {[30] *party*} partially complies with this discovery request now, and later the Court rules that {[31] *party*} must provide all the information requested, {[32] *party*} would be required to conduct a duplicative and burdensome search of records. {*See* ***O'Connor's Texas Rules****, "No compliance necessary," ch. 6-A, §18.10.2, p. 538.*}

Continued on next page

OBJECTION: {❸❸ *Party*} objects to this discovery request because it is outside the scope of permissible discovery. *See* Tex. R. Civ. P. 192.3; *In re Nat'l Lloyds Ins. Co.*, 532 S.W.3d 794, 808 (Tex. 2017); *In re CSX Corp.*, 124 S.W.3d 149, 152 (Tex. 2003). Specifically, the request is objectionable for the following reasons:

a. It seeks information that is not relevant. Tex. R. Civ. P. 192.3(a); *see In re Nat'l Lloyds*, 532 S.W.3d at 808; *Ford Motor Co. v. Leggat*, 904 S.W.2d 643, 649 (Tex. 1995); *Axelson, Inc. v. McIlhany*, 798 S.W.2d 550, 553 (Tex. 1990). {❸❹ *State basis for objection, e.g., the request seeks the engineering drawings for defendant's headlights, and this lawsuit involves an allegation that defendant's brake system was defective.*} {❸❺ *State any additional facts that support objection.*} {*See* ***O'Connor's Texas Rules***, *"Not relevant," ch. 6-A, §19.1.1(1), p. 538.*}

b. It would not lead to the discovery of admissible evidence. Tex. R. Civ. P. 192.3(a); *see In re Nat'l Lloyds*, 532 S.W.3d at 808; *Al Parker Buick Co. v. Touchy*, 788 S.W.2d 129, 130-31 (Tex. App.—Houston [1st Dist.] 1990, orig. proceeding). {❸❻ *State basis for objection, e.g., the request seeks information about defendant's net worth, and plaintiff has not made a claim for exemplary damages.*} {❸❼ *State any additional facts that support objection.*} {*See* ***O'Connor's Texas Rules***, *"Will not lead to admissible evidence," ch. 6-A, §19.1.1(3), p. 538.*}

OBJECTION: {❸❽ *Party*} objects to this discovery request because it seeks discovery of information that is not proportional to the needs of the case. *See* Tex. R. Civ. P. 192.4(b); *In re State Farm Lloyds*, 520 S.W.3d 595, 607 (Tex. 2017). {*See* ***O'Connor's Texas Rules***, *"Proportional," ch. 6-B, §2.1.1(2), p. 555; "Proportional," ch. 6-C, §6.1.2, p. 602.*} Specifically, the request is objectionable for the following reasons:

{*CHOOSE APPROPRIATE REASONS*}

a. The likely benefits of the requested discovery are minimal, and therefore any enhanced effort or expense in producing the information is undue. *See* Tex. R. Civ. P. 192.4(b); *In re State Farm*, 520 S.W.3d at 608. {❸❾ *Elaborate.*}

b. The requested discovery is not justified considering the needs of the case. *See* Tex. R. Civ. P. 192.4(b); *In re State Farm*, 520 S.W.3d at 608. {❹⓿ *Elaborate.*}

c. The requested discovery is not justified based on the amount in controversy. *See* Tex. R. Civ. P. 192.4(b); *In re State Farm*, 520 S.W.3d at 610. {❹❶ *Elaborate.*}

d. The requested discovery is not proportional to {42 *party*}'s resources. *See* Tex. R. Civ. P. 192.4(b); *In re State Farm*, 520 S.W.3d at 610-11. {43 *Explain how party's resources affect production, e.g., party does not have adequate resources to collect information and produce it in reasonably usable form.*}

e. The issues at stake are not of sufficient importance to justify the requested discovery. *See* Tex. R. Civ. P. 192.4(b); *In re State Farm*, 520 S.W.3d at 611. {44 *Elaborate.*}

f. The requested discovery is of low importance to resolving the issues in the case. *See* Tex. R. Civ. P. 192.4(b); *In re State Farm*, 520 S.W.3d at 611. {45 *Elaborate.*}

g. {46 *Identify any other reason that the requested discovery is not proportional to the needs of the case. See In re State Farm, 520 S.W.3d at 611-12.*}

OBJECTION: {47 *Party*} objects to this discovery request because it asks for a type of discovery not permitted by the rules of discovery. *See* Tex. R. Civ. P. 195.1; *In re Guzman*, 19 S.W.3d 522, 524-25 (Tex. App.—Corpus Christi 2000, orig. proceeding); *Moore v. Wood*, 809 S.W.2d 621, 623-24 (Tex. App.—Houston [1st Dist.] 1991, orig. proceeding). Specifically, the request is objectionable because {48 *state basis for objection, e.g., the request asks that plaintiff identify its testifying expert witness through an interrogatory answer*}. {49 *State any additional facts that support objection.*} {*See* ***O'Connor's Texas Rules****, "Not permissible form of discovery," ch. 6-A, §19.1.2, p. 539.*}

OBJECTION: {50 *Party*} objects to this discovery request because {51 *party*} and {52 *his/her/its*} attorney lack the information necessary to provide a response. *See* Tex. R. Civ. P. 193.1, 198.2(b). Specifically, the request is objectionable because {53 *party*} and {54 *his/her/its*} attorney have made a reasonable inquiry, but the information known or easily obtainable is insufficient to enable {55 *party*} to admit or deny the request. {56 *State any additional facts that support objection.*}

OBJECTION: {57 *Party*} objects to this discovery request because it seeks discovery of electronic information that is not reasonably available to {58 *party*} in the ordinary course of business. Tex. R. Civ. P. 196.4; *see In re State Farm Lloyds*, 520 S.W.3d 595, 600 (Tex. 2017); *In re Weekley Homes, L.P.*, 295 S.W.3d 309, 322 (Tex. 2009). Specifically, the requested information is not reasonably available, and thus the request is objectionable, because production of the information would be unduly {59 *burdensome/expensive/burdensome and expensive*}. *See* Tex. R. Civ. P. 192.4, 196.4; *In re State Farm*, 520 S.W.3d at 607; *In re Weekley Homes*, 295 S.W.3d at 322. {60 *State facts sup-*

Continued on next page

porting objection and show how production as requested would be unduly burdensome or expensive.} {*See **O'Connor's Texas Rules**, "Is electronic information reasonably available?," ch. 6-C, §6.2, p. 603.*}

OBJECTION: {61 *Party*} objects to this discovery request because it lacks specificity, and {62 *party*} has no means to identify the information requested. *Davis v. Pate*, 915 S.W.2d 76, 79 n.2 (Tex. App.—Corpus Christi 1996, orig. proceeding); *see* Tex. R. Civ. P. 196.1(b). Specifically, the request is objectionable because {63 *state basis for objection, e.g., the request seeks all evidence that supports plaintiff's allegations but does not identify any particular class or type of document*}. {64 *State any additional facts that support objection.*}

OBJECTION: {65 *Party*} objects to this discovery request because it exceeds the discovery permitted by the discovery-control plan. Tex. R. Civ. P. {66 *190.2(b)/190.3(b)*}. Specifically, the request is objectionable because {67 *state basis for objection, e.g., the request for interrogatories exceeds the 25-interrogatory limit of the Level 2 discovery-control plan*}. To the extent that {68 *party*} does not object to the discovery request, {69 *party*} serves the following answers: {70 *identify limit of compliance, e.g., defendant responds to the first 25 interrogatories but refuses to answer the rest*}. {*See **O'Connor's Texas Rules**, "Improper discovery request," ch. 6-A, §19.1.5(1), p. 539.*}

OBJECTION: {71 *Party*} objects to this discovery request because it seeks information previously produced. *See Sears, Roebuck & Co. v. Ramirez*, 824 S.W.2d 558, 559 (Tex. 1992). Specifically, the request is objectionable because {72 *state basis for objection, e.g., the request seeks defendant's tax returns to show net worth, and defendant has produced an audited, certified annual report*}. {73 *State any additional facts that support objection.*}

OBJECTION: {74 *Party*} objects to this discovery request because {75 *adverse party*}'s original pleading does not contain a specific statement of relief. *See* Tex. R. Civ. P. 47(c); *In re Greater McAllen Star Props., Inc.*, 444 S.W.3d 743, 750-51 (Tex. App.—Corpus Christi 2014, orig. proceeding). {76 *Elaborate.*} {77 *Adverse party*} cannot conduct discovery until {78 *he/she/it*} has filed an amended pleading that complies with Texas Rule of Civil Procedure 47. *See* Tex. R. Civ. P. 47; *In re Greater McAllen*, 444 S.W.3d at 750-51. {*See **O'Connor's Texas Rules**, "No specific statement of relief," ch. 6-A, §19.1.5(2), p. 539.*}

{*Continue until all discovery requests that party is objecting to have been identified.*}

SEE: Tex. R. Civ. P. 47, 190, 192, 193, 195, 196, 198
O'Connor's Texas Rules * Civil Trials (2019), "Types of Objections to Discovery," ch. 6-A, §19, p. 538

ADD: STYLE OF THE CASE – FORM 1B:2
SIGNATURE BLOCK – FORM 1B:3
CERTIFICATE OF SERVICE – FORM 1B:13

NOTE: The responding party's answers, objections, and other responses must be preceded by the request to which each applies. Tex. R. Civ. P. 193.1. For a motion for protection from discovery, see FORM 6A:10; for a motion for protection from a discovery subpoena, see FORM 6A:13; for claims of privilege, see FORMS 6A:19-22; for a motion to quash a deposition, see FORM 6F:2; for objections to interrogatories, see FORM 6G:3; for objections to requests for admissions, see FORM 6H:3; for objections to requests for production, see FORM 6I:3.

A party may object that a discovery request is unduly burdensome, harassing, or overbroad. See FORM 6A:10, ¶¶9-12.

The party must (1) object to the discovery request on or before the deadline to respond to it and (2) make a specific objection for each item it wishes to exclude from discovery. See ***O'Connor's Texas Rules***, "Making objections," ch. 6-A, §18.1, p. 533.

When a party amends its pleadings to include a specific statement of relief as required by Texas Rule of Civil Procedure 47(c), the time to respond to the discovery requests begins to run on the date the amended pleading is filed. ***In re Greater McAllen Star Props., Inc.***, 444 S.W.3d 743, 751 (Tex.App.—Corpus Christi 2014, orig. proceeding).

For most methods of service, the deadline for serving a request for discovery is 30 days before the end of the discovery period. See ***O'Connor's Texas Rules***, "Discovery Periods," ch. 6-A, §8, p. 523. But when service is by mail or fax, the request should be served at least 33 days (if mailed) or 31 days (if faxed after 5:00 p.m.) before the end of the discovery period. *See* Tex. R. Civ. P. 21a(b)(2), (c). Thus, a discovery request may need to provide at least 33 days to respond. See ***O'Connor's Texas Rules***, "Deadline to serve response," ch. 6-A, §14.1, p. 527.

For information to be discoverable, it must be both relevant and proportional to the needs of the case. *See* Tex. R. Civ. P. 192.3(a); ***In re State Farm Lloyds***, 520 S.W.3d 595, 607 (Tex.2017). The Court in ***In re State Farm*** set out factors for determining proportionality, which mirror the considerations under Texas Rule of Civil Procedure 192.4 for determining whether a discovery request is unduly burdensome. ***See In re State Farm***, 520 S.W.3d at 599-600. Although the Court discussed the proportionality guidelines in the context of electronic-discovery disputes, the Court emphasized that all discovery is subject to proportionality considerations. *Id.* at 599. See ***O'Connor's Texas Rules***, "Proportional," ch. 6-B, §2.1.1(2), p. 555; "Proportional," ch. 6-C, §6.1.2, p. 602.

{[1] *PARTY*}'S MOTION FOR PROTECTION FROM DISCOVERY

{[2] *Party*}, {[3] *name*}, asks the Court to protect {[4] *him/her/it*} from {[5] *adverse party*} {[6] *name*}'s request for {[7] *specify discovery from which protection is sought*}. {*See* ***O'Connor's Texas Rules****, "Motion for Protective Order," ch. 6-A, §20, p. 539.*}

INTRODUCTION

1. Plaintiff, {[8] *name*}, sued defendant, {[9] *name*}, for {[10] *state basis of suit*}.

2. Discovery in this suit is governed by a Level {[11] *1/2/3*} discovery-control plan. The discovery period {[12] *will end/ended*} on {[13] *date*}. {*See* ***O'Connor's Texas Rules****, "Discovery-Control Plans," ch. 6-A, §7, p. 520.*}

3. This case is set for trial on {[14] *date*}.

4. {[15] *State other relevant facts about the suit.*}

BACKGROUND

5. {[16] *Adverse party*} served the attached {[17] *identify type of discovery*}.

6. {[18] *State other facts relevant to the motion.*}

ARGUMENT & AUTHORITIES

7. A court has discretion to protect a party from discovery with a protective order. Tex. R. Civ. P. 192.6; *Axelson, Inc. v. McIlhany*, 798 S.W.2d 550, 553 (Tex. 1990). A court has the authority to limit the scope or distribution of discovery based on the needs and circumstances of the case. *See* Tex. R. Civ. P. 192 cmt. 7.

{*CHOOSE APPROPRIATE PARAGRAPHS 8-16*}

8. {[19] *Party*} asks the Court for a protective order because {[20] *adverse party*}'s discovery request is unreasonably cumulative or duplicative. Tex. R. Civ. P. 192.4(a); *see Brewer & Pritchard, P.C. v. Johnson*, 167 S.W.3d 460, 466 (Tex. App.—Houston [14th Dist.] 2005, pet. denied). {[21] *Elaborate.*} {*See* ***O'Connor's Texas Rules****, "Duplicative," ch. 6-A, §20.1.1(1), p. 540.*}

9. {[22] *Party*} asks the Court for a protective order because the information sought by {[23] *adverse party*}'s discovery request can be obtained from another source that is {[24] *more convenient/less burdensome/less expensive*}. Tex. R. Civ. P. 192.4(a); *In re Arras*, 24 S.W.3d 862, 864 (Tex. App.—El Paso 2000, orig. proceeding). {[25] *Elaborate.*} {*See* ***O'Connor's Texas Rules****, "Obtainable from alternative source," ch. 6-A, §20.1.1(2), p. 540.*}

10. {㉖ *Party*} asks the Court for a protective order because {㉗ *adverse party*}'s discovery request is not proportional to the needs of the case. *See* Tex. R. Civ. P. 192.4(b); *In re State Farm Lloyds*, 520 S.W.3d 595, 607 (Tex. 2017). {*See* ***O'Connor's Texas Rules****, "Proportional," ch. 6-B, §2.1.1(2), p. 555; "Proportional," ch. 6-C, §6.1.2, p. 602.*} Specifically, the request is not proportional for the following reasons:

{*CHOOSE APPROPRIATE REASONS*}

a. The likely benefits of the requested discovery are minimal, and therefore any enhanced effort or expense in producing the information is undue. *See* Tex. R. Civ. P. 192.4(b); *In re State Farm*, 520 S.W.3d at 608. {㉘ *Elaborate.*}

b. The requested discovery is not justified considering the needs of the case. *See* Tex. R. Civ. P. 192.4(b); *In re State Farm*, 520 S.W.3d at 608. {㉙ *Elaborate.*}

c. The requested discovery is not justified based on the amount in controversy. *See* Tex. R. Civ. P. 192.4(b); *In re State Farm*, 520 S.W.3d at 610. {㉚ *Elaborate.*}

d. The requested discovery is not proportional to {㉛ *party*}'s resources. *See* Tex. R. Civ. P. 192.4(b); *In re State Farm*, 520 S.W.3d at 610-11. {㉜ *Explain how party's resources affect production, e.g., party does not have adequate resources to collect information and produce it in reasonably usable form.*}

e. The issues at stake are not of sufficient importance to justify the requested discovery. *See* Tex. R. Civ. P. 192.4(b); *In re State Farm*, 520 S.W.3d at 611. {㉝ *Elaborate.*}

f. The requested discovery is of low importance to resolving the issues in the case. *See* Tex. R. Civ. P. 192.4(b); *In re State Farm*, 520 S.W.3d at 611. {㉞ *Elaborate.*}

g. {㉟ *Identify any other reason that the requested discovery is not proportional to the needs of the case. See In re State Farm, 520 S.W.3d at 611-12.*}

Continued on next page

11. {❸❻ *Party*} asks the Court for a protective order because {❸❼ *adverse party*}'s discovery request is harassing and annoying. Tex. R. Civ. P. 192.6(b). Specifically, {❸❽ *identify discovery request, e.g., plaintiff's request for production 9*} is harassing and annoying because {❸❾ *state basis for objection*}. {*See **O'Connor's Texas Rules**, "Harassing," ch. 6-A, §20.1.2, p. 540.*}

12. {❹⓿ *Party*} asks the Court for a protective order because {❹❶ *adverse party*}'s discovery request is overbroad. *See* Tex. R. Civ. P. 192 cmt. 1. A discovery request must be reasonably tailored to include only relevant matters. *In re Nat'l Lloyds Ins. Co.*, 507 S.W.3d 219, 223-24 (Tex. 2016); *In re Am. Optical Corp.*, 988 S.W.2d 711, 713 (Tex. 1998); *see In re Allstate Cty. Mut. Ins. Co.*, 227 S.W.3d 667, 669-70 (Tex. 2007). The Supreme Court has identified requests encompassing time periods, products, or activities as overbroad. *See, e.g., In re Ford Motor Co.*, 427 S.W.3d 396, 397 (Tex. 2014) (request to depose expert witnesses' corporate representatives on financial information for all cases their companies handled for defendant and other automobile manufacturers over 12-year period was overbroad); *In re Graco Children's Prods., Inc.*, 210 S.W.3d 598, 600-01 (Tex. 2006) (request for 20,000 pages of documents relating to defects in products that were not at issue in case was overbroad); *In re CSX Corp.*, 124 S.W.3d 149, 153 (Tex. 2003) (request to identify all safety employees of defendant over 30-year period was overbroad); *K Mart Corp. v. Sanderson*, 937 S.W.2d 429, 431 (Tex. 1996) (request for information about criminal conduct at location for seven years was overbroad). The request in this case is overbroad because {❹❷ *explain, e.g., it asks for "all documents relevant to the lawsuit"*}. The request should be limited to {❹❸ *specify suggested limits*}. {*See **O'Connor's Texas Rules**, "Overbroad," ch. 6-A, §20.1.3, p. 540.*}

13. {❹❹ *Party*} asks the Court for a protective order because {❹❺ *adverse party*}'s discovery request constitutes an invasion of {❹❻ *party*}'s {❹❼ *personal/constitutional/property*} rights. Tex. R. Civ. P. 192.6(b); *see Hoffman v. Fifth Court of Appeals*, 756 S.W.2d 723, 723 (Tex. 1988). Specifically, {❹❽ *identify discovery request, e.g., plaintiff's request for production number 9*} is objectionable because {❹❾ *identify right and why it will be violated without protective order*}.

14. {❺⓿ *Party*} asks the Court for a protective order to prevent the deposition of {❺❶ *name of corporate official*}, {❺❷ *identify corporate status, e.g., CEO*} of {❺❸ *name of corporation*}. {❺❹ *Adverse party*} has noticed {❺❺ *name of corporate official*} for a deposition, which is scheduled for {❺❻ *time*} on {❺❼ *date*}. Attached to this motion as Exhibit {❺❽ *letter*} is the affidavit of {❺❾ *name of corporate official*}, who states unequivocally that {❻⓿ *he/she*} has no personal knowledge of facts relevant to this lawsuit. {❻❶ *Adverse party*} seeks to depose {❻❷ *name of corporate official*} without showing

that the official has any unique or superior personal knowledge of discoverable information. *In re Alcatel USA, Inc.*, 11 S.W.3d 173, 176 (Tex. 2000); *Crown Cent. Petroleum Corp. v. Garcia*, 904 S.W.2d 125, 128 (Tex. 1995); *see In re BP Prods. N. Am., Inc.*, 244 S.W.3d 840, 842 n.2 (Tex. 2008). {63 *Adverse party*} has not made any attempt to secure the information {64 *he/she/it*} seeks through another, less intrusive discovery procedure. *In re Alcatel*, 11 S.W.3d at 176; *Crown Cent.*, 904 S.W.2d at 128. {*See **O'Connor's Texas Rules**, "To prevent apex deposition," ch. 6-F, §7.3, p. 645.*}

{*CHOOSE APPROPRIATE PARAGRAPH 15 IF APPLICABLE*}

{*If information is not reasonably available in requested form of production*}

15. {65 *Party*} asks the Court for a protective order because {66 *adverse party*} requests electronic information in {67 *a form/forms*} that {68 *is/are*} not reasonably available to {69 *party*} in the ordinary course of business. *See* Tex. R. Civ. P. 196.4; *In re State Farm Lloyds*, 520 S.W.3d 595, 600 (Tex. 2017); *In re Weekley Homes, L.P.*, 295 S.W.3d 309, 322 (Tex. 2009). Specifically, the requested information is not reasonably available because production of the information in {70 *identify requested form*} would be unduly {71 *burdensome/expensive/burdensome and expensive*}. *See* Tex. R. Civ. P. 192.4, 196.4; *In re State Farm*, 520 S.W.3d at 607; *In re Weekley Homes*, 295 S.W.3d at 322. {72 *State facts supporting objection and show how production as requested would be unduly burdensome or expensive.*} {73 *Party*} seeks to produce the information in a form that is {74 *reasonably available/as the information is ordinarily maintained*}. *See* Tex. R. Civ. P. 196.4. Specifically, {75 *party*} seeks to use {76 *specify form of production, e.g., Adobe Tagged Image File Format or Portable Document Format*}. {77 *State facts supporting party's identified form of production and show why that form should be ordered, e.g., the form is common and not specialized.*} {*See **O'Connor's Texas Rules**, "Is electronic information reasonably available?," ch. 6-C, §6.2, p. 603; "Object," ch. 6-C, §7.1.5(2)(b), p. 608.*}

{*If information itself is not reasonably available*}

15. {78 *Party*} asks the Court for a protective order because {79 *adverse party*} requests electronic information that is not reasonably available to {80 *party*} in the ordinary course of business. Tex. R. Civ. P. 196.4; *see In re State Farm Lloyds*, 520 S.W.3d 595, 600 (Tex. 2017); *In re Weekley Homes, L.P.*, 295 S.W.3d 309, 322 (Tex. 2009). Specifically, the requested information is not reasonably available because production of the information would be unduly {81 *burdensome/expensive/burdensome and expensive*}. *See* Tex. R. Civ. P. 192.4, 196.4; *In re State Farm*, 520 S.W.3d at 607; *In re Weekley Homes*, 295 S.W.3d at 322. {82 *State facts supporting objection and show how pro-*

Continued on next page

duction as requested would be unduly burdensome or expensive.} {*See* ***O'Connor's Texas Rules***, *"Is electronic information reasonably available?," ch. 6-C, §6.2, p. 603; "Object," ch. 6-C, §7.1.5(2)(b), p. 608.*}

{*If adverse party did not specify form of production*}

15. {83 *Party*} asks the Court for a protective order because {84 *adverse party*} requests electronic information but did not specify a form in which the information should be produced. Tex. R. Civ. P. 196.4. {85 *Party*} seeks to produce the information in a form that is {86 *reasonably available/as the information is ordinarily maintained*}. *See id.* Specifically, {87 *party*} seeks to use {88 *specify form of production, e.g., Adobe Tagged Image File Format or Portable Document Format*}. {89 *State facts supporting party's identified form of production and show why that form should be ordered, e.g., the form is common and not specialized.*}

16. {90 *Identify any other reason that information is exempt or protected from discovery, state facts supporting objection, and show how party will be unduly burdened by having to respond.*}

{*ADD FOLLOWING SECTION IF APPLICABLE*}

{91 *PARTIAL/NO*} COMPLIANCE

{*CHOOSE APPROPRIATE PARAGRAPH 17*}

17. {92 *Party*} refuses to provide some of the information requested by {93 *identify discovery request, e.g., interrogatory 3*} concerning {94 *identify request, e.g., criminal-activity reports for last 20 years for all of defendant's stores*}. However, {95 *party*} will provide the part of the information requested that is not subject to this motion. That is, {96 *party*} will provide {97 *identify limit of compliance, e.g., the criminal-activity reports for last five years for store where plaintiff was assaulted*}. {*See* ***O'Connor's Texas Rules***, *"Partial compliance necessary," ch. 6-A, §18.10.1, p. 538.*}

17. {98 *Party*} refuses to provide any of the information requested by {99 *identify discovery request, e.g., interrogatory 3*} concerning {100 *identify request, e.g., criminal-activity reports for last 20 years for all of defendant's stores*} because it is unreasonable to do so before obtaining a ruling on the motion. {101 *Explain why it is unreasonable, e.g., the request requires a search of thousands of records.*} If {102 *party*} partially complies with this discovery request now, and later the Court rules that {103 *party*} must provide all the information requested, {104 *party*} would be required to conduct a duplicative and burdensome search of records. {*See* ***O'Connor's Texas Rules***, *"No compliance necessary," ch. 6-A, §18.10.2, p. 538.*}

REQUESTED PROTECTION

18. A court has broad discretion to protect a person from discovery with a protective order. *See* Tex. R. Civ. P. 192.6(b). A court can (1) prohibit the discovery sought in whole or in part, (2) limit the extent or subject matter of discovery, (3) order that discovery not be undertaken at the time or place specified, (4) set terms or conditions on the discovery, (5) order the results of discovery to be sealed or otherwise protected, and (6) make any other order in the interest of justice. *Id.*

{*CHOOSE APPROPRIATE PARAGRAPHS 19-24*}

19. For the reasons described above, {105 *party*} asks the Court to sign a protective order that prohibits the discovery sought in {106 *whole/part*}.

20. For the reasons described above, {107 *party*} asks the Court to sign a protective order that limits the {108 *extent/subject matter*} of discovery. {109 *Specify the limits.*}

21. For the reasons described above, {110 *party*} asks the Court to sign a protective order that prohibits the discovery sought from being undertaken at the time and place specified. Instead, {111 *party*} asks the Court to set the discovery for {112 *specify new time and place*}.

22. For the reasons described above, {113 *party*} asks the Court to sign a protective order that {114 *limits the permissible methods of discovery/imposes certain terms and conditions on the discovery*}. {115 *Specify methods or terms and conditions.*}

23. For the reasons described above, {116 *party*} asks the Court to sign a protective order {117 *sealing/restricting the dissemination of and access to*} the results of the discovery sought. {118 *Elaborate.*}

24. For the reasons described above, {119 *party*} asks the Court to sign a protective order that {120 *add any other protection that is in the interest of justice*}.

CONCLUSION

25. {121 *Briefly summarize the motion.*}

PRAYER

26. For these reasons, {122 *party*} asks the Court to set this motion for protective order for hearing and, after the hearing, to issue an order protecting {123 *party*} from {124 *identify discovery from which protection is sought*} by granting the relief requested in this motion. {125 *Add if appropriate: Party refuses to comply with the part of the discovery request from which protection is sought until ordered to do so by the Court.*}

◄ *Continued on next page* ►

TEXAS CIVIL FORMS
CHAPTER 6. DISCOVERY
FORM 6A:10 MOTION FOR PROTECTION FROM DISCOVERY

SEE: Tex. R. Civ. P. 192.4, 192.6, 196.4, 199.4
O'Connor's Texas Rules * Civil Trials (2019), "Motion for Protective Order," ch. 6-A, §20, p. 539

ADD: STYLE OF THE CASE – FORM 1B:2
SIGNATURE BLOCK – FORM 1B:3
CERTIFICATE OF CONFERENCE – FORM 1B:12
CERTIFICATE OF SERVICE – FORM 1B:13

ATTACH: AFFIDAVIT – FORMS 1B:8 & 6A:15-18, if necessary
NOTICE OF HEARING OR SUBMISSION – FORM 1E:1
ORDER – FORM 6A:12
Copy of discovery request

NOTE: A person seeking a protective order must file the motion before the deadline to produce the requested discovery has passed. Tex. R. Civ. P. 192.6(a). A person should not seek a protective order when it is more appropriate to make an objection or claim of privilege, but a motion does not waive the objection or assertion of privilege. *Id.*

Once objections or claims of privilege have been served, the burden to secure a hearing on a discovery dispute is on the party seeking discovery. See ***O'Connor's Texas Rules***, "Burden to secure hearing & ruling," ch. 6-A, §18.6, p. 536.

A person can ask for temporary protection from discovery pending the resolution of threshold issues like venue, jurisdiction, forum non conveniens, and official immunity. ***In re Alford Chevrolet-Geo***, 997 S.W.2d 173, 181 (Tex.1999).

For information to be discoverable, it must be both relevant and proportional to the needs of the case. *See* Tex. R. Civ. P. 192.3(a); ***In re State Farm Lloyds***, 520 S.W.3d 595, 607 (Tex.2017). The Court in ***In re State Farm*** set out factors for determining proportionality, which mirror the considerations under Texas Rule of Civil Procedure 192.4 for determining whether a discovery request is unduly burdensome. *See* ***In re State Farm***, 520 S.W.3d at 599-600. Although the Court discussed the proportionality guidelines in the context of electronic-discovery disputes, the Court emphasized that all discovery is subject to proportionality considerations. *Id.* at 599. See ***O'Connor's Texas Rules***, "Proportional," ch. 6-B, §2.1.1(2), p. 555; "Proportional," ch. 6-C, §6.1.2, p. 602.

For general objections to discovery, see FORM 6A:9; for a motion for protection from a discovery subpoena, see FORM 6A:13; for claims of privilege, see FORMS 6A:19-22; for a motion to quash a deposition, see FORM 6F:2; for objections to interrogatories, see FORM 6G:3; for objections to requests for admissions, see FORM 6H:3; for objections to requests for production, see FORM 6I:3.

RESPONSE TO {❶ *ADVERSE PARTY*}'S
MOTION FOR PROTECTION FROM DISCOVERY

{❷ *{Party}/Intervenor*}, {❸ *name*}, asks the Court to deny {❹ *adverse party*} {❺ *name*}'s motion for a protective order because the motion seeks to {❻ *seal/restrict disclosure of*} documents that are considered "court records" as defined by Texas Rule of Civil Procedure 76a and thus {❼ *adverse party*} must meet the procedural and substantive requirements under Rule 76a to {❽ *seal/restrict disclosure of*} the records.

INTRODUCTION

1. Plaintiff, {❾ *name*}, sued defendant, {❿ *name*}, for {⓫ *state basis of suit*}.

{*ADD PARAGRAPH 2 IF APPLICABLE*}

2. Intervenor, {⓬ *name*}, is entitled to intervene in this suit as a matter of right. Tex. R. Civ. P. 76a(7); *Gen. Tire, Inc. v. Kepple*, 970 S.W.2d 520, 523 (Tex. 1998). {⓭ *Elaborate.*}

3. {⓮ *State other relevant facts about the suit.*}

BACKGROUND

4. On {⓯ *date*}, {⓰ *adverse party*} filed a motion for a protective order asking the Court to {⓱ *seal/restrict disclosure of*} the following documents: {⓲ *identify documents*}.

5. {⓳ *State other facts relevant to the response.*}

ARGUMENT & AUTHORITIES

6. Under Texas Rule of Civil Procedure 192.6(b)(5), a court may grant a protective order that seals or otherwise restricts the disclosure of documents produced through discovery. The court cannot, however, seal or restrict the disclosure of discovery without first complying with Rule 76a if the discovery is considered a "court record." *Gen. Tire, Inc. v. Kepple*, 970 S.W.2d 520, 524-25 (Tex. 1998) ("any restrictions on disclosure of … discovery must satisfy Rule 76a"). Before granting a protective order, the court must make a threshold determination whether the documents are court records when asked by a party or intervenor opposing the order. *Id.* at 525. {*See* ***O'Connor's Texas Rules****, "What Documents Are 'Court Records'," ch. 5-L, §2, p. 482; "Decision on court-records allegations," ch. 5-L, §8.3, p. 487.*} If the court finds that the documents are court records, the documents are presumed to be open to the general public and the party seeking to seal or restrict the disclosure of those records must meet the procedural and substantive requirements under Rule 76a. *See Kepple*, 970 S.W.2d at

Continued on next page

523; *Davenport v. Garcia*, 834 S.W.2d 4, 23-24 (Tex. 1992); *Upjohn Co. v. Freeman*, 906 S.W.2d 92, 96 (Tex. App.—Dallas 1995, no writ); *see, e.g., Clear Channel Commc'ns, Inc. v. United Servs. Auto. Ass'n*, 195 S.W.3d 129, 137 (Tex. App.—San Antonio 2006, no pet.) (court's protective order was reversed because it did not comply with procedural requirements under Rule 76a).

7. Under Rule 76a(2), court records include the following:

a. All documents of any nature filed in connection with any matter before any civil court. Tex. R. Civ. P. 76a(2)(a).

b. Unfiled settlement agreements that seek to restrict the disclosure of information concerning matters that have a probable adverse effect upon the general public health or safety, the administration of public office, or the operation of government. Tex. R. Civ. P. 76a(2)(b).

c. Unfiled discovery concerning matters that have a probable adverse effect upon the general public health or safety, the administration of public office, or the operation of government. Tex. R. Civ. P. 76a(2)(c).

{*CHOOSE APPROPRIATE PARAGRAPHS 8-10*}

8. {20 *Identify document*} is a court record under Rule 76a(2) because the document was filed with the court in connection with the matter. A document is filed when it is delivered or tendered to, or otherwise put under the custody or control of, the court clerk. *Jamar v. Patterson*, 868 S.W.2d 318, 319 (Tex. 1993). {21 *Add if applicable: This is true regardless of whether the document is file-stamped. Biffle v. Morton Rubber Indus., Inc., 785 S.W.2d 143, 144 (Tex. 1990).*} The documents were filed with court clerk when {22 *explain*}.

9. {23 *Identify document*} is a court record under Rule 76a(2) because the document is an unfiled settlement agreement that seeks to restrict the disclosure of information concerning matters that have a probable adverse effect on {24 *the general public health or safety/the administration of public office/the operation of government*}. The information in the unfiled settlement agreement concerns {25 *explain*}.

10. {26 *Identify document*} is a court record under Rule 76a(2) because the document is unfiled discovery concerning matters that have a probable adverse effect on {27 *the general public health or safety/the administration of public office/the operation of government*}. The unfiled discovery concerns {28 *explain*}.

CONCLUSION

11. {㉙ *Briefly summarize the response.*}

PRAYER

12. For these reasons, {㉚ *{party}/intervenor*} asks the Court to deny {㉛ *adverse party*}'s motion for a protective order.

SEE: Tex. R. Civ. P. 76a, 192.6(b)(5)
O'Connor's Texas Rules * Civil Trials (2019), "Motion to Seal Court Records," ch. 5-L, p. 482; "Motion for Protective Order," ch. 6-A, §20, p. 539

ADD: STYLE OF THE CASE – FORM 1B:2
SIGNATURE BLOCK – FORM 1B:3
CERTIFICATE OF SERVICE – FORM 1B:13

ATTACH: ORDER – FORM 6A:12

NOTE: The burden to prove that the documents are court records is on the party claiming the documents are open to the public (i.e., the party or intervenor opposing the protective order). ***Upjohn Co. v. Freeman***, 906 S.W.2d 92, 96 (Tex.App.—Dallas 1995, no writ).

If a party moves for a protective order, the party seeking discovery can file a motion to compel rather than a response to the motion for protective order. *See* ***Pace v. Jordan***, 999 S.W.2d 615, 622 (Tex. App.—Houston [1st Dist.] 1999, pet. denied). See FORM 6A:24.

ORDER ON {❶ *PARTY*}'S
MOTION FOR PROTECTION FROM DISCOVERY

After considering {❷ *party*} {❸ *name*}'s motion for protective order, the response, and arguments of counsel, the Court

{*CHOOSE APPROPRIATE ORDER*}

DENIES the motion and orders {❹ *party*} to comply with the discovery request.

GRANTS {❺ *party*}'s motion for protective order, finding that a protective order is necessary, and orders the following:

{*ADD APPROPRIATE RELIEF*}

a. The requested discovery of {❻ *identify discovery*} not be sought in {❼ *whole/part*}. {❽ *Elaborate.*}

b. The {❾ *extent/subject matter*} of discovery of {❿ *identify discovery*} be limited to {⓫ *specify the limits*}.

c. The discovery of {⓬ *identify discovery*} not be undertaken at the time or place specified. Instead, the discovery must be undertaken at {⓭ *specify time and place*}.

d. The discovery of {⓮ *identify discovery*} be undertaken only {⓯ *by the following method/on the following terms and conditions*}: {⓰ *specify methods or terms and conditions*}.

e. The discovery of {⓱ *identify discovery*} be {⓲ *sealed/{identify limits to distribution of discovery}*}.

f. {⓳ *Add any other protection that is in the interest of justice.*}

SIGNED on _______________, 20___.

____
PRESIDING JUDGE

SEE: Tex. R. Civ. P. 192.4, 192.6(b)
O'Connor's Texas Rules * Civil Trials (2019), "Order," ch. 6-A, §20.3, p. 541

ADD: STYLE OF THE CASE – FORM 1B:2
CERTIFICATE OF SERVICE – FORM 1B:13, if proposed order served separately from motion or response

{1 *{PARTY}'S/{NAME OF NONPARTY WITNESS}'S/{NAME OF AFFECTED NONPARTY}'S}*
MOTION FOR PROTECTION FROM DISCOVERY SUBPOENA

{2 *{Party}/{Name of nonparty witness}/{Name of affected nonparty}*} asks the Court for protection from {3 *adverse party*} {4 *name*}'s discovery subpoena that was served on a person who is not a party to this suit. {*See **O'Connor's Texas Rules**, "Motion for Protective Order," ch. 6-A, §20, p. 539.*}

INTRODUCTION

1. Plaintiff, {5 *name*}, sued defendant, {6 *name*}, for {7 *state basis of suit*}.

{*ADD PARAGRAPH 2 IF APPROPRIATE*}

2. {8 *Name of nonparty witness/name of affected nonparty*} is not a party to this suit. {9 *Describe nonparty witness's or affected nonparty's relationship to the suit.*}

3. Discovery in this suit is governed by a Level {10 *1/2/3*} discovery-control plan. The discovery period {11 *will end/ended*} on {12 *date*}. {*See **O'Connor's Texas Rules**, "Discovery-Control Plans," ch. 6-A, §7, p. 520.*}

4. This case is set for trial on {13 *date*}.

5. {14 *State other relevant facts about the suit.*}

BACKGROUND

6. {15 *Adverse party*} served the attached discovery subpoena on {16 *name of nonparty witness*}, seeking {17 *identify what adverse party seeks*}.

7. In the notice of subpoena, {18 *adverse party*} requests that {19 *name of nonparty witness*} comply with the subpoena on or before {20 *date*}. {21 *{Party}/{Name of nonparty witness}/{Name of affected nonparty}*} timely files this motion for protective order before the date of requested compliance.

8. {22 *State other facts relevant to the motion.*}

ARGUMENT & AUTHORITIES

9. A court may issue an order protecting a person served with or affected by a discovery subpoena from undue burden, unnecessary expense, harassment, annoyance, or invasion of personal, constitutional, or property rights. Tex. R. Civ. P. 192.6(b); *see* Tex. R. Civ. P. 176.6(e). A court has the authority to limit the scope of discovery based on the needs and circumstances of the case. Tex. R. Civ. P. 192 cmt. 7.

Continued on next page

{*CHOOSE APPROPRIATE PARAGRAPHS 10-24*}

10. The Court should issue a protective order because the subpoena was not dated and signed by a person authorized under Texas Rule of Civil Procedure 176.4 to issue subpoenas. Tex. R. Civ. P. 176.1(c), (h). {23 *Elaborate.*} {*See* ***O'Connor's Texas Rules****, "To challenge procedural defect," ch. 1-L, §4.3.1(1)(a), p. 106.*}

11. The Court should issue a protective order because the subpoena was not served by a sheriff, constable, or other person authorized by law. Tex. R. Civ. P. 176.5. {24 *Elaborate.*} {*See* ***O'Connor's Texas Rules****, "To challenge procedural defect," ch. 1-L, §4.3.1(1)(a), p. 106.*}

12. The Court should issue a protective order because the subpoena did not have a witness fee attached. Tex. Civ. Prac. & Rem. Code §22.001; Tex. R. Civ. P. 176.8(b); *Kieffer v. Miller*, 560 S.W.2d 431, 432 (Tex. App.—Beaumont 1977, writ ref'd n.r.e.). {25 *Elaborate.*} {*See* ***O'Connor's Texas Rules****, "To challenge procedural defect," ch. 1-L, §4.3.1(1)(a), p. 106.*}

13. The Court should issue a protective order because only one subpoena was issued for two or more witnesses. *See* Tex. R. Civ. P. 176.1(d). {26 *Elaborate.*} {*See* ***O'Connor's Texas Rules****, "To challenge procedural defect," ch. 1-L, §4.3.1(1)(a), p. 106.*}

14. The Court should issue a protective order because {27 *name of nonparty witness*} was served with a subpoena to appear in a county more than 150 miles from both the place where {28 *he/she*} was served with the subpoena and the place where {29 *he/she*} resides. Tex. R. Civ. P. 176.3(a). The subpoena was served at {30 *place*}; {31 *name of nonparty witness*} resides at {32 *place*}; the subpoena requires {33 *name of nonparty witness*} to appear at {34 *place*}. {*See* ***O'Connor's Texas Rules****, "TRCP 176.3," ch. 1-L, §3.2.1, p. 104.*}

15. The Court should issue a protective order because {35 *adverse party*} did not provide sufficient notice before serving the subpoena on {36 *name of nonparty witness*}. *See* Tex. R. Civ. P. 205.2. {37 *Elaborate.*} {*See* ***O'Connor's Texas Rules****, "Nonparty documents without deposition," ch. 6-I, §5.3.1, p. 686.*}

16. The Court should issue a protective order because the request for documents in {38 *adverse party*}'s subpoena is unreasonably cumulative and duplicative. Tex. R. Civ. P. 192.4(a). {39 *Elaborate.*} {*See* ***O'Connor's Texas Rules****, "Duplicative," ch. 6-A, §20.1.1(1), p. 540.*}

17. The Court should issue a protective order because the information requested by {40 *adverse party*}'s subpoena is obtainable from another source that is {41 *more convenient/less burdensome/less expensive*}. Tex. R. Civ. P. 192.4(a); *In re Arras*, 24 S.W.3d 862, 864 (Tex. App.—El Paso 2000, orig. proceeding). {42 *Elaborate.*} {*See **O'Connor's Texas Rules**, "Obtainable from alternative source," ch. 6-A, §20.1.1(2), p. 540.*}

18. The Court should issue a protective order because the request for information in {43 *adverse party*}'s subpoena is not proportional to the needs of the case. *See* Tex. R. Civ. P. 192.4(b); *In re State Farm Lloyds*, 520 S.W.3d 595, 607 (Tex. 2017). {*See **O'Connor's Texas Rules**, "Proportional," ch. 6-B, §2.1.1(2), p. 555; "Proportional," ch. 6-C, §6.1.2, p. 602.*} Specifically, the request is not proportional for the following reasons:

{*CHOOSE APPROPRIATE REASONS*}

a. The likely benefits of the requested discovery are minimal, and therefore any enhanced effort or expense in producing the information is undue. *See* Tex. R. Civ. P. 192.4(b); *In re State Farm*, 520 S.W.3d at 608. {44 *Elaborate.*}

b. The requested discovery is not justified considering the needs of the case. *See* Tex. R. Civ. P. 192.4(b); *In re State Farm*, 520 S.W.3d at 608. {45 *Elaborate.*}

c. The requested discovery is not justified based on the amount in controversy. *See* Tex. R. Civ. P. 192.4(b); *In re State Farm*, 520 S.W.3d at 610. {46 *Elaborate.*}

d. The requested discovery is not proportional to {47 *party*}'s resources. *See* Tex. R. Civ. P. 192.4(b); *In re State Farm*, 520 S.W.3d at 610-11. {48 *Explain how party's resources affect production, e.g., party does not have adequate resources to collect information and produce it in reasonably usable form.*}

e. The issues at stake are not of sufficient importance to justify the requested discovery. *See* Tex. R. Civ. P. 192.4(b); *In re State Farm*, 520 S.W.3d at 611. {49 *Elaborate.*}

f. The requested discovery is of low importance to resolving the issues in the case. *See* Tex. R. Civ. P. 192.4(b); *In re State Farm*, 520 S.W.3d at 611. {50 *Elaborate.*}

Continued on next page

g. {51 *Identify any other reason that the requested discovery is not proportional to the needs of the case. See In re State Farm, 520 S.W.3d at 611-12.*}

19. The Court should issue a protective order because the request for information in {52 *adverse party*}'s subpoena is harassing and annoying. Tex. R. Civ. P. 192.6(b). Specifically, the subpoena is harassing and annoying because {53 *state basis for objection*}. {*See* ***O'Connor's Texas Rules****, "Harassing," ch. 6-A, §20.1.2, p. 540.*}

20. The Court should issue a protective order because the request for documents in {54 *adverse party*}'s subpoena is overbroad. A discovery request must be reasonably tailored to include only relevant matters. *In re Am. Optical Corp.*, 988 S.W.2d 711, 713 (Tex. 1998). The Supreme Court has identified requests encompassing time periods, products, or activities as overbroad. *See, e.g., In re Graco Children's Prods., Inc.*, 210 S.W.3d 598, 600-01 (Tex. 2006) (request for 20,000 pages of documents relating to defects in products that were not at issue in case was overbroad); *In re CSX Corp.*, 124 S.W.3d 149, 153 (Tex. 2003) (request to identify all safety employees of defendant over 30-year period was overbroad); *In re Am. Optical*, 988 S.W.2d at 713 (request for almost every document relating to asbestos products that defendant produced over 50-year period was overbroad); *K Mart Corp. v. Sanderson*, 937 S.W.2d 429, 431 (Tex. 1996) (request for information about criminal conduct at location for seven years was overbroad). In this case, the subpoena requesting production of {55 *identify documents requested*} is objectionable because {56 *state basis for objection, e.g., it asks for "all documents relevant to the lawsuit"*}. Discovery should be limited to {57 *specify suggested limits*}. {*See* ***O'Connor's Texas Rules****, "Overbroad," ch. 6-A, §20.1.3, p. 540.*}

21. The Court should issue a protective order because the request for documents in {58 *adverse party*}'s subpoena served on {59 *name of nonparty witness*} constitutes an invasion of {60 *personal/constitutional/property*} rights. Tex. R. Civ. P. 192.6(b); *see Hoffman v. Fifth Court of Appeals*, 756 S.W.2d 723, 723 (Tex. 1988). Specifically, {61 *identify specific discovery request, e.g., request for production 9*} is objectionable because {62 *identify right and why it will be violated without protective order*}. {63 *Elaborate.*}

22. The Court should issue a protective order to prevent the deposition of {64 *name of nonparty witness who is a corporate official*}, {65 *identify corporate status, e.g., CEO*} of {66 *name of corporation*}. {67 *Adverse party*} has subpoenaed {68 *name of nonparty witness*} to appear for a deposition, which is scheduled for {69 *time*} on {70 *date*}. Attached to this motion as Exhibit {71 *letter*} is the affidavit of {72 *name of nonparty witness*}, who states unequivocally that {73 *he/she*} has no personal knowledge of facts relevant to this lawsuit. {74 *Adverse party*} seeks to depose {75 *name of*

nonparty witness} without showing that {76 *he/she*} has any unique or superior personal knowledge of discoverable information. *In re Alcatel USA, Inc.*, 11 S.W.3d 173, 176 (Tex. 2000); *Crown Cent. Petroleum Corp. v. Garcia*, 904 S.W.2d 125, 128 (Tex. 1995). {77 *Adverse party*} has not made any attempt to secure the information {78 *he/she/it*} seeks from another, less intrusive discovery procedure. *In re Alcatel*, 11 S.W.3d at 176; *Crown Cent.*, 904 S.W.2d at 128. {*See* ***O'Connor's Texas Rules***, *"To prevent apex deposition," ch. 6-F, §7.3, p. 645.*}

23. The Court should issue a protective order to {79 *prevent/limit*} the deposition of {80 *name of nonparty witness*}, who will be asked to testify about {81 *identify topic of deposition*}, a matter that is privileged as to {82 *{party}/{name of nonparty witness}/{name of affected nonparty}*}. {83 *Adverse party*} has subpoenaed {84 *name of nonparty witness*} to appear for a deposition, which is scheduled for {85 *time*} on {86 *date*}. Attached to this motion as Exhibit {87 *letter*} is the affidavit of {88 *name of nonparty witness*}, who states unequivocally that the only information {89 *he/she*} has about {90 *subject matter*} is privileged information relating to {91 *{party}/{name of nonparty witness}/{name of affected nonparty}*}. {92 *Elaborate.*} {*See* ***O'Connor's Texas Rules***, *"To cancel or limit because of privilege," ch. 6-F, §7.2, p. 645.*}

24. {93 *{Party}/{Name of nonparty witness}/{Name of affected nonparty}*} makes this withholding statement to notify {94 *adverse party*} that information or material responsive to the subpoena requesting production of {95 *identify documents or other tangible items sought*} is withheld under a claim of {96 *identify privilege*}. Tex. R. Civ. P. 193.3(a). {*See* ***O'Connor's Texas Rules***, *"Asserting privileges," ch. 1-L, §4.3.2, p. 107; "Withholding statement," ch. 6-A, §2.8, p. 516.*}

{*ADD FOLLOWING SECTION IF APPLICABLE*}

{97 *PARTIAL/NO*} COMPLIANCE

{*CHOOSE APPROPRIATE PARAGRAPH 25*}

25. {98 *Name of nonparty witness*} refuses to provide some of the information requested in the discovery subpoena concerning {99 *identify request for documents, e.g., criminal-activity reports for last 20 years for all of defendant's stores*}. However, {100 *name of nonparty witness*} will provide the part of the information requested that is not subject to this objection. That is, {101 *name of nonparty witness*} will provide {102 *identify limit of compliance, e.g., the criminal-activity reports for last five years for store where plaintiff was assaulted*}. {*See* ***O'Connor's Texas Rules***, *"Partial compliance necessary," ch. 6-A, §18.10.1, p. 538.*}

Continued on next page

25. {103 *Name of nonparty witness*} refuses to provide any of the information requested in the discovery subpoena concerning {104 *identify request for documents, e.g., criminal-activity reports for last 20 years for all of defendant's stores*} because it is unreasonable to do so before obtaining a ruling on the motion. {105 *Explain why it is unreasonable, e.g., the request requires a search of thousands of records.*} If {106 *name of nonparty witness*} partially complies with this discovery request now, and later the Court rules that {107 *name of nonparty witness*} must provide all the information requested, {108 *name of nonparty witness*} would be required to conduct a duplicative and burdensome search of records. {*See* ***O'Connor's Texas Rules****, "No compliance necessary," ch. 6-A, §18.10.2, p. 538.*}

{*ADD FOLLOWING SECTION IF APPLICABLE*}

COST OF COMPLIANCE

26. If this Court rules that {109 *name of nonparty witness*} must comply with the subpoena and produce documents to which objections have been raised regarding the expense of production, {110 *name of nonparty witness*} asks the Court to require {111 *adverse party*} to compensate {112 *him/her/it*} for the costs of production and for undue hardship. Tex. R. Civ. P. 176.7. {113 *Name of nonparty witness*} estimates the costs of production will be at least ${114 *amount*} and compliance with the subpoena will deprive {115 *him/her/it*} of income in the amount of ${116 *amount*}.

CONCLUSION

27. {117 *Briefly summarize the motion.*}

PRAYER

{*CHOOSE APPROPRIATE PARAGRAPH 28*}

28. For these reasons, {118 *name of nonparty witness*} refuses to comply with the part of the subpoena from which protection is sought until ordered to do so by the Court.

28. For these reasons, {119 *{party}/{name of affected nonparty}*} asks the Court to set this motion for protective order for hearing and, after the hearing, to issue an order protecting {120 *{party}/{name of affected nonparty}*} from {121 *identify discovery from which protection is sought*} by granting the relief requested in this motion.

FORM 6A:13 MOTION FOR PROTECTION FROM DISCOVERY SUBPOENA

SEE: Tex. R. Civ. P. 176, 192.4, 192.6
O'Connor's Texas Rules * Civil Trials (2019), "Subpoenas," ch. 1-L, p. 103; "Motion for Protective Order," ch. 6-A, §20, p. 539; "Challenging nonparty discovery subpoena," ch. 6-I, §5.5, p. 687

ADD: STYLE OF THE CASE – FORM 1B:2
SIGNATURE BLOCK – FORM 1B:3
CERTIFICATE OF CONFERENCE – FORM 1B:12
CERTIFICATE OF SERVICE – FORM 1B:13

ATTACH: AFFIDAVIT – FORMS 1B:8 & 6A:15-18, if necessary
NOTICE OF HEARING OR SUBMISSION – FORM 1E:1
ORDER – FORM 6A:14
Copy of subpoena

NOTE: A subpoenaed person, a party, or any person affected by the discovery subpoena may file a motion for protective order under Texas Rule of Civil Procedure 192.6. Tex. R. Civ. P. 176.6(e). The person from whom discovery is sought and any other person affected by the discovery request each have an independent right to challenge the subpoena—that is, one person's challenge to the subpoena will not affect another person's right to bring her own challenge. *See id.*; *see, e.g.*, ***In re Garza***, 544 S.W.3d 836, 841-42 (Tex.2018) (nonparty records custodians were permitted to seek protection from discovery subpoena even though P had already sought and been denied protection from same request).

The motion must be filed before the time specified for compliance and in the court where the action is pending or in a district court in the county where the subpoena was served. Tex. R. Civ. P. 176.6(e).

A nonparty who has been subpoenaed is not required to challenge the subpoena with a motion for protective order; the nonparty may simply file objections to the subpoena. See ***O'Connor's Texas Rules***, "Person subject to subpoena," ch. 1-L, §4.1.1, p. 106; "Types of challenges," ch. 1-L, §4.3, p. 106.

For information to be discoverable, it must be both relevant and proportional to the needs of the case. *See* Tex. R. Civ. P. 192.3(a); ***In re State Farm Lloyds***, 520 S.W.3d 595, 607 (Tex.2017). The Court in ***In re State Farm*** set out factors for determining proportionality, which mirror the considerations under Texas Rule of Civil Procedure 192.4 for determining whether a discovery request is unduly burdensome. *See* ***In re State Farm***, 520 S.W.3d at 599-600. Although the Court discussed the proportionality guidelines in the context of electronic-discovery disputes, the Court emphasized that all discovery is subject to proportionality considerations. *Id.* at 599. See ***O'Connor's Texas Rules***, "Proportional," ch. 6-B, §2.1.1(2), p. 555; "Proportional," ch. 6-C, §6.1.2, p. 602.

For general objections to discovery, see FORM 6A:9; for a motion for protection from discovery, see FORM 6A:10; for claims of privilege, see FORMS 6A:19-22; for a motion to quash a deposition, see FORM 6F:2; for objections to interrogatories, see FORM 6G:3; for objections to requests for admissions, see FORM 6H:3; for objections to requests for production, see FORM 6I:3.

ORDER ON {[1] *{PARTY}/{NAME OF NONPARTY WITNESS}/{NAME OF AFFECTED NONPARTY}*}'S
MOTION FOR PROTECTION FROM DISCOVERY SUBPOENA

After considering {[2] *{party}/{name of nonparty witness}/{name of affected nonparty}*}'s motion for protective order from a discovery subpoena, the response, and arguments of counsel, the Court

{*CHOOSE APPROPRIATE ORDER*}

DENIES the motion and orders {[3] *name of nonparty witness*} to comply with the discovery subpoena.

GRANTS the motion and orders the following:

{*ADD APPROPRIATE RELIEF*}

a. The requested discovery of {[4] *identify discovery*} not be sought in {[5] *whole/part*}. {[6] *Elaborate.*}

b. The {[7] *extent/subject matter*} of discovery of {[8] *identify discovery*} be limited to {[9] *specify the limits*}.

c. The documents sought not be produced at the time or place specified in the subpoena. Instead, the documents must be produced at {[10] *specify time and place*}.

d. The documents sought must be produced only {[11] *by the following method/on the following terms and conditions*}: {[12] *specify methods or terms and conditions*}.

e. The discovery of {[13] *identify discovery*} be {[14] *sealed/{identify limits to distribution of discovery}*}.

f. {[15] *Adverse party*} must compensate {[16] *name of nonparty witness*} in the amount of ${[17] *amount*} for the cost for producing the documents, as authorized by Texas Rule of Civil Procedure 176.7.

g. {[18] *Adverse party*} must compensate {[19] *name of nonparty witness*} {[20] *in the amount/at the rate*} of ${[21] *amount/amount per hour*} for {[22] *his/her/its*} undue hardship in complying with the subpoena.

h. {[23] *Add any other condition that is in the interest of justice.*}

SIGNED on _______________, 20___.

____
PRESIDING JUDGE

SEE: Tex. R. Civ. P. 176, 192.6
O'Connor's Texas Rules * Civil Trials (2019), "Subpoenas," ch. 1-L, p. 103; "Order," ch. 6-A, §20.3, p. 541; "Challenging nonparty discovery subpoena," ch. 6-I, §5.5, p. 687

ADD: STYLE OF THE CASE – FORM 1B:2
CERTIFICATE OF SERVICE – FORM 1B:13, if proposed order served separately from motion or response

☆

AFFIDAVIT OF {❶ *NAME*}

STATE OF TEXAS §
{❷ _______} COUNTY §

Before me, the undersigned notary, on this day personally appeared {❸ *name of affiant*}, the affiant, whose identity is known to me. After I administered an oath, affiant testified as follows:

1. "My name is {❹ *name of affiant*}, and I am {❺ *identify affiant's relationship to case, e.g., the defendant's attorney in this case*}. I am over 18 years of age, of sound mind, and capable of making this affidavit. The facts stated in this affidavit are within my personal knowledge and are true and correct.

2. "Plaintiff filed this suit on {❻ *date*}. {❼ *State facts to establish that the materials were prepared in anticipation of litigation, e.g., I prepared the attached handwritten notes during a conversation with defendant about the suit, which occurred after the suit was filed.*}

3. "{❽ *State facts to establish that the materials contain mental processes, conclusions, legal theories, etc., prepared by an attorney or at the direction of an attorney, e.g., I made these notes to prepare for the trial of this case.*}"

____
{❾ *Name of affiant*}

Sworn to and subscribed before me by {❿ *name of affiant*} on __________, 20___.

____
Notary Public in and for
the State of Texas

FORM 6A:15 AFFIDAVIT – WORK-PRODUCT PRIVILEGE

SEE: Tex. R. Civ. P. 192.5(a)
O'Connor's Texas Rules * Civil Trials (2019), "Affidavits," ch. 6-A, §18.7.1(1), p. 536; "Work-product privilege," ch. 6-B, §3.3, p. 569

ADD: STYLE OF THE CASE – FORM 1B:2

ATTACH: Motions resisting discovery and responses

NOTE: The work-product privilege includes the former party-communications privilege. *See* Tex. R. Civ. P. 192.5(a)(2). It is not necessary to assert a privilege in a withholding statement for materials created by or for attorneys for the litigation. Tex. R. Civ. P. 193.3(c). It is assumed such material will be withheld from virtually any request on the grounds of attorney-client or work-product privilege. Tex. R. Civ. P. 193 cmt. 3. The work-product privilege does not exempt from discovery the following: witness statements, potential parties, fact and testifying expert witnesses, photographs, trial exhibits ordered disclosed, material sought under the "need-and-hardship" exception, or matters listed in Texas Rule of Evidence 503(d) (crime, fraud, and other exceptions). Tex. R. Civ. P. 192.5(b), (c).

See notes under FORM 1B:8.

AFFIDAVIT OF {❶ *NAME*}

STATE OF TEXAS §
{❷ ______} COUNTY §

Before me, the undersigned notary, on this day personally appeared {❸ *name of affiant*}, the affiant, whose identity is known to me. After I administered an oath, affiant testified as follows:

1. "My name is {❹ *name of affiant*}, and I am {❺ *identify affiant's relationship to case, e.g., the defendant, the defendant corporation's CEO*}. I am over 18 years of age, of sound mind, and capable of making this affidavit. The facts stated in this affidavit are within my personal knowledge and are true and correct.

2. "On {❻ *date*}, {❼ *describe circumstances surrounding attorney-client communication, e.g., I sought legal services from Ms. Smith and received legal advice from her*}. {❽ *State facts surrounding the confidential communication, e.g., the services I sought and the advice I received are documented in my attached handwritten notes.*}

3. "The communications documented in the attached {❾ *describe document, e.g., handwritten notes*} were made for the purpose of facilitating the rendition of professional legal services for {❿ *myself/{party}*}. These communications were not intended to be disclosed, nor were they disclosed, to third persons other than those to whom disclosure was made in furtherance of the rendition of professional legal services for {⓫ *myself/{party}*}. Further, these communications were not intended to be disclosed, nor were they disclosed, to third persons other than those reasonably necessary for the transmission of the communication."

____
{⓬ *Name of affiant*}

Sworn to and subscribed before me by {⓭ *name of affiant*} on __________, 20___.

____
Notary Public in and for
the State of Texas

Form 6A:16 Affidavit – Attorney-Client Privilege

SEE: Tex. R. Civ. P. 193.3(c)
Tex. R. Evid. 503
O'Connor's Texas Rules * Civil Trials (2019), "Affidavits," ch. 6-A, §18.7.1(1), p. 536; "Attorney-client privilege," ch. 6-B, §3.4, p. 572

ADD: STYLE OF THE CASE – FORM 1B:2

ATTACH: Motions resisting discovery and responses
Notes or other documentation of the privileged communication

NOTE: It is not necessary to assert a privilege in a withholding statement for materials created by or for attorneys for the litigation. Tex. R. Civ. P. 193.3(c). It is assumed such material will be withheld from virtually any request on the grounds of attorney-client or work-product privilege. Tex. R. Civ. P. 193 cmt. 3.

See notes under FORM 1B:8.

AFFIDAVIT OF {❶ *NAME*}

STATE OF TEXAS §
{❷ _______} COUNTY §

Before me, the undersigned notary, on this day personally appeared {❸ *name of affiant*}, the affiant, whose identity is known to me. After I administered an oath, affiant testified as follows:

1. "My name is {❹ *name of affiant*}, and I am {❺ *identify affiant's relationship to case, e.g., a design engineer for the defendant in this case*}. I am over 18 years of age, of sound mind, and capable of making this affidavit. The facts stated in this affidavit are within my personal knowledge and are true and correct.

2. "I have reviewed {❻ *describe pleadings reviewed, e.g., plaintiff's original petition alleging that plaintiff was injured while operating defendant's bulldozer*}.

3. "I have reviewed {❼ *describe discovery reviewed, e.g., plaintiff's request for production to defendant and defendant's objections and responses to that request for production*}.

4. "{❽ *Describe discovery request, e.g., request for production 25 seeks blueprints, drawings, and other documents that refer to the design of the product.*}

5. "{❾ *Describe burdensome nature of request, e.g., the bulldozer consists of nearly 2,000 component parts. There are at least that many drawings associated with the bulldozer. Some of the component parts, such as nuts and bolts, are common to other products.*}

6. "{❿ *Describe burden of responding to request, e.g., the approximately 2,000 drawings associated with the bulldozer are not stored together in one location. Rather, the drawings pertaining to common component parts, such as the nuts and bolts, are in the custody of several sections or design groups who initially designed the particular component part. Our company does not employ a person whose responsibility includes the maintenance and custody of every drawing associated with every product. I estimate that at least four design engineers will be required to spend 100 hours each to identify the section or design group that initially designed each of the component parts and to locate the responsive drawings.*}

7. "The request for discovery is unduly burdensome because {⓫ *explain why request is unduly burdensome, not just burdensome*}."

____
{⓬ *Name of affiant*}

Sworn to and subscribed before me by {⓭ *name of affiant*} on _________, 20___.

____
Notary Public in and for
the State of Texas

SEE: Tex. R. Civ. P. 192.4
O'Connor's Texas Rules * Civil Trials **(2019), "Affidavits," ch. 6-A, §18.7.1(1), p. 536; "Undue burden," ch. 6-A, §20.1.1, p. 540**

ADD: STYLE OF THE CASE – FORM 1B:2

ATTACH: Motions resisting discovery and responses

NOTE: See notes under FORM 1B:8.

AFFIDAVIT OF {[1] *NAME*}

STATE OF TEXAS §
{[2] _______} COUNTY §

Before me, the undersigned notary, on this day personally appeared {[3] *name of affiant*}, the affiant, whose identity is known to me. After I administered an oath, affiant testified as follows:

1. "My name is {[4] *name of affiant*}, and I am {[5] *identify corporate status, e.g., CEO*} of {[6] *name of corporation*}. I am over 18 years of age, of sound mind, and capable of making this affidavit. The facts stated in this affidavit are within my personal knowledge and are true and correct.

2. "I have been {[7] *noticed/subpoenaed*} to appear for a deposition on {[8] *date*}, at {[9] *time*}, at {[10] *address*}, to testify about {[11] *state subject of deposition*}.

3. "{[12] *Adverse party*} has not made any attempt to secure the information {[13] *he/she/it*} seeks from another, less intrusive discovery procedure. The deposition will cause a serious inconvenience and hardship because {[14] *explain*}.

4. "I have no personal knowledge of facts relevant to {[15] *this lawsuit/the matter subject to the deposition*}. As an executive for {[16] *name of corporation*}, I do not supervise or control the activity related to {[17] *identify area about which deposition will be taken*}. That matter is delegated to {[18] *name of another corporate official*}, who can testify about the matter.

5. "I have no unique or superior personal knowledge of discoverable information relating to this lawsuit.

6. "{[19] *Include other reasons to avoid apex deposition.*}"

____
{[20] *Name of affiant*}

Sworn to and subscribed before me by {[21] *name of affiant*} on __________, 20___.

____
Notary Public in and for
the State of Texas

FORM 6A:18 AFFIDAVIT – APEX DEPOSITION

SEE: Tex. R. Civ. P. 192.6
O'Connor's Texas Rules * Civil Trials (2019), "Affidavits," ch. 6-A, §18.7.1(1), p. 536; "To prevent apex deposition," ch. 6-F, §7.3, p. 645

ADD: STYLE OF THE CASE – FORM 1B:2

ATTACH: Motions resisting discovery and responses

NOTE: To prevent an apex deposition, the corporation must file a motion for protective order or a motion to quash accompanied by the official's affidavit denying any personal knowledge of relevant facts. ***See In re Alcatel USA, Inc.***, 11 S.W.3d 173, 175 (Tex.2000). See FORMS 6A:10, 13, 6F:2. The "apex doctrine" allows corporate officials to potentially avoid unduly burdensome depositions based on their position in the company. ***In re Miscavige***, 436 S.W.3d 430, 435 (Tex.App.—Austin 2014, orig. proceeding). See ***O'Connor's Texas Rules***, "Application," ch. 6-F, §7.3.1, p. 645.

See notes under FORM 1B:8.

FORM 6A:19 WITHHOLDING STATEMENT

{❶ *PARTY*}'S WITHHOLDING STATEMENT

To: {❷ *Adverse party*}, {❸ *name*}, through {❹ *his/her/its*} attorney of record, {❺ *name*}, {❻ *address*}.

{❼ *Party*}, {❽ *name*}, timely serves the following withholding statement in response to {❾ *adverse party*}'s {❿ *identify discovery request, e.g., interrogatories*}.

1. {⓫ *Identify discovery request, e.g., INTERROGATORY 1*}: {⓬ *Restate discovery request.*}

WITHHOLDING STATEMENT: Information or material responsive to this request is withheld under a claim of {⓭ *identify privilege*}.

{*Continue until all withholding statements are asserted.*}

SEE: Tex. R. Civ. P. 193.3(a)
O'Connor's Texas Rules * Civil Trials (2019), "Withholding statement," ch. 6-A, §2.8, p. 516

ADD: STYLE OF THE CASE – FORM 1B:2
SIGNATURE BLOCK – FORM 1B:3
CERTIFICATE OF SERVICE – FORM 1B:13

NOTE: Generally, parties will not file a separate withholding statement but will include it as part of the response to the discovery request.

For general objections to discovery, see FORM 6A:9; for a motion for protection from discovery, see FORM 6A:10; for a motion for protection from a discovery subpoena, see FORM 6A:13; for a motion to quash a deposition, see FORM 6F:2; for objections to interrogatories, see FORM 6G:3; for objections to requests for admissions, see FORM 6H:3; for objections to requests for production, see FORM 6I:3.

{❶ *PARTY*}'S REQUEST FOR {❷ *ADVERSE PARTY*}'S PRIVILEGE LOG

To: {❸ *Adverse party*}, {❹ *name*}, through {❺ *his/her/its*} attorney of record, {❻ *name*}, {❼ *address*}.

Under Texas Rule of Civil Procedure 193.3(b), {❽ *adverse party*} is requested to identify, within 15 days of service of this request, the information or material withheld under claims of privilege in response to {❾ *party*}'s {❿ *identify each discovery request seeking privileged information, e.g., interrogatories 4, 7, and 10*}. {*See* ***O'Connor's Texas Rules****, "Request privilege log," ch. 6-A, §18.2.2, p. 534.*}

SEE: Tex. R. Civ. P. 193.3(b)
O'Connor's Texas Rules * Civil Trials (2019), "Request privilege log," ch. 6-A, §18.2.2, p. 534

ADD: STYLE OF THE CASE – FORM 1B:2
SIGNATURE BLOCK – FORM 1B:3
CERTIFICATE OF SERVICE – FORM 1B:13

{❶ *PARTY*}'S PRIVILEGE LOG

To: {❷ *Adverse party*}, {❸ *name*}, through {❹ *his/her/its*} attorney of record, {❺ *name*}, {❻ *address*}.

{❼ *Party*} timely serves the following privilege log in response to {❽ *adverse party*}'s request for a privilege log. Tex. R. Civ. P. 193.3(b). {*See **O'Connor's Texas Rules**, "Serve privilege log," ch. 6-A, §18.2.3, p. 534.*}

DISCOVERY REQUEST		BATES NO.	DESCRIPTION OF ITEM WITHHELD	PRIVILEGE
1	Request for Production 8	0001-0010	Letter, dated 10-11-12, authored by J.C. Smith to Laurie Johnson and copied to Frank Jones, regarding merger discussions of 10-2-12	Attorney-client
2	Request for Production 12	0011-0025	Handwritten notes authored by J.C. Smith regarding merger discussions of 10-2-12	Attorney-client
3	Request for Production 13	0025-0122	Engineering plans and production specifications for widget	Trade secret

SEE: Tex. R. Civ. P. 193.3(b)
O'Connor's Texas Rules * Civil Trials (2019), "Serve privilege log," ch. 6-A, §18.2.3, p. 534

ADD: STYLE OF THE CASE – FORM 1B:2
SIGNATURE BLOCK – FORM 1B:3
CERTIFICATE OF SERVICE – FORM 1B:13

NOTE: A party is not required to assert a privilege for materials created by or for attorneys for the litigation. Tex. R. Civ. P. 193.3(c). It is assumed such material will be withheld from virtually any request on the grounds of attorney-client or work-product privilege. Tex. R. Civ. P. 193 cmt. 3.

{❶ *PARTY*}'S AMENDED WITHHOLDING STATEMENT

To: {❷ *Adverse party*}, {❸ *name*}, through {❹ *his/her/its*} attorney of record, {❺ *name*}, {❻ *address*}.

Under Texas Rule of Civil Procedure 193.3(d), {❼ *party*}, {❽ *name*}, timely serves the following amended withholding statement in response to {❾ *adverse party*}'s {❿ *identify discovery request, e.g., request for production*}.

{⓫ *Identify discovery request, e.g., REQUEST FOR PRODUCTION 1*}: {⓬ *Restate request for information.*}

RESPONSE: On {⓭ *date*}, {⓮ *party*} accidentally produced {⓯ *identify specific documents or material produced, e.g., a letter dated October 11, 2012, authored by J.C. Smith to Laurie Johnson regarding merger discussions that took place on October 2, 2012*}. {⓰ *Party*} discovered the accidental production on {⓱ *state date of discovery, which must be no more than ten days before service of this amended withholding statement*}. This information is protected under the {⓲ *identify privilege*}, and {⓳ *party*} did not intend to waive that privilege. {⓴ *Party*} requests that all copies of the privileged information be returned pending a ruling by the Court. Tex. R. Civ. P. 193.3(d). {*See* ***O'Connor's Texas Rules****, "Use snap-back provision," ch. 6-A, §18.2.4, p. 535.*}

SEE: Tex. R. Civ. P. 193.3(d)
Tex. R. Evid. 511(b)(2)
O'Connor's Texas Rules * Civil Trials (2019), "Use snap-back provision," ch. 6-A, §18.2.4, p. 535

ADD: STYLE OF THE CASE – FORM 1B:2
SIGNATURE BLOCK – FORM 1B:3
CERTIFICATE OF SERVICE – FORM 1B:13

NOTE: The inadvertent disclosure of privileged material does not automatically waive a claim of privilege. Tex. R. Civ. P. 193.3(d) & cmt. 4; *see* Tex. R. Evid. 511(b)(2) (no waiver of attorney-client privilege or work-product protection if Texas Rule of Civil Procedure 193.3(d) is followed). By using the snap-back provision, a party can preserve the privilege for documents inadvertently disclosed to the other party. To claim a privilege after inadvertent production, serve this amended withholding statement on the other parties within ten days after discovering the accidental production. Tex. R. Civ. P. 193.3(d). See ***O'Connor's Texas Rules***, "Use snap-back provision," ch. 6-A, §18.2.4, p. 535.

When a party inadvertently discloses privileged materials to its own testifying expert, those materials generally cannot be retrieved by the party under Texas Rule of Civil Procedure 193.3(d). ***In re Christus Spohn Hosp. Kleberg***, 222 S.W.3d 434, 440-41 (Tex.2007). To retrieve the privileged materials, the party should argue that the disclosed material could not have influenced the expert's opinion. *Id.* at 441. In the alternative, the party can withdraw the expert's designation and name a new expert. *Id.* at 445. See ***O'Connor's Texas Rules***, "Inadvertent disclosure," ch. 6-D, §4.1.1(6)(b), p. 619. To designate an expert, see FORM 6E:3; to amend or supplement expert discovery, see FORMS 6D:2, 3.

STIPULATED PROTECTIVE ORDER

Plaintiff, {❶ *name*}, and defendant, {❷ *name*}, through their attorneys of record, stipulate to the following procedure for any claim of inadvertent disclosure of hard-copy documents or electronic or magnetic data (hereinafter "information") privileged under the attorney-client privilege or protected by the work-product doctrine. {*See Tex. R. Evid. 511(b)(4).*} The parties stipulate to this procedure because of the large amount of information that is in the possession, custody, or control of the parties and to provide protection against inadvertent disclosure of information subject to attorney-client privilege or work-product protection.

1. If a party inadvertently discloses information in connection with the pending litigation that the party later claims is privileged or protected, the disclosure will not waive any privilege or protection—in this litigation or any other—that would otherwise attach to the information and its subject matter.

2. If a disclosing party learns of an inadvertent disclosure of information, the disclosing party must promptly provide all parties with written notice of the inadvertent disclosure. The notice must identify the information and the date the information was disclosed.

3. If a disclosing party provides written notice of a claim of inadvertent disclosure, the receiving party must, within {❸ *number*} days of the notification, return the inadvertently disclosed information and any copies {❹ *he/she/it*} has. The receiving party must provide a certification that (1) {❺ *he/she/it*} is no longer reviewing, disseminating, or using the information, (2) the information has been returned, and (3) {❻ *he/she/it*} no longer has any copies of the information. If the receiving party distributed the information before receiving written notice from the disclosing party, the receiving party must take reasonable steps to retrieve the information and to prevent further distribution or use of the information until the claim is resolved.

4. Within {❼ *number*} days of the written notice of the claim of inadvertent disclosure, the disclosing party must produce a privilege log for the inadvertently disclosed information. {*See FORM 6A:21.*}

5. If the parties disagree about the claim of privilege or protection, the parties must meet and confer to resolve the dispute. If the dispute is not resolved, either party can present the inadvertently disclosed information to the Court for a determination of whether there has been a waiver of privilege or protection. The information must be filed under seal. Pending resolution of the dispute, the receiving party must not use the inadvertently disclosed information or disclose it to any person.

6. The disclosing party has the burden of establishing any claims of privilege or protection in connection with any dispute before the Court.

7. Any applicable claim of privilege or protection is not waived as to anyone who is not a party to this action by a disclosure connected with this action.

8. This stipulation is effective on the date it is signed by all parties and the Court.

SIGNED on _______________, 20___.

____
PRESIDING JUDGE

SEE: Tex. R. Evid. 511
O'Connor's Texas Rules * Civil Trials (2019), "Parties' agreement – attorney-related privileges," ch. 6-A, §25.3.2(3)(d), p. 551

ADD: STYLE OF THE CASE – FORM 1B:2
SIGNATURE BLOCK FOR AGREED MOTIONS – FORM 1B:4

NOTE: The parties can enter into an agreement to limit the effect of waiver by disclosure between them in any state proceeding. *See* Tex. R. Evid. 511(b)(4). The agreement applies only to communications or information covered by the attorney-client privilege or work-product doctrine. Tex. R. Evid. 511(b). For a stipulated plan under Texas Rule of Evidence 511 to be binding on nonparties and in other proceedings, it must be incorporated into a court order. *See* Tex. R. Evid. 511(b)(4).

{[1] *PARTY*}'S MOTION TO COMPEL {[2] *ADVERSE PARTY*} TO {[3] *RESPOND TO {IDENTIFY DISCOVERY REQUEST}/ {APPEAR/RESPOND TO A QUESTION} AT A DEPOSITION*}

{*CHOOSE APPROPRIATE OPENING PARAGRAPH*}

{[4] *Party*}, {[5] *name*}, asks the Court to compel {[6] *adverse party*}, {[7] *name*}, to respond to {[8] *party*}'s discovery requests. {*See* ***O'Connor's Texas Rules***, *"Motion to Compel Discovery," ch. 6-A, §22, p. 542.*}

{[9] *Party*}, {[10] *name*}, asks the Court to compel {[11] *adverse party*}, {[12] *name*}, to {[13] *appear/respond to a question*} at a deposition. {*See* ***O'Connor's Texas Rules***, *"Motion to Compel Discovery," ch. 6-A, §22, p. 542.*}

INTRODUCTION

1. Plaintiff, {[14] *name*}, sued defendant, {[15] *name*}, for {[16] *state basis of suit*}.

2. Discovery in this suit is governed by a Level {[17] *1/2/3*} discovery-control plan. The discovery period {[18] *will end/ended*} on {[19] *date*}. {*See* ***O'Connor's Texas Rules***, *"Discovery-Control Plans," ch. 6-A, §7, p. 520.*}

3. This case is set for trial on {[20] *date*}.

4. {[21] *State other relevant facts about the suit.*}

BACKGROUND

{*CHOOSE APPROPRIATE PARAGRAPH 5*}

5. On {[22] *date*}, {[23] *party*} served {[24] *adverse party*} with the discovery request in accordance with Texas Rules of Civil Procedure 21(a) and 21a.

5. On {[25] *date*}, {[26] *party*} served {[27] *adverse party*} with notice to appear at a deposition scheduled on {[28] *date*}.

{*CHOOSE APPROPRIATE PARAGRAPH 6*}

6. Although {[29] *adverse party*}'s responses were due on {[30] *date*}, {[31] *adverse party*} has not responded to {[32] *party*}'s discovery request. {[33] *Party*} attaches {[34] *identify document showing proof of service, e.g., the certified mail receipt*} to this motion as Exhibit {[35] *letter*} and incorporates it by reference.

6. {[36] *Adverse party*} responded by {[37] *describe response, including date served*}.

6. {(38) *Adverse party*} did not appear at the deposition scheduled on {(39) *date*}.

6. {(40) *Adverse party*} was deposed on {(41) *date*} but refused to answer a proper question asked at the deposition.

7. {(42) *State other facts relevant to the motion.*}

ARGUMENT & AUTHORITIES

8. The purpose of discovery is to seek the truth so that disputes may be decided by what facts are revealed, not by what facts are concealed. *Axelson, Inc. v. McIlhany*, 798 S.W.2d 550, 555 (Tex. 1990). A party may seek discovery of any matter that is relevant to the subject matter and proportional to the needs of the case. *See* Tex. R. Civ. P. 192.3(a), 192.4(b); *In re State Farm Lloyds*, 520 S.W.3d 595, 607 (Tex. 2017). Discovery can include evidence that may be inadmissible as long as it "appears reasonably calculated to lead to the discovery of admissible evidence." Tex. R. Civ. P. 192.3(a).

{*CHOOSE APPROPRIATE PARAGRAPH 9*}

{*Adverse party did not respond to discovery*}

9. A court may compel a party to respond to a discovery request. Tex. R. Civ. P. {(43) *215.1(b)/215.4*}. {(44) *Adverse party*} did not respond to {(45) *identify discovery request*} as required by Texas Rule of Civil Procedure 193.1. Therefore, the Court should compel {(46) *adverse party*} to respond to {(47) *identify discovery request*}. {(48) *Elaborate.*}

{*Adverse party made inadequate response to discovery*}

9. A court may compel a party to respond adequately to {(49) *identify type of discovery, e.g., interrogatories*}. Tex. R. Civ. P. {(50) *215.1(b), (c)/215.4*}. {(51) *Adverse party*} did not respond adequately to {(52) *identify discovery request*} as required by Texas Rule of Civil Procedure 193.1. Therefore, the Court should compel {(53) *adverse party*} to comply with the rule. {(54) *Adverse party*}'s responses are inadequate for the following reasons:

{*CHOOSE APPROPRIATE REASONS*}

a. {(55) *Adverse party*} refused to respond fully to {(56) *party*}'s requests for disclosure regarding expert witnesses. {(57) *Adverse party*} did not supply the following information required by Texas Rule of Civil Procedure 194.2(f): {(58) *identify information not provided about the testifying expert, e.g., the expert's identity and location, the subject matter on which the ex-*

Continued on next page

pert is expected to testify, the expert's mental impressions and opinions, the facts known to the expert}. {*See* ***O'Connor's Texas Rules****, "Testifying experts," ch. 6-E, §4.2.1(6), p. 631.*}

b. {59 *Adverse party*} did not {60 *verify/sign*} {61 *his/her/its*} response to interrogatories. Texas Rule of Civil Procedure 197.2(d) requires the interrogatories to be {62 *verified/signed*} by {63 *adverse party*}. {*See* ***O'Connor's Texas Rules****, "Signed & verified by party," ch. 6-G, §4.1.1(4), p. 666; "Object to formal defects," ch. 6-G, §8.2, p. 670.*}

c. {64 *Adverse party*} refused to respond fully to interrogatory {65 *number*}, regarding {66 *identify information requested in the interrogatory, e.g., impeachment or rebuttal evidence*}. Texas Rule of Civil Procedure 193.1 requires the party to make a "complete response" to a discovery request. {*See* ***O'Connor's Texas Rules****, "Answers," ch. 6-G, §4.2, p. 666; "Move to compel answers," ch. 6-G, §8.1, p. 669.*}

d. {67 *Adverse party*} refused to respond fully to request for admission {68 *number*}, regarding {69 *identify information requested for admission*}. Texas Rule of Civil Procedure 193.1 requires the party to make a "complete response" to a discovery request. {*See* ***O'Connor's Texas Rules****, "Challenging answers," ch. 6-H, §5.1.1, p. 675.*}

e. {70 *Adverse party*} refused to respond fully to request for production {71 *number*}, regarding {72 *identify information requested for production*}. Texas Rule of Civil Procedure 193.1 requires the party to make a "complete response" to a discovery request. {*See* ***O'Connor's Texas Rules****, "Production of things," ch. 6-I, §3.4.1(1), p. 684; "Motion to compel & for sanctions," ch. 6-I, §6.1, p. 688.*}

f. {73 *Adverse party*} {74 *refused to/did not adequately*} produce {75 *documents/tangible things/electronic data/magnetic data*} in response to request for production {76 *number*}, regarding {77 *identify information requested for production*}. {78 *Elaborate.*} The Court should require {79 *adverse party*} to produce the {80 *identify information requested for production*}. {*See* ***O'Connor's Texas Rules****, "Motion to compel," ch. 6-C, §8.1, p. 610; "Motion to compel & for sanctions," ch. 6-I, §6.1, p. 688.*}

g. {81 *Adverse party*} produced {82 *number*} boxes of documents that were not organized as they were kept in the ordinary course of business or seg-

regated and labeled according to each particular request, in violation of Texas Rule of Civil Procedure 196.3(c). The documents were shuffled before they were produced in order to make it difficult to analyze and evaluate them. The Court should require {83 *adverse party*} to produce the documents organized as they are ordinarily kept or segregated and labeled according to each request. {*See* ***O'Connor's Texas Rules****, "Organization of documents," ch. 6-I, §3.4.1(2), p. 684.*}

h. {84 *Adverse party*} produced documents in response to a request for production but did not serve a written response, as required by Texas Rule of Civil Procedure 196.2. The Court should require {85 *adverse party*} to serve a written response. {*See* ***O'Connor's Texas Rules****, "In writing," ch. 6-I, §3.3.1(1), p. 683.*}

i. {86 *Adverse party*} objected to {87 *identify request for discovery, e.g., request for production 13*} on the ground of {88 *identify ground for objection*}. Even though the objection was made to only part of the request, {89 *adverse party*} made no attempt to comply with the rest of the request. {90 *Adverse party*} had a duty to comply with the request to the extent that {91 *he/she/it*} made no objection. Tex. R. Civ. P. 193.2(b). {*See* ***O'Connor's Texas Rules****, "Partial compliance necessary," ch. 6-A, §18.10.1, p. 538.*}

j. {92 *Adverse party*} did not produce electronic information in response to request for production {93 *number*} in a format that is reasonably usable. *See* Tex. R. Civ. P. 196.4 & cmt. 3. {94 *Explain, e.g., adverse party produced information in native format that is specialized or uncommon.*} The Court should require {95 *adverse party*} to produce the electronic information in {96 *identify requested format*} because {97 *explain why requested format is reasonably usable*}. {*See* ***O'Connor's Texas Rules****, "Form of production," ch. 6-C, §7.1.5(1)(a), p. 605.*}

{*Adverse party refused to appear or answer at deposition*}

9. A court may compel a party to appear at a deposition the party previously refused to attend. Tex. R. Civ. P. 215.1(b)(2)(A). {98 *Adverse party*} was served with notice to appear at a deposition on {99 *date*}. {100 *Adverse party*} did not appear at the deposition. Therefore, the Court should compel {101 *adverse party*} to appear at a deposition. {102 *Elaborate.*} {*See* ***O'Connor's Texas Rules****, "Party witness," ch. 6-F, §7.6.1, p. 647.*}

◄ *Continued on next page* ►

9. A court may compel a party to respond to a question the party refused to answer at a deposition. Tex. R. Civ. P. 215.1(b)(2)(B); *see* Tex. R. Civ. P. 199.6. {103 *Adverse party*} did not respond to {104 *identify question from deposition*}. Therefore, the Court should compel {105 *adverse party*} to respond to that question. {106 *Elaborate.*} {*See* ***O'Connor's Texas Rules****, "Motion to compel answer," ch. 6-F, §9.4, p. 649.*}

{*Adverse party objected to discovery*}

9. {107 *Party*}'s discovery requests are within the scope of discovery permitted by Texas Rule of Civil Procedure 192.3. Even though {108 *party*}'s requests were proper, {109 *adverse party*} refused to comply with the rule and served the {110 *objections/motion for protective order/withholding statement*} to avoid discovery that is clearly authorized under the discovery rules. {111 *Elaborate, showing how objection or motion for protection is not appropriate.*} {*See* ***O'Connor's Texas Rules****, "After objection to discovery," ch. 6-A, §22.1.8, p. 543.*}

9. {112 *Adverse party*} asserted that information or material responsive to {113 *party*}'s discovery request was exempt from discovery and asserted the work-product privilege. {114 *Party*}, however, has a substantial need for the material and is unable without undue hardship to obtain the substantial equivalent of the material by other means. Tex. R. Civ. P. 192.5(b)(2); *see In re Nat'l Lloyds Ins. Co.*, 532 S.W.3d 794, 804 (Tex. 2017). {115 *State facts to establish substantial need and undue hardship.*} The material requested is noncore work product and thus is subject to the need-and-hardship exception in Texas Rule of Civil Procedure 192.5(b)(2). {*See* ***O'Connor's Texas Rules****, "Need & hardship exception," ch. 6-B, §2.13.2, p. 560.*}

9. {116 *Adverse party*} asserted that {117 *party*}'s discovery request is not proportional to the needs of the case because {118 *identify basis for adverse party's proportionality argument*}. However, {119 *party*}'s discovery request is proportional to the needs of the case. *See* Tex. R. Civ. P. 192.4(b); *In re State Farm*, 520 S.W.3d at 607. {*See* ***O'Connor's Texas Rules****, "Proportional," ch. 6-B, §2.1.1(2), p. 555; "Proportional," ch. 6-C, §6.1.2, p. 602.*} Specifically, the request is proportional for the following reasons:

{*CHOOSE APPROPRIATE REASONS*}

a. The likely benefits of the requested discovery outweigh any enhanced effort or expense in producing the information. *See* Tex. R. Civ. P. 192.4(b); *In re State Farm*, 520 S.W.3d at 608. {120 *Elaborate.*}

b. The requested discovery is justified considering the needs of the case. *See* Tex. R. Civ. P. 192.4(b); *In re State Farm*, 520 S.W.3d at 608. {121 *Elaborate.*}

c. The requested discovery is justified based on the amount in controversy. *See* Tex. R. Civ. P. 192.4(b); *In re State Farm*, 520 S.W.3d at 610. {122 *Elaborate.*}

d. The requested discovery is proportional to {123 *adverse party*}'s resources. *See* Tex. R. Civ. P. 192.4(b); *In re State Farm*, 520 S.W.3d at 610-11. {124 *Explain how adverse party's resources affect production, e.g., adverse party has significant resources to collect information and produce it in reasonably usable form.*}

e. The issues at stake in the case are extremely important. *See* Tex. R. Civ. P. 192.4(b); *In re State Farm*, 520 S.W.3d at 611. {125 *Elaborate.*}

f. The requested discovery is extremely important to resolving the issues in the case. *See* Tex. R. Civ. P. 192.4(b); *In re State Farm*, 520 S.W.3d at 611. {126 *Elaborate.*}

g. {127 *Identify any other reason that the requested discovery is proportional to the needs of the case. See In re State Farm, 520 S.W.3d at 611-12.*}

9. {128 *Adverse party*} asserted that information responsive to {129 *party*}'s request for discovery of electronic information is not reasonably available to {130 *adverse party*} in the ordinary course of business because of undue {131 *burden/expense/burden and expense*}. Specifically, {132 *adverse party*} alleged that {133 *state allegations supporting claim that the information is not reasonably available*}. Even if the requested information is not reasonably available, a court may still compel a party to produce the information when the proportional needs of the case outweigh any enhanced burden or expense in production and the information is not cumulative or obtainable from a less burdensome source. *See* Tex. R. Civ. P. 192.4; *In re State Farm*, 520 S.W.3d at 599-600; *In re Weekley Homes, L.P.*, 295 S.W.3d 309, 322 (Tex. 2009). {*See* ***O'Connor's Texas Rules****, "Is electronic information reasonably available?," ch. 6-C, §6.2, p. 603.*} In this case, the request is proportional for the following reasons:

{*CHOOSE APPROPRIATE REASONS*}

a. The likely benefits of the requested discovery outweigh any enhanced effort or expense in producing the information. *See* Tex. R. Civ. P. 192.4(b); *In re State Farm*, 520 S.W.3d at 608. {134 *Elaborate.*}

b. The requested discovery is justified considering the needs of the case. *See* Tex. R. Civ. P. 192.4(b); *In re State Farm*, 520 S.W.3d at 608. {135 *Elaborate.*}

Continued on next page

c. The requested discovery is justified based on the amount in controversy. *See* Tex. R. Civ. P. 192.4(b); *In re State Farm*, 520 S.W.3d at 610. {136 *Elaborate.*}

d. The requested discovery is proportional to {137 *adverse party*}'s resources. *See* Tex. R. Civ. P. 192.4(b); *In re State Farm*, 520 S.W.3d at 610-11. {138 *Explain how adverse party's resources affect production, e.g., adverse party has significant resources to collect information and produce it in reasonably usable form.*}

e. The issues at stake in the case are extremely important. *See* Tex. R. Civ. P. 192.4(b); *In re State Farm*, 520 S.W.3d at 611. {139 *Elaborate.*}

f. The requested discovery is extremely important to resolving the issues in the case. *See* Tex. R. Civ. P. 192.4(b); *In re State Farm*, 520 S.W.3d at 611. {140 *Elaborate.*}

g. {141 *Identify any other reason that the requested discovery is proportional to the needs of the case. See In re State Farm, 520 S.W.3d at 611-12.*}

{*Adverse party did not follow agreed schedule*}

9. A court may compel a party to comply with a Rule 11 agreement setting deadlines for discovery. *See Sullivan v. Bickel & Brewer*, 943 S.W.2d 477, 484 (Tex. App.—Dallas 1995, writ denied). Specifically, {142 *adverse party*} has not complied with {143 *explain how adverse party has not complied with Rule 11 agreement*}.

{*ADD FOLLOWING SECTION IF APPLICABLE*}

WAIVER

{*CHOOSE APPROPRIATE PARAGRAPH 10*}

10. {144 *Adverse party*} did not timely serve responses to {145 *party*}'s {146 *identify discovery request*} and therefore waived all objections. Tex. R. Civ. P. 193.2(e); *see Remington Arms Co. v. Canales*, 837 S.W.2d 624, 625 (Tex. 1992). On {147 *date*}, {148 *party*} served {149 *adverse party*} with the discovery in accordance with Texas Rules of Civil Procedure 21(a) and 21a. The responses were due on {150 *date*}. {151 *Party*} attaches {152 *identify document showing proof of service, e.g., the certified mail receipt*} to this motion as Exhibit {153 *letter*} and incorporates it by reference. The parties did not agree to an extension under Rule 11, and the Court did not grant an extension. *See* Tex. R. Civ. P. 191.1. {154 *Adverse party*} should not be relieved of the waiver because {155 *he/she/it*} cannot show good cause for not responding to the dis-

covery request. Tex. R. Civ. P. 193.2(e). {156 *Elaborate.*} {*See **O'Connor's Texas Rules**, "Timely objection," ch. 6-A, §18.1.1, p. 533.*}

10. {157 *Adverse party*} waived {158 *his/her/its*} objections because any valid objections are obscured by numerous unfounded objections. Tex. R. Civ. P. 193.2(e). Specifically, {159 *adverse party*} made {160 *number*} objections to {161 *identify discovery request, e.g., interrogatory 7*}. Some of those objections are completely unfounded. For example, {162 *adverse party*} objected to {163 *identify discovery request*} on the following grounds: {164 *identify grounds*}. Therefore, {165 *adverse party*} waived {166 *his/her/its*} objections, and the Court should strike {167 *adverse party*}'s objections to {168 *identify discovery request*}. {169 *Adverse party*} should not be relieved of the waiver because {170 *he/she/it*} cannot show good cause for not responding to the discovery request. *Id.* {171 *Elaborate.*}

EXPENSES OF MOTION

11. {172 *Party*} has incurred expenses in preparing and filing this motion to obtain relief. Under Texas Rule of Civil Procedure 215.1(d), {173 *party*} is entitled to reasonable expenses incurred in obtaining the order, including attorney fees. {*See **O'Connor's Texas Rules**, "Request for expenses," ch. 6-A, §22.3, p. 543.*}

CONCLUSION

12. {174 *Briefly summarize the motion.*}

PRAYER

13. For these reasons, {175 *party*} asks the Court to set this motion for hearing and, after the hearing, to compel {176 *adverse party*} to {177 *file adequate responses to {party}'s discovery requests/appear at a deposition/respond to the question asked at a deposition*} {178 *add if appropriate: , find that adverse party waived its objections,*} and order {179 *identify person or persons to be ordered to pay expenses, e.g., plaintiff, plaintiff's attorney, both plaintiff and plaintiff's attorney*} to pay {180 *party*} ${181 *amount*} for reasonable expenses incurred in filing this motion, including attorney fees.

SEE: Tex. R. Civ. P. 191.1, 192, 193, 194.2(f), 196.2, 197.2(d), 215
O'Connor's Texas Rules * Civil Trials (2019), "Motion to Compel Discovery," ch. 6-A, §22, p. 542

ADD: STYLE OF THE CASE – FORM 1B:2
SIGNATURE BLOCK – FORM 1B:3
CERTIFICATE OF CONFERENCE – FORM 1B:12
CERTIFICATE OF SERVICE – FORM 1B:13

◄ *Continued on next page* ►

ATTACH: AFFIDAVIT – FORM 1B:8, if necessary
NOTICE OF HEARING OR SUBMISSION – FORM 1E:1
AFFIDAVIT FOR ATTORNEY FEES – FORM 1H:14
ORDER – FORM 6A:26
Certified question from deposition or copy of deposition, if necessary
Discovery request, if necessary
Discovery responses, if necessary
Notice of deposition, if necessary
Proof of service of discovery request, if necessary

NOTE: The trial court can impose sanctions against a party for refusing to comply with proper discovery requests or violating deposition procedures, regardless of whether the party has disobeyed an order compelling discovery. *See* Tex. R. Civ. P. 215.1(b). Thus, the party seeking discovery can include a motion for sanctions in its first motion to compel discovery. *See* ***Lewis v. Illinois Empls. Ins.***, 590 S.W.2d 119, 120 (Tex.1979). A party may also pursue sanctions instead of filing a motion to compel. ***Adkins Servs. v. Tisdale Co.***, 56 S.W.3d 842, 844 (Tex.App.—Texarkana 2001, no pet.). See FORM 6A:27.

If a nonparty witness refuses to appear at a deposition, the party who subpoenaed the witness for deposition should file a motion to compel the witness to appear at the deposition and a motion to hold the witness in contempt of court. *See* Tex. R. Civ. P. 176.8(a). See ***O'Connor's Texas Rules***, "Nonparty witness," ch. 6-F, §7.6.2, p. 647.

If a party requested access to an opposing party's computer hard drive and the opposing party did not adequately produce the requested data, the requesting party can file a motion to compel. See ***O'Connor's Texas Rules***, "Accessing hard drive," ch. 6-C, §8.1.2, p. 610.

For information to be discoverable, it must be both relevant and proportional to the needs of the case. *See* Tex. R. Civ. P. 192.3(a); ***In re State Farm Lloyds***, 520 S.W.3d 595, 607 (Tex.2017). The Court in ***In re State Farm*** set out factors for determining proportionality, which mirror the considerations under Texas Rule of Civil Procedure 192.4 for determining whether a discovery request is unduly burdensome. *See* ***In re State Farm***, 520 S.W.3d at 599-600. Although the Court discussed the proportionality guidelines in the context of electronic-discovery disputes, the Court emphasized that all discovery is subject to proportionality considerations. *Id.* at 599. See ***O'Connor's Texas Rules***, "Proportional," ch. 6-B, §2.1.1(2), p. 555; "Proportional," ch. 6-C, §6.1.2, p. 602.

{❶ *PARTY*}'S RESPONSE TO
{❷ *ADVERSE PARTY*}'S MOTION TO COMPEL

{❸ *Party*}, {❹ *name*}, asks the Court to deny {❺ *adverse party*} {❻ *name*}'s motion to compel. {*See **O'Connor's Texas Rules**, "Response to motion to compel," ch. 6-A, §22.4, p. 543.*}

INTRODUCTION

1. Plaintiff, {❼ *name*}, sued defendant, {❽ *name*}, for {❾ *state basis of suit*}.

2. Discovery in this suit is governed by a Level {❿ *1/2/3*} discovery-control plan. The discovery period {⓫ *will end/ended*} on {⓬ *date*}. {*See **O'Connor's Texas Rules**, "Discovery-Control Plans," ch. 6-A, §7, p. 520.*}

3. This case is set for trial on {⓭ *date*}.

4. {⓮ *State other relevant facts about the suit.*}

BACKGROUND

{*CHOOSE APPROPRIATE PARAGRAPH 5*}

5. {⓯ *Adverse party*} served {⓰ *party*} with {⓱ *identify discovery request, e.g., a second set of interrogatories*}. The response was due on {⓲ *date*}.

5. {⓳ *Adverse party*} served {⓴ *party*} with notice to appear at a deposition scheduled on {㉑ *date*}.

{*CHOOSE APPROPRIATE PARAGRAPH 6*}

6. On {㉒ *date*}, {㉓ *party*} responded by serving {㉔ *the answers/the objections/the claims of privilege/a motion for protective order*}. On {㉕ *date*}, {㉖ *adverse party*} filed a motion to compel {㉗ *party*} to {㉘ *respond to the {describe type of discovery request, e.g., interrogatories}/appear at the deposition*}.

6. On {㉙ *date*}, {㉚ *adverse party*} filed a motion to compel {㉛ *party*} to {㉜ *respond to the {describe type of discovery request, e.g., interrogatories}/appear at the deposition*}. On {㉝ *date*}, {㉞ *party*} served {㉟ *his/her/its*} {㊱ *answers/objections/claims of privilege/motion for protective order*} {㊲ *add if appropriate: , which {are/is} attached to this response as Exhibit {letter}*}.

6. {㊳ *Adverse party*} asked the following question at the deposition: {㊴ *identify question from deposition*}. To {㊵ *preserve a privilege/comply with {a court order/the Texas Rules of Civil Procedure}/protect the deponent*}, {㊶ *party*}'s attorney objected

◄ *Continued on next page* ►

and instructed {42 *party*} not to answer {43 *adverse party*}'s question. On {44 *date*}, {45 *adverse party*} filed a motion to compel {46 *party*} to respond to the deposition question.

7. {47 *State other facts relevant to the response.*}

ARGUMENT & AUTHORITIES

{ADD SECTION A IF APPLICABLE}

A. No Waiver

{CHOOSE APPROPRIATE PARAGRAPHS 8-9}

8. {48 *Adverse party*} contends that {49 *party*} waived {50 *his/her/its*} objections to {51 *identify discovery request, e.g., plaintiff's request for production 9*} by making an untimely response. {52 *Party*}'s response was untimely, but {53 *party*} did not waive {54 *his/her/its*} objections. Under Texas Rule of Civil Procedure 193.2(e), untimely objections are not waived if the court excuses the waiver for good cause shown. In this case, the Court should excuse {55 *party*}'s untimeliness because {56 *explain good cause for late response*}.

9. {57 *Adverse party*} contends that {58 *party*} waived {59 *his/her/its*} objections to {60 *identify discovery request, e.g., plaintiff's request for production 9*} under Texas Rule of Civil Procedure 193.2(e) by obscuring {61 *his/her/its*} valid objections with numerous unfounded objections. However, {62 *party*} did not waive {63 *his/her/its*} objections because {64 *explain how objections are not unfounded*}.

B. Reasons for Denial

10. {65 *Adverse party*} contends that {66 *identify adverse party's contentions*}. Based on these contentions, {67 *adverse party*} asks the Court to sign an order compelling {68 *party*} to {69 *identify purpose of motion to compel*}. The Court should deny {70 *adverse party*}'s motion to compel.

{CHOOSE APPROPRIATE PARAGRAPHS 11-25}

11. {71 *Adverse party*}'s discovery request seeks information that is not relevant and is not reasonably calculated to lead to the discovery of admissible evidence. *See* Tex. R. Civ. P. 192.3; *In re CSX Corp.*, 124 S.W.3d 149, 152 (Tex. 2003); *Ford Motor Co. v. Leggat*, 904 S.W.2d 643, 649 (Tex. 1995); *Eli Lilly & Co. v. Marshall*, 850 S.W.2d 155, 160 (Tex. 1993). Specifically, {72 *identify discovery request, e.g., plaintiff's request for production 9*} is objectionable because {73 *state basis for objection,*

e.g., it seeks the engineering drawings for defendant's headlights, and this lawsuit involves an allegation that defendant's brake system was defective}. {*See* ***O'Connor's Texas Rules****, "Not within scope of discovery," ch. 6-A, §19.1.1, p. 538.*}

12. {74 *Adverse party*}'s discovery request seeks information that is not proportional to the needs of the case. *See* Tex. R. Civ. P. 192.4(b); *In re State Farm Lloyds*, 520 S.W.3d 595, 607 (Tex. 2017). {*See* ***O'Connor's Texas Rules****, "Proportional," ch. 6-B, §2.1.1(2), p. 555; "Proportional," ch. 6-C, §6.1.2, p. 602.*} Specifically, {75 *identify discovery request, e.g., plaintiff's request for production 9*} is objectionable for the following reasons:

{*CHOOSE APPROPRIATE REASONS*}

a. The likely benefits of the requested discovery are minimal, and therefore any enhanced effort or expense in producing the information is undue. *See* Tex. R. Civ. P. 192.4(b); *In re State Farm*, 520 S.W.3d at 608. {76 *Elaborate.*}

b. The requested discovery is not justified considering the needs of the case. *See* Tex. R. Civ. P. 192.4(b); *In re State Farm*, 520 S.W.3d at 608. {77 *Elaborate.*}

c. The requested discovery is not justified based on the amount in controversy. *See* Tex. R. Civ. P. 192.4(b); *In re State Farm*, 520 S.W.3d at 610. {78 *Elaborate.*}

d. The requested discovery is not proportional to {79 *party*}'s resources. *See* Tex. R. Civ. P. 192.4(b); *In re State Farm*, 520 S.W.3d at 610-11. {80 *Explain how party's resources affect production, e.g., party does not have adequate resources to collect information and produce it in reasonably usable form.*}

e. The issues at stake in the case are not of sufficient importance to justify the requested discovery. *See* Tex. R. Civ. P. 192.4(b); *In re State Farm*, 520 S.W.3d at 611. {81 *Elaborate.*}

f. The requested discovery is of low importance to resolving the issues in the case. *See* Tex. R. Civ. P. 192.4(b); *In re State Farm*, 520 S.W.3d at 611. {82 *Elaborate.*}

Continued on next page

g. {83 *Identify any other reason that the requested discovery is not proportional to the needs of the case. See In re State Farm, 520 S.W.3d at 611-12.*}

13. {84 *Adverse party*}'s discovery request asks for a type of discovery not permitted by the rules of discovery. *See* Tex. R. Civ. P. 192.1; *Moore v. Wood*, 809 S.W.2d 621, 623 (Tex. App.—Houston [1st Dist.] 1991, orig. proceeding). Specifically, {85 *identify discovery request, e.g., defendant's request for a mental examination of plaintiff*} is objectionable because {86 *state basis for objection, e.g., it asks that a vocational rehabilitation specialist examine plaintiff*}. {*See* ***O'Connor's Texas Rules****, "Not permissible form of discovery," ch. 6-A, §19.1.2, p. 539.*}

14. {87 *Adverse party*}'s discovery request seeks information that is privileged and exempt from discovery. *See* Tex. R. Civ. P. 192.3. Specifically, {88 *identify discovery request, e.g., plaintiff's request for production 9*} is objectionable because {89 *state basis for objection, e.g., it requests documents protected by the work-product privilege*}. {*See* ***O'Connor's Texas Rules****, "Asserting privileges," ch. 6-A, §18.2, p. 533.*}

15. {90 *Adverse party*}'s discovery request seeks information protected by the trade-secret privilege. *See* Tex. R. Evid. 507; *see also* Tex. Civ. Prac. & Rem. Code §134A.002(6) (definition of trade secret). Specifically, {91 *identify discovery request, e.g., plaintiff's request for production 9*} is objectionable because {92 *state basis for objection, e.g., it seeks a formula for a chemical compound used in defendant's business that gives defendant an opportunity to obtain an advantage over competitors who do not know or use the formula*}. {*See* ***O'Connor's Texas Rules****, "Asserting privileges," ch. 6-A, §18.2, p. 533; "Certain trade secrets," ch. 6-B, §2.24, p. 567; "Trade-secret privilege," ch. 6-B, §3.14, p. 581.*}

16. {93 *Adverse party*}'s discovery request is overbroad. *In re Nat'l Lloyds Ins. Co.*, 507 S.W.3d 219, 223 (Tex. 2016); *In re Graco Children's Prods., Inc.*, 210 S.W.3d 598, 600 (Tex. 2006); *In re CSX Corp.*, 124 S.W.3d 149, 153 (Tex. 2003); *In re Am. Optical Corp.*, 988 S.W.2d 711, 713 (Tex. 1998). Specifically, {94 *identify discovery request, e.g., plaintiff's request for production 9*} is objectionable because {95 *state basis for objection, e.g., it asks for "all documents relevant to this suit"*}. Discovery should be limited to {96 *specify suggested limits*}. {*See* ***O'Connor's Texas Rules****, "No compliance necessary," ch. 6-A, §18.10.2, p. 538; "Overbroad," ch. 6-A, §20.1.3, p. 540.*}

17. {97 *Adverse party*}'s discovery request is unduly burdensome. Tex. R. Civ. P. 192.4, 192.6(b). Specifically, {98 *identify discovery request, e.g., plaintiff's request for production 9*} is objectionable because it is unreasonably cumulative or duplica-

tive. Tex. R. Civ. P. 192.4(a). {99 *Elaborate.*} {*See* ***O'Connor's Texas Rules****, "No compliance necessary," ch. 6-A, §18.10.2, p. 538; "Duplicative," ch. 6-A, §20.1.1(1), p. 540.*}

18. {100 *Adverse party*}'s discovery request is unduly burdensome. Tex. R. Civ. P. 192.4, 192.6(b). Specifically, {101 *identify discovery request, e.g., plaintiff's request for production 9*} is objectionable because the information is obtainable from some other source that is {102 *more convenient/less burdensome/less expensive*}. Tex. R. Civ. P. 192.4(a). {103 *Elaborate.*} {*See* ***O'Connor's Texas Rules****, "No compliance necessary," ch. 6-A, §18.10.2, p. 538; "Obtainable from alternative source," ch. 6-A, §20.1.1(2), p. 540.*}

19. {104 *Adverse party*}'s discovery request is harassing and annoying. Tex. R. Civ. P. 192.6(b). Specifically, {105 *identify discovery request, e.g., plaintiff's request for production 9*} is objectionable because {106 *state basis for objection, e.g., it seeks documents reflecting net worth even though there is no claim for exemplary damages*}. {*See* ***O'Connor's Texas Rules****, "Harassing," ch. 6-A, §20.1.2, p. 540.*}

20. {107 *Adverse party*}'s discovery request seeks discovery of electronic information that is not reasonably available to {108 *party*} in the ordinary course of business. *See* Tex. R. Civ. P. 196.4; *In re State Farm Lloyds*, 520 S.W.3d 595, 600 (Tex. 2017); *In re Weekley Homes, L.P.*, 295 S.W.3d 309, 322 (Tex. 2009). Specifically, {109 *identify discovery request, e.g., plaintiff's request for production 9*} is objectionable because production of the requested information would be unduly {110 *burdensome/expensive/burdensome and expensive*}. *See* Tex. R. Civ. P. 192.4, 196.4; *In re State Farm*, 520 S.W.3d at 607; *In re Weekley Homes*, 295 S.W.3d at 322. {111 *State facts supporting objection and show how production as requested would be unduly burdensome or expensive.*} {*See* ***O'Connor's Texas Rules****, "Is electronic information reasonably available?," ch. 6-C, §6.2, p. 603.*}

21. {112 *Adverse party*}'s discovery request constitutes an invasion of a {113 *personal/constitutional/property*} right. Tex. R. Civ. P. 192.6(b); *see Hoffman v. Fifth Court of Appeals*, 756 S.W.2d 723, 723 (Tex. 1988). Specifically, {114 *identify discovery request, e.g., plaintiff's request for production 9*} is objectionable because {115 *identify right and why it will be violated without protective order*}.

Continued on next page

22. {116 *Adverse party*}'s deposition question seeks information that is privileged and exempt from discovery. *See* Tex. R. Civ. P. 199.5(f). Specifically, the question is objectionable because it seeks information that is protected by the {117 *identify privilege*}. {118 *Elaborate*}. {*See **O'Connor's Texas Rules**, "Preserve privileges," ch. 6-F, §9.2.1, p. 648.*}

23. Answering {119 *adverse party*}'s deposition question would cause {120 *party*} to violate {121 *a court order/the Texas Rules of Civil Procedure*}. *See* Tex. R. Civ. P. 199.5(f). Specifically, the question is objectionable because {122 *explain*}. {*See **O'Connor's Texas Rules**, "Comply with court order or TRCPs," ch. 6-F, §9.2.2, p. 648.*}

24. {123 *Adverse party*}'s deposition question is {124 *abusive/a question for which any answer would be misleading*}. *See* Tex. R. Civ. P. 199.5(f). Specifically, the question is objectionable because {125 *explain*}. {*See **O'Connor's Texas Rules**, "Protect a witness," ch. 6-F, §9.2.3, p. 649.*}

25. {126 *State any other basis for denying motion to compel.*} {*See FORMS 6A:9, 10; **O'Connor's Texas Rules**, "Valid objections to discovery requests," ch. 6-A, §19.1, p. 538; "Objecting Before Oral Deposition," ch. 6-F, §7, p. 644.*}

{*ADD FOLLOWING SECTION IF APPLICABLE*}

SEALED DOCUMENTS

26. {127 *Party*} relies on the following documents in support of its {128 *objections/assertions of privilege*} and tenders these documents in a sealed envelope for in camera inspection: {129 *list and generically describe each document for which an objection or privilege is claimed and include the corresponding discovery request and objection for each document*}. The sealed envelope, which is labeled with the cause number of this case, marked "SEALED – FOR IN CAMERA INSPECTION ONLY," and identified as Exhibit {130 *letter*}, is attached only to the Court's copy of this response. {*See **O'Connor's Texas Rules**, "Documents for inspection," ch. 6-A, §18.7.1(3), p. 537; "Produce documents for inspection," ch. 6-A, §18.8.3, p. 537.*}

EXPENSES OF RESPONSE

27. {131 *Party*} has incurred expenses in preparing and filing this response. Under Texas Rule of Civil Procedure 215.1(d), the Court may award {132 *party*} reasonable expenses incurred in opposing the motion to compel, including attorney fees. {*See **O'Connor's Texas Rules**, "Motion denied," ch. 6-A, §22.5.2(2), p. 543.*}

CONCLUSION

28. Because {133 *party*} complied with the rules, the Court should deny {134 *adverse party*}'s motion to compel.

PRAYER

29. For these reasons, {135 *party*} asks the Court to deny {136 *adverse party*}'s motion to compel and order {137 *adverse party/adverse party's attorney, {name},*} to pay {138 *party*} ${139 *amount*} for reasonable expenses incurred in opposing {140 *adverse party*}'s motion, including attorney fees.

SEE: Tex. R. Civ. P. 192, 215
Tex. R. Evid. 507
O'Connor's Texas Rules * Civil Trials (2019), "Motion to Compel Discovery," ch. 6-A, §22, p. 542

ADD: STYLE OF THE CASE – FORM 1B:2
SIGNATURE BLOCK – FORM 1B:3
CERTIFICATE OF SERVICE – FORM 1B:13

ATTACH: AFFIDAVIT – FORMS 1B:8 & 6A:15-18, if necessary
AFFIDAVIT FOR ATTORNEY FEES – FORM 1H:14
WITHHOLDING STATEMENT – FORM 6A:19, if necessary
PRIVILEGE LOG – FORM 6A:21, if necessary
ORDER – FORM 6A:26
Discovery responses, objections
Selected documents (to court's copy only), if necessary

NOTE: For information to be discoverable, it must be both relevant and proportional to the needs of the case. *See* Tex. R. Civ. P. 192.3(a); ***In re State Farm Lloyds***, 520 S.W.3d 595, 607 (Tex.2017). The Court in ***In re State Farm*** set out factors for determining proportionality, which mirror the considerations under Texas Rule of Civil Procedure 192.4 for determining whether a discovery request is unduly burdensome. *See* ***In re State Farm***, 520 S.W.3d at 599-600. Although the Court discussed the proportionality guidelines in the context of electronic-discovery disputes, the Court emphasized that all discovery is subject to proportionality considerations. *Id.* at 599. See ***O'Connor's Texas Rules***, "Proportional," ch. 6-B, §2.1.1(2), p. 555; "Proportional," ch. 6-C, §6.1.2, p. 602.

ORDER ON {❶ *PARTY*}'S MOTION TO COMPEL

After considering {❷ *party*} {❸ *name*}'s motion to compel, the response, and arguments of counsel, the Court

{*CHOOSE APPROPRIATE ORDER GRANTING OR DENYING MOTION*}

DENIES the motion.

GRANTS {❹ *party*}'s motion to compel and orders that the requested discovery of {❺ *identify discovery*} be produced by {❻ *adverse party*} by {❼ *date*}.

GRANTS {❽ *party*}'s motion to compel and orders {❾ *adverse party*} to appear for a deposition on {❿ *date*}, at {⓫ *time*}, at {⓬ *address*}.

GRANTS {⓭ *party*}'s motion to compel and orders {⓮ *adverse party*} to respond to the following question: {⓯ *identify question from deposition*}.

{*ADD PARAGRAPH BELOW*}

ORDERS {⓰ *identify person or persons to be ordered to pay expenses, e.g., plaintiff, plaintiff's attorney, both plaintiff and plaintiff's attorney*} to pay {⓱ *party/adverse party*} ${⓲ *amount*} for reasonable expenses, including attorney fees, incurred in preparing the {⓳ *motion/response*} and attending the hearing.

SIGNED on ________________, 20___.

____
PRESIDING JUDGE

SEE: Tex. R. Civ. P. 215.1(d)
O'Connor's Texas Rules * Civil Trials **(2019), "Ruling," ch. 6-A, §22.5, p. 543**

ADD: STYLE OF THE CASE – FORM 1B:2
CERTIFICATE OF SERVICE – FORM 1B:13, if proposed order served separately from motion or response

{1 *PARTY*}'S MOTION FOR DISCOVERY SANCTIONS

{2 *Party*}, {3 *name*}, asks the Court to sanction {4 *identify person or persons to be sanctioned, e.g., plaintiff, plaintiff's attorney, both plaintiff and plaintiff's attorney*} for discovery abuse and for impeding the discovery process. {*See* ***O'Connor's Texas Rules***, *"Discovery abuse," ch. 5-K, §5.1, p. 467.*}

INTRODUCTION

1. Plaintiff, {5 *name*}, sued defendant, {6 *name*}, for {7 *state basis of suit*}.

2. Discovery in this suit is governed by a Level {8 *1/2/3*} discovery-control plan. The discovery period {9 *will end/ended*} on {10 *date*}. {*See* ***O'Connor's Texas Rules***, *"Discovery-Control Plans," ch. 6-A, §7, p. 520.*}

3. This case is set for trial on {11 *date*}.

4. {12 *State other relevant facts about the suit.*}

BACKGROUND

5. {13 *State facts relevant to the motion.*}

ARGUMENT & AUTHORITIES

6. The purpose of discovery is to seek the truth, so disputes may be decided by what facts are revealed, not by what facts are concealed. *Axelson, Inc. v. McIlhany*, 798 S.W.2d 550, 555 (Tex. 1990). The purpose of sanctions is to secure compliance with the rules, to deter future violation of the rules, and to punish parties that violate the rules. *Chrysler Corp. v. Blackmon*, 841 S.W.2d 844, 849 (Tex. 1992).

{*CHOOSE APPROPRIATE PARAGRAPHS 7-22*}

7. A court can impose sanctions when a corporation or other entity does not designate a witness under Texas Rules of Civil Procedure 199.2(b)(1) or 200.1(b). Tex. R. Civ. P. 215.1(b)(1). The Court should impose sanctions against {14 *adverse party*} because {15 *adverse party*}, a {16 *identify type of entity, e.g., corporation*}, did not designate a witness in response to {17 *party*}'s notice of intent to depose {18 *adverse party*}. {19 *Elaborate.*}

8. A court can impose sanctions when a party or other deponent fails to appear for a properly noticed deposition. Tex. R. Civ. P. 215.1(b)(2)(A). The Court should impose sanctions against {20 *adverse party*} because {21 *{adverse party}/{name of person testifying on behalf of adverse party}*} did not appear for the deposition scheduled for {22 *date*}. {23 *Elaborate.*}

◄ *Continued on next page* ►

9. A court can impose sanctions when a party or other deponent fails to answer a deposition question. Tex. R. Civ. P. 215.1(b)(2)(B). The Court should impose sanctions against {24 *adverse party*} because {25 *{adverse party}/{name of person testifying on behalf of adverse party}*} did not answer certain deposition questions. {26 *Elaborate.*}

10. A court can impose sanctions when a party fails to serve answers or objections to interrogatories. Tex. R. Civ. P. 215.1(b)(3)(A). The Court should impose sanctions against {27 *adverse party*} because {28 *adverse party*} did not serve any answers or objections to {29 *identify interrogatories*}. {30 *Elaborate.*}

11. A court can impose sanctions when a party fails to answer an interrogatory. Tex. R. Civ. P. 215.1(b)(3)(B). The Court should impose sanctions against {31 *adverse party*} because {32 *adverse party*} did not answer {33 *identify interrogatories*}. {34 *Elaborate.*}

12. A court can impose sanctions when a party fails to serve a response to a request for inspection. Tex. R. Civ. P. 215.1(b)(3)(C). The Court should impose sanctions against {35 *adverse party*} because {36 *adverse party*} did not serve a response to {37 *party*}'s request for inspection. {38 *Elaborate.*}

13. A court can impose sanctions when a party served with a request for inspection fails to respond that it will permit the discovery requested or fails to permit the discovery requested. Tex. R. Civ. P. 215.1(b)(3)(D). The Court should impose sanctions against {39 *adverse party*} because {40 *adverse party*} neither permitted discovery nor indicated that it would permit discovery in response to {41 *party*}'s request for inspection. {42 *Elaborate.*}

14. A court can impose sanctions when a party fails to respond to a request for disclosure. *See* Tex. R. Civ. P. 215.2(b); *Magnuson v. Mullen*, 65 S.W.3d 815, 828 (Tex. App.—Fort Worth 2002, pet. denied). The Court should impose sanctions against {43 *adverse party*} because {44 *adverse party*} did not respond to {45 *party*}'s request for disclosure. {46 *Elaborate.*}

15. A court can impose sanctions when a party fails to serve a response to a request for admissions. *See* Tex. R. Civ. P. 215.2(b). The Court should impose sanctions against {47 *adverse party*} because {48 *adverse party*} did not serve a response to {49 *party*}'s request for admissions. {50 *Elaborate.*}

16. A court can impose sanctions when a party fails to serve a response to {51 *identify other type of discovery request, e.g., a request for medical records*}. *See* Tex. R. Civ. P. 215.2(b). The Court should impose sanctions against {52 *adverse party*} because {53 *adverse party*} did not serve a response to {54 *party*}'s {55 *identify discovery request*}. {56 *Elaborate.*}

17. A court can impose sanctions when a party gives evasive or incomplete answers during discovery. *See* Tex. R. Civ. P. 215.1(b), (c). The Court should impose sanctions against {57 *adverse party*} because {58 *adverse party*} gave evasive and incomplete answers to {59 *identify discovery request, e.g., plaintiff's request for production 9*}. {60 *Elaborate.*}

18. A court can impose sanctions when an attorney files frivolous objections to discovery. *See, e.g., Childs v. Argenbright*, 927 S.W.2d 647, 649-50 (Tex. App.—Tyler 1996, no writ) (attorney filed nine pages of objections to interrogatories without answering any of them). The Court should impose sanctions against {61 *adverse party*}'s attorney, {62 *name of attorney*}, for the frivolous objections made to {63 *identify discovery request, e.g., plaintiff's request for production 9*}. {64 *Elaborate.*}

19. A court can impose sanctions when a party intentionally gives false information under oath during discovery. *See In re Reece*, 341 S.W.3d 360, 368 (Tex. 2011) (court can impose sanctions for lying during deposition); *see, e.g., Schaver v. British Am. Ins. Co.*, 795 S.W.2d 875, 878-79 (Tex. App.—Beaumont 1990, no writ) (because plaintiff falsified his postinjury employment status in depositions and sworn answers to interrogatories, court imposed monetary sanctions). The Court should impose sanctions against {65 *adverse party*} because {66 *describe false information*}.

20. A court can impose sanctions when an attorney engages in improper discovery procedures. *See, e.g., Sanchez v. Brownsville Sports Ctr., Inc.*, 51 S.W.3d 643, 658-59 (Tex. App.—Corpus Christi 2001, pet. granted, judgm't vacated w.r.m.) (plaintiff's attorney went to defendant's store and pretended to be interested in buying vehicle). The Court should impose sanctions against {67 *adverse party*}'s attorney, {68 *name of attorney*}, for {69 *describe improper discovery procedures*}.

21. A court can impose sanctions for a general pattern of discovery abuse. *Vela v. Wagner & Brown, Ltd.*, 203 S.W.3d 37, 59 (Tex. App.—San Antonio 2006, no pet.). The Court should impose sanctions against {70 *adverse party*} because {71 *he/she/it*} has established a pattern of discovery abuse. {72 *Elaborate.*}

22. {73 *State any other reasons why the Court should impose sanctions.*}

APPROPRIATE SANCTIONS

23. When considering sanctions, a court should ensure that the punishment fits the crime. *TransAmerican Nat. Gas Corp. v. Powell*, 811 S.W.2d 913, 917 (Tex. 1991). When a court decides to sanction, the sanctions must have a direct relationship to the offensive conduct, measured by a direct nexus among the conduct, the offender, and the sanctions imposed. *Am. Flood Research, Inc. v. Jones*, 192 S.W.3d 581, 583 (Tex.

Continued on next page

2006); *Spohn Hosp. v. Mayer*, 104 S.W.3d 878, 882 (Tex. 2003); *TransAmerican*, 811 S.W.2d at 917. A court must not impose sanctions more severe than necessary to promote full compliance with the rules. *Am. Flood*, 192 S.W.3d at 583; *Spohn Hosp.*, 104 S.W.3d at 882; *Chrysler Corp.*, 841 S.W.2d at 849. {*See **O'Connor's Texas Rules**, "Regular sanctions," ch. 5-K, §3.1, p. 462.*}

24. {⓮ *Party*} asks the Court to impose sanctions of {75 *identify sanctions requested*}. These sanctions are justified because there is a direct relationship between the conduct of {76 *identify person or persons to be sanctioned*} and this request for sanctions. {77 *Identify conduct that justifies sanction and describe the relationship between the request for sanctions and the conduct, e.g., if the adverse party did not respond to a legitimate request for discovery and forced party to file a motion to compel, the motion should ask for attorney fees and expenses for preparing the motion and attending the hearing.*} {*See **O'Connor's Texas Rules**, "Direct relationship," ch. 5-K, §3.1.1, p. 462.*}

25. These sanctions are no more severe than necessary to promote full compliance with this and other discovery requests. {78 *Elaborate.*} {*See **O'Connor's Texas Rules**, "Necessary severity," ch. 5-K, §3.1.2, p. 463.*}

{*CHOOSE APPROPRIATE PARAGRAPH 26 IF APPLICABLE*}

26. Death-penalty sanctions are appropriate in this case because the Court has already used a lesser sanction to determine if it was adequate to secure {79 *adverse party*}'s compliance with discovery. {80 *Describe earlier sanctions and show how they were not effective.*} {*See **O'Connor's Texas Rules**, "Typical misconduct," ch. 5-K, §3.2.3(1), p. 464.*} {81 *Adverse party*}'s conduct justifies the presumption that {82 *his/her/its*} {83 *claims/defenses*} lack merit. {84 *Elaborate.*} {*See **O'Connor's Texas Rules**, "No merit," ch. 5-K, §3.2.4, p. 465.*}

26. Death-penalty sanctions are appropriate in this case because {85 *adverse party*} has committed egregious misconduct. {86 *Describe misconduct.*} Even though the Court has not used a lesser sanction, it has considered lesser sanctions and {87 *adverse party*}'s conduct justifies the presumption that {88 *his/her/its*} {89 *claims/defenses*} lack merit. *Cire v. Cummings*, 134 S.W.3d 835, 842 (Tex. 2004). {90 *Explain how the record reflects the Court's consideration of lesser sanctions and how those sanctions would have been ineffective.*} {*See **O'Connor's Texas Rules**, "Egregious misconduct," ch. 5-K, §3.2.3(2), p. 465; "No merit," ch. 5-K, §3.2.4, p. 465.*}

CONCLUSION

27. {91 *Briefly summarize the motion.*}

PRAYER

28. For these reasons, {92 *party*} asks the Court to set this motion for hearing and, after the hearing, to sanction {93 *identify person or persons to be sanctioned*} for abusing the discovery process and to sign an order for {94 *identify sanctions requested*} against {95 *identify person or persons to be sanctioned*}.

SEE: Tex. R. Civ. P. 192, 215
O'Connor's Texas Rules * Civil Trials (2019), "Standards for Imposing Sanctions," ch. 5-K, §3, p. 462; "Discovery abuse," ch. 5-K, §5.1, p. 467

ADD: STYLE OF THE CASE – FORM 1B:2
SIGNATURE BLOCK – FORM 1B:3
CERTIFICATE OF CONFERENCE – FORM 1B:12
CERTIFICATE OF SERVICE – FORM 1B:13

ATTACH: AFFIDAVIT – FORM 1B:8, if necessary
NOTICE OF HEARING OR SUBMISSION – FORM 1E:1
ORDER – FORM 6A:29

NOTE: The court is not required to hold an oral hearing; sanctions can be resolved by a hearing on submission. *See, e.g.*, ***Cire v. Cummings***, 134 S.W.3d 835, 843-44 (Tex.2004) (nothing in Tex. R. Civ. P. 215.3 requires an oral hearing).

The court has inherent power to impose sanctions for discovery abuse that is not covered by a rule or statute. *See* ***In re Bennett***, 960 S.W.2d 35, 40 (Tex.1997); ***Liles v. Contreras***, 547 S.W.3d 280, 290 (Tex. App.—San Antonio 2018, pet. denied). See ***O'Connor's Texas Rules***, "Inherent power," ch. 5-K, §2.2, p. 462. The standards for imposing sanctions under the court's inherent power are the same as those for imposing sanctions under a rule or statute. *See* ***Altesse Healthcare Solutions, Inc. v. Wilson***, 540 S.W.3d 570, 574-75 (Tex.2018). See ***O'Connor's Texas Rules***, "Standards for Imposing Sanctions," ch. 5-K, §3, p. 462.

{❶ *PARTY*}'S RESPONSE TO
{❷ *ADVERSE PARTY*}'S MOTION FOR DISCOVERY SANCTIONS

{❸ *Party*}, {❹ *name*}, asks the Court to deny {❺ *adverse party*} {❻ *name*}'s motion for discovery sanctions. {*See* ***O'Connor's Texas Rules****, "Discovery abuse," ch. 5-K, §5.1, p. 467.*}

INTRODUCTION

1. Plaintiff, {❼ *name*}, sued defendant, {❽ *name*}, for {❾ *state basis of suit*}.

2. Discovery in this suit is governed by a Level {❿ *1/2/3*} discovery-control plan. The discovery period {⓫ *will end/ended*} on {⓬ *date*}. {*See* ***O'Connor's Texas Rules****, "Discovery-Control Plans," ch. 6-A, §7, p. 520.*}

3. This case is set for trial on {⓭ *date*}.

4. {⓮ *State other relevant facts about the suit.*}

BACKGROUND

5. {⓯ *Adverse party*} asked the Court to sanction {⓰ *party*} because {⓱ *state conduct identified in adverse party's motion for sanctions*}.

6. {⓲ *State other facts relevant to the response.*}

ARGUMENT & AUTHORITIES

7. The purpose of sanctions is to secure compliance with the rules, to deter future violations of the rules, and to punish parties that violate the rules. *Chrysler Corp. v. Blackmon*, 841 S.W.2d 844, 849 (Tex. 1992). The Court should not sanction {⓳ *party*} because {⓴ *explain why adverse party's allegation that party violated the rules is incorrect, e.g., defendant answered each request as completely and as accurately as possible, defendant has produced all the documents in its custody or control*}.

8. If the Court determines that {㉑ *party*} violated the rules, it should not grant the sanction {㉒ *adverse party*} requests. When a court decides to sanction, the sanctions must have a direct relationship to the offensive conduct, measured by a direct nexus among the conduct, the offender, and the sanctions imposed. *Am. Flood Research, Inc. v. Jones*, 192 S.W.3d 581, 583 (Tex. 2006); *Spohn Hosp. v. Mayer*, 104 S.W.3d 878, 882 (Tex. 2003); *TransAmerican Nat. Gas Corp. v. Powell*, 811 S.W.2d 913, 917 (Tex. 1991). A court must not impose a sanction more severe than necessary to promote full compliance with the rules. *Am. Flood*, 192 S.W.3d at 583; *Spohn Hosp.*, 104 S.W.3d at 882; *Chrysler Corp.*, 841 S.W.2d at 849. {*See* ***O'Connor's Texas Rules****, "Regular sanctions," ch. 5-K, §3.1, p. 462.*}

9. In this case, {23 *adverse party*}'s request for sanctions is excessive. The only conduct {24 *adverse party*} complains of is {25 *identify and justify conduct adverse party complains of*}. Even though {26 *party*} only {27 *describe conduct complained of in light favorable to party*}, {28 *adverse party*} requests the excessive sanction of {29 *identify sanction sought*}. There is no direct relationship between {30 *party*}'s conduct and the sanction {31 *adverse party*} seeks. Thus, the sanction is unnecessary to ensure {32 *party*}'s future compliance with the rules, and the Court should deny the request.

{*CHOOSE APPROPRIATE PARAGRAPHS 10-15 IF APPLICABLE*}

10. {33 *Adverse party*} asked for death-penalty sanctions for {34 *party*}'s {35 *describe conduct complained of, e.g., failure to respond properly to discovery*}. The Court should deny {36 *adverse party*}'s motion and order a continuance of the trial to allow {37 *party*} to comply with {38 *adverse party*}'s discovery request because there is no direct relationship between the conduct and the sanction. *Chrysler Corp.*, 841 S.W.2d at 849; *see Am. Flood*, 192 S.W.3d at 583; *Spohn Hosp.*, 104 S.W.3d at 882; *TransAmerican*, 811 S.W.2d at 917. {39 *Elaborate.*} {*See* ***O'Connor's Texas Rules****, "Direct relationship," ch. 5-K, §3.1.1, p. 462.*}

11. {40 *Adverse party*} asked for death-penalty sanctions for {41 *party*}'s {42 *describe conduct complained of, e.g., failure to respond properly to discovery*}. The Court should deny {43 *adverse party*}'s motion and order a continuance of the trial to allow {44 *party*} to comply with {45 *adverse party*}'s discovery request because the requested sanction is more severe than necessary to promote full compliance with the Texas Rules of Civil Procedure. *Spohn Hosp.*, 104 S.W.3d at 882; *Chrysler Corp.*, 841 S.W.2d at 849; *see Am. Flood*, 192 S.W.3d at 583. {46 *Elaborate.*} {*See* ***O'Connor's Texas Rules****, "Necessary severity," ch. 5-K, §3.1.2, p. 463.*}

12. {47 *Adverse party*} asked for death-penalty sanctions for {48 *party*}'s {49 *describe conduct complained of, e.g., failure to respond properly to discovery*}. The Court should deny {50 *adverse party*}'s motion and order a continuance of the trial to allow {51 *party*} to comply with {52 *adverse party*}'s discovery request because the motion is {53 *adverse party*}'s first request for sanctions, and the Court must first consider a lesser sanction before imposing death-penalty sanctions. *GTE Commc'ns Sys. Corp. v. Tanner*, 856 S.W.2d 725, 729 (Tex. 1993). {54 *Elaborate.*} {*See* ***O'Connor's Texas Rules****, "Typical misconduct," ch. 5-K, §3.2.3(1), p. 464.*}

13. {55 *Adverse party*} asked for death-penalty sanctions for {56 *party*}'s {57 *describe conduct complained of, e.g., failure to respond properly to discovery*}. The Court should deny {58 *adverse party*}'s motion and order a continuance of the trial to allow

Continued on next page

{59 *party*} to comply with {60 *adverse party*}'s discovery request because {61 *party*}'s conduct is not so egregious as to alleviate the Court of the burden of using a lesser sanction first. *See Cire v. Cummings*, 134 S.W.3d 835, 842 (Tex. 2004). {62 *Describe conduct and explain how lesser sanctions would be effective.*} {*See* ***O'Connor's Texas Rules****, "Egregious misconduct," ch. 5-K, §3.2.3(2), p. 465.*}

14. {63 *Adverse party*} asked for death-penalty sanctions for {64 *party*}'s {65 *describe conduct complained of, e.g., failure to respond properly to discovery*}. The Court should deny {66 *adverse party*}'s motion and order a continuance of the trial to allow {67 *party*} to comply with {68 *adverse party*}'s discovery request because {69 *party*}'s conduct does not show lack of merit. A court should not impose a death-penalty sanction unless the party's conduct justifies the presumption that its claims or defenses lack merit. *Hamill v. Level*, 917 S.W.2d 15, 16 (Tex. 1996). {70 *Elaborate.*} {*See* ***O'Connor's Texas Rules****, "No merit," ch. 5-K, §3.2.4, p. 465.*}

15. {71 *Adverse party*} asked for death-penalty sanctions for {72 *party*}'s {73 *describe conduct complained of, e.g., failure to respond properly to discovery*}. The Court should deny {74 *adverse party*}'s motion and order a continuance of the trial to allow {75 *party*} to comply with {76 *adverse party*}'s discovery request because {77 *party*}'s attorney, {78 *name*}, was responsible for the conduct, and {79 *party*} was unaware of it. *See* Tex. R. Civ. P. 215.1(d), 215.2(b)(8); *Am. Flood*, 192 S.W.3d at 583; *TransAmerican*, 811 S.W.2d at 917; *Jones v. Andrews*, 873 S.W.2d 102, 106 (Tex. App.—Dallas 1994, no writ). {80 *Elaborate.*} {*See* ***O'Connor's Texas Rules****, "Attorney," ch. 5-K, §4.2, p. 466.*}

CONCLUSION

16. {81 *Briefly summarize the response.*}

PRAYER

17. For these reasons, {82 *party*} asks the Court to deny {83 *adverse party*}'s request for discovery sanctions.

FORM 6A:28 RESPONSE TO MOTION FOR DISCOVERY SANCTIONS

SEE: Tex. R. Civ. P. 192, 215
O'Connor's Texas Rules * Civil Trials (2019), "Standards for Imposing Sanctions," ch. 5-K, §3, p. 462; "Discovery abuse," ch. 5-K, §5.1, p. 467

ADD: STYLE OF THE CASE – FORM 1B:2
SIGNATURE BLOCK – FORM 1B:3
CERTIFICATE OF SERVICE – FORM 1B:13

ATTACH: AFFIDAVIT – FORM 1B:8, if necessary
ORDER – FORM 6A:29

NOTE: The court is not required to hold an oral hearing; sanctions can be resolved by a hearing on submission. *See, e.g.*, ***Cire v. Cummings***, 134 S.W.3d 835, 843-44 (Tex.2004) (nothing in Tex. R. Civ. P. 215.3 requires an oral hearing).

ORDER ON {❶ *PARTY*}'S MOTION FOR DISCOVERY SANCTIONS

After considering {❷ *party*} {❸ *name*}'s motion for discovery sanctions, the supporting affidavits, the response, and arguments of counsel, the Court

{*CHOOSE APPROPRIATE ORDER*}

DENIES the motion.

GRANTS the motion for discovery sanctions.

{*CHOOSE APPROPRIATE PROVISIONS*}

1. The Court imposes the following sanctions on {❹ *adverse party*}, {❺ *name*}: {❻ *list sanctions*}.

2. The Court imposes the following sanctions on {❼ *name*}, the attorney for {❽ *adverse party*}: {❾ *list sanctions*}.

3. The Court awards the following attorney fees and court costs to {❿ *party*}: {⓫ *list attorney fees and court costs*}.

FINDINGS OF FACT

The Court makes the following findings in support of the sanctions imposed for discovery abuse:

a. There is a direct relationship between the offensive conduct and the sanction in that {⓬ *describe conduct and identify relationship*}.

b. This sanction is no more severe than necessary to promote full compliance. {⓭ *Elaborate.*}

{*If imposing death-penalty sanctions, add paragraphs c-d*}

{*CHOOSE APPROPRIATE PARAGRAPH c*}

c. This Court imposed an earlier sanction on {⓮ *adverse party*}. {⓯ *Identify earlier conduct and sanction.*} That sanction was not sufficient to deter similar conduct.

c. A lesser sanction was not imposed because {⓰ *adverse party*} committed egregious misconduct. {⓱ *Describe misconduct.*} This Court considered lesser sanctions, but they would not have been effective. {⓲ *Elaborate.*}

d. {[19] *Adverse party*}'s conduct justifies the presumption that {[20] *his/her/its*} {[21] *claim/defense*} lacks merit. {[22] *Elaborate.*}

SIGNED on ______________, 20___.

____
PRESIDING JUDGE

SEE: Tex. R. Civ. P. 192, 215
O'Connor's Texas Rules * Civil Trials (2019), "Standards for Imposing Sanctions," ch. 5-K, §3, p. 462; "Order for discovery sanctions," ch. 5-K, §11.1, p. 478

ADD: STYLE OF THE CASE – FORM 1B:2
CERTIFICATE OF SERVICE – FORM 1B:13, if proposed order served separately from motion or response

NOTE: When judgment is rendered as a sanction for discovery abuse, the court should file separate findings of fact. See ***O'Connor's Texas Rules***, "After hearing on sanctions under TRCP 215," ch. 10-E, §2.2.1, p. 961.

{❶ *PARTY*}'S MOTION FOR SANCTIONS FOR SPOLIATION OF EVIDENCE

{❷ *Party*}, {❸ *name*}, asks the Court to sanction {❹ *adverse party*}, {❺ *name*} for spoliating discoverable evidence that {❻ *he/she/it*} could have reasonably preserved. {*See* ***O'Connor's Texas Rules****, "Spoliation," ch. 6-A, §24, p. 544.*}

INTRODUCTION

1. Plaintiff, {❼ *name*}, sued defendant, {❽ *name*}, for {❾ *state basis of suit*}.

2. Discovery in this suit is governed by a Level {❿ *1/2/3*} discovery-control plan. The discovery period {⓫ *will end/ended*} on {⓬ *date*}. {*See* ***O'Connor's Texas Rules****, "Discovery-Control Plans," ch. 6-A, §7, p. 520.*}

3. This case is set for trial on {⓭ *date*}.

4. {⓮ *State other relevant facts about the suit.*}

BACKGROUND

5. {⓯ *State facts relevant to the motion.*}

ARGUMENT & AUTHORITIES

6. The purpose of discovery is to seek the truth so disputes may be decided by what facts are revealed, not by what facts are concealed. *Axelson, Inc. v. McIlhany*, 798 S.W.2d 550, 555 (Tex. 1990). The purpose of sanctions is to secure compliance with the rules, to deter future violation of the rules, and to punish parties that violate the rules. *Chrysler Corp. v. Blackmon*, 841 S.W.2d 844, 849 (Tex. 1992).

7. In analyzing a claim of spoliation, a court must determine whether a party spoliated evidence—that is, did a party have a duty to preserve evidence and was that duty breached. *Brookshire Bros. v. Aldridge*, 438 S.W.3d 9, 14 (Tex. 2014). If the court determines that the party spoliated evidence, the court must assess an appropriate remedy after evaluating the culpability of the spoliating party (i.e., whether the spoliating party acted intentionally or negligently) and the prejudice to the nonspoliating party. *See id.*

A. {⓰ *Adverse party*} had duty to preserve evidence and breached that duty.

8. A court can impose sanctions when a party spoliates evidence—that is, when a party conceals, alters, or destroys evidence that it could have reasonably preserved. *See Wackenhut Corp. v. Gutierrez*, 453 S.W.3d 917, 921 (Tex. 2015); *Brookshire Bros.*, 438 S.W.3d at 18; *Cire v. Cummings*, 134 S.W.3d 835, 843 (Tex. 2004); *Miner Dederick Constr., LLP v. Gulf Chem. & Metallurgical Corp.*, 403 S.W.3d 451, 467 (Tex. App.—

Houston [1st Dist.] 2013), *pet. denied*, 455 S.W.3d 164 (Tex. 2015). For a court to determine that a party spoliated evidence, the spoliating party must have (1) had a duty to preserve the evidence and (2) breached that duty by not preserving the evidence. *Brookshire Bros.*, 438 S.W.3d at 20. {*See **O'Connor's Texas Rules**, "Requesting party's burden," ch. 6-A, §24.2.1(1), p. 545.*}

9. A party's duty to preserve evidence arises as soon as it knows or reasonably should know that (1) there is a substantial chance that a claim will be filed and (2) evidence in its possession or control will be material and relevant to that claim. *Brookshire Bros.*, 438 S.W.3d at 20; *Wal-Mart Stores, Inc. v. Johnson*, 106 S.W.3d 718, 722 (Tex. 2003). For there to be a substantial chance of a claim being filed, there must be more than the mere possibility or unwarranted fear of litigation. *Brookshire Bros.*, 438 S.W.3d at 20. {[17] *Adverse party*} had a duty to preserve evidence because {[18] *explain*}. {*See **O'Connor's Texas Rules**, "Duty to preserve," ch. 6-A, §24.2.1(1)(a), p. 545.*}

10. A party breaches its duty to preserve evidence if it does not exercise reasonable care. *Brookshire Bros.*, 438 S.W.3d at 20. Although extraordinary measures to preserve the evidence are not required, a party, in exercising reasonable care, has a duty to not alter the evidence's condition. *Miner Dederick Constr.*, 403 S.W.3d at 466-67. A party's breach can be either intentional or negligent. *Brookshire Bros.*, 438 S.W.3d at 20. An intentional breach occurs when a party acts with a subjective purpose to conceal, alter, or destroy discoverable evidence or allows for such spoliation of evidence, although the party does not directly conceal, alter, or destroy it; a negligent breach occurs when a party conceals, alters, or destroys evidence without deliberately doing so. *See id.* at 23-24. {[19] *Adverse party*} {[20] *intentionally/negligently*} breached {[21] *his/her/its*} duty to preserve evidence because {[22] *explain*}. {*See **O'Connor's Texas Rules**, "Breach of duty," ch. 6-A, §24.2.1(1)(b), p. 545; "Assess culpability," ch. 6-A, §24.2.2(1), p. 546.*}

B. {[23] *Party*} suffered prejudice as a result of {[24] *adverse party*}'s breach.

11. Before imposing a remedy for the spoliation of evidence, a court must evaluate any prejudice suffered by the nonspoliating party. *See Brookshire Bros.*, 438 S.W.3d at 21 & n.9. In assessing prejudice, a court will consider (1) the relevance of the missing evidence to key issues in the case, (2) whether the missing evidence would have been harmful to the spoliating party's case, or, alternatively, would have been helpful to the nonspoliating party's case, and (3) whether there is other competent evidence available to replace the missing evidence. *Id.* at 21-22. {[25] *Party*} has suffered prejudice as a result of {[26] *adverse party*}'s {[27] *intentional/negligent*} spoliation of evidence because {[28] *explain why the party has suffered prejudice, even if the missing evidence is cumu-*

Continued on next page

lative of other competent evidence, and identify what the missing evidence would show}. {*See* ***O'Connor's Texas Rules****, "Evaluate prejudice," ch. 6-A, §24.2.2(2), p. 546.*}

APPROPRIATE SANCTIONS

12. After assessing the spoliating party's culpability and the prejudice to the nonspoliating party, a court can impose appropriate sanctions. *See Brookshire Bros.*, 438 S.W.3d at 21. The sanctions must have a direct relationship to the spoliation of the evidence, measured by a direct nexus among the conduct, the offender, and the sanctions imposed, and must not be excessive. *See id.*; *Spohn Hosp. v. Mayer*, 104 S.W.3d 878, 882 (Tex. 2003); *TransAmerican Nat. Gas Corp. v. Powell*, 811 S.W.2d 913, 917 (Tex. 1991). That is, the sanctions must be proportionate to the culpability of the spoliating party and the prejudice to the nonspoliating party. *Brookshire Bros.*, 438 S.W.3d at 21. {*See* ***O'Connor's Texas Rules****, "Regular sanctions," ch. 5-K, §3.1, p. 462; "Standard," ch. 6-A, §24.2.2(3)(a), p. 547.*}

{*CHOOSE APPROPRIATE PARAGRAPH 13*}

{*Sanctions generally*}

13. {㉙ *Party*} asks the Court to impose sanctions of {㉚ *identify sanctions requested, e.g., attorney fees and costs, excluding certain evidence*}. These sanctions are justified because there is a direct relationship between the conduct of {㉛ *adverse party*} and the requested sanctions and because the sanctions are not excessive. {㉜ *Elaborate.*} {*See* ***O'Connor's Texas Rules****, "Sanctions," ch. 6-A, §24.2.2(3)(b)[1], p. 547.*}

{*Death-penalty sanctions*}

13. {㉝ *Party*} asks the Court to impose sanctions of {㉞ *identify sanctions requested, e.g., striking adverse party's pleadings, dismissing adverse party's claims*}. These sanctions are justified because there is a direct relationship between the conduct of {㉟ *adverse party*} and the requested sanctions and because the sanctions are not excessive. {㊱ *Elaborate.*} {*See* ***O'Connor's Texas Rules****, "Sanctions," ch. 6-A, §24.2.2(3)(b)[1], p. 547.*}

{*Spoliation jury instruction*}

13. {㊲ *Party*} asks the Court to give a spoliation instruction to the jury for it to presume that the missing evidence is relevant and harmful to the {㊳ *adverse party*}. A spoliation jury instruction is justified because there is a direct relationship between the

conduct of {39 *adverse party*} and the request for a jury instruction and because the jury instruction is not excessive. {40 *Elaborate.*} {*See **O'Connor's Texas Rules**, "Spoliation jury instruction," ch. 6-A, §24.2.2(3)(b)[2], p. 547.*}

{*Any other sanction or remedy*}

13. {41 *Identify any other sanction or remedy the court should impose and why it is directly related to adverse party's conduct and is not excessive. See Brookshire Bros., 438 S.W.3d at 21.*}

{*ADD PARAGRAPH 14 IF APPLICABLE*}

14. For {42 *death-penalty sanctions/a spoliation jury instruction*} to be proper, a party must have intentionally spoliated evidence or, if the party negligently spoliated evidence, the negligent spoliation must have irreparably prevented the nonspoliating party from presenting a claim or defense. *See Wackenhut Corp.*, 453 S.W.3d at 921; *Petroleum Sols., Inc. v. Head*, 454 S.W.3d 482, 489 (Tex. 2014); *Brookshire Bros.*, 438 S.W.3d at 24-26. Specifically, {43 *identify sanctions requested*} is proper in this case because {44 *adverse party*} {45 *intentionally spoliated evidence/negligently spoliated evidence such that {party} was irreparably prevented from presenting a {claim/defense}*}. {46 *Elaborate.*} {*See **O'Connor's Texas Rules**, "Types of remedies," ch. 6-A, §24.2.2(3)(b), p. 547.*}

{*CHOOSE APPROPRIATE PARAGRAPH 15 IF APPLICABLE*}

15. {47 *Death-penalty sanctions are/A spoliation jury instruction is*} appropriate in this case because the Court has already used a lesser sanction to determine if it was sufficient to secure {48 *adverse party*}'s compliance with discovery. *See Brookshire Bros.*, 438 S.W.3d at 25. {49 *Describe earlier sanctions and show how they were insufficient.*} {50 *Adverse party*}'s conduct justifies the presumption that {51 *his/her/its*} {52 *claims/defenses*} lack merit. {53 *Elaborate.*} {*See **O'Connor's Texas Rules**, "Typical misconduct," ch. 5-K, §3.2.3(1), p. 464; "No merit," ch. 5-K, §3.2.4, p. 465; "Types of remedies," ch. 6-A, §24.2.2(3)(b), p. 547.*}

15. {54 *Death-penalty sanctions are/A spoliation jury instruction is*} appropriate in this case because the Court, although it has not used a lesser sanction, has considered lesser sanctions and {55 *adverse party*}'s conduct justifies the presumption that {56 *his/her/its*} {57 *claims/defenses*} lack merit. *See Brookshire Bros.*, 438 S.W.3d at 25; *Cire*, 134 S.W.3d at 842. {58 *Explain how the record reflects the court's consideration of lesser sanctions and how those sanctions would have been insufficient to minimize the prejudice caused by the spoliating party.*} {*See **O'Connor's Texas Rules**, "Egregious misconduct," ch. 5-K, §3.2.3(2), p. 465; "No merit," ch. 5-K, §3.2.4, p. 465; "Types of remedies," ch. 6-A, §24.2.2(3)(b), p. 547.*}

Continued on next page

CONCLUSION

16. {59 *Briefly summarize the motion.*}

PRAYER

17. For these reasons, {60 *party*} asks the Court to set this motion for hearing and, after the hearing, to sanction {61 *adverse party*} for spoliating discoverable evidence and to sign an order for {62 *identify sanctions requested*} against {63 *adverse party*}.

SEE: Tex. R. Civ. P. 215
O'Connor's Texas Rules * Civil Trials (2019), "Standards for Imposing Sanctions," ch. 5-K, §3, p. 462; "Spoliation," ch. 6-A, §24, p. 544

ADD: STYLE OF THE CASE – FORM 1B:2
SIGNATURE BLOCK – FORM 1B:3
CERTIFICATE OF CONFERENCE – FORM 1B:12
CERTIFICATE OF SERVICE – FORM 1B:13

ATTACH: AFFIDAVIT – FORM 1B:8, if necessary
NOTICE OF HEARING OR SUBMISSION – FORM 1E:1
ORDER – FORM 6A:32

NOTE: **The court is not required to hold an oral hearing; sanctions can be resolved by a hearing on submission.** *See, e.g.*, ***Cire v. Cummings***, 134 S.W.3d 835, 843-44 (Tex.2004) (nothing in Tex. R. Civ. P. 215.3 requires an oral hearing). **If the court holds an evidentiary hearing, it must be outside the presence of the jury.** ***Brookshire Bros. v. Aldridge***, 438 S.W.3d 9, 20 (Tex.2014).

{1 *PARTY*}'S RESPONSE TO {2 *ADVERSE PARTY*}'S
MOTION FOR SANCTIONS FOR SPOLIATION OF EVIDENCE

{3 *Party*}, {4 *name*}, asks the Court to deny {5 *adverse party*} {6 *name*}'s motion for sanctions for spoliation of evidence. {*See* ***O'Connor's Texas Rules***, *"Spoliation," ch. 6-A, §24, p. 544.*}

INTRODUCTION

1. Plaintiff, {7 *name*}, sued defendant, {8 *name*}, for {9 *state basis of suit*}.

2. Discovery in this suit is governed by a Level {10 *1/2/3*} discovery-control plan. The discovery period {11 *will end/ended*} on {12 *date*}. {*See* ***O'Connor's Texas Rules***, *"Discovery-Control Plans," ch. 6-A, §7, p. 520.*}

3. This case is set for trial on {13 *date*}.

4. {14 *State other relevant facts about the suit.*}

BACKGROUND

5. {15 *Adverse party*} asked the Court to sanction {16 *party*} because {17 *state conduct identified in adverse party's motion for sanctions*}.

6. {18 *Adverse party*} asked the Court to impose the following sanctions on {19 *party*}: {20 *identify sanctions requested*}.

7. {21 *State other facts relevant to the response.*}

ARGUMENT & AUTHORITIES

8. A court can impose sanctions when a party spoliates evidence—that is, when a party conceals, alters, or destroys evidence that it could have reasonably preserved. *See Wackenhut Corp. v. Gutierrez*, 453 S.W.3d 917, 921 (Tex. 2015); *Brookshire Bros. v. Aldridge*, 438 S.W.3d 9, 18 (Tex. 2014). In this case, however, the Court should not {22 *impose sanctions/impose the sanctions requested by {adverse party}*}.

9. In analyzing a claim of spoliation, a court must determine whether a party spoliated evidence—that is, did a party have a duty to preserve evidence and was that duty breached. *Brookshire Bros.*, 438 S.W.3d at 14. If the court determines that the party spoliated evidence, the court must assess an appropriate remedy after evaluating the culpability of the spoliating party (i.e., whether the spoliating party acted intentionally or negligently) and the prejudice to the nonspoliating party. *See id.*

Continued on next page

{*CHOOSE APPROPRIATE SECTIONS A-C*}

A. {[23] *Party*} did not have a duty to preserve evidence.

10. For a court to determine that a party spoliated evidence, the party claiming spoliation must show that the allegedly spoliating party had a duty to preserve the evidence. *Brookshire Bros.*, 438 S.W.3d at 20. A party's duty to preserve evidence arises as soon as it knows or reasonably should know that (1) there is a substantial chance that a claim will be filed and (2) evidence in its possession or control will be material and relevant to that claim. *Id.*; *Wal-Mart Stores, Inc. v. Johnson*, 106 S.W.3d 718, 722 (Tex. 2003). For there to be a substantial chance of a claim being filed, there must be more than the mere possibility or unwarranted fear of litigation. *Brookshire Bros.*, 438 S.W.3d at 20. {*See* ***O'Connor's Texas Rules***, *"Duty to preserve," ch. 6-A, §24.2.1(1)(a), p. 545.*} {[24] *Party*} did not have a duty to preserve evidence because

{*CHOOSE APPROPRIATE STATEMENT*}

[A] {[25] *he/she/it*} did not know or reasonably should not have known that there was a substantial chance that a claim would be filed. *See id.*; *Wal-Mart Stores*, 106 S.W.3d at 722. {[26] *Elaborate.*} Thus, the Court should deny {[27] *adverse party*}'s motion for sanctions.

[B] {[28] *he/she/it*} did not know or reasonably should not have known that evidence in its possession or control would be material and relevant to a claim being filed. *See id.*; *Wal-Mart Stores*, 106 S.W.3d at 722. {[29] *Elaborate.*} Thus, the Court should deny {[30] *adverse party*}'s motion for sanctions.

[C] {[31] *he/she/it*} did not know or reasonably should not have known that there was a substantial chance that a claim would be filed or that evidence in {[32] *his/her/its*} possession or control would be material and relevant to a claim being filed. *See id.*; *Wal-Mart Stores*, 106 S.W.3d at 722. {[33] *Elaborate.*} Thus, the Court should deny {[34] *adverse party*}'s motion for sanctions.

{*ADD PARAGRAPH 11 IF APPLICABLE*}

11. Although {[35] *party*} {[36] *lost/altered/destroyed*} evidence, it was done in the ordinary course of {[37] *party*}'s business under a corporate retention policy and before any duty to preserve arose. *See Brumfield v. Exxon Corp.*, 63 S.W.3d 912, 920 (Tex. App.—Houston [14th Dist.] 2002, pet. denied); *Ordonez v. M.W. McCurdy & Co.*, 984 S.W.2d 264, 273-74 (Tex. App.—Houston [1st Dist.] 1998, no pet.); *Trevino v. Ortega*,

969 S.W.2d 950, 957 (Tex. 1998) (Baker, J., concurring). {❸❽ *Explain that the party's business has a reasonable retention policy of limited duration and that the duty to preserve evidence did not arise before evidence was lost, altered, or destroyed. See Brookshire Bros., 438 S.W.3d at 27 & n.19.*} {*See* ***O'Connor's Texas Rules****, "Destruction in ordinary course of business," ch. 6-A, §24.2.1(2)(b)[2], p. 545.*}

B. {❸❾ *Party*} did not breach {❹⓿ *his/her/its*} duty to preserve evidence.

12. For a court to determine that a party spoliated evidence, the party claiming spoliation must show that the allegedly spoliating party breached its duty to preserve evidence. *Brookshire Bros.*, 438 S.W.3d at 20. A party breaches its duty to preserve evidence if it does not exercise reasonable care. *Id.* Although extraordinary measures to preserve the evidence are not required, a party, in exercising reasonable care, has a duty to not alter the evidence's condition. *Miner Dederick Constr., LLP v. Gulf Chem. & Metallurgical Corp.*, 403 S.W.3d 451, 466-67 (Tex. App.—Houston [1st Dist.] 2013), *pet. denied*, 455 S.W.3d 164 (Tex. 2015). {*See* ***O'Connor's Texas Rules****, "Breach of duty," ch. 6-A, §24.2.1(1)(b), p. 545.*} {❹❶ *Party*} did not breach {❹❷ *his/her/its*} duty to preserve evidence because

{*CHOOSE APPROPRIATE REASON*}

Ⓐ {❹❸ *he/she/it*} exercised reasonable care. *See Brookshire Bros.*, 438 S.W.3d at 20. {❹❹ *Elaborate.*} Thus, the Court should deny {❹❺ *adverse party*}'s motion for sanctions.

Ⓑ the {❹❻ *loss/alteration/destruction*} of evidence was beyond {❹❼ *party*}'s control. *See Brookshire Bros.*, 438 S.W.3d at 21 n.8; *Walker v. Thomasson Lumber Co.*, 203 S.W.3d 470, 477 (Tex. App.—Houston [14th Dist.] 2006, no pet.); *Trevino v. Ortega*, 969 S.W.2d 950, 957 (Tex. 1998) (Baker, J., concurring). {❹❽ *Explain, e.g., the evidence was destroyed by an act of God and through no fault of the party.*} Thus, the Court should deny {❹❾ *adverse party*}'s motion for sanctions. {*See* ***O'Connor's Texas Rules****, "Loss or destruction beyond its control," ch. 6-A, §24.2.1(2)(b)[1], p. 545.*}

C. Requested sanctions are not appropriate.

13. If the Court determines that {❺⓿ *party*} spoliated evidence, it should not grant the sanctions {❺❶ *adverse party*} requests. Once a court determines that a party has spoliated evidence, it must assess the culpability of the spoliating party and evaluate any prejudice to the nonspoliating party before imposing an appropriate sanction. *See Brookshire Bros.*, 438 S.W.3d at 14. When a court decides to sanction, the sanctions

Continued on next page

must have a direct relationship to the offensive conduct, measured by a direct nexus among the conduct, the offender, and the sanctions imposed, and must not be excessive. *See id.* at 21; *Spohn Hosp. v. Mayer*, 104 S.W.3d 878, 882 (Tex. 2003); *TransAmerican Nat. Gas Corp. v. Powell*, 811 S.W.2d 913, 917 (Tex. 1991). That is, the sanctions must be proportionate to the culpability of the spoliating party and the prejudice to the non-spoliating party. *Brookshire Bros.*, 438 S.W.3d at 21. {*See* ***O'Connor's Texas Rules****, "Regular sanctions," ch. 5-K, §3.1, p. 462; "Assessing appropriate remedy," ch. 6-A, §24.2.2, p. 546.*}

14. A party's breach of its duty to preserve evidence can be either intentional or negligent. *Brookshire Bros.*, 438 S.W.3d at 20. An intentional breach occurs when a party acts with a subjective purpose to conceal, alter, or destroy discoverable evidence or allows for such spoliation of evidence, although the party does not directly conceal, alter, or destroy it; a negligent breach occurs when a party conceals, alters, or destroys evidence without deliberately doing so. *See id.* at 23-24. {❺❷ *Party*}'s breach of {❺❸ *his/her/its*} duty to preserve evidence was negligent because {❺❹ *explain*}. {*See* ***O'Connor's Texas Rules****, "Assess culpability," ch. 6-A, §24.2.2(1), p. 546.*}

15. In assessing prejudice suffered by the nonspoliating party, a court will consider (1) the relevance of the missing evidence to key issues in the case, (2) whether the missing evidence would have been harmful to the spoliating party's case, or, alternatively, would have been helpful to the nonspoliating party's case, and (3) whether there is other competent evidence available to replace the missing evidence. *Brookshire Bros.*, 438 S.W.3d at 21-22. {❺❺ *Adverse party*} has {❺❻ *not suffered/suffered minimal*} prejudice as a result of {❺❼ *party*}'s spoliation of evidence because {❺❽ *explain why the adverse party has not suffered or suffered only minimal prejudice and, if appropriate, that the type and quality of other competent evidence that is available negates or lessens a finding of prejudice*}. {*See* ***O'Connor's Texas Rules****, "Evaluate prejudice," ch. 6-A, §24.2.2(2), p. 546.*}

16. In this case, there is no direct relationship between {❺❾ *party*}'s conduct and the sanction {❻⓿ *adverse party*} requests. Even though {❻❶ *party*} only {❻❷ *describe conduct complained of in light favorable to party*}, {❻❸ *adverse party*} requests the excessive sanction of {❻❹ *identify sanctions requested*}. Thus, the sanction is not proportionate to the culpability of {❻❺ *party*} and the prejudice to {❻❻ *adverse party*}, and the Court should deny {❻❼ *adverse party*}'s motion for sanctions.

{*CHOOSE APPROPRIATE PARAGRAPHS 17-20 IF APPLICABLE*}

17. {68 *Adverse party*} asked for {69 *death-penalty sanctions/a spoliation jury instruction*} for {70 *party*}'s {71 *describe conduct complained of*}. For {72 *death-penalty sanctions/a spoliation jury instruction*} to be proper, a party must have intentionally spoliated evidence or, if the party negligently spoliated evidence, the negligent spoliation must have irreparably prevented the nonspoliating party from presenting a claim or defense. *See Wackenhut Corp.*, 453 S.W.3d at 921; *Petroleum Sols., Inc. v. Head*, 454 S.W.3d 482, 489 (Tex. 2014); *Brookshire Bros.*, 438 S.W.3d at 24-26. The Court should deny {73 *adverse party*}'s motion for sanctions because {74 *party*} did not intentionally spoliate evidence or negligently spoliate evidence such that {75 *adverse party*} was irreparably prevented from presenting a {76 *claim/defense*}. {77 *Elaborate.*} {*See* ***O'Connor's Texas Rules***, *"Types of remedies," ch. 6-A, §24.2.2(3)(b), p. 547.*}

18. {78 *Adverse party*} asked for {79 *death-penalty sanctions/a spoliation jury instruction*} for {80 *party*}'s {81 *describe conduct complained of*}. The Court should deny {82 *adverse party*}'s motion for sanctions because the motion is {83 *adverse party*}'s first request for sanctions, and the Court must first consider a lesser sanction before imposing {84 *death-penalty sanctions/a spoliation jury instruction*}. *See Brookshire Bros.*, 438 S.W.3d at 25; *Cire v. Cummings*, 134 S.W.3d 835, 842 (Tex. 2004); *GTE Commc'ns Sys. Corp. v. Tanner*, 856 S.W.2d 725, 729 (Tex. 1993). {85 *Elaborate.*} {*See* ***O'Connor's Texas Rules***, *"Typical misconduct," ch. 5-K, §3.2.3(1), p. 464; "Types of remedies," ch. 6-A, §24.2.2(3)(b), p. 547.*}

19. {86 *Adverse party*} asked for {87 *death-penalty sanctions/a spoliation jury instruction*} for {88 *party*}'s {89 *describe conduct complained of*}. The Court should deny {90 *adverse party*}'s motion for sanctions because {91 *party*}'s conduct is not so egregious as to alleviate the Court of the burden of using a lesser sanction first. *See Brookshire Bros.*, 438 S.W.3d at 25; *Cire v. Cummings*, 134 S.W.3d 835, 842 (Tex. 2004). {92 *Describe conduct and explain how lesser sanctions would be sufficient to minimize any prejudice caused by party.*} {*See* ***O'Connor's Texas Rules***, *"Egregious misconduct," ch. 5-K, §3.2.3(2), p. 465; "Types of remedies," ch. 6-A, §24.2.2(3)(b), p. 547.*}

20. {93 *Adverse party*} asked for {94 *death-penalty sanctions/a spoliation jury instruction*} for {95 *party*}'s {96 *describe conduct complained of*}. The Court should deny {97 *adverse party*}'s motion for sanctions because {98 *party*}'s conduct does not justify a presumption that {99 *party*}'s {100 *claims/defenses*} lack merit. *See Cire v. Cummings*, 134 S.W.3d 835, 839 (Tex. 2004); *Hamill v. Level*, 917 S.W.2d 15, 16 (Tex. 1996). {101 *Elaborate.*} {*See* ***O'Connor's Texas Rules***, *"No merit," ch. 5-K, §3.2.4, p. 465.*}

◄ *Continued on next page* ►

CONCLUSION

21. {(102) *Briefly summarize the response.*}

PRAYER

22. For these reasons, {(103) *party*} asks the Court to deny {(104) *adverse party*}'s motion for sanctions for spoliation of evidence.

SEE: Tex. R. Civ. P. 215
O'Connor's Texas Rules * Civil Trials (2019), "Standards for Imposing Sanctions," ch. 5-K, §3, p. 462; "Spoliation," ch. 6-A, §24, p. 544

ADD: STYLE OF THE CASE – FORM 1B:2
SIGNATURE BLOCK – FORM 1B:3
CERTIFICATE OF SERVICE – FORM 1B:13

ATTACH: AFFIDAVIT – FORM 1B:8, if necessary
ORDER – FORM 6A:32

NOTE: The court is not required to hold an oral hearing; sanctions can be resolved by a hearing on submission. *See, e.g.*, ***Cire v. Cummings***, 134 S.W.3d 835, 843-44 (Tex.2004) (nothing in Tex. R. Civ. P. 215.3 requires an oral hearing). If the court holds an evidentiary hearing, it must be outside the presence of the jury. ***Brookshire Bros. v. Aldridge***, 438 S.W.3d 9, 20 (Tex.2014).

ORDER ON {❶ *PARTY*}'S
MOTION FOR SANCTIONS FOR SPOLIATION OF EVIDENCE

After considering {❷ *party*}'s motion for sanctions for spoliation of evidence, the supporting affidavits, the response, and arguments of counsel, the Court

{*CHOOSE APPROPRIATE ORDER*}

DENIES the motion.

GRANTS the motion and imposes the following sanctions on {❸ *adverse party*}, {❹ *name*}: {❺ *list sanctions*}.

FINDINGS OF FACT

The Court makes the following findings in support of the sanctions imposed for spoliation of evidence:

1. There is a direct relationship between the offensive conduct and the sanction in that {❻ *describe conduct and identify relationship*}.

2. This sanction is not excessive. {❼ *Elaborate.*}

{*If imposing death-penalty sanctions or spoliation jury instruction, add paragraphs 3-5*}

{*CHOOSE APPROPRIATE PARAGRAPH 3*}

3. {❽ *Adverse party*} intentionally spoliated evidence. {❾ *Elaborate.*}

3. {❿ *Adverse party*} negligently spoliated evidence and as a result, {⓫ *party*} was irreparably prevented from presenting {⓬ *his/her/its*} {⓭ *claim/defense*}. {⓮ *Elaborate.*}

{*CHOOSE APPROPRIATE PARAGRAPH 4*}

4. This Court imposed an earlier sanction on {⓯ *adverse party*}. {⓰ *Identify earlier conduct and sanction.*} That sanction was not sufficient to deter similar conduct.

4. Although this Court has not imposed a lesser sanction, the Court considered lesser sanctions but determined they would have been insufficient to minimize the prejudice caused by {⓱ *adverse party*}. {⓲ *Elaborate.*}

◄ *Continued on next page* ►

5. {[19] *Adverse party*}'s conduct justifies the presumption that {[20] *his/her/its*} {[21] *claim/defense*} lacks merit. {[22] *Elaborate.*}

SIGNED on _______________, 20___.

____
PRESIDING JUDGE

SEE: Tex. R. Civ. P. 215
O'Connor's Texas Rules * Civil Trials (2019), "Standards for Imposing Sanctions," ch. 5-K, §3, p. 462; "Spoliation," ch. 6-A, §24, p. 544

ADD: STYLE OF THE CASE – FORM 1B:2
CERTIFICATE OF SERVICE – FORM 1B:13, if proposed order served separately from motion or response

{[1] *PARTY*}'S MOTION TO {[2] *AMEND/SUPPLEMENT*} RESPONSES TO {[3] *IDENTIFY TYPE OF DISCOVERY*}

{[4] *Party*}, {[5] *name*}, asks the Court to permit {[6] *him/her/it*} to {[7] *amend/supplement*} {[8] *his/her/its*} responses to {[9] *identify type of discovery, e.g., interrogatories*}, under the authority of Texas Rule of Civil Procedure 193.6. {*See* ***O'Connor's Texas Rules****, "Supplementing Discovery Responses," ch. 6-A, §17, p. 530.*}

INTRODUCTION

1. Plaintiff, {[10] *name*}, sued defendant, {[11] *name*}, for {[12] *state basis of suit*}.

2. Discovery in this suit is governed by a Level {[13] *1/2/3*} discovery-control plan. The discovery period {[14] *will end/ended*} on {[15] *date*}. {*See* ***O'Connor's Texas Rules****, "Discovery-Control Plans," ch. 6-A, §7, p. 520.*}

3. This case is set for trial on {[16] *date*}.

4. {[17] *State other relevant facts about the suit.*}

BACKGROUND

5. {[18] *Party*} served {[19] *his/her/its*} responses to {[20] *identify type of discovery, e.g., interrogatories*} on {[21] *date*}.

6. {[22] *State other facts relevant to the motion.*}

ARGUMENT & AUTHORITIES

7. A court may allow a party to amend or supplement a discovery response after the time to amend or supplement has passed if the court finds that there was good cause for the failure to timely amend or supplement or that the late amendment or supplementation will not unfairly surprise or prejudice the other parties. Tex. R. Civ. P. 193.6(a). {*See* ***O'Connor's Texas Rules****, "Deadline to supplement responses," ch. 6-A, §17.4, p. 531.*}

8. {[23] *Party*} asks the Court for permission to {[24] *amend/supplement*} {[25] *his/her/its*} {[26] *expert's report/expert's deposition testimony/responses to answers to the written discovery*} {[27] *less than 30 days before trial/after the date set by the Court to amend discovery responses*} because {[28] *state facts supporting either good cause for late amendment or supplementation, or lack of unfair surprise or prejudice to adverse party by the late amendment or supplementation*}.

◄ Continued on next page ►

CONCLUSION

9. {㉙ *Briefly summarize the motion.*}

PRAYER

10. For these reasons, {㉚ *party*} asks the Court for permission to file the attached {㉛ *amendment/supplement*} to {㉜ *identify type of discovery*}.

SEE: Tex. R. Civ. P. 193.5(b), 193.6
O'Connor's Texas Rules * Civil Trials (2019), "Supplementing Discovery Responses," ch. 6-A, §17, p. 530

ADD: STYLE OF THE CASE – FORM 1B:2
SIGNATURE BLOCK – FORM 1B:3
CERTIFICATE OF SERVICE – FORM 1B:13

ATTACH: AFFIDAVIT – FORM 1B:8, if necessary
NOTICE OF HEARING OR SUBMISSION – FORM 1E:1
ORDER – FORM 1G:1
AMENDMENT/SUPPLEMENT TO DISCOVERY – FORM 6A:34

NOTE: Generally, when a party serves an amended or supplemental response more than 30 days before trial and before the deadline set by the court to amend, it is not necessary to file a motion to supplement. See ***O'Connor's Texas Rules***, "Deadline to supplement responses," ch. 6-A, §17.4, p. 531. When in doubt, the party should either get a Rule 11 agreement with the other party or file this motion to seek the court's permission.

A party must timely supplement its discovery response to designate a witness before submitting evidence in a summary-judgment proceeding. *See* ***Fort Brown Villas III Condo. Ass'n v. Gillenwater***, 285 S.W.3d 879, 882 (Tex.2009) (exclusion of witnesses not timely identified under Tex. R. Civ. P. 193.6 applies equally to trial and summary-judgment proceedings). See ***O'Connor's Texas Rules***, "For summary-judgment witnesses," ch. 6-A, §17.1.3, p. 530.

To amend or supplement retained-expert discovery, see FORMS 6D:2, 3.

{❶ *PARTY*}'S {❷ *AMENDED/SUPPLEMENTAL*}
RESPONSE TO {❸ *IDENTIFY TYPE OF DISCOVERY*}

{❹ *Party*}, {❺ *name*}, serves {❻ *adverse party*}, {❼ *name*}, with the following {❽ *amendment/supplement*} to {❾ *his/her/its*} discovery. {*See* ***O'Connor's Texas Rules***, *"Supplementing Discovery Responses," ch. 6-A, §17, p. 530.*}

{*CHOOSE TYPE OF DISCOVERY*}

{*Request for disclosure*}

1. {❿ *Amended/Supplemental*} Response to Texas Rule of Civil Procedure {⓫ *identify rule, e.g., 194.2(b)*} Request: {⓬ *Provide amended or supplemental response, e.g., In addition to the names of potential parties furnished in the original response, defendant adds the following: {list the names, addresses (work and home), and telephone numbers (work and home) of additional potential parties}.*}

{*Interrogatories*}

1. Interrogatory No. {⓭ *number*}: {⓮ *Repeat interrogatory.*}

2. Original Answer: {⓯ *Repeat original answer.*}

3. {⓰ *Amended/Supplemental*} Answer: {⓱ *Provide amended or supplemental answer.*}

{*Request for admissions*}

1. Request for Admission No. {⓲ *number*}: {⓳ *Repeat request for admission.*}

2. Original Response: {⓴ *Repeat original response, e.g., Denied.*}

3. {㉑ *Amended/Supplemental*} Response: {㉒ *Provide amended or supplemental response, e.g., Admitted.*}

{*Request for production*}

1. Request for Production No. {㉓ *number*}: {㉔ *Repeat request.*}

2. {㉕ *Amended/Supplemental*} Response: {㉖ *Provide amended or supplemental response, e.g., In addition to the documents furnished in the original response, defendant produces the following documents and serves them with this response: {list the documents produced}.*}

{*Continue until each response is accurate.*}

◄ *Continued on next page* ►

TEXAS CIVIL FORMS
CHAPTER 6. DISCOVERY
FORM 6A:34 AMENDMENT/SUPPLEMENT TO DISCOVERY

SEE: Tex. R. Civ. P. 193.5(b), 193.6, 194.2
O'Connor's Texas Rules * Civil Trials (2019), "Supplementing Discovery Responses," ch. 6-A, §17, p. 530

ADD: STYLE OF THE CASE – FORM 1B:2
SIGNATURE BLOCK – FORM 1B:3
CERTIFICATE OF SERVICE – FORM 1B:13

ATTACH: MOTION TO AMEND/SUPPLEMENT DISCOVERY RESPONSE – FORM 6A:33

NOTE: Amended or supplemental answers to written discovery must be made in the same form as the original answers and be verified by the party if the original response was required to be verified. Tex. R. Civ. P. 193.5(b). See ***O'Connor's Texas Rules***, "Form of supplemental discovery," ch. 6-A, §17.6, p. 532.

If a party supplements documents to an original response to a request for production and the documents bear litigation numbers, the party should provide those numbers in the response. If possible, the documents produced should be attached to or accompany the response, or the response should state a reasonable time and place for production, inspection, and copying.

To amend or supplement retained-expert discovery, see FORMS 6D:2, 3.

REQUEST FOR COPY OF STATEMENT OF {❶ *NAME*}

To: {❷ *Adverse party*}, {❸ *name*}, through {❹ *his/her/its*} attorney of record, {❺ *name*}, {❻ *address*}.

{❼ *Name of party or witness*} gave a statement about the events that are the basis of this suit to {❽ *adverse party*} on {❾ *date*}.

{❿ *Name of party or witness*} asks that {⓫ *adverse party*} provide {⓬ *him/her/it*} with a copy of that statement.

SEE: Tex. R. Civ. P. 192.3(h)
O'Connor's Texas Rules * Civil Trials (2019), "Person's own statements," ch. 6-B, §2.7, p. 557

ADD: STYLE OF THE CASE – FORM 1B:2
SIGNATURE BLOCK – FORM 1B:3
CERTIFICATE OF SERVICE – FORM 1B:13

NOTE: This form can be used by a party or a witness to request her own statement, or by a party to request the statement of a witness. *See* Tex. R. Civ. P. 192.3(h). Witness statements, even if made or prepared in anticipation of litigation, are not protected by the work-product privilege. Tex. R. Civ. P. 192.5(c)(1). This does not mean all witness statements are discoverable; they are subject to the same rules concerning the scope of discovery and privileges applicable to other documents or tangible things. Tex. R. Civ. P. 192 cmt. 9; *see* Tex. R. Civ. P. 192.5(a) (definition of work product).

{[1] *PARTY*}'S MOTION FOR COURT-ORDERED EXPERT REPORT

{[2] *Party*}, {[3] *name*}, asks the Court to require {[4] *adverse party*}, {[5] *name*}, to produce a report from {[6] *his/her/its*} retained testifying expert, under the authority of Texas Rule of Civil Procedure 195.5. {*See* ***O'Connor's Texas Rules***, *"By court order," ch. 6-D, §7.2.2, p. 625.*}

INTRODUCTION

1. Plaintiff, {[7] *name*}, sued defendant, {[8] *name*}, for {[9] *state basis of suit*}.

2. Discovery in this suit is governed by a Level {[10] *1/2/3*} discovery-control plan. The discovery period {[11] *will end/ended*} on {[12] *date*}. {*See* ***O'Connor's Texas Rules***, *"Discovery-Control Plans," ch. 6-A, §7, p. 520.*}

3. This case is set for trial on {[13] *date*}.

4. {[14] *State other relevant facts about the suit.*}

BACKGROUND

5. {[15] *Party*} asked {[16] *adverse party*} to produce a report from {[17] *his/her/its*} retained testifying expert as part of {[18] *party*}'s request for disclosure. Tex. R. Civ. P. 194.2(f)(4)(A). {[19] *Adverse party*} declined to produce a report.

6. {[20] *Adverse party*}'s retained testifying expert has not recorded or reduced to tangible form {[21] *his/her*} discoverable factual observations, tests, supporting data, calculations, photographs, or opinions.

7. {[22] *State other facts relevant to the motion.*}

ARGUMENT & AUTHORITIES

8. This Court has the authority to order {[23] *adverse party*}'s expert to reduce {[24] *his/her*} opinion to tangible form and to produce it. Tex. R. Civ. P. 195.5.

{*CHOOSE APPROPRIATE PARAGRAPH 9*}

9. {[25] *Adverse party*}'s expert report is necessary to prepare for trial. {[26] *Elaborate.*}

9. A motion for summary judgment is pending, and {[27] *adverse party*}'s expert report is necessary for its resolution. {[28] *Elaborate.*}

9. {[29] *State any other reason the adverse party's expert report is necessary.*}

CONCLUSION

10. {㉚ *Briefly summarize the motion.*}

PRAYER

11. For these reasons, {㉛ *party*} asks the Court to require {㉜ *adverse party*} to produce a report from {㉝ *his/her/its*} retained testifying expert.

SEE: Tex. R. Civ. P. 195.5
O'Connor's Texas Rules * Civil Trials (2019), "By court order," ch. 6-D, §7.2.2, p. 625

ADD: STYLE OF THE CASE – FORM 1B:2
SIGNATURE BLOCK – FORM 1B:3
CERTIFICATE OF SERVICE – FORM 1B:13

ATTACH: AFFIDAVIT – FORM 1B:8, if necessary
NOTICE OF HEARING OR SUBMISSION – FORM 1E:1
ORDER – FORM 1G:1

{❶ *PARTY*}'S MOTION TO
{❷ *AMEND/SUPPLEMENT*} EXPERT DISCOVERY

{❸ *Party*}, {❹ *name*}, asks the Court for permission to {❺ *amend/supplement*} {❻ *his/her/its*} {❼ *expert's report/expert's deposition testimony/responses to request for disclosure/response to deposition notice of expert*} under the authority of Texas Rule of Civil Procedure 195.6. {*See* ***O'Connor's Texas Rules****, "Supplementing Expert Discovery," ch. 6-D, §5, p. 622.*}

INTRODUCTION

1. Plaintiff, {❽ *name*}, sued defendant, {❾ *name*}, for {❿ *state basis of suit*}.

2. Discovery in this suit is governed by a Level {⓫ *1/2/3*} discovery-control plan. The discovery period {⓬ *will end/ended*} on {⓭ *date*}. {*See* ***O'Connor's Texas Rules****, "Discovery-Control Plans," ch. 6-A, §7, p. 520.*}

3. This case is set for trial on {⓮ *date*}.

4. {⓯ *State other relevant facts about the suit.*}

BACKGROUND

{*CHOOSE APPROPRIATE PARAGRAPH 5*}

5. {⓰ *Party*} served {⓱ *his/her/its*} {⓲ *expert's report/response to request for disclosure/response to deposition notice of expert*} on {⓳ *date*}.

5. {⓴ *Party*}'s expert testified by deposition on {㉑ *date*}.

6. {㉒ *State other facts relevant to the motion.*}

ARGUMENT & AUTHORITIES

7. A court may allow a party to amend or supplement a discovery response less than 30 days before trial or after the date set by the court to amend discovery responses if the court finds that there was good cause for the failure to timely amend or supplement or that the late amendment or supplementation will not unfairly surprise or prejudice the other parties. *See* Tex. R. Civ. P. 193.5(b), 193.6(a). {*See* ***O'Connor's Texas Rules****, "Deadline to supplement responses," ch. 6-A, §17.4, p. 531.*}

8. {23 *Party*} asks the Court for permission to {24 *amend/supplement*} {25 *his/her/its*} {26 *expert's report/expert's deposition testimony/responses to request for disclosure/response to deposition notice of expert*} because {27 *state facts supporting either good cause for late amendment or supplementation, or lack of unfair surprise or prejudice to the adverse party by the late amendment or supplementation*}.

CONCLUSION

9. {28 *Briefly summarize the motion.*}

PRAYER

10. For these reasons, {29 *party*} asks the Court for permission to file the attached {30 *amendment/supplement*} to {31 *identify type of discovery*}.

SEE: Tex. R. Civ. P. 193.5(b), 193.6, 195.6
O'Connor's Texas Rules * Civil Trials (2019), "Supplementing Expert Discovery," ch. 6-D, §5, p. 622

ADD: STYLE OF THE CASE – FORM 1B:2
SIGNATURE BLOCK – FORM 1B:3
CERTIFICATE OF SERVICE – FORM 1B:13

ATTACH: AFFIDAVIT – FORM 1B:8, if necessary
NOTICE OF HEARING OR SUBMISSION – FORM 1E:1
ORDER – FORM 1G:1
AMENDMENT/SUPPLEMENT TO EXPERT DISCOVERY – FORM 6D:3

{[1] *PARTY*}'S {[2] *AMENDMENT/SUPPLEMENT*}
TO {[3] *IDENTIFY TYPE OF EXPERT DISCOVERY*}

{[4] *Party*}, {[5] *name*}, serves {[6] *adverse party*}, {[7] *name*}, with the following {[8] *amendment/supplement*} to {[9] *his/her/its*} discovery. {*See* ***O'Connor's Texas Rules***, *"Supplementing Expert Discovery," ch. 6-D, §5, p. 622.*}

{*CHOOSE TYPE OF DISCOVERY*}

{*Expert deposition/report*}

1. {[10] *Party*}'s testifying expert, {[11] *name*}, who was {[12] *retained by/employed by/under the control of*} {[13] *party*}, {[14] *testified by oral deposition/stated in a written report*} that {[15] *his/her*} {[16] *mental impressions/opinions*} were {[17] *identify mental impressions or opinions from the deposition or report*}. The basis for {[18] *his/her*} {[19] *mental impressions/opinions*} was {[20] *identify basis for mental impressions or opinions from the deposition or report*}. However, the testifying expert has now changed {[21] *his/her*} {[22] *mental impressions/opinions*} and the basis for them. The expert now {[23] *state present mental impressions or opinions and the basis for them*}. {*See* ***O'Connor's Texas Rules***, *"Supplementing discovery of retained testifying expert," ch. 6-D, §5.1, p. 622.*}

{*Response to request for disclosure*}

1. {[24] *Amended/Supplemental*} Response to Texas Rule of Civil Procedure {[25] *identify rule, e.g., 194.2(f)(2)*} Request: {[26] *Provide amended or supplemental response, e.g., In addition to the subjects on which the expert, {name}, will testify listed in defendant's original answer to plaintiff's request for disclosure, defendant adds the following subject: {identify other subject}.*}

{*Response to request for production for deposition*}

1. {[27] *Amended/Supplemental*} Response to Deposition Notice of Expert: {[28] *Provide amended or supplemental response, e.g., In addition to the documents listed in the response to the notice of deposition of defendant's retained expert, defendant produces the following documents, which are attached to this response: {list additional documents}.*}

{*Continue until each response is accurate.*}

Form 6D:3 Amendment/Supplement to Expert Discovery

SEE: Tex. R. Civ. P. 193.5(b), 193.6, 194.2, 195.6
O'Connor's Texas Rules * Civil Trials (2019), "Supplementing Expert Discovery," ch. 6-D, §5, p. 622

ADD: STYLE OF THE CASE – FORM 1B:2
SIGNATURE BLOCK – FORM 1B:3
VERIFICATION – FORM 1B:7, if necessary
CERTIFICATE OF SERVICE – FORM 1B:13

ATTACH: MOTION TO AMEND/SUPPLEMENT EXPERT DISCOVERY – FORM 6D:2

NOTE: A party must supplement the deposition testimony and the report of its testifying experts who are retained by, employed by, or otherwise under the control of the party. Tex. R. Civ. P. 195.6.

An amended or supplemental response must be verified by the party if the original response had to be verified. Tex. R. Civ. P. 193.5(b).

{❶ *PARTY*}'S REQUEST FOR DISCLOSURE TO {❷ *ADVERSE PARTY*}

To: {❸ *Adverse party*}, {❹ *name*}, through {❺ *his/her/its*} attorney of record, {❻ *name*}, {❼ *address*}.

Under Texas Rule of Civil Procedure 194, {❽ *adverse party*} is requested to disclose, within {❾ *30/50*} days of service of this request, the information or material described in Texas Rule of Civil Procedure 194.2 {❿ *identify subsections, e.g., (a), (c), and (f)*}. {*See **O'Connor's Texas Rules**, "Content of request," ch. 6-E, §3.2, p. 627.*}

{*ADD PARAGRAPH BELOW IF APPLICABLE*}

Under Texas Rule of Civil Procedure 190.2(b)(6), {⓫ *adverse party*} is requested to disclose, within {⓬ *30/50*} days of service of this request, all documents, electronic information, and tangible items that {⓭ *adverse party*} has in {⓮ *his/her/its*} possession, custody, or control and that {⓯ *he/she/it*} may use to support {⓰ *his/her/its*} {⓱ *claims/defenses*}. {*See **O'Connor's Texas Rules**, "Additional requests – Level 1 discovery," ch. 6-E, §3.2.3, p. 629.*}

SEE: Tex. R. Civ. P. 190.2, 192.3, 194
O'Connor's Texas Rules * Civil Trials (2019), "Making Requests for Disclosure," ch. 6-E, §3, p. 626

ADD: STYLE OF THE CASE – FORM 1B:2
SIGNATURE BLOCK – FORM 1B:3
CERTIFICATE OF SERVICE – FORM 1B:13

ATTACH: MEDICAL AUTHORIZATION – FORM 6J:1, if seeking medical records under Texas Rule of Civil Procedure 194.2(j)

NOTE: Except in cases filed in justice court, in addition to the requests for disclosure under Texas Rule of Civil Procedure 194.2, a party under a Level 1 discovery-control plan can request disclosure of all documents, electronic information, and tangible items that the disclosing party has in its possession, custody, or control and that it may use to support its claims or defenses. *See* Tex. R. Civ. P. 190.2(b)(6); Tex.Sup.Ct. Order, Misc. Docket No. 13-9022 (eff. Mar. 1, 2013).

Information under Texas Rule of Civil Procedure 194.2(j) and (k) should be requested only if the suit alleges physical or mental injury and damages from the occurrence that is the subject of the lawsuit. *See* Tex. R. Civ. P. 194.2(j), (k).

Requests for disclosure can be included in an original petition, an original answer, a letter, or a formal discovery request, such as this form. If a party includes requests for disclosure in its original pleading, it must change the name of the pleading to include the request. For example, for the plaintiff it would be "Plaintiff's Original Petition & Request for Disclosure." If a plaintiff serves a request with its original petition but as a separate document, it must list the request in both the citation and the return.

For most methods of service, the deadline for serving requests for disclosure is 30 days before the end of the discovery period. Tex. R. Civ. P. 194.1. See *O'Connor's Texas Rules*, "Discovery Periods," ch. 6-A, §8, p. 523. But when service is by mail or fax, the request for disclosure should be served at least 33 days (if mailed) or 31 days (if faxed after 5:00 p.m.) before the end of the discovery period. *See* Tex. R. Civ. P. 21a(b)(2), (c). See *O'Connor's Texas Rules*, "Deadline to serve response," ch. 6-A, §14.1, p. 527.

Special rules apply when calculating the deadline for responding to a request for information about testifying experts. *See* Tex. R. Civ. P. 194.3(b), 195.2.

{[1] *PARTY*}'S REQUESTS FOR DISCLOSURE TO {[2] *ADVERSE PARTY*}

To: {[3] *Adverse party*}, {[4] *name*}, through {[5] *his/her/its*} attorney of record, {[6] *name*}, {[7] *address*}.

Under Texas {[8] *Rule/Rules*} of Civil Procedure {[9] *194/194 and 190.2*}, {[10] *adverse party*} is requested to disclose the information or material set out below. {*See **O'Connor's Texas Rules**, "Targeted request," ch. 6-E, §3.2.2, p. 628.*}

{*CHOOSE APPROPRIATE REQUESTS 1-12*}

REQUEST 1: You are requested to disclose the correct names of the parties to the lawsuit as required by Rule 194.2(a) within {[11] *30/50*} days of service of this request.

REQUEST 2: You are requested to disclose the names, addresses (work and home), and telephone numbers (work and home) of potential parties as required by Rule 194.2(b) within {[12] *30/50*} days of service of this request. Please answer to the full extent authorized by the rule while including the names of all

{*CHOOSE INFORMATION REQUESTED*}

[A] individuals and entities with an ownership interest in the {[13] *identify the business, land, vehicle, or other thing made the basis of the suit*}.

[B] attending health-care providers for plaintiff during {[14] *identify period*} and all other patients who have similar claims for injuries after being treated by {[15] *adverse party*}.

[C] similarly situated individuals and entities who have similar claims against {[16] *adverse party*} for {[17] *identify nature of party's claim*}.

REQUEST 3: You are requested to disclose the name, addresses (work and home), and telephone numbers (work and home) of any person who may be designated as a responsible third party as required by Rule 194.2(*l*) within {[18] *30/50*} days of service of this request. {*See **O'Connor's Texas Rules**, "RTP," ch. 3-E, §7.4, p. 283.*}

REQUEST 4: You are requested to disclose the legal theories and, in general, the factual bases of your {[19] *claims/defenses/claims and defenses*} as required by Rule 194.2(c) within {[20] *30/50*} days of service of this request. {*See **O'Connor's Texas Rules**, "Contentions," ch. 6-E, §3.2.1(3), p. 627.*}

REQUEST 5: You are requested to disclose the amount of and any method of calculating economic damages as required by Rule 194.2(d) within {[21] *30/50*} days of service of this request.

REQUEST 6: You are requested to disclose the names, addresses (work and home), and telephone numbers (work and home) of persons having knowledge of relevant facts, with a brief statement of each person's connection with the case as required by Rule 194.2(e) within {㉒ *30/50*} days of service of this request. {*See* ***O'Connor's Texas Rules****, "Fact witnesses," ch. 6-E, §4.2.1(5), p. 630.*} Please answer to the full extent authorized by the rule while including the names of

{*CHOOSE INFORMATION REQUESTED*}

[A] any consulting experts who have firsthand knowledge of the facts of the case or who have knowledge of facts about the case that were not obtained in preparation for trial or in anticipation of litigation.

[B] employees who were present {㉓ *identify event made the basis of the suit, e.g., at the time of the accident, when plaintiff was terminated*}.

[C] all family members who are aware of the nature and extent of plaintiff's disability.

[D] all attending health-care providers for plaintiff, including doctors, nurses, physician assistants, pharmacists, and orderlies.

[E] any persons who have knowledge of {㉔ *adverse party*}'s electronic-information system.

REQUEST 7: You are requested to disclose the information about testifying experts as required by Rule 194.2(f) by either 30 days after the service of this request or {㉕ *60/90*} days before the end of the discovery period, whichever is later. A complete answer will include a list of all witness fees paid by you to each expert within the last four years. {*See* ***O'Connor's Texas Rules****, "Testifying experts," ch. 6-D, §4.1, p. 617; "Information about consulting expert + work reviewed," ch. 6-D, §4.2.2, p. 621.*} Please answer to the full extent authorized by the rule while including the following information:

a. For retained testifying experts:

(1) The expert's name, address, and telephone number.

(2) The subject matter on which the retained expert will testify.

(3) The general substance of the expert's mental impressions and opinions and a brief summary of the basis for them.

◄ *Continued on next page* ►

(4) All documents, tangible things, reports, models, or data compilations that have been provided to, reviewed by, or prepared by or for the expert in anticipation of the expert's testimony.

(5) The expert's current résumé and bibliography. The résumé should include a list of all other cases in which the expert has testified as an expert at trial or by deposition within the last four years.

b. For nonretained testifying experts:

(1) The expert's name, address, and telephone number.

(2) The subject matter on which the expert will testify.

(3) Either the general substance of the expert's mental impressions and opinions and a brief summary of the basis for them, or documents reflecting such information.

c. For consulting experts whose work was reviewed by a testifying expert, the same information as for retained testifying experts, as outlined above in section a.

REQUEST 8: You are requested to disclose the discoverable indemnity and insuring agreements as required by Rule 194.2(g) within {㉖ *30/50*} days of service of this request.

REQUEST 9: You are requested to disclose the discoverable settlement agreements as required by Rule 194.2(h) within {㉗ *30/50*} days of service of this request.

REQUEST 10: You are requested to disclose a list of all discoverable witness statements as required by Rule 194.2(i) within {㉘ *30/50*} days of service of this request. Please answer to the full extent authorized by the rule while including in your response the names of all witnesses who have given written statements or made oral statements that were recorded about the facts of the case to you or your agents, employees, representatives, insurance company's representatives, and attorneys. The only witness statement you are permitted to withhold is a witness statement made by {㉙ *adverse party*} and taken by {㉚ *adverse party*}'s attorney, which is privileged under Texas Rule of Evidence 503. Attach to your response all the witness statements listed in your response to this request. {*See* ***O'Connor's Texas Rules***, *"Witness statements," ch. 6-B, §2.6, p. 556.*}

REQUEST 11: Because this is a suit alleging physical or mental injury and damages from the occurrence made subject of the case, you are requested to disclose the medical records and bills reasonably related to the injuries or damages asserted in this case as required by Rule 194.2(j) within {❸❶ *30/50*} days of service of this request. Instead of the medical records and bills, you may provide an authorization permitting the disclosure of the medical records and bills. {*See* ***O'Connor's Texas Rules****, "Medical records," ch. 6-E, §3.2.1(9)(a), p. 628.*}

REQUEST 12: Because this is a suit alleging physical or mental injury and damages from the occurrence made subject of the case, you are requested to disclose all medical records and bills obtained by virtue of an authorization furnished by {❸❷ *party*} as required by Rule 194.2(k) within {❸❸ *30/50*} days of service of this request. {*See* ***O'Connor's Texas Rules****, "Medical records," ch. 6-E, §3.2.1(9)(b), p. 628.*}

{*ADD REQUEST 13 IF APPLICABLE*}

REQUEST 13: You are requested to disclose all documents, electronic information, and tangible items that you have in your possession, custody, or control and that you may use to support your {❸❹ *claims/defenses*} as required by Rule 190.2(b)(6) within {❸❺ *30/50*} days of service of this request. {*See* ***O'Connor's Texas Rules****, "Additional requests – Level 1 discovery," ch. 6-E, §3.2.3, p. 629.*}

SEE: Tex. R. Civ. P. 190.2, 192.3, 194
O'Connor's Texas Rules * Civil Trials (2019), "Making Requests for Disclosure," ch. 6-E, §3, p. 626

ADD: STYLE OF THE CASE – FORM 1B:2
SIGNATURE BLOCK – FORM 1B:3
CERTIFICATE OF SERVICE – FORM 1B:13

ATTACH: MEDICAL AUTHORIZATION – FORM 6J:1, if seeking medical records under Texas Rule of Civil Procedure 194.2(j)

NOTE: Except in cases filed in justice court, in addition to the requests for disclosure under Texas Rule of Civil Procedure 194.2, a party under a Level 1 discovery-control plan can request disclosure of all documents, electronic information, and tangible items that the disclosing party has in its possession, custody, or control and that it may use to support its claims or defenses. *See* Tex. R. Civ. P. 190.2(b)(6); Tex.Sup.Ct. Order, Misc. Docket No. 13-9022 (eff. Mar. 1, 2013).

Requests for disclosure can be included in an original petition, an original answer, a letter, or a formal discovery request, such as this form. If a party includes requests for disclosure in its original pleading, it must change the name of the pleading to include the request. For example, for the plaintiff it would be "Plaintiff's Original Petition & Request for Disclosure." If a plaintiff serves a request with its original petition but as a separate document, it must list the request in both the citation and the return.

◄ *Continued on next page* ►

For most methods of service, the deadline for serving requests for disclosure is 30 days before the end of the discovery period. Tex. R. Civ. P. 194.1. See *O'Connor's Texas Rules*, "Discovery Periods," ch. 6-A, §8, p. 523. But when service is by mail or fax, the request for disclosure should be served at least 33 days (if mailed) or 31 days (if faxed after 5:00 p.m.) before the end of the discovery period. *See* Tex. R. Civ. P. 21a(b)(2), (c). See *O'Connor's Texas Rules*, "Deadline to serve response," ch. 6-A, §14.1, p. 527.

{❶ *PARTY*}'S RESPONSES TO
{❷ *ADVERSE PARTY*}'S REQUESTS FOR DISCLOSURE

To: {❸ *Adverse party*}, {❹ *name*}, through {❺ *his/her/its*} attorney of record, {❻ *name*}, {❼ *address*}.

{❽ *Party*}, {❾ *name*}, serves these responses to {❿ *adverse party*}'s requests for disclosure made under Texas {⓫ *Rule/Rules*} of Civil Procedure {⓬ *194/194 and 190.2*}. {*See* ***O'Connor's Texas Rules****, "Responding to Requests for Disclosure," ch. 6-E, §4, p. 629.*}

{*CHOOSE APPROPRIATE RESPONSES*}

1. Response to request under Rule 194.2(a): The correct names of the parties to the lawsuit are as follows: {⓭ *list correct names of all parties*}. {*See* ***O'Connor's Texas Rules****, "Correct party name," ch. 6-E, §4.2.1(1), p. 630.*}

{*FOR POTENTIAL PARTIES, ADD APPROPRIATE PARAGRAPH 2*}

{*If known*}

2. Response to request under Rule 194.2(b): The names, addresses (work and home), and telephone numbers (work and home) of potential parties are as follows: {⓮ *provide information*}. {*See* ***O'Connor's Texas Rules****, "Potential parties," ch. 6-E, §4.2.1(2), p. 630.*}

{*If unknown*}

2. Response to request under Rule 194.2(b): {⓯ *Party*} knows of no other potential parties to this suit. {*See* ***O'Connor's Texas Rules****, "Potential parties," ch. 6-E, §4.2.1(2), p. 630.*}

{*FOR RESPONSIBLE THIRD PARTIES, ADD APPROPRIATE PARAGRAPH 3*}

{*If known*}

3. Response to request under Rule 194.2(*l*): The names, addresses (work and home), and telephone numbers (work and home) of persons who may be designated as responsible third parties are as follows: {⓰ *provide information*}. {*See* ***O'Connor's Texas Rules****, "RTP," ch. 3-E, §7.4, p. 283.*}

◄ *Continued on next page* ►

{*If unknown*}

3. Response to request under Rule 194.2(*l*): {[17] *Party*} does not know the identity of persons who may be designated as responsible third parties to this suit. {[18] *Elaborate.*} {*See **O'Connor's Texas Rules**, "Amended answer – RTP is unknown criminal," ch. 3-E, §7.4.2(1), p. 284.*}

3. Response to request under Rule 194.2(*l*): {[19] *Party*} knows of no persons who may be designated as responsible third parties to this suit. {*See **O'Connor's Texas Rules**, "RTP," ch. 3-E, §7.4, p. 283.*}

4. Response to request under Rule 194.2(c): The legal theories and, in general, the factual bases of {[20] *party*}'s {[21] *claims/defenses*} are as follows: {[22] *provide information*}. {*See **O'Connor's Texas Rules**, "Contentions," ch. 6-E, §4.2.1(3), p. 630.*}

5. Response to request under Rule 194.2(d): The amount and any method of calculating economic damages are as follows: {[23] *provide information*}. {*See **O'Connor's Texas Rules**, "Damages," ch. 6-E, §4.2.1(4), p. 630.*}

6. Response to request under Rule 194.2(e): The names, addresses (work and home), and telephone numbers (work and home) of persons having knowledge of relevant facts, with a brief statement of each person's connection with the case, are as follows: {[24] *list the parties, persons deposed, character witnesses, custodians of records, and any other witnesses*}. {[25] *Summarize their knowledge and opinions, if any.*} {*See **O'Connor's Texas Rules**, "Fact witnesses," ch. 6-E, §4.2.1(5), p. 630.*}

{*FOR EACH TESTIFYING EXPERT, ADD APPROPRIATE PARAGRAPH 7*}

{*No expert designated*}

7. Response to request under Rule 194.2(f): {[26] *Party*} has not yet designated an expert.

{*For expert subject to control of party*}

7. Response to request under Rule 194.2(f): {[27] *Party*} provides the following information about {[28] *his/her/its*} testifying expert, {[29] *identify expert*}, who is retained by, employed by, or subject to the control of {[30] *party*}. {*See **O'Connor's Texas Rules**, "Retained testifying experts," ch. 6-E, §4.2.1(6)(a), p. 631.*}

a. The expert's addresses (work and home) and telephone numbers (work and home) are as follows: {[31] *provide information*}.

b. The expert will testify on the following subject matter: {[32] *provide information*}.

c. The general substance of the expert's mental impressions and opinions and a brief summary of the basis for them are as follows: {33 *provide information*}.

d. The expert {34 *has/has not*} prepared a report {35 *add if appropriate: , which is attached as Exhibit {letter}*}.

e. The documents, tangible things, models, or data compilations that have been provided to, reviewed by, or prepared by or for the expert in anticipation of the expert's testimony are as follows: {36 *identify documents and tangible items*}. These documents and tangible items are {37 *attached as Exhibit {letter}/made available for copying at {identify location, time, and date}*}.

f. Attached as Exhibit {38 *letter*} are the expert's current résumé and bibliography.

{*Continue until all retained testifying experts or consulting experts whose work was reviewed by a testifying expert are identified.*}

{*For expert not subject to control of party*}

7. Response to request under Rule 194.2(f): {39 *Party*} provides the following information about {40 *his/her/its*} testifying expert, {41 *identify expert*}, who is not retained by, employed by, or subject to the control of {42 *party*}. {*See* ***O'Connor's Texas Rules***, *"Nonretained testifying experts," ch. 6-E, §4.2.1(6)(b), p. 631.*}

a. The expert's addresses (work and home) and telephone numbers (work and home) are as follows: {43 *provide information*}.

b. The expert will testify on the following subject matter: {44 *provide information*}.

{*CHOOSE APPROPRIATE PARAGRAPH c*}

c. The general substance of the expert's mental impressions and opinions and a brief summary of the basis for them are as follows: {45 *provide information*}.

c. The following documents reflect the expert's mental impressions and opinions and provide a brief summary of the basis for them: {46 *identify documents*}. These documents are {47 *attached as Exhibit {letter}/made available for copying at {identify location, time, and date}*}.

{*Continue until all nonretained testifying experts are identified.*}

Continued on next page

8. Response to request under Rule 194.2(g): The following are all the discoverable indemnity and insuring agreements: {㊽ *identify by name and date*}. These documents are {㊾ *attached as Exhibit {letter}/made available for copying at {identify location, time, and date}*}.

9. Response to request under Rule 194.2(h): The following are all the discoverable settlement agreements: {㊿ *identify by name of party and date*}. These documents are {51 *attached as Exhibit {letter}/made available for copying at {identify location, time, and date}*}.

10. Response to request under Rule 194.2(i): The following are all the discoverable witness statements: {52 *identify by name and date*}. These documents are {53 *attached as Exhibit {letter}/made available for copying at {identify location, time, and date}*}.

{FOR PARTY ALLEGING PHYSICAL OR MENTAL INJURY, ADD APPROPRIATE PARAGRAPH 11}

{If providing medical records & bills}

11. Response to request under Rule 194.2(j): The following are all the medical records and bills that are reasonably related to the injuries or damages asserted in this case: {54 *identify by name of patient, medical provider, and date*}. These documents are {55 *attached as Exhibit {letter}/made available for copying at {identify location, time, and date}*}. *{See* ***O'Connor's Texas Rules****, "Medical records," ch. 6-E, §4.2.1(8)(a), p. 632.}*

{If providing medical authorization}

11. Response to request under Rule 194.2(j): Attached as Exhibit {56 *letter*} is a medical authorization permitting {57 *adverse party*} to secure all the medical records and bills that are reasonably related to the injuries or damages asserted in this case. *{See* ***O'Connor's Texas Rules****, "Medical records," ch. 6-E, §4.2.1(8)(a), p. 632.}*

12. Response to request under Rule 194.2(k): The following is a list of all the medical records and bills that were acquired by {58 *party*} by the authorization furnished by {59 *name of person who furnished medical authorization*}: {60 *identify documents by name of patient, medical provider, and date*}. These documents are {61 *attached as Exhibit {letter}/made available for copying at {identify location, time, and date}*}. *{See* ***O'Connor's Texas Rules****, "Medical records," ch. 6-E, §4.2.1(8)(a), p. 632.}*

13. Response to request under Rule 190.2(b)(6): The following are all the documents, electronic information, and tangible items that {62 *party*} has in {63 *his/her/its*} possession, custody, or control and that {64 *he/she/it*} may use to support {65 *his/her/its*} {66 *claims/defenses*}: {67 *identify by name and date*}. {68 *Specify whether the documents, electronic information, and tangible items are attached as an exhibit, made available for copying—and if so, identify the location, time, and date—or both attached and made available for copying.*} {*See* ***O'Connor's Texas Rules****, "Additional requests – Level 1 discovery," ch. 6-E, §3.2.3, p. 629.*}

SEE: Tex. R. Civ. P. 190.2, 192.3, 194
O'Connor's Texas Rules * Civil Trials (2019), "Responding to Requests for Disclosure," ch. 6-E, §4, p. 629

ADD: STYLE OF THE CASE – FORM 1B:2
SIGNATURE BLOCK – FORM 1B:3
CERTIFICATE OF SERVICE – FORM 1B:13

ATTACH: MEDICAL AUTHORIZATION – FORM 6J:1, if necessary
Expert report, résumé, or other documents, if necessary

NOTE: Except in cases filed in justice court, in addition to the requests for disclosure under Texas Rule of Civil Procedure 194.2, a party under a Level 1 discovery-control plan can request disclosure of all documents, electronic information, and tangible items that the disclosing party has in its possession, custody, or control and that it may use to support its claims or defenses. *See* Tex. R. Civ. P. 190.2(b)(6); Tex.Sup.Ct. Order, Misc. Docket No. 13-9022 (eff. Mar. 1, 2013).

If the party seeking affirmative relief (generally the plaintiff) does not provide a report of the expert's factual observations, tests, supporting data, calculations, photographs, and opinions produced when the expert is designated, then the other party (generally the defendant) should immediately notice the deposition of the expert. *See* Tex. R. Civ. P. 195.3(a).

No objections or assertions of work product are permitted to requests for disclosure. Tex. R. Civ. P. 194.5. Disclosure under Rule 194 is designed to afford parties basic discovery of specific categories of information on request, without objection or assertion of work-product privilege. Tex. R. Civ. P. 194 cmt. 1. In those extremely rare cases when information ordinarily discoverable should be protected, such as when revealing a person's residence might result in harm to the person, a party may move for protection. *Id.* See FORM 6A:10.

Generally, a party responding to requests for disclosure has 30 days to respond. Tex. R. Civ. P. 194.3. But when the plaintiff serves requests for disclosure before the defendant's answer is due, the defendant has 50 days to respond rather than 30. Tex. R. Civ. P. 194.3(a). When service is by mail or fax, the responding party has an additional three days (if mailed) or one day (if faxed after 5:00 p.m.) to respond. *See* Tex. R. Civ. P. 21a(b)(2), (c). See ***O'Connor's Texas Rules***, "Deadline to serve response," ch. 6-A, §14.1, p. 527.

☆

{[1] *PARTY*}'S NOTICE OF ORAL DEPOSITION

{*CHOOSE APPROPRIATE INTRODUCTORY PARAGRAPH*}

To: {[2] *Adverse party*}, {[3] *name*}, through {[4] *his/her/its*} attorney of record, {[5] *name*}, {[6] *address*}.

To: {[7] *Name of nonparty deponent*}, {[8] *address*}.

{*CHOOSE APPROPRIATE PARAGRAPH 1*}

1. Please take notice that, under Texas Rule of Civil Procedure 199.2, {[9] *party*}, {[10] *name*}, will take the oral deposition of {[11] *name of adverse party*} on {[12] *date*}, at {[13] *time*}, at {[14] *address*}. {[15] *Add if appropriate: {Name of adverse party} is directed to designate a person or persons to testify on its behalf about the following matters: {identify matters, e.g., preliminary discussions, negotiations, and execution of the contract that is the basis of plaintiff's lawsuit}.*} {*See **O'Connor's Texas Rules**, "Party witness," ch. 6-F, §4.5.1(2)(a), p. 638.*}

1. Please take notice that, under Texas Rule of Civil Procedure 199.2, {[16] *party*}, {[17] *name*}, will take the oral deposition of {[18] *name of nonparty deponent*} on {[19] *date*}, at {[20] *time*}, at {[21] *address*}. {*See **O'Connor's Texas Rules**, "Nonparty witness," ch. 6-F, §4.5.1(2)(b), p. 638.*}

1. Please take notice that, under Texas Rule of Civil Procedure 199.2, {[22] *party*}, {[23] *name*}, will take the oral deposition of {[24] *name of nonparty entity, e.g., corporation, partnership*} on {[25] *date*}, at {[26] *time*}, at {[27] *address*}. {[28] *Name of entity*} is directed to designate a person or persons to testify on its behalf about the following matters: {[29] *identify matters, e.g., preliminary discussions, negotiations, and execution of the contract made the basis of plaintiff's lawsuit*}. {*See **O'Connor's Texas Rules**, "Unknown corporate witness," ch. 6-F, §4.5.1(2)(c), p. 638.*}

2. The deposition will continue from day to day until completed.

3. The deposition will be recorded

{*CHOOSE APPROPRIATE METHOD*}

[A] stenographically. The stenographic recording will be conducted by {[30] *identify court-reporting service that will provide the court reporter*}.

[B] stenographically and on videotape. The stenographic recording will be conducted by {[31] *identify court-reporting service that will provide the court reporter*}.

Ⓒ stenographically and on audiotape. The stenographic recording will be conducted by {㉜ *identify court-reporting service that will provide the court reporter*}.

Ⓓ stenographically and {㉝ *identify other means*}. The stenographic recording will be conducted by {㉞ *identify court-reporting service that will provide the court reporter*}.

Ⓔ on videotape and will not be recorded stenographically.

Ⓕ on audiotape and will not be recorded stenographically.

Ⓖ {㉟ *identify other means*} and will not be recorded stenographically.

{*CHOOSE APPROPRIATE PARAGRAPHS 4-6*}

4. Under Rule 199.2(b)(5), {㊱ *name of deponent*} is requested to produce at the deposition the documents listed on attached Exhibit {㊲ *letter*}. {*See* ***O'Connor's Texas Rules****, "Request for documents," ch. 6-F, §4.5.6, p. 640.*}

5. The deposition will be taken by telephone. The oath will be administered to the deponent at {㊳ *his/her/its*} location by a person who is authorized to administer oaths. {*See* ***O'Connor's Texas Rules****, "Deposition by Telephone," ch. 6-F, §14, p. 654.*}

6. {㊴ *Party*} gives notice, as required by Rule 199.2(b)(4), that the following persons will attend the deposition: {㊵ *identify any persons who will attend other than the deponent, parties, spouses of parties, counsel, employees of counsel, or the officer taking the deposition*}. {*See* ***O'Connor's Texas Rules****, "Additional attendee," ch. 6-F, §4.5.5, p. 640.*}

SEE: Tex. R. Civ. P. 199.2
O'Connor's Texas Rules * Civil Trials (2019), "Notice of oral deposition," ch. 6-F, §4.5, p. 638; "Discovery subpoena," ch. 6-I, §5.2, p. 686

ADD: STYLE OF THE CASE – FORM 1B:2
SIGNATURE BLOCK – FORM 1B:3
CERTIFICATE OF SERVICE – FORM 1B:13

ATTACH: SUBPOENA – FORM 1L:1, if deponent is a nonparty
COVER SHEET & DEFINITIONS – FORM 6I:1, if requesting deponent to produce documents

◄ *Continued on next page* ►

NOTE: If the notice includes a request for documents, the date for the deposition should be set at least 40 days after the date the notice is served, so the party noticing the deposition can reschedule it if the witness refuses to produce the documents. When a deposition with documents is set with only 30 days' notice, the responding party has no obligation to file objections or assertions of privileges before the deposition. A party cannot secure documents from another party in less than 30 days. *See* Tex. R. Civ. P. 196.2(a). See ***O'Connor's Texas Rules***, "For deposition with documents," ch. 6-F, §4.5.2(1), p. 639.

A party seeking information about an organization's sources of electronic information should consider deposing an information-technology employee or other person who knows about the organization's electronic-information system. See ***O'Connor's Texas Rules***, "Depositions," ch. 6-C, §7.1.2, p. 604.

{1 *{NAME OF SUBPOENAED WITNESS}'S/{PARTY}'S}*
MOTION TO QUASH DEPOSITION OF {2 *NAME OF DEPONENT*}

{3 *{Name of subpoenaed witness}/{Party}*} asks the Court to quash the deposition of {4 *name of deponent*} by {5 *deposing party*}. {*See* ***O'Connor's Texas Rules****, "Objecting Before Oral Deposition," ch. 6-F, §7, p. 644.*}

INTRODUCTION

1. Plaintiff, {6 *name*}, sued defendant, {7 *name*}, for {8 *state basis of suit*}.

{*ADD PARAGRAPH 2 IF APPROPRIATE*}

2. {9 *Name of subpoenaed witness*} is not a party to this suit. {10 *Describe subpoenaed witness's relationship to the suit.*}

3. Discovery in this suit is governed by a Level {11 *1/2/3*} discovery-control plan. The discovery period {12 *will end/ended*} on {13 *date*}. {*See* ***O'Connor's Texas Rules****, "Discovery-Control Plans," ch. 6-A, §7, p. 520.*}

4. This case is set for trial on {14 *date*}.

5. {15 *State other relevant facts about the suit.*}

BACKGROUND

6. On {16 *date*}, {17 *deposing party*} noticed the deposition of {18 *name of deponent*} for {19 *date*}, at {20 *time*}.

7. {21 *State other facts relevant to the motion.*}

ARGUMENT & AUTHORITIES

{*CHOOSE APPROPRIATE PARAGRAPHS 8-14*}

8. The Court should quash the deposition because the deposition notice is inadequate. Texas Rule of Civil Procedure 199.2(a) requires that the notice be served on the witness and the other parties "a reasonable time before the deposition is taken." {22 *Add if appropriate: Additionally, Texas Rule of Civil Procedure 205.2 requires that a deposition notice must be served before or at the same time that the subpoena is served.*} {23 *Deposing party*} served the deposition notice on {24 *date*}. This notice is inadequate because {25 *specify reasons notice is inadequate, e.g., witness lives out of town, witness is not available, notice was not served before or at the same time as the subpoena*}.

◄ *Continued on next page* ►

9. The Court should quash the deposition because the {㉖ *time/place/time and place*} designated for {㉗ *name of deponent*}'s oral deposition is unreasonable. Tex. R. Civ. P. 199.4. {㉘ *State basis for objection and include a reasonable time and place for the deposition.*} {*See **O'Connor's Texas Rules**, "To object to time or place," ch. 6-F, §7.1, p. 645.*}

10. The Court should quash the deposition because the discovery sought is {㉙ *overbroad/unlikely to produce relevant information*}. *In re Univar USA Inc.*, 311 S.W.3d 186, 189 (Tex. App.—Beaumont 2010, orig. proceeding). {㉚ *Elaborate.*}

11. The Court should quash the deposition because {㉛ *name of deponent*} is {㉜ *identify corporate status, e.g., CEO*} of {㉝ *name of corporation*}. Attached to this motion as Exhibit {㉞ *letter*} is the affidavit of {㉟ *name of deponent*}, who states unequivocally that {㊱ *he/she*} has no personal knowledge of facts relevant to this lawsuit. {㊲ *Deposing party*} seeks to depose {㊳ *name of deponent*} without showing that the official has any unique or superior personal knowledge of discoverable information. *In re Alcatel USA, Inc.*, 11 S.W.3d 173, 176 (Tex. 2000); *Crown Cent. Petroleum Corp. v. Garcia*, 904 S.W.2d 125, 128 (Tex. 1995); *see In re BP Prods. N. Am., Inc.*, 244 S.W.3d 840, 842 n.2 (Tex. 2008). {㊴ *Deposing party*} has not made any attempt to secure the information {㊵ *he/she/it*} seeks through another, less intrusive discovery procedure. *In re Alcatel*, 11 S.W.3d at 176; *Crown Cent.*, 904 S.W.2d at 128. {*See **O'Connor's Texas Rules**, "To prevent apex deposition," ch. 6-F, §7.3, p. 645.*}

12. The Court should quash the deposition because {㊶ *name of deponent*} will be asked to testify about {㊷ *identify topic of deposition*}, a matter that is privileged. Attached to this motion as Exhibit {㊸ *letter*} is the affidavit of {㊹ *name of deponent*}, who states unequivocally that the only information {㊺ *he/she*} has about {㊻ *subject matter*} is privileged. {㊼ *Elaborate.*} {*See **O'Connor's Texas Rules**, "To cancel or limit because of privilege," ch. 6-F, §7.2, p. 645.*}

13. The Court should quash the deposition because {㊽ *deposing party*} did not provide sufficient notice before serving {㊾ *his/her/its*} subpoena on {㊿ *name of deponent*}. Tex. R. Civ. P. 205.2. {(51) *Elaborate.*} {*See **O'Connor's Texas Rules**, "Deadlines to Serve Notice & Subpoena," chart 6-9, p. 641.*}

14. {(52) *State any other reasons why the Court should quash the deposition.*}

{ADD PARAGRAPH 15 IF APPLICABLE}

15. {53 *Deposing party*} served the notice of oral deposition on {54 *date*}. Because this motion is filed within three business days of the date the notice was served, this motion objecting to the {55 *time/place/time and place*} for the deposition stays the deposition until the motion can be determined by the Court. Tex. R. Civ. P. 199.4.

CONCLUSION

16. {56 *Briefly summarize the motion.*}

PRAYER

17. For these reasons, {57 *{name of subpoenaed witness}/{party}*} asks the Court to set this motion to quash for hearing and, after the hearing, to quash the deposition of {58 *name of deponent*} by {59 *deposing party*}.

SEE: Tex. R. Civ. P. 199.2, 199.4
O'Connor's Texas Rules * Civil Trials (2019), "Objecting Before Oral Deposition," ch. 6-F, §7, p. 644

ADD: STYLE OF THE CASE – FORM 1B:2
SIGNATURE BLOCK – FORM 1B:3
CERTIFICATE OF CONFERENCE – FORM 1B:12
CERTIFICATE OF SERVICE – FORM 1B:13

ATTACH: AFFIDAVIT – FORMS 1B:8 & 6A:18, if necessary
NOTICE OF HEARING OR SUBMISSION – FORM 1E:1
ORDER – FORM 1G:1

NOTE: To object to a deposition notice, a party or nonparty witness may file either a motion for protective order (see FORM 6A:13) or this motion to quash. *See* Tex. R. Civ. P. 199.4. Whichever motion is used, it must be filed before the date of the scheduled deposition. To object to the deposition subpoena, a subpoenaed person, a party, or any person affected by the subpoena should file a motion for protective order (see FORM 6A:13). *See* Tex. R. Civ. P. 176.6(e). See ***O'Connor's Texas Rules***, "Objecting to Trial & Discovery Subpoenas," ch. 1-L, §4, p. 106.

An objection under Texas Rule of Civil Procedure 199.4 does not delay the time for compliance with a document request served with a deposition notice; it only delays the time of the deposition itself.

For general objections to discovery, see FORM 6A:9; for a motion for protection from discovery, see FORM 6A:10; for a motion for protection from a discovery subpoena, see FORM 6A:13; for claims of privilege, see FORMS 6A:19-22; for objections to requests for production, see FORM 6I:3.

{❶ *PARTY*}'S MOTION TO SUPPRESS
DEPOSITION OF {❷ *NAME OF DEPONENT*}

{❸ *Party*}, {❹ *name*}, asks the Court to suppress the deposition of {❺ *name of deponent*}, as allowed by Texas Rule of Civil Procedure 203.5. {*See* ***O'Connor's Texas Rules****, "Motion to suppress," ch. 6-F, §9.5, p. 649.*}

INTRODUCTION

1. Plaintiff, {❻ *name*}, sued defendant, {❼ *name*}, for {❽ *state basis of suit*}.

2. Discovery in this suit is governed by a Level {❾ *1/2/3*} discovery-control plan. The discovery period {❿ *will end/ended*} on {⓫ *date*}. {*See* ***O'Connor's Texas Rules****, "Discovery-Control Plans," ch. 6-A, §7, p. 520.*}

3. This case is set for trial on {⓬ *date*}.

4. {⓭ *State other relevant facts about the suit.*}

BACKGROUND

5. On {⓮ *date*}, the deposition of {⓯ *name of deponent*} was taken.

6. {⓰ *Name of deposition officer*}, a certified shorthand court reporter, recorded deponent's testimony.

7. {⓱ *Party*} files and serves this motion to suppress before trial has commenced.

8. {⓲ *State other facts relevant to the motion.*}

ARGUMENT & AUTHORITIES

9. The Court should suppress {⓳ *the deposition/part of the deposition*} of {⓴ *name of deponent*} because there were errors and irregularities made by the deposition officer.

{*CHOOSE APPROPRIATE PARAGRAPHS 10-16*}

10. The deposition transcript is not a true record of the testimony given by the witness at the deposition. Tex. R. Civ. P. 203.2(a). {㉑ *Elaborate.*}

11. The deposition does not include changes made by the witness. Tex. R. Civ. P. 203.2(c); *see* Tex. R. Civ. P. 203.1(b). The witness reviewed the deposition and provided the deposition officer with a list of changes and a statement of the reasons for making the changes. Nothing in the deposition indicates that any of the witness's changes were made. The changes were material. {㉒ *Elaborate.*}

12. The deposition officer did not administer the oath to the witness. Tex. R. Civ. P. 203.2(a). Thus, the deposition was not taken under oath, as required by Rule 199.5(b). {[23] *Elaborate.*}

13. The deposition officer did not submit the original deposition transcript for signature to the witness or to the attorney of record for the party who was the witness. Tex. R. Civ. P. 203.2(b). {[24] *Elaborate.*}

14. The deposition officer did not certify the amount of time used by each party at the deposition. Tex. R. Civ. P. 203.2(e). {[25] *Elaborate.*}

15. The deposition officer did not serve a copy of the certificate on all parties in accordance with Texas Rule of Civil Procedure 21a(e). *See* Tex. R. Civ. P. 203.2(g). {[26] *Elaborate.*}

16. The deposition officer did not file a copy of the certificate with the Court. Tex. R. Civ. P. 203.2. {[27] *Elaborate.*}

CONCLUSION

17. {[28] *Briefly summarize the motion.*}

PRAYER

18. For these reasons, the Court should suppress the deposition of {[29] *name of deponent*}.

SEE: Tex. R. Civ. P. 21a, 199.5(b), 203
O'Connor's Texas Rules * Civil Trials (2019), "Motion to suppress," ch. 6-F, §9.5, p. 649

ADD: STYLE OF THE CASE – FORM 1B:2
SIGNATURE BLOCK – FORM 1B:3
CERTIFICATE OF CONFERENCE – FORM 1B:12
CERTIFICATE OF SERVICE – FORM 1B:13

ATTACH: AFFIDAVIT – FORM 1B:8, if necessary
NOTICE OF HEARING OR SUBMISSION – FORM 1E:1
ORDER – FORM 1G:1

NOTE: The motion to suppress must be served before the trial commences if the deposition officer delivered the deposition at least one entire day before the commencement of trial. Tex. R. Civ. P. 203.5; ***SAVA gumarska v. Advanced Polymer Sci., Inc.***, 128 S.W.3d 304, 316 (Tex.App.—Dallas 2004, no pet.).

{[1] *PARTY*}'S NOTICE OF DEPOSITION ON WRITTEN QUESTIONS

{*CHOOSE APPROPRIATE INTRODUCTORY PARAGRAPH*}

To: {[2] *Adverse party*}, {[3] *name*}, through {[4] *his/her/its*} attorney of record, {[5] *name*}, {[6] *address*}.

To: {[7] *Name of nonparty deponent*}, {[8] *address*}.

{*CHOOSE APPROPRIATE PARAGRAPH 1*}

1. Please take notice that, under Texas Rule of Civil Procedure 200.1, {[9] *party*}, {[10] *name*}, will take the deposition on written questions of {[11] *name of adverse party or custodian of records for adverse party*} on {[12] *date*}, at {[13] *time*}, at {[14] *address*}. {*See **O'Connor's Texas Rules**, "Notice of deposition on written questions," ch. 6-F, §15.3, p. 654.*}

1. Please take notice that, under Texas Rule of Civil Procedure 200.1, {[15] *party*}, {[16] *name*}, will take the deposition on written questions of {[17] *name of nonparty deponent*} on {[18] *date*}, at {[19] *time*}, at {[20] *address*}. {*See **O'Connor's Texas Rules**, "Notice of deposition on written questions," ch. 6-F, §15.3, p. 654.*}

1. Please take notice that, under Texas Rule of Civil Procedure 200.1, {[21] *party*}, {[22] *name*}, will take the deposition on written questions of {[23] *name of entity, e.g., corporation, partnership*} on {[24] *date*}, at {[25] *time*}, at {[26] *address*}. {[27] *Name of entity*} is directed to designate a person or persons to testify on its behalf about the following matters: {[28] *identify matters, e.g., custody of medical records for plaintiff, John Doe*}. {*See **O'Connor's Texas Rules**, "Notice of deposition on written questions," ch. 6-F, §15.3, p. 654.*}

2. The deposition will continue from day to day until completed.

3. The deposition will be taken by {[29] *identify deposition officer taking the deposition, e.g., court-reporting service or records-service company*}.

{*IF SEEKING DOCUMENTS, ADD APPROPRIATE PARAGRAPH 4*}

4. Under Rule 200.1(b), {[30] *name of deponent*} is requested to produce the following documents at the deposition: {[31] *list and number documents by individual item or category and describe with reasonable particularity each item or category*}.

4. Under Rules 176.2(b) and 200.1(b), {㉜ *name of nonparty deponent*} has been subpoenaed to produce the following documents at the deposition: {㉝ *list and number documents by individual item or category and describe with reasonable particularity each item or category*}. {*See* ***O'Connor's Texas Rules****, "Subpoena," ch. 6-F, §15.3.7, p. 655.*}

{IF ADDITIONAL PERSONS WILL ATTEND DEPOSITION, ADD PARAGRAPH 5}

5. {㉞ *Party*} gives notice, as required by Rule 200.1(b), that the following persons will attend the deposition: {㉟ *identify any persons who will attend other than the deponent, parties, spouses of parties, counsel, employees of counsel, or the officer taking the deposition*}. {*See* ***O'Connor's Texas Rules****, "Additional attendee," ch. 6-F, §4.5.5, p. 640.*}

SEE: Tex. R. Civ. P. 176.2, 200
O'Connor's Texas Rules * Civil Trials (2019), "Deposition on Written Questions," ch. 6-F, §15, p. 654; "Discovery subpoena," ch. 6-I, §5.2, p. 686

ADD: STYLE OF THE CASE – FORM 1B:2
SIGNATURE BLOCK – FORM 1B:3
CERTIFICATE OF SERVICE – FORM 1B:13

ATTACH: SUBPOENA – FORM 1L:1, if deponent is a nonparty
WRITTEN QUESTIONS – FORM 6F:5, if deponent is custodian of records
COVER SHEET & DEFINITIONS – FORM 6I:1, if requesting deponent to produce documents
Other written questions appropriate to the case

NOTE: A notice of intent to take a deposition on written questions must be served on the witness and all parties at least 20 days before the deposition is taken. Tex. R. Civ. P. 200.1(a). If the notice includes a request for documents, the date for the deposition should be set at least 40 days after the date the notice is served, so the party noticing the deposition can reschedule it if the witness refuses to produce the documents. When a deposition with documents is set with only 30 days' notice, the responding party has no obligation to file objections or assertions of privileges before the deposition. A party cannot secure documents from another party in less than 30 days. *See* Tex. R. Civ. P. 196.2(a). See ***O'Connor's Texas Rules***, "Date for deposition," ch. 6-F, §15.3.3, p. 655.

A copy of the notice and all written questions must be sent to the officer designated to take the deposition. Tex. R. Civ. P. 200.1(a). See ***O'Connor's Texas Rules***, "Provide to deposition officer," ch. 6-F, §15.3.9, p. 655.

DEPOSITION ON WRITTEN QUESTIONS

1. Please state your full name, occupation, official title, and business address.
Answer: ____

____

2. Are you the custodian of records for {❶ *name of entity, e.g., hospital, corporation, partnership*}?
Answer: ____

____

3. In your capacity as custodian of records for {❷ *name of entity*}, are you familiar with whether {❸ *name of entity*} maintains records of its business activities?
Answer: ____

____

4. Are the records of {❹ *name of entity*} kept under your care, supervision, custody, or control?
Answer: ____

____

5. Was it in the regular course of business activity of {❺ *name of entity*} for {❻ *identify employees of entity, e.g., doctors, nurses*} with personal knowledge of the act, event, condition, opinion, or diagnosis identified in the records to make such records or to transmit such information to be included in the records?
Answer: ____

____

6. Were the {❼ *identify requested records*} made at or near the time of the act, event, condition, opinion, or diagnosis identified in the records or within a reasonable time thereafter?
Answer: ____

____

7. Were the {❽ *identify requested records*} made and kept in the regular course of daily business activities by {❾ *name of entity*}?
Answer: ____

____

★

8. Were the {[10] *identify requested records*} transmitted to your files, and did you maintain the records as part of your official duties as the custodian of records for {[11] *name of entity*}?
Answer: ____
____

9. Please hand the originals or exact duplicates of {[12] *identify requested records*} to the {[13] *court reporter/notary public*} taking your deposition for photocopying and attachment to this deposition. Have you now given all {[14] *identify requested records*} to the {[15] *court reporter/notary public*} taking your deposition? If not, identify for the {[16] *court reporter/notary public*} the records and documents you did not produce and explain why you did not produce them.
Answer: ____
____

10. In the event you are unable to find any of the records requested in the subpoena you received, how long does {[17] *name of entity*} maintain its files, and does {[18] *name of entity*} ever destroy its files?
Answer: ____
____

11. Are you aware of any other {[19] *identify other types of entities or persons, e.g., hospital, clinic, physician, chiropractor, osteopath*} that may have possession of records pertaining to the subject matter of this lawsuit? If so, please state the name and address of such entity or person, if known.
Answer: ____
____

12. Have you been requested or directed by any person to withhold or protect, for any reason, the records identified in {[20] *party*}'s subpoena? Has any person suggested that you should withhold or protect the records identified in {[21] *party*}'s subpoena? If so, please state the name and address of the person who conveyed this information to you and when such event occurred.
Answer: ____
____

13. Do you know or have reason to believe that the records identified in {[22] *party*}'s subpoena have in any manner been edited, purged, culled, or otherwise altered? If so, please identify the records and explain why and how they were altered or removed.
Answer: ____
____

◄ *Continued on next page* ►

14. If any document responsive to this subpoena was, but is no longer, in your possession, custody, or control, or no longer exists, state whether (1) it is missing or lost, (2) it was destroyed, (3) it was transferred to others, or (4) it was otherwise disposed of, and explain the circumstances surrounding its disposition, including the date of such disposition.
Answer: ____
____

____
Custodian of records for
{23 *name of entity*}

STATE OF TEXAS §
{24 ______} COUNTY §

Before me, the undersigned {25 *officer/notary*}, on this day personally appeared {26 *name of custodian of records*}, the custodian of records for {27 *name of entity*}, whose identity is known to me. After I administered an oath, the custodian testified to the foregoing answers. I hereby certify that these answers were sworn to and subscribed before me by {28 *name of custodian of records*} on __________, 20___.

____
{29 *Identify title of officer/notary*}

SEE: Tex. R. Civ. P. 200
O'Connor's Texas Rules * Civil Trials (2019), "Deposition on Written Questions," ch. 6-F, §15, p. 654

ADD: STYLE OF THE CASE – FORM 1B:2

NOTE: These questions are generally acceptable to direct the custodian of records to produce records. If the custodian of records will agree to execute an affidavit proving up business records or the costs of services for the provider, and if a notice of deposition is not needed, the attorney should consider using a request for production under Texas Rule of Civil Procedure 205.3, as well as FORMS 8C:2 and 8C:4 or 8C:5, to avoid the expense of a deposition on written questions.

{❶ *PARTY*}'S OBJECTIONS & NOTICE OF CROSS-QUESTIONS FOR DEPOSITION ON WRITTEN QUESTIONS

To: {❷ *Adverse party*}, {❸ *name*}, through {❹ *his/her/its*} attorney of record, {❺ *name*}, {❻ *address*}.

{❼ *Party*}, {❽ *name*}, makes the following objections to {❾ *adverse party*}'s notice of deposition on written questions and serves the following cross-questions to be answered by deponent, {❿ *name of deponent*}, on {⓫ *date*}, at {⓬ *time*}, at {⓭ *address*}, as allowed by Texas Rule of Civil Procedure 200.3(b). {⓮ *Adverse party*} has five days after receipt of this notice to serve redirect questions. {*See* ***O'Connor's Texas Rules****, "Cross-questions," ch. 6-F, §15.4, p. 655; "Redirect questions," ch. 6-F, §15.5, p. 655.*}

OBJECTIONS TO WRITTEN QUESTIONS

1. {⓯ *Party*} objects to question {⓰ *number*} because {⓱ *state objection to question*}.

{*Continue until each objection is stated.*}

CROSS-QUESTIONS

1. {⓲ *State cross-question to be asked of witness.*}

{*Continue until each cross-question is stated.*}

SEE: Tex. R. Civ. P. 200
O'Connor's Texas Rules * Civil Trials (2019), "Cross-questions," ch. 6-F, §15.4, p. 655; "Redirect questions," ch. 6-F, §15.5, p. 655; "Recross questions," ch. 6-F, §15.6, p. 655; "Objections to questions," ch. 6-F, §15.7, p. 655; "Objections to assertions of privileges," ch. 6-F, §15.8, p. 656

ADD: STYLE OF THE CASE – FORM 1B:2
SIGNATURE BLOCK – FORM 1B:3
CERTIFICATE OF SERVICE – FORM 1B:13

NOTE: Cross-questions must be served within ten days after the notice and direct questions are served. Tex. R. Civ. P. 200.3(b).

{❶ *PARTY*}'S MOTION FOR LEAVE TO
TAKE DEPOSITION OUTSIDE THE DISCOVERY PERIOD

{❷ *Party*}, {❸ *name*}, asks the Court for permission to take the oral deposition of {❹ *name of deponent*} outside the discovery period, under the authority of Texas Rule of Civil Procedure 199.2(a).

INTRODUCTION

1. Plaintiff, {❺ *name*}, sued defendant, {❻ *name*}, for {❼ *state basis of suit*}.

2. Discovery in this suit is governed by a Level {❽ *1/2/3*} discovery-control plan. The discovery period {❾ *will end/ended*} on {❿ *date*}. {*See* ***O'Connor's Texas Rules***, *"Discovery-Control Plans," ch. 6-A, §7, p. 520.*}

3. This case is set for trial on {⓫ *date*}.

4. {⓬ *State other relevant facts about the suit.*}

BACKGROUND

5. {⓭ *State facts relevant to the motion.*}

ARGUMENT & AUTHORITIES

{*CHOOSE APPROPRIATE PARAGRAPH 6*}

{*Modification under Rule 190.5 – any action other than expedited action*}

6. Rule 199.2(a) specifically permits a court to grant leave to take the deposition of a witness outside the discovery period. Under Texas Rule of Civil Procedure 190.5, a court must modify a discovery-control plan and allow additional discovery when justice requires. {*See* ***O'Connor's Texas Rules***, *"Modification of discovery periods," ch. 6-A, §8.2, p. 524.*}

{*Modification under Rule 190.5 – expedited action*}

6. Rule 199.2(a) specifically permits a court to grant leave to take the deposition of a witness outside the discovery period. Under Texas Rule of Civil Procedure 190.5, a court may modify a discovery-control plan and allow additional discovery when certain conditions are met. {*See* ***O'Connor's Texas Rules***, *"Modification of discovery periods," ch. 6-A, §8.2, p. 524.*}

{*Modification under Rule 191.1 – any action other than expedited action*}

6. Rule 199.2(a) specifically permits a court to grant leave to take the deposition of a witness outside the discovery period. Under Texas Rule of Civil Procedure 191.1, a court can modify the discovery limitations when there is good cause, unless the modification is specifically prohibited. {*See* ***O'Connor's Texas Rules***, *"Modifying discovery by court order," ch. 6-A, §6.2, p. 519.*}

{*CHOOSE APPROPRIATE PARAGRAPHS 7-12*}

{*Modification under Rule 190.5 – any action other than expedited action*}

7. Justice requires that the Court permit {[14] *party*} to depose {[15] *name of deponent*} outside the discovery period because the witness's name was disclosed in {[16] *a new pleading/an amended pleading/a supplemental pleading/a discovery response*} filed after the discovery period, and {[17] *party*} would be unfairly prejudiced without the deposition. *See* Tex. R. Civ. P. 190.5(a). {[18] *Elaborate.*}

8. Justice requires that the Court permit {[19] *party*} to depose {[20] *name of deponent*} outside the discovery period because the witness's name was disclosed in {[21] *a new pleading/an amended pleading/a supplemental pleading/a discovery response*} filed so close to the end of the discovery period that {[22] *party*} {[23] *does/did*} not have an adequate opportunity to depose the witness, and {[24] *party*} would be unfairly prejudiced without the deposition. *See* Tex. R. Civ. P. 190.5(a). {[25] *Elaborate.*}

9. Justice requires that the Court permit {[26] *party*} to depose {[27] *name of deponent*} outside the discovery period because some matters have materially changed after the discovery cutoff, and the case will not reach trial for {[28] *three/more than three*} months after the discovery cutoff. *See* Tex. R. Civ. P. 190.5(b). {[29] *Elaborate.*}

{*Modification under Rule 190.5 – expedited action*}

10. The Court should permit {[30] *party*} to depose {[31] *name of deponent*} outside the discovery period because the witness's name was disclosed in {[32] *a new pleading/an amended pleading/a supplemental pleading/a discovery response*} filed after the discovery period, and {[33] *party*} would be unfairly prejudiced without the deposition. *See* Tex. R. Civ. P. 190.5(a) & cmt. (2013). {[34] *Elaborate.*} {*See* ***O'Connor's Texas Rules***, *"Modification of discovery periods," ch. 6-A, §8.2, p. 524.*}

11. The Court should permit {[35] *party*} to depose {[36] *name of deponent*} outside the discovery period because the witness's name was disclosed in {[37] *a new pleading/an amended pleading/a supplemental pleading/a discovery response*} filed so close to the end of the discovery period that {[38] *party*} {[39] *does/did*} not have an adequate

Continued on next page

opportunity to depose the witness, and {40 *party*} would be unfairly prejudiced without the deposition. *See* Tex. R. Civ. P. 190.5(a) & cmt. (2013). {41 *Elaborate.*} {*See* ***O'Connor's Texas Rules****, "Modification of discovery periods," ch. 6-A, §8.2, p. 524.*}

{*Modification under Rule 191.1 – any action other than expedited action*}

12. The Court should permit the oral deposition of {42 *name of deponent*} outside the discovery period because (1) there is good cause and (2) no rule prohibits it. {43 *Elaborate.*}

CONCLUSION

13. {44 *Briefly summarize the motion.*}

PRAYER

14. For these reasons, {45 *party*} asks the Court to set this motion for hearing and, after the hearing, to issue an order granting leave to take the oral deposition of {46 *name of deponent*} on {47 *date*}, at {48 *time*}, at {49 *address*}, before {50 *identify court-reporting service that will be taking the deposition*}.

SEE: Tex. R. Civ. P. 190.5, 191.1, 199.2(a)
O'Connor's Texas Rules * Civil Trials (2019), "Modification of discovery periods," ch. 6-A, §8.2, p. 524; "Depositions," ch. 6-F, p. 636

ADD: STYLE OF THE CASE – FORM 1B:2
SIGNATURE BLOCK – FORM 1B:3
CERTIFICATE OF CONFERENCE – FORM 1B:12
CERTIFICATE OF SERVICE – FORM 1B:13

ATTACH: AFFIDAVIT – FORM 1B:8, if necessary
NOTICE OF HEARING OR SUBMISSION – FORM 1E:1
ORDER – FORM 1G:1

NOTE: The court may modify a discovery period and allow for additional discovery at any time; it must do so when justice requires. Tex. R. Civ. P. 190.5. Expedited actions, however, are not subject to mandatory additional discovery, but the court may still allow additional discovery if the conditions of Texas Rule of Civil Procedure 190.5(a) are met. Tex. R. Civ. P. 190.5 & cmt. (2013). See ***O'Connor's Texas Rules***, "Expedited Actions," ch. 2-C, p. 134.

No. {❶ *docket number*}

IN RE {❷ *name of petitioner*},	§	IN THE {❸ _______} COURT
Petitioner.	§	
	§	
	§	OF {❹ _______} COUNTY, TEXAS
	§	
	§	
	§	{❺ ____} JUDICIAL DISTRICT

PETITIONER {❻ *NAME*}'S VERIFIED
PETITION TO TAKE DEPOSITION BEFORE SUIT

Petitioner, {❼ *name*}, asks the Court for permission to take a deposition by {❽ *oral examination/written questions*} to obtain testimony {❾ *in an anticipated suit/to investigate a potential claim*}, as allowed by Texas Rule of Civil Procedure 202. {*See* ***O'Connor's Texas Rules***, *"Petition," ch. 6-F, §16.1, p. 656.*}

INTRODUCTION

1. Petitioner is {❿ *identify status, e.g., an individual, a corporation*} {⓫ *who/that*} {⓬ *resides/does business*} in {⓭ _______} County, Texas.

2. The following {⓮ *persons/entities*} are sought to be deposed: {⓯ *identify names of deponents, their status (e.g., individuals, corporations), addresses, and telephone numbers*}. {*See* ***O'Connor's Texas Rules***, *"Deponent information," ch. 6-F, §16.1.3, p. 657.*}

BACKGROUND

{*CHOOSE APPROPRIATE PARAGRAPH 3*}

3. Petitioner seeks to {⓰ *perpetuate/obtain*} the deposition testimony of {⓱ *names of deponents*} for use in an anticipated suit in which petitioner may be a party. {*See* ***O'Connor's Texas Rules***, *"Anticipation of suit," ch. 6-F, §16.1.2(1), p. 656.*}

3. Petitioner seeks to take the deposition of {⓲ *names of deponents*} to investigate a potential claim {⓳ *by/against*} petitioner. {*See* ***O'Connor's Texas Rules***, *"Investigate claim," ch. 6-F, §16.1.2(2), p. 657.*}

◄ *Continued on next page* ►

{*IF DEPOSITION IN ANTICIPATION OF SUIT, ADD PARAGRAPHS 4-5*}

4. The subject matter of the anticipated suit is {[20] *identify subject matter*}. {[21] *Elaborate.*} {*See Tex. R. Civ. P. 202.2(e);* ***O'Connor's Texas Rules****, "Identify subject matter," ch. 6-F, §16.1.2(1)(a), p. 657.*}

5. Petitioner's interest in the anticipated suit is {[22] *state interest*}. {*See Tex. R. Civ. P. 202.2(e);* ***O'Connor's Texas Rules****, "Identify subject matter," ch. 6-F, §16.1.2(1)(a), p. 657.*}

{*IF DEPOSITION IN ANTICIPATION OF SUIT, CHOOSE APPROPRIATE PARAGRAPH 6*}

6. The following {[23] *persons/entities*} may have an interest adverse to that of petitioner in the anticipated suit: {[24] *list names, addresses, and telephone numbers*}. {*See* ***O'Connor's Texas Rules****, "Identify adverse persons," ch. 6-F, §16.1.2(1)(b), p. 657.*}

6. The names, addresses, and telephone numbers of the following {[25] *persons/entities*} that may have an interest adverse to that of petitioner in the anticipated suit cannot be determined through diligent inquiry: {[26] *describe persons or entities*}. {*See* ***O'Connor's Texas Rules****, "Identify adverse persons," ch. 6-F, §16.1.2(1)(b), p. 657.*}

{*CHOOSE APPROPRIATE PARAGRAPH 7*}

{*For deposition in anticipation of suit*}

7. This petition is filed in {[27] _______} County, Texas, where venue of the anticipated suit may lie. {*See Tex. R. Civ. P. 202.2(b)(1);* ***O'Connor's Texas Rules****, "Where to file," ch. 6-F, §16.2, p. 657.*}

{*For deposition to investigate claim*}

7. This petition is filed in {[28] _______} County, Texas, where {[29] *name of deponent*} resides. {*See Tex. R. Civ. P. 202.2(b)(2);* ***O'Connor's Texas Rules****, "Where to file," ch. 6-F, §16.2, p. 657.*}

8. The Court has subject-matter jurisdiction over the {[30] *anticipated suit/potential claim*}. {[31] *Elaborate.*} {*See In re DePinho, 505 S.W.3d 621, 623-24 (Tex. 2016); In re City of Dall., 501 S.W.3d 71, 73 (Tex. 2016); In re Doe, 444 S.W.3d 603, 608 (Tex. 2014);* ***O'Connor's Texas Rules****, "Subject-matter jurisdiction," ch. 6-F, §16.3.1, p. 658.*}

9. The Court has personal jurisdiction over {32 *names of deponents*}. Specifically, {33 *explain that deponents have sufficient minimum contacts with Texas for the court to exercise personal jurisdiction over them*}. {*See In re Doe, 444 S.W.3d at 610; FORM 3B:3, ¶¶7-10;* ***O'Connor's Texas Rules****, "No minimum contacts," ch. 3-B, §2.4.2, p. 226; "Personal jurisdiction," ch. 6-F, §16.3.2, p. 658.*}

REQUEST TO DEPOSE

10. Petitioner asks the Court to issue an order authorizing {34 *him/her/it*} to examine the following {35 *persons/entities*} by oral deposition: {36 *state names*}.

11. Petitioner expects to elicit the following testimony from the {37 *witness/witnesses*}: {38 *identify each deponent by name and state the substance of the testimony expected*}. {*See* ***O'Connor's Texas Rules****, "Deponent information," ch. 6-F, §16.1.3, p. 657.*}

12. Petitioner needs to depose {39 *names of deponents*} because {40 *state reasons testimony is necessary, e.g., the witness may move or disappear before the claim can be investigated*}. {*See* ***O'Connor's Texas Rules****, "Deponent information," ch. 6-F, §16.1.3, p. 657.*}

{*ADD PARAGRAPH 13 IF NECESSARY*}

13. Petitioner requests that the Court order the following {41 *persons/entities*} to produce documents at the deposition: {42 *identify each deponent by name, list documents by individual item or category, and describe with reasonable particularity each item or category*}. {*See* ***O'Connor's Texas Rules****, "Deponent information," ch. 6-F, §16.1.3, p. 657.*}

{*CHOOSE APPROPRIATE PARAGRAPH 14*}

{*For deposition in anticipation of suit*}

14. The requested deposition may prevent a failure or delay of justice in an anticipated suit. {43 *Explain.*} {*See Tex. R. Civ. P. 202.4(a)(1);* ***O'Connor's Texas Rules****, "Proof," ch. 6-F, §16.6.2, p. 660.*}

{*For deposition to investigate claim*}

14. The likely benefit of allowing the petitioner to take the requested deposition to investigate a potential claim outweighs the burden or expense of the procedure. {44 *Explain.*} {*See Tex. R. Civ. P. 202.4(a)(2);* ***O'Connor's Texas Rules****, "Proof," ch. 6-F, §16.6.2, p. 660.*}

◄ *Continued on next page* ►

HEARING

15. After service of this petition and notice, Rule 202.3(a) requires that the Court hold a hearing on the petition.

PRAYER

16. For these reasons, petitioner asks the Court to set this petition for hearing and, after the hearing, to order the deposition of {㊺ *names of deponents*} {㊻ *add if applicable: and the production of documents listed in this petition*}. {*See Tex. R. Civ. P. 202.2(h).*}

SEE: Tex. R. Civ. P. 202
O'Connor's Texas Rules * Civil Trials (2019), "Deposition Before Suit," ch. 6-F, §16, p. 656

ADD: SIGNATURE BLOCK – FORM 1B:3
VERIFICATION – FORM 1B:7
CERTIFICATE OF SERVICE – FORM 1B:13, on person to be deposed and any potential adverse party named in the petition

ATTACH: NOTICE OF HEARING OR SUBMISSION – FORM 1E:1
NOTICE TO DEPONENT – FORM 6F:9
NOTICE TO PERSONS WITH ADVERSE INTEREST – FORM 6F:10
ORDER – FORM 6F:11

NOTE: The person to be deposed and any potential adverse party named in the petition must be served at least 15 days before the hearing on the petition. Tex. R. Civ. P. 202.3(a). Service must be accomplished under Texas Rule of Civil Procedure 21a. Tex. R. Civ. P. 202.3(a). However, for the witness's attendance at the hearing to be secured, the witness must be served with a subpoena.

A presuit deposition under Texas Rule of Civil Procedure 202 cannot be taken to investigate a potential claim against a health-care provider until after an expert report is served. ***In re Jorden***, 249 S.W.3d 416, 418 (Tex.2008); *see* Tex. Civ. Prac. & Rem. Code §74.351(s). The filing of a Rule 202 deposition, however, does not trigger the 120-day deadline for serving an expert report. ***Drake v. Walker***, 529 S.W.3d 516, 526 (Tex.App.—Dallas 2017, no pet.); *see* Tex. Civ. Prac. & Rem. Code §74.351(a) (expert report must be served within 120 days after D's original answer is filed).

A presuit deposition under Texas Rule of Civil Procedure 202 generally cannot be taken to discover trade-secret information to determine if the petitioner has a potential claim. *See* ***In re Rockafellow***, ___ S.W.3d ___ & n.3 (Tex.App.—Amarillo 2011, orig. proceeding) (No. 07-11-00066-CV; 7-19-11) (undesignated op.). To take a presuit deposition to discover trade-secret information, a petitioner must satisfy the requirements of both Texas Rule of Evidence 507 and Texas Rule of Civil Procedure 202.4(a)(2). *See* ***In re PrairieSmarts LLC***, 421 S.W.3d 296, 305-06 (Tex. App.—Fort Worth 2014, orig. proceeding). See ***O'Connor's Texas Rules***, "Trade secret," ch. 6-F, §16.1.2(2)(b)[2], p. 657.

In ***In re DePinho***, the Supreme Court clarified that, even though a deposition under Texas Rule of Civil Procedure 202 can be used to investigate a potential claim, the claim must still be ripe for a court to have subject-matter jurisdiction. ***In re DePinho***, 505 S.W.3d 621, 624 (Tex.2016). For a claim to be ripe, the facts must be sufficiently developed so that an injury has occurred or is likely to occur, rather than being contingent or remote. *Id.*

At least two courts of appeals have held that a court cannot order production of documents in conjunction with a Texas Rule of Civil Procedure 202 deposition. *E.g.*, ***DeAngelis v. Protective Parents Coalition***, 556 S.W.3d 836, 858 (Tex.App.—Fort Worth 2018, no pet.); ***In re Pickrell***, No. 10-17-00091-CV (Tex.App.—Waco 2017, orig. proceeding) (memo op.; 4-19-17). But these holdings seem to contradict Rule 202, which states that presuit depositions are governed by the rules applicable to the depositions of nonparties. *See* Tex. R. Civ. P. 202.5. Texas Rule of Civil Procedure 205, which governs discovery from nonparties, allows a request for production to be served with a notice of deposition. Tex. R. Civ. P. 205.1(c). See ***O'Connor's Texas Rules***, "Subpoena for documents," ch. 6-F, §16.7.2(2), p. 660.

FORM 6F:9 NOTICE TO DEPONENT

No. {❶ *docket number*}

IN RE {❷ *name of petitioner*},	§	IN THE {❸ _______} COURT
Petitioner.	§	
	§	
	§	OF {❹ _______} COUNTY, TEXAS
	§	
	§	
	§	{❺ ___} JUDICIAL DISTRICT

NOTICE TO {❻ *NAME*} OF HEARING ON PETITIONER {❼ *NAME*}'S PETITION TO TAKE {❽ *NAME*}'S DEPOSITION

To: {❾ *Name of deponent*}, {❿ *address*}.

Petitioner, {⓫ *name*}, has filed the attached petition asking the Court for permission to take your deposition {⓬ *by oral examination/on written questions*} {⓭ *add if appropriate: and for the production of documents*} {⓮ *in an anticipated suit/to investigate a potential claim*} {⓯ *by/against*} petitioner.

You received this notice because you are the person whose deposition is sought by the petition.

A hearing is set on the petition on {⓰ *date*}, at {⓱ *time*}, in the courtroom of the Honorable {⓲ *name*}, presiding judge of the {⓳ *identify court*}, sitting in {⓴ *name of county*} County courthouse, located at {㉑ *address*}, {㉒ _______} County, Texas.

SEE: Tex. R. Civ. P. 202.3(a)
O'Connor's Texas Rules * Civil Trials (2019), "Notice & service," ch. 6-F, §16.4, p. 658

ADD: SIGNATURE BLOCK – FORM 1B:3
CERTIFICATE OF SERVICE – FORM 1B:13, on person to be deposed

NOTE: The person to be deposed must be served at least 15 days before the hearing on the petition. Tex. R. Civ. P. 202.3(a). Service must be accomplished under Texas Rule of Civil Procedure 21a. Tex. R. Civ. P. 202.3(a). However, for the witness's attendance at the hearing to be secured, the witness must be served with a subpoena.

No. {❶ *docket number*}

IN RE {❷ *name of petitioner*}, Petitioner.	§ § § § § § §	IN THE {❸ _______} COURT OF {❹ _______} COUNTY, TEXAS {❺ ____} JUDICIAL DISTRICT

NOTICE TO PERSONS
WITH ADVERSE INTEREST OF HEARING ON
PETITION TO TAKE DEPOSITION IN ANTICIPATION OF SUIT

To: {❻ *Name of interested person or entity*}, {❼ *address*}.

Petitioner, {❽ *name*}, has filed the attached petition to obtain the deposition testimony of {❾ *name of deponent*} {❿ *add if appropriate: and to request the production of documents*}.

You received this notice because you are a person or entity who potentially has an adverse interest in the anticipated litigation.

A hearing is set on the petition on {⓫ *date*}, at {⓬ *time*}, in the courtroom of the Honorable {⓭ *name*}, presiding judge of the {⓮ *identify court*}, sitting in {⓯ *name of county*} County courthouse, located at {⓰ *address*}, {⓱ _______} County, Texas.

SEE: Tex. R. Civ. P. 202.3(a)
O'Connor's Texas Rules * Civil Trials (2019), "Notice & service," ch. 6-F, §16.4, p. 658

ADD: SIGNATURE BLOCK – FORM 1B:3
CERTIFICATE OF SERVICE – FORM 1B:13, on person to be deposed and any potential adverse party named in the petition

NOTE: The person to be deposed and any potential adverse party named in the petition must be served at least 15 days before the hearing on the petition. Tex. R. Civ. P. 202.3(a). Service must be accomplished under Texas Rule of Civil Procedure 21a. Tex. R. Civ. P. 202.3(a).

No. {❶ *docket number*}

IN RE {❷ *name of petitioner*}, Petitioner.	§	IN THE {❸ _______} COURT
	§	
	§	
	§	OF {❹ _______} COUNTY, TEXAS
	§	
	§	
	§	{❺ ____} JUDICIAL DISTRICT

ORDER ON PETITIONER {❻ *NAME*}'S
VERIFIED PETITION TO TAKE DEPOSITION BEFORE SUIT

After considering {❼ *name*}'s petition asking the Court for permission to take the deposition {❽ *by oral examination/on written questions*} of {❾ *name of deponent*} {❿ *add if appropriate: and for the production of documents*} {⓫ *in an anticipated suit/to investigate a potential claim*}, the response, and arguments of counsel, the Court

{*CHOOSE APPROPRIATE ORDER*}

DENIES the request.

{*For deposition in anticipation of suit*}

GRANTS the request and finds that allowing petitioner to take the requested deposition may prevent a failure or delay of justice in an anticipated suit. It is therefore ordered that petitioner may take the deposition {⓬ *by oral examination/on written questions*} of {⓭ *name of deponent*}. {*See Tex. R. Civ. P. 202.4(a)(1);* ***O'Connor's Texas Rules****, "Required findings," ch. 6-F, §16.7.1, p. 660.*}

{*For deposition to investigate claim*}

GRANTS the request and finds that the likely benefit of allowing the petitioner to take the requested deposition to investigate a potential claim outweighs the burden or expense of the procedure. It is therefore ordered that petitioner may take the deposition {⓮ *by oral examination/on written questions*} of {⓯ *name of deponent*}. {*See Tex. R. Civ. P. 202.4(a)(2);* ***O'Connor's Texas Rules****, "Required findings," ch. 6-F, §16.7.1, p. 660.*}

{*ADD FOLLOWING PARAGRAPHS IF APPLICABLE*}

{16 *Name of entity, e.g., corporation, partnership*} is directed to designate a person or persons to testify on its behalf about the following matters: {17 *identify matters*}.

{18 *Name of deponent*} is ordered to produce the following documents at the deposition: {19 *list and number documents by individual item or category and describe with reasonable particularity each item or category*}.

CONDITIONS FOR THE DEPOSITION

{*CHOOSE APPROPRIATE PARAGRAPH 1*}

1. The deposition will be taken at {20 *address*}, on {21 *date*}, at {22 *time*}. {*See* ***O'Connor's Texas Rules****, "Deposition," ch. 6-F, §16.7.2(1), p. 660.*}

1. The petitioner will notice the deposition as required by Texas Rule of Civil Procedure {23 *199/200*}. {*See* ***O'Connor's Texas Rules****, "Notice & service," ch. 6-F, §16.4, p. 658.*}

2. {24 *Add provisions the Court deems necessary to protect the witness or any other person that might be affected by the deposition, or state that the Court finds no protection is necessary. See Tex. R. Civ. P. 202.4(b).*} {*See* ***O'Connor's Texas Rules****, "Protection for others," ch. 6-F, §16.7.3, p. 661.*}

SIGNED on ________________, 20___.

____
PRESIDING JUDGE

SEE: Tex. R. Civ. P. 202.4
O'Connor's Texas Rules * Civil Trials (2019), "Order," ch. 6-F, §16.7, p. 660

ADD: CERTIFICATE OF SERVICE – FORM 1B:13, if proposed order served separately from motion or response

{❶ *PARTY*}'S INTERROGATORIES TO {❷ *ADVERSE PARTY*}

To: {❸ *Adverse party*}, {❹ *name*}, by and through {❺ *his/her/its*} attorney of record, {❻ *name*}, {❼ *address*}.

{❽ *Party*}, {❾ *name*}, serves these interrogatories on {❿ *adverse party*}, as allowed by Texas Rule of Civil Procedure 197. {⓫ *Adverse party*} must answer each interrogatory separately, fully, in writing, and under oath, within 30 days after service. {*See* ***O'Connor's Texas Rules***, *"Serving Interrogatories," ch. 6-G, §3, p. 664.*}

INSTRUCTIONS

For any requested information about a document that no longer exists or cannot be located, identify the document, state how and when it passed out of existence or when it could no longer be located, and give the reasons for the disappearance. Also, identify each person having knowledge about the disposition or loss, and identify each document evidencing the existence or nonexistence of each document that cannot be located.

DEFINITIONS

1. "Plaintiff" or "defendant," as well as a party's full or abbreviated name or a pronoun referring to a party, means the party, and when applicable, the party's agents, representatives, officers, directors, employees, partners, corporate agents, subsidiaries, affiliates, or any other person acting in concert with the party or under the party's control, whether directly or indirectly, including any attorney.

2. "You" or "your" means {⓬ *adverse party*}, {⓭ *name*}, {⓮ *his/her/its*} successors, predecessors, divisions, subsidiaries, present and former officers, agents, employees, and all other persons acting on behalf of {⓯ *adverse party*} or {⓰ *his/her/its*} successors, predecessors, divisions, and subsidiaries.

3. "Document" means all written, typed, or printed matter and all magnetic, electronic, or other records or documentation of any kind or description in your actual possession, custody, or control, including those in the possession, custody, or control of any and all present or former directors, officers, employees, consultants, accountants, attorneys, or other agents, whether or not prepared by you, that constitute or contain matters relevant to the subject matter of the action. "Document" includes, but is not limited to, the following: letters, reports, charts, diagrams, correspondence, telegrams, memoranda, notes, records, minutes, contracts, agreements, records or notations of telephone or personal conversations or conferences, interoffice communications, e-mail, microfilm, bulletins, circulars, pamphlets, photographs, faxes, invoices, tape recordings, computer printouts, drafts, résumés, logs, worksheets, {⓱ *continue listing examples as necessary*}.

4. "Electronic or magnetic data" means electronic information that is stored in a medium from which it can be retrieved and examined. The term refers to the original (or identical duplicate when the original is not available) and any other copies of the data that may have attached comments, notes, marks, or highlighting of any kind. Electronic or magnetic data includes, but is not limited to, the following: computer programs; operating systems; computer activity logs; programming notes or instructions; e-mail receipts, messages, or transmissions; output resulting from the use of any software program, including word-processing documents, spreadsheets, database files, charts, graphs, and outlines; metadata; PIF and PDF files; batch files; deleted files; temporary files; Internet- or web-browser-generated information stored in textual, graphical, or audio format, including history files, caches, and cookies; {⓲ *continue listing examples as necessary*}; and any miscellaneous files or file fragments. Electronic or magnetic data includes any items stored on magnetic, optical, digital, or other electronic-storage media, such as hard drives, floppy disks, CD-ROMs, DVDs, tapes, smart cards, integrated-circuit cards (e.g., SIM cards), removable media (e.g., Zip drives, Jaz cartridges), microfiche, punched cards, {⓳ *continue listing examples as necessary*}. Electronic or magnetic data also includes the file, folder, tabs, containers, and labels attached to or associated with any physical storage device with each original or copy.

5. "Possession, custody, or control" of an item means that the person either has physical possession of the item or has a right to possession equal or superior to that of the person who has physical possession of the item.

6. "Person" means any natural person, corporation, firm, association, partnership, joint venture, proprietorship, governmental body, or any other organization, business, or legal entity, and all predecessors or successors in interest.

7. "Mobile device" means any cellular telephone, satellite telephone, pager, personal digital assistant, handheld computer, electronic rolodex, walkie-talkie, or any combination of these devices.

8. "Contract" means the agreement that is the subject of this lawsuit.

9. "Identify" or "describe," when referring to a person, means you must state the following:

a. The full name.

b. The present or last known residential address and residential telephone number.

c. The present or last known office address and office telephone number.

◄ *Continued on next page* ►

d. The occupation, job title, employer, and employer's address at the time of the event or period referred to in each particular interrogatory.

e. In the case of any entity, the identity of the officer, employee, or agent most closely connected with the subject matter of the interrogatory and the officer who is responsible for supervising that officer or employee.

10. "Identify" or "describe," when referring to a document, means you must state the following:

a. The nature of the document (e.g., letter, handwritten note).

b. The title or heading that appears on the document.

c. The date of the document and the date of each addendum, supplement, or other addition or change.

d. The identities of the author, signer of the document, and person on whose behalf or at whose request or direction the document was prepared or delivered.

e. The present location of the document and the name, address, position or title, and telephone number of the person or persons having custody of the document.

SEE: Tex. R. Civ. P. 197
*O'Connor's Texas Rules * Civil Trials* (2019), "Interrogatories," ch. 6-G, p. 663

ADD: STYLE OF THE CASE – FORM 1B:2
SIGNATURE BLOCK – FORM 1B:3
CERTIFICATE OF SERVICE – FORM 1B:13

NOTE: When a plaintiff serves interrogatories with its petition, the interrogatories should be addressed to the defendant. In such a case, delete "by and through its attorney of record." When the plaintiff serves interrogatories before the defendant's answer is due, the defendant has 50 days to respond rather than 30. Tex. R. Civ. P. 197.2(a).

For most methods of service, the deadline for serving interrogatories is 30 days before the end of the discovery period. Tex. R. Civ. P. 197.1. See ***O'Connor's Texas Rules***, "Discovery Periods," ch. 6-A, §8, p. 523. But when service is by mail or fax, the interrogatories should be served at least 33 days (if mailed) or 31 days (if faxed after 5:00 p.m.) before the end of the discovery period. *See* Tex. R. Civ. P. 21a(b)(2), (c). See ***O'Connor's Texas Rules***, "Deadline to serve response," ch. 6-A, §14.1, p. 527.

IDENTIFICATION & AUTHENTICATION INTERROGATORIES

The following identification and authentication interrogatories do not count against {❶ *party*}'s limit of {❷ *number*} interrogatories. *See* Tex. R. Civ. P. {❸ *190.2(b)(3)/ 190.3(b)(3)/190.4(b)*}.

INTERROGATORY 1: Identify all insurance policies relevant to this suit. {*Ask for documents in request for production.*}

ANSWER:

INTERROGATORY 2: Identify all invoices relevant to the contract that is the subject of this suit. {*Ask for documents in request for production.*}

ANSWER:

INTERROGATORY 3: Identify all documents relevant to {❹ *identify specific occurrence or transaction, e.g., the Master Sales Agreement that is attached as Exhibit A to Plaintiff's Original Petition*}.

ANSWER:

INTERROGATORY 4: Is the {❺ *identify document, e.g., contract*} attached to these interrogatories as Exhibit {❻ *letter*} a true and correct copy of the original?

ANSWER:

STANDARD INTERROGATORIES

The following standard interrogatories count against {❼ *party*}'s limit of {❽ *number*} interrogatories. *See* Tex. R. Civ. P. {❾ *190.2(b)(3)/190.3(b)(3)/190.4(b)*}.

INTERROGATORY 1: Identify each person answering these interrogatories, supplying information, or assisting in any way with the preparation of the answers to these interrogatories.

ANSWER:

INTERROGATORY 2: Identify every person who is expected to be called to testify at trial, including your experts. *See* Tex. R. Civ. P. 192.3(d). {*See* ***O'Connor's Texas Rules****, "Trial witnesses," ch. 6-G, §3.2.3, p. 665.*}

ANSWER:

Continued on next page

INTERROGATORY 3: Identify all discoverable consulting experts—that is, consulting experts whose work has been reviewed by a testifying expert. *See* Tex. R. Civ. P. 192.3(e). {*See* ***O'Connor's Texas Rules***, *"Consultant's work reviewed," ch. 6-G, §3.2.4(1), p. 665.*} For each expert identified, provide the following information:

a. The expert's name, address, and telephone number.

b. The expert's current résumé and bibliography.

c. The facts known to the expert that relate to or form the basis of the expert's mental impressions and opinions formed or made in connection with the case, regardless of when and how the factual information was acquired.

d. The mental impressions or opinions of the expert formed or made in connection with the case and any methods used to derive them.

e. Any bias of the expert.

f. A list of all documents and tangible things, including reports, models, or data compilations, that have been provided to, reviewed by, or prepared by or for the expert, so the documents or tangible things may properly be sought by a request for production. {*Ask for documents or tangible things in request for production.*}

ANSWER:

INTERROGATORY 4: Identify all experts who have firsthand factual information about the case and provide a brief statement of each expert's connection with the case. {*If the attorney believes opposing counsel has overlooked the names of experts with firsthand factual information about the case, add this question to the list of standard interrogatories. Otherwise, omit.*} {*See* ***O'Connor's Texas Rules***, *"Consultant with facts," ch. 6-G, §3.2.4(2), p. 665.*}

ANSWER:

INTERROGATORY 5: State the legal theories and describe in general the factual bases for your {⑩ *claims/defenses*}. *See* Tex. R. Civ. P. 192.3(j), 197.1. {*See* ***O'Connor's Texas Rules***, *"Party contentions," ch. 6-G, §3.2.5, p. 665.*}

ANSWER:

INTERROGATORY 6: Do you make the {⓫ *legal/factual*} contention that {⓬ *identify specific legal or factual contention*}? *See* Tex. R. Civ. P. 192.3(j), 197.1. {*See* ***O'Connor's Texas Rules****, "Party contentions," ch. 6-G, §3.2.5, p. 665.*}

ANSWER:

INTERROGATORY 7: Identify every person who has impeachment or rebuttal evidence and describe the evidence each person has. If you have enough information to anticipate the use of impeachment or rebuttal evidence or witnesses, you must provide that information. {*See* ***O'Connor's Texas Rules****, "Impeachment & rebuttal evidence," ch. 6-G, §3.2.6, p. 665.*} {*Ask for documents in request for production.*}

ANSWER:

INTERROGATORY 8: If you have ever been convicted of a felony or a crime involving moral turpitude, state the nature of the charge and the date and place of arrest and conviction. *See* Tex. R. Evid. 404(a)(2)(B), 609(a). {*See* ***O'Connor's Texas Rules****, "Impeaching by conviction," ch. 8-C, §6.4, p. 829.*}

ANSWER:

SEE: Tex. R. Civ. P. 192.3, 197
O'Connor's Texas Rules * Civil Trials (2019), "Interrogatories," ch. 6-G, p. 663

ADD: INTERROGATORIES – FORMS 6G:4-13, as appropriate

ATTACH: COVER SHEET & DEFINITIONS – FORM 6G:1

NOTE: The number of interrogatories each party is permitted to serve, excluding interrogatories asking a party to identify or authenticate specific documents, is governed by the discovery-control plan in effect. See ***O'Connor's Texas Rules***, "Discovery-Control Plans," ch. 6-A, §7, p. 520. Parties in a Level 1 case are limited to 15 interrogatories, parties in a Level 2 case are limited to 25 interrogatories, and parties in a Level 3 case are limited to either 15 interrogatories (if Level 1 limitations apply) or 25 interrogatories (if Level 2 limitations apply) unless expressly changed by court order. Tex. R. Civ. P. 190.2(b)(3), 190.3(b)(3), 190.4(b). See ***O'Connor's Texas Rules***, "Number of interrogatories," ch. 6-G, §3.1.3, p. 664.

Each "discrete subpart" of an interrogatory is considered a separate interrogatory. Tex. R. Civ. P. 190.2(b)(3), 190.3(b)(3). Discrete subparts of interrogatories are counted as single interrogatories, but not every separate factual inquiry is a discrete subpart. Tex. R. Civ. P. 190 cmt. 3 (1999). In general, a discrete subpart is a subpart that calls for information that is not logically or factually related to the primary interrogatory. *Id.*

Continued on next page

When seeking information about testifying experts, a party can use interrogatories only to discover the experts' identities. *See* Tex. R. Civ. P. 192.3(d), 195.1. Other information about a testifying expert must be sought through a request for disclosure or a deposition of the expert. Tex. R. Civ. P. 195.1. See ***O'Connor's Texas Rules***, "Trial witnesses," ch. 6-G, §3.2.3, p. 665. However, a party can use interrogatories to request discoverable information about consulting experts.

A party can combine more than one discovery form in the same document (e.g., requests for admissions, interrogatories, and requests for production). Tex. R. Civ. P. 192.2.

Instead of using an interrogatory, a party can use a request for admissions to have the adverse party admit or deny the genuineness of any document served with the request.

A party may use interrogatories to request information about the opposing party's electronic information. *See* Tex. R. Civ. P. 197.1. See ***O'Connor's Texas Rules***, "Interrogatories," ch. 6-C, §7.1.3, p. 605.

A party may file a motion to compel answers when the interrogatories are not answered, when they are not answered properly, or when objections are served. *See* Tex. R. Civ. P. 215.1(b). See FORM 6A:24.

☆

{[1] *PARTY*}'S RESPONSE TO {[2] *ADVERSE PARTY*}'S INTERROGATORIES

To: {[3] *Adverse party*}, {[4] *name*}, by and through {[5] *his/her/its*} attorney of record, {[6] *name*}, {[7] *address*}.

{[8] *Party*}, {[9] *name*}, serves these answers to {[10] *adverse party*}'s interrogatories. {*See* ***O'Connor's Texas Rules****, "Responding to Interrogatories," ch. 6-G, §4, p. 666.*}

ANSWERS & OBJECTIONS TO INTERROGATORIES

INTERROGATORY 1: {[11] *Restate interrogatory.*}

{*CHOOSE APPROPRIATE RESPONSE*}

ANSWER: {[12] *State answer to interrogatory.*}

ANSWER: {[13] *State answer to interrogatory.*} This interrogatory answer is based on information obtained from other persons, not on information that {[14] *party*} can verify under oath. Tex. R. Civ. P. 197.2(d).

WITHHOLDING STATEMENT: Material or information responsive to this interrogatory is withheld under the {[15] *identify privilege*}. *See* Tex. R. Civ. P. 193.3(a). {*See* ***O'Connor's Texas Rules****, "Withholding statement," ch. 6-A, §2.8, p. 516.*}

OBJECTION: {[16] *Party*} objects because the interrogatories exceed the {[17] *number*}-interrogatory limit for this Level {[18] *1/2/3*} case. {[19] *Elaborate.*} To the extent that {[20] *party*} does not object to the discovery request, {[21] *party*} serves the following answers: {[22] *identify limit of compliance, e.g., party responds to the first 15 interrogatories but refuses to answer the rest*}. {*See* ***O'Connor's Texas Rules****, "Number of questions," ch. 6-G, §6.2.1, p. 669.*}

OBJECTION: {[23] *Party*} objects because the interrogatory requests information about testifying experts, which is obtainable only through a request for disclosure under Texas Rule of Civil Procedure 194 or through a deposition of the expert. *See* Tex. R. Civ. P. 195.1, 197.1.

OBJECTION: {[24] *Party*} declines to give a narrative answer to this interrogatory because the interrogatory asks for information that is available from {[25] *his/her/its*} business records, and the burden of deriving the answer from the records is substantially the same for both parties. Instead, {[26] *party*} will make {[27] *his/her/its*} records available for inspection on {[28] *date*}, at {[29] *time*}, at {[30] *identify location*}. Tex. R. Civ. P. 197.2(c). {*See* ***O'Connor's Texas Rules****, "Evidence equally available," ch. 6-G, §4.2.2, p. 667.*}

◄ *Continued on next page* ►

OBJECTION: {31 *Party*} declines to give a narrative answer because the interrogatory asks for information that is available from public records, and the burden of deriving the answer from the records is substantially the same for both parties. Instead, {32 *party*} refers {33 *adverse party*} to the public records. {34 *State enough detailed information to permit the party asking the interrogatory to locate and identify the information.*} Tex. R. Civ. P. 197.2(c). {*See* ***O'Connor's Texas Rules****, "Evidence equally available," ch. 6-G, §4.2.2, p. 667.*}

OBJECTION: {35 *Party*} objects to this interrogatory because it is premature. *See* Tex. R. Civ. P. 193.1 (responding party must make complete response based on information available). An answer to this interrogatory will not be known until after additional discovery is completed. {36 *Elaborate, describing the additional discovery necessary.*} Once that discovery is completed, {37 *party*} will promptly respond to this interrogatory.

OBJECTION: {38 *Party*} objects because the interrogatory duplicates matters already produced in response to a request for disclosure under Texas Rule of Civil Procedure 194.2. {39 *Identify response to request for disclosure and explain how interrogatory duplicates the request.*}

SEE: Tex. R. Civ. P. 193.3, 197
O'Connor's Texas Rules * Civil Trials (2019), "Responding to Interrogatories," ch. 6-G, §4, p. 666; "Objecting to Questions," ch. 6-G, §6, p. 668

ADD: STYLE OF THE CASE – FORM 1B:2
SIGNATURE BLOCK – FORM 1B:3, for attorney
VERIFICATION – FORM 1B:7, for party, see note below for exceptions
CERTIFICATE OF SERVICE – FORM 1B:13

NOTE: The responding party's answers, objections, and other responses must be preceded by the interrogatory to which they apply. Tex. R. Civ. P. 193.1.

Most interrogatory answers must be verified under oath by the party. Tex. R. Civ. P. 197.2(d). However, a party is not required to verify its interrogatory answers when (1) the party's answer to the interrogatory states that the answer is based on information from other persons, or (2) the interrogatories ask about trial witnesses, legal contentions, and persons with knowledge of relevant facts. *Id.* The attorney is required to sign all interrogatory answers, even when some are verified by the party. *See* Tex. R. Civ. P. 191.3(a)(1), 197 cmt. 2.

The number of interrogatories each party is permitted to serve, excluding interrogatories asking a party to identify or authenticate specific documents, is governed by the discovery-control plan in effect. See ***O'Connor's Texas Rules***, "Discovery-Control Plans," ch. 6-A, §7, p. 520. Parties in a Level 1 case are limited to 15 interrogatories, parties in a Level 2 case are limited to 25 interrogatories, and parties in a Level 3 case are limited to either 15 interrogatories (if Level 1 limitations apply) or 25 interrogatories (if Level 2 limitations apply) unless expressly changed by court order. Tex. R. Civ. P. 190.2(b)(3), 190.3(b)(3), 190.4(b). See ***O'Connor's Texas Rules***, "Number of interrogatories," ch. 6-G, §3.1.3, p. 664.

Generally, a party responding to interrogatories has 30 days to respond. Tex. R. Civ. P. 197.2(a). But when the plaintiff serves interrogatories before the defendant's answer is due, the defendant has 50 days to respond rather than 30. *Id.* When service is by mail or fax, the responding party has an additional three days (if mailed) or one day (if faxed after 5:00 p.m.) to respond. *See* Tex. R. Civ. P. 21a(b)(2), (c). See ***O'Connor's Texas Rules***, "Deadline to serve response," ch. 6-A, §14.1, p. 527.

Each "discrete subpart" of an interrogatory is considered a separate interrogatory. Tex. R. Civ. P. 190.2(b)(3), 190.3(b)(3).

For general objections to discovery, see FORM 6A:9; for claims of privilege, see FORMS 6A:19-22.

{ADD TO STANDARD INTERROGATORIES – FORM 6G:2}

{Depending on the discovery-control plan, parties are generally limited to either 15 or 25 interrogatories. See the first note under FORM 6G:2.}

INTERROGATORY 9: Did you execute the written contract that is attached to plaintiff's original petition? If your answer is "no," describe the nature of your relationship with plaintiff.

ANSWER:

INTERROGATORY 10: If you contend the parties modified the terms of the contract, state how and when the parties modified the contract, including whether the modification was oral or written, the dates of modification, and the persons present during the modification. *{Ask for documents in request for production.}* *{See* ***O'Connor's Texas COA****, "Modification," ch. 5-B, §5.1.18, p. 104.}*

ANSWER:

INTERROGATORY 11: If you contend the contract on which plaintiff sues is not the original contract entered into between the parties on {❶ *date*}, state the factual basis for your contention. *{Ask for documents in request for production.}*

ANSWER:

INTERROGATORY 12: If you contend plaintiff did not {❷ *perform/tender performance*} as required by the contract, state the factual basis for your contention. *{Ask for documents in request for production.}*

ANSWER:

INTERROGATORY 13: If you contend plaintiff breached the contract, state the factual basis for your contention. *{Ask for documents in request for production.}* *{See* ***O'Connor's Texas COA****, "Discharge – plaintiff's repudiation or material breach," ch. 5-B, §5.1.26, p. 107.}*

ANSWER:

INTERROGATORY 14: If you contend defendant did not breach the contract, state the factual basis for your contention. *{Ask for documents in request for production.}*

ANSWER:

INTERROGATORY 15: If you contend either party to the contract rescinded or canceled the contract, state the factual basis for your contention. {*Ask for documents in request for production.*}

ANSWER:

INTERROGATORY 16: If you contend the contract was without consideration, state the factual basis for your contention. {*See* ***O'Connor's Texas COA****, "Consideration defenses," ch. 5-B, §5.1.9, p. 96.*}

ANSWER:

INTERROGATORY 17: If you contend plaintiff is estopped from suing on the contract, state the factual basis for your contention.

ANSWER:

INTERROGATORY 18: If you contend plaintiff did not perform {❸ *his/her/its*} contractual obligations, explain what part of plaintiff's contractual obligations {❹ *he/she/it*} did not perform, including a description of the obligation and the exact time, date, and place of plaintiff's failure to perform.

ANSWER:

INTERROGATORY 19: If you contend plaintiff did not suffer damages for the breach of the contract, state the factual basis for your contention.

ANSWER:

INTERROGATORY 20: If you contend plaintiff should have mitigated {❺ *his/her/its*} damages but did not, state the factual basis for your contention. {*See* ***O'Connor's Texas COA****, "Mitigation of damages," ch. 5-B, §5.1.21, p. 106.*}

ANSWER:

INTERROGATORY 21: If you contend the contract was illegal, state the factual basis for your contention. {*See* ***O'Connor's Texas COA****, "Illegality," ch. 5-B, §5.1.6, p. 94.*}

ANSWER:

◄ *Continued on next page* ►

INTERROGATORY 22: If you contend defendant lacked capacity to execute the contract, state the factual basis for your contention. {*See **O'Connor's Texas COA**, "Lack of capacity," ch. 5-B, §5.1.5, p. 93.*}

ANSWER:

INTERROGATORY 23: If you contend defendant revoked the offer before plaintiff accepted it, state the factual basis for your contention. {*See **O'Connor's Texas COA**, "Revocation," ch. 5-B, §5.1.4, p. 92.*}

ANSWER:

INTERROGATORY 24: If you contend the contract was void as against public policy, state the factual basis for your contention. {*See **O'Connor's Texas COA**, "Void as against public policy," ch. 5-B, §5.1.7, p. 95.*}

ANSWER:

INTERROGATORY 25: If you contend you were induced by fraud to enter into the contract, state the factual basis for your contention. {*See **O'Connor's Texas COA**, "Fraud," ch. 5-B, §5.1.8, p. 96.*}

ANSWER:

INTERROGATORY 26: If you contend you were forced by threats to enter into the contract, state the factual basis for your contention. {*See **O'Connor's Texas COA**, "Duress," ch. 5-B, §5.1.10, p. 97.*}

ANSWER:

INTERROGATORY 27: If you contend the parties entered into the contract under a mutual misconception or ignorance of a material fact, state the factual basis for your contention. {*See **O'Connor's Texas COA**, "Mutual mistake," ch. 5-B, §5.1.11(2), p. 99.*}

ANSWER:

INTERROGATORY 28: If you contend it was impossible for defendant to perform {❻ *his/her/its*} obligations under the contract, state the factual basis for your contention. {*See **O'Connor's Texas COA**, "Impossibility or impracticability of performance," ch. 5-B, §5.1.14, p. 100.*}

ANSWER:

INTERROGATORY 29: If you contend there was an accord and satisfaction that released defendant, state the factual basis for your contention. {*See* ***O'Connor's Texas COA***, *"Accord & satisfaction," ch. 5-B, §5.1.15, p. 102.*}

ANSWER:

INTERROGATORY 30: If you contend the enforcement of the contract would be unconscionable, state the factual basis for your contention. {*See* ***O'Connor's Texas COA***, *"Unconscionability," ch. 5-B, §5.1.17, p. 103.*}

ANSWER:

INTERROGATORY 31: If you contend plaintiff ratified the agreement, state the factual basis for your contention. {*See* ***O'Connor's Texas COA***, *"Ratification," ch. 5-B, §5.1.19, p. 105.*}

ANSWER:

SEE: Tex. R. Civ. P. 197
O'Connor's Texas Rules * Civil Trials (2019), "Interrogatories," ch. 6-G, p. 663
O'Connor's Texas Causes of Action (2019), "Breach of Contract," ch. 5-B, p. 69

ADD TO: STANDARD INTERROGATORIES – FORM 6G:2

NOTE: See notes under FORM 6G:2.

{ADD TO STANDARD INTERROGATORIES – FORM 6G:2}

{Depending on the discovery-control plan, parties are generally limited to either 15 or 25 interrogatories. See the first note under FORM 6G:2.}

INTERROGATORY 9: *{To establish plaintiff's breach of contract, see FORM 6G:4 and choose appropriate interrogatories, modifying them as necessary.}*

ANSWER:

INTERROGATORY 10: If you contend plaintiff mitigated {❶ *his/her/its*} damages, state the factual basis for your contention.

ANSWER:

INTERROGATORY 11: If you contend the oral contract is enforceable under the doctrine of promissory estoppel, state the factual basis for your contention. *{See **O'Connor's Texas COA**, "Promissory estoppel as equitable consideration," ch. 5-A, §2.5.3, p. 65.}*

ANSWER:

SEE: Tex. R. Civ. P. 197
O'Connor's Texas Rules * Civil Trials (2019), "Interrogatories," ch. 6-G, p. 663
O'Connor's Texas Causes of Action (2019), "General Concepts," ch. 5-A, p. 55; "Breach of Contract," ch. 5-B, p. 69

ADD TO: STANDARD INTERROGATORIES – FORM 6G:2

NOTE: See notes under FORM 6G:2.

{ADD TO STANDARD INTERROGATORIES – FORM 6G:2}

{Depending on the discovery-control plan, parties are generally limited to either 15 or 25 interrogatories. See the first note under FORM 6G:2.}

INTERROGATORY 9: Did you order the {❶ *describe goods or services*} described in the account attached to plaintiff's original petition?

ANSWER:

INTERROGATORY 10: If you contend you ordered {❷ *describe goods or services*} from plaintiff other than {❸ *that/those*} described in the account attached to plaintiff's original petition, state specifically what you ordered and how your order differs from the {❹ *item/items*} described in the account. {*Ask for documents in request for production.*}

ANSWER:

INTERROGATORY 11: Did plaintiff provide the {❺ *describe goods or services*} to you on an open-account basis?

ANSWER:

INTERROGATORY 12: If you contend plaintiff did not charge you {❻ *a price/prices*} in accordance with your agreement, provide the price you contend plaintiff agreed to charge for the {❼ *describe goods or services*} and the price plaintiff actually charged for the {❽ *describe goods or services*}.

ANSWER:

INTERROGATORY 13: Did you receive the {❾ *describe goods or services*} described in the account attached to plaintiff's original petition? If you did not, itemize and describe each good or service you claim you did not receive or accept.

ANSWER:

INTERROGATORY 14: If you rejected, contested, or returned any of the {❿ *describe goods or services*} described in the account attached to plaintiff's original petition, state the date and method of your rejection or contest (e.g., telephone, letter, fax) and, if you returned the {⓫ *describe goods or services*}, how you returned {⓬ *it/them*} (e.g., personally, courier, mail). {*Ask for documents in request for production.*}

ANSWER:

◄ *Continued on next page* ►

INTERROGATORY 15: If you contend you do not owe plaintiff for each item listed on the account attached to plaintiff's original petition, state the factual basis for your contention.

ANSWER:

INTERROGATORY 16: If you contend plaintiff has not allowed you a payment, credit, or offset against the account attached to plaintiff's original petition, provide the date, amount, and method of each payment, credit, or offset you allege plaintiff has not allowed. {*Ask for documents in request for production.*}

ANSWER:

INTERROGATORY 17: What balance, if any, do you acknowledge to be indebted to plaintiff?

ANSWER:

INTERROGATORY 18: If your answer to Interrogatory 17 was "zero" or less than the amount plaintiff alleged in the original petition and attached account, state the factual basis for your allegation that you owe less than the full amount of the account, including dates and amounts of payment and reasons for withholding full payment.

ANSWER:

INTERROGATORY 19: Did plaintiff present to you, your agent, or your representative a demand for payment of the account as alleged in plaintiff's original petition? If so, state the date you received the demand, who received it, the amount of the demand, and your response to the demand.

ANSWER:

INTERROGATORY 20: If you contend plaintiff has not performed any act, or a condition precedent has not occurred, necessary for plaintiff to file suit, state the act or event you allege has not occurred.

ANSWER:

INTERROGATORY 21: If you contend plaintiff should have mitigated {⓭ *his/her/its*} damages but did not, state the factual basis for your contention.

ANSWER:

SEE: Tex. R. Civ. P. 185, 197
O'Connor's Texas Rules * Civil Trials (2019), "Interrogatories," ch. 6-G, p. 663
O'Connor's Texas Causes of Action (2019), "Suit on Sworn Account," ch. 5-E, p. 126

ADD TO: STANDARD INTERROGATORIES – FORM 6G:2

NOTE: See notes under FORM 6G:2.

{ADD TO STANDARD INTERROGATORIES – FORM 6G:2}

{Depending on the discovery-control plan, parties are generally limited to either 15 or 25 interrogatories. See the first note under FORM 6G:2.}

INTERROGATORY 9: If you contend the {❶ *describe goods or services*} {❷ *was/were*} provided to defendant on an open-account basis, state the factual basis for your contention. {*Ask for documents in request for production.*}

ANSWER:

INTERROGATORY 10: If you presented to defendant or {❸ *his/her/its*} agent or representative a demand for payment of the account alleged in plaintiff's original petition, state the date you made the demand, who made it, and the amount of the demand. {*Ask for documents in request for production.*}

ANSWER:

INTERROGATORY 11: Identify the person who you contend received an order for the {❹ *describe goods or services*} described in the account attached to plaintiff's original petition.

ANSWER:

INTERROGATORY 12: Identify the {❺ *describe goods or services*} you contend {❻ *was/were*} purchased by defendant, the dates the {❼ *describe goods or services*} {❽ *was/were*} purchased, the person who {❾ *delivered the goods/performed the services*}, and the date the {❿ *describe goods or services*} {⓫ *was/were*} {⓬ *delivered/performed*}.

ANSWER:

INTERROGATORY 13: If you contend defendant agreed the account attached to plaintiff's original petition is an accurate record of the transaction between the parties and the balance due, identify the person who agreed to the account, the date of your conversation with the person, and whether the agreement was oral or in writing. {*Ask for documents in request for production.*}

ANSWER:

SEE: Tex. R. Civ. P. 185, 197
O'Connor's Texas Rules * Civil Trials (2019), "Interrogatories," ch. 6-G, p. 663
O'Connor's Texas Causes of Action (2019), "Suit on Sworn Account," ch. 5-E, p. 126

ADD TO: STANDARD INTERROGATORIES – FORM 6G:2

NOTE: See notes under FORM 6G:2.

{ADD TO STANDARD INTERROGATORIES – FORM 6G:2}

{Depending on the discovery-control plan, parties are generally limited to either 15 or 25 interrogatories. See the first note under FORM 6G:2.}

INTERROGATORY 9: Describe how the collision occurred and state specifically what you contend caused or contributed to the cause of the collision.

ANSWER:

INTERROGATORY 10: Describe what you were doing immediately before the collision occurred. If you were using a mobile device, identify the mobile device, and if you were speaking or texting with someone on the mobile device, identify the person with whom you were speaking or texting, the telephone number of your mobile device, and the telephone number of the other person.

ANSWER:

INTERROGATORY 11: Identify all mobile devices you regularly use, including those of family members and those of your employer, and include telephone numbers. *{Ask for telephone records in request for production.}*

ANSWER:

INTERROGATORY 12: Identify the owner of the vehicle you were driving and your relationship to the owner.

ANSWER:

INTERROGATORY 13: Identify each person who was in the vehicle you were driving at the time of the collision. For passengers under 21 years of age, also provide their ages and the identity of their parents. For passengers under eight years of age, state whether they were in a booster or child seat. *{Identification of fact witnesses and a brief statement of their connection should be secured by a request for disclosure, FORM 6E:2.}*

ANSWER:

INTERROGATORY 14: If you wear corrective lenses, contacts, glasses, hearing aids, or other devices that enable you to see or hear, were you wearing the corrective lenses, contacts, glasses, hearing aids, or other devices at the time of the collision? *{Ask for prescriptions of corrective eyewear or other devices in request for production.}*

ANSWER:

Continued on next page

INTERROGATORY 15: Describe the weather and road conditions at the time of the accident, including the amount of traffic on the road at the time of the collision.

ANSWER:

INTERROGATORY 16: Describe where each person was sitting in the vehicle and if and how each person was restrained by a seat belt or other safety device.

ANSWER:

INTERROGATORY 17: Identify when you first became aware of plaintiff's vehicle and, if it was before the collision occurred, include approximately how much time passed between the time you were aware of plaintiff's vehicle and the time the collision occurred.

ANSWER:

INTERROGATORY 18: What was your speed immediately before the impact and at the time of impact?

ANSWER:

INTERROGATORY 19: Did you apply your brakes before the impact?

ANSWER:

INTERROGATORY 20: Describe anything that obstructed your ability to see plaintiff's vehicle or distracted you immediately before the collision.

ANSWER:

INTERROGATORY 21: If you were holding anything at the time of the collision, identify the object and state its size and weight.

ANSWER:

INTERROGATORY 22: What, if anything, did you do to avoid the collision?

ANSWER:

INTERROGATORY 23: Describe what you and plaintiff did immediately after the collision.

ANSWER:

INTERROGATORY 24: Identify each place you had been in the five-hour period before the collision.

ANSWER:

INTERROGATORY 25: State whether you consumed any alcoholic beverage or took any prescription or nonprescription drug or medication in the 24-hour period before the collision, and identify the beverage or drug by brand name, time of consumption, and amount, and if a prescription drug, identify the prescribing doctor and the prescription number.

ANSWER:

INTERROGATORY 26: If you have ever suffered from any of the following conditions, please provide specific details, including duration of condition, names of treating physicians, and dates of treatment: blackouts, amnesia, sneezing spells, dizziness, back pain, or neck pain. In lieu of providing the information requested in this interrogatory, you may provide (1) a list of the medical providers, (2) the dates of treatment, and (3) an executed authorization permitting the disclosure of the medical records and bills, which is attached to these interrogatories. {*See FORM 6J:1; **O'Connor's Texas Rules**, "Medical authorization," ch. 6-J, §3.2, p. 692.*}

ANSWER:

INTERROGATORY 27: Describe in detail any conversations you have had with plaintiff or plaintiff's representative since the collision.

ANSWER:

INTERROGATORY 28: Describe in detail any conversations you have had with an insurance company or any of its agents since the collision. {*Ask for these statements in request for production.*}

ANSWER:

INTERROGATORY 29: If you contend any defect or failure on the part of any vehicle caused or contributed to the collision, describe the defect, the vehicle, and how the defect or failure contributed to the collision.

ANSWER:

◄ *Continued on next page* ►

INTERROGATORY 30: Identify all mechanical repairs performed on your {❶ *identify vehicle*} during the year before the collision. {*Ask for documents in request for production.*}

ANSWER:

INTERROGATORY 31: If you received a traffic citation as a result of the collision, identify the court involved, the violations for which you were cited, the date on which the citation was disposed, and the final disposition of the citation. {*Ask for document in request for production.*}

ANSWER:

INTERROGATORY 32: If you were acting within the course and scope of your employment or as an agent for any person or entity at the time of the collision, identify your employer or principal.

ANSWER:

INTERROGATORY 33: If you have been involved in any other vehicular collision before or since this collision, identify the date and nature of the collision, state whether you were injured, and state whether you filed suit or suit was filed against you. {*Ask for documents in request for production.*}

ANSWER:

INTERROGATORY 34: If you contend plaintiff should have mitigated {❷ *his/her/its*} damages but did not, state the factual basis for your contention.

ANSWER:

SEE: Tex. R. Civ. P. 197
O'Connor's Texas Rules * Civil Trials (2019), "Interrogatories," ch. 6-G, p. 663
O'Connor's Texas Causes of Action (2019), "Negligence Actions," ch. 21, p. 719

ADD TO: STANDARD INTERROGATORIES – FORM 6G:2

ATTACH: MEDICAL AUTHORIZATION – FORM 6J:1, if necessary

NOTE: See notes under FORM 6G:2.

{*ADD TO STANDARD INTERROGATORIES – FORM 6G:2*}

{*Depending on the discovery-control plan, parties are generally limited to either 15 or 25 interrogatories. See the first note under FORM 6G:2.*}

INTERROGATORY 9: {*To establish contributory negligence, see FORM 6G:8, ¶¶9-26 and choose appropriate interrogatories, modifying them as necessary.*}

ANSWER:

INTERROGATORY 10: Describe the nature and extent of the injury you allege you sustained as a result of the collision; list the name, address, and telephone number of each medical provider who treated you for the injury; describe the treatment you received; and state the charges for those services. {*Medical records for the injury from the accident should be secured by a request for disclosure, FORM 6E:2.*}

ANSWER:

INTERROGATORY 11: Itemize each element of damage for which you sue and state the dollar amount you seek for each element, both past and future. {*Information about economic damages should be secured by a request for disclosure, FORM 6E:2.*}

ANSWER:

INTERROGATORY 12: If you have been ill or have received any other injury since the collision, provide the name, address, and telephone number of each medical provider who treated you for the illness or injury, describe the illness or injury and treatment you received, and provide the cost for those services. In lieu of providing the information requested in this interrogatory, you may provide (1) a list of the medical providers, (2) the dates of treatment, and (3) an executed authorization permitting the disclosure of the medical records and bills, which is attached to these interrogatories. {*See FORM 6J:1;* ***O'Connor's Texas Rules****, "Medical authorization," ch. 6-J, §3.2, p. 692.*}

ANSWER:

INTERROGATORY 13: If you were hospitalized for any reason in the five-year period before the collision, for each hospitalization, provide the name and address of the facility, the date of each admission and discharge, the reason for the hospitalization, and the treatment received. In lieu of providing the information requested in this interrogatory, you may provide (1) a list of the medical providers, (2) the dates of treatment, and (3) an executed authorization permitting the disclosure of the medical records and bills,

Continued on next page

which is attached to these interrogatories. {*See FORM 6J:1;* ***O'Connor's Texas Rules,*** *"Medical authorization," ch. 6-J, §3.2, p. 692.*}

ANSWER:

INTERROGATORY 14: If anyone has stated that you will require surgery or that you will have any permanent disability, impairment, or limitation as a result of the collision, identify each person who made this statement, the date of the statement, and the content of the statement.

ANSWER:

INTERROGATORY 15: If your {❶ *identify vehicle*} was damaged in the collision, describe the damage, state whether it has been repaired, who repaired it, and the cost of the repairs. {*Amount and calculations for economic damages should be secured by a request for disclosure, FORM 6E:2.*}

ANSWER:

INTERROGATORY 16: If you contend you have incurred expenses as a result of the collision, provide an itemized list of your expenses, including medical expenses, lost income, and any other costs you allege you incurred. {*Amount and calculations for economic damages should be secured by a request for disclosure, FORM 6E:2.*}

ANSWER:

INTERROGATORY 17: If you have worked since the collision, provide the date you began working, a brief description of your job duties, and your rate of pay or salary.

ANSWER:

INTERROGATORY 18: If you contend you have missed work as a result of the collision, provide the dates you missed work, the reason for each day missed, and the amount of income you allege you lost for each day. {*Amount and calculations for economic damages should be secured by a request for disclosure, FORM 6E:2.*}

ANSWER:

INTERROGATORY 19: Provide the name and address of all your employers for the five-year period before the collision, the date you began and left each employer, your reason for leaving, a brief description of your job duties, and your rate of pay or salary for each employer.

ANSWER:

INTERROGATORY 20: If you contend defendant acted maliciously or with gross negligence, describe the act that was committed with malice or gross negligence.

ANSWER:

INTERROGATORY 21: If you have been involved in any other lawsuits within the last five years against any person or entity to recover damages as a result of personal injuries, state the date and nature of the accident, where the lawsuit was filed, the names of the parties involved, whether you were injured, whether you filed suit or suit was filed against you, and the outcome of the suit. {*Ask for documents in request for production.*}

ANSWER:

SEE: Tex. R. Civ. P. 197
O'Connor's Texas Rules * Civil Trials (2019), "Interrogatories," ch. 6-G, p. 663
O'Connor's Texas Causes of Action (2019), "Negligence Actions," ch. 21, p. 719

ADD TO: STANDARD INTERROGATORIES – FORM 6G:2

ATTACH: MEDICAL AUTHORIZATION – FORM 6J:1, if necessary

NOTE: See notes under FORM 6G:2.

{*ADD TO STANDARD INTERROGATORIES – FORM 6G:2*}

{*Depending on the discovery-control plan, parties are generally limited to either 15 or 25 interrogatories. See the first note under FORM 6G:2.*}

INTERROGATORY 9: State whether you owned, occupied, or controlled the premises at the time of the accident and identify any and all co-owners. {*Ask for documents in request for production.*}

ANSWER:

INTERROGATORY 10: If the premises were leased, identify the lessor and the terms and conditions of the lease, including any covenant to repair or maintain the premises. {*Ask for documents in request for production.*}

ANSWER:

INTERROGATORY 11: Identify any and all of your employees, servants, or agents who worked on the premises on the date of the accident.

ANSWER:

INTERROGATORY 12: Describe any communication either in words or gestures that took place between you and plaintiff immediately before the accident.

ANSWER:

INTERROGATORY 13: State the location on your premises where the accident occurred, giving the distance, in feet, to fixed objects or boundaries of the premises.

ANSWER:

INTERROGATORY 14: Describe any defective condition or foreign substances that caused or contributed to the accident. {*Ask for any photographs in request for production.*}

ANSWER:

INTERROGATORY 15: Describe the surface condition of the premises, including any repairs or maintenance performed to the surface before the accident.

ANSWER:

INTERROGATORY 16: If you knew of the defective condition of the premises before the accident occurred, when did you learn of the defect?

ANSWER:

INTERROGATORY 17: Describe in detail your regular procedure for maintaining and cleaning the premises. {*Ask for documents in request for production.*}

ANSWER:

INTERROGATORY 18: If you have employed a maintenance company to regularly service the premises, identify the name, address, and telephone number of the maintenance company and describe the service generally provided by the maintenance company.

ANSWER:

INTERROGATORY 19: Identify the last person who cleaned the area before the accident and the date and time it was cleaned.

ANSWER:

INTERROGATORY 20: What precautions do you take to prevent accidents of this type from happening?

ANSWER:

INTERROGATORY 21: Describe what warnings or signs were posted on your premises at the time of the accident in the specific area where the accident occurred.

ANSWER:

INTERROGATORY 22: Describe the lighting condition of the premises, including the amount of natural or artificial light that was present at the location and time of the accident.

ANSWER:

INTERROGATORY 23: Describe what you did immediately after the accident.

ANSWER:

Continued on next page

INTERROGATORY 24: If you monitor the area that is the subject of the lawsuit with a surveillance camera or other monitoring device, do you have a recording of the accident? {*Ask for tape in request for production.*}

ANSWER:

INTERROGATORY 25: If you prepared any written report of the accident, state the date and content for all such reports and identify to whom they were sent. {*Ask for documents in request for production.*}

ANSWER:

INTERROGATORY 26: If you contend plaintiff was negligent in causing {❶ *his/her/its*} own injuries, state the factual basis for your contention.

ANSWER:

INTERROGATORY 27: Describe in detail any conversations you have had with plaintiff since the accident.

ANSWER:

INTERROGATORY 28: Describe any accidents that occurred on the premises for the five-year period before the date of plaintiff's accident and include the name, address, and telephone number of any injured party.

ANSWER:

INTERROGATORY 29: If you have ever been sued before for an accident that occurred on the same premises, provide all information regarding the suit, including the name, address, and telephone number of each plaintiff and {❷ *his/her*} attorney.

ANSWER:

INTERROGATORY 30: If you contend that plaintiff did not mitigate {❸ *his/her/its*} damages, state the factual basis for your contention.

ANSWER:

SEE: Tex. R. Civ. P. 197
O'Connor's Texas Rules * Civil Trials (2019), "Interrogatories," ch. 6-G, p. 663
O'Connor's Texas Causes of Action (2019), "Liability to Invitees," ch. 23-B, p. 827

ADD TO: STANDARD INTERROGATORIES – FORM 6G:2

NOTE: Include in the cover sheet that the definition of the word "premises" is the premises at the defendant's address, where the plaintiff's accident occurred.

See notes under FORM 6G:2.

{*ADD TO STANDARD INTERROGATORIES – FORM 6G:2*}

{*Depending on the discovery-control plan, parties are generally limited to either 15 or 25 interrogatories. See the first note under FORM 6G:2.*}

INTERROGATORY 9: State the reasons why you were on defendant's premises at the time of the accident.

ANSWER:

INTERROGATORY 10: Describe how the accident occurred and state specifically what you contend caused or contributed to the cause of the accident.

ANSWER:

INTERROGATORY 11: If you were not alone at the time of the accident, identify each person accompanying you. For each person under 21 years of age, also provide their ages and the identity of their parents. {*Identification of fact witnesses and a brief statement of their connection should be secured by a request for disclosure, FORM 6E:2.*}

ANSWER:

INTERROGATORY 12: If you were holding or carrying anything at the time of the accident, identify the object and state its size and weight.

ANSWER:

INTERROGATORY 13: If you wear corrective lenses, contacts, glasses, hearing aids, or other devices that enable you to see or hear, were you wearing the corrective lenses, contacts, glasses, hearing aids, or other devices at the time of the accident? {*Ask for prescriptions of corrective eyewear or other devices in request for production.*}

ANSWER:

INTERROGATORY 14: Describe what you were doing immediately before the accident occurred. If you were using a mobile device, identify the mobile device, and if you were speaking or texting with someone on the mobile device, identify the person with whom you were speaking or texting, the telephone number of your mobile device, and the telephone number of the other person.

ANSWER:

INTERROGATORY 15: Identify all mobile devices you regularly use, including those of family members and those of your employer, and include telephone numbers. {*Ask for telephone records in request for production.*}

ANSWER:

INTERROGATORY 16: Describe the specific area on defendant's premises where the accident occurred.

ANSWER:

INTERROGATORY 17: Describe anything that obstructed your ability to see the alleged defect on the premises.

ANSWER:

INTERROGATORY 18: Identify the type of shoes you were wearing at the time of the accident, including brand name, size, and composition of the heel and sole.

ANSWER:

INTERROGATORY 19: Describe when you first became aware of the alleged defect on the premises, and if it was before the accident occurred, include approximately how much time passed between the time you were aware of the alleged defect and the time the accident occurred.

ANSWER:

INTERROGATORY 20: What, if anything, did you do to avoid the accident?

ANSWER:

INTERROGATORY 21: State whether you consumed any alcoholic beverage or took any prescription or nonprescription drug or medication in the 24-hour period before the accident, and identify the beverage or drug by brand name, time of consumption, and amount, and if a prescription drug, identify the prescribing doctor and the prescription number.

ANSWER:

INTERROGATORY 22: If you have ever suffered from any of the following conditions, please provide specific details, including duration of condition, names of treating physicians, and dates of treatment: blackouts, amnesia, sneezing spells, dizziness, back pain, or neck pain. In lieu of providing the information requested in this interrogatory,

Continued on next page

you may provide (1) a list of the medical providers, (2) the dates of treatment, and (3) an executed authorization permitting the disclosure of the medical records and bills, which is attached to these interrogatories. {*See FORM 6J:1; **O'Connor's Texas Rules**, "Medical authorization," ch. 6-J, §3.2, p. 692.*}

ANSWER:

INTERROGATORY 23: Describe in detail any conversations you have had with defendant since the accident.

ANSWER:

INTERROGATORY 24: If you have been involved in any other lawsuits within the last five years against any person or entity to recover damages as a result of personal injuries, state the date and nature of the accident, where the lawsuit was filed, the names of the parties involved, whether you were injured, whether you filed suit or suit was filed against you, and the outcome of the suit. {*Ask for documents in request for production.*}

ANSWER:

INTERROGATORY 25: Describe the nature and extent of the injury you allege you sustained as a result of the accident; list the name, address, and telephone number of each medical provider who treated you for the injury; describe the treatment you received; and state the charges for those services. {*Medical records for the injury from the accident should be secured by a request for disclosure, FORM 6E:2.*}

ANSWER:

INTERROGATORY 26: If you have been ill or have received any other injury since the accident, provide the name, address, and telephone number of each medical provider who treated you for the illness or injury, describe the illness or injury and treatment you received, and provide the cost for those services. In lieu of providing the information requested in this interrogatory, you may provide (1) a list of the medical providers, (2) the dates of treatment, and (3) an executed authorization permitting the disclosure of the medical records and bills, which is attached to these interrogatories. {*See FORM 6J:1; **O'Connor's Texas Rules**, "Medical authorization," ch. 6-J, §3.2, p. 692.*}

ANSWER:

INTERROGATORY 27: If you were hospitalized for any reason in the five-year period before the accident, for each hospitalization, provide the name and address of the facility, the date of each admission and discharge, the reason for hospitalization, and the treatment received. In lieu of providing the information requested in this interrogatory, you may provide (1) a list of the medical providers, (2) the dates of treatment, and (3) an executed authorization permitting the disclosure of the medical records and bills, which is attached to these interrogatories. {*See FORM 6J:1; **O'Connor's Texas Rules**, "Medical authorization," ch. 6-J, §3.2, p. 692.*}

ANSWER:

INTERROGATORY 28: If anyone has stated that you will require surgery or that you will have any permanent disability, impairment, or limitation, identify each person who made this statement, the date of the statement, and the content of the statement.

ANSWER:

INTERROGATORY 29: If you contend you incurred expenses as a result of the accident, provide an itemized list of your expenses, including medical expenses, lost income, and any other costs you allege you incurred. {*Amount and calculations for economic damages should be secured by a request for disclosure, FORM 6E:2.*}

ANSWER:

INTERROGATORY 30: If you have worked since the accident, provide the date you began working, a brief description of your job duties, and your rate of pay or salary.

ANSWER:

INTERROGATORY 31: If you contend you have missed work as a result of the accident, provide the dates you missed work, the reason for each day missed, and the amount of income you allege you lost for each day. {*Amount and calculations for economic damages should be secured by a request for disclosure, FORM 6E:2.*}

ANSWER:

INTERROGATORY 32: If you contend defendant acted maliciously or with gross negligence, describe the act that was committed with malice or gross negligence.

ANSWER:

Continued on next page

TEXAS CIVIL FORMS

CHAPTER 6. DISCOVERY

FORM 6G:11 D'S INTERROGATORIES – SLIP & FALL

SEE: Tex. R. Civ. P. 197
*O'Connor's Texas Rules * Civil Trials* (2019), "Interrogatories," ch. 6-G, p. 663
O'Connor's Texas Causes of Action (2019), "Liability to Invitees," ch. 23-B, p. 827

ADD TO: STANDARD INTERROGATORIES – FORM 6G:2

ATTACH: MEDICAL AUTHORIZATION – FORM 6J:1, if necessary

NOTE: Include in the cover sheet that the definition of the word "premises" is the premises at the defendant's address, where the plaintiff's accident occurred.

See notes under FORM 6G:2.

{ADD TO STANDARD INTERROGATORIES – FORM 6G:2}

{*Depending on the discovery-control plan, parties are generally limited to either 15 or 25 interrogatories. See the first note under FORM 6G:2.*}

INTERROGATORY 9: If you contend plaintiff waived the provisions of the Deceptive Trade Practices Act, state the factual basis for your contention.

ANSWER:

INTERROGATORY 10: If you contend plaintiff is not a consumer under the Deceptive Trade Practices Act, state the factual basis for your contention.

ANSWER:

INTERROGATORY 11: If you contend you are exempt from suit, state the factual basis for your contention.

ANSWER:

INTERROGATORY 12: If you contend plaintiff did not give proper presuit notice as required by the Deceptive Trade Practices Act, state with particularity the factual basis for your contention.

ANSWER:

INTERROGATORY 13: If you contend you attempted to correct the defects described in plaintiff's original petition, state the date of each attempt and describe what you did to remedy the defects on each date. {*Ask for documents in request for production.*}

ANSWER:

INTERROGATORY 14: Did you represent to plaintiff that {❶ *specify each false, misleading, and deceptive act and practice alleged in plaintiff's original petition*}?

ANSWER:

INTERROGATORY 15: If any other lawsuits have been filed against you within the last five years, state the date of the lawsuit, the nature of the claim, and the outcome of the suit.

ANSWER:

◄ *Continued on next page* ►

INTERROGATORY 16: If any person has complained to you that {❷ *his/her/its*} {❸ *describe goods or services*}, identical or similar to {❹ *that/those*} {❺ *purchased/leased*} by plaintiff, also {❻ *was/were*} defective, identify the person, the date the {❼ *describe goods or services*} {❽ *was/were*} {❾ *purchased/leased*}, and how the complaint was resolved.

ANSWER:

INTERROGATORY 17: State the amount of time the {❿ *describe goods*} {⓫ *was/were*} in your possession before the {⓬ *describe goods*} {⓭ *was/were*} {⓮ *purchased/leased*} by plaintiff.

ANSWER:

INTERROGATORY 18: If any inspections were performed on the {⓯ *describe goods or services*}, identify the date the inspection occurred, the person or entity that performed the inspection, the reason for the inspection, and the results of the inspection.

ANSWER:

INTERROGATORY 19: Identify all express or implied warranties applicable to the {⓰ *describe goods or services*}.

ANSWER:

INTERROGATORY 20: If you contend plaintiff should have mitigated {⓱ *his/her/its*} damages but did not, state the factual basis for your contention.

ANSWER:

SEE: Tex. R. Civ. P. 197
Tex. Bus. & Com. Code §17.41 et seq.
O'Connor's Texas Rules * Civil Trials (2019), "Interrogatories," ch. 6-G, p. 663
O'Connor's Texas Causes of Action (2019), "Deceptive Trade Practices Act," ch. 8, p. 209

ADD TO: STANDARD INTERROGATORIES – FORM 6G:2

NOTE: See notes under FORM 6G:2.

{ADD TO STANDARD INTERROGATORIES – FORM 6G:2}

{Depending on the discovery-control plan, parties are generally limited to either 15 or 25 interrogatories. See the first note under FORM 6G:2.}

INTERROGATORY 9: If you contend you {❶ *purchased/leased*} the {❷ *describe goods or services*} from defendant, state the date of {❸ *purchase/lease*} from defendant and identify the person from whom you {❹ *purchased/leased*} the {❺ *describe goods or services*} and any other persons present at the time of {❻ *purchase/lease*}. *{Ask for documents in request for production.}*

ANSWER:

INTERROGATORY 10: If you contend defendant made any oral or written representations regarding the {❼ *describe goods or services*}, list each representation. *{Ask for documents in request for production.}*

ANSWER:

INTERROGATORY 11: If you contend defendant breached any express or implied warranties, state the factual basis for your contention. *{Ask for documents in request for production.}*

ANSWER:

INTERROGATORY 12: If you contend defendant engaged in any action or course of conduct that was unconscionable, state the factual basis for your contention.

ANSWER:

INTERROGATORY 13: If you contend you lacked sufficient knowledge, ability, or experience, so that you relied on defendant's knowledge, ability, or experience in deciding to {❽ *purchase/lease*} the {❾ *describe goods or services*}, state the factual basis for your contention.

ANSWER:

INTERROGATORY 14: If you contend defendant took advantage of your lack of knowledge or experience to a grossly unfair degree, state the factual basis for your contention.

ANSWER:

◄ *Continued on next page* ►

INTERROGATORY 15: If you contend there is a gross disparity between the value of the {⑩ *describe goods or services*} received and the consideration paid, state the factual basis for your contention.

ANSWER:

INTERROGATORY 16: If you contend defendant acted knowingly or intentionally, describe the act that was committed knowingly or intentionally.

ANSWER:

INTERROGATORY 17: If you are claiming you suffered a physical injury, illness, or condition for which you seek damages in this lawsuit, describe the nature and extent of the injury, illness, or condition; provide the name, address, and telephone number of each medical provider who treated you for the injury; describe the treatment you received; and provide the charges for those services. {*Medical records for the injury from the DTPA violation should be secured by a request for disclosure, FORM 6E:2.*}

ANSWER:

INTERROGATORY 18: Identify the date you first noticed the defect or problem with the {⑪ *describe goods or services*}, the person who discovered the defect, and the circumstances surrounding the discovery of the defect.

ANSWER:

INTERROGATORY 19: If you contend that any inspections were performed on the {⑫ *describe goods or services*}, identify the date the inspection occurred, the person or entity that performed the inspection, the reason for the inspection, and the results of the inspection.

ANSWER:

INTERROGATORY 20: Identify each person who has used or come in contact with the {⑬ *describe goods or services*} since your initial {⑭ *purchase/lease*} and the reason the {⑮ *describe goods or services*} {⑯ *was/were*} used.

ANSWER:

INTERROGATORY 21: If you have been involved in any other lawsuits within the last five years, state the date of the lawsuit, where it was filed, the names of the parties involved, the nature of the claim, whether you filed the suit or the suit was filed against you, and the outcome of the suit.

ANSWER:

SEE: Tex. R. Civ. P. 197
Tex. Bus. & Com. Code §17.41 et seq.
O'Connor's Texas Rules * Civil Trials (2019), "Interrogatories," ch. 6-G, p. 663
O'Connor's Texas Causes of Action (2019), "Deceptive Trade Practices Act," ch. 8, p. 209

ADD TO: STANDARD INTERROGATORIES – FORM 6G:2

NOTE: See notes under FORM 6G:2.

{❶ *PARTY*}'S {❷ *NUMBER*} REQUEST
FOR ADMISSIONS TO {❸ *ADVERSE PARTY*}

To: {❹ *Adverse party*}, {❺ *name*}, by and through {❻ *his/her/its*} attorney of record, {❼ *name*}, {❽ *address*}.

{❾ *Party*}, {❿ *name*}, serves these requests for admissions on {⓫ *adverse party*}, as allowed by Texas Rule of Civil Procedure 198. {⓬ *Adverse party*} must admit or deny each request, in writing, within 30 days after service. {*See* ***O'Connor's Texas Rules***, *"Requests for Admissions," ch. 6-H, §3, p. 672.*}

DEFINITIONS

1. "Plaintiff" or "defendant," as well as a party's full or abbreviated name or a pronoun referring to a party, means the party, and when applicable, the party's agents, representatives, officers, directors, employees, partners, corporate agents, subsidiaries, affiliates, or any other person acting in concert with the party or under the party's control, whether directly or indirectly, including any attorney.

2. "You" or "your" means {⓭ *adverse party*}, {⓮ *name*}, {⓯ *his/her/its*} successors, predecessors, divisions, subsidiaries, present and former officers, agents, employees, and all other persons acting on behalf of {⓰ *adverse party*} or {⓱ *his/her/its*} successors, predecessors, divisions, and subsidiaries.

3. "Person" means any natural person, corporation, firm, association, partnership, joint venture, proprietorship, governmental body, or any other organization, business, or legal entity and all predecessors or successors in interest.

4. "Communication" means any oral or written communication of which {⓲ *adverse party*} has knowledge, information, or belief.

5. "Mobile device" means any cellular telephone, satellite telephone, pager, personal digital assistant, handheld computer, electronic rolodex, walkie-talkie, or any combination of these devices.

6. "Electronic or magnetic data" means electronic information that is stored in a medium from which it can be retrieved and examined. The term refers to the original (or identical duplicate when the original is not available) and any other copies of the data that may have attached comments, notes, marks, or highlighting of any kind. Electronic or magnetic data includes, but is not limited to, the following: computer programs; operating systems; computer activity logs; programming notes or instructions; e-mail receipts, messages, or transmissions; output resulting from the use of any software program, including word-processing documents, spreadsheets, database files, charts,

graphs, and outlines; metadata; PIF and PDF files; batch files; deleted files; temporary files; Internet- or web-browser-generated information stored in textual, graphical, or audio format, including history files, caches, and cookies; {⓳ *continue listing examples as necessary*}; and any miscellaneous files or file fragments. Electronic or magnetic data includes any items stored on magnetic, optical, digital, or other electronic-storage media, such as hard drives, floppy disks, CD-ROMs, DVDs, tapes, smart cards, integrated-circuit cards (e.g., SIM cards), removable media (e.g., Zip drives, Jaz cartridges), microfiche, punched cards, {⓴ *continue listing examples as necessary*}. Electronic or magnetic data also includes the file, folder, tabs, containers, and labels attached to or associated with any physical storage device with each original or copy.

SEE: Tex. R. Civ. P. 198
O'Connor's Texas Rules * Civil Trials (2019), "Requests for Admissions," ch. 6-H, p. 671

ADD: STYLE OF THE CASE – FORM 1B:2
SIGNATURE BLOCK – FORM 1B:3
CERTIFICATE OF SERVICE – FORM 1B:13

NOTE: When a plaintiff serves its request for admissions with its petition, the request should be addressed to the defendant. In such a case, delete "by and through its attorney of record." When the plaintiff serves the request before the defendant's answer is due, the defendant has 50 days to respond rather than 30. Tex. R. Civ. P. 198.2(a).

For most methods of service, the deadline for serving a request for admissions is 30 days before the end of the discovery period. Tex. R. Civ. P. 198.1. See ***O'Connor's Texas Rules***, "Discovery Periods," ch. 6-A, §8, p. 523. But when service is by mail or fax, the request should be served at least 33 days (if mailed) or 31 days (if faxed after 5:00 p.m.) before the end of the discovery period. *See* Tex. R. Civ. P. 21a(b)(2), (c). See ***O'Connor's Texas Rules***, "Deadline to serve response," ch. 6-A, §14.1, p. 527.

REQUESTS FOR ADMISSIONS

Admit or deny the truth of the following statements:

{*CHOOSE APPROPRIATE REQUESTS*}

REQUEST 1: Plaintiff {❶ *properly/improperly*} named defendant in plaintiff's original petition.

RESPONSE:

REQUEST 2: The document attached as Exhibit {❷ *letter*} is a genuine copy of that document.

RESPONSE:

REQUEST 3: The document attached as Exhibit {❸ *letter*} was received by {❹ *adverse party*} {❺ *on/after/before*} {❻ *date*}.

RESPONSE:

REQUEST 4: The document attached as Exhibit {❼ *letter*} was created {❽ *on/after/before*} {❾ *date*}.

RESPONSE:

REQUEST 5: The document attached as Exhibit {❿ *letter*} was signed {⓫ *on/after/before*} {⓬ *date*}.

RESPONSE:

REQUEST 6: The {⓭ *signature/initials*} on page {⓮ *number*} of the document attached as Exhibit {⓯ *letter*} {⓰ *was/were*} made by {⓱ *{adverse party}/{name of adverse party's employee}*}.

RESPONSE:

REQUEST 7: The original of the document attached as Exhibit {⓲ *letter*} is in the possession, custody, or control of {⓳ *adverse party*}. {*Ask for production of original in request for production here or in a separate document.*}

RESPONSE:

REQUEST 8: {[20] *{Adverse party}/{name of adverse party's employee}*} learned {[21] *on/before*} {[22] *date*}, that {[23] *state facts that would trigger limitations*}.

RESPONSE:

REQUEST 9: {[24] *{Adverse party}/{name of adverse party's employee}*} was convicted of a felony or a crime involving moral turpitude. {*Ask for more information in an interrogatory here or in a separate document.*}

RESPONSE:

REQUEST 10: The judgment attached as Exhibit {[25] *letter*} is a correct copy of the judgment of conviction rendered against {[26] *{adverse party}/{name of adverse party's employee}*} by the court {[27] *after a jury trial/upon a plea of guilty*}.

RESPONSE:

REQUEST 11: {[28] *Adverse party*} received proper presuit notice of {[29] *party*}'s claim, as required by {[30] *identify contract, statute, or rule that required presuit notice*}. {*Ask for more information in an interrogatory here or in a separate document.*}

RESPONSE:

REQUEST 12: {[31] *Name of adverse party's employee*} was acting in the course and scope of {[32] *his/her*} employment when {[33] *he/she*} {[34] *describe conduct*}.

RESPONSE:

SEE: Tex. R. Civ. P. 198
O'Connor's Texas Rules * Civil Trials (2019), "Requests for Admissions," ch. 6-H, p. 671

ADD: REQUESTS FOR ADMISSIONS – FORMS 6H:4-13, as appropriate

ATTACH: COVER SHEET & DEFINITIONS – FORM 6H:1

NOTE: A party in a Level 1 case can serve no more than 15 written requests for admissions on any other party. Tex. R. Civ. P. 190.2(b)(5). There is no limit on the number of requests for admissions or the number of sets of requests a party can serve in a Level 2 or 3 case. *See* Tex. R. Civ. P. 190.3(b), 190.4(b), 198. However, in a Level 3 case, the discovery limitations of Level 1 or 2 apply—depending on the damages sought and issues involved—unless expressly changed by court order. *See* Tex. R. Civ. P. 190.4(b). Thus, a party in a Level 3 case may also be limited to 15 written requests for admissions.

Each discrete subpart of a request for admissions is considered a separate request for admissions. Tex. R. Civ. P. 190.2(b)(5).

Continued on next page

When seeking information about testifying experts, a party can use requests only to discover the experts' identities. *See* Tex. R. Civ. P. 192.3(d), 195.1. Other information about a testifying expert must be sought through a request for disclosure or a deposition of the expert. Tex. R. Civ. P. 195.1. See ***O'Connor's Texas Rules***, "Standard requests," ch. 6-E, §3.2.1, p. 627. However, a party can use requests for admissions to request discoverable information about consulting experts.

A party may combine more than one discovery form in the same document (e.g., requests for admissions, interrogatories, and requests for production). Tex. R. Civ. P. 192.2.

A party should not pair a request with its mirror opposite; if both admissions are deemed admitted, the admissions establish both the positive and negative of the proposition, thus creating a fact issue. *E.g.*, ***CEBI Metal Sanayi ve Ticaret A.S. v. Garcia***, 108 S.W.3d 464, 466-67 (Tex.App.—Houston [14th Dist.] 2003, no pet.) (deemed admissions of requests paired with exact opposites could not support summary judgment); ***Noons v. Arabghani***, No. 13-03-628-CV (Tex.App.—Corpus Christi 2005, pet. denied) (memo op.; 8-25-05) (same).

A requesting party can ask the court to deem the answers admitted or to compel a proper response if a responding party does not comply with Texas Rule of Civil Procedure 198. *See* Tex. R. Civ. P. 215.4(a). See FORMS 6A:24, 6H:14.

{[1] *PARTY*}'S ANSWERS TO
{[2] *ADVERSE PARTY*}'S {[3] *NUMBER*} REQUEST FOR ADMISSIONS

To: {[4] *Adverse party*}, {[5] *name*}, by and through {[6] *his/her/its*} attorney of record, {[7] *name*}, {[8] *address*}.

{[9] *Party*}, {[10] *name*}, serves these responses to {[11] *adverse party*}'s requests for admissions. {*See* ***O'Connor's Texas Rules***, *"Responding to Requests for Admissions," ch. 6-H, §4, p. 673.*}

RESPONSES TO REQUESTS

REQUEST 1: {[12] *Restate request for admissions.*}

{*CHOOSE APPROPRIATE RESPONSE*}

RESPONSE: {[13] *Admitted/Denied.*}

RESPONSE: {[14] *Party*} admits part of this request, specifically {[15] *identify part that is admitted*}. {[16] *Party*}, however, denies the rest of the request. {*See* ***O'Connor's Texas Rules***, *"Denials," ch. 6-H, §4.2.2, p. 673.*}

RESPONSE: {[17] *Party*} cannot admit or deny this request because {[18] *party*} and {[19] *his/her/its*} attorney have insufficient information or knowledge of the request's subject matter to respond. A reasonable inquiry was made, but the information known or easily obtainable was insufficient to enable {[20] *party*} to admit or deny the matter. *See* Tex. R. Civ. P. 198.2(b). {[21] *Elaborate.*} {*See* ***O'Connor's Texas Rules***, *"Lack of information," ch. 6-H, §4.2.4, p. 674.*}

WITHHOLDING STATEMENT: Material or information responsive to this request is withheld under the {[22] *identify privilege*}. *See* Tex. R. Civ. P. 193.3(a). {*See* ***O'Connor's Texas Rules***, *"Withholding statement," ch. 6-A, §2.8, p. 516.*}

OBJECTION: {[23] *Party*} objects because the requests exceed the {[24] *number*}-request limit for this Level {[25] *1/3*} case. {[26] *Elaborate.*} To the extent that {[27] *party*} does not object to the discovery request, {[28] *party*} serves the following answers: {[29] *identify limit of compliance, e.g., party responds to the first 15 requests but refuses to answer the rest*}.

OBJECTION: {[30] *Party*} cannot admit or deny this request because the request is premature and the answer will not be known until after additional discovery is completed. *See* Tex. R. Civ. P. 193.1. {[31] *Elaborate, describing the additional discovery necessary.*} Once that discovery is completed, {[32] *party*} will respond to this request.

Continued on next page

OBJECTION: {33 *Party*} cannot admit or deny the genuineness of the document as requested because {34 *state reason, e.g., the copy is illegible*}.

OBJECTION: {35 *Party*} objects because this request asks that {36 *he/she/it*} admit a proposition of law. {*See* ***O'Connor's Texas Rules****, "Valid objections," ch. 6-H, §4.2.5(1)(a), p. 674.*}

OBJECTION: {37 *Party*} objects because the request asks that {38 *he/she/it*} admit matters that are hearsay. {*See* ***O'Connor's Texas Rules****, "Valid objections," ch. 6-H, §4.2.5(1)(a), p. 674.*}

SEE: Tex. R. Civ. P. 193.3, 198
O'Connor's Texas Rules * Civil Trials (2019), "Requests for Admissions," ch. 6-H, p. 671

ADD: STYLE OF THE CASE – FORM 1B:2
SIGNATURE BLOCK – FORM 1B:3
CERTIFICATE OF SERVICE – FORM 1B:13

NOTE: It is not necessary to verify answers to requests for admissions.

The responding party's answers, objections, and other responses must be preceded by the request to which they apply. Tex. R. Civ. P. 193.1.

A party in a Level 1 case can serve no more than 15 written requests for admissions on any other party. Tex. R. Civ. P. 190.2(b)(5). There is no limit on the number of requests for admissions or the number of sets of requests a party can serve in a Level 2 or 3 case. *See* Tex. R. Civ. P. 190.3(b), 190.4(b), 198. However, in a Level 3 case, the discovery limitations of Level 1 or 2 apply—depending on the damages sought and issues involved—unless expressly changed by court order. *See* Tex. R. Civ. P. 190.4(b). Thus, a party in a Level 3 case may also be limited to 15 written requests for admissions.

Each discrete subpart of a request for admissions is considered a separate request for admissions. Tex. R. Civ. P. 190.2(b)(5).

Generally, a party responding to a request for admissions has 30 days to respond. Tex. R. Civ. P. 198.2(a). But when the plaintiff serves a request for admissions before the defendant's answer is due, the defendant has 50 days to respond rather than 30. *Id.* When service is by mail or fax, the responding party has an additional three days (if mailed) or one day (if faxed after 5:00 p.m.) to respond. *See* Tex. R. Civ. P. 21a(b)(2), (c). See ***O'Connor's Texas Rules***, "Deadline to serve response," ch. 6-A, §14.1, p. 527.

To extend the time to respond to requests for admissions, a party may either ask the other party for a Rule 11 agreement or ask the court to extend the time. See FORM 6A:3. A motion filed with the court must be made before the date to answer. Once the time to respond expires, the answers are automatically deemed admitted against the defaulting party. Tex. R. Civ. P. 198.2(c). To avoid the effect of the deemed answers, the defaulting party must file a motion to strike, withdraw, or amend the deemed admissions. *See* ***Cherry v. North Am. Lloyds***, 770 S.W.2d 4, 5 (Tex.App.—Houston [1st Dist.] 1989, writ denied). See FORM 6H:17.

A party may file a motion for protective order under Texas Rule of Civil Procedure 192.6 to protect itself from undue burden, unnecessary expense, harassment, or annoyance. ***Reynolds v. Murphy***, 188 S.W.3d 252, 260 (Tex.App.—Fort Worth 2006, pet. denied). See ***O'Connor's Texas Rules***, "Motion for Protective Order," ch. 6-A, §20, p. 539. The party does not need to file a more specific objection to each request to prevent the requests from being deemed admitted. ***Reynolds***, 188 S.W.3d at 260.

For general objections to discovery, see FORM 6A:9; for claims of privilege, see FORMS 6A:19-22.

{ADD TO STANDARD REQUESTS FOR ADMISSIONS – FORM 6H:2}

{Depending on the discovery-control plan, parties may be limited to 15 requests. See the first note under FORM 6H:2.}

REQUEST 13: Defendant executed a written contract with plaintiff.

RESPONSE:

REQUEST 14: Defendant executed a written contract with plaintiff for adequate consideration.

RESPONSE:

REQUEST 15: Defendant executed the written contract attached to plaintiff's original petition.

RESPONSE:

REQUEST 16: Defendant signed the contract attached to plaintiff's original petition.

RESPONSE:

REQUEST 17: Defendant's signature on the contract attached to plaintiff's original petition is genuine.

RESPONSE:

REQUEST 18: Defendant authorized {❶ *name of person who signed contract*} to sign the written contract attached to plaintiff's original petition.

RESPONSE:

REQUEST 19: The contract attached to plaintiff's original petition is a true and correct copy of the contract executed and signed by defendant.

RESPONSE:

REQUEST 20: Plaintiff {❷ *fully/substantially*} performed all {❸ *his/her/its*} contractual obligations required by the contract attached to plaintiff's original petition.

RESPONSE:

INTERROGATORY 1: If your response to Request for Admission 20 is "denied," please explain what part of plaintiff's contractual obligations {❹ *he/she/it*} did not perform, including a description of the obligation and the start time, date, and place of plaintiff's nonperformance.

ANSWER:

REQUEST 21: Defendant did not substantially perform all {❺ *his/her/its*} contractual obligations required by the contract attached to plaintiff's original petition.

RESPONSE:

REQUEST 22: Defendant did not timely perform all {❻ *his/her/its*} contractual obligations required by the contract attached to plaintiff's original petition.

RESPONSE:

REQUEST 23: Defendant's performance of {❼ *his/her/its*} contractual obligations was not impossible.

RESPONSE:

REQUEST 24: Defendant's nonperformance constitutes a breach of the contract attached to plaintiff's original petition.

RESPONSE:

REQUEST 25: The parties did not modify the contract attached to plaintiff's original petition.

RESPONSE:

INTERROGATORY 2: If your response to Request for Admission 25 is "denied," please state how and when the parties modified the contract, including whether the modification was oral or written and the dates and persons present.

ANSWER:

REQUEST 26: Neither party rescinded the contract attached to plaintiff's original petition.

RESPONSE:

◄ *Continued on next page* ►

REQUEST 27: Plaintiff has performed all conditions precedent, or all conditions precedent have occurred, necessary for plaintiff to bring suit on the contract attached to plaintiff's original petition.

RESPONSE:

REQUEST 28: Plaintiff made a written demand for the sum sought in plaintiff's original petition more than 30 days before plaintiff filed suit.

RESPONSE:

REQUEST 29: Defendant refused to pay plaintiff the sum sought in the written demand referred to in Request for Admission 28.

RESPONSE:

REQUEST 30: Reasonable and necessary attorney fees for this suit are at least ${❽ *amount*}.

RESPONSE:

SEE: Tex. R. Civ. P. 198
O'Connor's Texas Rules * Civil Trials (2019), "Requests for Admissions," ch. 6-H, p. 671
O'Connor's Texas Causes of Action (2019), "Breach of Contract," ch. 5-B, p. 69

ADD TO: STANDARD REQUESTS FOR ADMISSIONS – FORM 6H:2

NOTE: In contract cases, many of the requests for admissions involve authenticating documents and signatures. For these requests, see FORM 6H:2.

See notes under FORM 6H:2.

{ADD TO STANDARD REQUESTS FOR ADMISSIONS – FORM 6H:2}

{Depending on the discovery-control plan, parties may be limited to 15 requests. See the first note under FORM 6H:2.}

REQUEST 13: Defendant did not execute a written contract with plaintiff.

RESPONSE:

REQUEST 14: There was no consideration for the contract attached to plaintiff's original petition.

RESPONSE:

REQUEST 15: Defendant did not sign the contract attached to plaintiff's original petition.

RESPONSE:

REQUEST 16: The contract attached to plaintiff's original petition is not a true and correct copy of the contract executed and signed by defendant.

RESPONSE:

REQUEST 17: Plaintiff has not performed all conditions precedent, or all conditions precedent have not occurred, necessary for plaintiff to bring suit on the contract attached to plaintiff's original petition.

RESPONSE:

REQUEST 18: Plaintiff did not {❶ *fully/substantially*} perform all the contractual obligations required by the contract attached to plaintiff's original petition.

RESPONSE:

REQUEST 19: Plaintiff's nonperformance was a breach of the contract attached to plaintiff's original petition.

RESPONSE:

REQUEST 20: The parties modified the contract attached to plaintiff's original petition when they agreed to {❷ *state agreement*}.

RESPONSE:

Continued on next page

REQUEST 21: {❸ *Plaintiff/Defendant*} rescinded the contract attached to plaintiff's original petition.

RESPONSE:

REQUEST 22: Defendant's performance of {❹ *his/her/its*} contractual obligations was impossible.

RESPONSE:

REQUEST 23: Plaintiff did not mitigate {❺ *his/her/its*} damages.

RESPONSE:

SEE: Tex. R. Civ. P. 198
O'Connor's Texas Rules * Civil Trials (2019), "Requests for Admissions," ch. 6-H, p. 671
O'Connor's Texas Causes of Action (2019), "Breach of Contract," ch. 5-B, p. 69

ADD TO: STANDARD REQUESTS FOR ADMISSIONS – FORM 6H:2

NOTE: In contract cases, many of the requests for admissions involve authenticating documents and signatures. For these requests, see FORM 6H:2.

See notes under FORM 6H:2.

{*ADD TO STANDARD REQUESTS FOR ADMISSIONS – FORM 6H:2*}

{*Depending on the discovery-control plan, parties may be limited to 15 requests. See the first note under FORM 6H:2.*}

REQUEST 13: Plaintiff provided defendant with the {❶ *describe goods or services*} identified in the account attached to plaintiff's original petition.

RESPONSE:

REQUEST 14: The account attached to plaintiff's original petition is just and true.

RESPONSE:

REQUEST 15: The account attached to plaintiff's original petition is due.

RESPONSE:

REQUEST 16: Defendant accepted the {❷ *describe goods or services*} identified in the account attached to plaintiff's original petition.

RESPONSE:

REQUEST 17: Defendant did not reject the {❸ *describe goods or services*} identified in the account attached to plaintiff's original petition.

RESPONSE:

REQUEST 18: The amount charged for the {❹ *describe goods or services*} listed in the account was the amount agreed to by plaintiff and defendant.

RESPONSE:

REQUEST 19: Defendant has not paid the amount due plaintiff on the account attached to plaintiff's original petition.

RESPONSE:

INTERROGATORY 1: If your response to Request for Admission 19 is "denied," provide complete information about payment, including but not limited to dates, amounts, and any reasons for withholding full payment.

ANSWER:

◄ *Continued on next page* ►

REQUEST 20: Defendant agreed to pay plaintiff for the {❺ *describe goods or services*} described in the account attached to plaintiff's original petition after the {❻ *describe goods or services*} {❼ *was/were*} delivered or provided to defendant.

RESPONSE:

REQUEST 21: Plaintiff made a written demand that defendant pay for the {❽ *describe goods or services*} identified in the account attached to plaintiff's original petition more than 30 days before plaintiff filed suit.

RESPONSE:

REQUEST 22: Defendant made no objection after receiving the written demand by plaintiff for payment.

RESPONSE:

REQUEST 23: Defendant refused to pay the sum sought in the written demand referred to in Request for Admission 21.

RESPONSE:

REQUEST 24: Reasonable and necessary attorney fees for this suit are at least ${❾ *amount*}.

RESPONSE:

SEE: Tex. R. Civ. P. 185, 198
O'Connor's Texas Rules * Civil Trials (2019), "Requests for Admissions," ch. 6-H, p. 671
O'Connor's Texas Causes of Action (2019), "Suit on Sworn Account," ch. 5-E, p. 126

ADD TO: STANDARD REQUESTS FOR ADMISSIONS – FORM 6H:2

NOTE: See notes under FORM 6H:2.

{ADD TO STANDARD REQUESTS FOR ADMISSIONS – FORM 6H:2}

{Depending on the discovery-control plan, parties may be limited to 15 requests. See the first note under FORM 6H:2.}

REQUEST 13: Defendant rejected the {❶ *describe goods or services*} identified in the account attached to plaintiff's original petition.

RESPONSE:

REQUEST 14: Plaintiff charged defendant an amount for the {❷ *describe goods or services*} not in accordance with the parties' agreement.

RESPONSE:

REQUEST 15: Defendant paid part of the amount plaintiff alleged is due on the account.

RESPONSE:

REQUEST 16: The {❸ *describe goods or services*} that plaintiff provided to defendant {❹ *is/are*} not the same {❺ *describe goods or services*} identified in the account attached to plaintiff's original petition.

RESPONSE:

REQUEST 17: Defendant disputed the charges for the {❻ *describe goods or services*} described in the summary of account at the time of delivery by plaintiff.

RESPONSE:

REQUEST 18: Plaintiff has not allowed defendant all lawful payments.

RESPONSE:

REQUEST 19: Plaintiff has not allowed defendant all lawful credits.

RESPONSE:

REQUEST 20: Plaintiff has not allowed defendant all lawful offsets.

RESPONSE:

Continued on next page

REQUEST 21: Plaintiff did not demand that defendant pay for the {❼ *describe goods or services*} identified in the account attached to plaintiff's original petition at least 30 days before filing suit.

RESPONSE:

SEE: Tex. R. Civ. P. 185, 198
O'Connor's Texas Rules * Civil Trials (2019), "Requests for Admissions," ch. 6-H, p. 671
O'Connor's Texas Causes of Action (2019), "Suit on Sworn Account," ch. 5-E, p. 126

ADD TO: STANDARD REQUESTS FOR ADMISSIONS – FORM 6H:2

NOTE: See notes under FORM 6H:2.

{ADD TO STANDARD REQUESTS FOR ADMISSIONS – FORM 6H:2}

{Depending on the discovery-control plan, parties may be limited to 15 requests. See the first note under FORM 6H:2.}

REQUEST 13: Defendant was driving {❶ *identify vehicle*} on {❷ *date of collision*}, when {❸ *he/she*} was involved in a collision.

RESPONSE:

REQUEST 14: On the date of the collision, defendant was operating a vehicle at {❹ *location of collision*}.

RESPONSE:

REQUEST 15: On the date of the collision, defendant's vehicle struck plaintiff's vehicle.

RESPONSE:

REQUEST 16: At the time of the collision, defendant owned the vehicle involved in the collision.

RESPONSE:

REQUEST 17: Defendant made an oral statement to an insurance company, conducted over the telephone and recorded by the agent for the insurance company.

RESPONSE:

REQUEST 18: On the date of the collision, defendant did not have a valid driver's license in any state.

RESPONSE:

REQUEST 19: On the date of the collision, defendant's driver's license was revoked or suspended.

RESPONSE:

REQUEST 20: On the date of the collision, defendant was violating a restriction placed on {❺ *his/her*} driver's license.

RESPONSE:

◄ Continued on next page ►

REQUEST 21: Defendant received a ticket as a result of the collision and was charged with the offense of {❻ *identify charge alleged in plaintiff's original petition*}.

RESPONSE:

REQUEST 22: Defendant entered a guilty plea to the charge described in Request for Admission 21.

RESPONSE:

REQUEST 23: Defendant entered a nolo contendere plea to the charge described in Request for Admission 21.

RESPONSE:

REQUEST 24: Defendant was found guilty of the charge described in Request for Admission 21.

RESPONSE:

REQUEST 25: The condition of the road surface did not contribute to the cause of the collision.

RESPONSE:

REQUEST 26: Lighting conditions did not contribute to the cause of the collision.

RESPONSE:

REQUEST 27: Weather conditions did not contribute to the cause of the collision.

RESPONSE:

REQUEST 28: A sudden emergency did not contribute to the cause of the collision.

RESPONSE:

REQUEST 29: An act of God did not contribute to the cause of the collision.

RESPONSE:

REQUEST 30: Defendant does not contend the collision was unavoidable.

RESPONSE:

REQUEST 31: No defect or malfunction in the vehicle that defendant was driving contributed to the cause of the collision.

RESPONSE:

REQUEST 32: Defendant does not have normal vision without the use of corrective lenses, contacts, glasses, or other devices.

RESPONSE:

REQUEST 33: Defendant was not wearing corrective lenses, contacts, glasses, or other devices at the time of the collision.

RESPONSE:

REQUEST 34: Defendant was not wearing {❼ *his/her*} hearing aid at the time of the collision.

RESPONSE:

REQUEST 35: Defendant was under the care of a medical practitioner or other practitioner of the healing arts during the month before the collision.

RESPONSE:

REQUEST 36: Defendant was under the influence of drugs or alcohol when the collision occurred.

RESPONSE:

REQUEST 37: Defendant had ingested or consumed drugs or alcohol within the 24 hours before the collision.

RESPONSE:

REQUEST 38: {❽ *Name of employee*} was acting within the course and scope of defendant's employment at the time of the collision.

RESPONSE:

REQUEST 39: Defendant was acting as an agent for another person or entity at the time of the collision.

RESPONSE:

Continued on next page

REQUEST 40: Defendant was not injured as a result of the collision.

RESPONSE:

REQUEST 41: Defendant did not maintain a proper lookout immediately before the collision.

RESPONSE:

REQUEST 42: Defendant's failure to maintain a proper lookout immediately before the collision was the proximate cause of defendant's vehicle striking plaintiff's vehicle.

RESPONSE:

REQUEST 43: Defendant did not timely apply {❾ *his/her*} brakes.

RESPONSE:

REQUEST 44: Defendant was using a mobile device when the collision occurred.

RESPONSE:

SEE: Tex. R. Civ. P. 198
O'Connor's Texas Rules * Civil Trials (2019), "Requests for Admissions," ch. 6-H, p. 671
O'Connor's Texas Causes of Action (2019), "Negligence Actions," ch. 21, p. 719

ADD TO: STANDARD REQUESTS FOR ADMISSIONS – FORM 6H:2

NOTE: See notes under FORM 6H:2.

{*ADD TO STANDARD REQUESTS FOR ADMISSIONS – FORM 6H:2*}

{*Depending on the discovery-control plan, parties may be limited to 15 requests. See the first note under FORM 6H:2.*}

REQUEST 13: Plaintiff was driving {❶ *identify vehicle*} on {❷ *date of collision*}, when {❸ *he/she*} was involved in a collision.

RESPONSE:

REQUEST 14: On the date of the collision, plaintiff was operating a vehicle at {❹ *location of collision*}.

RESPONSE:

REQUEST 15: On the date of the collision, plaintiff's vehicle struck defendant's vehicle.

RESPONSE:

REQUEST 16: Plaintiff owned the vehicle {❺ *he/she*} was driving at the time of the collision.

RESPONSE:

REQUEST 17: Plaintiff did not have a valid driver's license in any state on the date of the collision.

RESPONSE:

REQUEST 18: Plaintiff's driver's license was revoked or suspended on the date of the collision.

RESPONSE:

REQUEST 19: Plaintiff was violating a restriction placed on {❻ *his/her*} driver's license on the date of the collision.

RESPONSE:

REQUEST 20: The condition of the road surface contributed to the cause of the collision.

RESPONSE:

◄ *Continued on next page* ►

REQUEST 21: Lighting conditions contributed to the cause of the collision.

RESPONSE:

REQUEST 22: Weather conditions contributed to the cause of the collision.

RESPONSE:

REQUEST 23: A sudden emergency contributed to the cause of the collision.

RESPONSE:

REQUEST 24: An act of God contributed to the cause of the collision.

RESPONSE:

REQUEST 25: A defect or malfunction in the vehicle that plaintiff was driving contributed to the cause of the collision.

RESPONSE:

REQUEST 26: Plaintiff does not have normal vision without the use of corrective lenses, contacts, glasses, or other devices.

RESPONSE:

REQUEST 27: Plaintiff was not wearing corrective lenses, contacts, glasses, or other devices at the time of the collision.

RESPONSE:

REQUEST 28: Plaintiff was not wearing {❼ *his/her*} hearing aid at the time of the collision.

RESPONSE:

REQUEST 29: Plaintiff was under the care of a medical practitioner or other practitioner of the healing arts during the month before the collision.

RESPONSE:

REQUEST 30: Plaintiff was under the influence of drugs or alcohol when the collision occurred.

RESPONSE:

REQUEST 31: Plaintiff had ingested or consumed drugs or alcohol within the 24 hours before the collision.

RESPONSE:

REQUEST 32: Plaintiff has possession, custody, or control of a copy of a written statement or a recorded oral statement made by defendant relating to the collision.

RESPONSE:

REQUEST 33: {❽ *Name of employee*} was acting within the course and scope of plaintiff's employment at the time of the collision.

RESPONSE:

REQUEST 34: Plaintiff was acting as an agent for a person or entity at the time of the collision.

RESPONSE:

REQUEST 35: Plaintiff was not injured as a result of the collision.

RESPONSE:

REQUEST 36: Plaintiff did not maintain a proper lookout on the date of the collision.

RESPONSE:

REQUEST 37: Plaintiff's failure to maintain a proper lookout immediately before the collision was the proximate cause of plaintiff's vehicle striking defendant's vehicle.

RESPONSE:

REQUEST 38: Plaintiff received a ticket as a result of the collision and was charged with the offense of {❾ *identify charge*}.

RESPONSE:

REQUEST 39: Plaintiff entered a guilty plea as a result of the charge described in Request for Admission 38.

RESPONSE:

Continued on next page

REQUEST 40: Plaintiff entered a nolo contendere plea as a result of the charge described in Request for Admission 38.

RESPONSE:

REQUEST 41: Plaintiff was found guilty of the charge described in Request for Admission 38.

RESPONSE:

REQUEST 42: Plaintiff was not restrained by a seat belt.

RESPONSE:

REQUEST 43: The {⑩ *passenger/passengers*} in plaintiff's vehicle {⑪ *was/were*} not restrained by {⑫ *a seat belt/seat belts*} or other safety {⑬ *device/devices*}.

RESPONSE:

REQUEST 44: Plaintiff was using a mobile device when the collision occurred.

RESPONSE:

SEE: Tex. R. Civ. P. 198
O'Connor's Texas Rules * Civil Trials (2019), "Requests for Admissions," ch. 6-H, p. 671
O'Connor's Texas Causes of Action (2019), "Negligence Actions," ch. 21, p. 719

ADD TO: STANDARD REQUESTS FOR ADMISSIONS – FORM 6H:2

NOTE: See notes under FORM 6H:2.

{*ADD TO STANDARD REQUESTS FOR ADMISSIONS – FORM 6H:2*}

{*Depending on the discovery-control plan, parties may be limited to 15 requests. See the first note under FORM 6H:2.*}

REQUEST 13: Defendant owned the premises located at {❶ *address*}, at the time of the accident.

RESPONSE:

REQUEST 14: Defendant had control of the premises located at {❷ *address*}, at the time of the accident.

RESPONSE:

REQUEST 15: Defendant leased the premises.

RESPONSE:

REQUEST 16: The lease, a copy of which is attached to this request and marked as Exhibit {❸ *letter*}, is a genuine copy of the lease that is the subject of this litigation.

RESPONSE:

REQUEST 17: Defendant was in charge of maintaining the premises at {❹ *address*}, at the time of the accident.

RESPONSE:

INTERROGATORY 1: If your response to Request for Admission 17 is "denied," identify the person or entity responsible for maintaining the premises at the time of the accident.

ANSWER:

REQUEST 18: Defendant's business was open to the public at the time the accident occurred.

RESPONSE:

REQUEST 19: The floor of the premises contained a foreign substance, {❺ *identify substance*}, at the time of the accident.

RESPONSE:

Continued on next page

REQUEST 20: Defendant was notified of the condition on the floor before the accident occurred.

RESPONSE:

REQUEST 21: Defendant, after becoming aware of the condition on the floor, did not clean the floor until after the accident occurred.

RESPONSE:

REQUEST 22: Defendant caused the {❻ *identify substance*} to be on the floor.

RESPONSE:

REQUEST 23: Defendant was aware of the risk of injury created by the condition on the floor.

RESPONSE:

SEE: Tex. R. Civ. P. 198
O'Connor's Texas Rules * Civil Trials (2019), "Requests for Admissions," ch. 6-H, p. 671
O'Connor's Texas Causes of Action (2019), "Liability to Invitees," ch. 23-B, p. 827

ADD TO: STANDARD REQUESTS FOR ADMISSIONS – FORM 6H:2

NOTE: Include in the cover sheet that the definition of the word "premises" is the premises at the defendant's address, where the plaintiff's accident occurred.

See notes under FORM 6H:2.

{*ADD TO STANDARD REQUESTS FOR ADMISSIONS – FORM 6H:2*}

{*Depending on the discovery-control plan, parties may be limited to 15 requests. See the first note under FORM 6H:2.*}

REQUEST 13: Plaintiff noticed the substance on the floor before the accident occurred.

RESPONSE:

REQUEST 14: Plaintiff had a preexisting injury at the time of the accident.

RESPONSE:

REQUEST 15: Plaintiff was aware of warning signs posted in the area where the accident occurred.

RESPONSE:

REQUEST 16: Plaintiff was notified by defendant of the condition of the floor before the accident occurred.

RESPONSE:

REQUEST 17: Plaintiff was carrying {❶ *describe what plaintiff was carrying*} at the time the accident occurred.

RESPONSE:

REQUEST 18: Plaintiff was holding on to {❷ *describe object plaintiff was holding on to*} at the time the accident occurred.

RESPONSE:

REQUEST 19: Plaintiff was under the influence of drugs or alcohol when the accident occurred.

RESPONSE:

REQUEST 20: Plaintiff had ingested or consumed drugs or alcohol within the 24 hours before the accident occurred.

RESPONSE:

Continued on next page

REQUEST 21: Plaintiff caused the substance to be on the floor.

RESPONSE:

REQUEST 22: Plaintiff was on defendant's premises for the specific business purpose of {❸ *identify reason*}.

RESPONSE:

REQUEST 23: Plaintiff's business purpose for being on defendant's premises had ended at the time the accident occurred.

RESPONSE:

REQUEST 24: Plaintiff was using a mobile device at the time the accident occurred.

RESPONSE:

REQUEST 25: Plaintiff was {❹ *describe activity, e.g., listening to music through headphones, reading a magazine, running*} at the time the accident occurred.

RESPONSE:

REQUEST 26: Plaintiff was in {❺ *state unauthorized area where accident occurred, e.g., loading dock area*}, an unauthorized area on defendant's premises, at the time the accident occurred.

RESPONSE:

SEE: Tex. R. Civ. P. 198
O'Connor's Texas Rules * Civil Trials (2019), "Requests for Admissions," ch. 6-H, p. 671
O'Connor's Texas Causes of Action (2019), "Liability to Invitees," ch. 23-B, p. 827

ADD TO: STANDARD REQUESTS FOR ADMISSIONS – FORM 6H:2

NOTE: Include in the cover sheet that the definition of the word "premises" is the premises at the defendant's address, where the plaintiff's accident occurred.

See notes under FORM 6H:2.

{ADD TO STANDARD REQUESTS FOR ADMISSIONS – FORM 6H:2}

{Depending on the discovery-control plan, parties may be limited to 15 requests. See the first note under FORM 6H:2.}

REQUEST 13: On {❶ *date*}, plaintiff {❷ *purchased/leased*} the {❸ *describe goods or services*} from defendant.

RESPONSE:

REQUEST 14: Defendant represented to plaintiff that {❹ *specify each representation plaintiff contends defendant made that was false, misleading, or deceptive*}.

RESPONSE:

REQUEST 15: Defendant knew that {❺ *specify representations*} were false when {❻ *he/she/it*} made them.

RESPONSE:

REQUEST 16: Defendant warranted to plaintiff that {❼ *identify express warranty plaintiff contends defendant breached*}.

RESPONSE:

REQUEST 17: After plaintiff {❽ *purchased/leased*} the {❾ *describe goods or services*}, plaintiff complained to defendant that {❿ *identify defects in goods or services about which plaintiff complained to defendant*}.

RESPONSE:

REQUEST 18: Defendant did not correct the defects in the {⓫ *describe goods or services*} of which plaintiff complained.

RESPONSE:

REQUEST 19: Plaintiff is a consumer under the Deceptive Trade Practices Act.

RESPONSE:

REQUEST 20: Plaintiff gave defendant proper presuit notice before filing suit, as required by the Deceptive Trade Practices Act.

RESPONSE:

◄ *Continued on next page* ►

REQUEST 21: Defendant did not tender to plaintiff, within 30 days of receiving the presuit notice, the claimed amount of plaintiff's economic damages, mental-anguish damages, and expenses, including attorney fees, reasonably incurred in asserting the claim.

RESPONSE:

REQUEST 22: Plaintiff did not waive the provisions of the Deceptive Trade Practices Act.

RESPONSE:

REQUEST 23: Defendant is not exempt from suit under the Deceptive Trade Practices Act.

RESPONSE:

SEE: Tex. R. Civ. P. 198
Tex. Bus. & Com. Code §17.41 et seq.
O'Connor's Texas Rules * Civil Trials (2019), "Requests for Admissions," ch. 6-H, p. 671
O'Connor's Texas Causes of Action (2019), "Deceptive Trade Practices Act," ch. 8, p. 209

ADD TO: STANDARD REQUESTS FOR ADMISSIONS – FORM 6H:2

NOTE: See notes under FORM 6H:2.

{ADD TO STANDARD REQUESTS FOR ADMISSIONS – FORM 6H:2}

{Depending on the discovery-control plan, parties may be limited to 15 requests. See the first note under FORM 6H:2.}

REQUEST 13: When plaintiff {❶ *purchased/leased*} the {❷ *describe goods or services*}, defendant did not make any representations regarding {❸ *specify representations plaintiff alleged were false, misleading, or deceptive*}.

RESPONSE:

REQUEST 14: Plaintiff did not rely on defendant's knowledge, ability, or experience to {❹ *purchase/lease*} the {❺ *describe goods or services*}.

RESPONSE:

REQUEST 15: There is not a gross disparity between the value plaintiff received and the consideration paid for the {❻ *describe goods or services*}.

RESPONSE:

REQUEST 16: Plaintiff is not claiming {❼ *he/she*} suffered a physical injury, illness, or condition resulting directly or indirectly from the {❽ *purchase/lease*} of the {❾ *describe goods or services*}.

RESPONSE:

REQUEST 17: Defendant did not warrant to plaintiff that {❿ *identify express warranty plaintiff contends defendant made and breached*}.

RESPONSE:

REQUEST 18: After plaintiff {⓫ *purchased/leased*} the {⓬ *describe goods or services*} and complained of defects in {⓭ *it/them*} to defendant, defendant corrected the defects in the {⓮ *describe goods or services*}.

RESPONSE:

REQUEST 19: Plaintiff is not a consumer under the Deceptive Trade Practices Act.

RESPONSE:

◄ *Continued on next page* ►

REQUEST 20: Plaintiff did not give defendant proper presuit notice before filing suit, as required by the Deceptive Trade Practices Act.

RESPONSE:

REQUEST 21: Defendant tendered to plaintiff, within 30 days of receiving the presuit notice, the claimed amount of plaintiff's economic damages, mental-anguish damages, and expenses, including attorney fees, reasonably incurred in asserting the claim.

RESPONSE:

SEE: Tex. R. Civ. P. 198
Tex. Bus. & Com. Code §17.41 et seq.
O'Connor's Texas Rules * Civil Trials (2019), "Requests for Admissions," ch. 6-H, p. 671
O'Connor's Texas Causes of Action (2019), "Deceptive Trade Practices Act," ch. 8, p. 209

ADD TO: STANDARD REQUESTS FOR ADMISSIONS – FORM 6H:2

NOTE: See notes under FORM 6H:2.

{[1] *PARTY*}'S MOTION TO DEEM ANSWERS ADMITTED

{[2] *Party*}, {[3] *name*}, asks the Court to deem answers admitted, as allowed by Texas Rule of Civil Procedure 215.4. {*See **O'Connor's Texas Rules**, "Challenging the Response," ch. 6-H, §5, p. 675; "Motion to deem," ch. 6-H, §6.2, p. 676.*}

INTRODUCTION

1. Plaintiff, {[4] *name*}, sued defendant, {[5] *name*}, for {[6] *state basis of suit*}.

2. Discovery in this suit is governed by a Level {[7] *1/2/3*} discovery-control plan. The discovery period {[8] *will end/ended*} on {[9] *date*}. {*See **O'Connor's Texas Rules**, "Discovery-Control Plans," ch. 6-A, §7, p. 520.*}

3. This case is set for trial on {[10] *date*}.

4. {[11] *State other relevant facts about the suit.*}

BACKGROUND

5. On {[12] *date*}, {[13] *party*} served {[14] *his/her/its*} request for admissions on {[15] *adverse party*}, {[16] *name*}. The request for admissions is attached as Exhibit {[17] *letter*}. On {[18] *date*}, {[19] *adverse party*} timely served a response to the request. The response to the request for admissions is attached as Exhibit {[20] *letter*}.

6. {[21] *State other facts relevant to the motion.*}

ARGUMENT & AUTHORITIES

7. A court may deem timely served responses to a request for admissions admitted if the court finds the answers are evasive or incomplete or the responding party did not comply with the requirements of Texas Rule of Civil Procedure 198. Tex. R. Civ. P. 215.4(a); *In re RLS Legal Sols., L.L.C.*, 156 S.W.3d 160, 165-66 (Tex. App.—Beaumont 2005, orig. proceeding). {*See **O'Connor's Texas Rules**, "Challenging response to requests," ch. 6-H, §5.1, p. 675; "Necessary," ch. 6-H, §6.2.2, p. 676.*}

{*CHOOSE APPROPRIATE PARAGRAPHS 8-13*}

8. {[22] *Party*} asks the Court to grant {[23] *his/her/its*} motion to deem answers admitted because {[24] *adverse party*}'s response to request for admission {[25] *number*} is {[26] *evasive/incomplete*}. Tex. R. Civ. P. 215.4(a). {[27] *Elaborate.*} {*See **O'Connor's Texas Rules**, "Evasive answer," ch. 6-H, §5.1.1(1), p. 675.*}

◄ *Continued on next page* ►

9. {28 *Party*} asks the Court to grant {29 *his/her/its*} motion to deem answers admitted because {30 *adverse party*}'s {31 *qualified answer/denial in part*} to request for admission {32 *number*} was not made in good faith. *See* Tex. R. Civ. P. 198.2(b). {33 *Elaborate.*}

10. {34 *Party*} asks the Court to grant {35 *his/her/its*} motion to deem answers admitted because {36 *adverse party*}'s response to request for admission {37 *number*} is not proper. *See* Tex. R. Civ. P. 198.2(b). Specifically, {38 *adverse party*} stated that {39 *he/she/it*} lacked sufficient information or knowledge to admit or deny the request but did not state that a reasonable inquiry was made and that the information known or easily obtainable was insufficient to enable {40 *adverse party*} to admit or deny the request. {*See* ***O'Connor's Texas Rules**, "Refusal to answer," ch. 6-H, §5.1.1(3), p. 675.*}

11. {41 *Party*} asks the Court to grant {42 *his/her/its*} motion to deem answers admitted because {43 *adverse party*}'s objection to request for admission {44 *number*} is not proper. *See* Tex. R. Civ. P. 198.2(b). Specifically, {45 *adverse party*} stated that the request presents an issue for trial. *See id.*

12. {46 *Party*} asks the Court to grant {47 *his/her/its*} motion to deem answers admitted because {48 *adverse party*}'s objection to request for admission {49 *number*} is not proper. *See* Tex. R. Civ. P. 198.2(b). Specifically, {50 *adverse party*} stated that {51 *identify adverse party's invalid objection, e.g., the request relates to statements of opinion or of fact*}. {52 *Elaborate.*} {*See* ***O'Connor's Texas Rules**, "Invalid objections," ch. 6-H, §4.2.5(1)(b), p. 674; "Challenging objections," ch. 6-H, §5.1.2, p. 675.*}

13. {53 *Adverse party*}'s noncompliance with the discovery request thwarts {54 *party*}'s discovery efforts, prevents effective trial preparation, and conceals relevant facts. {55 *Party*} has incurred the cost of preparing and filing this motion to force {56 *adverse party*} to comply with the rules. {57 *Party*} attaches to this motion {58 *his/her/its*} affidavit for attorney fees and costs as Exhibit {59 *letter*} and incorporates it by reference.

CONCLUSION

14. {60 *Briefly summarize the motion.*}

PRAYER

15. For these reasons, {61 *party*} asks the Court to set this motion for hearing and, after the hearing and receiving evidence, to grant the motion to deem {62 *adverse party*}'s answers to requests for admissions {63 *numbers*} admitted {64 *add if appropriate: , and to award {party} attorney fees and costs*}.

SEE: Tex. R. Civ. P. 198, 215.4
O'Connor's Texas Rules * Civil Trials (2019), "Challenging the Response," ch. 6-H, §5, p. 675; "Deemed Admissions," ch. 6-H, §6, p. 675

ADD: STYLE OF THE CASE – FORM 1B:2
SIGNATURE BLOCK – FORM 1B:3
CERTIFICATE OF CONFERENCE – FORM 1B:12
CERTIFICATE OF SERVICE – FORM 1B:13

ATTACH: AFFIDAVIT – FORM 1B:8, if necessary
NOTICE OF HEARING OR SUBMISSION – FORM 1E:1
AFFIDAVIT FOR ATTORNEY FEES – FORM 1H:14
ORDER – FORM 6H:16
Request for admissions
Responses to the request for admissions

{1 *PARTY*}'S RESPONSE TO
{2 *ADVERSE PARTY*}'S MOTION TO DEEM ANSWERS ADMITTED

{3 *Party*}, {4 *name*}, asks the Court to deny {5 *adverse party*} {6 *name*}'s motion to deem answers admitted. {*See* ***O'Connor's Texas Rules****, "Response to motion to deem," ch. 6-H, §6.3, p. 676.*}

INTRODUCTION

1. Plaintiff, {7 *name*}, sued defendant, {8 *name*}, for {9 *state basis of suit*}.

2. Discovery in this suit is governed by a Level {10 *1/2/3*} discovery-control plan. The discovery period {11 *will end/ended*} on {12 *date*}. {*See* ***O'Connor's Texas Rules****, "Discovery-Control Plans," ch. 6-A, §7, p. 520.*}

3. This case is set for trial on {13 *date*}.

4. {14 *State other relevant facts about the suit.*}

BACKGROUND

5. On {15 *date*}, {16 *adverse party*} served {17 *his/her/its*} request for admissions on {18 *party*}. On {19 *date*}, {20 *party*} timely served a response to the request. {21 *Adverse party*} now asks the Court to deem {22 *party*}'s answers admitted.

6. {23 *State other facts relevant to the response.*}

ARGUMENT & AUTHORITIES

{*CHOOSE APPROPRIATE PARAGRAPHS 7-11*}

7. The Court should deny {24 *adverse party*}'s motion to deem answers admitted because {25 *party*}'s response to request for admission {26 *number*} is not {27 *evasive/incomplete*}. Tex. R. Civ. P. 215.4(a). {28 *Refute adverse party's basis for request to deem answer admitted.*} {*See* ***O'Connor's Texas Rules****, "Evasive answer," ch. 6-H, §5.1.1(1), p. 675.*}

8. The Court should deny {29 *adverse party*}'s motion to deem answers admitted because {30 *party*}'s {31 *qualified answer/denial in part*} in response to request for admission {32 *number*} was made in good faith. Tex. R. Civ. P. 198.2(b). {33 *State facts establishing good faith and refute adverse party's basis for request to deem answer admitted.*} {*See* ***O'Connor's Texas Rules****, "Denials," ch. 6-H, §4.2.2, p. 673.*}

9. The Court should deny {❸❹ *adverse party*}'s motion to deem answers admitted because {❸❺ *party*}'s response to request for admission {❸❻ *number*} is proper; {❸❼ *party*} made a reasonable inquiry, but the information known or easily obtainable was insufficient to enable {❸❽ *party*} to admit or deny the request. Tex. R. Civ. P. 198.2(b). {❸❾ *State facts and attach affidavits establishing that party made a reasonable inquiry and explain that the omission of a statement of reasonable inquiry was not intentional. See State v. Carrillo, 885 S.W.2d 212, 215 (Tex. App.—San Antonio 1994, no writ). If necessary, refute any additional facts relied on by adverse party as a basis for the request to deem answer admitted.*} {*See* ***O'Connor's Texas Rules****, "Lack of information," ch. 6-H, §4.2.4, p. 674.*}

10. Although {❹⓪ *party*}'s response to request for admission {❹❶ *number*} is not proper because {❹❷ *party*} stated that the request presents an issue for trial, the Court should not deem the answer admitted for the following reasons: {❹❸ *identify other valid objections to request for admissions*}. {*See* ***O'Connor's Texas Rules****, "Objections," ch. 6-H, §4.2.5(1), p. 674.*}

11. Although {❹❹ *party*}'s response to request for admission {❹❺ *number*} is not proper because {❹❻ *party*} stated that {❹❼ *identify party's objection to the request*}, the Court should not deem the answer admitted for the following reasons: {❹❽ *identify other valid objections to request for admissions*}. {*See* ***O'Connor's Texas Rules****, "Objections," ch. 6-H, §4.2.5(1), p. 674.*}

12. If the Court determines that {❹❾ *party*}'s answers to the request for admissions were evasive, incomplete, or improper or do not comply with the requirements of Texas Rule of Civil Procedure 198, before the Court deems the answer admitted, {❺⓪ *party*} requests permission to serve amended answers. *See* Tex. R. Civ. P. 215.4(a) (court may order either that the matter is admitted or that an amended answer be served); *Trans-American Nat. Gas Corp. v. Powell*, 811 S.W.2d 913, 917 (Tex. 1991) (courts must consider the availability of less stringent sanctions). {*See* ***O'Connor's Texas Rules****, "Amending or withdrawing answers," ch. 6-H, §4.3, p. 674.*}

CONCLUSION

13. {❺❶ *Briefly summarize the response.*}

PRAYER

14. For these reasons, {❺❷ *party*} asks the Court either to deny the motion to deem answers admitted or to sign an order allowing {❺❸ *party*} to amend {❺❹ *his/her/its*} answers to {❺❺ *adverse party*}'s request for admissions.

Continued on next page

TEXAS CIVIL FORMS

CHAPTER 6. DISCOVERY

FORM 6H:15 RESPONSE TO MOTION TO DEEM ANSWERS ADMITTED

SEE: Tex. R. Civ. P. 198, 215.4(a)
O'Connor's Texas Rules * Civil Trials (2019), "Deemed Admissions," ch. 6-H, §6, p. 675

ADD: STYLE OF THE CASE – FORM 1B:2
SIGNATURE BLOCK – FORM 1B:3
CERTIFICATE OF SERVICE – FORM 1B:13

ATTACH: AFFIDAVIT – FORM 1B:8, if necessary
ORDER – FORM 6H:16

ORDER ON {❶ *PARTY*}'S MOTION TO DEEM ANSWERS ADMITTED

After considering {❷ *party*} {❸ *name*}'s motion to deem answers admitted, the response, and arguments of counsel, the Court

{*CHOOSE APPROPRIATE ORDER*}

DENIES the motion.

ORDERS that {❹ *adverse party*}, {❺ *name*}, serve an amended response to {❻ *party*}'s request for admissions by {❼ *date*}.

GRANTS the motion and deems {❽ *adverse party*} {❾ *name*}'s responses to {❿ *party*}'s requests for admissions {⓫ *numbers*} admitted.

{*INSERT IF APPROPRIATE*}

ORDERS {⓬ *adverse party*} to pay {⓭ *party*} ${⓮ *amount*} for attorney fees and ${⓯ *amount*} for court costs incurred in preparing and filing the motion.

SIGNED on ____________________, 20___.

____
PRESIDING JUDGE

SEE: Tex. R. Civ. P. 198, 215.4(a)
O'Connor's Texas Rules * Civil Trials (2019), "Deemed Admissions," ch. 6-H, §6, p. 675

ADD: STYLE OF THE CASE – FORM 1B:2
CERTIFICATE OF SERVICE – FORM 1B:13, if proposed order served separately from motion or response

{1 *PARTY*}'S MOTION TO STRIKE DEEMED ADMISSIONS

{2 *Party*}, {3 *name*}, asks the Court to strike deemed admissions, as allowed by Texas Rule of Civil Procedure 198.3. {*See* ***O'Connor's Texas Rules****, "Motion to strike deemed admissions," ch. 6-H, §7.2.2, p. 676.*}

INTRODUCTION

1. Plaintiff, {4 *name*}, sued defendant, {5 *name*}, for {6 *state basis of suit*}.

2. Discovery in this suit is governed by a Level {7 *1/2/3*} discovery-control plan. The discovery period {8 *will end/ended*} on {9 *date*}. {*See* ***O'Connor's Texas Rules****, "Discovery-Control Plans," ch. 6-A, §7, p. 520.*}

3. This case is set for trial on {10 *date*}.

4. {11 *State other relevant facts about the suit.*}

BACKGROUND

5. On {12 *date*}, {13 *adverse party*}, {14 *name*}, served {15 *his/her/its*} request for admissions on {16 *party*}. The request for admissions is attached as Exhibit {17 *letter*}. {18 *Party*} did not timely serve a response to the request. A copy of {19 *party*}'s response is attached as Exhibit {20 *letter*}. Because the response was untimely, the requests were deemed admitted. {*See* ***O'Connor's Texas Rules****, "Answer deemed admitted," ch. 6-H, §6.1, p. 675.*}

6. There is good cause for the Court to strike the deemed admissions. Therefore, {21 *party*} asks the Court to strike the admissions and allow {22 *him/her/it*} to serve the attached responses.

7. {23 *State other facts relevant to the motion.*}

ARGUMENT & AUTHORITIES

8. A court may strike or allow a party to withdraw or amend its admissions if there is good cause and no undue prejudice to the adverse party. Tex. R. Civ. P. 198.3; *Marino v. King*, 355 S.W.3d 629, 633 (Tex. 2011); *Wheeler v. Green*, 157 S.W.3d 439, 442 (Tex. 2005); *Wal-Mart Stores, Inc. v. Deggs*, 968 S.W.2d 354, 356 (Tex. 1998). Good cause may be mere accident or mistake. *Marino*, 355 S.W.3d at 633; *Wheeler*, 157 S.W.3d at 442; *Wal-Mart Stores*, 968 S.W.2d at 356. {*See* ***O'Connor's Texas Rules****, "Motion to strike deemed admissions," ch. 6-H, §7.2.2, p. 676.*}

9. {㉔ *Party*}'s untimely serving of responses on {㉕ *adverse party*} was not intentional. Rather, {㉖ *show good cause for why party did not timely serve responses, e.g., calendaring mistake, drafted and typed responses and then inadvertently did not serve adverse party*}.

10. {㉗ *Party*} first became aware the responses were overdue on {㉘ *date*}. As soon as {㉙ *party*} discovered this, {㉚ *he/she/it*} filed this motion to strike along with the attached responses. {*See **O'Connor's Texas Rules**, "Deemed admissions set aside," ch. 6-H, §7.2.6(1), p. 679.*}

11. {㉛ *Adverse party*} will not be unduly prejudiced if the Court strikes the admissions. {㉜ *Elaborate.*}

12. If the Court strikes the admissions and allows {㉝ *party*} to serve the attached responses, the case will be resolved on the merits instead of by procedural default. Tex. R. Civ. P. 198.3(b); *see Wheeler*, 157 S.W.3d at 443 n.2; *In re Kellogg-Brown & Root, Inc.*, 45 S.W.3d 772, 777 (Tex. App.—Tyler 2001, orig. proceeding). {㉞ *Elaborate.*} {*See **O'Connor's Texas Rules**, "Presentation of merits will suffer if motion denied," ch. 6-H, §7.2.2(3), p. 678.*}

CONCLUSION

13. Because there is good cause for the Court to strike the admissions, and because {㉟ *adverse party*} will not be unduly prejudiced, the Court should strike the admissions and allow {㊱ *party*} to serve the attached responses.

PRAYER

14. For these reasons, {㊲ *party*} asks the Court to set this motion for hearing and, after the hearing and receiving evidence, to grant the motion to strike and allow {㊳ *party*} to serve the attached responses.

SEE: Tex. R. Civ. P. 198
O'Connor's Texas Rules * Civil Trials (2019), "Strike deemed admissions," ch. 6-H, §7.2, p. 676

ADD: STYLE OF THE CASE – FORM 1B:2
SIGNATURE BLOCK – FORM 1B:3
CERTIFICATE OF CONFERENCE – FORM 1B:12
CERTIFICATE OF SERVICE – FORM 1B:13

ATTACH: AFFIDAVIT – FORM 1B:8, if necessary
NOTICE OF HEARING OR SUBMISSION – FORM 1E:1
ORDER – FORM 1G:1
Request for admissions
Responses to the request for admissions

Continued on next page

NOTE: When merits-preclusive admissions (i.e., admissions that essentially ask a party to admit it has no cause of action or ground of defense) are deemed, it is unclear whether the party moving to strike the deemed admissions has the burden of proving no undue prejudice or the opposing party has the burden of proving undue prejudice. *See* ***In re Sewell***, 472 S.W.3d 449, 456 n.3 (Tex.App.—Texarkana 2015, orig. proceeding) (Supreme Court has not decided whether movant must show that striking merits-preclusive deemed admissions will not unduly prejudice nonmovant or whether nonmovant must show that it will be unduly prejudiced if admissions are struck), *disapproved on other grounds*, ***In re Bayview Loan Servicing, LLC***, 532 S.W.3d 510 (Tex.App.—Texarkana 2017, orig. proceeding); *see, e.g.*, ***Ramirez v. Noble Energy, Inc.***, 521 S.W.3d 851, 861-62 (Tex.App.—Houston [1st Dist.] 2017, no pet.) (motion to withdraw deemed admissions should have been granted when nonmovant did not prove bad faith or callous disregard and presented no evidence that withdrawal would cause it undue prejudice); ***Time Warner, Inc. v. Gonzalez***, 441 S.W.3d 661, 667 (Tex.App.—San Antonio 2014, pet. denied) (nonmovant argued that striking admissions would cause him undue prejudice). Until the issue of who has the burden is decided, both parties should address undue prejudice. See ***O'Connor's Texas Rules***, "Merits-preclusive deemed admissions," ch. 6-H, §7.2.2(1)(b), p. 676.

{1 *PARTY*}'S RESPONSE TO
{2 *ADVERSE PARTY*}'S MOTION TO STRIKE DEEMED ADMISSIONS

{3 *Party*}, {4 *name*}, asks the Court to deny {5 *adverse party*} {6 *name*}'s motion to strike deemed admissions.

INTRODUCTION

1. Plaintiff, {7 *name*}, sued defendant, {8 *name*}, for {9 *state basis of suit*}.

2. Discovery in this suit is governed by a Level {10 *1/2/3*} discovery-control plan. The discovery period {11 *will end/ended*} on {12 *date*}. {*See* ***O'Connor's Texas Rules****, "Discovery-Control Plans," ch. 6-A, §7, p. 520.*}

3. This case is set for trial on {13 *date*}.

4. {14 *State other relevant facts about the suit.*}

BACKGROUND

5. On {15 *date*}, {16 *party*} served {17 *his/her/its*} request for admissions on {18 *adverse party*}. Although {19 *number*} days passed, {20 *adverse party*} did not serve responses to the requests, and the requests were deemed admitted. {21 *Adverse party*} now asks the Court to strike the deemed admissions.

6. {22 *State other facts relevant to the response.*}

ARGUMENT & AUTHORITIES

{*CHOOSE APPROPRIATE PARAGRAPHS 7-8*}

{*If deemed admissions are not merits-preclusive*}

7. Before striking a party's deemed admissions or allowing a party to withdraw its admissions, a court must find that there is good cause and no undue prejudice to the adverse party. Tex. R. Civ. P. 198.3; *Marino v. King*, 355 S.W.3d 629, 633 (Tex. 2011); *Wheeler v. Green*, 157 S.W.3d 439, 442 (Tex. 2005); *Wal-Mart Stores, Inc. v. Deggs*, 968 S.W.2d 354, 356 (Tex. 1998). {*See* ***O'Connor's Texas Rules****, "Motion to strike deemed admissions," ch. 6-H, §7.2.2, p. 676.*}

8. In this case, there is no good cause supporting {23 *adverse party*}'s request to strike the admissions. In its motion to strike, {24 *adverse party*} alleged {25 *summarize reasons asserted by adverse party that constitute good cause*}. However, {26 *argue why this is not good cause or dispute adverse party's factual allegations, e.g., adverse party knew the requests had been served and refused to serve responses until a motion for summary judgment was filed*}.

◄ *Continued on next page* ►

{*If deemed admissions are merits-preclusive*}

7. Before striking a party's deemed admissions or allowing a party to withdraw its admissions, a court must find that there is good cause and no undue prejudice to the adverse party. Tex. R. Civ. P. 198.3; *Marino v. King*, 355 S.W.3d 629, 633 (Tex. 2011); *Wheeler v. Green*, 157 S.W.3d 439, 442 (Tex. 2005); *Wal-Mart Stores, Inc. v. Deggs*, 968 S.W.2d 354, 356 (Tex. 1998). The adverse party can prove there is no good cause for striking the deemed admissions by showing that the party moving to strike acted in flagrant bad faith or with callous disregard for the rules of civil procedure. *Time Warner, Inc. v. Gonzalez*, 441 S.W.3d 661, 666 (Tex. App.—San Antonio 2014, pet. denied); *see Marino*, 355 S.W.3d at 634. Bad faith is conscious wrongdoing for a dishonest, discriminatory, or malicious purpose. *Ramirez v. Noble Energy, Inc.*, 521 S.W.3d 851, 857 (Tex. App.—Houston [1st Dist.] 2017, no pet.); *Time Warner*, 441 S.W.3d at 666. {*See* ***O'Connor's Texas Rules***, *"Merits-preclusive deemed admissions," ch. 6-H, §7.2.4(2), p. 678.*}

8. In this case, there is no good cause supporting {㉗ *adverse party*}'s request to strike the deemed admissions because {㉘ *adverse party*} acted {㉙ *in flagrant bad faith/with callous disregard for the rules of civil procedure*}. In its motion to strike, {㉚ *adverse party*} alleged {㉛ *summarize reasons asserted by adverse party that allegedly constitute good cause*}. However, {㉜ *explain how adverse party acted in flagrant bad faith or with callous disregard for the rules*}.

9. {㉝ *Party*} will be unduly prejudiced if the Court strikes the admissions because {㉞ *explain*}.

CONCLUSION

{*CHOOSE APPROPRIATE PARAGRAPH 10*}

10. Because there is no good cause for the Court to strike the admissions, and because {㉟ *party*} will be unduly prejudiced if the Court does, the Court should deny the motion to strike and allow the admissions to stand.

10. Because {㊱ *adverse party*} acted {㊲ *in flagrant bad faith/with callous disregard for the rules of civil procedure*}, and because {㊳ *party*} will be unduly prejudiced if the Court strikes the admissions, the Court should deny the motion to strike and allow the admissions to stand.

PRAYER

11. For these reasons, {㊴ *party*} asks the Court to deny the motion to strike and allow the admissions to stand.

FORM 6H:18 RESPONSE TO MOTION TO STRIKE DEEMED ADMISSIONS

SEE: Tex. R. Civ. P. 198
O'Connor's Texas Rules * Civil Trials (2019), "Strike deemed admissions," ch. 6-H, §7.2, p. 676

ADD: STYLE OF THE CASE – FORM 1B:2
SIGNATURE BLOCK – FORM 1B:3
CERTIFICATE OF SERVICE – FORM 1B:13

ATTACH: AFFIDAVIT – FORM 1B:8, if necessary
ORDER – FORM 1G:1

NOTE: When a party attempts to use requests for admissions to compromise the other party's right to present the merits of the case (i.e., essentially asking the party to admit it has no cause of action or ground of defense), due process is implicated. *See* ***Marino v. King***, 355 S.W.3d 629, 634 (Tex.2011); ***Time Warner, Inc. v. Gonzalez***, 441 S.W.3d 661, 666 (Tex.App.—San Antonio 2014, pet. denied). Because merits-preclusive admissions implicate due-process concerns, courts must presume that requests for admissions are merits-preclusive unless the record affirmatively establishes that they are not. ***Ramirez v. Noble Energy, Inc.***, 521 S.W.3d 851, 858 (Tex.App.—Houston [1st Dist.] 2017, no pet.); ***In re Sewell***, 472 S.W.3d 449, 461 (Tex.App.—Texarkana 2015, orig. proceeding), *disapproved on other grounds*, ***In re Bayview Loan Servicing, LLC***, 532 S.W.3d 510 (Tex.App.—Texarkana 2017, orig. proceeding). For an opposing party to establish that the deemed admissions are not merits-preclusive, the record must show either that the admissions seek to authenticate or prove the admissibility of documents or that the admissions involve uncontroverted facts. ***Ramirez***, 521 S.W.3d at 858; ***In re Sewell***, 472 S.W.3d at 461.

When deemed admissions are merits-preclusive, the burden shifts to the party opposing the motion to strike to demonstrate that the moving party acted in flagrant bad faith or with callous disregard for the rules of civil procedure. *See* ***Marino***, 355 S.W.3d at 634; ***Time Warner***, 441 S.W.3d at 666. If the opposing party cannot demonstrate bad faith or callous disregard, the moving party is presumed to have established that there is good cause for granting the motion to strike and that presentation of the merits will be served. *See* ***In re Sewell***, 472 S.W.3d at 456.

When merits-preclusive admissions are deemed, it is unclear whether the party moving to strike the deemed admissions has the burden to prove no undue prejudice or the opposing party has the burden of proving undue prejudice. *See* ***In re Sewell***, 472 S.W.3d at 456 n.3 (Supreme Court has not decided whether movant must show that striking merits-preclusive deemed admissions will not unduly prejudice nonmovant or whether nonmovant must show that it will be unduly prejudiced if admissions are struck); *see, e.g.*, ***Ramirez***, 521 S.W.3d at 861-62 (motion to withdraw deemed admissions should have been granted when nonmovant did not prove bad faith or callous disregard and presented no evidence that withdrawal would cause it undue prejudice); ***Time Warner***, 441 S.W.3d at 667 (nonmovant argued that striking admissions would cause him undue prejudice). Until the issue of who has the burden is decided, both parties should address undue prejudice.

{❶ *PARTY*}'S {❷ *NUMBER*} REQUEST
FOR PRODUCTION TO {❸ *ADVERSE PARTY*}

To: {❹ *Adverse party*}, {❺ *name*}, by and through {❻ *his/her/its*} attorney of record, {❼ *name*}, {❽ *address*}.

{❾ *Party*}, {❿ *name*}, serves this request for production on {⓫ *adverse party*}, as allowed by Texas Rule of Civil Procedure 196. {⓬ *Adverse party*} must produce all requested documents (as they are kept in the ordinary course of business or organized and labeled to correspond with categories in each request) for inspection and copying, not more than 30 days after service, at {⓭ *specify location where adverse party is to produce documents*}. {*See* ***O'Connor's Texas Rules****, "Procedure," ch. 6-I, §3.1, p. 681.*}

INSTRUCTIONS

1. Answer each request for documents separately by listing the documents and by describing them as defined below. If documents produced in response to this request are numbered for production, in each response provide both the information that identifies the document and the document's number.

2. For a document that no longer exists or that cannot be located, identify the document, state how and when it passed out of existence or could no longer be located, and the reasons for the disappearance. Also, identify each person having knowledge about the disposition or loss of the document, and identify any other document evidencing the lost document's existence or any facts about the lost document.

a. When identifying the document, you must state the following:

(1) The nature of the document (e.g., letter, handwritten note).

(2) The title or heading that appears on the document.

(3) The date of the document and the date of each addendum, supplement, or other addition or change.

(4) The identities of the author, signer of the document, and person on whose behalf or at whose request or direction the document was prepared or delivered.

b. When identifying the person, you must state the following:

(1) The full name.

(2) The present or last known residential address and residential telephone number.

(3) The present or last known office address and office telephone number.

(4) The present occupation, job title, employer, and employer's address.

DEFINITIONS

1. "Plaintiff" or "defendant," as well as a party's full or abbreviated name or a pronoun referring to a party, means the party, and when applicable, the party's agents, representatives, officers, directors, employees, partners, corporate agents, subsidiaries, affiliates, or any other person acting in concert with the party or under the party's control, whether directly or indirectly, including any attorney.

2. "You" or "your" means {⓮ *adverse party*}, {⓯ *name*}, {⓰ *his/her/its*} successors, predecessors, divisions, subsidiaries, present and former officers, agents, employees, and all other persons acting on behalf of {⓱ *adverse party*} or {⓲ *his/her/its*} successors, predecessors, divisions, and subsidiaries.

3. "Document" means all written, typed, or printed matter and all magnetic, electronic, or other records or documentation of any kind or description in your actual possession, custody, or control, including those in the possession, custody, or control of any and all present or former directors, officers, employees, consultants, accountants, attorneys, or other agents, whether or not prepared by you, that constitute or contain matters relevant to the subject matter of the action. "Document" includes, but is not limited to, the following: letters, reports, charts, diagrams, correspondence, telegrams, memoranda, notes, records, minutes, contracts, agreements, records or notations of telephone or personal conversations or conferences, interoffice communications, e-mail, microfilm, bulletins, circulars, pamphlets, photographs, faxes, invoices, tape recordings, computer printouts, drafts, résumés, logs, worksheets, {⓳ *continue listing examples as necessary*}.

4. "Electronic or magnetic data" means electronic information that is stored in a medium from which it can be retrieved and examined. The term refers to the original (or identical duplicate when the original is not available) and any other copies of the data that may have attached comments, notes, marks, or highlighting of any kind. Electronic or magnetic data includes, but is not limited to, the following: computer programs; operating systems; computer activity logs; programming notes or instructions; e-mail receipts, messages, or transmissions; output resulting from the use of any software program, including word-processing documents, spreadsheets, database files, charts, graphs, and outlines; metadata; PIF and PDF files; batch files; deleted files; temporary files; Internet- or web-browser-generated information stored in textual, graphical, or audio format, including history files, caches, and cookies; {⓴ *continue listing examples*

◄ *Continued on next page* ►

as necessary}; and any miscellaneous files or file fragments. Electronic or magnetic data includes any items stored on magnetic, optical, digital, or other electronic-storage media, such as hard drives, floppy disks, CD-ROMs, DVDs, tapes, smart cards, integrated-circuit cards (e.g., SIM cards), removable media (e.g., Zip drives, Jaz cartridges), microfiche, punched cards, {21 *continue listing examples as necessary*}. Electronic or magnetic data also includes the file, folder, tabs, containers, and labels attached to or associated with any physical storage device with each original or copy.

5. "Possession, custody, or control" of an item means that the person either has physical possession of the item or has a right to possession equal or superior to that of the person who has physical possession of the item.

6. "Person" means any natural person, corporation, firm, association, partnership, joint venture, proprietorship, governmental body, or any other organization, business, or legal entity, and all predecessors or successors in interest.

7. "Mobile device" means any cellular telephone, satellite telephone, pager, personal digital assistant, handheld computer, electronic rolodex, walkie-talkie, or any combination of these devices.

SEE: Tex. R. Civ. P. 196
O'Connor's Texas Rules * Civil Trials (2019), "Securing Documents & Tangible Things," ch. 6-I, p. 681

ADD: STYLE OF THE CASE – FORM 1B:2
SIGNATURE BLOCK – FORM 1B:3
CERTIFICATE OF SERVICE – FORM 1B:13

NOTE: For most methods of service, the deadline for serving a request for production is 30 days before the end of the discovery period. Tex. R. Civ. P. 196.1(a). See ***O'Connor's Texas Rules***, "Discovery Periods," ch. 6-A, §8, p. 523. But when service is by mail or fax, the request should be served at least 33 days (if mailed) or 31 days (if faxed after 5:00 p.m.) before the end of the discovery period. *See* Tex. R. Civ. P. 21a(b)(2), (c). See ***O'Connor's Texas Rules***, "Deadline to serve response," ch. 6-A, §14.1, p. 527.

When a plaintiff serves its request for production with its petition, the request should be addressed to the defendant. In such a case, delete "by and through its attorney of record." When the plaintiff serves the request before the defendant's answer is due, the defendant has 50 days to respond rather than 30. Tex. R. Civ. P. 196.2(a).

A party seeking electronic information must specifically request it. Tex. R. Civ. P. 196.4 & cmt. 3. The request for production must specify the form in which the party wants the electronic information to be produced. Tex. R. Civ. P. 196.4 & cmt. 3. The request may ask for an opportunity to test or sample sources of electronic information to see if there is any relevant evidence. *See* Tex. R. Civ. P. 196.1(b). The request must also specify any extraordinary steps the producing party must take to retrieve, translate, and produce the electronic information. Tex. R. Civ. P. 196 cmt. 3. See ***O'Connor's Texas Rules***, "Request," ch. 6-C, §7.1.5(1), p. 605.

REQUEST FOR PRODUCTION

REQUEST 1: Produce {❶ *specify documents or other items to be produced or inspected, either by individual item or by category, and describe with reasonable particularity each item and category*}.

RESPONSE:

REQUEST 2: Produce the following {❷ *documents/tangible things*} for testing and sampling: {❸ *identify items for testing and sampling*}. The {❹ *documents/tangible things*} will be {❺ *sampled/tested*} by {❻ *describe specific means, manner, and procedure for testing or sampling and identify to what extent the testing or sampling will destroy the item*}.

RESPONSE:

REQUEST 3: Produce {❼ *medical/mental-health*} records regarding {❽ *name*}, a nonparty.

RESPONSE:

REQUEST 4: Produce all {❾ *electronic/magnetic*} data relating to {❿ *identify subject*} in the following form: {⓫ *specify the form in which data must be produced and any extraordinary steps necessary for retrieval and translation*}.

RESPONSE:

REQUEST 5: Produce any and all communications and documents sent to or received from, or exchanged by and between you and {⓬ *party*} and {⓭ *his/her/its*} agents, employees, or representatives concerning the subject matter of this lawsuit.

RESPONSE:

SEE: Tex. R. Civ. P. 196
O'Connor's Texas Rules * Civil Trials (2019), "Request," ch. 6-I, §3.2, p. 682

ADD: REQUESTS FOR PRODUCTION – FORMS 6I:4-11, as appropriate

ATTACH: COVER SHEET & DEFINITIONS – FORM 6I:1

◄ *Continued on next page* ►

NOTE: A party in a Level 1 case can serve no more than 15 written requests for production on any other party. Tex. R. Civ. P. 190.2(b)(4). There is no limit on the number of items a party can ask to have produced or the number of sets of requests a party can serve in a Level 2 or 3 case. *See* Tex. R. Civ. P. 190.3(b), 190.4(b), 196. However, in a Level 3 case, the discovery limitations of Level 1 or 2 apply—depending on the damages sought and issues involved—unless expressly changed by court order. *See* Tex. R. Civ. P. 190.4(b). Thus, a party in a Level 3 case may also be limited to 15 written requests for production.

Each discrete subpart of a request for production is considered a separate request for production. Tex. R. Civ. P. 190.2(b)(4).

Regarding request 3, when a party requests that another party produce the medical or mental-health records of a nonparty, the party who requests the records generally must serve the nonparty with the request for production under Texas Rule of Civil Procedure 21a. Tex. R. Civ. P. 196.1(c)(1); *see also* Tex. R. Civ. P. 196.1(c)(2) (exceptions to service requirement).

Regarding request 4, when a party requests that another party produce electronic information, the request must be clear and specific. Tex. R. Civ. P. 196.4; ***In re Weekley Homes, L.P.***, 295 S.W.3d 309, 314 (Tex.2009). For example, a party should expressly request deleted e-mails. ***In re Weekley Homes***, 295 S.W.3d at 314-15. See ***O'Connor's Texas Rules***, "Request," ch. 6-C, §7.1.5(1), p. 605.

A requesting party can move to compel production if a party or nonparty responding to the request refuses to produce the documents or tangible things. See FORM 6A:24.

{[1] *PARTY*}'S RESPONSES TO
{[2] *ADVERSE PARTY*}'S {[3] *NUMBER*} REQUEST FOR PRODUCTION

To: {[4] *Adverse party*}, {[5] *name*}, by and through {[6] *his/her/its*} attorney of record, {[7] *name*}, {[8] *address*}.

{[9] *Party*}, {[10] *name*}, serves these responses to {[11] *adverse party*}'s request for production. {*See* ***O'Connor's Texas Rules****, "Procedure to respond," ch. 6-I, §3.3, p. 683; "Contents of response," ch. 6-I, §3.4, p. 684.*}

RESPONSES TO REQUESTS

REQUEST 1: {[12] *Restate request.*}

{*CHOOSE APPROPRIATE RESPONSE*}

RESPONSE: The {[13] *identify requested action, e.g., production, inspection*} will be permitted as requested. Tex. R. Civ. P. 196.2(b)(1). {*See* ***O'Connor's Texas Rules****, "Party will comply," ch. 6-I, §3.4.1, p. 684.*}

RESPONSE: The following {[14] *documents/tangible things*} are produced as requested and are served with this response. Tex. R. Civ. P. 196.2(b)(2). {[15] *Provide a list of the documents or other items produced. If documents bear litigation numbers, provide them in the response. The documents must be organized as they are kept in the ordinary course of business or organized and labeled to correspond to the request.*} {*See* ***O'Connor's Texas Rules****, "Party will comply," ch. 6-I, §3.4.1, p. 684.*}

RESPONSE: Because this request requires the production of voluminous documents, they are not attached to this response. Instead, {[16] *party*} will provide {[17] *adverse party*} the opportunity to examine and copy the documents on {[18] *date*}, at {[19] *time*}, at {[20] *identify location*}. *See* Tex. R. Civ. P. 196.2(b)(3). {*See* ***O'Connor's Texas Rules****, "Objection to method of compliance," ch. 6-I, §3.4.2(2), p. 684.*}

RESPONSE: After a diligent search, no items have been identified that are responsive to the request. Tex. R. Civ. P. 196.2(b)(4).

RESPONSE: The following {[21] *electronic/magnetic*} data that are reasonably available to {[22] *party*} in {[23] *his/her/its*} ordinary course of business are produced as requested and are served with this response. Tex. R. Civ. P. 196.4. {[24] *Provide a list of the data produced in the form specified by the request.*} {*See* ***O'Connor's Texas Rules****, "Produce," ch. 6-C, §7.1.5(2)(a), p. 608; "Electronic or magnetic data," ch. 6-I, §3.4.1(3), p. 684.*}

Continued on next page

WITHHOLDING STATEMENT: Material or information responsive to this request is withheld under the {㉕ *identify privilege*}. Tex. R. Civ. P. 193.3(a). {*See **O'Connor's Texas Rules**, "Withholding statement," ch. 6-A, §2.8, p. 516; "Party asserts privileges," ch. 6-I, §3.4.5, p. 685.*}

OBJECTION: {㉖ *Party*} objects because the requests exceed the {㉗ *number*}-request limit for this Level {㉘ *1/3*} case. {㉙ *Elaborate.*} To the extent that {㉚ *party*} does not object to the discovery request, {㉛ *party*} serves the following answers: {㉜ *identify limit of compliance, e.g., party responds to the first 15 requests but refuses to answer the rest*}.

OBJECTION: {㉝ *Party*} objects to this request because {㉞ *state ground for objection*}. {㉟ *Elaborate.*} {㊱ *Party*} refuses to provide the information requested by request number {㊲ *number*}, concerning {㊳ *identify substance of request, e.g., criminal-activity reports for last 20 years for all of defendant's stores*}. {㊴ *Party*} refuses to provide

{*CHOOSE ONE OF THE FOLLOWING*}

Ⓐ some of the information requested by request number {㊵ *number*}. However, {㊶ *party*} will provide the information requested that is not subject to this objection. That is, {㊷ *party*} will provide {㊸ *identify limit of compliance, e.g., the criminal-activity reports for last five years for the store where plaintiff was assaulted*}. {*See **O'Connor's Texas Rules**, "Partial compliance necessary," ch. 6-A, §18.10.1, p. 538.*}

Ⓑ any of the information requested by request number {㊹ *number*} because it is unreasonable to do so before obtaining a ruling on the objection. {㊺ *Explain why it is unreasonable, e.g., the request requires a search of thousands of records.*} If {㊻ *party*} partially complies with this discovery request now, and later the Court rules that {㊼ *party*} must provide all the information requested, {㊽ *party*} would be required to conduct a duplicative and burdensome search of records. {*See **O'Connor's Texas Rules**, "No compliance necessary," ch. 6-A, §18.10.2, p. 538.*}

OBJECTION: {㊾ *Party*} objects to the request because it is not proportional to the needs of the case. *See* Tex. R. Civ. P. 192.4(b); *In re State Farm Lloyds*, 520 S.W.3d 595, 607 (Tex. 2017). {*See **O'Connor's Texas Rules**, "Proportional," ch. 6-B, §2.1.1(2), p. 555; "Proportional," ch. 6-C, §6.1.2, p. 602.*} Specifically, the request is not proportional for the following reasons:

{*CHOOSE APPROPRIATE REASONS*}

a. The likely benefits of the requested discovery are minimal, and therefore any enhanced effort or expense in producing the information is undue. *See* Tex. R. Civ. P. 192.4(b); *In re State Farm*, 520 S.W.3d at 608. {❺❿ *Elaborate.*}

b. The requested discovery is not justified considering the needs of the case. *See* Tex. R. Civ. P. 192.4(b); *In re State Farm*, 520 S.W.3d at 608. {51 *Elaborate.*}

c. The requested discovery is not justified based on the amount in controversy. *See* Tex. R. Civ. P. 192.4(b); *In re State Farm*, 520 S.W.3d at 610. {52 *Elaborate.*}

d. The requested discovery is not proportional to {53 *party*}'s resources. *See* Tex. R. Civ. P. 192.4(b); *In re State Farm*, 520 S.W.3d at 610-11. {54 *Explain how party's resources affect production, e.g., party does not have adequate resources to collect information and produce it in reasonably usable form.*}

e. The issues at stake are not of sufficient importance to justify the requested discovery. *See* Tex. R. Civ. P. 192.4(b); *In re State Farm*, 520 S.W.3d at 611. {55 *Elaborate.*}

f. The requested discovery is of low importance to resolving the issues in the case. *See* Tex. R. Civ. P. 192.4(b); *In re State Farm*, 520 S.W.3d at 611. {56 *Elaborate.*}

g. {57 *Identify any other reason that the requested discovery is not proportional to the needs of the case. See In re State Farm, 520 S.W.3d at 611-12.*}

OBJECTION: {58 *Party*} objects to the request because it seeks the discovery of data or information that exists in electronic or magnetic form but does not specify the type of data or information {59 *adverse party*} wants produced. Tex. R. Civ. P. 196.4; *see In re Shipman*, 540 S.W.3d 562, 566 (Tex. 2018); *In re Weekley Homes, L.P.*, 295 S.W.3d 309, 314-15 (Tex. 2009). {*See* ***O'Connor's Texas Rules****, "Request," ch. 6-C, §7.1.5(1), p. 605; "Object," ch. 6-C, §7.1.5(2)(b), p. 608.*}

◄ *Continued on next page* ►

OBJECTION: {60 *Party*} objects to the request because it seeks the discovery of data or information that exists in electronic or magnetic form but does not specify the form in which {61 *adverse party*} wants the data or information produced. Tex. R. Civ. P. 196.4. {*See **O'Connor's Texas Rules**, "Form of production," ch. 6-C, §7.1.5(1)(a), p. 605; "Object," ch. 6-C, §7.1.5(2)(b), p. 608.*}

OBJECTION: {62 *Party*} objects to the request for the discovery of data or information that exists in electronic or magnetic form because the requested information is not reasonably available to {63 *party*} in the ordinary course of business. Tex. R. Civ. P. 196.4; *see In re State Farm Lloyds*, 520 S.W.3d 595, 600 (Tex. 2017); *In re Weekley Homes, L.P.*, 295 S.W.3d 309, 322 (Tex. 2009). Specifically, the requested information is not reasonably available because production of the information would be unduly {64 *burdensome/expensive/burdensome and expensive*}. *See* Tex. R. Civ. P. 192.4, 196.4; *In re State Farm*, 520 S.W.3d at 607; *In re Weekley Homes*, 295 S.W.3d at 322. {65 *State facts supporting objection and show how production as requested will be unduly burdensome or expensive.*} {*See **O'Connor's Texas Rules**, "Is electronic information reasonably available?," ch. 6-C, §6.2, p. 603; "Object," ch. 6-C, §7.1.5(2)(b), p. 608.*}

OBJECTION: {66 *Party*} objects to the {67 *time/place/time and place*} for {68 *identify requested action, e.g., production, inspection, copying*} because the {69 *time/place/time and place*} designated for compliance is unreasonable. *See* Tex. R. Civ. P. 196.2(b)(3). A more reasonable {70 *time/place/time and place*} for {71 *party*} to comply is {72 *state alternative time and place for discovery*}. {73 *Party*} is willing to comply with the {74 *identify discovery request*} conducted at {75 *state alternative time and place for discovery*}. {*See **O'Connor's Texas Rules**, "Objection to time & place," ch. 6-I, §3.4.2(1), p. 684.*}

OBJECTION: {76 *Party*} objects to the request because the request asks for documents from testifying experts. Texas Rule of Civil Procedure 195.1 prohibits a party from learning about experts through a request for production. This information is available only through a request for disclosure under Texas Rule of Civil Procedure 194 or a deposition of the expert.

OBJECTION: {77 *Party*} objects to the request because the same information has been provided in response to {78 *identify other form of discovery*} that was served on {79 *adverse party*} on {80 *date*}. {81 *Elaborate.*}

OBJECTION: {82 *Party*} objects to the request because the request lacks specificity and is vague and unclear. {83 *Elaborate.*}

OBJECTION: {84 *Party*} objects to the request for {85 *party*}'s trial exhibits because {86 *adverse party*} is not entitled to ask for trial exhibits through a request for documents. Only the trial court can require a party to produce trial exhibits as part of discovery. *See* Tex. R. Civ. P. 166(*l*).

OBJECTION: {87 *Party*} objects to the request because it does not describe with sufficient specificity the means, manner, and procedure {88 *adverse party*} intends to use to {89 *inspect/test/sample*} {90 *identify items for inspection, testing, or sampling*}. Tex. R. Civ. P. 196.1(b). {91 *Elaborate.*}

OBJECTION: {92 *Party*} objects to the request because the {93 *inspection/testing/sampling*} {94 *adverse party*} intends to perform on {95 *identify items for inspection, testing, or sampling*} will destroy or materially alter the items. *See* Tex. R. Civ. P. 196.5. {96 *Elaborate.*} {*See* ***O'Connor's Texas Rules****, "Destruction by testing," ch. 6-I, §3.4.4(2), p. 684.*}

SEE: Tex. R. Civ. P. 166(*l*), 193.3, 195.1, 196
O'Connor's Texas Rules * Civil Trials (2019), "Procedure to respond," ch. 6-I, §3.3, p. 683; "Contents of response," ch. 6-I, §3.4, p. 684

ADD: STYLE OF THE CASE – FORM 1B:2
SIGNATURE BLOCK – FORM 1B:3
CERTIFICATE OF SERVICE – FORM 1B:13

NOTE: The responding party's answers, objections, and other responses must be preceded by the request to which they apply. Tex. R. Civ. P. 193.1. A party must comply with the request to the extent that the party has made no objection, unless it is unreasonable under the circumstances to do so before obtaining a ruling on the objection. Tex. R. Civ. P. 193.2(b) & cmt. 2. If the responding party objects to the requested time or place of production, the responding party must state a reasonable time and place for complying with the request and must comply with that time and place without further request or order. Tex. R. Civ. P. 193.2(b).

If the responding party can produce some but not all of the requested electronic information, it must object to the information it cannot retrieve or produce. *See* Tex. R. Civ. P. 193.2(b); Sedona Conference, *Sedona Conference Principles, Third Edition: Best Practices, Recommendations & Principles for Addressing Electronic Document Production*, 19 Sedona Conf.J. 1, 89 (2018), thesedonaconference.org/publications; Hecht, *Taking Point on E-Discovery: Texas Rule of Civil Procedure 196.4*, 51 The Advocate: State Bar Litigation Section Report 18, 20 (Summer 2010).

A party in a Level 1 case can serve no more than 15 written requests for production on any other party. Tex. R. Civ. P. 190.2(b)(4). There is no limit on the number of items a party can ask to have produced or the number of sets of requests a party can serve in a Level 2 or 3 case. *See* Tex. R. Civ. P. 190.3(b), 190.4(b), 196. However, in a Level 3 case, the discovery limitations of Level 1 or 2 apply—depending on the damages sought and issues involved—unless expressly changed by court order. *See* Tex. R. Civ. P. 190.4(b). Thus, a party in a Level 3 case may also be limited to 15 written requests for production.

◄ *Continued on next page* ►

Each discrete subpart of a request for production is considered a separate request for production. Tex. R. Civ. P. 190.2(b)(4).

Generally, a party responding to a request for production has 30 days to respond. Tex. R. Civ. P. 196.2(a). But when the plaintiff serves a request for production before the defendant's answer is due, the defendant has 50 days to respond rather than 30. *Id.* When service is by mail or fax, the responding party has an additional three days (if mailed) or one day (if faxed after 5:00 p.m.) to respond. *See* Tex. R. Civ. P. 21a(b)(2), (c). See ***O'Connor's Texas Rules***, "Deadline to serve response," ch. 6-A, §14.1, p. 527.

For information to be discoverable, it must be both relevant and proportional to the needs of the case. *See* Tex. R. Civ. P. 192.3(a); ***In re State Farm Lloyds***, 520 S.W.3d 595, 607 (Tex.2017). The Court in ***In re State Farm*** set out factors for determining proportionality, which mirror the considerations under Texas Rule of Civil Procedure 192.4 for determining whether a discovery request is unduly burdensome. *See* ***In re State Farm***, 520 S.W.3d at 599-600. Although the Court discussed the proportionality guidelines in the context of electronic-discovery disputes, the Court emphasized that all discovery is subject to proportionality considerations. *Id.* at 599. See ***O'Connor's Texas Rules***, "Proportional," ch. 6-B, §2.1.1(2), p. 555; "Proportional," ch. 6-C, §6.1.2, p. 602.

For general objections to discovery, see FORM 6A:9; for a motion for protection from discovery, see FORM 6A:10; for a motion for protection from a discovery subpoena, see FORM 6A:13; for claims of privilege, see FORMS 6A:19-22; for a motion to quash a deposition, see FORM 6F:2.

{ADD TO STANDARD REQUESTS FOR PRODUCTION – FORM 6I:2}

{Depending on the discovery-control plan, parties may be limited to 15 requests. See the first note under FORM 6I:2.}

REQUEST 6: Produce the original of the contract on which this suit is based.

RESPONSE:

REQUEST 7: Produce all drafts of the contract on which this suit is based.

RESPONSE:

REQUEST 8: Produce all communications between plaintiff and defendant relating to the contract on which this suit is based.

RESPONSE:

REQUEST 9: Produce all documents that relate to the contract on which this suit is based.

RESPONSE:

REQUEST 10: Produce the original of the guaranty of the contract on which this suit is based.

RESPONSE:

REQUEST 11: Produce all drafts of the guaranty of the contract on which this suit is based.

RESPONSE:

REQUEST 12: Produce all contracts entered into between plaintiff and defendant and signed by both parties.

RESPONSE:

REQUEST 13: Produce all documents pertaining to the parties' modification of the contract on which this suit is based.

RESPONSE:

Continued on next page

FORM 61:4 P'S OR D'S REQUEST FOR PRODUCTION – BREACH OF CONTRACT

SEE: Tex. R. Civ. P. 196
O'Connor's Texas Rules * Civil Trials (2019), "Securing Documents & Tangible Things," ch. 6-I, p. 681
O'Connor's Texas Causes of Action (2019), "Breach of Contract," ch. 5-B, p. 69

ADD TO: STANDARD REQUESTS FOR PRODUCTION – FORM 61:2

NOTE: These requests are appropriate for most breach-of-contract cases; however, the attorney should draft additional requests designed to discover information about the specific dispute.

See the first note under FORM 61:2.

{ADD TO STANDARD REQUESTS FOR PRODUCTION – FORM 6I:2}

{Depending on the discovery-control plan, parties may be limited to 15 requests. See the first note under FORM 6I:2.}

REQUEST 6: Produce all documents summarizing or reflecting payment on the account for which plaintiff sues.

RESPONSE:

REQUEST 7: Produce all documents relating to defendant's order of the {❶ *describe goods or services*} identified in the account attached to plaintiff's original petition.

RESPONSE:

REQUEST 8: Produce all documents relating to any price quotation or price agreement regarding the {❷ *describe goods or services*} identified in the account attached to plaintiff's original petition.

RESPONSE:

REQUEST 9: Produce all documents relating to the delivery and receipt of the {❸ *describe goods or services*} identified in the account attached to plaintiff's original petition.

RESPONSE:

REQUEST 10: Produce all ledgers, all statements, including accounts payable or receivable, and all other documents that relate to the account attached to plaintiff's original petition.

RESPONSE:

SEE: Tex. R. Civ. P. 185, 196
O'Connor's Texas Rules * Civil Trials **(2019), "Securing Documents & Tangible Things," ch. 6-I, p. 681**
O'Connor's Texas Causes of Action **(2019), "Suit on Sworn Account," ch. 5-E, p. 126**

ADD TO: STANDARD REQUESTS FOR PRODUCTION – FORM 6I:2

NOTE: These requests are appropriate for most suits on sworn accounts; however, the attorney should draft additional requests designed to discover information about the specific dispute.

See the first note under FORM 6I:2.

{ADD TO STANDARD REQUESTS FOR PRODUCTION – FORM 6I:2}

{Depending on the discovery-control plan, parties may be limited to 15 requests. See the first note under FORM 6I:2.}

REQUEST 6: Produce the title to the vehicle that defendant was driving when the collision occurred.

RESPONSE:

REQUEST 7: Produce defendant's driver's license.

RESPONSE:

REQUEST 8: Produce defendant's Social Security card.

RESPONSE:

REQUEST 9: Produce all photographs defendant has of the vehicle, parties, or scene of the collision.

RESPONSE:

REQUEST 10: Produce the damage appraisal of defendant's vehicle.

RESPONSE:

REQUEST 11: Produce the invoices or receipts for repairs to defendant's vehicle.

RESPONSE:

REQUEST 12: Produce all drawings, maps, or sketches of the scene of the collision.

RESPONSE:

REQUEST 13: Produce any surveillance movies, photographs, or videotapes of plaintiff or of the collision.

RESPONSE:

REQUEST 14: Produce the police report or other report of any governmental agency relating to the collision.

RESPONSE:

REQUEST 15: Produce all documents regarding any medicine prescribed for defendant by any medical doctor within the five-year period before the collision.

RESPONSE:

REQUEST 16: Produce the names and addresses for all medical providers who treated defendant during the five-year period before the collision.

RESPONSE:

REQUEST 17: Produce all documents relating to any inspection performed on the vehicle within the past five years.

RESPONSE:

REQUEST 18: Produce the personnel file of the driver who was driving the vehicle at the time of the collision. {*Ask this when defendant is a corporation.*}

RESPONSE:

REQUEST 19: Produce all telephone records and other documents reflecting the use of any mobile device that defendant regularly uses, including those of family members and those of defendant's employer, for the period beginning {❶ *date*}, at {❷ *time*}, and ending {❸ *date*}, at {❹ *time*}.

RESPONSE:

REQUEST 20: Produce all documents that defendant has, including all deposition testimony and trial transcripts, from any other lawsuits regarding personal injury in which defendant has been involved.

RESPONSE:

SEE: Tex. R. Civ. P. 196
O'Connor's Texas Rules * Civil Trials (2019), "Securing Documents & Tangible Things," ch. 6-I, p. 681
O'Connor's Texas Causes of Action (2019), "Negligence Actions," ch. 21, p. 719

ADD TO: STANDARD REQUESTS FOR PRODUCTION – FORM 6I:2

NOTE: These requests are appropriate for most auto-accident cases; however, the attorney should draft additional requests designed to discover information about the specific dispute.

See the first note under FORM 6I:2.

{*ADD TO STANDARD REQUESTS FOR PRODUCTION – FORM 61:2*}

{*Depending on the discovery-control plan, parties may be limited to 15 requests. See the first note under FORM 61:2.*}

REQUEST 6: Produce the title to the vehicle that plaintiff was driving when the collision occurred.

RESPONSE:

REQUEST 7: Produce plaintiff's driver's license.

RESPONSE:

REQUEST 8: Produce plaintiff's Social Security card.

RESPONSE:

REQUEST 9: Produce all photographs plaintiff has of the vehicle, parties, or scene of the collision.

RESPONSE:

REQUEST 10: Produce the damage appraisal of plaintiff's vehicle.

RESPONSE:

REQUEST 11: Produce the invoices or receipts for repairs to plaintiff's vehicle.

RESPONSE:

REQUEST 12: Produce all drawings, maps, or sketches of the scene of the collision.

RESPONSE:

REQUEST 13: Produce any surveillance movies, photographs, or videotapes in which defendant appears.

RESPONSE:

REQUEST 14: Produce the police report or other report of any governmental agency relating to the collision.

RESPONSE:

REQUEST 15: Produce all documents relating to any inspection performed on the vehicle within the past five years.

RESPONSE:

REQUEST 16: Produce plaintiff's income-tax returns for the five-year period before the collision.

RESPONSE:

REQUEST 17: Produce all employment records, workers' compensation records, unemployment insurance records, or welfare records made within the five-year period before the collision.

RESPONSE:

REQUEST 18: Produce all documents regarding any medicine prescribed for plaintiff by any medical doctor since the collision and within the five-year period before the collision.

RESPONSE:

REQUEST 19: Produce the names and addresses for all medical providers who have treated plaintiff since the collision and during the five-year period before the collision.

RESPONSE:

REQUEST 20: Produce all telephone records and other documents reflecting the use of any mobile device that plaintiff regularly uses, including those of family members and those of plaintiff's employer, for the period beginning {❶ *date*}, at {❷ *time*}, and ending {❸ *date*}, at {❹ *time*}.

RESPONSE:

REQUEST 21: Produce all documents that show plaintiff was restrained by a seat belt.

RESPONSE:

REQUEST 22: Produce all documents that show the {❺ *passenger/passengers*} in plaintiff's vehicle {❻ *was/were*} restrained by {❼ *a seat belt/seat belts*} or other safety {❽ *device/devices*}.

RESPONSE:

◄ *Continued on next page* ►

REQUEST 23: Produce all documents that plaintiff has, including all deposition testimony and trial transcripts, from any other lawsuits regarding personal injury in which plaintiff has been involved.

RESPONSE:

SEE: Tex. R. Civ. P. 196
O'Connor's Texas Rules * Civil Trials (2019), "Securing Documents & Tangible Things," ch. 6-I, p. 681
O'Connor's Texas Causes of Action (2019), "Negligence Actions," ch. 21, p. 719

ADD TO: STANDARD REQUESTS FOR PRODUCTION – FORM 6I:2

NOTE: These requests are appropriate for most auto-accident cases; however, the attorney should draft additional requests designed to discover information about the specific dispute.

See the first note under FORM 6I:2.

{*ADD TO STANDARD REQUESTS FOR PRODUCTION – FORM 6I:2*}

{*Depending on the discovery-control plan, parties may be limited to 15 requests. See the first note under FORM 6I:2.*}

REQUEST 6: Produce all documents and written reports made about the incident in anticipation of trial.

RESPONSE:

REQUEST 7: Produce all documents or reports that you possess of any accidents occurring within the last five years on any premises that you now own or previously owned.

RESPONSE:

REQUEST 8: Produce all lease agreements regarding the premises located at {❶ *address*}, and any lease agreements that defendant has or had with tenants of any premises that {❷ *he/she/it*} owns or previously owned for five years before the time of plaintiff's accident.

RESPONSE:

REQUEST 9: Produce all documents that pertain to the ownership of the premises located at {❸ *address*}.

RESPONSE:

REQUEST 10: Produce all documents in reference to any policies or procedures pertaining to the maintenance of the premises located at {❹ *address*}.

RESPONSE:

REQUEST 11: Produce all documents relating to any agreements employing a maintenance company to service your premises.

RESPONSE:

REQUEST 12: Produce all documents relating to the employees or agents of defendant who were in charge of the premises at the time of the accident.

RESPONSE:

Continued on next page

REQUEST 13: Produce all documents that defendant has, including all deposition testimony and trial transcripts, from any other lawsuits regarding premises liability in which defendant has been involved.

RESPONSE:

REQUEST 14: Produce all surveillance videos and any other recording used at the premises on {❺ *date*}, the date of plaintiff's accident.

RESPONSE:

REQUEST 15: Plaintiff, under Texas Rule of Civil Procedure 196.7, requests that defendant permit {❻ *identify person to enter property*} to enter defendant's premises at {❼ *address*}, to inspect, measure, survey, photograph, videotape, test, or sample the land. {❽ *Elaborate.*} Plaintiff further requests that such entry and inspection take place on {❾ *date*}, at {❿ *time*}, unless defendant designates another date which is agreed to by plaintiff.

RESPONSE:

SEE: Tex. R. Civ. P. 196
*O'Connor's Texas Rules * Civil Trials* (2019), "Securing Documents & Tangible Things," ch. 6-I, p. 681
O'Connor's Texas Causes of Action (2019), "Liability to Invitees," ch. 23-B, p. 827

ADD TO: STANDARD REQUESTS FOR PRODUCTION – FORM 6I:2

NOTE: Include in the cover sheet that the word "premises" is defined as the premises at the defendant's address, where the plaintiff's accident occurred.

These requests are appropriate for most slip-and-fall cases; however, the attorney should draft additional requests designed to discover information about the specific dispute.

See the first note under FORM 6I:2.

{ADD TO STANDARD REQUESTS FOR PRODUCTION – FORM 6I:2}

{Depending on the discovery-control plan, parties may be limited to 15 requests. See the first note under FORM 6I:2.}

REQUEST 6: Produce all employment records, workers' compensation records, unemployment-insurance records, or welfare records made within the five-year period before the accident.

RESPONSE:

REQUEST 7: Produce all documents regarding any medicine prescribed for plaintiff by any medical doctor within the five-year period before the accident.

RESPONSE:

REQUEST 8: Provide the names and addresses of all medical providers who treated plaintiff during the five-year period before the accident.

RESPONSE:

REQUEST 9: Produce all telephone records and other documents reflecting the use of any mobile device that plaintiff regularly uses, including those of family members and those of plaintiff's employer, for the period beginning {❶ *date*}, at {❷ *time*}, and ending {❸ *date*}, at {❹ *time*}.

RESPONSE:

REQUEST 10: Produce all documents that plaintiff has, including all deposition testimony and trial transcripts, from any other lawsuits regarding personal injury in which plaintiff has been involved.

RESPONSE:

SEE: Tex. R. Civ. P. 196
O'Connor's Texas Rules * Civil Trials (2019), "Securing Documents & Tangible Things," ch. 6-I, p. 681
O'Connor's Texas Causes of Action (2019), "Liability to Invitees," ch. 23-B, p. 827

ADD TO: STANDARD REQUESTS FOR PRODUCTION – FORM 6I:2

NOTE: These requests are appropriate for most slip-and-fall cases; however, the attorney should draft additional requests designed to discover information about the specific dispute.

See the first note under FORM 6I:2.

FORM 6I:10 P'S REQUEST FOR PRODUCTION – DTPA

{ADD TO STANDARD REQUESTS FOR PRODUCTION – FORM 6I:2}

{Depending on the discovery-control plan, parties may be limited to 15 requests. See the first note under FORM 6I:2.}

REQUEST 6: Produce all documents that relate to the {❶ *purchase/lease*} of the {❷ *describe goods or services*}.

RESPONSE:

REQUEST 7: Produce all documents that relate to any instructions or directions regarding the use of the {❸ *describe goods or services*}.

RESPONSE:

REQUEST 8: Produce all documents that reflect any warranties, either express or implied, regarding the {❹ *describe goods or services*}.

RESPONSE:

REQUEST 9: Produce all documents that reflect any attempt to correct the defects alleged by plaintiff in the {❺ *describe goods or services*}.

RESPONSE:

REQUEST 10: Produce all documents that relate to any inspections performed on the {❻ *describe goods or services*}.

RESPONSE:

SEE: Tex. R. Civ. P. 196
Tex. Bus. & Com. Code §17.41 et seq.
O'Connor's Texas Rules * Civil Trials (2019), "Securing Documents & Tangible Things," ch. 6-I, p. 681
O'Connor's Texas Causes of Action (2019), "Deceptive Trade Practices Act," ch. 8, p. 209

ADD TO: STANDARD REQUESTS FOR PRODUCTION – FORM 6I:2

NOTE: These requests are appropriate for most DTPA suits; however, the attorney should draft additional requests designed to discover information about the specific dispute.

See the first note under FORM 6I:2.

{ADD TO STANDARD REQUESTS FOR PRODUCTION – FORM 6I:2}

{Depending on the discovery-control plan, parties may be limited to 15 requests. See the first note under FORM 6I:2.}

REQUEST 6: Produce all documents that relate to the {❶ *purchase/lease*} of the {❷ *describe goods or services*}.

RESPONSE:

REQUEST 7: Produce all documents that reflect any instructions or directions plaintiff received regarding the use of the {❸ *describe goods or services*}.

RESPONSE:

REQUEST 8: Produce all documents plaintiff contends constitute a warranty, either express or implied, regarding the {❹ *describe goods or services*}.

RESPONSE:

REQUEST 9: Produce all documents that reflect any complaints plaintiff made to defendant regarding alleged defects in the {❺ *describe goods or services*}.

RESPONSE:

REQUEST 10: Produce the presuit notice you prepared and forwarded to defendant that you contend complies with the notice requirements of the Deceptive Trade Practices Act.

RESPONSE:

SEE: Tex. R. Civ. P. 196
Tex. Bus. & Com. Code §17.41 et seq.
O'Connor's Texas Rules * Civil Trials (2019), "Securing Documents & Tangible Things," ch. 6-I, p. 681
O'Connor's Texas Causes of Action (2019), "Deceptive Trade Practices Act," ch. 8, p. 209

ADD TO: STANDARD REQUESTS FOR PRODUCTION – FORM 6I:2

NOTE: These requests are appropriate for most DTPA suits; however, the attorney should draft additional requests designed to discover information about the specific dispute.

See the first note under FORM 6I:2.

FORM 6I:12 NOTICE FOR PRODUCTION FROM NONPARTY WITHOUT DEPOSITION

{❶ *PARTY*}'S NOTICE OF
REQUEST FOR PRODUCTION OF DOCUMENTS

To: {❷ *Name of nonparty*}, {❸ *address*}.

Please take notice that, under Texas Rule of Civil Procedure 205.3, {❹ *party*}, {❺ *name*}, intends to subpoena from {❻ *name of nonparty*} the documents in the attached Exhibit {❼ *letter*} to be produced on {❽ *date*}, at {❾ *time*}, at {❿ *address*}. {⓫ *Name of nonparty*} will be served with a subpoena after ten days from the date of service of this notice. {*See **O'Connor's Texas Rules**, "For documents only," ch. 6-I, §5.1.1(1), p. 685.*}

SEE: Tex. R. Civ. P. 176, 205.2, 205.3
O'Connor's Texas Rules * Civil Trials (2019), "Securing Things from a Nonparty," ch. 6-I, §5, p. 685

ADD: STYLE OF THE CASE – FORM 1B:2
SIGNATURE BLOCK – FORM 1B:3
CERTIFICATE OF SERVICE – FORM 1B:13

ATTACH: COVER SHEET & DEFINITIONS – FORM 6I:1
REQUEST FOR PRODUCTION – STANDARD REQUESTS – FORM 6I:2

NOTE: A party may subpoena the production of documents and tangible things from nonparties without the need for a motion or an oral or written deposition. Tex. R. Civ. P. 205 cmt.

A notice to produce documents or tangible things without a deposition must be served at least ten days before the subpoena compelling production is served. Tex. R. Civ. P. 205.2.

A request for the production of a nonparty's medical records must be served on the nonparty under Texas Rule of Civil Procedure 21a. Tex. R. Civ. P. 196.1(c)(1).

If testing or sampling is requested, the requesting party must provide information about the procedure, manner, and means of the testing or sampling. Tex. R. Civ. P. 205.3(b)(3).

{❶ *PARTY*}'S OBJECTION TO
AUTHENTICITY OF DOCUMENTS PRODUCED IN DISCOVERY

To: {❷ *Adverse party*}, {❸ *name*}, by and through {❹ *his/her/its*} attorney of record, {❺ *name*}, {❻ *address*}.

{❼ *Party*}, {❽ *name*}, serves this objection to the authenticity of documents produced by {❾ *party*} in discovery. {*See* ***O'Connor's Texas Rules***, *"Objection to authenticity," ch. 6-I, §8.3.1, p. 691.*}

INTRODUCTION

1. {⓾ *Party*}, in response to {⓫ *adverse party*}'s request for production of documents, produced the following documents: {⓬ *list documents produced to which party will object to authentication*}.

2. {⓭ *Party*} objects to the authenticity of these documents.

3. On {⓮ *date*}, {⓯ *party*} learned that {⓰ *adverse party*} intended to use documents produced by {⓱ *party*} against {⓲ *party*} at {⓳ *a pretrial hearing/trial*}.

ARGUMENTS

4. A party's production of documents in response to written discovery authenticates the documents for use against that party, unless the producing party objects to their use within ten days after the producing party has actual notice that the documents will be used. Tex. R. Civ. P. 193.7.

5. This motion is filed within ten days of the date that {⓴ *party*} learned that {㉑ *adverse party*} intended to use documents produced by {㉒ *party*} against {㉓ *party*} at {㉔ *a pretrial hearing/trial*}.

6. {㉕ *Party*} objects to the authenticity of documents {㉖ *he/she/it*} produced on the following grounds: {㉗ *identify each document and state specific objection to all or a specific part of each document*}.

7. {㉘ *Party*} has a good-faith factual and legal basis for making these objections. Tex. R. Civ. P. 193.7. {㉙ *Elaborate.*}

SEE: Tex. R. Civ. P. 193.7
O'Connor's Texas Rules * Civil Trials (2019), "Objection to authenticity," ch. 6-I, §8.3.1, p. 691

ADD: STYLE OF THE CASE – FORM 1B:2
SIGNATURE BLOCK – FORM 1B:3
CERTIFICATE OF SERVICE – FORM 1B:13

{❶ *PARTY*}'S NOTICE OF RECORDS REQUEST

{*CHOOSE APPROPRIATE INTRODUCTORY PARAGRAPH*}

To: {❷ *Adverse party*}, {❸ *name*}, through {❹ *his/her/its*} attorney of record, {❺ *name*}, {❻ *address*}.

To: {❼ *Name of nonparty*}, {❽ *address*}.

Please take notice that, under Texas Finance Code section 59.006(b), {❾ *party*}, {❿ *name*}, intends to subpoena from {⓫ *name of financial institution*} the following financial records to be produced on {⓬ *date*}, at {⓭ *time*}, at {⓮ *address*}: {⓯ *list records by individual item or category and describe with reasonable particularity each item or category*}. A copy of the proposed subpoena is included with this notice. {*See* ***O'Connor's Texas Rules****, "Securing Documents from a Financial Institution," ch. 6-I, §7, p. 688.*}

{*ADD FOLLOWING PARAGRAPHS IF REQUESTING RECORDS FROM NONPARTY*}

Before {⓰ *name of financial institution*} may release your records, {⓱ *party*} must obtain a signed authorization to release the records, as required by Texas Finance Code section 59.006(c)(3). A copy of the authorization is included with this notice. Please return the authorization, signed and notarized, in the self-addressed stamped envelope provided.

If you do not execute the authorization form, {⓲ *party*} will seek from the Court an in camera inspection of the requested records, as authorized by Texas Finance Code section 59.006(d). The Court may order {⓳ *name of financial institution*} to produce the requested records without your consent. Thus, you bear the burden of preventing or limiting {⓴ *name of financial institution*}'s compliance with the records request by seeking an appropriate remedy with the Court, including filing a motion to quash the record request or a motion for a protective order, as required by Texas Finance Code section 59.006(e).

SEE: Tex. Fin. Code §59.006
O'Connor's Texas Rules * Civil Trials (2019), "Securing Documents from a Financial Institution," ch. 6-I, §7, p. 688

ADD: STYLE OF THE CASE – FORM 1B:2
SIGNATURE BLOCK – FORM 1B:3
CERTIFICATE OF SERVICE – FORM 1B:13

ATTACH: SUBPOENA – FORM 1L:1
AUTHORIZATION TO RELEASE RECORDS – FORM 6I:15, if notice is for nonparty
Fee for costs
Self-addressed stamped envelope

NOTE: When seeking records about a nonparty-customer, the requesting party must serve this notice in the manner and within the time period provided by Texas Rule of Civil Procedure 21a. Tex. Fin. Code §59.006(c)(1). A certificate of service must be filed with the court and with the financial institution stating that the nonparty has been mailed or served with the notice and a copy of the record request. *Id.* §59.006(c)(2). See ***O'Connor's Texas Rules***, "Requesting records," ch. 6-I, §7.4.1, p. 689.

If a party-customer wants to prevent or limit a financial institution's compliance with a record request, it must file either a motion to quash the record request or a motion for a protective order. Tex. Fin. Code §59.006(e). Any motion filed must be served on the financial institution and the requesting party before the date for compliance. *Id.*

If a nonparty-customer wants to prevent or limit compliance by the financial institution, it only has to withhold written consent authorizing the institution's compliance with the request. *See* Tex. Fin. Code §59.006(d). If the nonparty-customer refuses to consent or does not respond to the request by the date for compliance, then the requesting party's sole means of obtaining access to the requested record is to file a motion for in camera inspection. *Id.* The court may then inspect the requested record to determine its relevance and order redaction of portions of the record. *Id.* To prevent production of the records, the nonparty-customer must file a motion to quash the record request or a motion for a protective order before the court's ruling. *See id.* §59.006(c)(1), (e).

Modify FORM 6A:13 to prevent production of the financial records.

AUTHORIZATION TO RELEASE FINANCIAL RECORDS

TO WHOM IT MAY CONCERN:

RE: {❶ *Name of nonparty-customer*}
{❷ *Address*}
{❸ *City, state, zip code*}
DOB: {❹ *Date of birth*}
SSN: {❺ *Social Security number*}

I, {❻ *name*}, authorize {❼ *name of party's attorney*} or the firm of {❽ *name of attorney's firm*} or their agents to inspect the originals of any and all financial or other information related to any account maintained by {❾ *name of financial institution*} in my name and to allow copies to be made of such records.

I understand that {❿ *name of financial institution*}, its officers, directors, and employees are released from legal responsibility or liability for the release of the requested records to the extent indicated and authorized in this document.

{⓫ *Name of financial institution*} is specifically and expressly authorized to accept a copy of this authorization as though it were an original.

Information obtained by this authorization is for use only in pending litigation and should not be disseminated for any other purpose.

____
{⓬ *Name of nonparty-customer*}

SEE: Tex. Fin. Code §59.006(c)(3)
O'Connor's Texas Rules * Civil Trials (2019), "Procedure to secure nonparty-customer records," ch. 6-I, §7.4, p. 689

ADD: STYLE OF THE CASE – FORM 1B:2
JURAT – FORM 1B:10

MEDICAL AUTHORIZATION FORM

TO THE CUSTODIAN OF MEDICAL RECORDS:

RE: {❶ *Name of patient*}
{❷ *Address*}
{❸ *City, state, zip code*}
DOB: {❹ *Date of birth*}
SSN: {❺ *Social Security number*}

{*CHOOSE APPROPRIATE PARAGRAPH 1*}

{*General release of records from all medical providers*}

1. I, {❻ *name of patient or legally authorized representative*}, authorize {❼ *name of person or law firm authorized to receive records*} to obtain a full and complete copy of the medical records relating to {❽ *my care and treatment/the care and treatment of {name of patient}*} held or maintained by any physician, dentist, psychiatrist, chiropractor, hospital, clinic, laboratory, physical therapist, or any other medical-care provider, including records relating to confidential information about HIV testing, drug or alcohol abuse, mental-health treatment, and any other sensitive medical information.

{*Release of records from specific medical provider*}

1. I, {❾ *name of patient or legally authorized representative*}, authorize {❿ *name of person or law firm authorized to receive records*} to obtain a full and complete copy of the medical records relating to {⓫ *my care and treatment/the care and treatment of {name of patient}*} held or maintained by {⓬ *name of medical-care provider*} {⓭ *add if appropriate: , including records relating to confidential information about HIV testing, drug or alcohol abuse, mental-health treatment, and any other sensitive medical information*}.

2. I authorize and direct the medical-care provider to discuss the records and {⓮ *my care and treatment/the care and treatment of {name of patient}*} with {⓯ *name of person or law firm authorized to receive records*} and to answer {⓰ *his/her/their*} questions.

3. This authorization is made at the request of the patient, {⓱ *name of patient*}.

4. This authorization can be revoked at any time with written notice to {⓲ *name of person or law firm authorized to receive records*}. However, any disclosures already made cannot be taken back and may no longer be protected.

◄ *Continued on next page* ►

5. This authorization is valid {19 *specify time period, e.g., until December 31, 2019, until the 180th day after the date it is signed, from the date of the accident through the date of last treatment*}.

6. My signing of this authorization is voluntary, and I understand that I may refuse to sign it. {20 *My/{Name of patient}'s*} treatment, payment, or enrollment or eligibility for benefits will not be conditioned on my signing of this authorization.

7. Information disclosed under this authorization could be redisclosed by the recipient, and the redisclosure may no longer be protected by federal or state law.

____
{21 *Name of patient or legally authorized representative*}
{22 *If signed by authorized representative, identify representative's capacity, e.g., Guardian of {name of patient}*}
Date: ____________________

SEE: 45 C.F.R. §164.508
Tex. R. Civ. P. 194.2(j), (k)
Tex. Health & Safety Code §241.152
O'Connor's Texas Rules * Civil Trials (2019), "Certain health-care information from hospital," ch. 6-B, §2.23, p. 567; "Medical authorization," ch. 6-J, §3.2, p. 692

ADD: STYLE OF THE CASE – FORM 1B:2
JURAT – FORM 1B:10

NOTE: Notice of a health-care-liability claim under Texas Civil Practice & Remedies Code §74.051 must be accompanied by a medical authorization in the form specified by Texas Civil Practice & Remedies Code §74.052. Tex. Civ. Prac. & Rem. Code §74.052(a). To determine whether a cause of action is a health-care-liability claim, see ***O'Connor's Texas Causes of Action*** (2019), "Medical Negligence Under the Medical Liability Act," ch. 20-A, p. 625.

{❶ *PARTY*}'S MOTION TO EXAMINE {❷ *NAME OF PERSON*}

{❸ *Party*}, {❹ *name*}, asks the Court to order {❺ *name of person*}, a {❻ *party/person under the party's control*}, to submit to a {❼ *physical/mental*} examination, as allowed by Texas Rule of Civil Procedure 204. {*See **O'Connor's Texas Rules**, "Motion to Examine the Person," ch. 6-J, §5, p. 694.*}

INTRODUCTION

1. Plaintiff, {❽ *name*}, sued defendant, {❾ *name*}, for {❿ *state basis of suit*}.

2. Discovery in this suit is governed by a Level {⓫ *1/2/3*} discovery-control plan. The discovery period {⓬ *will end/ended*} on {⓭ *date*}. {*See **O'Connor's Texas Rules**, "Discovery-Control Plans," ch. 6-A, §7, p. 520.*}

3. This case is set for trial on {⓮ *date*}.

4. {⓯ *State other relevant facts about the suit.*}

BACKGROUND

5. {⓰ *State facts relevant to the motion.*}

ARGUMENT & AUTHORITIES

6. A court may order the physical or mental examination of a party or a person under the party's control if the movant shows good cause and (1) the party's or person's physical or mental condition is in controversy, (2) the party has designated a psychologist as a testifying expert, or (3) the party has disclosed a psychologist's records for possible use at trial. Tex. R. Civ. P. 204.1(c). {*See **O'Connor's Texas Rules**, "Elements," ch. 6-J, §5.1.1, p. 694.*}

7. There is good cause for the Court to order the examination because the examination is relevant to the issues in controversy in the case. *In re H.E.B. Grocery Co., L.P.*, 492 S.W.3d 300, 303 (Tex. 2016); *see Coates v. Whittington*, 758 S.W.2d 749, 753 (Tex. 1988). Specifically, {⓱ *explain why examination is relevant or is likely to lead to the discovery of relevant evidence, e.g., physical examination of plaintiff who claims physical impairment that prevents him from working*}.

8. There is a reasonable nexus between the condition in controversy and the examination sought. *In re H.E.B. Grocery*, 492 S.W.3d at 303; *see Coates*, 758 S.W.2d at 753. Specifically, {⓲ *describe nexus, e.g., physical examination for physical impairment, psychological evaluation for claim for mental anguish*}.

◄ *Continued on next page* ►

9. It is not possible for {19 *party*} to obtain the information that would result from an examination through less intrusive means. *In re H.E.B. Grocery*, 492 S.W.3d at 303; *see Coates*, 758 S.W.2d at 753. {20 *Elaborate.*}

{*CHOOSE APPROPRIATE PARAGRAPHS 10-12*}

10. {21 *Name of person*}'s {22 *physical/mental*} condition is in controversy. Specifically, {23 *explain why person's physical or mental condition is in controversy, e.g., in medical-malpractice suit, plaintiff claims doctor was impaired by alcohol at the time of the operation*}. {*See* ***O'Connor's Texas Rules****, "In controversy," ch. 6-J, §5.1.1(2), p. 694.*}

11. {24 *Adverse party*} has designated a psychologist, {25 *name*}, as a testifying expert. {*See* ***O'Connor's Texas Rules****, "Other party's psychologist," ch. 6-J, §5.1.1(3), p. 695.*}

12. {26 *Adverse party*} has disclosed psychologist {27 *name*}'s records for possible use at trial. {*See* ***O'Connor's Texas Rules****, "Other party's psychologist," ch. 6-J, §5.1.1(3), p. 695.*}

13. The examination will be conducted by {28 *name of physician or psychologist*}.

CONCLUSION

14. {29 *Briefly summarize the motion.*}

PRAYER

15. For these reasons, {30 *party*} asks the Court to set this motion for hearing and, after the hearing, to order {31 *name of person*} to submit to a {32 *physical/mental*} examination.

Form 6J:2 Motion to Examine a Person

SEE: Tex. R. Civ. P. 204.1
O'Connor's Texas Rules * Civil Trials (2019), "Motion to Examine the Person," ch. 6-J, §5, p. 694

ADD: STYLE OF THE CASE – FORM 1B:2
SIGNATURE BLOCK – FORM 1B:3
CERTIFICATE OF CONFERENCE – FORM 1B:12
CERTIFICATE OF SERVICE – FORM 1B:13

ATTACH: AFFIDAVIT – FORM 1B:8, if necessary
NOTICE OF HEARING OR SUBMISSION – FORM 1E:1
ORDER – FORM 6J:4

NOTE: For most methods of service, the deadline to serve a motion to examine a person is 30 days before the end of the discovery period. Tex. R. Civ. P. 204.1(a). See ***O'Connor's Texas Rules***, "Discovery Periods," ch. 6-A, §8, p. 523. But when service is by mail or fax, the motion should be served at least 33 days (if mailed) or 31 days (if faxed after 5:00 p.m.) before the end of the discovery period. *See* Tex. R. Civ. P. 21a(b)(2), (c). See ***O'Connor's Texas Rules***, "Deadline to serve response," ch. 6-A, §14.1, p. 527.

{[1] *PARTY*}'S RESPONSE TO
{[2] *ADVERSE PARTY*}'S MOTION TO EXAMINE {[3] *NAME OF PERSON*}

{[4] *Party*}, {[5] *name*}, asks the Court to deny {[6] *adverse party*} {[7] *name*}'s motion to order {[8] *name of person*} to submit to a {[9] *physical/mental*} examination. {*See* ***O'Connor's Texas Rules****, "Motion to Examine the Person," ch. 6-J, §5, p. 694.*}

INTRODUCTION

1. Plaintiff, {[10] *name*}, sued defendant, {[11] *name*}, for {[12] *state basis of suit*}.

2. Discovery in this suit is governed by a Level {[13] *1/2/3*} discovery-control plan. The discovery period {[14] *will end/ended*} on {[15] *date*}. {*See* ***O'Connor's Texas Rules****, "Discovery-Control Plans," ch. 6-A, §7, p. 520.*}

3. This case is set for trial on {[16] *date*}.

4. {[17] *State other relevant facts about the suit.*}

BACKGROUND

5. {[18] *State facts relevant to the response.*}

ARGUMENT & AUTHORITIES

6. This is not a case in which the Court should order the {[19] *physical/mental*} examination of a {[20] *party/person under the party's control*}.

{*CHOOSE APPROPRIATE PARAGRAPHS 7-12*}

7. {[21] *Adverse party*} has not shown that there is good cause for the Court to order the examination. Specifically, {[22] *explain why examination is not relevant or is unlikely to lead to the discovery of relevant evidence, e.g., physical examination of plaintiff who was injured but who admits a full recovery and makes no claim for future impairment is unlikely to lead to the discovery of admissible evidence*}. {*See* ***O'Connor's Texas Rules****, "Good cause," ch. 6-J, §5.1.1(1)(a), p. 694.*}

8. {[23] *Adverse party*} has not shown that there is good cause for the Court to order the examination. Specifically, there is no reasonable nexus between the condition in controversy and the examination sought because {[24] *describe lack of nexus, e.g., defendant seeks psychological examination of plaintiff who claims only physical injuries*}. {*See* ***O'Connor's Texas Rules****, "Good cause," ch. 6-J, §5.1.1(1)(b), p. 694.*}

9. {㉕ *Adverse party*} has not shown that there is good cause for the Court to order the examination. Specifically, {㉖ *adverse party*} may obtain the same information that would result from an examination through less intrusive means. Specifically, {㉗ *explain less intrusive means, e.g., by ordering medical records from a disinterested medical provider who has already performed an examination*}. {*See* ***O'Connor's Texas Rules****, "Good cause," ch. 6-J, §5.1.1(1)(c), p. 694.*}

10. {㉘ *Adverse party*} contends that, as a result of the suit, {㉙ *name of person*}'s {㉚ *physical/mental*} condition is in controversy. However, {㉛ *name of person*}'s condition is not in controversy because {㉜ *explain why person's physical or mental condition is not in controversy*}. {*See* ***O'Connor's Texas Rules****, "In controversy," ch. 6-J, §5.1.1(2), p. 694.*}

11. {㉝ *Adverse party*} contends that a psychologist, {㉞ *name*}, has been designated as a testifying expert. That is not correct. {㉟ *Refute adverse party's contention.*} {*See* ***O'Connor's Texas Rules****, "Other party's psychologist," ch. 6-J, §5.1.1(3), p. 695.*}

12. {㊱ *Adverse party*} contends that psychologist {㊲ *name*}'s records have been disclosed for possible use at trial. That is not correct. {㊳ *Refute adverse party's contention.*} {*See* ***O'Connor's Texas Rules****, "Other party's psychologist," ch. 6-J, §5.1.1(3), p. 695.*}

CONCLUSION

13. {㊴ *Briefly summarize the response.*}

PRAYER

14. For these reasons, {㊵ *party*} asks the Court to deny {㊶ *adverse party*}'s motion that {㊷ *name of person*} submit to a {㊸ *physical/mental*} examination.

SEE: Tex. R. Civ. P. 204.1
O'Connor's Texas Rules * Civil Trials (2019), "Motion to Examine the Person," ch. 6-J, §5, p. 694

ADD: STYLE OF THE CASE – FORM 1B:2
SIGNATURE BLOCK – FORM 1B:3
CERTIFICATE OF SERVICE – FORM 1B:13

ATTACH: AFFIDAVIT – FORM 1B:8, if necessary
ORDER – FORM 6J:4

ORDER ON {❶ *PARTY*}'S MOTION TO REQUIRE {❷ *NAME OF PERSON*} TO SUBMIT TO A {❸ *PHYSICAL/MENTAL*} EXAMINATION

After considering {❹ *party*} {❺ *name*}'s motion to require {❻ *name of person*} to submit to a {❼ *physical/mental*} examination, the response, and arguments of counsel, the Court

{*CHOOSE APPROPRIATE ORDER*}

DENIES the motion.

GRANTS the motion because

{*CHOOSE APPROPRIATE REASON*}

[A] {❽ *name of person*}'s {❾ *physical/mental*} condition is in controversy, and there is good cause to order {❿ *name of person*} to submit to a {⓫ *physical/mental*} examination.

[B] {⓬ *adverse party*} designated a psychologist, {⓭ *name of psychologist*}, as a testifying expert, and there is good cause to order {⓮ *name of person*} to submit to a mental examination.

[C] {⓯ *adverse party*} disclosed the records of a psychologist, {⓰ *name of psychologist*}, for possible use at trial, and there is good cause to order {⓱ *name of person*} to submit to a mental examination.

Therefore, the Court orders {⓲ *name of person*} to submit to a {⓳ *physical/mental*} examination by {⓴ *name of physician or psychologist*} on {㉑ *date*}, at {㉒ *time*}, at {㉓ *address*}. The examination will be limited to {㉔ *specify scope and conditions of examination as appropriate, e.g., hearing examination on allegation of hearing loss*}.

SIGNED on _______________, 20___.

____
PRESIDING JUDGE

SEE: Tex. R. Civ. P. 204.1
O'Connor's Texas Rules * Civil Trials (2019), "Order," ch. 6-J, §5.4, p. 695

ADD: STYLE OF THE CASE – FORM 1B:2
CERTIFICATE OF SERVICE – FORM 1B:13, if proposed order served separately from motion or response

{[1] *PARTY*}'S REQUEST TO ENTER PROPERTY OF {[2] *ADVERSE PARTY*}

To: {[3] *Adverse party*}, {[4] *name*}, by and through {[5] *his/her/its*} attorney of record, {[6] *name*}, {[7] *address*}.

{[8] *Party*}, {[9] *name*}, serves this request to enter the {[10] *land/{identify other property}*} of {[11] *adverse party*}, located at {[12] *address*}, under the authority of Texas Rule of Civil Procedure 196.7. {*See* ***O'Connor's Texas Rules****, "Request," ch. 6-K, §3.1, p. 697.*}

1. {[13] *Party*} suggests that the inspection take place on {[14] *date*}, at {[15] *time*}, or at any other time agreeable to the parties.

2. {[16] *Party*} requests permission to {[17] *inspect/measure/survey/photograph/test/sample*} {[18] *the property/{identify item on the property}*}. {[19] *Elaborate.*}

3. The scope of the {[20] *inspection/measurement/survey/photographing/testing/sampling*} will be {[21] *identify scope*}.

4. The person who will conduct the {[22] *inspection/measurement/survey/photographing/testing/sampling*} is {[23] *name of person*}, who is qualified to perform the {[24] *inspection/measurement/survey/photographing/testing/sampling*} by {[25] *his/her*} training and education. {[26] *Elaborate.*}

5. {[27] *Party*} requests permission to allow {[28] *identify other persons who will attend, e.g., attorney*} to attend.

{*IF TESTING OR SAMPLING, ADD PARAGRAPH 6*}

6. The proposed means for {[29] *testing/sampling*} is {[30] *identify the specific means for testing or sampling*}. The {[31] *testing/sampling*} will not destroy or materially alter the item to be {[32] *tested/sampled*}. Tex. R. Civ. P. 196.5. {[33] *Elaborate, if necessary.*}

SEE: Tex. R. Civ. P. 196.7
O'Connor's Texas Rules * Civil Trials (2019), "Request to Enter Land of a Party," ch. 6-K, §3, p. 697

ADD: STYLE OF THE CASE – FORM 1B:2
SIGNATURE BLOCK – FORM 1B:3
CERTIFICATE OF SERVICE – FORM 1B:13

NOTE: For most methods of service, the deadline to serve a request to enter property is 30 days before the end of the discovery period. Tex. R. Civ. P. 196.7(a)(1). See ***O'Connor's Texas Rules***, "Discovery Periods," ch. 6-A, §8, p. 523. But when service is by mail or fax, the request should be served at least 33 days (if mailed) or 31 days (if faxed after 5:00 p.m.) before the end of the discovery period. *See* Tex. R. Civ. P. 21a(b)(2), (c). See ***O'Connor's Texas Rules***, "Deadline to serve response," ch. 6-A, §14.1, p. 527.

★

{[1] *PARTY*}'S RESPONSE TO
{[2] *ADVERSE PARTY*}'S REQUEST TO ENTER {[3] *PARTY*}'S PROPERTY

To: {[4] *Adverse party*}, {[5] *name*}, by and through {[6] *his/her/its*} attorney of record, {[7] *name*}, {[8] *address*}.

{[9] *Party*}, {[10] *name*}, responds to {[11] *adverse party*}'s request to enter the {[12] *land/{identify other property}*} of {[13] *party*}, located at {[14] *address*}, under the authority of Texas Rule of Civil Procedure 196.7. {*See* ***O'Connor's Texas Rules****, "Contents of response," ch. 6-K, §3.3.2, p. 697.*}

{*CHOOSE APPROPRIATE PARAGRAPHS 1-3*}

{*Entry permitted*}

1. {[15] *Party*} will permit {[16] *adverse party*} to enter the {[17] *land/{identify other property}*}

{*CHOOSE APPROPRIATE RESPONSE*}

[A] at the requested date of {[18] *date*}, at {[19] *time*}, to {[20] *inspect/measure/survey/photograph/test/sample*} {[21] *the property/{identify item on the property}*}.

[B] on {[22] *identify date and time different from that requested by adverse party*} to {[23] *inspect/measure/survey/photograph/test/sample*} {[24] *the property/{identify item on the property}*}.

2. {[25] *Party*} will permit {[26] *name of person*} to {[27] *inspect/measure/survey/photograph/test/sample*} {[28] *the property/{identify item on the property}*}, and will permit {[29] *identify other persons who will attend, e.g., attorney*} to attend. {[30] *Specify any other conditions or limitations to scope of entry.*}

{*Entry not permitted*}

3. {[31] *Party*} refuses to permit {[32] *adverse party*} to enter the {[33] *land/{identify other property}*}. {[34] *Elaborate, specifying reasons entry will not be permitted. Include any objections and claims of privilege.*}

SEE: Tex. R. Civ. P. 196.7
O'Connor's Texas Rules * Civil Trials (2019), "Response," ch. 6-K, §3.3, p. 697

ADD: STYLE OF THE CASE – FORM 1B:2
SIGNATURE BLOCK – FORM 1B:3
CERTIFICATE OF SERVICE – FORM 1B:13

NOTE: The response must include any objections and claims of privilege. Tex. R. Civ. P. 196.7(c)(2).

Generally, a party responding to a request to enter property has 30 days to respond. Tex. R. Civ. P. 196.7(c)(1). But when the plaintiff serves a request to enter the defendant's property before the defendant's answer is due, the defendant has 50 days to respond rather than 30. *Id.* When service is by mail or fax, the responding party has an additional three days (if mailed) or one day (if faxed after 5:00 p.m.) to respond. *See* Tex. R. Civ. P. 21a(b)(2), (c). See ***O'Connor's Texas Rules***, "Deadline to serve response," ch. 6-A, §14.1, p. 527.

{[1] *PARTY*}'S MOTION TO ENTER PROPERTY OF {[2] *NAME OF NONPARTY*}

{[3] *Party*}, {[4] *name*}, asks the Court to order {[5] *name of nonparty*} to permit {[6] *party*} to enter the property located at {[7] *address*}, as allowed by Texas Rule of Civil Procedure 196.7. {*See **O'Connor's Texas Rules**, "Motion," ch. 6-K, §4.1, p. 697.*}

INTRODUCTION

1. Plaintiff, {[8] *name*}, sued defendant, {[9] *name*}, for {[10] *state basis of suit*}.

2. Discovery in this suit is governed by a Level {[11] *1/2/3*} discovery-control plan. The discovery period {[12] *will end/ended*} on {[13] *date*}. {*See **O'Connor's Texas Rules**, "Discovery-Control Plans," ch. 6-A, §7, p. 520.*}

3. This case is set for trial on {[14] *date*}.

4. {[15] *State other relevant facts about the suit.*}

BACKGROUND

5. The property subject to this motion is owned by {[16] *name of nonparty*}, {[17] *a person/an entity*} who is not a party to this suit, whose address is {[18] *address*}, and whose telephone number is {[19] *number*}.

6. As a result of the suit, it is necessary for {[20] *party*} to enter the property located at {[21] *address*}, and owned by {[22] *name of nonparty*}, for the purpose of {[23] *inspecting/measuring/surveying/photographing/testing/sampling*} the property.

7. This motion is served more than 30 days before the end of the discovery period.

8. {[24] *State other facts relevant to the motion.*}

ARGUMENT & AUTHORITIES

9. A court may issue an order for entry on a nonparty's property if the movant shows good cause and that the property or an object on the property is relevant to the subject matter of the lawsuit. Tex. R. Civ. P. 196.7(d); *In re SWEPI L.P.*, 103 S.W.3d 578, 583 (Tex. App.—San Antonio 2003, orig. proceeding).

10. There is good cause for the Court to allow {[25] *party*} to enter {[26] *name of nonparty*}'s property because {[27] *specify facts supporting good cause*}.

11. {28 *Party*}'s entry on {29 *name of nonparty*}'s property is relevant to this lawsuit because {30 *explain why entry is relevant or is likely to lead to the discovery of relevant evidence*}.

TIME, PLACE & OTHER CONDITIONS

12. The order on a motion to enter the property of another must include the time, place, manner, conditions, and scope of the inspection; describe the desired means, manner, and procedure for testing or sampling; and describe the person or persons by whom the inspection, testing, or sampling is to be made. Tex. R. Civ. P. 196.7(b).

13. {31 *Party*} suggests that the inspection take place on {32 *date*}, at {33 *time*}, or at any other time agreeable to the parties and {34 *name of nonparty*}.

14. {35 *Party*} requests permission to {36 *inspect/measure/survey/photograph/test/sample*} {37 *the property/{identify item on the property}*}. {38 *Elaborate.*}

15. The scope of the {39 *inspection/measurement/survey/photographing/testing/sampling*} will be {40 *identify scope*}.

16. The person who will conduct the {41 *inspection/measurement/survey/photographing/testing/sampling*} is {42 *name of person*}, who is qualified to perform the {43 *inspection/measurement/survey/photographing/testing/sampling*} by {44 *his/her*} training and education. {45 *Elaborate.*}

17. {46 *Party*} asks the Court to allow {47 *identify other persons who will attend, e.g., attorney*} to attend.

{*IF TESTING OR SAMPLING, ADD PARAGRAPH 18*}

18. The proposed means for {48 *testing/sampling*} is {49 *identify the specific means for testing or sampling*}. The {50 *testing/sampling*} will not destroy or materially alter the item to be {51 *tested/sampled*}. Tex. R. Civ. P. 196.5. {52 *Elaborate, if necessary.*}

CONCLUSION

19. {53 *Briefly summarize the motion.*}

PRAYER

20. For these reasons, {54 *party*} asks the Court to set this motion for hearing and, after the hearing, to order {55 *name of nonparty*} to allow {56 *party*} to enter {57 *his/her/its*} property.

Continued on next page

TEXAS CIVIL FORMS

CHAPTER 6. DISCOVERY

FORM 6K:3 MOTION TO ENTER PROPERTY OF NONPARTY

SEE: Tex. R. Civ. P. 196.5, 196.7
O'Connor's Texas Rules * Civil Trials (2019), "Motion to Enter Land of a Nonparty," ch. 6-K, §4, p. 697

ADD: STYLE OF THE CASE – FORM 1B:2
SIGNATURE BLOCK – FORM 1B:3
CERTIFICATE OF CONFERENCE – FORM 1B:12
CERTIFICATE OF SERVICE – FORM 1B:13

ATTACH: AFFIDAVIT – FORM 1B:8, if necessary
NOTICE OF HEARING OR SUBMISSION – FORM 1E:1
ORDER – FORM 6K:5

NOTE: For most methods of service, the deadline to serve a motion to enter the property of a nonparty is 30 days before the end of the discovery period. Tex. R. Civ. P. 196.7(a)(2). See ***O'Connor's Texas Rules***, "Discovery Periods," ch. 6-A, §8, p. 523. But when service is by mail or fax, the motion should be served at least 33 days (if mailed) or 31 days (if faxed after 5:00 p.m.) before the end of the discovery period. *See* Tex. R. Civ. P. 21a(b)(2), (c). See ***O'Connor's Texas Rules***, "Deadline to serve response," ch. 6-A, §14.1, p. 527.

{1 *NAME OF NONPARTY*}'S RESPONSE TO
{2 *PARTY*}'S MOTION TO ENTER PROPERTY OF NONPARTY

{3 *Name of nonparty*} asks the Court to refuse {4 *name of party*}'s request to enter the property of {5 *name of nonparty*}, located at {6 *address*}, under Texas Rule of Civil Procedure 196.7. {*See* ***O'Connor's Texas Rules****, "Response," ch. 6-K, §4.4, p. 698.*}

INTRODUCTION

1. Plaintiff, {7 *name*}, sued defendant, {8 *name*}, for {9 *state basis of suit*}.

2. Discovery in this suit is governed by a Level {10 *1/2/3*} discovery-control plan. The discovery period {11 *will end/ended*} on {12 *date*}. {*See* ***O'Connor's Texas Rules****, "Discovery-Control Plans," ch. 6-A, §7, p. 520.*}

3. This case is set for trial on {13 *date*}.

4. {14 *State other relevant facts about the suit.*}

BACKGROUND

5. The property subject to this response is owned by {15 *name of nonparty*}, {16 *a person/an entity*} who is not a party to this suit, whose address is {17 *address*}, and whose telephone number is {18 *number*}.

6. {19 *Party*}, {20 *name*}, has filed a motion to enter the property located at {21 *address*} for the purpose of {22 *inspecting/measuring/surveying/photographing/testing/sampling*} the property.

7. {23 *State other facts relevant to the response.*}

ARGUMENT & AUTHORITIES

{*CHOOSE APPROPRIATE PARAGRAPHS 8-12*}

8. A court cannot issue an order for entry on a nonparty's property unless the movant shows good cause and that the property or an object on the property is relevant to the subject matter of the lawsuit. Tex. R. Civ. P. 196.7(d); *In re SWEPI L.P.*, 103 S.W.3d 578, 583 (Tex. App.—San Antonio 2003, orig. proceeding).

9. There is not good cause for the Court to allow {24 *party*} to enter {25 *name of nonparty*}'s property because {26 *specify facts showing lack of good cause*}.

◄ *Continued on next page* ►

10. {㉗ *Party*}'s entry on {㉘ *name of nonparty*}'s property will not produce evidence relevant to this lawsuit because {㉙ *explain why entry will not lead to the discovery of relevant evidence*}.

11. {㉚ *Name of nonparty*} cannot grant {㉛ *party*}'s request to enter the property because it does not belong to {㉜ *name of nonparty*}. {㉝ *Elaborate.*}

12. The proposed means for {㉞ *testing/sampling*} is {㉟ *identify the specific means for testing or sampling*}. The {㊱ *testing/sampling*} will destroy or materially alter the item to be {㊲ *tested/sampled*}. *See* Tex. R. Civ. P. 196.5. {㊳ *Elaborate.*}

CONCLUSION

13. {㊴ *Briefly summarize the response.*}

PRAYER

14. For these reasons, {㊵ *name of nonparty*} asks the Court to deny {㊶ *party*}'s request to enter {㊷ *name of nonparty*}'s property.

SEE: Tex. R. Civ. P. 196.5, 196.7
O'Connor's Texas Rules * Civil Trials (2019), "Response," ch. 6-K, §4.4, p. 698

ADD: STYLE OF THE CASE – FORM 1B:2
SIGNATURE BLOCK – FORM 1B:3
CERTIFICATE OF SERVICE – FORM 1B:13

ATTACH: AFFIDAVIT – FORM 1B:8, if necessary
ORDER – FORM 6K:5

NOTE: The nonparty may file a motion for protective order under Texas Rule of Civil Procedure 192.6 to protect itself from undue burden, unnecessary expense, harassment, annoyance, or invasion of personal, constitutional, or property rights. See FORM 6A:10.

The court cannot sign an order requiring inspection of a nonparty's property without a hearing. *See* Tex. R. Civ. P. 196.7(a)(2). At the hearing, the parties and the nonparty may assert objections. *See* Tex. R. Civ. P. 196.7(c)(2).

ORDER ON {1 *PARTY*}'S
MOTION TO ENTER PROPERTY OF NONPARTY

After considering {2 *party*} {3 *name*}'s motion to gain entry to the property of a nonparty, the response, and arguments of counsel, the Court

{*CHOOSE APPROPRIATE ORDER*}

DENIES the motion.

GRANTS the motion because there is good cause to allow {4 *party*} to gain entry to the property of {5 *name of nonparty*}, and the entry is relevant to the subject matter of the lawsuit. Therefore, the Court orders {6 *name of nonparty*} to allow {7 *party*} to enter {8 *his/her/its*} property located at {9 *address*}.

CONDITIONS FOR ENTRY

1. The inspection will take place on {10 *date*}, at {11 *time*}, or at any other time agreeable to the parties and {12 *name of nonparty*}.

2. The following persons may attend the inspection: {13 *identify other persons who will attend, e.g., attorney*}.

3. The purpose of the entry onto {14 *name of nonparty*}'s property is to {15 *inspect/measure/survey/photograph/test/sample*} {16 *the property/{identify item on the property}*}. {17 *Elaborate, if necessary.*}

4. The scope of the {18 *inspection/measurement/survey/photographing/testing/sampling*} is limited to {19 *identify scope*}.

{*IF TESTING OR SAMPLING, ADD PARAGRAPH 5*}

5. The {20 *testing/sampling*} must be conducted as follows: {21 *identify means, manner, or procedures to be used*}.

6. The person who will conduct the {22 *inspection/measurement/survey/photographing/testing/sampling*} is {23 *name of person*}.

7. {24 *Specify any other conditions or limitations to scope of entry.*}

SIGNED on _______________, 20___.

____
PRESIDING JUDGE

◄ *Continued on next page* ►

FORM 6K:5 ORDER ON MOTION TO ENTER PROPERTY OF NONPARTY

SEE: Tex. R. Civ. P. 196.5, 196.7
O'Connor's Texas Rules * Civil Trials (2019), "Order," ch. 6-K, §4.6, p. 698

ADD: STYLE OF THE CASE – FORM 1B:2
CERTIFICATE OF SERVICE – FORM 1B:13, **if proposed order served separately from motion or response**

Chapter 7. Disposition Without Trial

Table of Contents

PLAINTIFF'S MOTION FOR DEFAULT JUDGMENT

Plaintiff, {❶ *name*}, asks the Court to sign a default judgment against defendant, {❷ *name*}.

INTRODUCTION

1. Plaintiff, {❸ *name*}, sued defendant, {❹ *name*}, for {❺ *state basis of suit*}.

2. {❻ *State other relevant facts about the suit.*}

BACKGROUND

3. On {❼ *date*}, plaintiff filed {❽ *his/her/its*} {❾ *original/{identify other}*} petition in this suit.

4. On {❿ *date*}, defendant was served with citation and a copy of plaintiff's {⓫ *original/{identify other}*} petition by {⓬ *describe method of service*}.

{*ADD PARAGRAPH 5 IF APPLICABLE*}

5. Attached as Exhibit {⓭ *letter*} is a copy of the certificate from the Secretary of State certifying that process was forwarded to defendant by certified mail, return receipt requested, on {⓮ *date*}. {*See* ***O'Connor's Texas Rules****, "After Secretary of State served," ch. 7-A, §3.9.1(3), p. 707.*}

6. The citation and proof of service were filed on {⓯ *date*}, which was at least ten days before the filing of this motion.

{*ADD PARAGRAPHS 7-8 IF APPLICABLE*}

7. Defendant made an appearance before the Court on {⓰ *date*}. {⓱ *Elaborate.*} Attached as Exhibit {⓲ *letter*} is an affidavit showing that defendant was served with notice of the default hearing on liability.

8. On {⓳ *date*}, the Court granted defendant's motion to quash {⓴ *service/citation*}.

9. The deadline for defendant to file an answer was {㉑ *date*}. {㉒ *Elaborate.*} However, defendant did not file an answer or any other pleading constituting an answer.

10. {㉓ *State other facts relevant to the motion.*}

◄ *Continued on next page* ►

ARGUMENT & AUTHORITIES

11. The Court should render a default judgment against defendant because defendant was properly served and did not file an answer or any other pleading constituting an answer within the prescribed time period. *See* Tex. R. Civ. P. 239. {*See* ***O'Connor's Texas Rules***, *"Sufficiency of service," ch. 7-A, §3.4, p. 705; "Sufficiency of defendant's answer," ch. 7-A, §3.7, p. 706; "When to move for default," ch. 7-A, §3.9.1, p. 707.*}

{*ADD PARAGRAPH 12 IF APPLICABLE*}

12. In accordance with Texas Civil Practice & Remedies Code section 39.001, plaintiff sent a notice of intent to take a default judgment against defendant to the Texas Attorney General by certified mail, return receipt requested, on {㉔ *date*}, which was at least ten days before the filing of this motion. Attached as Exhibit {㉕ *letter*} is a copy of proof of receipt. {*See* ***O'Connor's Texas Rules***, *"After notice to Attorney General," ch. 7-A, §3.9.1(4), p. 708.*}

13. The last known address of defendant is {㉖ *address*}. Attached as Exhibit {㉗ *letter*} is a certificate of defendant's last known address. {*See* ***O'Connor's Texas Rules***, *"Certificate of last known address," ch. 7-A, §3.9.2(2), p. 708.*}

14. Defendant {㉘ *is/is not/may be*} in military service. Attached as Exhibit {㉙ *letter*} is an affidavit about defendant's military status. {㉚ *Add if appropriate: Because defendant is in the military, plaintiff asks the Court to appoint an attorney to represent defendant before rendering a default judgment. 50 U.S.C. §3931(b)(2).*} {*See* ***O'Connor's Texas Rules***, *"Servicemembers' affidavit," ch. 7-A, §3.9.2(3), p. 708.*}

DAMAGES

{*CHOOSE APPROPRIATE PARAGRAPH 15*}

15. Plaintiff asks the Court to render a default judgment establishing defendant's liability and, after a hearing, render a final judgment awarding plaintiff damages in the amount of ${㉛ *amount*} {㉜ *add if applicable: plus costs, attorney fees, and prejudgment interest*}. Plaintiff requests a court reporter to record the proceedings. {*See* ***O'Connor's Texas Rules***, *"Ask for court reporter," ch. 7-A, §3.13.2(1), p. 710.*}

15. Plaintiff asks the Court to render a default judgment establishing defendant's liability and awarding plaintiff damages in the amount of ${㉝ *amount*} {㉞ *add if applicable: plus costs, attorney fees, and prejudgment interest*}. No hearing is necessary to establish the amount of damages because

{*CHOOSE APPROPRIATE STATEMENT*}

Ⓐ the damages alleged in plaintiff's {㉟ *original/{identify other}*} petition are liquidated, are proved by a written instrument, and may be accurately calculated. *See* Tex. R. Civ. P. 241. {㊱ *Elaborate.*} {*See **O'Connor's Texas Rules**, "Liquidated damages – hearing not required," ch. 7-A, §3.13.1, p. 709.*}

Ⓑ the damages alleged in plaintiff's {㊲ *original/{identify other}*} petition are unliquidated. A court can award unliquidated damages based on affidavits without holding an evidentiary hearing. *Ingram Indus., Inc. v. U.S. Bolt Mfg., Inc.*, 121 S.W.3d 31, 37 (Tex. App.—Houston [1st Dist.] 2003, no pet.); *see Tex. Commerce Bank v. New*, 3 S.W.3d 515, 517 (Tex. 1999). Plaintiff attaches to this motion the following affidavits: {㊳ *identify each affidavit and the corresponding exhibit letter to establish damages, costs, attorney fees, and prejudgment interest as appropriate*}. {*See **O'Connor's Texas Rules**, "Unliquidated damages – hearing required," ch. 7-A, §3.13.2, p. 710.*}

CONCLUSION

16. Plaintiff is entitled to a default judgment for the reasons asserted in this motion. {㊴ *Briefly summarize the motion.*}

PRAYER

17. For these reasons, plaintiff asks the Court {㊵ *add if applicable: to sign a default judgment on liability, to set a hearing to establish the amount of damages, and after the hearing,*} to sign a default judgment for the amount of ${㊶ *amount*} {㊷ *add if applicable: plus costs, attorney fees, and prejudgment interest*}. {㊸ *Add if appropriate: Before the Court renders a default judgment, plaintiff asks the Court to appoint an attorney to represent defendant.*}

SEE: Tex. R. Civ. P. 107, 122, 238-241, 243, 244
Tex. Civ. Prac. & Rem. Code §30.004, §38.001 et seq., §§39.001, 39.002
11 U.S.C. §362; 50 U.S.C. §3931
O'Connor's Texas Rules * Civil Trials (2019), "No-Answer Default," ch. 7-A, §3, p. 704

◄ *Continued on next page* ►

ADD: STYLE OF THE CASE – FORM 1B:2
SIGNATURE BLOCK – FORM 1B:3
CERTIFICATE OF SERVICE – FORM 1B:13

ATTACH: AFFIDAVIT – FORM 1B:8, if necessary
NOTICE OF HEARING OR SUBMISSION – FORM 1E:1
AFFIDAVIT FOR ATTORNEY FEES – FORM 1H:14, if necessary
CERTIFICATE OF LAST KNOWN ADDRESS – FORM 7A:2
SERVICEMEMBERS' AFFIDAVIT – FORM 7A:3
AFFIDAVIT FOR DAMAGES – FORM 7A:4, if necessary
AFFIDAVIT TO PROVE NOTICE – FORM 7A:5, if necessary
ORDER – FORM 7A:6, if hearing on damages is requested
DEFAULT JUDGMENT – FORM 9C:2
Certificate from Secretary of State, if necessary
Proof of receipt of notice to Attorney General, if necessary

NOTE: Although most default judgments are granted on a motion, it is not necessary to file a motion for default judgment to obtain a default judgment. The plaintiff is entitled to have the judge or clerk call the case on appearance day and to ask the court to grant a default judgment. Tex. R. Civ. P. 238, 239. When the case is called, the court can grant a default judgment if no answer is on file and the citation has been on file with the clerk for at least ten days, not counting the day the citation was filed and the day of the default judgment. *See* Tex. R. Civ. P. 107(h), 239.

If the defendant does not make an appearance or file an answer (i.e., no-answer default), the plaintiff is not required to give the defendant notice of the hearing before the court renders a default judgment. *See* ***Long v. McDermott***, 813 S.W.2d 622, 623-24 (Tex.App.—Houston [1st Dist.] 1991, no writ); ***Olivares v. Cauthorn***, 717 S.W.2d 431, 434 (Tex.App.—San Antonio 1986, writ dism'd). If, however, the defendant appeared in the case but did not file an answer (i.e., post-appearance default), the plaintiff must give the defendant notice of the trial or dispositive default-judgment hearing as a matter of due process. See ***O'Connor's Texas Rules***, "Post-appearance default," ch. 7-A, §2.2.1, p. 704. The plaintiff must prove it gave this notice before the court can render a default judgment. See FORM 7A:5.

If the defendant was served by publication and has not answered, the plaintiff must follow the procedures for obtaining a judgment under Texas Rule of Civil Procedure 244. See ***O'Connor's Texas Rules***, "Trial," ch. 10-B, §10.1, p. 940.

To prove unliquidated damages in a no-answer default case, the plaintiff can (1) attach affidavits to the motion for default, (2) take a witness to the hearing on the motion, or (3) ask the court to sign a default judgment on liability and set a date for a hearing on damages. See ***O'Connor's Texas Rules***, "Instrument to prove damages," ch. 7-A, §3.9.2(1), p. 708; "Unliquidated damages," ch. 7-A, §3.9.2(5)(b), p. 709; "Unliquidated damages – hearing required," ch. 7-A, §3.13.2, p. 710. The trial court can award unliquidated damages based on affidavit testimony. See ***O'Connor's Texas Rules***, "Offer proof of damages," ch. 7-A, §3.13.2(2), p. 710.

If the plaintiff is taking a default judgment against one defendant in a multiple-defendant case, the plaintiff should file a motion for severance so that the default judgment can become final. ***Castano v. Foremost Cty. Mut. Ins.***, 31 S.W.3d 387, 388 (Tex.App.—San Antonio 2000, no pet.).

If the defendant learns about the plaintiff's motion for a no-answer default judgment before the court signs the judgment, the defendant should file its answer. If a defendant learns that the court rendered a default against it, the defendant should file a motion for new trial. See FORM 10B:3.

CERTIFICATE OF LAST KNOWN ADDRESS

Plaintiff, {❶ *name*}, certifies that the last known address of

Ⓐ defendant, {❷ *name*}, is {❸ *address*}.

{*Continue for each additional defendant.*}

SEE: Tex. R. Civ. P. 239a
O'Connor's Texas Rules * Civil Trials (2019), "Certificate of last known address," ch. 7-A, §3.9.2(2), p. 708

ADD: STYLE OF THE CASE – FORM 1B:2
SIGNATURE BLOCK – FORM 1B:3

PLAINTIFF'S SERVICEMEMBERS' AFFIDAVIT

STATE OF TEXAS §
{❶ _______} COUNTY §

Before me, the undersigned notary, on this day personally appeared {❷ *name of affiant*}, the affiant, whose identity is known to me. After I administered an oath, affiant testified as follows:

1. "My name is {❸ *name of affiant*}. I am over 18 years of age, of sound mind, and capable of making this affidavit. The facts stated in this affidavit are within my personal knowledge and are true and correct.

2. "I am {❹ *identify status of affiant, e.g., plaintiff, plaintiff's representative, plaintiff's attorney*}.

{*CHOOSE APPROPRIATE PARAGRAPH 3*}

3. "Defendant, {❺ *name*}, is not in military service. Attached as Exhibit {❻ *letter*} is a copy of the Military Status Report provided by the Department of Defense Manpower Data Center stating that {❼ *explain contents of report*}."

3. "I ask the Court to appoint an attorney to represent defendant, {❽ *name*}, because defendant is in military service. The Servicemembers Civil Relief Act, 50 U.S.C. section 3931(b)(2), requires the Court to appoint an attorney to represent defendant before a judgment may be rendered against {❾ *him/her*}."

3. "I am unable to determine whether defendant, {❿ *name*}, is in military service. {⓫ *State facts showing what affiant has done to determine defendant's military status.*}"

____
{⓬ *Name of affiant*}

Sworn to and subscribed before me by {⓭ *name of affiant*} on __________, 20___.

____
Notary Public in and for
the State of Texas

SEE: Tex. R. Civ. P. 239a
50 U.S.C. §3931
O'Connor's Texas Rules * Civil Trials (2019), "Servicemembers' affidavit," ch. 7-A, §3.9.2(3), p. 708

ADD: STYLE OF THE CASE – FORM 1B:2

NOTE: **If the court cannot determine whether the defendant is in military service, the court may require the plaintiff to file a bond before entering judgment. 50 U.S.C. §3931(b)(3).**

See notes under FORM 1B:8.

AFFIDAVIT OF {❶ *NAME*}

STATE OF TEXAS §
{❷ ________} COUNTY §

Before me, the undersigned notary, on this day personally appeared {❸ *name of affiant*}, the affiant, whose identity is known to me. After I administered an oath, affiant testified as follows:

1. "My name is {❹ *name of affiant*}. I am over 18 years of age, of sound mind, and capable of making this affidavit. The facts stated in this affidavit are within my personal knowledge and are true and correct.

2. "I am {❺ *identify status of affiant, e.g., plaintiff, plaintiff's representative, plaintiff's attorney*}.

3. "Plaintiff, {❻ *name*}, sued defendant, {❼ *name*}, for {❽ *state basis of suit*}, and defendant has not filed an answer or any other pleading constituting an answer.

4. "Plaintiff is entitled to unliquidated damages in the amount of ${❾ *amount*}. {❿ *State basis for determining this amount.*}

5. "Plaintiff incurred these damages because {⓫ *state facts supporting a causal nexus between defendant's conduct and plaintiff's damages*}."

____
{⓬ *Name of affiant*}

Sworn to and subscribed before me by {⓭ *name of affiant*} on __________, 20___.

____
Notary Public in and for
the State of Texas

SEE: Tex. R. Civ. P. 243
O'Connor's Texas Rules * Civil Trials (2019), "Instrument to prove damages," ch. 7-A, §3.9.2(1), p. 708

ADD: STYLE OF THE CASE – FORM 1B:2

NOTE: See notes under FORM 1B:8.

AFFIDAVIT OF {❶ *NAME*}

STATE OF TEXAS §
{❷ ______} COUNTY §

Before me, the undersigned notary, on this day personally appeared {❸ *name of affiant*}, the affiant, whose identity is known to me. After I administered an oath, affiant testified as follows:

1. "My name is {❹ *name of affiant*}. I am over 18 years of age, of sound mind, and capable of making this affidavit. The facts stated in this affidavit are within my personal knowledge and are true and correct.

2. "I am {❺ *identify status of affiant, e.g., plaintiff, plaintiff's representative, plaintiff's attorney*}.

3. "Plaintiff, {❻ *name*}, sued defendant, {❼ *name*}, for {❽ *state basis of suit*}, and defendant has not filed an answer or any other pleading constituting an answer.

4. "Plaintiff served defendant with notice of the default hearing on liability. Attached to this affidavit is the certificate of service from the notice of hearing sent to defendant. The certificate of service is part of the affidavit."

____
{❾ *Name of affiant*}

Sworn to and subscribed before me by {❿ *name of affiant*} on __________, 20___.

____
Notary Public in and for
the State of Texas

SEE: ***O'Connor's Texas Rules * Civil Trials*** (2019), "Post-appearance default," ch. 7-A, §2.2.1, p. 704

ADD: STYLE OF THE CASE – FORM 1B:2

ATTACH: Certificate of service from notice of default hearing

NOTE: If the defendant appeared but did not file an answer, the plaintiff must give the defendant notice of the trial or dispositive default-judgment hearing. *See* ***LBL Oil Co. v. International Power Servs.***, 777 S.W.2d 390, 390-91 (Tex.1989); ***Sedona Pac. Hous. Prtshp. v. Ventura***, 408 S.W.3d 507, 512 (Tex. App.—El Paso 2013, no pet.).

See notes under FORM 1B:8.

ORDER ON PLAINTIFF'S MOTION FOR DEFAULT JUDGMENT

After considering plaintiff {❶ *name*}'s motion for default judgment, the pleadings, and the affidavits, the Court

GRANTS plaintiff's motion for default judgment against defendant, {❷ *name*} as to liability. Because the damages are unliquidated and were not proved by affidavit, the Court will hear evidence of damages on _______________, 20___.

SIGNED on _______________, 20___.

____
PRESIDING JUDGE

FORM 7A:6

SEE: Tex. R. Civ. P. 21, 122, 238-241, 243, 245
O'Connor's Texas Rules * Civil Trials (2019), "No-Answer Default," ch. 7-A, §3, p. 704

ADD: STYLE OF THE CASE – FORM 1B:2
CERTIFICATION OF SERVICE – FORM 1B:13, if proposed order served separately from motion

NOTE: When the trial court awards unliquidated damages after a default judgment, the defendant should ask the court to file findings of fact and conclusions of law. *See* ***IKB Indus. v. Pro-Line Corp.***, 938 S.W.2d 440, 443 (Tex.1997). A request for findings of fact and conclusions of law accomplishes two things. First, it extends the time for the trial court to state the basis for its judgment. *Id.* at 442-43. Second, it extends the time for perfecting the appeal. Tex. R. App. P. 26.1(a)(4). Findings of fact and conclusions of law are not appropriate for a default judgment based on liquidated damages. ***IKB Indus.***, 938 S.W.2d at 443.

PLAINTIFF'S MOTION FOR DEFAULT JUDGMENT

Plaintiff, {❶ *name*}, asks the Court to sign a default judgment against defendant, {❷ *name*}.

INTRODUCTION

1. Plaintiff, {❸ *name*}, sued defendant, {❹ *name*}, for {❺ *state basis of suit*}.

2. Defendant answered asserting {❻ *identify answer and list defensive pleas, affirmative defenses, and counterclaims*}.

3. {❼ *State other relevant facts about the suit.*}

BACKGROUND

{*CHOOSE APPROPRIATE PARAGRAPH 4*}

4. This case was set for trial on {❽ *date*}.

4. This case was set for a dispositive hearing on {❾ *identify motion, e.g., a motion for sanctions*} on {❿ *date*}.

{*CHOOSE APPROPRIATE PARAGRAPH 5*}

5. {⓫ *The Court/Plaintiff*} gave defendant more than three days' notice of the hearing. Tex. R. Civ. P. 21(b). Attached as Exhibit {⓬ *letter*} is a copy of the notice. {*See* ***O'Connor's Texas Rules****, "First setting," ch. 1-E, §2.1, p. 47.*}

5. {⓭ *The Court/Plaintiff*} gave defendant 45 days' notice of the trial setting. Tex. R. Civ. P. 245. Attached as Exhibit {⓮ *letter*} is a copy of the notice and proof of receipt. {*See* ***O'Connor's Texas Rules****, "TRCP 245," ch. 7-A, §4.3.2, p. 713.*}

5. {⓯ *The Court/Plaintiff*} gave defendant {⓰ *number*} days' notice of the trial setting. Because this case had previously been set for trial, it was not necessary to give defendant 45 days' notice. Tex. R. Civ. P. 245. Attached as Exhibit {⓱ *letter*} is a copy of the notice and proof of receipt. {*See* ***O'Connor's Texas Rules****, "TRCP 245," ch. 7-A, §4.3.2, p. 713.*}

6. Even though defendant received notice of the {⓲ *trial/dispositive hearing*} on {⓳ *date*}, defendant did not appear in person or by counsel.

7. {⓴ *State other facts relevant to the motion.*}

Continued on next page

ARGUMENT & AUTHORITIES

8. A court may grant a post-answer default if the defendant received notice of the setting for, but does not appear at, the trial or other dispositive hearing. *See* Tex. R. Civ. P. 21a, 245; *$429.30 v. State*, 896 S.W.2d 363, 366 (Tex. App.—Houston [1st Dist.] 1995, no writ); *Matsushita Elec. Corp. v. McAllen Copy Data, Inc.*, 815 S.W.2d 850, 853 (Tex. App.—Corpus Christi 1991, writ denied). {*See* ***O'Connor's Texas Rules**, "Notice of trial or dispositive hearing," ch. 7-A, §4.3, p. 712.*}

9. Before granting a post-answer default, the Court must determine that defendant received notice. By the proof attached to this motion, plaintiff has proved that defendant received notice to appear.

10. Because plaintiff is requesting a post-answer default judgment, plaintiff is required to offer evidence and prove all aspects of the case. Plaintiff requests a hearing to prove all the elements of {21 *his/her/its*} cause of action and {22 *his/her/its*} damages and asks that a court reporter be present to record the proceedings. {*See* ***O'Connor's Texas Rules**, "Trial," ch. 7-A, §4.5, p. 713.*}

CONCLUSION

11. {23 *Briefly summarize the motion.*}

PRAYER

12. For these reasons, plaintiff asks the Court to set plaintiff's motion for post-answer default judgment for hearing and, after the hearing, to sign a judgment granting the relief requested in plaintiff's {24 *original/{identify other}*} petition and proved by the evidence.

SEE: Tex. R. Civ. P. 21, 21a, 238-241, 243, 245
O'Connor's Texas Rules * Civil Trials (2019), "Post-Answer Default," ch. 7-A, §4, p. 712

ADD: STYLE OF THE CASE – FORM 1B:2
SIGNATURE BLOCK – FORM 1B:3
CERTIFICATE OF SERVICE – FORM 1B:13

ATTACH: DEFAULT JUDGMENT – FORM 9C:3
Copy of notice of trial setting or hearing and proof of receipt, if necessary
Copy of order, agreement, or request setting case for trial or hearing, if necessary

NOTE: If, before the court signs a judgment, the defendant learns that the plaintiff filed a motion for a post-answer default, the defendant should file a response to the motion, incorporating the grounds from FORM 10B:4. If a defendant learns that the court rendered a post-answer default against it, the defendant should file a motion for new trial. See FORM 10B:4.

{❶ *PARTY*}'S SPECIAL EXCEPTIONS TO {❷ *ADVERSE PARTY*}'S {❸ *MOTION/RESPONSE TO MOTION*} FOR SUMMARY JUDGMENT

{❹ *Party*}, {❺ *name*}, specially excepts to {❻ *adverse party*} {❼ *name*}'s {❽ *motion/response to the motion*} for summary judgment and asks the Court to order {❾ *adverse party*} to cure the defects in the {❿ *motion/response*}.

INTRODUCTION

1. Plaintiff, {⓫ *name*}, sued defendant, {⓬ *name*}, for {⓭ *state basis of suit*}.

2. {⓮ *State other relevant facts about the suit.*}

SPECIAL EXCEPTIONS

3. {⓯ *Party*} specially excepts to paragraph {⓰ *number*} in {⓱ *adverse party*}'s {⓲ *motion/response*} because the {⓳ *grounds/objections*} stated are {⓴ *vague/ambiguous*}. {㉑ *Explain why the grounds or objections are vague or ambiguous.*} {*See* ***O'Connor's Texas Rules***, *"When necessary," ch. 7-B, §5.1, p. 723.*}

PRAYER

4. For these reasons, {㉒ *party*} asks the Court to sustain the special exceptions and order {㉓ *adverse party*} to cure the defects in the {㉔ *motion/response to the motion*} for summary judgment within a reasonable time.

SEE: Tex. R. Civ. P. 166a
O'Connor's Texas Rules * Civil Trials (2019), "Special Exceptions & Summary Judgments," ch. 3-G, §10, p. 305; "Special Exceptions in Summary-Judgment Procedure," ch. 7-B, §5, p. 723

ADD: STYLE OF THE CASE – FORM 1B:2
SIGNATURE BLOCK – FORM 1B:3
CERTIFICATE OF SERVICE – FORM 1B:13

ATTACH: NOTICE OF HEARING OR SUBMISSION – FORM 1E:1
ORDER – FORM 3G:2

NOTE: This form should be used only when attacking a motion for summary judgment (or a response to a motion for summary judgment) for being vague or lacking specificity. To attack a party's pleadings for failing to state a cause of action, or for some other curable defect, use FORM 3G:1.

Some attorneys prefer to file special exceptions with their objections to summary-judgment evidence, rather than filing a separate motion to strike. For the motion to strike, see FORM 7C:9. To include objections to summary-judgment evidence, add the appropriate objections from FORM 7C:11 and modify this form accordingly.

{[1] *PARTY*}'S MOTION TO RESET
HEARING ON MOTION FOR SUMMARY JUDGMENT

{[2] *Party*}, {[3] *name*}, asks the Court to reset the hearing on {[4] *adverse party*} {[5] *name*}'s motion for summary judgment until {[6] *date*}, because {[7] *party*} was not given the required notice under Texas Rule of Civil Procedure 166a(c).

INTRODUCTION

1. Plaintiff, {[8] *name*}, sued defendant, {[9] *name*}, for {[10] *state basis of suit*}.

2. The motion for summary judgment is set for {[11] *submission/hearing*} on {[12] *date*}.

3. {[13] *State other relevant facts about the suit.*}

BACKGROUND

{*CHOOSE APPROPRIATE PARAGRAPH 4*}

4. {[14] *Adverse party*} served {[15] *his/her/its*} motion for summary judgment and notice of {[16] *submission/hearing*} on {[17] *party*} on {[18] *date*}, by {[19] *identify type of service, e.g., e-service, mail, commercial delivery service, e-mail*}. The notice of {[20] *submission/hearing*} identified the date for the {[21] *submission/hearing*} as {[22] *date*}.

4. {[23] *Adverse party*} served {[24] *his/her/its*} motion for summary judgment on {[25] *party*} on {[26] *date*}. The motion was not set for {[27] *submission/hearing*} at that time. {[28] *Adverse party*} set the motion for {[29] *submission/hearing*} for {[30] *date*}, and sent {[31] *party*} a written notice of the {[32] *submission/hearing*} date on {[33] *date*}, by {[34] *identify type of service, e.g., e-service, mail, commercial delivery service, e-mail*}.

5. To support the facts in this motion, {[35] *party*} includes the {[36] *affidavit/declaration*} of {[37] *name of affiant or declarant*} and the exhibits attached to that {[38] *affidavit/declaration*} as Exhibits {[39] *letters*} and incorporates the evidence into this motion by reference.

{*ADD PARAGRAPH 6 IF APPLICABLE*}

6. A copy of {[40] *identify document that proves date of mailing, e.g., envelope*} is attached to the {[41] *affidavit/declaration*} in support of this motion as Exhibit {[42] *letter*}.

7. {[43] *State other facts relevant to the motion.*}

ARGUMENT & AUTHORITIES

8. Generally, a nonmovant is entitled to 21 days' notice of the date set for hearing or submission of the motion. Tex. R. Civ. P. 166a(c); *Lewis v. Blake*, 876 S.W.2d 314, 316 (Tex. 1994). But if the motion is served by mail, the nonmovant is entitled to 24 days' notice. *See* Tex. R. Civ. P. 4, 21a(c), 166a(c); *Lewis*, 876 S.W.2d at 315-16; *Chadderdon v. Blaschke*, 988 S.W.2d 387, 388 (Tex. App.—Houston [1st Dist.] 1999, no pet.). {*See **O'Connor's Texas Rules**, "By rule – 21 days before hearing," ch. 7-B, §6.1, p. 724.*}

9. Because summary judgment is a harsh remedy, the notice requirements of Rule 166a are strictly construed. *Chadderdon*, 988 S.W.2d at 388; *Luna v. Estate of Rodriguez*, 906 S.W.2d 576, 582 (Tex. App.—Austin 1995, no writ). The notice provisions of the rule are intended to prevent the rendition of a judgment without allowing the opposing party a full opportunity to respond on the merits. *Chadderdon*, 988 S.W.2d at 388.

10. Rule 166a(c) allows a party to file a late motion only "on leave of court, with notice to opposing counsel." Tex. R. Civ. P. 166a(c). {44 *Adverse party*} did not secure leave of court to file the motion with less than {45 *21 days'/24 days'*} notice. {*See **O'Connor's Texas Rules**, "By court order," ch. 7-B, §6.3, p. 726.*}

11. In computing the deadline to give proper notice, the day of the hearing is counted, but the day the motion and notice of hearing are served is not. Tex. R. Civ. P. 4; *Lewis*, 876 S.W.2d at 316; *see* Tex. R. Civ. P. 166a(c).

{*CHOOSE APPROPRIATE PARAGRAPH 12*}

12. Because the {46 *motion and notice of submission/motion and notice of hearing/notice of submission/notice of hearing*} {47 *was/were*} served electronically, {48 *party*} is entitled to 21 days' notice of the hearing, counting from the day after the {49 *notice/motion and notice*} {50 *was/were*} served. *See* Tex. R. Civ. P. 4, 21a(a)(1), 166a(c).

12. Because the {51 *motion and notice of submission/motion and notice of hearing/notice of submission/notice of hearing*} {52 *was/were*} served by {53 *personal delivery/commercial delivery service*}, {54 *party*} is entitled to 21 days' notice of the hearing, counting from the day after the {55 *notice/motion and notice*} {56 *was/were*} served. *See* Tex. R. Civ. P. 4, 21a(a)(2), 166a(c); *Lewis*, 876 S.W.2d at 315-16.

Continued on next page

FORM 7B:2

12. Because the {57 *motion and notice of submission/motion and notice of hearing/notice of submission/notice of hearing*} {58 *was/were*} served by mail, {59 *party*} is entitled to 24 days' notice of the hearing, counting from the day after the {60 *notice/motion and notice*} {61 *was/were*} mailed. *Lewis*, 876 S.W.2d at 315-16; *Chadderdon*, 988 S.W.2d at 388; *see* Tex. R. Civ. P. 4, 21a(c), 166a(c).

12. Because the {62 *motion and notice of submission/motion and notice of hearing/notice of submission/notice of hearing*} {63 *was/were*} served by fax, {64 *party*} is entitled to 21 days' notice of the hearing, counting from the day after the {65 *notice/motion and notice*} {66 *was/were*} served. *See* Tex. R. Civ. P. 4, 21a(a)(2), (b)(2), 166a(c); *Lewis*, 876 S.W.2d at 315. {*See* ***O'Connor's Texas Rules***, *"By fax," ch. 7-B, §6.1.1(1)(d), p. 725.*}

12. Because the {67 *motion and notice of submission/motion and notice of hearing/notice of submission/notice of hearing*} {68 *was/were*} served by e-mail, {69 *party*} is entitled to 21 days' notice of the hearing, counting from the day after the {70 *notice/motion and notice*} {71 *was/were*} served. *See* Tex. R. Civ. P. 4, 21a(a)(2), 166a(c).

13. {72 *Party*} did not receive the {73 *21/24*} days' notice of the summary-judgment {74 *submission/hearing*}; {75 *party*} was given only {76 *number*} days' notice. {77 *State facts about date for submission or hearing and show how party received less than 21 or 24 days' notice.*}

CONCLUSION

14. {78 *Briefly summarize the motion.*}

PRAYER

15. For these reasons, {79 *party*} asks the Court to reset the hearing on the motion for summary judgment until {80 *date*}.

SEE: Tex. R. Civ. P. 4, 21a, 166a(c), 247, 330(d)
O'Connor's Texas Rules * Civil Trials (2019), "Motion to reset SJ hearing for lack of 21 days' notice," ch. 5-D, §9.2, p. 421; "By rule – 21 days before hearing," ch. 7-B, §6.1, p. 724; "By court order," ch. 7-B, §6.3, p. 726

ADD: STYLE OF THE CASE – FORM 1B:2
SIGNATURE BLOCK – FORM 1B:3
CERTIFICATE OF SERVICE – FORM 1B:13

ATTACH: AFFIDAVIT TO RESET FOR INADEQUATE NOTICE – FORM 7B:3
ORDER – FORM 7B:4

NOTE: E-filing is mandatory for most courts in all counties. *See* Tex.Sup.Ct. Order, Misc. Docket No. 13-9164 (Dec. 9, 2013). See ***O'Connor's Texas Rules***, "E-filing," ch. 1-C, §4.1.1, p. 25. If a document is e-filed, a party must serve it electronically through the electronic-filing manager (EFM), as long as the EFM has on file the e-mail address of the attorney or unrepresented party to be served. Tex. R. Civ. P. 21a(a)(1). If the e-mail address is not on file or if the document was not e-filed, a party may serve the document by (1) mail, (2) personal delivery, (3) commercial delivery, (4) fax, (5) e-mail, or (6) any other method as ordered by the court. Tex. R. Civ. P. 21a(a)(2). See ***O'Connor's Texas Rules***, "Methods of service," ch. 1-D, §4.2, p. 41.

When the motion and notice of hearing are served by mail, they must be mailed at least 24 days before the hearing because Texas Rule of Civil Procedure 21a(c) extends the minimum notice by three days.

In computing the number of days before the hearing, the day the motion and notice of hearing are served is not counted (it is "day 0"), but the day of the hearing is counted (it is "day 21" or "day 24"). Tex. R. Civ. P. 4; ***Lewis v. Blake***, 876 S.W.2d 314, 316 (Tex.1994); *see* Tex. R. Civ. P. 166a(c). For fax service, service is complete upon receipt; however, a document received after 5:00 p.m. is deemed served on the next day. *See* Tex. R. Civ. P. 21a(b)(2). Thus, a faxed motion and notice of hearing received after 5:00 p.m. must have been faxed at least 22 days before the hearing. See ***O'Connor's Texas Rules***, "Computing time limits – days," ch. 1-C, §7.1, p. 32; "Filing & serving motion & notice," ch. 7-B, §6.1.1, p. 724.

AFFIDAVIT IN SUPPORT OF {[1] *PARTY*}'S MOTION
TO RESET HEARING ON MOTION FOR SUMMARY JUDGMENT

STATE OF TEXAS §
{[2] ________} COUNTY §

Before me, the undersigned notary, on this day personally appeared {[3] *name of affiant*}, the affiant, whose identity is known to me. After I administered an oath, affiant testified as follows:

1. "My name is {[4] *name of affiant*}. I am over 18 years of age, of sound mind, and capable of making this affidavit. The facts stated in this affidavit are within my personal knowledge and are true and correct.

2. "I am the attorney for {[5] *party*} in this case. I received the documents described below.

{*CHOOSE APPROPRIATE PARAGRAPH 3*}

3. "{[6] *Adverse party*} served the motion for summary judgment and notice of {[7] *submission/hearing*} on {[8] *party*} on {[9] *date*}, by {[10] *identify type of service, e.g., e-service, mail, commercial delivery service, e-mail*}. The notice of {[11] *submission/hearing*} identifies the date for the {[12] *submission/hearing*} as {[13] *date*}. The motion and notice were received by {[14] *party*} at {[15] *address*}, on {[16] *date*}. {[17] *Add if appropriate: Attached as Exhibit {letter} is a copy of {identify document, e.g., the envelope} that proves the date of service.*} {[18] *Party*} was given only {[19] *number*} days' notice of the {[20] *submission/hearing*}. {*See* ***O'Connor's Texas Rules****, "By rule – 21 days before hearing," ch. 7-B, §6.1, p. 724.*}

3. "{[21] *Adverse party*} served the motion for summary judgment on {[22] *party*} on {[23] *date*}. The motion was not set for {[24] *submission/hearing*} at that time. {[25] *Adverse party*} set the motion for {[26] *submission/hearing*} for {[27] *date*}, and served a written notice of the date for {[28] *submission/hearing*} on {[29] *party*} at {[30] *address*} on {[31] *date*}, by {[32] *identify type of service, e.g., e-service, mail, commercial delivery service, e-mail*}. {[33] *Add if appropriate: Attached as Exhibit {letter} is a copy of {identify document, e.g., the envelope} that proves the date of service.*} {[34] *Party*} was given only {[35] *number*} days' notice of the {[36] *submission/hearing*}. {*See* ***O'Connor's Texas Rules****, "Filing & serving motion & notice," ch. 7-B, §6.1.1, p. 724.*}

4. "{37 *State facts about service of notice of date for submission or hearing and show how party received less than 21 or 24 days' notice.*}"

____
{38 *Name of affiant*}

Sworn to and subscribed before me by {39 *name of affiant*} on __________, 20___.

____
Notary Public in and for
the State of Texas

SEE: Tex. R. Civ. P. 14, 166a(c)
Tex. Gov't Code §312.011(1)
O'Connor's Texas Rules * Civil Trials (2019), "Motion to reset SJ hearing for lack of 21 days' notice," ch. 5-D, §9.2, p. 421; "By rule – 21 days before hearing," ch. 7-B, §6.1, p. 724

ADD: STYLE OF THE CASE – FORM 1B:2

ATTACH: Copy of document that proves date of service, if possible

NOTE: See notes under FORM 1B:8.

ORDER ON {❶ *PARTY*}'S MOTION
TO RESET SUMMARY-JUDGMENT HEARING

After considering {❷ *party*} {❸ *name*}'s motion to reset the date for submission of the motion for summary judgment, the pleadings, the response, the affidavits, and other evidence on file, the Court

{*CHOOSE APPROPRIATE ORDER*}

DENIES {❹ *party*}'s motion to reset.

GRANTS {❺ *party*}'s motion to reset. The date for submission of the motion for summary judgment is reset until _______________, 20___. {❻ *Party*} must file {❼ *his/her/its*} response to the motion for summary judgment, supporting affidavits, and other summary-judgment evidence by _______________, 20___.

SIGNED on _______________, 20___.

____
PRESIDING JUDGE

SEE: Tex. R. Civ. P. 166a(c), 247, 330(d)
O'Connor's Texas Rules * Civil Trials (2019), "Motion to reset SJ hearing for lack of 21 days' notice," ch. 5-D, §9.2, p. 421; "By rule – 21 days before hearing," ch. 7-B, §6.1, p. 724; "By court order," ch. 7-B, §6.3, p. 726

ADD: STYLE OF THE CASE – FORM 1B:2
CERTIFICATE OF SERVICE – FORM 1B:13, if proposed order served separately from motion or response

{1 *PARTY*}'S {2 *ADD IF APPLICABLE: VERIFIED*} MOTION FOR CONTINUANCE

{3 *Party*}, {4 *name*}, asks the Court to continue the hearing on {5 *adverse party*} {6 *name*}'s {7 *traditional/no-evidence/traditional and no-evidence*} motion for summary judgment because {8 *identify reason for continuance, e.g., additional time is needed to obtain discovery, an adequate time for discovery has not passed*}.

INTRODUCTION

1. Plaintiff, {9 *name*}, sued defendant, {10 *name*}, for {11 *state basis of suit*}.

2. {12 *State other relevant facts about the suit.*}

BACKGROUND

3. On {13 *date*}, {14 *adverse party*} filed a {15 *traditional/no-evidence/traditional and no-evidence*} motion for summary judgment.

4. The motion for summary judgment is set for {16 *submission/hearing*} on {17 *date*}.

{*ADD PARAGRAPH 5 IF APPLICABLE*}

5. {18 *Party*} attaches {19 *affidavits/declarations*} as Exhibits {20 *letters*} in support of the facts stated in this motion and incorporates the evidence into this motion by reference. {*See* ***O'Connor's Texas Rules***, *"Unsworn declaration," ch. 1-B, §3.2.17, p. 14; "Affidavit," ch. 5-D, §9.3.3, p. 423.*}

6. {21 *State other facts relevant to the motion.*}

{*CHOOSE APPROPRIATE CONTINUANCE MOTIONS*}

CONTINUANCE TO OBTAIN ADDITIONAL DISCOVERY

7. Under Texas Rule of Civil Procedure 166a(g), a court can grant a continuance of a summary-judgment hearing if the party opposing summary judgment can establish by affidavit or verified motion that it has not had an adequate time for discovery. *Tenneco Inc. v. Enter. Prods. Co.*, 925 S.W.2d 640, 647 (Tex. 1996). To seek a continuance under Rule 166a(g), the affidavit or verified motion must identify the evidence sought, explain why it is material, and state with particularity the diligence used to obtain the evidence. *West v. SMG*, 318 S.W.3d 430, 443 (Tex. App.—Houston [1st Dist.] 2010, no pet.); *Rocha v. Faltys*, 69 S.W.3d 315, 319 (Tex. App.—Austin 2002, no pet.); *Dozier v. AMR Corp.*, No. 02-09-186-CV (Tex. App.—Fort Worth 2010, no pet.) (memo op.;

Continued on next page

8-5-10); *In re Estate of Mask*, No. 04-07-00667-CV (Tex. App.—San Antonio 2008, pet. denied) (memo op.; 10-15-08). If the basis for continuance is the need to take additional depositions, the affidavit or verified motion must also meet the additional requirements of Texas Rule of Civil Procedure 252. *Tri-Steel Structures, Inc. v. Baptist Found.*, 166 S.W.3d 443, 448 (Tex. App.—Fort Worth 2005, pet. denied); *Gundermann v. Buehring*, No. 13-05-278-CV (Tex. App.—Corpus Christi 2006, pet. denied) (memo op.; 2-2-06). To meet the additional requirements of Rule 252, the affidavit or verified motion must (1) explain the reasons for not obtaining the discovery earlier, if known, and (2) show that the discovery cannot be obtained from any other source if the party had previously applied for a continuance. Tex. R. Civ. P. 252; *see Mulcahy v. Wal-Mart Stores, Inc.*, No. 02-10-00074-CV (Tex. App.—Fort Worth 2010, no pet.) (memo op.; 12-16-10); *Gundermann*, No. 13-05-278-CV (memo op.).

8. If the affidavit or verified motion meets the requirements for a continuance, the court should consider the following nonexclusive factors in deciding whether to grant the motion: (1) the materiality and the purpose of the discovery sought, (2) whether the party exercised due diligence, and (3) the length of time the case has been on file. *West*, 318 S.W.3d at 443; *see Joe v. Two Thirty Nine Joint Venture*, 145 S.W.3d 150, 161 (Tex. 2004).

A. Evidence sought.

9. {22 *Party*} needs additional time to obtain the following evidence: {23 *specifically identify evidence needed to oppose motion for summary judgment, e.g., requests for production, deposition*}. {24 *Elaborate.*}

B. Evidence is material to opposition.

10. This evidence is material to {25 *party*}'s opposition to {26 *adverse party*}'s motion for summary judgment because {27 *explain*}.

C. {28 *Party*} has exercised diligence in attempting to obtain the evidence.

11. {29 *Party*} has been unable to obtain this evidence earlier even though {30 *he/she/it*} diligently used the discovery process. {31 *Summarize discovery attempts demonstrating diligence. If known, state why discovery attempts did not obtain evidence, e.g., witness is abroad and cannot be reached for two weeks, adverse party has not responded to discovery request, adverse party has objected to discovery request.*}

{ADD SECTION D IF REQUESTING DEPOSITION AND PARTY HAS PREVIOUSLY REQUESTED A CONTINUANCE}

D. Evidence cannot be obtained from another source.

12. {㉜ *Party*} cannot obtain the evidence from any other source. {㉝ *State facts that demonstrate inability to obtain evidence elsewhere.*}

E. Case has been on file for short period of time.

13. This case has been on file for a short period of time: only {㉞ *number*} {㉟ *weeks/months*}. {㊱ *Show the dates the suit and the motion for summary judgment were filed and the date the discovery period ended or will end.*} {*See* ***O'Connor's Texas Rules****, "Length of time suit has been on file," ch. 5-D, §9.3.2(5), p. 423.*}

CONTINUANCE TO PERMIT ADEQUATE TIME FOR DISCOVERY

14. Under Texas Rule of Civil Procedure 166a(i), a party cannot file a no-evidence motion for summary judgment until after an adequate time for discovery has passed. *In re Guardianship of Patlan*, 350 S.W.3d 189, 195 (Tex. App.—San Antonio 2011, no pet.). If a party contends that an adequate time for discovery has not passed, the party must file either an affidavit explaining the need for further discovery or a verified motion for continuance. *Watson v. Dall. Indep. Sch. Dist.*, 135 S.W.3d 208, 227 (Tex. App.—Waco 2004, no pet.), *disapproved on other grounds*, *Univ. of Tex. Med. Branch at Galveston v. Barrett*, 159 S.W.3d 631 (Tex. 2005); *Tempay, Inc. v. TNT Concrete & Constr., Inc.*, 37 S.W.3d 517, 520-21 (Tex. App.—Austin 2001, pet. denied); *see Davis v. West*, 317 S.W.3d 301, 313-14 (Tex. App.—Houston [1st Dist.] 2009, no pet.). To seek a continuance, the affidavit or verified motion must identify the evidence sought, explain why it is material, and state with particularity the diligence used to obtain the evidence. *See Hart v. Comstock*, No. 14-09-00657-CV (Tex. App.—Houston [14th Dist.] 2010, no pet.) (memo op.; 7-27-10). If the basis for continuance is the need to take additional depositions, the affidavit or verified motion must also meet the additional requirements of Texas Rule of Civil Procedure 252. *See Hart*, No. 14-09-00657-CV (memo op.). To meet the additional requirements of Rule 252, the affidavit or verified motion must (1) explain the reasons for not obtaining the discovery earlier, if known, and (2) show that the discovery cannot be obtained from any other source, if the party had previously applied for a continuance. Tex. R. Civ. P. 252.

◄ *Continued on next page* ►

15. If the affidavit or verified motion meets the requirements for a continuance, the court should consider the following nonexclusive factors for determining whether an adequate time for discovery has passed: (1) the nature of the suit, (2) the evidence necessary to controvert the motion, (3) the length of time the case has been on file, (4) the length of time the motion has been on file, (5) the amount of discovery that has already taken place, (6) whether the movant requested stricter deadlines for discovery, and (7) whether the discovery deadlines in place were specific or vague. *Cmty. Initiatives, Inc. v. Chase Bank*, 153 S.W.3d 270, 278 (Tex. App.—El Paso 2004, no pet.); *see McInnis v. Mallia*, 261 S.W.3d 197, 201 (Tex. App.—Houston [14th Dist.] 2008, no pet.). {*See **O'Connor's Texas Rules**, "During discovery period," ch. 7-D, §2.1.2, p. 762.*}

A. Evidence sought.

16. {㊲ *Party*} needs additional time to obtain the following evidence: {㊳ *specifically identify evidence needed to oppose motion for summary judgment, e.g., requests for production, deposition*}. {㊴ *Elaborate.*}

B. Evidence is material to opposition.

17. This evidence is material to {㊵ *party*}'s opposition to {㊶ *adverse party*}'s no-evidence motion for summary judgment because {㊷ *explain*}.

C. {㊸ *Party*} has exercised diligence in attempting to obtain the evidence.

18. {㊹ *Party*} has been unable to obtain this evidence earlier even though {㊺ *he/she/it*} diligently used the discovery process. {㊻ *Summarize discovery attempts demonstrating diligence. If known, state why discovery attempts did not obtain evidence, e.g., witness is abroad and cannot be reached, adverse party has not responded to discovery request, adverse party has objected to discovery request.*}

{*ADD SECTION D IF REQUESTING DEPOSITION AND PARTY HAS PREVIOUSLY REQUESTED A CONTINUANCE*}

D. Evidence cannot be obtained from another source.

19. {㊼ *Party*} cannot obtain the evidence from any other source. {㊽ *State facts that demonstrate inability to obtain evidence elsewhere.*}

E. Adequate time for discovery has not passed.

20. An adequate time for discovery has not passed in this case. {㊾ *Address the applicable factors and show that an adequate time for discovery has not passed.*}

CONTINUANCE UNTIL COURT RULES ON DISCOVERY MOTIONS

21. {50 *Party*} asks the Court to continue the summary-judgment hearing until after it rules on {51 *party*}'s outstanding discovery motions and {52 *party*} has a reasonable opportunity to review the Court's rulings. A party is entitled to a ruling on its discovery motions within a reasonable time. *Nelson v. PNC Mortg. Corp.*, 139 S.W.3d 442, 445 (Tex. App.—Dallas 2004, no pet.). Granting a summary judgment before ruling on a party's discovery motions forecloses any possibility that the party can exercise her right to obtain reasonable discovery before summary judgment. *Id.* For this reason, {53 *party*} asks the Court to continue the summary-judgment hearing until {54 *number*} days after it rules on the following discovery motions: {55 *list outstanding motions*}.

CONTINUANCE TO CURE DEFECT IN SUMMARY-JUDGMENT EVIDENCE

22. {56 *Party*} asks the Court to continue the summary-judgment hearing until after {57 *party*} cures a defect in {58 *his/her/its*} summary-judgment evidence. A motion to continue a summary-judgment hearing should be granted if a curable defect is identified in a party's summary-judgment evidence. *See* Tex. R. Civ. P. 166a(f); *Webster v. Allstate Ins. Co.*, 833 S.W.2d 747, 749-50 (Tex. App.—Houston [1st Dist.] 1992, no writ).

23. On {59 *date*}, {60 *adverse party*} raised an objection to {61 *identify summary-judgment evidence, e.g., plaintiff's affidavit*}. {62 *Adverse party*} alleged that {63 *identify summary-judgment evidence, e.g., the affidavit*} was defective because {64 *explain objection*}.

24. The Court should grant {65 *party*}'s motion for continuance because the defect in {66 *party*}'s summary-judgment evidence can be cured. {67 *Elaborate.*}

CONTINUANCE {68 *SPECIFY OTHER GROUNDS*}

25. {*For other grounds for continuance, insert appropriate paragraphs from FORM 5D:1 or FORM 5D:2.*}

CONCLUSION

26. {69 *Briefly summarize the motion.*}

PRAYER

27. For these reasons, {70 *party*} asks the Court to continue the hearing on {71 *adverse party*}'s {72 *traditional/no-evidence/traditional and no-evidence*} motion for summary judgment until {73 *date*}.

◄ *Continued on next page* ►

SEE: Tex. R. Civ. P. 5, 166a(g), 247, 251, 252
*O'Connor's Texas Rules * Civil Trials* (2019), "Motion to continue SJ hearing," ch. 5-D, §9.3, p. 422; "Motion to continue hearing," ch. 7-B, §6.10.1, p. 727; "Challenge timing of motion," ch. 7-D, §3.2.2, p. 764

ADD: STYLE OF THE CASE – FORM 1B:2
SIGNATURE BLOCK – FORM 1B:3
CERTIFICATE OF SERVICE – FORM 1B:13

ATTACH: AFFIDAVIT FOR CONTINUANCE OF SJ HEARING – FORM 7B:6, if necessary
ORDER – FORM 7B:8

NOTE: The request for additional time to respond to the motion for summary judgment can be included in the response to the motion for summary judgment (see FORMS 7C:3, 4) or made as a separate motion. A party should not file a motion for continuance without also filing the response to the motion for summary judgment. If the motion for continuance is denied, it may be too late to file the response.

To object to lack of the required 21 days' notice, a party should file a motion to reset, not a motion for continuance. See FORM 7B:2.

{❶ *PARTY*}'S AFFIDAVIT IN SUPPORT OF MOTION FOR CONTINUANCE

STATE OF TEXAS §
{❷ _______} COUNTY §

Before me, the undersigned notary, on this day personally appeared {❸ *name of affiant*}, the affiant, whose identity is known to me. After I administered an oath, affiant testified as follows:

1. "My name is {❹ *name of affiant*}. I am over 18 years of age, of sound mind, and capable of making this affidavit. The facts stated in this affidavit are within my personal knowledge and are true and correct.

2. "{❺ *Party*} cannot present facts essential to justify {❻ *his/her/its*} opposition to {❼ *adverse party*}'s motion for summary judgment and needs additional time to obtain the following evidence: {❽ *identify evidence*}.

3. "The evidence is material to {❾ *party*}'s {❿ *claim/defense*} of {⓫ *identify claim or defense*} because {⓬ *state facts showing materiality of evidence*}. {⓭ *Elaborate.*}

4. "{⓮ *Party*} was unable to obtain the evidence earlier even though {⓯ *he/she/it*} was diligent. {⓰ *Summarize efforts to obtain evidence, demonstrating diligence. If known, state why party could not obtain evidence.*}

{*CLOSE QUOTES OR ADD PARAGRAPH 5 IF PARTY IS SEEKING A DEPOSITION AND HAS PREVIOUSLY REQUESTED A CONTINUANCE*}

5. "This evidence cannot be obtained from any other source. {⓱ *State facts that demonstrate inability to obtain testimony elsewhere.*}"

____
{⓲ *Name of affiant*}

Sworn to and subscribed before me by {⓳ *name of affiant*} on __________, 20___.

____
Notary Public in and for
the State of Texas

◄ *Continued on next page* ►

SEE: Tex. R. Civ. P. 166a(g), 251, 252
O'Connor's Texas Rules * Civil Trials (2019), "Affidavit," ch. 5-D, §9.3.3, p. 423

ADD: STYLE OF THE CASE – FORM 1B:2

ATTACH: NOTICE OF ORAL DEPOSITION – FORM 6F:1, if necessary
Copy of discovery request, if necessary

NOTE: When requesting a continuance for additional time to conduct discovery, the request and the affidavit must be specific.

See notes under FORM 1B:8.

{[1] *PARTY*}'S RESPONSE TO
{[2] *ADVERSE PARTY*}'S MOTION FOR CONTINUANCE

{[3] *Party*}, {[4] *name*}, asks the Court to deny {[5] *adverse party*} {[6] *name*}'s motion to continue the hearing on {[7] *party*}'s {[8] *traditional/no-evidence/traditional and no-evidence*} motion for summary judgment.

INTRODUCTION

1. Plaintiff, {[9] *name*}, sued defendant, {[10] *name*}, for {[11] *state basis of suit*}.

2. {[12] *State other relevant facts about the suit.*}

BACKGROUND

3. On {[13] *date*}, {[14] *party*} filed a {[15] *traditional/no-evidence/traditional and no-evidence*} motion for summary judgment.

4. The motion for summary judgment is set for {[16] *submission/hearing*} on {[17] *date*}.

5. In response to {[18] *party*}'s motion for summary judgment, {[19] *adverse party*} asked the Court continue the hearing {[20] *identify grounds asserted for continuance, e.g., so she can conduct additional discovery*}.

{*ADD PARAGRAPH 6 IF APPLICABLE*}

6. {[21] *Party*} attaches {[22] *affidavits/declarations*} as Exhibits {[23] *letters*} in support of the facts stated in this response and incorporates the evidence into this response by reference. {*See* ***O'Connor's Texas Rules****, "Unsworn declaration," ch. 1-B, §3.2.17, p. 14; "Affidavit," ch. 5-D, §9.3.3, p. 423.*}

7. {[24] *State facts relevant to the response.*}

{*CHOOSE APPROPRIATE RESPONSES TO CONTINUANCE*}

RESPONSE TO CONTINUANCE TO OBTAIN ADDITIONAL DISCOVERY

8. Under Texas Rule of Civil Procedure 166a(g), a court can grant a continuance of a summary-judgment hearing if the party opposing summary judgment can establish by affidavit or verified motion that it has not had adequate time for discovery. *Tenneco Inc. v. Enter. Prods. Co.*, 925 S.W.2d 640, 647 (Tex. 1996). To seek a continuance under Rule 166a(g), the affidavit or verified motion must identify the evidence sought, explain why it is material, and state with particularity the diligence used to obtain the evidence. *West v. SMG*, 318 S.W.3d 430, 443 (Tex. App.—Houston [1st Dist.] 2010, no

◄ *Continued on next page* ►

pet.); *Rocha v. Faltys*, 69 S.W.3d 315, 319 (Tex. App.—Austin 2002, no pet.); *Dozier v. AMR Corp.*, No. 02-09-186-CV (Tex. App.—Fort Worth 2010, no pet.) (memo op.; 8-5-10); *In re Estate of Mask*, No. 04-07-00667-CV (Tex. App.—San Antonio 2008, pet. denied) (memo op.; 10-15-08). If the basis for continuance is the need to take additional depositions, the affidavit or verified motion must also meet the additional requirements of Texas Rules of Civil Procedure 252. *Tri-Steel Structures, Inc. v. Baptist Found.*, 166 S.W.3d 443, 448 (Tex. App.—Fort Worth 2005, pet. denied); *Gundermann v. Buehring*, No. 13-05-278-CV (Tex. App.—Corpus Christi 2006, pet. denied) (memo op.; 2-2-06). To meet the additional requirements of Rule 252, the affidavit or verified motion must (1) explain the reasons for not obtaining the discovery earlier, if known, and (2) show that the discovery cannot be obtained from any other source if the party had previously applied for a continuance. Tex. R. Civ. P. 252; *see Mulcahy v. Wal-Mart Stores, Inc.*, No. 02-10-00074-CV (Tex. App.—Fort Worth 2010, no pet.) (memo op.; 12-16-10); *Gundermann*, No. 13-05-278-CV (memo op.).

9. If the affidavit or verified motion meets the requirements for a continuance, the court can consider the following nonexclusive factors in deciding whether to grant the motion: (1) the materiality and the purpose of the discovery sought, (2) whether the party exercised due diligence, and (3) the length of time the case has been on file. *West*, 318 S.W.3d at 443; *see Joe v. Two Thirty Nine Joint Venture*, 145 S.W.3d 150, 161 (Tex. 2004).

{*CHOOSE APPROPRIATE SECTIONS A-F*}

A. {㉕ *Adverse party*}'s motion was not verified or supported by affidavit.

10. The Court should deny {㉖ *adverse party*}'s motion for continuance because the motion was not verified or supported by an affidavit. {㉗ *Elaborate.*}

B. {㉘ *Adverse party*} did not identify the evidence needed.

11. The Court should deny {㉙ *adverse party*}'s motion for continuance because {㉚ *adverse party*} did not identify in the {㉛ *affidavit/verified motion*} the specific evidence {㉜ *he/she/it*} needed to oppose the motion for summary judgment. {㉝ *Elaborate.*} Conclusory allegations that additional discovery is needed without identifying the specific evidence needed are not sufficient to support a motion for continuance. *Hart v. Comstock*, No. 14-09-00657-CV (Tex. App.—Houston [14th Dist.] 2010, no pet.) (memo op.; 7-27-10).

C. Evidence is not material to opposition.

{*CHOOSE APPROPRIATE PARAGRAPHS 12-13*}

12. The Court should deny {㉞ *adverse party*}'s motion for continuance because {㉟ *adverse party*} did not specify in the {㊱ *affidavit/verified motion*} how the evidence is material to the motion for summary judgment. {㊲ *Elaborate.*} Conclusory allegations that the evidence is material are insufficient to support a motion for continuance. *Carter v. MacFadyen*, 93 S.W.3d 307, 310 (Tex. App.—Houston [14th Dist.] 2002, pet. denied).

13. The Court should deny {㊳ *adverse party*}'s motion for continuance because the evidence sought to be obtained from {㊴ *his/her/its*} discovery is immaterial. {㊵ *Elaborate.*} When evidence is immaterial to a motion for summary judgment because it will not raise a fact issue, the court is permitted to render a summary judgment without allowing discovery to proceed. *See Doe v. Roman Catholic Archdiocese of Galveston-Hous.*, 362 S.W.3d 803, 812 (Tex. App.—Houston [14th Dist.] 2012, no pet.).

D. {㊶ *Adverse party*} has not been diligent in attempting to obtain evidence.

{*CHOOSE APPROPRIATE PARAGRAPHS 14-15*}

14. The Court should deny {㊷ *adverse party*}'s motion for continuance because {㊸ *adverse party*} did not identify in the {㊹ *affidavit/verified motion*} the specific steps {㊺ *he/she/it*} took to diligently obtain the evidence. {㊻ *Elaborate.*} Conclusory allegations that the party was diligent in trying to obtain the evidence are insufficient to support a motion for continuance. *Carter v. MacFadyen*, 93 S.W.3d 307, 310 (Tex. App.—Houston [14th Dist.] 2002, pet. denied).

15. The Court should deny {㊼ *adverse party*}'s motion for continuance because {㊽ *adverse party*} was not diligent in trying to obtain the evidence. {㊾ *Elaborate.*} When a party does not diligently use the rules of civil procedure for discovery purposes, the court does not abuse its discretion by denying the motion for continuance. *State v. Wood Oil Distrib., Inc.*, 751 S.W.2d 863, 865 (Tex. 1988).

{*ADD SECTION E IF PARTY IS SEEKING A DEPOSITION AND HAS PREVIOUSLY REQUESTED A CONTINUANCE*}

E. Evidence can be obtained from another source.

16. The Court should deny {㊿ *adverse party*}'s motion for continuance because {51 *adverse party*} can obtain the evidence from another source. {52 *Elaborate.*}

Continued on next page

F. {53 *Adverse party*} has had an adequate time for discovery.

17. The Court should deny {54 *adverse party*}'s motion for continuance because {55 *adverse party*} has had an adequate time for discovery.

{*CHOOSE APPROPRIATE REASONS*}

a. The case has been on file for {56 *number*} {57 *weeks/months*}, which is more than an adequate time for discovery. {58 *Elaborate.*}

b. When considering a request for a continuance, courts can presume that a plaintiff has sufficiently investigated her own case before filing suit. *Clemons v. Citizens Med. Ctr.*, 54 S.W.3d 463, 469 (Tex. App.—Corpus Christi 2001, no pet.).

c. Contrary to {59 *adverse party*}'s motion, a party can move for traditional summary judgment at any time; there is no requirement that the motion be brought after discovery deadlines have passed. *Lucio v. John G. & Marie Stella Kenedy Mem'l Found.*, 298 S.W.3d 663, 669 (Tex. App.—Corpus Christi 2009, pet. denied).

RESPONSE TO CONTINUANCE TO PERMIT ADEQUATE TIME FOR DISCOVERY

18. Under Texas Rule of Civil Procedure 166a(i), a party cannot file a no-evidence motion for summary judgment until after an adequate time for discovery has passed. *In re Guardianship of Patlan*, 350 S.W.3d 189, 195 (Tex. App.—San Antonio 2011, no pet.). If a party contends that an adequate time for discovery has not passed, the party must file either an affidavit explaining the need for further discovery or a verified motion for continuance. *Watson v. Dall. Indep. Sch. Dist.*, 135 S.W.3d 208, 227 (Tex. App.—Waco 2004, no pet.), *disapproved on other grounds*, *Univ. of Tex. Med. Center at Galveston v. Barrett*, 159 S.W.3d 631 (Tex. 2005); *Tempay, Inc. v. TNT Concrete & Constr., Inc.*, 37 S.W.3d 517, 520-21 (Tex. App.—Austin 2001, pet. denied); *see Davis v. West*, 317 S.W.3d 301, 313-14 (Tex. App.—Houston [1st Dist.] 2009, no pet.). To seek a continuance, the affidavit or verified motion must identify the evidence sought, explain why it is material, and state with particularity the diligence used to obtain the evidence. *See Hart v. Comstock*, No. 14-09-00657-CV (Tex. App.—Houston [14th Dist.] 2010, no pet.) (memo op.; 7-27-10). If the basis for continuance is the need to take additional depositions, the affidavit or verified motion must also meet the additional requirements of Texas Rules of Civil Procedure 252. *See Hart*, No. 14-09-00657-CV (memo op.). To meet the additional requirements of Rule 252, the affidavit or verified motion must (1) explain the reasons for not obtaining the discovery earlier, if known, and (2) show that the discovery cannot be obtained from any other source, if the party had previously applied for a continuance. Tex. R. Civ. P. 252.

19. If the affidavit or verified motion meets the requirements for a continuance, the court can consider the following nonexclusive factors for determining whether an adequate time for discovery has passed: (1) the nature of the suit, (2) the evidence necessary to controvert the motion, (3) the length of time the case has been on file, (4) the length of time the motion has been on file, (5) the amount of discovery that has already taken place, (6) whether the movant requested stricter deadlines for discovery, and (7) whether the discovery deadlines in place were specific or vague. *Cmty. Initiatives, Inc. v. Chase Bank*, 153 S.W.3d 270, 278 (Tex. App.—El Paso 2004, no pet.); *see McInnis v. Mallia*, 261 S.W.3d 197, 201 (Tex. App.—Houston [14th Dist.] 2008, no pet.). {*See* ***O'Connor's Texas Rules***, *"During discovery period," ch. 7-D, §2.1.2, p. 762.*}

{*CHOOSE APPROPRIATE SECTIONS A-F*}

A. {⓺⓪ *Adverse party*}'s motion was not verified or supported by affidavit.

20. The Court should deny {61 *adverse party*}'s motion for continuance because the motion was not verified or supported by an affidavit. {62 *Elaborate.*}

B. {63 *Adverse party*} did not identify the evidence needed.

21. The Court should deny {64 *adverse party*}'s motion for continuance because {65 *adverse party*} did not identify in the {66 *affidavit/verified motion*} the specific evidence she needed to oppose the motion for summary judgment. {67 *Elaborate.*} Conclusory allegations that additional discovery is needed without identifying the specific evidence needed are not sufficient to support a motion for continuance. *Hart*, No. 14-09-00657-CV (memo op.).

C. Evidence is not material to opposition.

{*CHOOSE APPROPRIATE PARAGRAPHS 22-23*}

22. The Court should deny {68 *adverse party*}'s motion for continuance because {69 *adverse party*} did not specify in the {70 *affidavit/verified motion*} how the evidence is material to the motion for summary judgment. {71 *Elaborate.*} Conclusory allegations that the evidence is material are insufficient to support a motion for continuance. *Carter v. MacFadyen*, 93 S.W.3d 307, 310 (Tex. App.—Houston [14th Dist.] 2002, pet. denied).

23. The Court should deny {72 *adverse party*}'s motion for continuance because the evidence sought to be obtained from {73 *his/her/its*} discovery is immaterial. {74 *Elaborate.*} When evidence is immaterial to a motion for summary judgment because it will not raise a fact issue, the court is permitted to render a summary judgment

Continued on next page

without allowing discovery to proceed. *See Doe v. Roman Catholic Archdiocese of Galveston-Hous.*, 362 S.W.3d 803, 812 (Tex. App.—Houston [14th Dist.] 2012, no pet.).

D. {⓻⓹ *Adverse party*} has not been diligent in attempting to obtain evidence.

{*CHOOSE APPROPRIATE PARAGRAPHS 24-25*}

24. The Court should deny {76 *adverse party*}'s motion for continuance because {77 *adverse party*} did not identify in the {78 *affidavit/verified motion*} the specific steps {79 *he/she/it*} took to diligently obtain the evidence. {80 *Elaborate.*} Conclusory allegations that the party was diligent in trying to obtain the evidence are insufficient to support a motion for continuance. *Carter v. MacFadyen*, 93 S.W.3d 307, 310 (Tex. App.—Houston [14th Dist.] 2002, pet. denied).

25. The Court should deny {81 *adverse party*}'s motion for continuance because {82 *adverse party*} was not diligent in trying to obtain the evidence. {83 *Elaborate.*} When a party does not diligently use the rules of civil procedure for discovery purposes, the court does not abuse its discretion by denying the motion for continuance. *State v. Wood Oil Distrib., Inc.*, 751 S.W.2d 863, 865 (Tex. 1988).

{*ADD SECTION E IF PARTY IS SEEKING A DEPOSITION AND HAS PREVIOUSLY REQUESTED A CONTINUANCE*}

E. Evidence can be obtained from another source.

26. The Court should deny {84 *adverse party*}'s motion for continuance because {85 *adverse party*} can obtain the evidence from another source. {86 *Elaborate.*}

F. Adequate time for discovery has passed.

27. An adequate time for discovery has passed in this case. {87 *Address the applicable factors that show that an adequate time for discovery has passed, e.g., the length of time the case was on file, the amount of discovery already conducted.*}

RESPONSE TO CONTINUANCE TO PERMIT RULING ON DISCOVERY MOTIONS

28. Contrary to {88 *adverse party*}'s motion, the Court should not continue the summary-judgment hearing until after it rules on {89 *party*}'s outstanding discovery motions. {90 *Explain, e.g., adverse party has not been diligent in seeking a ruling on her motions.*}

**RESPONSE TO CONTINUANCE
TO CURE DEFECT IN SUMMARY-JUDGMENT EVIDENCE**

29. Under Texas Rule of Civil Procedure 166a(f), a court may continue a summary-judgment hearing to allow a party to cure a defect in her summary-judgment evidence. A continuance under Rule 166a(f) is permitted, however, only if the defect in the evidence is related to form and not substance. A court is not required to give a party an opportunity to cure a defect that is substantive. *CA Partners v. Spears*, 274 S.W.3d 51, 63 (Tex. App.—Houston [14th Dist.] 2008, pet. denied).

30. The defect in {91 *adverse party*}'s evidence is substantive. {92 *Elaborate.*} Because the defect is substantive, the Court should deny {93 *adverse party*}'s motion for continuance.

**RESPONSE TO CONTINUANCE
{94 *SPECIFY OTHER GROUNDS ASSERTED IN MOTION*}**

31. {95 *For responses to other grounds for continuance, insert appropriate paragraphs from FORM 5D:3.*}

CONCLUSION

32. {96 *Briefly summarize the response.*}

PRAYER

33. For these reasons, {97 *party*} asks the Court to deny {98 *adverse party*}'s motion to continue the hearing on {99 *party*}'s {100 *traditional/no-evidence/traditional and no-evidence*} motion for summary judgment.

SEE: Tex. R. Civ. P. 5, 166a(f), (g), (i), 247, 251, 252
O'Connor's Texas Rules * Civil Trials (2019), "Motion to continue SJ hearing," ch. 5-D, §9.3, p. 422; "Motion to continue hearing," ch. 7-B, §6.10.1, p. 727; "Challenge timing of motion," ch. 7-D, §3.2.2, p. 764

ADD: STYLE OF THE CASE – FORM 1B:2
SIGNATURE BLOCK – FORM 1B:3
CERTIFICATE OF SERVICE – FORM 1B:13

ATTACH: ORDER – FORM 7B:8

ORDER ON {❶ *PARTY*}'S MOTION FOR
CONTINUANCE OF SUMMARY-JUDGMENT HEARING

After considering {❷ *party*} {❸ *name*}'s motion for continuance of the summary-judgment hearing, the pleadings, the response, the affidavits, and other evidence on file, the Court

{*CHOOSE APPROPRIATE ORDER*}

DENIES the motion for continuance.

GRANTS the motion for continuance. The date for the submission of the motion for summary judgment is continued until ______________, 20___. {❹ *Party*} must file {❺ *his/her/its*} response to the motion for summary judgment, supporting affidavits, and other summary-judgment evidence by ______________, 20___.

SIGNED on ______________, 20___.

____
PRESIDING JUDGE

SEE: Tex. R. Civ. P. 166a(g), 247, 251, 252, 330(d)
O'Connor's Texas Rules * Civil Trials (2019), "Motion to continue SJ hearing," ch. 5-D, §9.3, p. 422; "Motion to continue hearing," ch. 7-B, §6.10.1, p. 727

ADD: STYLE OF THE CASE – FORM 1B:2
CERTIFICATE OF SERVICE – FORM 1B:13, if proposed order served separately from motion or response

PLAINTIFF'S {❶ *TRADITIONAL/NO-EVIDENCE/ TRADITIONAL & NO-EVIDENCE*} MOTION FOR SUMMARY JUDGMENT

Plaintiff, {❷ *name*}, asks the Court to sign a summary judgment under Texas Rule of Civil Procedure 166a on {❸ *plaintiff's cause of action against defendant, {name}, for {identify cause of action}/defendant {name}'s counterclaim against plaintiff for {identify counterclaim}*}.

INTRODUCTION

1. Plaintiff, {❹ *name*}, sued defendant, {❺ *name*}, for {❻ *state basis of suit*}.

2. Defendant answered asserting {❼ *identify answer, defensive pleas, affirmative defenses, and counterclaims*}.

3. {❽ *State other relevant facts about the suit.*}

BACKGROUND

4. {❾ *State facts relevant to the motion with citations to evidence, if applicable.*}

{*ADD SECTION BELOW IF APPLICABLE*}

SUMMARY-JUDGMENT EVIDENCE

{*CHOOSE APPROPRIATE PARAGRAPH 5*}

5. To support the facts in this motion, plaintiff offers the following summary-judgment evidence attached to this motion and incorporates the evidence into this motion by reference. {*See* ***O'Connor's Texas Rules****, "Attached," ch. 7-B, §9.1.3, p. 731; "Attach to motion or response," ch. 7-B, §9.4.8(1), p. 735.*}

Exhibit 1: {❿ *identify evidence*}.

Exhibit 2: {⓫ *identify evidence*}.

{⓬ *Continue for all other exhibits.*}

5. To support the facts in this motion, plaintiff includes the summary-judgment evidence in an appendix filed with this motion and incorporates the evidence into this motion by reference. {*See* ***O'Connor's Texas Rules****, "Attached," ch. 7-B, §9.1.3, p. 731.*}

Continued on next page

{*CHOOSE APPROPRIATE SUMMARY-JUDGMENT MOTIONS*}

TRADITIONAL SUMMARY JUDGMENT
PLAINTIFF'S CAUSE OF ACTION FOR {[13] *IDENTIFY CAUSE OF ACTION*}

6. To succeed on a traditional motion for summary judgment on its cause of action, the plaintiff must show that there is no genuine issue of material fact and that it is entitled to summary judgment as a matter of law. Tex. R. Civ. P. 166a(c); *ConocoPhillips Co. v. Koopmann*, 547 S.W.3d 858, 865 (Tex. 2018); *Helix Energy Sols. Grp., Inc. v. Gold*, 522 S.W.3d 427, 431 (Tex. 2017); *Kachina Pipeline Co. v. Lillis*, 471 S.W.3d 445, 449 (Tex. 2015); *Amedisys, Inc. v. Kingwood Home Health Care, LLC*, 437 S.W.3d 507, 511 (Tex. 2014). To meet this burden, the plaintiff must conclusively prove all essential elements of its claim. *MMP, Ltd. v. Jones*, 710 S.W.2d 59, 60 (Tex. 1986). A matter is conclusively established if reasonable people could not differ on the conclusion to be drawn from the evidence. *City of Keller v. Wilson*, 168 S.W.3d 802, 816 (Tex. 2005). If the plaintiff establishes its right to summary judgment as a matter of law, the burden shifts to the defendant to present evidence that raises a genuine issue of material fact. *See Chavez v. Kan. City S. Ry. Co.*, 520 S.W.3d 898, 900 (Tex. 2017); *Amedisys, Inc.*, 437 S.W.3d at 511; *State v. $90,235*, 390 S.W.3d 289, 292 (Tex. 2013).

7. Plaintiff is entitled to summary judgment on {[14] *his/her/its*} cause of action for {[15] *identify cause of action*} because the undisputed facts in this case and plaintiff's summary-judgment evidence conclusively establish each essential element. The essential elements of plaintiff's cause of action for {[16] *identify cause of action*} are the following: {[17] *identify elements of cause of action*}. {*For lists of elements for various causes of action, see* ***O'Connor's Texas COA***, *"Causes of Action," Part 2, p. 7.*}

a. {[18] *Identify first element.*} {[19] *Show how each element is established as a matter of law by the summary-judgment evidence.*}

b. {[20] *Continue until all elements are established as a matter of law.*}

TRADITIONAL SUMMARY JUDGMENT
DEFENDANT'S COUNTERCLAIM FOR {[21] *IDENTIFY COUNTERCLAIM*}

{*CHOOSE APPROPRIATE SECTIONS A-E*}

A. Plaintiff can disprove defendant's counterclaim as a matter of law.

8. A plaintiff is entitled to summary judgment on a defendant's counterclaim if the plaintiff can disprove at least one element of the counterclaim as a matter of law. *Tello v. Bank One, N.A.*, 218 S.W.3d 109, 113 (Tex. App.—Houston [14th Dist.] 2007, no pet.);

see Sw. Elec. Power Co. v. Grant, 73 S.W.3d 211, 215 (Tex. 2002). {*See* ***O'Connor's Texas Rules***, *"When plaintiff moves for SJ on defendant's counterclaim," ch. 7-C, §4.4, p. 757.*}

9. Plaintiff is entitled to summary judgment on defendant's counterclaim for {[22] *identify counterclaim*} because plaintiff can disprove as a matter of law at least one element of the counterclaim. To prevail on a claim for {[23] *identify counterclaim*}, defendant must prove the following: {[24] *identify elements of counterclaim*}. {*For lists of elements for various causes of action, see* ***O'Connor's Texas COA***, *"Causes of Action," Part 2, p. 7.*}

a. {[25] *Identify element to be disproved.*} {[26] *Show how element can be disproved as a matter of law by the summary-judgment evidence.*}

b. {[27] *Continue for any other elements that can be disproved.*}

B. Defendant pleaded facts that negate {[28] *his/her/its*} counterclaim.

10. A plaintiff is entitled to summary judgment on a defendant's counterclaim if the defendant affirmatively pleads facts that conclusively negate its counterclaim. *See Tex. Dep't of Corr. v. Herring*, 513 S.W.2d 6, 9 (Tex. 1974); *see, e.g., Washington v. City of Hous.*, 874 S.W.2d 791, 794 (Tex. App.—Texarkana 1994, no writ) (pleading can negate claim when alleged facts demonstrate that statute of limitations has run or that a defense would bar recovery). If the pleading negates the claim, the court can grant a summary judgment without first giving the defendant an opportunity to amend its pleading. *See Tex. Dep't of Corr.*, 513 S.W.2d at 9.

11. Plaintiff is entitled to summary judgment on defendant's counterclaim for {[29] *identify counterclaim*} because defendant affirmatively pleaded the following facts: {[30] *identify facts pleaded that negate defendant's counterclaim as a matter of law, e.g., the fact that the statute of limitations has run*}. {[31] *Elaborate.*}

C. Defendant's counterclaim is not viable.

12. A plaintiff is entitled to summary judgment on a defendant's counterclaim if the defendant's pleading affirmatively demonstrates that no cause of action exists. *See Peek v. Equip. Serv. Co.*, 779 S.W.2d 802, 805 (Tex. 1989). If the pleading demonstrates that no cause of action exists, the court can grant a summary judgment without first giving the defendant an opportunity to amend its pleading. *Id.* {*See* ***O'Connor's Texas Rules***, *"Moving on the pleadings," ch. 7-C, §2.5.2, p. 750.*}

◄ *Continued on next page* ►

13. Plaintiff is entitled to summary judgment on defendant's counterclaim for {32 *identify counterclaim*} because defendant's pleading affirmatively demonstrates that it is not a viable claim. {33 *Elaborate.*}

D. Defendant's pleadings do not support {34 *his/her/its*} cause of action.

14. A plaintiff is entitled to summary judgment on a defendant's counterclaim if the defendant has not pleaded sufficient facts to state a cause of action and, even though the defendant was given an opportunity to amend, the pleading defect remains. *See Natividad v. Alexsis, Inc.*, 875 S.W.2d 695, 699 (Tex. 1994).

15. Plaintiff is entitled to summary judgment on defendant's counterclaim for {35 *identify counterclaim*} because the counterclaim fails to sufficiently state a cause of action and defendant did not cure the defect after plaintiff's challenge by special exceptions. {36 *Elaborate.*}

E. Plaintiff has an affirmative defense to defendant's counterclaim.

16. A plaintiff is entitled to summary judgment on a defendant's counterclaim if the plaintiff can prove as a matter of law that it has an affirmative defense to the counterclaim. *See KCM Fin. LLC v. Bradshaw*, 457 S.W.3d 70, 79 (Tex. 2015); *Johnson & Johnson Med., Inc. v. Sanchez*, 924 S.W.2d 925, 927 (Tex. 1996). To meet its burden, the plaintiff must show that there is no genuine issue of material fact on any of the elements of the affirmative defense. *See* Tex. R. Civ. P. 166a(c).

17. Plaintiff {37 *pleaded/asserts*} the affirmative defense of {38 *identify affirmative defense*} to defendant's counterclaim for {39 *identify counterclaim*}.

18. Plaintiff is entitled to summary judgment on defendant's counterclaim because the undisputed facts in this case and plaintiff's summary-judgment evidence conclusively establish each essential element of {40 *identify affirmative defense*}. To prevail on the affirmative defense of {41 *identify affirmative defense*}, plaintiff must establish the following: {42 *identify elements of affirmative defense*}. {*For elements of affirmative defenses, see* ***O'Connor's Texas COA***.}

a. {43 *Identify first element.*} {44 *Show how each element is established as a matter of law by the summary-judgment evidence.*}

b. {45 *Continue until all elements are established as a matter of law.*}

NO-EVIDENCE SUMMARY JUDGMENT
DEFENDANT'S COUNTERCLAIM FOR {46 *IDENTIFY COUNTERCLAIM*}

19. To succeed on a no-evidence motion for summary judgment against a defendant's counterclaim, the plaintiff must allege that, after an adequate time for discovery, there is no evidence of an essential element of the defendant's counterclaim. Tex. R. Civ. P. 166a(i); *Timpte Indus., Inc. v. Gish*, 286 S.W.3d 306, 310 (Tex. 2009); *see Boerjan v. Rodriguez*, 436 S.W.3d 307, 310 (Tex. 2014); *Fort Brown Villas III Condo. Ass'n v. Gillenwater*, 285 S.W.3d 879, 882 (Tex. 2009). If the plaintiff meets its burden, the burden shifts to the defendant to produce more than a scintilla of evidence to raise a genuine issue of material fact on the challenged element. Tex. R. Civ. P. 166a(i); *see Boerjan*, 436 S.W.3d at 312; *Forbes, Inc. v. Granada Biosciences, Inc.*, 124 S.W.3d 167, 172 (Tex. 2003). The evidence must be sufficient to allow reasonable and fair-minded people to differ in their conclusions on whether the challenged fact exists; evidence that raises only a speculation or surmise is insufficient. *Forbes, Inc.*, 124 S.W.3d at 172. If less than a scintilla of evidence is produced, the plaintiff is entitled to a summary judgment on the defendant's counterclaim.

A. Adequate time for discovery has passed.

20. Plaintiff is entitled to a no-evidence summary judgment on defendant's counterclaim for {47 *identify counterclaim*} because defendant has had an adequate time for discovery. To determine whether an adequate time for discovery has passed, courts consider the following nonexclusive factors: (1) the nature of the suit, (2) the evidence necessary to controvert the motion, (3) the length of time the case has been on file, (4) the length of time the motion has been on file, (5) the amount of discovery that has already taken place, (6) whether the movant requested stricter deadlines for discovery, and (7) whether the discovery deadlines in place were specific or vague. *McInnis v. Mallia*, 261 S.W.3d 197, 201 (Tex. App.—Houston [14th Dist.] 2008, no pet.); *Cmty. Initiatives, Inc. v. Chase Bank*, 153 S.W.3d 270, 278 (Tex. App.—El Paso 2004, no pet.). {*See* ***O'Connor's Texas Rules****, "When to file," ch. 7-D, §2.1, p. 762.*}

21. Defendant has had an adequate time for discovery. {48 *Show how the factors indicate that the time for discovery was adequate, e.g., the discovery deadline set by the court's docket-control order has passed. Identify the date the counterclaim was filed. Describe any completed discovery and any pending discovery.*}

B. No evidence on essential element of defendant's counterclaim.

22. Plaintiff is entitled to a no-evidence summary judgment on defendant's counterclaim for {49 *identify counterclaim*} because there is no evidence to support an essential element of {50 *his/her/its*} counterclaim. To prevail on a counterclaim for {51 *iden-*

Continued on next page

FORM 7C:1

tify counterclaim}, the defendant must prove the following: {❺❷ *identify elements of counterclaim*}. {*For lists of elements for various causes of action, see* ***O'Connor's Texas COA****, "Causes of Action," Part 2, p. 7.*}

a. {❺❸ *Identify element of counterclaim that lacks evidentiary support.*} The defendant cannot prevail on {❺❹ *his/her/its*} counterclaim for {❺❺ *identify counterclaim*} because there is no evidence of {❺❻ *identify element of counterclaim*}.

b. {❺❼ *Continue for all other elements that lack evidentiary support.*}

{*ADD SECTION BELOW IF DAMAGES ARE SOUGHT*}

DAMAGES

{*CHOOSE APPROPRIATE PARAGRAPH 23*}

23. The damages for plaintiff's cause of action are liquidated. Based on the facts stated in this motion and supported by summary-judgment evidence, plaintiff is entitled to damages in the amount of ${❺❽ *amount*}. {❺❾ *Elaborate.*}

23. The damages for plaintiff's cause of action are unliquidated. A plaintiff moving for summary judgment on its cause of action is not required to prove the amount of unliquidated damages, only that damages were incurred. *See* Tex. R. Civ. P. 166a(a); *Pinnacle Anesthesia Consultants, P.A. v. Fisher*, 309 S.W.3d 93, 100 (Tex. App.—Dallas 2009, pet. denied). Because plaintiff is entitled to summary judgment on liability and plaintiff proved the existence of damages, the Court should grant plaintiff an order for a summary judgment on liability and set the issue of damages for trial. *See, e.g., City of Hous. v. Socony Mobil Oil Co.*, 421 S.W.2d 427, 429-30 (Tex. App.—Houston [1st Dist.] 1967, writ ref'd n.r.e.) (after court rendered partial summary judgment, issue of damages was tried to jury).

{*ADD SECTION BELOW IF APPLICABLE*}

ATTORNEY FEES

24. As stated in plaintiff's petition, plaintiff is entitled under the authority of {❻⓿ *cite authority for attorney fees, e.g., contract, specific statute*} to reasonable and necessary attorney fees that were incurred in the prosecution of this suit {❻❶ *add if appropriate: and attorney fees for the appeal in the event of an appeal*}. The affidavit of plaintiff's attorney establishes the reasonable and necessary attorney fees that plaintiff is entitled to recover. {*See* ***O'Connor's Texas Rules****, "Attorney Fees from Adverse Party," ch. 1-H, §10, p. 74; "Attorney expert," ch. 7-B, §9.3.3(1), p. 733;* ***O'Connor's Texas COA****, "Attorney Fees," ch. 45, p. 1463.*}

{ADD SECTION BELOW IF APPLICABLE}

ALTERNATIVE RELIEF

25. In the alternative, if the Court denies any part of plaintiff's motion for summary judgment, plaintiff asks the Court to sign an order specifying the facts that are established as a matter of law and directing any further proceedings as are just. Tex. R. Civ. P. 166a(e).

CONCLUSION

26. {❻❷ *Briefly summarize the motion.*}

PRAYER

27. For these reasons, plaintiff asks the Court to grant this motion and sign {❻❸ *an order for partial summary judgment/a final summary judgment*}. {❻❹ *Add if requesting final summary judgment: Plaintiff asks for summary judgment on all issues, all claims, all theories of damages, and all parties. Plaintiff waives all causes of action and relief not requested in this motion.*} {❻❺ *Add if requesting alternative relief: In the alternative, plaintiff asks for an order specifying the facts that are established as a matter of law.*} {*See **O'Connor's Texas Rules**, "Request for final SJ," ch. 7-C, §2.6, p. 750.*}

SEE: Tex. R. Civ. P. 166a
Tex. Civ. Prac. & Rem. Code §38.001 et seq.
O'Connor's Texas Rules * Civil Trials (2019), "Summary-Judgment Evidence," ch. 7-B, §9, p. 730; "Traditional Motion for Summary Judgment," ch. 7-C, §2, p. 748; "Plaintiff's motion," ch. 7-C, §4.3.1, p. 755; "Plaintiff's motion," ch. 7-C, §4.4.1, p. 757; "No-Evidence Motion for Summary Judgment," ch. 7-D, §2, p. 762
O'Connor's Texas Causes of Action (2019), "Attorney Fees," ch. 45, p. 1463

ADD: STYLE OF THE CASE – FORM 1B:2
SIGNATURE BLOCK – FORM 1B:3
CERTIFICATE OF SERVICE – FORM 1B:13

ATTACH: AFFIDAVIT – FORM 1B:8, to verify summary-judgment facts
NOTICE OF HEARING OR SUBMISSION – FORM 1E:1
AFFIDAVIT FOR ATTORNEY FEES – FORM 1H:14, if necessary
NOTICE OF INTENT TO USE UNFILED DISCOVERY – FORM 7C:7, if necessary
APPENDIX OF EVIDENCE – FORM 7C:8, if necessary
ORDER – FORM 7C:12, for partial summary judgment
or
SUMMARY JUDGMENT – FORM 9C:4, for final summary judgment

◄ *Continued on next page* ►

NOTE: A motion for summary judgment that relies on multiple types of evidence (affidavits, declarations, deposition excerpts, and other documents) should include the summary-judgment evidence in an appendix. If the motion relies simply on a few affidavits or declarations, it is not necessary to submit them in an appendix. See ***O'Connor's Texas Rules***, "Attached," ch. 7-B, §9.1.3, p. 731.

Some courts have held that a party's motion for summary judgment may adopt and incorporate by reference grounds from a co-party's motion for summary judgment. *E.g.*, ***Lockett v. H.B. Zachry Co.***, 285 S.W.3d 63, 72-73 (Tex.App.—Houston [1st Dist.] 2009, no pet.); ***Chapman v. King Ranch, Inc.***, 41 S.W.3d 693, 699-700 (Tex.App.—Corpus Christi 2001), *rev'd on other grounds*, 118 S.W.3d 742 (Tex.2003). But other courts have rejected such incorporation by reference, holding that a motion for summary judgment must itself assert the grounds relied on. *E.g.*, ***Camden Mach. & Tool, Inc. v. Cascade Co.***, 870 S.W.2d 304, 310 (Tex.App.—Fort Worth 1993, no writ); ***Rentfro v. Cavazos***, No. 04-10-00617-CV (Tex.App.—San Antonio 2012, pet. denied) (memo op.; 2-15-12). See ***O'Connor's Texas Rules***, "Stated in motion," ch. 7-C, §2.4.1, p. 748.

DEFENDANT'S {❶ *TRADITIONAL/NO-EVIDENCE/ TRADITIONAL & NO-EVIDENCE*} MOTION FOR SUMMARY JUDGMENT

Defendant, {❷ *name*}, asks the Court to sign a summary judgment under Texas Rule of Civil Procedure 166a on {❸ *plaintiff {name}'s cause of action against defendant for {identify cause of action}/defendant's counterclaim against plaintiff, {name}, for {identify counterclaim}*}.

INTRODUCTION

1. Plaintiff, {❹ *name*}, sued defendant, {❺ *name*}, for {❻ *state basis of suit*}.

2. Defendant answered asserting {❼ *identify answer, defensive pleas, affirmative defenses, and counterclaims*}.

3. {❽ *State other relevant facts about the suit.*}

BACKGROUND

4. {❾ *State facts relevant to the motion with citations to evidence, if applicable.*}

{*ADD SECTION BELOW IF APPLICABLE*}

SUMMARY-JUDGMENT EVIDENCE

{*CHOOSE APPROPRIATE PARAGRAPH 5*}

5. To support the facts in this motion, defendant offers the following summary-judgment evidence attached to this motion and incorporates the evidence into this motion by reference. {*See* ***O'Connor's Texas Rules****, "Attached," ch. 7-B, §9.1.3, p. 731; "Attach to motion or response," ch. 7-B, §9.4.8(1), p. 735.*}

Exhibit 1: {❿ *identify evidence*}.

Exhibit 2: {⓫ *identify evidence*}.

{⓬ *Continue for all other exhibits.*}

5. To support the facts in this motion, defendant includes the summary-judgment evidence in an appendix filed with this motion and incorporates the evidence into this motion by reference. {*See* ***O'Connor's Texas Rules****, "Attached," ch. 7-B, §9.1.3, p. 731.*}

◄ *Continued on next page* ►

{*CHOOSE APPROPRIATE SUMMARY-JUDGMENT MOTIONS*}

TRADITIONAL SUMMARY JUDGMENT
PLAINTIFF'S CAUSE OF ACTION FOR {⓭ *IDENTIFY CAUSE OF ACTION*}

{*CHOOSE APPROPRIATE SECTIONS A-E*}

A. Defendant can disprove plaintiff's cause of action as a matter of law.

6. A defendant is entitled to summary judgment on a plaintiff's cause of action if the defendant can disprove at least one element of the plaintiff's cause of action as a matter of law. *Stanfield v. Neubaum*, 494 S.W.3d 90, 96 (Tex. 2016); *Boerjan v. Rodriguez*, 436 S.W.3d 307, 310 (Tex. 2014); *Nall v. Plunkett*, 404 S.W.3d 552, 555 (Tex. 2013); *Randall's Food Mkts., Inc. v. Johnson*, 891 S.W.2d 640, 644 (Tex. 1995); *see* Tex. R. Civ. P. 166a(c). {*See* ***O'Connor's Texas Rules****, "When defendant moves for SJ on plaintiff's cause of action," ch. 7-C, §4.5, p. 757.*}

7. Defendant is entitled to summary judgment on plaintiff's cause of action for {⓮ *identify cause of action*} because defendant can disprove as a matter of law at least one element of the cause of action. To prevail on a cause of action for {⓯ *identify cause of action*}, plaintiff must prove the following: {⓰ *identify elements of cause of action*}. {*For lists of elements for various causes of action, see* ***O'Connor's Texas COA****, "Causes of Action," Part 2, p. 7.*}

a. {⓱ *Identify element to be disproved.*} {⓲ *Show how element can be disproved as a matter of law by the summary-judgment evidence.*}

b. {⓳ *Continue for any other elements that can be disproved.*}

B. Plaintiff pleaded facts that negate {⓴ *his/her/its*} own cause of action.

8. A defendant is entitled to summary judgment on a plaintiff's cause of action if the plaintiff affirmatively pleads facts that conclusively negate its cause of action. *Tex. Dep't of Corr. v. Herring*, 513 S.W.2d 6, 9 (Tex. 1974); *see, e.g., Washington v. City of Hous.*, 874 S.W.2d 791, 794 (Tex. App.—Texarkana 1994, no writ) (pleading can negate claim when alleged facts demonstrate that statute of limitations has run or that a defense would bar recovery). If the pleading negates the claim, the court can grant a summary judgment without first giving the plaintiff an opportunity to amend its pleading. *Tex. Dep't of Corr.*, 513 S.W.2d at 9.

9. Defendant is entitled to summary judgment on plaintiff's cause of action for {[21] *identify cause of action*} because plaintiff affirmatively pleaded the following facts that negated {[22] *his/her/its*} claim: {[23] *identify facts pleaded that negate plaintiff's cause of action as a matter of law, e.g., the fact that the statute of limitations has run*}. {[24] *Elaborate.*}

C. Plaintiff's cause of action is not viable.

10. A defendant is entitled to summary judgment on a plaintiff's cause of action if the plaintiff's pleading affirmatively demonstrates that no cause of action exists. *Peek v. Equip. Serv. Co.*, 779 S.W.2d 802, 805 (Tex. 1989). If the pleading demonstrates that no cause of action exists, the court can grant a summary judgment without first giving the plaintiff an opportunity to amend its pleading. *Id.* {*See* ***O'Connor's Texas Rules***, *"Moving on the pleadings," ch. 7-C, §2.5.2, p. 750.*}

11. Defendant is entitled to summary judgment on plaintiff's cause of action for {[25] *identify cause of action*} because plaintiff's pleading affirmatively demonstrates that it is not a viable claim. {[26] *Elaborate.*}

D. Plaintiff's pleadings do not support {[27] *his/her/its*} cause of action.

12. A defendant is entitled to summary judgment on a plaintiff's cause of action if the plaintiff has not pleaded sufficient facts to state a cause of action and, even though the plaintiff was given an opportunity to amend, the pleading defect remains. *See Natividad v. Alexsis, Inc.*, 875 S.W.2d 695, 699 (Tex. 1994).

13. Defendant is entitled to summary judgment on plaintiff's cause of action for {[28] *identify cause of action*} because the claim fails to sufficiently state a cause of action and plaintiff did not cure the defect after defendant's challenge by special exceptions. {[29] *Elaborate.*}

E. Defendant has an affirmative defense to plaintiff's cause of action.

14. A defendant is entitled to summary judgment on a plaintiff's cause of action if the defendant can prove as a matter of law that it has an affirmative defense to the cause of action. *See Exxon Mobil Corp. v. Rincones*, 520 S.W.3d 572, 593 (Tex. 2017); *Long Distance Int'l, Inc. v. Telefonos de Mex., S.A. de C.V.*, 49 S.W.3d 347, 350-51 (Tex. 2001). To meet its burden, the defendant must show that there is no genuine issue of material fact on any of the elements of the affirmative defense. *See* Tex. R. Civ. P. 166a(c). {*See* ***O'Connor's Texas Rules***, *"When defendant moves for SJ on its affirmative defense," ch. 7-C, §4.6, p. 759.*}

Continued on next page

15. Defendant {30 *pleaded/asserts*} the affirmative defense of {31 *identify affirmative defense*} to plaintiff's cause of action for {32 *identify cause of action*}.

16. Defendant is entitled to summary judgment on plaintiff's cause of action because the undisputed facts in this case and defendant's summary-judgment evidence conclusively establish each essential element of {33 *identify affirmative defense*}. To prevail on the affirmative defense of {34 *identify affirmative defense*}, defendant must establish the following: {35 *identify elements of affirmative defense*}. {*For elements of affirmative defenses, see* ***O'Connor's Texas COA.***}

a. {36 *Identify first element.*} {37 *Show how each element is established as a matter of law by the summary-judgment evidence.*}

b. {38 *Continue until all elements are established as a matter of law.*}

NO-EVIDENCE SUMMARY JUDGMENT
PLAINTIFF'S CAUSE OF ACTION FOR {39 *IDENTIFY CAUSE OF ACTION*}

17. To succeed on a no-evidence motion for summary judgment against a plaintiff's cause of action, the defendant must allege that, after an adequate time for discovery, there is no evidence of an essential element of the plaintiff's cause of action. Tex. R. Civ. P. 166a(i); *Timpte Indus., Inc. v. Gish*, 286 S.W.3d 306, 310 (Tex. 2009); *see Boerjan v. Rodriguez*, 436 S.W.3d 307, 310 (Tex. 2014); *Fort Brown Villas III Condo. Ass'n v. Gillenwater*, 285 S.W.3d 879, 882 (Tex. 2009). If the defendant meets its burden, the burden shifts to the plaintiff to produce more than a scintilla of evidence to raise a genuine issue of material fact on the challenged element. Tex. R. Civ. P. 166a(i); *see Boerjan*, 436 S.W.3d at 312; *Forbes, Inc. v. Granada Biosciences, Inc.*, 124 S.W.3d 167, 172 (Tex. 2003). The evidence must be sufficient to allow reasonable and fair-minded people to differ in their conclusions on whether the challenged fact exists; evidence that raises only a speculation or surmise is insufficient. *Forbes, Inc.*, 124 S.W.3d at 172. If less than a scintilla of evidence is produced, the defendant is entitled to a summary judgment on the plaintiff's cause of action.

A. Adequate time for discovery has passed.

18. Defendant is entitled to a no-evidence summary judgment on plaintiff's cause of action for {40 *identify cause of action*} because plaintiff has had an adequate time for discovery. To determine whether an adequate time for discovery has passed, courts consider the following nonexclusive factors: (1) the nature of the suit, (2) the evidence necessary to controvert the motion, (3) the length of time the case has been on file, (4) the length of time the motion has been on file, (5) the amount of discovery that has already taken place, (6) whether the movant requested stricter deadlines for discovery, and

(7) whether the discovery deadlines in place were specific or vague. *McInnis v. Mallia*, 261 S.W.3d 197, 201 (Tex. App.—Houston [14th Dist.] 2008, no pet.); *Cmty. Initiatives, Inc. v. Chase Bank*, 153 S.W.3d 270, 278 (Tex. App.—El Paso 2004, no pet.). {*See **O'Connor's Texas Rules**, "When to file," ch. 7-D, §2.1, p. 762.*}

19. Plaintiff has had an adequate time for discovery. {❹❶ *Show how the factors indicate that the time for discovery was adequate, e.g., the discovery deadline set by the court's docket-control order has passed. Identify the date the cause of action was filed. Describe any completed discovery and any pending discovery.*}

B. No evidence of essential element of plaintiff's cause of action.

20. Defendant is entitled to a no-evidence summary judgment on plaintiff's cause of action for {❹❷ *identify cause of action*} because there is no evidence to support the essential elements of {❹❸ *his/her/its*} cause of action. To prevail on a cause of action for {❹❹ *identify cause of action*}, the plaintiff must prove the following: {❹❺ *identify elements of cause of action*}. {*For lists of elements for various causes of action, see **O'Connor's Texas COA**, "Causes of Action," Part 2, p. 7.*}

a. {❹❻ *Identify element of cause of action that lacks evidentiary support.*} Plaintiff cannot prevail on {❹❼ *his/her/its*} cause of action for {❹❽ *identify cause of action*} because there is no evidence of {❹❾ *identify element of cause of action*}.

b. {❺⓪ *Continue for all other elements that lack evidentiary support.*}

TRADITIONAL SUMMARY JUDGMENT
DEFENDANT'S COUNTERCLAIM FOR {❺❶ *IDENTIFY COUNTERCLAIM*}

21. To succeed on a traditional motion for summary judgment on its counterclaim, the defendant must show that there is no genuine issue of material fact and that it is entitled to summary judgment as a matter of law. Tex. R. Civ. P. 166a(c); *ConocoPhillips Co. v. Koopmann*, 547 S.W.3d 858, 865 (Tex. 2018); *Helix Energy Sols. Grp., Inc. v. Gold*, 522 S.W.3d 427, 431 (Tex. 2017); *Kachina Pipeline Co. v. Lillis*, 471 S.W.3d 445, 449 (Tex. 2015); *Amedisys, Inc. v. Kingwood Home Health Care, LLC*, 437 S.W.3d 507, 511 (Tex. 2014). To meet this burden, the defendant must conclusively prove all essential elements of its claim. *MMP, Ltd. v. Jones*, 710 S.W.2d 59, 60 (Tex. 1986). A matter is conclusively established if reasonable people could not differ on the conclusion to be drawn from the evidence. *City of Keller v. Wilson*, 168 S.W.3d 802, 816 (Tex. 2005). If the defendant establishes its right to summary judgment as a matter of law, the burden shifts to the plaintiff to present evidence that raises a genuine issue of material fact. *See*

Continued on next page

Chavez v. Kan. City S. Ry. Co., 520 S.W.3d 898, 900 (Tex. 2017); *Amedisys, Inc.*, 437 S.W.3d at 511; *State v. $90,235*, 390 S.W.3d 289, 292 (Tex. 2013).

22. Defendant is entitled to summary judgment on {52 *his/her/its*} counterclaim for {53 *identify counterclaim*} because the undisputed facts in this case and defendant's summary-judgment evidence conclusively establish each essential element. The essential elements of defendant's counterclaim for {54 *identify counterclaim*} are the following: {55 *identify elements of counterclaim*}. {*For lists of elements for various causes of action, see* ***O'Connor's Texas COA****, "Causes of Action," Part 2, p. 7.*}

a. {56 *Identify first element.*} {57 *Show how each element is established as a matter of law by the summary-judgment evidence.*}

b. {58 *Continue until all elements are established as a matter of law.*}

{*ADD SECTION BELOW IF DAMAGES ARE SOUGHT*}

DAMAGES

{*CHOOSE APPROPRIATE PARAGRAPH 23*}

23. The damages for defendant's counterclaim are liquidated. Based on the facts stated in this motion and supported by summary-judgment evidence, defendant is entitled to damages in the amount of ${59 *amount*}. {60 *Elaborate.*}

23. The damages for defendant's counterclaim are unliquidated. A defendant moving for summary judgment on a counterclaim is not required to prove the amount of unliquidated damages, only that damages were incurred. *See* Tex. R. Civ. P. 166a(a); *Pinnacle Anesthesia Consultants, P.A. v. Fisher*, 309 S.W.3d 93, 100 (Tex. App.—Dallas 2009, pet. denied). Because defendant is entitled to summary judgment on liability and defendant proved the existence of damages, the Court should grant defendant an order for a summary judgment on liability and set the issue of damages for trial. *See, e.g.*, *City of Hous. v. Socony Mobil Oil Co.*, 421 S.W.2d 427, 429-30 (Tex. App.—Houston [1st Dist.] 1967, writ ref'd n.r.e.) (after court rendered partial summary judgment, issue of damages was tried to jury).

{*ADD SECTION BELOW IF APPLICABLE*}

ATTORNEY FEES

24. As stated in defendant's answer, defendant is entitled under the authority of {61 *cite authority for attorney fees, e.g., contract, specific statute, equity*} to reasonable and necessary attorney fees that were incurred in the {62 *defense of this suit/prosecution*

of the counterclaim} {63 *add if appropriate: and attorney fees for the appeal in the event of an appeal*}. The affidavit of defendant's attorney establishes the reasonable and necessary attorney fees that defendant is entitled to recover. {*See* ***O'Connor's Texas Rules****, "Attorney Fees from Adverse Party," ch. 1-H, §10, p. 74; "Attorney expert," ch. 7-B, §9.3.3(1), p. 733;* ***O'Connor's Texas COA****, "Attorney Fees," ch. 45, p. 1463.*}

{*ADD SECTION BELOW IF APPLICABLE*}

ALTERNATIVE RELIEF

25. In the alternative, if the Court denies any part of defendant's motion for summary judgment, defendant asks the Court to sign an order specifying the facts that are established as a matter of law and directing any further proceedings as are just. *See* Tex. R. Civ. P. 166a(e).

CONCLUSION

26. {64 *Briefly summarize the motion.*}

PRAYER

27. For these reasons, defendant asks the Court to grant this motion and sign {65 *an order for partial summary judgment/a final summary judgment*}. {66 *Add if requesting final summary judgment: Defendant asks for summary judgment on all issues, all claims, all theories of damages, and all parties. Defendant waives all causes of action and relief not requested in this motion.*} {67 *Add if requesting alternative relief: In the alternative, defendant asks for an order specifying the facts that are established as a matter of law.*} {*See* ***O'Connor's Texas Rules****, "Request for final SJ," ch. 7-C, §2.6, p. 750.*}

SEE: Tex. R. Civ. P. 166a
Tex. Civ. Prac. & Rem. Code §38.001 et seq.
O'Connor's Texas Rules * Civil Trials (2019), "Summary-Judgment Evidence," ch. 7-B, §9, p. 730; "Traditional Motion for Summary Judgment," ch. 7-C, §2, p. 748; "Defendant's motion," ch. 7-C, §4.5.1, p. 758; "Defendant's motion," ch. 7-C, §4.6.1, p. 759; "Defendant's motion," ch. 7-C, §4.7.1, p. 760; "No-Evidence Motion for Summary Judgment," ch. 7-D, §2, p. 762
O'Connor's Texas Causes of Action (2019), "Attorney Fees," ch. 45, p. 1463

ADD: STYLE OF THE CASE – FORM 1B:2
SIGNATURE BLOCK – FORM 1B:3
CERTIFICATE OF SERVICE – FORM 1B:13

Continued on next page

ATTACH: AFFIDAVIT – FORM 1B:8, to verify summary-judgment facts
NOTICE OF HEARING OR SUBMISSION – FORM 1E:1
AFFIDAVIT FOR ATTORNEY FEES – FORM 1H:14, if necessary
NOTICE OF INTENT TO USE UNFILED DISCOVERY – FORM 7C:7, if necessary
APPENDIX OF EVIDENCE – FORM 7C:8, if necessary
ORDER – FORM 7C:12, for partial summary judgment
or
SUMMARY JUDGMENT – FORM 9C:4, for final summary judgment

NOTE: See notes under FORM 7C:1.

DEFENDANT'S RESPONSE TO
PLAINTIFF'S {❶ *TRADITIONAL/NO-EVIDENCE/*
TRADITIONAL & NO-EVIDENCE} MOTION FOR SUMMARY JUDGMENT

Defendant, {❷ *name*}, asks the Court to deny plaintiff {❸ *name*}'s motion for summary judgment.

INTRODUCTION

1. Plaintiff, {❹ *name*}, sued defendant, {❺ *name*}, for {❻ *state basis of suit*}.

2. Defendant answered asserting {❼ *identify answer, defensive pleas, affirmative defenses, and counterclaims*}.

3. {❽ *State other relevant facts about the suit.*}

BACKGROUND

4. {❾ *State facts relevant to the response with citations to evidence, if applicable.*}

{*ADD SECTION BELOW IF EVIDENCE IS NECESSARY FOR RESPONSE*}

SUMMARY-JUDGMENT EVIDENCE

{*CHOOSE APPROPRIATE PARAGRAPH 5*}

5. To support the facts in this response, defendant offers the following summary-judgment evidence attached to this response and incorporates the evidence into this response by reference. {*See **O'Connor's Texas Rules**, "Attached," ch. 7-B, §9.1.3, p. 731; "Attach to motion or response," ch. 7-B, §9.4.8(1), p. 735.*}

Exhibit 1: {❿ *identify evidence*}.

Exhibit 2: {⓫ *identify evidence*}.

{⓬ *Continue for all other exhibits.*}

5. To support the facts in this response, defendant includes the summary-judgment evidence in an appendix filed with this response and incorporates the evidence into this response by reference. {*See **O'Connor's Texas Rules**, "Attached," ch. 7-B, §9.1.3, p. 731.*}

Continued on next page

{*CHOOSE APPROPRIATE SUMMARY-JUDGMENT RESPONSES*}

RESPONSE TO TRADITIONAL SUMMARY JUDGMENT
PLAINTIFF'S CAUSE OF ACTION FOR {⓭ *IDENTIFY CAUSE OF ACTION*}

{*CHOOSE APPROPRIATE SECTIONS A-C*}

A. Plaintiff did not satisfy {⓮ *his/her/its*} burden under Texas Rule of Civil Procedure 166a(c).

6. To succeed on a traditional motion for summary judgment on its cause of action, the plaintiff must show that there is no genuine issue of material fact and that it is entitled to summary judgment as a matter of law. Tex. R. Civ. P. 166a(c); *ConocoPhillips Co. v. Koopmann*, 547 S.W.3d 858, 865 (Tex. 2018); *Helix Energy Sols. Grp., Inc. v. Gold*, 522 S.W.3d 427, 431 (Tex. 2017); *Kachina Pipeline Co. v. Lillis*, 471 S.W.3d 445, 449 (Tex. 2015); *Amedisys, Inc. v. Kingwood Home Health Care, LLC*, 437 S.W.3d 507, 511 (Tex. 2014); *Mann Frankfort Stein & Lipp Advisors, Inc. v. Fielding*, 289 S.W.3d 844, 848 (Tex. 2009). To meet this burden, the plaintiff must conclusively prove all essential elements of its claim. *MMP, Ltd. v. Jones*, 710 S.W.2d 59, 60 (Tex. 1986). A matter is conclusively established if reasonable people could not differ on the conclusion to be drawn from the evidence. *City of Keller v. Wilson*, 168 S.W.3d 802, 816 (Tex. 2005). If the plaintiff establishes its right to summary judgment as a matter of law, the burden shifts to the defendant to present evidence that raises a genuine issue of material fact. *See Chavez v. Kan. City S. Ry. Co.*, 520 S.W.3d 898, 900 (Tex. 2017); *Amedisys, Inc.*, 437 S.W.3d at 511; *State v. $90,235*, 390 S.W.3d 289, 292 (Tex. 2013). In deciding whether to grant plaintiff's motion, the court must take as true all competent evidence favorable to the defendant and indulge every reasonable inference and resolve any doubts in the defendant's favor. *Limestone Prods. Distrib., Inc. v. McNamara*, 71 S.W.3d 308, 311 (Tex. 2002); *Rhône-Poulenc, Inc. v. Steel*, 997 S.W.2d 217, 223 (Tex. 1999); *Nixon v. Mr. Prop. Mgmt. Co.*, 690 S.W.2d 546, 548-49 (Tex. 1985).

7. Plaintiff moved for summary judgment on {⓯ *his/her/its*} cause of action for {⓰ *identify cause of action*}, arguing that there is no genuine issue of material fact and that the summary-judgment evidence conclusively establishes all the elements of {⓱ *his/her/its*} cause of action as a matter of law.

8. To prevail on a cause of action for {⓲ *identify cause of action*}, plaintiff must prove the following: {⓳ *identify elements*}.

{*CHOOSE APPROPRIATE PARAGRAPHS 9-11*}

9. The Court should deny plaintiff's motion for summary judgment on {[20] *his/her/its*} cause of action because plaintiff did not carry {[21] *his/her/its*} burden of proving the element of {[22] *identify element*} as a matter of law. {[23] *Elaborate.*}

10. The Court should deny plaintiff's motion for summary judgment because there is a genuine issue of material fact on the following elements of plaintiff's cause of action: {[24] *identify elements and fact issues*}. {[25] *Elaborate.*}

11. The Court should deny plaintiff's motion for summary judgment on {[26] *his/her/its*} cause of action because the {[27] *identify type of evidence*} attached to plaintiff's motion is defective and does not present competent summary-judgment evidence. Specifically, {[28] *choose objections to evidence from FORM 7C:11*}.

B. Plaintiff's pleadings do not support {[29] *his/her/its*} cause of action.

12. For the movant to be entitled to a summary judgment, the grounds for summary judgment must be supported by the movant's pleadings. *See Daniels v. Daniels*, 45 S.W.3d 278, 282 (Tex. App.—Corpus Christi 2001, no pet.). Thus, an unpleaded cause of action cannot serve as the basis for a summary judgment if the nonmovant objects. *See Roark v. Stallworth Oil & Gas, Inc.*, 813 S.W.2d 492, 494 (Tex. 1991) (unpleaded affirmative defense); *Roadside Stations, Inc. v. 7HBF, Ltd.*, 904 S.W.2d 927, 930 (Tex. App.—Fort Worth 1995, no writ) (unpleaded cause of action). {*See **O'Connor's Texas Rules**, "Challenge movant's pleadings," ch. 7-C, §3.6.2, p. 753.*}

13. Accordingly, defendant objects to plaintiff's attempt to seek summary judgment on {[30] *identify cause of action*} because plaintiff has not pleaded that cause of action in {[31] *his/her/its*} petition.

C. Defendant has sufficient evidence to raise fact issue on {[32] *his/her/its*} affirmative defense.

14. A plaintiff is not entitled to summary judgment on a cause of action if the defendant is able to assert an affirmative defense in its response and provide sufficient summary-judgment evidence to create a fact issue on each element of the defense. *Bassett v. Am. Nat'l Bank*, 145 S.W.3d 692, 696 (Tex. App.—Fort Worth 2004, no pet.); *see Keenan v. Gibraltar Sav. Ass'n*, 754 S.W.2d 392, 393-94 (Tex. App.—Houston [14th Dist.] 1988, no writ). The defendant is not required to prove the affirmative defense by a preponderance of the evidence or as a matter of law; raising a fact issue is enough to defeat the summary judgment. *See Brownlee v. Brownlee*, 665 S.W.2d 111, 112 (Tex.

Continued on next page

1984). {*See **O'Connor's Texas Rules**, "Nonmovant's affirmative defense," ch. 7-C, §3.4.1(4), p. 752; "Create fact issue about affirmative defense," ch. 7-C, §4.3.2(2), p. 756.*}

15. The Court should deny plaintiff's motion for summary judgment on {㉝ *his/her/its*} cause of action for {㉞ *identify cause of action*} because of defendant's affirmative defense of {㉟ *identify affirmative defense*}. The elements of defendant's affirmative defense are the following: {㊱ *identify elements of affirmative defense*}. {㊲ *For elements of affirmative defenses, see **O'Connor's Texas COA**.*}

a. {㊳ *Identify first element.*} {㊴ *Show how the summary-judgment evidence creates a fact issue.*}

b. {㊵ *Continue until a fact issue is raised on all elements of affirmative defense.*}

RESPONSE TO TRADITIONAL SUMMARY JUDGMENT
DEFENDANT'S COUNTERCLAIM FOR {㊶ *IDENTIFY COUNTERCLAIM*}

{*CHOOSE APPROPRIATE SECTIONS A-F*}

A. Plaintiff did not disprove defendant's counterclaim as a matter of law.

16. A plaintiff is entitled to summary judgment on a defendant's counterclaim if the plaintiff can disprove at least one element of the counterclaim as a matter of law. *Tello v. Bank One, N.A.*, 218 S.W.3d 109, 113 (Tex. App.—Houston [14th Dist.] 2007, no pet.); *see Sw. Elec. Power Co. v. Grant*, 73 S.W.3d 211, 215 (Tex. 2002). {*See **O'Connor's Texas Rules**, "When plaintiff moves for SJ on defendant's counterclaim," ch. 7-C, §4.4, p. 757.*}

17. The elements of defendant's counterclaim for {㊷ *identify counterclaim*} are the following: {㊸ *identify elements*}. Plaintiff claims that {㊹ *he/she/it*} disproved {㊺ *identify elements*}.

{*CHOOSE APPROPRIATE PARAGRAPHS 18-19*}

18. The Court should deny plaintiff's motion for summary judgment on defendant's counterclaim because plaintiff did not disprove {㊻ *identify elements*} as a matter of law. There is a genuine issue of material fact on {㊼ *identify elements*}. {㊽ *Elaborate.*}

19. The Court should deny plaintiff's motion for summary judgment on defendant's counterclaim because the {㊾ *identify type of evidence*} attached to plaintiff's motion is defective and does not present competent summary-judgment evidence. Specifically, {㊿ *choose objections to evidence from FORM 7C:11*}.

B. Defendant did not plead facts that negate {51 *his/her/its*} counterclaim.

20. A plaintiff is entitled to summary judgment on a defendant's counterclaim if the defendant affirmatively pleads facts that conclusively negate its counterclaim. *See Tex. Dep't of Corr. v. Herring*, 513 S.W.2d 6, 9 (Tex. 1974); *see, e.g., Washington v. City of Hous.*, 874 S.W.2d 791, 794 (Tex. App.—Texarkana 1994, no writ) (pleading can negate claim when alleged facts demonstrate that statute of limitations has run or that a defense would bar recovery).

21. Plaintiff alleges that defendant conclusively negated the counterclaim when, in defendant's {52 *identify pleading, e.g., original answer*}, defendant pleaded the following: {53 *identify defendant's allegations that plaintiff claims negated the counterclaim*}.

22. The Court should deny plaintiff's motion for summary judgment on defendant's counterclaim for {54 *identify counterclaim*} because defendant did not affirmatively plead facts that negate the counterclaim. {55 *Elaborate.*}

C. Defendant has a viable counterclaim.

23. A plaintiff is entitled to summary judgment on a defendant's counterclaim if the defendant's pleading affirmatively demonstrates that no cause of action exists. *See Peek v. Equip. Serv. Co.*, 779 S.W.2d 802, 805 (Tex. 1989). If the pleading demonstrates that no cause of action exists, the court can grant a summary judgment without first giving the defendant an opportunity to amend its pleading. *See id.* However, if the pleading could be amended so that it does allege a viable cause of action, the court cannot grant a summary judgment without first giving the defendant an opportunity to amend. *See Sixth RMA Partners, L.P. v. Sibley*, 111 S.W.3d 46, 54-55 (Tex. 2003); *Pietila v. Crites*, 851 S.W.2d 185, 186 n.2 (Tex. 1993). {*See* ***O'Connor's Texas Rules****, "Moving on the pleadings," ch. 7-C, §2.5.2, p. 750.*}

24. Plaintiff claimed that {56 *he/she/it*} is entitled to summary judgment because defendant's pleadings show on their face that defendant's counterclaim is not viable.

{*CHOOSE APPROPRIATE PARAGRAPH 25*}

25. The Court should deny plaintiff's motion for summary judgment on defendant's counterclaim for {57 *identify counterclaim*} because the motion is an attempt to use the summary-judgment procedure to attack an alleged defect in defendant's pleadings that should have been challenged first by special exception. Plaintiff did not challenge defendant's pleadings by special exception, and defendant has not had an opportunity to

◄ Continued on next page ►

amend {58 *his/her/its*} pleading to cure any defect. {59 *Explain why the defect should have been challenged first by special exception.*}

25. The Court should deny plaintiff's motion for summary judgment on defendant's counterclaim for {60 *identify counterclaim*} because defendant amended {61 *his/her/its*} counterclaim to address the defect cited in plaintiff's motion. In the amended counterclaim, defendant pleaded a viable counterclaim for {62 *identify counterclaim*}. {63 *Show how the amended pleading asserts a viable counterclaim.*}

25. The Court should deny plaintiff's motion for summary judgment on defendant's counterclaim for {64 *identify counterclaim*} because, contrary to plaintiff's allegations, defendant has pleaded a viable claim. {65 *Show how the counterclaim is viable.*}

D. Defendant's pleading supports {66 *his/her/its*} cause of action.

26. A plaintiff is entitled to summary judgment on a defendant's counterclaim if the defendant has not pleaded sufficient facts to state a cause of action and, even though the defendant was given an opportunity to amend, the pleading defect remains. *See Natividad v. Alexsis, Inc.*, 875 S.W.2d 695, 699 (Tex. 1994).

27. Plaintiff claimed that {67 *he/she/it*} is entitled to summary judgment because defendant did not plead sufficient facts to state a cause of action.

{*CHOOSE APPROPRIATE PARAGRAPH 28*}

28. The Court should deny plaintiff's motion for summary judgment on defendant's counterclaim for {68 *identify counterclaim*} because the motion is an attempt to use the summary-judgment procedure to attack an alleged defect in defendant's pleadings that should have been challenged first by special exception. Plaintiff did not challenge defendant's pleadings by special exception, and defendant has not had an opportunity to amend {69 *his/her/its*} pleading to cure any defect. {70 *Explain why the defect should have been challenged first by special exception.*}

28. The Court should deny plaintiff's motion for summary judgment on defendant's counterclaim for {71 *identify counterclaim*} because defendant amended {72 *his/her/its*} counterclaim to address the defect cited in plaintiff's motion. In the amended counterclaim, defendant pleaded sufficient facts to state a cause of action. Attached to this response as Exhibit {73 *letter*} is a copy of defendant's {74 *identify pleading, e.g., second amended counterclaim*}. {75 *Show how the amended pleading alleges sufficient facts to state a cause of action.*}

28. The Court should deny plaintiff's motion for summary judgment on defendant's counterclaim for {76 *identify counterclaim*} because, contrary to plaintiff's allegations, defendant has pleaded sufficient facts to state a cause of action. {77 *Elaborate.*}

E. Plaintiff has not proved {78 *his/her/its*} affirmative defense as a matter of law.

29. A plaintiff is entitled to summary judgment on a defendant's counterclaim if the plaintiff can prove as a matter of law that it has an affirmative defense to the counterclaim. *See KCM Fin. LLC v. Bradshaw*, 457 S.W.3d 70, 79 (Tex. 2015); *Johnson & Johnson Med., Inc. v. Sanchez*, 924 S.W.2d 925, 927 (Tex. 1996). To meet its burden, the plaintiff must show that there is no genuine issue of material fact on any of the elements of the affirmative defense. *See* Tex. R. Civ. P. 166a(c).

30. In {79 *his/her/its*} motion for summary judgment, plaintiff asserted the affirmative defense of {80 *identify affirmative defense*} to defendant's counterclaim for {81 *identify counterclaim*}.

31. Plaintiff is not entitled to summary judgment on defendant's counterclaim because the undisputed facts in this case and plaintiff's summary-judgment evidence do not conclusively establish each essential element of {82 *identify affirmative defense*}. To prevail on the affirmative defense of {83 *identify affirmative defense*}, plaintiff must prove the following: {84 *identify elements of affirmative defense*}. {*For elements of affirmative defenses, see* ***O'Connor's Texas COA***.}

a. {85 *Identify first element.*} {86 *Show how the summary-judgment evidence creates a fact issue.*}

b. {87 *Continue for all other elements of affirmative defense where there is a fact issue.*}

F. Plaintiff's affirmative defense is not supported by {88 *his/her/its*} pleadings.

32. For the movant to be entitled to a summary judgment, the grounds for summary judgment must be supported by the movant's pleadings. *See Daniels v. Daniels*, 45 S.W.3d 278, 282 (Tex. App.—Corpus Christi 2001, no pet.). Thus, an unpleaded affirmative defense cannot serve as the basis for a summary judgment if the nonmovant objects. *Roark v. Stallworth Oil & Gas, Inc.*, 813 S.W.2d 492, 494 (Tex. 1991); *Downs v. Triad-Denton Hosp., L.P.*, No. 02-05-303-CV (Tex. App.—Fort Worth 2006, no pet.) (memo op.; 3-30-06).

Continued on next page

33. Accordingly, defendant objects to plaintiff's attempt to seek summary judgment on {89 *identify affirmative defense*} because plaintiff has not pleaded that defense in {90 *his/her/its*} answer to defendant's counterclaim.

RESPONSE TO NO-EVIDENCE SUMMARY JUDGMENT
DEFENDANT'S COUNTERCLAIM FOR {91 *IDENTIFY COUNTERCLAIM*}

{*CHOOSE APPROPRIATE SECTIONS A-B*}

A. Plaintiff's no-evidence motion is conclusory.

34. A no-evidence motion for summary judgment must be specific in challenging the evidentiary support for an element of a claim or defense. Tex. R. Civ. P. 166a(i); *Timpte Indus., Inc. v. Gish*, 286 S.W.3d 306, 310 (Tex. 2009). The rule does not authorize conclusory motions or general no-evidence challenges to an opponent's case. *Timpte Indus.*, 286 S.W.3d at 310; *see* Tex. R. Civ. P. 166a(i). When a no-evidence motion for summary judgment does not challenge specific elements, it should be treated as a traditional motion for summary judgment under Texas Rule of Civil Procedure 166a(c). *See Michael v. Dyke*, 41 S.W.3d 746, 751-52 (Tex. App.—Corpus Christi 2001, no pet.); *Amouri v. Sw. Toyota, Inc.*, 20 S.W.3d 165, 168 (Tex. App.—Texarkana 2000, pet. denied); *Weaver v. Highlands Ins. Co.*, 4 S.W.3d 826, 829 n.2 (Tex. App.—Houston [1st Dist.] 1999, no pet.). This switches the burden of proof from the nonmovant to the movant. *See* Tex. R. Civ. P. 166a(c), (i).

35. The Court should deny plaintiff's no-evidence motion for summary judgment, which must be treated as a traditional motion for summary judgment, because {92 *explain why plaintiff's motion fails as a traditional summary-judgment motion, e.g., plaintiff did not provide any summary-judgment evidence to support it*}. Plaintiff's motion for summary judgment alleges generally that there is no evidence to support defendant's counterclaim for {93 *identify counterclaim*}. Because plaintiff's motion does not challenge specific elements of defendant's counterclaim, the Court must treat plaintiff's motion as a traditional motion for summary judgment.

B. Defendant has sufficient evidence to raise fact issue on {94 *his/her/its*} counterclaim.

36. In a no-evidence motion for summary judgment, a plaintiff can challenge a defendant to produce evidence to support one or more elements of the defendant's counterclaim on which the defendant would have the burden of proof at trial after an adequate time for discovery has passed. Tex. R. Civ. P. 166a(i). To avoid a no-evidence summary judgment, the defendant is not required to marshal its proof; the defendant only needs to point out evidence that raises a fact issue on the elements challenged in

the plaintiff's motion. *Hamilton v. Wilson*, 249 S.W.3d 425, 426 (Tex. 2008); *see* Tex. R. Civ. P. 166a(i); *Boerjan v. Rodriguez*, 436 S.W.3d 307, 310 (Tex. 2014). To raise a genuine issue of material fact, the defendant must produce more than a scintilla of evidence in support of the challenged elements. *Smith v. O'Donnell*, 288 S.W.3d 417, 424 (Tex. 2009); *Ford Motor Co. v. Ridgway*, 135 S.W.3d 598, 600 (Tex. 2004); *see Boerjan*, 436 S.W.3d at 312. More than a scintilla of evidence is produced if the evidence is sufficient to allow reasonable and fair-minded people to differ in their conclusions on whether the challenged fact exists. *Forbes, Inc. v. Granada Biosciences, Inc.*, 124 S.W.3d 167, 172 (Tex. 2003); *see First United Pentecostal Church of Beaumont v. Parker*, 514 S.W.3d 214, 220 (Tex. 2017). In evaluating whether more than a scintilla of evidence exists, the court must view the evidence in the light most favorable to the defendant, crediting evidence favorable to the defendant if reasonable jurors could, and disregarding contrary evidence unless reasonable jurors could not. *Boerjan*, 436 S.W.3d at 311-12; *Timpte Indus., Inc. v. Gish*, 286 S.W.3d 306, 310 (Tex. 2009).

37. Plaintiff alleged that there is no evidence supporting essential elements of defendant's counterclaim for {95 *identify counterclaim*}. The elements of the counterclaim are the following: {96 *identify elements*}. Plaintiff contends that there is no evidence to support {97 *identify elements*}.

38. The Court should deny plaintiff's no-evidence motion for summary judgment because defendant has produced sufficient evidence to raise a fact issue on the {98 *element/elements*} challenged by plaintiff. {99 *Show how there is evidence to raise a fact issue on each element challenged.*}

{*ADD SECTION BELOW IF DAMAGES SOUGHT BY PLAINTIFF*}

RESPONSE TO DAMAGES

{*CHOOSE APPROPRIATE PARAGRAPHS 39-43*}

39. The Court should deny plaintiff's motion for summary judgment on damages because plaintiff did not prove that {100 *he/she/it*} incurred damages. {101 *Elaborate.*}

40. The Court should deny plaintiff's motion for summary judgment on damages because the damages in this case are unliquidated. {102 *Elaborate.*}

41. The Court should deny plaintiff's motion for summary judgment on liquidated damages in the amount of ${103 *amount*} because plaintiff did not prove the amount of damages. {104 *Elaborate.*}

Continued on next page

FORM 7C:3

42. The Court should deny plaintiff's motion for summary judgment on damages because the summary-judgment evidence raises a fact issue on the amount of damages. {105 *Elaborate.*}

43. The Court should deny plaintiff's motion for summary judgment on damages because plaintiff is not entitled to damages in this case. There is no authority under law, contract, or equity for damages for plaintiff's cause of action. {106 *Elaborate.*}

{*ADD SECTION BELOW IF ATTORNEY FEES SOUGHT BY PLAINTIFF*}

RESPONSE TO ATTORNEY FEES REQUEST

{*CHOOSE APPROPRIATE PARAGRAPH 44*}

44. The Court should deny plaintiff's request for attorney fees because plaintiff is not entitled to attorney fees in this case. Plaintiff moved for summary judgment on {107 *identify cause of action*}. That cause of action does not permit plaintiff to recover attorney fees. A plaintiff must show it is entitled to attorney fees under a specific statute, by the terms of the contract subject to the suit, or under equity. *See Akin, Gump, Strauss, Hauer & Feld, L.L.P. v. Nat'l Dev. & Research Corp.*, 299 S.W.3d 106, 120 (Tex. 2009); *Nationwide Mut. Ins. Co. v. Holmes*, 842 S.W.2d 335, 341 (Tex. App.—San Antonio 1992, writ denied). {108 *Elaborate.*} {*See* ***O'Connor's Texas COA***, *"Attorney Fees," ch. 45, p. 1463.*}

44. The Court should deny plaintiff's request for attorney fees because plaintiff did not prove that {109 *he/she/it*} is entitled to attorney fees as a matter of law. When attorney fees are authorized, the plaintiff claiming them must establish the following: (1) the plaintiff pleaded for attorney fees, (2) the plaintiff was represented by an attorney, (3) the plaintiff complied with the conditions precedent to recovery of attorney fees, (4) the plaintiff incurred or will incur attorney fees, and (5) the plaintiff established that the attorney fees were reasonable and necessary. Plaintiff did not prove {110 *identify element not established*}. {111 *Explain why plaintiff did not prove element. If fees are not reasonable and necessary, attach controverting affidavit showing why. See Am. 10-Minute Oil Change, Inc. v. Metro. Nat'l Bank-Farmers Branch, 783 S.W.2d 598, 602 (Tex. App.—Dallas 1989, no writ).*} Thus, plaintiff is not entitled to attorney fees. {*See* ***O'Connor's Texas COA***, *"Attorney Fees," ch. 45, p. 1463.*}

{*ADD SECTION BELOW IF OBJECTING TO A FINAL SUMMARY JUDGMENT*}

FINAL JUDGMENT NOT APPROPRIATE

45. Defendant asks the Court to deny plaintiff's request for a final summary judgment because the only judgment capable of being rendered on plaintiff's motion will

not dispose of {112 *all claims/all parties/all claims and parties/the damages*}. If the Court grants plaintiff's motion for summary judgment, the Court can only sign an order for a partial summary judgment because {113 *explain*}. {*See* ***O'Connor's Texas Rules,*** *"What judgments are final," ch. 9-C, §6.3, p. 910.*}

CONCLUSION

46. {114 *Briefly summarize the response.*}

PRAYER

47. For these reasons, defendant asks the Court to deny plaintiff's motion for summary judgment {115 *add if applicable: and grant defendant leave to amend {his/her/its} pleading*}. If the Court grants plaintiff's motion for summary judgment, defendant asks the Court to overrule defendant's objections so they will be preserved for appeal.

SEE: Tex. R. Civ. P. 166a
O'Connor's Texas Rules * Civil Trials (2019), "Nonmovant's Response to Traditional Motion for Summary Judgment," ch. 7-C, §3, p. 752; "Burden on nonmovant," ch. 7-C, §4.2, p. 754; "Defendant's response to plaintiff's motion," ch. 7-C, §4.3.2, p. 756; "Defendant's response to plaintiff's motion," ch. 7-C, §4.4.2, p. 757; "Nonmovant's Response to No-Evidence Motion for Summary Judgment," ch. 7-D, §3, p. 763
O'Connor's Texas Causes of Action (2019), "Attorney Fees," ch. 45, p. 1463

ADD: STYLE OF THE CASE – FORM 1B:2
SIGNATURE BLOCK – FORM 1B:3
CERTIFICATE OF SERVICE – FORM 1B:13

ATTACH: AFFIDAVIT – FORM 1B:8
NOTICE OF INTENT TO USE UNFILED DISCOVERY – FORM 7C:7, if necessary
APPENDIX OF EVIDENCE – FORM 7C:8, if necessary
ORDER – FORM 7C:12
Amended pleading, if necessary

NOTE: This form only permits a response to defeat a motion for summary judgment; it does not permit the defendant to seek a summary judgment of its own. To file its own motion for summary judgment, the defendant should use FORM 7C:2.

A nonmovant is entitled to at least 21 days' notice of the date set for hearing of a motion for summary judgment. Tex. R. Civ. P. 166a(c). If the nonmovant is not given proper notice, it can ask the court to reset the hearing. See FORM 7B:2.

A no-evidence motion for summary judgment can be made only after there has been adequate time for discovery. Tex. R. Civ. P. 166a(i). If the nonmovant has not had adequate time to conduct discovery, it should move for a continuance of the summary-judgment hearing. See FORM 7B:5.

PLAINTIFF'S RESPONSE TO
DEFENDANT'S {❶ *TRADITIONAL/NO-EVIDENCE/
TRADITIONAL & NO-EVIDENCE*} MOTION FOR SUMMARY JUDGMENT

Plaintiff, {❷ *name*}, asks the Court to deny defendant {❸ *name*}'s motion for summary judgment.

INTRODUCTION

1. Plaintiff, {❹ *name*}, sued defendant, {❺ *name*}, for {❻ *state basis of suit*}.

2. Defendant answered asserting {❼ *identify answer, defensive pleas, affirmative defenses, and counterclaims*}.

3. {❽ *State other relevant facts about the suit.*}

BACKGROUND

4. {❾ *State facts relevant to the response with citations to evidence, if applicable.*}

{*ADD SECTION BELOW IF EVIDENCE IS NECESSARY FOR RESPONSE*}

SUMMARY-JUDGMENT EVIDENCE

{*CHOOSE APPROPRIATE PARAGRAPH 5*}

5. To support the facts in this response, plaintiff offers the following summary-judgment evidence attached to this response and incorporates the evidence into this response by reference. {*See **O'Connor's Texas Rules**, "Attached," ch. 7-B, §9.1.3, p. 731; "Attach to motion or response," ch. 7-B, §9.4.8(1), p. 735.*}

Exhibit 1: {❿ *identify evidence*}.

Exhibit 2: {⓫ *identify evidence*}.

{⓬ *Continue for all other exhibits.*}

5. To support the facts in this response, plaintiff includes the summary-judgment evidence in an appendix filed with this response and incorporates the evidence into this response by reference. {*See **O'Connor's Texas Rules**, "Attached," ch. 7-B, §9.1.3, p. 731.*}

{*CHOOSE APPROPRIATE SUMMARY-JUDGMENT RESPONSES*}

RESPONSE TO TRADITIONAL SUMMARY JUDGMENT
PLAINTIFF'S CAUSE OF ACTION FOR {13 *IDENTIFY CAUSE OF ACTION*}

{*CHOOSE APPROPRIATE SECTIONS A-F*}

A. Defendant did not disprove plaintiff's cause of action as a matter of law.

6. A defendant is entitled to summary judgment on a plaintiff's cause of action if the defendant can disprove at least one element of the cause of action as a matter of law. *Painter v. Amerimex Drilling I, Ltd.*, 561 S.W.3d 125, 130 (Tex. 2018); *Sw. Elec. Power Co. v. Grant*, 73 S.W.3d 211, 215 (Tex. 2002). {*See* ***O'Connor's Texas Rules***, *"When defendant moves for SJ on plaintiff's cause of action," ch. 7-C, §4.5, p. 757.*}

7. The elements of plaintiff's cause of action for {14 *identify cause of action*} are the following: {15 *identify elements*}. Defendant claims that {16 *he/she/it*} disproved {17 *identify elements*}.

{*CHOOSE APPROPRIATE PARAGRAPHS 8-9*}

8. The Court should deny defendant's motion for summary judgment on plaintiff's cause of action because defendant did not disprove {18 *identify elements*} as a matter of law. There is a genuine issue of material fact on {19 *identify elements*}. {20 *Elaborate.*}

9. The Court should deny defendant's motion for summary judgment on plaintiff's cause of action because the {21 *identify type of evidence*} attached to defendant's motion is defective and does not present competent summary-judgment evidence. Specifically, {22 *choose objections to evidence from FORM 7C:11*}.

B. Plaintiff did not plead facts that negate {23 *his/her/its*} cause of action.

10. A defendant is entitled to summary judgment on a plaintiff's cause of action if the plaintiff affirmatively pleads facts that conclusively negate its cause of action. *Tex. Dep't of Corr. v. Herring*, 513 S.W.2d 6, 9 (Tex. 1974); *e.g., Washington v. City of Hous.*, 874 S.W.2d 791, 794 (Tex. App.—Texarkana 1994, no writ) (pleading can negate claim when alleged facts demonstrate that statute of limitations has run or that a defense would bar recovery).

11. Defendant alleges that plaintiff conclusively negated the cause of action when, in plaintiff's {24 *identify pleading, e.g., original petition*}, plaintiff pleaded the following: {25 *identify plaintiff's allegations that defendant claims negated the cause of action*}.

Continued on next page

12. The Court should deny defendant's motion for summary judgment on plaintiff's cause of action for {㉖ *identify cause of action*} because plaintiff did not affirmatively plead facts that negate the cause of action. {㉗ *Elaborate.*}

C. Plaintiff has a viable cause of action.

13. A defendant is entitled to summary judgment on a plaintiff's cause of action if the plaintiff's pleading affirmatively demonstrates that no cause of action exists. *Peek v. Equip. Serv. Co.*, 779 S.W.2d 802, 805 (Tex. 1989). If the pleading demonstrates that no cause of action exists, the court can grant a summary judgment without first giving the plaintiff an opportunity to amend its pleading. *Id.* However, if the pleading could be amended so that it does allege a viable cause of action, the court cannot grant a summary judgment without first giving the plaintiff an opportunity to amend. *See Sixth RMA Partners, L.P. v. Sibley*, 111 S.W.3d 46, 54-55 (Tex. 2003); *Pietila v. Crites*, 851 S.W.2d 185, 186 n.2 (Tex. 1993). {*See* ***O'Connor's Texas Rules***, *"Moving on the pleadings," ch. 7-C, §2.5.2, p. 750.*}

14. Defendant claimed that {㉘ *he/she/it*} is entitled to summary judgment because plaintiff's pleadings show on their face that plaintiff's cause of action is not viable.

{*CHOOSE APPROPRIATE PARAGRAPH 15*}

15. The Court should deny defendant's motion for summary judgment on plaintiff's cause of action for {㉙ *identify cause of action*} because the motion is an attempt to use the summary-judgment procedure to attack an alleged defect in plaintiff's pleadings that should have been challenged first by special exception. Defendant did not challenge plaintiff's pleadings by special exception, and plaintiff has not had an opportunity to amend {㉚ *his/her/its*} pleading to cure any defect. {㉛ *Explain why the defect should have been challenged first by special exception.*}

15. The Court should deny defendant's motion for summary judgment on plaintiff's cause of action for {㉜ *identify cause of action*} because plaintiff amended {㉝ *his/her/its*} petition to address the defect cited in defendant's motion. In the amended petition, plaintiff pleaded a viable cause of action for {㉞ *identify cause of action*}. Attached to this response as Exhibit {㉟ *letter*} is a copy of plaintiff's {㊱ *identify pleading, e.g., second amended petition*}. {㊲ *Show how the amended pleading asserts a viable cause of action.*}

15. The Court should deny defendant's motion for summary judgment on plaintiff's cause of action for {㊳ *identify cause of action*} because, contrary to defendant's allegations, plaintiff has pleaded a viable claim. {㊴ *Show how the cause of action is viable.*}

D. Plaintiff's pleading supports {40 *his/her/its*} cause of action.

16. A defendant is entitled to summary judgment on a plaintiff's cause of action if the plaintiff has not pleaded sufficient facts to state a cause of action and, even though the plaintiff was given an opportunity to amend, the pleading defect remains. *See Natividad v. Alexsis, Inc.*, 875 S.W.2d 695, 699 (Tex. 1994).

17. Defendant claimed that {41 *he/she/it*} is entitled to summary judgment because plaintiff did not plead sufficient facts to state a cause of action.

{*CHOOSE APPROPRIATE PARAGRAPH 18*}

18. The Court should deny defendant's motion for summary judgment on plaintiff's cause of action for {42 *identify cause of action*} because the motion is an attempt to use the summary-judgment procedure to attack an alleged defect in defendant's pleadings that should have been challenged first by special exception. Defendant did not challenge plaintiff's pleadings by special exception, and plaintiff has not had an opportunity to amend {43 *his/her/its*} pleading to cure any defect. {44 *Explain why the defect should have been challenged first by special exception.*}

18. The Court should deny defendant's motion for summary judgment on plaintiff's cause of action for {45 *identify cause of action*} because plaintiff amended {46 *his/her/its*} petition to address the defect cited in defendant's motion. In the amended petition, plaintiff pleaded sufficient facts to state a cause of action. Attached to this response as Exhibit {47 *letter*} is a copy of plaintiff's {48 *identify pleading, e.g., second amended petition*}. {49 *Show how the amended pleading alleges sufficient facts to state a cause of action.*}

18. The Court should deny defendant's motion for summary judgment on plaintiff's cause of action for {50 *identify cause of action*} because, contrary to defendant's allegations, plaintiff has pleaded sufficient facts to state a cause of action. {51 *Elaborate.*}

E. Defendant has not proved {52 *his/her/its*} affirmative defense as a matter of law.

19. A defendant is entitled to summary judgment on a plaintiff's cause of action if the defendant can prove as a matter of law that it has an affirmative defense to the cause of action. *See Exxon Mobil Corp. v. Rincones*, 520 S.W.3d 572, 593 (Tex. 2017); *Long Distance Int'l, Inc. v. Telefonos de Mex., S.A. de C.V.*, 49 S.W.3d 347, 350-51 (Tex. 2001). To meet its burden, the defendant must show that there is no genuine issue of material fact on any of the elements of the affirmative defense. *See* Tex. R. Civ. P. 166a(c). {*See* ***O'Connor's Texas Rules****, "When defendant moves for SJ on its affirmative defense," ch. 7-C, §4.6, p. 759.*}

Continued on next page

20. In {53 *his/her/its*} motion for summary judgment, defendant asserted the affirmative defense of {54 *identify affirmative defense*} to plaintiff's cause of action for {55 *identify cause of action*}.

21. Defendant is not entitled to summary judgment on plaintiff's cause of action because the undisputed facts in this case and defendant's summary-judgment evidence do not conclusively establish each essential element of {56 *identify affirmative defense*}. To prevail on the affirmative defense of {57 *identify affirmative defense*}, defendant must prove the following: {58 *identify elements of affirmative defense*}. {*For elements of affirmative defenses, see* ***O'Connor's Texas COA***.}

a. {59 *Identify first element.*} {60 *Show how the summary-judgment evidence creates a fact issue.*}

b. {61 *Continue for all other elements of affirmative defense where there is a fact issue.*}

F. Defendant's affirmative defense is not supported by {62 *his/her/its*} pleadings.

22. For the movant to be entitled to a summary judgment, the grounds for summary judgment must be supported by the movant's pleadings. *See Daniels v. Daniels*, 45 S.W.3d 278, 282 (Tex. App.—Corpus Christi 2001, no pet.). Thus, an unpleaded affirmative defense cannot serve as the basis for a summary judgment if the nonmovant objects. *Roark v. Stallworth Oil & Gas, Inc.*, 813 S.W.2d 492, 494 (Tex. 1991); *Downs v. Triad-Denton Hosp., L.P.*, No. 02-05-303-CV (Tex. App.—Fort Worth 2006, no pet.) (memo op.; 3-30-06).

23. Accordingly, plaintiff objects to defendant's attempt to seek summary judgment on {63 *identify affirmative defense*} because defendant has not pleaded that defense in {64 *his/her/its*} answer.

RESPONSE TO NO-EVIDENCE SUMMARY JUDGMENT
PLAINTIFF'S CAUSE OF ACTION FOR {65 *IDENTIFY CAUSE OF ACTION*}

{*CHOOSE APPROPRIATE SECTIONS A-B*}

A. Defendant's no-evidence motion is conclusory.

24. A no-evidence motion for summary judgment must be specific in challenging the evidentiary support for an element of a claim or defense. Tex. R. Civ. P. 166a(i); *Timpte Indus., Inc. v. Gish*, 286 S.W.3d 306, 310 (Tex. 2009). The rule does not authorize conclusory motions or general no-evidence challenges to an opponent's case. *Timpte Indus.*, 286 S.W.3d at 310; *see* Tex. R. Civ. P. 166a(i). When a no-evidence mo-

tion for summary judgment does not challenge specific elements, it should be treated as a traditional motion for summary judgment under Texas Rule of Civil Procedure 166a(c). *See Michael v. Dyke*, 41 S.W.3d 746, 751-52 (Tex. App.—Corpus Christi 2001, no pet.); *Amouri v. Sw. Toyota, Inc.*, 20 S.W.3d 165, 168 (Tex. App.—Texarkana 2000, pet. denied); *Weaver v. Highlands Ins. Co.*, 4 S.W.3d 826, 829 n.2 (Tex. App.—Houston [1st Dist.] 1999, no pet.). This switches the burden of proof from the nonmovant to the movant. *See* Tex. R. Civ. P. 166a(c), (i).

25. The Court should deny defendant's no-evidence motion for summary judgment, which must be treated as a traditional motion for summary judgment, because {66 *explain why defendant's motion fails as a traditional summary-judgment motion, e.g., defendant did not provide any summary-judgment evidence to support it*}. Defendant's motion for summary judgment alleges generally that there is no evidence to support plaintiff's cause of action for {67 *identify cause of action*}. Because defendant's motion does not challenge specific elements of plaintiff's cause of action, the Court must treat defendant's motion as a traditional motion for summary judgment.

B. Plaintiff has sufficient evidence to raise fact issue on {68 *his/her/its*} cause of action.

26. In a no-evidence motion for summary judgment, a defendant can challenge a plaintiff to produce evidence to support one or more elements of the plaintiff's cause of action on which the plaintiff would have the burden of proof at trial after an adequate time for discovery has passed. Tex. R. Civ. P. 166a(i). To avoid a no-evidence summary judgment, the plaintiff is not required to marshal its proof; the plaintiff only needs to point out evidence that raises a fact issue on the elements challenged in the defendant's motion. *Hamilton v. Wilson*, 249 S.W.3d 425, 426 (Tex. 2008); *see* Tex. R. Civ. P. 166a(i); *Boerjan v. Rodriguez*, 436 S.W.3d 307, 310 (Tex. 2014). To raise a genuine issue of material fact, the plaintiff must produce more than a scintilla of evidence in support of the challenged elements. *Smith v. O'Donnell*, 288 S.W.3d 417, 424 (Tex. 2009); *Ford Motor Co. v. Ridgway*, 135 S.W.3d 598, 600 (Tex. 2004); *see Boerjan*, 436 S.W.3d at 312. More than a scintilla of evidence is produced if the evidence is sufficient to allow reasonable and fair-minded people to differ in their conclusions on whether the challenged fact exists. *Forbes, Inc. v. Granada Biosciences, Inc.*, 124 S.W.3d 167, 172 (Tex. 2003); *see First United Pentecostal Church of Beaumont v. Parker*, 514 S.W.3d 214, 220 (Tex. 2017). In evaluating whether more than a scintilla of evidence exists, the court must view the evidence in the light most favorable to the plaintiff, crediting evidence favorable to the plaintiff if reasonable jurors could, and disregarding contrary evidence unless reasonable jurors could not. *Boerjan*, 436 S.W.3d at 311-12; *Timpte Indus., Inc. v. Gish*, 286 S.W.3d 306, 310 (Tex. 2009).

Continued on next page

27. Defendant alleged that there is no evidence supporting essential elements of plaintiff's cause of action for {69 *identify cause of action*}. The elements of the cause of action are the following: {70 *identify elements*}. Defendant contends that there is no evidence to support {71 *identify elements*}.

28. The Court should deny defendant's no-evidence motion for summary judgment because plaintiff has produced sufficient evidence to raise a fact issue on the {72 *element/elements*} challenged by defendant. {73 *Show how there is evidence to raise a fact issue on each element challenged.*}

RESPONSE TO TRADITIONAL SUMMARY JUDGMENT
DEFENDANT'S COUNTERCLAIM FOR {74 *IDENTIFY COUNTERCLAIM*}

{*CHOOSE APPROPRIATE SECTIONS A-C*}

A. Defendant did not satisfy {75 *his/her/its*} burden under Texas Rule of Civil Procedure 166a(c).

29. To succeed on a traditional motion for summary judgment on its counterclaim, the defendant must show that there is no genuine issue of material fact and that it is entitled to summary judgment as a matter of law. Tex. R. Civ. P. 166a(c); *ConocoPhillips Co. v. Koopmann*, 547 S.W.3d 858, 865 (Tex. 2018); *Kachina Pipeline Co. v. Lillis*, 471 S.W.3d 445, 449 (Tex. 2015); *Amedisys, Inc. v. Kingwood Home Health Care, LLC*, 437 S.W.3d 507, 511 (Tex. 2014); *Mann Frankfort Stein & Lipp Advisors, Inc. v. Fielding*, 289 S.W.3d 844, 848 (Tex. 2009). To meet this burden, the defendant must conclusively prove all essential elements of its claim. *MMP, Ltd. v. Jones*, 710 S.W.2d 59, 60 (Tex. 1986). A matter is conclusively established if reasonable people could not differ on the conclusion to be drawn from the evidence. *City of Keller v. Wilson*, 168 S.W.3d 802, 816 (Tex. 2005). If the defendant establishes its right to summary judgment as a matter of law, the burden shifts to the plaintiff to present evidence that raises a genuine issue of material fact. *See State v. $90,235*, 390 S.W.3d 289, 292 (Tex. 2013); *Casso v. Brand*, 776 S.W.2d 551, 556 (Tex. 1989). In deciding whether to grant defendant's motion, the court must take as true all competent evidence favorable to the plaintiff and indulge every reasonable inference and resolve any doubts in the plaintiff's favor. *Limestone Prods. Distrib., Inc. v. McNamara*, 71 S.W.3d 308, 311 (Tex. 2002); *Rhône-Poulenc, Inc. v. Steel*, 997 S.W.2d 217, 223 (Tex. 1999); *Nixon v. Mr. Prop. Mgmt. Co.*, 690 S.W.2d 546, 548-49 (Tex. 1985).

30. Defendant moved for summary judgment on {76 *his/her/its*} counterclaim for {77 *identify counterclaim*}, arguing that there is no genuine issue of material fact and that the summary-judgment evidence conclusively establishes all the elements of {78 *his/her/its*} counterclaim as a matter of law.

31. To prevail on a counterclaim for {79 *identify counterclaim*}, defendant must prove the following: {80 *identify elements*}.

{*CHOOSE APPROPRIATE PARAGRAPHS 32-34*}

32. The Court should deny defendant's motion for summary judgment on {81 *his/her/its*} counterclaim because defendant did not carry {82 *his/her/its*} burden of proving the element of {83 *identify element*} as a matter of law. {84 *Elaborate.*}

33. The Court should deny defendant's motion for summary judgment because there is a genuine issue of material fact on the following elements of defendant's counterclaim: {85 *identify elements and fact issues*}. {86 *Elaborate.*}

34. The Court should deny defendant's motion for summary judgment on {87 *his/her/its*} counterclaim because the {88 *identify type of evidence*} attached to defendant's motion is defective and does not present competent summary-judgment evidence. Specifically, {89 *choose objections to evidence from FORM 7C:11*}.

B. Defendant's pleadings do not support {90 *his/her/its*} counterclaim.

35. For the movant to be entitled to a summary judgment, the grounds for summary judgment must be supported by the movant's pleadings. *See Daniels v. Daniels*, 45 S.W.3d 278, 282 (Tex. App.—Corpus Christi 2001, no pet.). Thus, an unpleaded cause of action cannot serve as the basis for a summary judgment if the nonmovant objects. *See Roark v. Stallworth Oil & Gas, Inc.*, 813 S.W.2d 492, 494 (Tex. 1991); *Roadside Stations, Inc. v. 7HBF, Ltd.*, 904 S.W.2d 927, 930 (Tex. App.—Fort Worth 1995, no writ). {*See* ***O'Connor's Texas Rules***, *"Challenge movant's pleadings," ch. 7-C, §3.6.2, p. 753.*}

36. Accordingly, plaintiff objects to defendant's attempt to seek summary judgment on {91 *identify counterclaim*} because defendant has not asserted that counterclaim in {92 *his/her/its*} pleadings.

C. Plaintiff has sufficient evidence to raise fact issue on {93 *his/her/its*} affirmative defense.

37. A defendant is not entitled to summary judgment on a counterclaim if the plaintiff is able to assert an affirmative defense in its response and provide sufficient summary-judgment evidence to create a fact issue on each element of the defense. *See Bassett v. Am. Nat'l Bank*, 145 S.W.3d 692, 696 (Tex. App.—Fort Worth 2004, no pet.); *Keenan v. Gibraltar Sav. Ass'n*, 754 S.W.2d 392, 393-94 (Tex. App.—Houston [14th Dist.] 1988, no writ). The plaintiff is not required to prove the affirmative defense by a

◄ *Continued on next page* ►

preponderance of the evidence or as a matter of law; raising a fact issue is enough to defeat the summary judgment. *See Brownlee v. Brownlee*, 665 S.W.2d 111, 112 (Tex. 1984). {*See* ***O'Connor's Texas Rules***, *"Nonmovant's affirmative defense," ch. 7-C, §3.4.1(4), p. 752; "Create fact issue about affirmative defense," ch. 7-C, §4.3.2(2), p. 756.*}

38. The Court should deny defendant's motion for summary judgment on {94 *his/her/its*} counterclaim for {95 *identify counterclaim*} because of plaintiff's affirmative defense of {96 *identify affirmative defense*}. The elements of plaintiff's affirmative defense are the following: {97 *identify elements of affirmative defense*}. {*For elements of affirmative defenses, see* ***O'Connor's Texas COA***.}

a. {98 *Identify first element.*} {99 *Show how the summary-judgment evidence creates a fact issue.*}

b. {100 *Continue until a fact issue is raised on all elements of affirmative defense.*}

{*ADD SECTION BELOW IF DAMAGES SOUGHT BY DEFENDANT*}

RESPONSE TO DAMAGES

{*CHOOSE APPROPRIATE PARAGRAPHS 39-43*}

39. The Court should deny defendant's motion for summary judgment on damages because defendant did not prove that {101 *he/she/it*} incurred damages. {102 *Elaborate.*}

40. The Court should deny defendant's motion for summary judgment on damages because the damages in this case are unliquidated. {103 *Elaborate.*}

41. The Court should deny defendant's motion for summary judgment on liquidated damages in the amount of ${104 *amount*} because defendant did not prove the amount of damages. {105 *Elaborate.*}

42. The Court should deny defendant's motion for summary judgment on damages because the summary-judgment evidence raises a fact issue on the amount of damages. {106 *Elaborate.*}

43. The Court should deny defendant's motion for summary judgment on damages because defendant is not entitled to damages in this case. There is no authority under law, contract, or equity for damages for defendant's counterclaim. {107 *Elaborate.*}

{*ADD SECTION BELOW IF ATTORNEY FEES SOUGHT BY DEFENDANT*}

RESPONSE TO ATTORNEY FEES REQUEST

{*CHOOSE APPROPRIATE PARAGRAPH 44*}

44. The Court should deny defendant's request for attorney fees because defendant is not entitled to attorney fees in this case. Defendant moved for summary judgment on {108 *identify counterclaim*}. That counterclaim does not permit defendant to recover attorney fees. A defendant must show it is entitled to attorney fees under a specific statute, by the terms of the contract subject to the suit, or under equity. *See Akin, Gump, Strauss, Hauer & Feld, L.L.P. v. Nat'l Dev. & Research Corp.*, 299 S.W.3d 106, 120 (Tex. 2009); *Nationwide Mut. Ins. Co. v. Holmes*, 842 S.W.2d 335, 341 (Tex. App.—San Antonio 1992, writ denied). {109 *Elaborate.*} {*See **O'Connor's Texas COA**, "Attorney Fees," ch. 45, p. 1463.*}

44. The Court should deny defendant's request for attorney fees because defendant did not prove that {110 *he/she/it*} is entitled to attorney fees as a matter of law. When attorney fees are authorized, the defendant claiming them must establish the following: (1) the defendant pleaded for attorney fees, (2) the defendant was represented by an attorney, (3) the defendant complied with the conditions precedent to recovery of attorney fees, (4) the defendant incurred or will incur attorney fees, and (5) the defendant established that the attorney fees were reasonable and necessary. Defendant did not prove {111 *identify element not established*}. {112 *Explain why defendant did not prove element. If fees are not reasonable and necessary, attach controverting affidavit showing why. See Am. 10-Minute Oil Change, Inc. v. Metro. Nat'l Bank-Farmers Branch, 783 S.W.2d 598, 602 (Tex. App.—Dallas 1989, no writ).*} Thus, defendant is not entitled to attorney fees. {*See **O'Connor's Texas COA**, "Attorney Fees," ch. 45, p. 1463.*}

{*ADD SECTION BELOW IF OBJECTING TO A FINAL SUMMARY JUDGMENT*}

FINAL JUDGMENT NOT APPROPRIATE

45. Plaintiff asks the Court to deny defendant's request for a final summary judgment because the only judgment capable of being rendered on defendant's motion will not dispose of {113 *all claims/all parties/all claims and parties/the damages*}. If the Court grants defendant's motion for summary judgment, the Court can only sign an order for a partial summary judgment because {114 *explain*}. {*See **O'Connor's Texas Rules**, "What judgments are final," ch. 9-C, §6.3, p. 910.*}

CONCLUSION

46. {115 *Briefly summarize the response.*}

Continued on next page

PRAYER

47. For these reasons, plaintiff asks the Court to deny defendant's motion for summary judgment {116 *add if applicable: and grant plaintiff leave to amend {his/her/its} pleading*}. If the Court grants defendant's motion for summary judgment, plaintiff asks the Court to overrule plaintiff's objections so they will be preserved for appeal.

SEE: Tex. R. Civ. P. 166a
O'Connor's Texas Rules * Civil Trials (2019), "Nonmovant's Response to Traditional Motion for Summary Judgment," ch. 7-C, §3, p. 752; "Burden on nonmovant," ch. 7-C, §4.2, p. 754; "Plaintiff's response to defendant's motion," ch. 7-C, §4.5.2, p. 758; "Plaintiff's response," ch. 7-C, §4.6.2, p. 759; "Plaintiff's response," ch. 7-C, §4.7.2, p. 760; "Nonmovant's Response to No-Evidence Motion for Summary Judgment," ch. 7-D, §3, p. 763
O'Connor's Texas Causes of Action (2019), "Attorney Fees," ch. 45, p. 1463

ADD: STYLE OF THE CASE – FORM 1B:2
SIGNATURE BLOCK – FORM 1B:3
CERTIFICATE OF SERVICE – FORM 1B:13

ATTACH: AFFIDAVIT – FORM 1B:8
NOTICE OF INTENT TO USE UNFILED DISCOVERY – FORM 7C:7, if necessary
APPENDIX OF EVIDENCE – FORM 7C:8, if necessary
ORDER – FORM 7C:12
Amended pleading, if necessary

NOTE: **This form only permits a response to defeat a motion for summary judgment; it does not permit the plaintiff to seek a summary judgment of its own. To file its own motion for summary judgment, the plaintiff should use FORM 7C:1.**

A nonmovant is entitled to at least 21 days' notice of the date set for hearing on a motion for summary judgment. Tex. R. Civ. P. 166a(c). If the nonmovant is not given proper notice, it can ask the court to reset the hearing. See FORM 7B:2.

A no-evidence motion for summary judgment can be made only after there has been adequate time for discovery. Tex. R. Civ. P. 166a(i). If the nonmovant has not had adequate time to conduct discovery, it should move for a continuance of the summary-judgment hearing. See FORM 7B:5.

PLAINTIFF'S REPLY IN SUPPORT OF
{❶ *TRADITIONAL/NO-EVIDENCE/TRADITIONAL & NO-EVIDENCE*} MOTION FOR SUMMARY JUDGMENT

Plaintiff, {❷ *name*}, files this reply to defendant {❸ *name*}'s response to plaintiff's {❹ *traditional/no-evidence/traditional and no-evidence*} motion for summary judgment.

{*ADD SECTION BELOW IF APPLICABLE*}

SUMMARY-JUDGMENT EVIDENCE

{*CHOOSE APPROPRIATE PARAGRAPH 1*}

1. To support the facts in this reply, plaintiff relies on the summary-judgment evidence already on file in this case and incorporates the evidence into this reply by reference.

1. To support the facts in this reply, plaintiff relies on the summary-judgment evidence already on file and the evidence {❺ *attached to this reply as Exhibits {letters}/included in an appendix filed with this reply*}, and incorporates the evidence into this reply by reference. {*See **O'Connor's Texas Rules**, "Attached," ch. 7-B, §9.1.3, p. 731.*}

{*CHOOSE APPROPRIATE SUMMARY-JUDGMENT MOTIONS*}

TRADITIONAL SUMMARY JUDGMENT
PLAINTIFF'S CAUSE OF ACTION FOR {❻ *IDENTIFY CAUSE OF ACTION*}

{*CHOOSE APPROPRIATE SECTIONS A-F*}

A. Plaintiff satisfied {❼ *his/her/its*} burden under Texas Rule of Civil Procedure 166a(c).

2. In defendant's response to plaintiff's motion for summary judgment for {❽ *identify cause of action*}, defendant asserts that the motion should be denied because there is a genuine issue of material fact on the following elements of the cause of action: {❾ *identify elements*}. {❿ *Describe alleged fact issues.*}

3. Contrary to defendant's response, the Court should grant plaintiff's motion because there is no issue of fact on those elements. {⓫ *Elaborate.*}

Continued on next page

FORM 7C:5

B. Defendant's summary-judgment evidence is not competent.

4. In defendant's response to plaintiff's motion for summary judgment for {[12] *identify cause of action*}, defendant cited {[13] *identify summary-judgment evidence*} in support of {[14] *his/her/its*} opposition to the motion.

5. Contrary to defendant's response, the Court should grant plaintiff's motion because the evidence attached to defendant's response is defective and does not present competent summary-judgment evidence. Specifically, {[15] *identify evidence and assert appropriate objection from FORM 7C:11*}.

C. Plaintiff's pleadings support {[16] *his/her/its*} cause of action.

6. In defendant's response to plaintiff's motion for summary judgment for {[17] *identify cause of action*}, defendant claims that plaintiff's pleadings do not support {[18] *his/her/its*} cause of action.

7. Contrary to defendant's response, the Court should grant plaintiff's motion because plaintiff's pleadings do support {[19] *his/her/its*} cause of action for {[20] *identify cause of action*}. {[21] *Elaborate.*}

D. Defendant did not produce sufficient evidence to create a fact issue on {[22] *his/her/its*} affirmative defense.

8. In defendant's response to plaintiff's motion for summary judgment for {[23] *identify cause of action*}, defendant asserts the affirmative defense of {[24] *identify affirmative defense*}.

9. Contrary to defendant's response, the Court should grant plaintiff's motion because defendant did not introduce sufficient evidence to create fact issues on each element of {[25] *his/her/its*} affirmative defense. The elements of defendant's affirmative defense are as follows: {[26] *identify elements*}. Defendant did not introduce sufficient evidence to create fact issues on {[27] *identify elements on which defendant failed to raise a fact issue*}. {[28] *Negate fact issues raised by defendant.*}

E. Defendant's pleadings do not support {[29] *his/her/its*} affirmative defense.

10. In defendant's response to plaintiff's motion for summary judgment for {[30] *identify cause of action*}, defendant asserts for the first time the affirmative defense of {[31] *identify affirmative defense*}.

11. Contrary to defendant's response, the Court should grant plaintiff's motion because defendant did not plead this affirmative defense in {[32] *his/her/its*} answer. A de-

fendant cannot defeat a motion for summary judgment with an affirmative defense it did not plead. *See Kinnear v. Tex. Comm'n on Human Rights*, 14 S.W.3d 299, 300 (Tex. 2000) (affirmative defense must be pleaded or it is waived); *cf. Via Net v. TIG Ins. Co.*, 211 S.W.3d 310, 313 (Tex. 2006) (when plaintiff raised issue for first time in its summary-judgment response, defendant could have objected that issue had not been properly pleaded).

F. {33 *Add other grounds for reply.*}

12. {34 *Insert other grounds in reply to defendant's response.*}

TRADITIONAL SUMMARY JUDGMENT
DEFENDANT'S COUNTERCLAIM FOR {35 *IDENTIFY COUNTERCLAIM*}

{*CHOOSE APPROPRIATE SECTIONS A-E*}

A. Defendant's counterclaim can be disproved as a matter of law.

13. In defendant's response to plaintiff's motion for summary judgment on defendant's counterclaim for {36 *identify counterclaim*}, defendant asserts that the motion should be denied because plaintiff has not disproved any element of the counterclaim as a matter of law. {37 *Identify relevant facts asserted by defendant in response.*}

14. Contrary to defendant's response, the Court should grant plaintiff's motion because plaintiff has disproved {38 *identify elements plaintiff can disprove*}. {39 *Negate fact issues raised by defendant.*}

B. Defendant's summary-judgment evidence is not competent.

15. In defendant's response to plaintiff's motion for summary judgment on defendant's counterclaim for {40 *identify counterclaim*}, defendant cited {41 *identify summary-judgment evidence*} in support of {42 *his/her/its*} opposition to the motion.

16. Contrary to defendant's response, the Court should grant plaintiff's motion because the evidence attached to defendant's response is defective and does not present competent summary-judgment evidence. Specifically, {43 *choose objections to evidence from FORM 7C:11*}.

C. Plaintiff has proved {44 *his/her/its*} affirmative defense as a matter of law.

17. In defendant's response to plaintiff's motion for summary judgment on defendant's counterclaim for {45 *identify counterclaim*}, defendant asserted that plaintiff's affirmative defense of {46 *identify affirmative defense*} should be denied because there is a genuine issue of material fact on the following elements of that affirmative defense: {47 *identify elements*}.

Continued on next page

FORM 7C:5

18. Contrary to defendant's response, the Court should grant plaintiff's motion because there is no issue of fact on those elements. {48 *Elaborate.*}

D. Plaintiff's pleadings support {49 *his/her/its*} affirmative defense.

19. In defendant's response to plaintiff's motion for summary judgment on defendant's counterclaim for {50 *identify counterclaim*}, defendant asserted that plaintiff's pleadings did not support {51 *his/her/its*} affirmative defense of {52 *identify affirmative defense*}.

20. Contrary to defendant's response, the Court should grant plaintiff's motion because plaintiff's pleadings do support {53 *his/her/its*} affirmative defense of {54 *identify affirmative defense*}. {55 *Elaborate.*}

E. {56 *Add other grounds for reply.*}

21. {57 *Insert other grounds in reply to defendant's response.*}

NO-EVIDENCE SUMMARY JUDGMENT
DEFENDANT'S COUNTERCLAIM FOR {58 *IDENTIFY COUNTERCLAIM*}
{*CHOOSE APPROPRIATE SECTIONS A-C*}

A. Defendant did not produce sufficient evidence to defeat plaintiff's no-evidence motion for summary judgment.

22. In defendant's response to plaintiff's no-evidence motion for summary judgment on defendant's counterclaim for {59 *identify counterclaim*}, defendant asserts that there is a genuine issue of material fact supporting the {60 *element/elements*} challenged by the motion. Specifically, defendant contends that there is evidence to support {61 *identify each challenged element*}. {62 *Describe defendant's evidence.*}

23. Contrary to defendant's response, the Court should grant plaintiff's motion because defendant did not produce sufficient evidence to raise a fact issue on the challenged {63 *element/elements*}. {64 *Negate fact issues raised by defendant for each challenged element.*}

B. Defendant's summary-judgment evidence is not competent.

24. In defendant's response to plaintiff's no-evidence motion for summary judgment on defendant's counterclaim for {65 *identify counterclaim*}, defendant cited {66 *identify summary-judgment evidence*} in support of {67 *his/her/its*} opposition to the motion.

25. Contrary to defendant's response, the Court should grant plaintiff's motion because the evidence attached to defendant's response is defective and does not present competent summary-judgment evidence. Specifically, {68 *identify evidence and assert appropriate objection from FORM 7C:11*}.

C. {69 *Add other grounds for reply.*}

26. {70 *Insert other grounds in reply to defendant's response.*}

{*ADD SECTION BELOW IF DAMAGES SOUGHT BY PLAINTIFF*}

DAMAGES

{*CHOOSE APPROPRIATE PARAGRAPHS 27-31*}

27. In {71 *his/her/its*} response to plaintiff's motion for summary judgment, defendant claimed that the Court should deny plaintiff's motion because plaintiff did not prove that {72 *he/she/it*} incurred damages. {73 *Show how summary-judgment evidence proves that plaintiff incurred damages.*}

28. In {74 *his/her/its*} response to plaintiff's motion for summary judgment, defendant claimed that the Court should deny plaintiff's motion because the damages in this case are unliquidated. {75 *Show how summary-judgment evidence proves amount of liquidated damages.*}

29. In {76 *his/her/its*} response to plaintiff's motion for summary judgment, defendant claimed that the Court should deny plaintiff's motion on liquidated damages in the amount of ${77 *amount*} because plaintiff did not prove the amount of damages. {78 *Show how summary-judgment evidence proves amount of damages.*}

30. In {79 *his/her/its*} response to plaintiff's motion for summary judgment, defendant claimed that the Court should deny plaintiff's motion because the summary-judgment evidence raises a fact issue on the amount of damages. {80 *Negate fact issue on damages.*}

31. In {81 *his/her/its*} response to plaintiff's motion for summary judgment, defendant claimed that the Court should deny plaintiff's motion because plaintiff is not entitled to damages in this case. {82 *Show authority for damages for plaintiff's cause of action.*}

Continued on next page

{ADD SECTION BELOW IF ATTORNEY FEES SOUGHT BY PLAINTIFF}

ATTORNEY FEES

{CHOOSE APPROPRIATE PARAGRAPH 32}

32. In {83 *his/her/its*} response to plaintiff's motion for summary judgment, defendant claimed that plaintiff is not entitled to attorney fees in this case. {84 *Show how plaintiff is entitled to attorney fees under a specific statute, by the terms of the contract subject to the suit, or under equity.*}

32. In {85 *his/her/its*} response to plaintiff's motion for summary judgment, defendant claimed that plaintiff did not prove that {86 *he/she/it*} is entitled to attorney fees as a matter of law. When attorney fees are authorized, the party claiming them must establish the following: (1) the party pleaded for attorney fees, (2) the party was represented by an attorney, (3) the party complied with the conditions precedent to recovery of attorney fees, (4) the party incurred or will incur attorney fees, and (5) the attorney fees were reasonable and necessary. Plaintiff proved {87 *identify element challenged by defendant*}. {88 *Elaborate.*} {*See **O'Connor's Texas COA**, "Attorney Fees," ch. 45, p. 1463.*}

CONCLUSION

33. {89 *Briefly summarize the reply.*}

PRAYER

34. For these reasons, plaintiff asks the Court to grant plaintiff's motion for summary judgment and sign {90 *an order for partial summary judgment/a final summary judgment*}. {91 *Add if requesting alternative relief: In the alternative, plaintiff asks for an order specifying the facts that are established as a matter of law.*}

SEE: Tex. R. Civ. P. 166a
O'Connor's Texas Rules * Civil Trials (2019), "Plaintiff's reply to defendant's response," ch. 7-C, §4.3.3, p. 756; "Plaintiff's reply to defendant's response," ch. 7-C, §4.4.3, p. 757; "Movant's Reply to Nonmovant's Response," ch. 7-D, §4, p. 766

ADD: STYLE OF THE CASE – FORM 1B:2
SIGNATURE BLOCK – FORM 1B:3
CERTIFICATE OF SERVICE – FORM 1B:13

ATTACH: AFFIDAVIT – FORM 1B:8, if necessary
NOTICE OF INTENT TO USE UNFILED DISCOVERY – FORM 7C:7, if necessary
APPENDIX OF EVIDENCE – FORM 7C:8, if necessary

NOTE: This form contains some of the more common replies a plaintiff might make. Additional replies may be appropriate.

DEFENDANT'S REPLY IN SUPPORT OF
{❶ *TRADITIONAL/NO-EVIDENCE/TRADITIONAL & NO-EVIDENCE*} MOTION FOR SUMMARY JUDGMENT

Defendant, {❷ *name*}, files this reply to plaintiff {❸ *name*}'s response to defendant's {❹ *traditional/no-evidence/traditional and no-evidence*} motion for summary judgment.

{*ADD SECTION BELOW IF APPLICABLE*}

SUMMARY-JUDGMENT EVIDENCE

{*CHOOSE APPROPRIATE PARAGRAPH 1*}

1. To support the facts in this reply, defendant relies on the summary-judgment evidence already on file in this case and incorporates the evidence into this reply by reference.

1. To support the facts in this reply, defendant relies on the summary-judgment evidence already on file and the evidence {❺ *attached to this reply as Exhibits {letters}/ included in an appendix filed with this reply*}, and incorporates the evidence into this reply by reference. {*See* ***O'Connor's Texas Rules****, "Attached," ch. 7-B, §9.1.3, p. 731.*}

{*CHOOSE APPROPRIATE SUMMARY-JUDGMENT MOTIONS*}

TRADITIONAL SUMMARY JUDGMENT
PLAINTIFF'S CAUSE OF ACTION FOR {❻ *IDENTIFY CAUSE OF ACTION*}

{*CHOOSE APPROPRIATE SECTIONS A-E*}

A. Plaintiff's cause of action can be disproved as a matter of law.

2. In plaintiff's response to defendant's motion for summary judgment on plaintiff's cause of action for {❼ *identify cause of action*}, plaintiff asserts that the motion should be denied because defendant has not disproved any element of the cause of action as a matter of law. {❽ *Identify relevant facts asserted by plaintiff in response.*}

3. Contrary to plaintiff's response, the Court should grant defendant's motion because defendant has disproved {❾ *identify elements defendant can disprove*}. {❿ *Elaborate.*}

B. Plaintiff's summary-judgment evidence is not competent.

4. In plaintiff's response to defendant's motion for summary judgment on plaintiff's cause of action for {⓫ *identify cause of action*}, plaintiff cited {⓬ *identify summary-judgment evidence*} in support of {⓭ *his/her/its*} opposition to the motion.

◄ *Continued on next page* ►

5. Contrary to plaintiff's response, the Court should grant defendant's motion because the evidence attached to plaintiff's response is defective and does not present competent summary-judgment evidence. Specifically, {[14] *identify evidence and assert appropriate objection from FORM 7C:11*}.

C. Defendant has proved {[15] *his/her/its*} affirmative defense as a matter of law.

6. In plaintiff's response to defendant's motion for summary judgment on plaintiff's cause of action for {[16] *identify cause of action*}, plaintiff asserted that defendant's affirmative defense of {[17] *identify affirmative defense*} should be denied because there is a genuine issue of material fact on the following elements of that affirmative defense: {[18] *identify elements*}.

7. Contrary to plaintiff's response, the Court should grant defendant's motion because there is no issue of fact on those elements. {[19] *Elaborate.*}

D. Defendant's pleadings support {[20] *his/her/its*} affirmative defense.

8. In plaintiff's response to defendant's motion for summary judgment on plaintiff's cause of action for {[21] *identify cause of action*}, plaintiff asserted that defendant's pleadings did not support {[22] *his/her/its*} affirmative defense of {[23] *identify affirmative defense*}.

9. Contrary to plaintiff's response, the Court should grant defendant's motion because defendant's pleadings do support {[24] *his/her/its*} affirmative defense of {[25] *identify affirmative defense*}. {[26] *Elaborate.*}

E. {[27] *Add other grounds for reply.*}

10. {[28] *Insert other grounds in reply to plaintiff's response.*}

NO-EVIDENCE SUMMARY JUDGMENT
PLAINTIFF'S CAUSE OF ACTION FOR {[29] *IDENTIFY CAUSE OF ACTION*}

{*CHOOSE APPROPRIATE SECTIONS A-C*}

A. Plaintiff did not produce sufficient evidence to defeat defendant's no-evidence motion for summary judgment.

11. In plaintiff's response to defendant's no-evidence motion for summary judgment on plaintiff's cause of action for {[30] *identify cause of action*}, plaintiff asserts that there is a genuine issue of material fact supporting the {[31] *element/elements*} challenged by the motion. Specifically, plaintiff contends that there is evidence to support {[32] *identify each challenged element*}. {[33] *Describe plaintiff's evidence.*}

12. Contrary to plaintiff's response, the Court should grant defendant's motion because plaintiff did not produce sufficient evidence to raise a fact issue on the challenged {34 *element/elements*}. {35 *Negate fact issues raised by plaintiff for each challenged element.*}

B. Plaintiff's summary-judgment evidence is not competent.

13. In plaintiff's response to defendant's no-evidence motion for summary judgment on plaintiff's cause of action for {36 *identify cause of action*}, plaintiff cited {37 *identify summary-judgment evidence*} in support of {38 *his/her/its*} opposition to the motion.

14. Contrary to plaintiff's response, the Court should grant defendant's motion because the {39 *identify type of evidence*} attached to plaintiff's response is defective and does not present competent summary-judgment evidence. Specifically, {40 *identify evidence and assert appropriate objection from FORM 7C:11*}.

C. {41 *Add other grounds for reply.*}

15. {42 *Insert other grounds in reply to plaintiff's response.*}

TRADITIONAL SUMMARY JUDGMENT
DEFENDANT'S COUNTERCLAIM FOR {43 *IDENTIFY COUNTERCLAIM*}

{*CHOOSE APPROPRIATE SECTIONS A-F*}

A. Defendant satisfied {44 *his/her/its*} burden under Texas Rule of Civil Procedure 166a(c).

16. In plaintiff's response to defendant's motion for summary judgment on defendant's counterclaim for {45 *identify counterclaim*}, plaintiff asserted that defendant's motion should be denied because there is a genuine issue of material fact on the following elements of that counterclaim: {46 *identify elements*}. {47 *Describe alleged fact issues.*}

17. Contrary to plaintiff's response, the Court should grant defendant's motion because there are no issues of fact on those elements. {48 *Elaborate.*}

B. Plaintiff's summary-judgment evidence is not competent.

18. In plaintiff's response to defendant's motion for summary judgment on defendant's counterclaim for {49 *identify counterclaim*}, plaintiff cited {50 *identify summary-judgment evidence*} in support of {51 *his/her/its*} opposition to the motion.

Continued on next page

19. Contrary to plaintiff's response, the Court should grant defendant's motion because the {52 *identify type of evidence*} attached to plaintiff's response is defective and does not present competent summary-judgment evidence. Specifically, {53 *identify evidence and assert appropriate objection from FORM 7C:11*}.

C. Defendant's pleadings support {54 *his/her/its*} counterclaim.

20. In plaintiff's response to defendant's motion for summary judgment on defendant's counterclaim for {55 *identify counterclaim*}, plaintiff claims that defendant's pleadings do not support that counterclaim.

21. Contrary to plaintiff's response, the Court should grant defendant's motion because defendant's pleadings do support {56 *his/her/its*} counterclaim for {57 *identify counterclaim*}. {58 *Elaborate.*}

D. Plaintiff did not produce sufficient evidence to create a fact issue on {59 *his/her/its*} affirmative defense.

22. In plaintiff's response to defendant's motion for summary judgment on defendant's counterclaim for {60 *identify counterclaim*}, plaintiff asserts the affirmative defense of {61 *identify affirmative defense*}.

23. Contrary to plaintiff's response, the Court should grant defendant's motion because plaintiff did not introduce sufficient evidence to create fact issues on each element of {62 *his/her/its*} affirmative defense. The elements of plaintiff's affirmative defense are as follows: {63 *identify elements*}. Plaintiff did not introduce sufficient evidence to create fact issues on {64 *identify elements on which plaintiff failed to raise a fact issue*}. {65 *Negate fact issues raised by plaintiff.*}

E. Plaintiff's pleadings do not support {66 *his/her/its*} affirmative defense.

24. In plaintiff's response to defendant's motion for summary judgment on defendant's counterclaim for {67 *identify counterclaim*}, plaintiff asserts for the first time the affirmative defense of {68 *identify affirmative defense*}.

25. Contrary to plaintiff's response, the Court should grant defendant's motion because plaintiff did not plead this affirmative defense in {69 *his/her/its*} pleadings. A party cannot defeat a motion for summary judgment with an affirmative defense it did not plead. *See, e.g., Via Net v. TIG Ins. Co.*, 211 S.W.3d 310, 313 (Tex. 2006) (when plaintiff raised issue for first time in its summary-judgment response, defendant could have objected that issue had not been properly pleaded).

F. {⑦⓪ *Add other grounds for reply.*}

26. {⑦① *Insert other grounds in reply to plaintiff's response.*}

{*ADD SECTION BELOW IF DAMAGES SOUGHT BY DEFENDANT*}

DAMAGES

{*CHOOSE APPROPRIATE PARAGRAPHS 27-31*}

27. In {⑦② *his/her/its*} response to defendant's motion for summary judgment, plaintiff claimed that the Court should deny defendant's motion because defendant did not prove that {⑦③ *he/she/it*} incurred damages. {⑦④ *Show how summary-judgment evidence proves that defendant incurred damages.*}

28. In {⑦⑤ *his/her/its*} response to defendant's motion for summary judgment, plaintiff claimed that the Court should deny defendant's motion because the damages in this case are unliquidated. {⑦⑥ *Show how summary-judgment evidence proves amount of liquidated damages.*}

29. In {⑦⑦ *his/her/its*} response to defendant's motion for summary judgment, plaintiff claimed that the Court should deny defendant's motion on liquidated damages in the amount of ${⑦⑧ *amount*} because defendant did not prove the amount of damages. {⑦⑨ *Show how summary-judgment evidence proves amount of damages.*}

30. In {⑧⓪ *his/her/its*} response to defendant's motion for summary judgment, plaintiff claimed that the Court should deny defendant's motion because the summary-judgment evidence raises a fact issue on the amount of damages. {⑧① *Negate fact issue on damages.*}

31. In {⑧② *his/her/its*} response to defendant's motion for summary judgment, plaintiff claimed that the Court should deny defendant's motion because defendant is not entitled to damages in this case. {⑧③ *Show authority for damages for defendant's counterclaim.*}

{*ADD SECTION BELOW IF ATTORNEY FEES SOUGHT BY DEFENDANT*}

ATTORNEY FEES

{*CHOOSE APPROPRIATE PARAGRAPH 32*}

32. In {⑧④ *his/her/its*} response to defendant's motion for summary judgment, plaintiff claimed that defendant is not entitled to attorney fees in this case. {⑧⑤ *Show how defendant is entitled to attorney fees under a specific statute, by the terms of the contract subject to the suit, or under equity.*}

◄ *Continued on next page* ►

32. In {86 *his/her/its*} response to defendant's motion for summary judgment, plaintiff claimed that defendant did not prove that {87 *he/she/it*} is entitled to attorney fees as a matter of law. When attorney fees are authorized, the party claiming them must establish the following: (1) the party pleaded for attorney fees, (2) the party was represented by an attorney, (3) the party complied with the conditions precedent to recovery of attorney fees, (4) the party incurred or will incur attorney fees, and (5) the attorney fees were reasonable and necessary. Defendant proved {88 *identify element challenged by plaintiff*}. {89 *Elaborate.*} {*See* ***O'Connor's Texas COA****, "Attorney Fees," ch. 45, p. 1463.*}

CONCLUSION

33. {90 *Briefly summarize the reply.*}

PRAYER

34. For these reasons, defendant asks the Court to grant defendant's motion for summary judgment and sign {91 *an order for partial summary judgment/a final summary judgment*}. {92 *Add if requesting alternative relief: In the alternative, defendant asks for an order specifying the facts that are established as a matter of law.*}

SEE: Tex. R. Civ. P. 166a
O'Connor's Texas Rules * Civil Trials (2019), "When defendant moves for SJ on its own counterclaim," ch. 7-C, §4.7, p. 760; "Defendant's reply to plaintiff's response," ch. 7-C, §4.5.3, p. 758; "Movant's Reply to Nonmovant's Response," ch. 7-D, §4, p. 766

ADD: STYLE OF THE CASE – FORM 1B:2
SIGNATURE BLOCK – FORM 1B:3
CERTIFICATE OF SERVICE – FORM 1B:13

ATTACH: AFFIDAVIT – FORM 1B:8, if necessary
NOTICE OF INTENT TO USE UNFILED DISCOVERY – FORM 7C:7, if necessary
APPENDIX OF EVIDENCE – FORM 7C:8, if necessary

NOTE: This form contains some of the more common replies a defendant might make. Additional replies may be appropriate.

{❶ *PARTY*}'S NOTICE OF INTENT TO USE DISCOVERY
PRODUCTS NOT ON FILE IN A SUMMARY-JUDGMENT PROCEEDING

Under the authority of Texas Rule of Civil Procedure 166a(d), {❷ *party*}, {❸ *name*}, gives notice of {❹ *his/her/its*} intent to use the following unfiled discovery in support of {❺ *party*}'s {❻ *motion for summary judgment/response to {adverse party}'s motion for summary judgment*}. {❼ *List the unfiled discovery to be used as summary-judgment evidence. If the discovery is voluminous, provide specific references to the relevant material.*} {❽ *Party*} serves this notice and the attached discovery on all parties.

SEE: Tex. R. Civ. P. 166a(d)
O'Connor's Texas Rules * Civil Trials (2019), "Statement of intent," ch. 7-B, §9.5.2(1), p. 736

ADD: STYLE OF THE CASE – FORM 1B:2
SIGNATURE BLOCK – FORM 1B:3
CERTIFICATE OF SERVICE – FORM 1B:13

ATTACH: Discovery products not on file

NOTE: A party may satisfy the requirement in Texas Rule of Civil Procedure 166a(d)—to provide a "statement of intent" to use unfiled discovery—by attaching the discovery to the motion or response and clearly relying on the attached discovery in the motion or response. See ***O'Connor's Texas Rules***, "Unfiled discovery," ch. 7-B, §9.5.2, p. 736.

APPENDIX OF SUMMARY-JUDGMENT EVIDENCE

{❶ *Party*}, {❷ *name*}, files this appendix of evidence in support of {❸ *his/her/its*} {❹ *motion/response*} for {❺ *partial/final*} summary judgment and incorporates the evidence into the {❻ *motion/response*} by reference. {*See* ***O'Connor's Texas Rules***, *"Attached," ch. 7-B, §9.1.3, p. 731.*}

{*CHOOSE APPROPRIATE TYPES OF EVIDENCE*}

1. Affidavit of {❼ *name of affiant*}, {❽ *plaintiff/defendant/plaintiff's expert/defendant's expert/fact witness*} .... Tab A
2. Affidavit of {❾ *name of affiant*}, business-records custodian of {❿ *identify source of records*} .... Tab B
3. Sworn copy of {⓫ *identify evidence, e.g., contract, medical records*} .... Tab C
4. Declaration of {⓬ *name of declarant*}, {⓭ *plaintiff/defendant/plaintiff's expert/defendant's expert/fact witness*} .... Tab D
5. Interrogatories to {⓮ *adverse party*} .... Tab E
6. Excerpt of deposition of {⓯ *name of deponent*}, {⓰ *plaintiff/defendant/plaintiff's expert/defendant's expert/fact witness*} .... Tab F
7. Response of {⓱ *adverse party*} to request for disclosure .... Tab G
8. Response of {⓲ *adverse party*} to request for admissions .... Tab H
9. Certified copy of {⓳ *identify evidence, e.g., public records*} .... Tab I
10. Stipulation of the parties .... Tab J
11. {⓴ *Other evidence*} .... Tab K

{*Continue with list until all evidence is identified.*}

SEE: Tex. R. Civ. P. 166a(d)
O'Connor's Texas Rules * Civil Trials (2019), "Attached," ch. 7-B, §9.1.3, p. 731

ADD: STYLE OF THE CASE – FORM 1B:2
VERIFICATION – FORM 1B:7
CERTIFICATE OF SERVICE – FORM 1B:13

{❶ *PARTY*}'S MOTION TO STRIKE {❷ *ADVERSE PARTY*}'S SUMMARY-JUDGMENT EVIDENCE

{❸ *Party*}, {❹ *name*}, asks the Court to strike evidence submitted by {❺ *adverse party*}, {❻ *name*}, in connection with {❼ *adverse party*}'s summary-judgment {❽ *motion/response/reply*}.

INTRODUCTION

1. Plaintiff, {❾ *name*}, sued defendant, {❿ *name*}, for {⓫ *state basis of suit*}.

2. {⓬ *State other relevant facts about the suit.*}

BACKGROUND

3. On {⓭ *date*}, {⓮ *plaintiff/defendant*} filed a {⓯ *traditional/no-evidence/traditional and no-evidence*} motion for summary judgment.

4. The motion for summary judgment is set for {⓰ *submission/hearing*} on {⓱ *date*}.

5. {⓲ *State other facts relevant to the motion.*}

ARGUMENT & AUTHORITIES

6. {⓳ *Party*} objects to Exhibit {⓴ *identify exhibit*} on the ground that {㉑ *choose objections to evidence from FORM 7C:11*}.

7. {㉒ *Continue until all objections to adverse party's summary-judgment evidence are made.*}

CONCLUSION

8. {㉓ *Briefly summarize the motion.*}

PRAYER

9. For these reasons, {㉔ *party*} asks the Court to strike {㉕ *adverse party*}'s evidence.

Continued on next page

FORM 7C:9 MOTION TO STRIKE SUMMARY-JUDGMENT EVIDENCE

SEE: Tex. R. Civ. P. 166a(f)
O'Connor's Texas Rules * Civil Trials (2019), "Unsworn declaration," ch. 1-B, §3.2.17, p. 14; "Affidavits," ch. 7-B, §9.4, p. 733; "Discovery products," ch. 7-B, §9.5, p. 736; "Objections to Summary-Judgment Evidence," ch. 7-B, §10, p. 738

ADD: STYLE OF THE CASE – FORM 1B:2
SIGNATURE BLOCK – FORM 1B:3
CERTIFICATE OF SERVICE – FORM 1B:13

ATTACH: AFFIDAVIT – FORM 1B:8, if necessary
ORDER – FORM 7C:10

NOTE: For specific objections to summary-judgment evidence, see FORM 7C:11.

ORDER ON {❶ *PARTY*}'S MOTION TO STRIKE
{❷ *ADVERSE PARTY*}'S SUMMARY-JUDGMENT EVIDENCE

After considering {❸ *party*} {❹ *name*}'s motion to strike {❺ *adverse party*}'s summary-judgment evidence, the Court orders as follows:

1. Exhibit {❻ *identify exhibit*}: SUSTAINED ___ OVERRULED ___
2. Exhibit {❼ *identify exhibit*}: SUSTAINED ___ OVERRULED ___
3. {❽ *Continue as necessary.*}

The Court strikes from the summary-judgment record each exhibit where the objection is sustained.

SIGNED on _______________, 20___.

____
PRESIDING JUDGE

SEE: Tex. R. Civ. P. 166a
O'Connor's Texas Rules * Civil Trials (2019), "Unsworn declaration," ch. 1-B, §3.2.17, p. 14; "Affidavits," ch. 7-B, §9.4, p. 733; "Discovery products," ch. 7-B, §9.5, p. 736; "Objections to Summary-Judgment Evidence," ch. 7-B, §10, p. 738

ADD: STYLE OF THE CASE – FORM 1B:2
CERTIFICATE OF SERVICE – FORM 1B:13, if proposed order served separately from motion or response

NOTE: A court may reduce its rulings on objections to writing either at the same time it rules on the motion for summary judgment or sometime afterward. *See* ***Crocker v. Paulyne's Nursing Home, Inc.***, 95 S.W.3d 416, 420-21 (Tex.App.—Dallas 2002, no pet.); ***Dolcefino v. Randolph***, 19 S.W.3d 906, 926 (Tex.App.—Houston [14th Dist.] 2000, pet. denied). If it is done at the same time the court rules on the motion for summary judgment, the court may state its rulings in the order on summary judgment rather than in a separate order. See FORM 7C:12.

Before the Supreme Court's ruling in ***Seim v. Allstate Tex. Lloyds***, the courts of appeals were split on whether a trial court's implicit ruling on objections to summary-judgment evidence was sufficient to preserve error. ***Seim v. Allstate Tex. Lloyds***, 551 S.W.3d 161, 165-66 (Tex.2018). Although the Court suggested than an implicit ruling might be sufficient when the implication is "clear" from the record, it rejected the view that a ruling on the summary-judgment motion alone constitutes an implicit ruling on the objections. *See id.* The Court similarly rejected the idea that error is preserved as long as the record indicates "in some way" that the trial court ruled on the objections. *See, e.g., id.* (SJ order stating that court considered motions, briefs, and all competent SJ evidence was not sufficient to show implicit ruling on objections). Until the Court defines what constitutes a clearly implied ruling, a party should obtain an express ruling on any objections in order to avoid waiving error. See ***O'Connor's Texas Rules***, "Secure ruling on objections," ch. 7-B, §10.2, p. 742.

{*CHOOSE APPROPRIATE GENERAL OBJECTIONS*}

{*Evidence is irrelevant*}

1. {❶ *Party*} objects to {❷ *identify evidence, e.g., Exhibit A*} on the ground that it is not relevant. {❸ *Show why the evidence is not relevant.*} To be admissible, evidence must be relevant. Tex. R. Evid. 402; *see E.I. du Pont de Nemours & Co. v. Robinson*, 923 S.W.2d 549, 556 (Tex. 1995). Because the evidence is not competent summary-judgment evidence, the Court should strike it. {*See* ***O'Connor's Texas Rules***, *"Relevance of opinion," ch. 5-N, §2.3.2, p. 503.*}

{*Evidence is not authenticated*}

2. {❹ *Party*} objects to {❺ *identify evidence, e.g., Exhibit A*} on the ground that it has not been properly authenticated. {❻ *Identify defect, e.g., the affidavit does not contain the proper predicate for admissibility, the evidence was filed without an affidavit verifying its authenticity.*} Evidence that is not properly authenticated is not competent summary-judgment evidence. *See Blanche v. First Nationwide Mortg. Corp.*, 74 S.W.3d 444, 451-52 (Tex. App.—Dallas 2002, no pet.); *Banowsky v. State Farm Mut. Auto. Ins. Co.*, 876 S.W.2d 509, 513 (Tex. App.—Amarillo 1994, no writ); *see, e.g., Seidner v. Citibank (S.D.) N.A.*, 201 S.W.3d 332, 334-35 (Tex. App.—Houston [14th Dist.] 2006, pet. denied) (business-record affidavit must meet requirements of Tex. R. Evid. 902(10)); *Cottrell v. Carrillon Assocs., Ltd.*, 646 S.W.2d 491, 494 (Tex. App.—Houston [1st Dist.] 1982, writ ref'd n.r.e.) (affidavit did not lay proper predicate required by Business Records Act). Because the evidence is not competent summary-judgment evidence, the Court should strike it. {*See* ***O'Connor's Texas Rules***, *"Discovery responses," ch. 7-B, §9.5.3(1), p. 737; "Failure to lay predicate," ch. 7-B, §10.1.1(6), p. 740; "Lack of authentication," ch. 7-B, §10.1.2(7), p. 741.*}

{*Evidence contains hearsay*}

3. {❼ *Party*} objects to {❽ *identify evidence, e.g., Exhibit A*} on the ground that it contains hearsay. {❾ *Identify statements and show why they are hearsay.*} Hearsay statements are not competent summary-judgment evidence. *Kerlin v. Arias*, 274 S.W.3d 666, 668 (Tex. 2008) (affidavits); *Southland Corp. v. Lewis*, 940 S.W.2d 83, 85 (Tex. 1997) (same); *Fid. & Cas. Co. v. Burts Bros.*, 744 S.W.2d 219, 224 (Tex. App.—Houston [1st Dist.] 1987, writ denied) (same). Because hearsay statements are not competent summary-judgment evidence, the Court should strike them. {*See* ***O'Connor's Texas Rules***, *"Hearsay evidence," ch. 7-B, §10.1.1(5), p. 740.*}

{*Witness is not competent to testify*}

4. {[10] *Party*} objects to {[11] *identify evidence, e.g., Exhibit A*} on the ground that the {[12] *affiant/declarant/deponent*}, {[13] *name*}, is not competent to testify. {[14] *State why the person is not competent to testify, e.g., person is insane, person is a child who lacks sufficient intellect to testify. See, e.g., Kokes v. College, 148 S.W.3d 384, 389-90 (Tex. App.—Beaumont 2004, no pet.) (party who attacked witness's competency in summary-judgment proceeding had burden of proving incompetency).*} A statement by a witness who is not competent to testify cannot support a summary judgment. *See* Tex. R. Civ. P. 166a(f); Tex. R. Evid. 601(a). Because {[15] *name of affiant, declarant, or deponent*} is not competent to testify, the Court should strike {[16] *his/her*} {[17] *affidavit/declaration/deposition*}. {*See* ***O'Connor's Texas Rules****, "Lack of competence," ch. 7-B, §10.1.1(2), p. 739.*}

{*Testimony is not based on personal knowledge*}

5. {[18] *Party*} objects to {[19] *identify evidence, e.g., Exhibit A*} on the ground that the testimony is not based on personal knowledge. Testimony is not competent summary-judgment evidence unless evidence shows that it is based on the witness's personal knowledge. *See* Tex. R. Civ. P. 166a(f); Tex. R. Evid. 602; *Kerlin v. Arias*, 274 S.W.3d 666, 668 (Tex. 2008); *Ryland Grp., Inc. v. Hood*, 924 S.W.2d 120, 122 (Tex. 1996); *Garner v. Long*, 106 S.W.3d 260, 267 (Tex. App.—Fort Worth 2003, no pet.); *Geiselman v. Cramer Fin. Grp., Inc.*, 965 S.W.2d 532, 537 (Tex. App.—Houston [14th Dist.] 1997, no writ). {[20] *Identify statements and explain why the witness lacks personal knowledge.*} Because these statements are not competent summary-judgment evidence, the Court should strike them. {*See* ***O'Connor's Texas Rules****, "Personal knowledge," ch. 7-B, §9.4.4, p. 733.*}

{*Testimony contains legal conclusions*}

6. {[21] *Party*} objects to {[22] *identify evidence, e.g., Exhibit A*} on the ground that it contains legal conclusions. {[23] *Identify statements and show how they are merely legal conclusions without factual support.*} When a legal conclusion is not based on any facts, it is not competent summary-judgment evidence. *See Brownlee v. Brownlee*, 665 S.W.2d 111, 112 (Tex. 1984) (affidavits); *Larsen v. Santa Fe Indep. Sch. Dist.*, 296 S.W.3d 118, 132 (Tex. App.—Houston [14th Dist.] 2009, pet. denied) (deposition testimony); *see, e.g., Rizkallah v. Conner*, 952 S.W.2d 580, 587 (Tex. App.—Houston [1st Dist.] 1997, no writ) (statements that defendant was negligent and deceptive were legal conclusions and incompetent as summary-judgment evidence). Because these statements are not competent summary-judgment evidence, the Court should strike them. {*See* ***O'Connor's Texas Rules****, "Not legal conclusions," ch. 7-B, §9.4.5, p. 734.*}

◄ *Continued on next page* ►

{*Testimony contains factual conclusions*}

7. {㉔ *Party*} objects to {㉕ *identify evidence, e.g., Exhibit A*} on the ground that it contains factual conclusions. {㉖ *Identify statements and show how they are merely factual conclusions without factual support.*} A factual conclusion without supporting facts is not competent summary-judgment evidence. *See Elizondo v. Krist*, 415 S.W.3d 259, 264-65 (Tex. 2013) (affidavits); *Ryland Grp., Inc. v. Hood*, 924 S.W.2d 120, 122 (Tex. 1996) (affidavits); *Hovorka v. Cmty. Health Sys., Inc.*, 262 S.W.3d 503, 511 (Tex. App.—El Paso 2008, no pet.) (deposition testimony); *see, e.g., Haynes v. City of Beaumont*, 35 S.W.3d 166, 178 (Tex. App.—Texarkana 2000, no pet.) (affidavit that plaintiff was fired because of unacceptable behavior was factual conclusion and incompetent as summary-judgment evidence); *Rizkallah v. Conner*, 952 S.W.2d 580, 587-88 (Tex. App.—Houston [1st Dist.] 1997, no writ) (affidavit that defendant caused problem with plaintiff's car by steam cleaning engine was factual conclusion and incompetent as summary-judgment evidence). Because these statements are not competent summary-judgment evidence, the Court should strike them. {*See **O'Connor's Texas Rules**, "Not factual conclusions," ch. 7-B, §9.4.6, p. 734.*}

{*Testimony is from interested witness*}

8. {㉗ *Party*} objects to {㉘ *identify evidence, e.g., Exhibit A*} on the ground that the {㉙ *affiant/declarant/deponent*}, {㉚ *name*}, is an interested witness and {㉛ *his/her*} testimony is not clear, positive, direct, credible, free from contradiction, and susceptible to being readily controverted. To be competent summary-judgment evidence, an interested witness's testimony must be all of these things. *See* Tex. R. Civ. P. 166a(c); *New Times, Inc. v. Isaacks*, 146 S.W.3d 144, 164 (Tex. 2004); *Trico Techs. Corp. v. Montiel*, 949 S.W.2d 308, 310 (Tex. 1997); *Casso v. Brand*, 776 S.W.2d 551, 558 (Tex. 1989). The statements made by {㉜ *name of affiant, declarant, or deponent*} are not competent summary-judgment evidence. {㉝ *Identify statements of interested witness and explain why they are defective.*} Because these statements are not competent summary-judgment evidence, the Court should strike them. {*See **O'Connor's Texas Rules**, "Interested witness," ch. 7-B, §9.3.2, p. 732.*}

{*Testimony contradicts previous statement*}

9. {㉞ *Party*} objects to {㉟ *identify evidence, e.g., Exhibit A*} on the ground that it contradicts a statement previously made by the same witness. {㊱ *Identify conflicting statements.*} A statement contradicted by the same witness who made the statement is not competent summary-judgment evidence. *See* Tex. R. Civ. P. 166a(c); *Dillard v. NCNB Tex. Nat'l Bank*, 815 S.W.2d 356, 360-61 (Tex. App.—Austin 1991, no writ), *disapproved on other grounds, Amberboy v. Societe de Banque Privee*, 831 S.W.2d 793 (Tex. 1992). Because these statements are not competent summary-judgment evidence, the Court should strike them.

{*Testimony about disputed factual matter is from party's attorney*}

10. {37 *Party*} objects to {38 *identify evidence, e.g., Exhibit A*} on the ground that the testimony of {39 *adverse party*}'s attorney is not proper summary-judgment evidence. A person who is an attorney for one of the parties cannot act as a witness about disputed factual matters. *See* Tex. Disc. R. Prof. Conduct 3.08; *Mauze v. Curry*, 861 S.W.2d 869, 870 (Tex. 1993). {40 *Identify attorney's statements and show how they attempt to establish facts.*} Because {41 *name of attorney*}'s statements are not competent summary-judgment evidence, the Court should strike them. {*See **O'Connor's Texas Rules**, "Rule 3.08 – attorney as witness," ch. 1-H, §8.2.1(3), p. 70.*}

{*Evidence violates parol-evidence rule*}

11. {42 *Party*} objects to {43 *identify evidence, e.g., Exhibit A*} on the ground that it contains statements that violate the parol-evidence rule. Under the parol-evidence rule, a party cannot offer evidence of an oral agreement if it was made before or at the same time as a contradictory written agreement. *Albritton Dev. Co. v. Glendon Invs., Inc.*, 700 S.W.2d 244, 246 (Tex. App.—Houston [1st Dist.] 1985, writ ref'd n.r.e.). {44 *Identify statements and explain why they violated the parol-evidence rule.*} A statement that violates the parol-evidence rule is not competent summary-judgment evidence. *See Nat'l Union Fire Ins. Co. v. CBI Indus., Inc.*, 907 S.W.2d 517, 520 (Tex. 1995); *Albritton Dev. Co.*, 700 S.W.2d at 246. Because these statements are not competent summary-judgment evidence, the Court should strike them. {*See **O'Connor's Texas COA**, "Parol-evidence rule," ch. 5-B, §7.2, p. 109.*}

{*Evidence violates best-evidence rule*}

12. {45 *Party*} objects to {46 *identify evidence, e.g., Exhibit A*} on the ground that it violates the best-evidence rule. {47 *Identify the document that is not in evidence and the statements made to prove its contents.*} Statements about the contents of a document (or a copy of the document) are not admissible if the original document is not produced, its contents are disputed, and its absence is unexplained. *See Mercer v. Daoran Corp.*, 676 S.W.2d 580, 584 (Tex. 1984). The original {48 *identify the document*} has not been produced, its contents are disputed, and its absence is unexplained. {49 *Explain dispute about document.*} The purpose of the best-evidence rule is to allow admission of the best obtainable evidence of a document's contents. *Doe v. Mobile Video Tapes, Inc.*, 43 S.W.3d 40, 56 (Tex. App.—Corpus Christi 2001, no pet.). Because there is no proof that the original document cannot be produced, the statements are not competent summary-judgment evidence about the contents of the document, and the Court should strike them. {*See **O'Connor's Texas Rules**, "Not best evidence," ch. 7-B, §10.1.1(7), p. 740.*}

◄ *Continued on next page* ►

{*Evidence is not on file or attached to motion, response, or reply*}

13. {❺⓿ *Party*} objects to {❺❶ *identify provision in motion, response, or reply*} on the ground that the evidence it refers to is not on file with the Court or attached to the {❺❷ *motion/response/reply*}. Evidence that is not on file with the court or attached to the {❺❸ *motion/response/reply*} cannot be used to {❺❹ *support/oppose*} a summary judgment. *See* Tex. R. Civ. P. 166a(d); *Lance v. Robinson*, 543 S.W.3d 723, 732 (Tex. 2018); *McConathy v. McConathy*, 869 S.W.2d 341, 342 n.2 (Tex. 1994). Because {❺❺ *identify evidence*} is not before the Court, the Court should strike {❺❻ *identify provision in motion, response, or reply*}. {*See* ***O'Connor's Texas Rules***, *"Generally," ch. 7-B, §9.1, p. 730; "Unfiled discovery," ch. 7-B, §9.5.2, p. 736.*}

{*Party cannot use its own discovery responses as summary-judgment evidence*}

14. {❺❼ *Party*} objects to {❺❽ *identify evidence, e.g., Exhibit A*} on the ground that a party cannot use {❺❾ *his/her/its*} own discovery responses to support a motion for summary judgment. {❻⓿ *Identify paragraph in motion, response, or reply that relies on adverse party's own discovery responses.*} A party cannot use its own answers to discovery as summary-judgment evidence. *See* Tex. R. Civ. P. 197.3 (answers to interrogatories); *Yates v. Fisher*, 988 S.W.2d 730, 731 (Tex. 1998) (same); *Americana Motel, Inc. v. Johnson*, 610 S.W.2d 143, 143 (Tex. 1980) (responses to request for admissions); *Schulz v. State Farm Mut. Auto. Ins. Co.*, 930 S.W.2d 872, 876 (Tex. App.—Houston [1st Dist.] 1996, no writ) (same). Because the evidence supporting {❻❶ *adverse party*}'s {❻❷ *motion/response/reply*} is {❻❸ *his/her/its*} own responses to discovery, that evidence is not competent summary-judgment evidence, and the Court should strike it.

{*Evidence from other case submitted without certified copy of reporter's record*}

15. {❻❹ *Party*} objects to the use of sworn testimony from {❻❺ *identify other case that adverse party is referencing sworn testimony from*}. To rely on sworn testimony received in another case, the party must file a certified copy of the reporter's record from that case in the summary-judgment proceeding. *See Austin Bldg. Co. v. Nat'l Union Fire Ins. Co.*, 432 S.W.2d 697, 698 (Tex. 1968); *Murillo v. Valley Coca-Cola Bottling Co.*, 895 S.W.2d 758, 761-62 (Tex. App.—Corpus Christi 1995, no writ). Because {❻❻ *adverse party*} did not file a certified copy of the reporter's record from {❻❼ *identify other case that adverse party is referencing sworn testimony from*}, the Court should strike all references to the testimony in {❻❽ *adverse party*}'s {❻❾ *motion/response/reply*}.

{*Affidavit or declaration is based on knowledge and belief*}

16. {⑦⓪ *Party*} objects to {⑦① *identify evidence, e.g., Exhibit A*} on the ground that the testimony is based on {⑦② *affiant/declarant*}'s knowledge and belief. {⑦③ *Identify statements that show mere knowledge and belief.*} Testimony based on a witness's best knowledge and belief is not competent summary-judgment evidence. *Kerlin v. Arias*, 274 S.W.3d 666, 668 (Tex. 2008); *Ryland Grp., Inc. v. Hood*, 924 S.W.2d 120, 122 (Tex. 1996); *Price v. Am. Nat'l Ins. Co.*, 113 S.W.3d 424, 429-30 (Tex. App.—Houston [1st Dist.] 2003, no pet.); *see* Tex. R. Civ. P. 166a(f). Because a statement based on "best knowledge and belief" is not competent summary-judgment evidence, the Court should strike the entire {⑦④ *affidavit/declaration*}. {*See **O'Connor's Texas Rules**, "Personal knowledge," ch. 7-B, §9.4.4, p. 733.*}

{*Evidence does not qualify as either an affidavit or a declaration*}

17. {⑦⑤ *Party*} objects to {⑦⑥ *identify evidence, e.g., Exhibit A*} on the ground that it does not qualify as an affidavit or an unsworn declaration and thus is incompetent summary-judgment evidence. The statement fails as an affidavit because it does not comply with Texas Government Code section 312.011(1), which defines an affidavit as "a statement in writing of a fact or facts signed by the party making it, sworn to before an officer authorized to administer oaths, and officially certified to by the officer under his seal of office." *See Mansions in the Forest, L.P. v. Montgomery Cty.*, 365 S.W.3d 314, 316-17 (Tex. 2012). Specifically, {⑦⑦ *describe defect, e.g., the statement was not properly certified*}. The statement also fails as an unsworn declaration because it does not comply with Texas Civil Practice & Remedies Code section 132.001. Specifically, {⑦⑧ *describe defect, e.g., the statement was not subscribed under the penalty of perjury*}. Thus, the statement is merely an unsworn statement, and an unsworn statement is not competent summary-judgment proof. *See Mansions in the Forest*, 365 S.W.3d at 316-17; *Perkins v. Crittenden*, 462 S.W.2d 565, 568 (Tex. 1970). Because the statement is not competent summary-judgment proof, the Court should strike it. {*See **O'Connor's Texas Rules**, "Unsworn declaration," ch. 1-B, §3.2.17, p. 14; "Affidavits," ch. 7-B, §9.4, p. 733; "Absence of jurat," ch. 7-B, §10.1.1(1)(c), p. 739.*}

{*Evidence does not qualify as an affidavit*}

18. {⑦⑨ *Party*} objects to {⑧⓪ *identify evidence, e.g., Exhibit A*} on the ground that it does not qualify as an affidavit and thus is incompetent summary-judgment evidence. The statement fails as an affidavit because it does not comply with Texas Government Code section 312.011(1), which defines an affidavit as "a statement in writing of a fact or facts signed by the party making it, sworn to before an officer authorized to administer oaths, and officially certified to by the officer under his seal of office." *See Man-*

Continued on next page

sions in the Forest, L.P. v. Montgomery Cty., 365 S.W.3d 314, 316-17 (Tex. 2012). Specifically, {81 *describe defect, e.g., the statement was not properly certified*}. {*See* ***O'Connor's Texas Rules****, "Affidavits," ch. 7-B, §9.4, p. 733; "Absence of jurat," ch. 7-B, §10.1.1(1)(c), p. 739.*}

{*Evidence does not qualify as a declaration*}

19. {82 *Party*} objects to {83 *identify evidence, e.g., Exhibit A*} on the ground that it does not qualify as an unsworn declaration and thus is incompetent summary-judgment evidence. The statement fails as an unsworn declaration because it does not comply with Texas Civil Practice & Remedies Code section 132.001. Specifically, {84 *describe defect, e.g., the statement was not subscribed under the penalty of perjury*}. Thus, the statement is merely an unsworn statement, and an unsworn statement is not competent summary-judgment proof. *See Mansions in the Forest, L.P. v. Montgomery Cty.*, 365 S.W.3d 314, 316-17 (Tex. 2012); *Perkins v. Crittenden*, 462 S.W.2d 565, 568 (Tex. 1970). Because the statement is not competent summary-judgment proof, the Court should strike it. {*See* ***O'Connor's Texas Rules****, "Unsworn declaration," ch. 1-B, §3.2.17, p. 14.*}

{*Contents of affidavit are defective*}

20. {85 *Party*} objects to {86 *identify evidence, e.g., Exhibit A*} on the ground that it contains defective statements. *See Haynes v. Haynes*, 178 S.W.3d 350, 355 (Tex. App.—Houston [14th Dist.] 2005, pet. denied). Specifically, {87 *identify defective statements and state reasons for objection, e.g., the statements are hearsay*}. Because the affidavit is not competent summary-judgment evidence, the Court should strike it. {*See* ***O'Connor's Texas Rules****, "Defective content of affidavit," ch. 7-B, §10.1.1(1)(a), p. 739.*}

{*Jurat is defective*}

21. {88 *Party*} objects to {89 *identify evidence, e.g., Exhibit A*} on the ground that it includes a defective jurat. *See Ford Motor Co. v. Leggat*, 904 S.W.2d 643, 645-46 (Tex. 1995). Specifically, {90 *describe defect, e.g., there is an error in the date of the jurat*}. Because the evidence is not competent summary-judgment proof, the Court should strike it. {*See* ***O'Connor's Texas Rules****, "Defect in jurat," ch. 7-B, §10.1.1(1)(d), p. 739.*}

{*Affidavit or declaration lacks supporting evidence*}

22. {91 *Party*} objects to {92 *identify evidence, e.g., Exhibit A*} on the ground that it references facts in {93 *identify document being referenced in affidavit or declaration*}, which is not attached as an exhibit to the {94 *affidavit/declaration*}. Sworn or certified

copies of all papers or parts of papers referred to in a summary-judgment affidavit or declaration must be attached to and served with the affidavit or declaration. *See* Tex. R. Civ. P. 166a(f) (affidavit); *see, e.g., Brown v. Brown*, 145 S.W.3d 745, 752 (Tex. App.—Dallas 2004, pet. denied) (lack of exhibits made affidavit conclusory); *see also* Tex. Civ. Prac. & Rem. Code §132.001(a) (unsworn declaration can be used instead of affidavit). Because {95 *identify document being referenced in affidavit or declaration*} is not attached, the Court should strike the {96 *affidavit/declaration*}. {*See **O'Connor's Texas Rules**, "Failure to attach exhibit," ch. 7-B, §10.1.1(1)(b), p. 739; "Failure to attach exhibit," ch. 7-B, §10.1.2(1), p. 741.*}

{*CHOOSE APPROPRIATE OBJECTIONS TO EXPERTS*}

{*Expert was not timely designated*}

23. {97 *Party*} objects to {98 *identify evidence, e.g., Exhibit A*} on the ground that {99 *name of expert*} was not timely designated as an expert. When an expert is not timely designated, the expert's opinion is not admissible as summary-judgment evidence unless the offering party can show good cause or lack of unfair surprise. *Fort Brown Villas III Condo. Ass'n v. Gillenwater*, 285 S.W.3d 879, 881 (Tex. 2009); *Total Clean, LLC v. Cox Smith Matthews Inc.*, 330 S.W.3d 657, 663-64 (Tex. App.—San Antonio 2010, pet. denied). The Court's scheduling order called for {100 *adverse party*} to designate experts by {101 *date*}. {102 *Adverse party*} did not designate {103 *name of expert*} as a testifying expert by that date. {104 *Elaborate.*} Because {105 *adverse party*} did not timely designate {106 *name of expert*} and made no showing of good cause or lack of unfair surprise, the Court should strike {107 *name of expert*}'s {108 *affidavit/declaration/deposition*}. {*See **O'Connor's Texas Rules**, "On procedure for SJ," ch. 5-A, §6.2, p. 399.*}

{*Expert's qualifications were not established*}

24. {109 *Party*} objects to {110 *identify evidence, e.g., Exhibit A*} on the ground that it does not include the expert's qualifications. If a party attempts to offer an expert's opinion into evidence, it must first establish the expert's qualifications. *United Blood Servs. v. Longoria*, 938 S.W.2d 29, 30-31 (Tex. 1997); *see* Tex. R. Evid. 104(a), 702; *Estorque v. Schafer*, 302 S.W.3d 19, 26 (Tex. App.—Fort Worth 2009, no pet.). {111 *Name of expert*}'s {112 *affidavit/declaration/deposition*} does not include {113 *his/her*} qualifications, and no such information has been provided by {114 *adverse party*}. The Court should strike the entire {115 *affidavit/declaration/deposition*} of the expert. {*See **O'Connor's Texas Rules**, "Expert witness," ch. 7-B, §9.3.3, p. 732.*}

◄ *Continued on next page* ►

{*Expert is not qualified to give opinion on subject*}

25. {116 *Party*} objects to {117 *identify evidence, e.g., Exhibit A*} on the ground that it does not establish that the expert is qualified to give an opinion on {118 *identify subject matter*}. The expert's {119 *affidavit/declaration/deposition*} does not demonstrate that {120 *he/she*} is qualified to give an opinion on that subject. {121 *Show why the expert is not qualified.*} An expert must be qualified to give an opinion as an expert "by knowledge, skill, experience, training, or education." Tex. R. Evid. 702; *Gammill v. Jack Williams Chevrolet, Inc.*, 972 S.W.2d 713, 718 (Tex. 1998); *e.g., United Blood Servs. v. Longoria*, 938 S.W.2d 29, 30-31 (Tex. 1997) (expert was not qualified to testify about standard of care for blood-banking industry because he had no medical training or experience relating to blood transfusions); *see, e.g., Leitch v. Hornsby*, 935 S.W.2d 114, 119 (Tex. 1996) (coworker was not qualified to testify that lift belt would have prevented back injury); *Broders v. Heise*, 924 S.W.2d 148, 153 (Tex. 1996) (emergency-room doctor was not qualified to testify in wrongful-death case about cause of brain injury). Because the expert is not shown to be qualified to give an expert's opinion, the Court should strike the entire {122 *affidavit/declaration/deposition*} of the expert. {*See* ***O'Connor's Texas Rules***, *"Qualifications test," ch. 5-N, §2.1, p. 499.*}

{*Expert's opinion is not reliable*}

26. {123 *Party*} objects to {124 *identify evidence, e.g., Exhibit A*} on the ground that {125 *name of expert*}'s opinion is not reliable. {126 *Show why the opinion is not reliable.*} To be admissible, an expert's opinion must be reliable. *E.I. du Pont de Nemours & Co. v. Robinson*, 923 S.W.2d 549, 557 (Tex. 1995); *see* Tex. R. Evid. 702. An expert's opinion is not admissible if it is based on flawed reasoning and methodology. *Merrell Dow Pharms., Inc. v. Havner*, 953 S.W.2d 706, 714 (Tex. 1997); *see, e.g., Marathon Corp. v. Pitzner*, 106 S.W.3d 724, 729 (Tex. 2003) (expert opinion was mere speculation not based on evidence); *Robinson*, 923 S.W.2d at 558-59 (expert's opinion was not based on reliable foundation because he did not conduct test to exclude other causes). Because the expert's opinion is not reliable and is not competent summary-judgment evidence, the Court should strike the entire {127 *affidavit/declaration/deposition*}. {*See* ***O'Connor's Texas Rules***, *"Reliability of opinion," ch. 5-N, §2.3.1, p. 501.*}

{*Expert's opinion does not involve specialized knowledge*}

27. {128 *Party*} objects to {129 *identify evidence, e.g., Exhibit A*} on the ground that {130 *name of expert*}'s opinion does not involve scientific, technical, or other specialized knowledge. {131 *Elaborate.*} To be admissible, an expert's opinion must be based on the expert's special knowledge, skill, experience, training, or education. *GTE Sw., Inc. v. Bruce*, 998 S.W.2d 605, 620 (Tex. 1999); *see* Tex. R. Evid. 702. When an issue

involves only general knowledge and experience, it is not a proper subject for expert opinion. *GTE Sw., Inc.*, 998 S.W.2d at 620. Because the testimony of {132 *name of expert*} on {133 *identify expert's opinion*} does not require specialized knowledge, the Court should strike the opinion. {*See* ***O'Connor's Texas Rules***, *"Knowledge test," ch. 5-N, §2.2, p. 500.*}

{*Expert's opinion is conclusory*}

28. {134 *Party*} objects to {135 *identify evidence, e.g., Exhibit A*} on the ground that {136 *name of expert*}'s opinion is conclusory because it does not include the facts on which the opinion was based. {137 *Elaborate.*} A conclusory statement by an expert witness without supporting facts is not competent summary-judgment evidence. *McIntyre v. Ramirez*, 109 S.W.3d 741, 749-50 (Tex. 2003). Because a conclusory statement is not competent summary-judgment evidence, the Court should strike the expert's entire {138 *affidavit/declaration/deposition*}. {*See* ***O'Connor's Texas Rules***, *"Expert witness," ch. 7-B, §9.3.3, p. 732; "Not legal conclusions," ch. 7-B, §9.4.5, p. 734.*}

{*Expert's opinion is not clear, positive, and controvertible*}

29. {139 *Party*} objects to {140 *identify evidence, e.g., Exhibit A*} on the ground that {141 *name of expert*}'s opinion is not clear, positive, direct, credible, free from contradiction, and susceptible to being readily controverted. To be competent summary-judgment evidence, an expert's opinion must be all of these things. *See* Tex. R. Civ. P. 166a(c); *Anderson v. Snider*, 808 S.W.2d 54, 55 (Tex. 1991). The statements made by {142 *name of expert*} are not competent summary-judgment evidence. {143 *Identify expert's statements and explain why they are defective.*} Because these statements are not competent summary-judgment evidence, the Court should strike them. {*See* ***O'Connor's Texas Rules***, *"Interested witness," ch. 7-B, §9.3.2, p. 732; "Expert witness," ch. 7-B, §9.3.3, p. 732.*}

{*Expert not qualified to testify in a medical-malpractice case about physician's standard of care*}

30. {144 *Party*} objects to {145 *identify evidence, e.g., Exhibit A*} on the ground that {146 *name of expert*} does not meet the statutory qualifications to testify as an expert about the standard of care of a physician. To meet the qualifications, the expert must (1) be a physician practicing medicine at the time the testimony is given or at the time the claim arose, (2) have knowledge of the accepted standards of medical care for the diagnosis, care, or treatment of the plaintiff's illness, injury or condition, and (3) be qualified on the basis of training or experience at the time the testimony is given or at the time the claim arose. Tex. Civ. Prac. & Rem. Code §74.401(a). To determine if the

Continued on next page

expert is qualified on the basis of training or experience, the court must consider whether the expert (1) is board-certified or has other substantial training or experience in an area of medical practice relevant to the claim and (2) is actively practicing medicine by rendering medical-care services relevant to the claim. *Id.* §74.401(c). {147 *Name of expert*} does not qualify because {148 *explain how expert does not meet the qualifications*}. Because {149 *name of expert*} is not qualified, the Court should strike {150 *identify evidence*}. {*See* ***O'Connor's Texas COA***, *"Objecting to experts," ch. 20-A, §8.5, p. 696.*}

{Expert not qualified to testify in a medical-malpractice case about health-care provider's standard of care}

31. {151 *Party*} objects to {152 *identify evidence, e.g., Exhibit A*} on the ground that {153 *name of expert*} does not meet the statutory qualifications to testify as an expert about the standard of care of a health-care provider. To meet the qualifications, the expert must (1) be practicing health care in a field of practice that involves the same type of care or treatment delivered by the defendant, if the defendant is an individual, at the time the expert's testimony is given or at the time the claim arose, (2) have knowledge of the standard of care for health-care providers for the diagnosis, care, or treatment of the plaintiff's illness, injury, or condition, and (3) be qualified on the basis of training or experience. Tex. Civ. Prac. & Rem. Code §74.402(b). To determine if the expert is qualified on the basis of training or experience the court must consider whether the expert (1) is certified by a licensing agency of one or more states of the United States or by a national professional-certifying agency, or has other substantial training or experience in the area of health care relevant to the plaintiff's claim, and (2) is actively practicing health care by rendering health-care services relevant to the claim. *Id.* §74.402(c). {154 *Name of expert*} does not qualify because {155 *explain how expert does not meet the qualifications*}. Because {156 *name of expert*} is not qualified, the Court should strike {157 *identify evidence*}. {*See* ***O'Connor's Texas COA***, *"Objecting to experts," ch. 20-A, §8.5, p. 696.*}

{Expert not qualified to render an opinion about causation in a medical-malpractice case}

32. {158 *Party*} objects to {159 *identify evidence, e.g., Exhibit A*} on the ground that {160 *name of expert*} does not meet the statutory qualifications to render an opinion about causation in a suit against a {161 *physician/health-care provider*}. The statutory qualifications are set out in Texas Civil Practice & Remedies Code section 74.403(a)-(c). Specifically, {162 *explain why expert is not qualified to render an opinion on causation under the statute*}. Because the {163 *affidavit/declaration/deposition*} of {164 *name of expert*} does not meet the statutory requirements, the Court should strike it. {*See* ***O'Connor's Texas COA***, *"Objecting to experts," ch. 20-A, §8.5, p. 696.*}

FORM 7C:11

SEE: Tex. R. Civ. P. 166a(f)
Tex. R. Evid. 104(a), 402, 601, 602, 702, 901, 902
Tex. Gov't Code §312.011(1)
Tex. Civ. Prac. & Rem. Code §§74.401-74.403
O'Connor's Texas Rules * Civil Trials (2019), "Unsworn declaration," ch. 1-B, §3.2.17, p. 14; "*Daubert-Robinson* Test for Expert Testimony," ch. 5-N, §2, p. 499; "Types of witnesses," ch. 7-B, §9.3, p. 732; "Affidavits," ch. 7-B, §9.4, p. 733; "Discovery products," ch. 7-B, §9.5, p. 736; "Reporter's record," ch. 7-B, §9.7, p. 737; "Objections to Summary-Judgment Evidence," ch. 7-B, §10, p. 738
O'Connor's Texas Causes of Action (2019), "Parol-evidence rule," ch. 5-B, §7.2, p. 109; "Objecting to experts," ch. 20-A, §8.5, p. 696

NOTE: Before the Supreme Court's ruling in ***Seim v. Allstate Tex. Lloyds***, the courts of appeals were split on whether a trial court's implicit ruling on objections to summary-judgment evidence was sufficient to preserve error. ***Seim v. Allstate Tex. Lloyds***, 551 S.W.3d 161, 165-66 (Tex.2018). Although the Court suggested than an implicit ruling might be sufficient when the implication is "clear" from the record, it rejected the view that a ruling on the summary-judgment motion alone constitutes an implicit ruling on the objections. *See id.* The Court similarly rejected the idea that error is preserved as long as the record indicates "in some way" that the trial court ruled on the objections. *See, e.g., id.* (SJ order stating that court considered motions, briefs, and all competent SJ evidence was not sufficient to show implicit ruling on objections). Until the Court defines what constitutes a clearly implied ruling, a party should obtain an express ruling on any objections in order to avoid waiving error. See ***O'Connor's Texas Rules***, "Secure ruling on objections," ch. 7-B, §10.2, p. 742.

ORDER ON {1 *PARTY*}'S MOTION FOR SUMMARY JUDGMENT

After considering {2 *party*} {3 *name*}'s motion for summary judgment, the pleadings, the response, the reply, the affidavits, and other evidence on file, the Court

{*CHOOSE APPROPRIATE ORDER*}

DENIES {4 *party*}'s motion for summary judgment.

DENIES {5 *party*}'s motion for summary judgment, but orders that the following facts are established as a matter of law: {6 *identify facts established as matter of law*}.

GRANTS {7 *party*}'s motion for partial summary judgment on {8 *identify cause of action resolved by summary judgment*}.

{*CHOOSE APPROPRIATE PARAGRAPH 1*}

1. Accordingly, the Court orders {9 *adverse party*} to take nothing on {10 *his/her/its*} cause of action against {11 *party*} for {12 *identify cause of action*}.

1. Accordingly, the Court orders {13 *party*} to recover the following from the {14 *adverse party*}:

{*CHOOSE APPROPRIATE PARAGRAPHS a-f*}

a. Actual damages in the amount of ${15 *amount*}.

b. Prejudgment interest on the actual damages awarded at the rate of {16 *specify rate of interest*} from {17 *date interest began to accrue*} until the date of this judgment, in the amount of ${18 *amount of prejudgment interest*}.

c. Reasonable and necessary attorney fees in the amount of ${19 *amount*} for the prosecution of this case through this judgment.

d. {20 *State any other damages or penalties that are recoverable.*}

e. Court costs.

f. Postjudgment interest on all of the above at the rate of {21 *specify rate of interest*}, compounded annually, from the date this judgment is entered until all amounts are paid in full.

{ADD IF APPLICABLE}

After considering {㉒ *party*}'s objections to summary-judgment evidence, the Court also orders as follows:

1. {㉓ *Party*}'s objections to {㉔ *identify evidence, e.g., Exhibit A*} are {㉕ *sustained/overruled*}.

2. {㉖ *Continue as necessary.*}

SIGNED on ________________, 20___.

____
PRESIDING JUDGE

SEE: Tex. R. Civ. P. 166a(f)
O'Connor's Texas Rules * Civil Trials (2019), "Judgment or order?," ch. 7-B, §12.2, p. 743

ADD: STYLE OF THE CASE – FORM 1B:2
CERTIFICATE OF SERVICE – FORM 1B:13, if proposed order served separately from motion or response

NOTE: This form should be used if the court is granting a partial summary judgment or denying a final or partial summary judgment. If the court is granting a final summary judgment, prepare a judgment, not an order. See FORM 9C:4.

An order granting a partial summary judgment is not appealable or immediately enforceable because it is interlocutory. A trial court, on its own initiative or on a party's motion, can allow an appeal from an order that is not otherwise appealable if the following conditions are met: (1) the order to be appealed involves a controlling question of law about which there is a substantial ground for difference of opinion and (2) an immediate appeal from the order may materially advance the ultimate termination of the litigation. Tex. Civ. Prac. & Rem. Code §51.014(d); Tex. R. Civ. P. 168. Permission must be stated in the order being appealed rather than in a separate order. Tex. R. Civ. P. 168 & cmt. See ***O'Connor's Texas Rules***, "Interlocutory appeal," ch. 7-B, §14.3.4, p. 746. To make a partial summary judgment final and appealable, a party should ask the court to sever the adjudicated claims from the claims that remain. *See, e.g.*, ***B.Z.B., Inc. v. Clark***, 273 S.W.3d 899, 901 (Tex.App.—Houston [14th Dist.] 2008, no pet.) (trial court granted motion to sever after granting motion for partial summary judgment).

A court may rule on objections either at the same time it rules on the motion for summary judgment or sometime afterward. *See* ***Crocker v. Paulyne's Nursing Home, Inc.***, 95 S.W.3d 416, 420-21 (Tex. App.—Dallas 2002, no pet.); ***Dolcefino v. Randolph***, 19 S.W.3d 906, 926 (Tex.App.—Houston [14th Dist.] 2000, pet. denied). If the court rules on objections at the same time the court rules on the motion for summary judgment, the court may state its rulings in the order on summary judgment rather than in a separate order. For the separate order, see FORM 7C:10.

◄ *Continued on next page* ►

Before the Supreme Court's ruling in ***Seim v. Allstate Tex. Lloyds***, the courts of appeals were split on whether a trial court's implicit ruling on objections to summary-judgment evidence was sufficient to preserve error. ***Seim v. Allstate Tex. Lloyds***, 551 S.W.3d 161, 165-66 (Tex.2018). Although the Court suggested than an implicit ruling might be sufficient when the implication is "clear" from the record, it rejected the view that a ruling on the summary-judgment motion alone constitutes an implicit ruling on the objections. *See id.* The Court similarly rejected the idea that error is preserved as long as the record indicates "in some way" that the trial court ruled on the objections. *See, e.g., id.* (SJ order stating that court considered motions, briefs, and all competent SJ evidence was not sufficient to show implicit ruling on objections). Until the Court defines what constitutes a clearly implied ruling, a party should obtain an express ruling on any objections in order to avoid waiving error. See ***O'Connor's Texas Rules***, "Secure ruling on objections," ch. 7-B, §10.2, p. 742.

A party may file a motion to reconsider the court's summary-judgment ruling. When a party files a motion requesting reconsideration of a motion for summary judgment that was granted, the motion is effectively a motion for new trial. See FORM 10B:6; ***O'Connor's Texas Rules***, "MNT After Summary Judgment," ch. 10-B, §11, p. 941. When a party files a motion requesting reconsideration of a motion for summary judgment that was denied, the party should reurge all the grounds raised in the original motion for summary judgment and summarize any objections to the other party's motion or response. *See, e.g.*, ***State Farm Lloyds v. Page***, 315 S.W.3d 525, 531-32 (Tex.2010) (because motion for reconsideration was limited to grounds in traditional summary-judgment motion and did not reurge no-evidence grounds in motion for summary judgment, D's no-evidence arguments were not preserved).

MOTION FOR JUDGMENT ON AGREED STATEMENT OF FACTS

{❶ *Party*}, {❷ *name*}, and {❸ *adverse party*}, {❹ *name*}, ask the Court to sign a judgment in this case on their agreed statement of facts, in accordance with Texas Rule of Civil Procedure 263.

INTRODUCTION

1. Plaintiff, {❺ *name*}, sued defendant, {❻ *name*}, for {❼ *state basis of suit*}.

2. Defendant answered asserting {❽ *identify answer and list defensive pleas, affirmative defenses, and counterclaims*}.

3. {❾ *State other relevant facts about the suit.*}

BACKGROUND

4. On {❿ *date*}, plaintiff and defendant executed an agreed statement of facts under Rule 263.

5. The agreed statement of facts is attached to this motion as Exhibit {⓫ *letter*} and incorporated by reference.

6. {⓬ *State other facts relevant to the motion.*}

ARGUMENT & AUTHORITIES

7. The purpose of a motion for judgment on an agreed statement of facts is to ask the trial court to render a decision on the law when the facts are not in controversy. *See* Tex. R. Civ. P. 263; *State Bar v. Faubion*, 821 S.W.2d 203, 205 (Tex. App.—Houston [14th Dist.] 1991, writ denied). A court should grant the motion when the parties agree on all ultimate facts essential for the determination of the lawsuit and file a written agreement setting out the agreed facts. *See* Tex. R. Civ. P. 263; *Perry v. Aetna Life Ins. Co.*, 380 S.W.2d 868, 874-75 (Tex. App.—Tyler 1964, writ ref'd n.r.e.).

8. The Court should grant this motion because the parties agree on all ultimate facts essential for the determination of the lawsuit. They agree that the facts in the attached agreed statement are all the facts of the case, and they agree that those are the facts on which this case must be decided. *See Cummins & Walker Oil Co. v. Smith*, 814 S.W.2d 884, 886 (Tex. App.—San Antonio 1991, no writ). No other facts are relevant to the disposition of this lawsuit.

CONCLUSION

9. {⓭ *Briefly summarize the motion.*}

◄ *Continued on next page* ►

PRAYER

10. For these reasons, {⓮ *party*} and {⓯ *adverse party*} ask the Court to certify the agreed statement of facts and resolve the controversy between the parties by signing a judgment on the agreed facts.

SEE: Tex. R. Civ. P. 11, 263
O'Connor's Texas Rules * Civil Trials (2019), "Motion," ch. 7-E, §3, p. 769

ADD: STYLE OF THE CASE – FORM 1B:2
SIGNATURE BLOCK FOR AGREED MOTIONS – FORM 1B:4

ATTACH: AGREED STATEMENT OF FACTS & CERTIFICATION – FORM 7E:2
JUDGMENT ON AGREED STATEMENT OF FACTS – FORM 9C:5

NOTE: **Each party should attach its proposed judgment to the motion so the court can choose between them and sign the appropriate one.**

AGREED STATEMENT OF FACTS

In accordance with Texas Rule of Civil Procedure 263, {1 *party*}, {2 *name*}, and {3 *adverse party*}, {4 *name*}, agree to the following facts:

{5 *State the specific facts on which the parties agree.*}

Executed on ______________, 20___.

____
{6 *Name of attorney for party*}
Texas Bar No. {7 _____}
{8 *Address 1*}
{9 *Address 2*}
{10 *City, state, zip code*}
Tel. {11 __________}
Fax {12 __________}
{13 *E-mail address*}

ATTORNEY FOR {14 *PARTY*},
{15 *NAME OF PARTY*}

____
{16 *Name of attorney for adverse party*}
Texas Bar No. {17 _____}
{18 *Address 1*}
{19 *Address 2*}
{20 *City, state, zip code*}
Tel. {21 __________}
Fax {22 __________}
{23 *E-mail address*}

ATTORNEY FOR {24 *ADVERSE PARTY*},
{25 *NAME OF ADVERSE PARTY*}

Continued on next page

CERTIFICATION OF AGREED STATEMENT OF FACTS

The Court has read the agreed statement of facts filed under Texas Rule of Civil Procedure 263 and certifies it to be correct. The Court will render a judgment based on the agreed facts.

SIGNED on _______________, 20___.

____
PRESIDING JUDGE

SEE: Tex. R. Civ. P. 11, 263
O'Connor's Texas Rules * Civil Trials (2019), "Certificate for judge," ch. 7-E, §3.5, p. 769

ADD: STYLE OF THE CASE – FORM 1B:2

{❶ *PARTY*}'S NONSUIT AGAINST {❷ *ADVERSE PARTY*}

{❸ *Party*}, {❹ *name*}, gives written notice of {❺ *his/her/its*} nonsuit on all claims against {❻ *adverse party*}, {❼ *name*}. {*See* ***O'Connor's Texas Rules****, "Service of notice," ch. 7-F, §2.6, p. 772.*}

INTRODUCTION

1. Plaintiff, {❽ *name*}, sued defendant, {❾ *name*}, for {❿ *state basis of suit*}.

2. {⓫ *State other relevant facts about the suit.*}

NOTICE OF NONSUIT

{*CHOOSE APPROPRIATE PARAGRAPH 3*}

3. Plaintiff asks the Court to sign an order of nonsuit on all {⓬ *his/her/its*} claims against defendant.

3. Defendant asks the Court to sign an order of nonsuit on all {⓭ *his/her/its*} counterclaims against plaintiff.

4. {⓮ *Party*} requests a dismissal {⓯ *with/without*} prejudice.

SEE: Tex. R. Civ. P. 162
O'Connor's Texas Rules * Civil Trials (2019), "Motion," ch. 7-F, §2, p. 771

ADD: STYLE OF THE CASE – FORM 1B:2
SIGNATURE BLOCK – FORM 1B:3
CERTIFICATE OF SERVICE – FORM 1B:13

ATTACH: ORDER – FORM 1G:1
Consent of guardian ad litem, if necessary

NOTE: A nonsuit in a trial must be taken before the plaintiff introduces all of its evidence other than rebuttal evidence (i.e., before it rests). Tex. R. Civ. P. 162; ***Epps v. Fowler***, 351 S.W.3d 862, 868 (Tex.2011); *e.g.*, ***UTMB v. Estate of Blackmon***, 195 S.W.3d 98, 100 (Tex.2006) (P had right to nonsuit during interlocutory appeal to court of appeals). A nonsuit in a summary-judgment proceeding must be taken before the court grants ("renders") a summary judgment. ***Pace Concerts, Ltd. v. Resendez***, 72 S.W.3d 700, 702 (Tex.App.—San Antonio 2002, pet. denied); ***Taliaferro v. Smith***, 804 S.W.2d 548, 550 (Tex.App.—Houston [14th Dist.] 1991, no writ).

The plaintiff can nonsuit some parties without nonsuiting others, as long as doing so will not prejudice another party. *See* Tex. R. Civ. P. 162, 163; ***C/S Solutions, Inc. v. Energy Maint. Servs. Grp.***, 274 S.W.3d 299, 306 (Tex.App.—Houston [1st Dist.] 2008, no pet.).

Continued on next page

The plaintiff cannot nonsuit only some of the claims against a party, but instead must nonsuit the entire case. *See* Tex. R. Civ. P. 162, 163; ***C/S Solutions***, 274 S.W.3d at 306. Although the plaintiff cannot nonsuit only some of her claims, she can voluntarily dismiss certain claims either by filing an amended pleading that omits a claim under Texas Rule of Civil Procedure 63 or by abandoning a claim under Texas Rule of Civil Procedure 165. ***C/S Solutions***, 274 S.W.3d at 306. If the plaintiff files a written "nonsuit" that abandons certain claims, it is actually an amended pleading voluntarily dismissing the claims, and it will be treated as such, despite the fact that the word "nonsuit" appears. *Id.* at 306-07. The distinction between a nonsuit under Texas Rule of Civil Procedure 162 and an amended pleading that voluntarily dismisses some claims has no practical effect unless the "nonsuit" violates the timing requirements of Rule 63. ***C/S Solutions***, 274 S.W.3d at 306. See ***O'Connor's Texas Rules***, "Motion to Amend Pleadings—Pretrial," ch. 5-F, p. 432.

<u>{[1] *PARTY*}'S OBJECTION TO {[2] *ADVERSE PARTY*}'S NONSUIT</u>

{[3] *Party*}, {[4] *name*}, objects to {[5] *adverse party*} {[6] *name*}'s nonsuit.

INTRODUCTION

1. Plaintiff, {[7] *name*}, sued defendant, {[8] *name*}, for {[9] *state basis of suit*}.

2. {[10] *State other relevant facts about the suit.*}

BACKGROUND

3. {[11] *Adverse party*} asked this Court to sign an order of nonsuit on {[12] *his/her/its*} claims against {[13] *party*}.

4. {[14] *State other facts relevant to the objection.*}

ARGUMENT & AUTHORITIES

{*CHOOSE APPROPRIATE PARAGRAPH 5*}

5. A party cannot take a nonsuit after it rests. Tex. R. Civ. P. 162; *Epps v. Fowler*, 351 S.W.3d 862, 868 (Tex. 2011). The Court should deny {[15] *adverse party*}'s nonsuit because {[16] *adverse party*} filed {[17] *his/her/its*} notice of nonsuit after {[18] *he/she/it*} had rested.

5. A party cannot take a nonsuit after the court grants summary judgment. *Pace Concerts, Ltd. v. Resendez*, 72 S.W.3d 700, 702 (Tex. App.—San Antonio 2002, pet. denied); *Taliaferro v. Smith*, 804 S.W.2d 548, 550 (Tex. App.—Houston [14th Dist.] 1991, no writ). The Court should deny {[19] *adverse party*}'s nonsuit because {[20] *adverse party*} filed {[21] *his/her/its*} notice of nonsuit after the Court granted summary judgment.

5. A party cannot take a nonsuit on any issues resolved by a partial summary judgment. *Hyundai Motor Co. v. Alvarado*, 892 S.W.2d 853, 855 (Tex. 1995). The Court should deny {[22] *adverse party*}'s nonsuit on the issue of {[23] *identify issue*} because {[24] *adverse party*} filed {[25] *his/her/its*} notice of nonsuit after the Court granted a partial summary judgment on the issue of {[26] *identify issue*}.

CONCLUSION

6. {[27] *Briefly summarize the objection.*}

PRAYER

7. For these reasons, {[28] *party*} asks the Court to deny the nonsuit.

◄ *Continued on next page* ►

SEE: Tex. R. Civ. P. 162
O'Connor's Texas Rules * Civil Trials (2019), "Objections to Nonsuit," ch. 7-F, §4, p. 773

ADD: STYLE OF THE CASE – FORM 1B:2
SIGNATURE BLOCK – FORM 1B:3
CERTIFICATE OF SERVICE – FORM 1B:13

ATTACH: AFFIDAVIT – FORM 1B:8, if necessary
ORDER – FORM 1G:1

{❶ *PARTY*}'S MOTION TO SET ASIDE NONSUIT & REINSTATE CASE

{❷ *Party*}, {❸ *name*}, asks the Court to set aside the nonsuit in this case and reinstate {❹ *list causes of action, counterclaims, or cross-claims to be reinstated*}.

INTRODUCTION

1. Plaintiff, {❺ *name*}, sued defendant, {❻ *name*}, for {❼ *state basis of suit*}.

2. {❽ *State other relevant facts about the suit.*}

BACKGROUND

3. {❾ *Plaintiff/Defendant*}, {❿ *name*}, moved for a nonsuit on {⓫ *his/her/its*} {⓬ *cause of action/counterclaim/cross-claim*} against {⓭ *plaintiff/defendant*}.

4. On {⓮ *date*}, the Court signed an order of nonsuit.

5. {⓯ *State other facts relevant to the motion.*}

ARGUMENT & AUTHORITIES

A. Motion timely.

6. A trial court can reinstate a case dismissed by voluntary nonsuit upon the filing of a timely motion. *Missouri Pac. R.R. v. Whitaker*, 815 S.W.2d 348, 349 n.2 (Tex. App.—Tyler 1991, orig. proceeding); *McClendon v. State Farm Mut. Auto. Ins. Co.*, 796 S.W.2d 229, 233 (Tex. App.—El Paso 1990, writ denied). A motion to set aside a nonsuit and reinstate a case is timely if it is filed while the court still has jurisdiction over the order of nonsuit. *See Whitaker*, 815 S.W.2d at 349 n.2. Although an order of nonsuit does not divest the court of jurisdiction over the case, the duration of the court's jurisdiction depends on whether the order is interlocutory or final. *See In re Romero*, 956 S.W.2d 659, 660 (Tex. App.—San Antonio 1997, orig. proceeding); *Quanto Int'l Co. v. Lloyd*, 897 S.W.2d 482, 485 (Tex. App.—Houston [1st Dist.] 1995, orig. proceeding). If the order does not dispose of all the claims in the case, the order is interlocutory and remains subject to the court's continuing control. *In re Romero*, 956 S.W.2d at 660. If the order disposes of all the claims, the order is final and the court retains plenary power over the order for 30 days after the court signed it. *Id.*

7. This motion is timely because the Court still has jurisdiction over the order of nonsuit. {⓰ *Explain, e.g., the nonsuit asked for the dismissal of only certain claims, and thus the order of nonsuit was interlocutory and is presently subject to the Court's continuing control.*}

◄ *Continued on next page* ►

{*CHOOSE APPROPRIATE SECTIONS B-E*}

B. Nonsuit prejudicial.

8. The Court should set aside the nonsuit granted to {[17] *plaintiff/defendant*} because it prejudiced the right of {[18] *party*} to be heard on {[19] *his/her/its*} claim for {[20] *identify claim*}, which is a pending claim for affirmative relief. A nonsuit cannot prejudice an adverse party's pending claim for affirmative relief. Tex. R. Civ. P. 162; *Epps v. Fowler*, 351 S.W.3d 862, 868 (Tex. 2011); *Tex. Mut. Ins. Co. v. Ledbetter*, 251 S.W.3d 31, 38 (Tex. 2008). To qualify as a claim for affirmative relief under Texas Rule of Civil Procedure 162, the claim must allege a cause of action on which the adverse party can recover independent of the nonsuited claim. *Univ. of Tex. Med. Branch v. Estate of Blackmon*, 195 S.W.3d 98, 101 (Tex. 2006). {[21] *Elaborate.*} {*See* ***O'Connor's Texas Rules****, "Effect on defendant's claims," ch. 7-F, §6.3, p. 775.*}

C. Nonsuit overly broad.

9. The Court should set aside the nonsuit granted to {[22] *plaintiff/defendant*} on {[23] *party*}'s {[24] *cause of action/counterclaim/cross-claim*} because {[25] *plaintiff/defendant*} had no right to nonsuit it. A party has an absolute right to nonsuit its own claims, but it cannot nonsuit the independent claims of other parties. *Tex. Mut. Ins. Co. v. Ledbetter*, 251 S.W.3d 31, 37 (Tex. 2008). {[26] *Party*}'s {[27] *cause of action/counterclaim/cross-claim*} is independent of {[28] *plaintiff/defendant*}'s nonsuited claim, and the dismissal of {[29] *plaintiff/defendant*}'s claim cannot dispose of {[30] *party*}'s {[31] *cause of action/counterclaim/cross-claim*}. {[32] *Elaborate.*}

D. Parties' agreement.

10. The Court should set aside the nonsuit granted to {[33] *plaintiff/defendant*} because the parties have agreed to reinstate {[34] *list causes of action, counterclaims, or cross-claims to be reinstated*}. A court can reinstate a case based on the agreement of the parties. *See, e.g., McClendon*, 796 S.W.2d at 233 (parties agreed to reinstate plaintiff's cause of action). {[35] *Elaborate.*}

E. {[36] *Add appropriate heading for other ground.*}

11. {[37] *State any other reason the nonsuit should be set aside.*}

CONCLUSION

12. {[38] *Briefly summarize the motion.*}

PRAYER

13. For these reasons, {39 *party*} asks the Court to set aside the nonsuit and reinstate the {40 *list causes of action, counterclaims, or cross-claims to be reinstated*}.

SEE: Tex. R. Civ. P. 162
O'Connor's Texas Rules * Civil Trials (2019), "Reinstatement of Nonsuited Case," ch. 7-F, §7, p. 778

ADD: STYLE OF THE CASE – FORM 1B:2
SIGNATURE BLOCK – FORM 1B:3
CERTIFICATE OF SERVICE – FORM 1B:13

ATTACH: AFFIDAVIT – FORM 1B:8, if necessary
ORDER – FORM 1G:1

NOTE: The motion to set aside a nonsuited case can be labeled a motion to reinstate after nonsuit, a motion to set aside the nonsuit, a motion to withdraw the nonsuit, or even a motion for new trial. See ***O'Connor's Texas Rules***, "Reinstatement of Nonsuited Case," ch. 7-F, §7, p. 778.

An intervenor's claim for affirmative relief cannot be affected by a nonsuit. *See, e.g.*, ***Texas Mut. Ins. v. Ledbetter***, 251 S.W.3d 31, 38 (Tex.2008) (intervening insurance carrier's subrogation claim was claim for affirmative relief).

DEFENDANT'S MOTION TO DISMISS

Defendant, {❶ *name*}, asks the Court to dismiss plaintiff {❷ *name*}'s suit.

INTRODUCTION

1. Plaintiff, {❸ *name*}, sued defendant, {❹ *name*}, for {❺ *state basis of suit*}.

2. Defendant answered asserting {❻ *identify answer and list defensive pleas, affirmative defenses, and counterclaims*}.

3. {❼ *State other relevant facts about the suit.*}

BACKGROUND

4. {❽ *State facts relevant to the motion.*}

ARGUMENT & AUTHORITIES

{*CHOOSE APPROPRIATE SECTIONS A-G*}

A. Plaintiff did not appear at {❾ *trial/hearing*}.

5. A court can dismiss a plaintiff's suit if the plaintiff did not appear at a trial or hearing after receiving notice of the setting. Tex. R. Civ. P. 165a(1); *In re Conner*, 458 S.W.3d 532, 535 (Tex. 2015); *Alexander v. Lynda's Boutique*, 134 S.W.3d 845, 852 (Tex. 2004). {*See* ***O'Connor's Texas Rules****, "Failure to appear," ch. 7-G, §2.2.1(1), p. 781.*}

6. The Court should dismiss plaintiff's suit because plaintiff did not appear at {❿ *trial/a hearing*} after receiving notice of the setting. {⓫ *Elaborate.*}

B. Plaintiff has not disposed of suit within time standards.

7. A court can dismiss a suit if the suit is not disposed of within the Supreme Court's time standards for disposition. Tex. R. Civ. P. 165a(2); *In re Conner*, 458 S.W.3d 532, 535 (Tex. 2015); *Steward v. Colonial Cas. Ins. Co.*, 143 S.W.3d 161, 164 (Tex. App.—Waco 2004, no pet.). A civil case (other than a family-law case) in which {⓬ *a/no*} jury has been requested should be brought to trial or final disposition within {⓭ *18/12*} months from the appearance date. Tex. R. Jud. Admin. 6.1(b). {*See* ***O'Connor's Texas Rules****, "Failure to comply with time standards," ch. 7-G, §2.2.1(2), p. 781.*}

8. The Court should dismiss plaintiff's suit because the suit was not disposed of within the Supreme Court's disposition time standards. {14 *A/No*} jury has been requested in this case. Defendant's appearance date was {15 *date*}. More than {16 *number*} months have elapsed since defendant's appearance date, and this case is still awaiting trial. {17 *Elaborate.*}

C. Plaintiff has not diligently prosecuted suit.

9. A court can dismiss a plaintiff's suit under its inherent power if the plaintiff has not been diligent in the prosecution of its suit. *Villarreal v. San Antonio Truck & Equip.*, 994 S.W.2d 628, 630 (Tex. 1999); *Veterans' Land Bd. v. Williams*, 543 S.W.2d 89, 90 (Tex. 1976). Considerations include (1) the length of time the case was on file, (2) the extent of activity in the case, (3) whether a trial setting was requested, and (4) the existence of reasonable excuses for delay. *Tex. Mut. Ins. Co. v. Olivas*, 323 S.W.3d 266, 274 (Tex. App.—El Paso 2010, no pet.); *Polk v. Sw. Crossing Homeowners Ass'n*, 165 S.W.3d 89, 97 (Tex. App.—Houston [14th Dist.] 2005, pet. denied). {*See* ***O'Connor's Texas Rules****, "Inherent power," ch. 7-G, §2.2.2, p. 781.*}

10. The Court should dismiss plaintiff's suit because plaintiff has not diligently prosecuted {18 *his/her/its*} suit. {19 *Elaborate.*}

D. Plaintiff did not replead after special exceptions.

11. A court should dismiss a plaintiff's suit if the plaintiff does not replead after the court sustains special exceptions to the plaintiff's petition. *See Baca v. Sanchez*, 172 S.W.3d 93, 97 (Tex. App.—El Paso 2005, no pet.). {*See* ***O'Connor's Texas Rules****, "Bar to suit," ch. 7-G, §5.1, p. 784.*}

12. The Court should dismiss plaintiff's suit because plaintiff did not replead after the Court sustained defendant's special exceptions. Defendant filed special exceptions on {20 *date*}. The Court sustained the special exceptions on {21 *date*} and ordered plaintiff to replead by {22 *date*}, but plaintiff did not comply with the order. {23 *Elaborate.*}

E. Plaintiff did not provide expert report.

13. In a medical-malpractice suit, a court must dismiss a plaintiff's suit with prejudice and award the defendant its reasonable attorney fees and costs if the plaintiff does not serve the defendant with a report and résumé of its expert within 120 days after the defendant filed its original answer. *See* Tex. Civ. Prac. & Rem. Code §74.351(a), (b). {*See* ***O'Connor's Texas COA****, "Did not meet 120-day deadline," ch. 20-A, §7.2.3(3), p. 683.*}

Continued on next page

14. The Court should dismiss with prejudice plaintiff's suit and award defendant {㉔ *his/her/its*} reasonable attorney fees and costs because plaintiff did not timely provide defendant with the report and résumé of {㉕ *his/her/its*} expert. {㉖ *Elaborate.*}

F. Plaintiff provided inadequate expert report.

15. In a medical-malpractice suit, a court must dismiss a plaintiff's suit with prejudice and award the defendant its reasonable attorney fees and costs if the plaintiff does not serve the defendant with a report and résumé of its expert within 120 days after the defendant filed its original answer. *See* Tex. Civ. Prac. & Rem. Code §74.351(a), (b). A plaintiff who serves an expert report within 120 days is considered not to have served an expert report if (1) the plaintiff did not initially make a good-faith effort to comply with statutory requirements of an expert report or (2) after initially making a good-faith effort to comply, the plaintiff has not cured the defects after being granted an opportunity to cure. *See id.* §74.351(c); *Scoresby v. Santillan*, 346 S.W.3d 546, 554 (Tex. 2011). {*See* ***O'Connor's Texas COA****, "Did not meet 120-day deadline," ch. 20-A, §7.2.3(3), p. 683; "Challenging adequacy of report," ch. 20-A, §7.2.6, p. 688.*}

{*CHOOSE APPROPRIATE PARAGRAPH 16*}

16. The Court should dismiss plaintiff's suit with prejudice and award costs and attorney fees because the plaintiff did not initially make a good-faith effort to comply with statutory requirements of an expert report. To constitute a good-faith effort, the initial report must, at a minimum, contain an expert's opinion that the claim has merit and implicate the defendant's conduct. *Scoresby*, 346 S.W.3d at 557. Because plaintiff's report does {㉗ *not contain an expert opinion that the claim has merit/not implicate the defendant's conduct/neither*}, the plaintiff should not be given an opportunity to amend {㉘ *his/her/its*} report, and {㉙ *his/her/its*} case should be dismissed with prejudice. {㉚ *Elaborate.*}

16. The Court should dismiss plaintiff's suit with prejudice and award costs and attorney fees because plaintiff has not cured the deficiencies in {㉛ *his/her/its*} expert's report after being granted a 30-day extension. {㉜ *Elaborate.*}

G. Plaintiff {㉝ *is not indigent/filed frivolous or malicious claim*}.

17. A court can dismiss a suit filed by an indigent if the trial court finds {㉞ *the allegation of poverty in the affidavit is false/the action is frivolous or malicious*}. Tex. Civ. Prac. & Rem. Code §13.001.

18. The Court should dismiss the suit because plaintiff's {㉟ *allegation of poverty is false/claim is frivolous/claim is malicious*}. {㊱ *Elaborate.*}

CONCLUSION

19. {㊲ *Briefly summarize the motion.*}

PRAYER

20. For these reasons, defendant asks the Court to dismiss plaintiff's suit {㊳ *with/ without*} prejudice. {*See* ***O'Connor's Texas Rules****, "Type of dismissal," ch. 7-G, §6.2, p. 784.*}

SEE: Tex. R. Civ. P. 143, 161, 165a
Tex. Civ. Prac. & Rem. Code §§13.001, 74.351(a), (b)
Tex. R. Jud. Admin. 6
O'Connor's Texas Rules * Civil Trials (2019), "Grounds for Dismissal," ch. 7-G, §2, p. 780
O'Connor's Texas Causes of Action (2019), "Expert report," ch. 20-A, §7.2, p. 680

ADD: STYLE OF THE CASE – FORM 1B:2
SIGNATURE BLOCK – FORM 1B:3
CERTIFICATE OF SERVICE – FORM 1B:13

ATTACH: AFFIDAVIT – FORM 1B:8, if necessary
ORDER – FORM 1G:1

NOTE: A trial court generally cannot dismiss a suit without giving the plaintiff notice of its intent to dismiss. ***Ginn v. Forrester***, 282 S.W.3d 430, 432 (Tex.2009); ***Alexander v. Lynda's Boutique***, 134 S.W.3d 845, 852 (Tex.2004). See ***O'Connor's Texas Rules***, "Notice of Intent to Dismiss," ch. 7-G, §3, p. 782.

PLAINTIFF'S {❶ *MOTION TO RETAIN/RESPONSE TO MOTION TO DISMISS*}

Plaintiff, {❷ *name*}, asks the Court to retain {❸ *his/her/its*} suit on the Court's docket {❹ *add if appropriate: and deny defendant's motion to dismiss*}.

INTRODUCTION

1. Plaintiff, {❺ *name*}, sued defendant, {❻ *name*}, for {❼ *state basis of suit*}.

2. Defendant {❽ *made an appearance/filed an answer*} on {❾ *date*}.

3. {❿ *State other relevant facts about the suit.*}

BACKGROUND

{*CHOOSE APPROPRIATE PARAGRAPH 4*}

4. On {⓫ *date*}, defendant filed and served a motion to dismiss the suit.

4. On {⓬ *date*}, the Court sent a notice that it intended to dismiss the suit.

{*CHOOSE APPROPRIATE STATEMENT*}

Ⓐ because {⓭ *state the reasons for the dismissal*}.

Ⓑ if plaintiff did not {⓮ *state the conditions for retaining case*}.

5. {⓯ *State other facts relevant to the motion.*}

ARGUMENT & AUTHORITIES

{*CHOOSE APPROPRIATE SECTIONS A-D*}

A. Failure to appear.

6. A court can dismiss a plaintiff's suit if the plaintiff did not appear at a trial or hearing. Tex. R. Civ. P. 165a(1). The court should not, however, dismiss a case if (1) the plaintiff did not receive notice of the setting or (2) there is good cause for the case to be maintained on the docket. *See id.* {*See* ***O'Connor's Texas Rules****, "Motion to retain," ch. 7-G, §4.1, p. 783.*}

{*CHOOSE APPROPRIATE PARAGRAPHS 7-8*}

7. The Court should not dismiss plaintiff's suit because plaintiff did not have notice of the {⓰ *trial/hearing*}. {⓱ *Elaborate.*}

8. The Court should not dismiss plaintiff's suit because there is good cause to maintain it on the docket. {18 *Elaborate.*}

B. Failure to comply with time standards.

9. A court can dismiss a plaintiff's suit if the plaintiff does not prosecute its case within the time standards set by the Supreme Court. Tex. R. Civ. P. 165a(2); *see* Tex. R. Jud. Admin. 6.1; *In re Conner*, 458 S.W.3d 532, 535 (Tex. 2015).

{*CHOOSE APPROPRIATE PARAGRAPH 10*}

{*If outside of time standard*}

10. Although this case is no longer within the Supreme Court's disposition time standards, the Court should retain the case because plaintiff has a reasonable excuse for not timely prosecuting the case. {19 *Elaborate.*}

{*If still within time standard*}

10. The Supreme Court's disposition time standards are measured from the date the defendant made its appearance. *See* Tex. R. Jud. Admin. 6.1(b). Defendant made an appearance on {20 *date*}. Under the time standards, a civil {21 *jury/nonjury*} case not involving family law should be brought to trial or final disposition within {22 *18/12*} months. *Id.* The case has been on the docket for only {23 *number*} months. The Court should retain the case on the docket because the case is still within the time standards.

C. Diligent prosecution of suit.

11. A court should not dismiss a case if the plaintiff shows that it has diligently prosecuted its suit. *See Villarreal v. San Antonio Truck & Equip.*, 994 S.W.2d 628, 630 (Tex. 1999); *Tex. Mut. Ins. Co. v. Olivas*, 323 S.W.3d 266, 274 (Tex. App.—El Paso 2010, no pet.).

12. The Court should retain this case because plaintiff has diligently prosecuted the case. {24 *Elaborate.*}

D. {25 *Add appropriate heading for other ground.*}

13. {26 *State any other reason the Court should retain the case.*}

CONCLUSION

14. {27 *Briefly summarize the motion.*}

◄ *Continued on next page* ►

PRAYER

15. For these reasons, plaintiff asks the Court to retain {㉘ *his/her/its*} suit on the docket {㉙ *add if appropriate: and deny defendant's motion to dismiss*}.

SEE: Tex. R. Civ. P. 165a
Tex. R. Jud. Admin. 6
O'Connor's Texas Rules * Civil Trials (2019), "Motion to retain," ch. 7-G, §4.1, p. 783

ADD: STYLE OF THE CASE – FORM 1B:2
SIGNATURE BLOCK – FORM 1B:3
VERIFICATION – FORM 1B:7, if necessary
CERTIFICATE OF SERVICE – FORM 1B:13

ATTACH: AFFIDAVIT – FORM 1B:8, if necessary
ORDER – FORM 1G:1

NOTE: A motion to retain should be filed if the case is already set on the court's dismissal docket. File a response to the motion to dismiss if the case is not yet on the dismissal docket.

A motion to retain should comply with any requirements stated in the notice of dismissal. *See, e.g.*, ***Villarreal v. San Antonio Truck & Equip.***, 994 S.W.2d 628, 632 (Tex.1999) (notice of dismissal only required D to appear and announce ready for trial; D did not have to show good cause); ***Nabelek v. Aldrich***, No. 14-04-00886-CV (Tex.App.—Houston [14th Dist.] 2006, no pet.) (memo op.; 6-22-06) (if court wanted D to argue good cause in motion to retain, court must have stated so in notice). If the court retains the case, it must assign a trial date, and any continuances must be by court order. Tex. R. Civ. P. 165a(1). If the court dismisses the case, the plaintiff should file a motion to reinstate. See FORM 10F:1; ***O'Connor's Texas Rules***, "Motion to Reinstate After Dismissal for Want of Prosecution," ch. 10-F, p. 970.

The motion to retain informs the court why the case should not be dismissed. The motion to reinstate informs the court why the dismissal was wrong.

DEFENDANT'S DECLARATION
INVOKING OFFER-OF-SETTLEMENT PROCEDURE

Defendant, {❶ *name*}, files this declaration to invoke the procedure for making an offer of settlement under Texas Rule of Civil Procedure 167.

INTRODUCTION

1. Plaintiff, {❷ *name*}, sued defendant, {❸ *name*}, for {❹ *state basis of suit*}.

2. This case is set for trial on {❺ *date*}.

3. {❻ *State other relevant facts about the suit.*}

DECLARATION

4. The offer-of-settlement procedure is available in this case. Tex. Civ. Prac. & Rem. Code §42.002(b), (c); Tex. R. Civ. P. 167.1. {❼ *Elaborate.*} {*See* ***O'Connor's Texas Rules****, "Availability," ch. 7-H, §2.1, p. 787.*}

5. This case involves a claim for monetary damages against defendant. Tex. Civ. Prac. & Rem. Code §42.002(a); Tex. R. Civ. P. 167.1. {❽ *Elaborate.*} {*See* ***O'Connor's Texas Rules****, "Available," ch. 7-H, §2.1.1, p. 787.*}

6. Defendant files this declaration invoking the procedure for making an offer of settlement at least 45 days before the case is set for trial. Tex. R. Civ. P. 167.2(a). {❾ *Elaborate.*} {*See* ***O'Connor's Texas Rules****, "Deadline," ch. 7-H, §3.3, p. 788.*}

SEE: Tex. R. Civ. P. 167
Tex. Civ. Prac. & Rem. Code §§42.001-42.005
O'Connor's Texas Rules * Civil Trials (2019), "Availability & Election of Settlement Procedure," ch. 7-H, §2, p. 787; "Defendant's Declaration," ch. 7-H, §3, p. 788

ADD: STYLE OF THE CASE – FORM 1B:2
SIGNATURE BLOCK – FORM 1B:3

NOTE: Only a defendant can file a declaration invoking the offer-of-settlement procedure. Tex. R. Civ. P. 167.2(a). A "defendant" includes a counterdefendant, cross-defendant, third-party defendant, or any person from whom a party seeks monetary damages. Tex. Civ. Prac. & Rem. Code §42.001(3). In a case with multiple defendants, each defendant must file a separate declaration for the procedure to apply to that defendant. *See id.* §42.002(c).

On a motion based on good cause, the court may modify the 45-day deadline by signing a pretrial order. Tex. R. Civ. P. 167.5(a).

Nothing in Texas Rule of Civil Procedure 167 provides for the withdrawal or revocation of a declaration once it has been filed.

{❶ *PARTY*}'S OFFER OF SETTLEMENT

{❷ *Party*}, {❸ *name*}, offers to settle {❹ *identify claim to be settled*} in accordance with Texas Civil Practice & Remedies Code chapter 42 and Texas Rule of Civil Procedure 167. {*See* ***O'Connor's Texas Rules****, "Settlement Offer," ch. 7-H, §4, p. 788.*}

INTRODUCTION

1. Plaintiff, {❺ *name*}, sued defendant, {❻ *name*}, for {❼ *state basis of suit*}.

2. {❽ *State other relevant facts about the suit.*}

BACKGROUND

3. This case is set for trial on {❾ *date*}.

4. On {❿ *date*}, defendant, {⓫ *name*}, filed a declaration invoking the offer-of-settlement procedure.

5. {⓬ *Party*} makes this offer of settlement more than 60 days after both {⓭ *party*} and {⓮ *adverse party*}, {⓯ *name*}, have appeared in the case. {⓰ *Elaborate.*} Tex. R. Civ. P. 167.2(e)(2).

{*CHOOSE APPROPRIATE PARAGRAPH 6*}

6. {⓱ *Party*} makes this offer of settlement more than 14 days before the case is set for a conventional trial on the merits. {⓲ *Elaborate.*} Tex. R. Civ. P. 167.2(e)(3).

6. {⓳ *Party*} makes this offer of settlement in response to an earlier settlement offer made on {⓴ *date*}. This settlement offer is made within seven days of the earlier offer. {㉑ *Elaborate.*} Tex. R. Civ. P. 167.2(e)(3).

OFFER OF SETTLEMENT

7. {㉒ *Party*} offers to settle with {㉓ *adverse party*} the following claims in accordance with Texas Civil Practice & Remedies Code chapter 42 and Texas Rule of Civil Procedure 167:

   a. {㉔ *Describe claim*} for $\{㉕ *amount*}, which represents all monetary damages claimed—including attorney fees, costs, and interest that would be recoverable as of the date of this offer—between {㉖ *party*} and {㉗ *adverse party*}. Tex. R. Civ. P. 167.2(b)(4). {*See* ***O'Connor's Texas Rules****, "Monetary claims," ch. 7-H, §4.3.2, p. 789.*}

   b. {㉘ *Continue with other claims that party offers to settle.*}

{ADD PARAGRAPH 8 IF APPLICABLE}

8. {㉙ *Party*}'s offer of settlement is subject to the following conditions: {㉚ *describe reasonable conditions for settlement, including executing releases, indemnities, or other documents*}. {*See* ***O'Connor's Texas Rules****, "Other conditions," ch. 7-H, §4.3.4, p. 789.*}

ACCEPTANCE OF OFFER

9. {㉛ *Adverse party*} may accept this settlement offer by serving written notice on {㉜ *party*} before {㉝ *state deadline for acceptance, which must be at least 14 days after the offer is served*}. Tex. Civ. Prac. & Rem. Code §42.003(a)(4); Tex. R. Civ. P. 167.2(b)(5). If the offer is not accepted by {㉞ *state deadline*}, it is deemed rejected and can serve as the basis for litigation costs under Texas Civil Practice & Remedies Code chapter 42 and Texas Rule of Civil Procedure 167. *See* Tex. Civ. Prac. & Rem. Code §42.004(a); Tex. R. Civ. P. 167.3(c), 167.4(a).

SEE: Tex. R. Civ. P. 167
Tex. Civ. Prac. & Rem. Code §§42.001-42.005
O'Connor's Texas Rules * Civil Trials (2019), "Settlement Offer," ch. 7-H, §4, p. 788

ADD: STYLE OF THE CASE – FORM 1B:2
SIGNATURE BLOCK – FORM 1B:3
CERTIFICATE OF SERVICE – FORM 1B:13

NOTE: The offer must be served on all parties to whom it is made, but it is not filed with the court. *See* Tex. Civ. Prac. & Rem. Code §42.003(a)(5), (b); Tex. R. Civ. P. 167.2(b)(6); *see also* Tex. R. Civ. P. 21a(a) (methods of service).

An offeror may designate a responsible third party or join another party after making a Rule 167 offer. *See* Tex. R. Civ. P. 167.3(d).

An offeror can recover litigation costs from a rejecting offeree if the judgment to be rendered on the claim is significantly less favorable to the offeree than the rejected offer. See ***O'Connor's Texas Rules***, "Litigation Costs," ch. 7-H, §6, p. 790.

{[1] *PARTY*}'S NOTICE OF
{[2] *WITHDRAWAL OF/OBJECTIONS TO/*
ACCEPTANCE OF/REJECTION OF} OFFER OF SETTLEMENT

{[3] *Party*}, {[4] *name*}, gives written notice of {[5] *his/her/its*} {[6] *withdrawal of/objections to/acceptance of/rejection of*} the offer of settlement. {*See* ***O'Connor's Texas Rules****, "Withdrawal, Acceptance, Objections & Rejection," ch. 7-H, §5, p. 789.*}

INTRODUCTION

1. Plaintiff, {[7] *name*}, sued defendant, {[8] *name*}, for {[9] *state basis of suit*}.

2. {[10] *State other relevant facts about the suit.*}

BACKGROUND

3. On {[11] *date*}, {[12] *plaintiff/defendant*} served an offer of settlement on {[13] *defendant/plaintiff*}.

4. The acceptance deadline stated in the offer of settlement is {[14] *date*}.

5. {[15] *State other facts relevant to the notice.*}

{[16] *WITHDRAWAL OF/OBJECTIONS TO/ACCEPTANCE OF/ REJECTION OF*} OFFER OF SETTLEMENT

{*CHOOSE APPROPRIATE PARAGRAPH 6*}

{*For withdrawal*}

6. {[17] *Party*} gives notice of the withdrawal of {[18] *his/her/its*} offer of settlement. Tex. R. Civ. P. 167.3(a). The withdrawal is effective upon service of this notice. *Id.*; *see* Tex. R. Civ. P. 21a. This notice of withdrawal is served on {[19] *adverse party*} before the offer has been accepted.

{*For objections*}

6. {[20] *Party*} gives notice of {[21] *his/her/its*} objections to the following conditions in {[22] *adverse party*}'s offer of settlement: {[23] *identify conditions and explain why they are unreasonable*}. Tex. R. Civ. P. 167.2(c). This notice of objections to the offer of settlement is served on {[24] *adverse party*} before the acceptance deadline.

{*For acceptance*}

6. {㉕ *Party*} gives notice of {㉖ *his/her/its*} acceptance of {㉗ *adverse party*}'s offer of settlement. Tex. R. Civ. P. 167.3(b). This notice of acceptance of the offer of settlement is served on {㉘ *adverse party*} before the acceptance deadline and before the offer is withdrawn. *Id.*

{*For rejection*}

6. {㉙ *Party*} gives notice of {㉚ *his/her/its*} rejection of {㉛ *adverse party*}'s offer of settlement. Tex. R. Civ. P. 167.3(c). This notice of rejection of the offer of settlement is served on {㉜ *adverse party*} before the acceptance deadline. *Id.*

SEE: Tex. R. Civ. P. 167
O'Connor's Texas Rules * Civil Trials (2019), "Withdrawal, Acceptance, Objections & Rejection," ch. 7-H, §5, p. 789

ADD: STYLE OF THE CASE – FORM 1B:2
SIGNATURE BLOCK – FORM 1B:3
CERTIFICATE OF SERVICE – FORM 1B:13

NOTE: If an offeror joins another party or designates a responsible third party after making an offer, litigation costs will not be awarded against the offeree for rejecting the offer if the offeree files an objection to the offer within 15 days after service of the pleading or designation. Tex. R. Civ. P. 167.3(d).

When the offer is accepted, either party may file the offer and acceptance and ask the court to enforce the settlement. Tex. R. Civ. P. 167.3(b).

An offeror can recover litigation costs from a rejecting offeree if the judgment to be rendered on the claim is significantly less favorable to the offeree than the rejected offer. See ***O'Connor's Texas Rules***, "Litigation Costs," ch. 7-H, §6, p. 790.

SETTLEMENT AGREEMENT & MUTUAL RELEASE

This settlement agreement and mutual release ("Agreement") is made by {❶ *party*}, {❷ *name*}, and {❸ *adverse party*}, {❹ *name*}, effective on {❺ *date*}.

RECITALS

1. Plaintiff, {❻ *name*}, sued defendant, {❼ *name*}, for {❽ *state basis of suit*} in {❾ *identify the court, cause number, and style of the case*} ("Litigation").

2. Defendant filed an answer to the suit and denied and continue to deny all the allegations made in the Litigation.

3. To avoid the uncertainties, annoyance, and expense of further litigation, the parties have agreed, without any party making any admission to any other party, to settle the disputes and controversies that are the subject of the Litigation.

AGREEMENT & RELEASES

4. Defendant, in consideration for the execution of the Agreement, agrees to pay plaintiff ${❿ *amount*} by {⓫ *date*} in full and final settlement of all of plaintiff's claims in the Litigation. {*See* ***O'Connor's Texas Rules****, "Release," ch. 7-I, §2.1, p. 792.*}

5. Defendant, in consideration for the execution of the Agreement, forever releases, acquits, and discharges plaintiff, together with plaintiff's

{*CHOOSE APPROPRIATE STATEMENT*}

{*Add if person*}

Ⓐ heirs, executors, administrators, legal representatives, successors, employees, agents, and assigns,

{*Add if partnership*}

Ⓑ owners, partners, shareholders, employees, agents, legal representatives, insurers, and assigns,

{*Add if corporation*}

Ⓒ officers, directors, employees, agents, legal representatives, subsidiary organizations, parent organizations, successor corporations, insurers, and assigns,

and all other persons, firms, or corporations who might be liable, from all claims, demands, charges, and costs of court, including but not limited to attorney fees and causes of action of whatever nature, on any legal theory arising from the circumstances described in plaintiff's last live pleading, and from all liability and damages of any kind, known or unknown, arising from the events that gave rise to the Litigation, whether in contract or in tort.

{*ADD PARAGRAPH 6 IF APPLICABLE*}

6. Plaintiff, in consideration for the execution of the Agreement and defendant's agreement to pay the settlement amount, agrees to voluntarily dismiss the Litigation with prejudice.

7. Plaintiff, in consideration for the execution of the Agreement and defendant's agreement to pay the settlement amount, forever releases, acquits, and discharges defendant, together with defendant's

{*CHOOSE APPROPRIATE STATEMENT*}

{*Add if person*}

A heirs, executors, administrators, legal representatives, successors, employees, agents, and assigns,

{*Add if partnership*}

B owners, partners, shareholders, employees, agents, legal representatives, insurers, and assigns,

{*Add if corporation*}

C officers, directors, employees, agents, legal representatives, subsidiary organizations, parent organizations, successor corporations, insurers, and assigns,

and all other persons, firms, or corporations who might be liable, from all claims, demands, charges, and costs of court, including but not limited to attorney fees and causes of action of whatever nature, on any legal theory arising from the circumstances described in plaintiff's last live pleading, and from all liability and damages of any kind, known or unknown, arising from the events that gave rise to the Litigation, whether in contract or in tort.

Continued on next page

8. Plaintiff accepts the consideration in full satisfaction of all damages or claims that are owed to {12 *him/her/it*} or that may be owed to {13 *him/her/it*} by defendant. Plaintiff understands this is a compromise and settlement of all matters alleged by plaintiff in {14 *his/her/its*} petition against defendant.

9. Plaintiff understands {15 *his/her/its*} acceptance of the consideration is in full accord and satisfaction of the claims made in the Litigation, and defendant's payment of consideration is not an admission of defendant's liability.

10. In executing the Agreement, plaintiff acknowledges that {16 *he/she/it*} is not relying on any statement or representation of defendant or any of {17 *his/her/its*} agents regarding the matters in dispute. Plaintiff is relying on {18 *his/her/its*} own judgment and is represented by an attorney in this matter. Plaintiff's attorney read and explained the contents of the Agreement to plaintiff and explained the legal consequences of the Agreement. Plaintiff understands that the Agreement will operate as a full, complete, and final release and settlement of all claims in the Litigation.

11. Plaintiff acknowledges that {19 *he/she/it*} read the Agreement and that it is a complete, written statement of the terms and conditions of the settlement. Plaintiff signs the Agreement under {20 *his/her/its*} own free will and accord.

{*ADD PARAGRAPH 12 IF APPLICABLE*}

12. The parties agree to {21 *memorialize this release by an agreed judgment that will be filed in the records of the case/dismiss this suit with prejudice*}.

13. Each party will be responsible for its own attorney fees and court costs.

OTHER PROVISIONS

14. The Agreement reflects the entire agreement between the parties. There are no other agreements, either written or oral, and the execution of the Agreement supersedes all earlier representations, negotiations, or agreements about the Litigation.

15. The Agreement will be governed and construed by the laws of the State of Texas.

16. {*For other provisions that can be included in a settlement agreement, see* ***O'Connor's Texas Rules****, "Other provisions," ch. 7-I, §2.2, p. 794.*}

Executed on _______________, 20___.

____
{22 *Name of party*}

____
{23 *Name of attorney for party*}
Texas Bar No. {24 _____}
{25 *Address 1*}
{26 *Address 2*}
{27 *City, state, zip code*}
Tel. {28 __________}
Fax {29 __________}
{30 *E-mail address*}

ATTORNEY FOR {31 *PARTY*},
{32 *NAME OF PARTY*}

____
{33 *Name of adverse party*}

____
{34 *Name of attorney for adverse party*}
Texas Bar No. {35 _____}
{36 *Address 1*}
{37 *Address 2*}
{38 *City, state, zip code*}
Tel. {39 __________}
Fax {40 __________}
{41 *E-mail address*}

ATTORNEY FOR {42 *ADVERSE PARTY*},
{43 *NAME OF ADVERSE PARTY*}

Continued on next page

SEE: Tex. R. Civ. P. 11
O'Connor's Texas Rules * Civil Trials (2019), "Provisions in Settlement Agreement," ch. 7-I, §2, p. 792

ADD: STYLE OF THE CASE – FORM 1B:2

NOTE: When the release is a separate instrument from the settlement agreement, the description of the released claims must be stated in identical language in both documents.

If the parties agree to memorialize the settlement in an agreed judgment, the judgment should accurately state the terms of the settlement, but it is not necessary for the judgment to incorporate all the terms of the settlement agreement; even unincorporated terms can be enforced. ***Compania Financiara Libano, S.A. v. Simmons***, 53 S.W.3d 365, 368 (Tex.2001).

A release is not a covenant not to sue and does not bar future suits. *See* ***National Prop. Holdings, L.P. v. Westergren***, 453 S.W.3d 419, 428-29 (Tex.2015). If the parties want the settlement agreement to include a contractual obligation not to sue in the future such that any suit by one party would entitle the other party to damages for breach of the agreement, the agreement or the release must specifically include language to that effect. *See id.* at 428.

Settlement with an incapacitated person, which includes minors and adults who are unable to care for themselves, must be judicially approved. *See* Tex. R. Civ. P. 44(2), 173.4(c).

Chapter 8. The Trial

Table of Contents

{❶ *PARTY*}'S MOTION TO REALIGN PARTIES

{❷ *Party*}, {❸ *name*}, asks the Court to make a proper alignment of the parties. {*See* ***O'Connor's Texas Rules****, "Multiparty case," ch. 8-A, §7.2.2, p. 813.*}

INTRODUCTION

1. Plaintiff, {❹ *name*}, sued defendant, {❺ *name*}, for {❻ *state basis of suit*}.

2. Defendant answered, asserting the defenses of {❼ *identify defenses and specify any other parties, defenses, or claims involved in the case*}.

3. {❽ *State other relevant facts about the suit.*}

BACKGROUND

4. This case is set for trial on {❾ *date*}.

5. {❿ *State other facts relevant to the motion.*}

ARGUMENT & AUTHORITIES

6. In a case involving multiple parties on either or both sides of the dispute, the court must determine whether the parties are properly aligned before it can allocate peremptory strikes. *See* Tex. R. Civ. P. 233; *Scurlock Oil Co. v. Smithwick*, 724 S.W.2d 1, 5 (Tex. 1986); *Pojar v. Cifre*, 199 S.W.3d 317, 324 (Tex. App.—Corpus Christi 2006, pet. denied). A "side" is made up of all parties who have common interests on the matters to be submitted to the jury, and does not depend on designations such as "plaintiff" or "defendant." Tex. R. Civ. P. 233. Thus, opposing parties may be realigned to the same side when there is an issue on which they have a common interest such that they may no longer be considered adversaries. *See, e.g.*, *Moore v. Altra Energy Techs. Inc.*, 321 S.W.3d 727, 747 (Tex. App.—Houston [14th Dist.] 2010, pet. denied) (trial court should have aligned codefendant with plaintiff and given each side same number of strikes); *Am. Cyanamid Co. v. Frankson*, 732 S.W.2d 648, 651 (Tex. App.—Corpus Christi 1987, writ ref'd n.r.e.) (codefendants expected to settle with plaintiff were aligned with plaintiff and received no jury strikes). {*See* ***O'Connor's Texas Rules****, "Are parties properly aligned?," ch. 8-A, §7.2.2(1), p. 813.*}

7. {⓫ *Party*} asks the Court to realign {⓬ *coparty*}, {⓭ *name*}, on the same side as {⓮ *plaintiff(s)/defendant(s)*} for purposes of allocating peremptory strikes because the parties have a common interest on the matters to be submitted to the jury. {⓯ *Elaborate.*}

◄ *Continued on next page* ►

CONCLUSION

8. {⑯ *Briefly summarize the motion.*}

PRAYER

9. For these reasons, {⑰ *party*} asks the Court to grant this motion and realign the parties.

SEE: Tex. R. Civ. P. 233
O'Connor's Texas Rules * Civil Trials (2019), "Multiparty case," ch. 8-A, §7.2.2, p. 813

ADD: STYLE OF THE CASE – FORM 1B:2
SIGNATURE BLOCK – FORM 1B:3
CERTIFICATE OF CONFERENCE – FORM 1B:12, if necessary
CERTIFICATE OF SERVICE – FORM 1B:13

ATTACH: AFFIDAVIT – FORM 1B:8, if necessary
NOTICE OF HEARING OR SUBMISSION – FORM 1E:1
ORDER – FORM 1G:1

NOTE: A court will not determine whether parties on the same side of the suit are antagonistic to each other until after voir dire. ***Garcia v. Central Power & Light Co.***, 704 S.W.2d 734, 737 (Tex.1986). See ***O'Connor's Texas Rules***, "Are aligned parties antagonistic to each other?," ch. 8-A, §7.2.2(2), p. 814.

If the court decides that the parties on the same side are not antagonistic to each other, each side must receive the same number of strikes—that is, six strikes for district court or three strikes for county court. *See* Tex. R. Civ. P. 233; ***Garcia***, 704 S.W.2d at 736. If the court decides that the parties on the same side are antagonistic to each other, each party gets its own set of strikes. *See* ***Patterson Dental Co. v. Dunn***, 592 S.W.2d 914, 918 (Tex.1979) (it is error to require antagonistic parties on same side to share six strikes).

If the allocation of strikes would result in one party or side gaining an unfair advantage, a party can—before the exercise of strikes—make a motion to equalize the peremptory strikes. Tex. R. Civ. P. 233. The motion should be made orally after voir dire. *See, e.g.*, ***Patterson Dental***, 592 S.W.2d at 917 (party objected to court's allocation of strikes and made oral motion to equalize); ***Texas Commerce Bank Reagan v. Lebco Constructors, Inc.***, 865 S.W.2d 68, 77-78 (Tex.App.—Corpus Christi 1993, writ denied) (pretrial motion to equalize did not preserve error when no objection to court's allocation of strikes was made after voir dire).

{1 *PARTY*}'S RESPONSE TO {2 *COPARTY*}'S MOTION TO REALIGN PARTIES

{3 *Party*}, {4 *name*}, asks the Court to deny {5 *coparty*} {6 *name*}'s motion to realign the parties.

INTRODUCTION

1. Plaintiff, {7 *name*}, sued defendant, {8 *name*}, for {9 *state basis of suit*}.

2. Defendant answered, asserting the defenses of {10 *identify defenses and specify any other parties, defenses, or claims involved in the case*}.

3. {11 *State other relevant facts about this suit.*}

BACKGROUND

4. This case is set for trial on {12 *date*}.

5. On {13 *date*}, {14 *coparty*}, {15 *name*}, filed a motion to align {16 *party*}, {17 *name*}, with {18 *plaintiff(s)/defendant(s)*}.

6. {19 *State other facts relevant to the response.*}

ARGUMENT & AUTHORITIES

7. In a case involving multiple parties on either or both sides of the dispute, the court must determine whether the parties are properly aligned before it can allocate peremptory strikes. *See* Tex. R. Civ. P. 233; *Scurlock Oil Co. v. Smithwick*, 724 S.W.2d 1, 5 (Tex. 1986); *Pojar v. Cifre*, 199 S.W.3d 317, 324 (Tex. App.—Corpus Christi 2006, pet. denied). A "side" is made up of all parties who have common interests on the matters to be submitted to the jury. Tex. R. Civ. P. 233. When allocating strikes, a court should presume that the litigants on the same side of the docket are one "party," and should not realign opposing parties unless they have a common interest on jury issues. *See Patterson Dental Co. v. Dunn*, 592 S.W.2d 914, 917 (Tex. 1979); *see, e.g., Am. Cyanamid Co. v. Frankson*, 732 S.W.2d 648, 652 (Tex. App.—Corpus Christi 1987, writ ref'd n.r.e.) (Mary Carter agreement that was not accepted by plaintiff was insufficient to align codefendant with plaintiff). {*See* ***O'Connor's Texas Rules***, *"Are parties properly aligned?," ch. 8-A, §7.2.2(1), p. 813.*}

8. The Court should not realign {20 *party*} with {21 *plaintiff(s)/defendant(s)*} because the parties do not have a common interest on the matters to be submitted to the jury. Specifically, {22 *explain why parties do not have common interest, e.g., parties have no settlement agreement*}.

◄ *Continued on next page* ►

FORM 8A:2

CONCLUSION

9. {[23] *Briefly summarize the response.*}

PRAYER

10. For these reasons, {[24] *party*} asks the Court to deny {[25] *coparty*}'s motion to realign the parties.

SEE: Tex. R. Civ. P. 233
O'Connor's Texas Rules * Civil Trials (2019), "Multiparty case," ch. 8-A, §7.2.2, p. 813

ADD: STYLE OF THE CASE – FORM 1B:2
SIGNATURE BLOCK – FORM 1B:3
CERTIFICATE OF CONFERENCE – FORM 1B:12, if necessary
CERTIFICATE OF SERVICE – FORM 1B:13

ATTACH: AFFIDAVIT – FORM 1B:8, if necessary
ORDER – FORM 1G:1

NOTE: A court will not determine whether parties on the same side of the suit are antagonistic to each other until after voir dire. ***Garcia v. Central Power & Light Co.***, 704 S.W.2d 734, 737 (Tex.1986). See ***O'Connor's Texas Rules***, "Are aligned parties antagonistic to each other?," ch. 8-A, §7.2.2(2), p. 814.

If the court decides that the parties on the same side are not antagonistic to each other, each side must receive the same number of strikes—that is, six strikes for district court or three strikes for county court. *See* Tex. R. Civ. P. 233; ***Garcia***, 704 S.W.2d at 736. If the court decides that the parties on the same side are antagonistic to each other, each party gets its own set of strikes. *See* ***Patterson Dental Co. v. Dunn***, 592 S.W.2d 914, 918 (Tex.1979) (it is error to require antagonistic parties on same side to share six strikes).

DEFENDANT'S MOTION TO OPEN & CLOSE

Defendant, {❶ *name*}, asks the Court to allow {❷ *him/her/it*} to open and close the argument and evidence in the trial of this case.

INTRODUCTION

1. Plaintiff, {❸ *name*}, sued defendant, {❹ *name*}, for {❺ *state basis of suit*}.

2. Defendant answered, asserting the defenses of {❻ *identify defenses*}.

3. {❼ *State other relevant facts about the suit.*}

BACKGROUND

4. {❽ *State facts relevant to the motion.*}

ARGUMENT & AUTHORITIES

{*CHOOSE APPROPRIATE PARAGRAPHS 5-8*}

{*When defendant has burden on entire case*}

5. A defendant has the right to open and close the argument and evidence when the defendant has the burden of proof on the entire case under the pleadings. *See* Tex. R. Civ. P. 265(a), (b), 266, 269(a); *Pace Corp. v. Jackson*, 284 S.W.2d 340, 350 (Tex. 1955). {*See* ***O'Connor's Texas Rules****, "Burden of proof," ch. 8-B, §2.2.1, p. 822.*}

6. The Court should permit defendant to open and close the argument and evidence in this case because {❾ *he/she/it*} has the burden of proof on the entire case under the pleadings. Specifically, defendant has the burden on {❿ *list issues*}.

{*When defendant admits plaintiff's right to recover, subject to its defenses*}

7. A defendant has the right to open and close the argument and evidence if, before trial begins, defendant admits that plaintiff is entitled to recover, except to the extent defendant proves the defensive allegations. Tex. R. Civ. P. 266; *see Seigler v. Seigler*, 391 S.W.2d 403, 404 (Tex. 1965). {*See* ***O'Connor's Texas Rules****, "Admission under TRCP 266," ch. 8-B, §2.2.2, p. 822.*}

8. Defendant admits that plaintiff will recover for the claims in {⓫ *his/her/its*} {⓬ *identify petition, e.g., original, second amended*} petition unless those claims are defeated by proof at trial supporting defendant's defensive allegations in {⓭ *his/her/its*} answer. Defendant asks that this admission be entered on record.

◄ Continued on next page ►

CONCLUSION

9. {⓮ *Briefly summarize the motion.*}

PRAYER

10. For these reasons, defendant asks the Court to allow defendant to open and close the argument and evidence in the trial of this case.

SEE: Tex. R. Civ. P. 265(a), (b), 266, 269(a)
O'Connor's Texas Rules * Civil Trials (2019), "Right to Make First Opening Statement," ch. 8-B, §2, p. 822

ADD: STYLE OF THE CASE – FORM 1B:2
SIGNATURE BLOCK – FORM 1B:3
CERTIFICATE OF CONFERENCE – FORM 1B:12, if necessary
CERTIFICATE OF SERVICE – FORM 1B:13

ATTACH: AFFIDAVIT – FORM 1B:8, if necessary
NOTICE OF HEARING OR SUBMISSION – FORM 1E:1
ORDER – FORM 1G:1

PLAINTIFF'S RESPONSE TO DEFENDANT'S MOTION TO OPEN & CLOSE

Plaintiff, {❶ *name*}, asks the Court to deny defendant's motion to open and close the argument and evidence in the trial of this case.

INTRODUCTION

1. Plaintiff, {❷ *name*}, sued defendant, {❸ *name*}, for {❹ *state basis of suit*}.

2. Defendant answered, asserting the defenses of {❺ *identify defenses*}.

3. {❻ *State other relevant facts about the suit.*}

BACKGROUND

4. {❼ *State facts relevant to the response.*}

ARGUMENT & AUTHORITIES

5. A defendant does not have the right to open and close the argument and evidence unless (1) the defendant bears the burden of proof on the entire case under the pleadings or (2) before trial begins, the defendant admits that the plaintiff is entitled to recover on the plaintiff's claims, except to the extent that the defendant proves {❽ *his/her/its*} defensive allegations. *See* Tex. R. Civ. P. 265(a), (b), 266, 269(a); *Seigler v. Seigler*, 391 S.W.2d 403, 404 (Tex. 1965); *Pace Corp. v. Jackson*, 284 S.W.2d 340, 350 (Tex. 1955); *Ocean Transp., Inc. v. Greycas, Inc.*, 878 S.W.2d 256, 269 (Tex. App.—Corpus Christi 1994, writ denied). {*See* ***O'Connor's Texas Rules****, "Burden of proof," ch. 8-B, §2.2.1, p. 822; "Admission under TRCP 266," ch. 8-B, §2.2.2, p. 822.*}

{*CHOOSE APPROPRIATE PARAGRAPHS 6-10*}

{*When defendant claims to have burden on entire case*}

6. Defendant should not be granted the right to open and close the argument and evidence in this case because {❾ *he/she/it*} does not bear the burden of proof on the entire case. Specifically, defendant does not bear the burden of proof on {❿ *identify issues on which plaintiff has the burden of proof, e.g., request for attorney fees*}. Plaintiff bears the burden of proof on {⓫ *this issue/these issues*}.

◄ Continued on next page ►

FORM 8B:2

{*When defendant admits plaintiff's right to recover, subject to its defenses*}

7. Defendant filed {⓬ *his/her/its*} admission of liability {⓭ *state when admission was filed, e.g., after the parties had announced ready, after voir dire had begun*}. Thus, the trial had begun, and defendant's admission was too late under Texas Rule of Civil Procedure 266.

8. Contrary to defendant's allegations, all issues of fact in this case are not settled. Tex. R. Civ. P. 266. {⓮ *Specify fact issues that have not been settled.*} Thus, defendant is not entitled to invoke Texas Rule of Civil Procedure 266.

9. Contrary to defendant's allegations, defendant has not admitted unequivocally that plaintiff is entitled to recover on all {⓯ *his/her/its*} theories of liability. Specifically, defendant has not admitted {⓰ *specify issues defendant has not admitted*}.

10. Even when a defendant stipulates liability, a plaintiff may still be permitted to open and close the argument and evidence if the plaintiff has pleaded for attorney fees. *See 4M Linen & Unif. Supply Co. v. W.P. Ballard & Co.*, 793 S.W.2d 320, 324-25 (Tex. App.—Houston [1st Dist.] 1990, writ denied). Plaintiff pleaded for attorney fees and bears the burden of proof on that issue.

CONCLUSION

11. {⓱ *Briefly summarize the response.*}

PRAYER

12. For these reasons, plaintiff asks the Court to deny defendant's motion and allow plaintiff to open and close the argument and evidence in the trial of this case.

SEE: Tex. R. Civ. P. 265(a), (b), 266, 269(a)
O'Connor's Texas Rules * Civil Trials (2019), "Right to Make First Opening Statement," ch. 8-B, §2, p. 822

ADD: STYLE OF THE CASE – FORM 1B:2
SIGNATURE BLOCK – FORM 1B:3
CERTIFICATE OF SERVICE – FORM 1B:13

ATTACH: AFFIDAVIT – FORM 1B:8, if necessary
ORDER – FORM 1G:1

STIPULATION ON {❶ *IDENTIFY STIPULATION ON EVIDENCE*}

{❷ *Party*}, {❸ *name*}, and {❹ *adverse party*}, {❺ *name*}, through their attorneys, have agreed to the following stipulations:

{*CHOOSE APPROPRIATE STIPULATIONS*}

1. The parties agree that {❻ *identify document or other exhibit*} is authentic and no custodian of records or other witness is needed to testify about its authenticity.

2. The parties agree that {❼ *identify document or other exhibit*} will be admitted into evidence without objection.

3. The parties agree that {❽ *name of expert*} is qualified to give expert testimony on the subject of {❾ *identify subject of testimony*}.

4. {❿ *Identify other stipulations agreed to by the parties.*}

SEE: Tex. R. Civ. P. 11 (agreements between attorneys)
O'Connor's Texas Rules * Civil Trials (2019), "Distinction Between Agreed Statement & Stipulations," ch. 7-E, §2, p. 768

ADD: STYLE OF THE CASE – FORM 1B:2
SIGNATURE BLOCK FOR AGREED MOTIONS – FORM 1B:4

NOTE: **Although this form can be used to stipulate to evidence, it is not the correct form to submit a case on an agreed statement of facts under Texas Rule of Civil Procedure 263. For that form, see FORM 7E:1. For agreements on discovery matters, see FORMS 6A:1, 6A:3, 6A:6, and 6A:23.**

BUSINESS-RECORDS AFFIDAVIT

STATE OF TEXAS §
{❶_______} COUNTY §

Before me, the undersigned notary, on this day personally appeared {❷ *name of affiant*}, the affiant, whose identity is known to me. After I administered an oath, affiant testified as follows:

1. "My name is {❸ *name of affiant*}. I am over 18 years of age, of sound mind, and capable of making this affidavit. The facts stated in this affidavit are within my personal knowledge and are true and correct.

2. "I am the {❹ *identify qualified witness, e.g., custodian of the records*} of {❺ *name of business entity*} and am familiar with the manner in which its records are created and maintained by virtue of my duties and responsibilities.

3. "Attached to this affidavit are {❻ *number*} pages of records from {❼ *name of business entity*}. These are the original records or exact duplicates of the original records.

{*CHOOSE APPROPRIATE PARAGRAPH 4*}

4. "The records were made at or near the time of each act, event, condition, opinion, or diagnosis that was recorded.

4. "It is the regular practice of {❽ *name of business entity*} to make this type of record at or near the time of each act, event, condition, opinion, or diagnosis that was recorded.

{*CHOOSE APPROPRIATE PARAGRAPH 5*}

5. "The records were made by, or from information transmitted by, persons with knowledge of the matters set forth in the record.

5. "It is the regular practice of {❾ *name of business entity*} for this type of record to be made by, or from information transmitted by, persons with knowledge of the matters set forth in the record.

{*CHOOSE APPROPRIATE PARAGRAPH 6*}

6. "The records were kept in the course of regularly conducted business activity.

6. "It is the regular practice of {❿ *name of business entity*} to keep this type of record in the course of regularly conducted business activity.

7. "It is the regular practice of the business activity to make the records."

____
{⓫ *Name of affiant*}

Sworn to and subscribed before me by {⓬ *name of affiant*} on __________, 20___.

____
Notary Public in and for
the State of Texas

SEE: Tex. R. Evid. 803(6), (7), 902(10)(B)
O'Connor's Texas Rules * Civil Trials (2019), "Business records by affidavit," ch. 8-C, §8.4.4(1), p. 833

ADD: STYLE OF THE CASE – FORM 1B:2
CERTIFICATE OF SERVICE – FORM 1B:13

ATTACH: Business records

NOTE: A party can prove specific information from business records with an affidavit from the custodian of the records. *See* Tex. R. Evid. 803(6)(D), 902(10).

A party must serve the affidavit and business records on each party to the case at least 14 days before trial. Tex. R. Evid. 902(10)(A). Even if the service requirements are not met, the court may order that a business record be treated as presumptively authentic if good cause is shown. Tex. R. Evid. 902(10).

See notes under FORM 1B:8.

FORM 8C:2

AFFIDAVIT OF COST OF SERVICES BY PROVIDER

STATE OF TEXAS §
{❶ _______} COUNTY §

Before me, the undersigned notary, on this day personally appeared {❷ *name of affiant*}, the affiant, whose identity is known to me. After I administered an oath, affiant testified as follows:

1. "My name is {❸ *name of affiant*}. I am over 18 years of age, of sound mind, and capable of making this affidavit. The facts stated in this affidavit are within my personal knowledge and are true and correct.

2. "On {❹ *date*}, I provided a service to {❺ *name of recipient of the service*}. An itemized statement of the service and the charge for the service is attached to this affidavit and is a part of this affidavit.

3. "The service I provided was necessary, and the amount I charged for the service was reasonable at the time and place the service was provided."

____
{❻ *Name of affiant*}

Sworn to and subscribed before me by {❼ *name of affiant*} on __________, 20___.

____
Notary Public in and for
the State of Texas

SEE: Tex. Civ. Prac. & Rem. Code §§18.001, 18.002(a)
O'Connor's Texas Rules * Civil Trials (2019), "Affidavit for past expenses," ch. 8-C, §8.4.4(2), p. 834

ADD: STYLE OF THE CASE – FORM 1B:2
CERTIFICATE OF SERVICE – FORM 1B:13

ATTACH: Itemized statement of services and charges

Form 8C:3 Affidavit of Cost of Services by Provider

NOTE: A party can prove the necessity of services and the reasonableness of the cost of the services with an affidavit from the provider of the services. *See* Tex. Civ. Prac. & Rem. Code §18.001(b), (c)(2)(A).

The statutory form from Texas Civil Practice & Remedies Code §18.002 cannot be used to establish the causal link between the event that the case is based on and the resulting damages. ***Hong v. Bennett***, 209 S.W.3d 795, 804 n.4 (Tex.App.—Fort Worth 2006, no pet.); *see* ***Barrajas v. VIA Metro. Transit Auth.***, 945 S.W.2d 207, 208 n.1 (Tex.App.—San Antonio 1997, no writ); ***Beauchamp v. Hambrick***, 901 S.W.2d 747, 749 (Tex.App.—Eastland 1995, no writ).

The affidavit must be served on each party at least 30 days before evidence is first presented at trial. Tex. Civ. Prac. & Rem. Code §18.001(d).

Records attached to the affidavit do not need to be filed with the court clerk before trial begins, except as provided by the Texas Rules of Evidence. Tex. Civ. Prac. & Rem. Code §18.001(d).

This affidavit cannot be used in a suit on a sworn account. Tex. Civ. Prac. & Rem. Code §18.001(a).

See notes under FORM 1B:8.

☆

AFFIDAVIT OF COST OF SERVICES BY CUSTODIAN

STATE OF TEXAS §
{❶ ______} COUNTY §

Before me, the undersigned notary, on this day personally appeared {❷ *name of affiant*}, the affiant, whose identity is known to me. After I administered an oath, affiant testified as follows:

1. "My name is {❸ *name of affiant*}. I am over 18 years of age, of sound mind, and capable of making this affidavit. The facts stated in this affidavit are within my personal knowledge and are true and correct.

2. "I am the person in charge of the records for {❹ *name of person who provided the service*}. Attached to this affidavit are records that provide an itemized statement of the service and the charge for the service that {❺ *name of person who provided the service*} provided to {❻ *name of recipient of the service*} on {❼ *date*}. The attached records are a part of the affidavit.

3. "The attached records are kept by me in the regular course of business. The information contained in the records was transmitted to me in the regular course of business by {❽ *name of person who provided the service*} or an employee or representative of {❾ *name of person who provided the service*}, who had personal knowledge of the information. The records were made at or near the time or reasonably soon after the time the service was provided. The records are the originals or exact duplicates of the originals.

4. "The service provided was necessary, and the amount charged for the service was reasonable at the time and place the service was provided."

____
{❿ *Name of affiant*}

Sworn to and subscribed before me by {⓫ *name of affiant*} on __________, 20___.

____
Notary Public in and for
the State of Texas

FORM 8C:4

SEE: Tex. Civ. Prac. & Rem. Code §§18.001, 18.002(b)
O'Connor's Texas Rules * Civil Trials (2019), "Affidavit for past expenses," ch. 8-C, §8.4.4(2), p. 834

ADD: STYLE OF THE CASE – FORM 1B:2
CERTIFICATE OF SERVICE – FORM 1B:13

ATTACH: Records, including itemized statement of services and charges

NOTE: A party can prove the necessity of services and the reasonableness of the cost of the services with an affidavit from the custodian of the records. *See* Tex. Civ. Prac. & Rem. Code §18.001(b), (c)(2)(B).

This statutory form from Texas Civil Practice & Remedies Code §18.002 cannot be used to establish the causal link between the event that the case is based on and the resulting damages. ***Hong v. Bennett***, 209 S.W.3d 795, 804 n.4 (Tex.App.—Fort Worth 2006, no pet.); *see* ***Barrajas v. VIA Metro. Transit Auth.***, 945 S.W.2d 207, 208 n.1 (Tex.App.—San Antonio 1997, no writ); ***Beauchamp v. Hambrick***, 901 S.W.2d 747, 749 (Tex.App.—Eastland 1995, no writ).

The affidavit must be served on each party at least 30 days before evidence is first presented at trial. Tex. Civ. Prac. & Rem. Code §18.001(d).

Records attached to the affidavit do not need to be filed with the court clerk before trial begins, except as provided by the Texas Rules of Evidence. Tex. Civ. Prac. & Rem. Code §18.001(d).

This affidavit cannot be used in a suit on a sworn account. Tex. Civ. Prac. & Rem. Code §18.001(a).

See notes under FORM 1B:8.

AFFIDAVIT OF COST OF SERVICES – MEDICAL RECORDS

STATE OF TEXAS §
{❶ _______} COUNTY §

Before me, the undersigned notary, on this day personally appeared {❷ *name of affiant*}, the affiant, whose identity is known to me. After I administered an oath, affiant testified as follows:

1. "My name is {❸ *name of affiant*}. I am over 18 years of age, of sound mind, and capable of making this affidavit. The facts stated in this affidavit are within my personal knowledge and are true and correct.

2. "I am the custodian of records for {❹ *name of medical provider*}.

3. "Attached to this affidavit are records that contain an itemized statement of the service and the charge for the service that {❺ *name of medical provider*} provided to {❻ *name of patient*} on {❼ *date service was provided*}. The attached records are a part of this affidavit.

4. "These records are kept by {❽ *name of medical provider*} in the regular course of business, and it was the regular course of business of {❾ *name of medical provider*} for an employee or representative of {❿ *name of medical provider*}, with knowledge of the service provided, to make these records or to transmit the information to be included in them. The records were made at or near the time of the service or reasonably soon after it was provided. The records attached to this affidavit are the originals or duplicates of the originals.

5. "The service provided was necessary, and the amount charged for the service was reasonable at the time and place that the service was provided.

6. "The total amount of the charge for the service was ${⓫ *amount*}.

7. "The amount adjusted or credited was ${⓬ *amount*}.

8. "The total amount paid for the service was ${⓭ *amount*}. The amount currently unpaid but for which {⓮ *name of medical provider*} has a right to be paid after any adjustments or credits is ${⓯ *amount*}."

____
{⓰ *Name of affiant*}

Sworn to and subscribed before me by {⓱ *name of affiant*} on __________, 20___.

____
Notary Public in and for
the State of Texas

SEE: Tex. Civ. Prac. & Rem. Code §18.002(b-1)
O'Connor's Texas Rules * Civil Trials (2019), "Affidavit for past expenses," ch. 8-C, §8.4.4(2), p. 834

ADD: STYLE OF THE CASE – FORM 1B:2
CERTIFICATE OF SERVICE – FORM 1B:13

ATTACH: Records, including itemized statement of services and charges

NOTE: A party can prove the necessity of past medical services and the reasonableness of the expenses for those services with an affidavit from the provider of the services or from a custodian of the records that show the services provided and the charges incurred. *See* Tex. Civ. Prac. & Rem. Code §18.001(c)(2). If the affiant is a custodian of records, she does not have to be the custodian for the medical provider who performed the services. *E.g.*, ***Gunn v. McCoy***, 554 S.W.3d 645, 672 (Tex.2018) (affidavits from subrogation agents for health-insurance carriers that paid P's medical expenses were sufficient evidence). See ***O'Connor's Texas Rules***, "For medical expenses," ch. 8-C, §8.4.4(2)(a)[3], p. 834.

The affidavit must be served on each party at least 30 days before evidence is first presented at trial. Tex. Civ. Prac. & Rem. Code §18.001(d).

Records attached to the affidavit do not need to be filed with the court clerk before trial begins, except as provided by the Texas Rules of Evidence. Tex. Civ. Prac. & Rem. Code §18.001(d).

See notes under FORM 1B:8.

COUNTERAFFIDAVIT TO COST-OF-SERVICES AFFIDAVIT

STATE OF TEXAS §
{❶ _______} COUNTY §

Before me, the undersigned notary, on this day personally appeared {❷ *name of affiant*}, the affiant, whose identity is known to me. After I administered an oath, affiant testified as follows:

1. "My name is {❸ *name of affiant*}. I am over 18 years of age, of sound mind, and capable of making this affidavit. The facts stated in this affidavit are within my personal knowledge and are true and correct.

2. "My education, training, experience, and other expertise qualify me to make this affidavit. {❹ *Describe how affiant's training and experience qualify the affiant to give an opinion about the reasonableness and necessity of the particular services and charges. E.g., the services received by plaintiff, as documented in the affidavit of William Willis, custodian of records for Willis Pharmacy, involved the proper filling and dispensing of medications according to a physician's prescription. I am a licensed pharmacist in the State of Texas and have had over ten years of experience in dispensing prescription medications to customers, including the medication prescribed to plaintiff.*} I attach to this affidavit a copy of my résumé, incorporate that résumé into this affidavit by reference, and attest that every statement in that résumé is true and correct.

3. "I have read the affidavit filed in this case by {❺ *name of affiant in affidavit being controverted*}, including the itemized statement of the service and the charge for the service.

{*CHOOSE APPROPRIATE PARAGRAPHS 4-5 & CLOSE QUOTES*}

4. "The service that {❻ *name of person who provided the service*} provided to {❼ *name of recipient of the service*} was not necessary because {❽ *specifically explain why service was not necessary*}.

FORM 8C:6

5. "The charge for the service that {❾ *name of person who provided the service*} provided to {❿ *name of recipient of the service*} was not reasonable because {⓫ *specifically explain why charge was not reasonable*}.

____
{⓬ *Name of affiant*}

Sworn to and subscribed before me by {⓭ *name of affiant*} on __________, 20___.

____
Notary Public in and for
the State of Texas

SEE: Tex. Civ. Prac. & Rem. Code §18.001(e), (f)
O'Connor's Texas Rules * Civil Trials (2019), "Affidavit for past expenses," ch. 8-C, §8.4.4(2), p. 834

ADD: STYLE OF THE CASE – FORM 1B:2
CERTIFICATE OF SERVICE – FORM 1B:13

ATTACH: Résumé of affiant

NOTE: To controvert a claim in an affidavit concerning cost and necessity of services, the counteraffidavit must show (1) the affiant is qualified as an expert to contravene the particular service and charge involved and (2) the specific reason why the service was not necessary or why the charge was unreasonable. *See* Tex. Civ. Prac. & Rem. Code §18.001(f); ***Turner v. Peril***, 50 S.W.3d 742, 747 (Tex.App.—Dallas 2001, pet. denied). The counteraffidavit must be served on each party or each party's attorney (1) no later than 30 days after receipt of a copy of the affidavit of cost of services and at least 14 days before evidence is first presented at the trial, or (2) with leave of the court, anytime before the commencement of evidence at trial. Tex. Civ. Prac. & Rem. Code §18.001(e).

See notes under FORM 1B:8.

FORMAL BILL OF EXCEPTION

{*CHOOSE APPROPRIATE OPENING PARAGRAPH*}

{❶ *Party*}, {❷ *name*}, presents this bill of exception to the Court and asks the Court to approve, sign, and file the bill as part of the record in this case. {*See **O'Connor's Texas Rules**, "Formal Bill of Exception," ch. 8-E, §4, p. 847.*}

{❸ *Party*}, {❹ *name*}, and {❺ *adverse party*}, {❻ *name*}, present this bill of exception to the Court and ask the Court to approve, sign, and file the bill as part of the record in this case. {*See **O'Connor's Texas Rules**, "Formal Bill of Exception," ch. 8-E, §4, p. 847.*}

1. On {❼ *date*}, during the trial of this case, {❽ *describe the action, order, or ruling of the court to which movant objected, including the circumstances or the evidence necessary to explain the objection and to exclude any reasonable hypothesis on which the decision of the trial court could be based*}.

2. {❾ *Party*} objected in open court to {❿ *state the action, order, or ruling of the court*}.

3. The evidence the Court ruled inadmissible related to {⓫ *briefly describe the evidence ruled inadmissible*}.

{*CHOOSE APPROPRIATE PARAGRAPHS 4-7*}

4. Attached as Exhibit {⓬ *letter*} is an affidavit of {⓭ *name of witness*}, which presents a summary of what {⓮ *his/her*} testimony would have been if the Court had not ruled the testimony inadmissible.

5. Attached as Exhibit {⓯ *letter*} is a copy of the deposition of {⓰ *name of deponent*}, which the Court ruled inadmissible.

6. Attached as Exhibit {⓱ *letter*} is a copy of the {⓲ *describe document*}, which the Court ruled inadmissible.

7. {⓳ *State other facts relevant to the bill of exception.*}

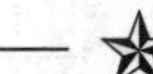

{ADD JUDGE'S FINDINGS IF BILL NOT AGREED TO}

___ The Court finds that the bill is correct, approves it, and orders the clerk of the Court to file the bill of exception as part of the record in this case.

___ The Court refuses to approve the bill.

SIGNED on ______________, 20___.

____
PRESIDING JUDGE

SEE: Tex. R. Evid. 103
Tex. R. App. P. 33.2
*O'Connor's Texas Rules * Civil Trials* (2019), "Formal Bill of Exception," ch. 8-E, §4, p. 847

ADD: STYLE OF THE CASE – FORM 1B:2
SIGNATURE BLOCK – FORM 1B:3, if contested bill
SIGNATURE BLOCK FOR AGREED MOTIONS – FORM 1B:4, if agreed bill
CERTIFICATE OF SERVICE – FORM 1B:13

ATTACH: AFFIDAVIT – FORM 1B:8, if necessary
BYSTANDERS' BILL OF EXCEPTION – FORM 8E:2, if necessary
AFFIDAVIT FOR BYSTANDERS' BILL – FORM 8E:3, if necessary
Exhibits

NOTE: If the judge finds that the bill is incorrect, the judge may suggest a correction or amendment to accurately reflect the trial-court proceedings. Tex. R. App. P. 33.2(c)(2)(B). If the complaining party agrees with the suggested corrections, the changes can be made, and the judge will sign the amended bill and file it with the trial-court clerk. *Id.*

BYSTANDERS' BILL OF EXCEPTION

We, the undersigned bystanders and citizens of this state, have read {❶ *party*} {❷ *name*}'s bill of exception. Each of us was present at the time of the proceedings and rulings of the Court described in {❸ *party*}'s bill of exception. We attest to the correctness of the bill as presented by {❹ *party*}. {❺ *Party*}'s bill of exception and the affidavit supporting this bystanders' bill of exception are attached and incorporated into this bill by reference.

SIGNED on ______________, 20___.

____
{❻ *Bystander's name*}

____
{❼ *Bystander's name*}

____
{❽ *Bystander's name*}

SEE: Tex. R. Evid. 103
Tex. R. App. P. 33.2(c)(3)
O'Connor's Texas Rules * Civil Trials (2019), "Bystanders' bill," ch. 8-E, §4.2.2(3)(c), p. 848

ADD: STYLE OF THE CASE – FORM 1B:2
CERTIFICATE OF SERVICE – FORM 1B:13

ATTACH: AFFIDAVIT FOR BYSTANDERS' BILL – FORM 8E:3

NOTE: To preserve error when a bill is refused by the court, the party attempting to make a bill must file the refused bill and a "bystanders' bill." The bystanders' bill is an attestation to the correctness of the refused bill by at least three bystanders who are not interested in the outcome of the case and who were present and observed the matters addressed in the refused bill. *See* Tex. R. App. P. 33.2(c)(3); *see, e.g.*, ***Circle Y v. Blevins***, 826 S.W.2d 753, 755 (Tex.App.—Texarkana 1992, writ denied) (bystanders' bill not valid because all affiants were attorneys interested in the outcome of the case).

AFFIDAVIT

STATE OF TEXAS §
{❶ _______} COUNTY §

Before me, the undersigned notary, on this day personally appeared {❷ *name of affiant*}, the affiant, whose identity is known to me. After I administered an oath, affiant testified as follows:

1. "My name is {❸ *name of affiant*}. I am over 18 years of age, of sound mind, and capable of making this affidavit. The facts stated in this affidavit are within my personal knowledge and are true and correct.

2. "I am a citizen of Texas.

3. "I have no concern with the outcome of this case.

4. "On {❹ *date*}, I was a bystander at the time of the proceedings and rulings in this case, in the {❺ *name of court*} of {❻ _______} County, Texas.

5. "I witnessed the following proceedings: {❼ *set out facts as stated in bill of exception*}.

6. "I read and signed the bystanders' bill of exception, and state that the bill correctly describes the proceedings and is true and correct in all respects."

____
{❽ *Name of affiant*}

Sworn to and subscribed before me by {❾ *name of affiant*} on __________, 20___.

____
Notary Public in and for
the State of Texas

SEE: Tex. R. Evid. 103
Tex. R. App. P. 33.2(c)(3)
O'Connor's Texas Rules * Civil Trials (2019), "Bystanders' bill," ch. 8-E, §4.2.2(3)(c), p. 848

ADD: STYLE OF THE CASE – FORM 1B:2

NOTE: See notes under FORM 1B:8.

{1 *PARTY*}'S MOTION FOR
LEAVE TO FILE {2 *NAME OF AMENDED PLEADING*}

{3 *Party*}, {4 *name*}, asks the Court to allow {5 *him/her/it*} to file {6 *his/her/its*} {7 *name of amended pleading*}. {*See* ***O'Connor's Texas Rules****, "Motion for Leave to Amend," ch. 8-F, §2, p. 849.*}

INTRODUCTION

1. Plaintiff, {8 *name*}, sued defendant, {9 *name*}, for {10 *state basis of suit*}.

2. {11 *State other relevant facts about the suit.*}

BACKGROUND

3. On {12 *date*}, {13 *party*} filed {14 *his/her/its*} {15 *identify last live pleading, e.g., Second Amended Petition*}.

4. During trial,

{*CHOOSE APPROPRIATE STATEMENT*}

[A] {16 *party*} discovered a {17 *defect/omission*} in {18 *his/her/its*} pleading that can be cured by amendment.

[B] {19 *adverse party*}, {20 *name*}, objected to the {21 *introduction of evidence/submission of a jury question*} on an issue that was not included in {22 *party*}'s pleading.

5. {23 *Party*} now seeks leave to file {24 *his/her/its*} {25 *name of amended pleading*}. {26 *Party*} files {27 *his/her/its*} {28 *name of amended pleading*} simultaneously with this motion.

6. {29 *State other facts relevant to the motion.*}

ARGUMENT & AUTHORITIES

{*CHOOSE APPROPRIATE SECTIONS A-C*}

A. Procedural defect.

7. A court should permit a trial amendment that corrects formal, procedural defects and does not change the substantive issues. *Chapin & Chapin, Inc. v. Tex. Sand & Gravel Co.*, 844 S.W.2d 664, 665 (Tex. 1992). {*See* ***O'Connor's Texas Rules****, "TRCP 63 & 66," ch. 8-F, §2.4.1, p. 851.*}

FORM 8F:1

8. The Court should grant leave for {30 *party*} to file {31 *his/her/its*} {32 *name of amended pleading*} because the amendment does not change the substantive issues in this case but merely corrects a procedural defect. Specifically, {33 *describe how amendment cures defect without changing substantive issues*}.

B. Trial by consent.

9. A court should permit a trial amendment that conforms the pleadings to the evidence on an issue that was tried by consent. *See* Tex. R. Civ. P. 67. If an issue that should have been pleaded is tried by consent, it will be treated as if it had been raised by the pleadings. *Id.* An issue is tried by consent when (1) a party introduces evidence to support an unpleaded issue and (2) the opposing party does not object to the admission of that evidence or to the submission of a jury question on that issue. *See* Tex. R. Civ. P. 66, 67; *Ingram v. Deere*, 288 S.W.3d 886, 893 (Tex. 2009); *Pine Trail Shores Owners' Ass'n v. Aiken*, 160 S.W.3d 139, 146 (Tex. App.—Tyler 2005, no pet.). {*See **O'Connor's Texas Rules**, "TRCP 67," ch. 8-F, §2.4.2, p. 851.*}

10. The Court should grant leave for {34 *party*} to file {35 *his/her/its*} {36 *name of amended pleading*} because the amendment does not change the substantive issues in this case but merely conforms the pleadings to the evidence on an issue that was tried by consent. {37 *Elaborate, identifying the evidence that was introduced without objection.*}

C. No surprise or prejudice.

11. A court may refuse a trial amendment only if the opposing party (1) presents evidence of surprise or prejudice or (2) establishes that the amendment asserts a new cause of action or defense that is prejudicial on its face. *State Bar v. Kilpatrick*, 874 S.W.2d 656, 658 (Tex. 1994); *see* Tex. R. Civ. P. 63, 66. An amendment is prejudicial on its face if it (1) asserts a new substantive matter that reshapes the nature of the lawsuit, (2) could not have been anticipated by the opposing party, and (3) will detrimentally affect the opposing party's ability to present its case. *Hampden Corp. v. Remark, Inc.*, 331 S.W.3d 489, 498 (Tex. App.—Dallas 2010, pet. denied); *Apodaca v. Rios*, 163 S.W.3d 297, 301 (Tex. App.—El Paso 2005, no pet.). {*See **O'Connor's Texas Rules**, "Prove surprise or prejudice," ch. 8-F, §3.2, p. 852.*}

12. The Court should grant leave for {38 *party*} to file {39 *his/her/its*} {40 *name of amended pleading*} because {41 *adverse party*}, {42 *name*}, cannot present evidence of surprise or prejudice or establish that the amendment asserts a new cause of action or defense that is prejudicial on its face. {43 *Elaborate.*}

◄ *Continued on next page* ►

FORM 8F:1

CONCLUSION

13. {㊹ *Briefly summarize the motion.*}

PRAYER

14. For these reasons, {㊺ *party*} asks the Court to grant leave to file {㊻ *his/her/its*} {㊼ *name of amended pleading*}.

SEE: Tex. R. Civ. P. 62-67, 278
O'Connor's Texas Rules * Civil Trials (2019), "Motion for Leave to Amend," ch. 8-F, §2, p. 849

ADD: STYLE OF THE CASE – FORM 1B:2
SIGNATURE BLOCK – FORM 1B:3
CERTIFICATE OF CONFERENCE – FORM 1B:12, if necessary
CERTIFICATE OF SERVICE – FORM 1B:13

ATTACH: AFFIDAVIT – FORM 1B:8, if necessary
ORDER – FORM 1G:1
Amended pleading

NOTE: The motion for leave to amend pleadings during trial may be dictated into the record. *See* ***Pennington v. Gurkoff***, 899 S.W.2d 767, 771 (Tex.App.—Fort Worth 1995, writ denied).

{1 *PARTY*}'S MOTION FOR LEAVE
TO FILE {2 *NAME OF AMENDED PLEADING*}

{3 *Party*}, {4 *name*}, asks the Court to allow {5 *party*} to file {6 *his/her/its*} {7 *name of amended pleading*}.

INTRODUCTION

1. Plaintiff, {8 *name*}, sued defendant, {9 *name*}, for {10 *state basis of suit*}.

2. {11 *State other relevant facts about the suit.*}

BACKGROUND

3. On {12 *date*}, {13 *party*} filed {14 *his/her/its*} {15 *identify last live pleading, e.g., Second Amended Petition*}.

4. After a verdict was returned,

{*CHOOSE APPROPRIATE STATEMENT*}

[A] {16 *party*} discovered a {17 *defect/omission*} in {18 *his/her/its*} pleading that can be cured by amendment.

[B] {19 *adverse party*}, {20 *name*}, objected to {21 *identify objection*} because an issue was not included in {22 *party*}'s pleading.

5. {23 *Party*} now seeks leave to file {24 *his/her/its*} {25 *name of amended pleading*} to conform the pleadings to the verdict and the evidence presented at trial. {26 *Party*} files {27 *his/her/its*} {28 *name of amended pleading*} simultaneously with this motion.

6. {29 *State other facts relevant to the motion.*}

ARGUMENT & AUTHORITIES

{*CHOOSE APPROPRIATE ARGUMENTS*}

{*If trial by consent*}

7. A court should permit a post-trial amendment that conforms the pleadings to the evidence on an issue that was tried by consent. *See* Tex. R. Civ. P. 67. If an issue that should have been pleaded is tried by consent, it will be treated as if it had been raised by the pleadings. *Id.* An issue is tried by consent when (1) a party introduced evidence to support an unpleaded issue and (2) the opposing party did not object to the admission of

Continued on next page

FORM 8F:2

that evidence or to the submission of a jury question on that issue. *See* Tex. R. Civ. P. 66, 67; *Ingram v. Deere*, 288 S.W.3d 886, 893 (Tex. 2009); *Pine Trail Shores Owners' Ass'n v. Aiken*, 160 S.W.3d 139, 146 (Tex. App.—Tyler 2005, no pet.). {*See* ***O'Connor's Texas Rules***, *"TRCP 67," ch. 8-F, §2.4.2, p. 851.*}

{*CHOOSE APPROPRIATE PARAGRAPHS 8-10*}

8. {㉚ *Party*} asks for leave to file {㉛ *his/her/its*} {㉜ *name of amended pleading*} to add a cause of action that was tried by consent. *See Bell v. Meeks*, 725 S.W.2d 179, 179 (Tex. 1987); *Grp. Hosp. Servs., Inc. v. Daniel*, 704 S.W.2d 870, 876 (Tex. App.—Corpus Christi 1985, no writ). {㉝ *Demonstrate how issue was tried by consent.*}

9. {㉞ *Party*} asks for leave to file {㉟ *his/her/its*} {㊱ *name of amended pleading*} to add a new defense that was tried by consent. *Allstate Prop. & Cas. Ins. Co. v. Gutierrez*, 281 S.W.3d 535, 539-40 (Tex. App.—El Paso 2008, no pet.). {㊲ *Demonstrate how issue was tried by consent.*}

10. {㊳ *Party*} asks for leave to file {㊴ *his/her/its*} {㊵ *name of amended pleading*} to add a request for damages that was tried by consent. *Centroplex Ford, Inc. v. Kirby*, 736 S.W.2d 261, 265 (Tex. App.—Austin 1987, no writ) (mental-anguish damages). {㊶ *Demonstrate how issue was tried by consent.*}

{*If no trial by consent*}

11. A court should refuse a post-trial amendment only if the opposing party shows (1) it is surprised or prejudiced by the amendment or (2) the amendment asserts a new cause of action or defense that is prejudicial on its face. *State Bar v. Kilpatrick*, 874 S.W.2d 656, 658 (Tex. 1994); *see* Tex. R. Civ. P. 63, 66. {*See* ***O'Connor's Texas Rules***, *"Prove surprise or prejudice," ch. 8-F, §3.2, p. 852.*}

{*CHOOSE APPROPRIATE PARAGRAPHS 12-16*}

12. {㊷ *Party*} asks for leave to file {㊸ *his/her/its*} {㊹ *name of amended pleading*} to {㊺ *explain purpose of amendment, e.g., add a new claim for relief*}. The Court should grant leave because {㊻ *adverse party*}, {㊼ *name*}, cannot show that {㊽ *he/she/it*} is surprised or prejudiced by the amendment. {㊾ *Elaborate.*}

13. {㊿ *Party*} asks for leave to file {51 *his/her/its*} {52 *name of amended pleading*} to add a new {53 *cause of action/defense*}. An amendment that adds a new cause of action or defense is not prejudicial on its face if it (1) does not assert any new substantive matter, (2) could have been anticipated by the opposing party, or (3) will not detrimentally affect the opposing party's ability to present its case. *Hampden Corp. v. Remark*,

FORM 8F:2

Inc., 331 S.W.3d 489, 498 (Tex. App.—Dallas 2010, pet. denied); *Apodaca v. Rios*, 163 S.W.3d 297, 301 (Tex. App.—El Paso 2005, no pet.). The new {54 *cause of action/defense*} is not prejudicial on its face because {55 *demonstrate how the amendment is not prejudicial, e.g., it has common elements with pleaded matters and the evidentiary proof required to support it is the same for an already pleaded cause of action or defense. Smith Detective Agency & Nightwatch Serv., Inc. v. Stanley Smith Sec., Inc., 938 S.W.2d 743, 749 (Tex. App.—Dallas 1996, writ denied)*}. Thus, the Court should grant leave for {56 *party*} to file {57 *his/her/its*} {58 *name of amended pleading*}.

14. {59 *Party*} asks for leave to file {60 *his/her/its*} {61 *name of amended pleading*} to conform the pleadings to the damages awarded, which was a higher amount than requested in {62 *party*}'s pleadings. The Court should grant leave because (1) the suit was governed by a Level {63 *2/3*} discovery-control plan, and (2) {64 *adverse party*}, {65 *name*}, cannot show that {66 *he/she/it*} is surprised or prejudiced by the amendment. *See* Tex. R. Civ. P. 169 cmt. 4, 190 cmt. 2 (1999). {67 *Elaborate, e.g., Before trial, adverse party had acknowledged the amount in dispute was greater than what party had pleaded for, and the difference was not enough to require a different trial strategy. Greenhalgh v. Serv. Lloyds Ins. Co., 787 S.W.2d 938, 940-41 (Tex. 1990); Minn. Life Ins. Co. v. Vasquez, 133 S.W.3d 320, 331 (Tex. App.—Corpus Christi 2004), rev'd on other grounds, 192 S.W.3d 774 (Tex. 2006); Weidner v. Sanchez, 14 S.W.3d 353, 376-77 (Tex. App.—Houston [14th Dist.] 2000, no pet.).*}

15. {68 *Party*} asks for leave to file {69 *his/her/its*} {70 *name of amended pleading*} to add a claim for prejudgment interest. The Court should grant leave for {71 *party*} to file {72 *his/her/its*} {73 *name of amended pleading*} because an amendment seeking to add a claim for prejudgment interest requires no evidentiary proof at trial and thus cannot be the basis of a claim for surprise or prejudice. *Benavidez v. Isles Constr. Co.*, 726 S.W.2d 23, 26 (Tex. 1987); *Firefighters' & Police Officers' Civil Serv. Comm'n v. Herrera*, 981 S.W.2d 728, 734-35 (Tex. App.—Houston [1st Dist.] 1998, pet. denied).

16. {74 *Party*} asks for leave to file {75 *his/her/its*} {76 *name of amended pleading*} to add a claim for attorney fees. The Court should grant leave because {77 *adverse party*}, {78 *name*}, cannot show that {79 *he/she/it*} is surprised or prejudiced by the amendment. *Swate v. Medina Cmty. Hosp.*, 966 S.W.2d 693, 701-02 (Tex. App.—San Antonio 1998, pet. denied). {80 *Elaborate.*}

CONCLUSION

17. {81 *Briefly summarize the motion.*}

Continued on next page

FORM 8F:2

PRAYER

18. For these reasons, {82 *party*} asks the Court to grant leave to file {83 *his/her/its*} {84 *name of amended pleading*}.

SEE: Tex. R. Civ. P. 62-67, 278
O'Connor's Texas Rules * Civil Trials (2019), "Motion to Amend Pleadings—Trial & Post-trial," ch. 8-F, p. 849

ADD: STYLE OF THE CASE – FORM 1B:2
SIGNATURE BLOCK – FORM 1B:3
CERTIFICATE OF CONFERENCE – FORM 1B:12, if necessary
CERTIFICATE OF SERVICE – FORM 1B:13

ATTACH: AFFIDAVIT – FORM 1B:8, if necessary
NOTICE OF HEARING OR SUBMISSION – FORM 1E:1
ORDER – FORM 1G:1
Amended pleading

{1 *PARTY*}'S RESPONSE TO {2 *ADVERSE PARTY*}'S
MOTION FOR LEAVE TO FILE {3 *NAME OF AMENDED PLEADING*}

{4 *Party*}, {5 *name*}, asks the Court to deny {6 *adverse party*} {7 *name*}'s motion for leave to file {8 *his/her/its*} {9 *name of amended pleading*}. {*See* ***O'Connor's Texas Rules****, "Response to Motion for Leave to Amend," ch. 8-F, §3, p. 852.*}

INTRODUCTION

1. Plaintiff, {10 *name*}, sued defendant, {11 *name*}, for {12 *state basis of suit*}.

2. {13 *State other relevant facts about the suit.*}

BACKGROUND

3. On {14 *date*}, {15 *adverse party*}, {16 *name*}, filed {17 *his/her/its*} {18 *identify last live pleading, e.g., Second Amended Petition*}.

4. {19 *Adverse party*} has asked the Court to grant {20 *him/her/it*} leave to file a {21 *trial/post-trial*} amendment to {22 *identify purpose of amendment*}.

5. {23 *State other facts relevant to the response.*}

ARGUMENT & AUTHORITIES

{*CHOOSE APPROPRIATE SECTIONS A-G*}

A. Issue not tried by consent.

6. The Court should deny {24 *adverse party*}'s motion for leave to file {25 *his/her/its*} {26 *name of amended pleading*} because the unpleaded issue that is the subject of the amendment was not tried by consent. The evidence {27 *adverse party*} claims was in support of the unpleaded issue was introduced in support of a pleaded issue. {28 *Identify pleaded issue on which same evidence was relevant.*} An unpleaded issue is not tried by consent if the evidence introduced that is relevant to the unpleaded issue is also relevant to a pleaded issue. *Marrs & Smith P'ship v. D.K. Boyd Oil & Gas Co.*, 223 S.W.3d 1, 18-19 (Tex. App.—El Paso 2005, pet. denied); *Harrison v. City of San Antonio*, 695 S.W.2d 271, 278 (Tex. App.—San Antonio 1985, no writ). {*See* ***O'Connor's Texas Rules****, "Evidence relevant to pleaded issue," ch. 8-F, §2.4.2(2)(c), p. 851.*}

7. The Court should deny {29 *adverse party*}'s motion for leave to file {30 *his/her/its*} {31 *name of amended pleading*} because the unpleaded issue that is the subject of the amendment was not tried by consent. Even though some evidence came in without objection, the issue was not developed. *Whatley v. City of Dall.*, 758 S.W.2d 301,

Continued on next page

FORM 8F:3

306-07 (Tex. App.—Dallas 1988, writ denied). {32 *Elaborate.*} {*See* ***O'Connor's Texas Rules***, *"Issue not developed," ch. 8-F, §2.4.2(2)(b), p. 851.*}

B. Party surprised or prejudiced by amendment.

8. The Court should deny {33 *adverse party*}'s motion for leave to file {34 *his/her/its*} {35 *name of amended pleading*} because {36 *party*} is surprised or prejudiced by it. *See* Tex. R. Civ. P. 63 (surprise), 66 (prejudice); *Greenhalgh v. Serv. Lloyds Ins. Co.*, 787 S.W.2d 938, 939 (Tex. 1990) (surprise or prejudice). {37 *Elaborate, e.g., party's pretrial preparation was made in reliance on the pleadings on file, party decided not to pursue other avenues of pretrial investigation it would have pursued under the proposed amended pleading.*} {*See* ***O'Connor's Texas Rules***, *"Show surprise or prejudice," ch. 8-F, §3.2.1, p. 852.*}

C. Amendment prejudicial on its face.

9. The Court should deny {38 *adverse party*}'s motion for leave to file {39 *his/her/its*} {40 *name of amended pleading*} because the pleading asserts a new {41 *cause of action/defense*} that is prejudicial on its face. *See* Tex. R. Civ. P. 66; *Greenhalgh v. Serv. Lloyds Ins. Co.*, 787 S.W.2d 938, 939 (Tex. 1990). {*See* ***O'Connor's Texas Rules***, *"Show prejudice on its face," ch. 8-F, §3.2.2, p. 853.*} The amended pleading is prejudicial on its face for the following reasons:

a. The pleading asserts a new substantive matter that reshapes the nature of the lawsuit. *Hampden Corp. v. Remark, Inc.*, 331 S.W.3d 489, 498-99 (Tex. App.—Dallas 2010, pet. denied); *Apodaca v. Rios*, 163 S.W.3d 297, 301 (Tex. App.—El Paso 2005, no pet.); *Smith Detective Agency & Nightwatch Serv., Inc. v. Stanley Smith Sec., Inc.*, 938 S.W.2d 743, 749 (Tex. App.—Dallas 1996, writ denied). {42 *Elaborate.*} A court may refuse to permit an amendment asserting a new cause of action or defense that alters the nature of the trial itself. *Chapin & Chapin, Inc. v. Tex. Sand & Gravel Co.*, 844 S.W.2d 664, 665 (Tex. 1992).

b. The new matter could not have been anticipated by {43 *party*} in light of the development of the case. *Hampden Corp.*, 331 S.W.3d at 498-99; *Apodaca*, 163 S.W.3d at 301; *Smith Detective Agency*, 938 S.W.2d at 749. {44 *Elaborate.*}

c. {45 *Party*}'s presentation of the case will be adversely affected if the amendment is permitted. *Hampden Corp.*, 331 S.W.3d at 498-99; *Apodaca*, 163 S.W.3d at 301; *Smith Detective Agency*, 938 S.W.2d at 749. {46 *Elaborate.*}

FORM 8F:3

D. Amendment made after judgment.

{*CHOOSE APPROPRIATE PARAGRAPH 10*}

{*When leave requested to amend to add new party or claim*}

10. The Court should deny {47 *adverse party*}'s motion for leave to file {48 *his/her/its*} {49 *name of amended pleading*} to add new parties or claims because the Court has rendered judgment. *See Mitchell v. LaFlamme*, 60 S.W.3d 123, 132 (Tex. App.—Houston [14th Dist.] 2000, no pet.); *Cantu v. Martin*, 934 S.W.2d 859, 860-61 (Tex. App.—Corpus Christi 1996, no writ). It is therefore too late for {50 *adverse party*} to ask the Court for leave to amend the pleadings to add a new {51 *party/claim*}. {52 *Elaborate.*} {*See* ***O'Connor's Texas Rules****, "No new claims," ch. 8-F, §4.1, p. 853.*}

{*When leave requested to amend to conform judgment to damages award of more than $100,000 – expedited action*}

10. The Court should deny {53 *adverse party*}'s motion for leave to file {54 *his/her/its*} {55 *name of amended pleading*} to conform the judgment to a damages award over $100,000 because {56 *adverse party*} prosecuted this suit as an expedited action. *See* Tex. R. Civ. P. 169 & cmt. 4. Under Texas Rule of Civil Procedure 169, {57 *adverse party*} cannot recover a judgment greater than $100,000, excluding postjudgment interest. Tex. R. Civ. P. 169(b). {58 *Elaborate.*}

E. Amendment made after plenary power expired.

11. The Court should deny {59 *adverse party*}'s motion for leave to file {60 *his/her/its*} {61 *name of amended pleading*} to conform it to the evidence because the Court has rendered judgment and its plenary power has expired. *See Boarder to Boarder Trucking, Inc. v. Mondi, Inc.*, 831 S.W.2d 495, 500 (Tex. App.—Corpus Christi 1992, no writ) (Hinojosa, J., concurring). The Court therefore has no power to grant leave to amend the pleadings. {62 *Elaborate.*} {*See* ***O'Connor's Texas Rules****, "Conform pleadings to evidence," ch. 8-F, §4.2, p. 854.*}

F. Request for additional discovery.

12. In the alternative, if the Court grants {63 *adverse party*}'s motion for leave to file {64 *name of amended pleading*}, {65 *party*} asks the Court to allow {66 *him/her/it*} to conduct additional discovery for evidence to respond to the new issue. *See* Tex. R. Civ. P. 66. {67 *Explain what additional discovery is necessary.*}

— Continued on next page —

G. Request for continuance.

13. In the alternative, if the Court grants {68 *adverse party*}'s motion for leave to file {69 *his/her/its*} {70 *name of amended pleading*}, {71 *party*} asks the Court to continue the trial until {72 *date*}, to allow {73 *party*} to secure evidence to respond to the new issue. *See* Tex. R. Civ. P. 66. {74 *Explain what evidence is necessary and the time needed to obtain the evidence.*} {*See* ***O'Connor's Texas Rules****, "Motion for continuance," ch. 8-F, §3.4, p. 853.*}

CONCLUSION

14. {75 *Briefly summarize the response.*}

PRAYER

15. For these reasons, {76 *party*} asks the Court to deny {77 *adverse party*}'s motion for leave to file {78 *his/her/its*} {79 *name of amended pleading*}.

{*ADD PARAGRAPH 16 IF APPLICABLE*}

16. If the Court grants {80 *adverse party*}'s motion for leave to file {81 *his/her/its*} {82 *name of amended pleading*}, {83 *party*} asks the Court to

{*CHOOSE APPLICABLE RELIEF*}

A grant a trial continuance until {84 *date*}.

B grant additional discovery—specifically, {85 *state discovery desired*}.

SEE: Tex. R. Civ. P. 62-67, 278
O'Connor's Texas Rules * Civil Trials (2019), "Response to Motion for Leave to Amend," ch. 8-F, §3, p. 852; "Amendments After Judgment," ch. 8-F, §4, p. 853

ADD: STYLE OF THE CASE – FORM 1B:2
SIGNATURE BLOCK – FORM 1B:3
CERTIFICATE OF SERVICE – FORM 1B:13

ATTACH: AFFIDAVIT – FORM 1B:8, if necessary
ORDER – FORM 1G:1

{❶ *PARTY*}'S MOTION FOR DIRECTED VERDICT

{❷ *Party*}, {❸ *name*}, asks the Court to {❹ *return/instruct the jury to return*} a verdict in {❺ *his/her/its*} favor. {*See **O'Connor's Texas Rules**, "Motion," ch. 8-G, §3, p. 855.*}

INTRODUCTION

1. Plaintiff, {❻ *name*}, sued defendant, {❼ *name*}, for {❽ *state basis of suit*}.

2. Defendant answered, asserting the defenses of {❾ *identify defenses*}.

3. {❿ *State other relevant facts about the suit.*}

BACKGROUND

4. {⓫ *State facts relevant to the motion.*}

ARGUMENT & AUTHORITIES

{*CHOOSE APPROPRIATE PARAGRAPHS 5-9*}

5. The Court should grant a directed verdict because {⓬ *adverse party*} {⓭ *name*}'s pleadings contain a specific defect that renders them incapable of supporting a judgment for {⓮ *adverse party*}. *Double Ace, Inc. v. Pope*, 190 S.W.3d 18, 26 (Tex. App.—Amarillo 2005, no pet.). Specifically, {⓯ *describe defect*}. {*See **O'Connor's Texas Rules**, "Defect in pleadings," ch. 8-G, §4.3, p. 856.*}

6. The Court should grant a directed verdict because the substantive law does not permit {⓰ *plaintiff to recover on {his/her/its} cause of action/defendant to assert {his/her/its} defense*}. *See, e.g., Dietrich v. Goodman*, 123 S.W.3d 413, 419-20 (Tex. App.—Houston [14th Dist.] 2003, no pet.) (court directed verdict because, under Water Code, flood water did not qualify as "surface water"); *Arguelles v. UT Family Med. Ctr.*, 941 S.W.2d 255, 257-58 (Tex. App.—Corpus Christi 1996, no writ) (court directed verdict because Texas does not recognize the "lost chance of survival" doctrine in medical-malpractice suits). Specifically, {⓱ *discuss law that prevents recovery or defense*}. {*See **O'Connor's Texas Rules**, "Defect in pleadings," ch. 8-G, §4.3, p. 856.*}

7. The Court should grant a directed verdict because the evidence conclusively proves a fact that establishes {⓲ *party*}'s right to judgment as a matter of law. *Double Ace, Inc. v. Pope*, 190 S.W.3d 18, 26 (Tex. App.—Amarillo 2005, no pet.); *Cortez v. HCCI-San Antonio, Inc.*, 131 S.W.3d 113, 120 (Tex. App.—San Antonio 2004), *aff'd*, 159 S.W.3d 87 (Tex. 2005); *see Envtl. Processing Sys., L.C. v. FPL Farming Ltd.*, 457 S.W.3d 414, 425-26 (Tex. 2015); *Prudential Ins. Co. of Am. v. Fin. Review Servs., Inc.*,

◄ *Continued on next page* ►

29 S.W.3d 74, 77 (Tex. 2000). Specifically, {⓳ *identify facts that evidence conclusively establishes*}. {*See* ***O'Connor's Texas Rules***, *"Conclusive evidence," ch. 8-G, §4.2, p. 855.*}

8. The Court should grant a directed verdict because the evidence conclusively proves a fact that negates as a matter of law {⓴ *adverse party*} {㉑ *name*}'s right to judgment. *Westchester Fire Ins. Co. v. Admiral Ins. Co.*, 152 S.W.3d 172, 191 (Tex. App.—Fort Worth 2004, pet. denied); *Rowland v. City of Corpus Christi*, 620 S.W.2d 930, 932 (Tex. App.—Corpus Christi 1981, writ ref'd n.r.e.). Specifically, {㉒ *identify facts that negate right to judgment*}. {*See* ***O'Connor's Texas Rules***, *"Conclusive evidence," ch. 8-G, §4.2, p. 855.*}

9. The Court should grant a directed verdict because the evidence does not raise a fact issue on one or more material issues that {㉓ *adverse party*}, {㉔ *name*}, must establish to be entitled to a judgment. *Cherqui v. Westheimer St. Festival Corp.*, 116 S.W.3d 337, 343 (Tex. App.—Houston [14th Dist.] 2003, no pet.); *see Prudential Ins. Co. of Am. v. Fin. Review Servs., Inc.*, 29 S.W.3d 74, 77 (Tex. 2000); *Double Ace, Inc. v. Pope*, 190 S.W.3d 18, 26 (Tex. App.—Amarillo 2005, no pet.). Specifically, there is no fact issue on {㉕ *explain*}. {*See* ***O'Connor's Texas Rules***, *"No evidence," ch. 8-G, §4.1, p. 855.*}

CONCLUSION

10. {㉖ *Briefly summarize the motion.*}

PRAYER

11. For these reasons, {㉗ *party*} asks the Court to {㉘ *return/instruct the jury to return*} a verdict for {㉙ *party*} for {㉚ *describe desired verdict*}.

SEE: Tex. R. Civ. P. 268
O'Connor's Texas Rules * Civil Trials (2019), "Motion," ch. 8-G, §3, p. 855; "Grounds for Directed Verdict," ch. 8-G, §4, p. 855

ADD: STYLE OF THE CASE – FORM 1B:2
SIGNATURE BLOCK – FORM 1B:3
CERTIFICATE OF CONFERENCE – FORM 1B:12, if necessary
CERTIFICATE OF SERVICE – FORM 1B:13

ATTACH: AFFIDAVIT – FORM 1B:8, if necessary
ORDER – FORM 1G:1

FORM 8G:1

Form 8G:1 Motion for Directed Verdict

NOTE: A motion for directed verdict asks the court to render judgment without submitting the charge to the jury because there is nothing for the jury to decide. ***C.B. v. TDFPS***, 440 S.W.3d 756, 769 (Tex.App.—El Paso 2013, no pet.). In a nonjury trial, the correct procedure is to make a motion for judgment, rather than a motion for directed verdict, because there is no jury to "direct." This form can be modified to make it a motion for judgment for a nonjury trial. See ***O'Connor's Texas Rules***, "Purpose," ch. 8-G, §1.2, p. 854.

A motion for directed verdict may be made orally. ***Dillard v. Broyles***, 633 S.W.2d 636, 645 (Tex.App.—Corpus Christi 1982, writ ref'd n.r.e.). If the motion is made orally, it preserves the grounds only if it is recorded by the court reporter and included in the reporter's record.

{❶ *PARTY*}'S RESPONSE TO {❷ *ADVERSE PARTY*}'S MOTION FOR DIRECTED VERDICT

{❸ *Party*}, {❹ *name*}, asks the Court to deny {❺ *adverse party*} {❻ *name*}'s motion for directed verdict. {*See* ***O'Connor's Texas Rules****, "Response," ch. 8-G, §5, p. 856.*}

INTRODUCTION

1. Plaintiff, {❼ *name*}, sued defendant, {❽ *name*}, for {❾ *state basis of suit*}.

2. Defendant answered, asserting the defenses of {❿ *identify defenses*}.

3. {⓫ *State other relevant facts about the suit.*}

BACKGROUND

4. {⓬ *State facts relevant to the response.*}

ARGUMENT & AUTHORITIES

{*CHOOSE APPROPRIATE PARAGRAPHS 5-9*}

5. A court should not direct a verdict when a party's pleadings support a judgment. *See Double Ace, Inc. v. Pope*, 190 S.W.3d 18, 26 (Tex. App.—Amarillo 2005, no pet.). Specifically, the Court should not direct a verdict in this case because {⓭ *explain*}. {*See* ***O'Connor's Texas Rules****, "Defect in pleadings," ch. 8-G, §4.3, p. 856.*}

6. A court should not direct a verdict if the evidence does not conclusively prove a fact that establishes or negates as a matter of law a party's right to judgment. *Prudential Ins. Co. of Am. v. Fin. Review Servs., Inc.*, 29 S.W.3d 74, 77 (Tex. 2000); *Westchester Fire Ins. Co. v. Admiral Ins. Co.*, 152 S.W.3d 172, 191 (Tex. App.—Fort Worth 2004, pet. denied); *see Envtl. Processing Sys., L.C. v. FPL Farming Ltd.*, 457 S.W.3d 414, 425-26 (Tex. 2015). Specifically, the Court should not direct a verdict in this case because {⓮ *explain*}. {*See* ***O'Connor's Texas Rules****, "Conclusive evidence," ch. 8-G, §4.2, p. 855.*}

7. A court should not direct a verdict if the evidence raises a fact issue on all material issues that a party must establish to be entitled to judgment. *Prudential Ins. Co. of Am. v. Fin. Review Servs., Inc.*, 29 S.W.3d 74, 77 (Tex. 2000); *Double Ace, Inc. v. Pope*, 190 S.W.3d 18, 26 (Tex. App.—Amarillo 2005, no pet.). Specifically, the Court should not direct a verdict in this case because {⓯ *explain*}. {*See* ***O'Connor's Texas Rules****, "No evidence," ch. 8-G, §4.1, p. 855.*}

8. The Court should not direct a verdict because of the defect in {16 *party*}'s pleadings that {17 *adverse party*} asserted in {18 *his/her/its*} motion for directed verdict. Instead, the Court should allow {19 *party*} to amend {20 *his/her/its*} pleadings to cure the defect. {21 *Party*} files a motion to amend {22 *his/her/its*} pleadings simultaneously with this response and incorporates that motion into this response. {*See* ***O'Connor's Texas Rules****, "Motion for Leave to Amend," ch. 8-F, §2, p. 849.*}

9. The Court should not direct a verdict based on the lack of evidence on the issue of {23 *specify issue*}. Instead, the Court should allow {24 *party*} to reopen the evidence to prove the issue. {25 *Party*} files a motion to reopen the evidence simultaneously with this response and incorporates that motion into this response. {*See* ***O'Connor's Texas Rules****, "Motion to Reopen," ch. 8-H, §2, p. 858.*}

CONCLUSION

10. {26 *Briefly summarize the response.*}

PRAYER

11. For these reasons, {27 *party*} asks the Court to deny {28 *adverse party*}'s motion for directed verdict.

SEE: Tex. R. Civ. P. 268
O'Connor's Texas Rules * Civil Trials (2019), "Grounds for Directed Verdict," ch. 8-G, §4, p. 855; "Response," ch. 8-G, §5, p. 856

ADD: STYLE OF THE CASE – FORM 1B:2
SIGNATURE BLOCK – FORM 1B:3
CERTIFICATE OF SERVICE – FORM 1B:13

ATTACH: AFFIDAVIT – FORM 1B:8, if necessary
ORDER – FORM 1G:1
MOTION TO AMEND PLEADING – FORM 8F:1, if necessary
MOTION TO REOPEN – FORM 8H:1, if necessary

{❶ *PARTY*}'S MOTION TO REOPEN THE EVIDENCE

{❷ *Party*}, {❸ *name*}, asks the Court to allow {❹ *him/her/it*} to reopen the evidence to present additional evidence in this case. {*See **O'Connor's Texas Rules**, "Motion to Reopen," ch. 8-H, §2, p. 858.*}

INTRODUCTION

1. Plaintiff, {❺ *name*}, sued defendant, {❻ *name*}, for {❼ *state basis of suit*}.

2. {❽ *State other relevant facts about the suit.*}

BACKGROUND

3. Although all parties have rested, it is necessary for {❾ *party*} to present additional relevant evidence of {❿ *describe the issue for which the evidence is necessary*}.

4. The evidence that {⓫ *party*} seeks to offer is {⓬ *identify evidence*}. {⓭ *Party*} attaches {⓮ *identify evidence*} to this motion as Exhibit(s) {⓯ *letter(s)*} in support of the motion and incorporates {⓰ *it/them*} by reference.

5. {⓱ *State other facts relevant to the motion.*}

ARGUMENT & AUTHORITIES

6. A trial court should reopen the evidence when the introduction of additional evidence clearly appears to be necessary to the administration of justice. Tex. R. Civ. P. 270. The decision to reopen the case to permit additional evidence is within the trial court's sound discretion. *Poag v. Flories*, 317 S.W.3d 820, 828 (Tex. App.—Fort Worth 2010, pet. denied); *Lopez v. Lopez*, 55 S.W.3d 194, 201 (Tex. App.—Corpus Christi 2001, no pet.); *In re Hawk*, 5 S.W.3d 874, 876-77 (Tex. App.—Houston [14th Dist.] 1999, no pet.). The trial court should liberally exercise that discretion to permit the full development of the case. *Lopez*, 55 S.W.3d at 201; *In re Hawk*, 5 S.W.3d at 877. {*See **O'Connor's Texas Rules**, "Standard," ch. 8-H, §4, p. 858.*}

7. In deciding whether to allow additional evidence, a court should consider (1) whether the movant has been diligent in obtaining the evidence, (2) whether the receipt of additional evidence will cause undue delay or injustice, and (3) whether the evidence will be decisive. *Moore v. Jet Stream Invs., Ltd.*, 315 S.W.3d 195, 201 (Tex. App.—Texarkana 2010, pet. denied); *Hernandez v. Lautensack*, 201 S.W.3d 771, 779 (Tex. App.—Fort Worth 2006, pet. denied); *Lopez*, 55 S.W.3d at 201.

8. The Court should reopen the evidence in this case for the following reasons: {*See* ***O'Connor's Texas Rules****, "Grounds," ch. 8-H, §2.2, p. 858.*}

a. {[18] *Party*} was diligent in obtaining evidence. Specifically, {[19] *specify evidence party produced*}.

b. The receipt of evidence will not cause undue delay because {[20] *explain*}.

c. The receipt of evidence will not cause an injustice because {[21] *explain*}.

d. The evidence is decisive because it establishes {[22] *describe what evidence establishes*}.

CONCLUSION

9. {[23] *Briefly summarize the motion.*}

PRAYER

10. For these reasons, {[24] *party*} asks the Court to reopen the evidence.

SEE: Tex. R. Civ. P. 270
O'Connor's Texas Rules * Civil Trials (2019), "Motion to Reopen for Additional Evidence," ch. 8-H, p. 857

ADD: STYLE OF THE CASE – FORM 1B:2
SIGNATURE BLOCK – FORM 1B:3
CERTIFICATE OF SERVICE – FORM 1B:13

ATTACH: AFFIDAVIT – FORM 1B:8, if necessary
ORDER – FORM 1G:1

{❶ *PARTY*}'S RESPONSE TO
{❷ *ADVERSE PARTY*}'S MOTION TO REOPEN THE EVIDENCE

{❸ *Party*}, {❹ *name*}, asks the Court to deny {❺ *adverse party*} {❻ *name*}'s motion to reopen the evidence to present additional evidence in this case. {*See* ***O'Connor's Texas Rules***, *"Motion to Reopen," ch. 8-H, §2, p. 858.*}

INTRODUCTION

1. Plaintiff, {❼ *name*}, sued defendant, {❽ *name*}, for {❾ *state basis of suit*}.

2. {❿ *State other relevant facts about the suit.*}

BACKGROUND

3. {⓫ *State facts relevant to the response.*}

ARGUMENT & AUTHORITIES

{*ADD PARAGRAPH 4 IF APPROPRIATE*}

4. In a jury trial, the court cannot admit evidence on a controversial matter after the jury returns the verdict. Tex. R. Civ. P. 270. The Court should deny {⓬ *adverse party*}'s motion to reopen the evidence because {⓭ *adverse party*} seeks to offer evidence on a controversial matter after the jury has returned a verdict. *Guerrero v. Standard Alloys Mfg. Co.*, 598 S.W.2d 656, 658 (Tex. App.—Beaumont 1980, writ ref'd n.r.e.). {⓮ *Elaborate.*}

5. A trial court should deny a motion to reopen the evidence when the introduction of additional evidence does not clearly appear to be necessary to the administration of justice. *See* Tex. R. Civ. P. 270. In deciding whether to allow additional evidence, a court should consider (1) whether the movant has been diligent in obtaining the evidence, (2) whether the receipt of additional evidence will cause undue delay or injustice, and (3) whether the evidence will be decisive. *Moore v. Jet Stream Invs., Ltd.*, 315 S.W.3d 195, 201 (Tex. App.—Texarkana 2010, pet. denied); *Hernandez v. Lautensack*, 201 S.W.3d 771, 779 (Tex. App.—Fort Worth 2006, pet. denied); *Lopez v. Lopez*, 55 S.W.3d 194, 201 (Tex. App.—Corpus Christi 2001, no pet.). {*See* ***O'Connor's Texas Rules***, *"Grounds," ch. 8-H, §2.2, p. 858.*}

{*CHOOSE APPROPRIATE PARAGRAPHS 6-9*}

6. The Court should deny {⓯ *adverse party*}'s motion to reopen the evidence because {⓰ *adverse party*} was not diligent in obtaining the evidence. *Poag v. Flories*, 317 S.W.3d 820, 828 (Tex. App.—Fort Worth 2010, pet. denied). {⓱ *Elaborate.*}

7. The Court should deny {18 *adverse party*}'s motion to reopen the evidence because receipt of the evidence that {19 *adverse party*} seeks to offer will cause undue delay. {20 *Elaborate.*}

8. The Court should deny {21 *adverse party*}'s motion to reopen the evidence because receipt of the evidence that {22 *adverse party*} seeks to offer will cause an injustice. {23 *Elaborate.*}

9. The Court should deny {24 *adverse party*}'s motion to reopen the evidence because the evidence that {25 *adverse party*} seeks to offer is not decisive. *Naguib v. Naguib*, 137 S.W.3d 367, 373 (Tex. App.—Dallas 2004, pet. denied). {26 *Elaborate.*}

CONCLUSION

10. {27 *Briefly summarize the response.*}

PRAYER

11. For these reasons, {28 *party*} asks the Court to deny {29 *adverse party*}'s motion to reopen the evidence.

SEE: Tex. R. Civ. P. 270
O'Connor's Texas Rules * Civil Trials (2019), "Motion to Reopen for Additional Evidence," ch. 8-H, p. 857

ADD: STYLE OF THE CASE – FORM 1B:2
SIGNATURE BLOCK – FORM 1B:3
CERTIFICATE OF SERVICE – FORM 1B:13

ATTACH: AFFIDAVIT – FORM 1B:8, if necessary
ORDER – FORM 1G:1
Proposed evidence

WRITTEN INSTRUCTIONS FROM THE COURT

{❶ *Members of the Jury/Ladies and Gentlemen of the Jury*}:

After the closing arguments, you will go to the jury room to decide the case, answer the questions that are attached, and reach a verdict. You may discuss the case with other jurors only when you are all together in the jury room.

Remember my previous instructions: Do not discuss the case with anyone else, either in person or by any other means. Do not do any independent investigation about the case or conduct any research. Do not look up any words in dictionaries or on the Internet. Do not post information about the case on the Internet. Do not share any special knowledge or experiences with the other jurors. Do not use your phone or any other electronic device during your deliberations for any reason. {❷ *Add if appropriate: I will give you a telephone number where others may contact you in case of an emergency.*}

{*ADD THE FOLLOWING TWO PARAGRAPHS ON JURY NOTES IF APPROPRIATE*}

Any notes you have taken are for your own personal use. You may take your notes back into the jury room and consult them during deliberations, but do not show or read your notes to your fellow jurors during your deliberations. Your notes are not evidence. Each of you should rely on your independent recollection of the evidence and not be influenced by the fact that another juror has or has not taken notes.

You must leave your notes with the bailiff when you are not deliberating. The bailiff will give your notes to me promptly after collecting them from you. I will make sure your notes are kept in a safe, secure location and not disclosed to anyone. After you complete your deliberations, the bailiff will collect your notes. When you are released from jury duty, the bailiff will promptly destroy your notes so that nobody can read what you wrote.

Here are the instructions for answering the questions.

1. Do not let bias, prejudice, or sympathy play any part in your decision.

2. Base your answers only on the evidence admitted in court and on the law that is in these instructions and questions. Do not consider or discuss any evidence that was not admitted in the courtroom.

3. You are to make up your own minds about the facts. You are the sole judges of the credibility of the witnesses and the weight to give their testimony. But on matters of law, you must follow all of my instructions.

4. If my instructions use a word in a way that is different from its ordinary meaning, use the meaning I give you, which will be a proper legal definition.

5. All the questions and answers are important. No one should say that any question or answer is not important.

6. Answer "yes" or "no" to all questions unless you are told otherwise. A "yes" answer must be based on a preponderance of the evidence {❸ *add if appropriate: unless you are told otherwise*}. Whenever a question requires an answer other than "yes" or "no," your answer must be based on a preponderance of the evidence {❹ *add if appropriate: unless you are told otherwise*}.

The term "preponderance of the evidence" means the greater weight of credible evidence presented in this case. If you do not find that a preponderance of the evidence supports a "yes" answer, then answer "no." A preponderance of the evidence is not measured by the number of witnesses or by the number of documents admitted in evidence. For a fact to be proved by a preponderance of the evidence, you must find that the fact is more likely true than not true.

7. Do not decide who you think should win before you answer the questions and then just answer the questions to match your decision. Answer each question carefully without considering who will win. Do not discuss or consider the effect your answers will have.

8. Do not answer questions by drawing straws or by any method of chance.

9. Some questions might ask you for a dollar amount. Do not agree in advance to decide on a dollar amount by adding up each juror's amount and then figuring the average.

10. Do not trade your answers. For example, do not say, "I will answer this question your way if you answer another question my way."

11. The answers to the questions must be based on the decision of at least {❺ *10 of the 12/5 of the 6*} jurors. The same {❻ *10/5*} jurors must agree on every answer. Do not agree to be bound by a vote of anything less than {❼ *10/5*} jurors, even if it would be a majority. {❽ *Add instruction if answers to any questions require the jury to vote unanimously.*}

As I have said before, if you do not follow these instructions, you will be guilty of juror misconduct, and I might have to order a new trial and start this process over again. This would waste your time and the parties' money, and would require the taxpayers of

Continued on next page

this county to pay for another trial. If a juror breaks any of these rules, tell that person to stop and report it to me immediately.

{❾ *Insert the definitions, questions, and special instructions for the jury.*}

DEFINITIONS & SPECIAL INSTRUCTIONS

You are instructed that {❿ *insert definitions or instructions that apply to all questions, e.g., the parties in this case have entered into a number of stipulations. This means that both sides agree that the stipulated matters are facts. You must therefore treat each stipulated fact as having been proved*}. {⓫ *Repeat for each additional definition or instruction.*}

QUESTION NO. 1

{⓬ *Insert question.*}

{⓭ *Insert definitions if applicable.*}

{⓮ *Insert special instructions if applicable.*}

Answer "Yes" or "No"
ANSWER: ____________

{⓯ *Insert conditioning language if applicable, e.g., If your answer to Question 1 is "Yes," then answer the following question. Otherwise, do not answer the following question and proceed to Question 5.*}

QUESTION NO. 2

{⓰ *Insert question.*}

{⓱ *Insert definitions if applicable.*}

{⓲ *Insert special instructions if applicable.*}

Answer "Yes" or "No"
ANSWER: ____________

{*Repeat for each additional question.*}

{*ADD IF PLAINTIFF SEEKS EXEMPLARY DAMAGES*}

QUESTION NO. {19 *NUMBER*}

{20 *Insert question about defendant's liability on at least one claim for actual damages that will support an award of exemplary damages.*}

Answer "Yes" or "No"

ANSWER: ____________

Answer Question {21 *number*} for {22 *name of defendant*} only if you unanimously answered "Yes" to Question {23 *number*} regarding {24 *name of defendant*}. Otherwise, do not answer Question {25 *number*} regarding {26 *name of defendant*}.

{*Repeat for each additional defendant.*}

You are instructed that in order to answer "Yes" to {27 *add if applicable: any part of*} Question {28 *number*}, your answer must be unanimous. You may answer "No" to {29 *add if applicable: any part of*} Question {30 *number*} only upon a vote of {31 *10/5*} or more jurors. Otherwise, you must not answer {32 *add if applicable: that part of*} Question {33 *number*}.

QUESTION NO. {34 *NUMBER*}

{35 *Insert question about any additional conduct, such as malice or gross negligence, required for an award of exemplary damages.*}

Answer "Yes" or "No"

ANSWER: ____________

Answer Question {36 *number*} for {37 *name of defendant*} only if you answered "Yes" to Question {38 *number*} for {39 *name of defendant*}. Otherwise, do not answer Question {40 *number*} for {41 *name of defendant*}.

{*Repeat for each additional defendant.*}

You are instructed that you must unanimously agree on the amount of any award of exemplary damages.

QUESTION NO. {42 *NUMBER*}

{43 *Insert question about the amount of exemplary damages to be awarded.*}

ANSWER: ____________

◄ *Continued on next page* ►

PRESIDING JUROR

1. When you go into the jury room to answer the questions, the first thing you will need to do is choose a presiding juror.

2. The presiding juror has these duties:

   a. Have the complete charge read aloud if it will be helpful to your deliberations.

   b. Preside over your deliberations, meaning manage the discussions, and see that you follow these instructions.

   c. Give written questions or comments to the bailiff, who will give them to the judge.

   d. Write down the answers you agree on.

   e. Get the signatures for the verdict certificate.

   f. Notify the bailiff that you have reached a verdict.

Do you understand the duties of the presiding juror? If you do not, please tell me now.

INSTRUCTIONS FOR SIGNING THE VERDICT CERTIFICATE

1. You may answer the questions on a vote of {44 *10/5*} jurors. The same {45 *10/5*} jurors must agree on every answer in the charge. This means you may not have one group of {46 *10/5*} jurors agree on one answer and a different group of {47 *10/5*} jurors agree on another answer. {48 *Add instruction if answers to any questions require the jury to vote unanimously.*}

2. If {49 *10/5*} jurors agree on every answer, those {50 *10/5*} jurors sign the verdict. {51 *Add if appropriate: If 11 jurors agree on every answer, those 11 jurors sign the verdict.*} If all {52 *12/6*} of you agree on every answer, you are unanimous, and only the presiding juror signs the verdict.

3. All jurors should deliberate on every question. You may end up with all {53 *12/6*} of you agreeing on some answers, while only {54 *10 or 11/5*} of you agree on other answers. But when you sign the verdict, only those {55 *10/5*} who agree on every answer will sign the verdict.

{ADD IF THE CHARGE REQUIRES SOME UNANIMOUS ANSWERS}

4. There are some special instructions before Questions {56 *numbers*} explaining how to answer those questions. Please follow the instructions. If all {57 *12/6*} of you answer those questions, you will need to complete a second verdict certificate for those questions.

Do you understand these instructions? If you do not, please tell me now.

____
PRESIDING JUDGE

SEE: Tex. R. Civ. P. 226a, 292
O'Connor's Texas Rules * Civil Trials (2019), "Charge Submitted to Jury," ch. 8-I, §6, p. 871

ADD: STYLE OF THE CASE – FORM 1B:2

ATTACH: VERDICT CERTIFICATE – FORM 8I:2

NOTE: These instructions, which are given to the jury panel as part of the charge, may be modified "as the circumstances of the particular case may require." Tex. R. Civ. P. 226a, "Court's Charge," §III.

For an instruction to be proper, it must (1) assist the jury in its deliberations, (2) accurately state the law, and (3) be supported by the pleadings and the evidence. ***Gunn v. McCoy***, 554 S.W.3d 645, 675 (Tex. 2018); ***Thota v. Young***, 366 S.W.3d 678, 687 (Tex.2012); ***Columbia Rio Grande Healthcare, L.P. v. Hawley***, 284 S.W.3d 851, 855 (Tex.2009).

The parties generally must make all objections to the charge before the court reads the charge to the jury. Tex. R. Civ. P. 272; ***King Fisher Mar. Serv. v. Tamez***, 443 S.W.3d 838, 843 (Tex.2014); ***Cruz v. Andrews Restoration, Inc.***, 364 S.W.3d 817, 830 (Tex.2012). But Texas Rule of Civil Procedure 272 allows a court to set a deadline for the parties to object to the charge that expires before the charge is read to the jury as long as the parties had a reasonable time to examine and object to the charge. ***King Fisher Mar.***, 443 S.W.3d at 843. See ***O'Connor's Texas Rules***, "General rule," ch. 8-I, §4.2.1(1), p. 865. The parties do not have to object before the charge is read to the jury when the parties are (1) challenging the legal sufficiency of the evidence, (2) objecting that a certain legal theory precludes recovery, or (3) objecting to an immaterial jury question. See ***O'Connor's Texas Rules***, "Exceptions," ch. 8-I, §4.2.1(2), p. 866.

If a plaintiff seeks exemplary damages against a defendant, the jury must unanimously find, for that defendant, (1) liability on at least one claim for actual damages that will support an award of exemplary damages, (2) any additional conduct, such as malice or gross negligence, required for an award of exemplary damages, and (3) the amount of exemplary damages. Tex. R. Civ. P. 226a, "Court's Charge," §III. The jury is not required to be unanimous on the amount of actual damages. *Id.*

VERDICT CERTIFICATE

{*CHECK APPROPRIATE OPTION BELOW*}

____ Our verdict is unanimous. All {❶ *12/6*} of us have agreed to each and every answer. The presiding juror has signed the certificate for all {❷ *12/6*} of us.

____
PRESIDING JUROR

____
PRINTED NAME OF
PRESIDING JUROR

____ Our verdict is not unanimous. Eleven of us have agreed to each and every answer and have signed the certificate below.

____ Our verdict is not unanimous. {❸ *Ten/Five*} of us have agreed to each and every answer and have signed the certificate below.

Jurors' Signatures | Jurors' Printed Names

{❹ *Insert appropriate number of lines for signatures and printed names.*}

{*ADD THE FOLLOWING SENTENCE IF CHARGE INCLUDES QUESTION ON EXEMPLARY-DAMAGES AMOUNT*}

If you have answered Question No. {❺ *number*}, then you must sign this certificate also.

{ADD THE ADDITIONAL CERTIFICATE IF SOME OF THE JURY'S ANSWERS MUST BE UNANIMOUS}

ADDITIONAL CERTIFICATE

I certify that the jury was unanimous in answering the following questions. All {❻ *12/6*} of us agreed to each of the answers. The presiding juror has signed the certificate for all {❼ *12/6*} of us.

{❽ *List questions that require a unanimous answer, including the predicate liability question.*}

____
PRESIDING JUROR

____
PRINTED NAME OF PRESIDING JUROR

SEE: Tex. R. Civ. P. 226a, 292

ADD: STYLE OF THE CASE – FORM 1B:2

DEFENDANT'S MOTION TO OPEN & CLOSE FINAL ARGUMENT

Defendant, {❶ *name*}, asks the Court to allow {❷ *him/her/it*} to open and close the final argument in this case. {*See **O'Connor's Texas Rules**, "Defendant opens & closes," ch. 8-J, §2.2, p. 879.*}

INTRODUCTION

1. Plaintiff, {❸ *name*}, sued defendant, {❹ *name*}, for {❺ *state basis of suit*}.

2. {❻ *State other relevant facts about the suit.*}

BACKGROUND

3. The parties have entered all of their evidence, and the charge has been prepared and read to the jury.

4. {❼ *State other facts relevant to the motion.*}

ARGUMENT & AUTHORITIES

5. A defendant has the right to open and close the final argument if the defendant has the burden of proof on all matters submitted in the court's charge to the jury or on the entire case. Tex. R. Civ. P. 269(a).

{*CHOOSE APPROPRIATE PARAGRAPH 6*}

6. The Court should grant defendant the right to open and close the final argument in this case because {❽ *he/she/it*} has the burden of proof on all matters submitted in the Court's charge to the jury. Specifically, defendant has the burden of proof on {❾ *list issues on which defendant has the burden of proof*}. {*See **O'Connor's Texas Rules**, "Burden in the charge," ch. 8-J, §2.2.2, p. 879.*}

6. The Court should grant defendant the right to open and close the final argument in this case because {❿ *he/she/it*} has the burden of proof on the entire case. {⓫ *Elaborate.*} {*See **O'Connor's Texas Rules**, "Burden of proof," ch. 8-J, §2.2.1, p. 879.*}

CONCLUSION

7. {⓬ *Briefly summarize the motion.*}

PRAYER

8. For these reasons, defendant asks the Court to grant this motion and allow defendant to open and close the final argument in this case.

FORM 8J:1

FORM 8J:1 MOTION TO OPEN & CLOSE FINAL ARGUMENT

SEE: Tex. R. Civ. P. 269(a)
O'Connor's Texas Rules * Civil Trials (2019), "Defendant opens & closes," ch. 8-J, §2.2, p. 879

ADD: STYLE OF THE CASE – FORM 1B:2
SIGNATURE BLOCK – FORM 1B:3
VERIFICATION – FORM 1B:7
CERTIFICATE OF SERVICE – FORM 1B:13

ATTACH: AFFIDAVIT – FORM 1B:8, if necessary
NOTICE OF HEARING OR SUBMISSION – FORM 1E:1
ORDER – FORM 1G:1

PLAINTIFF'S RESPONSE TO
DEFENDANT'S MOTION TO OPEN & CLOSE FINAL ARGUMENT

Plaintiff, {❶ *name*}, asks the Court to deny defendant's motion to open and close the final argument in this case.

INTRODUCTION

1. Plaintiff, {❷ *name*}, sued defendant, {❸ *name*}, for {❹ *state basis of suit*}.

2. Defendant answered, asserting the defenses of {❺ *identify defenses*}.

3. {❻ *State other relevant facts about the suit.*}

BACKGROUND

4. {❼ *State facts relevant to the response.*}

ARGUMENT & AUTHORITIES

5. A defendant has the right to open and close the final argument only if the defendant bears the burden of proof on all matters submitted in the court's charge to the jury or on the entire case. Tex. R. Civ. P. 269(a); *see Ocean Transp., Inc. v. Greycas, Inc.*, 878 S.W.2d 256, 269 (Tex. App.—Corpus Christi 1994, writ denied); *First State Bank v. Fatheree*, 847 S.W.2d 391, 397 (Tex. App.—Amarillo 1993, writ denied); *Horton v. Dental Capital Leasing Corp.*, 649 S.W.2d 655, 657 (Tex. App.—Texarkana 1983, no writ).

{*CHOOSE APPROPRIATE PARAGRAPH 6*}

6. Defendant should not be granted the right to open and close the final argument in this case because {❽ *he/she/it*} does not bear the burden of proof on all matters submitted in the Court's charge to the jury. Specifically, defendant does not bear the burden of proof on {❾ *identify issues on which plaintiff has the burden of proof, e.g., request for attorney fees*}. Plaintiff bears the burden of proof on {❿ *this issue/these issues*}. {*See* ***O'Connor's Texas Rules****, "Burden in the charge," ch. 8-J, §2.2.2, p. 879.*}

6. Defendant should not be granted the right to open and close the final argument in this case because {⓫ *he/she/it*} does not bear the burden of proof on the entire case. Specifically, defendant does not bear the burden of proof on {⓬ *identify issues on which plaintiff has the burden of proof, e.g., request for attorney fees*}. Plaintiff bears the burden of proof on {⓭ *this issue/these issues*}. {*See* ***O'Connor's Texas Rules****, "Burden of proof," ch. 8-J, §2.2.1, p. 879.*}

CONCLUSION

7. {⓮ *Briefly summarize the response.*}

PRAYER

8. For these reasons, plaintiff asks the Court to deny defendant's motion and allow plaintiff to open and close the final argument in this case.

SEE: Tex. R. Civ. P. 269(a)
O'Connor's Texas Rules * Civil Trials (2019), "Right to Open & Close Final Argument," ch. 8-J, §2, p. 879

ADD: STYLE OF THE CASE – FORM 1B:2
SIGNATURE BLOCK – FORM 1B:3
CERTIFICATE OF SERVICE – FORM 1B:13

ATTACH: AFFIDAVIT – FORM 1B:8, if necessary
ORDER – FORM 1G:1

CHAPTER 9. THE JUDGMENT

TABLE OF CONTENTS

{[1] *PARTY*}'S MOTION FOR JUDGMENT

{[2] *Party*}, {[3] *name*}, asks the Court to sign a judgment based on the {[4] *jury's findings/decision announced after a nonjury trial*}. {*See* ***O'Connor's Texas Rules****, "Winner," ch. 9-A, §2.1.1, p. 891.*}

INTRODUCTION

1. Plaintiff, {[5] *name*}, sued defendant, {[6] *name*}, for {[7] *state basis of suit*}.

2. {[8] *State other relevant facts about the suit.*}

BACKGROUND

{*CHOOSE APPROPRIATE PARAGRAPH 3*}

3. After a trial on the merits, the Court submitted this case to the jury. {[9] *Party*} attaches as Exhibit {[10] *letter*} the questions the jury considered and its answers. The jury's findings entitle {[11] *party*} to a judgment against {[12] *adverse party*}, {[13] *name*}.

3. After a nonjury trial, the Court announced that it was rendering judgment for {[14] *party*} against {[15] *adverse party*}, {[16] *name*}.

4. The trial ended on {[17] *date*}. On that date, the Court {[18] *accepted the jury's verdict/announced its decision*}. No judgment has been signed even though {[19] *number*} {[20] *weeks/months*} have passed.

5. {[21] *State other facts relevant to the motion.*}

DAMAGES & INTEREST

6. The Court should sign a judgment for {[22] *party*} against {[23] *adverse party*} for the sum of ${[24] *amount*}, {[25] *add if allowed: prejudgment interest on that sum at the annual rate of {specify rate of interest}, in the sum of ${amount},*} postjudgment interest on the total sum at the annual rate of {[26] *specify rate of interest*}, {[27] *add if applicable: attorney fees,*} and court costs. {*See* ***O'Connor's Texas Rules****, "Winner," ch. 9-A, §2.1.1, p. 891.*}

PRAYER

7. For these reasons, {[28] *party*} asks the Court to sign a judgment, attached as Exhibit {[29] *letter*}.

Continued on next page

FORM 9A:1 MOTION FOR JUDGMENT – WINNING PARTY

SEE: Tex. R. Civ. P. 300-314
Tex. Fin. Code §304.001 et seq., §304.101 et seq.
O'Connor's Texas Rules * Civil Trials (2019), "Motion for judgment on the verdict," ch. 9-A, §2.1, p. 891
O'Connor's Texas Causes of Action (2019), "Damages & Other Compensation," Part 4, p. 1343

ADD: STYLE OF THE CASE – FORM 1B:2
SIGNATURE BLOCK – FORM 1B:3
CERTIFICATE OF SERVICE – FORM 1B:13

ATTACH: NOTICE OF HEARING OR SUBMISSION – FORM 1E:1
JUDGMENT – FORM 9C:1
Jury charge, if necessary

NOTE: It is not necessary to hold a hearing on a motion for judgment. If a party wants a hearing, it should request one in writing.

{[1] *PARTY*}'S MOTION FOR JUDGMENT

{[2] *Party*}, {[3] *name*}, asks the Court to sign a judgment based on the {[4] *jury's findings/decision announced after a nonjury trial*}. {*See* ***O'Connor's Texas Rules****, "Loser," ch. 9-A, §2.1.2, p. 891.*}

INTRODUCTION

1. Plaintiff, {[5] *name*}, sued defendant, {[6] *name*}, for {[7] *state basis of suit*}.

2. {[8] *State other relevant facts about the suit.*}

BACKGROUND

{*CHOOSE APPROPRIATE PARAGRAPH 3*}

3. After a trial on the merits, the Court submitted this case to the jury. {[9] *Party*} attaches as Exhibit {[10] *letter*} the questions the jury considered and its answers.

3. After a nonjury trial, the Court announced that it was rendering judgment for {[11] *adverse party*}, {[12] *name*}, against {[13] *party*}.

4. The trial ended on {[14] *date*}. On that date, the Court {[15] *accepted the jury's verdict/announced its decision*}. No judgment has been signed even though {[16] *number*} {[17] *weeks/months*} have passed.

5. {[18] *State other facts relevant to the motion.*}

ARGUMENT & AUTHORITIES

6. {[19] *Party*} asks the Court to sign the proposed judgment {[20] *filed by {adverse party}/attached as Exhibit {letter}*} so that the appellate deadlines may begin to run.

7. {[21] *Party*} agrees only with the form of the proposed judgment, disagrees with the content and result of the proposed judgment, and plans to challenge the proposed judgment on appeal. *See First Nat'l Bank v. Fojtik*, 775 S.W.2d 632, 633 (Tex. 1989). {*See* ***O'Connor's Texas Rules****, "On the verdict," ch. 9-A, §2.1.2(1), p. 891.*}

PRAYER

8. For these reasons, {[22] *party*} asks the Court to sign a judgment.

◄ Continued on next page ►

FORM 9A:2 MOTION FOR JUDGMENT – LOSING PARTY

SEE: Tex. R. Civ. P. 300-314
*O'Connor's Texas Rules * Civil Trials* (2019), "Motion for judgment on the verdict," ch. 9-A, §2.1, p. 891
O'Connor's Texas Causes of Action (2019), "Damages & Other Compensation," Part 4, p. 1343

ADD: STYLE OF THE CASE – FORM 1B:2
SIGNATURE BLOCK – FORM 1B:3
CERTIFICATE OF SERVICE – FORM 1B:13

ATTACH: NOTICE OF HEARING OR SUBMISSION – FORM 1E:1
JUDGMENT – FORM 9C:1
Jury charge, if necessary

NOTE: This form is for the party who lost the case but wants the court to sign a judgment so that the party can begin the appeal. By including paragraph 7, the losing party preserves the right to challenge the judgment even though the party is asking the court to sign an adverse judgment. The reservation of the right to appeal should be contained in this motion; the reservation is not effective if it is contained in some other document, like a brief. See *O'Connor's Texas Rules*, "On the verdict," ch. 9-A, §2.1.2(1), p. 891.

If the losing party is entitled to limit damages, or if the winning party prevailed on two theories of recovery and is required to elect damages, the losing party should include these objections in the motion for judgment. See FORM 9A:3, ¶¶7-11.

{1 *PARTY*}'S OBJECTIONS TO
{2 *ADVERSE PARTY*}'S PROPOSED JUDGMENT

{3 *Party*}, {4 *name*}, objects to {5 *adverse party*} {6 *name*}'s proposed judgment.

INTRODUCTION

1. Plaintiff, {7 *name*}, sued defendant, {8 *name*}, for {9 *state basis of suit*}.

2. {10 *State other relevant facts about the suit.*}

BACKGROUND

{*CHOOSE APPROPRIATE PARAGRAPH 3*}

3. After a trial on the merits, the Court submitted this case to the jury. {11 *Party*} attaches to this objection as Exhibit {12 *letter*} the questions the jury considered and its answers.

3. After a nonjury trial, the Court announced that it was rendering judgment for {13 *adverse party*} against {14 *party*}.

4. {15 *Adverse party*} filed a motion asking the Court to sign a judgment based on the {16 *jury's answers/decision announced after a nonjury trial*}. {17 *Party*} attaches to this objection as Exhibit {18 *letter*} {19 *adverse party*}'s proposed judgment.

5. {20 *State other facts relevant to the objection.*}

ARGUMENT & AUTHORITIES

{*CHOOSE APPROPRIATE PARAGRAPHS 6-23*}

{*General objections*}

6. {21 *Party*} objects to the proposed judgment because {22 *state objections to proposed judgment, e.g., the proposed judgment misapplies the law to the facts*}. {23 *Elaborate.*}

{*Objections to damages*}

7. {24 *Party*} objects to the proposed judgment because the damages are not properly calculated. {25 *Identify specific objections to damages, e.g., party is entitled to a limitation on damages because adverse party seeks a recovery of exemplary damages that exceeds the maximum allowed under Texas Civil Practice & Remedies Code section 41.008(b).*} {26 *Elaborate.*} {*See* ***O'Connor's Texas Rules****, "To limit damages," ch. 9-A, §2.1.2(2), p. 892.*}

Continued on next page

FORM 9A:3

8. {㉗ *Party*} objects to the proposed judgment because {㉘ *adverse party*} cannot receive a double recovery for the same injury. At trial, {㉙ *adverse party*} prevailed on {㉚ *identify theories of recovery*}. Two of those theories of recovery represent damages for the same injury. {㉛ *Explain how damages for both theories are for the same injury.*} Thus, {㉜ *adverse party*} must be required to elect between the remedies because {㉝ *he/she/it*} is not entitled to a double recovery. *Waite Hill Servs., Inc. v. World Class Metal Works, Inc.*, 959 S.W.2d 182, 184 (Tex. 1998). {*See* ***O'Connor's Texas Rules***, *"To force election of remedies," ch. 9-A, §2.1.2(3), p. 892; "Alternative recoveries," ch. 9-C, §4.4.2(1), p. 902.*}

9. {㉞ *Party*} objects to {㉟ *adverse party*}'s proposed judgment because {㊱ *adverse party*} is not entitled to damages in the amount of ${㊲ *amount*}. This is a suit under the Texas Deceptive Trade Practices Act in which {㊳ *adverse party*} rejected {㊴ *party*}'s offer of settlement made in compliance with Texas Business & Commerce Code section 17.5052(a), (d), and (f). Attached as Exhibit {㊵ *letter*} is a copy of {㊶ *party*}'s affidavit certifying rejection of the settlement offer. The terms of the settlement offer were the following: {㊷ *state amount or terms of settlement offer*}. The {㊸ *jury/Court*} found damages for {㊹ *adverse party*} to be {㊺ *state amount of damages*}. The amount of the settlement offer, reduced to cash value, was {㊻ *the same as/substantially the same as/more than*} the amount of the damages found by the {㊼ *jury/Court*}. Under Texas Business & Commerce Code section 17.5052(g), {㊽ *adverse party*}'s recovery is limited to the lesser of (1) the amount of damages tendered in the settlement offer or (2) the amount of damages found by the trier of fact. Therefore, {㊾ *adverse party*}'s recovery is limited to ${㊿ *amount*}. {*See* ***O'Connor's Texas COA***, *"Offers of settlement," ch. 8, §7.1, p. 249.*}

10. {51 *Party*} objects to {52 *adverse party*}'s proposed judgment because {53 *adverse party*} is not entitled to damages in the amount of ${54 *amount*}. This is a suit in which {55 *adverse party*} rejected {56 *party*}'s offer of settlement made in compliance with Texas Civil Practice & Remedies Code chapter 42 and Texas Rule of Civil Procedure 167. Attached as Exhibit {57 *letter*} is a copy of {58 *adverse party*}'s written notice rejecting the offer of settlement. The terms of the settlement offer were the following: {59 *state amount or terms of settlement offer*}. The {60 *jury/Court*} found damages for {61 *adverse party*} to be {62 *state amount of damages*}. The amount of damages found by the {63 *jury/Court*}, reduced to cash value, was significantly less favorable to {64 *adverse party*} than {65 *party*}'s offer of settlement. {66 *Elaborate.*} {67 *Party*} is entitled to recover {68 *his/her/its*} litigation costs incurred after rejection of the offer as an offset against {69 *adverse party*}'s recovery. Tex. Civ. Prac. & Rem. Code §42.004(a), (c), (g); Tex. R. Civ. P. 167.4(a), (g). A hearing is requested to determine the amount and reasonableness of {70 *party*}'s litigation costs to be incorporated with the

{71 *jury/Court*}'s finding of damages in the final judgment. Tex. R. Civ. P. 167.5(c). {*See* ***O'Connor's Texas Rules**, "Litigation Costs," ch. 7-H, §6, p. 790.*}

11. {72 *Party*} objects to {73 *adverse party*}'s proposed judgment because {74 *adverse party*} is not entitled to damages in the amount of ${75 *amount*}. Damages in this suit are limited under {76 *state statute that limits damages and explain how statute applies in the suit*}.

{*Objections to interest*}

12. {77 *Party*} objects to the proposed judgment because the {78 *prejudgment/postjudgment*} interest was not properly calculated. {79 *Explain how interest was not properly calculated.*} {*See* ***O'Connor's Texas Rules**, "Calculating prejudgment interest," ch. 9-C, §4.5.2, p. 903; "Calculating postjudgment interest," ch. 9-C, §4.6.2, p. 905.*}

13. {80 *Party*} objects to the proposed judgment because {81 *adverse party*} is not entitled to prejudgment interest. {82 *Explain why no prejudgment interest is permissible, citing statute or case law.*} {*See* ***O'Connor's Texas Rules**, "Prejudgment interest not permitted," ch. 9-C, §4.5.3, p. 904.*}

{*General objection to attorney fees*}

14. {83 *Party*} objects to the proposed judgment because {84 *adverse party*} is not entitled to attorney fees in this case under {85 *cite rule, statute, or contract under which the adverse party claims attorney fees*}. {86 *Elaborate.*} Attorney fees must be authorized by statute or contract; common law does not provide a right to attorney fees. *Hill v. Heritage Res., Inc.*, 964 S.W.2d 89, 143 (Tex. App.—El Paso 1997, pet. denied); *see Holland v. Wal-Mart Stores, Inc.*, 1 S.W.3d 91, 95 (Tex. 1999). {*See* ***O'Connor's Texas COA**, "Attorney Fees," ch. 45, p. 1463.*}

{*Objections to attorney fees under Tex. Civ. Prac. & Rem. Code ch. 38*}

15. {87 *Party*} objects to the proposed judgment because {88 *adverse party*} is not entitled to attorney fees in this case under Texas Civil Practice & Remedies Code chapter 38. Specifically, the claim is not listed in Texas Civil Practice & Remedies Code section 38.001. *See 1/2 Price Checks Cashed v. United Auto. Ins. Co.*, 344 S.W.3d 378, 383 (Tex. 2011); *London v. London*, 94 S.W.3d 139, 147-48 (Tex. App.—Houston [14th Dist.] 2002, no pet.); *see, e.g., Henry v. Ins. Co. of N. Am.*, 879 S.W.2d 366, 368-69 (Tex. App.—Houston [14th Dist.] 1994, no writ) (garnishment action does not entitle party to attorney fees under §38.001). {89 *Elaborate.*} {*See* ***O'Connor's Texas Rules**, "Requirements," ch. 1-H, §10.4.1(1)(a)[3], p. 76.*}

Continued on next page

FORM 9A:3

16. {90 *Party*} objects to the proposed judgment because {91 *adverse party*} is not entitled to attorney fees in this case under Texas Civil Practice & Remedies Code chapter 38. Specifically, {92 *adverse party*} did not present {93 *his/her/its*} claim as required by Texas Civil Practice & Remedies Code section 38.002(2). *Note Inv. Grp., Inc. v. Assocs. First Capital Corp.*, 476 S.W.3d 463, 483 (Tex. App.—Beaumont 2015, no pet.); *Goodin v. Jolliff*, 257 S.W.3d 341, 349 (Tex. App.—Fort Worth 2008, no pet.); *see Great Am. Ins. Co. v. N. Austin Mun. Util. Dist.*, 908 S.W.2d 415, 427 n.10 (Tex. 1995). {94 *Elaborate.*} {*See* ***O'Connor's Texas Rules***, *"Requirements," ch. 1-H, §10.4.1(1)(a)[6], p. 76.*}

17. {95 *Party*} objects to the proposed judgment because {96 *adverse party*} is not entitled to attorney fees in this case under Texas Civil Practice & Remedies Code chapter 38. Specifically, {97 *adverse party*} is not a "prevailing party" in this suit. *See In re Nalle Plastics Family Ltd. P'ship*, 406 S.W.3d 168, 172-73 (Tex. 2013); *State Farm Life Ins. Co. v. Beaston*, 907 S.W.2d 430, 437 (Tex. 1995). {98 *Elaborate.*} {*See* ***O'Connor's Texas Rules***, *"Requirements," ch. 1-H, §10.4.1(1)(a)[8], p. 76.*}

18. {99 *Party*} objects to the proposed judgment because {100 *adverse party*} is not entitled to attorney fees in this case under Texas Civil Practice & Remedies Code chapter 38. Specifically, {101 *adverse party*} is not entitled to judicial notice of attorney fees because the case was not tried either to the Court as a nonjury case or to a jury. *See Coward v. Gateway Nat'l Bank*, 525 S.W.2d 857, 859 (Tex. 1975) (dicta; judicial notice of attorney fees under former Tex. Rev. Civ. Stat. art. 2226 not appropriate in summary-judgment case); *Gen. Elec. Supply Co. v. Gulf Electroquip, Inc.*, 857 S.W.2d 591, 601 (Tex. App.—Houston [1st Dist.] 1993, writ denied) (in summary-judgment case, fact issue about attorney fees cannot be resolved by judicial notice). {102 *Elaborate.*} {*See* ***O'Connor's Texas Rules***, *"Section 38.004 hearings," ch. 1-H, §10.4.1(1)(b)[2], p. 77.*}

19. {103 *Party*} objects to the proposed judgment because {104 *adverse party*} is not entitled to attorney fees in this case under Texas Civil Practice & Remedies Code chapter 38. Specifically, {105 *adverse party*} was not represented by an attorney as required by Texas Civil Practice & Remedies Code section 38.002(1). *See Great Am. Ins. Co. v. N. Austin Mun. Util. Dist.*, 908 S.W.2d 415, 427 n.10 (Tex. 1995). {106 *Elaborate.*} {*See* ***O'Connor's Texas Rules***, *"Requirements," ch. 1-H, §10.4.1(1)(a)[4], p. 76.*}

20. {107 *Party*} objects to the proposed judgment because {108 *adverse party*} is not entitled to attorney fees in this case under Texas Civil Practice & Remedies Code chapter 38. Specifically, {109 *list any other reasons why adverse party is not entitled to attorney fees under Texas Civil Practice & Remedies Code chapter 38, e.g., adverse party did not tender payment of the claim*}. {*See* ***O'Connor's Texas Rules***, *"CPRC ch. 38," ch. 1-H, §10.4.1(1), p. 75;* ***O'Connor's Texas COA***, *"Claim not covered by §38.001," ch. 45-B, §3.3, p. 1495.*}

{*Objection to unsegregated attorney fees*}

21. {110 *Party*} objects to the proposed judgment because {111 *adverse party*} is not entitled to the amount of attorney fees claimed. A party seeking recovery of attorney fees has the burden to show that the claim is one for which attorney fees are permitted and that the fees were incurred against the particular defendant sought to be charged. *See Koch Oil Co. v. Wilber*, 895 S.W.2d 854, 867 (Tex. App.—Beaumont 1995, writ denied).

{*CHOOSE APPROPRIATE REASONS*}

22. In this case, {112 *adverse party*} did not show proof at trial that {113 *he/she/it*} properly segregated the attorney fees incurred in {114 *his/her/its*} dispute against {115 *party*} because this case involves multiple claims, only some of which permit the recovery of attorney fees. {116 *Identify all the claims and argue that a substantial amount of attorney fees were spent prosecuting a claim for which attorney fees are not allowed, e.g., a tort.*} When a case involves more than one claim, fees may be recovered only for those claims falling within the statute or contract. *Tony Gullo Motors I, L.P. v. Chapa*, 212 S.W.3d 299, 310-11 (Tex. 2006); *AU Pharm., Inc. v. Boston*, 986 S.W.2d 331, 336 (Tex. App.—Texarkana 1999, no pet.). {117 *Elaborate.*} {*See* ***O'Connor's Texas Rules****, "Fees were segregated," ch. 1-H, §10.5.4, p. 80.*}

23. In this case, {118 *adverse party*} did not show proof at trial that {119 *he/she/it*} properly segregated the attorney fees incurred in {120 *his/her/its*} dispute against {121 *party*} because this case involves claims against multiple defendants. {122 *Identify all defendants and the different claims asserted against each.*} When a plaintiff seeks to charge multiple defendants with liability in one suit, the plaintiff must segregate the fees so that the defendants are charged only for the fees for which they are responsible. *Stewart Title Guar. Co. v. Sterling*, 822 S.W.2d 1, 10-11 (Tex. 1991), *modified on other grounds*, *Tony Gullo Motors I, L.P. v. Chapa*, 212 S.W.3d 299 (Tex. 2006). {123 *Elaborate.*}

CONCLUSION

24. {124 *Briefly summarize the objections.*}

PRAYER

25. For these reasons, {125 *party*} asks the Court to refuse to sign {126 *adverse party*}'s proposed judgment.

Continued on next page

SEE: Tex. R. Civ. P. 167, 300-314
Tex. Civ. Prac. & Rem. Code §38.001 et seq., §41.008(b), §42.001 et seq.
Tex. Bus. & Com. Code §17.5052
Tex. Fin. Code §304.001 et seq., §304.101 et seq.
O'Connor's Texas Rules * Civil Trials (2019), "Attorney Fees from Adverse Party," ch. 1-H, §10, p. 74; "Litigation Costs," ch. 7-H, §6, p. 790; "Judgment," ch. 9-C, p. 897
O'Connor's Texas Causes of Action (2019), "Offers of settlement," ch. 8, §7.1, p. 249; "Damages & Other Compensation," Part 4, p. 1343

ADD: STYLE OF THE CASE – FORM 1B:2
SIGNATURE BLOCK – FORM 1B:3
CERTIFICATE OF SERVICE – FORM 1B:13

ATTACH: DTPA AFFIDAVIT CERTIFYING REJECTION OF SETTLEMENT OFFER – FORM 3A:5, if necessary
Written notice of rejection of settlement offer, if necessary
Jury charge, if necessary
Other party's proposed judgment

NOTE: This form can be modified for an objection after the rendition of a judgment.

FORM 9A:3

{❶ *PARTY*}'S MOTION FOR
JUDGMENT NOTWITHSTANDING THE VERDICT

{❷ *Party*}, {❸ *name*}, asks the Court to disregard all the jury findings and sign a judgment notwithstanding the verdict. {*See* ***O'Connor's Texas Rules****, "Motion," ch. 9-B, §2, p. 893.*}

INTRODUCTION

1. Plaintiff, {❹ *name*}, sued defendant, {❺ *name*}, for {❻ *state basis of suit*}.

2. {❼ *State other relevant facts about the suit.*}

BACKGROUND

3. After a trial on the merits, the Court submitted this case to the jury. The jury returned a verdict for {❽ *adverse party*}, {❾ *name*}. {❿ *Party*} attaches as Exhibit {⓫ *letter*} the questions the jury considered and its answers.

4. {⓬ *Party*} asks the Court to disregard all the jury findings and sign a judgment notwithstanding the verdict that {⓭ *describe desired judgment*}. {⓮ *Party*} attaches the proposed judgment as Exhibit {⓯ *letter*}.

ARGUMENT & AUTHORITIES

5. A court may disregard all the jury findings and grant a motion for judgment notwithstanding the verdict if a directed verdict would have been proper. *See* Tex. R. Civ. P. 301; *Fort Bend Cty. Drainage Dist. v. Sbrusch*, 818 S.W.2d 392, 394 (Tex. 1991).

{*CHOOSE APPROPRIATE PARAGRAPHS 6-13*}

{*No evidence to support answer*}

6. A court may disregard the jury's answer to a question if there is no evidence to support it. Tex. R. Civ. P. 301; *Tiller v. McLure*, 121 S.W.3d 709, 713 (Tex. 2003); *Wal-Mart Stores, Inc. v. Miller*, 102 S.W.3d 706, 709 (Tex. 2003). {*See* ***O'Connor's Texas Rules****, "No evidence," ch. 9-B, §3.1, p. 893.*}

7. The Court should disregard the jury's answers in this case because {⓰ *explain how there is no evidence to support the jury's answers*}.

◄ *Continued on next page* ►

{*Evidence establishes contrary fact*}

8. A court may disregard the jury's answer to a question if the evidence establishes a fact to the contrary as a matter of law. *Gallas v. Car Biz, Inc.*, 914 S.W.2d 592, 593 (Tex. App.—Dallas 1995, writ denied); *John Masek Corp. v. Davis*, 848 S.W.2d 170, 173 (Tex. App.—Houston [1st Dist.] 1992, writ denied); *see TRT Dev. Co.-KC v. Meyers*, 15 S.W.3d 281, 285 (Tex. App.—Corpus Christi 2000, no pet.). {*See **O'Connor's Texas Rules**, "Conclusive evidence," ch. 9-B, §3.2, p. 894.*}

9. The Court should disregard the jury's answers in this case because {⓱ *explain how the evidence establishes a contrary fact as a matter of law*}.

{*Legal principle precludes recovery*}

10. Even when a party proves all the allegations in its pleadings, a court may disregard the jury's answers if a legal principle precludes the party's recovery and justifies a judgment notwithstanding the verdict. *United Parcel Serv., Inc. v. Tasdemiroglu*, 25 S.W.3d 914, 916 n.4 (Tex. App.—Houston [14th Dist.] 2000, pet. denied); *Purina Mills, Inc. v. Odell*, 948 S.W.2d 927, 932 (Tex. App.—Texarkana 1997, pet. denied). {*See **O'Connor's Texas Rules**, "Legal bar," ch. 9-B, §3.3, p. 894.*}

11. The Court should disregard the jury's answers in this case because {⓲ *explain how a legal principle precludes adverse party's recovery*}.

{*Question is immaterial*}

12. A court may disregard the jury's answer to an immaterial question. *Spencer v. Eagle Star Ins. Co. of Am.*, 876 S.W.2d 154, 157 (Tex. 1994); *see Salinas v. Rafati*, 948 S.W.2d 286, 288 (Tex. 1997). A jury question is immaterial if (1) the question was improperly submitted, (2) even though properly submitted, the question was rendered immaterial by other findings, (3) the answer to the question can be found elsewhere in the verdict, or (4) the answer to the question cannot change the effect of the verdict. *BP Am. Prod. Co. v. Red Deer Res., LLC*, 526 S.W.3d 389, 402 (Tex. 2017) (#3, 4); *Salinas*, 948 S.W.2d at 288 (#1, 2); *City of Brownsville v. Alvarado*, 897 S.W.2d 750, 752 (Tex. 1995) (#3, 4); *Spencer*, 876 S.W.2d at 157 (#1, 2). {*See **O'Connor's Texas Rules**, "Immaterial jury finding," ch. 9-B, §3.4, p. 894.*}

13. The Court should disregard the jury's answers in this case because {⓳ *explain how the disputed questions are immaterial*}.

☆

{ADD PARAGRAPH 14 IF APPROPRIATE}

14. In the alternative, {[20] *party*} asks the Court to grant a new trial so this case may be retried. {[21] *Elaborate.*} {[22] *Party*} filed a motion for new trial with this Court on {[23] *date*}.

CONCLUSION

15. Because {[24] *restate reasons for disregarding jury findings*}, the Court should disregard all of the jury findings and sign a judgment in favor of {[25] *party*}.

PRAYER

16. For these reasons, {[26] *party*} asks the Court to grant this motion and sign the proposed judgment notwithstanding the verdict that {[27] *describe desired judgment*} {[28] *add if applicable: or, in the alternative, grant {party}'s request for a new trial so this case may be retried*}.

SEE: Tex. R. Civ. P. 301
O'Connor's Texas Rules * Civil Trials (2019), "Motion," ch. 9-B, §2, p. 893; "Grounds for JNOV," ch. 9-B, §3, p. 893

ADD: STYLE OF THE CASE – FORM 1B:2
SIGNATURE BLOCK – FORM 1B:3
CERTIFICATE OF SERVICE – FORM 1B:13

ATTACH: NOTICE OF HEARING OR SUBMISSION – FORM 1E:1
JUDGMENT – FORM 9C:1
Jury charge

NOTE: Courts disagree about the deadline to file a motion for JNOV. *Compare* ***BCY Water Sup. v. Residential Invs.***, 170 S.W.3d 596, 604-05 (Tex.App.—Tyler 2005, pet. denied) (motion for JNOV can be filed as long as trial court has jurisdiction over case), *and* ***Needville ISD v. S.P.J.S.T. Rest Home***, 566 S.W.2d 40, 42 (Tex.App.—Beaumont 1978, no writ) (same), *with* ***Commonwealth Lloyd's Ins. v. Thomas***, 825 S.W.2d 135, 141 (Tex.App.—Dallas 1992) (motion for JNOV must be filed within 30 days after signing of judgment), *writ granted w.r.m.*, 843 S.W.2d 486 (Tex.1993). To be safe, a motion for JNOV should be filed within the deadline for a motion for new trial (i.e., 30 days after the court signs the judgment). See ***O'Connor's Texas Rules***, "To file motion," ch. 9-B, §4.1, p. 895.

{❶ *PARTY*}'S RESPONSE TO {❷ *ADVERSE PARTY*}'S
MOTION FOR JUDGMENT NOTWITHSTANDING THE VERDICT

{❸ *Party*}, {❹ *name*}, asks the Court to deny {❺ *adverse party*} {❻ *name*}'s motion to sign a judgment notwithstanding the verdict.

INTRODUCTION

1. Plaintiff, {❼ *name*}, sued defendant, {❽ *name*}, for {❾ *state basis of suit*}.

2. {❿ *State other relevant facts about the suit.*}

BACKGROUND

3. After a trial on the merits, the Court submitted this case to the jury. The jury returned a verdict for {⓫ *party*}. {⓬ *Party*} attaches as Exhibit {⓭ *letter*} the questions the jury considered and its answers.

4. {⓮ *State other facts relevant to the response.*}

ARGUMENT & AUTHORITIES

5. A court cannot disregard all the jury findings and grant a motion for judgment notwithstanding the verdict unless a directed verdict would have been proper. *See* Tex. R. Civ. P. 301; *Fort Bend Cty. Drainage Dist. v. Sbrusch*, 818 S.W.2d 392, 394 (Tex. 1991).

{*CHOOSE APPROPRIATE PARAGRAPHS 6-13*}

{*Evidence supports answer*}

6. A court may disregard the jury's answer to a question if there is no evidence to support it; however, this is not a case in which the Court should do so. *See Tiller v. McLure*, 121 S.W.3d 709, 713 (Tex. 2003); *Wal-Mart Stores, Inc. v. Miller*, 102 S.W.3d 706, 709 (Tex. 2003). {*See* ***O'Connor's Texas Rules****, "No evidence," ch. 9-B, §3.1, p. 893.*}

7. The Court should not disregard the jury's answers in this case because {⓯ *explain how there is more than a scintilla of evidence to support the jury's answers*}. {*See Mancorp, Inc. v. Culpepper, 802 S.W.2d 226, 228 (Tex. 1990).*}

{*Evidence does not establish contrary fact*}

8. A court may disregard the jury's answer to a question if the evidence establishes a fact to the contrary as a matter of law; however, this is not a case in which the Court should do so. *See TRT Dev. Co.-KC v. Meyers*, 15 S.W.3d 281, 285 (Tex. App.—Corpus Christi 2000, no pet.); *Gallas v. Car Biz, Inc.*, 914 S.W.2d 592, 593 (Tex. App.—Dallas 1995, writ denied); *John Masek Corp. v. Davis*, 848 S.W.2d 170, 173 (Tex. App.—Houston [1st Dist.] 1992, writ denied). {*See* ***O'Connor's Texas Rules***, *"Conclusive evidence," ch. 9-B, §3.2, p. 894.*}

9. The Court should not disregard the jury's answers in this case because {⓰ *explain how the evidence does not establish a contrary fact as a matter of law*}.

{*Legal principle does not preclude recovery*}

10. A court may disregard the jury's answers even when a party proves all the allegations in its pleadings if a legal principle precludes the party's recovery; however, this is not a case in which the Court should do so. *See United Parcel Serv., Inc. v. Tasdemiroglu*, 25 S.W.3d 914, 916 n.4 (Tex. App.—Houston [14th Dist.] 2000, pet. denied); *Purina Mills, Inc. v. Odell*, 948 S.W.2d 927, 932 (Tex. App.—Texarkana 1997, pet. denied). {*See* ***O'Connor's Texas Rules***, *"Legal bar," ch. 9-B, §3.3, p. 894.*}

11. The Court should not disregard the jury's answers in this case because {⓱ *explain how no legal principle precludes party's recovery*}.

{*Question is material*}

12. A court may disregard the jury's answer to an immaterial question; however, this is not a case in which the Court should do so. *Spencer v. Eagle Star Ins. Co. of Am.*, 876 S.W.2d 154, 157 (Tex. 1994); *see Salinas v. Rafati*, 948 S.W.2d 286, 288-89 (Tex. 1997). A jury question is immaterial only if (1) the question was improperly submitted, (2) even though properly submitted, the question was rendered immaterial by other findings, (3) the answer to the question can be found elsewhere in the verdict, or (4) the answer to the question cannot change the effect of the verdict. *BP Am. Prod. Co. v. Red Deer Res., LLC*, 526 S.W.3d 389, 402 (Tex. 2017) (#3, 4); *Salinas*, 948 S.W.2d at 288 (#1, 2); *City of Brownsville v. Alvarado*, 897 S.W.2d 750, 752 (Tex. 1995) (#3, 4); *Spencer*, 876 S.W.2d at 157 (#1, 2). {*See* ***O'Connor's Texas Rules***, *"Immaterial jury finding," ch. 9-B, §3.4, p. 894.*}

13. The Court should not disregard the jury's answers in this case because {⓲ *explain how the disputed jury questions are material*}.

◄ *Continued on next page* ►

CONCLUSION

14. Because {19 *restate the reasons the Court should not disregard the jury findings*}, the Court should not disregard all of the jury findings and should not sign a judgment notwithstanding the verdict.

PRAYER

15. For these reasons, {20 *party*} asks the Court to deny {21 *adverse party*}'s motion for judgment notwithstanding the verdict and to sign a judgment for {22 *party*} in accordance with the jury's verdict.

SEE: Tex. R. Civ. P. 301
O'Connor's Texas Rules * Civil Trials (2019), "Grounds for JNOV," ch. 9-B, §3, p. 893; "Response," ch. 9-B, §5, p. 895

ADD: STYLE OF THE CASE – FORM 1B:2
SIGNATURE BLOCK – FORM 1B:3
CERTIFICATE OF SERVICE – FORM 1B:13

ATTACH: ORDER – FORM 1G:1
Jury charge

{[1] *PARTY*}'S MOTION TO DISREGARD JURY FINDINGS

{[2] *Party*}, {[3] *name*}, asks the Court to disregard the jury's {[4] *finding/findings*} and render a judgment on the remaining issues for {[5] *party*}. {*See **O'Connor's Texas Rules**, "Motion," ch. 9-B, §2, p. 893.*}

INTRODUCTION

1. Plaintiff, {[6] *name*}, sued defendant, {[7] *name*}, for {[8] *state basis of suit*}.

2. {[9] *State other relevant facts about the suit.*}

BACKGROUND

3. After a trial on the merits, the Court submitted this case to the jury. The jury returned a verdict for {[10] *name of party*}. {[11] *Party*} attaches as Exhibit {[12] *letter*} the questions the jury considered and its answers.

4. {[13] *Party*} asks the Court to disregard the jury's {[14] *finding/findings*} on {[15] *list jury questions by number*}, and render judgment on the remaining findings for {[16] *party*}. {[17] *Party*} attaches the proposed judgment as Exhibit {[18] *letter*}.

ARGUMENT & AUTHORITIES

{*CHOOSE APPROPRIATE PARAGRAPHS 5-10*}

{*No evidence to support answer*}

5. A court may disregard the jury's answer to a question if there is no evidence to support it. Tex. R. Civ. P. 301; *Tiller v. McLure*, 121 S.W.3d 709, 713 (Tex. 2003); *Wal-Mart Stores, Inc. v. Miller*, 102 S.W.3d 706, 709 (Tex. 2003). {*See **O'Connor's Texas Rules**, "No evidence," ch. 9-B, §3.1, p. 893.*}

6. The Court should disregard the following jury {[19] *answer/answers*}: {[20] *list jury questions and corresponding answers*}. Specifically, {[21] *explain how there is no evidence to support each answer*}.

{*Evidence establishes contrary fact*}

7. A court may disregard the jury's answer to a question if the evidence establishes a fact to the contrary as a matter of law. *Gallas v. Car Biz, Inc.*, 914 S.W.2d 592, 593 (Tex. App.—Dallas 1995, writ denied); *John Masek Corp. v. Davis*, 848 S.W.2d 170, 173 (Tex. App.—Houston [1st Dist.] 1992, writ denied); *see TRT Dev. Co.-KC v. Meyers*, 15 S.W.3d 281, 285 (Tex. App.—Corpus Christi 2000, no pet.). {*See **O'Connor's Texas Rules**, "Conclusive evidence," ch. 9-B, §3.2, p. 894.*}

◄ *Continued on next page* ►

8. The Court should disregard the following jury {[22] *answer/answers*}: {[23] *list jury questions and corresponding answers*}. Specifically, {[24] *explain how the evidence establishes a contrary fact as a matter of law*}.

{*Question is immaterial*}

9. A court may disregard the jury's answer to an immaterial question. *Spencer v. Eagle Star Ins. Co. of Am.*, 876 S.W.2d 154, 157 (Tex. 1994); *see Salinas v. Rafati*, 948 S.W.2d 286, 288 (Tex. 1997). A jury question is immaterial if (1) the question was improperly submitted, (2) even though properly submitted, the question was rendered immaterial by other findings, (3) the answer to the question can be found elsewhere in the verdict, or (4) the answer to the question cannot change the effect of the verdict. *BP Am. Prod. Co. v. Red Deer Res., LLC*, 526 S.W.3d 389, 402 (Tex. 2017) (#3, 4); *Salinas*, 948 S.W.2d at 288 (#1, 2); *City of Brownsville v. Alvarado*, 897 S.W.2d 750, 752 (Tex. 1995) (#3, 4); *Spencer*, 876 S.W.2d at 157 (#1, 2). {*See **O'Connor's Texas Rules**, "Immaterial jury finding," ch. 9-B, §3.4, p. 894.*}

10. The Court should disregard the following jury {[25] *answer/answers*}: {[26] *list jury questions and corresponding answers*}. Specifically, {[27] *explain how the questions are immaterial*}.

11. If the Court disregards the jury's answers to these questions, the remaining findings mandate a judgment for {[28] *party*} because {[29] *explain*}.

CONCLUSION

12. {[30] *Briefly summarize the motion.*}

PRAYER

13. For these reasons, {[31] *party*} asks the Court to disregard the jury's answers to {[32] *list questions*} and sign a judgment for {[33] *party*} on the remaining jury findings for {[34] *state desired judgment*}.

FORM 9B:3 MOTION TO DISREGARD JURY FINDINGS

SEE: Tex. R. Civ. P. 301
*O'Connor's Texas Rules * Civil Trials* (2019), "Motion," ch. 9-B, §2, p. 893; "Grounds for JNOV," ch. 9-B, §3, p. 893

ADD: STYLE OF THE CASE – FORM 1B:2
SIGNATURE BLOCK – FORM 1B:3
CERTIFICATE OF SERVICE – FORM 1B:13

ATTACH: NOTICE OF HEARING OR SUBMISSION – FORM 1E:1
JUDGMENT – FORM 9C:1
Jury charge

NOTE: A motion for JNOV and a motion to disregard jury findings both ask the court to disregard all or some of the jury's answers to the jury questions and to render judgment for the movant. The only distinction between the two motions is that the motion for JNOV asks the trial court to disregard all the jury findings and to sign a judgment contrary to the jury findings; the motion to disregard asks the trial court to disregard only some of the jury answers and to sign a judgment on the remaining ones. *See* ***Teston v. Miller***, 349 S.W.2d 296, 299 (Tex.App.—Beaumont 1961, writ ref'd n.r.e.).

Texas Rule of Civil Procedure 301 does not state a filing deadline for a motion to disregard jury findings; however, the motion should be filed within the deadline for a motion for new trial (i.e., 30 days after the court signs the judgment). See ***O'Connor's Texas Rules***, "To file motion," ch. 9-B, §4.1, p. 895.

{❶ *PARTY*}'S RESPONSE TO
{❷ *ADVERSE PARTY*}'S MOTION TO DISREGARD JURY FINDINGS

{❸ *Party*}, {❹ *name*}, asks the Court to deny {❺ *adverse party*} {❻ *name*}'s motion to disregard the jury's findings and to sign a judgment on the verdict.

INTRODUCTION

1. Plaintiff, {❼ *name*}, sued defendant, {❽ *name*}, for {❾ *state basis of suit*}.

2. {❿ *State other relevant facts about the suit.*}

BACKGROUND

3. After a trial on the merits, the Court submitted this case to the jury. The jury returned a verdict for {⓫ *name of party*}. {⓬ *Party*} attaches as Exhibit {⓭ *letter*} the questions the jury considered and its answers.

4. {⓮ *State other facts relevant to the response.*}

ARGUMENT & AUTHORITIES

{*CHOOSE APPROPRIATE PARAGRAPHS 5-10*}

{*Evidence supports answer*}

5. A court may disregard the jury's answer to a question if there is no evidence to support it; however, this is not a case in which the Court should do so. *USAA Tex. Lloyds Co. v. Menchaca*, 545 S.W.3d 479, 505 (Tex. 2018); *see Tiller v. McLure*, 121 S.W.3d 709, 713 (Tex. 2003); *Wal-Mart Stores, Inc. v. Miller*, 102 S.W.3d 706, 709 (Tex. 2003). {*See* ***O'Connor's Texas Rules****, "No evidence," ch. 9-B, §3.1, p. 893.*}

6. The Court should not disregard the following jury {⓯ *answer/answers*}: {⓰ *list jury questions and corresponding answers*}. Specifically, {⓱ *explain how there is more than a scintilla of evidence to support the jury's answers*}. {*See Mancorp, Inc. v. Culpepper, 802 S.W.2d 226, 228 (Tex. 1990).*}

{*Evidence does not establish contrary fact*}

7. A court may disregard the jury's answer to a question if the evidence establishes a fact to the contrary as a matter of law; however, this is not a case in which the Court should do so. *See TRT Dev. Co.-KC v. Meyers*, 15 S.W.3d 281, 285 (Tex. App.—Corpus Christi 2000, no pet.); *Gallas v. Car Biz, Inc.*, 914 S.W.2d 592, 593 (Tex. App.—Dallas 1995, writ denied); *John Masek Corp. v. Davis*, 848 S.W.2d 170, 173 (Tex. App.—Houston [1st Dist.] 1992, writ denied). {*See* ***O'Connor's Texas Rules****, "Conclusive evidence," ch. 9-B, §3.2, p. 894.*}

d. Reasonable and necessary attorney fees in the amount of ${❷❶ *amount*} for the prosecution of this case through this judgment.

e. {❷❷ *State any other damages or penalties that are recoverable.*}

f. Court costs.

g. Postjudgment interest on all of the above at the rate of {❷❸ *specify rate of interest*}, compounded annually, from the date this judgment is rendered until all amounts are paid in full.

1. Accordingly, the Court orders that plaintiff take nothing and that defendant recover court costs from plaintiff.

1. Accordingly, the Court orders that plaintiff take nothing and that defendant recover the following from plaintiff:

{*CHOOSE APPROPRIATE PARAGRAPHS a-g*}

a. Actual damages in the amount of ${❷❹ *amount*}.

b. Exemplary damages in the amount of ${❷❺ *amount*}.

c. Prejudgment interest on the actual damages awarded at the rate of {❷❻ *specify rate of interest*} from {❷❼ *date interest began to accrue*} until the date of this judgment, in the amount of ${❷❽ *amount*}.

d. Reasonable and necessary attorney fees in the amount of ${❷❾ *amount*} for defending this case through this judgment.

e. {❸⓿ *State any other damages or penalties that are recoverable.*}

f. Court costs.

g. Postjudgment interest on all of the above at the rate of {❸❶ *specify rate of interest*}, compounded annually, from the date this judgment is rendered until all amounts are paid in full.

{*ADD PARAGRAPH 2 IF APPLICABLE*}

2. {❸❷ *State any other relief awarded in the judgment, e.g., permanent injunction.*}

{*ADD PARAGRAPHS 3-4 IF APPLICABLE*}

3. The Court further orders that if {❸❸ *party*} prevails in an appeal of this judgment to an intermediate court of appeals, {❸❹ *party*} will additionally recover from {❸❺ *ad-*

Continued on next page

verse party} the amount of ${㊱ *amount of attorney fees*}, representing the anticipated reasonable and necessary attorney fees that would be incurred by {㊲ *party*} in {㊳ *defending/prosecuting*} the appeal. {㊴ *Party*} will also recover from {㊵ *adverse party*} postjudgment interest on the appellate attorney fees at the rate of {㊶ *specify rate of interest*}, compounded annually, from the date the appellate award is made final until the amount is paid in full.

4. The Court further orders that if {㊷ *party*} prevails in an appeal of this judgment to the Texas Supreme Court, {㊸ *party*} will additionally recover from {㊹ *adverse party*} the amount of ${㊺ *amount of attorney fees*}, representing the anticipated reasonable and necessary attorney fees that would be incurred by {㊻ *party*} in {㊼ *defending/prosecuting*} the appeal. {㊽ *Party*} will also recover from {㊾ *adverse party*} postjudgment interest on the appellate attorney fees at the rate of {㊿ *specify rate of interest*}, compounded annually, from the date the appellate award is made final until the amount is paid in full.

5. This judgment {51 *finally disposes/does not dispose*} of all claims and all parties, and {52 *is/is not*} appealable. {*See* ***O'Connor's Texas Rules****, "Final Judgment," ch. 9-C, §6, p. 909.*}

{*ADD PARAGRAPH 6 IF APPLICABLE*}

6. The Court orders execution to issue for this judgment.

SIGNED on _______________, 20___.

FORM 9C:1

SEE: Tex. R. Civ. P. 131, 167, 300-314
Tex. Bus. & Com. Code §17.5052
Tex. Civ. Prac. & Rem. Code §38.001 et seq., §42.001 et seq.
Tex. Fin. Code §304.001 et seq., §304.101 et seq.
O'Connor's Texas Rules * Civil Trials (2019), "Litigation Costs," ch. 7-H, §6, p. 790; "Judgment," ch. 9-C, p. 897
O'Connor's Texas Causes of Action (2019), "Offers of settlement," ch. 8, §7.1, p. 249; "Damages & Other Compensation," Part 4, p. 1343

ADD: STYLE OF THE CASE – FORM 1B:2
SIGNATURE LINES FOR JUDGMENT – FORM 1B:5

ATTACH: Jury charge, if necessary

NOTE: Joint and several liability. Joint and several liability refers to a defendant who is liable both jointly with other defendants and separately. When the acts of two or more wrongdoers join to produce an indivisible injury, all the wrongdoers are jointly and severally liable for the entire amount of damages (after a reduction for the plaintiff's percentage of responsibility or for any settlement credit). *See* ***Amstadt v. U.S. Brass Corp.***, 919 S.W.2d 644, 654 (Tex.1996); ***Landers v. East Tex. Salt Water Disposal Co.***, 248 S.W.2d 731, 734 (Tex.1952). See ***O'Connor's Texas Rules***, "Joint & several liability," ch. 2-F, §4.3, p. 158.

Interest rates. All money judgments must specify the applicable postjudgment- and prejudgment-interest rates. *See* Tex. Fin. Code §304.001 (judgment must specify postjudgment-interest rate), §304.103 (prejudgment-interest rate is the same as postjudgment rate). See ***O'Connor's Texas Rules***, "Prejudgment interest," ch. 9-C, §4.5, p. 902; "Postjudgment interest," ch. 9-C, §4.6, p. 905. If possible, the judgment should be drafted to state the exact amount of prejudgment and postjudgment interest awarded so no interpretation is necessary to execute the judgment. If the exact amount of prejudgment interest is not available, the judgment should state the dates for which prejudgment interest accrued. See ***O'Connor's Texas Rules***, "Accrual," ch. 9-C, §4.5.2(3), p. 904. When facts outside the judgment determine the dates for which prejudgment interest accrued (e.g., when offers of settlement are made in personal-injury, wrongful-death, or property-damage cases), the clerk cannot calculate the amount of prejudgment interest without evidence of those dates. *See, e.g.*, ***Zamarripa v. Sifuentes***, 929 S.W.2d 655, 657 (Tex. App.—San Antonio 1996, no writ) (calculation of prejudgment interest is not a ministerial act if written settlement offers were exchanged and record is not clear on dates and amounts).

Postjudgment interest begins to accrue on the day the judgment is rendered (i.e., the day the final judgment is signed) and stops accruing on the day the judgment is satisfied. Tex. Fin. Code §304.005(a); ***Ventling v. Johnson***, 466 S.W.3d 143, 149 (Tex.2015); ***Long v. Castle Tex. Prod.***, 426 S.W.3d 73, 78 (Tex.2014); ***Phillips v. Bramlett***, 407 S.W.3d 229, 239 (Tex.2013). The date postjudgment interest begins to accrue may be affected by whether the judgment is the trial court's original judgment or a judgment on remand or appeal. See ***O'Connor's Texas Rules***, "Accrual," ch. 9-C, §4.6.2(3), p. 906.

Final judgment. There is a presumption that a judgment signed following a conventional trial on the merits disposes of all parties and claims and is final. ***Vaughn v. Drennon***, 324 S.W.3d 560, 561 (Tex. 2010). As a general rule, however, a judgment should clearly state whether it disposes of all issues and parties and whether it is intended to be final and appealable. *See* ***In re Elizondo***, 544 S.W.3d 824, 825-26 (Tex.2018); ***Farm Bur. Cty. Mut. Ins. v. Rogers***, 455 S.W.3d 161, 163 (Tex.2015); ***In re Daredia***, 317 S.W.3d 247, 248 (Tex.2010); ***Lehmann v. Har-Con Corp.***, 39 S.W.3d 191, 205-06 (Tex.2001). See ¶5, above; ***O'Connor's Texas Rules***, "Statement of finality," ch. 9-C, §4.3, p. 901; "What judgments are final," ch. 9-C, §6.3, p. 910.

Attorney fees. A party cannot recover attorney fees from an adverse party unless permitted by a statute or a rule of procedure, by a contract between the parties, or under equity. See ***O'Connor's Texas Rules***, "Attorney Fees from Adverse Party," ch. 1-H, §10, p. 74.

A party that prevails in the trial court can also ask the court to award conditional appellate attorney fees. *See* ***Ventling***, 466 S.W.3d at 154. See ***O'Connor's Texas Rules***, "Note," ch. 9-C, §4.7, p. 907. In most cases, a prevailing party in the trial court seeks recovery of appellate attorney fees for successfully defending a judgment on appeal; however, a prevailing party can recover appellate attorney fees for successfully prosecuting an appeal as well. *See* ***Ventling***, 466 S.W.3d at 154-55. To be entitled to appellate attorney fees, the party must at least partially prevail on appeal. *See id.* at 155. The party can recover postjudgment interest on the appellate attorney fees, accruing from the date the appellate award is made final. *Id.* at 156.

Costs. The judgment should state that costs are awarded against a certain party, not the amount of the costs awarded. A trial court is not required to assess costs for its judgment to be final. See ***O'Connor's Texas Rules***, "Costs," ch. 9-C, §4.9, p. 907.

{❶ *FINAL/PARTIAL*} DEFAULT JUDGMENT

{*CHOOSE APPROPRIATE INTRODUCTORY PARAGRAPH*}

{*For oral hearing on motion*}

On {❷ *date*}, plaintiff, {❸ *name*}, moved for default judgment after defendant, {❹ *name*}, failed to file an answer in this case. A hearing on plaintiff's motion was held on {❺ *date*}. Plaintiff appeared {❻ *in person/through {his/her/its} representative*} and through {❼ *his/her/its*} attorney. Defendant, having been duly served with citation and a copy of plaintiff's {❽ *original/{identify other}*} petition, did not appear and answer.

{*For motion heard on submission*}

On {❾ *date*}, plaintiff, {❿ *name*}, moved for default judgment after defendant, {⓫ *name*}, failed to file an answer in this case. Plaintiff's motion was heard on submission on {⓬ *date*}. Plaintiff has appeared {⓭ *in person/through {his/her/its} representative*} and through {⓮ *his/her/its*} attorney. Defendant, having been duly served with citation and a copy of plaintiff's {⓯ *original/{identify other}*} petition, has not appeared or answered.

{⓰ *At the hearing/On submission*}, the Court determined it had jurisdiction over the subject matter and the parties in this proceeding, and the citation and proof of service were on file for at least ten days before the motion was filed. After considering the pleadings, the papers on file in this case, and the evidence plaintiff presented on liability, {⓱ *add when necessary: damages, and attorney fees,*} the Court grants plaintiff's motion for default judgment. {*See **O'Connor's Texas Rules**, "No-Answer Default," ch. 7-A, §3, p. 704.*}

The Court

{*CHOOSE APPROPRIATE STATEMENT*}

Ⓐ hereby RENDERS judgment for {⓲ *party*}. {*See **O'Connor's Texas Rules**, "Rendition," ch. 9-C, §3.1, p. 898.*}

Ⓑ orally RENDERED judgment for {⓳ *party*} on {⓴ *date*}. This written judgment memorializes that rendition. {*See **O'Connor's Texas Rules**, "Signing," ch. 9-C, §3.2, p. 899.*}

1. Accordingly, the Court orders that plaintiff recover the following from {21 *defendant/defendants, jointly and severally*}:

{*CHOOSE APPROPRIATE PARAGRAPHS a-g*}

a. Actual damages in the amount of ${22 *amount*}.

b. Exemplary damages in the amount of ${23 *amount*}.

c. Prejudgment interest on the actual damages awarded at the rate of {24 *specify rate of interest*} from {25 *date interest began to accrue*} until the date of this judgment, in the amount of ${26 *amount*}.

d. Reasonable and necessary attorney fees in the amount of ${27 *amount*} for the prosecution of this case through this judgment.

e. {28 *State any other damages or penalties that are recoverable.*}

f. Court costs.

g. Postjudgment interest on all of the above at the rate of {29 *specify rate of interest*}, compounded annually, from the date this judgment is rendered until all amounts are paid in full.

{*ADD PARAGRAPHS 2-3 IF APPLICABLE*}

2. The Court further orders that if {30 *party*} prevails in an appeal of this judgment to an intermediate court of appeals, {31 *party*} will additionally recover from {32 *adverse party*} the amount of ${33 *amount of attorney fees*}, representing the anticipated reasonable and necessary attorney fees that would be incurred by {34 *party*} in {35 *defending/prosecuting*} the appeal. {36 *Party*} will also recover from {37 *adverse party*} postjudgment interest on the appellate attorney fees at the rate of {38 *specify rate of interest*}, compounded annually, from the date the appellate award is made final until the amount is paid in full.

3. The Court further orders that if {39 *party*} prevails in an appeal of this judgment to the Texas Supreme Court, {40 *party*} will additionally recover from {41 *adverse party*} the amount of ${42 *amount of attorney fees*}, representing the anticipated reasonable and necessary attorney fees that would be incurred by {43 *party*} in {44 *defending/prosecuting*} the appeal. {45 *Party*} will also recover from {46 *adverse party*} postjudgment interest on the appellate attorney fees at the rate of {47 *specify rate of interest*}, compounded annually, from the date the appellate award is made final until the amount is paid in full.

Continued on next page

4. This judgment {㊽ *finally disposes/does not dispose*} of all claims and all parties, and {㊾ *is/is not*} appealable. {*See **O'Connor's Texas Rules**, "Final Judgment," ch. 9-C, §6, p. 909.*}

{*ADD PARAGRAPH 5 IF APPLICABLE*}

5. The Court orders execution to issue for this judgment.

SIGNED on _______________, 20___.

SEE: Tex. R. Civ. P. 131, 239, 239a, 300-314
Tex. Civ. Prac. & Rem. Code §38.001 et seq.
Tex. Fin. Code §304.001 et seq., §304.101 et seq.
O'Connor's Texas Rules * Civil Trials (2019), "No-Answer Default," ch. 7-A, §3, p. 704; "Drafting Default Judgment," ch. 7-A, §5, p. 714; "Notice of Default Judgment," ch. 7-A, §6, p. 714; "Litigation Costs," ch. 7-H, §6, p. 790; "Judgment," ch. 9-C, p. 897
O'Connor's Texas Causes of Action (2019), "Damages & Other Compensation," Part 4, p. 1343

ADD: STYLE OF THE CASE – FORM 1B:2
SIGNATURE LINES FOR JUDGMENT – FORM 1B:5

NOTE: Joint and several liability. See "Joint and several liability" note under FORM 9C:1.

Interest rates. See "Interest rates" note under FORM 9C:1.

Final judgment. As a general rule, a judgment should clearly state whether it disposes of all issues and parties and whether it is intended to be final and appealable. *See **In re Elizondo***, 544 S.W.3d 824, 825-26 (Tex.2018); ***In re Daredia***, 317 S.W.3d 247, 248 (Tex.2010); ***Lehmann v. Har-Con Corp.***, 39 S.W.3d 191, 205-06 (Tex.2001). See ¶4, above; ***O'Connor's Texas Rules***, "No-answer default," ch. 7-A, §5.3.1, p. 714; "Statement of finality," ch. 9-C, §4.3, p. 901.

If you are suing multiple defendants, one who has answered and another who has not, and you are seeking a default judgment against only the nonanswering defendant, do not draft the default judgment to say that it "disposes of all parties and all claims and is therefore final." *See **In re Daredia***, 317 S.W.3d at 248-49. Otherwise, you may lose your right to obtain a judgment against the answering defendant because it has been unequivocally, even though inadvertently, dismissed from the case. *See id.* See ***O'Connor's Texas Rules***, "Statement of finality," ch. 9-C, §4.3, p. 901.

Attorney fees. See "Attorney fees" note under FORM 9C:1.

Costs. See "Costs" note under FORM 9C:1.

FORM 9C:2

{❶ *FINAL/PARTIAL*} DEFAULT JUDGMENT

On {❷ *date*}, this case was called for {❸ *trial/a hearing on {name of dispositive motion}*}. Plaintiff, {❹ *name*}, appeared {❺ *in person/through {his/her/its} representative*} and through {❻ *his/her/its*} attorney. Defendant, {❼ *name*}, had notice of the {❽ *trial/hearing*} setting but did not attend. Plaintiff moved for default judgment. The Court determined it had jurisdiction over the subject matter and the parties in this proceeding. After considering the pleadings, the papers on file in this case, and the evidence plaintiff presented on liability, damages, and attorney fees, the Court grants plaintiff's motion for default judgment. {*See* ***O'Connor's Texas Rules****, "Post-Answer Default," ch. 7-A, §4, p. 712.*}

The Court

{*CHOOSE APPROPRIATE STATEMENT*}

Ⓐ hereby RENDERS judgment for {❾ *party*}. {*See* ***O'Connor's Texas Rules****, "Rendition," ch. 9-C, §3.1, p. 898.*}

Ⓑ orally RENDERED judgment for {❿ *party*} on {⓫ *date*}. This written judgment memorializes that rendition. {*See* ***O'Connor's Texas Rules****, "Signing," ch. 9-C, §3.2, p. 899.*}

1. Accordingly, the Court orders that plaintiff recover the following from {⓬ *defendant/defendants, jointly and severally*}:

{*CHOOSE APPROPRIATE PARAGRAPHS a-g*}

a. Actual damages in the amount of ${⓭ *amount*}.

b. Exemplary damages in the amount of ${⓮ *amount*}.

c. Prejudgment interest on the actual damages awarded at the rate of {⓯ *specify rate of interest*} from {⓰ *date interest began to accrue*} until the date of this judgment, in the amount of ${⓱ *amount*}.

d. Reasonable and necessary attorney fees in the amount of ${⓲ *amount*} for the prosecution of this case through this judgment.

e. {⓳ *State any other damages or penalties that are recoverable.*}

f. Court costs.

◄ *Continued on next page* ►

g. Postjudgment interest on all of the above at the rate of {⓴ *specify rate of interest*}, compounded annually, from the date this judgment is rendered until all amounts are paid in full.

{*ADD PARAGRAPHS 2-3 IF APPLICABLE*}

2. The Court further orders that if {㉑ *party*} prevails in an appeal of this judgment to an intermediate court of appeals, {㉒ *party*} will additionally recover from {㉓ *adverse party*} the amount of ${㉔ *amount of attorney fees*}, representing the anticipated reasonable and necessary attorney fees that would be incurred by {㉕ *party*} in {㉖ *defending/prosecuting*} the appeal. {㉗ *Party*} will also recover from {㉘ *adverse party*} postjudgment interest on the appellate attorney fees at the rate of {㉙ *specify rate of interest*}, compounded annually, from the date the appellate award is made final until the amount is paid in full.

3. The Court further orders that if {㉚ *party*} prevails in an appeal of this judgment to the Texas Supreme Court, {㉛ *party*} will additionally recover from {㉜ *adverse party*} the amount of ${㉝ *amount of attorney fees*}, representing the anticipated reasonable and necessary attorney fees that would be incurred by {㉞ *party*} in {㉟ *defending/prosecuting*} the appeal. {㊱ *Party*} will also recover from {㊲ *adverse party*} postjudgment interest on the appellate attorney fees at the rate of {㊳ *specify rate of interest*}, compounded annually, from the date the appellate award is made final until the amount is paid in full.

4. This judgment {㊴ *finally disposes/does not dispose*} of all claims and all parties, and {㊵ *is/is not*} appealable. {*See* ***O'Connor's Texas Rules****, "Final Judgment," ch. 9-C, §6, p. 909.*}

{*ADD PARAGRAPH 5 IF APPLICABLE*}

5. The Court orders execution to issue for this judgment.

SIGNED on ______________, 20___.

SEE: Tex. R. Civ. P. 131, 167, 300-314
Tex. Bus. & Com. Code §17.5052
Tex. Civ. Prac. & Rem. Code §38.001 et seq.
Tex. Fin. Code §304.001 et seq., §304.101 et seq.
O'Connor's Texas Rules * Civil Trials (2019), "Post-Answer Default," ch. 7-A, §4, p. 712; "Drafting Default Judgment," ch. 7-A, §5, p. 714; "Notice of Default Judgment," ch. 7-A, §6, p. 714; "Litigation Costs," ch. 7-H, §6, p. 790; "Judgment," ch. 9-C, p. 897
O'Connor's Texas Causes of Action (2019), "Offers of settlement," ch. 8, §7.1, p. 249; "Damages & Other Compensation," Part 4, p. 1343

ADD: STYLE OF THE CASE – FORM 1B:2
SIGNATURE LINES FOR JUDGMENT – FORM 1B:5

NOTE: Joint and several liability. See "Joint and several liability" note under FORM 9C:1.

Interest rates. See "Interest rates" note under FORM 9C:1.

Final judgment. As a general rule, a judgment should clearly state whether it disposes of all issues and parties and whether it is intended to be final and appealable. *See* ***In re Elizondo***, 544 S.W.3d 824, 825-26 (Tex.2018); ***Farm Bur. Cty. Mut. Ins. v. Rogers***, 455 S.W.3d 161, 163 (Tex.2015); ***In re Daredia***, 317 S.W.3d 247, 248 (Tex.2010); ***Lehmann v. Har-Con Corp.***, 39 S.W.3d 191, 205-06 (Tex.2001). See ¶4, above; ***O'Connor's Texas Rules***, "Statement of finality," ch. 9-C, §4.3, p. 901. Because a post-answer default judgment can be rendered only after notice to defendant and a trial of the issues, a post-answer default judgment is presumed to dispose of all issues. See ***O'Connor's Texas Rules***, "Post-answer default," ch. 7-A, §5.3.2, p. 714.

Attorney fees. See "Attorney fees" note under FORM 9C:1.

Costs. See "Costs" note under FORM 9C:1.

FINAL SUMMARY JUDGMENT

On {❶ *date*}, the Court heard {❷ *party*} {❸ *name*}'s motion for summary judgment. The parties appeared before the Court for the hearing on the motion. After considering the pleadings, motion, response, evidence on file, and arguments of counsel, the Court grants the motion.

The Court

{*CHOOSE APPROPRIATE STATEMENT*}

Ⓐ hereby RENDERS judgment for {❹ *party*}. {*See* ***O'Connor's Texas Rules****, "Rendition," ch. 9-C, §3.1, p. 898.*}

Ⓑ orally RENDERED judgment for {❺ *party*} on {❻ *date*}. This written judgment memorializes that rendition. {*See* ***O'Connor's Texas Rules****, "Signing," ch. 9-C, §3.2, p. 899.*}

{*CHOOSE APPROPRIATE PARAGRAPH 1*}

1. Accordingly, the Court orders that plaintiff recover the following from {❼ *defendant/defendants, jointly and severally*}:

{*CHOOSE APPROPRIATE PARAGRAPHS a-g*}

a. Actual damages in the amount of ${❽ *amount*}.

b. Exemplary damages in the amount of ${❾ *amount*}.

c. Prejudgment interest on the actual damages awarded at the rate of {❿ *specify rate of interest*} from {⓫ *date interest began to accrue*} until the date of this judgment, in the amount of ${⓬ *amount*}.

d. Reasonable and necessary attorney fees in the amount of ${⓭ *amount*} for the prosecution of this case through this judgment.

e. {⓮ *State any other damages or penalties that are recoverable.*}

f. Court costs.

g. Postjudgment interest on all of the above at the rate of {⓯ *specify rate of interest*}, compounded annually, from the date this judgment is rendered until all amounts are paid in full.

1. Accordingly, the Court orders that plaintiff take nothing and that defendant recover court costs from plaintiff.

1. Accordingly, the Court orders that plaintiff take nothing and that defendant recover the following from plaintiff:

{*CHOOSE APPROPRIATE PARAGRAPHS a-g*}

a. Actual damages in the amount of ${[16] *amount*}.

b. Exemplary damages in the amount of ${[17] *amount*}.

c. Prejudgment interest on the actual damages awarded at the rate of {[18] *specify rate of interest*} from {[19] *date interest began to accrue*} until the date of this judgment, in the amount of ${[20] *amount*}.

d. Reasonable and necessary attorney fees in the amount of ${[21] *amount*} for defending this case through this judgment.

e. {[22] *State any other damages or penalties that are recoverable.*}

f. Court costs.

g. Postjudgment interest on all of the above at the rate of {[23] *specify rate of interest*}, compounded annually, from the date this judgment is rendered until all amounts are paid in full.

{*ADD PARAGRAPH 2 IF APPLICABLE*}

2. {[24] *State any other relief awarded in the judgment.*}

{*ADD PARAGRAPHS 3-4 IF APPLICABLE*}

3. The Court further orders that if {[25] *party*} prevails in an appeal of this judgment to an intermediate court of appeals, {[26] *party*} will additionally recover from {[27] *adverse party*} the amount of ${[28] *amount of attorney fees*}, representing the anticipated reasonable and necessary attorney fees that would be incurred by {[29] *party*} in {[30] *defending/prosecuting*} the appeal. {[31] *Party*} will also recover from {[32] *adverse party*} postjudgment interest on the appellate attorney fees at the rate of {[33] *specify rate of interest*}, compounded annually, from the date the appellate award is made final until the amount is paid in full.

Continued on next page

4. The Court further orders that if {㉞ *party*} prevails in an appeal of this judgment to the Texas Supreme Court, {㉟ *party*} will additionally recover from {㊱ *adverse party*} the amount of ${㊲ *amount of attorney fees*}, representing the anticipated reasonable and necessary attorney fees that would be incurred by {㊳ *party*} in {㊴ *defending/prosecuting*} the appeal. {㊵ *Party*} will also recover from {㊶ *adverse party*} post-judgment interest on the appellate attorney fees at the rate of {㊷ *specify rate of interest*}, compounded annually, from the date the appellate award is made final until the amount is paid in full.

5. This judgment finally disposes of all claims and all parties, and is appealable. {*See* ***O'Connor's Texas Rules****, "Final SJ," ch. 7-B, §12.3.2(1), p. 744.*}

6. The Court orders execution to issue for this judgment.

SIGNED on _______________, 20___.

SEE: Tex. R. Civ. P. 131, 166a, 167, 300-314
Tex. Bus. & Com. Code §17.5052
Tex. Civ. Prac. & Rem. Code §38.001 et seq.
Tex. Fin. Code §304.001 et seq., §304.101 et seq.
O'Connor's Texas Rules * Civil Trials (2019), "Motion for Summary Judgment—General Rules," ch. 7-B, p. 722; "Judgment," ch. 9-C, p. 897
O'Connor's Texas Causes of Action (2019), "Damages & Other Compensation," Part 4, p. 1343

ADD: STYLE OF THE CASE – FORM 1B:2
SIGNATURE LINES FOR JUDGMENT – FORM 1B:5

NOTE: Joint and several liability. See "Joint and several liability" note under FORM 9C:1.

Interest rates. See "Interest rates" note under FORM 9C:1.

Final judgment. As a general rule, a judgment should clearly state whether it disposes of all issues and parties and whether it is intended to be final and appealable. *See* ***In re Elizondo***, 544 S.W.3d 824, 825-26 (Tex.2018); ***Farm Bur. Cty. Mut. Ins. v. Rogers***, 455 S.W.3d 161, 163 (Tex.2015); ***In re Daredia***, 317 S.W.3d 247, 248 (Tex.2010); ***Lehmann v. Har-Con Corp.***, 39 S.W.3d 191, 205-06 (Tex.2001). See ¶5, above; ***O'Connor's Texas Rules***, "State whether final or partial," ch. 7-B, §12.3.2, p. 744. There is no presumption of finality for summary-judgment orders. *See* ***Crites v. Collins***, 284 S.W.3d 839, 840 (Tex. 2009).

Attorney fees. See "Attorney fees" note under FORM 9C:1.

Costs. See "Costs" note under FORM 9C:1.

FORM 9C:4

{❶ *FINAL/PARTIAL*} JUDGMENT ON AGREED FACTS

On {❷ *date*}, this case was heard. Plaintiff, {❸ *name*}, appeared {❹ *in person/through {his/her/its} representative*} and through {❺ *his/her/its*} attorney and announced ready for trial. Defendant, {❻ *name*}, appeared {❼ *in person/through {his/her/its} representative*} and through {❽ *his/her/its*} attorney and announced ready for trial. The case was tried to this Court on the parties' agreed statement of facts filed in this case in accordance with Texas Rule of Civil Procedure 263. After reviewing the agreed statement of facts and hearing the arguments of counsel, the Court

{*CHOOSE APPROPRIATE STATEMENT*}

[A] hereby RENDERS judgment for {❾ *party*}. {*See* ***O'Connor's Texas Rules****, "Rendition," ch. 9-C, §3.1, p. 898.*}

[B] orally RENDERED judgment for {❿ *party*} on {⓫ *date*}. This written judgment memorializes that rendition. {*See* ***O'Connor's Texas Rules****, "Signing," ch. 9-C, §3.2, p. 899.*}

1. Accordingly, the Court orders under Agreed Fact {⓬ *number*} that {⓭ *state relief awarded*}. {*See* ***O'Connor's Texas Rules****, "Judgment," ch. 7-E, §5, p. 770.*}

{*Continue until all relief rendered is specified.*}

{*ADD PARAGRAPHS 2-3 IF APPLICABLE*}

2. The Court further orders that if {⓮ *party*} prevails in an appeal of this judgment to an intermediate court of appeals, {⓯ *party*} will additionally recover from {⓰ *adverse party*} the amount of ${⓱ *amount of attorney fees*}, representing the anticipated reasonable and necessary attorney fees that would be incurred {⓲ *party*} in {⓳ *defending/prosecuting*} the appeal. {⓴ *Party*} will also recover from {㉑ *adverse party*} postjudgment interest on the appellate attorney fees at the rate of {㉒ *specify rate of interest*}, compounded annually, from the date the appellate award is made final until the amount is paid in full.

3. The Court further orders that if {㉓ *party*} prevails in an appeal of this judgment to the Texas Supreme Court, {㉔ *party*} will additionally recover from {㉕ *adverse party*} the amount of ${㉖ *amount of attorney fees*}, representing the anticipated reasonable and necessary attorney fees that would be incurred by {㉗ *party*} in {㉘ *defending/prosecuting*} the appeal. {㉙ *Party*} will also recover from {㉚ *adverse party*} postjudgment interest on the appellate attorney fees at the rate of {㉛ *specify rate of interest*}, compounded annually, from the date the appellate award is made final until the amount is paid in full.

Continued on next page

4. This judgment {㉜ *finally disposes/does not dispose*} of all claims and all parties, and {㉝ *is/is not*} appealable. {*See* ***O'Connor's Texas Rules****, "Final Judgment," ch. 9-C, §6, p. 909.*}

{*ADD PARAGRAPH 5 IF APPLICABLE*}

5. The Court orders execution to issue for this judgment.

SIGNED on ______________, 20____.

SEE: Tex. R. Civ. P. 131, 167, 263, 300-314
Tex. Bus. & Com. Code §17.5052
Tex. Civ. Prac. & Rem. Code §38.001 et seq.
Tex. Fin. Code §304.001 et seq., §304.101 et seq.
O'Connor's Texas Rules * Civil Trials (2019), "Judgment," ch. 7-E, §5.2, p. 770; "Judgment," ch. 9-C, p. 897
O'Connor's Texas Causes of Action (2019), "Damages & Other Compensation," Part 4, p. 1343

ADD: STYLE OF THE CASE – FORM 1B:2
SIGNATURE LINES FOR JUDGMENT – FORM 1B:5

NOTE: Interest rates. See "Interest rates" note under FORM 9C:1.

Final judgment. As a general rule, a judgment should clearly state whether it disposes of all issues and parties and whether it is intended to be final and appealable. *See* ***In re Elizondo***, 544 S.W.3d 824, 825-26 (Tex.2018); ***Farm Bur. Cty. Mut. Ins. v. Rogers***, 455 S.W.3d 161, 163 (Tex.2015); ***In re Daredia***, 317 S.W.3d 247, 248 (Tex.2010); ***Lehmann v. Har-Con Corp.***, 39 S.W.3d 191, 205-06 (Tex.2001). See ¶4, above; ***O'Connor's Texas Rules***, "Statement of finality," ch. 9-C, §4.3, p. 901.

Attorney fees. See "Attorney fees" note under FORM 9C:1.

Costs. See "Costs" note under FORM 9C:1.

CHAPTER 10. POSTJUDGMENT MOTIONS

TABLE OF CONTENTS

TEXAS CIVIL FORMS

CHAPTER 10. POSTJUDGMENT MOTIONS

{❶ *PARTY*}'S MOTION FOR NEW TRIAL

{❷ *Party*}, {❸ *name*}, asks the Court to grant a new trial in the interest of justice and fairness.

INTRODUCTION

1. Plaintiff, {❹ *name*}, sued defendant, {❺ *name*}, for {❻ *state basis of suit*}.

2. {❼ *State other relevant facts about the suit.*}

BACKGROUND

3. After a trial on the merits, the Court submitted this cause to the jury. The jury returned a verdict for {❽ *plaintiff/defendant*}. The Court signed a judgment for {❾ *plaintiff/defendant*} on {❿ *date*}.

4. {⓫ *State other facts relevant to the motion.*}

ARGUMENT & AUTHORITIES

{*CHOOSE APPROPRIATE SECTIONS A-O*}

A. Sufficiency of the evidence.

{*CHOOSE APPROPRIATE PARAGRAPHS 5-8*}

{*To challenge jury findings on which the movant had burden of proof*}

5. The Court should grant a motion for new trial because the jury's answer to question number {⓬ *number*} is against the great weight and preponderance of the evidence and is manifestly unjust. {⓭ *Elaborate.*} *See Pool v. Ford Motor Co.*, 715 S.W.2d 629, 635 (Tex. 1986). {*See* ***O'Connor's Texas Rules****, "Standard challenges," ch. 10-B, §13.1.4, p. 944.*}

6. The Court should grant a motion for new trial because the evidence proves conclusively, as a matter of law, that {⓮ *state what the evidence proves*}. Thus, the jury's answer to question number {⓯ *number*} is wrong, and the Court erred by overruling {⓰ *objections to the charge/the motion for directed verdict/the motion for judgment notwithstanding the verdict*}. {⓱ *Elaborate.*} {*See* ***O'Connor's Texas Rules****, "Standard challenges," ch. 10-B, §13.1.4, p. 944.*}

Continued on next page

{*To challenge jury findings on which the movant did not have burden of proof*}

7. The Court should grant a motion for new trial because the evidence is insufficient to support the jury's answer to question number {[18] *number*}. {[19] *Elaborate.*} {*See* ***O'Connor's Texas Rules***, *"Standard challenges," ch. 10-B, §13.1.4, p. 944.*}

8. The Court should grant a motion for new trial because there is no evidence to support the jury's answer to question number {[20] *number*}, and the Court erred by overruling {[21] *objections to the charge/the motion for directed verdict/the motion for judgment notwithstanding the verdict*}. {[22] *Elaborate.*} {*See* ***O'Connor's Texas Rules***, *"Standard challenges," ch. 10-B, §13.1.4, p. 944.*}

B. Immaterial jury finding.

9. The Court should disregard the jury's answer to question number {[23] *number*} because the finding is immaterial. A jury finding is immaterial if the question was one that should not have been submitted or, even though properly submitted, was rendered immaterial by other findings. *Spencer v. Eagle Star Ins. Co. of Am.*, 876 S.W.2d 154, 157 (Tex. 1994). The jury's finding on question number {[24] *number*} is immaterial because {[25] *explain*}. {*See* ***O'Connor's Texas Rules***, *"Immaterial jury finding," ch. 10-B, §13.4, p. 944.*}

C. Damages.

{*CHOOSE APPROPRIATE PARAGRAPHS 10-14*}

{*To challenge jury finding of zero damages*}

10. The Court should grant a new trial because the great weight and preponderance of the evidence supports a finding that {[26] *party*} incurred some damages, and the jury's answer of zero damages is manifestly unjust. {[27] *Elaborate.*} {*See* ***O'Connor's Texas Rules***, *"When MNT necessary," ch. 10-B, §2.1.3, p. 930.*}

11. The Court should grant a new trial because {[28] *party*} proved as a matter of law that some damages are appropriate. {[29] *Elaborate.*} {*See* ***O'Connor's Texas Rules***, *"When MNT necessary," ch. 10-B, §2.1.3, p. 930.*}

{*To challenge jury finding of inadequate damages*}

12. The Court should grant a new trial because the great weight and preponderance of the evidence supports a finding that {[30] *party*} incurred greater damages than what the jury awarded, and thus the jury's award of ${[31] *amount*} in damages is manifestly unjust. {[32] *Elaborate.*} {*See* ***O'Connor's Texas Rules***, *"When MNT necessary," ch. 10-B, §2.1.3, p. 930.*}

13. The Court should grant a new trial because {33 *party*} proved as a matter of law that greater damages are appropriate. {34 *Elaborate.*} {*See* ***O'Connor's Texas Rules****, "When MNT necessary," ch. 10-B, §2.1.3, p. 930.*}

{*To challenge jury finding of excessive damages*}

14. The Court should suggest a remittitur to {35 *adverse party*} because the jury's award of ${36 *amount*} in damages is grossly excessive. The standard for a request for remittitur is factual sufficiency of the evidence. *Torrington Co. v. Stutzman*, 46 S.W.3d 829, 851 (Tex. 2000); *Mar. Overseas Corp. v. Ellis*, 971 S.W.2d 402, 406 (Tex. 1998); *Rose v. Doctors Hosp.*, 801 S.W.2d 841, 848 (Tex. 1990). A court must examine all the evidence to determine if there is sufficient evidence to support the damages award. *Pope v. Moore*, 711 S.W.2d 622, 624 (Tex. 1986). A court should suggest a remittitur when the evidence to support the damages award is so factually insufficient, or when the damages award is so against the great weight and preponderance of the evidence, that it is manifestly unjust. *Id.*; *Gainsco Cty. Mut. Ins. Co. v. Martinez*, 27 S.W.3d 97, 108 (Tex. App.—San Antonio 2000, pet. granted, judgm't vacated w.r.m.). In this case the award is manifestly unjust. {37 *Elaborate.*} If {38 *adverse party*} does not file a remittitur in the amount of at least ${39 *amount*}, the Court should grant a new trial. {*See FORM 10C:3;* ***O'Connor's Texas Rules****, "When MNT necessary," ch. 10-B, §2.1.3, p. 930; "Motion for Remittitur," ch. 10-C, p. 954.*}

D. Erroneous charge.

{*CHOOSE APPROPRIATE PARAGRAPHS 15-18*}

15. The Court erred by submitting question number {40 *number*} to the jury because the question was defective. Specifically, {41 *state how it was defective*}.

16. The Court erred by submitting the {42 *instruction on/definition of*} {43 *identify instruction or definition*} because it was defective. Specifically, {44 *state how it was defective*}.

17. The Court erred by refusing to submit requested question number {45 *number*} because {46 *party*} tendered the question in substantially correct form, and the question was supported by the pleadings and the evidence. {47 *Elaborate.*}

18. The Court erred by refusing to submit requested instruction number {48 *number*} because the instruction was supported by evidence and was necessary to assist the jury in answering the question as submitted. {49 *Elaborate.*}

Continued on next page

E. Improper jury argument.

19. The Court should grant a new trial because {50 *adverse party*} made an improper and prejudicial jury argument. *See Standard Fire Ins. Co. v. Reese*, 584 S.W.2d 835, 839-40 (Tex. 1979). {51 *Identify jury argument and explain why it was improper.*} {*See **O'Connor's Texas Rules**, "Test for reversible jury argument," ch. 8-J, §6.2, p. 883.*}

20. The jury argument was not invited or provoked. *Living Ctrs. of Tex., Inc. v. Peñalver*, 256 S.W.3d 678, 680 (Tex. 2008); *see Standard Fire*, 584 S.W.2d at 839. {52 *Elaborate.*} {*See **O'Connor's Texas Rules**, "Record of argument," ch. 8-J, §6.1, p. 883.*}

21. By its nature, degree, and extent, the argument constituted reversible, harmful error. *Living Ctrs.*, 256 S.W.3d at 680-81; *see Standard Fire*, 584 S.W.2d at 839. {53 *Elaborate.*} {*See **O'Connor's Texas Rules**, "Test for reversible jury argument," ch. 8-J, §6.2.5, p. 883.*}

{*CHOOSE APPROPRIATE PARAGRAPH 22*}

{*When error preserved*}

22. The error in the improper jury argument was preserved by

{*CHOOSE APPROPRIATE FACTS*}

A an objection, which was overruled.

B an objection, which was sustained, and a request for an instruction to disregard, which was denied.

C an objection, which was sustained, a request for an instruction to disregard, which was given, and a motion for mistrial, which was denied.

{*When error not preserved*}

22. Although the error was not properly preserved, the error was so prejudicial that it was not curable by an instruction to disregard, prompt withdrawal of the statement, or a reprimand from the Court. *See Living Ctrs.*, 256 S.W.3d at 680-81; *Standard Fire*, 584 S.W.2d at 839; *Otis Elevator Co. v. Wood*, 436 S.W.2d 324, 333 (Tex. 1968). {54 *Elaborate.*} {*See **O'Connor's Texas Rules**, "Incurable argument," ch. 8-J, §5.2, p. 882; "When MNT necessary," ch. 10-B, §2.1.4, p. 930.*}

23. The improper jury argument had a probable effect on a material finding. *See Standard Fire*, 584 S.W.2d at 840. {55 *Elaborate.*} {*See* ***O'Connor's Texas Rules****, "Test for reversible jury argument," ch. 8-J, §6.2.6, p. 884.*}

F. Evidence of jury or bailiff misconduct.

24. A court should grant a new trial if the jury or bailiff engaged in misconduct, the misconduct was material, and the misconduct probably caused injury. Tex. R. Civ. P. 327(a); *see In re Health Care Unlimited, Inc.*, 429 S.W.3d 600, 602 (Tex. 2014); *Golden Eagle Archery, Inc. v. Jackson*, 24 S.W.3d 362, 372 (Tex. 2000); *Redinger v. Living, Inc.*, 689 S.W.2d 415, 419 (Tex. 1985). To prove materiality, the moving party must show the misconduct is reasonably calculated to prejudice its rights. *Sharpless v. Sim*, 209 S.W.3d 825, 829 (Tex. App.—Dallas 2006, pet. denied). To prove probable injury, the moving party generally must show the misconduct likely caused a juror to vote differently on one or more issues vital to the judgment. *In re Health Care Unlimited*, 429 S.W.3d at 603; *Redinger*, 689 S.W.2d at 419. {*See* ***O'Connor's Texas Rules****, "Allegations in MNT," ch. 10-B, §14.1.1, p. 945.*}

{*CHOOSE APPROPRIATE PARAGRAPHS 25-28*}

25. The Court should grant a new trial because there was material jury misconduct that caused injury to {56 *party*}. Tex. R. Civ. P. 327(a). Specifically, an outside influence, originating from a source other than the jurors themselves, affected the verdict. *See* Tex. R. Civ. P. 327(b); *Golden Eagle*, 24 S.W.3d at 370. {57 *Explain the misconduct, e.g., evidence was tampered with, conversations occurred between the judge and a juror, a juror was threatened, and how it was material and caused probable injury.*} {*See* ***O'Connor's Texas Rules****, "Jury misconduct during deliberations," ch. 10-B, §14.1.1(1)(a), p. 945.*}

26. The Court should grant a new trial because there was material jury misconduct that caused injury to {58 *party*}. Tex. R. Civ. P. 327(a). Specifically, a juror responded to a question during voir dire with an untruthful, erroneous, or incomplete answer. *See id.* {59 *Explain the misconduct and how it was material and caused probable injury.*} {*See* ***O'Connor's Texas Rules****, "Erroneous juror answer during voir dire," ch. 10-B, §14.1.1(1)(d), p. 947.*}

27. The Court should grant a new trial because there was material jury misconduct that caused injury to {60 *party*}. Tex. R. Civ. P. 327(a). Specifically, a juror had improper {61 *contact/communication*} with {62 *identify person who had improper contact or communication with juror, e.g., an attorney, a party, a witness, any person connected with or interested in the case*}. *See id.*; *In re Health Care Unlimited*, 429 S.W.3d at

Continued on next page

602. {63 *Explain the misconduct, e.g., a juror requested a ride home from the plaintiff's attorney, and how it was material and caused probable injury.*} {*See **O'Connor's Texas Rules**, "Improper contact or communication with juror," ch. 10-B, §14.1.1(1)(c), p. 947.*}

28. The Court should grant a new trial because there was material bailiff misconduct that caused injury to {64 *party*}. Tex. R. Civ. P. 327(a). Specifically, {65 *explain the misconduct and how it was material and caused probable injury*}. The bailiff is prohibited from communicating with the jury except to ask if they have agreed to a verdict or to make a communication as ordered by the Court. Tex. R. Civ. P. 283; *Pharo v. Chambers Cty.*, 922 S.W.2d 945, 950 (Tex. 1996). {*See **O'Connor's Texas Rules**, "Bailiff misconduct," ch. 10-B, §14.1.1(1)(b), p. 947.*}

{*CHOOSE APPROPRIATE PARAGRAPH 29*}

29. {66 *Party*} attaches the affidavit of {67 *name*}, a juror in the trial of this case, to establish facts not apparent from the record, and incorporates it by reference. {*See **O'Connor's Texas Rules**, "Affidavits," ch. 10-B, §14.1.2(1), p. 948.*}

29. {68 *Party*} attaches the affidavit of {69 *name*}, a person with knowledge of jury misconduct in this case, to establish facts not apparent from the record, and incorporates it by reference. {*See **O'Connor's Texas Rules**, "Affidavits," ch. 10-B, §14.1.2(2), p. 948.*}

29. {70 *Party*} attaches the affidavit of {71 *name*} and incorporates it by reference to explain the unavailability of other affidavits and the diligence used in attempting to procure affidavits to prove jury misconduct. {*See **O'Connor's Texas Rules**, "Affidavits," ch. 10-B, §14.1.2(3), p. 948.*}

G. Newly discovered evidence.

30. After the jury returned a verdict, {72 *party*} discovered evidence that {73 *describe newly discovered evidence*}. Because of this newly discovered evidence, the Court should grant a new trial. {*See **O'Connor's Texas Rules**, "Motion," ch. 10-B, §16.1, p. 950.*}

31. This admissible, competent evidence was discovered after trial. *See Jackson v. Van Winkle*, 660 S.W.2d 807, 809-10 (Tex. 1983), *overruled on other grounds*, *Moritz v. Preiss*, 121 S.W.3d 715 (Tex. 2003); *Dankowski v. Dankowski*, 922 S.W.2d 298, 305 (Tex. App.—Fort Worth 1996, writ denied). {74 *Elaborate.*} {*See **O'Connor's Texas Rules**, "Motion," ch. 10-B, §16.1.1, p. 950.*}

32. {75 *Party*} could not have discovered this evidence sooner because {76 *he/she/it*} had no notice before trial of the existence of the evidence even though {77 *he/she/it*} diligently used the discovery process. *See Jackson*, 660 S.W.2d at 809-10; *Dankowski*, 922 S.W.2d at 305. {78 *Party*}'s late discovery of the evidence was not because of a lack of diligence. {79 *Elaborate.*} {*See* ***O'Connor's Texas Rules****, "Motion," ch. 10-B, §16.1.2, p. 950.*}

33. This evidence is not merely cumulative of other evidence. *See Jackson*, 660 S.W.2d at 809-10; *In re Marriage of Yarbrough*, 719 S.W.2d 412, 415 (Tex. App.—Amarillo 1986, no writ). {80 *Elaborate.*} {*See* ***O'Connor's Texas Rules****, "Motion," ch. 10-B, §16.1.3, p. 950.*}

34. This evidence is not merely for impeachment. *See New Amsterdam Cas. Co. v. Jordan*, 359 S.W.2d 864, 866 (Tex. 1962); *Eckert v. Smith*, 589 S.W.2d 533, 538 (Tex. App.—Amarillo 1979, writ ref'd n.r.e.). {81 *Elaborate.*} {*See* ***O'Connor's Texas Rules****, "Motion," ch. 10-B, §16.1.4, p. 951.*}

35. This evidence is material and would probably produce a different result at a new trial. *See Jackson*, 660 S.W.2d at 809-10. {82 *Elaborate.*} {*See* ***O'Connor's Texas Rules****, "Motion," ch. 10-B, §16.1.5, p. 951.*}

H. Discovery sanctions.

36. The Court abused its discretion in {83 *dismissing the suit/granting a default judgment*} for discovery abuse because the Court did not impose a lesser sanction first. {84 *Elaborate.*} Sanctions that terminate or inhibit the presentation of the merits must be reserved for circumstances in which the party has so abused the rules of procedure that it would be unjust to permit the party to present the substance of its position before the Court. *Braden v. Downey*, 811 S.W.2d 922, 929 (Tex. 1991); *see Cire v. Cummings*, 134 S.W.3d 835, 842 (Tex. 2004); *Spohn Hosp. v. Mayer*, 104 S.W.3d 878, 883 (Tex. 2003). {85 *Elaborate.*} {*See* ***O'Connor's Texas Rules****, "Death-penalty sanctions," ch. 5-K, §3.2, p. 464.*}

I. Ruling on {86 *adverse party*}'s pleadings.

37. The Court abused its discretion when it allowed {87 *adverse party*} to file {88 *identify amended pleading*} because {89 *party*} proved {90 *he/she/it*} was surprised and prejudiced by the late amendment to the pleading. *See Stevenson v. Koutzarov*, 795 S.W.2d 313, 321 (Tex. App.—Houston [1st Dist.] 1990, writ denied). {91 *Elaborate.*} {*See* ***O'Connor's Texas Rules****, "Prove surprise or prejudice," ch. 8-F, §3.2, p. 852.*}

Continued on next page

J. Ruling on {92 *party*}'s pleadings.

38. The Court abused its discretion when it refused to permit {93 *party*} to file {94 *identify amended pleading*} because {95 *adverse party*} did not show {96 *he/she/it*} would be surprised and prejudiced by the late amendment to the pleading. *Hardin v. Hardin*, 597 S.W.2d 347, 349-50 (Tex. 1980). {97 *Elaborate.*} {*See* ***O'Connor's Texas Rules****, "Prove surprise or prejudice," ch. 8-F, §3.2, p. 852.*}

K. Motion for continuance.

39. The Court abused its discretion by denying {98 *party*}'s motion for continuance because counsel {99 *restate grounds from motion for continuance*}. {100 *Elaborate.*} {*See* ***O'Connor's Texas Rules****, "Motion for Continuance," ch. 5-D, p. 417.*}

L. Evidence rulings.

{*CHOOSE APPROPRIATE PARAGRAPHS 40-42*}

40. The Court abused its discretion by admitting {101 *identify the testimony or documentary evidence*} because the evidence was inadmissible, was crucial to a key issue, and was not merely cumulative of other evidence. *See Reliance Steel & Aluminum Co. v. Sevcik*, 267 S.W.3d 867, 873 (Tex. 2008); *Nissan Motor Co. v. Armstrong*, 145 S.W.3d 131, 144 (Tex. 2004). {102 *Elaborate.*} The admission of this evidence probably caused the rendition of an improper judgment. Tex. R. App. P. 44.1(a)(1); *Reliance Steel*, 267 S.W.3d at 871. {*See* ***O'Connor's Texas Rules****, "Harmless-error review," ch. 8-D, §8.3.1, p. 844.*}

41. The Court abused its discretion by excluding {103 *identify the excluded testimony, documentary evidence, or witness*}, which was offered to {104 *state purpose*}, because the evidence was admissible, was crucial to a key issue, and was not merely cumulative of other evidence. *See Diamond Offshore Servs. v. Williams*, 542 S.W.3d 539, 551 (Tex. 2018); *Caffe Ribs, Inc. v. State*, 487 S.W.3d 137, 145 (Tex. 2016); *Williams Distrib. Co. v. Franklin*, 898 S.W.2d 816, 817 (Tex. 1995). {105 *Elaborate.*} The exclusion of this evidence probably caused the rendition of an improper judgment. Tex. R. App. P. 44.1(a)(1); *Diamond Offshore*, 542 S.W.3d at 551; *McCraw v. Maris*, 828 S.W.2d 756, 758 (Tex. 1992). {*See* ***O'Connor's Texas Rules****, "Harmless-error review," ch. 8-D, §8.3.1, p. 844.*}

42. The Court abused its discretion by allowing {106 *name of witness*} to testify; {107 *adverse party*} did not identify that witness in response to a request for disclosure of the identity of persons with knowledge of relevant facts, and {108 *adverse party*} did not show good cause for allowing the testimony. *See* Tex. R. Civ. P. 193.6(a)(1); *Snider*

v. Stanley, 44 S.W.3d 713, 715 (Tex. App.—Beaumont 2001, pet. denied). The sanction for not timely designating a witness in response to a discovery request is the automatic exclusion of the witness's testimony, unless a court finds good cause for the failure to timely respond. *Gonzalez v. Stevenson*, 791 S.W.2d 250, 252-53 (Tex. App.—Corpus Christi 1990, no writ); *see Morrow v. H.E.B., Inc.*, 714 S.W.2d 297, 297-98 (Tex. 1986). {109 *Elaborate.*} {*See **O'Connor's Texas Rules**, "Exclude witness," ch. 6-E, §10.2, p. 634.*}

M. Attorney fees.

{*CHOOSE APPROPRIATE PARAGRAPHS 43-48*}

43. The Court erred by awarding attorney fees because this suit involves {110 *identify type of suit*}, and no rule, statute, or case permits the award of attorney fees in this type of suit. *See Holland v. Wal-Mart Stores, Inc.*, 1 S.W.3d 91, 95 (Tex. 1999). {111 *Elaborate.*} {*See **O'Connor's Texas Rules**, "Attorney Fees from Adverse Party," ch. 1-H, §10, p. 74.*}

44. The Court erred by awarding attorney fees because {112 *adverse party*} has no pleadings to support an award of attorney fees. *See Swate v. Medina Cmty. Hosp.*, 966 S.W.2d 693, 701-02 (Tex. App.—San Antonio 1998, pet. denied). {113 *Elaborate.*} {*See **O'Connor's Texas Rules**, "Pleadings required," ch. 1-H, §10.1, p. 75.*}

45. The Court erred by awarding attorney fees because there is no evidence or, in the alternative, insufficient evidence to support the Court's award of ${114 *amount*} as attorney fees. {115 *Elaborate.*} {*See **O'Connor's Texas Rules**, "Elements of proof for attorney fees," ch. 1-H, §10.5, p. 77.*}

46. The Court erred by taking judicial notice of attorney fees under Texas Civil Practice & Remedies Code section 38.004. A court is permitted to take judicial notice of attorney fees only if the suit is for a claim listed in Texas Civil Practice & Remedies Code section 38.001. *Coward v. Gateway Nat'l Bank*, 525 S.W.2d 857, 859 (Tex. 1975); *Gorman v. Gorman*, 966 S.W.2d 858, 866 (Tex. App.—Houston [1st Dist.] 1998, pet. denied); *Hasty Inc. v. Inwood Buckhorn Joint Venture*, 908 S.W.2d 494, 503 (Tex. App.—Dallas 1995, writ denied). The underlying claim is not listed in section 38.001. {116 *Elaborate.*} {*See **O'Connor's Texas Rules**, "Section 38.001 claim," ch. 1-H, §10.4.1(1)(b)[1], p. 77.*}

47. The Court erred by awarding attorney fees under Texas Civil Practice & Remedies Code section 38.001. Before a party is entitled to attorney fees, the party must present the claim to the opposing party or its agent. Tex. Civ. Prac. & Rem. Code §38.002(2); *Great Am. Ins. Co. v. N. Austin Mun. Util. Dist.*, 908 S.W.2d 415, 427 n.10

Continued on next page

FORM 10B:1

(Tex. 1995). {117 *Adverse party*} did not present the claim as required by section 38.002(2). {118 *Elaborate.*} {*See* ***O'Connor's Texas Rules****, "Requirements," ch. 1-H, §10.4.1(1)(a)[6], p. 76.*}

48. The Court erred by awarding attorney fees under Texas Civil Practice & Remedies Code section 38.001. A party is entitled to attorney fees only if it prevails on a cause of action for which attorney fees are recoverable. *State Farm Life Ins. Co. v. Beaston*, 907 S.W.2d 430, 437 (Tex. 1995); *London v. London*, 94 S.W.3d 139, 149 n.5 (Tex. App.—Houston [14th Dist.] 2002, no pet.). {119 *Adverse party*} did not prevail on a cause of action for which attorney fees were recoverable. {120 *Elaborate.*} {*See* ***O'Connor's Texas Rules****, "Requirements," ch. 1-H, §10.4.1(1)(a)[8], p. 76.*}

N. Fees to guardian ad litem.

49. The Court erred by granting fees to the guardian ad litem because there is no evidence or, in the alternative, insufficient evidence to support the Court's award of ${121 *amount*} as ad litem fees. *See* Tex. R. Civ. P. 173.6(b); *Jocson v. Crabb*, 133 S.W.3d 268, 270-71 (Tex. 2004). {122 *Elaborate.*} {*See* ***O'Connor's Texas Rules****, "Objection to fees," ch. 1-I, §6.2, p. 93; "Hearing on application," ch. 1-I, §6.3, p. 94.*}

O. No consent to agreed judgment.

50. The Court erred by rendering an agreed judgment because {123 *party*} {124 *never consented/revoked its consent*} to the agreed judgment before it was rendered by the Court. *Sohocki v. Sohocki*, 897 S.W.2d 422, 424 (Tex. App.—Corpus Christi 1995, no writ). {125 *Elaborate.*} The parties must be in agreement when the judgment is rendered, or the judgment is void. *Id.*

CONCLUSION

51. {126 *Briefly summarize the motion.*}

PRAYER

52. For these reasons, and in the interest of justice and fairness, {127 *party*} asks the Court to {128 *if requesting a new trial on the ground of jury misconduct or newly discovered evidence, include: conduct a hearing with a court reporter, receive evidence, and, after the hearing,*} grant a new trial. {*See* ***O'Connor's Texas Rules****, "Prayer," ch. 10-B, §2.4, p. 930.*}

SEE: Tex. R. Civ. P. 271-279, 320-329b
Tex. R. Evid. 606(b)
Tex. Civ. Prac. & Rem. Code §38.001 et seq.
O'Connor's Texas Rules * Civil Trials (2019), "Motion for New Trial," ch. 10-B, p. 929

ADD: STYLE OF THE CASE – FORM 1B:2
SIGNATURE BLOCK – FORM 1B:3
VERIFICATION – FORM 1B:7, if based on grounds in Tex. R. Civ. P. 324(b)(1)
CERTIFICATE OF SERVICE – FORM 1B:13

ATTACH: AFFIDAVIT – FORM 1B:8, if necessary
NOTICE OF HEARING OR SUBMISSION – FORM 1E:1
ORDER – FORM 10B:8

NOTE: The appellant should include in the motion any complaints not previously brought to the trial court's attention and not waived. See ***O'Connor's Texas Rules***, "When MNT necessary," ch. 10-B, §2.1.5, p. 930.

To challenge the sufficiency of the evidence to support a verdict when the charge asked only a broad-form question, the appellant must assume that the jury found against it on all elements of the cause of action and thus must challenge all of the elements. See ***O'Connor's Texas Rules***, "Challenging broad-form jury question," ch. 10-B, §13.2, p. 944.

When alleging jury misconduct, newly discovered evidence, failure to set aside a default judgment, or any other ground that requires the presentation of evidence at a hearing, the motion must be verified and should include affidavits supporting each element. See ***O'Connor's Texas Rules***, "When verification required," ch. 10-B, §3.1, p. 931.

In most cases alleging jury misconduct, the movant must prove that, based on the entire record, the misconduct probably resulted in injury to the movant. *See* Tex. R. Civ. P. 327(a). Some acts, however, are so prejudicial to fairness that the movant must show only that the improper act occurred; by doing so, prima facie proof of injury is met. *E.g.*, ***Texas Empls. Ins. v. McCaslin***, 317 S.W.2d 916, 921 (Tex.1958) (harm presumed when party went to juror's office and asked her to do all she could to help party). See ***O'Connor's Texas Rules***, "Misconduct resulted in injury," ch. 10-B, §14.1.1(3), p. 947.

A request for remittitur can be made as part of a motion for new trial. See FORMS 10C.

{❶ *PARTY*}'S MOTION FOR NEW TRIAL

{❷ *Party*}, {❸ *name*}, asks the Court to grant a new trial in the interest of justice and fairness.

INTRODUCTION

1. Plaintiff, {❹ *name*}, sued defendant, {❺ *name*}, for {❻ *state basis of suit*}.

2. {❼ *State other relevant facts about the suit.*}

BACKGROUND

3. After a trial to the Court, the Court signed a judgment for {❽ *adverse party*}, {❾ *name*}, on {❿ *date*}.

4. {⓫ *State other facts relevant to the motion.*}

CHALLENGING THE FINDINGS & CONCLUSIONS

5. The Court should grant a new trial because it erred by making the following rulings:

{*CHOOSE APPROPRIATE PARAGRAPHS 6-12*}

{*To challenge findings on which movant had burden of proof*}

6. The Court erred by finding that {⓬ *state the finding*} because that finding is against the great weight and preponderance of the evidence and is manifestly unjust. {⓭ *Elaborate.*}

7. The Court erred by finding that {⓮ *state the finding*} because the evidence proves conclusively, as a matter of law, that {⓯ *state what the evidence proves*}. {⓰ *Elaborate.*}

{*To challenge findings on which movant did not have burden of proof*}

8. The Court erred by finding that {⓱ *state the finding*} because the evidence is insufficient to support the finding. {⓲ *Elaborate.*}

9. The Court erred by finding that {⓳ *state the finding*} because there is no evidence to support the finding. {⓴ *Elaborate.*}

{To challenge failure to file findings}

10. The Court erred by refusing to file findings of fact and conclusions of law because {[21] *party*} cannot ascertain the facts and grounds for {[22] *recovery/defense*} on which the Court based its judgment. When a party timely requests findings of fact and conclusions of law and the Court does not file them, the failure is presumed harmful on appeal unless the record affirmatively shows that the party suffered no injury. *Tenery v. Tenery*, 932 S.W.2d 29, 30 (Tex. 1996). In this case, {[23] *party*} can show injury because {[24] *explain*}. *{See* ***O'Connor's Texas Rules****, "When findings are requested but not filed," ch. 10-E, §6.2.7, p. 969.}*

{To challenge implicit findings}

11. Even though the Court did not make an express finding, the Court erred by implicitly finding that {[25] *identify implicit findings*} because there is no evidence or, in the alternative, insufficient evidence to support that finding on the issue of {[26] *identify issue*}. {[27] *Elaborate.*} *{See* ***O'Connor's Texas Rules****, "When findings are not requested or filed," ch. 10-E, §6.2.8, p. 970.}*

{To challenge conclusions of law}

12. The Court erred by concluding that {[28] *state specific legal conclusion*}. {[29] *Elaborate, stating specific error.*}

{ADD SECTION BELOW IF APPROPRIATE}

OTHER GROUNDS

13. {[30] *State other appropriate grounds. See FORM 10B:1, §§H-O, for various challenges that can be asserted.*}

CONCLUSION

14. {[31] *Briefly summarize the motion.*}

PRAYER

15. For these reasons, and in the interest of justice and fairness, {[32] *party*} asks the Court to grant a new trial.

◄ Continued on next page ►

SEE: Tex. R. Civ. P. 296-299a, 320-329b
O'Connor's Texas Rules * Civil Trials (2019), "MNT After Nonjury Trial," ch. 10-B, §15, p. 950

ADD: STYLE OF THE CASE – FORM 1B:2
SIGNATURE BLOCK – FORM 1B:3
CERTIFICATE OF SERVICE – FORM 1B:13

ATTACH: AFFIDAVIT – FORM 1B:8, if necessary
NOTICE OF HEARING OR SUBMISSION – FORM 1E:1
ORDER – FORM 10B:8

NOTE: After a nonjury trial, a motion for new trial is necessary to preserve error for appeal only when the party has not made its objection known to the trial court. *See* Tex. R. Civ. P. 324(a); Tex. R. App. P. 33.1(a).

There is no need to complain in a motion for new trial about factual or legal insufficiency of the evidence. *See* Tex. R. Civ. P. 324(b)(2), (b)(4); ***In re Marriage of Parker***, 20 S.W.3d 812, 816 (Tex.App.—Texarkana 2000, no pet.); ***Strickland v. Coleman***, 824 S.W.2d 188, 191 (Tex.App.—Houston [1st Dist.] 1991, no writ). See ¶¶6-9, this form. For a civil nonjury trial, these issues can be raised for the first time on appeal. Tex. R. App. P. 33.1(d).

DEFENDANT'S MOTION FOR NEW TRIAL

Defendant, {❶ *name*}, asks the Court to grant a new trial in the interest of justice and fairness.

INTRODUCTION

1. Plaintiff, {❷ *name*}, sued defendant, {❸ *name*}, for {❹ *state basis of suit*}.

2. {❺ *State other relevant facts about the suit.*}

BACKGROUND

3. The Court signed a default judgment for plaintiff on {❻ *date*}.

4. {❼ *State other facts relevant to the motion.*}

ARGUMENT & AUTHORITIES

{*CHOOSE APPROPRIATE SECTIONS A-J*}

A. Defective citation.

5. A court should grant a new trial if the citation is not in strict compliance with all applicable rules. *See Verlander Enters., Inc. v. Graham*, 932 S.W.2d 259, 262 (Tex. App.—El Paso 1996, no writ).

{*CHOOSE APPROPRIATE PARAGRAPHS 6-22*}

6. The Court should grant a new trial because the citation was not styled "The State of Texas." Tex. R. Civ. P. 15, 99(b)(1). {❽ *Elaborate.*} {*See **O'Connor's Texas Rules**, "Style of process," ch. 2-I, §2.1, p. 189.*}

7. The Court should grant a new trial because the citation did not contain the {❾ *name/location*} of the Court. Tex. R. Civ. P. 99(b)(3). {❿ *Elaborate.*} {*See **O'Connor's Texas Rules**, "Identification of court," ch. 2-I, §2.3.1, p. 189.*}

8. The Court should grant a new trial because the citation did not contain the address of the court clerk. Tex. R. Civ. P. 99(b)(11). {⓫ *Elaborate.*} {*See **O'Connor's Texas Rules**, "Identification of court," ch. 2-I, §2.3.1, p. 189.*}

9. The Court should grant a new trial because the citation was not signed by the court clerk. Tex. R. Civ. P. 15, 99(b)(2); *e.g.*, *Verlander Enters.*, 932 S.W.2d at 262 (return attached to citation without clerk's signature or seal did not confer jurisdiction). {⓬ *Elaborate.*} {*See **O'Connor's Texas Rules**, "Signature & seal," ch. 2-I, §2.3.2, p. 189.*}

◄ *Continued on next page* ►

10. The Court should grant a new trial because the citation did not contain the seal of the Court. Tex. R. Civ. P. 15, 99(b)(2); *e.g.*, *Verlander Enters.*, 932 S.W.2d at 262 (return attached to citation without clerk's signature or seal did not confer jurisdiction). {[13] *Elaborate.*} {*See* ***O'Connor's Texas Rules****, "Signature & seal," ch. 2-I, §2.3.2, p. 189.*}

11. The Court should grant a new trial because the citation {[14] *did not contain the/contained the wrong*} cause number. Tex. R. Civ. P. 99(b)(6); *Medeles v. Nunez*, 923 S.W.2d 659, 662-63 (Tex. App.—Houston [1st Dist.] 1996, writ denied), *overruled on other grounds, Barker CATV Constr., Inc. v. Ampro, Inc.*, 989 S.W.2d 789 (Tex. App.—Houston [1st Dist.] 1999, no pet.); *Martinez v. Wilber*, 810 S.W.2d 461, 463 (Tex. App.—San Antonio 1991, writ denied). {[15] *Elaborate.*} {*See* ***O'Connor's Texas Rules****, "Information about suit," ch. 2-I, §2.2, p. 189.*}

12. The Court should grant a new trial because the citation did not properly identify plaintiff. Tex. R. Civ. P. 99(b)(7). {[16] *Elaborate.*} {*See* ***O'Connor's Texas Rules****, "Identification of P," ch. 2-I, §2.4.1, p. 189.*}

13. The Court should grant a new trial because the citation did not contain {[17] *the name and address of plaintiff's attorney/plaintiff's address*}. Tex. R. Civ. P. 99(b)(9). {[18] *Elaborate.*} {*See* ***O'Connor's Texas Rules****, "P's attorney," ch. 2-I, §2.4.2, p. 189.*}

14. The Court should grant a new trial because the citation did not properly identify defendant. *E.g.*, *Werner v. Colwell*, 909 S.W.2d 866, 870 (Tex. 1995) (judgment could not be rendered against defendant as trustee when she was sued only as individual); *Amato v. Hernandez*, 981 S.W.2d 947, 949 (Tex. App.—Houston [1st Dist.] 1998, pet. denied) (citation was defective because defendant's name was incorrect). {[19] *Elaborate.*} {*See* ***O'Connor's Texas Rules****, "Identification of D," ch. 2-I, §2.5.1, p. 189.*}

15. The Court should grant a new trial because the citation was not directed to defendant but instead was directed to {[20] *identify person to whom citation was directed*}. Tex. R. Civ. P. 99(b)(8). Therefore, the citation was void. *ISO Prod. Mgmt. 1982, Ltd. v. M & L Oil & Gas Expl., Inc.*, 768 S.W.2d 354, 355-56 (Tex. App.—Waco 1989, no writ); *see Barker CATV Constr., Inc. v. Ampro, Inc.*, 989 S.W.2d 789, 792 (Tex. App.—Houston [1st Dist.] 1999, no pet.). {[21] *Elaborate.*} {*See* ***O'Connor's Texas Rules****, "Citation directed to D," ch. 2-I, §2.5.2, p. 190.*}

16. The Court should grant a new trial because the citation did not properly identify the agent for service. The citation must state the name of the agent for service and the agent's address for service even though the citation must be directed to the defendant. *See Barker CATV Constr., Inc. v. Ampro, Inc.*, 989 S.W.2d 789, 792 (Tex. App.—

Houston [1st Dist.] 1999, no pet.). {❷❷ *Elaborate.*} {*See* ***O'Connor's Texas Rules***, *"Identification of D's agent for service," ch. 2-I, §2.6, p. 190.*}

17. The Court should grant a new trial because the citation did not identify the date plaintiff filed the petition. Tex. R. Civ. P. 99(b)(4); *Mansell v. Insurance Co. of the W.*, 203 S.W.3d 499, 501 (Tex. App.—Houston [14th Dist.] 2006, no pet.); *Hance v. Cogswell*, 307 S.W.2d 277, 278-79 (Tex. App.—Austin 1957, no writ). {❷❸ *Elaborate.*} {*See* ***O'Connor's Texas Rules***, *"Date petition filed," ch. 2-I, §2.7.1, p. 191.*}

18. The Court should grant a new trial because the citation did not identify the date the citation was issued. Tex. R. Civ. P. 15, 99(b)(5); *see London v. Chandler*, 406 S.W.2d 203, 204 (Tex. 1966). {❷❹ *Elaborate.*} {*See* ***O'Connor's Texas Rules***, *"Date citation issued," ch. 2-I, §2.7.2, p. 191.*}

19. The Court should grant a new trial because the citation did not state that defendant is required to file a written answer on or before 10:00 a.m. on the first Monday after the expiration of 20 days from the date of service. Tex. R. Civ. P. 99(b)(10), (c). {❷❺ *Elaborate.*} {*See* ***O'Connor's Texas Rules***, *"Time to answer," ch. 2-I, §2.7.3, p. 191.*}

20. The Court should grant a new trial because the citation did not warn defendant that if {❷❻ *he/she/it*} does not file an answer, a default judgment may be rendered against {❷❼ *him/her/it*} on the petition. Tex. R. Civ. P. 99(b)(12), (c). {❷❽ *Elaborate.*} {*See* ***O'Connor's Texas Rules***, *"Warning of default," ch. 2-I, §2.8, p. 191.*}

21. The Court should grant a new trial because the citation did not include a notice to defendant that {❷❾ *he/she/it*} has been sued, as required by Texas Rule of Civil Procedure 99(c). {❸⓿ *Elaborate.*}

22. The Court should grant a new trial because the citation was void because {❸❶ *explain*}. When a defendant is served with a void citation, the service is ineffective. *Nat'l Sur. Corp. v. Anderson*, 809 S.W.2d 313, 316 (Tex. App.—Houston [1st Dist.] 1991, no writ). {❸❷ *Elaborate.*}

B. Defective service of citation.

23. If a court signs a default judgment against a defendant who was not properly served, the defendant is deprived of due process. *See Peralta v. Heights Med. Ctr., Inc.*, 485 U.S. 80, 84 (1988); *LBL Oil Co. v. Int'l Power Servs., Inc.*, 777 S.W.2d 390, 390-91 (Tex. 1989). A court should grant a new trial if the service of citation is not in strict compliance with all applicable rules. *See Primate Constr., Inc. v. Silver*, 884 S.W.2d 151, 152 (Tex. 1994).

Continued on next page

{*CHOOSE APPROPRIATE PARAGRAPHS 24-26*}

24. The Court should grant a new trial because defendant was served by substitute service by {33 *describe method of substitute service*}, which the Court did not authorize. *See* Tex. R. Civ. P. 106(b). {34 *Elaborate.*} {*See* ***O'Connor's Texas Rules****, "Substituted service," ch. 2-I, §4.3, p. 193.*}

25. The Court should grant a new trial because defendant was served by substitute service by {35 *describe method of substitute service*}, but plaintiff did not comply with the appropriate statutes and rules for substitute service. *See* Tex. R. Civ. P. 106(b). {36 *Elaborate.*} A default judgment rendered following substituted service is void if the plaintiff did not strictly comply with the rules for service of citation. *Westcliffe, Inc. v. Bear Creek Constr., Ltd.*, 105 S.W.3d 286, 290 (Tex. App.—Dallas 2003, no pet.); *Lozano v. Hayes Wheels Int'l, Inc.*, 933 S.W.2d 245, 247 (Tex. App.—Corpus Christi 1996, no writ). {*See* ***O'Connor's Texas Rules****, "Sufficiency of service," ch. 7-A, §3.4, p. 705.*}

26. The Court should grant a new trial because defendant was served on a Sunday, in violation of Texas Rule of Civil Procedure 6. *Nichols v. Nichols*, 857 S.W.2d 657, 659 (Tex. App.—Houston [1st Dist.] 1993, no writ). {37 *Elaborate.*} {*See* ***O'Connor's Texas Rules****, "Note," ch. 2-I, §4, p. 192.*}

C. Untimely notice.

27. If a court signs a default judgment against a defendant who was not given proper notice of the trial or dispositive hearing, the defendant is deprived of due process. *See LBL Oil Co. v. Int'l Power Servs., Inc.*, 777 S.W.2d 390, 390-91 (Tex. 1989).

{*CHOOSE APPROPRIATE PARAGRAPHS 28-30*}

28. The Court should grant a new trial because defendant did not receive timely notice of {38 *trial/a dispositive hearing*}. {39 *Elaborate.*}

29. The Court should grant a new trial because, although defendant is {40 *a person who/an entity that*} must be represented by the Attorney General according to Texas Civil Practice & Remedies Code chapter 104, plaintiff did not send a notice of intent to take a default judgment to the Texas Attorney General by certified mail, return receipt requested, at least ten days before filing the motion for default judgment. Tex. Civ. Prac. & Rem. Code §§30.004(d), 39.001. {41 *Elaborate.*} {*See* ***O'Connor's Texas Rules****, "After notice to Attorney General," ch. 7-A, §3.9.1(4), p. 708.*}

30. The Court should grant a new trial because the Court rendered a default judgment after remand from federal court even though defendant did not have 15 days' notice of the filing of the federal court's order of remand with the Court. Tex. R. Civ. P. 237a. {㊷ *Elaborate.*}

D. Answer filed in federal court.

31. The Court should grant a new trial because the Court rendered a default judgment after remand from federal court even though defendant filed an answer in federal court during removal. Tex. R. Civ. P. 237a. {㊸ *Elaborate.*}

E. Bankruptcy stay in effect.

32. The Court should grant a new trial because the Court rendered a default judgment less than 30 days after a request for relief from a bankruptcy stay was made, at which time the stay was still in effect. *See* 11 U.S.C. §362(e)(1). {㊹ *Elaborate.*}

F. Defective return of service.

33. A court should grant a new trial if the return of service was defective. *See Primate Constr., Inc. v. Silver*, 884 S.W.2d 151, 152 (Tex. 1994). {㊺ *Elaborate.*} The return of service must be in strict compliance with all applicable rules. *Id.*

{*CHOOSE APPROPRIATE PARAGRAPHS 34-58*}

{*General*}

34. The Court should grant a new trial because the return does not identify the case name. Tex. R. Civ. P. 107(b)(1). {㊻ *Elaborate.*}

35. The Court should grant a new trial because the return does not identify the cause number. Tex. R. Civ. P. 107(b)(1). {㊼ *Elaborate.*}

36. The Court should grant a new trial because the return does not identify the court where the case was filed. Tex. R. Civ. P. 107(b)(2). {㊽ *Elaborate.*}

37. The Court should grant a new trial because the return does not show the address of service. Tex. R. Civ. P. 16, 107(b)(6); *see Jacksboro Nat'l Bank v. Signal Oil & Gas Co.*, 482 S.W.2d 339, 341-42 (Tex. App.—Tyler 1972, no writ). {㊾ *Elaborate.*}

38. The Court should grant a new trial because the Supreme Court, by order, certified a person to serve process and the return does not show {㊿ *that person's identification number/the expiration date of that person's certification/that person's identification number and the expiration date of {his/her} certification*}. Tex. R. Civ. P. 107(b)(10). {51 *Elaborate.*}

Continued on next page

39. The Court should grant a new trial because the return does not state the date it was filed with the Court. *HB & WM, Inc. v. Smith*, 802 S.W.2d 279, 282 (Tex. App.—San Antonio 1990, no writ); *Melendez v. John R. Schatzman, Inc.*, 685 S.W.2d 137, 138 (Tex. App.—El Paso 1985, no writ); *see* Tex. R. Civ. P. 107(h). {❺❷ *Elaborate.*} {*See* ***O'Connor's Texas Rules***, *"Filing date," ch. 2-I, §9.4.9, p. 203.*}

40. The Court should grant a new trial because the return does not include {❺❸ *identify any other information required by rule or law to be included in the return*}. Tex. R. Civ. P. 107(b)(11). {❺❹ *Elaborate.*}

41. The Court should grant a new trial because there is no return on file among the papers of this case. Tex. R. Civ. P. 107(g). {❺❺ *Elaborate.*}

{*When service completed*}

42. The Court should grant a new trial because the return does not include a description of what was served. Tex. R. Civ. P. 107(b)(3). Specifically, the Court should grant a new trial because the return did not state that a copy of the citation and a copy of the petition were served on defendant. Tex. R. Civ. P. 106(a)(1); *Woodall v. Lansford*, 254 S.W.2d 540, 541 (Tex. App.—Fort Worth 1953, no writ). The return must correctly identify the petition served on the defendant. *See Primate Constr.*, 884 S.W.2d at 152. {❺❻ *Elaborate.*} {*See* ***O'Connor's Texas Rules***, *"Description of documents," ch. 2-I, §9.4.3, p. 201.*}

43. The Court should grant a new trial because the person who served the citation did not endorse it with the date and time {❺❼ *he/she*} received it. Tex. R. Civ. P. 16, 105, 107(b)(4); *Ins. Co. of Pa. v. Lejeune*, 297 S.W.3d 254, 256 (Tex. 2009); *TAC Americas, Inc. v. Boothe*, 94 S.W.3d 315, 319 (Tex. App.—Austin 2002, no pet.). {❺❽ *Elaborate.*}

44. The Court should grant a new trial because the return does not identify the exact person or entity that was served. Tex. R. Civ. P. 107(b)(5); *e.g., Uvalde Country Club v. Martin Linen Supply Co.*, 690 S.W.2d 884, 884 (Tex. 1985) (return invalid because it did not include "Jr."). {❺❾ *Elaborate.*} {*See* ***O'Connor's Texas Rules***, *"Person or entity served," ch. 2-I, §9.4.4, p. 201.*}

45. The Court should grant a new trial because the return does not state the manner of delivery of service. Tex. R. Civ. P. 107(b)(8). {❻⓿ *Elaborate.*} {*See* ***O'Connor's Texas Rules***, *"Manner of service or attempted service," ch. 2-I, §9.4.6, p. 202.*}

46. The Court should grant a new trial because the return does not identify who served defendant. Tex. R. Civ. P. 107(b)(9). {❻❶ *Elaborate.*} {*See* ***O'Connor's Texas Rules***, *"Name of server," ch. 2-I, §9.4.7, p. 202.*}

47. The Court should grant a new trial because the name of the person identified on the return as the person who served process does not match the name of the person identified in the trial-court order authorizing service. *See* Tex. R. Civ. P. 107(b)(9); *see, e.g., Mega v. Anglo Iron & Metal Co.*, 601 S.W.2d 501, 504 (Tex. App.—Corpus Christi 1980, no writ) (return was invalid because order appointed "A.R. 'Tony' Martinez" to serve process and return was signed by "A.R. Martinez, Jr."). {62 *Elaborate.*}

48. The Court should grant a new trial because the return does not state the date of service. Tex. R. Civ. P. 16, 107(b)(7). {63 *Elaborate.*} {*See* ***O'Connor's Texas Rules****, "Date of service or attempted service," ch. 2-I, §9.4.8, p. 203.*}

49. The Court should grant a new trial because the return, which was served by registered or certified mail, does not contain the return receipt with the addressee's signature. Tex. R. Civ. P. 107(c); *Ramirez v. Consol. HGM Corp.*, 124 S.W.3d 914, 916 (Tex. App.—Amarillo 2004, no pet.); *All Commercial Floors, Inc. v. Barton & Rasor*, 97 S.W.3d 723, 726-27 (Tex. App.—Fort Worth 2003, no pet.); *Fowler v. Quinlan Indep. Sch. Dist.*, 963 S.W.2d 941, 944 (Tex. App.—Texarkana 1998, no pet.). {64 *Elaborate.*} {*See* ***O'Connor's Texas Rules****, "Addressee's signature," ch. 2-I, §9.5, p. 203.*}

50. The Court should grant a new trial because the person who served the citation did not sign the return. Tex. R. Civ. P. 16, 107(e). {65 *Elaborate.*} {*See* ***O'Connor's Texas Rules****, "Signature of server," ch. 2-I, §9.6, p. 204.*}

51. The Court should grant a new trial because the person who served the citation did not sign the return under penalty of perjury. Tex. Civ. Prac. & Rem. Code §17.030(c); Tex. R. Civ. P. 107(e). The return must be signed under penalty of perjury if it is signed by an authorized person other than a sheriff, constable, or court clerk. Tex. R. Civ. P. 107(e). {66 *Elaborate.*}

52. The Court should grant a new trial because the person who served the citation did not verify the return. Tex. R. Civ. P. 107(e). The return must be verified if it (1) is signed by an authorized person other than a sheriff, constable, or court clerk and (2) is not signed under penalty of perjury. *Id.* {67 *Elaborate.*}

{*When service not completed*}

53. The Court should grant a new trial because the return does not state the manner of delivery of the attempted service. Tex. R. Civ. P. 107(b)(8). {68 *Elaborate.*} {*See* ***O'Connor's Texas Rules****, "Manner of service or attempted service," ch. 2-I, §9.4.6, p. 202.*}

◄ *Continued on next page* ►

54. The Court should grant a new trial because the return does not identify who attempted to serve defendant. Tex. R. Civ. P. 107(b)(9). {69 *Elaborate.*} {*See* ***O'Connor's Texas Rules***, *"Name of server," ch. 2-I, §9.4.7, p. 202.*}

55. The Court should grant a new trial because the return does not state the date of attempted service. Tex. R. Civ. P. 16, 107(b)(7). {70 *Elaborate.*} {*See* ***O'Connor's Texas Rules***, *"Date of service or attempted service," ch. 2-I, §9.4.8, p. 203.*}

56. The Court should grant a new trial because the return does not show the diligence used by the officer or other authorized person in attempting service. Tex. R. Civ. P. 107(d). {71 *Elaborate.*}

57. The Court should grant a new trial because the return does not show the reason service was not accomplished. Tex. R. Civ. P. 107(d). {72 *Elaborate.*}

58. The Court should grant a new trial because the return does not identify defendant's location, which is known. Tex. R. Civ. P. 107(d). {73 *Elaborate.*}

G. Citation & proof of service not on file.

59. The Court should grant a new trial because it rendered a default judgment before the citation and proof of service were on file for ten days. Tex. R. Civ. P. 107(h); *Webb v. Oberkampf Supply of Lubbock, Inc.*, 831 S.W.2d 61, 64 (Tex. App.—Amarillo 1992, no writ). {74 *Elaborate.*}

H. Petition does not support default judgment.

60. A plaintiff's petition will support a default judgment only if it (1) states a cause of action within a court's jurisdiction against a defendant who is amenable to process, (2) gives fair notice to the defendant of the claim asserted, and (3) does not affirmatively disclose the invalidity of the claim. *See Paramount Pipe & Supply Co. v. Muhr*, 749 S.W.2d 491, 494 (Tex. 1988); *Stoner v. Thompson*, 578 S.W.2d 679, 684-85 (Tex. 1979). {*See* ***O'Connor's Texas Rules***, *"Defects in plaintiff's petition," ch. 10-B, §9.1.1(1)(d), p. 936.*}

{*CHOOSE APPROPRIATE PARAGRAPHS 61-64*}

61. The Court should grant a new trial because plaintiff's petition does not state a cause of action. *See Fairdale, Ltd. v. Sellers*, 651 S.W.2d 725, 726 (Tex. 1982). Specifically, {75 *explain*}. Thus, plaintiff's petition does not support the default judgment.

62. The Court should grant a new trial because plaintiff's petition does not give fair notice of the claim asserted. *See Stoner*, 578 S.W.2d at 683-85. Specifically, {76 *explain*}. Thus, plaintiff's petition does not support the default judgment.

63. The Court should grant a new trial because plaintiff's petition discloses on its face that the claim is invalid. *See Arnold v. Allen Ctr. Co. #2*, 747 S.W.2d 17, 19 (Tex. App.—Houston [14th Dist.] 1988, writ denied). Specifically, {77 *explain*}. Thus, plaintiff's petition does not support the default judgment.

64. The Court should grant a new trial because plaintiff's petition does not allege facts that, if true, would make defendant responsible for filing an answer. *See Whitney v. L & L Realty Corp.*, 500 S.W.2d 94, 95-96 (Tex. 1973). Specifically, {78 *explain, e.g., the allegations are not sufficient under Texas Civil Practice & Remedies Code section 17.042, the long-arm statute*}. Thus, plaintiff's petition does not support the default judgment.

I. Mistake or accident.

65. When a defendant does not file an answer because of a mistake or an accident, a court should set aside the default judgment and grant a new trial if the defendant can meet the requirements of *Craddock v. Sunshine Bus Lines, Inc.*, 133 S.W.2d 124 (Tex. 1939). *Craddock* requires a defendant to do all of the following:

a. Demonstrate that the failure to file an answer was not intentional or the result of conscious indifference, but was a mistake or an accident. *Sutherland v. Spencer*, 376 S.W.3d 752, 754-55 (Tex. 2012); *In re R.R.*, 209 S.W.3d 112, 114-15 (Tex. 2006); *Estate of Pollack v. McMurrey*, 858 S.W.2d 388, 391 (Tex. 1993); *Craddock*, 133 S.W.2d at 126. {*See* ***O'Connor's Texas Rules****, "Not intentional but accidental," ch. 10-B, §9.1.3(1), p. 937.*}

b. Set up a meritorious defense. *In re R.R.*, 209 S.W.3d at 114-15; *Ivy v. Carrell*, 407 S.W.2d 212, 214 (Tex. 1966); *Craddock*, 133 S.W.2d at 126. To set up a meritorious defense, the defendant must allege facts that constitute a defense to the plaintiff's cause of action and support the allegations with affidavits or other evidence. *Estate of Pollack*, 858 S.W.2d at 392; *Ivy*, 407 S.W.2d at 214. {*See* ***O'Connor's Texas Rules****, "Meritorious defense," ch. 10-B, §9.1.3(2), p. 939.*}

c. Demonstrate that granting a new trial will not cause delay or otherwise injure the plaintiff. *In re R.R.*, 209 S.W.3d at 114-15; *Craddock*, 133 S.W.2d at 126. {*See* ***O'Connor's Texas Rules****, "No delay or injury," ch. 10-B, §9.1.3(3), p. 939.*}

66. The Court should grant a new trial because defendant's failure to answer was not intentional, but was accidental. Specifically, {79 *explain failure to answer*}.

◄ *Continued on next page* ►

67. The Court should grant a new trial because defendant has a meritorious defense. Specifically, {80 *set up prima facie defense supported by affidavits*}.

68. The Court should grant a new trial because a new trial will not cause delay or otherwise injure plaintiff. Defendant is ready for trial and willing to reimburse plaintiff for all reasonable expenses incurred in obtaining the default judgment.

J. Defendant in the military.

{*CHOOSE APPROPRIATE PARAGRAPH 69*}

69. The Court should grant a new trial because plaintiff did not attach an affidavit of defendant's military status. 50 U.S.C. §3931(b)(1). Defendant attaches an affidavit as Exhibit {81 *letter*} concerning {82 *his/her*} military status at the time of judgment and incorporates it by reference. {*See **O'Connor's Texas Rules**, "Servicemembers' affidavit," ch. 7-A, §3.9.2(3), p. 708.*}

69. The Court should grant a new trial because plaintiff averred that defendant was not in the military when, in fact, defendant was in the armed forces on active duty. *See* 50 U.S.C. §3931(b)(1). Defendant attaches an affidavit as Exhibit {83 *letter*} concerning {84 *his/her*} military status at the time of judgment and incorporates it by reference. {*See **O'Connor's Texas Rules**, "Servicemembers' affidavit," ch. 7-A, §3.9.2(3), p. 708.*}

69. The Court should grant a new trial because plaintiff filed an affidavit of defendant's military status that indicated plaintiff knew defendant was in the military, but the Court did not appoint an attorney to represent defendant before it signed an order directing the entry of a default judgment. 50 U.S.C. §3931(b)(2). {*See **O'Connor's Texas Rules**, "Servicemembers' affidavit," ch. 7-A, §3.9.2(3), p. 708.*}

69. The Court should grant a new trial because plaintiff filed an affidavit of defendant's military status that indicated plaintiff was unsure of defendant's military status, but plaintiff did not file a bond in the amount of ${85 *amount*}, which was approved by the Court, before the Court signed an order directing the entry of a default judgment. 50 U.S.C. §3931(b)(3). {*See **O'Connor's Texas Rules**, "Servicemembers' affidavit," ch. 7-A, §3.9.2(3), p. 708.*}

CONCLUSION

70. {86 *Briefly summarize the motion.*}

PRAYER

71. For these reasons, and in the interest of justice and fairness, defendant asks the Court to grant a new trial.

SEE: Tex. R. Civ. P. 15, 16, 99, 105-107, 237a, 320-329b
Tex. Civ. Prac. & Rem. Code §§17.030, 30.004, 39.001
11 U.S.C. §362; 50 U.S.C. §3931
O'Connor's Texas Rules * Civil Trials (2019), "Serving the Defendant with Suit," ch. 2-I, p. 188; "Default Judgment," ch. 7-A, p. 703; "MNT After Default Judgment," ch. 10-B, §9, p. 936

ADD: STYLE OF THE CASE – FORM 1B:2
SIGNATURE BLOCK – FORM 1B:3
VERIFICATION – FORM 1B:7, if necessary
CERTIFICATE OF SERVICE – FORM 1B:13

ATTACH: AFFIDAVIT – FORM 1B:8, if necessary
NOTICE OF HEARING OR SUBMISSION – FORM 1E:1
SERVICEMEMBERS' AFFIDAVIT – FORM 7A:3, if necessary
ORDER – FORM 10B:8

NOTE: If the defendant asserts that it did not file an answer because of improper service and proves that service was improper, the defendant does not need to establish the ***Craddock*** factors to be entitled to a new trial. *See* ***Sutherland v. Spencer***, 376 S.W.3d 752, 755 (Tex.2012); ***Fidelity & Guar. Ins. v. Drewery Constr. Co.***, 186 S.W.3d 571, 574 (Tex.2006). If the defendant is uncertain whether the court will sustain its argument that it did not receive proper service or notice, the defendant should allege and prove the three ***Craddock*** factors as an alternative ground for reversal (see §I, this form). See ***O'Connor's Texas Rules***, "*Craddock* factors," ch. 10-B, §9.1.1(2), p. 936.

The Supreme Court has held that service of a new citation is not required when serving a more onerous amended petition on a nonanswering defendant; however, the plaintiff must serve the amended petition before taking a default judgment. ***In re E.A.***, 287 S.W.3d 1, 6 (Tex.2009). Because the Court held that Texas Rule of Civil Procedure 21a, which applies to all pleadings required to be served under Rule 21 other than the original petition, does not require the plaintiff to serve a new citation for amended petitions, failure to serve a new citation for an amended petition is not a ground for a new trial. ***See In re E.A.***, 287 S.W.3d at 4. See ***O'Connor's Texas Rules***, "Adding claims or damages – service required," ch. 7-A, §3.2.1(1), p. 705.

DEFENDANT'S MOTION FOR NEW TRIAL

Defendant, {❶ *name*}, asks the Court to grant a new trial in the interest of justice and fairness.

INTRODUCTION

1. Plaintiff, {❷ *name*}, sued defendant, {❸ *name*}, for {❹ *state basis of suit*}.

2. {❺ *State other relevant facts about the suit.*}

BACKGROUND

3. Defendant filed an answer on {❻ *date*}.

4. The Court signed a default judgment for plaintiff on {❼ *date*}.

5. {❽ *State other facts relevant to the motion.*}

ARGUMENT & AUTHORITIES

{*CHOOSE APPROPRIATE SECTIONS A-B*}

A. No notice of {❾ *trial/hearing*}.

6. A post-answer default is valid only if the defendant received notice of the setting for the trial or other dispositive hearing at which the default was rendered. *$429.30 v. State*, 896 S.W.2d 363, 366 (Tex. App.—Houston [1st Dist.] 1995, no writ); *see* Tex. R. Civ. P. 21a, 245; *Matsushita Elec. Corp. v. McAllen Copy Data, Inc.*, 815 S.W.2d 850, 853 (Tex. App.—Corpus Christi 1991, writ denied). Before rendering a default judgment against a defendant who has answered but who did not appear for trial or for a dispositive hearing, the trial court must determine if the defendant received notice. *See, e.g., Cliff v. Huggins*, 724 S.W.2d 778, 779 (Tex. 1987) (reversed; defendant did not receive notice of trial setting); *Murphree v. Ziegelmair*, 937 S.W.2d 493, 495 (Tex. App.—Houston [1st Dist.] 1995, no writ) (reversed; defendants did not receive notice that failure to attend pretrial conference could result in immediate disposition). {*See* ***O'Connor's Texas Rules***, *"Notice of trial or dispositive hearing," ch. 7-A, §4.3, p. 712.*}

{*CHOOSE APPROPRIATE PARAGRAPHS 7-8*}

7. Once a defendant makes an appearance in a case, it is entitled to notice of the trial setting or other dispositive hearing as a matter of due process. *LBL Oil Co. v. Int'l Power Servs., Inc.*, 777 S.W.2d 390, 390-91 (Tex. 1989). If a defendant did not receive notice of the trial setting or a dispositive hearing, it is entitled to a new trial without hav-

ing to show a meritorious defense. *Mathis v. Lockwood*, 166 S.W.3d 743, 744 (Tex. 2005); *Lopez v. Lopez*, 757 S.W.2d 721, 723 (Tex. 1988); *see Peralta v. Heights Med. Ctr., Inc.*, 485 U.S. 80, 86-87 (1988). {*See* ***O'Connor's Texas Rules***, *"Due process," ch. 7-A, §4.3.1, p. 713; "Allege no notice," ch. 10-B, §9.1.2(1), p. 936.*}

8. A court must give the parties at least 45 days' notice of the trial setting. Tex. R. Civ. P. 245. If a trial is held without notice to a party as required by Rule 245, the judgment must be set aside. {*See* ***O'Connor's Texas Rules***, *"TRCP 245," ch. 7-A, §4.3.2, p. 713.*}

9. Defendant did not receive notice of the {⑩ *trial setting/hearing*} at which the Court granted the default judgment. {⑪ *Elaborate.*}

B. Mistake or accident.

10. When a defendant does not appear for trial or for a dispositive hearing because of a mistake or an accident, a court should set aside a default judgment and grant a new trial if a defendant can meet the requirements of *Craddock v. Sunshine Bus Lines, Inc.*, 133 S.W.2d 124 (Tex. 1939). *Craddock* requires the defendant to do all of the following:

a. Demonstrate the failure to appear at a hearing or trial was not intentional or the result of conscious indifference, but was a mistake or an accident. *Dolgencorp of Tex., Inc. v. Lerma*, 288 S.W.3d 922, 925 (Tex. 2009); *In re R.R.*, 209 S.W.3d 112, 114-15 (Tex. 2006); *Estate of Pollack v. McMurrey*, 858 S.W.2d 388, 391 (Tex. 1993); *Craddock*, 133 S.W.2d at 126. {*See* ***O'Connor's Texas Rules***, *"Not intentional but accidental," ch. 10-B, §9.1.3(1), p. 937.*}

b. Set up a meritorious defense. *Dolgencorp of Tex.*, 288 S.W.3d at 925; *In re R.R.*, 209 S.W.3d at 114-15; *Ivy v. Carrell*, 407 S.W.2d 212, 214 (Tex. 1966); *Craddock*, 133 S.W.2d at 126. To set up a meritorious defense, the defendant must allege facts that constitute a defense to the plaintiff's cause of action and support the allegations with affidavits or other evidence. *Dolgencorp of Tex.*, 288 S.W.3d at 928; *Estate of Pollack*, 858 S.W.2d at 392; *Ivy*, 407 S.W.2d at 214. {*See* ***O'Connor's Texas Rules***, *"Meritorious defense," ch. 10-B, §9.1.3(2), p. 939.*}

c. Demonstrate that granting a new trial will not cause delay or otherwise injure the plaintiff. *Dolgencorp of Tex.*, 288 S.W.3d at 925; *In re R.R.*, 209 S.W.3d at 114-15; *Craddock*, 133 S.W.2d at 126. {*See* ***O'Connor's Texas Rules***, *"No delay or injury," ch. 10-B, §9.1.3(3), p. 939.*}

— Continued on next page —

11. The Court should grant a new trial because defendant's failure to appear was not intentional, but was accidental. Specifically, {⓬ *explain failure to appear*}.

12. The Court should grant a new trial because defendant has a meritorious defense. Specifically, {⓭ *set up prima facie defense*}.

13. The Court should grant a new trial because a new trial will not cause delay or otherwise injure plaintiff. Defendant is ready for trial and willing to reimburse plaintiff for all reasonable expenses incurred in obtaining the default judgment.

CONCLUSION

14. {⓮ *Briefly summarize the motion.*}

PRAYER

15. For these reasons, and in the interest of justice and fairness, defendant asks the Court to grant a new trial.

SEE: Tex. R. Civ. P. 320-329b
O'Connor's Texas Rules * Civil Trials (2019), "Notice of trial or dispositive hearing," ch. 7-A, §4.3, p. 712; "Failure to answer or appear after proper notice," ch. 10-B, §9.1.3, p. 937

ADD: STYLE OF THE CASE – FORM 1B:2
SIGNATURE BLOCK – FORM 1B:3
VERIFICATION – FORM 1B:7, if necessary
CERTIFICATE OF SERVICE – FORM 1B:13

ATTACH: AFFIDAVIT – FORM 1B:8, if necessary
NOTICE OF HEARING OR SUBMISSION – FORM 1E:1
ORDER – FORM 10B:8

NOTE: If a defendant is able to prove lack of notice of the trial or hearing (see §A, this form), the defendant does not need to establish the remaining ***Craddock*** factors to be entitled to a new trial. ***See Mathis v. Lockwood***, 166 S.W.3d 743, 744 (Tex.2005) (if first ***Craddock*** element is established, D does not have to prove meritorious defense). If the defendant is uncertain whether the court will sustain its argument that it did not receive proper notice, the defendant should allege and prove the three ***Craddock*** factors as an alternative ground for reversal (see §B, this form). See ***O'Connor's Texas Rules***, "No notice of trial + post-answer default," ch. 10-B, §9.1.2, p. 936.

DEFENDANT'S MOTION FOR NEW TRIAL

Defendant, {❶ *name*}, asks the Court to grant a new trial in the interest of justice and fairness.

INTRODUCTION

1. Plaintiff, {❷ *name*}, sued defendant, {❸ *name*}, for {❹ *state basis of suit*}.

2. {❺ *State other relevant facts about the suit.*}

BACKGROUND

3. Plaintiff served defendant by publication by {❻ *identify method of publication*}.

4. On {❼ *date*}, the Court signed a judgment against defendant.

5. {❽ *State other facts relevant to the motion.*}

ARGUMENT & AUTHORITIES

{*CHOOSE APPROPRIATE PARAGRAPH 6*}

6. When judgment has been rendered after valid service by publication and the defendant has not appeared, a court may grant a new trial if the defendant (1) files a motion for new trial within two years after judgment was rendered and (2) shows good cause why a new trial should be granted. *See* Tex. R. Civ. P. 329(a); *In re E.R.*, 385 S.W.3d 552, 563 (Tex. 2012). {*See* ***O'Connor's Texas Rules****, "Service valid," ch. 10-B, §10.2.1, p. 941; "Deadline," ch. 10-B, §10.4, p. 941.*}

6. When judgment has been rendered after invalid service by publication and the defendant has not appeared, a court may grant a new trial if the defendant (1) files a motion for new trial within two years after judgment was rendered and (2) shows that service was invalid. *See* Tex. R. Civ. P. 329(a); *In re E.R.*, 385 S.W.3d 552, 563 (Tex. 2012). If service was invalid, the defendant does not need to show good cause. *In re E.R.*, 385 S.W.3d at 563. {*See* ***O'Connor's Texas Rules****, "Service invalid," ch. 10-B, §10.2.2, p. 941; "Deadline," ch. 10-B, §10.4, p. 941.*}

{*CHOOSE APPROPRIATE PARAGRAPHS 7-13*}

{*Grounds when service valid*}

7. The Court should grant a new trial because it did not appoint an attorney to defend the suit on defendant's behalf. Tex. R. Civ. P. 244; *Isaac v. Westheimer Colony Ass'n*, 933 S.W.2d 588, 590-91 (Tex. App.—Houston [1st Dist.] 1996, writ denied); *see*

◄ *Continued on next page* ►

Cahill v. Lyda, 826 S.W.2d 932, 933 (Tex. 1992). {❾ *Elaborate.*} {*See* ***O'Connor's Texas Rules***, *"Trial," ch. 10-B, §10.1, p. 940.*}

8. The Court should grant a new trial because it did not approve and sign a statement of the evidence and file it with the records of the case. Tex. R. Civ. P. 244. {❿ *Elaborate.*}

9. The Court should grant a new trial because plaintiff did not present sufficient evidence to support the trial court's judgment. Specifically, {⓫ *explain*}.

10. The Court should grant a new trial because the Court erred in applying the law to the facts. {⓬ *Elaborate.*}

{*Grounds when service invalid*}

11. The Court should grant a new trial because plaintiff served citation by publication without conducting a diligent search for defendant; thus, the service was invalid. *In re E.R.*, 385 S.W.3d at 564. {⓭ *Elaborate.*} {*See* ***O'Connor's Texas Rules***, *"Diligent search," ch. 2-I, §4.3.2(1)(a)[2], p. 194.*}

12. The Court should grant a new trial because the citation was defective. *See Wood v. Brown*, 819 S.W.2d 799, 800 (Tex. 1991); *Wiebusch v. Wiebusch*, 636 S.W.2d 540, 542 (Tex. App.—San Antonio 1982, no writ); *Fleming v. Hernden*, 564 S.W.2d 157, 159 (Tex. App.—El Paso 1978, writ ref'd n.r.e.). The citation by publication was defective because {⓮ *state how the citation did not comply with TRCP 15, 99, or 109-117a, e.g., the citation did not contain a brief statement of the nature of the suit, as required by Texas Rule of Civil Procedure 114*}.

13. The Court should grant a new trial because plaintiff procured the service of citation and the default judgment by fraud. *See Morris v. Morris*, 759 S.W.2d 707, 708-09 (Tex. App.—San Antonio 1988, writ denied). {⓯ *Explain, e.g., plaintiff knew where defendant was and could have obtained personal service.*}

CONCLUSION

14. {⓰ *Briefly summarize the motion.*}

PRAYER

15. For these reasons, and in the interest of justice and fairness, defendant asks the Court to grant a new trial.

FORM 10B:5 MOTION FOR NEW TRIAL – JUDGMENT AFTER SERVICE BY PUBLICATION

SEE: Tex. R. Civ. P. 244, 320-329b
O'Connor's Texas Rules * Civil Trials (2019), "TRCP 109 – service by publication," ch. 2-I, §4.3.2(1), p. 193; "MNT After Service by Publication," ch. 10-B, §10, p. 940

ADD: STYLE OF THE CASE – FORM 1B:2
SIGNATURE BLOCK – FORM 1B:3
VERIFICATION – FORM 1B:7, if necessary
CERTIFICATE OF SERVICE – FORM 1B:13

ATTACH: AFFIDAVIT – FORM 1B:8, if necessary
NOTICE OF HEARING OR SUBMISSION – FORM 1E:1
ORDER – FORM 10B:8

FORM 10B:5

{[1] *PARTY*}'S MOTION FOR NEW TRIAL

{[2] *Party*}, {[3] *name*}, asks the Court to grant a new trial in the interest of justice and fairness.

INTRODUCTION

1. Plaintiff, {[4] *name*}, sued defendant, {[5] *name*}, for {[6] *state basis of suit*}.

2. {[7] *State other relevant facts about the suit.*}

BACKGROUND

3. {[8] *Adverse party*}, {[9] *name*}, filed a motion for summary judgment based on {[10] *summarize grounds*}.

4. {[11] *Party*} filed a response to the motion for summary judgment that {[12] *summarize response*}.

5. The Court granted the motion for summary judgment and signed a summary judgment for {[13] *adverse party*} on {[14] *date*}.

6. {[15] *State other facts relevant to the motion.*}

ARGUMENT & AUTHORITIES

7. The Court should grant a new trial because it erred by granting the motion for summary judgment.

{*CHOOSE APPROPRIATE PARAGRAPHS 8-38*}

{*Procedural defects*}

8. The Court erred by granting the motion for summary judgment because {[16] *plaintiff/defendant*} did not {[17] *file the motion/receive notice of the motion*} at least 21 days before the hearing. Tex. R. Civ. P. 166a(c). {[18] *Elaborate.*} {*See* ***O'Connor's Texas Rules****, "Challenge movant's notice," ch. 7-C, §3.6.4, p. 753.*}

9. The Court erred by granting the motion for summary judgment because {[19] *adverse party*} used the motion for summary judgment to circumvent special-exception practice. *See Tex. Dep't of Corr. v. Herring*, 513 S.W.2d 6, 10 (Tex. 1974). {[20] *Party*} made this objection in response to the motion for summary judgment and was entitled to amend {[21] *his/her/its*} pleadings. {[22] *Elaborate.*} {*See* ***O'Connor's Texas Rules****, "Defective pleadings," ch. 7-C, §3.6.2(1), p. 753.*}

10. The Court erred by granting {23 *adverse party*}'s no-evidence motion for summary judgment because there had not been adequate time for discovery. Tex. R. Civ. P. 166a(i). {24 *Identify additional discovery needed and why it is material to the summary judgment.*} {*See* ***O'Connor's Texas Rules****, "When to file," ch. 7-D, §2.1, p. 762.*}

{*Substantive defects*}

11. The Court erred by granting the motion for summary judgment because there is a disputed fact issue about {25 *state exactly what fact issues preclude summary judgment*}, which must be submitted to the jury. *See Park Place Hosp. v. Estate of Milo*, 909 S.W.2d 508, 510-11 (Tex. 1995). {26 *Elaborate.*} {*See* ***O'Connor's Texas Rules****, "Moving on the facts," ch. 7-C, §2.5.1, p. 749.*}

12. The Court erred by granting the motion for summary judgment because {27 *adverse party*} did not meet {28 *his/her/its*} burden of proving, as a matter of law, the element of {29 *identify element*} for {30 *identify cause of action or defense*}. *See Kachina Pipeline Co. v. Lillis*, 471 S.W.3d 445, 449 (Tex. 2015); *Provident Life & Accident Ins. Co. v. Knott*, 128 S.W.3d 211, 215-16 (Tex. 2003); *M.D. Anderson Hosp. & Tumor Inst. v. Willrich*, 28 S.W.3d 22, 23 (Tex. 2000). Unless the movant meets its burden, the burden never shifts to the nonmovant. *M.D. Anderson*, 28 S.W.3d at 23; *Casso v. Brand*, 776 S.W.2d 551, 556 (Tex. 1989); *City of Hous. v. Clear Creek Basin Auth.*, 589 S.W.2d 671, 678 (Tex. 1979). {31 *Elaborate.*} {*See* ***O'Connor's Texas Rules****, "Burden of Proof," ch. 7-C, §4, p. 754.*}

13. The Court erred by granting the motion for summary judgment because {32 *party*} raised a fact issue on the element of {33 *identify element*} of {34 *adverse party*}'s affirmative defense. *See Jones v. Tex. Pac. Indem. Co.*, 853 S.W.2d 791, 794 (Tex. App.—Dallas 1993, no writ). {35 *Elaborate.*} {*See* ***O'Connor's Texas Rules****, "Create fact issue," ch. 7-C, §4.6.2(1), p. 759.*}

14. The Court erred by granting the motion for summary judgment because {36 *party*} asserted the affirmative defense of {37 *identify affirmative defense*} in {38 *his/her/its*} original answer and response and provided summary-judgment evidence that raised a fact issue on each element of the affirmative defense. *See Brownlee v. Brownlee*, 665 S.W.2d 111, 112 (Tex. 1984); *Brown v. Aztec Rig Equip., Inc.*, 921 S.W.2d 835, 845 (Tex. App.—Houston [14th Dist.] 1996, writ denied). {39 *Elaborate.*} {*See* ***O'Connor's Texas Rules****, "Create fact issue about affirmative defense," ch. 7-C, §4.3.2(2), p. 756.*}

Continued on next page

15. The Court erred by denying {㊵ *party*}'s cross-motion for summary judgment because {㊶ *party*} proved {㊷ *he/she/it*} was entitled to summary judgment as a matter of law. *See M.D. Anderson Hosp. & Tumor Inst. v. Willrich*, 28 S.W.3d 22, 23 (Tex. 2000); *Lear Siegler, Inc. v. Perez*, 819 S.W.2d 470, 471 (Tex. 1991). {㊸ *Elaborate.*} {*See* ***O'Connor's Texas Rules****, "Burden on movant," ch. 7-C, §4.1, p. 754.*}

16. The Court erred by granting {㊹ *adverse party*}'s no-evidence motion for summary judgment because {㊺ *party*} provided summary-judgment evidence that raised a fact issue on {㊻ *identify challenged elements*} of {㊼ *party*}'s {㊽ *cause of action/defense*}. Tex. R. Civ. P. 166a(i). {㊾ *Elaborate.*} {*See* ***O'Connor's Texas Rules****, "Sufficiency of evidence," ch. 7-D, §3.6, p. 766.*}

17. The Court erred by granting a summary judgment purporting to be final because {㊿ *adverse party*}'s motion did not ask for judgment {51 *on all claims/against all parties*}. {52 *Elaborate.*} In a summary-judgment proceeding, a judgment is not final for purposes of appeal unless it actually disposes of every pending claim and party or it clearly and unequivocally states that it finally disposes of all claims and all parties. *Farm Bureau Cty. Mut. Ins. Co. v. Rogers*, 455 S.W.3d 161, 163 (Tex. 2015); *Lehmann v. Har-Con Corp.*, 39 S.W.3d 191, 205 (Tex. 2001); *see Nash v. Harris Cty.*, 63 S.W.3d 415, 416 (Tex. 2001). In this case, the judgment did not dispose of all {53 *claims/parties*}, and it did not unequivocally state that it finally disposed of all claims and all parties. {*See* ***O'Connor's Texas Rules****, "Request for final SJ," ch. 7-C, §2.6, p. 750; "Judgments that are final," ch. 9-C, §6.3.1, p. 910.*}

18. The Court erred by denying attorney fees on {54 *party*}'s {55 *motion/cross-motion*} for summary judgment because {56 *party*} requested attorney fees and supported the request with proper summary-judgment evidence. {57 *Elaborate.*} {*See* ***O'Connor's Texas Rules****, "Other matters," ch. 10-B, §11.1.2(3), p. 942;* ***O'Connor's Texas COA****, "Attorney Fees," ch. 45, p. 1463.*}

{*Defects in affidavits*}

19. The Court erred by granting the motion for summary judgment because the affidavit of {58 *name of affiant*} was not based on personal knowledge. Specifically, {59 *state what affiant did not have personal knowledge of*}. Thus, the affiant's evidence was not adequate summary-judgment evidence. Tex. R. Civ. P. 166a(f); *see Ryland Grp., Inc. v. Hood*, 924 S.W.2d 120, 122 (Tex. 1996). {60 *Elaborate.*} {*See* ***O'Connor's Texas Rules****, "Personal knowledge," ch. 7-B, §9.4.4, p. 733.*}

20. The Court erred by granting the motion for summary judgment because the affidavit of {61 *name of affiant*} was based only on the best of {62 *his/her*} knowledge and belief and thus was not adequate summary-judgment evidence. *Price v. Am. Nat'l Ins. Co.*, 113 S.W.3d 424, 429-30 (Tex. App.—Houston [1st Dist.] 2003, no pet.). {63 *Elaborate.*} {*See* ***O'Connor's Texas Rules****, "Personal knowledge," ch. 7-B, §9.4.4, p. 733.*}

21. The Court erred by granting the motion for summary judgment because the affidavit of {64 *name of affiant*} stated a mere legal conclusion and did not provide any summary-judgment evidence. *Brownlee v. Brownlee*, 665 S.W.2d 111, 112 (Tex. 1984); *Life Ins. Co. v. Gar-Dal, Inc.*, 570 S.W.2d 378, 381-82 (Tex. 1978); *801 Nolana, Inc. v. RTC Mortg. Tr.*, 944 S.W.2d 751, 754 (Tex. App.—Corpus Christi 1997, writ denied). {65 *Elaborate.*} {*See* ***O'Connor's Texas Rules****, "Not legal conclusions," ch. 7-B, §9.4.5, p. 734.*}

22. The Court erred by granting the motion for summary judgment because the affidavit of {66 *name of affiant*} contained unsubstantiated opinion and thus was not adequate summary-judgment evidence. *See McIntyre v. Ramirez*, 109 S.W.3d 741, 749-50 (Tex. 2003); *Ryland Grp., Inc. v. Hood*, 924 S.W.2d 120, 122 (Tex. 1996). {67 *Elaborate.*} {*See* ***O'Connor's Texas Rules****, "Not factual conclusions," ch. 7-B, §9.4.6, p. 734.*}

23. The Court erred by granting the motion for summary judgment because the affidavit of {68 *name of affiant*} was based on hearsay and thus was not adequate summary-judgment evidence. *See Southland Corp. v. Lewis*, 940 S.W.2d 83, 85 (Tex. 1997). {69 *Elaborate.*} {*See* ***O'Connor's Texas Rules****, "Hearsay evidence," ch. 7-B, §10.1.1(5), p. 740.*}

24. The Court erred by granting the motion for summary judgment because the affidavit of {70 *name of affiant*}, who is an {71 *interested/expert*} witness, was not clear, positive, direct, credible, and free from contradiction and could not be easily controverted. Tex. R. Civ. P. 166a(c); *see McIntyre v. Ramirez*, 109 S.W.3d 741, 749-50 (Tex. 2003); *Ryland Grp., Inc. v. Hood*, 924 S.W.2d 120, 122 (Tex. 1996). {72 *Elaborate.*} {*See* ***O'Connor's Texas Rules****, "Interested witness," ch. 7-B, §9.3.2, p. 732; "Expert witness," ch. 7-B, §9.3.3, p. 732.*}

25. The Court erred by granting the motion for summary judgment based on the affidavit of {73 *name of affiant*} because the affidavit does not lay the proper predicate for the admissibility of {74 *identify evidence*}. *See Seidner v. Citibank (S.D.) N.A.*, 201 S.W.3d 332, 334-35 (Tex. App.—Houston [14th Dist.] 2006, pet. denied); *Cottrell v.*

Continued on next page

Carrillon Assocs., Ltd., 646 S.W.2d 491, 494 (Tex. App.—Houston [1st Dist.] 1982, writ ref'd n.r.e.). {❺ *Elaborate.*} {*See* ***O'Connor's Texas Rules***, *"Failure to lay predicate," ch. 7-B, §10.1.1(6), p. 740.*}

26. The Court erred by granting the motion for summary judgment based on the affidavit of {❻ *name of affiant*} because the affidavit is not the best evidence of the contents of {❼ *specify document*}. *See Mercer v. Daoran Corp.*, 676 S.W.2d 580, 583 (Tex. 1984). {❽ *Elaborate.*} {*See* ***O'Connor's Texas Rules***, *"Not best evidence," ch. 7-B, §10.1.1(7), p. 740.*}

27. The Court erred by granting the motion for summary judgment based on an affidavit that violates the parol-evidence rule. *Albritton Dev. Co. v. Glendon Invs., Inc.*, 700 S.W.2d 244, 246 (Tex. App.—Houston [1st Dist.] 1985, writ ref'd n.r.e.). If an oral agreement was made before or at the same time as a written agreement, and it contradicts the written agreement, a party cannot offer evidence of the oral agreement. *Id.* {❾ *Elaborate.*}

28. The Court erred by granting the motion for summary judgment based on an affidavit without a jurat or other evidence showing that the affidavit was sworn to before an authorized officer. *See Mansions in the Forest, L.P. v. Montgomery Cty.*, 365 S.W.3d 314, 316-17 (Tex. 2012). {80 *Elaborate.*}

29. The Court erred by granting the motion for summary judgment based on the affidavit of {81 *name of affiant*}, {82 *adverse party*}'s expert, because the affidavit does not demonstrate that the expert's opinion is relevant to the issues in this case and is based on a reliable foundation. *See Ryland Grp., Inc. v. Hood*, 924 S.W.2d 120, 122 (Tex. 1996); *E.I. du Pont de Nemours & Co. v. Robinson*, 923 S.W.2d 549, 556 (Tex. 1995). {83 *Elaborate.*} {*See* ***O'Connor's Texas Rules***, *"Daubert-Robinson Test for Expert Testimony," ch. 5-N, §2, p. 499; "Underlying methodology to expert opinion," ch. 7-B, §10.1.1(8), p. 740.*}

30. The Court erred by granting the motion for summary judgment based on the affidavit of {84 *name of affiant*}, {85 *adverse party*}'s expert, because the affidavit is based on {86 *records not attached to the affidavit/records not included in the summary-judgment evidence*}. *See Guthrie v. Suiter*, 934 S.W.2d 820, 824-25 (Tex. App.—Houston [1st Dist.] 1996, no writ). {87 *Elaborate.*} {*See* ***O'Connor's Texas Rules***, *"Failure to attach exhibit," ch. 7-B, §10.1.1(1)(b), p. 739.*}

31. The Court erred by granting the motion for summary judgment based on the affidavit of {88 *name of affiant*}, {89 *adverse party*}'s expert, because the affidavit does not include {90 *his/her*} qualifications. {*See* ***O'Connor's Texas Rules****, "Expert witness," ch. 7-B, §9.3.3, p. 732.*}

32. The Court erred by granting the motion for summary judgment based on the affidavit of {91 *name of affiant*}, {92 *adverse party*}'s expert, because the affidavit does not include the facts on which the expert based {93 *his/her*} opinion. {*See* ***O'Connor's Texas Rules****, "Expert witness," ch. 7-B, §9.3.3, p. 732.*}

33. The Court erred by granting the motion for summary judgment based on the affidavit of {94 *name of affiant*}, {95 *adverse party*}'s expert, because the affidavit does not include the reasoning on which the expert based {96 *his/her*} opinion. {*See* ***O'Connor's Texas Rules****, "Expert witness," ch. 7-B, §9.3.3, p. 732.*}

34. The Court erred by granting the motion for summary judgment based on the affidavit of Dr. {97 *name of affiant*}, {98 *adverse party*}'s expert, because the affidavit does not meet the requirements of Texas Civil Practice & Remedies Code section 74.401(a). Specifically, the affidavit does not demonstrate that the doctor was a physician, as the term "physician" is defined in section 74.401(g), when {99 *the doctor made the affidavit/the incident occurred*}. {100 *Elaborate.*} {*See* ***O'Connor's Texas COA****, "Physician," ch. 20-A, §8.3.1(1)(a)[1][a], p. 692.*}

35. The Court erred by granting the motion for summary judgment based on the affidavit of Dr. {101 *name of affiant*}, {102 *adverse party*}'s expert, because the affidavit does not meet the requirements of Texas Civil Practice & Remedies Code section 74.401(a). Specifically, the affidavit does not demonstrate that the doctor was practicing medicine when {103 *the doctor made the affidavit/the incident occurred*}, as the term "practicing medicine" is defined in section 74.401(b). {104 *Elaborate.*} {*See* ***O'Connor's Texas COA****, "Practicing medicine," ch. 20-A, §8.3.1(1)(a)[1][b], p. 692.*}

36. The Court erred by granting the motion for summary judgment based on the affidavit of Dr. {105 *name of affiant*}, {106 *adverse party*}'s expert, because the affidavit does not meet the requirements of Texas Civil Practice & Remedies Code section 74.401(a). Specifically, the affidavit does not demonstrate that the doctor has knowledge of accepted standards of medical care for the diagnosis, care, or treatment of the illness, injury, or condition involved in this suit. {107 *Elaborate.*} {*See* ***O'Connor's Texas COA****, "Knowledge of standard of care," ch. 20-A, §8.3.1(1)(a)[2], p. 693.*}

Continued on next page

37. The Court erred by granting the motion for summary judgment based on the affidavit of Dr. {108 *name of affiant*}, {109 *adverse party*}'s expert, because the affidavit does not meet the requirements of Texas Civil Practice & Remedies Code section 74.401(a). Specifically, the affidavit does not demonstrate that the doctor is qualified on the basis of training or experience to offer an expert opinion on accepted standards of medical care. {110 *Elaborate.*} {*See **O'Connor's Texas COA**, "Qualified by training or experience," ch. 20-A, §8.3.1(1)(a)[3], p. 693.*}

38. The Court erred by granting attorney fees as part of the summary judgment because {111 *party*} challenged the amount of the fees, and the affidavit of {112 *adverse party*}'s attorney could not be easily controverted as to the actual time spent on this case. *See AU Pharm., Inc. v. Boston*, 986 S.W.2d 331, 337-38 (Tex. App.—Texarkana 1999, no pet.). {113 *Elaborate.*} {*See **O'Connor's Texas Rules**, "Not readily controvertible," ch. 7-B, §10.1.1(4), p. 740; "Proof of attorney fees," ch. 7-C, §2.9.1, p. 751.*}

CONCLUSION

39. {114 *Briefly summarize the motion.*}

PRAYER

40. For these reasons, and in the interest of justice and fairness, {115 *party*} asks the Court to grant a new trial.

SEE: Tex. R. Civ. P. 166a, 320-329b
Tex. Civ. Prac. & Rem. Code §74.401
O'Connor's Texas Rules * Civil Trials (2019), "Motion for Summary Judgment—General Rules," ch. 7-B, p. 722; "Traditional Motion for Summary Judgment," ch. 7-C, p. 748; "Judgments that are final," ch. 9-C, §6.3.1, p. 910; "MNT After Summary Judgment," ch. 10-B, §11, p. 941
O'Connor's Texas Causes of Action (2019), "General rule," ch. 20-A, §8.3.1(1)(a), p. 692; "Attorney Fees," ch. 45, p. 1463

ADD: STYLE OF THE CASE – FORM 1B:2
SIGNATURE BLOCK – FORM 1B:3
VERIFICATION – FORM 1B:7, if necessary
CERTIFICATE OF SERVICE – FORM 1B:13

ATTACH: AFFIDAVIT – FORM 1B:8, if necessary
NOTICE OF HEARING OR SUBMISSION – FORM 1E:1
ORDER – FORM 10B:8

NOTE: In a response to a motion for summary judgment, the nonmovant must object to any defect in the form or substance of the motion or pleadings. If the nonmovant does not make any objections in its response, its objections are waived. On appeal, it can argue only that the grounds presented to the trial court are insufficient as a matter of law to support the summary judgment. See ***O'Connor's Texas Rules***, "Objections to SJ motion," ch. 7-C, §3.6, p. 753. If the movant's affidavits contain evidence that would not be admissible at trial, the nonmovant should object and move to strike the inadmissible evidence. As a general rule, unless a party objects in writing to the formal deficiencies in the summary-judgment proof, the party waives the objection. See ***O'Connor's Texas Rules***, "Generally," ch. 7-B, §10.1, p. 738.

If the nonmovant did not have an opportunity to file a response to a motion for summary judgment, seek a continuance, or ask for permission to file a late response before summary judgment was rendered, the nonmovant should file a sworn motion for new trial, probably relying on the factors from ***Craddock v. Sunshine Bus Lines, Inc.***, 133 S.W.2d 124, 126 (Tex.1939). See FORMS 10B:3, §I; 10B:4, §B. In the rare situations when summary judgment is rendered before a nonmovant discovers a procedural mistake that should have been included in the response, the nonmovant can raise the issue in a motion for new trial. See ***O'Connor's Texas Rules***, "No opportunity to file response," ch. 10-B, §11.1.2(2), p. 942.

Paragraphs 34-37 in this form apply to health-care-liability claims against a physician. These paragraphs can be modified to apply to health-care-liability claims against a health-care provider, using Texas Civil Practice & Remedies Code §74.402. See ***O'Connor's Texas COA***, "For claims against health-care providers," ch. 20-A, §8.3.1(2), p. 694.

{❶ *PARTY*}'S RESPONSE TO
{❷ *ADVERSE PARTY*}'S MOTION FOR NEW TRIAL

{❸ *Party*}, {❹ *name*}, asks the Court to deny {❺ *adverse party*} {❻ *name*}'s motion for new trial.

INTRODUCTION

1. Plaintiff, {❼ *name*}, sued defendant, {❽ *name*}, for {❾ *state basis of suit*}.

2. {❿ *State other relevant facts about the suit.*}

BACKGROUND

3. The Court signed a judgment for {⓫ *party*} on {⓬ *date*}.

4. {⓭ *State other facts relevant to the response.*}

ARGUMENT & AUTHORITIES
{*CHOOSE APPROPRIATE PARAGRAPHS 5-25*}

{*Sufficiency of the evidence*}

5. The Court should deny the motion for new trial because there is ample evidence in the record to support the jury's answer to question number {⓮ *number*} that {⓯ *state the substance of the jury's answer*}. {⓰ *Elaborate.*} {*See* ***O'Connor's Texas Rules****, "Challenging sufficiency of evidence," ch. 10-B, §13.1, p. 943.*}

{*Default judgment*}

6. The Court should deny the motion for new trial because plaintiff's petition contains the necessary factual allegations to make defendant amenable to service. *See Paramount Pipe & Supply Co. v. Muhr*, 749 S.W.2d 491, 494 (Tex. 1988). The petition supports the default judgment. {⓱ *Elaborate.*} {*See* ***O'Connor's Texas Rules****, "Defects in plaintiff's petition," ch. 10-B, §9.1.1(1)(d), p. 936.*}

7. The Court should deny the motion for new trial because defendant was properly served with valid citation. {⓲ *Elaborate.*} {*See* ***O'Connor's Texas Rules****, "Requirements for the Citation," ch. 2-I, §2, p. 189; "Proof of Service – The Return," ch. 2-I, §9, p. 200; "Sufficiency of service," ch. 7-A, §3.4, p. 705.*}

{*Summary judgment*}

8. The Court should deny the motion for new trial because, as a matter of law, there is no fact issue in the case, and {[19] *party*} was entitled to summary judgment. *See City of Hous. v. Clear Creek Basin Auth.*, 589 S.W.2d 671, 678 & n.5 (Tex. 1979). {[20] *Elaborate.*} {*See* ***O'Connor's Texas Rules****, "Moving on the facts," ch. 7-C, §2.5.1, p. 749.*}

9. The Court should deny the motion for new trial because {[21] *adverse party*}, in {[22] *his/her/its*} response to the motion for summary judgment, did not object to any defects in the {[23] *identify summary-judgment evidence, e.g., motion, affidavits*}; therefore, {[24] *adverse party*} waived those complaints. *See Lee v. Braeburn Valley W. Civic Ass'n*, 786 S.W.2d 262, 263 (Tex. 1990). {[25] *Elaborate.*} {*See* ***O'Connor's Texas Rules****, "Waivable objections to evidence," ch. 7-B, §10.1.1, p. 738.*}

{*Motion for continuance*}

10. The Court should deny the motion for new trial because {[26] *adverse party*} did not verify {[27] *his/her/its*} motion for continuance. *See Taherzadeh v. Ghaleh-Assadi*, 108 S.W.3d 927, 928 (Tex. App.—Dallas 2003, pet. denied); *Rhima v. White*, 829 S.W.2d 909, 912 (Tex. App.—Fort Worth 1992, writ denied). A court has the discretion to deny an unverified motion for continuance. {*See* ***O'Connor's Texas Rules****, "Verification & affidavits," ch. 5-D, §2.3, p. 418.*}

{*Newly discovered evidence*}

11. The Court should deny the motion for new trial on the ground of newly discovered evidence because the "newly discovered evidence" is neither admissible nor competent. *See Waffle House, Inc. v. Williams*, 313 S.W.3d 796, 813 (Tex. 2010); *Dankowski v. Dankowski*, 922 S.W.2d 298, 305 (Tex. App.—Fort Worth 1996, writ denied). {[28] *Elaborate.*} {*See* ***O'Connor's Texas Rules****, "Motion," ch. 10-B, §16.1.1, p. 950.*}

12. The Court should deny the motion for new trial on the ground of newly discovered evidence because {[29] *adverse party*} did not prove that {[30] *he/she/it*} exercised due diligence in attempting to discover the evidence before trial. *Jackson v. Van Winkle*, 660 S.W.2d 807, 809-10 (Tex. 1983), *overruled on other grounds*, *Moritz v. Preiss*, 121 S.W.3d 715 (Tex. 2003); *Dankowski v. Dankowski*, 922 S.W.2d 298, 305 (Tex. App.—Fort Worth 1996, writ denied). {[31] *Elaborate.*} {*See* ***O'Connor's Texas Rules****, "Motion," ch. 10-B, §16.1.2, p. 950.*}

◄ *Continued on next page* ►

13. The Court should deny the motion for new trial on the ground of newly discovered evidence because the "newly discovered evidence" is merely cumulative of other evidence introduced at trial. *See Jackson v. Van Winkle*, 660 S.W.2d 807, 809 (Tex. 1983), *overruled on other grounds, Moritz v. Preiss*, 121 S.W.3d 715 (Tex. 2003); *In re Marriage of Yarbrough*, 719 S.W.2d 412, 415 (Tex. App.—Amarillo 1986, no writ). {㉜ *Elaborate.*} {*See **O'Connor's Texas Rules**, "Motion," ch. 10-B, §16.1.3, p. 950.*}

14. The Court should deny the motion for new trial on the ground of newly discovered evidence because the "newly discovered evidence" is merely for the impeachment of a witness. *See New Amsterdam Cas. Co. v. Jordan*, 359 S.W.2d 864, 866 (Tex. 1962); *Eckert v. Smith*, 589 S.W.2d 533, 538 (Tex. App.—Amarillo 1979, writ ref'd n.r.e.). {㉝ *Elaborate.*} {*See **O'Connor's Texas Rules**, "Motion," ch. 10-B, §16.1.4, p. 951.*}

15. The Court should deny the motion for new trial on the ground of newly discovered evidence because the "newly discovered evidence" is not so material that it would probably produce a different result at a new trial. *See Jackson v. Van Winkle*, 660 S.W.2d 807, 809 (Tex. 1983), *overruled on other grounds, Moritz v. Preiss*, 121 S.W.3d 715 (Tex. 2003). {㉞ *Elaborate.*} {*See **O'Connor's Texas Rules**, "Motion," ch. 10-B, §16.1.5, p. 951.*}

{*Procedural defects*}

16. The Court should deny the motion for new trial because {㉟ *adverse party*} waived any complaint about the submission of jury question number {㊱ *number*} by not objecting to the question in writing or at the charge conference. *Mitchell v. Bank of Am.*, 156 S.W.3d 622, 627-28 (Tex. App.—Dallas 2004, pet. denied). {㊲ *Elaborate.*} {*See **O'Connor's Texas Rules**, "Formal Charge Conference," ch. 8-I, §4, p. 863.*}

17. The Court should deny the motion for new trial because {㊳ *adverse party*} waived the complaint that {㊴ *identify adverse party's complaint*} by not objecting and getting a ruling on the objection during trial. *Hur v. City of Mesquite*, 893 S.W.2d 227, 231 (Tex. App.—Amarillo 1995, writ denied). {㊵ *Elaborate.*} {*See **O'Connor's Texas Rules**, "Trial objections," ch. 8-D, §2.2, p. 836; "When jury hears inadmissible evidence," ch. 8-D, §6.7, p. 841.*}

18. The Court should deny the motion for new trial because it was not timely filed. *See* Tex. R. Civ. P. 329b(a); *Padilla v. LaFrance*, 907 S.W.2d 454, 458 (Tex. 1995). The judgment was signed on {㊶ *date*}, and the 30 days to file a motion for new trial expired on {㊷ *date*}. The motion for new trial was filed on {㊸ *date*}. The Court cannot extend the time to file a motion for new trial. Tex. R. Civ. P. 5. {*See **O'Connor's Texas Rules**, "Original MNT," ch. 10-B, §5.1, p. 932.*}

19. The Court should deny the motion for new trial because it contains evidence not in the record, and the motion was neither verified nor accompanied by an affidavit. *See Dir., State Emps. Workers' Comp. Div. v. Evans*, 889 S.W.2d 266, 268 (Tex. 1994). {44 *Elaborate.*} {*See **O'Connor's Texas Rules**, "When verification required," ch. 10-B, §3.1, p. 931.*}

{*Improper jury argument*}

20. The Court should deny the motion for new trial because {45 *party*}'s attorney did not make an improper and prejudicial jury argument. *Standard Fire Ins. Co. v. Reese*, 584 S.W.2d 835, 839-40 (Tex. 1979). {46 *Elaborate.*} {*See **O'Connor's Texas Rules**, "Test for reversible jury argument," ch. 8-J, §6.2, p. 883.*}

21. The Court should deny the motion for new trial because the jury argument was invited or provoked. *See Standard Fire Ins. Co. v. Reese*, 584 S.W.2d 835, 839 (Tex. 1979). {47 *Elaborate.*} {*See **O'Connor's Texas Rules**, "Record of argument," ch. 8-J, §6.1, p. 883.*}

22. The Court should deny the motion for new trial because the jury argument did not constitute reversible error. *Standard Fire Ins. Co. v. Reese*, 584 S.W.2d 835, 839-40 (Tex. 1979). {48 *Elaborate.*} {*See **O'Connor's Texas Rules**, "Test for reversible jury argument," ch. 8-J, §6.2.5, p. 883.*}

23. The Court should deny the motion for new trial because {49 *adverse party*} did not preserve error and the jury argument was not so prejudicial as to be incurable. *Phillips v. Bramlett*, 288 S.W.3d 876, 883 (Tex. 2009). {50 *Elaborate.*} {*See **O'Connor's Texas Rules**, "Incurable argument," ch. 8-J, §5.2, p. 882.*}

{*Jury or bailiff misconduct*}

24. The Court should deny the motion for new trial because {51 *adverse party*} did not prove that the jury or bailiff engaged in misconduct, that the misconduct was material, and that the misconduct caused injury. *See* Tex. R. Civ. P. 327(a); *In re Health Care Unlimited, Inc.*, 429 S.W.3d 600, 602 (Tex. 2014); *Golden Eagle Archery, Inc. v. Jackson*, 24 S.W.3d 362, 372 (Tex. 2000); *Redinger v. Living, Inc.*, 689 S.W.2d 415, 419 (Tex. 1985). {52 *Elaborate.*} {*See **O'Connor's Texas Rules**, "Allegations in MNT," ch. 10-B, §14.1.1, p. 945.*}

{*Any other ground*}

25. The Court should deny the motion for new trial because {53 *refute any other ground asserted in adverse party's motion for new trial*}.

Continued on next page

CONCLUSION

26. {54 *Briefly summarize the response.*}

PRAYER

27. For these reasons, {55 *party*} asks the Court to deny {56 *adverse party*}'s motion for new trial.

SEE: Tex. R. Civ. P. 320-329b
O'Connor's Texas Rules * Civil Trials (2019), "Motion for Summary Judgment—General Rules," ch. 7-B, p. 722; "Motion for New Trial," ch. 10-B, p. 929

ADD: STYLE OF THE CASE – FORM 1B:2
SIGNATURE BLOCK – FORM 1B:3
CERTIFICATE OF SERVICE – FORM 1B:13

ATTACH: AFFIDAVIT – FORM 1B:8, if necessary to controvert the allegations in the motion for new trial
ORDER – FORM 10B:8

NOTE: When the movant files a motion with affidavits, the nonmovant should consider filing controverting affidavits. When there is no recorded hearing on a motion for new trial and no controverting affidavits, the movant's uncontroverted affidavit is taken as true. ***Director, State Empls. Workers' Comp. Div. v. Evans***, 889 S.W.2d 266, 268 (Tex.1994); ***Onyeanu v. Rivertree Apts.***, 920 S.W.2d 397, 398 (Tex.App.—Houston [1st Dist.] 1996, no writ).

Generally, it is not necessary for the nonmovant to file a response when the movant files an unsworn motion for new trial. However, because some local rules infer acquiescence when the nonmovant does not file a response, the attorney should always check the local rules. *See, e.g.*, Harris Cty. Loc. R. 3.3.2.

ORDER ON {❶ *PARTY*}'S MOTION FOR NEW TRIAL

After considering {❷ *party*} {❸ *name*}'s motion for new trial, the response, the pleadings, and arguments of counsel, the Court

{*CHOOSE APPROPRIATE ORDER*}

DENIES the motion.

GRANTS the motion and orders a new trial {❹ *add if applicable: on part of the case*}. {❺ *Identify legally appropriate and reasonably specific reasons for granting a new trial.*}

{*Add if granting partial new trial*}

In granting a partial new trial, the Court makes the following findings and conclusions:

1. The matter is separable without unfairness to the parties. {❻ *Elaborate.*}

{*CHOOSE APPROPRIATE PARAGRAPH 2*}

2. The damages in this case are liquidated.

2. The damages in this case are unliquidated, and liability is not contested.

SIGNED on _______________, 20___.

____
PRESIDING JUDGE

SEE: Tex. R. Civ. P. 320-329b
O'Connor's Texas Rules * Civil Trials (2019), "Order," ch. 10-B, §8, p. 934

ADD: STYLE OF THE CASE – FORM 1B:2
CERTIFICATE OF SERVICE – FORM 1B:13, if proposed order served separately from motion or response

NOTE: The court's stated reasons for granting the new trial must be legally appropriate and reasonably specific. ***In re Bent***, 487 S.W.3d 170, 176 (Tex.2016); ***In re Toyota Motor Sales, U.S.A., Inc.***, 407 S.W.3d 746, 757 (Tex.2013); ***In re United Scaffolding, Inc.***, 377 S.W.3d 685, 688-89 (Tex.2012). A broad statement like "in the interest of justice and fairness" is not an adequate reason for granting a new trial. ***In re Bent***, 487 S.W.3d at 176; ***In re United Scaffolding***, 377 S.W.3d at 689-90; ***In re Columbia Med. Ctr.***, 290 S.W.3d 204, 215 (Tex.2009). See ***O'Connor's Texas Rules***, "Facial review – stated reasons not legally appropriate or specific," ch. 10-B, §17.5.1, p. 952. Even if the stated reasons are legally appropriate and reasonably specific, the trial court's order is reviewable by mandamus to determine if the reasons are not substantively valid or correct. *See* ***In re Toyota Motor Sales***, 407 S.W.3d at 758. See ***O'Connor's Texas Rules***, "Reasons stated in order not substantively valid or correct," ch. 10-B, §17.5.2(3), p. 953.

DEFENDANT'S MOTION FOR REMITTITUR

Defendant, {❶ *name*}, asks the Court to reduce the damages awarded in the judgment in this case.

INTRODUCTION

1. Plaintiff, {❷ *name*}, sued defendant, {❸ *name*}, for {❹ *state basis of suit*}.

2. {❺ *State other relevant facts about the suit.*}

BACKGROUND

3. On {❻ *date*}, the Court signed a judgment against defendant awarding the following damages to plaintiff: {❼ *specify the damages in the judgment*}.

4. {❽ *State other facts relevant to the motion.*}

ARGUMENT & AUTHORITIES

5. The standard for a request for remittitur is factual sufficiency of the evidence. *Torrington Co. v. Stutzman*, 46 S.W.3d 829, 851 (Tex. 2000); *Mar. Overseas Corp. v. Ellis*, 971 S.W.2d 402, 406 (Tex. 1998); *Rose v. Doctors Hosp.*, 801 S.W.2d 841, 848 (Tex. 1990). A court must examine all the evidence to determine if there is sufficient evidence to support the damages award. *Pope v. Moore*, 711 S.W.2d 622, 624 (Tex. 1986). A court should suggest a remittitur when the evidence to support the damages award is so factually insufficient, or when the damages award is so against the great weight and preponderance of the evidence, that it is manifestly unjust. *Id.*; *Gainsco Cty. Mut. Ins. Co. v. Martinez*, 27 S.W.3d 97, 108 (Tex. App.—San Antonio 2000, pet. granted, judgm't vacated w.r.m.). {*See* ***O'Connor's Texas Rules****, "Standard," ch. 10-C, §5.1, p. 955.*}

6. The damages of ${❾ *amount*} for {❿ *specify type of damages*} should be reduced because there is insufficient evidence to support the award of those damages. {⓫ *Elaborate.*}

CONCLUSION

7. {⓬ *Briefly summarize the motion.*}

PRAYER

8. For these reasons, defendant asks the Court to suggest that plaintiff file a remittitur for ${⓭ *amount*} by {⓮ *date*}, and if plaintiff does not comply with the Court's order, to grant a new trial.

SEE: Tex. R. Civ. P. 315, 320
Tex. R. App. P. 46
O'Connor's Texas Rules * Civil Trials (2019), "Motion for Remittitur," ch. 10-C, p. 954

ADD: STYLE OF THE CASE – FORM 1B:2
SIGNATURE BLOCK – FORM 1B:3
CERTIFICATE OF SERVICE – FORM 1B:13

ATTACH: NOTICE OF HEARING OR SUBMISSION – FORM 1E:1
ORDER – FORM 10C:3

NOTE: A request for a remittitur can be made as part of a motion for new trial. *See* ***C.M. Asfahl Agency v. Tensor, Inc.***, 135 S.W.3d 768, 797 (Tex.App.—Houston [1st Dist.] 2004, no pet.). See FORM 10B:1. If the request for remittitur is filed as a separate document, it should be filed with the motion for new trial. At the latest, the request must be filed within 30 days after the judgment was signed and before the motion for new trial is overruled. *See* Tex. R. Civ. P. 320, 329b(b).

PLAINTIFF'S RESPONSE TO
DEFENDANT'S MOTION FOR REMITTITUR

Plaintiff, {❶ *name*}, asks the Court to deny defendant {❷ *name*}'s motion for remittitur.

INTRODUCTION

1. Plaintiff, {❸ *name*}, sued defendant, {❹ *name*}, for {❺ *state basis of suit*}.

2. {❻ *State other relevant facts about the suit.*}

BACKGROUND

3. On {❼ *date*}, the Court signed a judgment for plaintiff awarding {❽ *him/her/it*} the following damages: {❾ *specify the damages in the judgment*}.

4. {❿ *State other facts relevant to the response.*}

ARGUMENT & AUTHORITIES

5. The standard for a request for remittitur is factual sufficiency of the evidence. *Torrington Co. v. Stutzman*, 46 S.W.3d 829, 851 (Tex. 2000); *Mar. Overseas Corp. v. Ellis*, 971 S.W.2d 402, 406 (Tex. 1998); *Rose v. Doctors Hosp.*, 801 S.W.2d 841, 848 (Tex. 1990). A court must examine all the evidence to determine if there is sufficient evidence to support the damages award. *Pope v. Moore*, 711 S.W.2d 622, 624 (Tex. 1986). Only if the evidence is so factually insufficient, or the damages award is so against the great weight and preponderance of the evidence that it is manifestly unjust, should a court suggest a remittitur. *Id.*; *Gainsco Cty. Mut. Ins. Co. v. Martinez*, 27 S.W.3d 97, 108 (Tex. App.—San Antonio 2000, pet. granted, judgm't vacated w.r.m.). That is not the case here. {*See* ***O'Connor's Texas Rules****, "Standard," ch. 10-C, §5.1, p. 955.*}

6. The Court should not suggest that plaintiff file a remittitur because there is sufficient evidence to support the damages award in the judgment. {⓫ *Elaborate.*}

CONCLUSION

7. {⓬ *Briefly summarize the response.*}

PRAYER

8. For these reasons, plaintiff asks the Court to deny defendant's motion for remittitur.

Form 10C:2 Response to Motion for Remittitur

SEE: Tex. R. Civ. P. 315, 320
Tex. R. App. P. 46
O'Connor's Texas Rules * Civil Trials (2019), "Motion for Remittitur," ch. 10-C, p. 954

ADD: STYLE OF THE CASE – FORM 1B:2
SIGNATURE BLOCK – FORM 1B:3
CERTIFICATE OF SERVICE – FORM 1B:13

ATTACH: ORDER – FORM 10C:3

ORDER ON DEFENDANT'S MOTION FOR REMITTITUR

After considering defendant {❶ *name*}'s motion for remittitur, the response, the pleadings, and arguments of counsel, the Court

{*CHOOSE APPROPRIATE ORDER*}

DENIES the motion.

SUGGESTS that plaintiff file a remittitur of ${❷ *amount 1*}, reducing the amount awarded for damages of ${❸ *amount 2*} for {❹ *specify type of damages*} to ${❺ *amount 3*}. If plaintiff does not file a remittitur of ${❻ *amount 1*} by {❼ *date*}, a new trial is granted on the day following that deadline.

SIGNED on _______________, 20___.

____
PRESIDING JUDGE

SEE: Tex. R. Civ. P. 315, 320
Tex. R. App. P. 46
O'Connor's Texas Rules * Civil Trials (2019), "Order," ch. 10-C, §5, p. 955

ADD: STYLE OF THE CASE – FORM 1B:2
CERTIFICATE OF SERVICE – FORM 1B:13, if proposed order served separately from motion or response

NOTE: The appellate timetable begins to run on the date the trial court signs the order suggesting remittitur. See ***O'Connor's Texas Rules***, "Appellate timetable begins," ch. 10-C, §7.1, p. 955.

PLAINTIFF'S CONSENT TO {❶ *MOTION FOR/SUGGESTION OF*} REMITTITUR

Plaintiff, {❷ *name*}, consents to the reduction of plaintiff's damages in response to {❸ *the Court's suggestion of/defendant's motion for*} remittitur.

Plaintiff agrees that the damages awarded by the jury for {❹ *identify type of injury*} may be reduced by the Court to ${❺ *amount*}, and that the Court may render {❻ *judgment/an amended judgment*} for that amount.

If defendant appeals the judgment rendered by the Court, plaintiff reserves the right to appeal this remittitur. {*See* ***O'Connor's Texas Rules****, "Right to appeal," ch. 10-C, §7.2, p. 955.*}

SEE: Tex. R. Civ. P. 315, 320
Tex. R. App. P. 46
O'Connor's Texas Rules * Civil Trials (2019), "Acceptance," ch. 10-C, §6.1, p. 955

ADD: STYLE OF THE CASE – FORM 1B:2
SIGNATURE BLOCK – FORM 1B:3
VERIFICATION – FORM 1B:7
CERTIFICATE OF SERVICE – FORM 1B:13

{❶ *PARTY*}'S MOTION TO MODIFY JUDGMENT UNDER TEXAS RULE OF CIVIL PROCEDURE 329b

{❷ *Party*}, {❸ *name*}, asks the Court to modify the judgment.

INTRODUCTION

1. Plaintiff, {❹ *name*}, sued defendant, {❺ *name*}, for {❻ *state basis of suit*}.

2. {❼ *State other relevant facts about the suit.*}

BACKGROUND

3. The Court signed a judgment on {❽ *date*}.

4. {❾ *State other facts relevant to the motion.*}

{*CHOOSE APPROPRIATE PARAGRAPH 5*}

5. This motion is timely because it is filed within 30 days after the Court signed the judgment. *See* Tex. R. Civ. P. 329b(a), (g). {*See* ***O'Connor's Texas Rules***, *"Deadlines," ch. 10-D, §3, p. 958.*}

5. Even though this motion is filed more than 30 days after the date the Court signed the judgment, it is filed during the period the Court has plenary power over the judgment. The judgment was signed on {❿ *date*}, and the Court's plenary power expires on {⓫ *date*}. Even though this motion will not extend the appellate timetables or preserve error should the Court overrule it, the Court retains the power to change its judgment until its plenary power expires. {*See* ***O'Connor's Texas Rules***, *"Late motion," ch. 10-D, §3.4, p. 958.*}

ARGUMENT & AUTHORITIES

6. The Court should modify the judgment because it is incorrect. A court has the power to modify the judgment as long as it retains plenary power over the judgment. *See* Tex. R. Civ. P. 329b(g); *L.M. Healthcare, Inc. v. Childs*, 929 S.W.2d 442, 443-44 (Tex. 1996). The Court retains plenary power over the judgment in this case until {⓬ *date*}.

{*CHOOSE APPROPRIATE PARAGRAPHS 7-11*}

7. The judgment is incorrect because it does not award {13 *prejudgment interest/the correct amount of prejudgment interest*}. *See Bulgerin v. Bulgerin*, 724 S.W.2d 943, 946 (Tex. App.—San Antonio 1987, no writ), *overruled on other grounds*, *Trinity Universal Ins. Co. v. Cowan*, 945 S.W.2d 819 (Tex. 1997). {14 *Explain why the calculation is incorrect, and state the correct amount.*} {*See* ***O'Connor's Texas Rules****, "Prejudgment interest," ch. 10-D, §2.1.1, p. 957.*}

8. The judgment is incorrect because it does not award {15 *attorney fees/the correct amount of attorney fees*}. *See Tex. Educ. Agency v. Maxwell*, 937 S.W.2d 621, 623 (Tex. App.—Eastland 1997, writ denied); *Am. Bank v. Waco Airmotive, Inc.*, 818 S.W.2d 163, 178 (Tex. App.—Waco 1991, writ denied). {16 *Elaborate and specify the amount of attorney fees proved in the case.*} {*See* ***O'Connor's Texas Rules****, "Attorney fees," ch. 10-D, §2.1.2, p. 958.*}

9. The judgment is incorrect because it does not award {17 *costs/the correct amount of costs/costs to the correct party*}. {18 *Elaborate and specify the amount of costs the judgment should award or the party that should be awarded costs.*} {*See* ***O'Connor's Texas Rules****, "Costs," ch. 10-D, §2.1.3, p. 958.*}

10. The judgment is incorrect because it states that the dismissal was with prejudice even though the dismissal should be without prejudice. *See L.M. Healthcare*, 929 S.W.2d at 443. {19 *Elaborate and specify why dismissal should be without prejudice.*} {*See* ***O'Connor's Texas Rules****, "Any other error or omission in judgment," ch. 10-D, §2.1.4, p. 958.*}

11. The judgment is incorrect because {20 *specify any defect or omission in the judgment*}. {21 *Elaborate.*} {*See* ***O'Connor's Texas Rules****, "Any other error or omission in judgment," ch. 10-D, §2.1.4, p. 958.*}

CONCLUSION

12. {22 *Briefly summarize the motion.*}

PRAYER

13. For these reasons, {23 *party*} asks the Court to grant this motion and sign a corrected judgment that {24 *describe requested modification*}.

◄ *Continued on next page* ►

SEE: Tex. R. Civ. P. 329b(g)
O'Connor's Texas Rules * Civil Trials (2019), "Motion to Modify the Judgment," ch. 10-D, p. 957

ADD: STYLE OF THE CASE – FORM 1B:2
SIGNATURE BLOCK – FORM 1B:3
CERTIFICATE OF SERVICE – FORM 1B:13

ATTACH: NOTICE OF HEARING OR SUBMISSION – FORM 1E:1
ORDER – FORM 1G:1
Modified judgment

NOTE: A party can file a motion to modify the judgment after the court has overruled a motion for new trial, as long as the motion to modify is filed within 30 days after the date the judgment was signed. ***In re Brookshire Grocery Co.***, 250 S.W.3d 66, 72 (Tex.2008); ***L.M. Healthcare, Inc. v. Childs***, 929 S.W.2d 442, 443-44 (Tex.1996).

{❶ *PARTY*}'S REQUEST FOR
FINDINGS OF FACT & CONCLUSIONS OF LAW

{❷ *Party*}, {❸ *name*}, asks the Court to file findings of fact and conclusions of law.

INTRODUCTION

1. Plaintiff, {❹ *name*}, sued defendant, {❺ *name*}, for {❻ *state basis of suit*}.

2. The Court signed a judgment on {❼ *date*}.

REQUEST

3. {❽ *Party*} asks the Court to file findings of fact and conclusions of law and require the court clerk to mail copies to all parties, as required by Texas Rule of Civil Procedure 297.

4. {❾ *Party*} files this request within 20 days after the Court signed the judgment. Tex. R. Civ. P. 296. {*See* ***O'Connor's Texas Rules***, *"Deadline," ch. 10-E, §3.1.1, p. 964.*}

SEE: Tex. R. Civ. P. 296, 297
O'Connor's Texas Rules * Civil Trials (2019), "First request," ch. 10-E, §3.1, p. 964

ADD: STYLE OF THE CASE – FORM 1B:2
SIGNATURE BLOCK – FORM 1B:3
CERTIFICATE OF SERVICE – FORM 1B:13

NOTE: Findings of fact are appropriate in nonjury cases and cases in which the findings can properly be considered by the appellate court. See ***O'Connor's Texas Rules***, "Availability of Findings of Fact," ch. 10-E, §2, p. 961. A request for findings does not always extend appellate deadlines. See ***O'Connor's Texas Rules***, "Effect on appellate timetable," ch. 10-E, §6.1, p. 968.

The losing party should always request findings of fact; otherwise, all findings are deemed in favor of the judgment. ***Worford v. Stamper***, 801 S.W.2d 108, 109 (Tex.1990). Although the winning party probably does not want to ask for findings of fact, once the losing party makes the proper request for findings, the winning party should make sure they are filed.

{❶ *PARTY*}'S RESPONSE TO {❷ *ADVERSE PARTY*}'S
REQUEST FOR FINDINGS OF FACT & CONCLUSIONS OF LAW

{❸ *Party*}, {❹ *name*}, files this response to {❺ *adverse party*} {❻ *name*}'s request for findings of fact and conclusions of law.

INTRODUCTION

1. Plaintiff, {❼ *name*}, sued defendant, {❽ *name*}, for {❾ *state basis of suit*}.

2. The Court signed a judgment on {❿ *date*}.

FINDINGS OF FACT & CONCLUSIONS OF LAW

{*CHOOSE APPROPRIATE PARAGRAPH 3*}

3. {⓫ *Party*} attaches proposed findings of fact and conclusions of law to this response and asks that the Court sign and file them.

3. Findings of fact and conclusions of law are inappropriate in this case because {⓬ *state reasons, e.g., all issues were tried to a jury, the case was resolved by summary judgment*}. {*See* ***O'Connor's Texas Rules****, "Findings of fact are not appropriate," ch. 10-E, §2.4, p. 963.*} The Court should therefore deny the request and decline to file findings of fact and conclusions of law.

PRAYER

4. For these reasons, {⓭ *party*} asks the Court to {⓮ *file/decline to file*} findings of fact and conclusions of law.

SEE: Tex. R. Civ. P. 296, 297
O'Connor's Texas Rules * Civil Trials (2019), "Response," ch. 10-E, §4, p. 966

ADD: STYLE OF THE CASE – FORM 1B:2
SIGNATURE BLOCK – FORM 1B:3
CERTIFICATE OF SERVICE – FORM 1B:13

ATTACH: Findings and conclusions, if appropriate

NOTE: See notes under FORM 10E:1.

{❶ *PARTY*}'S NOTICE OF PAST-DUE FINDINGS OF FACT & CONCLUSIONS OF LAW

{❷ *Party*}, {❸ *name*}, gives the Court notice that its findings of fact and conclusions of law are past due and asks the Court to file findings of fact and conclusions of law.

INTRODUCTION

1. Plaintiff, {❹ *name*}, sued defendant, {❺ *name*}, for {❻ *state basis of suit*}.

2. The Court signed a judgment on {❼ *date*}.

FIRST REQUEST

3. {❽ *Party*} filed a timely request for findings of fact and conclusions of law on {❾ *date*}.

4. The findings of fact and conclusions of law were due on {❿ *date*}, 20 days after the request was filed. Tex. R. Civ. P. 297.

SECOND REQUEST

5. {⓫ *Party*} files this notice of past-due findings of fact and conclusions of law within 30 days after {⓬ *his/her/its*} original request. {*See* ***O'Connor's Texas Rules****, "Second request," ch. 10-E, §3.3, p. 964.*}

6. This notice extends the date the findings of fact and conclusions of law are due until {⓭ *date*}, 40 days after the original request.

7. {⓮ *Party*} asks the Court to file findings of fact and conclusions of law and require the court clerk to mail copies to all parties, as required by Texas Rule of Civil Procedure 297. {*See* ***O'Connor's Texas Rules****, "Court files findings," ch. 10-E, §3.4, p. 964.*}

SEE: Tex. R. Civ. P. 296, 297
O'Connor's Texas Rules * Civil Trials (2019), "Second request," ch. 10-E, §3.3, p. 964; "Court files findings," ch. 10-E, §3.4, p. 964

ADD: STYLE OF THE CASE – FORM 1B:2
SIGNATURE BLOCK – FORM 1B:3
CERTIFICATE OF SERVICE – FORM 1B:13

FORM 10E:3

◄ *Continued on next page* ►

NOTE: If a party does not file a notice of past-due findings of fact and conclusions of law, it waives the right to complain about the trial court's failure to file findings and conclusions. ***AD Villarai, LLC v. Chan Il Pak***, 519 S.W.3d 132, 137 (Tex.2017); ***Sonnier v. Sonnier***, 331 S.W.3d 211, 214 (Tex.App.—Beaumont 2011, no pet.); *see* ***Gnerer v. Johnson***, 227 S.W.3d 385, 389 (Tex.App.—Texarkana 2007, no pet.).

Several courts have held that a premature notice of past-due findings is not timely. *E.g.*, ***Estate of Gorski v. Welch***, 993 S.W.2d 298, 301 (Tex.App.—San Antonio 1999, pet. denied); ***Echols v. Echols***, 900 S.W.2d 160, 161-62 (Tex.App.—Beaumont 1995, writ denied); ***Nisby v. Dentsply Int'l***, No. 05-14-00814-CV (Tex.App.—Dallas 2015, no pet.) (memo op.; 5-11-15); ***Joseph v. Joseph***, No. 01-11-01096-CV (Tex.App.—Houston [1st Dist.] 2012, no pet.) (memo op.; 5-3-12). These courts have held that Texas Rule of Civil Procedure 306c, which states that a request for findings of fact is not ineffective because it is prematurely filed, does not apply to notices of past-due findings. ***Estate of Gorski***, 993 S.W.2d at 301; ***Echols***, 900 S.W.2d at 161; ***Nisby***, No. 05-14-00814-CV (memo op.); ***Joseph***, No. 01-11-01096-CV (memo op.).

{[1] *PARTY*}'S REQUEST FOR
{[2] *ADDITIONAL/AMENDED/ADDITIONAL & AMENDED*} FINDINGS OF FACT & CONCLUSIONS OF LAW

{[3] *Party*}, {[4] *name*}, asks the Court to file {[5] *additional/amended/additional and amended*} findings of fact and conclusions of law.

INTRODUCTION

1. Plaintiff, {[6] *name*}, sued defendant, {[7] *name*}, for {[8] *state basis of suit*}.

2. The Court signed a judgment on {[9] *date*}.

3. On {[10] *date*}, the Court filed findings of fact and conclusions of law.

4. {[11] *State other relevant facts about the suit.*}

REQUEST

5. {[12] *Party*} makes this request within ten days after the Court filed the original findings and conclusions. Tex. R. Civ. P. 298.

{*CHOOSE APPROPRIATE PARAGRAPHS 6-7*}

6. {[13] *Party*} asks the Court to make an additional {[14] *finding of fact/conclusion of law*}. {[15] *Specify the proposed finding or legal conclusion.*} The proposed {[16] *finding of fact/conclusion of law*} concerns a controlling issue because {[17] *state reason*}.

7. {[18] *Party*} asks the Court to amend {[19] *finding of fact/conclusion of law*} number {[20] *number*} to read as follows: {[21] *specify the proposed amended finding or conclusion*}. The Court should amend the {[22] *finding of fact/conclusion of law*} because {[23] *state reason*}.

CONCLUSION

{*CHOOSE APPROPRIATE PARAGRAPH 8*}

{*If winning party*}

8. {[24] *Briefly summarize the request.*}

{*If losing party*}

8. {[25] *Party*} makes this request because a material, disputed issue arose during the trial that was not {[26] *properly addressed/addressed*} in the findings of fact. Although {[27] *party*} does not agree with these requested {[28] *additional/amended*} find-

Continued on next page

ings of fact, the request is necessary so {㉙ *party*} may challenge the lack of these findings on appeal if the Court does not make a finding.

PRAYER

9. {㉚ *Party*} attaches {㉛ *his/her/its*} requested {㉜ *additional/amended*} findings of fact and conclusions of law to this request and asks that the Court file them on or before {㉝ *date*}, ten days from the date of this request.

SEE: Tex. R. Civ. P. 298, 299
O'Connor's Texas Rules * Civil Trials (2019), "Third request – for additional or amended findings," ch. 10-E, §3.5, p. 965

ADD: STYLE OF THE CASE – FORM 1B:2
SIGNATURE BLOCK – FORM 1B:3
CERTIFICATE OF SERVICE – FORM 1B:13

ATTACH: Additional or amended findings and conclusions

NOTE: One court has held that a request for additional findings made before the trial court makes any findings is ineffective. *See* ***Mohnke v. Greenwood***, 915 S.W.2d 585, 590 (Tex.App.—Houston [14th Dist.] 1996, no writ). *But see* Tex. R. Civ. P. 306c (no premature request for findings shall be ineffective).

PLAINTIFF'S VERIFIED MOTION TO REINSTATE

Plaintiff, {❶ *name*}, asks the Court to reinstate this case on its docket, under the authority of Texas Rule of Civil Procedure 165a.

INTRODUCTION

1. Plaintiff, {❷ *name*}, sued defendant, {❸ *name*}, for {❹ *state basis of suit*}.

2. {❺ *State other relevant facts about the suit.*}

BACKGROUND

3. On {❻ *date*}, the Court dismissed the case.

{*CHOOSE APPROPRIATE PARAGRAPH 4*}

4. The Court dismissed the case for want of prosecution because of plaintiff's failure to appear at {❼ *a hearing/trial*} on {❽ *date*}.

4. The Court dismissed the case for failure to diligently prosecute the suit.

4. The Court dismissed the case for failure to comply with the Supreme Court's time standards.

5. Plaintiff files this motion while the Court has plenary power, within 30 days of {❾ *dismissal/receipt of notice of the dismissal*}. The Court therefore has jurisdiction to reinstate this case. Tex. R. Civ. P. 165a(3).

6. {❿ *State other facts relevant to the motion.*}

ARGUMENT & AUTHORITIES

{*CHOOSE APPROPRIATE SECTIONS A-D*}

A. Failure to appear.

{*CHOOSE APPROPRIATE PARAGRAPHS 7-9*}

{*No notice of trial or hearing*}

7. A party must be given proper notice of a trial or hearing before a court may dismiss for failure to appear. *See* Tex. R. Civ. P. 165a(1). The Court should grant the motion to reinstate because plaintiff did not receive notice of the {⓫ *trial/hearing*}, as required by Rule 165a(1). {⓬ *Elaborate.*} {*See* ***O'Connor's Texas Rules****, "Communications from Court," ch. 1-H, §6, p. 64; "No notice of trial or hearing," ch. 10-F, §3.4.1(1), p. 971.*}

◄ *Continued on next page* ►

{Failure to appear not intentional}

8. A court should grant a motion to reinstate if the plaintiff's failure to appear at a trial or hearing was not intentional or the result of conscious indifference, but was the result of a mistake or an accident or can otherwise be reasonably explained. Tex. R. Civ. P. 165a(3); *Smith v. Babcock & Wilcox Constr. Co.*, 913 S.W.2d 467, 468 (Tex. 1995); *Melton v. Ryander*, 727 S.W.2d 299, 301-02 (Tex. App.—Dallas 1987, writ ref'd n.r.e.). A party's failure to appear is not intentional or due to conscious indifference within the meaning of Rule 165a merely because it is deliberate. *Smith*, 913 S.W.2d at 468. To support a dismissal, the failure to appear must be without adequate justification. *Id.* Proof of such justification—accident, mistake, or other reasonable explanation—negates the intent or conscious indifference for which reinstatement can be denied. *Id.*; *Bank One v. Moody*, 830 S.W.2d 81, 84 (Tex. 1992). {*See* ***O'Connor's Texas Rules,*** *"Mistake or accident," ch. 10-F, §3.4.1(3), p. 972.*}

9. The Court should reinstate this case because plaintiff's failure to appear was neither intentional nor the result of conscious indifference. Plaintiff's failure was due to {⓭ *a mistake/an accident/{identify other reasonable explanation}*}. Specifically, {⓮ *explain*}.

B. Failure to comply with time standards.

{ADD PARAGRAPHS 10-11 IF TIME STANDARDS DID NOT EXPIRE}

10. A court should grant a motion to reinstate if the suit was dismissed before the appropriate time standards expired. *See Johnson-Snodgrass v. KTAO, Inc.*, 75 S.W.3d 84, 87 (Tex. App.—Fort Worth 2002, pet. dism'd). {*See* ***O'Connor's Texas Rules,*** *"Failure to comply with time standards," ch. 10-F, §3.4.2(2), p. 972.*}

11. The Court should reinstate the case because the case is still within the Supreme Court's disposition time standards. *See Johnson-Snodgrass*, 75 S.W.3d at 87. The time standards are measured from the date defendant made {⓯ *his/her/its*} appearance. Tex. R. Jud. Admin. 6.1(b). Defendant made an appearance on {⓰ *date*}. Under the time standards, a civil {⓱ *jury/nonjury*} case not involving family law should be brought to trial or final disposition within {⓲ *18/12*} months. *Id.* The case has been on the docket for only {⓳ *number*} months. The Court should retain the case on the docket because the case is still within the time standards.

{*ADD APPROPRIATE PARAGRAPH 12 IF TIME STANDARDS EXPIRED BUT THERE IS REASONABLE EXCUSE*}

{*Conscious-indifference standard*}

12. A court should grant a motion to reinstate if the plaintiff's failure to prosecute the case before the appropriate time standards expired was not intentional or the result of conscious indifference, but was the result of a mistake or an accident or can otherwise be reasonably explained. *See* Tex. R. Civ. P. 165a(3); *Cappetta v. Hermes*, 222 S.W.3d 160, 166-67 (Tex. App.—San Antonio 2006, no pet.); *Polk v. Sw. Crossing Homeowners Ass'n*, 165 S.W.3d 89, 96-97 (Tex. App.—Houston [14th Dist.] 2005, pet. denied). The Court should reinstate this case because plaintiff's failure to prosecute before the disposition time standards expired was neither intentional nor the result of conscious indifference. Plaintiff's failure was due to {⓴ *a mistake/an accident/{identify other reasonable explanation}*}. Specifically, {㉑ *explain*}. {*See **O'Connor's Texas Rules**, "Failure to comply with time standards," ch. 10-F, §3.4.2(2), p. 972; "Caution," ch. 10-F, §3.4.2(3), p. 973.*}

{*Good-cause standard*}

12. A court should grant a motion to reinstate if the plaintiff shows good cause for its failure to prosecute within the appropriate time standards. *See Steward v. Colonial Cas. Ins. Co.*, 143 S.W.3d 161, 164-65 (Tex. App.—Waco 2004, no pet.); *Maida v. Fire Ins. Exch.*, 990 S.W.2d 836, 840-41 (Tex. App.—Fort Worth 1999, no pet.). The Court should reinstate this case because {㉒ *explain how there was good cause for failure*}. {*See **O'Connor's Texas Rules**, "Failure to comply with time standards," ch. 10-F, §3.4.2(2), p. 972; "Caution," ch. 10-F, §3.4.2(3), p. 973.*}

C. Failure to diligently prosecute suit.

{*CHOOSE APPROPRIATE PARAGRAPHS 13-16*}

{*Failure to diligently prosecute not intentional*}

13. A court should grant a motion to reinstate if the plaintiff's failure to diligently prosecute the case was not intentional or the result of conscious indifference, but was the result of a mistake or an accident or can otherwise be reasonably explained. *See* Tex. R. Civ. P. 165a(3); *Zarychta v. Montgomery Cty. Dist. Attorney*, 398 S.W.3d 260, 264-65 (Tex. App.—Corpus Christi 2011, pet. dism'd); *Cappetta v. Hermes*, 222 S.W.3d 160, 166-67 (Tex. App.—San Antonio 2006, no pet.). The Court should reinstate this case because plaintiff's failure to diligently prosecute was neither intentional nor the result of conscious indifference. Plaintiff's failure was due to {㉓ *a mistake/an*

◄ *Continued on next page* ►

accident/{identify other reasonable explanation}}. Specifically, {㉔ *explain*}. {*See* ***O'Connor's Texas Rules****, "Caution," ch. 10-F, §3.4.2(3), p. 973.*}

{*Plaintiff was reasonably diligent in prosecuting suit*}

14. After a case is dismissed for failure to diligently prosecute, if the plaintiff files a motion to reinstate showing that it was in fact reasonably diligent in prosecuting the suit, a court should grant the motion and reinstate the case. *See MacGregor v. Rich*, 941 S.W.2d 74, 76 (Tex. 1997). A motion to reinstate provides a plaintiff with an opportunity to explain its diligence and to request that a court reconsider the order of dismissal. *Ellmossallamy v. Huntsman*, 830 S.W.2d 299, 302 (Tex. App.—Houston [14th Dist.] 1992, no writ). {*See* ***O'Connor's Texas Rules****, "Inherent power," ch. 10-F, §3.4.2(3), p. 972.*}

15. The Court should reinstate this case because plaintiff has diligently prosecuted the case.

a. This case was filed on {㉕ *date*}.

b. Plaintiff diligently pursued discovery. {㉖ *Elaborate.*}

c. Plaintiff complied with all of defendant's requests for discovery. {㉗ *Elaborate.*}

d. Plaintiff is ready to proceed to trial. {㉘ *State whether a trial setting has been requested.*}

16. The only discovery that remains outstanding is {㉙ *describe necessary discovery and explain why it was not completed sooner*}.

D. No notice of intent to dismiss.

17. A party must be given notice and an opportunity to be heard before a court may dismiss a case for want of prosecution under Rule 165a or under its inherent power. *Villarreal v. San Antonio Truck & Equip.*, 994 S.W.2d 628, 630 (Tex. 1999); *see* Tex. R. Civ. P. 165a(1). The court clerk must send notice of intent to dismiss to each attorney of record and to each party not represented by an attorney. Tex. R. Civ. P. 165a(1). If the party did not appear at a trial or hearing, this notice and opportunity to be heard are not required if the notice of trial or hearing stated that the party's failure to appear could result in dismissal. *Alexander v. Lynda's Boutique*, 134 S.W.3d 845, 852 (Tex. 2004). {*See* ***O'Connor's Texas Rules****, "No notice of intent to dismiss," ch. 10-F, §3.4.2(1), p. 972.*}

18. Plaintiff did not receive proper notice of the Court's intent to dismiss {30 *add if appropriate: , nor did the notice for the {trial/hearing} state that plaintiff's failure to appear could result in dismissal*}. {31 *Elaborate if necessary.*}

{*CHOOSE APPROPRIATE PARAGRAPHS 19-23*}

19. The court clerk did not send the notice of intent to dismiss to {32 *either attorney of record/plaintiff's attorney of record/plaintiff*}. Tex. R. Civ. P. 165a(1); *Rohus v. Licona*, 942 S.W.2d 111, 112 (Tex. App.—Houston [1st Dist.] 1997, no writ). {33 *Elaborate.*}

20. The court clerk did not send the notice of intent to dismiss to each attorney of record for plaintiff. Tex. R. Civ. P. 165a(1); *Cannon v. ICO Tubular Servs., Inc.*, 905 S.W.2d 380, 388 (Tex. App.—Houston [1st Dist.] 1995, no writ), *overruled on other grounds, Lane Bank Equip. Co. v. Smith S. Equip., Inc.*, 10 S.W.3d 308 (Tex. 2000). The notice was sent only to {34 *name of attorney*}. Plaintiff was also represented by {35 *another attorney/other attorneys*} of record, {36 *names of other attorneys*}, who did not receive the notice of intent to dismiss.

21. The court clerk did not send the notice of intent to dismiss by U.S. Postal Service. Tex. R. Civ. P. 165a(1). Instead, the notice was {37 *identify how notice was given*}.

22. The notice of intent to dismiss did not state the date and place of the dismissal hearing. Tex. R. Civ. P. 165a(1); *Brown v. Brookshires Grocery Store*, 10 S.W.3d 351, 353-54 (Tex. App.—Dallas 1999, pet. denied). {38 *Elaborate.*}

23. The notice of intent to dismiss stated a ground for dismissal different from the ground for which the case was actually dismissed. *See, e.g., Villarreal*, 994 S.W.2d at 631-32 (notice under Rule 165a(1) does not support dismissal under Rule 165a(2) or inherent power). {39 *Elaborate.*}

REQUEST FOR HEARING

24. Plaintiff requests that the Court conduct an oral hearing. Rule 165a requires an oral hearing on any timely filed motion to reinstate. Tex. R. Civ. P. 165a(3); *Gulf Coast Inv. Corp. v. NASA 1 Bus. Ctr.*, 754 S.W.2d 152, 153 (Tex. 1988). The trial court must set a hearing on the motion to reinstate as soon as practicable. Tex. R. Civ. P. 165a(3); *Thordson v. City of Hous.*, 815 S.W.2d 550, 550 (Tex. 1991). {*See* ***O'Connor's Texas Rules****, "Requesting hearing," ch. 10-F, §3.6, p. 973.*}

CONCLUSION

25. {40 *Briefly summarize the motion.*} This case should be decided on the merits, not on a procedural default.

Continued on next page

PRAYER

26. For these reasons, plaintiff asks the Court to set this motion for hearing and, after the hearing, grant the motion and reinstate this case on the docket.

SEE: Tex. R. Civ. P. 165a, 306a
Tex. R. Jud. Admin. 6.1
O'Connor's Texas Rules * Civil Trials (2019), "Motion to Reinstate After Dismissal for Want of Prosecution," ch. 10-F, p. 970

ADD: STYLE OF THE CASE – FORM 1B:2
SIGNATURE BLOCK – FORM 1B:3
VERIFICATION – FORM 1B:7
CERTIFICATE OF SERVICE – FORM 1B:13

ATTACH: AFFIDAVIT – FORM 1B:8, if necessary
NOTICE OF HEARING OR SUBMISSION – FORM 1E:1
ORDER – FORM 1G:1

NOTE: When a plaintiff files a motion to reinstate more than 30 days after the date of dismissal, the plaintiff must also demonstrate that it received late notice of the dismissal. *See* Tex. R. Civ. P. 306a(4), (5). See FORM 10G:1.

If the court dismissed the suit for failure to prosecute without giving the plaintiff notice of its intent to dismiss, the plaintiff must (1) prove lack of proper notice and (2) refute the grounds for failure to prosecute. The court can overrule the motion if the plaintiff merely proves lack of notice and does not address the failure to prosecute. *See* ***Texas Sting, Ltd. v. R.B. Foods, Inc.***, 82 S.W.3d 644, 649 (Tex. App.—San Antonio 2002, pet. denied).

If the trial court's order mistakenly dismissed the suit "with prejudice" or stated that plaintiff "take nothing," that statement must be challenged in the motion to reinstate or in a motion for new trial; otherwise, the error is waived and the suit cannot be refiled. *See* ***El Paso Pipe & Sup. Co. v. Mountain States Leasing, Inc.***, 617 S.W.2d 189, 190 (Tex.1981). See ***O'Connor's Texas Rules***, "Challenging language of dismissal order," ch. 10-F, §3.5, p. 973.

Although a hearing on a motion to reinstate is mandatory, the plaintiff should still include a request for a hearing in its motion. *See* Tex. R. Civ. P. 165a(3); ***Thordson v. City of Houston***, 815 S.W.2d 550, 550 (Tex.1991). Even when a plaintiff does not ask for a hearing, the trial court must conduct one unless the plaintiff actually waives it. *See* ***Parker v. Cain***, 505 S.W.3d 119, 122-23 (Tex.App.—Amarillo 2016, no pet.); ***Enriquez v. Livingston***, 400 S.W.3d 610, 618-19 (Tex.App.—Austin 2013, pet. denied); ***Matheson v. American Carbonics***, 867 S.W.2d 146, 147-48 & n.2 (Tex.App.—Texarkana 1993, no writ); *see, e.g.*, ***Kelly v. Cunningham***, 848 S.W.2d 370, 371 (Tex.App.—Houston [1st Dist.] 1993, no writ) (Ps waived right to oral hearing by setting motion to reinstate on court's submission docket). Some courts, however, have held that the burden is on the plaintiff to request a hearing on the motion. *See, e.g.*, ***Johnson v. Sepulveda***, 178 S.W.3d 117, 119 (Tex.App.—Houston [14th Dist.] 2005, no pet.) (relying on precedent that based its reasoning on cases predating 1983 version of Tex. R. Civ. P. 165a, court held P was required to alert court of need for hearing); ***Rainbow Home Health, Inc. v. Schmidt***, 76 S.W.3d 53, 57 (Tex.App.—San Antonio 2002, pet. denied) (same).

An affidavit by the plaintiff's attorney can act as a substitute for verification. *See* ***Andrews v. Stanton***, 198 S.W.3d 4, 8-9 (Tex.App.—El Paso 2006, no pet.). An unverified motion does not extend the trial court's plenary power or the deadlines for perfecting an appeal. *See* ***Guest v. Dixon***, 195 S.W.3d 687, 688-89 (Tex.2006) (dicta). See ***O'Connor's Texas Rules***, "Verified," ch. 10-F, §3.3, p. 971.

The courts are split on whether the conscious-indifference standard of Texas Rule of Civil Procedure 165a(3) applies only to dismissal for failure to appear or whether it also applies when the case is dismissed for noncompliance with the Supreme Court's disposition time standards or when the court exercises its inherent power to dismiss for lack of diligence. *Compare* ***Zarychta v. Montgomery Cty. Dist. Atty.***, 398 S.W.3d 260, 264-65 (Tex.App.—Corpus Christi 2011, pet. dism'd) (conscious-indifference standard applies to all three grounds), ***Cappetta v. Hermes***, 222 S.W.3d 160, 166-67 (Tex.App.—San Antonio 2006, no pet.) (same), *and* ***Beames v. Hooks***, No. 01-14-00103-CV (Tex.App.—Houston [1st Dist.] 2015, no pet.) (memo op.; 1-13-15) (same), *with* ***Steward v. Colonial Cas. Ins.***, 143 S.W.3d 161, 164-65 (Tex.App.—Waco 2004, no pet.) (conscious-indifference standard only applies to cases dismissed for failure to appear), ***Maida v. Fire Ins. Exch.***, 990 S.W.2d 836, 840-41 (Tex.App.—Fort Worth 1999, no pet.) (same), *and* ***Burton v. Hoffman***, 959 S.W.2d 351, 354 (Tex.App.—Austin 1998, no pet.) (same).

DEFENDANT'S RESPONSE TO PLAINTIFF'S MOTION TO REINSTATE

Defendant, {❶ *name*}, asks the Court to deny plaintiff {❷ *name*}'s motion to reinstate this case on its docket.

INTRODUCTION

1. Plaintiff, {❸ *name*}, sued defendant, {❹ *name*}, for {❺ *state basis of suit*}.

2. {❻ *State other relevant facts about the suit.*}

BACKGROUND

3. On {❼ *date*}, the Court dismissed the case for want of prosecution.

4. {❽ *State other facts relevant to the response.*}

ARGUMENT & AUTHORITIES

{*CHOOSE APPROPRIATE SECTIONS A-E*}

A. Untimely motion.

5. A court should grant a motion to reinstate only if the plaintiff filed the motion within 30 days after the court signed the order of dismissal or within 30 days after receiving notice of dismissal. Tex. R. Civ. P. 165a(3), 306a(4), (5); *Mem'l Hosp. v. Gillis*, 741 S.W.2d 364, 365 (Tex. 1987). Plaintiff filed the motion to reinstate on {❾ *date*}, more than 30 days after {❿ *the dismissal/receipt of notice of the dismissal*}. The Court lost plenary power over the judgment on {⓫ *date*}. Therefore, the Court has no jurisdiction to reinstate this case. *See* Tex. R. Civ. P. 165a(3). {*See* ***O'Connor's Texas Rules***, *"Deadline," ch. 10-F, §4, p. 974.*}

B. Failure to appear was intentional.

6. A court should grant a motion to reinstate only if the plaintiff's failure to appear was not intentional or the result of conscious indifference, but was the result of a mistake or an accident or can otherwise be reasonably explained. Tex. R. Civ. P. 165a(3); *Smith v. Babcock & Wilcox Constr. Co.*, 913 S.W.2d 467, 468 (Tex. 1995); *Melton v. Ryander*, 727 S.W.2d 299, 301-02 (Tex. App.—Dallas 1987, writ ref'd n.r.e.). The Court should not reinstate this case because plaintiff's failure to appear was intentional or the result of conscious indifference. Plaintiff's motion to reinstate does not establish that the failure to appear was a mistake or an accident, nor does it otherwise reasonably explain the nonappearance. {⓬ *Elaborate.*} {*See* ***O'Connor's Texas Rules***, *"Mistake or accident," ch. 10-F, §3.4.1(3), p. 972.*}

C. Noncompliance with disposition time standards.

{*CHOOSE APPROPRIATE PARAGRAPH 7*}

7. A court should grant a motion to reinstate only when (1) the suit was dismissed before the appropriate time standards expired or (2) the plaintiff's failure to have the case disposed of within the appropriate time standards was not intentional or the result of conscious indifference, but was the result of a mistake or an accident or can otherwise be reasonably explained. *See* Tex. R. Civ. P. 165a(2), (3); *Cappetta v. Hermes*, 222 S.W.3d 160, 167 (Tex. App.—San Antonio 2006, no pet.); *Polk v. Sw. Crossing Homeowners Ass'n*, 165 S.W.3d 89, 96-97 (Tex. App.—Houston [14th Dist.] 2005, pet. denied). {*See **O'Connor's Texas Rules**, "Failure to comply with time standards," ch. 10-F, §3.4.2(2), p. 972; "Caution," ch. 10-F, §3.4.2(3), p. 973.*} The Court should not reinstate this case because the case was dismissed after the Supreme Court's disposition time standards expired, and plaintiff's failure to have the case disposed of within the time standards was intentional or the result of conscious indifference. {⓭ *Elaborate.*}

7. A court should grant a motion to reinstate only when (1) the suit was dismissed before the appropriate time standards expired or (2) the plaintiff shows good cause for its failure to prosecute within the time standards. *See Steward v. Colonial Cas. Ins. Co.*, 143 S.W.3d 161, 164-65 (Tex. App.—Waco 2004, no pet.); *Maida v. Fire Ins. Exch.*, 990 S.W.2d 836, 840-41 (Tex. App.—Fort Worth 1999, no pet.). {*See **O'Connor's Texas Rules**, "Failure to comply with time standards," ch. 10-F, §3.4.2(2), p. 972; "Caution," ch. 10-F, §3.4.2(3), p. 973.*} The Court should not reinstate this case because the case was dismissed after the Supreme Court's disposition time standards expired and plaintiff does not have a reasonable excuse for not prosecuting the case within the time standards. {⓮ *Elaborate.*}

D. Proper notice.

8. A court should grant a motion to reinstate only when the plaintiff was not given notice and an opportunity to be heard before the court dismissed the case for want of prosecution under Rule 165a. Tex. R. Civ. P. 165a(1); *Villarreal v. San Antonio Truck & Equip.*, 994 S.W.2d 628, 630 (Tex. 1999). {*See **O'Connor's Texas Rules**, "No notice of intent to dismiss," ch. 10-F, §3.4.2(1), p. 972.*} The Court should not reinstate this case because plaintiff received proper notice of the Court's intent to dismiss. Plaintiff had proper notice of the Court's intent to dismiss for the following reasons:

a. The court clerk sent the notice of intent to dismiss to {⓯ *each attorney of record/plaintiff's attorney of record/plaintiff*}. Tex. R. Civ. P. 165a(1); *see Rohus v. Licona*, 942 S.W.2d 111, 112 (Tex. App.—Houston [1st Dist.] 1997, no writ). {⓰ *Elaborate.*}

Continued on next page

b. The court clerk sent the notice of intent to dismiss by U.S. Postal Service. Tex. R. Civ. P. 165a(1).

c. The notice of intent to dismiss stated the date and place of the dismissal hearing. Tex. R. Civ. P. 165a(1); *see Brown v. Brookshires Grocery Store*, 10 S.W.3d 351, 353-54 (Tex. App.—Dallas 1999, pet. denied). {[17] *Elaborate.*}

d. The case was dismissed for the specific reason stated in the notice of intent to dismiss. *See Villarreal*, 994 S.W.2d at 631-32. {[18] *Elaborate.*}

E. {[19] *Add appropriate subheading for additional grounds.*}

9. The Court should not reinstate this case because {[20] *refute any other ground asserted in plaintiff's motion to reinstate*}.

CONCLUSION

10. {[21] *Briefly summarize the response.*}

PRAYER

11. For these reasons, defendant asks the Court to deny the motion to reinstate.

SEE: Tex. R. Civ. P. 165a, 306a
O'Connor's Texas Rules * Civil Trials (2019), "Motion to Reinstate After Dismissal for Want of Prosecution," ch. 10-F, p. 970

ADD: STYLE OF THE CASE – FORM 1B:2
SIGNATURE BLOCK – FORM 1B:3
VERIFICATION – FORM 1B:7
CERTIFICATE OF SERVICE – FORM 1B:13

ATTACH: AFFIDAVIT – FORM 1B:8, if necessary
ORDER – FORM 1G:1

NOTE: The courts are split on whether the conscious-indifference standard of Texas Rule of Civil Procedure 165a(3) applies only to dismissal for failure to appear or whether it also applies when the case is dismissed for noncompliance with the Supreme Court's disposition time standards or when the court exercises its inherent power to dismiss for lack of diligence. *Compare* ***Zarychta v. Montgomery Cty. Dist. Atty.***, 398 S.W.3d 260, 264-65 (Tex.App.—Corpus Christi 2011, pet. dism'd) (conscious-indifference standard applies to all three grounds), ***Cappetta v. Hermes***, 222 S.W.3d 160, 166-67 (Tex.App.—San Antonio 2006, no pet.) (same), *and* ***Beames v. Hooks***, No. 01-14-00103-CV (Tex.App.—Houston [1st Dist.] 2015, no pet.) (memo op.; 1-13-15) (same), *with* ***Steward v. Colonial Cas. Ins.***, 143 S.W.3d 161, 164-65 (Tex.App.—Waco 2004, no pet.) (conscious-indifference standard only applies to cases dismissed for failure to appear), ***Maida v. Fire Ins. Exch.***, 990 S.W.2d 836, 840-41 (Tex.App.—Fort Worth 1999, no pet.) (same), *and* ***Burton v. Hoffman***, 959 S.W.2d 351, 354 (Tex.App.—Austin 1998, no pet.) (same).

{❶ *PARTY*}'S MOTION TO EXTEND POSTJUDGMENT DEADLINES

{❷ *Party*}, {❸ *name*}, asks the Court to determine the date {❹ *party*} {❺ *received notice/acquired actual knowledge*} of the Court's judgment, under the authority of Texas Rule of Civil Procedure 306a(4).

INTRODUCTION

1. Plaintiff, {❻ *name*}, sued defendant, {❼ *name*}, for {❽ *state basis of suit*}.

2. {❾ *State other relevant facts about the suit.*}

BACKGROUND

3. On {❿ *date*}, the Court signed a judgment.

4. {⓫ *Party*} did not {⓬ *receive notice/acquire actual knowledge*} of the judgment until {⓭ *date*}, more than 20 days after the Court signed the judgment.

5. {⓮ *Party*} filed this motion during the Court's plenary power over the judgment. *See* Tex. R. Civ. P. 306a(5). {*See* ***O'Connor's Texas Rules****, "Plenary-power limits," ch. 10-G, §4.1, p. 979.*}

6. {⓯ *State other facts relevant to the motion.*}

ARGUMENT & AUTHORITIES

7. Throughout this case, {⓰ *party*} was represented by {⓱ *name of attorney*}.

{*CHOOSE APPROPRIATE PARAGRAPH 8*}

8. {⓲ *Name of attorney*} first learned of the Court's judgment on {⓳ *date*}, when {⓴ *state how the attorney learned of the judgment, including who gave notice and the type of notice, or how actual knowledge was acquired*}. That date was more than 20 days but less than 90 days after the Court signed the judgment. The affidavit of {㉑ *name of attorney*}, attached as Exhibit {㉒ *letter*}, supports this claim. {*See* ***O'Connor's Texas Rules****, "Date of notice or actual knowledge," ch. 10-G, §3.2.1, p. 977; "Description of notice or actual knowledge," ch. 10-G, §3.2.2, p. 977; "Attorney," ch. 10-G, §3.4.2(1), p. 978.*}

8. {㉓ *Party*} first learned of the Court's judgment on {㉔ *date*}, when {㉕ *state how party learned of the judgment, including who gave notice and the type of notice, or how actual knowledge was acquired*}. That date was more than 20 days but less than 90 days after the Court signed the judgment. The affidavit of {㉖ *party*}, attached as Exhibit {㉗ *letter*}, supports this claim. {*See* ***O'Connor's Texas Rules****, "Date of notice or*

Continued on next page

actual knowledge," ch. 10-G, §3.2.1, p. 977; "Description of notice or actual knowledge," ch. 10-G, §3.2.2, p. 977; "Party," ch. 10-G, §3.4.2(2), p. 979.}

9. Neither {㉘ *party*} nor {㉙ *his/her/its*} attorney learned by any other means, formal or informal, of the Court's judgment within 20 days after the judgment was signed. The attached affidavits of {㉚ *party*} and {㉛ *his/her/its*} attorney support this claim. {*See **O'Connor's Texas Rules**, "No earlier actual knowledge," ch. 10-G, §3.2.3, p. 978; "Affidavits," ch. 10-G, §3.4.2, p. 978.*}

{*CHOOSE APPROPRIATE PARAGRAPH 10*}

10. Neither {㉜ *party*} nor {㉝ *his/her/its*} attorney ever received any notice of the judgment from the court clerk. {*See **O'Connor's Texas Rules**, "No earlier notice from clerk," ch. 10-G, §3.2.4, p. 978.*}

10. The only notice of the judgment that either {㉞ *party*} or {㉟ *his/her/its*} attorney received from the court clerk was on {㊱ *date*}, in the form of {㊲ *describe type of notice*}. {*See **O'Connor's Texas Rules**, "No earlier notice from clerk," ch. 10-G, §3.2.4, p. 978.*}

{*CHOOSE APPROPRIATE PARAGRAPHS 11-13*}

11. The court clerk, in an affidavit attached to this motion as Exhibit {㊳ *letter*}, states that a {㊴ *postcard notice of the judgment/copy of the judgment*} was sent to {㊵ *{party}/{name of attorney}*} at {㊶ *address*}. {㊷ *If known, explain why the notice was not received, e.g., the attorney moved.*} {*See **O'Connor's Texas Rules**, "Clerk," ch. 10-G, §3.4.2(3), p. 979.*}

12. Other attorneys of record for {㊸ *party*} include {㊹ *names of other attorneys*}. None of the other attorneys of record learned of the Court's judgment until {㊺ *date*}, when {㊻ *state how they learned of the judgment, including who gave notice and the type of notice, or how actual knowledge was acquired*}. That date was more than 20 days but less than 90 days after the Court signed the judgment. The affidavits of {㊼ *names of other attorneys*}, attached as Exhibits {㊽ *letters*}, support this claim. {*See **O'Connor's Texas Rules**, "Date of notice or actual knowledge," ch. 10-G, §3.2.1, p. 977; "Description of notice or actual knowledge," ch. 10-G, §3.2.2, p. 977; "Attorney," ch. 10-G, §3.4.2(1), p. 978.*}

13. {㊾ *Name of attorney*} confirmed that {㊿ *his/her*} law firm's mail room did not receive any notice of the judgment from the court clerk. The law firm's office procedure is to log all mail in the mail room before distributing it to the attorneys. The law office has no record of having received any document from this Court on or about {51 *date*}, the date the court clerk indicated {52 *he/she*} mailed the copies of the judgment to the parties. Attached to the affidavit of {53 *name of attorney*} are copies of the log from the law office's mail room covering the period from the date the court clerk mailed the judgment to three weeks later. {*See* ***O'Connor's Texas Rules***, *"Attorney," ch. 10-G, §3.4.2(1), p. 978.*}

REQUEST FOR HEARING

14. Plaintiff asks the Court to set this motion for an oral hearing as soon as possible. A hearing on a motion to extend postjudgment deadlines is required. *See Cantu v. Longoria*, 878 S.W.2d 131, 132 (Tex. 1994). {*See* ***O'Connor's Texas Rules***, *"Request hearing," ch. 10-G, §3.3, p. 978.*}

CONCLUSION

15. {54 *Party*} asks the Court to find that {55 *he/she/it*} did not {56 *receive notice/acquire actual knowledge*} of the Court's judgment until {57 *date*}.

PRAYER

16. For these reasons, {58 *party*} asks the Court to set this motion for hearing and, after the hearing, grant the motion, determine the date {59 *party*} {60 *received notice/acquired actual knowledge*} of the judgment, and order that date to be considered the new date the judgment was signed.

SEE: Tex. R. Civ. P. 306a(4), (5)
Tex. R. App. P. 4.2
O'Connor's Texas Rules * Civil Trials (2019), "Motion to Extend Postjudgment Deadlines," ch. 10-G, p. 976

ADD: STYLE OF THE CASE – FORM 1B:2
SIGNATURE BLOCK – FORM 1B:3
VERIFICATION – FORM 1B:7
CERTIFICATE OF SERVICE – FORM 1B:13

ATTACH: AFFIDAVIT – FORM 1B:8, if necessary for court clerk
NOTICE OF HEARING OR SUBMISSION – FORM 1E:1
PARTY'S AFFIDAVIT – FORM 10G:2
ATTORNEY'S AFFIDAVIT – FORM 10G:3
ORDER – FORM 10G:5

◄ *Continued on next page* ►

NOTE: A motion to extend the postjudgment deadlines (MEPD) may be made as part of a motion for new trial or a motion to reinstate, or it may be filed as a separate motion. *See* ***In re Lynd Co.***, 195 S.W.3d 682, 686 (Tex.2006); ***John v. Marshall Health Servs.***, 58 S.W.3d 738, 739-40 (Tex.2001). See ***O'Connor's Texas Rules***, "Form," ch. 10-G, §3.1, p. 977.

Texas Rule of Civil Procedure 306a does not address the deadline for receiving late notice or acquiring actual knowledge of the judgment. The courts have interpreted the statement in Rule 306a(4) that "in no event shall such periods [in Rule 306a(1)] begin more than 90 days after" the judgment as preventing an MEPD when notice is received or actual knowledge is acquired more than 90 days after the judgment is signed. *See, e.g.*, ***Estate of Howley v. Haberman***, 878 S.W.2d 139, 140 (Tex.1994) (too late to file MEPD because P learned of DWOP more than 90 days after dismissal); ***Levit v. Adams***, 850 S.W.2d 469, 470 (Tex.1993) (same, because P learned of DWOP 91 days after dismissal).

When a party receives notice of judgment too late to file an MEPD, the party may be able to challenge the judgment by a restricted appeal or bill of review. *See* ***Levit***, 850 S.W.2d at 470. See ***O'Connor's Texas Rules***, "Direct attacks on default judgment," ch. 7-A, §7.1, p. 715.

Even though Texas Rule of Civil Procedure 306a does not require the trial court to issue a written finding designating the actual date the party received notice or acquired actual knowledge of the judgment, Texas Rule of Appellate Procedure 4.2(c) does; therefore, the party should request one. *See* ***In re Lynd Co.***, 195 S.W.3d at 686. See ***O'Connor's Texas Rules***, "Written finding," ch. 10-G, §7.1, p. 981.

AFFIDAVIT OF {❶ *PARTY*} {❷ *NAME*}

STATE OF TEXAS §
{❸ _______} COUNTY §

Before me, the undersigned notary, on this day personally appeared {❹ *name of affiant*}, the affiant, whose identity is known to me. After I administered an oath, affiant testified as follows:

1. "My name is {❺ *name of affiant*}. I am over 18 years of age, of sound mind, and capable of making this affidavit. The facts stated in this affidavit are within my personal knowledge and are true and correct.

2. "I am the {❻ *party*} in this case. I did not know that the Court signed a judgment until {❼ *date*}. Before that date, I had no notice or actual knowledge of the judgment. If I had received notice or acquired knowledge of the Court's judgment, I would have instructed my attorney to {❽ *file a timely motion for new trial/perfect the appeal*}.

3. "I learned of the Court's judgment when {❾ *state how party learned of the judgment, e.g., when my attorney called me*}."

____
{❿ *Name of affiant*}

Sworn to and subscribed before me by {⓫ *name of affiant*} on _________, 20___.

____
Notary Public in and for
the State of Texas

SEE: Tex. R. Civ. P. 306a(4), (5)
O'Connor's Texas Rules * Civil Trials (2019), "Party," ch. 10-G, §3.4.2(2), p. 979

ADD: STYLE OF THE CASE – FORM 1B:2

NOTE: See notes under FORM 1B:8.

★

AFFIDAVIT OF {❶ *PARTY*}'S ATTORNEY

STATE OF TEXAS §
{❷ _______} COUNTY §

Before me, the undersigned notary, on this day personally appeared {❸ *name of affiant*}, the affiant, whose identity is known to me. After I administered an oath, affiant testified as follows:

1. "My name is {❹ *name of affiant*}. I am over 18 years of age, of sound mind, and capable of making this affidavit. The facts stated in this affidavit are within my personal knowledge and are true and correct.

2. "I am the attorney for the {❺ *party*} in this case. I did not know that the Court signed a judgment until {❻ *date*}. Before that date, I had no notice or actual knowledge of the judgment. If I had received notice or acquired knowledge of this Court's judgment, I would have {❼ *filed a timely motion for new trial/perfected the appeal*}.

3. "I learned of this Court's judgment when {❽ *state how attorney learned of the judgment*}.

{*CLOSE QUOTES OR ADD PARAGRAPH 4 IF APPROPRIATE*}

4. "I have confirmed that my law firm's mail room did not receive a notice of the judgment from the court clerk. The office procedure is to log all mail in the mail room before distributing it to the attorneys. Our office has no record of having received any document from this Court on or about {❾ *date*}, the date the court clerk indicated {❿ *he/she*} mailed the copies of the judgment to the parties. Attached to this affidavit are copies of the log from our mail room from the date the court clerk mailed the judgment to three weeks later."

____
{⓫ *Name of affiant*}

Sworn to and subscribed before me by {⓬ *name of affiant*} on __________, 20___.

____
Notary Public in and for
the State of Texas

SEE: Tex. R. Civ. P. 306a(4), (5)
O'Connor's Texas Rules * Civil Trials **(2019), "Attorney," ch. 10-G, §3.4.2(1), p. 978**

ADD: STYLE OF THE CASE – FORM 1B:2

ATTACH: Mail-room logs, if necessary

NOTE: See notes under FORM 1B:8.

{[1] *PARTY*}'S RESPONSE TO {[2] *ADVERSE PARTY*}'S
MOTION TO EXTEND POSTJUDGMENT DEADLINES

{[3] *Party*}, {[4] *name*}, asks the Court to deny {[5] *adverse party*} {[6] *name*}'s motion to determine that {[7] *adverse party*} {[8] *received notice/acquired actual knowledge*} of the judgment of this Court more than 20 days after the Court signed the judgment. {*See* ***O'Connor's Texas Rules***, *"Response," ch. 10-G, §5, p. 981.*}

INTRODUCTION

1. Plaintiff, {[9] *name*}, sued defendant, {[10] *name*}, for {[11] *state basis of suit*}.

2. {[12] *State other relevant facts about the suit.*}

BACKGROUND

3. On {[13] *date*}, this Court signed a judgment.

4. {[14] *Adverse party*} states that {[15] *he/she/it*} did not {[16] *receive notice/acquire actual knowledge*} of the judgment until {[17] *date*}.

5. {[18] *State other facts relevant to the response.*}

6. {[19] *Party*} attaches affidavits to this response as Exhibits {[20] *letters*} to establish facts not apparent from the record and incorporates them by reference.

ARGUMENT & AUTHORITIES

{*CHOOSE APPROPRIATE PARAGRAPHS 7-9*}

7. {[21] *Party*} gave {[22] *adverse party*} notice of the Court's judgment on {[23] *date*}, by {[24] *state how party gave adverse party notice of the judgment*}. The affidavit of {[25] *party*}, attached as Exhibit {[26] *letter*}, supports this claim. Because {[27] *adverse party*} received notice of the judgment within 20 days after the judgment was signed, the Court should deny {[28] *adverse party*}'s motion. {*See* ***O'Connor's Texas Rules***, *"Allegations," ch. 10-G, §3.2, p. 977.*}

8. {[29] *Adverse party*} acquired actual knowledge of the Court's judgment on or about {[30] *date*}, when {[31] *state how adverse party acquired knowledge of the judgment*}. The affidavit of {[32] *affiant*}, attached as Exhibit {[33] *letter*}, supports this claim. Because {[34] *adverse party*} acquired actual knowledge of the judgment within 20 days after the judgment was signed, the Court should deny {[35] *adverse party*}'s motion. {*See* ***O'Connor's Texas Rules***, *"Allegations," ch. 10-G, §3.2, p. 977.*}

9. {36 *Adverse party*} filed the motion on {37 *date*}, outside the limits of the Court's plenary power. *See* Tex. R. Civ. P. 306a(5); *John v. Marshall Health Servs., Inc.*, 58 S.W.3d 738, 741 (Tex. 2001). Because the Court's plenary power expired on {38 *date*}, and the motion was filed on {39 *date*}, the Court should deny the motion. {*See* ***O'Connor's Texas Rules***, *"Plenary-power limits," ch. 10-G, §4.1, p. 979.*}

CONCLUSION

10. {40 *Briefly summarize the response.*}

PRAYER

11. For these reasons, {41 *party*} asks the Court to deny the motion to extend post-judgment deadlines {42 *add if appropriate: and find that {adverse party} {received notice/acquired actual knowledge} of the judgment on {date}*}.

SEE: Tex. R. Civ. P. 306a(4), (5)
Tex. R. App. P. 4.2
O'Connor's Texas Rules * Civil Trials (2019), "Response," ch. 10-G, §5, p. 981

ADD: STYLE OF THE CASE – FORM 1B:2
SIGNATURE BLOCK – FORM 1B:3
VERIFICATION – FORM 1B:7
CERTIFICATE OF SERVICE – FORM 1B:13

ATTACH: AFFIDAVIT – FORM 1B:8, if necessary
ORDER – FORM 10G:5

ORDER ON {❶ *PARTY*}'S MOTION
TO EXTEND POSTJUDGMENT DEADLINES

After considering {❷ *party*}'s motion to extend postjudgment deadlines, the response, the pleadings, and arguments of counsel, the Court

{*CHOOSE APPROPRIATE ORDER*}

DENIES the motion. {❸ *Party*} {❹ *received notice/acquired actual knowledge*} of the judgment on {❺ *date*}. The date of the judgment is {❻ *date*}, which is the date the judgment was signed.

GRANTS the motion. {❼ *Party*} {❽ *received notice/acquired actual knowledge*} of the judgment on {❾ *date*}. This date was more than 20 days after the judgment was signed. The new date for the judgment is {❿ *date*}.

SIGNED on _______________, 20___.

____
PRESIDING JUDGE

SEE: Tex. R. Civ. P. 306a(4), (5)
Tex. R. App. P. 4.2(c)
O'Connor's Texas Rules * Civil Trials (2019), "Order," ch. 10-G, §7, p. 981

ADD: STYLE OF THE CASE – FORM 1B:2
CERTIFICATE OF SERVICE – FORM 1B:13, if proposed order served separately from motion or response

NOTE: Texas Rule of Appellate Procedure 4.2(c) requires the trial court to sign an order and make a finding of the date of notice or actual knowledge of the judgment. ***In re Bokeloh***, 21 S.W.3d 784, 792 (Tex.App.—Houston [14th Dist.] 2000, orig. proceeding). By comparison, Texas Rule of Civil Procedure 306a does not require the trial court to sign an order with such a finding. ***In re Lynd Co.***, 195 S.W.3d 682, 686 (Tex. 2006). If the court grants the motion but does not identify the date of notice or actual knowledge, the date may be implied from the order granting the motion, unless there is no evidence to support the implied finding or the party establishes an alternate notice date as a matter of law. *Id.*

{❶ *PARTY*}'S MOTION FOR JUDGMENT
NUNC PRO TUNC UNDER TEXAS RULE OF CIVIL PROCEDURE 316

{❷ *Party*}, {❸ *name*}, asks the Court to sign a judgment nunc pro tunc, under the authority of Texas Rule of Civil Procedure 316. {*See **O'Connor's Texas Rules**, "Motion," ch. 10-H, §2, p. 983.*}

INTRODUCTION

1. Plaintiff, {❹ *name*}, sued defendant, {❺ *name*}, for {❻ *state basis of suit*}.

2. {❼ *State other relevant facts about the suit.*}

BACKGROUND

3. On {❽ *date*}, the Court signed a judgment.

4. The judgment signed by the Court contains a clerical error. Specifically, {❾ *describe clerical error*}.

5. {❿ *State other facts relevant to the motion.*}

ARGUMENT & AUTHORITIES

6. A court can correct a clerical error in the judgment at any time, even after it loses plenary power over the judgment. *See Tex. Dep't of Transp. v. A.P.I. Pipe & Supply, LLC*, 397 S.W.3d 162, 167 (Tex. 2013); *Escobar v. Escobar*, 711 S.W.2d 230, 231 (Tex. 1986). A clerical error is a discrepancy between the entry of a judgment in the official record and the judgment as it was actually rendered. *Universal Underwriters Ins. Co. v. Ferguson*, 471 S.W.2d 28, 29-30 (Tex. 1971); *Morris v. O'Neal*, 464 S.W.3d 801, 810 (Tex. App.—Houston [14th Dist.] 2015, no pet.).

{*CHOOSE APPROPRIATE PARAGRAPHS 7-17*}

7. The error in the judgment is a clerical error, which can be corrected by a judgment nunc pro tunc, because the error was in the date the judgment was signed. *Claxton v. (Upper) Lake Fork Water Control & Improvement Dist. No. 1*, 220 S.W.3d 537, 543 (Tex. App.—Texarkana 2006, pet. denied). {⓫ *Elaborate.*}

8. The error in the judgment is a clerical error, which can be corrected by a judgment nunc pro tunc, because the error was a discrepancy between the judgment actually signed and the judgment the Court intended to sign. *E.g.*, *Andrews v. Koch*, 702 S.W.2d 584, 586 (Tex. 1986) (probate order to sell was different from order confirming sale). {⓬ *Elaborate.*}

◄ *Continued on next page* ►

9. The error in the judgment is a clerical error, which can be corrected by a judgment nunc pro tunc, because the error was in a written judgment that did not reflect the settlement agreement made in open court. *Delaup v. Delaup*, 917 S.W.2d 411, 413 (Tex. App.—Houston [14th Dist.] 1996, no writ). {⓭ *Elaborate.*}

10. The error in the judgment is a clerical error, which can be corrected by a judgment nunc pro tunc, because the error was a mathematical error in the amount of damages. *See Travelers Cos. v. Wolfe*, 838 S.W.2d 708, 710 & n.2 (Tex. App.—Amarillo 1992, no writ). {⓮ *Elaborate.*}

11. The error in the judgment is a clerical error, which can be corrected by a judgment nunc pro tunc, because the error was a mistake in the party designations. *E.g.*, *Dickens v. Willis*, 957 S.W.2d 657, 659-60 (Tex. App.—Austin 1997, no pet.) ("respondent" should have been "petitioner"). {⓯ *Elaborate.*}

12. The error in the judgment is a clerical error, which can be corrected by a judgment nunc pro tunc, because the error was a mistake in a party's name in the judgment. *See, e.g.*, *Gonzalez v. Doctors Hosp.—E. Loop*, 814 S.W.2d 536, 537 (Tex. App.—Houston [1st Dist.] 1991, no writ) (changed plaintiff's name from John to Juan). {⓰ *Elaborate.*}

13. The error in the judgment is a clerical error, which can be corrected by a judgment nunc pro tunc, because the error was a discrepancy in the acreage description of land. *See Escobar*, 711 S.W.2d at 231-32. {⓱ *Elaborate.*}

14. The error in the judgment is a clerical error, which can be corrected by a judgment nunc pro tunc, because the error was a discrepancy between the body of the judgment actually rendered and the title of the document. *See, e.g.*, *Butler v. Cont'l Airlines, Inc.*, 31 S.W.3d 642, 647-48 (Tex. App.—Houston [1st Dist.] 2000, pet. denied) (only reference to motion for sanctions was in title of order). {⓲ *Elaborate.*}

15. The error in the judgment is a clerical error, which can be corrected by a judgment nunc pro tunc, because the error was an unintended judgment of dismissal caused by the court clerk. *Knox v. Long*, 257 S.W.2d 289, 292-93 (Tex. 1953), *overruled on other grounds*, *Jackson v. Hernandez*, 285 S.W.2d 184 (Tex. 1955). {⓳ *Elaborate.*}

16. The error in the judgment is a clerical error, which can be corrected by a judgment nunc pro tunc, because the error was a judgment that granted a nonsuit with prejudice when the moving party requested a nonsuit without prejudice. *See Thompson v. Tex. Dept. of Human Res.*, 859 S.W.2d 482, 485 (Tex. App.—San Antonio 1993, no writ).

17. The error in the judgment is a clerical error, which can be corrected by a judgment nunc pro tunc, because the error was {20 *describe other clerical error*}. {21 *Elaborate.*}

CONCLUSION

18. {22 *Briefly summarize the motion.*}

PRAYER

19. For these reasons, and in the interest of justice and fairness, {23 *party*} asks the Court to grant the motion and sign a judgment nunc pro tunc.

SEE: Tex. R. Civ. P. 316
*O'Connor's Texas Rules * Civil Trials* (2019), "Ground," ch. 10-H, §2.1, p. 983

ADD: STYLE OF THE CASE – FORM 1B:2
SIGNATURE BLOCK – FORM 1B:3
VERIFICATION – FORM 1B:7, if motion contains evidence outside the record
CERTIFICATE OF SERVICE – FORM 1B:13

ATTACH: AFFIDAVIT – FORM 1B:8, if necessary
NOTICE OF HEARING OR SUBMISSION – FORM 1E:1
ORDER – FORM 1G:1

NOTE: There is no deadline to file a motion for judgment nunc pro tunc. *See* Tex. R. Civ. P. 316. The earliest date to file the motion is the day after the court loses plenary power over the judgment. *See* ***Riner v. Briargrove Park Prop. Owners, Inc.***, 976 S.W.2d 680, 682 (Tex.App.—Houston [1st Dist.] 1997, no writ).

The movant must give all interested parties notice of the motion for judgment nunc pro tunc, or else the correction is a nullity. ***West Tex. State Bank v. General Res. Mgmt.***, 723 S.W.2d 304, 307 (Tex.App.—Austin 1987, writ ref'd n.r.e.); *see* Tex. R. Civ. P. 316.

{❶ *PARTY*}'S RESPONSE TO
{❷ *ADVERSE PARTY*}'S MOTION FOR JUDGMENT NUNC PRO TUNC

{❸ *Party*}, {❹ *name*}, asks the Court to deny {❺ *adverse party*} {❻ *name*}'s motion for judgment nunc pro tunc. {*See* ***O'Connor's Texas Rules****, "Response," ch. 10-H, §4, p. 984.*}

INTRODUCTION

1. Plaintiff, {❼ *name*}, sued defendant, {❽ *name*}, for {❾ *state basis of suit*}.

2. {❿ *State other relevant facts about the suit.*}

BACKGROUND

3. On {⓫ *date*}, the Court signed a judgment.

4. {⓬ *State other facts relevant to the response.*}

ARGUMENT & AUTHORITIES

5. The judgment signed by the Court does not contain a clerical error. The error about which {⓭ *adverse party*} complains is a judicial error. *See Tex. Dep't of Transp. v. A.P.I. Pipe & Supply, LLC*, 397 S.W.3d 162, 167 (Tex. 2013); *In re Daredia*, 317 S.W.3d 247, 249 (Tex. 2010); *Comet Aluminum Co. v. Dibrell*, 450 S.W.2d 56, 58 (Tex. 1970); *Finlay v. Jones*, 435 S.W.2d 136, 138 (Tex. 1968); *Hernandez v. Lopez*, 288 S.W.3d 180, 184-85 (Tex. App.—Houston [1st Dist.] 2009, no pet.). A judicial error cannot be corrected by a judgment nunc pro tunc filed after the judgment is final. *Finlay*, 435 S.W.2d at 138. {*See* ***O'Connor's Texas Rules****, "Ground," ch. 10-H, §2.1, p. 983.*}

6. The error in the judgment was a judicial error because {⓮ *explain why error is not a clerical error but a judicial error, e.g., the judgment contained a mistake in the award of prejudgment interest. Comet Aluminum, 450 S.W.2d at 59*}. {*See* ***O'Connor's Texas Rules****, "Judicial error," ch. 10-H, §2.1.2(2), p. 984.*}

7. The Court does not have power to correct a judicial error in the judgment because it no longer has plenary power over the judgment. *See Tex. Dep't of Transp.*, 397 S.W.3d at 167; *Bd. of Trs. v. Toungate*, 958 S.W.2d 365, 367 (Tex. 1997); *Dikeman v. Snell*, 490 S.W.2d 183, 186 (Tex. 1973). The Court lost plenary power over the judgment on {⓯ *date*}. {⓰ *Elaborate.*} {*See* ***O'Connor's Texas Rules****, "Incorrect judgment nunc pro tunc," ch. 10-H, §6.2, p. 985.*}

CONCLUSION

8. {⓱ *Briefly summarize the response.*}

PRAYER

9. For these reasons, and in the interest of justice and fairness, {⓲ *party*} asks the Court to deny {⓳ *adverse party*}'s motion for judgment nunc pro tunc.

SEE: Tex. R. Civ. P. 316
O'Connor's Texas Rules * Civil Trials (2019), "Response," ch. 10-H, §4, p. 984

ADD: STYLE OF THE CASE – FORM 1B:2
SIGNATURE BLOCK – FORM 1B:3
CERTIFICATE OF SERVICE – FORM 1B:13

ATTACH: AFFIDAVIT – FORM 1B:8, if necessary
ORDER – FORM 1G:1

INDEX

INDEX

Page numbers in ***boldface italic***

INDEX

Page numbers in ***boldface italic***

Page numbers in ***boldface italic***

INDEX

Page numbers in ***boldface italic***

Page numbers in ***boldface italic***

Page numbers in ***boldface italic***

Page numbers in ***boldface italic***

INDEX

Page numbers in ***boldface italic***

INDEX

Page numbers in ***boldface italic***

INDEX

Page numbers in ***boldface italic***

Page numbers in ***boldface italic***